THE APOCRYPHAL OLD TESTAMENT

Edited by

H. F. D. SPARKS

CLARENDON PRESS · OXFORD

Oxford University Press, Walton Street, Oxford OX2 6DP

Oxford New York Toronto
Delhi Bombay Calcutta Madras Karachi
Petaling Jaya Singapore Hong Kong Tokyo
Nairobi Dar es Salaam Cape Town
Melbourne Auckland

and associated companies in
Berlin Ibadan

Oxford is a trade mark of Oxford University Press

Published in the United States
by Oxford University Press, New York

First published in cloth and paperback 1985
Reprinted 1987, 1989, 1990

British Library Cataloguing in Publication Data

[Bible, O.T. 1984] The Apocryphal Old Testament.
1. Bible (Texts, versions, etc.)
I. Sparks, H. F. D.
229'.05'2   BS1692
ISBN 0–19–826177–2

Library of Congress Cataloging in Publication Data
Main entry under title:
The Apocryphal Old Testament.
Includes bibliographies and index.
1. Apocryphal books (Old Testament)—
Criticism, interpretation, etc.   I. Sparks,
H. F. D. (Hedley Frederick Davis)
BS1692 1984   229'.91052   82–22569
ISBN 0–19–826177–2

Printed in Great Britain by
Biddles Ltd, Guildford & King's Lynn

CONTENTS

PREFACE

The Apocryphal Old Testament was originally planned as a companion volume to M. R. James's *The Apocryphal New Testament*, first published as long ago as 1924.

When, in the mid-1950s, the stocks of R. H. Charles's well-known two-volume work, *The Apocrypha and Pseudepigrapha of the Old Testament* (1913), were running low there was discussion at the Press about what should be done. Would a simple reprint be sufficient? Ought a revised 'second edition' to be undertaken? Or ought a completely new work to be commissioned to replace it?

There were a number of conflicting factors. After the lapse of nearly half a century there was an obvious need to up-date some of the information: many of the critical opinions expressed seemed less certain than once they did; and questions, too, might be asked about the items selected for inclusion in the second volume – why this, and if this, why not that? On the other hand, Charles's two volumes were one of the outstanding achievements of British biblical scholarship in the early years of the twentieth century: they had been widely used, and continued to be widely used; *but* they were both bulky and expensive. Further, it was clear that there was a much greater popular demand for the second (Pseudepigrapha) volume than for the first (Apocrypha), presumably because the books in the Apocrypha volume were readily available in several standard translations, whereas those in the Pseudepigrapha volume were not. The upshot was that the Press decided to reprint both volumes, as and when circumstances required, and at the same time to commission a much smaller, handier, and less expensive volume, designed on much the same lines as James's.

The idea was to ignore the books in Charles's first volume (the Apocrypha proper) and concentrate on those in the second. But it was agreed that some latitude in selection must be allowed – some of the books included by Charles might be omitted, while others, omitted by Charles, might be included. A volume of translations was the primary end in view: each translation was to be preceded by an Introduction and a Bibliography; and such footnotes as there were, were to be limited to points of text and translation. Since the Press were the publishers of Charles and were also to publish the new volume, there would be no difficulty in taking over a number of Charles's translations with only, perhaps, minor revision; though, of course, for the books not in Charles, which it was hoped to include, fresh translations would have to be obtained. So a team of translators and revisers was got together. I was appointed Editor, and, in addition to general editorial duties, I assumed personal responsibility for writing the Introductions and compiling the Bibliographies, in order to secure as much consistency as possible.

As with so many undertakings of this kind, the completion of the volume has been delayed beyond expectation. Some of the translators and revisers sent me their contributions within two or three years: others took longer; and a few of them very much longer. But this was not the major problem. A great deal of work had been done in the field since Charles's day, and it continued to be done; and this inevitably had an unfortunate effect on our rate of progress. At first glance it might seem that to revise one of the translations already in Charles was not a very time-consuming task. It might be assumed (especially in the light of the undisputed wealth of scholarship which lay behind Charles's two volumes) that no more than a cursory check-over was required. Yet when a new edition of the text in question had appeared in the interval (based, perhaps, on freshly discovered manuscripts, or on a different recension), or there had been more than one new edition, 'revision' began to take on a new meaning. And the same considerations applied sometimes to those contributors from whom fresh translations had been commissioned. In several instances a contribution was well under way, or even complete and sent to me, when new textual evidence was brought to light, or a new edition appeared, which, although it might not necessarily have to be made the base of the translation, nevertheless had to be taken full account of.

A further problem that became increasingly pressing as the work proceeded was that of translation-style. The style of the translations in Charles is what used to be called 'biblical' – i.e. a style which imitated the Authorized Version of 1611 and the Revised Version of 1881–1894 (and the same is also true of James's *The Apocryphal New Testament*, though less obviously so). Inasmuch as part of our original plan was to reprint as many as possible of the translations in Charles with only minor revision, it followed that we also were committed to 'biblical style'. In the 1950s there seemed no serious objection to this, and all contributors were instructed accordingly. But as time went on it became clear that our decision was questionable. The 1960s and 1970s witnessed the appearance, not only of The New English Bible and The Jerusalem Bible, but also of several other versions of the Bible (or parts of it) in modern idiom, which found a ready welcome from the Bible-reading public. Hence by the mid-1970s 'biblical style' did not mean what it had meant fifteen or twenty years earlier; and anything deliberately written in old-fashioned 'biblical style' was bound to seem tiresomely dated and artificial.

The issue came to a head over 1 Enoch. A revision of Charles's translation of 1 Enoch was ready when it was learned that Dr. M. A. Knibb was engaged on a new edition of the Ethiopic text, which was to be accompanied by a fresh translation, together with a full Introduction and (mainly textual) Commentary. The Press was to publish it;[1] and Dr. Knibb most generously agreed that we should be allowed to use his translation instead of the revision of Charles's translation we had ready. But Dr. Knibb's translation was in modern idiom. Very naturally he was unwilling to archaize, in order to make his contribution conform in style with the others. The only alternative was to modernize the others. And I undertook to do this as part of my overall responsibility as Editor: I can only hope that the result will not be judged too aggressively modern. Throughout, the convention that God is addressed directly in the second person singular has been retained (as in the first edition of The New English Bible). Also retained from time to time, though not necessarily universally, are certain well-known 'biblical' expressions such as 'And it came to pass . . .': the purpose in retaining them is to indicate that the text translated is itself not

---

[1] It appeared, in two volumes, in 1978.

without an antique flavour; for there is much to be said for translations in a volume such as ours preserving something of the style of the originals instead of all being reduced to a dead level of uniformity.

Any reader of any translation is apt to assume that there is no need for him to bother about the original behind the translation unless there is some special reason for his doing so. This may not matter so long as no serious questions can be raised about the reliability of the text of the original. But when, as is the case with some of the documents we are concerned with, there are a number of manuscripts available which regularly differ from one another, there are, perhaps, three or four versions in as many different languages, and also, maybe, several distinct recensions,[2] the identification of an 'original' text is no easy matter. Experts are often deeply divided. In these circumstances it is essential that the user of a translation should be plainly informed about *what the translator has translated*. We have always tried to do this. In each Introduction will be found a precise explanatory statement (usually at the end, or towards the end); and this statement, when read in conjunction with the details given elsewhere in the Introduction about the authorities available for the text, should provide the necessary information.

More particularized information about any significant textual variants, as well as about possible translational alternatives, will be found in the notes underneath the translations. These notes, as already indicated, have been limited to points of text and translation, and make no attempt to discuss any of the often highly controversial literary-critical, historical, or theological issues involved.

The Bibliographies are constructed in three sections. First in each comes a list of editions of the text – in chronological order: then a list of the existing translations in English, French, and

---

[2] Since it is a relatively short work, The Ladder of Jacob has been chosen to illustrate in its simplest form the situation when there is more than one recension of the text of the same document extant. On pp. 455–463 (below) will be found translations of both extant recensions of The Ladder, printed one after the other, so that whoever is so minded can compare the two and form some estimate of the kind of problems that arise.

German – also in chronological order; and last of all, a section headed 'General', whose function is to draw attention to some of the scholarly treatments that have been offered of the work concerned (not necessarily by the most modern authors), which in one way or another assist in its understanding and appreciation. The items in this last section are arranged, not chronologically, but alphabetically. No attempt has been made to be all-inclusive.

Few of our readers, who have been brought up on Charles, will fail to notice, not only a difference in the contents, but also a fundamental difference in general approach. These are not unconnected.

When deciding on the contents of his second volume, Charles seems to have been guided by no exactly definable principle of selection, except in so far as he regarded all the items he included as Jewish in origin, written in the so-called 'intertestamental period', and therefore of the greatest value, first to students of the Judaism of this period, and secondly to students of early Christianity, since they illustrated the Jewish background both of the primitive Church and also of many of the New Testament books.

In his general Preface Charles wrote:

For students both of the Old and New Testaments the value of the non-Canonical Jewish literature from 200 BC to AD 100 is practically recognized on every side alike by Jewish and Christian scholars. But hitherto no attempt has been made to issue an edition of this literature as a whole in English.[3]

and elsewhere:

This literature was written probably for the most part in Galilee, the home of the religious seer and mystic. Not only was the development of a religious but also of an ethical character. In both these respects the way was prepared by this literature for the advent of Christianity, while a study of the New Testament makes it clear that its writers had been brought up in the atmosphere created by these books and were themselves directly acquainted with many of them.[4]

---

[3] *APOT* i, p. iii and ii, p. iii.
[4] *Religious Development between the Old and the New Testaments* (The Home University Library of Modern Knowledge; London, 1914), p. 9.

To-day an approach along these lines is barely possible. Despite Charles's ascription of all the items in his second volume to the centuries between 200 BC and AD 100, and his conviction that all of them were Jewish in origin, the fact remains that the textual tradition in nearly every case is Christian.[5] Here lies the major difficulty.

About the Jewish origin of many of them there can be no doubt; and some of these would seem to have come down to us in very much the same form as their authors wrote them – Jubilees is a case in point. Most of the others, however, have been transmitted to us as what would appear to be an amalgam of Jewish and Christian elements, which to the unpractised eye are not very easily separable. But Charles, committed as he was to the view that all were Jewish originally, had no scruples in explaining the Christian elements as either later additions to, or interpolations into, what were once purely Jewish texts. And in his translations he repeatedly enclosed several words, or a verse, or verses, or a whole chapter, or more, within square brackets, and added in his notes such a comment as, 'The words in brackets are a Christian interpolation, as is evident from . . .'.

For Charles's successors much of this has seemed nothing like so evident. In many instances of alleged Christian addition or interpolation Charles may well have been quite right. We know that Christians did take over Jewish writings, and there is every reason for supposing that from time to time they added to them and interpolated into them bits and pieces here and there, in order to make them more acceptable for Christian use. But there is also evidence to suggest that they sometimes recast a Jewish text altogether, so that for us to think purely in terms of 'additions' and 'interpolations' is irrelevant – such a work will have been a Christian work, though based on a Jewish foundation. We have also to allow for the likelihood that Christians also wrote works with a traditionally Jewish background: they may have been influenced by Jewish legends they had come across, either written

---

[5] The exceptions are (i) The Zadokite Fragments, (ii) The Story of Ahikar, and (iii) Pirke Aboth. But Charles made it clear that he did not number these works among 'the Pseudepigrapha' as he understood the term: see his remarks to this effect in his Preface (*APOT* i, p. iv, and ii, p. iv).

or oral, or the influence may have been no more than what they had read for themselves in the Old Testament, expanded by a liberal use of their own imagination (in much the same way as some of the already existing Jewish works had come into being); but again these will have been Christian works from the beginning, and the appearance in them of Christian theological expressions, or what may look like quotations from the New Testament, should occasion no surprise.

In other words, the problem has proved to be much more complicated than Charles imagined, and his approach in consequence was much too narrow. We have, therefore, when considering which items to include in our own volume, thought it best to abandon the concept of 'background literature' entirely. Our single criterion for inclusion has been whether or not any particular item is attributed to (or is primarily concerned with the history or activities of) an Old Testament character (or characters). And we have tried to include all the more important and interesting items that satisfy this criterion, irrespective of date, and irrespective, too, of whether or not a convincing claim can be put forward on behalf of any one of them for a respectable Jewish pedigree.

To have included everything which satisfies this criterion would have been impossible. In making our choices we have been guided principally by a desire to produce a collection as representative as possible of the various types of literature within the field – i.e. History (and Legend), Testament, Apocalypse, Psalms, etc. A number of items, such as 1 Enoch, selected themselves. With others a decision sometimes was more difficult. The extant fragments of the apocryphal Ezekiel, for example, were thought too insubstantial to merit inclusion; and some readers might maintain, not unreasonably, that the same argument should have been applied to the fragmentary Apocalypse of Zephaniah, which has been included (see below, pp. 919–20). And so one might go on.

In practice the differences in content between our volume and Charles's second volume are nothing like so great as the above remarks might suggest. We have naturally dropped The Fragments of a Zadokite Work, The Story of Ahikar, The Sibylline Oracles, and The Letter of Aristeas, as failing to satisfy our criterion: 4 Ezra belongs, strictly speaking, to the Apocrypha (= 2 Esdras), and it has therefore also been dropped: 4 Maccabees is a doubtful case, and we have decided against it. On the other hand, we have added a number of other items – The Apocalypse of Abraham, The Testament of Abraham, The Testament of Isaac, The Testament of Jacob, The Ladder of Jacob, Joseph and Aseneth, The Testament of Job, The Odes of Solomon, The Testament of Solomon, The Apocalypse of Elijah, The Paraleipomena of Jeremiah, The Apocalypse of Zephaniah, The 'Anonymous' Apocalypse, The Apocalypse of Esdras, The Vision of Esdras, and The Apocalypse of Sedrach. Even so, there is an essential core common to both volumes.

The difference in general approach, which has been alluded to, can most satisfactorily be illustrated by comparing the two treatments of the text of The Ascension of Isaiah. Charles explained the existing text as a 2nd cent. AD putting together of three previously independent constituents, one of which was Jewish and the other two Christian: the first (Jewish) constituent he identified as the fragmentary 'Martyrdom of Isaiah' (i. 1–2*a*, 6*b*–13*a*, ii. 1–8, 10–iii. 12, v. 1*b*–14), the second as the 'Testament of Hezekiah' (iii. 13*b*–iv. 18), and the third as the 'Vision of Isaiah (vi. 1–xi. 40) – the remaining verses were 'editorial additions' (i. 2*b*–6*a*, 13*b*, ii. 9, iii. 13*a*, iv. 19–v. 1*a*, 15–16, xi. 41–43), inserted to give cohesion to the whole. Charles, accordingly, in his second volume printed the text of 'The Martyrdom of Isaiah' only, and he described it as such. In our Introduction to the work we have, of course, discussed the various literary-critical hypotheses that have been put forward; but we have preferred to give a translation of the text entire (and we have described it as a translation of 'The Ascension of Isaiah') on the ground that this is the form in which the work was popularly known, and the title by which it was popularly known, in the Church.

Occasionally this difference in approach may have a more obviously practical consequence. For example, in Charles's view The Testaments of the Twelve Patriarchs were a Jewish work which had suffered heavily from Christian interpolation. Before Charles most scholars had thought of it as Christian in origin, though no doubt modelled on earlier Jewish 'Testaments'; and some still do.

In three separate passages in the Testaments as we have received them the two commandments, 'Thou shalt love the Lord, thy God' and 'Thou shalt love thy neighbour as thyself', are associated together. Charles's comment here was that the Testaments were the 'earliest literary authority for conjoining love to God and love to one's neighbour'.[6] If Charles was right and the Testaments are Jewish (*c.* 100 BC), then Our Lord's so-called 'Summary of the Law' (Matt. xxii. 37–40; Mark xii. 29–31) was anticipated; but if Charles was wrong and the Testaments are Christian, then the passages in question are likely to be no more than the reflection of the teaching in the Gospels (and the same would also be true, of course, if the passages were three additional Christian interpolations into his originally Jewish Testaments, which had escaped Charles's eagle-eye!).

And finally, the term 'Pseudepigrapha' has been avoided altogether. Pseudepigrapha is, in any case, an ugly word. And when used in association with 'Apocrypha', as it so frequently is, it can be very misleading. Strictly it is 'a collective term for books or writings bearing a false title, or ascribed to another than the true author'.[7] Many of the books commonly grouped together and alluded to as 'the Pseudepigrapha' are indeed pseudepigraphical – no doubt a majority. But there is nothing distinctive about this: there are pseudepigraphical books in the Apocrypha (e.g. The Wisdom of Solomon), and there are pseudepigraphical books in the Old Testament itself (e.g. Daniel). To refer to '*the* Pseudepigrapha', without further definition or qualification, creates the impression in the popular mind that alongside the 'canonical' Old Testament and the 'deutero-canonical' Apocrypha there is a third, universally recognized, 'trito-canonical' collection of books – when there is not. Any collection of books of this kind, however chosen, is bound to mirror the predilections and the prejudices of its editor(s); and it is well that this should be realized. The term therefore, though ancient, is best avoided.

It only remains for me to record my personal thanks: first, to my team of translators and revisers, and to express the hope that

---

[6] *APOT* ii, p. 334.   [7] *OED* viii, p. 1542.

ABBREVIATIONS AND SYMBOLS

AjSaB²   P. RIESSLER, *Altjüdisches Schrifttum ausserhalb der Bibel*. 2. Auflage (Heidelberg, 1966).

AL   C. C. TORREY, *The Apocryphal Literature: A Brief Introduction* (New Haven, 1945: reprinted Hamden, Conn., 1963).

ALGhJ   *Arbeiten zur Literatur und Geschichte des hellenistischen Judentums* (Leiden, 1968–   ).

APAT   E. KAUTZSCH (ed.), *Die Apokryphen und Pseudepigraphen des Alten Testaments*. 2 vols. (Tübingen, 1900).

APOT   R. H. CHARLES (ed.), *The Apocrypha and Pseudepigrapha of the Old Testament in English, with Introductions and Critical and Explanatory Notes to the several Books, edited in conjunction with many scholars*. 2 vols. (Oxford, 1913).

CBQ   *Catholic Biblical Quarterly*.

ChOIDR   *Chteniya v Imperatorskom Obshchestve istorii i drevnostei rossiiskikh pri Moskovskom universitete*.

CSCO   *Corpus Scriptorum Christianorum Orientalium*.

CSEL   *Corpus Scriptorum Ecclesiasticorum Latinorum*.

DBSup   L. PIROT *et al.* (eds.), *Dictionnaire de la Bible: Suppléments* (Paris, 1928–   ).

EATAP   L. ROST, *Einleitung in die alttestamentlichen Apokryphen und Pseudepigraphen* (Heidelberg, 1971).

EUX   H. WEINEL, 'Die spätere christliche Apokalyptik' in H. SCHMIDT (ed.), *Εὐχαριστήριον: Studien zur Religion und Literatur des Alten und Neuen Testaments Hermann Gunkel . . . dargebracht*, ii (= *Forschungen zur Religion und Literatur des Alten und Neuen Testaments*, N.F., xix. 2; Göttingen, 1923).

GCS   *Griechischen christlichen Schriftsteller der ersten drei Jahrhunderte.*

GjVZJC⁴ iii   E. SCHÜRER, *Geschichte des jüdischen Volkes im Zeitalter Jesu Christi.* 4. Auflage. 3. Band (Leipzig, 1909).

HJPTJC II. iii   E. SCHÜRER, *A History of the Jewish People in the Time of Jesus Christ* (Pt. II, vol. iii, Translated by SOPHIA TAYLOR and PETER CHRISTIE; Edinburgh, 1886).

HSM   *Harvard Semitic Monographs.*

HTR   *Harvard Theological Review.*

HUCA   *Hebrew Union College Annual.*

IPGAT   A.-M. DENIS, *Introduction aux pseudépigraphes grecs d'Ancien Testament* (= *Studia in Veteris Testamenti Pseudepigrapha*, i; Leiden, 1970).

JAOS   *Journal of the American Oriental Society.*

JBL   *Journal of Biblical Literature.*

JE   *Jewish Encyclopedia.*

JJS   *Journal of Jewish Studies.*

JQR   *Jewish Quarterly Review.*

JSh-rZ   W. G. KÜMMEL (ed.), *Jüdische Schriften aus hellenistisch-römischer Zeit* (Gütersloh, 1973–   ).

JTS   *Journal of Theological Studies.*

LAOT   M. R. JAMES, *The Lost Apocrypha of the Old Testament: Their Titles and Fragments* (= S.P.C.K., *Translations of Early Documents*; London, 1920).

NTA   R. Mc L. WILSON (ed.), *New Testament Apocrypha.* 2 vols. (London, 1963 and 1965).

NTS   *New Testament Studies.*

OTI   O. EISSFELDT, *The Old Testament: An Introduction,*
                including the Apocrypha and Pseudepigrapha, and also the
                works of similar type from Qumran (Translated by
                PETER R. ACKROYD; Oxford, 1966).

Peshiṭta   *The Old Testament in Syriac according to the Peshiṭta*
                Version (Leiden, 1972–   ).
PG   J. P. MIGNE (ed.), *Patrologia Graeca.*
PL   J. P. MIGNE (ed.), *Patrologia Latina.*
PO   *Patrologia Orientalis.*
PVTG   *Pseudepigrapha Veteris Testamenti Graece* (Leiden,
                1964–   ).

R Bén   *Revue Bénédictine.*
R Bibl   *Revue Biblique.*

SBL   Society of Biblical Literature.
SCS   *Septuagint and Cognate Studies.*
SORYaS   *Sbornik Otdeleniya russkogo yazyka i slovesnosti*
                Imperatorskoi Akademii nauk.
SPB   *Studia Post Biblica.*
SVTP   *Studia in Veteris Testamenti Pseudepigrapha* (Leiden,
                1970–   ).

TS   *Texts and Studies.*
TU   *Texte und Untersuchungen.*
TZ   *Theologische Zeitung.*

UWOT²   J. ISSAVERDENS, *The Uncanonical Writings of the*
                Old Testament found in the Armenian MSS of the Library
                of St. Lazarus, translated into English. 2nd edition
                (Venice, 1934).

VT   *Vetus Testamentum.*

ZAW   *Zeitschrift für die altestamentliche Wissenschaft.*

| ZDMG | *Zeitschrift der deutschen morgenländischen Gesellschaft.* |
| ZNW | *Zeitschrift für die neutestamentliche Wissenschaft.* |

† †	indicates that the word or words so enclosed are corrupt.
[ ]	indicates that the word or words so enclosed, though part of the text being translated, are in all probability an intrusion into the original.
⟨ ⟩	indicates that the word or words so enclosed are a restoration into the text of what is conjectured to have fallen out of the original.
thick type	indicates that the word or words so printed are a conjectural emendation.
italics	indicate that the word or words so printed are not actually found in the text being translated, but they have been added to improve the sense.

JUBILEES

INTRODUCTION

Jubilees describes itself in the Prologue as 'the account of the division of the days of the law and of the testimony, of the events of the years, according to their *year*-weeks and their jubilees, through all the years of the world, as the Lord gave it to Moses on mount Sinai, when he went up to receive the stone tablets of the law and of the commandment, in accordance with God's command, as he said to him, Go up to the top of the mount'.

The scene is accordingly set in the biblical context of Exod. xxiv. 12–18. During the forty days and forty nights that Moses is on the mount 'the angel of the presence' recounts to him all the significant events from the Creation to the Exodus (including the circumstances of his own birth and early history, the passage of the Red Sea, and the celebration of the first Passover) and also initiates him into the mysteries of the secret traditions which had already been communicated to certain of the patriarchs. These traditions had been handed down from father to son, in some instances in writing;[1] and Moses is now instructed to write what is revealed to him 'in a book'[2] – an instruction obviously inspired by the statement at Exod. xxiv. 4 ('Moses wrote down all the words of the Lord') and the definite instruction at Exod. xxxiv. 27 ('Write these words down'). But the 'book' referred to in Jubilees is not 'the book of the covenant', from which Moses reads at Exod. xxiv. 7. Nor is it one of the books of the Pentateuch, traditionally ascribed to Moses. It is the Book of Jubilees itself. Whereas the Pentateuch, 'the first law',[3] had been published by Moses openly, Jubilees is represented as a kind of 'second law' (although the actual phrase does not occur), which Moses is commissioned to write and preserve for the generations in the last times ('. . . till I descend and dwell with them through all eternity'[4]).

Jubilees is thus in content for the most part a parallel version of Gen. i. 1 – Exod. xv. 22; and it stands in much the same sort of

---

[1] e.g. vii. 38, xxxix. 6, xlv. 16. [2] i. 5: cp. ii. 1.
[3] vi. 22. [4] i. 26.

relationship to its primary biblical sources as do the Books of Chronicles to the Books of Samuel and Kings. Just as the Chronicler has rewritten Samuel and Kings, concentrating on the religious aspects of Israel's history, especially on the Temple and its worship, and on the part that David played in the preparations for its building, so the author of Jubilees has rewritten the material in Gen. i. 1 – Exod. xv. 22, partly in order to bring it up to date from the point of view of the beliefs and practices of his own day, but more particularly in order to bring it into line with his own special theological outlook and interests.

Many of his additions to the Genesis–Exodus narrative would seem to have been derived from traditional Jewish folklore, since parallels are found elsewhere. His account of how Abraham protested to his father Terah about his worship of idols, how one night Abraham set fire to 'the idols' house', and how his brother Nahor perished in trying to save the idols,[5] has parallels not only in The Apocalypse of Abraham,[6] but also in Rabbinic sources;[7] and, similarly, 'Tharmuth', the name given to Pharaoh's daughter, who rescued Moses from the bullrushes,[8] is paralleled by the 'Thermuthis' of Josephus.[9] No doubt, too, many of the names of the patriarchal wives[10] were also derived from tradition. But in any case, whether such details were traditional in origin, or whether the author himself invented them, there is abundant evidence of his concern throughout to trace all the social and religious institutions of which he most approved back to the earliest times, to uphold and assert the eternal validity of the Law, and to present the patriarchs as the exemplary saints of Israel's past, who had in fact observed the Law in all its particulars before it was formally promulgated.

The wearing of clothes, for example, is said to have originated in a specific obligation laid by God on Adam when he left the Garden of Eden, in accordance with the prescription 'on the heavenly tablets that all those familiar with the provisions of the law should cover their shame and not uncover themselves as the Gentiles

---

[5] xii. 1–14.   [6] Apoc. Abrah. i–viii (see below pp. 369 – 75).
[7] e.g. Midrash *Bereshith Rabbah*, xxxviii. 13, xxxix. 1, 8; T.B. *Erubin*, 53a.
[8] xlvii. 5.   [9] *Ant.* II. ix. 5 (§224).
[10] e.g. iv. 9–33, xxxiv. 20–21.

uncover themselves.'[11] Again, the annual celebration of the Feast of Weeks was 'ordained and written on the heavenly tablets': Weeks had been celebrated in heaven from the Creation: Noah had observed it: so had Abraham, Isaac, Jacob, and Jacob's children; and it was the feast celebrated by Moses and the elders on Mount Sinai at the time of the giving of the Law.[12] And, so that no one might think that anything any of the patriarchs did was discreditable, the deceptions practised by Abraham and Isaac on Pharaoh and Abimelech, described at length in Genesis,[13] are in Jubilees passed over in silence;[14] and the motivation of Abraham's attempted sacrifice of Isaac is ascribed, neither to God nor to Abraham himself, but to the evil prince Mastema, who prompts God to test Abraham (much as in the Bible Satan prompts God to test Job) and in the event is put to shame by Abraham's faithfulness in obeying the Divine command.[15]

By far the most notable feature about the book, however, is the author's very evident interest in chronology and calendars. A calendar of some kind was, of course, an essential requisite for the correct regulation of the various feasts; and the calendar followed in Jubilees seems to presuppose a year divided into 12 months of 30 days each, with an extra day added at the end of every third month (or, more accurately, at the beginning of every fourth – or first). Such an arrangement results in a year of 4 quarters, each of 91 days (or exactly 13 weeks), making 52 weeks and 364 days in all.[16] This calendar was not the only calendar in use in the author's day, as he himself clearly recognized;[17] but it had the advantage of simplicity, in that the days of the week and of the month were the same in each successive year, and that the feasts always fell regularly on the first day of the week in which they occurred.

Fundamental to any calendar must be the week of seven days ordained by God at the Creation. In Lev. xxv the idea of the seven-day week had already been extended to cover not only an additional time-period of seven years (i.e. a week of years), but also a further one of 'seven times seven' (i.e. forty-nine) years, with a

[11] iii. 30–31.
[12] vi. 17–19.
[13] Gen. xii. 10–20, xx. 1–18, xxvi. 1–17.
[14] At xiii. 11, xvi. 10, xxiv. 8–17.
[15] xvii. 15 – xviii. 11.
[16] See especially vi. 23–35.
[17] vi. 36–38.

fiftieth 'year of jubilee'[18] at the end. It was this extension that caught our author's fancy (or, perhaps, the fancy of some other member of the religious community to which he belonged) and prompted him to extend it even further and adapt it to provide the basis for a complete chronological scheme. In the process the word 'jubilee' changed its meaning. No longer was it just a descriptive epithet applied to every fiftieth year, as it was in Leviticus. Now it was used as a standard technical term to mean the whole of a forty-nine-year period; and so it became the most significant of all the units for the measurement of time – presumably because it was the longest. Consequently, the entire course of history could be divided into jubilees and events dated by reference to a particular jubilee and its appropriate sub-divisions (i.e. weeks of years, years, months, weeks, and days).

Thus, the very first week of the first jubilee of all was occupied with creation and the giving of the 'great sign' – the sabbath.[19] The first five days of the second week were taken up with Adam's review of the animals and his naming of them;[20] and Eve was created during the night between the fifth day and the sixth.[21] The temptation by the serpent is assigned to the seventeenth day of the second month after the conclusion of the first seven-year period (in modern terms '17.2.8')[22] and the expulsion from Eden to the first of the fourth month of the same year (i.e. '1.4.8').[23] Cain was born in the third seven-year period (or 'week' according to the author's terminology) of the second jubilee (i.e. between 64 and 70), Abel in the fourth (between 71 and 77);[24] and Cain murdered Abel in the first 'week' of the third jubilee (between 99 and 105).[25] The birth of Abraham is dated in the seventh year of the second 'week' of the thirty-ninth jubilee (i.e. 1876),[26] the death of Isaac in the sixth year of the first 'week' of the forty-fifth jubilee (i.e. 2162),[27] and the descent of Jacob and his sons into Egypt ten years later – 'on the new moon of the fourth month, in the second year of the third week of the forty-fifth jubilee' (i.e. '1.4.2172').[28] Finally, the Exodus, the

[18] Lit. 'year of the ram's horn (or cornet)' – i.e. the year whose beginning was announced by a ceremonial blast on the ram's horn (Lev. xxv. 9–10).

[19] ii. 1–17.   [20] iii. 1–3.   [21] iii. 4–6.   [22] iii. 17.

[23] iii. 32.   [24] iv. 1.   [25] iv. 2.   [26] xi. 14–15.

[27] xxxvi. 1–18.   [28] xlv. 1.

passage of the Red Sea, and the revelation on Sinai, are dated to the year 2410 (and the completion of the forty-ninth jubilee nine years previously is remarked on in passing): there are yet forty years to run before Israel enters Canaan (on the completion of the fiftieth jubilee, i.e. in 2450); after which 'the jubilees shall pass by till Israel is cleansed from all guilt . . . and the land shall be clean from that day forward for evermore.'[29]

There can be no doubt in the light of all this that the author was a Jew, who lived in one of the later centuries BC; and scholarly opinion has varied between the fifth century and the first, most preferring a date about 100 BC. The earliest evidence for the existence of Jubilees is to be found in the so-called 'Zadokite Fragments' or 'Damascus Document', associated with the sect at Qumran. There are several apparent allusions to Jubilees in the course of this work, and in one passage it is referred to explicitly – 'And the exact statement of the epochs of Israel's blindness to all these [i.e. the ordinances of the Law], behold it can be learned in the Book of the Divisions of Times into their Jubilees and their Weeks.'[30] Some would argue that both Jubilees and the Damascus Document were products of the Qumran sect. But whether this be so or not, we are no better informed about the date of the Damascus Document than we are about the date of Jubilees, and so the reference to Jubilees in the Document does no more than establish the priority of Jubilees. In the Rabbinic literature there is no certain reference to it anywhere.

Among Christians the book seems to have been known comparatively early. So far as our evidence goes, the first Christian to refer to it by name was the blind Alexandrian scholar Didymus (4th cent.); and he calls it 'The Little Genesis'.[31] This was the most popular name for it in the Church, being used, for example, by Jerome (†420).[32] The name 'Jubilees' is first found in Epiphanius (†403), who gives 'Jubilees' and 'The Little Genesis' as alternatives.[33] Another alternative, according to the Gelasian Decree,

---

[29] 1. 4–5.
[30] *Damascus Document*, xvi. 2–4.
[31] Didymus, *Enarr. in I Ioann*. iii. 12. [32] Jerome, *Ep*. lxxviii. 20.
[33] Epiph. *Haer*. XXXIX. vi. 1.

was 'The Book about the Daughters of Adam'.[34] Yet another appears
to have been 'The Apocalypse of Moses,'[35] and another, perhaps,
'The Life of Adam'[36] – though this last work may have been no
more than an abstract, consisting only of parts of the opening
chapters.

Since the book first became known in modern times it has been
argued on purely internal and circumstantial grounds that it was
originally written in Hebrew, though some (notably C. C. Torrey)
have suggested Aramaic. The arguments in favour of Hebrew have
recently been considerably strengthened, not merely by the evidence
of the Damascus Document, but also by the fact that a number of
fragments of Jubilees, from some ten different manuscripts, have
been found in four of the Qumran caves, and all of them are in
Hebrew. A further fragment, also in Hebrew, has been found at
Masada.

At a date unknown a Greek version was made, of which only
extracts now survive, mainly in Epiphanius and the Byzantine
chroniclers Syncellus and Cedrenus. Later on, the Greek version
was translated into both Latin and Ethiopic. Of the Latin there are
substantial surviving fragments, preserved in the same 6th cent.
MS that contains also The Assumption of Moses: these fragments
were edited by Ceriani in 1861, and cover more than a quarter of
the complete text; and according to Rönsch (their next editor), the
date of the Latin version itself was about a hundred years earlier
than the MS – i.e. mid-5th cent. It is probable that there was also a
Syriac version; and if the results of Tisserant's study of what are
apparently extensive extracts preserved in an anonymous late 12th
cent. chronicle are accepted, then the Syriac version was made
direct from the Hebrew, without reference to the Greek, and about
the same time as the Peshitta.

The Ethiopic version alone has preserved the complete text of
the book. Dillmann, the first editor of it, worked from two MSS
only, one in Tübingen (19th cent.) and one in Paris (17th cent.).
Charles, for his edition of 1895, added two more of the 16th and

[34] *Decr. Gel.* v. 4: 'Liber de filiabus Adae, [hoc est] Leptogeneseos, apocryphus'.
[35] Syncellus, *Chronographia* (= *Corpus Scriptorum Historiae Byzantinae*; ed.
W. Dindorf, Bonn, 1829), i, p. 5.
[36] Ibid., p. 7.

15th cents. (in London and Paris). Since Charles's day at least half a dozen other MSS have come to light, of which two are probably of the 14th cent. – the oldest yet discovered.

The translation which follows is a thoroughgoing revision of Charles's translation of his own Ethiopic text. Any conflict of any importance between this text and the text of the Latin fragments (where they are extant) has attention drawn to it in the notes; and it will be found that overall, in these instances, we have preferred the Latin rather more frequently than did Charles. Unfortunately, none of the Hebrew fragments so far available is sufficiently substantial to enable us to establish anything like a continuous text in any part of the book. What does emerge, however, from a detailed study of these fragments is the impression that the Ethiopic version, despite the fact that it is a secondary version, is nevertheless to be accepted as a generally trustworthy and reliable guide to the Hebrew original.

BIBLIOGRAPHY

EDITIONS

Ethiopic

C. F. A. DILLMANN, *Maṣḥafa kufale sive Liber Jubilaeorum, qui idem a Graecis Ἡ Λεπτὴ Γένεσις inscribitur . . . aethiopice ad duorum librorum manuscriptorum fidem primum edidit* (Kiel and London, 1859).

R. H. CHARLES, *The Ethiopic Version of the Hebrew Book of Jubilees, otherwise known among the Greeks as Ἡ Λεπτὴ Γένεσις, edited from four manuscripts, and critically revised through a continuous comparison of the Massoretic and Samaritan Texts, and the Greek, Syriac, Vulgate and Ethiopic Versions of the Pentateuch, and further emended and restored in accordance with the Hebrew, Syriac, Greek and Latin fragments of this Book, which are here published in full* (= *Anecdota Oxoniensia*, Semitic Series viii; Oxford, 1895).

Hebrew

D. BARTHÉLEMY and J. T. MILIK, *Discoveries in the Judaean Desert*, I: *Qumran Cave I* (Oxford, 1955), pp. 82–84.

M. BAILLET, J. T. MILIK and R. DE VAUX, *Discoveries in the Judaean Desert*, III: *Les 'Petites Grottes' de Qumran* (Oxford, 1962), pp. 77–79.

Greek

R. H. CHARLES, *The Ethiopic Version* . . . [as above].
A.-M. DENIS, *Fragmenta Pseudepigraphorum quae supersunt Graeca* (= *PVTG* iii (Leiden, 1970), pp. 70–102).

Latin

A. M. CERIANI, *Monumenta sacra et profana*, I. i (Milan, 1861), pp. 9–54, 63–64.
H. RÖNSCH, *Das Buch der Jubiläen oder Die Kleine Genesis, unter Beifügung des revidirten Textes der in der Ambrosiana aufgefundenen lateinischen Fragmente, so wie einer von Dr. August Dillmann aus zwei äthiopischen Handschriften gefertigten lateinischen Übertragung erläutert, untersucht und herausgegeben* (Leipzig, 1874; reprinted Amsterdam, 1970).
R. H. CHARLES, *The Ethiopic Version* . . . [as above].

Syriac

E. TISSERANT, 'Fragments syriaques du Livre des Jubilés' in *Rev. Bibl.* xxx (1921), pp. 55–86, 206–232 (reprinted in *Recueil Cardinal Eugène Tisserant 'Ab Oriente et Occidente'*, i (Louvain, 1955), pp. 25–87).
    also
A. M. CERIANI, *Monumenta sacra et profana*, II. i (Milan, 1863), pp. ix–x.
R. H. CHARLES, *The Ethiopic Version* . . . [as above], p. 183.

TRANSLATIONS

English

G. H. SCHODDE, 'The Book of Jubilees translated from the Ethiopic' in *Bibliotheca Sacra* (Oberlin, Ohio), xlii (1885), pp. 629–645; xliii (1886), pp. 56–72, 356–371, 455–486; xliv (1887), pp. 426–459, 602–611, 727–745.

R. H. CHARLES, *The Book of Jubilees or the Little Genesis, translated from the Editor's Ethiopic Text, and edited with Introduction, Notes, and Indices* (London, 1902).

——, *APOT* ii, pp. 1–82.

——, *The Book of Jubilees or the Little Genesis* (= S.P.C.K. *Translations of Early Documents*; London, 1917).

German

C. F. A. DILLMANN, 'Das Buch der Jubiläen oder die kleine Genesis, aus dem Aethiopischen übersetzt' in *Jahrbücher der biblischen Wissenschaft*, ii (1850), pp. 230–256 and iii (1851), pp. 1–96.

E. LITTMANN in E. KAUTZSCH, *APAT* ii, pp. 31–119.

P. RIESSLER, *AjSaB*², pp. 539–666.

K. BERGER in *JSh-rZ* II. 3 (1982), pp. 275–575.

GENERAL

G. H. BOX, in R. H. CHARLES, *The Book of Jubilees or the Little Genesis* (London, 1917), pp. vii–xxxiii.

G. L. DAVENPORT, *The Eschatology of the Book of Jubilees* (= *SPB* xx; Leiden, 1971).

A.-M. DENIS, *IPGAT*, pp. 150–162.

O. EISSFELDT, *OTI*, pp. 606–608.

L. FINKELSTEIN, 'The Book of Jubilees and the Rabbinic Halaka' in *HTR* xvi (1923), pp. 39–61.

——, 'The Date of the Book of Jubilees' in *HTR* xxxvi (1943), pp. 19–24.

J.-B. FREY, art. 'Apocryphes de l'Ancien Testament' in *DB Sup* i, cols. 371–380.

K. KOHLER, 'Jubilees, Book of' in *JE* vii (New York, 1904), pp. 301–304.

J. MORGENSTERN, 'The Calendar of the Book of Jubilees: Its Origin and its Character' in *VT* v (1955), pp. 34–76.

P. RIESSLER, *AjSaB*², pp. 1304–1311.

H. RÖNSCH, *Das Buch der Jubiläen* . . . [as above].

L. ROST, *EATAP*, pp. 98–101.

H. H. ROWLEY, 'Criteria for the Dating of Jubilees' in *JQR* N.S.
    xxxvi (1945–6), pp. 183–187.
E. SCHÜRER, *HJPTJC* II. iii, pp. 134–141.
——, *GjVZJC*[4] iii, pp. 371–384.
M. TESTUZ, *Les Idées religieuses du Livre des Jubilés* (Geneva and
    Paris, 1960).
C. C. TORREY, *AL*, pp. 126–129.
J. C. VANDERKAM, *Textual and Historical Studies in the Book of
    Jubilees* (= *HSM* 14; Missoula, 1977).
E. WIESENBERG, 'The Jubilee of Jubilees' in *Revue de Qumran*, III.
    1 (1961–1962), pp. 3–40.
S. ZEITLIN, 'The Book of Jubilees: Its Character and its Signi-
    ficance' in *JQR* N.S. xxx (1939–40), pp. 1–31.
——, 'Criteria for the Dating of Jubilees' in *JQR* N.S. xxxvi (1945–
    6), pp. 187–189.

PROLOGUE

This is the account of the division of the days of the law and of the
testimony, of the events of the years, according to their *year*-weeks
and their jubilees, through all the years of the world, as the Lord
gave it to Moses on mount Sinai, when he went up to receive the
stone tablets of the law and of the commandment, in accordance
with God's command, as he said to him, Go up to the top of the
mount.

I. And it came to pass in the first year of the exodus of the Israelites
from Egypt, in the third month, on the sixteenth day of the month,
that God spoke to Moses, saying, Come up to me on the mount,
and I will give you the two stone tablets of the law and of the
commandment, which I have written so that you may teach them.
2 And Moses went up into the mount of God, and the glory of the
Lord rested on mount Sinai and a cloud overshadowed it for six
3 days. And on the seventh day he called to Moses in[1] the cloud; and
the glory of the Lord looked like a flaming fire on the mountain-

---

[1] Lit. 'in the middle of': Charles would emend to 'out of' to accord with Exod.
xxiv. 16.

4 top. And Moses was on the mount forty days and forty nights; and God taught him the first things and the last things, *and* the division of all the days of the law and of the testimony.

5 And he said, Listen carefully to everything that I tell you on this mountain, and write it in a book so that the generations *to come* may see how I have not forsaken them on account of all the evil they have done in **transgressing** the covenant that I am establishing between me and you on mount Sinai today for *all* their generations.

6 And so, when all these things have happened to them, they will recognize that I am more righteous than they are in all they think and do,[2] and they will recognize that I have kept faith with them.

7 Write down everything, then, that I tell you today; for I know how defiant and stubborn they are, *even* before I lead them into the land about which I swore an oath to their fathers, Abraham, Isaac, and Jacob, saying, To your descendants will I give a land flowing

8 with milk and honey. And they will eat and be satisfied, and they will turn to foreign gods that are powerless to rescue them in their distress; and *then* this evidence will serve as evidence against them.

9 For they will forget all my commandments that I give them and copy the Gentiles, their uncleanness and their shame, and worship their gods; and these will prove a stumbling-block to them, a *source*

10 *of* distress and misery, and a snare. And many will perish; and *others* will be taken captive and fall into the enemy's hands, because they have forsaken my law and commandment, and the festivals of my covenant and my sabbaths, and my holy offerings which I have hallowed for myself in their midst, and my tabernacle and my sanctuary which I have hallowed for myself in the midst of the land

11 to make it the dwelling-place for my name.[3] And they will make hill-shrines and sacred poles and carved images, and each one will worship his own *carved image* and go astray; and they will sacrifice their children to demons and to all the idols they have made in[4] the

12 error of their hearts. And I will send witnesses to them to witness against them; but they will not listen, and they will kill the witnesses and persecute those who seek the law, and they will abrogate and

13 change everything and do what is evil in my sight. And I will hide

---

[2] Lit. 'in all their judgements and in all their actions'.
[3] Lit. 'that I should set my name upon it and that it should dwell *there*'.
[4] Lit. 'and to all the works of'.

my face from them and hand them over to the Gentiles to be taken captive and **to be preyed upon** and to be devoured;[5] and I will drive
14 them out of the land and scatter them among the Gentiles. And they will forget all my law and all my commandments and all my precepts and go astray as regards new moons and sabbaths and
15 festivals and jubilees and *the other* ordinances.[6] And after this they will turn to me from among the Gentiles with all their heart and with all their soul and with all their strength; and I will gather them from among all the Gentiles, and they will seek me, and I will
16 let them find me.[7] And when they seek me with all their heart and with all their soul, I will grant them an age of peace and righteous-ness[8] and set them apart as an upright plant,[9] with all my heart and with all my soul; and they shall be a blessing and not a curse, the
17 head and not the tail. And I will build my sanctuary in their midst, and I will dwell with them and be their God, and they shall be my
18 people in truth and righteousness. And I will not forsake them nor fail them; for I am the Lord their God.

19   And Moses prostrated himself and prayed and said, O Lord my God, do not forsake thy people and thine own possession, and let them not wander in the error of their hearts: deliver them not into the hands of their enemies, the Gentiles, and let them not rule over
20 them and make them sin against thee. Let thy mercy, O Lord, watch over[10] thy people, and create in them an upright spirit; and let not the spirit of Beliar rule over them to accuse them before thee and ensnare them from all the paths of righteousness, so that they
21 perish from thy sight. For they are thy people and thine own possession, whom thou hast delivered with thy great power from the hands of the Egyptians. Create in them a pure heart and a holy spirit, and let them not be ensnared in their sins now or ever.

22   And the Lord said to Moses, I know their contrariness, their thoughts, and their stubbornness, and they will not be obedient till
23 they ackowledge their own sin and the sin of their fathers. And

---

[5] Text 'for captivity and for injustice and for devouring'.

[6] Lit. 'new moon . . . ordinance' (i.e. singulars not plurals).

[7] Lit. 'so that I shall be found by them'.

[8] Lit. 'I will reveal to them abounding peace of righteousness'.

[9] Or 'and set apart for them an upright plant' (i.e. the latter-day community of saints).

[10] Lit. 'be lifted up upon'.

after this they will turn to me in all uprightness and with all their heart and soul; and I will circumcise the foreskin of their heart and the foreskin of the heart of their sons,[11] and I will create in them a holy spirit, and I will cleanse them so that they shall not turn away
24 from me *again*, from that day till eternity. And they will hold fast to me and to all my commandments, and fulfil my commandments;
25 and I will be their father, and they shall be my children. And they all shall be called children of the living God; and every angel and spirit shall know (they shall know indeed) that these are my children, and that I am truly and genuinely their father,[12] and that I love them.

26   And do you write down[13] everything I tell you on this mountain, the first *things* and the last *things* that shall come to pass in all the divisions of the days, in the law and in the testimony, and in the weeks of the jubilees till eternity, till I descend and dwell with them through all eternity.

27   And he said to the angel of the presence, Write for Moses *the account* from the beginning of creation[14] till *the time when* my
28 sanctuary shall be built among them for all eternity, and the Lord appear in the sight of all, and all know that I am the God of Israel and the father of all the sons of Jacob and king on mount Zion for
29 all eternity, and Zion and Jerusalem shall be established.[15] And the angel of the presence, who used to go before the camp of Israel, took the tablets of the divisions of the years, from the time of the creation of the law and of the testimony[16] – *the tablets, that is,* of the weeks of the jubilees according to *their* years, according to all the number of the jubilees according to *their* years,[17] from the day of the creation **until** *the day when* the heavens and the earth are renewed and *with them* all created things both in heaven and on earth,[18] until

[11] Lit. 'seed'.   [12] Lit. 'I am their father in uprightness and righteousness'.
[13] Following two MSS which read 'Do you write down for yourself': the others read 'I will write down for you'.
[14] Lit. 'from the first creation'.   [15] Alternative reading 'holy'.
[16] The reference here is to the idea that the Law was created before the world.
[17] One MS omits the second 'according to *their* years' and Charles bracketed it as an interpolation. This is probably not the only dittograph in the verse; and in several places both text and translation are highly uncertain.
[18] Lit. 'and all their creation according to the powers of heaven and according to all the creation of the earth'.

the day when the sanctuary of the Lord is created in Jerusalem on mount Zion and all the luminaries are renewed as instruments of healing and of peace and of blessing for all the elect of Israel, and that so it may be from that day on as long as the earth lasts.

II. And the angel of the presence spoke to Moses in accordance with the Lord's command, saying, Write the complete history of the creation, how the Lord God finished all his works and all that he created on the sixth day, and kept sabbath on the seventh day, and hallowed it for all ages and appointed it as a sign for all his

2 works. For on the first day he created the heavens which are above, and the earth, and the waters, and every spirit that serves before him – the angels of the presence, and the angels of holiness, and the angels of the spirit of fire,[1] and the angels of the spirit of the winds, and the angels of the spirit of the clouds and of darkness and of snow and of hail and of hoar-frost, and the angels of the depths and of thunders and lightnings, and the angels of the cold winds and the hot *winds* and of winter and spring and autumn and summer, and the spirits of his creatures in the heavens and on the earth and in all the abysses, and the deep darkness and the light and the dawn and the morning and the evening, which he had already

3 prepared and planned.[2] And then we saw his works, and we blessed him and sang praises before him because of all his works;

4 for on the first day he created seven great works. And on the next day he created the vault between[3] the waters, and the waters were divided on that day – half of them went up above and half of them went down below the vault *that was* between[3] them over the earth;

5 and this was the only work he did on the second day. And on the third day he commanded the waters to be gathered together from the surface of the earth into one place, and the dry land to appear.

6 And the waters did so, just as he commanded them; and they receded from the surface of the earth into one place outside the

7 vault, and the dry land appeared. And on that day he created all the seas in their separate gathering-places, and all the rivers, and

---

[1] One MS omits 'and the angels of the spirit of fire'.
[2] Lit. 'which he had prepared in the knowledge of his heart'.
[3] Lit. 'in the middle of'.

the gatherings of the waters in the mountains and all over the earth, and all the lakes, and all the dew of the earth, and the seed that is sown, and all plants that grow, and the trees that bear fruit, and the trees of the wood, and the garden of Eden in Eden;[4] and all
8 these four great works God created on the third day. And on the fourth day he created the sun and moon and stars, and he set them in the vault of heaven to give light on earth, to have charge over day
9 and night, and to separate light from darkness. And God appointed the sun as a great sign on earth to mark the days and weeks[5] and months[6] and festivals and years and weeks[5] of years and jubilees
10 and all the seasons of the years; and it separates light from darkness, and is the source of health, so that everything may be healthy that sprouts and grows on earth. These three kinds *of lights*[7] he
11 made on the fourth day. And on the fifth day he created great sea-monsters in the depths of the waters (these were the first living creatures[8] that were created by his hands), and all the fish that
12 swim in the waters, and all kinds of birds that fly. And the sun rose over them *all* to give them health, over everything that was on the earth – all plants and trees and living creatures. These three kinds
13 *of living creatures* he created on the fifth day. And on the sixth day he created all the wild animals of the earth, and all the cattle, and
14 everything that moves on the earth. And after all this he created man: a man and a woman he created; and he made him master over everything that is on the earth and in the seas, and over everything that flies, and over the wild animals and the cattle, and over everything that moves on the earth, and over the whole earth:
15 over all this he made him master. And these four kinds *of creatures* he created on the sixth day. And there were altogether twenty-two kinds.
16 And he finished all his work on the sixth day – all that is in the heavens and on the earth, and in the seas and the abysses, and in
17 the light and the darkness, and in everything. And he gave us a

---

[4] All MSS add 'for delight' – doubtless a translational variant of 'in Eden', which itself may well be a dittograph of the preceding '(garden) of Eden'.
[5] Or 'sabbaths'.   [6] Or 'new-moon days'.
[7] i.e. sun, moon, and stars.   [8] Lit. 'things of flesh'.

great sign, the sabbath day,[9] that we should work for six days,[10] but
18 keep sabbath from all work on the seventh day. And all the angels
of the presence and all the angels of holiness, these two great
classes – he has commanded us to keep the sabbath with him in
19 heaven and on earth. And he said to us, Behold, I will set apart for
myself a people out of all the peoples, and they shall keep the
sabbath day; and I will hallow them as my own people, and I will
bless them: as I have hallowed the sabbath day and do hallow *it* as
mine,[11] even so will I bless them, and they shall be my people and I
20 will be their God. And I have chosen Jacob's descendants **out of** all
the peoples[12] (for I have seen *him,* and I have marked him down as
my eldest son and hallowed him as mine[11] for evermore); and I will
teach them *the law of* the sabbath day, that they may keep sabbath
21 on it from all work. And so he created in it a sign *that they should be*
like him, *and* that they should keep sabbath with us on the seventh
day, and eat and drink and bless him who created all things, as he
blessed and hallowed as his own[13] a special people out of all
22 peoples, and that they should keep sabbath together with us, and
the doing of his commands should ascend before him for ever like a
23 pleasant soothing odour.[14] There *were* twenty-two patriarchs from
Adam to Jacob, and twenty-two kinds of created things[15] were
made before the seventh day: this *day* is blessed and holy; and
Jacob[16] also is blessed and holy; and so the two together are
24 hallowed and blessed.[17] And to Jacob and his descendants[18] it was
granted that they should always be the blessed and holy ones of the
first covenant and law, even as he had hallowed and blessed the

[9] Lit. 'the day of the sabbaths'.
[10] Or 'keep on working on the sixth day'. If this is the meaning, it may be a
polemic against the Rabbinic custom of beginning the sabbath an hour before
sunset on Friday.
[11] Lit. 'to myself'.   [12] Text '. . . descendants in everything'.
[13] Lit 'to himself'.
[14] Several references to this passage in Christian writers (confirmed by Jewish
tradition) suggest that there is a lacuna in the text here and that the original ran, 'As
there were twenty-two letters, and twenty-two sacred books, and twenty-two
patriarchs from Adam to Jacob, so . . .'
[15] Lit. 'kinds of work'.   [16] Lit. 'that' (i.e. 'the former').
[17] Lit. 'this one serves with that one for hallowing and blessing'.
[18] Lit. 'And to this'.

25 sabbath on the seventh day.[19] In six days he created heaven and earth and everything that he created, and the seventh day God made holy for all his works: that is why he gave the command that whoever does any work on it shall die, and that whoever defiles it

26 shall most surely die. And so you must command the sons of Israel to observe this day to keep it holy and not do any work on it and not

27 defile it, for it is holier than all other days. And whoever profanes it shall most surely die, and whoever does any work on it shall most surely die eternally, so that Israel's sons may observe this day in every generation and not be uprooted from the land; for it is a holy

28 day and a blessed day. And every man who observes it and keeps sabbath on it from all his work, will be holy and blessed for all time,

29 like us. Proclaim the law of this day to the sons of Israel and tell them to keep sabbath on it, and not to make the mistake of thinking they can ignore it,[20] *and* that it is not lawful to do any work that is **unseemly** or do business[21] on it, or draw water, or carry any heavy load through their gates on it, either in or out, and that they should not prepare on it anything to eat or drink that they have not prepared for themselves already in their homes on the sixth day.[22]

30 And they shall not bring in or take out *anything* from one house to another on that day, for that day is more holy and blessed than any jubilee day:[23] that is why we kept sabbath in the heavens before it was made known to any mortal[24] to keep sabbath on it on earth.

31 And the creator of all things blessed it, but he did not hallow all peoples and nations to keep sabbath on it, but Israel only: them alone on earth did he allow to eat and drink and keep sabbath on it.

32 And the creator of all things blessed this day, which he had created

33 for blessing and holiness and glory above all days. This law and statute was given to Israel's sons as a law for ever, for all their generations.

III. And on the six days of the second week, in accordance with God's command, we brought to Adam all the wild animals, and all

[19] Some MSS read 'even as it had been hallowed and blessed on the seventh day'.
[20] Lit. 'not forsake it in the error of their hearts'.
[21] Lit. 'do their own pleasure'. Cp. Isa. lviii. 13.
[22] In the latter part of this verse Charles's suggested re-arrangement of the clauses has been followed.
[23] Text adds 'of the jubilees'.   [24] Lit. 'flesh'.

the cattle, and all the birds, and everything that moves on the earth, and everything that swims in the water, according to their kinds, and according to their species – the wild animals on the first day, the cattle of the second day, the birds on the third day, everything that moves on the earth on the fourth day, and what

2 swims in the water on the fifth day. And Adam gave them all their
3 names; and what he called them, those were their names. And on these five days Adam saw all of them, male and female, according to every kind that was on the earth; but he was alone and had[1] no partner like himself.

4   And the Lord said to us, it is not good for the man to be alone: let
5 us make a partner for him like himself. And the Lord our God made him fall into a deep sleep, and he slept; and he took one of his bones to make a woman[2] (and so the origin of woman was this rib *taken* from Adam's[3] bones), and he built the flesh up *again* in its

6 place and built the woman. And he woke Adam up from his sleep; and he awoke and got up on the sixth day. And he brought her to him;[4] and he recognized[5] her and said to her,

> This is bone from my bones,
> And flesh from my flesh:
> She shall be called my wife,
> Because she was taken from her husband.

7 That is why man and wife are one; and that is why a man leaves his father and his mother and is united to his wife, and they become a

8 single body.[6] In the first week Adam was created, and the rib – his wife:[7] in the second week he showed her to him; and that is why the commandment was given *for women* to keep in their uncleanness –

9 seven days for a male and fourteen days for a female. And after Adam had been in the land where he had been created for forty days, we brought him into the garden of Eden to till *it* and guard it; but his wife they brought in on the eightieth day (only then[8] did she

---

[1] Lit. 'found'.

[2] Lit. 'and he took (for) the woman one bone from among his bones'.

[3] Lit. 'his'.

[4] An alternative reading is 'And he came to her'; but both Gen. ii. 22 and the statement 'he shewed her to him' in verse 8 below support the reading preferred.

[5] Lit. 'knew'.   [6] Lit. 'one flesh'.

[7] Or 'the woman'.   [8] Lit. 'and after this'.

10 enter the garden of Eden). And that is why the commandment is written on the heavenly tablets about a woman that gives birth – If she bears a male, she shall wait in her uncleanness seven days (that is a week to begin with[9]), and *then another* thirty-three days shall she wait for her blood to be purified,[10] and she shall touch nothing that is holy, nor enter the sanctuary, until she completes these days *that

11 are appointed* in the case of a male child. But in the case of a female child she shall wait in her uncleanness fourteen days (that is a fortnight to begin with[11]), and *then another* sixty-six days for her

12 blood to be purified,[10] eighty days in all. And when she had completed these eighty days, we brought her into the garden of Eden; for it is holier than any other place on earth,[12] and every tree

13 that is planted in it is holy. That is why the rule was laid down about *a woman* that bears a child, whether male or female, that she should touch nothing that is holy, nor enter the sanctuary, until these days *that are appointed* for the male or female child are com-

14 pleted. This is the law and the statute which was written down for Israel, that they should observe *it* always.

15 And in the first week of the first jubilee Adam and his wife were in the garden of Eden for seven years tilling it and guarding it; and we gave him work *to do* and taught him all the details of the

16 gardener's craft. And he tilled *the garden*; and he was naked and did not realize it and was not ashamed. And he protected the garden from the birds and wild animals and cattle; and he gathered its fruit, and ate, and put aside what was left over for himself and his wife.[13]

17 And when he had completed seven years there, seven years exactly, in the second month, on the seventeenth day *of the month*, the serpent came and approached the woman; and the serpent said

18 to the woman, Has God commanded you, saying, You are not to eat *the fruit* of every tree of the garden? And she said to it, Of all the fruit of the trees in the garden God said to us, Eat; but of the fruit of the tree in the middle of the garden God said to us, You shall not

[9] Lit. 'according to the first week of days'.
[10] Lit. 'in the blood of her purifying'.
[11] Lit. 'according to the first two weeks'.
[12] Lit. 'than all the earth besides'.
[13] The text adds (through dittography) 'and put aside what was being kept'.

19 eat of it, nor shall you touch it: if you do, you will die. And the
serpent said to the woman, Of course you will not die: God knows
that on the day you do eat of it, your eyes will be opened, and you
20 will be like gods and know good and evil. And the woman looked at
the tree *and saw* that it was agreeable and pleasant to the eye and
21 that its fruit was good to eat, and she took some of it and ate. And
when she had covered her shame with fig-leaves[14] she gave some to
Adam and he ate; and his eyes were opened, and he saw that he
22 was naked. And he took fig-leaves and sewed them together, and
23 made a loin-cloth for himself, and covered his shame. And God
24 cursed the serpent and was angry with it for ever.[15] And he was
angry with the woman because she had listened to the serpent and
eaten; and he said to her,

> I will increase your labour and your pains:
> In sorrow you shall bear children.
> On your husband you shall rely.[16]
> And he shall be your master.

25 And to Adam he said,

> Because you have listened to your wife,
> And have eaten from the tree, from which I commanded
>   you not to eat,
> Accursed shall be the ground on your account:
> Thorns and thistles it shall produce for you,
> And you shall eat your bread by the sweat of your brow,
> Till you return to the earth from which you **were taken**;
> For earth you are, and to earth you shall return.

26 And he made them coats of skin and clothed them, and sent them
out of the garden of Eden.
27 And on the day that Adam went out of the garden he offered
frankincense, galbanum, and stacte, and spices, as a food-offering

---

[14] More exactly 'with the leaves of the aforementioned fig'. According to Jewish
tradition the tree of knowledge was a fig-tree.
[15] Charles was of the opinion that there is a lacuna here and that the text
originally described the punishment of the serpent by the cutting off of his four feet
by the ministering angels.
[16] Lit. 'And your return shall be to your husband'.

of soothing odour; *and so he did every day* in the morning, at sunrise,
28 from the day he covered his shame. And on that day the mouths of
all the wild animals and the cattle and the birds, and of everything
that walks or moves, were shut, so that they could no longer speak
(for *up till then* they had all spoken with one another in a common
29 tongue[17]). And he sent out of the garden of Eden all creatures[18] that
were in it; and they were scattered to the places naturally suited to
30 them,[19] according to their kinds and species. And Adam alone, as
distinct from all the wild animals and the cattle, did he cause to
31 cover his shame. That is why it is prescribed on the heavenly
tablets that all those familiar with the provisions[20] of the law should
cover their shame and not uncover themselves as the Gentiles
uncover themselves.

32   And Adam and his wife went out of the garden of Eden on *the day
of* the new moon of the fourth month; and they settled in the land of
33 Elda (in the land of their creation). And Adam called his wife Eve.
34 And they had no son till the first jubilee; and after this he had
35 intercourse with her. And he tilled the land, as he had been taught
in the garden of Eden.

IV.   And in the third week of the second jubilee she gave birth to
Cain, and in the fourth she gave birth to Abel, and in the fifth she
2 gave birth to her daughter Awan. And in the first *week* of the third
jubilee Cain killed Abel because God[1] had accepted Abel's sacrifice,
3 but had not accepted his.[2] And he killed him out in the open; and his
blood cried from the ground to heaven, accusing him of murder.[3]
4 And the Lord reproved Cain for Abel's murder and **made him a
fugitive**[4] on the earth because of his brother's blood; and he cursed
5 him on the earth. And that is why it is written on the heavenly
tablets, Cursed is the man who strikes another man in secret,[5] and
let all who have seen and heard *it* say, Amen; and the man who has

[17] Lit. 'with one lip and one tongue'.
[18] Lit. 'flesh'.
[19] Or 'the places that had been created for them'.
[20] Lit. 'judgement'.

[1] Text 'he' (or, alternatively, 'we').
[2] Lit. 'but as for Cain, he had not accepted his offering'.
[3] Lit. 'complaining because he had killed him'.
[4] The text reads 'he made him for length'.
[5] Or 'wickedly' or 'treacherously'.

6 seen *it* and not disclosed *it*, let him be *as* accursed as the other. And this is why, when we come before the Lord our God, we report all the sin that is committed in heaven and on earth, and in light and darkness, everywhere.

7   And Adam and his wife mourned for Abel four weeks of years. And in the fourth year of the fifth week their zest for life returned; and Adam had intercourse with his wife once more, and she bore him a son, and he called him Seth – for he said, God has given us another son[6] on earth instead of Abel, because Cain killed him.

8,9 And in the sixth week he begot his daughter Azura. And Cain took his sister Awan as his wife, and she bore him Enoch[7] at the close of the fourth jubilee. And in the first year of the first week of the fifth jubilee houses were built on earth; and Cain built a city and named
10 it after his son Enoch. And Adam had intercourse with his wife Eve, and she bore *him* nine more children.

11   And in the fifth week of the fifth jubilee Seth took his sister Azura as his wife, and in the fourth *year of the sixth week* she bore him Enos.
12,13 He was the first on earth to invoke the Lord by name. And in the seventh jubilee, in the third week, Enos took his sister Noam as his wife, and she bore him a son in the third year of the fifth week, and
14 he called him Kenan. And at the close of the eighth jubilee Kenan took his sister Mualeleth as his wife, and she bore him a son in the ninth jubilee (in the first week, in the third year of that week), and
15 he called him Mahalalel. And in the second week of the tenth jubilee Mahalalel took as his wife Dinah, the daughter of Barakiel, his father's **brother**'s[8] daughter, and she bore him a son in the third week, in the sixth year, and he called him Jared; and in his days the angels of the Lord (those who were called Watchers) came down to earth to teach men to do[9] what is just and right on earth.

16   And in the eleventh jubilee Jared took a wife, in the fourth week of this jubilee, and her name was Berakhah, the daughter of Rasuel, a daughter of his father's **brother**,[10] and she bore him a son in the fifth week, in the fourth year of the jubilee, and he called him
17 Enoch.[11] And he was the first among men born on earth to learn to

---

6 Lit. 'raised up another seed to us'.   7 Spelled *Henoḥ*.
8 The MSS read 'sister's'.   9 Text 'and to do'.
10 The MSS read 'sister'.   11 Spelled *Henok*.

write and *to acquire* knowledge and wisdom; and he wrote down in a book *details about* the signs of heaven according to the order of their months, so that men might know the seasons of the years according

18 to the order of their several months. And he was the first to write a testimony; and he warned the sons of men about what would happen in future generations on the earth,[12] and recounted the weeks of the jubilees, and made known the days of the years, and set in order the months, and recounted the sabbaths of the years,

19 just as we made *them* known to him. And what was and what will be he saw in a vision in his sleep, just as it will happen to the sons of men in every generation till the day of judgement: he saw and knew all of it; and he wrote his testimony and left it[13] as a testimony on

20 earth for[14] all the sons of men for every generation. And in the twelfth jubilee, in the seventh week of it, he took a wife, and her name was Edni, the daughter of Danel, his father's **brother**'s[15] daughter; and in the sixth year in that week she bore him a son, and

21 he called him Methuselah. And he was with the angels of God these six jubilees of years, and they showed him everything on earth and in the heavens, and the power of the sun;[16] and he wrote

22 down everything. And he bore witness to[17] the Watchers, who had sinned with the daughters of men – for these had begun to form unions with the daughters of men[18] and so defile themselves; and

23 Enoch bore witness against *them* all. And he was taken away from the sons of men, and we conducted him into the garden of Eden in[19] majesty and honour; and there he records the condemnation and the judgement of the world, and all the wickedness of the sons of

24 men. And because of him the water of the flood **did not reach** the land of Eden;[20] for he was established there as a sign to bear witness against all the sons of men *and* keep a record of all the deeds

---

[12] Lit. 'and he testified to the sons of men concerning the generations of the earth'.

[13] Lit. 'and placed it'.

[14] Lit. 'upon'. Or, perhaps, we should translate 'and left it as a witness on earth against'.   [15] The MSS. read 'sister's'.

[16] Or 'and they showed him all the power of the sun on the earth and in the heavens'.   [17] Or 'against'.

[18] Alternative reading 'daughters of the earth' (or 'of the land').

[19] Alternative reading 'to'.

[20] That is, Enoch was spared in the flood. The text reads 'And because of him (or 'it') he (i.e. God) brought the water of the flood upon all the land of Eden'.

25 of every generation till the day of judgement. And he burned the incense of the sanctuary, *which is* acceptable before the Lord, on the
26 mount.[21] For the Lord has four *holy* places on earth – the garden of Eden, the mount of the east, this mountain on which you are to-day (mount Sinai), and mount Zion, which in the new creation will be set apart[22] for the hallowing of the earth: through it the earth will be purified[22] from all *its* guilt and its uncleanness in each successive generation.

27 And in the fourteenth jubilee Methuselah took a wife, Ednah, the daughter of Azariel, his father's **brother**'s[15] daughter, in the third week, in the first year of this week, and he begot a son, and
28 called him Lamech. And in the fifteenth jubilee, in the third week, Lamech took a wife, and her name was Betenos, the daughter of Barachel, his father's **brother**'s[15] daughter; and in this week she bore him a son, and he called him Noah, saying, The one who will comfort me for my trouble and all my work, and for the ground which the Lord has cursed.

29 And at the close of the nineteenth jubilee, in the seventh week, in the sixth year of it, Adam died; and all his children buried him in the land of his creation (and he was the first on earth to be buried).
30 And he was seventy years short of a thousand; for in the testimony of the heavens a thousand years are as one day, and this explains why it was written about the tree of knowledge, On the day that you eat from it, you will die. So he did not complete the years of this
31 day, but died during it. After him, at the close of this jubilee, Cain was killed, in the same year: his house fell on him, and he died inside it and was killed by the stones of it; for with a stone he had killed Abel, and by a just retribution he was killed by a stone
32 himself. There is a rule about this on the heavenly tablets, With the instrument with which one man kills another man, with the same *instrument* shall he be killed: if he has done a particular injury to another man, the same *injury* shall be done to him.

33 And in the twenty-fifth jubilee Noah took a wife, and her name was Emzara, the daughter of Rakeel, his father's **brother**'s[15] daughter, in the first year, in the fifth week; and in the third year of it she bore him Shem, in the fifth year of it she bore him Ham, and in the first year in the sixth week she bore him Japheth.

[21] Most MSS add 'of the midday' (or 'of the south').   [22] Lit 'will be hallowed'.

V. And it came to pass when the sons of men began to increase on the earth, and daughters were born to them, that in the first year of this jubilee the angels of God looked on them and saw that they were beautiful; and they took wives from as many of them as they

2 chose. And they bore them sons; and they were giants. And lawlessness increased on the earth, and the way *of life* of every creature[1] became corrupted – men, cattle, wild animals, and birds alike, everything that lives[2] on earth: corrupt were the ways of all of them and of the whole natural order;[3] and they began to devour one another. And lawlessness increased on the earth, and men's

3 thoughts and inclinantions *were* never anything but evil. And God looked on the earth and behold, it was corrupt: the whole natural order was corrupt;[4] and all *creatures* on earth had **done every kind of**

4 **evil** before his eyes. And he said he would destroy[5] man and all

5 creatures[6] on the earth, which he had created.[7] Noah alone found

6 favour with the Lord. And against the angels he had sent on earth his anger was so great that he uprooted them from *the place of* their dominion and commanded us to imprison them in the depths of the earth; and behold, they are in prison there and *kept in a* separate *place.*

7 And against their sons a commandment went forth from him[8] that they should die by the sword and be removed from under

8 heaven. And he said, My spirit shall not remain in men for ever; for they are mortal[6] too, and their life-span[9] shall be a hundred and

9 twenty years. And he sent his sword[10] among them, so that they should kill each other; and they began to kill each other, till all of them had fallen by the sword and were destroyed from the earth.

10 And their fathers were witnesses *of their destruction*; and after this they were imprisoned in the depths of the earth for ever – till the great judgement-day, when sentence will be passed on all whose

[1] Lit. 'of all flesh'.   [2] Lit. 'walks'.
[3] Lit. 'all of them corrupted their way and their order'.
[4] Lit. 'and all flesh had corrupted its order'.
[5] Alternative reading 'I will destroy'.   [6] Lit. 'flesh'.
[7] Alternative reading 'which has been created'.
[8] Lit. 'a voice went from his face'.
[9] Lit. 'their days'.   [10] Alternative reading 'the sword'.

11 way *of life* and behaviour[11] have been corrupt before the Lord. And
    he **will destroy**[12] all of them from their places, and not one **shall be**
12 **left**[12] that he **will not judge**[12] as their wickedness deserves. And he
    will create[12] a new and righteous nature for all his creatures,[13] so
    that in their nature they will never sin again, but all be righteous,
13 each in his kind, always. And the judgement of every one is
    ordained and written on the heavenly tablets, and there is no
    injustice in it: all who stray from the path marked out for them to
    follow, and do not follow it — judgement is written down *for them,* for
14 every creature and for every kind *of creature*. And there is nothing in
    heaven or earth, or in light or darkness, or in Sheol or in the depth,
    or in the place of darkness, which will not be judged; and all their
15 judgements are ordained and written and engraved.[14] From every
    angle he will judge *them,* the great man as a great man, the small
16 man as a small man, and each according to his way *of life*. And he is
    not one to respect persons, nor is he one who will accept bribes,
    when he says he will pass sentence on everyone: if one were to give
    him everything on earth, he would not take notice of the bribes or of
    the person *of anyone,* nor would he accept anything at his hands; for
17 he is a righteous judge. And about the sons of Israel it has been
    written and ordained, If they repent in righteousness, he will
18 forgive all their transgressions and pardon all their sins. It is
    written and ordained that he will show mercy to all who repent of
    all their sins they have committed inadvertently, once every year.

19   And as for all those whose way *of life* and thoughts had become
    corrupt before the flood, no man had mercy shown him but Noah
    only: he had mercy shown him,[15] together with his sons,[16] whom
    God saved from the waters of the flood because of him; for his heart
    was righteous in all his ways *and his life* in accord with what he had
    been commanded, and he had not strayed in any way from the
20 path marked out for him.[17] And the Lord said he would destroy

---

[11] Alternative reading 'thoughts' (as in verse 19).

[12] All these verbs are perfects in the Ethiopic, in all probability through failure on
the part of the translator of the Greek version (from which the Ethiopic was made)
to appreciate the sequence of tenses in the Hebrew original.

[13] Lit. 'works'.   [14] Or 'decided'.

[15] The phrase translated 'show mercy to' in this verse (lit. 'lift the face of') is the
same as that translated 'respect the person of' in verse 16 above.

[16] Lit. 'concerning his sons'.   [17] Lit. 'from anything ordained for him'.

everything on the dry land, men and cattle, wild animals and
21 birds, and everything that moves on earth. And he commanded
Noah to make an ark, to save himself[18] from the waters of the flood.
22 And Noah made the ark in all respects as he commanded him, in
the twenty-**seventh**[19] jubilee of years, in the fifth week in the fifth
23 year. And he went in in the sixth year of it, in the second month,
from the new moon of the second month till the sixteenth *day*. And
he and all that we brought him went into the ark; and the Lord
closed it from the outside on the seventeenth evening.
24 And the Lord opened seven flood-gates of heaven, and the
mouths of the springs of the great abyss (seven mouths in number).
25 And the flood-gates began to pour down water from heaven forty
days and forty nights, and the springs of the abyss also sent up
26 waters, till the whole world was full of water. And the waters
increased over the earth: fifteen cubits higher than the highest
mountains did the waters rise;[20] and the ark was lifted up above the
27 earth, and it floated[21] on the surface of the waters. And the water
remained on the surface of the earth five months – for a hundred
28 and fifty days. And the ark ran aground[22] on the top of Lubar, one of
29 the mountains of Ararat. And in the fourth month the springs of
the great abyss were exhausted and the flood-gates of heaven were
restrained; and on the new moon of the seventh month all the
mouths of the abysses of the earth were opened, and the water
30 began to descend into the depths below.[23] And on the new moon of
the tenth month the tops of the mountains were seen; and on the
31 new moon of the first month the earth became visible. And the
waters dried up from the surface of[24] the earth in the fifth week, in
the seventh year of it; and on the seventeenth day in the second
32 month the earth was dry. And on the twenty-seventh of it he
opened the ark and let out the wild animals and cattle[25] and birds
and every living creature.[26]

[18] Alternative reading 'that he might save him'.
[19] So Charles, in accord with the Samaritan Chronicle and with the support of the dates at the end of chap. iv. All MSS read 'twenty-second'.
[20] Lit. 'fifteen cubits did the waters rise above every mountain'.
[21] Lit. 'moved'.   [22] Lit. 'went and rested'.
[23] Lit. 'into the uttermost (or 'western') deep'.
[24] Or 'the higher parts of' (lit. 'above').
[25] Most MSS om. 'and cattle'.   [26] Lit. 'every moving thing'.

VI. And on the new moon[1] of the third month he went out of the ark
2 and built an altar on that mountain.[2] And he made atonement for
the earth, and took a kid and made atonement by its blood for all
the guilt of the earth; for everything on it had been destroyed, apart
3 from what was in the ark with Noah. And he put its fat on the altar;
and he took an ox, and a he-goat, and a sheep, and kids, and salt,
and a turtle-dove, and young pigeons, and offered *them as* a whole-
offering on the altar, and poured an offering mixed with oil on it,
and sprinkled wine and scattered frankincense over everything,
4 and made a soothing odour, **acceptable** before the Lord. And the
Lord smelt the soothing odour; and he made a covenant with him
that there should never again be a flood to destroy the earth, that
while the earth lasts seed-time and harvest should never cease, *and
that* cold and heat, summer and winter, and day and night, should
5 not change their order or ever cease. And *he said to Noah,* Be fruitful
and multiply on the earth, increase in number on it, and be a
blessing in it. I will inspire the fear and dread of you in everything
6 on earth and in the sea. And behold, I give you for food all the wild
animals and birds,[3] and everything that moves on earth, and the
fish in the waters[4] – *that is,* all things: as *once I gave you* the green
7 plants, *so now* I give you all things to eat. But you must not eat flesh
with its life *still* in it – that is, its blood[5] (for the life of every
creature[6] is in its blood), lest your own blood[7] be required. From
every man, from every **animal**,[8] will I require the blood of man.
8 Whoever sheds man's blood, by man shall his blood be shed; for in
9 the image of God he made man. And do you be fruitful and
10 multiply on the earth. And Noah and his sons swore they would
not eat any blood in any flesh; and in this month he made a
covenant before the Lord God for ever, for every generation of the
earth.
11   It was for this reason that in this month he told you too to make a
covenant with the sons of Israel on the mountain, with an oath,

---

[1] Alternative reading 'on the tenth day'.
[2] Alternative reading 'in that land'.
[3] Lit. 'all winged things'.   [4] Some MSS add 'and cattle'.
[5] Lit. 'flesh with its life, with the blood'.
[6] Lit. 'the life of all flesh'.   [7] Lit. 'your blood in your lives'.
[8] So Charles on the basis of Gen. ix. 5. The MSS read 'everyone'.

and to sprinkle blood on them to ratify the terms of the covenant,[9]

12 which the Lord made[10] with them for ever. And this provision is written *there* for you to observe continually, *namely*, that you should never eat any blood of wild animals or birds or cattle as long as the earth lasts;[11] and anyone who does eat the blood of wild animals or cattle or birds at any time,[11] he and his offspring[12] shall be up-

13 rooted from the land. Command the sons of Israel never to eat any blood at all, so that their names and their descendants[12] may be

14 before the Lord our God continually. And for this law there is no time-limit: it is for ever. They shall observe it in every generation, so that regularly every day they may make atonement on their[13] behalf with blood before the altar: in the morning and in the evening they shall seek forgiveness on their[14] behalf perpetually before the Lord, that they may keep it and not be rooted up.

15 And he gave Noah and his sons a sign that there should never

16 again be a flood on the earth. He set his bow in the cloud as a sign of the eternal covenant that there should never again be a flood on the

17 earth to destroy it. That is why it is ordained and written on the heavenly tablets that they should celebrate the feast of weeks in this month once a year – so as to renew the covenant each year.

18 And this whole festival was always celebrated in heaven from the day of creation till Noah's days (for twenty-six jubilees and five weeks of years); and Noah and his sons observed it for seven jubilees and a week of years, till the day of Noah's death, but after Noah's death his sons became corrupt and ate blood, till the days

19 of Abraham. Yet Abraham observed it, and Isaac and Jacob and his children observed it, till your days; but in your days the sons of

20 Israel forgot *it*, till I restored *it to* them[15] at this mountain. Command the sons of Israel, then, to observe this festival in every generation as a commandment *binding* on them: on one day[16] in the

---

[9] Lit. '. . . on them because of all the words of the covenant'.
[10] Alternative reading 'I will make'.
[11] Lit. 'during all the days of the earth'.
[12] Lit. 'seed'.   [13] Alternative reading 'your'.
[14] Alternative readings 'your' and 'its'.
[15] Alternative reading 'till you restored it'.
[16] So the text, literally translated. The meaning, however, is probably 'on the first day (of the week), in this month, every year' – i.e. always on a Sunday (as we would say in English).

21 year, in this month, shall they celebrate the festival. It is the feast of weeks and the feast of first-fruits, a twofold and double festival:

22 celebrate it, then, as you have been instructed.[17] For I have written in the book of the first law, which I have written for you, that you should celebrate it at its proper time, on one day[16] in the year, and I have explained to you *the details of* its sacrifices, so that the sons of Israel may remember *it* and celebrate it in every generation, in this month, on one day[16] in every year.

23 And on the new moon of the first month, and on the new moon of the fourth month, and on the new moon of the seventh month, and on the new moon of the tenth month are the days of remembrance, festive days also, marking[18] the four divisions of the year: these are

24 written and ordained as a testimony for ever. And Noah observed them himself and ordained them as feasts for future generations,[19]

25 so that they have become a memorial to him. On the new moon of the first month he was told to make himself an ark, and on that *day too* the earth was dry and he opened *the window of the ark* and saw the

26 earth: on the new moon of the fourth month the mouths of the depths of the abyss below were closed: on the new moon of the seventh month the mouth of the depths of the earth was opened,

27 and the waters began to descend into it; and on the new moon of the tenth month the tops of the mountains were seen, and Noah

28 rejoiced. So it was that he observed them and ordained them as feasts[20] as a memorial for ever; and so they are ordained.

29 And they are on record[21] on the heavenly tablets: there is an interval of thirteen weeks between each feast and the next,[22] from the first to the second, from the second to the third, and from the

30 third to the fourth. This makes in all fifty-two weeks,[23] and together they make up a complete year: thus is it engraved and

31 ordained on the heavenly tablets. And no year ever exceeds it.

32 Command, then, the sons of Israel to observe the years according to this reckoning – three hundred and sixty-four days; and these

[17] Lit. 'according to what is written and engraved concerning it'.

[18] Lit. 'in'.

[19] Lit. 'And Noah ordained them for himself as feasts for the generations for ever'.

[20] Lit. 'he ordained them for himself as feasts'.

[21] Lit. 'And they placed them'.

[22] Lit. 'each has thirteen weeks, from one to another is their memorial'.

[23] Lit. 'And all the days of the commandment are fifty-two weeks of days'.

shall make up a complete year. And they shall not change the times of its days or its feasts (for everything must follow in its appointed place); and they shall not leave out any day or pass over any feast.

33 But if they neglect the proper order and fail to observe them as he commanded them, then all their seasons will get out of order and

34 the sequence of the year will be disturbed.[24] Yet all the sons of Israel will forget and be ignorant of the progression of the years:[25] they will forget new moon and festival and sabbath, and so go

35 wrong about the order of the years. For I know, and I tell you now, and it is not something I have imagined; for the book lies written before me, and on the heavenly tablets the division of the days is ordained, so that they should not forget the feasts of the covenant and keep[26] the feasts of the Gentiles, and show themselves equally

36 misguided and ignorant. There will be those who make careful observations of the moon (*despite the fact that* it upsets the seasons

37 and comes in from year to year ten days too soon). Thus the years will come to them all wrong: they will make the day of testimony *a day* of no consequence[27] and an ordinary[28] day a feast day; and they will mix up all the days, the holy with the ordinary,[28] and the ordinary[28] with the holy, and go wrong about the months and

38 sabbaths and feasts and jubilees. This is why I am giving you this command and solemn warning, so that you may pass it on to them; for after your death your sons will upset *everything* through not making *the length of* the year three hundred and sixty-four days only, and so they will go wrong about the new moons and seasons and sabbaths and festivals; and they will eat all kinds of flesh with the blood still in it.[29]

---

[24] The above is a free (perhaps over-free) rendering of a very difficult passage, made even more difficult by the inclusion of an obvious dittograph. Charles's original for verses 32b and 33 ran, 'And they will not disturb its time from its days and from its feasts; for everything will fall out in them according to their testimony, and they will not leave out any day nor disturb any feasts. But if they do neglect and do not observe them according to his commandment, then they will disturb all their seasons, and the years will be dislodged from this *order,* [and theywill disturb the seasons and the years will be dislodged] and they will neglect their ordinances'.

[25] Lit. 'and will not find the path of the years'.

[26] Lit. 'walk according to'.

[27] Lit. '*a day* despised'.   [28] Lit. 'unclean'.

[29] Lit. 'all kinds of blood with all kinds of flesh'.

VII. And in the seventh week of this jubilee, in the first year of it,
Noah planted a vine[1] on the mountain called Lubar, on which the
ark had run aground (one of the Ararat mountains); and it produced
fruit in the fourth year, and he looked after its fruit and gathered it
2 in this year, in the seventh month. And he made wine from it and
put it in a vessel and kept it till the fifth year, till the first day of the
3 new moon of the first month. And he celebrated this feast-day with
rejoicing; and he offered a whole-offering to the Lord – one young
ox, one ram, seven sheep (each a year old), and a he-goat, to make
4 atonement with it for himself and for his sons. And he prepared the
kid first and put some of its blood on the flesh that was on the altar
he had made, and all the fat he laid on the altar where he offered
the whole-offering; and *so he did also with* the ox and the ram and the
5 sheep, and he laid all their flesh on the altar. And he put all the
offerings,[2] mixed with oil, on it. And afterwards he sprinkled wine
on the fire he had previously made on the altar, and put incense on
the altar,[3] and made a soothing odour **acceptable** before the Lord
6 his God. And he rejoiced and drank of this wine, he and his
children with joy.
7   And it was evening, and he went into his tent and lay down in a
drunken stupor and went to sleep; and he lay in his tent naked, as
8 he slept. And Ham saw his father Noah naked, and went outside
9 and told his two brothers. And Shem took his cloak and got up, he
and Japheth, and they put the cloak on their shoulders and **went
10 backwards and**[4] covered their father's shame. And Noah woke up
from his sleep and learnt what his younger son had done to him;
and he cursed his son and said,

> Cursed be Canaan:
> A servant enslaved to his brothers shall he be.

11 And he blessed Shem and said,

> Blessed be the Lord God of Shem,

[1] Or, possibly, 'the vine' (which Adam had brought with him from Paradise: cp.
Midrash *Bereshith Rabbah*, xxxvi. 3).   [2] Lit. 'their offerings'.
[3] Alternative reading '. . . on the fire he made on the altar, and he had previously
put incense on the altar'.
[4] Text 'and with their faces turned backwards they'.

> And Canaan shall be his servant:
12 > God shall enlarge[5] Japheth;
> And God shall dwell in the dwelling of Shem,
> And Canaan shall be his[6] servant.

13 And Ham learnt that his father had cursed his younger son, and he was displeased because he had cursed his son; and he parted from his father, he and his sons with him – Cush and Mizraim and 14 Put[7] and Canaan. And he built himself a city and called it after his 15 wife, Neelatamauk. And Japheth saw it, and envied his brother, and he too built himself a city and called it after his wife, Adata-16 neses. And Shem lived with his father Noah; and he built a city under his father's authority by the mountain, and he too called it 17 after his wife, Sedeqatelebab. And behold, these three cities are near mount Lubar. Sedeqatelebab facing the mountain on its east, Naeltamauk on the south, and Adataneses towards the west.

18 And these are the sons of Shem – Elam and Asshur and Arpach-19 shad (**born** two years after the flood) and Aram and Lud: the sons of Japheth – Gomer and Magog and Madai and Javan,[8] Tubal[9] and Meshech and Tiras. These are the sons of Noah.

20 And in the twenty-eight jubilee Noah began to instruct his grandsons in the precepts and commandments, and in all the statutes that he knew; and he exhorted his sons to do what is right, to cover the shame of their flesh, to bless their creator, to honour father and mother, to love each his neighbour, and to keep them-21 selves from fornication and uncleanness and all iniquity. For it was because of these three things, *Noah told them,* that the flood came on the earth – because of the fornication of the Watchers, who, contrary to the law of their nature, lusted after the daughters of men and took for themselves such wives as they chose: that was[10] 22 the beginning of uncleanness. And they begot sons, the Naphidim, and they were all unalike one another,[11] and they devoured one

[5] Alternative reading 'God shall enlarge the land for'.
[6] Alternative reading 'their'.   [7] Eth. 'Mestrem and Fud'.
[8] Eth. 'Iyuaya' or (alternatively) 'Iyoiya'.   [9] Eth. 'Tobel'.
[10] Lit. 'and they made'.
[11] Or, by a slight emendation, 'they all quarrelled with one another'. However, the text is probably right and refers to the three different kinds of giants mentioned in the latter part of the verse, and even more explicitly in Syncellus's Gk. version of 1 Enoch vii. 1–2.

another: the giant killed the Naphil, the Naphil killed the Eljo,[12]

23 and the Eljo[12] human kind, and one man another man. And everyone sold himself to do what is wrong and to shed much blood;

24 and the earth was filled with iniquity. And after this **they sinned against** the wild animals and birds and everything that moves and walks on the earth; and much blood was shed on the earth, and all men's inclinations and desires were towards what is worthless and

25 evil continually. And the Lord destroyed everything from the earth, because of the wickedness of their deeds; and because of the

26 blood they had shed in the earth he destroyed everything. And we were left, I and you, my sons, and everything that went in with us into the ark.

And behold, I can see what you are doing before my eyes,[13] that you are not following the way of righteousness, for you have begun to tread the path to destruction: you are separating from one another and are envious of one another, and *so it comes about*, my

27 sons, that you are not in harmony, each *of you* with his brother. I can see the demons have begun *their* seductions against you and against your children; and I am afraid for you, that after my death you will shed men's blood on the earth, and that you too will be

28 destroyed from the earth. For whoever sheds man's blood, and whoever eats the blood of any living creature,[14] shall be destroyed

29 altogether from the earth. And no man that eats blood shall be left on the earth, or that sheds the blood of man,[15] nor shall there be left to him any offspring or descendants[16] under heaven; for to Sheol shall they go, and into the place of punishment shall they go down, and to the darkness of the deep shall they all be removed by a

30 violent death. There shall be no blood seen on you of any of the blood shed when you kill any animals or cattle or birds on the earth; and do *then* what is right[17] and cover what has been shed on

31 the earth. And you shall not be like the man that eats *meat* with the blood *still in it,* and take care that no one eats blood in your

[12] Alternative reading 'Iliyo'. In Syncellus 'Elioud'.

[13] Lit 'your works before me': alternative reading 'the beginning of your works'.

[14] Lit. 'any flesh'.

[15] Alternative reading 'the blood of any man'.

[16] Lit. 'any seed or descendants': alternative reading 'any seed of his descendants.'

[17] Lit. 'and do a good work to your souls'.

company: cover the blood, for so I have been commanded to
32 instruct you and your children and all mankind.[18] Never allow the
life[19] to be eaten with the flesh, so that your blood (which is your
life[19]) may not be asked for from any creature[18] that sheds it on the
33 earth. For the earth will not be clean from the blood that has been
shed on it: *only* through the blood of him that shed it will the earth
be purified through all its generations.

34 And now, my children, listen: act justly[20] and do what is right, so
that you **may be planted** in righteousness over the whole earth and
your glory exalted before my God, who saved me[21] from the waters
of the flood. And behold, you will go and build yourselves cities,
and you will plant in them all the plants that there are upon the
36 earth, and also all trees that bear fruit. For three years the fruit of
everything that can be eaten must not be gathered; and in the
fourth year its fruit shall be reckoned holy,[22] and they shall offer the
first-fruits, acceptable before the Most High God, who created
heaven and earth and all things.[23] Let them offer it sprinkled with
the first of the wine and the oil *as* first-fruits on the altar of the Lord,
who receives it; and what is left let the servants of the Lord's house
37 eat before the altar which receives *it*. And in the fifth year[24] let *the
land* lie fallow, so that you let it lie fallow in righteousness and
honestly; and you will be righteous, and all your orchards will be
38 ritually pure. For so your great-great-grandfather,[25] Enoch, commanded his son Methuselah, and Methuselah his son Lamech,
and Lamech commanded me *to observe* everything his fathers had
39 commanded him. And I also give you commandment, my sons, as
Enoch commanded his son in the first jubilees: while still living,
the seventh in his generation, he commanded and instructed his
son and his grandsons till the day of his death.

VIII. In the twenty-ninth jubilee, in the first week, in the beginning
of it, Arpachshad took a wife, and her name was Rasuejah, the

---

[18] Lit. 'flesh'.   [19] Lit. 'soul'.
[20] Alternative reading 'honestly'.   [21] Alternative reading 'us'.
[22] Alternative reading 'its fruit may be gathered'.
[23] Some MSS om. 'and all things'.
[24] Charles supposed that there was a lacuna here, since what follows would seem
to be appropriate to the seventh year.
[25] Lit. 'the father of your father'.

daughter of Susan, Elam's daughter; and she bore him a son in the
2 third year in this week, and he called him Kainam. And the boy
grew up, and his father taught him writing;[1] and he went to look for
3 a place where he could found a city. And he came upon a writing
which some men of old time had carved on a rock, and he read
what was on it and transcribed it;[2] and he sinned because of it, for it
contained the teaching of the Watchers, in accordance with which
they used to observe the omens of[3] the sun and moon and stars in
4 all the signs of heaven. And he wrote it down and said nothing
about it; for he was afraid to tell Noah about it in case he might be
angry with him because of it.

5 And in the thirtieth jubilee, in the second week, in the first year
of it, he took a wife, and her name was Melka, the daughter of
Madai,[4] Japheth's son; and in the fourth year she bore him a son,
6 and he called him Shelah, for he said, Truly I have been sent. And
Shelah grew up and took a wife, and her name was Muak, the
daughter of Kesed, his father's brother: *this was* in the thirty-first
7 jubilee, in the fifth week, in the first year of it. And she bore him a
son in the fifth year of it, and he called him Eber; and he took a wife,
and her name was Azurad, the daughter of Nimrod[5] – in the
thirty-second jubilee, in the seventh week, in the third year of it.
8 And in the sixth year of it, she bore him a son, and he called him
Peleg,[6] for in the days when he was born Noah's sons began to
divide the earth among themselves (that is why he called him
9 Peleg). And they divided *it* secretly[7] among themselves, and they
told Noah.

10 And it was at the beginning of the thirty-third jubilee that they
divided the earth into three parts, *one part* for Shem and *one* for Ham
and *one* for Japheth, a share for each,[8] in the first year, in the first
week, while one of us, who had been sent to them, was with them.
11 And he called his sons and they came to him, they and their

---

[1] Or '(the) book(s)'.

[2] Or 'translated it': or, by a slight emendation, 'it led him astray' (so Charles).

[3] Alternative readings 'the chariot of' or 'the wheel of' (with reference to the Zodiac?).

[4] So Syr. and a Gk. scholion: Eth. 'Abadai'. Cp. vii. 19, ix. 9, x. 35 – 36.

[5] Eth. 'Nebrod'.   [6] Eth. 'Falek'.

[7] Or 'in wickedness'.   [8] Lit. 'according to the inheritance of each'.

children; and he[9] divided the earth by drawing lots *to decide* what *each of* his three sons should have, and they stretched out their hands and took their lot[10] out of their father Noah's lap.

12 And Shem drew as his lot[11] the middle of the earth, to take *it* as his patrimony and his sons' patrimony for ever – from the middle of the mountain range of Rafa, from the mouth of the river Tina;[12] and his share goes westwards through the middle of this river and extends as far as the water of the abysses, out of which this river rises and pours its waters into the sea *of* Miot,[13] and this river flows into the great sea (and all that is on the north is Japheth's and all

13 that is on the south belongs to Shem). And it extends as far as

14 Karaso[14] – this is in the heart[15] of the tongue that faces south. And his share extends along the great sea in a straight line till it reaches the west of the tongue that faces south; for this sea is called the

15 tongue of the Egyptian sea. And it turns from here southwards, towards the mouth of the great sea, on the shores of *its* waters; and it extends to the west to[16] Afra[17] as far as the waters of the river Gihon, and to the south of the waters of Gihon, to the banks of this

16 river. And it extends eastwards as far as the garden of Eden, to the south of it, [to the south] and from the east of the whole land of Eden and of the whole east, and it turns to the east and goes on till it reaches the east of the mountain called Rafa, and it goes down to

17 the bank of the mouth of the river Tina.[18] This share fell by lot to Shem and to his sons as an eternal possession for his descendants for ever.

18 And Noah rejoiced that this share had fallen to Shem and to his sons, and he remembered everything he had uttered with his mouth in his prophecy; for he had said,

---

[9] Alternative reading 'they'. [10] Lit. 'took the writing'.
[11] Lit. 'And there came out on the writing as Shem's lot'.
[12] Lit. 'from the mouth of the water from the river Tina'.
[13] Alternative reading 'Meat'. [14] Alternative reading 'Karan'.
[15] Lit. 'bosom'. [16] Alternative reading 'of'.
[17] Alternative readings 'Afara', 'Arafa', 'Wafara'.
[18] There is obviously some geographical confusion in this verse. Charles proposed to read 'north' for 'south' (and also 'west' for 'east' in the clause 'and it turns to the east'). In later Ethiopic tradition, and in some of the following chapters of Jubilees, the words for 'north' and 'south' were often given contrary meanings.

> Blessed be the Lord God of Shem,
> And may the Lord dwell in the dwelling of Shem.

19 And he knew that the garden of Eden is the holy of holies and the Lord's dwelling place, and mount Sinai the centre of the desert, and mount Zion the centre of the navel of the earth: these three
20 were created as holy places facing one another. And he blessed the God of gods, who had put the Lord's word into his mouth, even the
21 Lord for evermore. And he knew that Shem and his sons were blessed[19] for ever – the whole land of Eden, and the whole land of the Red Sea, and the whole land of the east, and India, and Bairetra[20] and its mountains, and all the land of Bashan,[21] and all the land of Lebanon and the islands of Caphtor, and all the mountains of Senir and Amana, and the mountains of Asshur in the north, and all the land of Elam, Asshur, and Babel, and Susa, and Media, and all the mountains of Ararat, and all the region beyond the sea, which is beyond the mountains of Asshur northwards, a blessed and spacious land, and all that is in it is very good.

22 And Ham drew the second share – *what lies* beyond the Gihon southwards, to the right of the garden; and it extends southwards as far as all the fiery mountains; and it extends westwards to the sea of Atel, and further still[22] till it reaches the sea of Mauk (that *is the*
23 *sea* into which everything that does not[23] perish descends). And it goes northwards to the boundaries of Gadir and out to the coast of the waters of the sea, to the waters of the great sea, till it reaches the river Gihon, and the river Gihon goes along till it reaches the right
24 of the garden of Eden. And this is the land that fell to Ham in the division, which he was to occupy for ever, he and his sons, generation after generation for ever.

25 And Japheth drew the third share – *what lies* beyond the river Tina, to the north of its waters' outflow; and it extends on the north-east to the whole region of Gog and to all the country east of

---

[19] Lit. 'that a share of blessing and a blessed one had come to Shem and to his sons'.

[20] Perhaps (through the Gk. 'Ερυθρά) a mistranslation of Edom.

[21] Eth. 'Basa': alternative readings 'Bala' and 'Basor'.

[22] Lit. 'and it extends westwards'.

[23] One MS omits 'not'. According to Charles the sense required is 'if anything descends into it, it perishes' – this sea being Oceanus in the extreme west.

26 it. And it extends northwards as far as the mountains of Qelt[24] and
to the sea of Mauk; and it goes to the east of Gadir as far as the
27 region of the waters of the sea. And it goes on until it reaches the
west of Fara[25] and returns towards Aferag;[26] and it extends east-
28 wards to the waters of the sea of Meat. And in a north-easterly
direction it extends to the region of the river Tina till it reaches the
boundary of its waters towards the mountain Rafa; and *then* it turns
29 round towards the north. This is the land that fell to Japheth and
his sons as the share for them to hold as their patrimony, generation after generation for ever – five large islands, and a large *tract of*
30 land in the north. But it is cold. Ham's land is hot. And Shem's is
neither hot nor cold, but a blend of cold and heat.

IX. And Ham divided *his land* among his sons; and the first share
fell to Cush – *that is* the eastern part, and to the west of him was
Mizraim, and to the west of him Put, and to the west of him
Canaan, and to the west of him the sea.[1]
2 And Shem also divided *his land* among his sons; and the first
share fell to Elam and his sons – *what lies* east of the river Tigris till
it reaches the east, the whole land of India, and the Red Sea coast[2],
and the waters of Dedan, and all the mountains of Mebri and Ela[3],
and all the land of Susa, and all that is on the side of Pharnak[4] to
3 the Red Sea and the river Tina. And the second share fell to Asshur
– all the land of Asshur and Nineveh and Shinar as far as the
4 border of India, and it goes up to the river Wadafa. And the third
share fell to Arpachshad – all the land of the region of the Chaldees
to the east of the Euphrates, that borders on the Red Sea, and all

[24] Text 'And it extends northwards to the north, and it extends to the mountains of Qelt towards the north'.
[25] Alternative readings 'Fera' and 'Fereg'.
[26] Alternative reading 'Afreg'.

[1] The translation of this verse is uncertain. Charles rendered '. . . Put, and to the west of him [and to the west thereof] on the sea for Canaan', and understood the sense to be that Canaan's allotted share extended from Libya (= Put) to the Atlantic (cp. x. 28 ff.).
[2] Lit. 'and on the Red Sea on its coast'.
[3] Alternative reading 'Mazbara and Elam'.
[4] Alternative readings 'Phernak' and 'Pherernak'.

the waters of the desert close to the tongue of the sea that looks towards Egypt, all the land of Lebanon and Senir and Amana to
5 the border of the Euphrates. And the fourth share fell to Aram – all the land of Mesopotamia between the Tigris and the Euphrates to the north of the Chaldees, to where it reaches the mountains of
6 Asshur and the land of Ararat. And the fifth share fell to Lud – the mountains of Asshur and all that belongs to them till it reaches the great sea, and till it reaches the east of Asshur his brother.

7   And Japheth also divided the land of his patrimony among his
8 sons. And the first share fell to Gomer – *what lies* to the east, from the north side to the river Tina. And in the north there fell to Magog all the inner parts of the north, till it reaches the sea of
9 Meat. And to Madai fell as his share to occupy *what lies* west[5] of his
10 two brothers to the islands and the coasts of the islands. And the fourth share fell to Javan – all the islands[6] towards the border of
11 Lud. And the fifth share fell to Tubal – *what lies* in the middle of the tongue that runs towards the border of Lud's share, as far as the second tongue, as far as the region beyond the second tongue, as far
12 as the third tongue. And the sixth share fell to Meshech – all the
13 region beyond the third tongue till it reaches the east of Gadir. And the seventh share fell to Tiras – four great islands in the middle of the sea, which stretch as far as Ham's share. (And the islands of Kamaturi fell by lot to the sons of Arpachshad as *part of* his patrimony[7].)

14   And so Noah's sons divided *their lands* among their sons in the presence of their father Noah; and he bound them all by an oath, putting a curse on anyone that tried to seize what[8] had not fallen *to*
15 *him* by lot. And they all said, So be it, So be it, for themselves and their sons for ever, in every generation till the day of judgement, when the Lord God will judge them with sword and fire for all their uncleanness and the wickedness of their misdeeds,[9] with which they have filled the earth – with transgression and uncleanness and fornication and sin.

---

[5] Lit. 'from the west'.   [6] Lit. 'every island and the islands'.
[7] Charles square-bracketed this sentence as an interpolation, on the grounds that the text is here dealing with the sons of Japheth, whereas Arpachshad was a son of Shem and has already been mentioned in verse 4 above.
[8] Lit. 'the share which'.   [9] Lit. 'for all the unclean wickedness of their errors'.

X. And in the third week of this jubilee the unclean demons began to lead the children of Noah's sons astray and to mislead them and
2 destroy them. And Noah's sons came to their father Noah and told him about the demons that were misleading and blinding and
3 killing his grandsons. And he prayed before the Lord his God, and said,

> God of the spirits of all mankind, who hast shown
>   mercy to me,
> And hast saved me and my sons from the waters of the
>   flood,
> And didst not leave me to perish[1] as thou didst those
>   doomed to perdition;[2]
> For thy grace has been great towards me,
> And great has been thy mercy to my soul.
> Let thy grace be exalted upon my sons,
> And let not wicked spirits rule over them
> And destroy them from the earth.

4 But do thou bless me and my sons, that we may be fruitful and
5 increase and fill the earth. And thou knowest what thy Watchers, the fathers of these spirits, did in my day; and as for these spirits which are now alive, imprison them and hold them securely in the place of punishment, and let them not bring destruction on thy servant's sons, my God, for these are malevolent and created in
6 order to destroy. And let them have no dominion over the spirits of the living, for thou alone knowest how to deal with them;[3] and let them have no power over the sons of the righteous, either now or ever.

7,8   And the Lord our God ordered us to bind *them* all. And Mastema, the chief of the spirits, came and said, O Lord, creator, let some of them remain before me, and let them listen to what I say and do everything I tell them; for if some are not left me, I shall not be able to exercise over men the authority I want; for these are *destined* for corruption and to be led astray[4] before my judgement, for great is

---

[1] Alternative reading 'And hast not forgotten me so that I perished'.
[2] Lit. 'the sons of perdition'.   [3] Lit. 'their judgement (nature)'.
[4] Lit. 'and leading astray'.

9 the wickedness[5] of men. And he said, let a tenth of them remain before him, and let nine tenths go down into the place of punish-
10 ment. And he commanded one of us to teach Noah all the remedies against them (for he knew they would not live upright lives, nor
11 even try to do what is right). And we did as he told us: all the malevolent *and* evil ones we imprisoned in the place of punishment, and a tenth we left as agents of punishment under Satan[6] on the
12 earth. And we explained to Noah all the remedies against their diseases, together with their seductions,[7] *and* how to heal them with
13 herbs.[8] And Noah wrote down everything in a book, as we instructed him about every kind of remedy: thus were the evil spirits kept
14 from *doing harm to* Noah's sons. And he gave everything he had written to Shem, his eldest son; for he loved him most of all his sons.

15   And Noah slept with his fathers and was buried on mount Lubar
16 in the land of Ararat. He completed nine hundred and fifty years in
17 all – nineteen jubilees, two weeks, and five years. And in his life on earth he surpassd *all* mortal men in achieving perfect righteous-ness, except Enoch; for Enoch had a special function to be a witness to the world's generations and report all the deeds of each generation till the day of judgement.

18   And in the thirty-third jubilee, in the first year, in the second week, Peleg took a wife, whose name was Lomna, the daughter of Shinar;[9] and she bore him a son in the fourth year of this week, and he called him Reu,[10] for he said, Behold the sons of men have become evil through their wicked purpose of building a city and a
19 tower in the land of Shinar. (For they had left the land of Ararat and moved eastwards to Shinar; and in his days they built the city
20 and the tower, saying, Come, let us go up into heaven by it.) And they began to build; and in the fourth week they baked *bricks* in the fire, and the bricks served them for stone; and the clay they bonded them with was asphalt, which comes out of the sea and out of the
21 fountains of water in the land of Shinar. And they were forty-three

[5] Alternative reading 'judgement'.
[6] Lit. 'that they might punish before Satan'.
[7] Alternative reading 'evil effects'.
[8] Lit. 'the trees of the earth'.   [9] Eth. 'Sinaar'.
[10] Eth. 'Ragau'. The name in the original was, of course, a pun on the Hebrew for 'evil'.

years building it: they built it entirely of bricks (each *brick* was
†thirteen cubits† wide, and the height *of each* a third of its width):
its height *altogether* amounted to five thousand, four hundred, and
thirty-three cubits, and two palms, and *the extent of one wall was*
22 thirteen stades, *and of the other thirty stades*.[11] And the Lord our God
said to us, Behold, they are one people: they have begun to do this,
and now they will not stop. Come, let us go down and confound
their tongues, so that they cannot understand one another, and be
dispersed into cities and nations, and thus have no common
23 purpose[12] till the day of judgement. And the Lord went down, and
we went down with him, to inspect the city and the tower that the
24 sons of men had built. And he confounded all their tongues,[13] and
in consequence they no longer understood one another's speech
25 and left off building the city and the tower. This is why the whole
land of Shinar is called Babel, because the Lord confounded there
all men's tongues; and from there they were dispersed to their
26 *various* cities, each according to his language and his nation. And
the Lord sent a violent wind against the tower and levelled it with
the ground (its site is between Asshur and Babylon in the land of
27 Shinar), and they called it, Collapse. *It was* in the fourth week of the
first year, at the beginning of it, in the thirty-fourth jubilee, that
they were dispersed from the land of Shinar.

28   And Ham and his sons went into the land set aside for him,
which he had been allotted as his share in the land of the south.[14]
29 And Canaan saw the land of Lebanon as far as the river of Egypt,
that it was very good, and did not go to the land that had fallen to
him in the west by the sea, but settled in the land of Lebanon
30 between the Jordan region and the sea.[15] And his father Ham, and
Cush and Mizraim, his brothers, said to him, You have settled in a
land that is not yours and that did not fall to us by lot. Do not do it.

[11] The details of the text of this passage are very problematical; and in the
translation the final clause (about the walls) has been filled out from the description
in Nicephorus's *Catena* (i. 175), which seems to be directly dependent on Jubilees.
Several Christian writers give similar, though not identical, particulars about the
construction and size of the building.

[12] Lit. 'and thus one purpose will no longer remain with them'.

[13] Lit. 'all speech of their tongues'.   [14] Or 'north': see note on viii. 16.

[15] Charles rendered '. . . Lebanon, eastward and westward from the border of
Jordan and from the border of the sea'.

If you do, you and your sons will be reduced to ruin in the land and bring a curse upon yourselves because of *your* rebellious act; for as a rebel you have settled, and by rebellion will your children be
31 reduced to ruin and you will be rooted up for ever. Do not encroach on Shem's patrimony,[16] for to Shem and his sons it fell by lot.
32 Cursed you are, and cursed you will be more than all the sons of Noah, as a result of the curse by which we bound ourselves with an oath in the presence of the holy prince and in the presence of our
33 father Noah. But he took no notice of them and settled in the land of Lebanon, from Hamath to the entrance of Egypt, he and his sons
34 till this day. And this is why that land is called Canaan.
35   And Japheth and his sons went towards the sea and settled in the land allotted to them;[17] and Madai looked at the land of the sea and was not pleased with it, and he begged a share from Elam and Asshur and Arpachshad, his wife's brother, and settled in the land
36 of Media, near his wife's brother, till this day. And they called the place where he and his sons settled, Media, after the name of their father Madai.

XI.   And in the thirty-fifth jubilee, in the third week, in the first year of it, Reu took a wife, and her name was Ora, the daughter of Ur, the son of Chesed; and she bore him a son, and he called him Serug, in the seventh year of this week in this jubilee.
2   And Noah's sons began to make war on each other, to take one another captive, and to kill each other, and to shed men's blood on the earth, and to eat blood, and to build strong cities and walls and towers; and certain individuals *began* to exalt themselves above the rest,[1] and to set themselves up as kings,[2] and to go to war – people against people, and nation against nation, and city against city. And all *of them began* to do evil, to get arms, and to teach their sons to fight; and they began to capture cities, and to sell men and
3 women as slaves. And Ur, the son of Chesed, built the city of Era[3]

[16] Lit. 'Dwell not in the dwelling of Shem'.
[17] Lit. 'the land of their share'.

[1] Lit. 'the people'.   [2] Lit. 'to found the beginnings of kingship'.
[3] Alternative reading 'Ara': possibly we should read 'Eraha' (taking the final *-ha* as part of the name and not as an accusative ending). The more normal form 'Ur' occurs in verses 7 and 8 and subsequently.

of the Chaldees, and called it after his own name and his father's
4 name. And men made for themselves images of cast metal, and
each man worshipped his own image that he had cast for himself;[4]
and they began to make carved images *too*, and unclean figures.
And malevolent spirits egged *them* on and seduced them, so that
5 they indulged in *every kind of* sin and uncleanness. And the prince
Mastema exerted himself to do all this, and he sent out as agents
the spirits that were under his control to do all kinds of wrong and
sin, and all kinds of transgression, to corrupt and to destroy, and to
6 shed blood on the earth. And so they called Serug's name Seruk,[5]
for everyone turned aside after all kinds of sin and transgression.

7   And he grew up and lived in Ur of the Chaldees, near his wife's
mother's father, and he worshipped idols; and he took a wife in the
thirty-sixth jubilee, in the fifth week, in the first year of it, and her
name was Milcah, the daughter of Heber, his father's brother's
8 daughter. And she bore him Nahor, in the first year of this week;
and he grew up and lived in Ur of the Chaldees, and his father
instructed him in the learning of the Chaldees, *how* to divine and
foretell the future from the signs of heaven.

9   And in the thirty-seventh jubilee, in the sixth week, in the first
year of it, he took a wife, and her name was Iscah, the daughter of
10 Nestag of the Chaldees. And she bore him Terah in the seventh
11 year of this week. And the prince Mastema sent ravens and *other*
birds to eat up the seed that had been sown in the land, in order to
destroy the land and rob men of *the fruit of* their labours: before they
could plough the seed in, the ravens pecked *it* from the surface of
12 the ground. And that is why he called him Terah, because the
ravens and *other* birds had reduced them to destitution and had
13 eaten up their seed.[6] And the years became sterile, owing to the
birds, and they ate up all the fruit on the trees: it was only with
great effort that they could save any at all of the earth's fruits in
those[7] days.

14   And in this thirty-ninth jubilee, in the second week, in the first

---

[4] Lit. 'and they worshipped each the idol he had made for himself as an image of
cast metal'.
[5] From the Heb. root *s-r-k*, 'twist, turn' (cp. Jer. ii. 23).
[6] No satisfactory explanation of this reason for the name has so far been given.
[7] Lit. 'their'.

year, Terah took a wife, the daughter of Abram, his father's sister's
15 daughter. And in the seventh year of this week she bore him a son,
and he called him Abram, after his mother's father (for he had died
16 before his daughter had conceived a son). And the child began to
understand the errors of the earth, how all went astray after carved
17 images and uncleanness; and his father taught him writing. And
when he was two weeks of years old, he separated himself from his
father, so that he might not worship idols with him; and he began
to pray to the creator of all things, that he might save him from the
errors of mankind, and that it should not be his lot to go astray after
the unclean and the degrading.

18 And the seed time came for sowing on the land, and they all went
out together to protect their seed from the ravens; and Abram went
19 out with them[8] (and he was a lad of fourteen). And a cloud of
ravens came to eat up the seed; and Abram ran to meet them before
they settled on the ground, and he shouted to them before they
settled on the ground to eat up the seed and said, Keep off:[9] go back
20 to where you came from. And they turned and went away. And he
did this to the cloud of ravens seventy times that day; and not a
21 single raven settled on any of the fields where Abram was. And all
who were with him in the fields saw him shout out and all the
ravens turn back; and his fame spread through all the land of the
22 Chaldees. And all those that wished to sow that year came to him,
and he went with them until the time for sowing was over; and they
sowed their land, and that year they brought home grain in
plenty,[10] and they ate their fill.

23 And in the first year of the fifth week Abram gave instructions to
the carpenters who made the agricultural implements, and they
made a container above ground-level, facing the frame of the
plough, to put the seed in, and the seed fell down from it onto the
ploughshare and was hidden in the earth; and *so* they were no longer
24 frightened of the ravens. And they made *containers* like this above
ground-level on all the frames of the ploughs; and they sowed all
the land and tilled it, exactly as Abram told them, and they were no
longer frightened of the birds.

---

[8] Lit. 'those that went'.
[9] Lit. 'Do not come down'.
[10] Lit. 'sufficient grain'.

XII. And it came to pass in the sixth week, in the seventh year of it,
2 that Abram spoke to Terah his father, saying, Father! And he said,
Behold, here I am, my son. And he said, What profit or advantage
do we gain from those idols that you worship and prostrate yourself
3 in front of? For there is no spirit in[1] them: dumb things they are
4 that only lead us into error;[2] so do not worship them. Worship the
God of heaven, who makes the rain and the dew come down on the
earth, and does everything on the earth, and has created all things
5 by his word, and all life is from him.[3] Why do you worship things
that have no spirit in[1] them, for they are the work of *men's* hands?
You carry them on your shoulders, and you get no help from them.
Rather do they bring no small shame on those who make them, and
mislead the minds of those who worship them. So do not worship
6 them. And his father said to him, I know *it* too, my son; but what
7 shall I do about the people that I serve?[4] If I tell them the truth,
they will kill me; for they cling to them to worship them and honour
8 them. Keep quiet, my son, in case they kill you. And he said the
same to his two brothers, and they were angry with him, so he said
no more.

9   And in the fortieth jubilee, in the second week, in the seventh
year of it, Abram took a wife, and her name was Sarai,[5] his father's
10 daughter; and she became his wife. And Haran, his brother, took a
wife in the third year of the third week; and she bore him a son in
11 the seventh year of this week, and he called him Lot. And his *other*
brother, Nahor, *also* took a wife.

12   And in the sixtieth[6] year of Abram's life, that is, in the fourth
week, in the fourth year of it, Abram got up at night and set fire to

---

[1] Lit. 'upon'.
[2] Lit. 'for they are dumbness and a misleading of the heart'.
[3] Lit. 'from before his face'.
[4] Charles rendered 'but what shall I do with a people who have made me to serve
before them?', which implies that Terah was not just a private craftsman, but either
a municipal employee or under some other external compulsion to make his idols;
and this last interpretation is reinforced by the alternative reading '. . . who have
commanded me to serve . . .'. The translation offered is sufficiently imprecise as to
leave all possibilities open.
[5] Eth. 'Sora' (as in the Eth. Old Testament).
[6] Alternative readings 'second' and 'thirtieth'.

the idols' house and burnt everything that was in the house; and no

13 one knew *about* it. And they got up in the night and tried to save

14 their gods from the fire. And Haran rushed in to save them, but the flames overcame him, and he was burnt in the fire and died in Ur of the Chaldees before the eyes of his father Terah; and they buried

15 him in Ur of the Chaldees. And Terah left Ur of the Chaldees, he and his sons, and set out for the land of Lebanon and the land of Canaan, and he settled in the land of Haran; and Abram lived in Haran with Terah, his father, two weeks of years.

16   And in the sixth week, in the fifth year of it, Abram sat up all through the night of the new moon of the seventh month to observe the stars from evening till morning, in order to discover how the rains would fall that year; and he was alone as he sat and observed.

17 And a thought struck him, and he said, All the signs of the stars and the signs of the moon and sun are in the hand of the Lord.

18 Why, then, should I enquire into them? If he so wills, he makes it rain evening and morning, and if he so wills, he withholds the rain;

19 and all things are in his hand. And he prayed that night and said, My God, God Most High, thou alone for me art God: thou hast created all things, and all things that are are the work of thy hands;

20 and thee and thy dominion have I chosen. Deliver me from the evil spirits who have dominion over the thoughts and minds of men, and let them not lead me astray from thee, my God; and establish me and my descendants for ever, that we go not astray either now

21 or ever. And I ask thee, should I return to Ur of the Chaldees, *to those* who beg me[7] to return to them? Or should I rather remain here in this place? Help thy servant to choose[8] whatever is the right path before thee, and let me not walk in the error of my heart, O my God.

22   And he finished speaking and praying, and behold, the word of the Lord was sent to him through me, saying, Leave your country and your kinsmen and your father's house, and go to a land that I will show you; and I will make you a great and numerous nation.

23 And I will bless you and make your name great, and you shall be blessed in the earth, and in you shall all fathers[9] of the earth be blessed; and I will bless those that bless you and curse those that

---

[7] Lit. 'who seek my face'.   [8] Lit. 'do'.

[9] Alternative reading 'nations' (as in the Eth. Old Testament).

24 curse you. And I will be a God to you, and to your son, and to your grandson, and to all your descendants: do not be afraid: from now, and for all time, I am your God.

25 And the Lord God said to me, Open his mouth and his ears, so that he may hear and may speak with his mouth the language which shall be revealed (for it had never been spoken by men since

26 the day of the collapse *of the tower of Babel*). And I opened his mouth and his ears and his lips, and I began to speak to him in Hebrew –

27 the original language.¹⁰ And he took his fathers' books, which were written in Hebrew, and transcribed them and began from then on to study them, and I explained to him everything he could not *understand*; and he¹¹ studied them during the six rainy months.

28 And it came to pass in the seventh year of the sixth week that he spoke to his father and told him that he wanted to leave Haran and

29 go into the land of Canaan to inspect it and come back to him. And Terah his father said to him, Go in peace: may the eternal God make your path straight, and the Lord *be* with you and protect you from all evil, and grant you grace, mercy, and favour, with those who see you, and may no man have power over you to harm you: go

30 in peace. And if it seems to you a pleasant land, and suitable to settle in, then come back and fetch me: take Lot with you *now*, your brother Haran's son, *and treat him* as if he were your own; and the

31 Lord be with you. And leave your *other* brother Nahor *here* with me, till you come back in peace, and *then* we can all go with you together.

XIII. And Abram journeyed from Haran and took Sarai, his wife, and Lot, his brother Haran's son, to the land of Canaan; and he came to Asshur,¹ and wandered about till he came to Shechem,

2 and settled *there* near a lofty oak.² And he looked, and behold, the land was very pleasant from the entrance of Hamath to the lofty

3 oak.² And the Lord said to him, To you and your descendants will I

4 give this land. And he built an altar there and offered on it a whole-offering to the Lord, who had appeared to him.

---

¹⁰ Or 'the natural language'. Alternative readings 'the language that was natural to him' or 'the language of his family'.

¹¹ Alternative reading 'we'.

¹ Alternative reading 'Sur' (= Tyre?).   ² As in the LXX at Gen. xii. 6.

5 And he moved on from there to the hill-country ⟨east of Bethel⟩, *with* Bethel on the west and Ai on the east; and there he pitched his
6 tent. And he looked, and behold, the land was spacious and very good, and everything grew there – vines and figs and pomegranates, oaks and ilexes, and terebinths and olive trees, and cedars and cypresses and frankincense trees,[3] and all the trees of the
7 countryside; and there was water in the hill-country. And he blessed the Lord, who had led him out of Ur of the Chaldees and
8 brought him to this land.[4] And it came to pass in the first year, in the seventh week, on the new moon of the first month, that he built an altar on the hill there[5] and invoked the Lord, Thou art my God,
9 the eternal God. And he offered a whole-offering to the Lord on the altar, so that he might be with him and not forsake him all the days of his life.

10 And he moved on from there and went southwards and came to Hebron (Hebron was built at that time); and he stayed there two years. And he went *on from there* into the land of the south, to Bealoth.

11 And there was a famine in the land; and Abram went into Egypt in the third year of the week and lived in Egypt five years before his
12 wife was torn away from him. (Tanais in Egypt was built at that
13 time – seven years after Hebron.) And it came to pass, when Pharaoh seized Sarai, Abram's wife, the Lord struck Pharaoh and his entire household with severe diseases because of Sarai, Abram's
14 wife. And Abram was held in high esteem on account of his possessions in sheep, and cattle, and asses, and horses, and camels, and male and female slaves, and abundance of silver and gold; and
15 Lot, his brother's son, was also wealthy. And Pharaoh gave back Sarai, Abram's wife, and sent him out of the land of Egypt; and he made his way to the place where he had pitched his tent in the beginning, to the place of the altar, with Ai on the east and Bethel on the west. And he blessed the Lord his God, who had brought him back in peace.

16 And it came to pass in the forty-first jubilee, in the third year of the first week, that he returned to this place and offered there a

---

[3] Or, by a slight emendation, 'date-palms'.
[4] Alternative reading 'hill' or 'mountain'.
[5] Lit. 'on this hill (mountain)'.

whole-offering, and he invoked the Lord by name and said, Thou
17 art the Most High God, my God for ever and ever. And in the
fourth year of this week Lot parted from him; and Lot settled in
18 Sodom (and the men of Sodom were great sinners). And it grieved
him that his brother's son had parted from him; for he had no
19 children. In that year, when Lot was taken captive, the Lord spoke
to Abram (after Lot had parted from him) in the fourth year of this
week, and said to him, Look up from the place you are living in,
20 northwards and southwards, and westwards and eastwards. For
all the land you can see I will give to you and your descendants for
ever, and I will make your descendants as the sand of the sea:[6] even
though a man might count the dust of the earth,[7] your descendants
21 will not *be able to* be[8] counted. Rise up, walk through the length and
breadth of *the land*, and look at all of it; for to your descendants will
I give it. And Abram went to Hebron and settled there.
22   And in this year came Chedorlaomer, king of Elam, and Amraphel,
king of Shinar, and Arioch, king of Sellasar, and Tergal, king of
nations, and killed the king of Gomorrah; and the king of Sodom
fled, and many fell wounded in the **valley of Siddim**, by the Salt Sea.[9]
23 And they captured Sodom and Adam and Zeboim; and they took
Lot captive also, Abram's brother's son, and all his possessions,
24 and **they**[10] went as far as Dan. And a fugitive came and told Abram
25 that his brother's son had been taken captive. And he armed his
household servants . . . for Abram,[11] and for his descendants, the
first tenth to the Lord; and the Lord ordained it as a rule for all time
that they should give it to the priests who serve before him, that it
26 should be theirs for ever. And to this law there is no time-limit; for
he has ordained that in every generation they should give to the

---

⁶ Alternative reading 'of the earth'.   ⁷ Alternative reading 'of the sea'.
⁸ Alternative reading 'will be' – i.e. without the negative (in which case the whole
setence should be translated 'if a man could count the dust of the earth, then your
descendants could be counted').
⁹ Most MSS 'in the salt (or 'desert') country'.   ¹⁰ The MSS read 'he'.
¹¹ The existing text, transmitted by nearly all MSS makes no sense at all. Charles
supposed that although there is no direct evidence for it in the MSS, there is in fact a
lacuna here and that the original text described Abram's pursuit of the four kings,
his attack on them, his recovery of the spoil, and his meeting with Melchizedek – as
in Gen. xiv. 14–20. The scribe of one MS, however, by a slight change in the word
translated 'armed', managed to achieve at least some sense with 'And his household
servants made atonement for Abram'.

Lord the tenth of everything,[12] of seed and wine and oil and cattle
27 and sheep. And he has given *it* to his priests to eat and drink with
28 joy before him. And the king of Sodom came and prostrated himself before him and said, Our lord Abram, grant us the people you
29 have rescued, but let the spoil be yours. And Abram said to him, I
lift up my hands to the Most High God *on oath*, that I will take
nothing that is yours, so that you cannot say, I have made Abram
rich: I will take only what the young men have eaten, and the share
of the men who went with me — Aunan, Eschol, and Mamre. These
shall have their share.

XIV. And after these things, in the fourth year of this week, on the
new moon of the third month, the word of the Lord came to Abram
in a dream, saying, Do not be afraid, Abram: I am your defender,
2 and your reward will indeed be great. And he said, Lord, Lord,
what will you give me, for I have no children, and the son of
Maseq, my slave-girl's son, Eliezer of Damascus, will be my heir:
3 to me you have given no children. And he said to him, This *man*
4 shall not be your heir, but your own son[1] shall be your heir. And he
took him outside and said to him, Look up to heaven and count the
5 stars of heaven, if you can count them. And he looked up to heaven
and surveyed the stars; and he said to him, So shall your descen-
6 dants be. And he believed in the Lord; and it was counted to him as
righteousness.

7 And he said to him, I am the Lord that brought you out of Ur of
the Chaldees, to give you the land of the Canaanites[2] as a possession for ever, and to be[3] your God and your descendants' *God* after
8 you. And he said, Lord, Lord, how shall I know that I shall inherit
9 *it*? And he said to him, Bring me[4] a heifer three years old, and a
goat three years old, and a sheep three years old, and a turtle-dove,
10 and a pigeon. And he took all these in the middle of the month,
11 while he was living by the oak of Mamre, near Hebron. And he
built an altar there and sacrificed all of them; and he poured their

---

[12] Some MSS om. 'of everything'.

[1] Lit. 'one that shall come out of your own bowels'.
[2] Alternative reading 'land of Canaan'.
[3] Alternative reading 'and I will be'.
[4] Alternative reading 'Take'.

blood on the altar and cut *each of* them in two, and laid the pieces[5]
12 out opposite each other; but the birds he did not cut in two. And
birds *of prey* came down on the **pieces**;[6] and Abram drove them
away, and would not allow the birds to touch them.

13   And it came to pass, as the sun went down, a trance came over
Abram; and lo, a horror *of the* darkness came upon him, and a voice
said[7] to Abram, Know for certain that your descendants will be
aliens in a foreign land, and they will be reduced to slavery there
14 and oppressed for four hundred years. But I will punish[8] the nation
that enslaves them, and afterwards they will come out with great
15 possessions. You shall go to your fathers in peace and be buried in
16 a good old age. And in the fourth generation they shall return here;
for the Amorites will not be ripe for punishment till then.

17   And he woke up from his sleep and got up: the sun had set; and
there was a flame, and behold, a smoking brazier, and a flame of
18 fire passed between the **pieces**. And on that day the Lord made a
covenant with Abram, saying, To your descendants will I give this
land, from the river of Egypt, to the great river, *the river* Euphrates —
the Kenites, the Kenizzites, the Kadmonites, the Perizzites, and
the Rephaim, the Phakorites,[9] and the Hivites, and the Amorites,
19 and the Canaanites, and the Girgashites, and the Jebusites. And
that day passed,[10] and Abram offered the **pieces** and the birds and
their cereal-offerings and their drink-offerings, and the fire con-
20 sumed them. And on that day we made a covenant with Abram,
just as we had covenanted with Noah in this month; and Abram
renewed the festival and rule for himself for ever.

21   And Abram rejoiced and told his wife Sarai everything; and he
believed he was to be a father,[11] although *as yet* she had borne *him*

---

[5] Lit. 'laid them'.
[6] The Eth. here, and in verses 17 and 19, literally means 'the things spread out'.
Charles conjectured corruption in the underlying Gk. and suggested two possibilities, either 'pieces' (as in the translation above) or 'carcases'. In this connection it is worth noting that the Heb. text of Genesis has 'carcases' at xv. 11. (parallel
to our verse 12) and '*cut* pieces' at xv. 17 (parallel to our verse 17): to our verse 19 it
has no parallel.
[7] Lit. 'and it was said'.   [8] Lit. 'judge'.
[9] Alternative readings 'Phakerites' and 'Phekarites'. They replace here the
Hittites, included at Gen. xv. 20.
[10] Most MSS 'And he passed'.   [11] Lit. 'that he would have seed'.

22 no *children*. And Sarai counselled her husband Abram and said to him, Take Hagar, my Egyptian maid: perhaps I can found a family
23 for you through her. And Abram listened to what Sarai his wife told him, and he said, Do *as you think best*; and Sarai took Hagar, her Egyptian maid, and gave her to her husband Abram as his wife.
24 And he lay with her, and she conceived and bore a son; and he called him Ishmael, in the fifth year of this week. And Abram was in his eighty-sixth year at the time.

XV. And in the fifth year of the †fourth†[1] week of this jubilee, in the third month, in the middle of the month, Abram celebrated the
2 feast of the first-fruits of the grain[2] harvest. And he offered to the Lord on the altar new offerings, the first-fruits of the produce – a heifer and a he-goat and a sheep as a whole-offering to the Lord on the altar: their cereal-offerings and their drink-offerings he also
3 offered on the altar with frankincense. And the Lord appeared to
4 Abram and said to him, I am God Almighty: prove yourself before
5 me and be perfect. And I will make my covenant between myself
6 and you, and I will multiply you greatly. And Abram fell on his
7 face; and God talked with him and said, Behold, I have decreed a future for you,[3] and you shall be[4] the father of many nations. Your name therefore shall not be Abram, but from now on, till eternity, your name shall be Abraham; for the father of many nations have I
8 appointed you. And I will make you very great, and I will make
9 nations of you, and kings shall spring from you. And I will establish my covenant between myself and you, and your descendants after you, generation after generation, an eternal covenant, that I may be a God to you, and to your descendants after you, generation
10 after generation. ⟨And I will give you and your descendants after you⟩[5] the land where you have been an alien, the land of Canaan, as a possession for ever; and I will be their God.
11 And the Lord said to Abraham, You for your part must keep my covenant, you and your descendants after you: circumcise every

---

[1] So most MSS: one has 'seventh'. Probably 'third' should be read both here and at xvi. 15.
[2] Or 'wheat'.   [3] Lit. 'Behold my decree is with you'.
[4] Alternative reading 'and I will make you'.
[5] Restored by Charles on the basis of Gen. xvii. 8.

male among you, and circumcise your foreskins; and it shall be a
12 sign of my eternal covenant between myself and you. And you shall
circumcise every male child on the eighth day, generation after
generation, *whether* born in your house, or bought with money from
a foreigner – one you have come by, who is not of your own stock.[6]
13 *Every male* born in your house shall be circumcised, and those you
have bought with money shall be circumcised; and *the sign of* my
14 covenant shall be in your flesh as a rule[7] for all time. And every
uncircumcised male, who is not circumcised in the flesh of his
foreskin on the eighth day, shall be cut off from his father's kin; for
he has broken my covenant.

15 And God said to Abraham, As for your wife Sarai, she shall no
16 more be called Sarai, but Sarah shall be her name. And I will bless
her and give you a son by her; and I will bless him, and he shall
17 become a nation, and kings of nations spring from him. And
Abraham threw himself down on his face and rejoiced and said to
himself, Shall a son *indeed* be born to a man a hundred years old,
18 and shall Sarah, who is ninety, bear *a child*? And Abraham said to
19 God, If only Ishmael might live under thy special care![8] And God
said, He shall;[9] and Sarah also shall bear you a son, and you shall
call him Isaac; and I will establish my covenant with him as an
20 everlasting covenant, and with his descendants after him. And as
for Ishmael, I have heard your prayer; and behold, I will bless him
and make him great and multiply him greatly, and he shall be
21 father of twelve princes, and I will make him a mighty nation. But
my covenant I will establish with Isaac, whom Sarah will bear you
22 at this time next year. And he left off talking with him; and God
went up from Abraham.

23 And Abraham did as God had told him, and he took his son
Ishmael, and all those born in his house, and those he had bought
with money, every male in his house, and circumcised the flesh of
24 their foreskins. And on the very same day Abraham *himself* was
circumcised; and all the men of his house, and all those he had
bought with money from foreigners, were circumcised with him.

25 This law is for all generations for ever; and there can be no
reduction in the number of the days, nor omission of even a single

---

[6] Lit. 'seed'.   [7] Alternative reading 'shoot' or 'germ'.
[8] Lit. 'before thee'.   [9] Lit. 'Yes'.

day out of the eight,[10] for it is a rule for all time, ordained and
26 written on the heavenly tablets. And every one that is born, the
flesh of whose foreskin is not circumcised **on**[11] the eighth day, does
not belong among the sons of the covenant which the Lord made
with Abraham, but is marked out for destruction:[12] there is no sign
on him that he is the Lord's; and *his destiny is* to be destroyed and to
perish and to be uprooted from the earth, because he has broken
27 the covenant of the Lord our God. For all the angels of the presence
and all the angels of holiness have been created as they are[13] from
the day of their creation; and, just as *the Lord God hallowed* the angels
of the presence and the angels of holiness, so he has hallowed
28 Israel, that they should be with him and with his holy angels. And
you, for your part, command the sons of Israel to observe the sign
of this covenant in every generation as a rule for all time, so that
29 they are not uprooted from the land. The command is binding on
all the sons of Israel: it is part of the covenant they must observe.
30 For the Lord did not admit into his presence either Ishmael and his
sons and brothers, or Esau, and he did not choose them, although
they were children of Abraham, because he knew them; but he
31 chose Israel as his people. And he hallowed it and gathered it from
all mankind; for there are many nations and many peoples, and all
are his, and he has set spirits in authority over all *of them* to lead
32 them astray from him. But over Israel he appointed no angel or
spirit, for he alone is their ruler; and he will preserve them and hold
his angels and spirits and all his **powers**[14] answerable for them, so
that he may preserve them and bless them, and that they may be
his and he theirs, now and for ever.

33 But I warn you that the sons of Israel will not keep this rule,
neither will they circumcise their sons in accordance with this law;
for, though circumcised themselves,[15] they will neglect the
circumcision of their sons, and the miscreants,[16] all of them, will
34 leave their sons uncircumcised, just as they were born. And great

---

[10] Lit. 'and there is no circumcision (alternative reading 'closure') of the days,
and no omission of one day out of the eight days'.
[11] All Eth. MSS, supported by Lat., read 'till'.
[12] Lit. 'for he is of the sons of destruction'.
[13] Lit. 'have been so created'.   [14] Text 'commands'.
[15] Lit. 'for in the flesh of their circumcision'.   [16] Lit. 'sons of Beliar'.

will be the Lord's wrath against the sons of Israel, because they have forsaken his covenant and turned aside from his word, and provoked *him* and shown their contempt *for him* by not observing the rule as regards this law; for they have treated their members like the Gentiles and will be removed and uprooted from the land. And although there is forgiveness and pardon for all sins, they will never be pardoned or forgiven for this transgression, *not even* in eternity.[17]

XVI. And on the new moon of the fourth month we appeared to Abraham at the oak of Mamre; and we talked with him and told
2 him that a son would be given him by his wife Sarah. And Sarah laughed, for she heard that we had said this to Abraham; and we rebuked her, and she was frightened, and denied she had laughed
3 at what we said. And we told her her son's name, Isaac – just as his
4 name is ordained and written on the heavenly tablets. And *we told her that* when we returned to her at the time appointed, she would have conceived a son.[1]

5 And in this month the Lord executed his judgements on[2] Sodom and Gomorrah and Zeboim and all the Jordan region; and he burned them with fire and brimstone and destroyed them till this day (I have told you *already* everything they did, how they were very wicked and great sinners, and how they defiled themselves and committed fornication in their flesh and abandoned them-
6 selves to *every kind of* vice[3] *there is* on earth. And God will execute a like judgement on places where men imitate the vices[3] of the
7 Sodomites, just as he judged Sodom. But Lot we saved; for God remembered Abraham, and he rescued him from the disaster.
8 Nevertheless, he and his daughters committed sin on the earth, such as there had not been on the earth from the days of Adam till
9 his time – that a man should lie with his daughter.[4] And behold, it was commanded and engraved on the heavenly tablets about all his descendants, that they should be removed and uprooted, and

---

[17] Eth. obscure. The translation represents the most probable sense.

[1] Or 'And when we returned . . . she had . . .'
[2] Lit. 'the judgements of'.   [3] Lit. 'uncleanness(es)'.
[4] Alternative Eth. reading 'daughters', and also Lat.

that judgement should be executed on them exactly as it was on Sodom, and that he should be left no descendants on earth on the *final* judgement-day.

10 And in this month Abraham moved from Hebron and went and
11 settled between Kadesh and Shur in the mountains[5] of Gerar. And in the middle of the fifth month he moved from there and settled at the Well of the Oath.

12 And in the middle of the sixth month the Lord showed Sarah favour and made good his promise to her, and she conceived and
13 bore a son in the third month. And in the middle of the month, at the time the Lord had promised Abraham, on the festival of the
14 first-fruits of the harvest, Isaac was born. And Abraham circumcised his son on the eighth day: he was the first to be circumcised in accordance with *the rule of* the covenant, which is ordained for ever.

15 And in the sixth year of the fourth[6] week we went to meet Abraham at the Well of the Oath, and we appeared to him [as we had told Sarah that we would return to her, and she would have
16 conceived a son. And we returned in the seventh month and found Sarah with child before our eyes], and we blessed him[7] and told him[7] everything that had been decreed concerning him – that he should not die till he was the father of six sons more and *that* he should see *them* before he died, but *that* it was through Isaac that his
17 true descent would be traced.[8] And *we told him that* all the descendants of his *other* sons would be Gentiles, and be reckoned with the Gentiles, although one of Isaac's sons would become a
18 holy seed, and not be reckoned with the Gentiles: he would become the Most High's portion, and all his descendants settled in that *land* which belongs to God, so as to be the Lord's **special possession**,[9] *chosen* out of all nations, and to be a kingdom of priests[10] and a holy
19 nation. And we went our way and repeated to Sarah all we had told him; and they were both overjoyed.

---

[5] So Eth.: Lat. 'boundaries'.
[6] Probably 'third' should be read. Cp. xv. 1.   [7] So Lat.: Eth. 'her'.
[8] Lit. 'in Isaac should name and seed be called for him'.
[9] Eth. lit. 'to be to the Lord a people of glory' (the word translated 'glory' could also mean 'adoption'): Lat. lit. 'to be to the Lord a hallowed people'. The emendation assumes that an allusion in the original to Exod. xix. 5, Deut. vii. 6, etc., has been either misunderstood or mistranslated in both Eth. and Lat. Cp. xix. 18.
[10] So Lat.: Eth. 'a kingdom and priests'. Cp. Exod. xix. 6.

20   And he built an altar there to the Lord who had delivered him and was the cause of his joy in the land where he was an alien; and he celebrated a festival of joy in this month, lasting seven days,

21 near the altar he had built at the Well of the Oath. And he built booths for himself and for his servants at this festival and he was

22 the first man on earth to celebrate the feast of Tabernacles. And during these seven days he brought to the altar each day a whole-offering to the Lord, two oxen, two rams, seven sheep, *and* one he-goat for a sin-offering (to make atonement by it for himself and

23 his descendants). And as a thank-offering *he brought* seven rams, seven kids, seven sheep, and seven he-goats, and their fruit-offerings and their drink-offerings; and burnt all their fat on the

24 altar – a choice offering to the Lord as a soothing odour. And every morning and evening he burnt fragrant substances – frankincense, and galbanum, and stacte, and nard, and myrrh, and spice, and costum: all these seven he offered, crushed, in exactly equal parts,

25 mixed, *and* pure. And he celebrated this feast for seven days, rejoicing with all his heart and soul, he and all his household; and

26 there was no alien with him, nor anyone uncircumcised. And he blessed his creator who had created him in his generation (for he had created him in accordance with his purpose),[11] since he perceived and understood that from him would sprout the plant of righteousness for the generations to eternity, and *that* from him *would come* a holy seed to be like him who created all things.

27   And he blessed *the Lord* and rejoiced; and he called this festival

28 the Lord's festival,[12] a joy[13] acceptable to the Most High God. And we blessed him for ever, and all his descendants after him[14] for all the generations of the earth, because he celebrated this festival at its appointed time, according to what is prescribed on the heavenly

29 tablets. This is why it is prescribed on the heavenly tablets concerning Israel, that they shall celebrate the feast of Tabernacles for seven days with joy, in the seventh month, *which is* acceptable before the Lord – a precept for ever, for every generation, every

30 year. And to this there is no time-limit; for it is ordained for ever concerning Israel, that they should celebrate it and live in booths,

---

[11] Lit. 'according to his good pleasure'.

[12] So Eth.: Lat. 'the festive day' or (as in later Hebrew) simply 'the festival'.

[13] So Eth.: Lat. 'a day of joy'.   [14] So Eth.: Lat. 'with him'.

and put wreaths on their heads, and take leafy boughs, and willows
31 from the brook. And Abraham took palm-**branches** and fruit from
the choicest trees, and he went round the altar every day with the
branches, seven times a day[15] in the morning, and he praised and
gave thanks to his God with all joy.

XVII. And in the first year of the fifth[1] week in this jubilee Isaac
was weaned; and Abraham gave a great feast in the third month,
2 on the day his son Isaac was weaned. And Ishmael, the son of
Hagar, the Egyptian, was *present* in his place opposite[2] his father
Abraham; and Abraham rejoiced and blessed God because he had
3 seen his sons and had not died childless. And he remembered the
words he had spoken to him on the day Lot parted from him; and
he rejoiced because the Lord had given him offspring on the earth
to possess it, and he blessed and praised[3] the creator of all things.
4 And Sarah saw Ishmael playing and dancing,[4] and Abraham
rejoicing with great joy; and a fit of jealousy came over her, and she
said to Abraham, Drive out this slave-girl and her son, for this
5 slave-girl's son shall not be heir with my son Isaac. And Abraham
was distressed by her demand that he should drive them out, both
6 on his slave-girl's account and on his son's. And God said to
Abraham, Do not distress yourself, either on the child's account, or
on the slave-girl's: do everything Sarah has told you to do; for
7 through Isaac shall your true descent be traced.[5] As for this
slave-girl's son, I will make *of* him a great nation, because he is a
child of your's.
8 And Abraham got up early in the morning and took bread and a
bottle of water, and he put them and the child on Hagar's
9 shoulders, and he sent her away. And she went and wandered in
the wilderness of Beersheba; and the water in the bottle was

[15] So most Eth. MSS and Lat.: one Eth. MS has 'on the seventh day'.

[1] Probably 'fourth' should be read. Cp. xvi. 15.
[2] Lit. 'before the face of'.
[3] Eth. 'blessed with all his heart': Lat. 'blessed with all his mouth'.
[4] So Eth.: Lat. 'playing with Isaac' (i.e. playfully teasing him? – as in the
Midrash).
[5] Lit. 'shall your name and seed be called'.

finished, and the child was thirsty and not able to go on, and he fell
10 to the ground. And his mother carried him and went and laid him
under an olive tree; and she herself went and sat down some way
off, *about* a bowshot's distance away, for she said, How can I watch
11 my child die?[6] And she sat and wept. And an angel of God (one of
the holy ones) said to her, Why are you weeping, Hagar? Get up,
take the child, and hold him in your arms; for God has heard your
12 cry and has seen the child. And she opened her eyes and saw a well
of water, and she went and filled her bottle with water and gave her
child a drink; and she rose and went in the direction of the
13 wilderness of Paran. And the child grew up and became an archer,
and God was with him; and his mother found him a wife from
14 among the women of Egypt. And she bore him a son, and he called
him Nebaioth, for she said, The Lord was near me when I invoked
him.

15 And it came to pass in the seventh week, in the first year of it, in
the first month in this jubilee, on the twelfth of this month, it was
said[7] in heaven about Abraham, that he had been faithful in doing
everything the Lord[8] had told him *to do*, and that he loved the Lord,
16 and that in every affliction he had been faithful. And the prince
Mastema came and said in God's presence, Behold, Abraham
loves his son Isaac *dearly* and dotes on him more than on anything
else: tell him to offer him as a whole-offering on the altar, and see if
he will carry out this order; and *then* you will know if he is *really*
17 faithful in every test you subject him to. But the Lord knew that
Abraham was faithful in all his afflictions; for he had tested him
through *the command to leave* his country and with famine, and he
had tested him with the wealth of kings, and he had tested him
again through his wife (when she was torn away *from him*) and with
circumcision, and he had tested him through Ishmael and Hagar,
18 his slave-girl (when he sent them away). And in every test to which
the Lord subjected him, he had been found faithful, and he was not
impatient, nor was he slow to act; for he was faithful and loved the
Lord.

---

[6] Lit. 'Let me not see the death of my child'.
[7] Lit. 'there were voices'.   [8] Text 'he'.

XVIII.   And God said to him, Abraham, Abraham;[1] and he said,
2 Behold, here I am. And he said, Take Isaac your beloved son,
whom you love, and go into the highlands, and offer him on one of
3 the hills I will show you *there*. And he got up in the morning at
dawn, and he saddled his ass, and took two of his young men with
him, and his son Isaac, and he split the wood for the whole-
offering; and he came near the place on the third day and saw it in
4 the distance.[2] And he came to a well of water and said to his young
men, Stay here with the ass, and the child and I will go *further*, and
5 when we have worshipped we will come back to you. And he took
the wood for the whole-offering and put it on his son Isaac's
shoulders, and he carried the fire and the knife himself; and both of
6 them went on together to the place appointed.[3] And Isaac said to
his father, Father. And he said, Here I am my son. And he said to
him, Behold, *here are* the fire and the knife and the wood; but where
7 is the sheep for the whole-offering, father? And he said, God will
provide a sheep for a whole-offering himself, my son. And he
8 approached the place of the mount of God. And he built an altar
and placed the wood on the altar, and he bound his son Isaac and
placed him on top of the wood on the altar, and he stretched out for
9 the knife to kill his son Isaac. And I was standing in the Lord's
presence (and the prince Mastema was there also),[4] and the Lord
said, Tell him not to lay his hand[5] on the child, nor to do anything
10 to him, for *now* I know that he is a man who fears the Lord. And I
called to him from heaven and said to him, Abraham, Abraham;
11 and he was terrified and said, Behold, here I am. And I said to him,
Lay no hand on the child, and do nothing to him; for now I know[6]
that you are a man who fears the Lord and have not withheld from
me your son, your first-born son. And the prince Mastema was put
12 to shame. And Abraham looked up, and behold, a[7] ram caught **in a**

[1] Alternative reading 'said to Abraham, Abraham'.
[2] Lit. 'And he went to the place on the third day, and he saw the place afar off'.
[3] Lit. 'to that place'.
[4] Lit. 'And I stood before him and before the prince Mastema'.
[5] Alternative reading 'Tell him not to hurry, and not to raise the knife, and not to lay his hand'.
[6] So Eth.: Lat. 'I have clearly shown' (The Lat. is not extant in verse 9: cp. also verse 16).   [7] Lit. 'one'.

thicket[8] by its horns; and Abraham went and took the ram and
13 offered it as a whole-offering instead of his son. And Abraham
called that place, The Lord has seen (hence the saying, On the
mount the Lord has seen[9]) – that is mount Sion.

14 And the Lord called Abraham by name from heaven a second
15 time, and he told us[10] to speak to him in the Lord's name. And he
said, By myself I swear, says the Lord, Because you have carried
out this command and have not withheld from me your son, your
own dear son,[11] I will bless you abundantly, and I will greatly
multiply your descendants, *and I will make them as numerous* as the
stars of heaven and as the *grains of* sand on the seashore; and your
16 descendants shall take possession of their enemies' cities. And in
your descendants shall all the nations of the earth be blessed; and
this because you have obeyed me, and I have made known[12] to all
your faithfulness in *doing* everything I told you. Go in peace.

17 And Abraham went *back* to his young men, and they got up and
went together to Beersheba; and Abraham stayed *there*, by the Well
18 of the Oath. And he celebrated this festival with joy, every year for
seven days; and he called it the Lord's festival of[13] the seven days,
19 during which he went and returned in peace. And that is why it
was ordained and written on the heavenly tablets about Israel and
his descendants, that they should observe this festival for seven
days with festal joy.

XIX. And in the first year of the first week in the forty-second
jubilee Abraham returned and lived two weeks of years opposite
2 Hebron (that is Kirjath -Arba). And in the first year of the third[1]
week of this jubilee the time came for Sarah to die; and she died in
3 Hebron. And Abraham went to mourn over her and bury her; and
we tested him to see if he was patient in demeanour and free from

---

[8] Emended on the basis of the Heb. of Gen. xxii. 13. All Eth. MSS read 'and he
came': Lat. has no equivalent.

[9] Eth. simply 'The Lord has seen' (omitting 'On the mount'): Lat. 'On the
mount the Lord has been seen'.

[10] Lit. 'as he caused us to appear'.

[11] Alternative reading 'your son, your first-born son, whom you love': Lat. 'your
son, your only son, whom you love'.

[12] So Eth.: Lat. 'clearly shown'.   [13] Lit. 'according to'.

[1] Probably 'second' should be read.

rancour in what he said, and he was found patient too in this and
4 undisturbed. For with consistent patience he conducted the
negotiations with the sons of Heth and asked them to give him a
5 place where he could bury his dead. And the Lord made all who
saw him well-disposed towards him; and he pleaded gently with
the sons of Heth, and they gave him the *plot of* land of the double
cave opposite Mamre (that is Hebron) for four hundred[2] pieces of
6 silver. And they begged him, saying, We will give it you for
nothing. But he would not take it from them for nothing: he paid
the price of the place in full, in ready money, and bowed before
them twice; and after this he buried his dead in the double cave.
7 And Sarah was a hundred and twenty-seven years old – that is, two
jubilees, four weeks, and a year: so long had Sarah's life lasted.
8 This is the tenth test by which Abraham was tested; and he was
9 found faithful and consistently patient. And he said not a single
word about the rumour in the land,[3] how that God had said that he
would give it to him and to his descendants after him, but begged a
place in it to bury his dead; for he was found faithful and
recorded on the heavenly tablets as the friend of God.

10 And in the fourth year of it he took a wife for his son Isaac; and
her name was Rebecca, [the daughter of Bethuel, the son of Nahor,
Abraham's brother,] the sister of Laban and daughter of Bethuel
(and Bethuel was the son of Milcah, Abraham's brother Nahor's
11 wife).[4] And Abraham took a third wife, whose name was Keturah,
from among his household servants (for Hagar had died before
12 Sarah). And she bore him six sons, Zimram, and Jokshan, and
Medan, and Midian, and Ishbak, and Shuah, in two weeks of
13 years. And in the sixth[5] week, in the second year of it, Rebecca bore
Isaac two sons, Jacob and Esau; and Jacob was a mild[6] and
upright man, while Esau was ruthless, a man of the field, and
14 hairy; and Jacob stayed by the tents. And the boys grew up, and
Jacob learned to write,[7] but Esau did not learn *to write*, for he was a

---

[2] So Lat.: Eth. 'forty'. [3] Or 'the promise concerning the land'.

[4] There is doubtless some dittography here. The translation follows the Lat., which gives a clearer overall sense than the Eth.

[5] Probably 'fifth' should be read.

[6] Or 'smooth': so Lat. (*lenis* – cp. Gen. xxvii. 11). Of the various Eth. readings 'perfect' goes back to the Heb. and 'misshapen' to the LXX at Gen. xxv. 27, while 'happy' is an easily intelligible scribal emendation. [7] Lit. 'books'.

man of the field and a hunter: he learned to fight,[8] and all his deeds
15 were ruthless. And Abraham loved Jacob, but Isaac loved Esau.

16 And Abraham saw what Esau did and he realized that it was
through Jacob that his promised heirs would come;[9] and he called
Rebecca and gave *her* instructions about Jacob, for he saw that she
17 *too* loved Jacob much more than Esau. And he said to her, My
daughter, watch over my son Jacob; for he shall take my place on
earth, and be a blessing among the sons of men, and the glory of the
18 whole line of Shem. For I know that the Lord will choose him to be
19 his **special possession**[10] from all the peoples on the earth. And
behold, my son Isaac loves Esau more than Jacob, but I can see
20 there is no doubt that you love Jacob. Increase yet more your
concern for him, and may your eyes watch over him in love, for he
shall be a blessing to us on the earth from now on and for evermore.
21 May your hands be strong and your heart rejoice in your son
Jacob, for I love him far more than any of my sons: he shall be
22 blessed for ever, and his descendants shall fill the earth. If anyone
is ever able to count the *grains of* sand on the earth, then his
23 descendants shall be counted too. And all the blessings that the
Lord has promised me and my descendants shall be Jacob's and
24 his descendants' always. And by his descendants shall my name be
blessed, and the name of my fathers, Shem, and Noah, and Enoch,
25 and Mahalalel, and Enosh, and Seth, and Adam. And these shall
serve to lay the foundations of heaven, and to strengthen the earth,
and to renew all the luminaries that are upon the vault *of heaven*.[11]

26 And he summoned Jacob in the presence of his mother Rebecca
27 and kissed him, and he blessed him and said, Jacob, my beloved
son, whom my soul loves, may God bless you from above the vault
of heaven, and may he give you all the blessings he showered on
Adam and Enoch and Noah and Shem; and may he bestow on[12]
you, and on your descendants for ever, all the things about which

[8] Lit. 'war'.

[9] Lit. 'that in Jacob would his name and seed be called'.

[10] There is much variation between the Eth. MSS, though no one of them gives a
tolerable sense. Lat. has 'to be a holy people to himself'. However, the verse is very
evidently an adaptation of Deut. vii. 6 – hence the emendation. Cp. xvi. 18.

[11] So Eth.: Lat. 'so that all the luminaries of the vault *of heaven* may be
recognized'.

[12] Lit. 'cause to cling to'.

he told me and all the things he promised to give me, unfailing as[13]
28 the days of heaven above the earth. And the spirits of Mastema
shall not have power over you or over your descendants to turn you
29 from the Lord, who is your God from now on, and for ever. And
may the Lord God be a father to you, and *may* you *be* the first-born
30 son and a people always. Go in peace my son. And they both left
31 Abraham together.[14] And Rebecca loved Jacob with all her heart
and soul, very much more than Esau; but Isaac loved Esau much
more than Jacob.

XX. And in the forty-second jubilee, in the first year of the
seventh[1] week, Abraham called Ishmael and his twelve sons, and
Isaac and his two sons, and the six sons of Keturah and their sons.
2 And he commanded them to observe the way of the Lord, to act
righteously and love each his neighbour, and to behave like this **to
all men**,[2] and to live in relation to them so that each acted justly and
3 righteously on earth. *And he commanded them* to circumcise their sons
in accordance with the covenant which the Lord[3] had made with
them, and not deviate either to the right or to the left from any of
the paths which the Lord had commanded us; and that we should
keep ourselves from all fornication and uncleanness, and let them
4 have no place among us.[4] And if any woman or girl among you
commits fornication, *he said*, burn her with fire: see that no woman
commits fornication with her eyes or her heart; and see that no
man takes a wife[5] from the women of Canaan — for the stock of
Canaan will be uprooted from the land.
5 And he told them about the judgement of the giants and the
judgement of the Sodomites, how they had been judged because of
their wickedness, and had died because of their fornication and
6 uncleanness and mutual corruption through fornication. And do

---

[13] Lit. 'according to'.
[14] So most MSS (lit. 'And they both went out together from Abraham'): alternative reading 'And they both went out together with him'.

[1] Probably 'sixth' should be read.
[2] Text 'in every war'.   [3] Lit. 'he'.
[4] Lit. 'and renounce from among us all fornication and uncleanness'.
[5] Lit. '. . . with fire, and let them (*fem.*) not commit fornication with their eyes and their heart; and let them (*masc.*) not take wives'.

you keep yourselves, *he said*, from all fornication and uncleanness, and from all pollution of sin, lest you make our name a curse and your whole life a terror,[6] and *cause* all your sons to be destroyed by the sword, and you yourselves become accursed like Sodom and all your remnant as the sons of Gomorrah. I implore you,[7] my sons, love the God of heaven, and hold fast to all his commandments; and do not go after their idols and after their uncleannesses. And do not make gods for yourselves, either cast in metal or carved, for they are empty things, and there is no spirit in them whatever: they are the work of *men's* hands, and all who trust in them, trust in nothing at all. Do not serve them or worship them, but serve the Most High God and worship him continually; and hope for his favour[8] always, and do what is upright[9] and righteous in his sight, that he may have pleasure in you[10] and grant you his mercy, and send rain upon you morning and evening, and bless all your works which you have done upon the earth, and bless your bread and your water, and bless the fruit of your womb and the fruit of your land, and your herds of cattle and your flocks of sheep. And you will be a blessing on the earth, and all the nations of the earth will have pleasure in you[11] and will bless your sons in my name, that they may be blessed even as I am.

And he gave gifts to Ishmael and his sons and to the sons of Keturah, and he sent them away from his son Isaac; and he gave his son Isaac everything. And Ishmael and his sons, and the sons of Keturah and their sons, went together and settled between Paran and the borders of Babylon,[12] in all the land that is to the east, facing the desert. And these mingled with each other, and they were called Arabs and Ishmaelites.[13]

XXI. And in the sixth year of the seventh[1] week of this jubilee Abraham called his son Isaac and instructed him, saying, I am old

---

[6] So Eth.: Lat. 'hissing'.　　　　　　　[7] Lit. 'I bear witness before you'.
[8] Lit. 'countenance'.　　　　　　　　　[9] So Eth.: Lat. 'true'.
[10] So Eth.: Lat. 'that he may guide you'.　　[11] So Eth.: Lat. 'desire you'.
[12] Lit. 'from Faramon to the entering in of Babylon'.
[13] So Eth: Lat. '. . . each other, and their name stuck to the Arabs, and the Ishmaelites *survive* till to-day'.

[1] Probably 'sixth' should be read.

2 and full of years, and I do not know when I shall die. Behold, I am a hundred and seventy-five years old, and throughout my life I have remembered the Lord and set my heart on the doing of his will and
3 walking straight in all his paths. My soul has hated idols, and I have despised those that serve them; and I have devoted my heart
4 and spirit[2] to observe and do the will of him who created me. For he is the living God, and holy and faithful and righteous above all: he does not respect persons and he cannot be bribed; for he is a righteous God and executes judgement on all who transgress his commandments and despise his covenant.

5 And as for you, my son, observe his commandments and his precepts and his judgements, and do not go astray after idols[3] and
6 after images, whether carved or cast in metal. And do not eat the blood of any of the wild animals or cattle, nor of any bird that flies
7 in heaven. And if you kill a victim as a peace-offering *that is to be* acceptable *to God*, kill it and pour out its blood on the altar, and all the fat offer on the altar as an offering with fine flour, and the meat-offering,[4] mixed with oil, with its drink-offering – offer them all together on the altar as a whole-offering:[5] it is a soothing odour
8 before the Lord. And you shall put the fat of the sacrifice of thank-offerings on the fire which is on the altar – the fat that is on the belly, and all the fat that is on the entrails and the two kidneys, and all the fat that is on them and that is on the loins; and the liver
9 you shall remove together with the kidneys.[6] And offer all these as a soothing odour, acceptable before the Lord, with its meat-offering and with its drink-offering, as a soothing odour, as food offered to
10 the Lord. And eat the meat of it on that day and on the second day, and do not let sunset on the second day find any of it still uneaten. Let none of it be left over till the third day; for it is not *by then* acceptable, nor is it desirable. Let none of it, therefore, be eaten then; and all who do eat of it *then* will bring sin upon themselves – for so I have found it written in the books of my forefathers (in the words of Enoch and in the words of Noah).

[2] Eth. om. 'and I have despised . . . spirit'.
[3] So Lat. (lit. 'abominations'): Eth. 'those who are unclean'.
[4] Lat. om. 'and the meat-offering'.   [5] So Eth.: Lat. 'on the altar of fruits'.
[6] So Lat.: Eth. '. . . on the loins and envelops the liver and the kidneys'. Cp. Lev. iii. 9–10.

11   And on all your offerings you shall sprinkle salt, and do not let the **salt of the covenant**[7] be lacking on any of your offerings before the Lord.

12   And as regards the wood of the sacrifices, on no account use *any other kinds of* wood apart from these – cypress, bay, almond, fir,
13   pine, cedar, savin, fig, olive, myrrh, laurel, aspalathus.[8] And of these kinds of wood place under the sacrifice on the altar *only* such *pieces* as have been inspected first;[9] and do not use[10] any wood that is split or spotted, *but only what is* hard and clean, without any spots, and of recent growth – no old wood, for old wood has lost its
14   fragrance, and there is no fragrance in it as there once was. Besides these there are no other kinds of wood you should put *on the altar*, for their smell[11] is not pleasant (and their smell[11] ascends to heaven).
15   Observe this commandment and carry it out, my son, that you may be upright in everything you do.

16   And at all times keep your body clean: wash yourself with water before you approach the altar to make an offering on it, and wash your hands and your feet before you come near it;[12] and when you
17   have done sacrificing, wash your hands and your feet again. And see there is no blood, either on you or on your clothes: be careful about blood, my son, be very careful indeed: cover it with dust.
18   And do not eat any blood, for it is the soul: do not eat any blood at
19   all. And accept no bribe for the blood of man, lest it be shed to no profit *and* unjustly; for it is the blood that is shed that makes the earth to sin, and **the earth**[13] cannot be cleansed from the blood of
20   man except by the blood of the man that shed it. Accept no bribe or gift for the blood of man: blood for blood is *what is* required[14] before the Lord, the Most High God; and hold fast to what is good,[15] so that you may be preserved from all evil and he may keep you safe from every kind of death.

[7] All MSS read 'the covenant of salt'. Cp. Lev. ii. 13.
[8] Several renderings in this list are uncertain.
[9] Lit. 'such as have been tested as to their appearance'.   [10] Lit. 'place'.
[11] Lit. 'fragrance . . . and the smell of their fragrance'. In the last clause Charles, following Littmann, inserted a negative ('and their smell does not ascend . . .').
[12] Lit. 'the altar'.
[13] The MSS read 'its blood'. For the emendation cp. vii. 33.
[14] Lit. 'is acceptable'. There is some variation between the MSS here.
[15] Lit. 'and let there be keeping of the good'.

21   I see, my son, that all the works of the sons of men are sin and
wickedness, and all their deeds are uncleanness and an abomination and a pollution, and there is no righteousness with them.
22   Beware, lest you walk in their way and tread in their footsteps; and
commit no deadly sin before the Most High God, or he will hide his
face from you, and give you back into the hands of your transgression, and uproot you from the land, and your descendants also
from under heaven, and your name and your posterity shall perish
23   from the whole earth. Turn away from all their deeds and all their
uncleanness, and keep the commandment[16] of the Most High God,
24   and do his will, and be upright in all things. And he will bless you
in all you do, and he will raise up from you a plant of righteousness
through all the earth, in every generation of the earth, and my
name and your name will never at any time be forgotten[17] under
25   heaven. Go, my son, in peace: may the Most High God, my God
and your God, strengthen you to do what he wills, and may he
bless all your descendants and your posterity, in every generation
for ever, with every righteous blessing, that you may be a blessing
in all the earth.
26   And he went out from him rejoicing.

XXII. And it came to pass in the first week in the forty-fourth
jubilee, in the second year,[1] that is the year in which Abraham
died, that Isaac and Ishmael came from the Well of the Oath to
celebrate the feast of weeks (that is, the feast of the first-fruits of the
harvest) to Abraham, their father; and Abraham rejoiced because
2   his two sons had come. For Isaac had many possessions in
Beersheba, and Isaac's habit was to go and look to his possessions
3   and *then* return to his father. And in those days Ishmael came to see
his father, and they both[2] came together; and Isaac sacrificed a
whole-offering and offered it on his father's altar that he had made
4   in Hebron. And he offered a thank-offering and prepared a joyful
feast in his brother Ishmael's presence; and Rebecca made a new
cake from the new grain, and she gave it to her son Jacob to take to

---

[16] Lit. 'keep the keeping'.   [17] Lit. 'be silenced'.

[1] Probably '. . . sixth . . . forty-second . . . seventh . . .' should be read.
[2] So Lat.

his father Abraham, from the first fruits of the land, so that he
5 might eat it and bless the creator of all things before he died. And
Isaac, too, sent Abraham a thank-offering by Jacob's hand, that he
6 might eat and drink. And he ate and drank, and he blessed the
Most High God, who created heaven and earth, who made all the
good things on the earth, and gave them to the sons of men so that
they might eat and drink and bless their creator.

7 And now, *he said*, I give thee thanks, my God, because thou hast
let me see this day: behold, I am a hundred and seventy-five years
old, an old man with a long life-span, and I have prospered all my
8 days.[3] The enemy's sword has never at any time prevailed against
9 me, nor against my children. My God, may thy mercy and thy
peace be upon thy servant, and upon his descendants,[4] that they
may be to thee a chosen nation and a possession out of all the
nations of the earth, now and in every generation on the earth for
evermore.

10 And he called Jacob and said, Jacob, my son, may the God of all
bless you and strengthen you to do rightousness, and *to do* his will
before him; and may he choose you and your seed to be always a
people for his own possession according to his will. And *now*, Jacob
my son, come near and kiss me.

11 And he came near and kissed him; and he said, May God Most
High bless you, Jacob my son, and all your sons for ever: may God
give you righteous offspring, and through your sons **may he be
hallowed** in all the earth:[5] may nations serve you, and may all
12 nations bow down before your sons.[6] Be strong in the presence of
men, and have authority among all the sons[6] of Seth: then your
ways and your sons' ways will be justified, so that they may
13 become a holy nation. May the Most High God give you all the
blessings with which he has blessed me, and with which he blessed
Noah and Adam: may they rest on the hallowed heads of your
14 descendants in every generation for ever. And may he cleanse you
from all unrighteousness[7] and impurity, so that you may be forgiven
all your transgressions and your errors committed in ignorance;

---

[3] Lit. 'and all my days have been peace to me'.
[4] So Lat.: Eth. 'his sons' descendants'.
[5] Text 'and from your sons may he hallow in the midst of the whole earth'.
[6] Lit. 'seed'.　　[7] So Lat.: Eth. 'defilement'.

and may he strengthen you and bless you, and may you possess the
15 whole earth. And may he renew his covenant with you, that you
may be to him a nation for his own possession always, and that he
may be to you and your descendants a God in truth and righteousness as long as the earth shall last.

16   And do you, Jacob my son, remember my words, and observe
the commands of your father Abraham. Keep yourself separate
from the nations, and do not eat with them; and do not imitate
their rites,[8] nor associate yourself with them; for their rites[9] are
unclean and all their practices[10] polluted, an abomination and
17 unclean. They offer their sacrifices to the dead and worship demons,
and they eat among the graves; yet all their rites[9] are worthless and
18 to no purpose. They have no mind[11] to understand, and their eyes
do not see what it is they really do,[12] and how great is their error
when they say to a piece of wood, You are my god, and to a stone,
You are my lord, and, You are my deliverer. They have no mind[11]
to understand.

19   And as for you, Jacob my son, may the Most High God help you
and the God of heaven bless you and keep you from their unclean-
20 ness and all their error. On no account, Jacob my son, take as a
wife a woman descended from Canaan; for all his descendants are
21 to be uprooted from the earth. For through Ham's transgression
Canaan *also* went astray, and all his descendants will be destroyed
from the earth: there will be no survivors;[13] and none of them will
22 be saved on the day of judgement. And as for all those who make
idols their gods, and the **profane**,[14] there shall be no hope for them
in the land of the living; for they shall descend into Sheol, and into
the place of punishment shall they go, and there shall be no memory
of them on the earth. As the sons of Sodom were taken away from
the earth, so will all those be taken away who make idols their gods.

23   Have no fear, Jacob my son, and do not be dismayed, you son of
Abraham: may the Most High God keep you from destruction, and
24 may he preserve you from all erroneous paths. This house have I
built for myself that I might put my name on it on the earth: it is

---

[8] Lit. 'and do not according to their works'.
[9] Lit. 'works'.   [10] Lit. 'ways'.   [11] Lit. 'heart'.
[12] Lit. 'what their works are'.   [13] Lit. 'and all the residue of them'.
[14] The MSS vary here between 'the hated ones' and 'the perverse'.

given to you and your descendants for ever; and it shall be called the house of Abraham. It is given to you and your descendants for ever; for you shall build my house and establish my name before God for ever. Your descendants and your name shall endure through all the generations of the earth.

5,26   And he finished his charge and his blessing of him. And the two were lying together on one bed, and Jacob was asleep in his grandfather Abraham's lap; and he kissed him seven times, and his
27 heart and soul[15] rejoiced over him. And he blessed him with all his heart and said, The Most High God, the God of all and creator of all, who brought me out of Ur of the Chaldees, that he might give me this land as a possession for ever, and that I might establish a holy race,[6] so that the Most High may be blessed for ever, and so
28 that Jacob may bless him . . .[16] My son, over whom I rejoice with all my heart and soul . . . may thy grace and thy mercy be on him and
29 on his descendants always. And do not forsake him or abandon him from now until eternity; and may thine eyes be on him and on his descendants, that thou mayest preserve him, and bless him,
30 and hallow him as a nation for thine own possession. And bless him with all thy blessings from now until eternity; and renew thy covenant and thy grace with him and with his descendants in accordance with thy chosen purpose in every generation on the earth.

XXIII.   And he placed two of Jacob's fingers on his eyes, and he blessed the God of gods, and he covered his face and stretched out his feet, and he slept the eternal sleep and was gathered to his
2 fathers. And despite all this Jacob was lying asleep in his lap and
3 was not aware that his grandfather Abraham was dead. And Jacob

[15] Lit. 'his affection and his heart' – and similarly in verse 28.
[16] So, following the majority of MSS, and with a slight emendation. In any case, something has gone radically wrong in this passage, and the probability is that some words have fallen out of the text, not only here, but also later on in the middle of verse 28. Charles, well aware that as things stand there is no main verb, solved the difficulty here by offering an admittedly inexact translation (' . . . and that I might establish a holy seed – blessed be the Most High for ever.[28] And he blessed Jacob and said, My son . . .') and suggesting that verse 27 is an interpolation: he made no comment, however, on the seemingly very abrupt change of address in the middle of verse 28.

woke up from his sleep, and behold Abraham was as cold as ice; and he said, Father, father. But he did not speak; and he realized

4 that he was dead. And he got up from where he was[1] and ran and told his mother Rebecca, and Rebecca went to Isaac in the night and told him; and they went together, and Jacob with them, with a lamp in his hand, and they went in and found Abraham lying dead.

5,6 And Isaac bent over his father,[2] and wept and kissed him. And *their* voices were heard in Abraham's house, and his son Ishmael got up and went to his father Abraham, and wept over his father Abraham, he and all Abraham's household; and they wept with a great

7 weeping. And his sons Isaac and Ishmael buried him in the double cave, near his wife Sarah; and they wept for him forty days, all the men of his household, and Isaac and Ishmael, and all their sons, and all Keturah's sons in their place. And the weeping[3] for Abraham came to an end.

8 And he lived three jubilees and four weeks of years – that is, a

9 hundred and seventy-five years, and he died at a good old age.[4] For the length of the lives of the ancients was nineteen jubilees; but after the flood it began to be less than nineteen jubilees, and *men* grew old more quickly, and the length of their lives decreased as a result of *their* manifold tribulations and the wickedness of their

10 ways, except Abraham only.[5] For Abraham was perfect in all his dealings with the Lord and gained favour by his righteousness[6] throughout his life, yet even he did not complete four jubilees in his life, but grew old as a result of the wickedness *of others* and died.[7]

11 And all the generations from this time till the day of judgement will grow old quickly, before they complete two jubilees, and old

12 age will impair their powers of mind.[5] And in those days, if a man live a jubilee and a half of years, it will be said about him, He has lived a long time; and the greater part of his days have been pain

13 and sorrow and tribulation, and he has had no peace. For calamity follows on calamity, and wound on wound, and tribulation on

---

[1] Lit. 'his lap'.　　　[2] Lit. 'fell on his father's face'.

[3] Other readings 'the wailing and weeping', 'the wailing of the weeping'.

[4] Lit. 'and he completed the days of his life, being old and full of days'.

[5] In this verse Eth. and Lat. differ not a little in detail, although the general sense is plain enough. The translation offered inclines to Lat.

[6] Lit. 'being well-pleasing in righteousness'.

[7] Lit. 'and was full of his days'.

tribulation, and bad news on bad news, and illness on illness, and all such painful punishments as these, one after another – illness, and disaster, and snow, and frost, and ice, and fever, and chills, and torpor, and famine, and death, and sword, and captivity, and

14 all kinds of calamities and pains. And all these will come on an evil generation that transgresses on the earth[8] and practices unclean-

15 ness[8] and fornication and pollution and abominations. Then it will be said, The lives of the ancients were long – *even* up to a thousand years, and they were pleasant *years*; but behold, the length of our lives is seventy years at the most, and, if a man's strength holds, *perhaps* eighty, but there is no pleasure in them and no peace at all in the days of this evil generation.

16 And in that generation the sons will convict their fathers and their elders of sin and unrighteousness, and because of the words that they utter and the great evils that they perpetrate, and because they forsake the covenant which the Lord made between them and him, that they should keep and observe all his command-ments and his rules and all his laws, without going astray either to

17 the right hand or the left. For all have done evil, and every mouth utters iniquity, and everything they do is unclean and an abomina-tion, and all their ways are pollution, uncleanness, and corruption.

18 Behold, the earth will perish because of all they do, and there will be no seed of the vine, and no oil; for the works of all of them are faithless, and they will all perish together – wild animals and cattle and birds, and all the fish in the sea, because of the sons of men.

19 And they will quarrel with one another, the young with the old, and the old with the young, the poor with the rich, the lowly with the great, and the beggar with the prince, because of the law and the covenant; for they will forget[9] commandment, and covenant, and feasts, and new moons, and sabbaths, and jubilees, and all the

20 customary observances.[10] And *some among them* will[11] take their stand with bows and swords and *other weapons of* war to restore *their kinsmen*[11] to the *accustomed* path; but they will not return until much

21 blood has been shed on the earth on either side. And those who have escaped will not return from their wickedness to the path of righteousness; but they will all attempt to enrich themselves by

---

[8] So Lat.   [9] Lit. 'they have forgotten'.
[10] Lit. 'all the judgements'.   [11] Lit. 'And they will . . . restore them'.

dishonest means and filch all they can from their neighbours,[12] and they will call themselves by the great name,[13] but not in truth and not in righteousness,[14] and they will defile the holy of holies with their uncleanness and the corruption of their pollution.

22 And the deeds of that generation will bring on them a mighty retribution from the Lord; and he will abandon them to the sword and to judgement and to captivity, and to be plundered and

23 devoured. And he will stir up against them the sinners of the Gentiles,[15] who have neither mercy nor compassion and will show favour to no one, neither to old nor young, nor to anyone, for they are more wicked and intent on evil than any of the sons of men. And they will use violence against Israel and treachery[16] against Jacob; and much blood will be shed upon the earth, and there will

24 be no one to gather *them* up and no one to bury *them*. In those days they will cry aloud, and call and pray that they may be saved from

25 the sinful Gentiles; but none will be saved. And the heads of the children will be white with grey hair, and a child three weeks old will look like a man who is a hundred, and their growth will be stunted by *their* misery and distress.

26 But[17] in those days the children will begin to study the laws, and to seek the commandments, and return to the path of righteous-

27 ness. And *then* men's lives will begin to get longer and *the number of* their years increase, generation by generation and day by day, till they approach a thousand, and the number of *their* years becomes

28 greater than *once* was the number of their days. And there will be no old man, nor any who is burdened by his years,[18] for all will be *like*

29 infants and young children. And they will live out all their days in peace and joy, and there will be no Satan[19] nor any evil agent to corrupt them;[20] for all their days will be days of blessing and of healing.

---

[12] Lit. 'but they will all exalt themselves to deceit and riches, so that they may each take all that is his neighbour's'.

[13] So Eth.: Lat. 'name the great name'.

[14] i.e. they will not in reality be worshippers of the God whose name they take in vain.

[15] Or 'the most sinful among the nations'.

[16] Lit. 'transgression'.

[17] Lit. 'And'.

[18] Lit. 'nor one who is sated with his days'.

[19] Or 'adversary'.

[20] Lit. 'nor any evil corrupter'.

30   And at that time the Lord will heal his servants, and they shall be exalted and prosper greatly;[21] and they shall drive out their adversaries. And the righteous shall see *it* and be thankful, and rejoice with joy for ever and ever; and they shall see all the punishments and curses that had been their lot falling on their
31   enemies.[22] And their bones shall rest in the earth, and their spirits shall have much joy; and they shall know that the Lord is one who executes judgement, and shows mercy to hundreds, and to tens of thousands, and to all that love him.

32   And do you, Moses, write down these words; for so are they written and recorded on the heavenly tablets as a testimony for each generation for ever.

XXIV. And it came to pass after the death of Abraham that the Lord blessed his son Isaac; and he left Hebron and went and dwelt at the Well of the Vision, in the first year of the third week of this jubilee, seven years.

2   And in the first year of the fourth week a famine began in the land (distinct from the first famine there had been in Abraham's
3   time). And Jacob made a lentil stew; and Esau came in hungry from the country. And he said to his brother Jacob, Give me *some* of this **red**[1] stew. And Jacob said to him, Give me your birthright in exchange (that is your right as first-born),[2] and I will give you
4   bread and also some of this lentil stew. And Esau thought to himself,[3] I am at death's door: of what use is this birthright to me?
5   And he said to Jacob, I give it you. And Jacob said, Give me your
6   oath to-day; and he gave him his oath. And Jacob gave his brother Esau the bread and the stew, and he ate till he was satisfied – so little did Esau value his birthright; and Esau was called Edom because of the **red**[1] stew that Jacob gave him in exchange for his

---

[21] Lit. 'see great peace'.
[22] Lit. '. . . all their judgements and all their curses on their enemies'.

[1] Text 'wheaten'. The emendation follows the Heb. of Gen. xxv. 30 and presupposes either a misreading of the Gk. πυρροῦ as πυροῦ by the Ethiopic translator, or an earlier corruption in the Gk. text from which he worked.
[2] Charles supposed that we have two alternative renderings of τὰ πρωτοτόκιά σου here.
[3] Lit. 'said in his heart'.

7 birthright. And *thus* Jacob became the elder, and Esau was demoted.

8 And the famine spread through all the land, and Isaac started out for Egypt in the second year of this week and came to

9 Abimelech, king of the Philistines, to Gerar. And the Lord appeared to him and said to him, Do not go down into Egypt: dwell in the land that I shall tell you of, and stay in this land *now* as an alien,

10 and I will be with you and bless you. For to you and your descendants will I give all this land, and I will fulfil my oath, which I swore to Abraham your father, and I will make your descendants as numerous as the stars of heaven, and I will give them all this

11 land. And in your descendants shall all the nations of the earth be blessed, because your father obeyed me and kept my charge and my commandments and my laws and my rules and my covenant;

12 and now, do you obey me and dwell in this land. And he dwelt in

13 Gerar three weeks of years. And Abimelech issued a warning about him, and about his property, that no one should molest either him or his property on pain of death.

14 And Isaac prospered among the Philistines and acquired great possessions – oxen and sheep and camels and asses and a large

15 retinue of servants.[4] And he sowed *seed* in the land of the Philistines and gathered in a hundred-fold. And Isaac prospered more and

16 more, and the Philistines envied him. Now all the wells, which Abraham's servants had dug during Abraham's lifetime, the Philistines had stopped up after his death and filled them with

17 earth. And Abimelech said to Isaac, Go away from us, for you are much stronger than we are; so Isaac left them in the first year of the

18 seventh week and settled in the valleys of Gerar. And they dug again[5] the wells which his father Abraham's servants had dug, and which the Philistines had filled in after Abraham's death, and he called them by the same names as his father Abraham had called

19 them. And Isaac's servants dug a well in a valley and found running water, and the shepherds of Gerar started a dispute with Isaac's shepherds, saying, This water is ours; and Isaac called the well Perversity, Because, *he said*, they have been perverse with us.

---

[4] So Lat. (*ministerium magnum*), as in the Heb. of Gen. xxvi. 14: Eth. 'a great possession'.

[5] Lit. 'And as they went round about they dug'.

20 And they dug a second well, and they disputed about that too; and he called it Enmity.[6] And he moved on from there and they dug another well, and about that there was no dispute; and he called it Plenty of Room,[7] and Isaac said, Now has the Lord made room for us, and we are increased in numbers in the land.

21 And he went up from there to the Well of the Oath, in the first
22 year of the first week in the forty-fourth jubilee. And the Lord appeared to him that night, on the new moon of the first month, and said to him, I am the God of Abraham your father: do not be afraid, for I am with you, and I will bless you and make your descendants as many in number as the sand on the sea-shore,[8] for
23 Abraham my servant's sake. And he built an altar there, where his father Abraham had built one before;[9] and he invoked the Lord by
24 name and offered sacrifice to his father Abraham's God. And
25 they[10] dug a well and found running water. And Isaac's servants dug another well and found no water, and they went and told Isaac that they had found no water; and Isaac said, I have sworn an oath to the Philistines to-day, and this is what[11] has happened to us.
26 And he called that place the Well of the Oath, for there he had sworn an oath to Abimelech, and Ahuzzath his friend, and Phicol
27 the commander of his army.[12] And Isaac realized that day that he had done wrong in swearing to them to make peace with them.

28 And Isaac cursed the Philistines that day and said, Accursed be the Philistines, more than all the nations, till the day of wrath and indignation: may God make them a laughing-stock and curse, and an object of wrath and indignation, in the hands of the sinful
29 Gentiles and in the hands of the Kittim. And whoever *of them* escapes the sword of the enemy and of the Kittim, may the righteous nation root *him* up in judgement from under heaven; for they shall be my children's enemies and foes in every generation on the earth.
30 And no remnant shall be left them, nor *shall there be* one that shall be saved on the day of the wrath of judgement: for destruction and

---

[6] So Lat.: Eth. 'narrow'. [7] So Lat. (*capacitas*): Eth. 'spacious'.
[8] Lit. 'sand of the earth'.
[9] Lit. 'which his father Abraham had first built'.
[10] One Eth. MS reads 'he' against all the other Eth. MSS and Lat. If this is the original reading, it is possible that the reference is to Abraham, who according to Gen. xxi. 25 and 30 had dug a well at Beersheba (and hence the name).
[11] Lit. 'this thing' or 'this word'. [12] So Lat.: Eth. 'Phicol his commander'.

rooting up and expulsion from the earth is the whole brood[13] of the Philistines *reserved*; and there shall not be left for any of those from

31 Caphtor[14] either name or posterity on earth. For though he ascend to heaven, from there shall he be brought down; and though he make himself strong on earth, from there shall he be pulled out; and though he hide himself among the nations, even from there shall he be rooted up; and though he descend into Sheol, there also shall relentless judgement be his lot, and there also he shall have no

32 peace at all. And if he go into captivity, by the hands of those that seek his life he shall be struck down while on the way, and neither name nor posterity shall be left him in all the earth; for into eternal

33 malediction he shall depart. And so it is written and engraved concerning him on the heavenly tablets, that this should be his fate on the day of judgement, so that he may be uprooted from the earth.

XXV. And in the second year of this week in this jubilee Rebecca summoned her son Jacob and admonished him, saying, My son, do not marry a Canaanite woman, like Esau your brother, who has married two Canaanite women, and they have been a constant source of distress to me[1] with all their wanton ways; for they are utterly debauched and dissolute, and there is no righteousness in

2 them whatever – *everything they do* is evil. But I am devoted to you, my son, and I bless you with all my heart and soul[2] every hour of

3 the day and through the watches of the night. And now, my son, listen to what I say, and do what your mother wants: do not marry a woman from here, but choose someone from my father's house and of my father's kin. If you do marry someone from my father's house, then[3] the Most High God will bless you and your children will be a righteous generation and a holy stock.[4]

4 And Jacob answered his mother Rebecca and said to her, Behold, mother, I am nine weeks of years old, and I have neither known nor touched any woman, nor have I pledged myself in marriage to

---

[13] Lit. 'seed'.   [14] Lit. 'for all the Caphtorim'.

[1] Lit. 'they have embittered my soul'.
[2] Lit. 'and my heart and my affection bless you'.
[3] Lit. 'You shall marry . . ., and'   [4] Lit. 'seed'.

anyone, nor have I even thought of marrying a Canaanite woman.

5 For I remember, mother, what our father Abraham said, how he commanded me not to marry a Canaanite woman, but to choose a

6 wife from my father's clan[5] and from my own kith and kin. I heard long ago that your brother Laban had some daughters, and I have

7 set my heart on them, to find a wife among them. And that is why I have kept myself from sinning or being corrupted in any way at any time in my life; for my father Abraham gave me many warnings to

8 beware of lust and fornication. And in spite of all his warnings to me, for twenty-two years my brother has argued with me and said to me time and time again, My brother, take a sister of *one of* my

9 two wives as a wife; but I refuse to do as he did. I swear before you, mother, that never while I live will I marry a woman of Canaanite

10 ancestry, and I will not do what is wrong as my brother did. Do not be afraid mother: be assured I will do what you want and live a blameless life and keep myself always from wicked ways.

11 And at this she looked up to heaven and spread out the fingers of her hands, and opened her mouth, and blessed the Most High God who created heaven and earth, and gave him thanks and praise.

12 And she said, Blessed be the Lord God, and may his holy name be blessed for ever and ever, he who has given me Jacob as a pure son and a holy offspring; for he is thine, and thine shall his offspring be

13 continually and in every generation for evermore. Bless him, O Lord, and put in my mouth the blessing of righteousness, that I may bless him.

14 And at that very moment, when the spirit of righteousness[6] came down upon her mouth, she placed both her hands on Jacob's head

15 and said, Blessed art thou, Lord of righteousness and God of the ages; and as for you, *Jacob*, may he bless you more than all the generations of men: may he set you, my son, on the path of

16 righteousness, and reveal righteousness to your descendants. And may he multiply your sons while you are still alive, and may they equal in number the months of the year; and may their sons multiply and surpass in number the stars of heaven, and their

17 numbers be more than the sand of the sea. And may he give them this goodly land (as he said he would give it for all time to Abraham

---

[5] Lit. 'from the seed of my father's house'.
[6] One MS reads 'the holy spirit'.

and his descendants after him), and may they hold it as a posses-
18 sion for ever. And while I am still alive, my son, may I see blessed
children *born* to you; and a blessed and holy race may all your
19 descendants be. And as you have refreshed your mother's spirit
while she was still alive, the womb of her that bore you blesses you
thus: my bosom[7] and my breasts bless you, and my mouth and my
20 tongue extol you. May you increase and spread over the earth, and
may your descendants be perfect in the joy of heaven and earth for
ever; and may those who spring from you rejoice, and on the day of
21 great peace may they have peace. May your name and your line
endure through every age, and may the Most High God be their
God; and may the God of righteousness dwell with them, and by
them may his sanctuary be built *and stand* for ever. Blessed be the
22 man that blessses you, and any man that curses you without due
cause, may he be cursed.
23   And she kissed him and said to him, May the Lord of the world
love you *as much* as your mother's heart and her affection *for you*
rejoice in you and bless you. And she brought her blessing to an
end.

XXVI. And in the seventh year of this week Isaac called Esau, his
elder son, and said to him, I am old, my son, and behold my eyes
2 have failed, and I do not know when I shall die. And now, take
your hunting gear, your quiver and your bow, and go out into the
country, and go hunting and get *some venison* for me, my son, and
make me a dish[1] of the kind I like, and bring it to me to eat, so that I
3 may give you my blessing before I die. But Rebecca heard Isaac
4 talking to Esau. And Esau went out early into the country to go
hunting and get *the venison* and bring *it* home to his father.
5   And Rebecca called her son Jacob and said to him, Behold, I
heard your father Isaac talking to your brother Esau, saying, Go
out hunting for me, and make me a dish[1] of the kind I like, and
6 bring *it* to me, so that I may give you my blessing before I die. And

---

[7] Or 'my natural affections'. The word in the Heb. original was probably
raḥᵃmim, usually explained as an intensive plural of the word previously translated
'womb' (*reḥem*).

[1] Lit. 'make me food'.

now, my son, listen to me and do what I tell you: go to your flock
and fetch me two choice kids from the goats, and I will make them
into a dish[2] for your father of the kind he likes, and you shall take *it*
to your father, so that he may eat *it* and bless you in the Lord's
7 presence before he dies, and you may be blessed *instead of Esau*. And
Jacob said to his mother Rebecca, Mother, I am not being niggardly
about *providing* what my father likes to eat and what would please
him: I am only afraid, mother, that he will recognise my voice and
8 want to touch me. And you know that I am smooth, but my brother
Esau is hairy, and he will think I am a blackguard and doing
something he has not told me to do; and he will be angry with me,
9 and I shall bring a curse on myself and not a blessing. And his
mother Rebecca said to him, Let your curse fall on me, my son:
only do what I say.

10 And Jacob did as his mother Rebecca told him, and he went and
fetched two choice fat kids from the goats and brought them to his
mother, and his mother made them into a dish[3] of the kind that
11 *Isaac* liked, And Rebecca took her elder son Esau's best clothes that
were with her in the house, and clothed her younger son Jacob in
them, and she put the skins of the kids on his hands and the
12 exposed parts of his neck. And she gave her son Jacob the dish she
13 had cooked and the bread she had baked.[4] And Jacob went in to his
father and said, I am your son: I have done as you told me: come
and sit and eat what I have got *for you*, father, so that you may give
14 me your blessing. And Isaac said to his son, How have you found it
15 so quickly, my son? And Jacob said, Because the Lord your God[5]
16 helped me to find *it*.[6] And Isaac said to him, Come close to me, so
that I can feel you, my son, *to make sure* whether you are my son
17 Esau or not. And Jacob came close to his father Isaac; and he felt
him and said, The voice is Jacob's voice, but the hands are Esau's
18 hands. And he did not recognize him, for it was a dispensation
from heaven to remove his powers of perception;[7] and Isaac did not
recognize him because his hands were hairy like Esau's, and so he

---

[2] Lit. 'make them into food'. [3] Lit. 'made them into food'.
[4] Lit. 'prepared'. [5] So Lat.: Eth. 'Because your God'.
[6] Other Eth. readings 'caused me to find *it*' and 'showed *it* to me': Lat. 'directed *it*
before me'.
[7] Lit. 'his spirit'.

19 blessed him. And he said, Are you my son Esau? And he said, I am your son. And he said, Bring me *the venison* that you have found, my
20 son, so that I may eat *some* of it and give you my blessing. And he brought it to him, and he ate it; and he brought him wine and he
21 drank. And his father Isaac said to him, Come close and kiss me, my son. And he came close and kissed him.

22 And he smelled the smell of his clothes, and he blessed him and said,

> Behold, the smell of my son is like the smell of a field[8] which the Lord has blessed.
23 And may the Lord give you in abundance of the dew of heaven
> And of the dew of the earth,
> And corn and oil in plenty:
> May nations serve you
> And the people bow down to you.
24 Be lord over your brothers,
> And may your mothers sons bow down to you;
> And may all the blessings which the Lord has bestowed on me and on my father Abraham,
> Be bestowed on you and on your descendants for ever.
> Accursed be the man that curses you,
> And blessed be the man that blesses you.

25 And it came to pass after Isaac had finshed blessing his son Jacob, and after Jacob had left his father Isaac, [he hid himself;
26 and][9] his brother Esau came in from his hunting. And he also made a dish[10] and brought *it* to his father; and he said to his father, Come, father, and eat of my venison, so that you may give me your
27 blessing. And his father Isaac said to him, Who are you? And he said to him, I am your elder son Esau: I have done as you told me.
28 And Isaac was greatly astonished and said, Who is it then that has gone out hunting and got *venison* and brought *it* to me? I ate all of it before you came in, and I have blessed him, *and so* he will indeed be blessed, *he* and all his descendants for ever.

---

[8] So Eth.: Lat. 'a full field'.
[9] A later addition according to Charles.
[10] Lit. 'made food'.

29 And it came to pass, when Esau heard what his father Isaac said,
he gave a loud and bitter cry, and said to his father, Bless me also,
30 father. And he said to him, Your brother has treacherously come
and taken away your blessing. And he said, Now I realize why he is
called Jacob: behold, he has tricked me twice: he took away my
31 birthright, and now he has taken away my blessing. And he said,
Have you no blessing left over for me, father? And Isaac answered
and said to Esau, Behold, I have made him lord over you, and all
his brothers have I given him as servants, and with plenty of corn
and wine and oil have I enriched him; and now what can I do for
32 you, my son? And Esau said to his father Isaac, Have you only one
blessing,[11] father? Bless me also, father. And Esau cried aloud and
33 wept. And Isaac answered and said to him,

> Behold, of the dew of the earth shall your dwelling be,
> And of the dew of heaven from above.
34 > And by your sword you shall live,
> And you shall serve your brother.
> And it shall come to pass, when you have the power,[12]
> And shake his yoke from your neck,
> It will be counted against you as a deadly sin,[13]
> And your offspring will be uprooted from under heaven.

35 And Esau kept threatening Jacob because of the blessing his father
had given him; and he said to himself, I wish the time of mourning
for my father would come, so that I can kill my brother Jacob.

XXVII. And what Esau, her elder son, was saying was told
2 Rebecca in a dream. And Rebecca sent for Jacob, her younger son,
and said to him, Behold, your brother Esau is planning to get his
3 own back on you and kill you. So now, my son, do what I tell you,
and make your escape and go to Laban, my brother in Haran, and
stay with him awhile, till your brother's anger cools, and he thinks
no more about it,[1] and forgets all you have done *to him*: then I will
4 send and fetch you back. And Jacob said, I am not afraid *of him*: if

---

[11] Lit. 'Is your blessing only one?'
[12] Lit. 'become great'.   [13] Lit. 'You will sin a complete sin unto death'.

[1] Lit. 'and he removes his anger from you'.

5 he wants to kill me, I will kill him. But she said to him, Do not be
6 the cause of my losing both my sons the same day. And Jacob said
to his mother Rebecca, Behold, you know how old my father is, and
he cannot see because his eyes have failed: if I leave him, he will
think it wrong of me to leave him and go away from you, and my
father will be angry and curse me. I will not go: only if he sends me
7 will I go. And Rebecca said to Jacob, I will go in and talk to him,
and he will send you away.

8 And Rebecca went in and said to Isaac, I am sick to death of[2] the
two Hittite women that Esau has married; and if Jacob marries a
local girl like them, I shall find life unendurable,[3] for Canaanite
women are insufferable.[4]

9 And Isaac called Jacob and blessed him and admonished him
and said to him, Do not choose a wife from among the Canaanites.
10 Go now to Mesopotamia, to the house of Bethuel, your mother's
father, and find a wife there, one of Laban your mother's brother's
11 daughters. And God Almighty bless you, and make you fruitful,
and multiply you, so that you may become a host of nations; and
may he bestow on you the blessings of my father Abraham, and on
your descendants after you, so that you may take possession of the
land you live in now, even all the land that God gave to Abraham.
12 Go, my son, in peace. And Isaac sent Jacob away; and he went to
Mesopotamia, to Laban, the son of Bethuel the Syrian, the brother
of Rebecca, Jacob's mother.

13 And it came to pass after Jacob had gone away to Mesopotamia,
14 Rebecca fretted after her son and wept. And Isaac said to Rebecca,
My sister do not weep on my son Jacob's account; for he has gone
15 in peace, and he will return in peace. The Most High God will keep
him from all evil and be with him and never fail him at any time.
16 For I know that his paths will be prospered[5] in every way, wherever
17 he goes, till he returns to us in peace. Have no fear on his account,
my sister, for he is upright in all his dealings, and a man of integrity
18 and faithful,[6] and he will come to no harm *at all*. Do not weep. And
Isaac comforted Rebecca on account of her son Jacob; and he
blessed him.

---

[2] Lit. 'I loathe my life because of'.
[3] Lit. 'to what purpose shall I live further'.   [4] Lit. 'evil'.
[5] So Lat.: Eth. 'that he will prosper'.   [6] Or 'truthful'.

19   And Jacob left the Well of the Oath for Haran in the first year of the second week in the forty-fourth jubilee, and he came to Luz among the mountains (that is Bethel) on the new moon of the first month of this week; and he came to the place in the evening, and turned aside off the road, towards the west, for the night, and he lay

20 down to sleep there[7] – for the sun had set. And he took one of the stones of that place and laid it at his head,[8] under the tree;[9] and he was journeying on his own, and went to sleep.

21   And that night he had a dream, and behold, a ladder was set up on the ground, and the top of it reached to heaven, and the angels of the Lord were going up and down on it; and behold the Lord was

22 standing on it. And he spoke to Jacob and said, I am the Lord, the God of your father Abraham, and the God of Isaac: the land on which you are sleeping will I give to you and your descendants

23 after you. And your descendants shall be as *numerous as* the *specks of* dust on the ground, and you shall spread west and east, *and* north and south, and in you and your descendants shall all the tribes of

24 the earth[10] be blessed. And behold, I will be with you, and I will protect you wherever you go, and I will bring you back to this land in peace; for I will never leave you until I have done everything I promised you.

25   And Jacob **woke up from his sleep**[11] and said, Truly this place is the house of the Lord, and I did not know it. And he was afraid and said, *How* awesome is this place, which is no other than the house of

26 the Lord, and this is the gate of heaven. And Jacob got up in the morning early, and he took the stone he had put under his head and set it up as a pillar for a sign, and he poured oil on the top of it; and he named that place Bethel (but the country's name before

27 was Luz). And Jacob made a vow[12] to the Lord saying, If the Lord will be with me and protect me on my journey, and give me bread to eat and clothes to wear, and I come back to my father's house in peace, then shall the Lord be my God, and this stone I have set up as a pillar for a sign in this place shall be the Lord's house; and of all that thou givest me, I will give a tenth to thee, my God.

---

[7] Lit. 'he slept there'.   [8] So Lat.: Eth. om. 'at his head'.
[9] Presumably the '*asherah* at the 'place' (= 'sanctuary').
[10] So Lat.: Eth. 'countries of the nations'.
[11] Text 'slept a sleep'.   [12] Or 'prayer'.

XXVIII. And he resumed his journey and came to the land of the East, to Laban, Rebecca's brother; and he stayed with him and
2 became his servant for his daughter Rachel, one week. And in the first year of the third week he said to him, Give me my wife, for whom I have served you seven years; and Laban said to Jacob, I
3 will give you your wife. And Laban prepared a feast, and he took Leah, his elder daughter, and gave *her* to Jacob as *his* wife (and he gave her Zilpah his *own* slave-girl as *her* slave-girl); and Jacob did
4 not realize it, but thought she was Rachel. And he slept with her, and *when morning came*, behold, she was Leah; and Jacob was angry with Laban and said to him, Why have you done this to me? Did I not *agree to* serve you for Rachel and not for Leah? Why have you
5 done me this wrong? Take your daughter, and I will go: you have tricked me.[1] (For Jacob loved Rachel more than Leah, for Leah's eyes had no sparkle, despite her shapely figure, whereas Rachel had attractive eyes as well as an attractive and very shapely figure.)
6 And Laban said to Jacob, In our country it is not the custom to give the younger *sister in marriage* before the elder. (And *indeed*, it is not right to do this; for so it is ordained and written on the heavenly tablets, that no one should give his younger daughter *in marriage* before the elder, but the elder should be given first; and the man who does so has it entered to his discredit in heaven, and no one is righteous that does it, for to do such a thing is abhorrent to the
7 Lord. And give the sons of Israel orders that they should not do it: see that they neither take nor give the younger *in marriage* without
8 having given the elder first, for *to do so* is very wicked.) And Laban said to Jacob, Let the seven days of Leah's feast[2] run their course, and *then* I will give you Rachel *on the understanding* that you serve me another seven years and pasture my sheep as you did in the
9 previous week. And on *one of* the days, when the seven days of Leah's feast were over, Laban gave Rachel to Jacob, that he might serve him another seven years (and he gave Rachel as *her* slave-girl
10 Bilhah, Zilpah's sister). And he served seven years more for Rachel, for Leah had been given him to no purpose.
11 And the Lord made Leah fruitful, and she conceived and bore

---

[1] Lit. 'you have done evil to me'.
[2] Lit. 'of the feast of this one'.

Jacob a son, and he called him Reuben, on the fourteenth day of
12 the ninth month, in the first year of the third week. But Rachel had
no children, for the Lord saw that Leah was neglected[3] and Rachel
13 loved. And Jacob slept with Leah again, and she conceived and
bore Jacob a second son, and he called him Simeon, on the twenty-
14 first of the tenth month, and in the third year of this week. And
again Jacob slept with Leah, and she conceived and bore him a
third son, and he called him Levi, on the new moon of the first
15 month in the sixth year of this week. And again Jacob slept with
her, and she conceived and bore him a fourth son, and he called
him Judah, on the fifteenth of the third month, in the †first† year of
the †fourth† week.

16 And because of all this Rachel was jealous of Leah (for she
herself had no children), and she said to Jacob, Give me children;
17 and Jacob said, Have I denied you children? Have I deserted you?
And when Rachel saw that Leah had borne Jacob four sons,
Reuben and Simeon and Levi and Judah, she said to him, Sleep
with my slave-girl Bilhah, and she will conceive and bear me a son.
18 And she gave *him* her slave-girl Bilhah as a wife; and he slept with
her, and she conceived and bore him a son, and he called him Dan,
on the ninth of the sixth month, in the †sixth† year of the †third†
19 week. And Jacob slept with Bilhah again, a second time, and she
conceived and bore Jacob another son, and Rachel called him
Naphtali, on the fifth of the seventh month, in the second year of
the fourth week.

20 And when Leah saw that she had no more children, she became
jealous of Rachel; and she also gave her slave-girl, Zilpah, to Jacob
as a wife, and she conceived and bore a son, and Leah called him
Gad, on the twelfth of the eighth month, in the third year of the
21 fourth week. And he slept with her again, and she conceived and
bore him a second son, and Leah called him Asher, on the second
22 of the eleventh month, in the †fifth† year of the fourth week. And
Jacob slept with Leah, and she conceived and bore a son and she
called him Issachar, on the fourth of the fifth month, in the
23 †fourth† year of the fourth week; and she gave him to a nurse. And
Jacob slept with her again, and she conceived and bore twins, a son

---

[3] Lit. 'hated'.

and a daughter, and she called the son Zabulon and the daughter
Dinah, on the seventh of the seventh month, in the sixth year of the
24 fourth week. And the Lord showed Rachel favour and made her
fruitful, and she conceived and bore a son, and she called him
Joseph, on the new moon of the fourth month, in the †sixth† year in
this fourth week.

25 And at the time Joseph was born, Jacob said to Laban, Give me
my wives and sons, and let me go to my father Isaac and let me set
up my household *there;*[4] for I have completed my years of service to
26 you for your two daughters, and I will go to my father's house. And
Laban said to Jacob, **Tell me what wages you want from me,**[5] and
27 pasture my flock for me again, and I will pay your wages.[6] And
they agreed with one another that he should give him as his wages
the lambs and the kids that were born either grey or spotted or
28 speckled: *these* were to be his wages. And all the sheep produced
lambs that were either spotted or speckled or grey, and they again
produced lambs like themselves; and all that were spotted were
29 Jacob's and those that were not were Laban's.[7] And Jacob's
possessions increased more and more – oxen and sheep and asses
30 and camels, and male slaves and female slaves. And Laban and his
sons were jealous of Jacob; and Laban withdrew his sheep from
him, and eyed him with evil intent.

XXIX.   And it came to pass, after Rachel had given birth to Joseph,
Laban went to shear his sheep (a three day's journey each way).
2 And Jacob saw that Laban was going to shear his sheep; and Jacob

---

⁴ Lit. 'let me make a house'.
⁵ Emended in the light of Gen. xxx. 28. Eth. has 'Wait with me for your wages'
and Lat. '*Expecta me in mercede*', neither of which Charles considered satisfactory.
⁶ So Lat.: Eth. 'and take your wages'.
⁷ Both the text and the precise meaning of some of the Eth. words used to indicate
differences of colour in this passage are uncertain. However, the general sense, that
things turned out very much to Jacob's advantage, is plain. Gen. xxx. 32–42
describes in detail how Jacob arranged this himself; and part of the obscurity of the
Jubilees version is due to the fact that the author, by abbreviating so drastically the
Genesis account, has confused the details in Genesis that apply to the sheep with
others that apply to the goats – unless, perhaps, several lines have at some stage in
the copying fallen out of the original text.

called Leah and Rachel and persuaded them to go[1] with him to the
3 land of Canaan. He told them how he had seen everything in a
dream, and how *the Lord* had given him instructions to return to his
father's house; and they said, Wherever you go, we will go with
4 you. And Jacob blessed the God of his father Isaac, and the God of
his grandfather Abraham, and he made his preparations, and
mounted his wives and his children, and took all his possessions,
and crossed the river, and came to the land of Gilead; and Jacob
kept his plan secret from Laban and did not tell him.

5 And *it was* in the seventh year of the fourth week *that* Jacob
started out for Gilead, in the first month, on the twenty-first *day* of
the month. And Laban went after him and overtook Jacob in the
highlands of Gilead, in the third month, on the thirteenth *day* of *the*
6 *month*. And the Lord did not allow him to injure Jacob (for he
appeared to him in a dream by night); and Laban talked with
Jacob.

7 And on the fifteenth *day* of the month[2] Jacob prepared a feast for
Laban and all those who had come with him; and Jacob and Laban
made an agreement that day under oath that neither would cross
8 the highlands of Gilead with hostile intent against the other. And
he erected a cairn there *to stand* as a witness: that is why that place is
9 called The Cairn of Witness – after the cairn. (At one time[3] they
used to call the land of Gilead the land of the Rephaim; for it was
the land of the Rephaim, and the Rephaim originated *there*[4] –
giants, whose height was ten, nine, eight down to seven, cubits.
10 And their settlements extended from the land of the Ammonites to
Mount Hermon; and the seats of their kingdom were Karnaim and
11 Ashtaroth and Edrei and Misur and Beon. And the Lord destroyed
them because of the wickedness of their doings, for they were very
wicked; and the Amorites replaced them, *so* wicked and sinful *were*
they – there is no people in existence to-day that can compete with
them in sin,[5] and that is why they perished.[6])

12 And Jacob sent Laban away, and he went back to Mesopotamia,
13 the land of the East; and Jacob returned to the land of Gilead. And

---

[1] Lit. 'and spoke kindly to them that they should go'.
[2] Lit. 'of those days'.   [3] Or 'previously'.
[4] Lit. 'were born *there*'.   [5] Lit. 'that has filled up all their sins'.
[6] Lit. 'and they had (have) no longer length of life on earth'.

he crossed the Jabbok in the ninth month, on the eleventh *day* of *the month*. And on that day his brother Esau came to him, and was reconciled,[7] and left him for the land of Seir; and Jacob was living in tents.

14 And in the first year of the fifth week in this jubilee he crossed the Jordan, and settled beyond the Jordan, and pastured his sheep

15 from. . . .[8] And he sent to his father Isaac from his household goods, clothing and food and meat and drink and milk and butter and

16 cheese and some dates of the valley (and to his mother Rebecca also), four times a year – between the times of the months, between ploughing and reaping, between autumn and winter,[9]

17 and between winter and spring,[10] to the tower of Abraham. (For Isaac had left the Well of the Oath and moved to the tower of his father Abraham and was living there, separately from his son

18 Esau. For after Jacob had gone to Mesopotamia, Esau had married *another* wife, Mahalath, Ishmael's daughter, and had taken all his father's flocks, and his wives, and had gone and settled in the hill-country of Seir and left his father Isaac at the Well of the

19 Oath alone. And Isaac had moved from the Well of the Oath and was living in the tower of his father Abraham on the highlands by

20 Hebron.) And there Jacob sent everything he sent from time to time to his father and his mother, all they needed; and they blessed Jacob heart and soul.

XXX. And in the first year of the sixth week he went up to Salem,

2 to the east of Shechem, in peace, in the fourth month. And there they carried off Dinah, Jacob's daughter, to the house of Shechem, the son of Hamor, the Hivite, the prince of the land; and he lay with her and defiled her (and she was a little girl, a child, *only* twelve

3 years old). And he asked his father and her brothers that she might

---

[7] So Lat.: Eth. 'they were reconciled with one another'.

[8] Eth. 'from the sea of the cairn to Bethshan and to Dothan and to (one MS adds 'the forest of') Akrabbim': Lat. '*a mare salso usque (Bethasan et usque Dothaim et usque) agruum Acrabin*'. The area described would appear to lie west of the Jordan and the Dead Sea, and to extend from Bethshan and Dothan in the north to 'the ascent of Akrabbim' (cp. Num. xxxiv. 4; Josh. xv. 3), bordering on Edomite territory, in the south.

[9] Lit. 'the rain'.

[10] Jacob, that is, sent his gifts on the first day of the first, fourth, seventh, and tenth months (cp. vi. 23 above).

be given him as his wife. And Jacob and his sons were furious with the Shechemites because they had defiled their sister Dinah, and they determined on revenge, but they kept their counsel and dissimulated.[1]

4 And Simeon and Levi came to Shechem without warning,[2] and executed judgement on all the Shechemites, and killed every man they found *there*, and left not a single survivor: they killed them all without mercy,[3] because they had dishonoured their sister Dinah. 5 And let no Israelite girl ever be defiled in this way again; for judgement was ordained in heaven against them — that all the Shechemites should perish by the sword, because they had com-6 mitted an outrage in Israel. And the Lord delivered them into the hands of Jacob's sons, so that they might exterminate them with the sword and execute judgement on them, and so that it might not happen again in Israel that an Israelite virgin should be *thus* defiled.

7 And if there is ever a man in Israel who is desirous of giving his daughter or his sister *in marriage* to a man who is a Gentile, he shall be stoned to death, for he has committed an outrage in Israel, and the woman shall be burned *alive*, because she has defiled the name 8 of her father's house, and she shall be rooted out of Israel. And let no harlot nor any uncleanness be found in Israel at any time;[4] for Israel is holy to the Lord, and every man who causes defilement 9 shall be stoned to death. For so it has been decreed and written on the heavenly tablets about the stock of Israel in perpetuity[5] — a man 10 who causes defilement shall be stoned to death. And to this law there is no time limit, neither *can there be any* relaxation *of it* nor substitute[6] *for it*; but the man who has defiled his daughter shall be rooted out before the whole people of Israel,[7] because he has given of his offspring to Moloch, and acted profanely and so defiled it.

11 And do you, Moses, command the sons of Israel and exhort

[1] Lit. '. . . Dinah, and they spoke to them with evil intent, and dealt deceitfully with them and beguiled them'.

[2] So Eth.: Lat. 'determined to exterminate them'.

[3] So Eth. (lit. 'in torment'): Lat. 'in judgement'.

[4] Lit. 'throughout all the days of the generations of the earth'.

[5] Lit. 'about all the seed of Israel'.

[6] Lit. 'atonement' (Lat. *propitiatio*).

[7] Lit. 'in the midst of all Israel'.

them not to give their daughters *in marriage* to the Gentiles, and not to take for their sons[8] *wives* of the Gentiles' daughters, for this is
12 abominable to the Lord. For this reason I have written for you in the words of the law all the details of what the Shechemites did to Dinah, and how Jacob's sons spoke up and said, We will not give our daughter to a man who is uncircumcised, for that would be a
13 disgrace for us. And it is a disgrace for an Israelite[9] to give *his daughter to the Gentiles in marriage* and to take the Gentiles' daughters *as wives for his sons* – for this is unclean and abominable in Israel.
14 And Israel will not be free from this uncleanness if anyone has a wife of the Gentiles' daughters, or has given any of his own daugh-
15 ters to a man who is a Gentile. For there will follow plague on plague and curse on curse, and every judgement and plague and curse will fall **on Israel**[10] if they[11] do this thing or hide their[11] eyes from those responsible for the uncleanness,[12] or who defile the Lord's sanctuary or profane his holy name: *thus* the whole nation will be judged together for all this uncleanness and profanation.[13]
16 And there will be no respect of persons and no consideration of persons, and no receiving at anyone's hands of fruits and offerings and whole-offerings and fat, nor will the sweet smell of his sooth-ing sacrifices be accepted; and so will every man or woman in
17 Israel fare who defiles the sanctuary. For this reason I have com-manded you, saying, Give Israel this solemn warning: see how the Shechemites fared and their sons: *see* how they were delivered into the hands of two of Jacob's sons, and how they killed them without mercy,[14] and it was reckoned to them as righteousness and accounted to their credit.
18 And the descendants of Levi were chosen for the priesthood, and to be Levites, that they might minister before the Lord (as we[15] *do*) continually; and Levi and his sons are blessed for ever, for he showed zeal to execute righteousness and judgement and ven-
19 geance on all those who rose up against Israel. And so blessing and

---

[8] So Lat.: one Eth. MS reads 'for themselves', the rest om. altogether.
[9] Lit. 'for Israel'.
[10] Supplied on the basis of the Latin 'on him'.
[11] Lit. 'it (he) . . . its (his)'.
[12] Lit. 'those who commit uncleanness'.
[13] So Eth.: Lat. 'for all the abominations and contaminations of this man'.
[14] See verse 4 above.   [15] i.e. the angels.

righteousness are inscribed on the heavenly tablets as a testimony
20 in his favour before the God of all. And we remember the righteous
acts[16] which the man did in his lifetime, at every period of the year:
for a thousand generations they[16] will be recorded, and the blessings resulting from them[17] will come upon him and upon his
descendants after him; and he has been described in the record on
21 the heavenly tablets as a friend and a righteous man. All this
account I have written for you, and I have commanded you to tell
the sons of Israel not to commit sin nor transgress the commandments nor break the covenant that has been ordained for them, *but*
22 to keep it and be *themselves* described as friends. But if they transgress and engage in unclean practices of any kind,[18] they will be
described as adversaries and their names[19] erased from the book of
life, and they will be recorded in the book of those who are to be
23 destroyed and uprooted from the earth. And on the day when
Jacob's sons killed Shechem it was recorded in their favour in
heaven that they had executed righteousness and justice and vengeance on the sinners; and it was written as a blessing.

24   And they brought their sister Dinah out of Shechem's house,
and they laid their hands on everything there was in Shechem,
their sheep and their oxen and their asses, and all their flocks and
all their wealth, and they brought them all to their father Jacob.
25 And he reproached them[20] for putting the city to the sword,
because he was afraid of the Canaanites and the Perizzites who
26 were living in the land. And the dread of the Lord was on all the
cities in the neighbourhood of Shechem; and they made no attempt
to pursue[21] Jacob's sons, for terror had fallen on them.

XXXI.   And on the new moon of the month Jacob spoke to all the
members of his household, saying, Purify yourselves and change
your clothes, and let us get up and go to Bethel, where I vowed a
vow to the Lord[1] on the day I fled from my brother Esau, because

---

[16] Lit. 'righteousness . . . it'.   [17] Lit. 'and it'.
[18] Lit. 'act in any of the ways of uncleanness'.
[19] Lit. 'and they will be'.   [20] Lit. 'spoke to them'.
[21] So Lat.: Eth. 'expel'.

[1] Lit. 'to him'.

he has been with me and brought me into this land in peace; and do
2 you rid yourselves of the foreign gods that are among you. And
they **gave up**[2] the foreign gods, and *the ornaments* that were in their
ears and on their necks; and Rachel gave to Jacob all the idols that
she had stolen from her father Laban. And he burnt *them* and broke
them in pieces and destroyed[3] them, and he hid them under an oak
near[4] Shechem.

3 And he went up on the new moon of the seventh month to
Bethel. And he built an altar at the place where he had slept, and
he set up a pillar there; and he sent word to his father Isaac to come
4 to him to his sacrifice, and to his mother Rebecca. And Isaac said,
Let my son Jacob come *to me*, and let me see him *here* before I die.
5 And Jacob went to his father Isaac and to his mother Rebecca, to
the house of his father Abraham; and he took two of his sons with
him, Levi and Judah, and came to his father Isaac and his mother
Rebecca.

6 And Rebecca came out from the tower, to the gate of the tower,
to kiss Jacob and embrace him (for her spirit revived when she
heard *the words*, Behold, Jacob your son has come), and she kissed
7 him. And she saw his two sons, and she recognized them and said
to him, Are these your sons, my son? And she embraced them
and kissed them and blessed them, saying, Through you shall
Abraham's line become famous, and you shall be a blessing on the
earth.

8 And Jacob went in to his father Isaac, into the room where he
was lying, and his two sons were with him; and he took his father's
hand, and stooping down he kissed him; and Isaac clung to his son
9 Jacob's neck, and wept upon his neck. And the darkness left
Isaac's eyes, and he saw Jacob's two sons, Levi and Judah, and he
10 said, Are these your sons, my son, for they are like you? And he told
him that they were indeed his sons (You have rightly seen, *he said*,
11 that they are indeed my sons). And they came near him, and he
12 turned and kissed them and embraced them both together. And
the spirit of prophecy came down upon his mouth, and he took
Levi by his right hand and Judah by his left.

---

[2] So Charles, by a slight change in the Eth. ('they melted down'). The Lat. is not
extant at this point.
[3] Lit. 'defaced'.   [4] Lit. 'in the land of'.

13   And he turned to Levi first, and began to bless him first, and said to him, May the God of all, the very Lord of all the ages, bless you
14 and your children through all the ages. And may the Lord give you and your descendants greatness and great glory,[5] and set you and your descendants apart from all mankind to minister to him and to serve[6] *him* in his sanctuary like the angels of the presence and the holy ones: like them your sons' descendants shall be accounted glorious, and great, and holy; and may he make them great for
15 ever. And they shall be judges and princes and chiefs of all the descendants of Jacob's sons. They shall speak the Lord's word in righteousness, and dispense all his judgements in righteousness; and they shall declare my ways to Jacob and my paths to Israel: the blessing of the Lord shall be given by their mouths, to bless all the
16 descendants of the beloved one. Your mother has named you Levi, and rightly she has named you: you shall be joined to the Lord, and be the companion of all the sons of Jacob. May his table be yours, and you and your sons eat of it; and may your table be full in every
17 generation, and your food never fail to eternity. And may all who hate you fall down before you, and may all your adversaries be uprooted and perish; and blessed shall the man be that blesses you, and accursed every nation that curses you.

18   And to Judah he said, May the Lord give you strength and power to tread down all that hate you: a prince shall you be (you and one of your sons) over the sons of Jacob: may your name and your sons' name go out and spread through every land and region. Then shall the Gentiles fear you, and all nations quake, and all
19 peoples stand in awe *of you*.[7] In you shall be Jacob's help, and in
20 you shall be found Israel's salvation. And when you sit on the throne of honour, your righteousness will bring[8] great peace for all the offspring of the sons of the beloved one. Blessed shall the man be that blesses you; and all that hate you and afflict you and curse

---

[5] So one Eth. MS: the others differ among themselves and from the Latin (*magno intellegere gloriam eius*).

[6] Lit. 'and cause you and your seed from among all flesh to approach him to serve'.

[7] Lit. 'quake', as in the preceding clause. Charles bracketed this clause as a dittograph.

[8] Lit. 'will be'. Another reading is 'And when you sit on the throne of the honour of your righteousness there shall be . . .'.

you shall be uprooted and destroyed from the earth and be accursed.

21 And he turned and kissed him again and embraced him, and rejoiced greatly (for he had seen his son Jacob's sons in very

22 truth[9]). And he disengaged himself[10] and fell down and bowed himself before him. And he blessed them. And he stayed there with

23 his father Isaac that night; and they ate and drank with joy. And he made Jacob's two sons sleep, one on his right hand and the other

24 on his left, and it was counted to him as righteousness. And during the night Jacob told his father everything, how the Lord had shown him great mercy, and how he had prospered *him in* every way and

25 protected him from all evil. And Isaac blessed the God of his father Abraham, who had not withdrawn his mercy and his righteousness from his servant Isaac's sons.

26 And in the morning Jacob told his father Isaac about the vow he had vowed to the Lord and the vision he had seen, and that he had built an altar, and that everything was ready for the sacrifice to be made before the Lord as he had vowed, and that he had come to set

27 him on an ass *and take him with him.* And Isaac said to his son Jacob, I cannot go with you, for I am too old and unable to stand the journey: go, my son, in peace, for I am a hundred and sixty-five years old today. My travelling days are done: set your mother *on the*

28 *ass* and let her go with you. And I know, my son, that you have come because of me; and blessed be this day on which you have

29 seen me *still* alive, and I also have seen you, my son. May you prosper and fulfil the vow that you have vowed; and do not put it[11] off, for you will be called to account in respect of it,[12] so make haste and fulfil it now, and may the maker of all things, to whom you have vowed the vow, be pleased.

30 And he said to Rebecca, Go with your son Jacob. And Rebecca went with her son Jacob, and Deborah with her, and they came to

31 Bethel. And Jacob remembered the prayer with which his father had blessed him and his two sons, Levi and Judah; and he rejoiced

32 and blessed the God of his fathers, Abraham and Isaac. And he

---

[9] Or 'in righteousness'.
[10] Lit. 'he went forth from between his feet'.
[11] Lit. 'your vow'.
[12] Lit. 'the vow'.

said, Now I know that I have an eternal hope, and my sons also, before the God of all.

And so it was decreed concerning the two; and how Isaac blessed them is recorded on the heavenly tablets as an eternal testimony.

XXXII. And he spent[1] that night at Bethel. And Levi dreamed that they had ordained him and made him the priest of the Most High God, him and his sons for ever; and he woke up from his sleep and 2 blessed the Lord. And Jacob got up early in the morning, on the fourteenth of this month, and gave a tithe of everything that had come with him, of men and cattle, of gold, and of every vessel and 3 garment: he gave tithes of all. And in these days Rachel was pregnant with her son Benjamin. And Jacob counted his sons from him upwards, and *so it was that* Levi was chosen to minister to the Lord;[2] and his father clothed him in the garments of the priesthood and installed him.[3]

4 And on the fifteenth of this month he brought to the altar fourteen oxen from the cattle, and twenty-eight rams, and forty-nine sheep, and seven[4] lambs, and twenty-one[4] kids from the goats, as a whole-offering on the altar, a sacrifice acceptable as a soothing 5 odour before God. This was his offering in fulfilment of the vow he had vowed that he would give a tenth, with their fruit-offerings and 6 their drink-offerings. And when the fire had consumed it he burnt incense on the fire over it, and for a thank-offering *he offered* two oxen, and four rams, and four sheep, four he-goats, and two sheep of a year old, and two kids from the goats; and so he did daily for 7 seven days. And he and all his sons and his men ate there with joy for seven days, and he blessed and thanked the Lord who had delivered him from all his distress and granted him his prayer.[5]

8 And he tithed all the clean animals and made a whole-offering, but

---

[1] So Eth.: Lat. 'they slept'.
[2] Lit. 'and Levi fell to the portion (or 'lot') of the Lord'. The idea seems to be that as Levi was the third of Jacob's sons (so xxviii. 14 above) he would be the tenth if the count were started from the bottom with Benjamin.
[3] Or 'consecrated him' (lit. 'filled his hands').
[4] So Lat.: Eth. '. . . sixty . . . twenty-nine'.
[5] Lit. 'vow'.

the unclean animals he gave to his son Levi,[6] and he gave him *also*
9 all the souls of men. And Levi discharged the priestly office at
Bethel before his father Jacob in preference to his ten brothers, and
he was a priest there. And Jacob fulfilled his vow; in this way he
tithed again the tithe to the Lord and hallowed it, and it became
holy to him.

10 And for this reason it is decreed on the heavenly tablets as a law
for the tithing again the tithe to eat before the Lord from year to
year in the place chosen as a dwelling for his name; and to this law
11 there is no time limit whatever. This decree is written that it may
be fulfilled from year to year, and that the second tithe may be
eaten before the Lord in the place chosen, and nothing of it shall be
12 left over from one year to the next. For in its own year shall the seed
be eaten till the time when the seed of that year is harvested, and
the wine *be drunk* till the time when the grapes are gathered in,[7] and
13 the oil similarly.[8] And whatever of it is left over and becomes stale –
14 let it be treated as polluted: let it be burnt, for it is unclean. And so
let *all of* them eat it together in the sanctuary and not allow it to
15 become stale. And all the tithes of the oxen and sheep shall be holy
to the Lord, and shall belong to his priests: they shall eat them
before him from year to year; for it is so decreed and engraved
about the tithe on the heavenly tablets.

16 And on the following night, on the twenty-second of this month,
Jacob decided to start building *at* that place, and to surround the
court with a wall, and to hallow it and make it holy for ever, for
17 himself and his children after him. And the Lord appeared to him
by night and blessed him and said to him, Your name shall no
18 longer be Jacob, but Israel shall be your name. And he said to him
again, I am the Lord who created heaven and earth, and I will
increase you and multiply you greatly, and kings shall spring from
you, and they shall sit in judgement in every land wherever men
19 have set their feet. And I will give to your descendants all the earth
that is[9] under heaven, and they shall judge all the nations in
accordance with their desires, and after that they shall gain possession of the entire earth and inherit it for ever.

---

[6] Charles supplied a negative in this clause ('. . . he gave not to his son Levi').
[7] Lit. 'till the days of the wine'.   [8] Lit. 'till the days of its season'.
[9] So Eth.: Lat. 'all the blessings that are'.

20 And he finished speaking with him and went up from him; and
21 Jacob looked *after him* till he had gone up into heaven. And that
night he saw a vision, and behold, an angel came down from
heaven with seven tablets in his hands, and he gave them to Jacob;
and he read them and understood[10] everything that was written on
22 them — what would befall him and his sons in every age. And he
showed him everything that was written on the tablets, and said to
him, Do not start building *at* this place and do not make it either an
eternal sanctuary or a permanent abode; for this is not the *chosen*
place. Go to your father Abraham's house and live *there* with your
23 father Isaac till the day of your father's death. You will die in peace
in Egypt, but you will be buried in this land with honour in your
24 fathers' grave, with Abraham and Isaac. Do not be afraid, for as
you have seen and read it, so shall it all be; and write down
25 everything, just as you have seen *it* and read *it*. And Jacob said,
Lord, how can I remember all that I have read and seen? And he
said to him, I will see that you remember everything; and he went
26 up from him. And he woke up from his sleep and remembered
everything he had read and seen, and he wrote down every word.[11]

27 And he celebrated an extra day there, and he offered sacrifices
on it, just as he had on the previous days; and he called it
Addition[12] (because it was an additional day[13]), and the previous
28 days he called The Feast. And it was made plain that it should be
so, and it is written on the heavenly tablets; and that is why it was
revealed to him that he should celebrate it and add[14] it to the seven
29 days of the feast. And it was called Addition because it was
recorded among the feast days according to the number of the days
of the year.[15]

30 And on the twenty-third of this month, in the night, Deborah,

[10] So Lat. ('got to know'): Eth. 'read'.
[11] Lit. 'he wrote down all the words that he had read and seen'.
[12] So Eth.: Lat. 'Keeping back' (*retentatio*). The allusion is to the 'closing ceremony' (Heb. '*aṣereth*) of the feast of Tabernacles (cp. Lev. xxiii. 36, Num. xxix. 35, and Neh. viii. 18).
[13] Lit. 'because this day was added (Lat. 'kept back' = *retentus est*)'.
[14] So both Eth. and Lat. (*adicere*).
[15] The Eth. and Lat. are in essential agreement on the text of this verse. Charles conjectured an original 'And it was called '*Aṣereth* when it was recorded among the feast days in the number of the days of the year.'

Rebecca's nurse, died, and they buried her below the city, under
the oak by the river; and he[16] called the place, Deborah's River,
31   and the oak, The oak of mourning for Deborah. And Rebecca
returned home to his father Isaac; and Jacob sent with her rams
and sheep and he-goats, so that she could prepare food for his
32   father of the kind he liked. And he went after his mother till he
came to the land of Kabratan, and he settled there.

33   And Rachel gave birth to a son in the night, and she called him
Son of my sorrow (for her birth-pangs were severe), but his father
called him Benjamin – on the eleventh of the eighth month in the
34   first year of the sixth week of this jubilee. And Rachel died there
and was buried in the land of Ephratha (that is Bethlehem); and
Jacob set up a pillar over Rachel's grave, by the road above her
grave.

XXXIII.   And Jacob moved and settled to the south of Migdal-
Eder-Ephrata. And he went to *visit* his father Isaac, he and his wife
2   Leah, on the new moon of the tenth month. And Reuben saw
Bilhah, Rachel's maid, his father's concubine, bathing in water in
3   a secluded place, and he became enamoured of her. And he hid
himself and went into Bilhah's house at night and found her asleep
4   alone on her bed in her house; and he lay with her. And she woke
up and looked round, and behold Reuben was lying with her on the
bed; and she lifted the edge of her coverlet and took hold of him,
5   and when she realized it was Reuben she cried out aloud. And she
was ashamed because of him,[1] and she let go of him, and he fled.
6   And she was much upset by what had happened and said nothing
7   to any one about it. And when Jacob returned and asked for[2] her,
she said to him, I am not clean for you, for I have been defiled:[3]
Reuben defiled me and lay with me in the night, when I was asleep,

---

[16] So Eth.: Lat. 'they'.

[1] So Eth.: Lat. 'he was ashamed because of her'. As the texts of this passage now
stand, this is the only clear case of confusion about who was doing what. It is
probable, however, that at earlier stages in the tradition there were more; and in the
original it may well have been Reuben who lifted the edge of the coverlet and took
hold of Bilhah, and then, when she cried out, let go of her, rather than *vice versa*.
[2] Lit. 'sought'.   [3] Lit. 'defiled as regards you'.

and I did not realize *who it was* until he had uncovered my shame[4]
8 and had intercourse with me. And Jacob was very angry with
Reuben because he had lain with Bilhah – because he had uncovered his father's shame. And Jacob did not approach her again
because Reuben had defiled her.

9   And any man who uncovers his father's shame – what he does is
wicked beyond measure, for he is abominable in the Lord's sight.
10 That is why it is written and decreed on the heavenly tablets that a
man should not lie with his father's wife and should not uncover his
father's shame, for *to do* this is unclean: they shall be put to death
together, the man who lies with his father's wife and the woman
11 also, for they are guilty of uncleanness on the earth. And there shall
be nothing unclean before our God in the nation that he has chosen
12 for himself as a possession. And again, it is written a second time,
Cursed be the man who lies with his father's wife, for he has
uncovered his father's shame; and all the Lord's holy ones said,
Amen, Amen.

13   And do you, Moses, command the sons of Israel to observe this
injunction,[5] for *transgression of* it *entails* the punishment of death,
and it *concerns what* is unclean; and there is no atonement that can
ever atone for the man who has committed this *sin*, but he must be
killed and put to death by stoning and uprooted from among the
14 people of our God. For no man who does this in Israel should be
allowed to remain alive a single day on the earth, for he is abomin-
15 able and unclean. And let no one say, Reuben was granted life and
forgiveness after he had lain with his father's concubine, and so
also was Bilhah,[6] although she had a husband, and her husband
16 Jacob (Reuben's[7] father) was still alive. For at that time the
ordinance and the decree and the law in its completeness, to cover
every case,[8] had not been revealed; but in your days *it has been
revealed* as a law for *all* times and seasons, and as an everlasting law
17 for all generations for ever. And for this law there is no time limit,
neither can there be atonement for *transgression of* it, but both *the*

----

[4] Lit. 'skirt' and so also in verses 8, 9, 10 and 12.
[5] Lit. 'this word'.
[6] Lit. 'To Reuben was granted . . . and to her also'.
[7] Lit. 'his'.
[8] Lit. 'for all'.

man and the woman must be uprooted from the nation: on the day on which they committed the sin[9] they shall be put to death.

18   And do you, Moses, write *it* down for Israel, that they may observe it, and not do such a thing, and not commit a mortal sin; for the Lord our God is a judge who neither respects persons nor

19   accepts bribes. And tell them these words of the covenant, that they may hear *them*, and observe *them*, and be on their guard in relation to them, and *take care* not to be destroyed and uprooted from the land; for all on the earth who commit this sin[10] are an uncleanness and an abomination and a contamination and a pollu-

20   tion before our God. And there is no sin on earth they can commit greater than fornication, for Israel is a holy nation to the Lord its God, and a special nation of his own, and a priestly and royal nation for his possession; and no such uncleanness should be seen in a holy nation.

21   And in the third year of this sixth week Jacob and all his sons went and lived in Abraham's house near his father Isaac and his

22   mother Rebecca. And these were the names of Jacob's sons: Reuben (the eldest), Simeon, Levi, Judah, Issachar, Zebulon – *all* sons of Leah; and the sons of Rachel – Joseph and Benjamin; and the sons of Bilhah – Dan and Naphtali; and the sons of Zilpah – Gad and Asher; and Dinah, the daughter of Leah (Jacob's only

23   daughter). And they came and bowed themselves before Isaac and Rebecca; and when they saw them they blessed Jacob and all his sons. And Isaac rejoiced greatly when he saw his younger son Jacob's sons; and he blessed them.

XXXIV. And in the sixth year of this week of this fourty-fourth jubilee Jacob sent his sons to pasture their sheep in the pastures of

2   Shechem, and his servants with them. And the seven kings of the Amorites banded together against them and took up their posi-tions in a wood,[1] with the intention of killing them and taking their

3   cattle as spoil. And Jacob and Levi and Judah and Joseph were at home with their father Isaac (for he was in a sorry state and they

---

[9] Lit. 'committed it'.
[10] Lit. 'commit it'.

[1] So Lat.: Eth. 'hiding themselves under the trees'.

could not leave him); and Benjamin was the youngest, and for this
4 reason remained with his father. And the king of Tappuah came,
and the king of Aresa, and the king of Seragan, and the king of Selo,
and the king of Gaash, and the king of Beth-horon, and the king of
Maanisakir, and all who live in these mountains *and* in the woods
5 in the land of Canaan. And Jacob was told, Behold, the kings of the
Amorites have surrounded your sons and plundered their herds.
6 And he left his house, he and his three sons and all his father's
servants and his own servants, and he went against them with six
7 thousand men armed with swords. And he cut them down in the
pastures of Shechem, and he pursued the fugitives and put them to
the sword; and he killed *the kings of* Aresa and Tappuah and
Saregan and Selo and Amanisakir and Gaash and recovered his
8 herds. And he gained the mastery over them and imposed tribute
on them, and he made them pay him as tribute five fruit products
9 of their land; and he built[2] Robel and Timnath-heres. And he
returned in peace; and he made peace with them, and they became
his servants till the day that he and his sons went down to Egypt.
10   And in the seventh year of this week he sent Joseph from home to
the land of Shechem to see how his brothers were faring; and he
11 found them in the land of Dothan. And they conspired against
him[3] and hatched a plot to kill him, but they changed their minds
and sold him to Ishmaelite merchants; and they took him down to
Egypt and sold him to Potiphar, a eunuch of Pharaoh's *and his* chief
12 cook, priest of the city of Elew.[4] And Jacob's sons slaughtered a kid
and dipped Joseph's coat in the blood and sent *it* to their father
13 Jacob on the tenth of the seventh month. And he mourned all that
night (for they had brought it to him in the evening), and he was
beside himself with grief[5] and said, An evil beast has devoured
Joseph; and all his household mourned with him that day, and
14 they mourned and lamented with him the whole day. And his sons
and his daughter tried to comfort him, but he refused to be comforted for his son.
15   And on that day Bilhah heard that Joseph was dead, and she

---

[2] Or 'restored'.
[3] Lit. 'behaved treacherously towards him'.
[4] i.e. Heliopolis.
[5] Lit. 'he became feverish with mourning for his death'.

died while mourning for him, and she was living in Qafratef; and Dinah, Jacob's[6] daughter, also died when *she heard that* Joseph was
16 dead. And so Israel suffered three losses[7] in a single month. And they buried Bilhah opposite Rachel's tomb; and they buried
17 Jacob's[6] daughter Dinah there too. And Jacob[8] mourned for Joseph for a whole year and would not desist, for he said, Let me go
18 down to the grave mourning for my son. This is why it is decreed that the sons of Israel should mortify themselves on the tenth of the seventh month (on the day that the news which made him weep for Joseph came to his father Jacob), *and* that on it they should make expiation for themselves with a young goat – on the tenth of the seventh month, once a year, for their sin (for they had resented
19 their father's affection for his son Joseph[9]). And this day has been set apart so that on it they should grieve for their sins and for all their transgressions and for all their misdeeds, *and* so cleanse themselves, once a year, on that day.
20 And after Joseph was taken away, Jacob's sons married wives. The name of Reuben's wife was Ada; and the name of Simeon's wife Adibaa, a Canaanite; and the name of Levi's wife Melka, an Aramaean,[10] a descendant of the sons of Terah; and the name of Judah's wife Betasuel, a Canaanite; and the name of Issachar's wife Hezaqa; and the name of Zebulon's wife Niiman; and the name of Dan's wife Egla; and the name of Naphtali's wife Rasuu, from Mesopotamia; and the name of Gad's wife Maka; and the name of Asher's wife Ijona; and the name of Joseph's wife Asenath,
21 the Egyptian; and the name of Benjamin's wife Ijasaka. And Simeon repented and took a second wife from Mesopotamia, like his brothers.

XXXV. And in the first year of the first week of the forty-fourth jubilee Rebecca summoned her son Jacob and gave him instructions to honour his father and his brother all the days of his life.
2 And Jacob said, I will do everything you tell me; for to honour

---

6 Lit. 'his'.
7 Lit. 'And there came these three mournings on Israel'.
8 Lit. 'he'.
9 Lit. 'for they had grieved the affection of their father regarding his son Joseph'.
10 Lit. 'of the daughters of Aram'.

them will bring me honour, and greatness, and credit with[1] the
3 Lord. And you know, mother, all my deeds and thoughts from the
day of my birth till now; *and you know* that I am always well-
4 disposed towards everyone.[2] How, then, should I not do what you
5 tell me, and honour my father and my brother? Point out to me,
mother, anything[3] you have observed in me that is evil, and I will
6 set my face against it, and ask for mercy. And she said to him, I
have never at any time, my son, seen you do anything that is evil
but *only* what is good.[4] And I will tell you the truth, my son: this
year I shall die, and I shall not survive this present year; for I have
seen the day of my death in a dream, *and I know* that I shall not live
more than a hundred and fifty-five years: I have *now all but* com-
7 pleted the span of life allotted to me.[5] And Jacob laughed at his
mother's words, because his mother told him that she was about to
die, when she was sitting opposite him in full possession of all her
faculties and was not in any way infirm; for she went in and out, her
sight was good, her teeth were strong, and she had never had an
8 illness in her life. And Jacob said to her, I should indeed be blessed,
mother, if the span of my life were to be anywhere near what yours
is, and I were to retain my faculties as you have: you are not dying:
it is only an idle dream you are telling me about your death.

9 And she went in to Isaac and said to him, One thing I would ask
you: make Esau swear that he will not injure Jacob or maintain a
feud with him; for you know Esau's disposition, how savage he has
been from his youth up, and there is nothing good about him, and
10 he is *only* waiting for your death to kill Jacob.[6] And you know
everything he has done from the day his brother Jacob went to
Haran until to-day, how he deliberately left us[7] and has done us
evil: he has appropriated your flocks and stripped you of all your
11 possessions. And when we implored and besought him for what
12 was our own he assumed the role of someone taking pity on us. And
he is embittered against you because you blessed Jacob, your

---

[1] Lit. 'and righteousness before'.
[2] Eth. 'that I always think good concerning all': Lat. 'that I always (have the
intention) to do good to all'.
[3] Lit. 'what'.   [4] Lit. 'upright'.
[5] Lit. 'all the days of my life which I am to live'.
[6] Lit. 'for he desires after your death to kill him'.
[7] Lit. 'how he forsook us with all his heart'.

perfect and upright son; for in Jacob[8] there is nothing evil, but only
what is good, and since he came back from Haran until to-day he
has not let us lack for anything, but brings us everything in its
season always, and rejoices with all his heart when we take *it* at his
hands, and blesses us and has not left us since he came back from
Haran until to-day, and he remains with us continually at home
and honours us.

13　　And Isaac said to her, I too know and see what Jacob does, how
he stays by us,[9] *and* how he honours us with all his heart: at one
time I loved Esau more than Jacob, because he was the firstborn;
but now I love Jacob more than Esau, for Esau[10] has done all kinds
of evil, and there is no righteousness in him *at all* – everything he
does is vicious[11] and violent, and there is no righteousness about

14　　him whatsoever. But now I am troubled in mind because of what
he does: neither he nor his descendants will be saved, for they are
destined to perish from the earth and be uprooted from under
heaven; for he has forsaken the God of Abraham and followed his
wives and their uncleanness and their misdeeds, he and his

15　　children. And *now* you ask me to make him swear that he will not

16　　kill his brother Jacob: even if he does swear, he will not abide by his
oath; and he will do no good, but evil only. But if he does want to
kill his brother Jacob, he will be given into Jacob's hands and will

17　　not escape his hands [, for he will fall into his hands]. Have no fear
on Jacob's account; for Jacob's guardian is great and powerful and
honourable, and much more glorious than Esau's guardian.

18　　And Rebecca sent and summoned Esau; and he came to her, and

19　　she said to him, I have something to ask you, my son: promise me

20　　you will do it, my son. And he said, I will do everything you tell me
and not refuse you what you ask. And she said to him, I ask that
when I die, you will take me and bury me near Sarah, your father's
mother. And *I ask too* that you and Jacob will love one another, and
that neither will harbour evil desires against the other, but mutual
love only, and *so* you will prosper, my sons, and be honoured in the
land, and no enemy will rejoice over you, and you will be a blessing

21　　and a mercy in the eyes of all that love you. And he said, I will do
everything you have told me, and on the day you die I will bury you

---

near Sarah, my father's mother, since you want her bones to be
22 near your bones. And I will, too, love my brother Jacob more than
any other living creature;[12] for I have no *other* brother anywhere in
the world, but him only. It is no great virtue in me if I love him, for
he is my brother: we were sown together in your womb, and we
came forth together from your womb,[13] and if I do not love my
23 brother, whom shall I love? And I, for my part, would ask you to
appeal to Jacob on my behalf and on my sons' behalf, for I know
that he must rule over me and *over* my sons; for on the day my father
24 blessed him he made him the senior and me the junior. And I swear
to you that I will love him and not harbour any evil desires against
him, but good only, all my life. And he swore an oath to her in these
terms.

25 And she summoned Jacob in Esau's presence and gave him the
26 same instructions she had given Esau. And he said, I will do as you
would have me do:[14] believe me, no evil shall come to Esau either
from me or from my sons, and I will be the first in nothing, but in
27 love only. And they ate and drank, she and her sons that night.
And that night she died, three jubilees and one week and one year
old; and her two sons, Esau and Jacob, buried her in the double
cave near Sarah, their father's mother.

XXXVI. And in the sixth year of this week Isaac summoned his
two sons, Esau and Jacob; and they came to him, and he said to
them, My sons, I am going the way of my fathers, to the eternal
2 house where my fathers are. Bury me near my father Abraham, in
the double cave in the field of Ephron the Hittite, which Abraham
bought as a burial place: bury me there, in the grave that I dug for
3 myself. And this command I lay upon you, my sons, that you are
just and upright in your dealings on the earth, so that the Lord may
bring upon you all that the Lord said he would do to Abraham and
4 his descendants. And love one another, my sons, as a man loves his
own soul, and let each see what he can to do to help his brother and
act together *with him* on the earth; and let each love the other as his
own soul.

5 And as for idols, I command *you* and I warn you to keep them

---

[12] Lit. 'above all flesh'.   [13] Lit. 'navel'.
[14] Lit. 'I will do your pleasure'.

from you and hate them, and love them not; for they are a delusion and a snare[1] to those who worship them and bow down to them.

6 Remember the Lord, my sons, the God of Abraham your father, and **how** I too made him my God and served him in righteousness and joy, that he might multiply you and increase the number of your descendants *till they were* like the stars of heaven, and that he might establish you on the earth as the plant of righteousness which will not be uprooted for all generations for ever.

7 And now I will make you swear a great oath (for there is no oath greater) by the Name, glorious and honoured and great and splendid and wonderful, *the Name of him* who created the heavens and the earth and all things together – that you will fear him and

8 worship him; and that each *of you* will love his brother in affection and righteousness, and that neither *of you* will harbour any evil desires against his brother either now or at any future time, so that you may prosper in everything you do and may not be destroyed.

9 And if either of you plans any evil against his brother, know now that whoever does plan evil against his brother will fall into his hand and be uprooted from the land of the living, and his progeny

10 will perish from the earth.[2] But on the day of turmoil and execration and indignation and anger, just as the Lord[3] burned Sodom with flaming *and* devouring fire, so will he burn that man's[4] land and his city and all that is his, and he will be blotted out of the book of the discipline of mortal men, and not be recorded in the book of life, but rather in that which is[5] appointed for destruction; and he will depart into eternal execration – so that their condemnation may be always renewed in hate and execration and wrath and

11 torment and indignation, and in plagues and disease for ever. I tell you *this* and testify to you, my sons, that judgement will come[6] upon the man who lays plans to injure his brother.

12 And on that day he divided all his possessions between the two *of them*; and he gave the larger part to the elder – the tower and all that was round about it, and everything that had belonged to Abraham

13 at the Well of the Oath. And he said, I will **give** the elder this larger

---

[1] Lit. 'they are full of deception'.
[2] Lit. 'from under heaven'.
[3] Lit. 'he'.   [4] Lit. 'his'.   [5] Or 'that of those'.
[6] Lit. 'according to the judgement that will come'.

14 portion. And Esau said, I sold Jacob my portion as elder brother and have given it to him: let it *therefore* be given him: I have no
15 claim on it,[7] for it is his. And Isaac, said, May a blessing rest upon you, my sons, and upon your descendants this day; for you have set my mind at rest, and I have no anxiety about the elder's portion,
16 that you will come to blows about it. May the Most High God bless the man that does what is right, *may he bless* him and his
17 descendants for ever. And he finished instructing them and blessing them; and they ate and drank together in his presence, and he rejoiced at the harmony between them. And they went out from
18 him and rested that day and slept. And Isaac slept on his bed that day rejoicing; and he slept the eternal sleep and died, a hundred and eighty years old. He *thus* completed twenty-five weeks and five years; and his sons Esau and Jacob buried him.

19 And Esau went to the land of Edom, to the mountains of Seir,
20 and lived there. And Jacob lived in the mountains of Hebron, in the tower in the country where his father Abraham had lived; and he worshipped the Lord with all his heart and in accordance with the commandments that had been revealed at the time of his
21 birth.[8] And his wife Leah died in the fourth year of the second week of the forty-fifth jubilee; and he buried her in the double cave near Rebecca his mother, on the left of the grave of Sarah his father's
22 mother. And all her sons and his sons came to mourn over his wife Leah with him, and to comfort him on her account, because he was
23 making lamentation for her. For after her sister Rachel died he loved her all the more,[9] for she was perfect and upright in all her ways and honoured[10] Jacob; and all the time she lived with him he never heard a harsh word from her mouth, for she was gentle and
24 peaceable and upright and honourable. And he remembered everything she had done during her lifetime; and he made a great lamentation for her, for he loved her heart and soul.

XXXVII. And on the day that Jacob and Esau's father Isaac died, Esau's sons heard that Isaac had given the elder's portion to Jacob

---

[7] Lit. 'I have not a single word to say regarding it'.

[8] Both the text and the meaning are uncertain here: the Eth. MSS differ among themselves as well as from the Lat.

[9] Lit. 'he loved her exceedingly'.　　　　[10] One Eth. MS reads 'loved'.

2 his younger son; and they were very angry. And they started a dispute with their father, saying, why has your father given Jacob the elder's portion and passed you over, although you are the elder

3 and Jacob the younger? And he said to them, Because I sold my birthright to Jacob for a modest lentil stew; and on the day my father sent me out hunting to bring him back something, so that he could eat *of it* and bless me, Jacob[1] treacherously came and brought my father food and drink, and my father blessed him and

4 made me his subordinate.[2] And now our father has made us swear, both of us, that we will plan no evil against each other, either *of us* against his brother, and that we will persevere in love and peace,

5 each with his brother, and not be led astray.[3] And they said to him, we will not listen to you and make peace with him, for our strength is greater than his strength, and we are more powerful than he is: we will attack him and kill him, and we will destroy his sons;[4] and if

6 you will not go with us, we will do you some damage too. Listen now to us: let us send to Aram and Philistia and Moab and Ammon and choose for ourselves picked men, ardent for battle, and let us attack him and do battle with him and exterminate him from the earth before he takes root and grows strong.

7 And their father said to them, Do not go and make war with him

8 in case you fall before him. And they said to him, This is exactly how you always have behaved from your youth till now: you submit your neck to his yoke; but we will not listen to such talk.

9 And they sent to Aram, and to Aduram, their father's friend, and they hired along with them a thousand fighting men, picked war-

10 riors *all of them*. And there came to them from Moab and from the Ammonites a thousand picked mercenaries, and from Philistia a thousand picked warriors, and from Edom and the Horites a thousand picked fighting men, and from the Kittim mighty war-

11 riors. And they said to their father, Take the field with them and

12 lead them, or we will kill you. And he was furious and indignant when he saw his sons were forcing him to take command of them

13 and lead them against his brother Jacob. But afterwards he recol-

---

[1] Lit. 'he'.   [2] Lit. 'put me under his hand'.
[3] Lit. 'and not make our ways corrupt'.
[4] So the majority of Eth. MSS: Lat. and (it would seem) one Eth. MS read 'him and his sons'.

lected all the evil *thoughts* about his brother Jacob that lay hidden in his heart; and he forgot the oath he had sworn to his father and his mother that he would never plan evil against his brother Jacob at any time.

14 And in spite of all this Jacob was unaware that they were coming against him to battle (for he was mourning for his wife Leah) until they came very near to the tower with four thousand warriors and

15 picked fighting men. And the men of Hebron sent to him, saying, Behold your brother has come against you to fight you, with four thousand men armed with swords and with shields and other weapons. (They told him because they much preferred Jacob to Esau, for Jacob was a much kinder and more generous man than

16 Esau.) But Jacob would not believe *it* until they came very near the

17 tower. And he shut the gates of the tower and stood on the battlements and addressed his brother Esau and said, This is fine comfort you come with to comfort me for my wife's death. Is this the oath that you swore to your father and again to your mother before they died? You have broken the oath; and at the very moment you swore to your father you were condemned.

18 And Esau answered immediately and said to him, Neither man nor beast knows of any oath that is inviolable, which when once sworn, is valid for ever;[5] but they plan evil against each other every

19 day, how they can kill their rivals and *their* enemies. You hate me and my children always; and there is no *possibility of* observing the

20 tie of brotherhood with you. Listen now to this,[6]

> If the boar can change his skin and make his bristles as soft as wool,
> Or if he can make horns to sprout out of his head like the horns of a stag or a sheep,
> Then will I observe the tie of brotherhood with you.[7]

[5] Lit. 'Neither the sons of men nor the beasts of the earth have any oath of righteousness, which in swearing they have sworn for ever'.

[6] Lit. 'Hear these words which I declare to you'.

[7] All the Eth. MSS add an extra line at this point, which does not fit well into the context. Charles rendered it 'And if the breasts separated themselves from their mother, for you have not been a brother to me' and supposed it to be a wandering fragment from verse 19. After transposing the two distinct clauses in the line, and some further emendation, he suggested as the original for verse 19, 'You hate me

21   And if the wolves can make peace with the lambs so as not to
       devour them or do them violence,
     And if their hearts are inclined towards them for good,
     Then shall there be peace in my heart towards you.

22   And if the lion becomes the friend of the ox and makes peace
       with him,[8]
     And if he is joined under one yoke with him and ploughs with
       him,
     Then will I make peace with you.

23   And when the raven becomes white like the raza,[9]
     Then know that I am well disposed towards you,
     And that I will make peace with you.
     But now you shall be rooted up, and your sons shall be rooted
       up,
     And you shall have no peace.

24   And when Jacob saw that he was *so* evilly disposed towards him
     and was determined at all costs to kill him, and that he had come
     charging *at him* like a wild boar that hurls itself without flinching
25   against the spear that pierces and kills it, he gave the order to his
     household and his servants to attack him and all his associates.

XXXVIII.   And Judah spoke up at once and said to his father Jacob,

     Bend your bow, father, and let fly your arrows,
     And bring low the adversary and slaughter the enemy;
     And may you have the power,
     For we will not kill your brother because he is your *brother*,
     And we owe him as much honour as *we owe* to you.

2   Then Jacob bent his bow and let fly an arrow and shot his brother
3   Esau in the right breast, and killed him. And he let fly another

---

and my children always; for you have never been a brother to me since the twins
were separated from their mother, and there is no *possibility of* observing the tie of
brotherhood with you'.

[8] In some MSS 'and makes peace with him' is placed after 'and ploughs with
him': in others it is omitted.

[9] According to Charles this was the local name for 'a large white bird'.

arrow and shot Adoran the Aramaean in the left breast, and knocked him off his feet and killed him.

4 And then Jacob's sons went out with their servants, divided into
5 companies on the four sides of the tower. And Judah went out in front, and Naphtali and Gad with him and fifty servants, on the south side of the tower; and they killed everyone they found before
6 them, and not a single one escaped. And Levi and Dan and Asher went out on the east side of the tower, and fifty men with them; and
7 they killed the fighting men of Moab and Ammon. And Reuben and Issachar and Zebulon went out on the north side of the tower, and fifty men with them; and they killed the fighting men of the
8 Philistines. And Simeon and Benjamin and Enoch, Reuben's son, went out on the west side of the tower, and fifty men with them; and they killed four hundred men of Edom and the Horites (stout warriors *all of them*), and six hundred fled; and four of Esau's sons fled with them and left their father lying dead, just as he had fallen
9 on the hill in Aduram. And Jacob's sons pursued them to the mountains of Seir. And Jacob buried his brother on the hill in Aduram and returned home.

10 And Jacob's sons pressed hard on[1] Esau's sons in the mountains in Seir and subdued them,[2] so that they became their servants.[3]
11 And they sent to their father asking whether they should make
12 peace with them or kill them. And Jacob sent word to his sons that they should make peace; and they made peace with them and laid on them the yoke of servitude, so that they paid tribute to Jacob
13 and his sons in perpetuity. And they continued to pay tribute to
14 Jacob till the day he went down into Egypt. And the Edomites have not got quit of the yoke of servitude that Jacob's twelve sons imposed on them to this day.

15 And these are the kings that reigned in Edom before there
16 reigned any king over Israel – to this day in the land of Edom.[4] And Balak, the son of Beor, reigned in Edom, and the name of his city
17 was Dinhaba. And Balak died, and was succeeded by Jobab, the

---

[1] So Eth.: Lat. 'surrounded'.
[2] Lit. 'made them bow their necks'.
[3] Lit. 'became servants of Jacob's sons'.
[4] Charles bracketed 'to this day' as an insertion. Perhaps both phrases are dittographs.

18 son of Zerah of Bosra. And Jobab died, and was succeeded by
19 Husham from Teman. And Husham died, and was succeeded by
Adath, the son of Barad, who defeated Midian in Moabite terri-
20 tory, and the name of his city was Avith. And Adath died, and
21 was succeeded by Salman from Amaseqa. And Salman died,
22 and was succeeded by Saul of Rehoboth *by the* river. And Saul
23 died, and was succeeded by Baal-Hanan, the son of Achbor. And
Baal-Hanan, the son of Achbor, died, and was succeeded by
Adath; and the name of his wife was Maitabith, the daughter of
24 Matarat, the daughter of Metabedzaab. These are the kings that
reigned in the land of Edom.

XXXIX. And Jacob lived in the country[1] where his father had
2 settled, in the land of Canaan. This is the story of his family.[2]

Joseph was seventeen years old when they took him down to the
land of Egypt, and Potiphar, one of Pharaoh's eunuchs and *his*
3 chief cook, bought him. And he put Joseph in charge of his household; and the Lord blessed the Egyptian's household because of
Joseph, and the Lord made him successful in everything he did.
4 And the Egyptian left everything in Joseph's **hands**,[3] for he saw that
the Lord was with him and made him successful in everything he
did.

5 And Joseph was handsome and very good-looking, and his
6 master's wife eyed him and took notice of him; and she fell in love
with him and begged him to lie with her. But he would not
surrender himself, for he remembered the Lord and what[4] his
father Jacob used to read from the commandments[5] of Abraham,
that no man should commit fornication with a woman that has a
husband, that for the man who does[6] the punishment of death has
been ordained in the heavens before the Most High God, and that
his sin will be recorded against him in the eternal books before the
7 Lord for ever. And Joseph remembered this and refused to lie with

[1] Or 'land'.
[2] Lit. 'These are the generations of Jacob'.
[3] All Eth. MSS 'in Joseph's presence': the emendation is based on the Lat. of verse 12 and the Heb. of Gen. xxxix. 6.
[4] Lit. 'the words which'.   [5] Lit. 'the words'.
[6] Lit. 'for him'.

8   her. And she pleaded with him for a *whole* year, and *then* for another
    year; but he refused to listen.

9   At last,[7] when they were indoors, she caught hold of him and
    clung to him, to try and force him to lie with her, and she locked the
    doors of the house and clung tightly to him; but he fled, leaving his
10 cloak in her hands, and broke open the doors and escaped. And the
    woman saw that he would not lie with her,[8] and she told his master
    lies about him, saying, Your Hebrew servant that you are *so* fond of
    tried to force me and lie with me; and when I screamed out he fled
    and left his cloak I had taken hold of in my hands and broke open
11 the door. And the Egyptian saw Joseph's cloak and the broken
    door and believed what his wife had told him;[9] and he put Joseph
    in prison, in the place where the king's prisoners were kept.

12   And he was there in the prison. And the Lord made the governor
    of the prison well-disposed towards Joseph and treat him kindly
    (for he saw that the Lord was with him and that the Lord made
    him successful in everything he did); and he left everything in his
13 hands.[10] And the governor of the prison knew of nothing that was
    happening in the prison,[11] for Joseph did everything; and the Lord
    made it *all* succeed. And he remained there two years.

14   And in those days Pharaoh, king of Egypt, was angry with two of
    his eunuchs, the chief butler and the chief baker, and he put them
    in custody in the chief cook's house, in the prison where Joseph was
15 kept. And the governor of the prison appointed Joseph to attend to
16 them; and he waited on them. And they both dreamed a dream,[12]
    the chief butler and the chief baker, and they told it[12] to Joseph.
17 And as he interpreted *it* to them, so it happened to them: the chief
    butler Pharaoh restored to his office, and the chief baker he
18 hanged[13] – just as Joseph had interpreted to them. But the chief
    butler forgot Joseph in the prison, although he had told him what
    would happen to him; and he did not remember to tell Pharaoh
    how Joseph had told him,[14] but forgot.

---

[7] Lit. 'But'.   [8] So Eth.: Lat. 'that he despised her'.
[9] Lit. 'heard the words of his wife'.   [10] So Lat.: Eth. 'in his presence'.
[11] So Lat.: Eth. 'nothing that was with him'.
[12] So Eth.: Lat. 'dreamed dreams . . . them'.
[13] So Lat.: Eth. 'the baker he killed'.
[14] So Eth.: Lat. 'and did not remember *to ask* that Pharaoh the king might
intervene and release Joseph'.

XL. And in those days Pharaoh had two dreams in one night, about a famine there was to be in all the land; and he woke up from his sleep and called all the interpreters of dreams there were in Egypt, and the magicians, and he told them his two dreams, and

2 they were not able to interpret *them*. Then the chief butler remembered Joseph and spoke to the king about him; and he had him fetched from the prison and repeated his two dreams to him.

3 And he told Pharaoh that his two dreams were one; and he said to him, There will be seven years of plenty throughout the land of Egypt, and after that seven years of famine, such as there have

4 never been *before* in all the land. Pharaoh should now appoint controllers[1] in all the land of Egypt, who can store up food in every city during the seven years[2] of plenty, so that there will be food for the seven years of famine, and the land will not perish through the famine, for it will be very severe.

5 And the Lord made Pharaoh look favourably on what Joseph said,[3] and Pharaoh said to his servants, we shall not find *anywhere* such a wise and knowledgeable man as this man; for the spirit of

6 the Lord is with him. And he appointed him viceroy[4] in all his kingdom, and gave him authority over the whole of Egypt, and

7 mounted him in Pharaoh's viceroy's chariot. And he dressed him in fine linen and put a gold chain on his neck, and he was acclaimed El El wa Abirer.[5] And Pharaoh[6] put a ring on his finger[7] and placed his household in his charge; and he made a great man of him and said to him, Only as regards the throne will I be greater than you.

8 And Joseph ruled over all the land of Egypt; and all Pharaoh's princes and all his servants and all who did the king's business loved him, for he was straight in his dealings, without pride or arrogance, and he showed favour to no one and accepted no bribes, but decided every case that was brought before him with strict

9 impartiality.[8] And the land of Egypt lived at peace under Pharaoh

---

[1] The Eth. MSS differ among themselves: Lat. '*speculatores*'.
[2] So Lat.: Eth. 'throughout the days of the years'.
[3] Lit. 'And the Lord gave Joseph grace and mercy in the eyes of Pharaoh'.
[4] Lit. 'the second'.
[5] So Eth. (God, God, the Mighty One of God'): Lat. '*Elel et Habirel*'.
[6] Lit. 'he'.   [7] Lit. 'hand'.
[8] Lit. 'but judged in uprightness all the peoples of the land'.

because of Joseph, for the Lord was with him and made all those that knew him and had heard about him look with favour on him and on his family; and Pharaoh's kingdom was well ordered, and

10 there was no adversary[9] nor any evil person in it. And the king named Joseph Zaphnath-paaneah; and he gave Joseph as a wife the daughter of Potiphar (the daughter, that is, of the priest of Heliopolis, the chief cook).

11 And Joseph was thirty years old the day that he entered Pharaoh's service;[10] and *it was* in that *same* year *in which* Isaac died.

12 And it came to pass as Joseph had foretold in the interpretation of Pharaoh's[11] two dreams, just as he had foretold it, there were seven years of plenty throughout the land of Egypt, and the land of Egypt produced abundantly, one measure *producing* eighteen hundred

13 measures. And Joseph gathered food in every city until each one was stacked so full of corn that it was no longer possible to keep a record of how much there was.

XLI. And in the fourty-fifth jubilee, in the second week, in the second year, Judah found a wife for his eldest son Er, a woman of

2 Aram named Tamar. But he took a dislike to her and would not lie with her, because his mother was a woman of Canaan and he wanted a wife from his mother's kinsfolk, but his father, Judah,

3 would not allow it. And this Er, Judah's eldest son, was wicked,

4 and the Lord took his life. And Judah said to Onan, his brother, Take your brother's wife and do your duty as her brother-in-law

5 and raise offspring for your brother. And Onan knew that the offspring would not be his, *but* his brother's only, and he went into his sister-in-law's house and spilled his seed on the ground; and he

6 *too* was wicked in the Lord's sight, and he took his life *as well*. And Judah said to his daughter-in-law Tamar, Remain in your father's house as a widow till my son Shelah grows up, and I will give you to

7 him as his wife. And he grew up; but Bath-Shua, Judah's wife, would not allow her son Shelah to marry her. And Bath-Shua, Judah's wife, died in the fifth year of this week.

8 And in the sixth year Judah set off for Timnathah to shear his

---

[9] Or 'Satan'.

[10] All MSS add 'when he entered Pharaoh's service' – clearly a dittograph.

[11] Lit. 'his'.

sheep. And they said to Tamar, Behold your father-in-law is going

9 up to Timnathah to shear his sheep. And she set aside her widow's
weeds, and put on a veil, and adorned herself, and sat in the gate by

10 the Timnathah road. And as Judah was on his way he came upon
her and thought she was a harlot and said to her, Let me come in to

11 you; and she said to him, Come in; and he went in. And she said to
him, Give me my fee; and he said to her, I have nothing with me[1]
but the ring on my finger, my bracelet, and the staff in my hand.

12 And she said to him, Give me them till you send me my fee; and he
said to her, I will send you a kid; and he gave them to her and went

13 in to her,[2] and she conceived by him. And Judah went to his sheep,
and she went to her father's house.

14 And Judah sent his shepherd, an Adullamite, with the kid, but
he could not find her; and he asked the people of the place, saying,

15 Where is the harlot here?[3] And they said to him, We have no harlot
here. And he returned and told Judah[4] that he could not find her
and said to him, I asked the people of the place, and they said to
me, There is no harlot here. And he said, Let her keep them,[5] or we
shall become a laughing-stock.

16 And when she had completed three months it became obvious
that she was with child; and they told Judah, saying, Behold,

17 Tamar, your daughter-in-law, is with child by harlotry. And
Judah went to her father's house and said to her father and her
brothers, Bring her out and let her be burnt, for she has committed

18 an outrage[6] in Israel. And it came to pass when they brought her
out to burn her, she sent her father-in-law the ring and the bracelet
and the staff, saying, Do you recognize whose these are? By him I

19 am with child. And Judah realized *that they were his* and said, Tamar

20 is more in the right than I am, so let her not be burnt. And for that
reason she was not given to Shelah;[7] and he did not approach her

---

[1] Lit. 'in my hand'.
[2] So Lat.: Eth. om. 'and went in to her'.
[3] Eth. 'who is here': Lat. 'who was here'.
[4] So Lat.: Eth. 'him'.   [5] So Lat.: Eth. '*You* keep *it*'.
[6] Lit. 'wrought uncleanness'.
[7] This sentence fits in very oddly here. In Gen. xxxviii. 26 Judah gives no explicit
counter-instructions that Tamar should not be burnt, and the statement about her
not being given to Shelah is part of Judah's declaration, explaining why he thought
she was more in the right than he was. The probability is that Judah's counter-

21 again. And after that she bore two sons, Perez and Zerah, in the
22 seventh year of this second week. (And it was then that the seven
years of plenty came to an end, about which Joseph had spoken to
Pharaoh.)

23 And Judah realized that what he had done was wrong (for he
had had intercourse with his daughter-in-law), and he despised
himself because of it[8] and realized he had transgressed and done
something shameful (for he had dishonoured his son's bed), and he
began to lament and make supplication before the Lord because of
24 his transgression. And we told him in a dream that it would be
forgiven him because his supplication and his lamentation were
25 sincere, and *provided* he did not transgress again. And he received
forgiveness because he repented of his sin and because he had done
it without knowing what it was he did (although his transgression
was very great before our God, and everyone that behaves like this,
and everyone that has intercourse with his mother-in-law, must be
burnt with fire and destroyed,[9] for they are unclean and polluted:
26 let them be burnt with fire. And do you give instructions to the sons
of Israel that there be no uncleanness among them, for everyone
that has intercourse with his daughter-in-law or his mother-in-law
brings on himself[10] uncleanness: let them be burnt with fire, *both*
the man who has had intercourse with her and the woman also;
and the Lord[11] will turn back *his* wrath and *avert* the punishment
27 from Israel.) And we assured Judah that inasmuch as his two sons
had not had intercourse with Tamar,[12] his own offspring *by her*
were established as a second family and would not be rooted up.
28 For he had honestly sought *her* punishment, and, in accordance
with Abraham's ruling that he had given to his sons, Judah had
tried to have her burnt with fire.

instruction (whether added by the author of Jubilees himself or by a later source)
had been accidentally inserted in the wrong place in the text, and that we should
reverse the clauses in verses 19–20 and read 'And Judah realized *that they were his*
and said, "Tamar is more in the right than I am, because she was not given to
Shelah: so let her not be burnt". And he did not approach her again'.

[8] Lit. 'and he esteemed it hateful in his eyes'.
[9] Lit. 'burnt with fire that he may burn in it'.
[10] Lit. 'has wrought'.
[11] Lit. 'he'.   [12] Lit. 'her'.

XLII. And in the first year of the third week of the forty-fifth jubilee the famine struck the land; and the rain failed,[1] for none whatever
2 fell. And the *whole* earth was parched; but in the land of Egypt there was food, for Joseph had gathered the produce of the land in the
3 seven years of plenty and had preserved it. And the Egyptians came to Joseph to provide them with food; and he opened the granaries where the first year's grain was *stored*, and he sold it to the people of the land for gold.
4   Now in the land of Canaan the famine was very severe indeed;[2] and Jacob heard there was food in Egypt, and he sent ten of his sons to buy food for him in Egypt (Benjamin he did not send), and they arrived[3] together with others that had come *to buy corn there*.
5 And Joseph recognized them, but they did not recognize him; and he spoke harshly to them[4] and said to them, You are spies and have
6 come to spy on our defences.[5] And he put them in prison. And afterwards he set them free, but kept Simeon behind and sent off
7 his nine brothers. And he filled their sacks with corn; and he put
8 their money in their sacks *as well*, and they did not know *it*. And he ordered them to bring *him* their younger brother – for they had told him their father was still living and *about* their younger brother.
9   And they went up from the land of Egypt and came to the land of Canaan; and they told their father all that had happened to them, and how the lord of the country had spoken harshly to them and
10 had kept Simeon behind till they should bring him Benjamin. And Jacob said, You have robbed me of my children! Joseph is no more, and Simeon too is no more, and *now* you would take Benjamin
11 away: on me has your wickedness fallen.[6] And he said, My son shall not go down with you: he might fall ill;[7] for his[8] mother gave birth to two sons, and one is dead, and *now* you would take this one from me: if he was taken ill on the way, you would bring down my
12 grey hairs with sorrow to the grave. (For he saw[9] that their money

---

[1] Lit. 'refused to be given to the land'.
[2] 'Now . . . indeed' is read by the Lat. only.
[3] So Eth.: Lat. 'and the ten sons of Jacob arrived in Egypt'.
[4] So Lat.: Eth. 'spoke to them and questioned them'.
[5] Eth. 'to spy out the approaches of the land': Lat. 'to spy out the land'.
[6] So Eth.: Lat. differs substantially.
[7] Lat. adds 'on the way'.   [8] Lit. 'their'.
[9] So Eth.: Lat. 'for they had told him'.

had been returned to each of them in their sacks, and it was for this reason that he was afraid to send him.)

13 And the famine became even more severe in the land of Canaan, and in all *other* lands, though not in the land of Egypt, for many of the Egyptians had *of their own accord* been storing their produce for food ever since they saw Joseph gathering it and putting it in
14 granaries to preserve it for the years of famine. And the people of
15 Egypt fed themselves on it in the first year of their famine. And when Israel saw that the famine was so severe in the land and that there was no relief, he said to his sons, Go again and buy food for us
16 to keep ourselves alive. And they said, We will not go: unless our
17 youngest brother goes with us, we will not go. And Israel saw that
18 if he did not send him with them they would all starve.[10] And Reuben said, Entrust him to me, and if I do not bring him back to you, you can kill both my sons in exchange for him.[11] And he said
19 to him, He shall not go with you. And Judah came forward and said, Send him with me, and if I do not bring him back to you, you
20 can hold me guilty all my life. And he sent him with them in the second year of this week, on the first day of the month, and they came to the land of Egypt with all *the others* who had come *to buy*; and *they took* presents with them, stacte and almonds and terebinth nuts and pure honey.

21 And they came and stood before Joseph. And he saw his brother Benjamin and recognized him; and he said to them, Is this your youngest brother? And they said to him, It is. And he said, May the Lord be gracious to you, my son! And he sent him into his house.
22 And he brought Simeon out to them, and he made a feast for them;
23 and they gave him the present they had brought with them. And they ate in his presence; and he gave them each a portion, but
24 Benjamin's portion was seven times larger than any of theirs. And
25 they ate and drank and returned to[12] their asses. And Joseph devised a plan to test them out,[13] and he said to the steward who was in charge of his household, Fill all their sacks with food, and

[10] Lit. 'perish through famine'.
[11] Lit. 'instead of his soul'.
[12] Lit. 'remained with'.
[13] Lit. 'a plan by which he might learn their thoughts as to whether thoughts of peace prevailed among them'.

put their money back in their sacks,[14] and put my cup (the silver cup I drink out of) in the youngest's sack, and send them away.

XLIII. And he did as Joseph had told him, and he filled all their sacks for them with food and put their money in their sacks, and he put the cup in Benjamin's sack; and early in the morning they
2 departed. And it came to pass, after they had started, Joseph said to the steward of his household, Hurry after them[1] and accuse them, saying, You have repaid me evil for good: you have stolen from me the silver cup my lord drinks out of. And bring me back their youngest brother – and fetch *him* quickly before I go out to
3 court. And he ran after them and said what he had been told to
4 them. And they said to him, God forbid that your servants should do such a thing as to steal anything[2] from your lord's house. Even the money we found in our sacks the first time, your servants brought back from the land of Canaan: how then could we steal
5 anything? Behold, here are we and our sacks: search *us*, and in whoever's sack among us you find the cup, let him be put to death, and we and our asses will become your lord's slaves. And he said to
6 them, No! I will take as a slave only the man in whose possession I
7 find *it*, and *the rest* of you shall go home in peace. And he searched in their sacks,[3] starting with the eldest and finishing with the
8 youngest; and it was found in Benjamin's sack. And they rent their clothes and loaded their asses and returned to the city and came to Joseph's house; and they all prostrated themselves before him with their faces to the ground.

9   And Joseph said to them, You have done a wicked thing. And they said, What shall we say and how shall we defend ourselves? Our lord has discovered his servants' sin: behold, we are our lord's
10 slaves and our asses also. And Joseph said to them, No![4] You shall go home, and your brother shall be my slave (for you have done a wicked thing). Did it not occur to you that a man could be as fond
11 of his cup as I am of this cup?[5] – and yet you stole it from me. And

---

[14] Lit. 'vessels'.

[1] Lit. 'Pursue them and run'.   [2] Lit. 'any vessel'.
[3] Lit. 'vessels'.   [4] Lit. 'No, I am afraid'.
[5] Lit. 'Do you not know that a man delights in his cup as I with this cup'.

Judah said, Let *the blame* be on me; *and* let your servant explain to your lordship.[6] Your servant's mother bore to our father two brothers: one went away and was lost, and has not been found, and this one[7] is his mother's only remaining child, and your servant our

12 father loves him, and his life is bound up with this *lad's* life. And if we go back to your servant our father, and the lad is not with us, then he will die, and we shall bring down our father with sorrow to

13 the grave. Let me, your servant, remain instead of the boy as my lord's slave, and let the lad go with his brothers; for I went surety for him with your servant our father, and if I do not take him back our father will hold your servant guilty for ever.

14 And Joseph saw there was a common bond of good-will and unity between them, and he could not control himself; and he told

15 them he was Joseph. And he talked with them in Hebrew and embraced them and wept. But they did not recognize him; and

16 they began to weep. And he said to them, Do not weep over me, but hurry back and bring my father to me, so that I can see him before

17 we die and my brother Benjamin can see him too.[8] For behold, this is *but* the second year of the famine, and there will be another five

18 years without harvest or fruit on the trees or ploughing. Come down quickly, you and your households, so that you do not perish in the famine; and do not be worried about *leaving* your possessions, for the Lord sent me ahead of you to arrange things so that many

19 lives may be saved. And tell my father that I am still alive, as you can see for yourselves, and that the Lord has made me like a father to Pharaoh, and ruler over his household and over all the land of

20 Egypt. And tell my father of all my glory and all the riches and

21 glory that the Lord has given me. And on Pharaoh's instructions[9] he gave them wagons and provisions for the journey; and he gave

22 them all clothes of many colours and silver. And to their father he sent clothes and silver and ten asses laden with corn; and he sent them away.

---

[6] Lit. '*and* let your servant speak a word in my lord's ear'.

[7] Lit. 'he'.

[8] Lit. 'and while the eyes of my brother Benjamin see'. Charles proposed a radical emendation of the whole passage, based on Gen. xlv. 12 – ' . . . father to me; and you see that it is my mouth that speaks, and the eyes of my brother Benjamin see'.

[9] Lit. 'And by the command of the mouth of Pharaoh'.

23   And they went up and told their father that Joseph was alive and measuring out corn to all the nations of the earth, and that he was
24 ruler over all the land of Egypt. And their father did not believe it, for he was stunned; but when he saw the wagons that Joseph had sent, his spirit[10] revived, and he said, It is enough for me if Joseph is still alive: I will go down and see him before I die.

XLIV.   And Israel set out from his house in **Hebron**[1] on the new moon of the third month; and he went by way of the Well of the Oath and offered a sacrifice to the God of his father Isaac on the
2 seventh of this month. And Jacob remembered the dream he had
3 had at Bethel, and he was afraid to go down to Egypt. And he thought of sending word to Joseph to come to him, *saying* that he would not go down; and he stayed there seven days in the hope that he might see a vision *telling him* either to stay *where he was* or go down
4 *to Egypt*. And he kept the harvest festival of the first-fruits with old grain, for in all the land of Canaan, there was not *even* a handful of seed in the land, for the famine had affected all the wild animals and cattle and birds as well as men.

5   And on the sixteenth the Lord appeared to him and said to him, Jacob, Jacob. And he said, Here I am. And he said to him, I am the God of your fathers, the God of Abraham and Isaac: do not be afraid to go down to Egypt, for I will make you a great nation there.
6 I will go down with you, and I will bring you up *again*, and in this land you shall be buried, and Joseph shall close your eyes.[2] Do not
7 be afraid: go down to Egypt. And he got up, and his sons and his grandsons, and they put their father and their possessions on the
8 wagons. And Israel left the Wall of the Oath on the sixteenth of this third month and set out for the land of Egypt.

9   And Israel sent Judah before him to his son Joseph to inspect the land of Goshen, for Joseph had told his brothers to come and settle
10 there so that they could be near him. And this was the finest *region* in the land of Egypt, and near to him – *the best* for all *of them* and also for *their* cattle.

---

[10] Lit: 'the life of his spirit'.

[1] Text 'Haran'.
[2] Lit. 'put his hand upon your eyes'.

11   And these are the names of Jacob's sons who entered Egypt with
12 their father Jacob. Reuben, Israel's eldest; and these are the
names of his sons – Enoch and Pallu and Hezron and Carmi (five
13 *altogether*). Simeon and his sons; and these are the names of his sons
– Jemuel and Jamin and Ohad and Jachin and Zohar and Saul, the
14 son of a Phoenician[3] woman (seven *altogether*). Levi and his sons;
and these are the names of his sons – Gershon and Kohath and
15 Merari (four *altogether*). Judah and his sons; and these are the
names of his sons – Shelah and Perez and Zerah (four *altogether*).
16 Issachar and his sons; and these are the names of his sons – Tola
17 and Phua and Jasub and Shimron (five *altogether*). Zebulon and his
sons; and these are the names of his sons – Saar and Elon and
18 Jahleel (four *altogether*). And these are Jacob's sons (and their
sons), whom Leah bore to Jacob in Mesopotamia – six *sons*, and
their only sister Dinah; and Leah's sons, and their sons, who
entered Egypt with their father Jacob, were twenty-nine in all, and
19 including their father Jacob there were thirty of them. And the sons
of Zilpah, Leah's slave-girl, Jacob's wife, that she bore to Jacob,
20 *were* Gad and Asher. And these are the names of their sons who
entered Egypt with him: the sons of Gad – Ziphion and Haggi and
Shuni and Ezbon ⟨and Eri⟩ and Areli and Arodi (eight *altogether*);
21 and the sons of Asher – Imnah and Ishvah ⟨and Ishvi⟩ and Beriah
22 and Serah, their only sister (six *altogether*). Zilpah thus had fourteen descendants; and so Leah's total was forty-four.[4]

23   And the sons of Jacob's wife Rachel *were* Joseph and Benjamin.
24 And there were born to Joseph in Egypt, before his father came
into Egypt, the two sons that[5] Asenath the daughter of Potiphar,
priest of Heliopolis, bore to him – Manasseh and Ephraim (three
25 *altogether*). And the sons of Benjamin – Bela and Becher and Ashbel
and Guad and Naaman and Abdeyo and Rosh and Senanim and
26 Huppim and Gaam (eleven *altogether*). Rachel thus had fourteen
27 descendants.[6] And the sons of Bilhah, Rachel's slave-girl, Jacob's

---

[3] So the majority of MSS ('*Fenesawit*'). Charles, following Rönsch, preferred the reading of a single MS ('*Sifnawat*'), which, in the light of the mention of Zephath at Judges i. 17, he rendered 'Zephathite'.

[4] Lit. 'All the souls were fourteen; and all those of Leah were forty-four'.

[5] Lit. 'those whom'.

[6] Lit. 'And all the souls of Rachel were fourteen'.

28 wife, that she bore to Jacob, were Dan and Naphtali. And these are
the names of their sons who entered Egypt with them. The sons of
Dan were Hushim and Samon and Asudi and Ijaka and Salomon
29 (six *altogether*). And the last four of them[7] died in the year they
30 entered Egypt, and Dan had Hushim only left. And these are the
names of the sons of Naphtali – Jahziel and Guni and Jezer and
31 Shallum and Iv. And Iv, who was born after the year of famine,
32 died in Egypt. Thus Rachel's total altogether was twenty-six.[8]

33 So Jacob's household, when it entered Egypt, numbered seventy
– that is his children and his grandchildren numbered seventy in
all; but five died in Egypt before Joseph,[9] and they had no children.
34 And two of Judah's sons, Er and Onan, had died *already* in the land
of Canaan, and they had no children. And Israel's sons buried
those who had died, and they were reckoned among the seventy
Gentile nations.

XLV. And Israel came into Egypt, into the land of Goshen, on the
new moon of the fourth month, in the second year of the third week
2 of the forty-fifth jubilee. And Joseph went to the land of Goshen to
meet his father Jacob; and he threw his arms round his father's
3 neck and wept. And Israel said to Joseph, Now I can die *in peace*, for
I have seen you *again alive*; and now may the Lord God of Israel be
blessed, the God of Abraham and the God of Isaac, who has not
4 held back his mercy and his grace from his servant Jacob. It is
enough for me that I have seen your face while I am[1] still alive.
True indeed is the vision that I saw at Bethel. Blessed be the Lord
5 my God for ever and ever, and blessed be his name. And Joseph
and his brothers ate in their father's presence and drank wine; and
Jacob was overjoyed to see Joseph eating with his brothers and
drinking in his presence, and he blessed the Creator of all things,
who had preserved him and had preserved his twelve sons.

6 And Joseph had given his father and brothers the right to settle
in the land of Goshen, and in Rameses[2] and the surrounding region

---

7 Lit. 'And they'.
8 Lit. 'And all the souls of Rachel were twenty-six'.
9 Alternative reading 'before they married'.

1 Charles would emend 'I am' to 'you are' to accord with Gen. xlvi. 30.
2 Eth. 'Ramesina'.

which he ruled as Pharaoh's viceroy.[3] And Israel and his sons
settled in the land of Goshen, the best part of the land of Egypt; and
Israel was a hundred and thirty years old when he entered Egypt.
7 And Joseph supported his father and his brothers, and also their
possessions, with as much as they needed during the seven years of
8 the famine. And the land of Egypt suffered because of the famine.
And Joseph acquired all the land for Pharaoh in return for food,
and he gained possession of the people and their cattle, and he
acquired everything for Pharaoh.

9   And the years of famine came to an end, and in the eighth year
Joseph gave the people in the land seed-corn[4] to sow the land,[5] for
10 the river had overflowed all the land of Egypt (in the seven years of
the famine it had not[6] overflowed and had irrigated only a few
places on the banks of the river, but now it overflowed *once more*);
and the Egyptians sowed the land, and it produced much corn that
11 year. And this was the first year of the fourth week of the forty-fifth
12 jubilee. And Joseph took a fifth part of all the harvest[7] for the king
and left four parts for them as seed and food; and Joseph established
it as a law for the land of Egypt – *a law that has survived* till to-day.

13   And Israel lived in the land of Egypt seventeen years; and he
lived altogether for three jubilees, *that is for* a hundred and forty
seven years, and he died in the fourth year of the fifth week of the
14 forty-fifth jubilee. And Israel blessed his sons before he died and
told them everything that would happen to them in the land of
Egypt, and made known to them what would come upon them in
the last days; and he blessed them and gave Joseph two portions in
15 the land. And he slept with his fathers and was buried in the double
cave in the land of Canaan, near Abraham his father, in the grave
which he dug for himself in the double cave in the neighbourhood[8]
16 of Hebron. And he gave all his books and his fathers' books to his
son Levi, to preserve them and keep them in repair[9] for his children
till to-day.

[3] Lit. 'before Pharaoh'.   [4] Lit. 'seed and food'.
[5] So Lat.: Eth. om. 'the land'.   [6] So Lat.: Eth. om. 'not'.
[7] So Lat.: Eth. 'of the corn of the harvest'.
[8] Lit. 'land'.
[9] Or 'have fresh copies made of them': lit. 'renew them'.

XLVI. And it came to pass after Jacob died the number of Israelites in the land of Egypt increased, and they became a great nation; and they were united in heart and mind, so that each one loved his brother and helped his brother. And their numbers increased more and more and multiplied greatly, ten weeks of years, all the time
2 that Joseph was alive. And there was no adversary[1] nor any evil *to afflict them* all the time that Joseph lived after his father Jacob's *death*, for while Joseph lived all the Egyptians held the Israelites in high esteem.

3 And Joseph died at the age of a hundred and ten: for seventeen years he lived in the land of Canaan, for ten years he was a servant, for three years he was in prison, and for eighty years he was viceroy
4 and ruled the whole of the land of Egypt. And he died, and *so did* all
5 his brothers and all that generation. And before he died he gave instructions to the Israelites to take his bones with them when they
6 went out of the land of Egypt. And he put them on oath regarding his bones, for he knew that the Egyptians would not take him and bury him in the land of Canaan (for Makamaron,[2] king of Canaan, while living in the land of Assyria, fought in the valley with the king of Egypt and killed him there, and pursued the Egyptians to the
7 gates of Ermon.[3] But he was not able to get inside, because another king, a new one, had become king of Egypt, and he was stronger than he was, and *so* he returned to the land of Canaan; and the gate of Egypt was shut, and no one went out of Egypt and no one went
8 in). And Joseph died in the forty-sixth jubilee, in the sixth week, in the second year; and they buried him in the land of Egypt. And all his brothers died after him.

9 And the king of Egypt went out to war with the king of Canaan in the forty-seventh jubilee, in the second week in the second year; and the Israelites brought out all the bones of Jacob's children except Joseph's, and they buried them in the country, in the double
10 cave in the mountain. And most *of them* returned to Egypt, but a few of them remained in the mountains of Hebron; and your father
11 Amram remained among them. And the king of Canaan was victorious over the king of Egypt; and he shut the gate of Egypt.

[1] Or 'Satan'.   [2] Alternative reading 'Mamkeron'.
[3] According to Charles this is Heroonpolis, near the desert, on the canal of Ramses.

12   And he devised an infamous plan to afflict the Israelites; and he
13 said to the Egyptians, Behold the Israelite people have increased *in
    number* and multiplied more than we *have*. Come then, let us take
    steps to curb them[4] before they become too many, and let us wear
    them down with heavy labour,[5] in case war comes on us and they
    join our enemies[6] and fight against us too and leave our land
    altogether (for their hearts and faces are *always turned* towards the
14 land of Canaan). And he set over them taskmasters[7] to wear them
    down with heavy labour. And they built strong cities for Pharaoh,
    Pithom and Raamses; and they built all the walls and all the
15 fortifications which had fallen in the cities[8] of Egypt. And they
    forced them into slavery; but the more harshly they treated them,
16 the more *their numbers* increased and multiplied. And the Egyptians
    despised[9] the Israelites.

XLVII.   And in the seventh week, in the seventh year, in the forty-
seventh jubilee, your father left the land of Canaan, and you were
born in the fourth week, in its sixth year, in the forty-eighth jubilee:
2 this was a time of great distress for the Israelites. And Pharaoh,
king of Egypt, issued an order that they should throw all male
3 children born to them into the river. And for seven months they
threw them in; and your mother hid you for three months, but
4 information was laid against her.[1] So she made a basket for you,
and covered it with tar and pitch, and put it among the reeds by the
river's bank, and put you in it; *and you were there for* seven days, and
your mother came by night and suckled you, and by day your sister
Miriam kept you from the birds.

5   And in those days Tharmuth, Pharaoh's daughter, came to
bathe in the river, and she heard your voice crying; and she told her
6 **maids**[2] to fetch you out, and they brought you to her. And she lifted

---

[4] Eth. 'let us act cleverly against them': Lat. 'let us afflict them'.
[5] Eth. 'let us afflict them with slavery': Lat. 'let us humble them by (in) their
works' – and similarly in verse 14.   [6] So Lat.: Eth. 'the enemy'.
[7] Eth. lit. 'elders of workmen': Lat. 'executors of works'.
[8] So Lat.: Eth. 'city'.   [9] Lit. 'regarded as an abomination'.

[1] Lit. 'and they told concerning her'.
[2] Lat. 'maid': Eth. 'Hebrew women' (by a misreading of a presumed Gk. original
ἄβραις as 'Εβραίαις).

7 you out of the basket and took pity on you. And your sister said to her, Shall I go and call you one of the Hebrew women to nurse this
8 babe and suckle *him* for you? And she said to her, Please do.[3] And she went and called your mother Jochebed; and she paid her for
9 nursing you. And afterwards, when you were old enough,[4] they brought you to Pharaoh's **daughter**[5] and you became her son, and your father Amram taught you to write; and three weeks after that they took you to the royal court.
10 And you were three weeks of years at court, until one day you went out from the royal court and saw an Egyptian belabouring one of your fellow-Israelites, and you killed him and hid him in the
11 sand. And on the next day you found two Israelites fighting, and
12 you asked the culprit,[6] why are you hitting your brother? And he was angry and indignant and said, Who made you a chief and judge over us? Do you want to kill me as you killed the Egyptian yesterday? And you were frightened by what he said and fled.

XLVIII. And in the sixth year of the third week of the forty-ninth jubilee you went and lived in the land of Midian;[1] *and you stayed there for* five weeks and a year. And you returned to Egypt in the second
2 week, in the second year, in the fiftieth jubilee. And you yourself know what the Lord said to you on Mount Sinai, and what the prince Mastema tried to do with you when you were returning to
3 Egypt, on the way when you met him at the lodging-place.[2] Did he not try his very best to kill you and deliver the Egyptians from you, when he saw that you were sent to execute judgement and ven-
4 geance on the Egyptians? And I delivered you from him; and you performed the signs and portents which you were sent to perform in Egypt against Pharaoh, and against his whole household, and against his servants, and against his people.

[3] Lit. 'Go'.
[4] Lit. 'when you were grown'.
[5] Both Eth. and Lat. 'Pharaoh's house'.
[6] So Eth. (lit. 'said to him who was doing the wrong'): Lat. 'said to him who was hitting his neighbour'.

[1] Eth. om. 'in the land of Midian'.
[2] So Lat.: Eth. corrupt (though it might mean 'on the way, at Elath, in the lodging-place').

5 And the Lord took a fearful vengeance on them for Israel's sake. And he plagued them[3] with blood and frogs, lice and dog-flies, and with festering boils: their cattle died: he destroyed with hail-stones everything they had that grew, and locusts ate what the hail had left: *he plagued them* with darkness and ⟨the death⟩[4] of their first-born, of men and of animals; and on all their gods[5] the Lord

6 took vengeance and burned them with fire. And everything was arranged through you,[6] that you should **declare**[7] *these things* before they were done; and you spoke with the king of Egypt in the presence of all his servants and in the presence of his people. And

7 everything happened just as you had said: ten great and terrible judgements came on the land of Egypt to execute vengeance on it

8 for Israel. And the Lord did everything for Israel's sake, and in accordance with his covenant that he had made with Abraham, that he would take vengeance on them because they had enslaved them.

9 And the prince Mastema set himself against you and tried to get you into Pharaoh's clutches; and he helped the Egyptian sorcerers, and they set themselves up against you and did the best they

10 could.[8] (For, although we let them do the evils, we did not allow

11 them to effect their cure.) And the Lord struck them with the boils, and they were not able to stand against you (for we destroyed them so that they could not perform a single sign).

12 Yet in spite of all *these* signs and marvels the prince Mastema was not put to shame **because**[9] he encouraged the Egyptians[10] to pursue you with all the might of Egypt, with their chariots and with their

13 horses and with all the forces of the people of Egypt. And I stood between the Egyptians and Israel; and we delivered Israel from him and from his people, and the Lord brought them through the

14 middle of the sea, as if it were dry land. And all the people he had brought in pursuit of Israel, the Lord our God threw them into the sea — into the depths of the abyss beneath the Israelites, just as the

---

[3] Lit. 'he struck them': Eth. adds 'and killed them'.
[4] Omitted by both Eth. and Lat.
[5] So Eth.: Lat. 'all the gods of the Egyptians'.
[6] Lit. 'was sent through your hand'. [7] Text 'do'.
[8] Lit. 'and wrought before you'. [9] Text 'until'.
[10] Lit. 'he took courage and cried to the Egyptians'.

people of Egypt had thrown their children into the river. He took vengeance on a million of them; and a thousand strong and active men were destroyed for each babe in arms from among your people

15 that they had thrown into the river. (On the fourteenth day, and on the fifteenth, and on the sixteenth, and on the seventeenth, and on the eighteenth, the prince Mastema had been kept bound and in chains[11] behind the Israelites, so that he could not harass[12] them.

16 And on the nineteenth we let them[13] loose so that they could help

17 the Egyptians and *encourage them to* pursue the Israelites. And he made them obstinate and stubborn – the plan was devised by the Lord our God so that he could strike the Egyptians down and

18 throw them into the sea. And we bound him on the fourteenth *day*[14] so that he could not harass[12] the Israelites on the day they asked the Egyptians for ornaments[15] and clothing – ornaments[15] of silver and gold and bronze, in order to despoil the Egyptians in return for

19 the slavery they had forced upon them. And *so* we did not bring the Israelites out of Egypt empty-handed.)

XLIX. Remember the commandment which the Lord gave you concerning the Passover, that you should celebrate it in its season on the fourteenth of the first month, that you should slaughter the lamb[1] before the evening, and that it should be eaten at night on

2 the evening of the fifteenth after sunset. For on this night (the beginning of the festival and the beginning of the rejoicing) you were eating the Passover in Egypt, when all the powers of Mastema had been let loose to kill all the first-born in the land of Egypt, from the first-born of Pharaoh to the first-born of the captive maid-servant at the mill and to the cattle.

3 And this is the sign that the Lord gave them – they should not enter any house *with intent* to kill, on the door-posts of which they saw the blood of a yearling lamb, but should pass *it* by, so that all those in the house might be preserved because the sign of the blood

---

[11] Lit. 'locked up'.   [12] Or 'accuse'.
[13] i.e. Mastema and his minions.
[14] The MSS vary between 'fourteenth', 'fifteenth', and 'seventeenth'.
[15] Or 'articles', 'objects'.

[1] Lit. 'it'.

4 was on its door-posts. And the powers of the Lord did everything just as the Lord commanded them, and they passed over all the Israelites, and the plague did not touch them and destroyed not so
5 much as a single man or beast or dog among them. But among the Egyptians[2] the plague struck savagely, and there was not a house
6 in Egypt without its dead and weeping and lamentation. And *meanwhile* all Israel was eating the flesh of the paschal lamb, and drinking the wine, and singing praises, and blessing and giving thanks to the Lord God of their fathers, *all* ready to escape from the yoke of Egypt and the shackles of their slavery.[3]

7 And remember this day all the days of your life and observe it regularly, once a year, on its *appointed* day, in accordance with all its regulations;[4] and do not change its date, either from one day to
8 another, or from one month to another. For it is a rule for all time, and *it is* written on the heavenly tablets concerning all Israelites, that they should observe it every year on its *appointed* day, once a year, in every generation; and there is no time limit, for it is decreed
9 for ever. And whoever is not unclean and fails to come and observe it on its proper day, and to bring an acceptable offering in the Lord's presence, and to eat and drink in the Lord's presence, on the day it is celebrated, that man, if he is clean and near at hand, shall be rooted up: inasmuch as he has not offered the Lord's offering at the proper time, he must accept responsibility for his sin.[5]

10 Let the Israelites come and celebrate the Passover[6] at the time appointed, on the fourteenth day of the first month at dusk,[7] from the third part of the day to the third part of the night (for two parts of the day are given to the light and a third part to the evening).
11 This is what the Lord commanded you – that you should celebrate
12 it[8] at dusk.[7] And the lamb[1] should not be slaughtered at any time during the daylight, but *only* towards the evening; and it should be eaten between the time when evening comes and the third part of

---

[2] Lit. 'in Egypt'.
[3] Lit. 'the evil bondage'.   [4] Lit. 'law'.
[5] Lit. 'that man will bear his sin'.
[6] Or 'offer the paschal lamb': lit. 'do the Passover'.
[7] Eth. lit. 'between the evenings' (as in the Heb. at Exod. xii. 6): Lat. lit. 'at eventide' (as in the Gk. at Exod. xii. 6).   [8] Lit. 'do it'.

the night, and if afterwards[9] any of its flesh is left over, it must be burnt in the fire.

13   And it shall not be boiled in water, nor shall it be eaten raw, but roast on the fire: it must be eaten[10] with care:[11] its head with its entrails and its feet shall be roasted on the fire; and no bone of it

14   shall be broken (for of Israelites no bone shall be crushed[12]). That is why the Lord commanded Israelites to celebrate the Passover[6] at the time appointed, and not to break any of the lamb's bones;[13] for it is a festal day, and a day *he has* commanded, and there can be no changing it from day to day, and from month to month, but *only*

15   on its proper day[14] must it be celebrated.[15] And command the Israelites to celebrate the Passover[6] generation after generation, every year, once a year at the time appointed; and it will serve as a reminder, acceptable to the Lord, and no plague shall come upon them to harm *them* or destroy them in any year in which they celebrate the Passover[6] at the proper time *and* in every way in accordance with what he has commanded.

16   And the lamb[1] shall not be eaten outside the Lord's sanctuary, but within its precincts;[16] and the whole community of Israel shall

17   offer it[17] at the time appointed. And every one who comes then shall eat it[18] in the sanctuary of your[19] God in the Lord's presence, from twenty years old and upwards; for so it is written and decreed that they should eat it in the Lord's sanctuary.

18   And when the Israelites come into the land they are to occupy, the land of Canaan, and set up the Lord's tabernacle in one of their

---

[9] Lit. 'from the third part of the night'.

[10] Eth. obscure: Lat. 'you shall eat it'.

[11] So both Eth. and Lat. here, understanding the Gk. μετὰ σπουδῆς at Exod. xii. 11 in this sense. At verse 23 below, however, Eth. (Lat. is not extant) takes the sense 'in haste', which is clearly preferable in both places in the light of the underlying Heb. *bᵉhippazon* (cp. also Deut. xvi. 3).

[12] So Eth.: Lat. 'and there shall be no tribulation among Israelites in that day'.

[13] Lit. 'break any bone of it'.

[14] Eth. 'on the day of its festival': Lat. 'at its own time'.

[15] Or 'offered'.

[16] Eth. 'within view of the Lord's sanctuary': Lat. 'alongside the Lord's tabernacle'.   [17] Or 'celebrate the Passover': lit. 'do it'.

[18] Eth. 'And every man who has come on its day shall eat it': Lat. is difficult and presumably corrupt ('*et omnis homo quicumque praetermiserit in visitatione manducare illud*').   [19] So Eth.: Lat. 'our'.

tribes, till the Lord's sanctuary is built in the land, they shall come and celebrate the Passover[6] in the Lord's tabernacle and slaughter

19 the lamb[1] in the Lord's presence from year to year. And when the house is built in the Lord's name in the land of their heritage, they shall go there and slaughter the paschal lamb in the evening, at

20 sunset, at the third part of the day. And they shall offer its blood at the base of the altar, and they shall place its fat on the fire that is on the altar, and they shall eat its flesh roast on the fire in the court of

21 the house which has been hallowed in the Lord's name. And they may not celebrate the Passover[6] in their cities, nor in any *other* place, but only within the precincts of the Lord's tabernacle, or within the precincts of his house where his name dwells; and they shall not go astray from the Lord.

22 And as for you, Moses, command the Israelites to keep the rules of the Passover, as you yourself have received them: draw their attention to them[20] every year on the day appointed and during the Feast of unleavened bread;[21] *and command them* to eat unleavened bread for seven days, *and* to keep the feast and make an offering every day during those seven days of joy in the Lord's presence on

23 the altar of your God. For you celebrated this feast in haste when you set out from Egypt, till you entered the wilderness of Shur, and it was *only* on the sea-shore that you completed it.

L. And after this law I made known to you *the laws of* the sabbath

2 days in the desert of Sinai, which is between Elim and Sinai. And I told you about the sabbaths of the land on mount Sinai, and I told you about the jubilee years in the sabbaths of years; but its year

3 have we not told you till you enter the land you are to occupy. And the land also shall keep its sabbaths while the sons of Israel[1] are

4 living in it; and *then* shall they know the jubilee year. And so I have set in order for you the year-weeks, and the years, and the jubilees: there are forty-nine jubilees, one week, and two years, from the days of Adam until to-day; and there are forty years yet to come,[2]

---

[20] So one Eth. MS and Lat.: the other Eth. MSS differ but give the general sense 'you shall perform it'.

[21] This seems the sense required, though neither Eth. nor Lat. are completely intelligible by themselves.

[1] Lit. 'they'. [2] Lit. 'distant'.

in which to learn the commandments of the Lord, before they pass
5 over into the land of Canaan and cross the Jordan to the west. And
the jubilees shall pass by till Israel is cleansed from all guilt of
fornication, and uncleanness, and pollution, and sin, and error,
and dwells in safety in all the land; and there shall no longer be an
adversary[3] or any evil power[4] *to afflict them*, and the land shall be
clean from that day forward for evermore.

6   And behold, the commandment about the sabbaths, and all the
7 rules and regulations,[5] I have written down for you. Six days you
shall work, but on the seventh day is the sabbath of the Lord your
God: on it you shall do no work, neither you, nor your sons, nor
your slaves, nor your slave-girls, nor any of your cattle, nor the
8 alien who is among you. And the man that does any work on it shall
die: whoever desecrates that day, whoever lies with a woman, or
whoever talks on it about anything he intends to do (what, *for
example*, he will buy or sell next day), and whoever draws water on
it because he did not remember to draw it on the sixth day,[6] or
whoever lifts any load to carry it out of his tent or out of his house,
9 shall die. You shall do no work whatever on the sabbath day: only
what you have prepared for yourselves on the sixth day *shall you eat
and drink*, so that you may eat and drink and rest and keep sabbath
from all work on that day, and bless the Lord your God who has
given you a festal day and a holy day; and this day shall be a day of
10 the holy kingdom for all Israel among their days for ever. For great
is the honour which the Lord has given Israel, to eat and drink
their fill on this festal day, and to rest on it from all the work men
have to do, except to burn frankincense and present offerings and
sacrifices in the Lord's presence every day and every sabbath.[7]
11 This work alone shall be done on the sabbath days in the sanctuary
of the Lord your God, that atonement may be made for Israel with
offerings continually, day by day, as a reminder, aceptable to the
Lord, and that he may receive them always, day by day, just as you
12 have been commanded. And any man who does any work on the
sabbath days,[8] or goes on a journey or tills a field (whether at home

---

[3] Or 'a Satan'.   [4] Lit. 'any evil one'.
[5] Lit. 'and all the judgements of its laws'.
[6] Lit. 'which he has not prepared for himself on the sixth day'.
[7] Lit. 'for days and for sabbaths'.   [8] Lit. 'on them'.

or elsewhere), and whoever lights a fire or loads any beast or travels by ship on the sea, and whoever shoots or kills anything or slaughters a beast or bird or takes[9] an animal or a bird or a fish, or 13 whoever fasts or makes war on the sabbath – the man who does any of these things on the sabbath shall die, so that the sons of Israel may observe the sabbaths in accordance with the commandments concerning the sabbaths of the land, as it is written on the tablets which he gave into my hands to write out for you the laws of the seasons, and the seasons according to the division of their days.

And with this the account of the division of the days is complete.

[9] Or 'catches'.

THE LIFE OF ADAM AND EVE

INTRODUCTION

The Life of Adam and Eve here translated is the Latin version of
the story of Adam and Eve from the time of their expulsion from
Paradise until their deaths.

Jewish legends connected with Adam and Eve and their children
abound. So much is clear from the Rabbinic literature. Yet there is
no direct evidence for the existence of any pre-Christian written
collection of these legends in either Hebrew or Aramaic. The
Church, however, seems to have known a number of apparently
different Adam books from a comparatively early date: Epiphanius,
for example, says that 'many' Gnostic books were attributed to
Seth and 'revelations' to Adam,[1] the Apostolic Constitutions
mentions Adam along with Moses and Enoch as one of the 'ancients'
who wrote apocryphal books,[2] and the Gelasian Decree includes in
its list of apocrypha 'the book that is called The Penitence of
Adam'.[3]

The Adam books which have survived have various titles: they
have been preserved in a variety of forms and recensions, and in a
variety of languages. Some are distinct: others are interrelated,
some obviously so, others less obviously. Thus, the Coptic
'Apocalypse of Adam', discovered near Nag Hammadi in 1945,
has no points of contact at all with the Syriac 'Testament of Adam'
(apart from its form), nor with the Ethiopic 'Conflict of Adam and
Eve with Satan': on the other hand, our Latin 'Life of Adam and
Eve' has a number of points of contact with the Ethiopic 'Conflict',
but nothing like as many as it has with the Armenian 'Book of
Adam'. No attempt will be made, therefore, either to summarize
the contents of these books individually, or to disentangle the very
complicated interrelationships where they exist. Fundamental to
the group most closely related to our 'Life' would appear to be the

---

[1] Epiph. *Haer*. XXVI. viii. 1.
[2] *Const. Apost*. VI. xvi. 3.
[3] *Decr. Gelas*. v. 6.

Greek work edited by Tischendorf in 1866 (under the title 'The Apocalypse of Moses'[4]) and again by Ceriani two years later.[5]

Despite the very considerable differences in detail, Tischendorf's 'Apocalypse' covers in all essentials the same ground as our 'Life'. On the debit side it lacks the account of the penitence of Adam and Eve contained in Life i–xxi, as well as the vision of Adam in Life xxv–xxix: on the credit side, it puts into the mouth of Eve a much more elaborate account of the Fall, a translation of which, because of its inherent interest, is printed in full as an appendix at the end of our translation of the Life.[6]

So far as the origin of the Apocalypse is concerned, there is nothing in it that is necessarily Christian; and for this reason many regard it as a purely Jewish work, some even going as far as to claim that it is a translation from a Semitic original. But for this last view there is no sound evidence. Against it is the presence of certain Greek terms and expressions, which are unlikely to be found in a translation, and the fact that references and allusions to the Old Testament betray dependence on the Septuagint. All that can safely be said about it is that the author, whether Jew or Christian, constructed his narrative making use of such Jewish traditions or written sources as were known to him: that he almost certainly wrote in Greek; and that in all probability he is to be dated within the first three Christian centuries. Wells, for instance, saw the author as a Jew of the Dispersion, who wrote perhaps at Alexandria, 'between AD 60 and 300, and probably in the earliest years of this period'. Wells reckoned, however, with the possibility that the extant Greek text may be 'a slightly revised version'.[7]

The Latin text of the Life, with which we are more immediately concerned, was first published by Meyer in 1878 from twelve MSS, all (with one exception) at Munich and dating from the 9th to 15th

[4] This title was Tischendorf's own. His four MSS all gave as title (with minor variations) 'The Story and Life of Adam and Eve, revealed by God to Moses his servant, when he received the tables of the Law of the Covenant from the Lord's hand, being taught by the archangel Michael'.

[5] Ceriani printed only the text of Cod. Ambrosianus C. 237 Inf. (11th cent., = Tischendorf's 'D'), which unfortunately has a lacuna of eighteen chapters in the middle. To-day more than twenty MSS are known.

[6] See below, pp. 161 – 67.

[7] L.S.A. Wells in R. H. Charles, *APOT* ii, pp. 129 and 130.

cents. In 1929 J. H. Mozley printed a text based on twelve 13th–15th cent. English MSS. This text does not differ markedly from Meyer's in content: it only makes even more clear what is already evident from Meyer, namely that the mediaeval copyists of the Life had no scruples about altering and expanding the phraseology of their original whenever they felt so inclined, or about incorporating odd scraps of additional material that came their way wherever it seemed appropriate.

As already indicated, it is the presence of not a little of such additional material in the Latin Life which particularly differentiates it from the Greek 'Apocalypse'. Some of this additional material is undoubtedly Jewish – as, for example, the legend which appears in Life l–li, that, in accordance with Eve's final instructions before her death, Seth wrote down the story of Adam and Eve and 'all that he had heard and seen from them' both on 'tablets of stone' and on 'tablets of clay', so that whatever form the threatened judgement took, whether fire or flood, the record on one or other might survive.[8] Some of the additional material, however, is undoubtedly Christian – as, for example, the speech of Michael in xli.2–xlii.5 prophesying the coming upon earth of 'the most beloved King, Christ, the son of God', which is almost verbally identical with Michael's speech as given in the 'Latin A' recension of the Acts of Pilate (Gospel of Nicodemus) chap. xix. The Life is thus a typical compound of Jewish and Christian elements, but with the Jewish predominating. It has come down to us in Latin, yet the occurrence from time to time of transliterated Greek words (e.g. *cinnamomum et calaminthen et nardum* at xliii.3) makes it as reasonably certain as anything can be that it is basically a translation of a Greek original. It is best explained as the translation either of a later recension of the 'Apocalypse', or, possibly but less probably, of one of the sources behind the 'Apocalypse'.

The English translation which follows is based on the Latin as printed by Meyer.

---

[8] Cp. Josephus, *Ant.* I. ii. 3 (70–71).

BIBLIOGRAPHY

EDITIONS

Latin

W. MEYER, *Vita Adae et Evae* (= *Abhandlungen der philosopisch-philologischen Classe der königlich Bayerischen Akademie der Wissenschaften*, xiv. 3 (Munich, 1878), pp. 185–250).

J. H. MOZLEY, 'The "Vita Adae" ' in *JTS* xxx (1929), pp. 121–149.

also:

Greek

C. TISCHENDORF, *Apocalypses apocryphae* (Leipzig, 1866), pp. 1–23.

A. M. CERIANI, *Monumenta sacra et profana*, V. i (Milan, 1868), pp. 19–24.

and:

M. R. JAMES, 'A Fragment of the Apocalypse of Adam in Greek' in *Apocrypha Anecdota: A Collection of Thirteen Apocryphal Books and Fragments* (= *TS* ii. 3; Cambridge, 1893), pp. 138–145.

Syriac

M. KMOSKO, *Testamentum patris nostri Adam* (= *Patrologia Syriaca*, I. ii (Paris, 1907), pp. 1306–1360). [Together with a Latin translation.]

E. RENAN, 'Fragments du livre gnostique inutilé, Apocalypse d'Adam, ou Pénitance d'Adam, ou Testament d'Adam, publiés d'après deux versions syriaques' in *Journal asiatique*, v. 2 (Paris, 1853), pp. 427–471. [Together with a French translation.]

also:

C. BEZOLD, *Die Schatzhöhle, syrisch und deutsch herausgegeben*, II. *Texte* (Leipzig, 1888).

Armenian

S. HOVSEPHEANTZ, *A Treasury of Old and New Primitive Writers*. Vol. I (*Uncanonical Books of the Old Testament*; Venice, 1896), pp. 1–26 and 307–332.

Coptic

A. BÖHLIG and P. LABIB, *Koptisch-gnostische Apokalypsen aus Codex V von Nag Hammadi* (Halle-Wittenberg, 1963), pp. 86–117.

Ethiopic

E. TRUMPP, *Der Kampf Adams: Aethiopischer Text, verglichen mit dem arabischen Originaltext* (= *Abhandlungen der philosophisch-philologischen Classe der königlich Bayerischen Akademie der Wissenschaften*, xv. 3 (Munich, 1881), pp. 1–172.)

Georgian

C. KURCIK'IDZE in *P'ilologiuri dziebani*, i (Tiflis, 1964), pp. 97–136.

Slavonic

V. JAGIĆ, *Slavische Beiträge zu den biblischen Apocryphen*, I. *Die altkirchen-slavischen Texte des Adambuches* (= *Denkschriften der kaiserlichen Akademie der Wissenschaften. Philos.-hist. Classe*, xlii (Vienna, 1893), pp. 1–104.)

I. IVANOV, *Bogomilski knigi i legendi* (Sófia, 1925), pp. 207–227.

TRANSLATIONS

English

L. S. A. WELLS in R. H. CHARLES, *APOT* ii, pp. 123–154. [Of the Latin.]

A. WALKER, *Apocryphal Gospels, Acts, and Revelations* (= *Ante-Nicene Christian Library*, vol. xvi; Edinburgh, 1870), pp. 454–467. [Of the Greek Apocalypse of Moses.]

E. A. WALLIS BUDGE, *The Book of the Cave of Treasures . . . Translated from the Syriac text of the British Museum MS. Add. 25875* (London, 1927), pp. 51–74.

F. C. CONYBEARE, 'On the Apocalypse of Moses' in *JQR* vii (London, 1895), pp. 216–235. [Of the Armenian.]

J. ISSAVERDENS, *UWOT*,[2] pp. 31–78. [Of the Armenian.]

S. C. MALAN, *The Book of Adam and Eve, also called The Conflict of Adam and Eve with Satan* (London, 1882). [Of the Ethiopic.]

French

E. RENAN, 'Fragments du livre gnostique . . .'. [as above: of the Syriac.]

J.-P. MAHÉ in *Studies in Gnosticism and Hellenistic Religions* (ed. R. VAN DEN BROEK and M. J. VERMASEREN; Leiden, 1981), pp. 227–260. [Of the Georgian.]

German

C. FUCHS in E. KAUTZSCH, *APAT* ii, pp. 506–528.

P. RIESSLER, *AjSaB*,[2] pp. 668–681 [of the Latin]; pp. 138–155 [of the Greek Apocalypse of Moses]; pp. 1084–1090 [of the Syriac Testament of Adam]; pp. 944–951 [of the Syriac Cave of Treasures].

C. BEZOLD, *Die Schatzhöhle, syrisch und deutsch herausgegeben*, I. *Übersetzung* (Leipzig, 1883).

E. PREUSCHEN, 'Die apokryphen gnostischen Adamschriften aus dem armenischen übersetzt und untersucht' in *Festgruss für Bernhard Stade* (Giessen, 1900), pp. 163–252.

C. F. A. DILLMANN, *Das christliche Adambuch des Morgenlandes aus dem Äthiopischen mit Bemerkungen übersetzt* (Göttingen, 1853).

GENERAL

A.-M. DENIS, *IPGAT*, pp. 3–14.

O. EISSFELDT, *OTI*, pp. 636–637.

L. GINZBERG, art. 'Adam, Book of' in *JE* i (New York, 1901), pp. 179–180.

——, *The Legends of the Jews*, i (Philadelphia, 1909), pp. 86–102 and v (Philadelphia, 1925), pp. 114–131.

F. J. A. HORT, art. 'Adam, Books of' in W. SMITH and H. WACE, *A Dictionary of Christian Biography*, i (London, 1877), pp. 34–39

M. R. JAMES, *LAOT*, pp. 1–8.

P. RIESSLER, *AjSaB*,[2] pp. 1273–1274, 1311–1312, 1325–1326, 1332.

L. ROST, *EATAP*, pp. 114–116.

E. SCHÜRER, *HJPTJC* II. iii, pp. 147–148.

——, *GjVZJC*[4] iii, pp. 396–399.

J. L. SHARPE, 'The Second Adam in the Apocalypse of Moses' in *CBQ* xxxv (1973), pp. 35–46.

C. C. TORREY, *AL*, pp. 131–133.

É. TURDEANU, 'Apocryphes bogomiles et apocryphes pseudo-bogomiles' in *Revue de l'histoire des religions*, cxxxviii (1950), pp. 187–194.

I. When they were driven out of Paradise they made a booth for themselves and spent seven days mourning and lamenting in great grief.

II. But after seven days they began to be hungry and started to
2 look for food to eat, and they did not find it. Then Eve said to Adam, My lord, I am hungry. Go *and* look *for something* for us to eat. Perhaps the Lord God will relent and pity us and recall us to the place where we were before.

III. And Adam got up and roamed for seven days through all that
2 land and found no food of the kind they had had in Paradise. And Eve said to Adam, Would you kill me and have me dead? Then, perhaps, the Lord God will take you back into Paradise, for *it was*
3 because of me *that* you were driven out of it. Adam answered, Do not say such things, Eve, lest the Lord God bring on us some other curse. How could I stretch out my hand against my own flesh? Rather let us bestir ourselves and look for something to keep ourselves alive on.

IV. And they wandered about and searched for nine days; and they found nothing of the kind they had had in Paradise, but found only
2 animals' food. And Adam said to Eve, This *kind of food* the Lord has provided for the animals and beasts to eat, but we had angels' food.
3 Yet it is right and proper for us to lament in the sight of God who made us. Let us be truly penitent.[1] Perhaps the Lord God will be gracious to us and pity us and give us something to live on.

V. And Eve said to Adam, What is penitence?[1] Tell me, my lord,
2 what sort of penitence[1] should I do? Let us not impose on ourselves

---

[1] Lit. 'Let us repent with a great repentance'.

[1] Or 'penance'.

too great a strain so that we cannot bear it, with the result that the Lord will not listen to our prayers, and turn his face away from us

3 because we have not done what we promised. My lord, how much penitence[1] have you in mind? I have indeed brought trouble and tribulation on you.

VI. And Adam said to Eve, You cannot do as much as I *can*, so do only as much as you have strength for. I will spend forty days fasting. As for you, get up and go to the River Tigris and take a stone and stand on it in the water up to your neck in the deep *part* of the river. And let no words pass your lips,[1] since we are unworthy to entreat the Lord, for our lips are unclean because of the unlawful

2 and forbidden tree. And stand in the water of the river for thirty-seven days. I will spend *my* forty days in the water of Jordan. Perhaps the Lord God will take pity on us.

VII. And Eve made her way to the River Tigris and did as Adam

2 had told her. So, too, Adam made his way to the River Jordan and stood on a stone up to his neck in water.

VIII. And Adam said, I bid you, water of Jordan, share my grief; and assemble for me all *those creatures* in you that swim, and let

2 them surround me and mourn together with me. Let them lament, not for themselves, but for me; for it is not they that have sinned,

3 but I. Immediately all living things came and surrounded him. And from that moment[1] the water of Jordan stood *still* and stopped its flow.

IX. And eighteen days passed by. Then Satan in anger transformed himself into the brightness of the angels, and went off to the

2 River Tigris, to Eve, and found her weeping. And the devil pretended to share her grief himself; and he began to weep and said to her, Come out of the river and lament no more. Cease now from *your* sorrow and *your* groans. Why are you anxious, *you* and your

3 husband Adam? The Lord God has heard your groans and accepted

---

[1] Or 'penance'.

[1] Lit. 'And speech shall not go out of your mouth.'

[1] Lit. 'hour'.

your penitence;[1] and all we angels have entreated *him* on your
4 behalf and made supplication to the Lord, and he has sent me to
fetch you out of the water and give you the food[2] you had in
5 Paradise, *the loss of* which has caused your *present* wails. So come out
of the water now, and I will take you to the place where your food
has been made ready.

X. Eve heard this and believed it, and she got out of the water of
2 the river; and her body was blue with cold from the water.[1] And
when she had got out she collapsed. And the devil helped her to her
3 feet and led her to Adam. But when Adam saw her, and the devil
with her, he wept and cried aloud and said, O Eve, Eve, where is
4 the fruit[2] of your penitence?[3] How *is it that* you have been again
ensnared by our adversary? *It was* through him we were driven out
of our dwelling-place in Paradise as aliens and *deprived of* all
spiritual joy.

XI. When she heard this, Eve realized *it was* the devil *who* had
persuaded her to get out of the river; and she fell on her face on the
earth, and her sorrow and groaning and wailing were redoubled.
2 And she cried out and said Woe to you, devil. Why do you attack us
for no reason? Why do you interfere with us?[1] What have we done
3 to you that you pursue us with *such* craft?[2] Or why is your malice
directed against us?[3] Have we taken away your glory and caused
you to be dishonoured? Why, enemy, do you persecute us to the
death with *such* malice and *such* spite?

XII. And with a heavy sigh the devil said, O Adam! all my
hostility, envy, and sorrow is in consequence of you, for it is

---

¹ Or 'penance'.   ² Lit. 'nourishment'.

¹ Or 'she was quivering all over with cold from the water'. The force of the simile
in the text as it stands (lit. 'her flesh was like grass from the cold of the water') is
obscure.
² Lit. 'work'.   ³ Or 'penance'.

¹ Lit. 'What have you to do with us?'
² Reading with the text *dolose*: some emend to *dolore* ('with *such* pain').
³ Lit. 'Or what has your malice to do with us?'

because of you that I was driven from my glory, which I had in
heaven among the angels, and because of you I was thrown out
2 onto the earth. Adam answered, What have I done to you, or what
can you blame me for? We have done you no harm or injury. Why,
then, do you pursue us?

XIII. The devil replied, Adam, what are you saying to me? It was
2 on account of you that I was thrown out of heaven.[1] When you
were formed I was expelled from the presence of God and banished
from the company of the angels. When God breathed into you the
breath of life, and your face and likeness was made in the image of
God, Michael brought you and made us worship you in the sight of
God; and the Lord God said, Here is Adam. I have made **him**[2] in
our image and likeness.

XIV. And Michael went out and called all the angels, saying,
2 Worship the image of God as the Lord God has commanded. And
3 Michael himself worshipped first. And *then* he called me and said,
Worship the image of God. And I answered, I have no *duty* to
worship Adam. And since Michael kept urging me to worship, I
said to him, Why do you urge me? I will not worship an inferior
and a younger *being than I am*. I am his senior in creation: before he
was made I was already made: he ought to worship me.

XV. When the rest of the angels, who were under me, heard this,
2 they *too* refused to worship him. And Michael said, Worship the
image of God; and, if you will not worship him, you will make the
3 Lord God very angry. And I said, If he is angry with me, I will set
my seat above the stars of heaven and I will be like the Most High.

XVI. And the Lord God was angry with me and banished me and
my angels from our glory; and on your account were we driven
from our dwelling-places into this world and thrown out onto the
2 earth. At this we were overcome with grief, since we had been
3 deprived of so great glory. And we were pained to see you in such
4 joy and luxury. So I beguiled your wife and caused you to be driven

---

[1] Lit. 'thence'.   [2] The MSS read 'you'.

from your joy and luxury through her, just as I was driven from my glory.

XVII.   When Adam heard the devil say this, he cried out and wept; and he said, O Lord my God, my life is in your hands. Put far from me this adversary, who seeks to destroy my soul, and give me his
2 glory which he himself has lost. And immediately the devil vanished
3 from him. But Adam persevered for forty days, standing in penitence[1] in the water of Jordan.

XVIII.   And Eve said to Adam, Live *out your life*, my lord. You are granted life, since you are guilty of neither the first nor the second error. But I have erred and been led astray, for I have not kept God's commandment. Cut me off now from the light of your life,
2 and I will go westwards[1] and remain[2] there till I die. And she began to make her way towards the regions of the west and to
3 mourn and weep bitterly and groan aloud. And she made there a booth, having been pregnant for about three months.

XIX.   And when the time came for the child to be born she was seized with pains; and she cried aloud to the Lord and said, Have
2 mercy on me, Lord, *and* help me. But she was not heard and God's
3 mercy was denied her.[1] And she said to herself, Who will tell my lord Adam? I implore you, luminaries of heaven, on your way back to the east, bear a message to my lord Adam.

XX.   At that very moment[1] Adam said, A cry of woe from Eve[2] has
2 reached me: perhaps the serpent has attacked her once again. And he went and found her in great distress. And Eve said, As soon as I saw you, my lord, my grief-stricken soul was refreshed. And now entreat the Lord God for me, that he may listen to you, and look on

---

[1] Or 'penance'.

[1] Lit. 'to the sunset'.   [2] Lit. 'be'.

[1] Lit. 'was not around her'.

[1] Lit. 'hour'.   [2] Or 'Eve's cry of woe'.

3 me and free me from my awful pains. And Adam entreated the
Lord for Eve.

XXI. And behold, twelve angels came and two powers, and they
stood on Eve's right and on her left. And Michael was standing on
2 the right. And he stroked her on the face as far down as her breast;
and he said to Eve, You are blessed, Eve, for Adam's sake. In
answer to his fervent prayers and intercessions[1] I have been sent to
you to give you our help. Get up now and prepare to give birth.
3 And she bore a son; and he was beautiful.[2] And at once the babe
got up and ran and brought a blade of grass in his hands and gave it
to his mother. And his name was called Cain.[3]

XXII. And Adam took Eve and the boy and led them towards the
2 east. And the Lord God sent Michael the archangel with different
kinds of seeds and gave *them* to Adam and showed him how to work
and till the ground so that they might have fruit on which they and
3 all their descendants could live. After this Eve conceived and bore
another son, whose name was Abel. And Cain and Abel lived
4 together. And Eve said to Adam, My lord, while I was asleep I
saw a vision. The blood of our son Abel was in Cain's hand, and he
5 was gulping it down with his mouth. I am worried by it. And Adam
said, Cain surely could not murder Abel![1] Yet let us separate them
from one another and give each of them a separate place to live in.

XXIII. And they made Cain a farmer *and* Abel they made a
2 shepherd, so that they were separate from one another. And after
this Cain murdered Abel (Adam was then a hundred and thirty
years old, and Abel, when he was murdered, was **twenty-two**[1]).

---

[1] Lit. 'Since his prayers and intercessions are great'.

[2] Or 'shining' (*lucidus*).

[3] a blade of grass . . . Cain: a Hebrew word-play would seem to be involved here
(*qaneh* . . . *Qayyin*), parallel to, but different from, that at Gen. iv. 1.

[1] Lit. 'Alas, if Cain should kill Abel'.

[1] The text reads 'a hundred and twenty-two'. The emendation depends partly on
common sense and partly on the information in Syncellus (*Chron.* – ed. Dindorf, i,
p. 14) that Abel was twenty-two when he offered his sacrifice.

3 And after this Adam had intercourse with his wife; and he became the father of *another* son and called his name Seth.

XXIV. And Adam said to Eve, Behold, I have fathered a son in
2 place of Abel, whom Cain murdered. And after Adam had fathered Seth he lived eight hundred years and fathered thirty sons *more* and thirty daughters – in all, sixty-three children. And they increased in numbers and spread everywhere in the earth and became nations.[1]

XXV. And Adam said to Seth, Listen, Seth my son, and I will tell you what I heard and saw after your mother and I had been driven
2 out of Paradise. When we were at prayer, Michael the archangel, a
3 messenger of God, came to me. And I saw a chariot like the wind, and its wheels were fiery; and I was caught up into the Paradise of righteousness. And I saw the Lord sitting; and his face was a flaming fire that no man could endure. And many thousands of angels were on the right and on the left of that chariot.

XXVI. When I saw this I was thrown into confusion: terror seized me; and I prostrated myself before God with my face to the ground.
2 And God said to me, Behold, you shall die, because you have transgressed the commandment of God; for you chose to listen to your wife, over whom I gave you authority, in order that you might control her, and you have listened to her and have ignored what I said.

XXVII. And when I heard these words of God I fell prone on the ground and worshipped the Lord and said, My Lord, all-powerful and merciful God, Holy and Righteous One, let not the name that is mindful of thy majesty be blotted out; but renew my life,[1] for I am at the point of death and my breath is about to leave my mouth.
2 Do not drive me from thy presence, *even me*, whom thou didst form from the clay of the earth. Do not banish from thy favour him
3 whom thou didst rear. And lo, a word concerning you came to me,

---

[1] Lit. 'And they were multiplied over the earth in their nations'.

[1] Lit. 'convert my soul'.

and the Lord said to me, Since your days **were fashioned**[2] you have been created with a love of knowledge: your descendants, therefore, shall never lose *the right* to serve me.

XXVIII. And when I heard these words I threw myself to the ground and adored the Lord God and said, Thou art the eternal and supreme God, and all creatures give thee honour and praise.
2 Thou art the True Light, which shines above every light, the Living Life, the Infinite Mighty Power. To thee the spiritual powers give honour and praise. Thou workest on the race of men the miracles of thy mercy.

XXIX. After I had worshipped the Lord, Michael, God's arch-angel, took hold of my hand immediately and led me out[1] of the
2 Paradise of God's Reckoning.[2] And Michael had a rod in his hand and touched the waters that surrounded Paradise, and they froze
3 hard. And I went across. And Michael the archangel went across with me and led me back to the place from which he had caught me
4 up. Listen, Seth my son, to the rest of the secrets also, and the mysteries that are to be, which were revealed to me when I had eaten from the tree of knowledge and learned and understood what
5 is to come to pass in this age, and what God intends to do to the
6 human race he has created. The Lord will appear in a flame of fire, *and* from the mouth of his majesty will issue commandments and precepts: from his mouth *also* will proceed a two-edged sword; and
7 men will hallow him in the house where his majesty dwells. And he will show them the marvellous place of his majesty. And then will they build a house to the Lord their God in the land he will prepare for them; and there will they disobey his precepts. And their sanctuary will be burnt up, their land deserted, and they them-
8 selves dispersed, because they have aroused the wrath of God. And once more he will bring them back from their dispersion; and again
9 they will build God's house. And in the last time God's house will

---

[2] So Meyer (= *figurantur*): all MSS are corrupt.

[1] Lit. 'threw me out'.
[2] Both text and interpretation are highly uncertain: the MSS vary between *visitationis, visionis, visitationis et visionis,* and *visitationis et iussionis.*

be exalted *even* higher than before. And once more iniquity will exceed righteousness. And after that God will dwell with men on the earth in visible form; and then will righteousness begin to shine. And God's house will be honoured for ever.[3] And the adversary will be able no more to harm men who believe in God. And God will raise up for himself a faithful people that he will keep safe for evermore. And the impious will be punished by God their

10 King – *that is* those who have refused to love his law. Heaven and earth, nights and days, and all creatures will obey him and neither transgress his commandment nor change their ways.[4] But men will

11 be changed and forsake the law of the Lord. Therefore the Lord will drive away the wicked from him, but the righteous will shine

12 like the sun before him.[5] And at that time men will be purified by water from their sins; but those who will not be purified will be condemned. And happy shall that man be who has reformed his life[6] when the judgement comes, and God's mighty power is seen among men, and their deeds are inquired into by God the righteous judge.

XXX. When Adam was nine hundred and thirty years old and knew that his end was near, he said, Let all my sons come together

2 to me, so that I can bless them before I die and talk with them. And they came together into his presence in three groups, in the house

3 of prayer where they used to worship the Lord God. And they asked him, *saying*, Why is it, father, you have called us together?

4 And why are you lying on your bed? Then Adam answered and said, My sons, I am ill and in pain. And all his sons said to him, What do illness and pain mean, father?

XXXI. Then his son Seth said, You have been pining, perhaps, for the fruit of Paradise, which you used to eat *once*, and that is why you are lying in such a sorry state. *Only* tell me, and I will go to the nearest of the gates of Paradise and put dust on my head and prostrate myself on the ground before the gates of Paradise and lament and entreat the Lord with a loud and bitter lament: perhaps

---

[3] Or 'in *that* age'. [4] Lit. 'works'.
[5] Lit. 'in the sight of God'.
[6] Or 'learned discipline': lit. 'corrected his soul'.

he will listen to me and send his angel to fetch me the fruit you have
2 been pining for. Adam answered and said, No, my son, I have not
been pining *for that fruit*; but I feel weak and am in great pain in my
body. Seth answered, What is pain, my lord father? I do not
understand. But explain it to us and[1] tell us *about it*.

XXXII.   And Adam answered and said, Listen to me my sons.
When God made us, me and your mother, and placed us in
Paradise, and gave us every tree that bears fruit to eat, he laid a
prohibition on us concerning the tree of the knowledge of good and
2 evil that is in the middle of Paradise, saying, Do not eat of it. And
God gave a part of Paradise to me and *a part* to your mother: the
trees of[1] the eastern part and the north he gave to me, and he gave
the south and the western part to your mother.

1,2 **XXXIII.**   *Also*, the Lord God gave us two angels to guard us. The
time came when the angels had gone up to worship in God's
presence; *and* at once the adversary, the devil, took the opportunity, while the angels were away, and led your mother astray *and*
3 *persuaded her* to eat of the unlawful and forbidden tree. And she ate
of it herself and gave *some* to me.

XXXIV.   And immediately the Lord God was angry with us. And
the Lord said to me, Because you have forsaken my commandment
and have not kept my word, which I made binding on you, behold
I will afflict your body with seventy ills.[1] With all kinds of different
pains will you be tormented in every limb, from your head and eyes
2 and ears right down to your toe-nails. These *ills* he appointed for us
as a punishment.[2] All of them has the Lord laid on me and all our
race.

---

   [1] Lit. 'But do not hide it from us, but'.

   [1] Some MSS read 'the authority over'.

   [1] Lit. 'I will bring upon your body seventy blows (or 'strokes' – of the rod)'.
   [2] All MSS have an additional phrase here. They differ widely from one another,
but not one makes even tolerable sense.

XXXV. So did Adam speak to his sons. And he was seized with violent pains and cried out loudly, What shall I do? I am exhausted,
2 so cruel are the pains that grip me. And when Eve saw him weeping, she also began to weep herself and said, O Lord, my God,
3 transfer to me his pain, for it was I who sinned. And Eve said to Adam, My lord, let me share your pains,[1] for it is my fault they have come on you.

XXXVI. And Adam said to Eve, Get up and go with my son Seth to the neighbourhood of Paradise, and put dust on your heads and prostrate yourselves on the ground and lament in the sight of God.
2 Perhaps he will pity you and send his angel across to the tree of mercy, from which flows the oil of life; and *perhaps* he will give you a drop of it to anoint me with, so that I can get some respite from these pains by which I am consumed.

XXXVII. Then Seth and his mother went off towards the gates of Paradise. And while they were going, suddenly a beast appeared, a
2 serpent, and it attacked and bit Seth. And as soon as Eve saw it, she wept and said, Alas, wretched woman that I am. I am accursed
3 because I have not kept God's commandment. And Eve shouted at the serpent, Accursed beast! How *is it* you are not afraid to let yourself loose against the image of God but dare to fight it?

XXXVIII. The beast answered in human speech, Is it not against you, Eve, that our malice *is directed*? Are not you the objects of our
2 spite? Tell me, Eve, how came it that your mouth was open to eat the fruit? Yet now, if I should *even* begin to reproach you, you could not endure it.

XXXIX. Then Seth said to the beast, The Lord God rebuke you! Be silent, be dumb, shut your mouth, accursed enemy of truth, confounder and destroyer! Keep your distance from the image of God till the day when the Lord God orders you to be brought to the
2 *final* trial. And the beast said to Seth, See I leave the presence of

---

[1] Lit. 'give me a part of your pains'.

God's image as you have told me to. At this, he left Seth with the marks of his teeth upon him.[1]

XL. But Seth and his mother continued their journey to the regions of Paradise, *looking* for the oil of mercy to anoint the ailing Adam; and they arrived at the gates of Paradise. They took dust from the ground and put it on their heads and they prostrated 2 themselves and began to lament with loud moans, supplicating the Lord God to pity Adam in his pains and to send his angel to give him the oil from the tree of his mercy.

XLI. And when they had been praying and making supplication for many hours, behold, the angel Michael appeared to them and 2 said, I have been sent to you by the Lord. I am appointed by God 3 to look after men's bodies; *and I am to* tell you, Seth, *since you are* a man of God, not to weep or pray or make supplication for the oil of the tree of mercy, so as to anoint your father Adam and ease the pains in his body.

XLII. For, I tell you, you can never have it, except in the last days. 2 When five thousand five hundred years have been completed, then will come upon earth the most beloved King, Christ, the Son of God, to revive the body of Adam, and to revive the bodies of the 3 dead with him. He himself, the Son of God, will be baptized at his coming in the River Jordan; and when he comes out of the water of Jordan, then will he anoint with the oil of mercy all that believe in 4 him. And the oil of mercy will be *given* generation after generation to those who are ready to be born again to life eternal by water and 5 the Holy Spirit. Then, when the most beloved Son of God, Christ, descends to earth, he will take your father Adam into Paradise *and lead him* to the tree of mercy.[1]

---

[1] Lit. 'wounded by his teeth'.

[1] Michael's speech up to here (i.e. xli.2–xlii.5) is almost verbally identical with his speech as given in the Latin 'A' recension of the Acts of Pilate (Gospel of Nicodemus) xix, where, at Adam's request, Seth recounts the incident to his 'sons' the patriarchs and prophets' in Hell. The Greek and the Latin 'B' recensions of the Acts also include the speech, but in slightly different forms. Neither the Greek nor either of the Latin recensions, however, has the concluding verse in the Life (i.e. xliii. 1). See M. R. James, *The Apocryphal New Testament* (Oxford, 1924), pp. 126–8.

XLIII. But as for you, Seth, go to your father Adam, for his life-span is complete. Six days from now his soul will leave his body; and, when it goes out, you will see great marvels in the heaven and
2 on the earth and in the luminaries of heaven. *And* with these words
3 Michael left Seth immediately. And Eve and Seth returned, carry-ing with them sweet-smelling herbs — nard, and crocus, and calamus, and cinnamon.

XLIV. And when Seth and his mother reached Adam, they told
2 him how the serpent-beast had bitten Seth. And Adam said to Eve, What *is it that* you did? A great plague have you brought on us —
3 transgression and sin for all our generations. After my death tell your children what you did;[1] for our descendants[2] will toil and not
4 make a living, they will be in want and curse us and say, Our first
5 parents brought all *these* evils on us. *And* when Eve heard what he said, she began to weep and moan.

XLV. And after six days came Adam's death, just as the archangel
2 Michael had foretold. When Adam realized that the hour of his death was near he said to all his sons, Behold, I am nine hundred and thirty years old; and after I am dead bury me towards the
3 sunrising † in the field that belongs to the house over there†. And it came to pass, when he had finished speaking, he breathed his last. *Then* was the sun darkened, and the moon and the stars *also*, for seven days.

XLVI. And Seth bent over his father's body, mourning, and embraced it;[1] and Eve stared at the ground with hands folded over

---

[1] The Apocalypse of Moses puts this charge of Adam to Eve in the form of a command to summon their children and grandchildren immediately and, when assembled in a group round Adam's deathbed, to 'tell them the manner of our transgression'. The Apocalypse then continues with Eve's account of the fall (chaps. xv–xxx), which thus *precedes* Adam's death. It consequently lacks Eve's speech in Life xlix.1–l.2, which accords with Adam's instructions here to Eve to tell her story *after* his death. The account of the Fall in the Apocalypse will be found printed in full as an Appendix (pp. 161–67, below).

[2] Lit. 'those who arise from us'.

[1] Lit. 'And Seth in his mourning embraced from above his father's body'.

2 her head, and all her children wept most bitterly. And behold,
   Michael the angel appeared and stood at Adam's head and said to
3 Seth, Get up and leave your father's body, and come to me and see
   what the Lord God has in store for him. His creature he is, and he
   has had pity on him.

XLVII. And all the angels blew their trumpets and cried, Blessed
art thou, O Lord, for thou hast had pity on thy creature.

XLVIII. Then Seth saw God's hand stretched out *and* holding
2 Adam; and he delivered him over to Michael, saying, Let him be in
   your charge till the day of judgement in punishment, till the last
3 years when I will turn his sorrow into joy. Then shall he sit on the
4 throne of his supplanter.[1] And the Lord said again to the angels
   Michael and Uriel, Bring me three linen sheets and spread them
   out over Adam, and *spread* other sheets over his son Abel, and bury
5 Adam and his son. And all the angelic powers marched in proces-
   sion in front of Adam; and the sleep of the dead was consecrated.
6 And the angels Michael and Uriel buried Adam and Abel in the
   regions of Paradise, before the eyes of Seth and his mother and no
7 one else. And Michael and Uriel said, Just as you have seen *us
   doing*, so do you also bury your dead.

XLIX. Six days after Adam died, Eve, realizing *that* her own death
was near, called all her sons and daughers together — that is, Seth
2 with *his* thirty brothers and thirty sisters. And Eve said to all *of
   them*, Listen to me, my children, and I will tell you what the
   archangel Michael said to us when your father and I transgressed
3 the command of God. Because of your transgression, *he said*, our
   Lord will bring on your race the anger of his judgement, first by
   water, the second time by fire: by these two things will the Lord
   judge the whole human race.

L. But listen to me, my children. Make *two kinds of* tablets, *some o*
stone and others of clay, and record on them everything that has
happened in my life and your father's, what you have heard from

---

[1] Or, according to some MSS, 'of his seducer'.

2 us and *what you* have seen *yourselves*. If the Lord judges our race by water, the clay tablets will become mud,[1] but the stone ones will be preserved; but if he judges our race by fire, *then* the stone tablets 3 will be shattered,[1] but the clay ones baked *hard*. When Eve had said this to her children, she spread out her hands to heaven in prayer, and bent her knees to the earth; and while she was worshipping the Lord and giving him thanks she breathed her last. *And* afterwards all her children buried her with loud lamentation.

LI. When they had been mourning four days the archangel 2 Michael appeared and said to Seth, Man of God, never mourn for your dead more than six days, because on the seventh day is the sign of the resurrection *and* the rest of the age to come, for on the 3 seventh day the Lord rested from all his works. Then Seth made the tablets.[1]

APPENDIX

EVE'S ACCOUNT OF THE FALL FROM THE APOCALYPSE OF MOSES XV–XXX

[As noted above (p. 142, n. 6) this account corresponds to the short speech of Eve to 'all her sons and daughters' in Life xlix.1–l.2, though it differs in that (1) it is placed in the Apocalypse *before* and not *after* the death of Adam, and (2) it is very much more elaborate. In fact, it incorporates the only considerable body of matter contained in the Apocalypse that is not also contained in some form in the Life. It is printed partly for this reason, and partly on account of its intrinsic interest.]

[1] Lit. 'will be dissolved'.

[1] Some MSS add an account of how these tablets survived the Flood, but no one could read them: Solomon, however, had the secret of the script revealed to him by the same angel who had 'held the hand' of Seth when he wrote them. The account concludes by stating that 'on these stones was found what Enoch, the seventh from Adam, had prophesied before the Flood about the advent of Christ'; and then follows the well-known passage from 1 Enoch i. 9, quoted at Jude 14 and 15. Still other MSS have further additions, including information about the materials out of which Adam's body was made and the statement that he was fashioned 'in that place in which Jesus was born, that is to say in Bethlehem, which is in the middle of the world'.

XIV. 3 . . . And he said to her, Call all our children and our children's children, and tell them how it was that we transgressed.

XV. Then Eve said to them, Listen, my children and children's children, all of you, and I will tell you how the enemy deceived us.
2 It happened when we were guarding Paradise, each of us the part allotted to us by God. I was on guard in my lot, the south and the
3 west. But the devil went to Adam's lot, where the male creatures were (for God had divided the creatures: all the males he had given to your father, and all the females he had given to me; and we each looked after our own).

XVI. And the devil spoke to the serpent, saying, Get up *and* come *here* to me, and I will tell you something that could be to your
2 advantage. And he got up and came to him. And the devil said to him, I hear you are the wisest of all the animals, and I have come to
3 talk to you. Why do you eat Adam's tares and not the fruits of Paradise? Come, and let us see to it that he is thrown out of
4 Paradise, just as we were thrown out because of him. The serpent
5 said to him, I am afraid the Lord will be angry with me. The devil said to him, Do not be afraid, only be my tool, and I will put into your mouth such words as will deceive him.

XVII. And he *went* immediately *and* hung from the wall of Paradise. And when the angels went up to worship God, then Satan appeared
2 in the form of an angel and sang hymns like the angels. And I bent over the wall and saw him *looking* just like an angel. And he said to
3 me, Are you Eve? And I said to him, I am. And he said to me, What do you do in Paradise?[1] And I said to him, God set us to guard *it*
4 and to eat from it. The devil answered through the serpent's
5 mouth, You do well; yet you do not eat from every plant. And I said, Yes, we do eat from every plant, except only one – the one that is in the middle of Paradise, about which God commanded us not to eat from it. For on the day you do eat from it, he said to us, you will certainly die.

---

[1] Or 'what are you doing in Paradise?'

XVIII. Then the serpent said to me, As God lives, I am grieved about you, because you are like the animals; and I would not have you remain in ignorance. Come, listen to me and eat, and learn the
2 value of that tree. But I said to him, I am afraid that God will be
3 angry with me, as he told us *he would*. And he said to me, Do not be afraid, for as soon as you eat from it, you too will be like God,[1]
4 knowing good and evil. God realized this, that you would be like
5 him, so he envied you and said, You must not eat from it. But *go and*
6 look at the plant and you will see how splendid it is.[2] Yet I was afraid to take *any* of the fruit. And he said to me, Come, and I will give it you: follow me.

XIX. And I opened *the gate* for him, and he came inside, into Paradise, and went on in front of me. And when he had gone a little way he turned and said to me, I have changed my mind: I will not give you *any of the fruit* to eat till you swear to me that you will give
2 *some* also to your husband. I said to him, I do not know what sort of oath I should swear to you by; yet, so far as my knowledge goes, I promise you, By the Throne of Majesty, and by the Cherubim, and by the Tree of Life, I will give *some of the fruit* also to my husband to
3 eat. And as soon as he had the oath from me, he went and put on the fruit the poison of his wickedness – that is to say, lust, the root and origin of every sin. And he bent the branch down to the ground; and I took *some* of the fruit and ate *it*.

XX. And at that very moment my eyes were opened; and I knew immediately that I had been stripped[1] of the righteousness I had
2 been clothed with. And I wept and said to him, Why have you done
3 this to me and deprived me of my glory? And I wept also because of the oath I had sworn. But he got down from the tree and vanished.
4 And in my nakedness I began to look in my part *of Paradise* for leaves to hide my shame, but I could not find any; for, as soon as I had eaten, the leaves dropped off all the trees in my part *of Paradise*,

---

[1] Or 'like gods'.
[2] Lit 'the great glory concerning it'.

[1] Lit. 'was naked'.

except the fig-tree. So I took some leaves from it and made myself a
5 girdle. And it was from that very same tree that I had eaten.

XXI. And I cried out loud, saying, Adam, Adam, where are you?
2 Get up *and* come to me, and I will show you a great secret. But
when your father came I spoke wicked words to him – words that
3 brought us down from our pinnacle of glory. For, when he came, I
opened my mouth and began to exhort him and said (it was the
devil speaking), Come here, my lord Adam: listen to me, and eat
some of the fruit of the tree God told us not to eat of, and you will be
4 like God.[1] And your father answered and said, I am afraid that
God will be angry with me. And I said to him, Do not be afraid, for
5 as soon as you have eaten you will know good and evil. And I
quickly persuaded him; and he ate. And his eyes were opened
6 immediately, and he too became aware of his nakedness. And he
said to me, You wicked woman! What have I done to you that you
have deprived me of the glory of God?

XXII. And at that very moment we heard the archangel Michael
blowing with his trumpet and calling to the angels and saying,
2 Thus says the Lord, Come with me to Paradise and hear the
judgement with which I am about to judge Adam. And when we
heard the archangel trumpeting, we said, Behold, God is coming
3 into Paradise to judge us. And we were afraid and hid. And when
God appeared in Paradise, mounted on the chariot of the cherubim,
with the angels going before him and singing hymns of praise, all
the plants of Paradise, both of your father's lot and mine, burst into
4 flower. And God's throne was set up where the Tree of Life was.

XXIII. And God called Adam, saying, Adam where are you? Can
2 the house be hidden from its builder? Then your father answered,
We have not hidden, Lord, because we think thou canst not find
us; but I was afraid, because I am naked, and overawed, Lord, by
3 thy might. God said to him, Who showed you that you are naked?
Have you forsaken my commandment which I told you to observe?
4 Then Adam remembered my promise to him, I will protect you if

---

[1] Or 'like a god'.

God is angry;[1] and he turned to me and said, Why have you done
5 this? And I said, The serpent deceived me.

XXIV. God said to Adam, Because you have disregarded my
commandment and have listened to your wife, cursed shall the
2 ground be by your labours. You will work it and it will not yield its
wealth: thorns and thistles will it grow for you; and by the sweat of
your brow you shall eat your bread. Manifold will be your toils:
you will be crushed by bitterness; and of sweetness you will have no
3 taste. Weary you will be and yet find no rest, by heat exhausted
and by cold distraught. You will labour incessantly, but not be
4 rich; and you will grow fat, yet come to no *good* end.[1] Even the
beasts, over whom you were given the dominion, will rise up in
rebellion against you, because you have not kept my commandment.

XXV. And the Lord turned to me and said, Because you listened to
the serpent and turned a deaf ear to my commandment, you shall
2 suffer **the pangs of child birth**[1] and agonizing pains. You shall bear
children in much **trembling**,[2] and within a single hour you shall come *to
the point of birth* and lose your life, so intense will be your anguish and
3 *your* pangs. *Then* will you make confession and say, Lord, Lord, save
4 me, and I will turn no more to carnal sin. And so, by your own words
will I judge you, because of the enmity which the enemy has planted
in you.

XXVI. And he turned to the serpent in great wrath and said, Because
you have done this and become a graceless creature[1] and have
deceived the innocent in heart, accursed shall you be more than all
beasts. You shall be deprived of the food you used to eat and shall feed
on dust all the days of your life. On your breast and your belly shall

[1] Lit. 'I will make you safe before God'.

[1] The MSS vary in this catalogue both in the ordering, and in the inclusion or
omission, of some of the details.

[1] Text 'you shall be in vain things'.
[2] = τρόμοις. Text 'in many ways (= τρόποις)'.

[1] Lit. 'vessel, thing'.

you crawl and lose your hands and feet. There shall be left to you neither ear nor wing nor any limb that in your malice you ensnared them with and caused them to be thrown out of Paradise. And I will put enmity between you and human kind:[2] they shall watch out for your head and you shall watch out for their heel till the day of judgement.

XXVII. So he spoke and gave orders to his angels that we should be 2 thrown out of Paradise. And as we were being driven out, with loud lamentations, your father Adam pleaded with the angels, saying, Spare me a moment, so that I may entreat the Lord to have compassion on me and pity me, for only I have sinned. And they left off 3 driving him. And Adam cried out with tears and said, Forgive me, 4 Lord, for what I did. Then the Lord said to the angels, Why have you stopped driving Adam out of Paradise? Is it I who have done wrong? 5 Or is my judgement faulty? Then the angels fell to the ground and worshipped the Lord, saying, Thou art righteous, Lord, and thou judgest rightly.

XXVIII. And the Lord turned to Adam and said, I will allow you to 2 remain in Paradise no longer. And Adam answered and said, Grant 3 me, Lord, to eat from the Tree of Life before I am thrown out. Then the Lord spoke to Adam, *saying*, You shall not have *any* of it now, for because of you I have commanded the Cherubim to guard it with the flaming sword that turns *every way*, so that you should not taste *it* and thereby gain immortality for ever: you must endure instead the 4 conflict that the enemy has brought upon you. Yet after you have gone out of Paradise, if you can keep yourself from all evil (as one about to die), at the resurrection[1] I will raise you up, and then shall you be given *to eat* from the Tree of Life, you shall be immortal for evermore.

XXIX. So the Lord spoke and ordered us to be thrown out of 2 Paradise. But your father Adam wept in the angels' presence in[1]

---

[2] Lit. 'and his seed'.

[1] Lit. 'when the resurrection has again come into being'.

[1] Lit. 'opposite, over against'.

Paradise; and the angels said to him, What would you have us do for
3 you, Adam? And your father said to them, Behold, you are driving me
out: I beg you, let me take away *some* sweet-smelling *herbs* from
Paradise so that I can make an offering to God after I have gone out of
4 Paradise, and God may listen to me. And the angels approached God
and said, Jael, eternal king, give orders that Adam be given sweet-
5 smelling incense from Paradise. And God ordered Adam to go and
take sweet-smelling spices from Paradise *and also some seeds* for his food.
6 And the angels let him go; and he gathered both kinds – crocus and
7 nard and calamus and cinnamon, and other seeds for his food. And,
taking them *with him*, he went out of Paradise. And we found ourselves
on earth.

XXX. So now, my children, I have shown you how it was we were
deceived. And as for you, see to it that you do not abandon what is
good.

XXXI. And when Eve had said this, surrounded by her sons, and
Adam was lying ill and about to die the following day . . .

1 ENOCH

INTRODUCTION

The patriarch Enoch was well known in pre-Christian Judaism and in the primitive Church, not merely as a paragon of righteousness, but also as an author whose writings had a wide circulation and in some quarters were accepted as 'scripture'. The Book of Jubilees represents him as the inventor of writing, and it refers to his having written several apparently quite unrelated works dealing with 'the signs of heaven', his own vision of 'what will happen to the sons of men in every generation', and certain angelic revelations concerning 'everything on earth and in the heavens':[1] later on, his 'special function' is described as 'to be a witness to the world's generations and report all the deeds of each generation till the day of judgement';[2] and, later still, the dying Abraham is reported as telling Isaac that he had found certain regulations about sacrifice 'written . . . in the words of Enoch'.[3] In the New Testament, the Epistle of Jude explicitly quotes Enoch and introduces the quotation with the formula 'Enoch, the seventh from Adam, prophesied, saying . . .'[4] Thereafter quotations and references are frequent. Thus, the Epistle of Barnabas quotes him ('. . . concerning which it is written, as Enoch says, . . .'),[5] and the Testaments of the Twelve Patriarchs have no less than nine references to material contained in the 'words', or 'writing', or 'book', or 'books', 'of Enoch'.[6]

Among the Fathers, Tertullian, although he himself accepted Enoch, knew of some who did not.[7] Origen quoted and referred to Enoch, but he had reservations;[8] and he was at pains to point out to Celsus that 'the books entitled "Enoch" are not generally held to

[1] Jub. iv. 17–21.   [2] Jub. x. 17.
[3] Jub. xxi. 10.   [4] Jude 14–15.
[5] *Ep. Barn.* iv. 3 (the quotation at xvi. 5 is attributed to 'Scripture', and that at xvi. 6 is introduced by 'it is written': in neither case is Enoch mentioned by name).
[6] It should be noted, however, that there is textual uncertainty in five of these instances.
[7] Tert. *cult. fem.* I. iii. 1.
[8] Orig. *In Ioann.* VI. xlii (25); *in Num. hom.* xxviii. 2.

be divine by the churches'.[9] For Jerome Enoch was certainly apocryphal.[10] And so too for Augustine: Augustine admitted that Enoch had written 'not a little' by divine inspiration, but he himself found the writings then circulating under Enoch's name so full of incredible fables and other undesirable matter that they could not possibly be genuine: they were quite rightly rejected by both Jews and Christians.[11]

'Enoch' is listed among the works outside the Canon in the Stichometry of Nicephorus, in the List of Sixty Books, and in the pseudo-Athanasian Synopsis; but it is not mentioned in the Gelasian Decree. This presumably means that writings attributed to Enoch passed out of circulation in the West rather earlier than they did in the East. The last Eastern writer to show personal acquaintance with the writings of Enoch is Georgius Syncellus (*c*.800). In his *Chronography* Syncellus gives (in Greek) four extracts 'from the first book of Enoch', and later on he refers to certain astronomical information which the archangel Uriel had given Enoch 'as Enoch records in his book'.[12]

After the lapse of more than a thousand years the Enoch literature was re-introduced to the West at the end of the eighteenth century by James Bruce as a result of his travels in Abyssinia. Among the Ethiopic manuscripts that Bruce brought back were three containing what is now known as 1 Enoch or 'Ethiopian Enoch'. One of these manuscripts (now in the Bodleian Library at Oxford) contained 1 Enoch only: the second (also in the Bodleian) contained 1 Enoch, followed by Job, Isaiah, the Twelve, Proverbs, Wisdom, Ecclesiastes, Canticles and Daniel: the third (now in the Bibliothèque Nationale in Paris) is a transcript of the second. In all three the work was entitled 'the Book of Enoch the Prophet'. Richard Laurence, Regius Professor of Hebrew at Oxford and subsequently Archbishop of Cashel, issued a translation of the text of the first of the Bodleian manuscripts in 1821 and followed this in 1838 by printing the text itself. Meanwhile, more manuscripts

---

[9] Orig. *c. Cel*. v. 54.

[10] Hieron. *vir. inl.* 4; *Comm. in Tit.* i. 12: cp. *Tract. de Ps.* cxxxii. 3.

[11] Aug. *Civ. Dei*, xv. 23, xviii. 38.

[12] Syncellus, *Chronographia* (ed. Dindorf = *Corp. Scr. Hist. Byz.*, vol i (Bonn, 1829), pp. 20–23, 42–47, 60).

were being brought back by other travellers, and three of these, along with the two in the Bodleian, were used by Dillmann for the first critical edition of the Ethiopic text, published in 1851.

In 1886–7 workers attached to the French Archaeological Museum at Cairo discovered in a monk's tomb at Akhmim two extensive parchment fragments of Enoch in Greek, bound up together with fragments of the Gospel and the Revelation of Peter (also in Greek). The larger of the two Enoch fragments was found to correspond to 1 Enoch i. 1–xxxii. 6 in the Ethiopic, and the smaller to xix. 3–xxi. 9. They are to be assigned to either the fifth or the sixth centuries. They were published by U. Bouriant and A. Lods in 1892–3 and were consequently not available to R. H. Charles for use in the first edition of his *The Book of Enoch* (English translation, with Introduction and Commentary), which appeared in 1893. However, when Charles produced his full critical edition of the Ethiopic text in 1906 (based on twenty-three MSS), he printed opposite the Ethiopic text at the appropriate points, not only the complete Greek text of the Akhmim fragments, but also the Greek extracts from Syncellus, a Greek fragment corresponding to lxxxix. 42–49 from Vat. Cod. Gr. 1809 (which had been published by A. Mai in 1844 in the second volume of his *Patrum Nova Bibliotheca*), and a Latin fragment corresponding to cvi. 1–18 discovered in the British Museum by M. R. James in 1893 and published in the Cambridge *Texts and Studies* in the same year. All this additional material was assimilated in the 'wholly recast, enlarged, and re-written' second edition of Charles's *The Book of Enoch* in 1912.

Since Charles's day there have been two major discoveries.[13]

First, in 1930 the University of Michigan acquired six leaves of a papyrus codex, written in Greek and dating from the fourth or early fifth century. Shortly afterwards it appeared that eight more leaves and three fragments, all belonging to the same codex as the Michigan leaves, were included in the very valuable collection of papyri acquired by A. Chester Beatty about the same time. When reconstructed, this codex was found to contain a complete Greek

[13] Among minor discoveries should be mentioned the 6th–7th cent. fragment, which appears to contain a text of 1 Enoch xciii. 3–8 in Coptic, and which was discovered during the excavations at Antinoë in 1937 and published in 1960.

text (apart from the inevitable minor deficiencies) of 1 Enoch xcvii. 6–civ. 13 and cvi. 1–cvii. 3, followed by the Greek text of the otherwise lost *Homily on the Passion* of Melito of Sardis. It was clear at once that the text of Enoch offered by the codex differed from the Ethiopic in lacking both chap. cv and the final chap. cviii (chaps. civ and cvi are continuous, and after cvii. 3 is written the colophon 'Epistle of Enoch', with Melito's *Homily* following immediately). What was not clear was how much had been lost before xcvii. 6. Campbell Bonner, who was entrusted with the task of editing both texts, was of the opinion, for technical reasons, that it was most unlikely that the codex had ever contained the whole of 1 Enoch: in his view it included only chaps. xci–cvii (minus cv), and these chapters were preceded by another short work of which the three fragments were the sole extant remains. These fragments he assigned to an apocryphal 'Ezekiel'.

The second major discovery since Charles's day is that of the Aramaic fragments found in Cave IV at Qumran. The first of these was identified as belonging to 1 Enoch by J. T. Milik at the beginning of September 1952: the identification of others soon followed; and Milik published a sumptuous edition of all of them, with extended commentary, explanatory essays, and plates, in 1976. Altogether there are some hundreds of fragments, which Milik interpreted as the remains of eleven different manuscripts, the oldest of which he assigned to the first half of the second century BC; and they cover all parts of the book as we know it with the exception of chaps. xxxvii–lxxi. This is clear proof that the greater part of what is now 1 Enoch, if not all of it, was known and was popular at Qumran in pre-Christian times. On the other hand, since all the fragments are so small (many of them minute), the amount of continuous Aramaic text preserved is effectively very little: this means that the value of the Aramaic evidence for text-critical purposes is far less than might be expected.

In 1978, two years after Milik, came M. A. Knibb's *The Ethiopic Book of Enoch: A new Edition in the Light of the Aramaic Dead Sea Fragments*. In Volume 1 (Text and Apparatus) Knibb printed as his base text photographs of Rylands Ethiopic MS 23 and assembled in his apparatus the variants of twenty-five other Ethiopic MSS together with the variants of the Greek witnesses: Volume 2 contained the Introduction, Translation, and Commentary. As explained in the Introduction, the Translation was intended as a translation of the Ethiopic version and not of an Ethiopic version corrected or revised in the light of the Greek or Aramaic, where they exist. Furthermore, the translation follows the base text (Ryl. Eth. MS 23) very closely and only diverges from it where, for example, it seems to make no sense. Thus, Knibb made no attempt to reconstruct a supposed 'original' text of the Ethiopic, nor of an 'original' Enoch, either in its Aramaic or its Greek forms. Those who wish to try their hands at this must resort first to the Apparatus in volume 1 and then to the Commentary in volume 2, which is throughout textual and not exegetical.

When, towards the middle of the nineteenth century, 1 Enoch became known generally, most of the scholars who studied it very naturally treated it as a unity – as 'the Book of Enoch the Prophet' as the manuscripts described it. But it was soon realized that it was composite; and to-day it is commonly agreed that it is in fact a collection of several previously independent writings, or 'books', that have been put together and edited. These, we may suppose, already circulated under Enoch's name before they were put together, though there is reason to think that some bits and pieces have been incorporated to which the name of Noah was previously attached (e.g. chaps. cvi–cvii), and perhaps some others as well. But leaving aside the details, 1 Enoch, in its present form, is plainly divisible into five subsidiary 'books':–

Book I, chaps. i–xxxvi;
Book II, chaps. xxxvii–lxxi;
Book III, chaps. lxxii–lxxxii;
Book IV, chaps. lxxxiii–xc; and
Book V, chaps. xci–cviii.

A parallel has frequently been noted between this five-fold division and the five books ascribed to Moses and the five books of the Psalter. If such an arrangement was intentional, then 1 Enoch is not just a collection of writings ascribed to Enoch: it is an Enochic Pentateuch.

It will be convenient to make a few comments on each 'book' separately.

Book I is commonly known as 'The Book of Watchers', because three out of Syncellus's four extracts were certainly taken from it, and he says they were 'from the first book of Enoch, concerning the Watchers'. This book is undoubtedly ancient, probably the most ancient of the five. It was well known to the Fathers: it was quoted as scripture by the author of the Epistle of Jude:[14] the Akhmim fragments, together with Syncellus's extracts, are evidence for the existence of a complete Greek version of it; and there were no less than five copies of it in Aramaic at Qumran. The oldest of these copies is assigned by Milik to the first half of the 2nd cent. BC, which takes back the date of the book itself to the 3rd cent., if not earlier.

Book II (The Book of Parables – cp. xxxviii. 1, xlv. 1, etc.) provides a complete contrast. No Aramaic fragments of it were found at Qumran: no traces of any version of it (apart from the Ethiopic) have survived; and there are no quotations from it in the Fathers. Indeed, there is no convincing proof that it ever existed before the 15th cent. AD, when it was copied as a constituent part of 1 Enoch in the earliest of the Ethiopic MSS. No one, however, has proposed a date for the Parables anything like as late as this. Representative dates proposed are the first half of the last century BC (Charles), the end of the first century AD (Knibb), and the end of the 3rd cent. AD (Milik).

Such wide variations in the dating of the Parables pose an awkward problem for the New Testament scholar, inasmuch as the Parables are noteable, not only for the number of verbal parallels with the New Testament that are to be found in them (cp., e.g., 1 Enoch lxix. 27 with Matt. xxv. 31 and John v. 22, 27), but also for their use of several of the well-known New Testament Christological titles, particularly 'the Son of Man'. It has been customary to explain this (on the assumption that Charles's dating was correct) by supposing that Our Lord and his earliest followers were very much influenced by the Parables, and that the Parables are therefore of primary importance for the study of Christian origins. Charles himself wrote:

---

[14] 1 Enoch i. 9 is quoted at Jude 14–15.

'This definite title [i.e. Son of Man] is found in 1 Enoch for the first time in Jewish literature, and is, historically, the source of the New Testament designation, and contributes to it some of its most characteristic contents'.[15]

But if Charles's dating is wrong and the Parables are to be dated in the Christian era, then the parallels and the common use of the Christological titles will have to be explained in some other way – it may be, for example, that it was the New Testament that influenced the Parables, and not *vice versa*. In any case, it looks as if much that has been written during the twentieth century about these matters will have to be re-written.

Book III (The Astronomical Book). Fragments of four MSS of this book were found at Qumran, but they attest a much fuller text than the eleven chapters now preserved in the Ethiopic version. Jubilees records that Enoch 'wrote down in a book *details about* the signs of heaven according to the order of their months';[16] and since the author of Jubilees places this first among the works of Enoch known to him, it is probable that he regarded it as the most significant part of the Enoch corpus, and in consequence he may well have known it in its longer form. At any rate, the length of the book, as read at Qumran, was such as to require a complete roll of parchment for each copy.

The oldest of the Qumran copies is dated by Milik to the end of the 3rd or the beginning of the 2nd cent. BC, which takes back the date of the book itself to sometime in the 3rd cent. at the latest – as is the case with the Book of Watchers. For the existence of a Greek version there is no incontrovertible evidence. But several considerations converge to make it likely that there was a Greek version: (1) the Ethiopic version was presumably made from one; (2) Origen's remarks in his *Homilies on Numbers* seem to refer to the final chapter of the Astronomical Book,[17] while Syncellus's reference to the astronomical information that the archangel Uriel had given Enoch is in effect a brief-summary of the entire book,[18] and both Origen and Syncellus are likely to have known a text in Greek rather than any other language; and (3) Milik claimed to have

[15] Charles, *APOT* ii, p. 185.   [16] Jub. iv. 17.
[17] See above p. 169.   [18] See above p. 170.

identified two scraps of a Greek text of lxxvii. 7–lxxviii. 1 and of lxxviii. 8 on an Oxyrhynchus fragment published in 1927.

Even so, the absence of any representative sections of continuous Greek text is a serious handicap in trying to decide whether the abridgement preserved in the Ethiopic was made when the Aramaic was translated into Greek, or, alternatively, when the Greek was translated into Ethiopic, or at some other stage in the transmission. Yet are we certainly dealing with an abridgement? Charles held that the Astronomical Book was originally written in Hebrew. If so, then it is possible to argue that the Hebrew had the shorter text and that the Aramaic represents an expansion when the Hebrew was translated into Aramaic, but that the Greek version was made from the Hebrew – in which case the Ethiopic will in general be a more faithful witness to the text of the book as the author wrote it than the Aramaic from Qumran!

Book IV (The Book of Dreams) is represented by fragments from four of the Qumran MSS, the oldest of which is to be dated to the third quarter of the 2nd cent. The book was known to the author of Jubilees;[19] and its origin is securely anchored within the last years of the Maccabaean revolt by the details in xc. 6–19. Since Judas (the ram with the 'big horn') is apparently still active, this section must have been written before his death in 161 BC – more exactly (according to Milik) in the few weeks that followed the battle of Bethsur in 164. The existence of a Greek version is made virtually certain, not only by the existence of the Ethiopic version, but also by the fragment containing lxxxix. 42–49, discovered and published by Mai, and by the quotation in *Ep. Barn.* xvi. 5. It should be noted, however, that the Mai 'fragment' is not a fragment in the technical sense (like the Qumran fragments), but rather an 'extract', comparable with the extracts preserved by Syncellus. Furthermore, despite the author's use of the quotation-formula 'the scripture says', Barnabas is so inexact as to raise doubts whether the reference is to lxxxix. 66–67, or to xc. 26–28, or is merely general: it is, it seems, an 'allusion' and not a true quotation.[20]

---

[19] Jub. iv. 19.
[20] Unless, of course, the author was quoting from a Greek text different from the one that underlies the Ethiopic.

Book V (The Epistle of Enoch). The title derives from the colophon at the end of the Chester Beatty-Michigan papyrus; and it is supported by the Greek text offered at c. 6 ('. . . these words of this epistle') as against the Ethiopic ('. . . the words of this book'). As previously mentioned, Campbell Bonner, who edited the papyrus, thought that Book V was the only part of 1 Enoch that it contained. Fragments in Aramaic from two MSS are available from Qumram: the fragments from one of these MSS (to be dated *c*.50 BC) correspond to parts of chaps. xci–xciv and those from the other (to be dated *c*.100 BC) to parts of chaps. civ–cvii. From the Aramaic evidence two points stand out: (1) As with the Astronomical Book, the text of the earlier part of the Epistle as read at Qumran was much fuller than that preserved in the Ethiopic; and (2) Although chaps. cvi–cvii were undoubtedly included in the second of the Qumran MSS, they were separated from the preceding text by a gap of a line and a half. All in all, it looks very much as if the text of Book V had suffered more than ordinarily at the hands of its editors, particularly through their additions and re-ordering of the material in the last few chapters. And in this connection it is interesting to observe that several of the suggestions made by the earlier source-critics, such as Charles, purely on the basis of internal evidence, have been confirmed by the more recent manuscript discoveries.

When the five separate Books were put together we do not know. Nor do we know the dates of the Greek or the Ethiopic translations. Nor, again, do we know whether there were translations initially of the separate Books made independently, or of the five books together, or of earlier collections containing two, three, or four of the Books.

According to Milik, the idea of an Enochic Pentateuch can be traced back at least as far as Qumran. At Qumran the works attributed to Enoch were copied in two volumes: the first volume contained the (much fuller) text of the Astronomical Book; and the second the texts of the Book of Watchers, the Book of Giants (a work that told the story of the Watchers in some detail and foretold their future destruction by the waters of the Flood and by eternal fire), the Book of Dreams, and the Epistle of Enoch. When, some-

time in the later third or fourth century AD, the Book of Giants fell
into disfavour in the Church, perhaps because of its popularity
with the Manichees, it was replaced by the Book of Parables; and
thus 1 Enoch took its present shape. So Milik. But obviously the
almost complete lack of evidence does not enable us either to prove
or to disprove such a detailed reconstruction.

As we have seen, quotations in Greek begin to appear from
about AD 100 onwards. The difficulty here is that since nearly all of
them are quotations of isolated passages, they give no help in
deciding whether they were taken from a text containing only one
or more of the Books. Nevertheless, there are some pointers. *Ep.
Barn.* xvi. 6, for example, which offers a combined quotation of 1
Enoch xci. 13 and xciii. 7, follows immediately on the 'allusion' to 1
Enoch lxxxix and xc, to which attention was drawn in our discussion of Book IV: from this it may be inferred that the author read 1
Enoch lxxxix–xc and xci–xciii continuously – i.e. that in the text
he was familiar with Books IV and V stood side by side. Similarly,
Tertullian (*idol.* iv. 2–3) connects an apparent allusion to 1 Enoch
xix. 1 and an explicit quotation of xcix. 6–7: from this again it
might be inferred, though perhaps with less justification, that for
Tertullian Books I and V belonged together. In other words,
although without a doubt separate copies were made of individual
Books, and continued to be made for some time, there is good
reason to suspect that from early times a Greek Enoch corpus also
circulated in the Church, which, apart from the fact that it lacked
Book II, otherwise closely resembled the 1 Enoch we know to-
day.[21]

For the Ethiopic translation various dates have been suggested:
Burkitt suggested the fourth century AD, Milik thought 'hardly
earlier than the sixth century', Knibb 'before the end of the sixth
century', and Charles suggested either the sixth or the seventh
century. If there is anything in Ullendorff's suggestion that the
Ethiopic translators had access to an Aramaic text as well as a
Greek one, then we must be prepared to treat their version with

---

[21] Whether or not this corpus was a Pentateuch and included the Book of Giants
as Book II is impossible to say, since we have no detailed knowledge of the text of
Giants. If it was, it may be that some of the patristic quotations, which are
attributed to Enoch and difficult to place, are actually quotations from it.

greater respect than perhaps we otherwise would and occasionally prefer its readings when these differ from the Greek.

Our English translation is, with only very slight alterations, a reprint of the translation in Knibb's *The Ethiopic Book of Enoch*. It is important, therefore, to repeat that what the reader is offered is a straight translation of the Ethiopic text as found in Ryl. Eth. MS 23, the only exceptions being in passages where this particular MS seems to make no sense. The reader is not offered either a translation of an 'original' Ethiopic text or of an 'original' Enoch. The more important variants of the other Ethiopic MSS are mentioned from time to time in the notes, and all readings in the extant Greek evidence which differ from the Ethiopic are recorded there; but it must not be thought that any of such information implies a value judgement unless explicitly stated – e.g. 'adds' or 'omits' indicates nothing more than 'has' or 'does not have'. Since the Aramaic evidence is for the most part so fragmentary it has only been referred to in those places where it seems to cast a clear light on the Greek and Ethiopic.

The two main families of the Ethiopic MSS are designated Eth. I and Eth. II respectively. The capitals used for the MSS are the same as the letters used by Dillmann, Charles, and Flemming, though two more MSS have been added, viz:–

D′ = Lake Tana MS 9 (15th cent.).
C′ = an early 18th cent. MS in the possession of Edward Ullendorff.

(D′ belongs to Eth. I and C′ to Eth. II).

The Greek authorities are differentiated as follows:–

Gk.ᵃ = the Akhmim fragments.
Gk.ᵐ = the Chester Beatty-Michigan fragments.
Gk.ˢ = the extracts in Syncellus.
Gk.ᵛ = the Vatican fragment.

(Gk.ᵃ¹ and Gk.ᵃ², Gk.ˢ¹ and Gk.ˢ², indicate variations in text where either Gkᵃ or Gk.ˢ offer the same passage more than once in slightly different forms).

BIBLIOGRAPHY

EDITIONS

Ethiopic

R. LAURENCE, *Libri Enochi Prophetæ Versio Aethiopica* (Oxford, 1838).

C. F. A. DILLMANN, *Liber Henoch aethiopice, ad quinque codicum fidem editus cum variis lectionibus* (Leipzig, 1851).

J. FLEMMING, *Das Buch Henoch: Äthiopischer Text mit Einleitung und Commentar* (= *TU* N.F. vii. 1; Leipzig, 1902).

R. H. CHARLES, *The Ethiopic Version of the Book of Enoch edited from twenty-three MSS, together with the fragmentary Greek and Latin Versions* (Oxford, 1906).

M. A. KNIBB, *The Ethiopic Book of Enoch: A New Edition in the Light of the Aramaic Dead Sea Fragments*. I. Text and Apparatus (Oxford, 1978).

Greek

(i) The Akhmim fragments

U. BOURIANT, *Fragments du texte grec du livre d'Énoch et de quelques écrits attribués à Saint Pierre* (= *Mémoires publiés par les membres de la Mission archéologique française au Caire*, ix. 1 (Paris, 1892), pp. 91–147).

A. LODS, *Le Livre d'Hénoch: Fragments grecs découverts à Akhmîm (Haute-Égypte), publiés avec les variantes du texte éthiopien, traduits et annotés* (Paris, 1892).

——, *Reproduction en héliogravure du manuscrit d'Énoch et des écrits attribués à Saint Pierre* (= *Mémoires publiés par les membres de la Mission archéologique française au Caire*, ix. 3; Paris, 1893).

(ii) The Vatican fragment

A. MAI, *Patrum Nova Bibliotheca*, tom. ii (Rome, 1844), p. iv.

J. GILDEMEISTER, 'Ein Fragment des Griechischen Henoch' in *ZDMG* ix (1855), pp. 621–624.

(iii) The Chester Beatty-Michigan fragments

CAMPELL BONNER, with the collaboration of HERBERT C.
YOUTIE, *The Last Chapters of Enoch in Greek* (= *Studies and Documents*, viii; London, 1937 – reprinted Darmstadt 1968).

F. G. KENYON, *The Chester Beatty Biblical Papyri*, fasc. viii
(London, 1941). [A brief Preface and plates.]

(iv) The Syncellus fragments

W. DINDORF, *Georgius Syncellus et Nicephorus* (= *Corpus Scriptorum Historiae Byzantinae*, i (Bonn, 1829, pp. 20–23, 42–46, 46–47, 47).

(v) *a*

H. B. SWETE, *The Old Testament in Greek*,[4] iii (Cambridge, 1912),
pp. 789–809.

——, *The Psalms of Solomon with the Greek fragments of the Book of Enoch*
(Cambridge, 1899), pp. 25–45. [Reprinted from the above.]

(v) *b*

M. BLACK, *Apocalypsis Henochi Graece* (= *PVTG* iii (Leiden, 1970),
pp. 1–44).

Latin

M. R. JAMES, 'A Fragment of the Book of Enoch in Latin' in
Apocrypha Anecdota (= *TS* ii. 3; Cambridge, 1893), pp. 146–150.

Aramaic

J. T. MILIK, *The Books of Enoch: Aramaic Fragments of Qumran, Cave
4* (Oxford, 1976).

Syriac

S. P. BROCK, 'A Fragment of Enoch in Syriac' in *JTS* N.S. xix
(1968), pp. 626–631.

TRANSLATIONS

English

R. LAURENCE, *The Book of Enoch the Prophet: An apocryphal production . . . now first translated from an Ethiopic MS in the Bodleian Library* (Oxford, 1821; reprinted with an *Introduction* of 45 pages by the Author of 'The Evolution of Christianity', London, 1883).

R. H. CHARLES, *The Book of Enoch translated from Professor Dillmann's Ethiopic Text emended and revised . . ., edited with Introduction, Notes, Appendices, and Indices* (Oxford, 1893).

——, *The Book of Enoch, or I Enoch, translated from the Editor's Ethiopic Text, and edited with the Introduction, Notes, and Indexes of the First Edition wholly recast, enlarged, and rewritten* (Oxford, 1912).

——, in *APOT* ii, pp. 163–281.

——, *The Book of Enoch* (= S.P.C.K. *Translations of Early Documents*; London, 1917 – with an Introduction by W. O. E. OESTERLEY).

M. A. KNIBB, *The Ethiopic Book of Enoch: A New Edition in the Light of the Aramaic Dead Sea Fragmento*. II. Introduction, Translation, and Commentary (Oxford, 1978).

French

F. MARTIN, *Le Livre d'Hénoch traduit sur le texte éthiopien* (= *Documents pour l'étude de la Bible: Les apocryphes de l'Ancien Testament*; Paris, 1906).

German

C. F. A. DILLMANN, *Das Buch Henoch übersetzt und erklärt* (Leipzig, 1853).

G. BEER in E. KAUTZSCH, *APAT* ii, pp. 217–310.

J. FLEMMING and L. RADERMACHER, *Das Buch Henoch* (= *GCS* v; Leipzig, 1901).

P. RIESSLER, *AjSaB*,[2] pp. 355–451.

GENERAL

F. C. BURKITT, 'On the Greek Text of Enoch' (= Appendix I in *Jewish and Christian Apocalypses* (London, 1914), pp. 53–71).

A.-M. DENIS, *IPGAT*, pp. 15–30.

O. EISSFELDT, *OTI*, pp. 617–622.

J.-B. FREY, art. 'Apocryphes de l'Ancien Testament' in *DB Sup* i, cols. 357–371.

L. GINZBERG, *The Legends of the Jews*, i (Philadelphia, 1909), pp. 130–137 and v (Philadelphia, 1925), pp. 158–162.

J. G. GREENFIELD and M. E. STONE, 'The Enochic Pentateuch and the Date of the Similitudes' in *HTR* lxx (1977), pp. 51–65.

P. GRELOT, 'La Légende d'Hénoch dans les Apocryphes et dans la Bible: Origin et signification' in *Recherches de science religieuse*, xlvi (1958), pp. 5–26 and 181–210.

J. C. HINDLEY, 'Towards a Date for the Similitudes of Enoch: An Historical Approach' in *NTS* xiv (1967–8), pp. 551–565.

H. J. LAWLOR, 'Early Citations from the Book of Enoch' in *The Journal of Philology*, xxv (1897), pp. 164–225.

E. LITTMANN, art. 'Enoch, Books of: I Ethiopic Enoch' in *JE* v (1903), pp. 179–181.

J. T. MILIK, 'Problèmes de la Littérature Hénochique à la Lumière des Fragments arameéns de Qumrân' in *HTR* lxiv (1971), pp. 333–378.

P. RIESSLER, *AjSab*,[2] pp. 1291–1297.

L. ROST, *EATAP*, pp. 101–106.

N. SCHMIDT, 'The Original Language of the Parables of Enoch' in *Old Testament and Semitic Studies in memory of William Rainey Harper*, ii (ed. R. F. HARPER, F. BROWN, and G. F. MOORE; Chicago, 1908), pp. 327–349.

E. SCHÜRER, *HJPTJC* II. iii, pp. 54–73.

——, *GjVZJC*[4] iii, pp. 268–290.

C. C. TORREY, *AL*, pp. 110–114.

E. ULLENDORFF, 'An Aramaic "Vorlage" of the Ethiopic Text of Enoch?' (= *Atti del Convegno Internazionale di Studi Etiopici* (Rome, 1960), pp. 259–267).

G. ZUNTZ, 'Notes on the Greek Enoch' in *JBL* lxi (1942), pp. 193–204.

——, 'Enoch on the Last Judgement (ch. cii. 1–3)' in *JTS* xlv (1944), pp. 161–170.

I. The words of the blessing of Enoch according to which he blessed the chosen and righteous who must be[1] present on the day of distress *which is appointed* for the removal of all the wicked and
2 impious.[2] And Enoch answered[3] and said, *There was* a righteous man whose eyes were opened by the Lord,[4] and he saw a holy vision in the heavens[5] which the angels showed to me. And I heard everything from them, and I understood what I saw,[6] but not for this generation,[7] but for a distant generation which will come.[8]
3 Concerning the chosen I spoke, and I uttered a parable[9] concerning them, The Holy and Great One[10] will come out from his
4 dwelling, and the Eternal God will tread from there[11] upon mount Sinai, and he will appear with his host,[12] and will appear in the
5 strength of his power from heaven.[13] And all will be afraid, and the Watchers will shake,[14] and fear and great trembling will seize them
6 unto the ends of the earth. And the high mountains will be shaken,[15] and the high hills will be made low,[16] and will melt like wax before

[1] Gk.ᵃ 'will be'.

[2] the wicked and impious: UD′ 'the impious'; Gk.ᵃ 'the enemies, and the righteous will be saved'.

[3] Gk.ᵃ 'took up his parable', and so probably Aram.

[4] whose eyes . . . the Lord: Gk.ᵃ 'to whom a vision from God was disclosed'.

[5] GMD′BY 'a vision of the Holy One in the heavens'; Gk.ᵃ 'a vision of the Holy One and of heaven'.

[6] which the angels . . . what I saw: Gk.ᵃ 'He showed *it* to me, and the holy ones speaking holy things I heard; and when I heard everything from them, I understood as I looked'.

[7] Gk.ᵃ adds 'did I take thought'.

[8] Gk.ᵃ 'but to a distant one I will speak', and so probably Aram.

[9] Gk.ᵃ 'and I took up my parable'.   [10] Gk.ᵃ 'My Holy Great One'.

[11] from there: Gk.ᵃ 'upon earth'.   [12] with his host: Gk.ᵃ 'from his camp'.

[13] Gk.ᵃ 'from the heaven of heavens'.

[14] will shake: Gk.ᵃ 'will believe, and they will sing hidden things in all the ends of the ⟨earth⟩, and all the ends of the earth will shake'.

[15] D′ 'will fall and be shaken'; Gk.ᵃ 'will be shaken and fall and be broken up'.

[16] Gk.ᵃ adds 'so that the mountains will waste away'.

7   the flame. And the earth will sink[17] and everything that is on the
earth will be destroyed, and there will be judgement upon all, and
8   upon all the righteous.[18] But for the righteous he will make peace,
and he will keep safe the chosen,[19] and mercy will be upon them.
They will all belong to God, and will prosper and be blessed,[20] and
9   the light of God[21] will shine upon them.[22] And behold![23] He[24]
comes with ten thousand holy ones[25] to execute judgement upon
them,[26] and to destroy the impious, and to contend with[27] all flesh[28]
concerning everything which the sinners and the impious have
done and wrought against him.[29]

II. Contemplate[1] all the events in heaven, how the lights in heaven
do not change their courses, how[2] each rises and sets in order, each
2   at its proper time,[3] and they do not transgress their law. Consider

[17] GQT²D′ Gk.ᵃ 'will be split open'.

[18] and upon all the righteous: Gk.ᵃ om.

[19] and he will keep safe the chosen: Gk.ᵃ 'and upon the chosen will be protection
and peace'.

[20] and will prosper and be blessed: Gk.ᵃ 'and he will show (lit. 'give') favour to
them and will bless them all, and he will help them all and will help us'.

[21] of God: Gk.ᵃ om.

[22] Gk.ᵃ adds 'and he will make peace with them'.

[23] And behold: Gk.ᵃ 'For'. This verse is cited in Jude 14f.

[24] Jude 'The Lord'.

[25] Gk.ᵃ 'with his ten thousands and his holy ones'; Jude 'with his holy ten
thousands'.

[26] D′ Gk.ᵃ Jude 'upon all'.

[27] contend with: Eth I (cp. Gk.ᵃ Jude) 'reprove'.

[28] and to destroy . . . all flesh: Gk.ᵃ 'and he will destroy all the impious and will
reprove all flesh'; Jude 'and to reprove all the impious'. Some Eth. MSS follow Gk.ᵃ
in having a future construction.

[29] concerning . . . him: Gk.ᵃ 'concerning all the deeds of their impiety which they
have impiously committed, and the hard words which they have spoken, and
concerning all the things which the impious sinners have spoken against him'; Jude
'concerning all the deeds of their impiety which they have impiously committed,
and concerning all the hard things which the impious sinners have spoken against
him'. Aram., like Gk.ᵃ and Jude, probably also had a clause referring to the 'hard
words' spoken by the impious.

[1] So D′ Gk.ᵃ: all other Eth. MSS 'I contemplated'; Aram. 'Consider'.

[2] Gk.ᵃ 'how they do not change their courses, and the lights in heaven, how'.

[3] Gk.ᵃ adds 'and they appear at their feasts'.

the earth, and understand[4] from the work which is done upon it, from the beginning to the end,[5] that no work of God changes as 3 it becomes manifest.[6] Consider[7] the summer and the winter, how the whole earth is full of water, and clouds and dew and rain rest upon it.[8]

III.   Contemplate and see[1] how all the trees[2] appear withered, and *how* all their leaves are stripped, with the exception of fourteen trees which are not stripped, which remain with the old *foliage* until the new comes after two or three years.

IV. And again, contemplate[1] the days of summer, how at its beginning[2] the sun is above it.[3] You seek shelter and shade because of the heat of the sun, and the earth burns with a scorching heat, and you cannot tread upon the earth, or upon a rock, because of its heat.

V.   Contemplate[1] how the trees are covered with green leaves,[2] and bear fruit.[3] And understand in respect of everything and perceive[4] how he who lives for ever made all these things for you;[5]

[4] Q 'I considered the earth and understood'.
[5] Gk.[a] adds 'they are corrupt'.
[6] Gk.[a] 'that nothing upon earth changes, but all the works of God become manifest to you'.
[7] QD′ 'I considered'.   [8] how . . . upon it: Gk.[a] om.

[1] So UD′ Gk.[a]: all other Eth. MSS 'I contemplated and saw'; Aram. 'Consider'.
[2] Gk.[a] om. iiib – v.1a by homoioteleuton and reads only 'Contemplate and see all the trees . . . how the green leaves etc.'.

[1] So U: all other Eth. MSS 'I contemplated'; Aram. 'consider'.
[2] at its beginning: so GQU; D′ corrupt; all other Eth. MSS 'opposite it', viz. 'how the sun is above it, opposite it'.
[3] above it: i.e. the earth.

[1] So GU: Q 'I contemplated and saw'; all other Eth. MSS 'I contemplated'.
[2] Gk.[a] 'how the green leaves on them cover the trees'.
[3] Gk.[a] 'and all their fruit *is* for honour and glory', and so probably Aram.
[4] Gk.[a] 'Understand and know in respect of all his works and perceive'.
[5] GMQT′U 'how you made all these things who live for ever'; D′ corrupt; Gk.[a] 'how the living God made these *things* so, and he lives for all eternity'.

2 and *how* his works *are* before him in each succeeding year,[6] and all his works serve him and do not change,[7] but as God has decreed,[8]
3 so everything is done. And consider how the seas and rivers
4 together[9] complete[10] their tasks.[11] But you have not persevered, nor observed the law of the Lord.[12] But you have transgressed, and have spoken proud and hard words with your unclean mouth against his majesty.[13] You hard of heart! You will not have peace!
5 And because of this you will curse your days, and the years of your life you will destroy.[14] And the eternal curse will increase,[15] and
6 you will not receive mercy.[16] In those days you will transform your name[17] into an eternal curse[18] to all the righteous, and they will
7 curse you sinners for ever[19] – you together with the sinners.[20] For the chosen there will be light and joy[21] and peace, and they will inherit the earth. But for you, the impious, there will be a curse.
8 When[22] wisdom is given to the chosen,[23] they will all live, and will

[6] Gk.ᵃ 'and *how* his works, all the things which he has made for ever, all are thus brought into being from year to year'.

[7] and all . . . change: Gk.ᵃ 'and all the tasks which they complete for him, and their tasks do not change'.

[8] Gk.ᵃ 'but in accordance with the decree'.

[9] Gk.ᵃ 'likewise'.   [10] Gk.ᵃ adds 'and do not change'.

[11] Gk.ᵃ adds 'from his words'.   [12] Gk.ᵃ 'his commandments'.

[13] Gk.ᵃ adds 'because you have spoken with your lies'.

[14] C'Gk.ᵃ 'will be destroyed'.

[15] GTUD' 'And it will increase in an eternal curse'; M 'in an eternal curse'; Gk.ᵃ 'and the years of your destruction will increase in an eternal curse', and so probably Aram.

[16] Gk.ᵃ adds 'or peace'.

[17] So GQT¹UD': M is corrupt; T² Eth. II 'peace'.

[18] In those days . . . curse: Gk.ᵃ 'Then your names will become an eternal curse'.

[19] The Ethiopic could also be translated 'and the sinners will curse you for ever'; Gk.ᵃ 'and all those who curse will curse by you'.

[20] you . . . the sinners: Gk.ᵃ 'and all the sinners and impious will swear by you. And all the sinless (?) will rejoice, and there will be for them forgiveness of sins and all mercy and peace and graciousness, there will be for them salvation, a good light, and they will inherit the earth. And for all you sinners there will be no salvation, but upon you all will rest a curse'.

[21] Gk.ᵃ 'grace'.   [22] Some Eth. MSS 'If'; D' Gk.ᵃ 'Then'.

[23] D' 'Then there will be given to the chosen wisdom, and'; Gk.ᵃ repeats some material from verse 7 by homoioteleuton, viz. 'Then there will be given to the chosen light and grace, and they will inherit the earth. Then there will be given to all the chosen wisdom, and'.

not again do wrong, either through forgetfulness, or through pride.
9 But those who possess wisdom will be humble.[24] They will not
again do wrong, and they will not be judged[25] all the days of their
life, and they will not die of *the divine* wrath or anger. But they will
complete the number of the days of their life, and their life will
grow in peace, and the years of their joy will increase in gladness
and in eternal peace all the days of their life.

VI. And it came to pass, when the sons of men had increased, that
in those days[1] there were born to them[2] fair and beautiful[3]
2 daughters. And the angels, the sons of heaven, saw them and
desired them.[4] And they said to one another, Come,[5] let us choose
for ourselves wives from the children of men,[6] and let us beget for
3 ourselves children.[7] And Semyaza, who was their leader, said to
them, I fear that you may not wish this deed to be done,[8] and *that* I
4 alone will pay for this great sin.[9] And they all answered him and
said,[10] Let us all swear an oath, and bind[11] one another with curses
5 not to alter this plan, but to carry out this plan effectively.[12] Then
they all swore together and all[13] bound one another with curses to
6 it.[14] And they were in all two hundred, and they came down on

[24] Gk.[a] 'But there will be to the enlightened man light, and to the wise man perception'.

[25] Gk.[a] 'and they will not sin'.

[1] in those days: Gk.[s] om.

[2] to them: Gk.[a] om.

[3] and beautiful: Gk.[s] om.

[4] And the angels . . . desired them: Gk.[s] 'And the Watchers desired them and went astray after them'.

[5] Come: Gk.[s] om.

[6] Gk.[a] 'from men', i.e. 'from among mankind'; Gk.[s] 'from the daughters of the men of the earth'.

[7] and let us beget . . . children: Gk.[s] om.

[8] Gk.[a s] 'to do this deed'.

[9] GMT[1](?) U Gk.[a s] 'a great sin'; D' corrupt.

[10] and said: GMD' Gk.[a] om.

[11] GMTD' Gk.[a] 'and all bind'; Q is defective.

[12] but . . . effectively: C'D' 'but to do this deed'; U is defective; Gk.[a] 'until we have accomplished it and have done this deed'; Gk.[s] 'until we have accomplished it'.

[13] all: Eth.I AD Gk.[a s] om.   [14] to it: Gk.[s] om.

Ardis which is the summit of Mount Hermon.[15] And they called
the mountain Hermon, because on it they swore and bound one
7 another with curses. And these *are* the names of their leaders:[16]
Semyaza,[17] who was their leader, Urakiba, Ramiel,[18] Kokabiel,[19]
Tamiel,[20] Ramiel, Daniel,[21] Ezeqiel,[22] Baraqiel,[23] Asael,[24]
Armaros,[25] Batriel,[26] Ananel, Zaqiel,[27] Samsiel, Sartael,[28] . . . ,[29]
8 Turiel, Yomiel, Araziel.[30] These are the leaders of the two hundred
angels, and of all the others with them.[31]

VII. And they took wives for themselves, and everyone chose for
himself one each.[1] And they began to go in to them and were

[15] Gk.[s] 'And they were two hundred who came down in the days of Jared on the
summit of Mount Hermon', and so probably Aram.; Gk.[a] omits the entire verse by
hmt.

[16] The following list of names was copied out in the wrong order in Gk.[a] through
an easily recognisable mistake, but the evidence of Gk.[a] is given in the correct order
in the notes. The list also occurs, with some variations, in lxix.2 and is partially
reproduced in viii.3. Many of the names suffered corruption during the course of
their transmission, and the versions now offer a large number of variants, not all of
which are recorded below.   [17] Aram. 'Shemihazah'.

[18] Urakiba (or 'Arakiba'), Ramiel: most Eth. MSS in vi. 7 write these two names
as one word; the division into two follows D', and external evidence confirms that its
division is correct. Gk.[s] 'Atarqouph, Araqiel'; Gk.[a] 'Arathak, Kimbra, Sammane'.
For the second name in the list Aram. apparently read 'Arataqqiph' or 'Arataqoph'.

[19] Eth.II 'Akibeel'.   [20] Gk.[s] 'Horammame'; Aram. defective.
[21] Gk.[s] 'Sampsich'.   [22] Gk.[s] 'Zaqiel'; Aram. 'Ziqiel'.
[23] Eth.II 'Saraqiel'; Gk.[s] 'Balqiel'.   [24] Gk.[s] 'Azalzel'; Gk.[a] 'Aseal'.
[25] Gk.[s] 'Pharmaros'; Gk.[a] 'Arearos'; Aram. 'Hermoni'.
[26] Gk.[s] 'Amariel'; Aram. 'Matarel'.

[27] So D'N: other Eth. readings in vi. 7 appear to be corruptions of Zaqiel. Gk.[s]
'Thausael'; Gk.[a] 'Raqiel'; Aram. 'Satherel' or 'Sathawel'.

[28] So most Eth. MSS: GM 'Satarel'; other Eth. readings are corruptions of Sartael
or Satarel; Gk.[s] 'Sarinas'; Gk.[a] 'Sathiel'; Aram. 'Sahriel'.

[29] The seventeenth name has dropped out of the list in Eth; Gk.[s] 'Eumiel'; Gk.[a]
'Thoniel'; Aram. defective.

[30] Gk.[s] 'Sariel'; Gk.[a] 'Atriel'; Aram. uncertain.

[31] So T[2] Eth.II: G 'These are their leaders of tens, and of all the others with them',
and this is probably what is intended by the other Eth.I MSS; Gk.[a] 'These are their
leaders ⟨over⟩ tens'; Gk.[s] 'These and all the others (vii.i. in the . . .)'.

[1] Gk.[a] 'And they took wives for themselves; each of them chose for himself a wife';
Gk.[s] '(vi. 8 . . . the others) in the one thousand, one hundred and seventieth year of the
world took wives for themselves'.

promiscuous with them.[2] And they taught them charms and spells,
2 and showed to them the cutting of roots and trees.[3] And they
became pregnant[4] and bore large giants, and their height *was* three
3 thousand cubits.[5] These[6] devoured all the toil of men,[7] until[8] men
4 were unable to sustain them. And the giants turned against them
5 in order to devour men.[9] And they began to sin against birds, and
against animals, and against reptiles and against fish, and they
6 devoured[10] one another's flesh and drank the blood from it.[11] Then
the earth complained about the lawless ones.

VIII. And Azazel taught men to make swords,[1] and daggers, and
shields and breastplates.[2] And he showed them the things after
these, and the art of making them: bracelets,[3] and ornaments,[4] and

[2] Gk.[a] 'And they began to go in to them and to defile themselves with them'; Gk.[s] 'And they began to defile themselves with them until the flood'.

[3] GQT[1](?)NY Gk.[a] 'And they taught them charms and spells and the cutting of roots, and showed to them trees (Gk.[a] 'plants')'; Gk.[s] om. (but Aram. supports Eth. Gk.[a]).

[4] And they became pregnant: so Eth. Gk.[a] Aram.; Gk.[s] om., and then instead of verse 2 continues 'And they bore to them three kinds: first large giants, and the giants begat the Naphilim, and to the Naphilim were born the Elioud. And they grew according to their greatness, and they taught themselves and their wives charms and spells'.

[5] and their . . . cubits: Gk.[a] 'three thousand cubits *in height*'.

[6] MFC' Gk.[a] 'who'; Gk.[s] om. vii. 3–6.

[7] all the toil of men: Gk.[a] om. 'all'; C' Aram. 'the toil of all men'.

[8] Gk.[a] 'And when'.

[9] And the giants . . . men: Gk.[a] 'the giants acted with effrontery against them and devoured men'; Aram., whose text is incomplete and in part uncertain, used the verb 'to kill', not 'to devour'.

[10] ABCX Gk.[a] 'and to devour'.

[11] from it: D' Gk.[a] om.

[1] Gk.[a] 'Azael taught men to make swords'; Gk.[s] 'First Azael, the tenth of the leaders, taught the making of swords'.

[2] Gk.[a] 'and arms, and shields and breastplates, teachings of angels'; Gk.[s] 'and breastplates and all military equipment'.

[3] Eth.I (cp. Gk.[a]) 'and bracelets'.

[4] Gk.[a] 'And he showed them metals, and the art of working them, and bracelets, and ornaments'; Gk.[s] 'and the metals of the earth and gold, how they work *them* and make them into ornaments for women, and silver. And he showed to them'. In Eth. 'the things after these' possibly derives from a corrupt translation of the word for 'metals'.

the art of making up the eyes and of beautifying the eyelids,[5] and the most precious and choice stones, and all *kinds of* coloured dyes.
2 And the world was changed.[6] And there was great impiety and much fornication,[7] and they went astray,[8] and all their ways
3 became corrupt.[9] Amezarak[10] taught all[11] those who cast spells and cut roots,[12] Armaros the release of spells,[13] and Baraqiel astrologers,[14] and Kokabel portents,[15] and Tamiel taught
4 astrology,[16] and Asradel[17] taught the path of the moon.[18] And at

[5] So Eth., lit. 'and *how* to make up *the eyes* with antimony and *how* to beautify the eyelids': Gk.[a] 'and antimony and eyepaint' (cp. Aram. 'concerning antimony and concerning eye-paint'); Gk.[s] is in part corrupt, but should probably be read 'both *how* to make up *the eyes* with antimony and *how* to beautify the face'.

[6] And the world was changed: so G; Q is corrupt; D' 'and the changing of the world'; all other Eth. MSS 'and eternal change'. But Gk.[a s] om., and Eth. is probably a second rendering (more precisely, a corrupt transliteration) of 'the metals (of the earth)'. Gk.[s] adds 'And the sons of men made *these things* for themselves and their wives, and they transgressed and led astray the holy ones'.

[7] MT[1]U 'And there was great and widespread (lit. 'much') impiety, and they committed fornication' (GD' are similar); Gk.[a] 'And there was much impiety, and they committed fornication'; Gk.[s] 'And there was much impiety on the earth'.

[8] and they went astray: Q Gk.[s] om.

[9] Gk.[a] 'and became corrupt in all their ways'; Gk.[s] 'and they made all their ways corrupt'.

[10] So Eth. II: Eth. I 'Amizaras' or similar. Both forms are corrupt for 'Semyaza'.

[11] GMQT[1]UD' om.

[12] Gk.[a] 'Semyaza taught spells and the cutting of roots'; Gk.[s] 'And furthermore their leader, Semyaza, taught spells (so I correct Gk.[s]) against the mind, and the roots of the plants of the earth'.

[13] Gk.[s] 'the eleventh, Pharmaros, taught charms, spells, *magical* skills and the release of spells'. Aram. is incomplete, but appears to have had a long text comparable to that of Gk.[s].

[14] Gk.[a] '[Ba]raqiel astrology'; Gk.[s] 'the ninth taught astrology'.

[15] Gk.[s] 'the fourth taught astrology'.

[16] Gk.[a] 'Sathiel astrology': Gk.[s] 'the eighth taught aeroscopy'. Eth. 'Tamiel' and Gk.[a] 'Sathiel' are corrupt for 'Ziqiel' which is attested by Aram. here and is the eighth name in vi. 7. – Gk.[s] adds 'the third taught the portents of the earth; the seventh taught the portents of the sun'; correspondingly Aram. adds 'Arataqqiph (or 'Arataqoph') taught the portents of the earth; Shamshiel taught the portents of the sun'. Arataqqiph and Shamshiel are second and fifteenth in vi. 7, not third and seventh, but in Gk.[s] in vi. 7 the third name ('Araqiel') appears to be an alternative form of the second, and the seventh ('Sampsich') of the fifteenth.

[17] Corrupt; the name originally was 'Sahriel' ('Moon of God').

[18] Gk.[a] 'Seriel the course of the moon'; Gk.[s] 'the twentieth taught the portents of the moon'. Sahriel is sixteenth in vi. 7, not twentieth, but Gk.[s] appears to presuppose this

the destruction of men[19] they cried out,[20] and their voices reached heaven.[21]

IX. And then Michael, Gabriel, Suriel and Uriel[1] looked down from heaven and saw[2] the mass of blood that was being shed on the
2 earth and all the iniquity that was being done on the earth.[3] And they said[4] to one another, Let the devastated earth cry out with the
3 sound of their cries unto the gate of heaven.[5] And now, to you O holy ones of heaven,[6] the souls of men complain, saying,[7] Bring our
4 suit[8] before the Most High.[9] And they said to their Lord, the

name for the twentieth angel, as well as for the sixteenth. Gk.[s] further adds 'All these began to reveal mysteries to their wives and their children. After this the giants began to devour the flesh of men'; Aramaic evidence has survived corresponding to the first of these sentences, but not to the second.

[19] And at . . . men: Gk.[s] 'And men began to decrease on the earth'.

[20] they cried out: Gk.[a s] om.

[21] and their . . . heaven: Gk.[a] 'a cry went up to heaven'; Gk.[s1] 'and the rest cried out to heaven concerning their mistreatment, saying that the remembrance of them should be brought before the Lord'; Gk.[s2] 'Then men cried out to heaven, saying, Bring our suit before the Most High, and our destruction before the Great Glory, before the Lord of all the lords in majesty'.

[1] So Eth.II, but B²NX add 'Raphael' after 'Gabriel': M 'Michael, Raphael, Suriel and Gabriel'; other Eth.I MSS abbreviate the list.

[2] Gk.[a] 'Then looking down, Michael, Uriel, Raphael and Gabriel saw from heaven'; Gk.[s1 s2] 'And hearing *this*, the four great archangels, Michael, Uriel, Raphael and Gabriel, looked down on the earth from the sanctuary of heaven; and seeing'. In Aram. the list of names was probably 'Michael, Sariel, Raphael and Gabriel'.

[3] and all the iniquity . . . the earth: Gk.[a] om. (hmt.); Gk.[s1s2] 'and all the impiety and iniquity that was being done on it'.

[4] And they said: Gk.[s1 s2] 'entering, they said'.

[5] Let . . . heaven: Gk.[a] 'The sound of those who cry out on the earth *reaches* unto the gates of heaven'; Gk.[s1 s2] om.; Aram is incomplete, but appears to support Eth. Gk.[a].

[6] And now . . . of heaven: Gk.[a s1 s2] om. (hmt. ?).

[7] Gk.[s1s2] 'The spirits and souls of men groan, complaining and saying'.

[8] Gk.[s2] 'petition'.

[9] Gk.[s1] adds 'and our destruction before the Great Glory, before the Lord of all the Lords in majesty'.

King,[10] Lord of Lords, God of Gods, King of Kings![11] Your[12]
glorious throne *endures* for all the generations of the world, and your
name *is* holy[13] and praised for all the generations of the world[14] and
5 blessed and praised![15] You have made everything, and power over
everything is yours. And everything is uncovered and open before
you, and you see everything, and there is nothing which can be
6 hidden from you. See then[16] what Azazel[17] has done,[18] how he[19] has
taught all iniquity on the earth[20] and revealed the eternal secrets
7 which were made in heaven. And Semyaza has made known spells,
he to whom[21] you gave authority to rule over those who are with
8 him. And they went in to the daughters of men together,[22] and lay
with those women,[23] and became unclean,[24] and revealed to them
9 these[25] sins.[26] And the women[27] bore giants,[28] and thereby[29] the

[10] Eth.I 'And they said to the Lord of the Kings'; Gk.[a] 'And they said to the
Lord'; Gk.[s1] 'And they said to the Lord of the ages'; Gk.[s2] 'And entering, the four
archangels said to the Lord'.
[11] Gk.[a] 'You are Lord of Lords, God of Gods, King of the ages'; Gk.[s1 s2] 'You are
God of gods, Lord of Lords, King of Kings, God of the ages'.
[12] So ABX Gk.[a s1 s2] Aram.: other Eth. MSS 'His'.
[13] D' adds 'and blessed'; Gk.[a] adds 'and great'.
[14] Eth.I Gk.[a s1 s2] 'for all eternity'.
[15] and blessed and praised: D'C' Gk.[a s] om.; BX 'and you *are* blessed and
praised'.
[16] and there is nothing . . . See then: Gk.[a] om. (hmt.). GMQTD'N Gk.[s] read 'You
see' for 'See then'.   [17] Gk.[a s] 'Azael'.
[18] Gk.[s] adds 'and what he has introduced'.   [19] how he: NA' Gk.[a] 'who'.
[20] how he . . . the earth: Gk.[s] '*and* what he has taught, wickedness and sin on the
earth and all craftiness on the dry ground'.
[21] and revealed . . . to whom: so Eth.II; GMT'U 'and they have revealed the
eternal secrets which were made in heaven. *And* Semyaza has brought knowledge to
men, *he* to whom'; QD' are untranslatable, but in part agree with Gk.[a]; Gk.[a] 'and
has revealed the eternal secrets, the things in heaven which men practice ⟨and⟩
know. And *what* Semyaza *has done*, to whom'; Gk.[s] 'For he has taught the secrets and
revealed to the world the things in heaven. And the sons of men practise his
practices in order to know the secrets. To Semyaza'. No version inspires complete
confidence.
[22] of men together: UEXC' om. 'together'; GMT corrupt; QD' 'of men on the
earth'; Gk.[a s] 'of the men of the earth'.   [23] Gk.[a s] 'with them'.
[24] Gk.[s] adds 'with the women'.   [25] GMQTD' Gk.[a s] 'all'; U om.
[26] Gk.[s] adds 'and taught them to make charms for producing hatred'.
[27] Gk.[s] 'And now behold the daughters of men'.
[28] Gk.[a] 'titans'; Gk.[s] 'by them giant sons'.
[29] and thereby: GD' Gk.[a] 'through whom'.

10 whole earth has been filled with blood and iniquity.[30] And now behold the souls which have died cry out[31] and complain unto the gate of heaven, and their[32] lament has ascended, and they[33] cannot go out in the face of the iniquity which is being committed on the

11 earth. And you know everything before it happens, and you know this[34] and what concerns each of them.[35] But you say nothing to us. What ought we to do with them about this?[36]

X. And then the Most High, the Great and Holy One, spoke[1] and

2 sent Arsyalalyur[2] to the son of Lamech, and said to him,[3] Say[4] to him in my name, Hide yourself, and reveal to him the end which is coming, for the whole earth will be destroyed, and a deluge[5] is about to come on all the earth, and what is in it will be destroyed.[6]

3 And now[7] teach him that he may escape, and *that* his offspring may

4 survive for the whole earth.[8] And further the Lord said[9] to Raphael,

[30] and thereby . . . iniquity: Gk.ˢ 'Deceitfulness has been poured out on the men of the earth, and the whole earth has been filled with iniquity'.

[31] GMQT'U BOXB'C' Gk.ᵃ 'the souls of those who have died cry out'; D' corrupt; Gk.ˢ 'the spirits of the souls of the men who have died complain'.

[32] and complain . . . and their: Gk.ˢ 'and unto the gates of heaven their'.

[33] GQT¹(?)U Gk.ᵃ ˢ 'it'.

[34] and you know this: Gk.ᵃ 'and you see these things'; Gk.ˢ 'and you see them'.

[35] and what concerns each of them: Gk.ᵃ ˢ 'but you leave them alone'.

[36] Gk.ᵃ 'And you do not tell us what *we* ought to do with them about these things'; Gk.ˢ 'And you say nothing. What ought *we* to do with them about this?'

[1] Gk.ᵃ 'Then the Most High talked about these things, the Great Holy One, and he spoke and talked'; Gk.ˢ 'Then the Most High talked, and the Great Holy One spoke'.

[2] So Eth.II: D' 'Asuryal'; G 'Asaryalyor' and other Eth.I MSS similarly; Gk.ᵃ 'Istrael'; Gk.ˢ 'Uriel'. All Eth. readings probably corruptions of 'Istrael'.

[3] and said to him: Eth.I Gk.ᵃ om.; Gk.ˢ 'saying'.

[4] Eth.I prefixes 'And'; Gk.ˢ prefixes 'Go to Noah and'.

[5] and a deluge: Gk.ˢ 'And say to him that a deluge'.

[6] D' 'and everything that is in it will be destroyed'; Gk.ᵃ 'and it will destroy everything that is on it'; Gk.ˢ 'to destroy everything from the face of the earth'.

[7] And now: Gk.ᵃ 'And'; Gk.ˢ om. and reads for this verse 'Teach the righteous one, the son of Lamech, what he should do, and he will preserve his soul alive and will escape through the world, and from him a plant will be planted and will be established for all the generations of the world'.

[8] for the whole earth: so Eth.II, but N adds 'for ever'; Eth.I 'for all generations'; Gk.ᵃ ˢ 'for all the generations of the world'. [9] Gk.ᵃ ˢ 'And he said'.

Bind[10] Azazel[11] by his hands and his feet,[12] and throw him into the darkness. And split open the desert which is in Dudael,[13] and
5 throw him there.[14] And throw on him[15] jagged and sharp stones, and cover him with darkness; and let him stay there for ever, and
6 cover his face, that he may not see light,[16] and that on the great day
7 of judgement he may be hurled[17] into the fire. And restore the earth[18] which the angels[19] have ruined, and announce the restoration of the earth,[20] for I shall restore the earth,[21] so that not all the sons of men shall be destroyed through the mystery of everything[22]
8 which the Watchers **made known**[23] and taught to their sons. And the whole earth has been ruined[24] by the teaching of the works of
9 Azazel,[25] and against him[26] write down all sin. And the Lord said[27] to Gabriel, Proceed[28] against the bastards[29] and the reprobates and against the sons of the fornicators,[30] and destroy the sons of the fornicators and[31] the sons of the Watchers from amongst men.[32] And send them out, and send them against one another, and let

[10] Gk.[s] prefixes 'Go, Raphael, and'.

[11] Gk.[a s] 'Azael'.

[12] by his hands and his feet: Gk.[s] 'tie him hand and foot'.

[13] Gk.[a] 'in Dadouel'; Gk.[s] 'in the desert Doudael'.

[14] Gk.[s] 'and having gone there, throw him *in*'.

[15] Gk.[a s] 'And place under him'.

[16] Gk.[a s] 'and let him not see light'.

[17] Gk.[a s] 'And on the day of the great (Gk.[s] om. 'great') judgement he will be hurled'.

[18] Gk.[a] 'And the earth will be restored'.

[19] Gk.[s] 'the Watchers'.

[20] the restoration of the earth: Gk.[s] 'the healing of the plague'.

[21] for I shall restore the earth: GMUD 'that the earth may be restored' (lit. 'that one may restore the earth'); Gk.[a s] 'that they may heal the plague'.

[22] D' Gk.[a] 'through the entire mystery'; Gk.[s] 'through the mystery'.

[23] Eth. 'killed'; Gk.[a] 'struck'; Gk.[s] 'spoke'. All three are impossible, but Eth. and Gk.[a] probably derive from a confusion of the Aramaic verbs 'to strike' and 'to show, make known'; hence the above translation. Gk.[s] 'spoke' is an *ad hoc* correction of an already corrupt text.

[24] Gk.[a] adds 'having been corrupted'.

[25] Gk.[a s] 'by the works taught by Azael'.

[26] Gk.[s] 'against it'.

[27] Gk.[s] 'and he said'.

[28] Gk.[s] adds 'Gabriel'.

[29] Gk.[s] 'the giants'.

[30] Gk.[a s] 'of fornication'.

[31] the sons of the fornicators and: Gk.[a s] om.; GAK om. by hmt. 'and destroy the sons of the fornicators'.

[32] Gk.[s] 'the sons of men'.

them destroy themselves in battle,[33] for they will not have length of
10 days. And they will all petition you, but their fathers will gain
    nothing in respect of them,[34] for they hope for eternal life,[35] and
11 that each of them will live life for five hundred years. And the Lord
    said[36] to Michael, Go,[37] inform[38] Semyaza and the others with him
    who have associated with the women[39] to corrupt themselves with
12 them in all[40] their uncleanness. When[41] all[42] their sons kill each
    other, and when[43] they see the destruction of their beloved ones,
    bind them for seventy generations under the hills[44] of the earth
    until the day of their judgement and of their consummation, until
13 the judgement which is for all eternity is accomplished. And in
    those days[45] they will lead them to the abyss of fire; in torment and
14 in prison they will be shut up for all eternity.[46] And then he[47] will be
    burnt and from then on destroyed with them; together they will be
15 bound until the end of all generations.[48] And destroy all the souls of
    lust[49] and the sons of the Watchers, for they have wronged men.
16 Destroy all wrong from the face of the earth, and every evil work
    will cease.[50] And let the plant of righteousness and truth appear,

[33] And send them out . . . in battle: Gk.[a] 'Send them in a battle of destruction';
Gk.[s] 'Send them against one another, *some* of them against *the rest of* them, in battle
and in destruction.'

[34] And they . . . of them: Gk.[a] corrupt, but probably 'And ⟨no⟩ petition will be
granted to their fathers even in respect of them'; Gk.[s] 'And no petition will be (lit. 'is')
granted to their fathers'.

[35] for eternal life: GMTUD′ Gk.[a s] 'to live an eternal life'.

[36] Gk.[a s] 'And he said'.   [37] Go: some Eth. MSS om.; Gk.[s] adds 'Michael'.

[38] Gk.[s] 'bind'.   [39] Gk.[s] 'the daughters of men'.

[40] Q Gk.[a s] om.   [41] Eth.I Gk.[a s] 'And when'.

[42] Gk.[a s] om., and so apparently Aram.

[43] U Gk.[a s] om., and so apparently Aram.

[44] under the hills: Gk.[a s] 'in the valleys'.   [45] And in those days: Gk.[a s] 'Then'.

[46] in torment . . . all eternity: Gk.[a s] 'and to torment and to the prison of eternal
confinement'.

[47] i.e. Semyaza, but see below.

[48] GMQT¹UD′ Gk.[a] 'And when *anyone* is burnt and destroyed from now on, he
will be bound together with them until the end of all generations (Gk.[a] 'the
generation')'; Gk.[s] 'And whoever is condemned and destroyed from now on will be
bound with them until the end of their generation'. Aram. 'And whoever . . .' agrees
with Gk.[s].

[49] Gk.[a] 'the spirits of the reprobate'.

[50] So GMQD′ and some Eth.II MSS: Gk.[a] and other Eth. MSS 'and let every
evil work cease'.

and the deed will become a blessing; righteousness and truth[51] will
17 they plant[52] in joy for ever. And now all the righteous will be
humble,[53] and will live until they beget thousands; and all the days
18 of their youth and their sabbaths[54] they will fulfil in peace. And in
those days[55] the whole earth will be tilled in righteousness, and all
of it will be planted with trees,[56] and it will be filled with blessing.
19 And all pleasant trees they will plant on it,[57] and they will plant on
it[58] vines, and the vine which is planted[59] on it will produce fruit[60]
in abundance;[61] and every seed which is sown on it, each measure
20 will produce a thousand, and each measure of olives will produce
ten baths of oil.[62] And you, cleanse the earth from all wrong,[63] and
from all iniquity, and from all sin, and from all[64] impiety, and from
all the uncleanness which is brought about on the earth; remove
21 them from the earth.[65] And all the sons of men shall be righteous,[66]
and all the nations shall serve and bless me, and all shall worship
22 me. And the earth[67] will be cleansed from all corruption, and from

[51] and the deed . . . and truth: GTU 'and it will become a blessing; deeds of
righteousness and truth'; Q corrupt; D' Gk.ᵃ om. (hmt.).

[52] Some Eth. MSS 'will be planted'; D' 'will he plant'; M corrupt; Gk.ᵃ 'will he
plant for himself', but most correct to 'will be planted'.

[53] So Eth.II: Eth.I Gk.ᵃ Aram. 'will escape'.

[54] and their sabbaths: so Eth. Gk.ᵃ, but long recognised to be a mistranslation of
an Aramaic 'and their old age'; Aram. now confirms this.

[55] And in those days: Gk.ᵃ 'Then'.

[56] and all . . . with trees: so Eth. and apparently Aram.; Gk.ᵃ 'and a tree will be
planted in it'.

[57] And all . . . on it: Gk.ᵃ 'And all the trees of the earth will rejoice; they will be
planted'.

[58] on it: Gk.ᵃ om.

[59] Some Eth. MSS 'which *a man* plants'.

[60] GMQTD' 'wine'; U corrupt.

[61] and the vine . . . in abundance: Gk.ᵃ 'and the vine which they plant, they will
produce thousands of jars of wine'.

[62] and every seed . . . of oil: Gk.ᵃ defective.

[63] Gk.ᵃ 'uncleanness'; D' adds 'and from all uncleanness'.

[64] from all: Gk.ᵃ om.

[65] and from all the uncleanness . . . from the earth: Gk.ᵃ 'and wipe away all the
uncleanness which is brought about on the earth'.

[66] And all . . . be righteous: Gk.ᵃ om. In the remainder of the verse Gk.ᵃ has a
strange word order and differs slightly from Eth.

[67] Gk.ᵃ 'And the whole earth'.

all sin, and from all wrath, and from all torment;[68] and I will not
again send a flood[69] upon it[70] for all generations for ever.

XI. And in those days[1] I will open the storehouses of blessing
which *are* in heaven that I may send them down upon the earth,[2]
2 upon the work and upon the toil of the sons of men. Peace and
truth[3] will be united for all the days of eternity and for all the
generations of eternity.[4]

XII. And before everything[1] Enoch had been hidden,[2] and none of
the sons of men[3] knew where he was hidden,[4] or where he was, or
2 what had happened.[5] And all[6] his[7] doings *were* with the Holy Ones
3 and with the Watchers[8] in his days.[9] And I Enoch was blessing[10]
the Great Lord[11] and the King of Eternity, and behold the
Watchers[12] called to me, Enoch the scribe, and said to me,
4 Enoch,[13] scribe of righteousness, go, inform[14] the Watchers of
heaven who have left the high heaven and the holy eternal place,[15]
and have corrupted[16] themselves with the women, and have done
as the sons of men[17] do, and have taken wives for themselves, and
5 have become completely corrupt on the earth.[18] They[19] will have

---

[68] and from all sin . . . all torment: Gk.[a] 'and from all uncleanness and wrath and
torment'.

[69] a flood: GMQT[1]UD' Gk.[a] om.   [70] Gk.[a] 'upon them'.

[1] Gk.[a] 'And then'.   [2] upon the earth: Gk.[a] om.
[3] Gk.[a] 'And then truth and peace'.   [4] Gk.[a] 'of men'.

[1] D' Gk.[a] 'Before these things'.   [2] Gk.[a] 'taken'.
[3] Gk.[a] 'and none of mankind'.   [4] Gk.[a] 'taken'.
[5] Gk.[a] adds 'to him'.   [6] Gk.[a] om.
[7] Gk.[a] 'their', but corrupt for 'his'.
[8] Holy Ones . . . Watchers: Eth.I Gk.[a] transpose.
[9] in his days: Gk.[a] '*were* his days'.   [10] Gk.[a] 'standing blessing'.
[11] D' Gk.[a] 'the Lord of majesty'; GMT[1]U corrupt.
[12] Gk.[a] adds 'of the Holy Great One'.
[13] the scribe . . . Enoch: Gk.[a] om. (hmt.), D' omits 'the scribe'.
[14] Gk.[a] 'and say to'.
[15] and the holy eternal place: Gk.[a] 'the sanctuary of the eternal place'.
[16] Gk.[a] 'defiled'.   [17] Gk.[a] 'of the earth'.
[18] and have become completely . . . earth: Gk.[a] 'You have completely ruined the
earth!'   [19] Gk.[a] 'You'.

on earth[20] neither peace nor forgiveness of sin,[21] for they will not
6 rejoice in their sons. The slaughter[22] of their beloved ones they will
see, and over the destruction of their sons they will lament and
petition for ever. But they will have neither mercy nor peace.

XIII. And Enoch went and said to Azazel,[1] You will not have
peace. A severe sentence has come out against you that you should
2 be bound. And you will have neither rest,[2] nor mercy,[3] nor *the
granting of any* petition, because of the wrong which you have
taught, and because of all the works of blasphemy[4] and wrong and
3 sin which you have shown to the sons of men.[5] Then I went and
spoke to them all together,[6] and they were all afraid; fear and
4 trembling seized them. And they asked me to write out for them the
record of a petition that they might receive forgiveness, and to take
5 the record of their petition up[7] to[8] the Lord in heaven.[9] For they
themselves were not able from then on to speak, and they did not
raise[10] their eyes to heaven out of shame for the sins for which they
6 had been condemned. And then I wrote out the record of their
petition and their[11] supplication in regard to their spirits[12] and the
deeds of each one of them,[13] and in regard to what they asked,
7 *namely* that they should obtain absolution and forbearance. And I
went and sat down by the waters of Dan in Dan[14] which is south-
west of Hermon; and I read out the record of their petition until I
8 fell asleep. And behold a dream[15] came to me, and visions fell upon

---

[20] on earth: GMTUD′N Gk.ᵃ om.   [21] of sin: Gk.ᵃ om.
[22] for they will . . . slaughter: so T Eth.II; GMQUD′ corrupt; Gk.ᵃ 'And
concerning their sons in whom they rejoice, the slaughter'.

[1] Gk.ᵃ (corrupt) 'And Enoch said to Azael, Go'.
[2] Gk.ᵃ 'clemency'; GMQD′ corrupt.
[3] nor mercy: Eth.I Gk.ᵃ om.   [4] Gk.ᵃ 'impiety'.
[5] GMQT¹UD′P¹ Gk.ᵃ 'to men'.   [6] together: Gk.ᵃ om.
[7] Gk.ᵃ 'and to read the record of the petition out'.
[8] Eth.I AKP¹ Gk.ᵃ 'before'.
[9] GMTUD′ Gk.ᵃ 'of heaven'.   [10] Gk.ᵃ 'or to raise'.
[11] GMT¹UD′ Gk.ᵃ 'the', but Aram. apparently read 'their'.
[12] in regard to their spirits: so Eth. Gk.ᵃ, but possibly a mistranslation of 'in
regard to themselves'.
[13] and the deeds of each one of them: Gk.ᵃ om., but Aram. supports Eth.
[14] in Dan: Gk.ᵃ 'in the land of Dan'.   [15] Gk.ᵃ 'dreams'.

me, and I saw a vision[16] of wrath, *namely* that I should speak to the
9 sons of heaven and reprove them.[17] And I woke up and went to
them, and they were all sitting gathered together as they mourned
in Ubelseyael,[18] which is between Lebanon and Senir, with their
10 faces covered. And I spoke before them[19] all the visions which I
had seen in my[20] sleep, and I began to speak these[21] words of
righteousness and to reprove[22] the Watchers of heaven.

XIV. This book *is* the word[1] of righteousness and of reproof for the
Watchers who *are* from eternity, as the Holy and[2] Great One
2 commanded in that vision. I saw in my sleep what I will now tell
with the tongue of flesh and with my breath which the Great One
has given to men in the mouth,[3] that they might speak with it and
3 understand with the heart.[4] As he has created and appointed men
to understand the word of knowledge, so he created and appointed
4 me[5] to reprove the Watchers, the sons of heaven. And I wrote out
your petition,[6] but in my vision thus it appeared, that your petition
will not be *granted* to you[7] for all the days of eternity; and complete
judgement *has been decreed* against you,[8] and you will not have

---

[16] U Gk.[a] Aram. 'visions'.

[17] *namely* that I . . . reprove them: Gk.[a] 'and a voice came, saying, Speak to the
sons of heaven to reprove them'.

[18] Gk.[a] 'Ebelsata'. The forms in Eth. and Gk.[a] are possibly corruptions of
'Abilene'.

[19] And I spoke before them: so Eth. Aram.; Gk.[a] (corrupt) 'Before them and I
reported to them'.

[20] GMT[1]UD'KP[1] Gk.[a] om.

[21] Gk.[a] 'the'.

[22] and to reprove: Gk.[a] 'reproving'.

[1] QD' 'This *is* the book of the words'; Gk.[a] Aram. 'The book of the words'.

[2] Gk.[a] om.

[3] and with my breath . . . in the mouth: so Eth.II; GMQTU corrupt; D' Gk.[a]
'with (D' 'and with') the breath of my (D' 'the') mouth which the Great One has
given to men'.

[4] Gk.[a] 'with them and *with* understanding of heart'.

[5] men to understand . . . appointed me: Gk.[a] om. (hmt.).

[6] Gk.[a] 'the petition of you angels'.

[7] Gk.[a] 'but in my vision this appeared; and your petition has not been accepted'.

[8] for all the days . . . against you: Gk.[a] om., but Aram. supports Eth.

5 peace.[9] And from now on you will not ascend[10] into heaven for all eternity, and it has been decreed that you are to be bound in the 6 earth[11] for all the days[12] of eternity. And before this you will have seen[13] the destruction of your beloved sons, and you will not be 7 able to enjoy them,[14] but they will fall before you by the sword. And your petition will not be *granted* in respect of them, nor in respect of yourselves. And while you weep and supplicate, you do not speak a 8 single word from the writing which I have written. And the vision appeared to me as follows:[15] Behold clouds called me[16] in the vision, and mist called me, and the path of the stars and flashes of lightning hastened me and drove me,[17] and in the[18] vision winds caused me to fly and hastened me and lifted me up into heaven.[19] 9 And I proceeded until I came near to a wall which was built of hail stones, and a tongue of fire surrounded it, and it began to make me 10 afraid.[20] And I went into the tongue[21] of fire and came near to a large house which was built of hail stones, and the wall of that house *was* like a mosaic *made* of hail stones,[22] and its floor *was* 11 snow.[23] Its roof *was*[24] like the path of the stars and flashes of lightning, and among them *were* fiery Cherubim, and their heaven 12 *was like* water. And *there was* a fire burning around its wall,[25] and its 13 door was ablaze[26] with fire. And I went into that house, and *it was*

[9] and you will not have peace: so NP²; all other Eth. MSS 'and you will have nothing'; Gk.ᵃ om., and so probably Aram.

[10] Gk.ᵃ 'that you should no longer ascend'.

[11] Gk.ᵃ 'in the bonds of the earth'.

[12] days: so Eth. Aram.; Gk.ᵃ 'generations'.

[13] Gk.ᵃ 'and that before these things you should see'.

[14] and you . . . enjoy them: Gk.ᵃ 'and that you will have no enjoyment in them'.

[15] Gk.ᵃ 'And in the vision thus it appeared to me'.

[16] me: Gk.ᵃ om.

[17] Gk.ᵃ 'and confused me'.   [18] Gk.ᵃ 'my'.

[19] and hastened me . . . into heaven: Gk.ᵃ 'and lifted me up and brought me into heaven'.

[20] which was built . . . me afraid: so Eth., but D′ reads 'tongues' instead of 'a tongue'; Gk.ᵃ 'of a building *built* of hail stones and tongues of fire around them, and they began to make me afraid'.   [21] D′ Gk.ᵃ 'tongues'.

[22] and the wall . . . of hail stones: Gk.ᵃ 'and the walls of the house *were* like slabs of stone, and all *the slabs* were of snow'.

[23] Gk.ᵃ 'and the foundations *were* of snow'.   [24] Gk.ᵃ 'And the roofs *were*'.

[25] Eth.I N 'around the wall'; Gk.ᵃ 'around the walls'.

[26] Gk.ᵃ 'and the doors were ablaze'.

hot as fire and cold as snow, and there was neither pleasure nor
14 life[27] in it. Fear covered me and trembling took hold of me. And as I
was shaking and trembling, I fell on my face.[28] And I saw in the[18]
15 vision, and behold, another house, which was larger than the
former, and all its doors *were* open before me, and *it was* built[29] of a
16 tongue[30] of fire. And in everything it so excelled[31] in glory and
splendour and size that I am unable to describe to you its glory and
17 its size. And its floor *was* fire, and above *were* lightning[32] and the
18 path of the stars, and its roof also *was* a burning fire. And I looked
and I saw in it[33] a high throne, and its appearance *was* like ice and
its surrounds like the shining sun[34] and the sound of Cherubim.[35]
19 And from underneath the high[36] throne there flowed out rivers of
20 burning fire[37] so that it was impossible to look[38] at it.[39] And He who
is great in glory[40] sat on it, and his raiment was brighter than the
21 sun, and whiter than any snow.[41] And no angel could enter,[42] and
at the appearance of the face of him who is honoured and praised
22 no *creature of* flesh could look.[43] A sea of fire[44] burnt around him,
and a great fire stood before him, and none of those around him
came near to him. Ten thousand times ten thousand *stood* before

---

27 GMQU 'no pleasure of life'; D' 'nothing'; Gk.[a] 'no food of life'.

28 on my face: Gk.[a] om.

29 another house . . . and *it was* built: D' 'a door before me, ⟨and⟩ another house,
which was larger than the former, and all of it *was* built'; Gk.[a] 'another door open
before me, and a house larger than the former, and all of it *was* built'. Aram
probably had the same order as D' Gk.[a].

30 GMUD' Gk.[a] 'of tongues'.   31 Gk.[a] 'and all of it *so* excelling'.

32 GMTUD' Gk.[a] 'flashes of lightning'.   33 in it: Gk.[a] om.

34 and its surrounds . . . sun: Gk.[a] 'and a wheel as of the shining sun'.

35 and the sound of Cherubim: so Eth. The text does not inspire confidence, but
Gk.[a] is corrupt.

36 high: Eth.I Gk.[a] om.   37 Gk.[a] 'burning rivers of fire'.

38 T[2] Gk.[a] 'so that I could not look'.   39 at it: GMTUAKP[1]C' Gk.[a] om.

40 GMQT[1]UD'Y Gk.[a] 'And the Great Glory'.

41 and his raiment . . . snow: Gk.[a] 'his raiment *was* like the appearance of the sun,
brighter and whiter than any snow'.

42 Gk.[a] adds 'into this house'.

43 and at the appearance . . . look: GTUD' 'and look at the face of him who is
honoured and praised, and no *creature of* flesh could look at him'; Gk.[a] 'and look at
his face because of the magnificence and glory, and no *creature of* flesh could look at
him'.

44 Eth. I some Eth. II MSS Gk.[a] 'A fire'.

23 him,[45] but he needed no holy counsel. And the Holy Ones[46] who
were near to him did not leave by night or day,[47] and did not depart
24 from him. And until then I had a covering on my face,[48] as I
trembled. And the Lord called me with his own mouth and said to
me, Come hither, Enoch, to my holy word. And he lifted me up[49]
and brought me near to the door. And I looked,[50] with my face
down.

XV. And he answered me and said to me with his voice, Hear![1] Do
not be afraid, Enoch, *you* righteous man and scribe of righteous-
2 ness.[2] Come hither and hear my voice. And go, say to the Watchers
of heaven who sent you[3] to petition on their behalf,[4] You ought to
3 petition on behalf of men, not men on behalf of you. Why have you
left the high, holy and eternal heaven, and lain with the women
and become unclean with the daughters of men, and taken wives
for yourselves, and done as the sons of the earth and begotten[5]
4 giant sons? And you *were* spiritual, holy, living an eternal life, *but*
you became unclean upon the women,[6] and begat *children* through
the blood of flesh, and lusted after the blood of men, and produced
5 flesh and blood as they do[7] who die and are destroyed. And for this

[45] and none . . . before him: Gk.[a] 'and no one came near to him. In a circle ten
thousand times ten thousand stood before him'.

[46] but he needed . . . Holy Ones: so T Eth.II; D′ 'but he needed no counsel. And
the holiness of the Holy Ones (i.e. 'And the most Holy Ones')'; GMQU corrupt;
Gk.[a] 'and his every word *was* deed. And the most holy angels'. No version inspires
complete confidence.

[47] or day: GMQT[1]UD ′ Gk.[a] om.

[48] Gk.[a] 'I had been prostrate on my face'.

[49] to my holy word. And he lifted me up: Gk.[a] 'and hear my word. And one of the
Holy Ones came to me, and raised me, and stood me up'.

[50] Gk.[a] 'And I bowed'.

[1] and said . . . Hear: GMQD′ 'and said to me, ⟨and ⟩ his voice I heard'; U
defective; Gk.[a] 'and said to me, O upright man! Man of uprightness! Scribe! And his
voice I heard'.

[2] righteous . . . righteousness: Gk.[a] 'upright . . . uprightness'.

[3] Gk.[a] 'to those who sent you'.   [4] to petition on their behalf: Gk.[a] om.

[5] Gk.[a] add 'children for yourselves'.

[6] upon the women: so Eth., but corrupt for Gk.[a] 'through the blood of the
women'.

[7] and produced . . . as they do: D′ Gk.[a] 'as they produce flesh and blood'.

reason I gave them wives, *namely* that they might sow seed in them and *that* children might be born by them,[8] that thus deeds might be
6 done on the earth.[9] But you formerly[10] were spiritual, living an
7 eternal, immortal life for all the generations of the world. For this reason I did not arrange wives for you because[11] the dwelling of the
8 spiritual ones[12] *is* in heaven. And now the giants who were born from body and flesh[13] will be called evil spirits[14] upon the earth,
9 and on the earth will be their dwelling. And evil spirits came out[15] from their flesh[16] because from above[17] they were created; from the holy Watchers was their origin and first foundation.[18] Evil spirits they will be on the earth, and spirits of the evil ones[19] they will be
10 called.[20] And the dwelling of the spirits of heaven is in heaven, but the dwelling of the spirits of earth,[21] who were born on the earth, *is*
11 on earth. And the spirits of the giants † the clouds † which do wrong[22] and are corrupt,[23] and attack and fight and break[24] on the earth,[25] and cause sorrow;[26] and they eat no food[27] and do not

---

[8] Gk.[a] 'and thus beget children by them'.

[9] that thus . . . on the earth: so Eth.II; Eth.I defective and corrupt, but GTUD' are similar to Gk.[a] 'that nothing might be lacking to them on the earth'.

[10] formerly: Gk.[a] om.   [11] because: Gk.[a] om.

[12] Eth.I Gk.[a] add 'of heaven'.

[13] G 'from souls and flesh'; Q 'from the spirits of flesh'; D' Gk.[a s] 'from the spirits and flesh'.

[14] will be called evil spirits: Gk.[a] defective and reads 'strong' for 'evil'.

[15] Gk.[s] 'And evil spirits they will be, the spirits which have come out'.

[16] Gk.[a] 'from their bodies' (and so Eth. could also be translated); Gk.[s] 'from the bodies of their flesh'.

[17] Gk.[s] 'from men'.

[18] was their . . . foundation: Gk.[a s] '*was* the beginning of their creation and the beginning of *their* foundation'.

[19] they will be . . . the evil ones: Q Gk.[a] om. (hmt.); some Eth. MSS read 'and evil spirits' for 'and spirits of the evil ones'.

[20] and spirits . . . will be called: Gk.[s] om. together with verse 10.

[21] of earth: Gk.[a] om.

[22] So Eth.: D' Gk.[a] 'And the spirits of the giants wrong the clouds'; Gk.[s] 'The spirits of the giants lay waste, do wrong'. No version is satisfactory, but it is possible that 'clouds' in Eth. Gk.[a] ('lay waste' in Gk.[s]) is a corruption of 'the Nephilim', viz. 'The spirits of the giants, the Nephilim, do wrong'.

[23] GQ Gk.[a s] 'and cause corruption' *or* 'and cause destruction'.

[24] Gk.[a s] 'and throw'(?).   [25] Gk.[a] adds 'harsh spirits of giants'.

[26] Gk.[a s] 'and cause running'(?).

[27] Gk.[a s] 'and they do not eat, but fast'; Gk.[s] adds 'and cause apparitions'.

12 thirst,[28] and are not observed.[29] And these spirits will rise[30] against
the sons of men and against the[31] women because they came out
from them.[32] In the days[33] of slaughter and destruction

XVI. and the death of the giants, wherever the spirits have gone
out from *their* bodies,[1] their flesh shall be destroyed before the
judgement;[2] thus they will be destroyed[3] until the day of the great
consummation is accomplished upon the great age,[4] upon the
2 Watchers and the impious ones.[5] And now to the Watchers who
sent you to petition on their behalf, who were formerly[6] in heaven –
3 and now[7] *say*, You were in heaven, but *its* secrets had not yet been
revealed to you and a worthless mystery you knew.[8] This you made
known to the women in the hardness of your hearts, and through
this mystery the women and the men cause evil to increase on the
4 earth. Say to them therefore, You will not have peace.

XVII. And they took[1] me to a place where they[2] were like burning
fire, and, when they wished, they made themselves look like men.

[28] MXY Gk.[a s] 'and thirst'.
[29] D' 'and do not cause offence'; Gk.[a s] 'and cause offence'.
[30] So MT'UP[1] Gk.[a s]: all other Eth. MSS 'will not rise'.
[31] against the: Gk.[a s] 'of'.
[32] from them: so Gk.[a s]; Eth. om.   [33] QD' 'From the days'.

[1] ENY 'from *their* souls'; MQTUD' corrupt or defective.
[2] In the days . . . the judgement: Gk.[a] corrupt, but perhaps translate 'From the
day of the slaughter and destruction and death ⟨of the giants⟩ the spirits, having
gone out from the souls of their flesh, will destroy without judgement'; Gk.[s] 'And
from the day of the time of the slaughter and destruction and death of the giant
Nephilim, the mighty ones of the earth, the great famous ones, the spirits that have
gone out from their souls as from the flesh, will destroy without judgement'.
[3] Gk.[a s] 'they will destroy'.
[4] Gk.[a s] 'until the day of the consummation, (Gk.[s] adds 'until') the great judgement in which the great age will be brought to an end'.
[5] upon the Watchers and the impious ones: Gk.[a s] om., but Gk.[s] adds 'once for all
at the same time it will be brought to an end'; GQTUD' add 'all will be
accomplished', and GQT make further additions.
[6] Gk.[a] om.   [7] and now: Gk.[a] om.
[8] Gk.[a] (corrupt) 'but every mystery which had not been revealed to you and a
mystery which was from God you knew'.

[1] Gk.[a] adds 'and brought'.   [2] GMQ Gk.[a] 'those who were there'.

2 And they[3] led me to a place of storm,[4] and to a mountain the tip of[5]
3 whose summit reached to heaven. And I saw lighted places[6] and
thunder[7] in the outermost ends, in its depths,[8] a bow of fire and
arrows and their quivers, and a sword of fire,[9] and all the flashes of
4 lightning. And they took me to the water of life,[10] as it is called,[11]
and to the fire of the west which receives[12] every setting of the sun.
5 And I[13] came to a river of fire whose fire flows like water and pours
6 out into the great sea which *is* towards the west.[14] And I saw all[15]
the great rivers, and I reached the great[16] darkness and went where
7 all[17] flesh walks. And I saw the mountains[18] of the darkness of
winter and the place where the water of all the deep pours out.[19]
8 And I saw the mouths of all the rivers of the earth and the mouth of
the deep.

XVIII.   And I saw the storehouses of all the winds, and I saw how
with them he has adorned all creation, and *I saw* the foundations of
2 the earth. And I saw the cornerstone of the earth, and I saw the
four winds which support the earth and the firmament of heaven.
3 And I saw how the winds stretch out the height of heaven[1] and *how*
they position themselves between heaven and earth;[2] they are the
4 pillars of heaven.[3] And I saw the winds which turn heaven and
5 cause the disk of the sun and all the stars to set. And I saw the
winds on the earth which support the clouds, and I saw the paths of

---

[3] So G Gk.[a]: all other Eth. MSS 'he'.
[4] Gk.[a] 'to a dark place'.   [5] the tip of: Gk.[a] om.
[6] MQD′ 'the places of light'; G corrupt; Gk.[a] 'the place of the lights'.
[7] and thunder: Gk.[a] 'and the storehouses of the stars and of the thunder'.
[8] in the outermost . . . depths: Gk.[a] 'and in the depths of air'; GMQT'UD'AK
Gk.[a] add 'where *were*'.
[9] and a sword of fire: Gk.[a] om.
[10] GQTUD′ 'the waters of life'; M corrupt; Gk.[a] 'the living waters'.
[11] as it is called: Gk.[a] om.
[12] Gk.[a] (corrupt) 'produces'.   [13] Gk.[a] 'we'.
[14] which *is* towards the west: Gk[a] 'of the west'.
[15] MQU Gk.[a] om.   [16] Gk.[a] adds 'river and the great'.
[17] Gk.[a] 'no'.   [18] Gk.[a] 'the winds'.
[19] Gk.[a] 'all the waters of the deep pour out'.

[1] And I saw how . . . heaven: Gk.[a] om. (hmt.).
[2] Gk.[a] 'between earth and heaven'.   [3] they are . . . heaven: Gk.[a] om. (hmt.).

the angels. I saw[4] at the end[5] of the earth the firmament of heaven
6 above. And I went towards the south – and it was burning day and
night[6] – where *there were* seven mountains of precious stones, three
7 towards the east and three towards the south. And *those* towards
the east *were* of coloured stone, and one *was* of pearl and one of
8 healing stone;[7] and those towards the south *were* of red stone. And
the middle one reached to heaven, like the throne of the Lord,[8] of
9 stibium, and the top of the throne *was* of sapphire. And I saw a
10 burning fire and what was in all the[9] mountains. And I saw there a
place beyond the great earth;[10] there the waters were gathered
11 together.[11] And I saw a deep chasm of the earth[12] with pillars of
heavenly fire, and I saw among them fiery pillars of heaven,[13]
which were falling,[14] and as regards both height and depth they
12 were immeasurable. And beyond this chasm I saw a place and *it
had* neither the firmament of heaven above it, nor the foundation of
earth below it; there was no water on it,[15] and no birds, but it was a
13 desert place. And a terrible thing I saw there[16] – seven stars like
great burning mountains. And like a spirit questioning me[17] the
14 angel said, This is the place of the end of heaven and earth; this is
15 the prison for the stars of heaven[18] and the host of heaven. And the
stars which roll over[19] the fire, these are the ones which transgressed the command of the Lord from[19] the beginning of their
16 rising[20] because they did not come out at their proper times. And

---

[4] the paths . . . I saw: Gk.^a om. (hmt.).   [5] Gk.^a '⟨at⟩ the ends'.
[6] Gk.^a 'And I proceeded and saw a place *which was* burning night and day'.
[7] healing stone: so Eth., but the text is very doubtful; Gk.^a corrupt.
[8] Gk.^a 'of God'.   [9] all the: D' 'these'.
[10] and what was . . . the great earth: Gk.^a 'And beyond these mountains there is a
place *which is* the end of the great earth'.
[11] GMQT¹U¹D' 'the heavens were gathered together'; Gk.^a 'the heavens were
finished'.
[12] of the earth: GMQT¹UD' Gk.^a om.   [13] of heaven: GT²D' om.
[14] with pillars . . . falling: Gk.^a 'with pillars of fire which were falling'.
[15] Gk.^a 'under it'.
[16] QD' 'but it was a desert place, and terrible. I saw there'; Gk.^a 'but the place
was desolate and terrible. There I saw'.
[17] And like . . . me: Gk.^a 'concerning which to me, when I inquired'.
[18] of heaven: GMTUD' Gk.^a om.   [19] Gk.^a 'in'.
[20] Gk.^a adds 'because the place outside heaven is empty'.

he was angry with them and bound them until the time of the consummation of their sin in the year of mystery.[21]

XIX. And Uriel said to me, The spirits of the angels who were promiscuous with the women will stand here; and they, assuming many forms, made men unclean[1] and will lead men[2] astray so that they sacrifice to demons as gods[3] – *that is*, until the great judgement day on[4] which they will be judged so that an end will be made of
2 them. And their wives, having led astray the angels of heaven,[5] will
3 become peaceful.[6] And I, Enoch, alone saw the sight, the ends of everything; and no man has seen[7] what I have seen.

XX. And these are the names of the holy angels who keep watch.[1]
2 Uriel, one of the holy angels, namely *the angel* of thunder and of
3 tremors.[2] Raphael, one of the holy angels, *the angel* of[3] the spirits of
4 men. Raguel, one of the holy angels, who takes vengeance on the
5 world and on the lights.[4] Michael, one of the holy angels, namely the one put in charge of the best part of mankind,[5] in charge of the
6 nation.[6] Saraqael,[7] one of the holy angels, who *is* in charge of the
7 spirits of men who cause the spirits to sin.[8] Gabriel, one of the holy

[21] in the year of mystery: Gk.[a] 'for ten thousand years'.

[1] made men unclean: Gk.[a] 'harm men'.
[2] GMTUD' Gk.[a] 'them'.   [3] as gods: Gk.[a] om.
[4] So MTD' and some Eth.II MSS: other Eth. MSS corrupt; Gk.[a] 'until the great judgement in'.
[5] So Eth., but GMQT'UD' om. 'of heaven': Gk.[a] 'And the wives of the angels who went astray'.
[6] So Eth., but a mistake: Gk.[a] 'sirens'.
[7] GMQUD' 'will see'.

[1] And these . . . keep watch: Gk.[a1] 'Angels of the powers'; Gk.[a2] om. together with 'Uriel' in verse 2.
[2] GQD' 'namely the eternal one and *the angel* of tremors'; Gk.[a1 a2] 'the one in charge of the world and of Tartarus'.
[3] of: Gk.[a1 a2] 'in charge of'.   [4] Gk.[a1 a2] 'the world of the lights'.
[5] Gk.[a1 a2] 'of the nation'.
[6] D' 'and in charge of the nations'; Gk.[a1 a2] 'and in charge of chaos'.
[7] Gk.[a1 a2] 'Sariel'.
[8] who *is* in charge . . . sin: Gk.[a1 a2] 'the one in charge of the spirits who sin against the spirit'.

angels, who *is* in charge of the serpents and the Garden⁹ and the Cherubim.¹⁰

XXI. And I went round to a place¹ where there was nothing
2 made.² And I saw there a terrible thing³ – neither the high heaven,⁴
nor the *firmly* founded earth,⁵ but a desert place, prepared and
3 terrible.⁶ And there I saw seven stars of heaven bound on it
4 together,⁷ like great mountains, and burning like⁸ fire. Then I said,
For what sin have they been bound, and why⁹ have they been
5 thrown here? And¹⁰ Uriel, one of the holy angels who was with me
and led me,¹¹ spoke to me and said,¹² Enoch, about whom do you
6 ask? About whom do you inquire and ask¹³ and care?¹⁴ These are
some of the stars¹⁵ which transgressed the command of the Lord
Most High,¹⁶ and they have been bound here until ten thousand
7 ages¹⁷ are completed, the number of the days of their sin.¹⁸ And
from there I went to another place, more terrible than this, and I
saw a terrible thing: *there was* a great fire there¹⁹ which burnt and
blazed, and the place²⁰ had a cleft reaching to the abyss, full of
great pillars of fire²¹ which were made to fall; neither its extent nor

⁹ Eth.I Gk.ᵃ¹ ᵃ² 'the Garden and the serpents'.
¹⁰ Gk.ᵃ¹ adds 'Seven names of archangels'; Gk.ᵃ² adds 'Remiel, one of the holy angels, whom God put in charge of those who rise. Seven names of archangels'.

¹ a place: GMQT'UD' Gk.ᵃ¹ ᵃ² om.　　² i.e. a place of chaos.
³ GT Gk.ᵃ¹ ᵃ² add 'I saw'; Q adds 'And I saw'.
⁴ GMQUD' Gk.ᵃ¹ ᵃ² 'neither heaven above'.　　⁵ Gk.ᵃ¹ adds 'did I see'.
⁶ GMQT'U 'but a prepared and terrible place'; D' Gk.ᵃ¹ ᵃ² 'but a chaotic and terrible place'.
⁷ Gk.ᵃ¹ ᵃ² 'bound and thrown down on it'.　　⁸ GMQUD' Gk.ᵃ¹ ᵃ² 'with'.
⁹ Gk.ᵃ¹ 'For what reason . . . and why'; Gk.ᵃ² 'For what reason . . . and for what reason'.　　¹⁰ Gk.ᵃ¹ 'Then'.
¹¹ and led me: so Eth., but all MSS except G om. 'and'; Gk.ᵃ¹ ᵃ² 'and was the leader of them'.
¹² D' Gk.ᵃ¹ ᵃ² add 'to me'.　　¹³ and ask: GMQD' om.
¹⁴ do you inquire . . . and care: Gk.ᵃ¹ ᵃ² 'are you eager for the truth'.
¹⁵ D' Gk.ᵃ¹ ᵃ² add 'of heaven'.
¹⁶ Most High: Eth.I Gk.ᵃ¹ ᵃ² om.　　¹⁷ D' Gk.ᵃ¹ ᵃ² 'years'.
¹⁸ D' 'the number of their sins'; Gk.ᵃ¹ ᵃ² 'the time of their sins'.
¹⁹ there: D' and some Eth.II MSS om.
²⁰ So GMQT'UD' Gk.ᵃ¹ ᵃ²: T² Eth.II 'the boundary'.
²¹ Gk.ᵃ¹ ᵃ² 'of pillars of a great fire'.

8   its size could I see, nor could I see its source.[22] Then I said, How
9   terrible this place *is*, and *how* painful[23] to look at! Then Uriel,[24] one
    of the holy angels who was with me, answered me. He answered
    me[25] and said to me, Enoch, why do you have such fear and terror[26]
10 because of this terrible place, and before this pain?[27] And he said to
    me,[28] This place *is* the prison of the angels, and there[29] they will be
    held for ever.

XXII.   And from there I went to another place, and he showed me
    in the west a large and high mountain, and a hard rock and four
2   beautiful[1] places, and inside it was deep and wide and very
    smooth.[2] How smooth *is* that which rolls,[3] and deep and dark to
3   look at! Then Raphael, one of the holy angels who was with me,
    answered me[4] and said to me, These beautiful[5] places *are intended
    for this*, that the spirits, the souls[6] of the dead, might be gathered
    into them; for them[7] they were created,[8] *that* here they might gather
4   all the souls of the sons of men.[9] And these places they made where
    they will keep them[10] until the day of their judgement and until

---

[22]   nor could I see its scource: so T[2] Eth.II; GQ corrupt; D′ Gk.[a1 a2] 'nor could I
(Gk.[a1 a2] om. 'could I') guess *them*', and this text is supported by the otherwise
impossible MT[1]U.

[23]   G 'horrible'; Gk.[a1 a2] 'fearful'.   [24]   Uriel: Gk.[a1 a2] om.

[25]   He answered me: QAKX Gk.[a] om.

[26]   Gk.[a] adds 'And ⟨I⟩ answered'.

[27]   and before this pain: Gk.[a] 'and because of the fearful spectacle'.

[28]   to me: Gk.[a] om.   [29]   and there: D′ Gk.[a] 'here'.

---

[1]   beautiful: so Eth., but a misreading of the Greek word for 'hollow'.

[2]   a large . . . very smooth: Gk.[a] 'another large and high mountain, of hard rock.
And *there were* four hollow places in it, deep and very smooth: three of them *were*
dark, and one bright, and *there was* a spring of water in the middle of it. And I said'.

[3]   *is* that which rolls: so Eth., but a mistranslation of the Greek; Gk.[a] 'are these
hollow places'.

[4]   me: GMQ[2]T[1]U Gk.[a] om.

[5]   beautiful: so Eth., but a misreading; Gk.[a] 'hollow'.

[6]   GT[1]D′H Gk.[a] 'the spirits of the souls'; Q corrupt; OB′ om. 'the souls'.

[7]   GQUD′ Gk.[a] 'for this'; MT corrupt.   [8]   Gk.[a] (corrupt) 'judged'.

[9]   Gk.[a] 'all the souls of men'; Aram. '[the soul]s of all the sons of men'.

[10]   where they will keep them: Gk.[a] 'for their reception'; Aram. uncertain, but
probably 'And behold, these are the pits for their prison house [which] they have
thus made'.

their appointed time – and that appointed time *will be* long[11] – until
5 the great judgement *comes* upon them.[12] And I saw the spirits of the sons of men who were dead,[13] and their voice reached heaven and
6 complained.[14] Then[15] I asked Raphael, the angel[16] who was with me, and said to him, Whose is this spirit whose voice thus reaches
7 heaven[17] and complains?[18] And he answered me and said to me,[19] saying, This spirit is the one which came out of Abel whom Cain, his brother, killed. And he[20] will complain about him until his[21] offspring is destroyed from the face of the earth, and from amongst
8 the offspring of men his offspring perishes. Then I asked about him and[22] about the judgement on all[23] and I said,[24] Why is one
9 separated from another? And he answered me and said to me,[25] These three[26] *places* were made in order that they might separate the spirits of the dead. And thus the souls[27] of the righteous have been separated;[28] this is the spring of water *and* on it *is* the light.[29]

[11] and that appointed time *will be* long: so Eth., but probably an attempt to deal with an impossible text; Gk.[a] has a dittograph of the previous phrase.

[12] and until their appointed time . . . upon them: so Eth., but QD′ have abbreviated texts; Gk.[a] 'and until the appointed time and the time appointed at which the great judgement will be *executed* upon them'; Aram. 'and until the appointed time of the day of the end of the great judgement which will be executed upon them'.

[13] And I saw . . . were dead: so Eth., but fairly clearly only one spirit was mentioned originally (cp. verses 6ff.); Gk.[a] corrupt, but perhaps read 'I saw ⟨the spirit⟩ of a dead man complaining'; Aram. 'There I saw the spirit of a dead man complaining'.

[14] and their voice . . . complained: so Eth. Gk.[a], but Gk.[a] reads 'his' for 'their'; Aram. 'and his lamentation going up to heaven and crying out and complaining'.

[15] Gk.[a] 'And'.   [16] Aram. 'the Watcher and holy one'.

[17] heaven: so C′; all other Eth. MSS om.

[18] Gk.[a] 'Whose is this spirit which is complaining? Therefore his voice thus reaches and complains to heaven'.

[19] and said to me: QD′ AD Gk.[a] om.; C′ om. 'saying'.   [20] Gk.[a] 'Abel'.

[21] Eth.I 'all his'.   [22] about him and: Gk.[a] om.

[23] about the judgement on all: so Eth.; Gk.[a] 'about all the circular places'; both are perhaps corrupt for 'about all the hollow places'.

[24] and I said: GMQT′UD′ Gk.[a] om.   [25] and said to me: Gk.[a] 'saying'.

[26] three: so Eth. Gk.[a], but we expect 'four' because four places are mentioned in verse 1 and four seem to be described in verses 9b–13.   [27] N 'the spirits'.

[28] C′ Gk.[a] 'And thus *a place* has been separated for the souls (Gk.[a] 'the spirits') of the righteous'.

[29] this is . . . the light: Gk.[a] 'in which *there is* the bright spring of water'.

10 Likewise[30] *a place* has been created for sinners[31] when they die and
are buried in the earth and judgement has not come upon them
11 during their life. And here their souls[32] will be separated for this
great torment, until the great day of judgement and punishment
and torment for those who curse for ever, and of vengeance on their
souls,[33] and there he will bind them for ever. Verily he is from the
12 beginning of the world.[34] And thus *a place* has been separated for
the souls[32] of those who complain and give information about *their*
13 destruction, when they were killed in the days of the sinners. Thus
a place has been created for the souls[32] of men who are not righteous,[35] but sinners, accomplished in wrongdoing,[36] and with the
wrongdoers will be their lot.[37] But their souls will not be killed on
14 the day of judgement,[38] nor will they rise from here. Then I blessed
the Lord of Glory and said, Blessed be my Lord, the Lord of Glory
and Righteousness,[39] who rules everything for ever.[40]

XXIII.   And from there I went to another place towards the west, to
2   the ends[1] of the earth. And I saw a fire which burnt and[2] ran
without resting or ceasing from running[3] by day or night, but
3   *continued* in exactly the same way.[4] And I asked saying, What is this
4   which has no rest? Then Raguel, one of the holy angels who was

[30] D' Gk.ᵃ 'And thus'.
[31] D' 'And thus the sinners have been separated'.
[32] Gk.ᵃ 'spirits'.
[33] for those . . . their souls: Gk.ᵃ in part corrupt, but perhaps read 'for those who
are cursed for ever, that *there may be* vengeance on *their* spirits'.
[34] Verily . . . the world: an Eth. gloss; Gk.ᵃ om.
[35] Gk.ᵃ 'will not be holy'.
[36] accomplished in wrongdoing: Gk.ᵃ 'who *will be* impious'.
[37] Lit. 'and with the wrongdoers they will be like them'; Gk.ᵃ 'and of the lawless
they will be companions'.
[38] Gk.ᵃ 'But *their* spirits, because those who are afflicted here are punished less
than them, will not be punished on the day of judgement'.
[39] GMTUD' 'Blessed by my Lord, the Lord of Righteousness'; Gk.ᵃ 'Blessed are
you, Lord of Righteousness'; Aram. 'Blessed be the Judge of Righteousness'.
[40] Eth.I and some Eth.II MSS 'who rules for ever'; Gk.ᵃ 'who rules the world'.

[1] Gk.ᵃ 'of the ends'.
[2] burnt and: Gk.ᵃ om.
[3] Lit. 'from its running' or 'from its course'; Gk.ᵃ om. 'its'.
[4] Gk.ᵃ uncertain, but perhaps emend to read 'but remained constant'.

with me, answered me and said to me,[5] This burning fire whose course you saw, towards the west, is *the fire of* all the lights of heaven.[6]

XXIV.   And from there I went to another place of the earth,[1] and he
2 showed me a mountain[2] of fire which blazed day and night.[3] And I went towards it[4] and saw seven magnificent mountains, and all were different from one another, and precious and beautiful stones, and all *were* precious and their appearance glorious and their form beautiful;[5] three *of the mountains* towards[6] the east, one fixed firmly on another, and three towards the south, one on another, and deep
3 and rugged valleys, no one *of which* was near another. And *there was* a seventh mountain in the middle of these, and in their height they were all like the seat of a throne,[7] and fragrant[8] trees surrounded it.
4 And there was among them a tree such as I have never smelt, and none of them nor any others were like it:[9] it smells more fragrant than any fragrance, and its leaves and its flowers and its wood never wither; its fruit[10] *is* good, and its fruit[11] *is* like the bunches of
5 dates on a palm. And then I said, Behold,[12] this beautiful tree! Beautiful to look at and pleasant *are* its leaves, and its fruit very[13]
6 delightful in appearance.[14] And then Michael, one of the holy and

[5] and said to me: Gk.[a] om.

[6] Gk.[a] 'This course of fire is the fire towards the west which persecutes all the lights of heaven'. Neither version inspires complete confidence, but Gk.[a] 'persecutes' may be corrupt for 'takes vengeance', cp. xx. 4.

[1] And from . . . earth: Gk.[a] om.
[2] Gk.[a] 'mountains'.
[3] day and night: HKOB′ 'by day'; Gk.[a] 'by night'.
[4] Gk.[a] 'beyond them'.
[5] seven magnificent . . . form beautiful: Gk.[a] 'seven mountains, all magnificent, each differing from the other, whose stones *were* precious in *their* beauty, and all *were* precious and glorious and beautiful'.
[6] three . . . towards: Gk.[a] om.
[7] Gk.[a] 'and it was superior in height, like the seat of a throne'.
[8] Gk.[a] (corrupt) 'beautiful'.
[9] Gk.[a] 'and no one else had enjoyed it, and no other one *was* like it'.
[10] its fruit: Gk.[a] corrupt.   [11] *is* good, and its fruit: Gk.[a] om.
[12] Behold: Eth.I om.   [13] and its fruit very: D′ 'and its flowers'.
[14] Behold . . . in appearance: Gk.[a] 'How beautiful this tree is, and fragrant, and the leaves pleasant, and its flowers pleasant in appearance'.

honoured[15] angels who was with me and *was* in charge of them,[16] answered me

XXV. and said to me, Enoch, why do you ask me[1] about the
2   fragrance of this tree, and *why* do you inquire to learn?[2] Then I,
Enoch,[3] answered him, saying,[4] I wish to learn about everything,
3   but especially about this tree. And he answered me,[5] saying, This
high mountain which you saw,[6] whose summit is like the throne of
the Lord,[7] is the throne where the Holy and Great One, the Lord of
Glory, the Eternal King,[8] will sit when he comes down to visit the
4   earth for good. And this beautiful[9] fragrant tree – and no *creature of*
flesh has authority to touch it until the great judgement when he
will take vengeance on all and will bring *everything* to a consummation[10] for ever[11] – this[12] will be given to the righteous and humble.[13]
5   From its fruit life will be given to the chosen; towards the north[14] it
will be planted, in[15] a holy place, by the house of the Lord, the
6   Eternal King.[16] Then they will rejoice with joy and be glad in[17] the
holy *place*; they[18] will each[19] draw the fragrance of it into their

[15] and honoured: Gk.[a] om.
[16] Gk.[a] 'and was the leader of them'.

[1] me: D′AOXB′ Gk.[a] om.; Gk.[a] adds 'and why did you wonder'.
[2] Gk.[a] 'and why do you wish to learn the truth?'
[3] Enoch: QD′ Gk.[a] om.
[4] saying: Gk.[a] om.   [5] me: GD′ Gk.[a] om.
[6] which you saw: Gk.[a] om.   [7] Gk.[a] 'of God'.
[8] the Holy . . . King: Gk.[a] 'the Great Lord, the Holy One of Glory, the King of Eternity'.
[9] beautiful: GMQT¹UD′ Gk.[a] (below) om.
[10] So GTD′: other Eth. MSS 'and *everything* is brought to a consummation'.
[11] Gk.[a] 'And as for this fragrant tree, no *creature of* flesh has authority to touch it until the great judgement when *there will be* vengeance on all and a consummation for ever'.
[12] this: so Eth.I (literally 'this therefore'); Eth.II 'that'.
[13] Gk.[a] 'Then it will be given to the righteous and holy'.
[14] From its fruit . . . towards the north: Gk.[a] 'Its fruit *will be* to the chosen as food for life'; D′ is corrupt, but in part supports Gk.[a]. The difference in Greek between 'towards the north' (all Eth. MSS) and 'as food' (Gk.[a]) is only one letter.
[15] Gk.[a] 'and it will be transplanted to'.
[16] Gk.[a] 'of God, the King of Eternity'.   [17] D′ 'and in'.
[18] GQOB′C′ 'and they'.   [19] each: GMQT¹UD′K¹N om.

bones,[20] and they will live a long life on earth, as your fathers lived, and in their days sorrow and pain and toil[21] and punishment[22] will
7 not touch them. Then I blessed the Lord[23] of Glory, the Eternal King,[24] because he[25] has prepared such things for righteous men, and has created such things[26] and said that they are to be given to them.

XXVI. And from there I went to the middle of the earth and saw a blessed, *well*-watered,[1] place[2] which had branches which remained
2 *alive* and sprouted from a tree which had been cut down. And there I saw a holy mountain, and under the mountain, to the east of it,
3 *there was* water and it flowed towards the south. And I saw towards the east another mountain which was of the same height,[3] and between them *there was* a deep and narrow valley; and in it a stream
4 ran by[4] the mountain. And to the west of this one *was* another mountain which was lower than it, and not high; and under it *there was* a valley between them, and *there were* other deep and dry
5 valleys[5] at the end of the three mountains.[6] And all the valleys *were* deep and narrow,[7] of hard rock, and trees were[8] planted on them.
6 And I was amazed at the rock and I was amazed[9] at the valley; I was very much amazed.

---

[20] and be glad . . . their bones: Gk.ᵃ 'and be glad and into the holy *place* they will enter; the fragrance of it *will be* in their bones'.

[21] Eth.I 'and torment'.

[22] sorrow . . . punishment: Gk.ᵃ 'torment and plague and punishment'.

[23] MTUD' Gk.ᵃ 'the God'; C' om. 'of glory'.

[24] Gk.ᵃ 'the King of Eternity'.

[25] because he: Gk.ᵃ 'who'.

[26] such things: Gk.ᵃ 'them'.

[1] *well*-watered: Gk.ᵃ om.; Q om. 'a blessed, *well*-watered, place'.

[2] Gk.ᵃ adds 'where *there were* trees'.

[3] Q Gk.ᵃ 'which was higher than this'; D' is corrupt, but supports Q Gk.ᵃ.

[4] Gk.ᵃ 'under'.

[5] and under . . . dry valleys: Gk.ᵃ 'and *there was* a deep and dry valley between them, and another deep and dry valley'; GMQUD' partially support the reading 'and another deep and dry valley'.

[6] mountains: so Gk.ᵃ; Eth. om.

[7] and narrow: Gk.ᵃ om.

[8] Gk.ᵃ 'were not'.

[9] at the rock and I was amazed: Gk.ᵃ om.

XXVII.   Then[1] I said, What *is* the purpose of this blessed land
which is completely full of trees and of this accursed valley[2] in the
2   middle of them? Then Raphael,[3] one of the holy angels who was
with me, answered me and said to me, This[4] accursed valley[5] is for
those who are cursed for ever; here will be gathered together all[6]
who speak with their mouths against the Lord words that are not
fitting and say hard things about his glory. Here they will gather
3   them together, and here *will be* their place of judgement.[7] And in
the last days there will be the spectacle of the righteous judgement
upon them before the righteous for ever, for evermore; here the
4   merciful[8] will bless the Lord of Glory, the Eternal King.[9] And in
the days of the judgement on them they will bless him[10] on account
of *his* mercy, according as he has assigned to them *their lot*. Then I
5   myself[11] blessed the Lord of Glory and I addressed him,[12] and I
remembered his majesty, as was fitting.[13]

XXVIII.   And from there I went towards the east[1] to the middle of
2   the mountain[2] of the wilderness, and I saw only desert. But *it was*
full of trees[3] from this seed, and[4] water gushed out over it[5] from

---

[1] Gk.[a] 'And'.

[2] and of this accursed valley: Gk.[a] 'and *why is* this valley accursed?'

[3] Raphael: so OP²B'; all other Eth. MSS 'Uriel'.

[4] in the middle . . . to me, This: Gk.[a] om.

[5] valley: Gk.[a] 'land', but Gk.[a] has probably transliterated the original Semitic
word instead of translating it.

[6] D' Gk.[a] add 'the accursed'.   [7] Gk.[a] 'will be *their* dwelling'.

[8] Gk.[a] 'In the last ages, in the days of the true judgement before the righteous for
ever, here the impious'.

[9] Gk.[a] 'the King of Eternity'.   [10] him: Gk.[a] om.

[11] myself: GMQT¹UD' Gk.[a] om.

[12] and I addressed him: Gk.[a] 'and I proclaimed his glory'.

[13] and I remembered . . . fitting: so Eth., but probably corrupt; Gk.[a] 'and I sang
his praises in a way befitting *his* majesty'.

---

[1] towards the east: Gk.[a] om.   [2] of the mountain: Gk.[a] om.

[3] and I saw . . . full of trees: so Eth.II, although the text is awkward (lit. 'and I
saw it only desert etc.'); GMQT¹U Gk.[a] 'and I saw it desert, and *it was* isolated, full
of trees'; D' 'and I saw a desert, and *it was* isolated, full of trees'.

[4] D' 'and from this seed'; Gk.[a] 'and from the seeds'. But the text appears to be
corrupt.   [5] over it: Q om.

3 above. The torrent, which flowed towards the north-west, seemed copious, and from all sides there went up[6] . . . water and dew.[7]

XXIX. And I went[1] to another place *away* from[2] the wilderness; I[3]
2 came near to the east of this mountain. And there[4] I saw trees of judgement,[5] especially vessels of the fragrance of incense and myrrh,[6] and the[7] trees were not alike.[8]

XXX. And above it, above these, above the mountains of the east, and not far away,[1] I saw another[2] place, valleys of water[3] like that
2 which does not fail.[4] And I saw a beautiful tree and its fragrance
3 *was* like that of the mastic.[5] And by the banks of these valleys I saw fragrant cinnamon. And beyond those[6] *valleys* I came near towards the east.

[6] All Eth. MSS add 'and from there', but the words may have been misplaced from the beginning of xxix. 1.
[7] water gushed . . . and dew: Gk.[a] 'water gushed out from above; flowing like a copious watercourse towards the north-west from all sides it sent up water and dew'.

[1] Gk.[a] 'From there I went yet'.
[2] *away* from: Gk.[a] 'in'.
[3] D' Gk.[a] 'and I'.
[4] there: Q Gk.[a] om.
[5] trees of judgement: so Eth. Gk.[a], but perhaps a corruption in the original Aramaic of 'fragrant trees'.
[6] especially . . . myrrh: so Eth., but the text is corrupt; Gk.[a] 'which smelt of the fragrance of incense and myrrh'.
[7] D' Gk.[a] 'their'.
[8] GMQT¹UD' 'were alike'; Gk.[a] '*were* like the almond tree'.

[1] And above it . . . not far away: so Eth, but corrupt; Gk.[a] 'And beyond these I went towards the east, far away, and'; Aram. (so far as it exists) supports Gk.[a]. Eth.I and some Eth.II MSS read 'and' before 'I saw'.
[2] Gk.[a] adds 'large'.
[3] GMQT¹D' Gk.[a] 'a valley of water'; U defective.
[4] like that . . . not fail: Gk.[a] om.
[5] So Eth.II: QT 'And I saw a beautiful tree which was like a fragrant tree like the mastic'; other Eth.I MSS corrupt or defective; Gk.[a] (?) 'where also *there was* a tree, the colour of fragrant plants like the mastic'. Underlying Eth. 'beautiful tree', 'fragrant tree' is the O.T. 'sweet cane' or 'aromatic cane' as the fragmentary Aram. makes clear.
[6] Gk.[a] 'these'.

XXXI. And I saw another mountain[1] on which there were trees,[2] and there flowed out water, and there flowed out[3] from it[4] as it were[5] a nectar whose name is styrax and galbanum. And beyond this mountain[6] I saw another mountain, and on it *there were* aloe trees,[7] and those trees *were* full of *a fruit* which *is* like an almond and *is* hard.[8] And when they take[9] this fruit, it is better than any fragrance.[10]

XXXII. And after these fragrances, to the north,[1] as I looked over the mountains,[2] I saw seven mountains[3] full of fine hard and fragrant trees[4] and cinnamon[5] and pepper. And from there I went over the summits of those mountains,[6] far away to the east,[7] and I

---

[1] Eth.I EKNP[1] Gk.ᵃ Aram. 'other mountains'.

[2] Gk.ᵃ 'and on them *there were* groves of trees'; Aram. 'and also on them I saw trees'.

[3] water, and there flowed out: GT²UD′ Gk.ᵃ om.; AC′ om. 'and there flowed out'; MQ defective.

[4] from it (the mountain?): so Eth., but might perhaps also be translated 'from them'; Gk.ᵃ 'from them'.

[5] as it were: Gk.ᵃ om.   [6] D′ Gk.ᵃ Aram. 'these mountains'.

[7] and on it . . . aloe trees: Gk.ᵃ om., but has instead 'to the east of the ends of the earth'.

[8] and those trees . . . hard: Gk.ᵃ 'and all the trees *were* full immediately (?) in the likeness of almonds. Only the latter part of Aram. can be clearly read, '. . . and it is like the husks of (or 'the bark of') . . .': in the Aramaic original underlying Gk.ᵃ the word for 'fruit' may have been confused with the word for 'thereupon, immediately'.

[9] So Eth., but corrupt for 'crush' (Gk.ᵃ Aram.).

[10] Gk.ᵃ is partially corrupt, 'When they crush *it*; therefore *it is* more fragrant than any fragrance'.

[1] And after . . . the north: Gk.ᵃ 'To the north-east'; Aram. 'And beyond these [. . .], to the north-east of them'.

[2] as I looked . . . mountains: Gk.ᵃ Aram. om.

[3] Aram. 'I was shown other mountains'.

[4] fragrant trees: so Eth. (representing here the O.T. 'aromatic cane'?); Gk.ᵃ 'mastic'; Aram.(?) 'pepperwort'.

[5] Aram. 'cardamon'.

[6] Gk.ᵃ 'over the beginnings of all these mountains'; Aram. 'to the east of all these mountains'.

[7] D′ Gk.ᵃ 'far away to the east of the earth'; Aram. 'far from them to the east of the earth'.

went over the Red Sea and I was far from it,[8] and I went over the
3 angel Zotiel.[9] And I came to the Garden of Righteousness, and I
saw beyond those trees many large trees[10] growing[11] there, sweet-
smelling, large, very beautiful and glorious,[12] and the tree of
4 wisdom[13] from which they[14] eat and know great wisdom.[13] And it is
like the carob-tree,[15] and its fruit *is* like the bunches of grapes on a
vine, very beautiful, and the smell of this tree spreads and pene-
5 trates afar.[16] And[17] I said, This tree *is* beautiful! How beautiful[18]
6 and pleasing *is* its appearance![19] And[17] the holy angel Raphael,
who was with me, answered me and said to me,[20] This is the tree of
wisdom from which your old father and your aged mother, who
were before you, ate[21] and learnt wisdom; and their eyes were
opened, and they knew that they were naked, and they were driven
from the garden.

XXXIII. And from there I went to the ends of the earth and I saw
there large animals, each different from the other, and also birds
which differed in form, beauty and call – each different from the
2 other. And to the east of these animals I saw the ends of the earth
3 on which heaven rests, and the open gates of heaven. And I saw

---

[8] and I was far from it: Gk.[a] (?) 'and I went to the outermost ends', but probably
corrupt for 'and I went far away'; Aram. 'and I went far from it'.

[9] Gk.[a] 'and from this I went over Zotiel'; Aram. 'and I went over the darkness,
far from it'.

[10] beyond those trees . . . trees: Gk.[a] 'from far away more trees than these trees,
and large'.

[11] growing: Gk.[a] (corrupt) 'two'.

[12] sweet-smelling . . . glorious: Gk.[a] 'very large, beautiful, and glorious, and
magnificent'.

[13] Gk.[a] 'knowledge'.

[14] from which they: Gk.[a] 'whose fruit the holy ones'.

[15] Gk.[a] 'That tree *is* like the fir in height, but its leaves *are* like *those of* the
carob-tree'.

[16] Q 'and the smell of this tree spreads very far'; Gk.[a] 'and its smell spreads far
from the tree'.

[17] Gk.[a] 'Then'.   [18] How beautiful: Q om.

[19] This tree . . . its appearance: Gk.[a] 'How beautiful the tree *is*, and how pleasing
in appearance!'

[20] me and said to me: Gk.[a] om.

[21] Gk.[a] 'This *is* the tree of knowledge from which your father ate' (Gk.[a] ends
here).

how the stars of heaven come out, and counted the gates out of which they come, and wrote down all their outlets, for each one individually according to their number and their names, according to their constellations, their positions, their times and their

4 months, as the angel Uriel, who was with me,[1] showed me. And he showed me everything and wrote it down, and also their names he wrote down for me, and their laws and their functions.[2]

XXXIV. And from there I went towards the north to the ends of the earth, and there I saw a great and glorious wonder[1] at the ends of

2 the whole earth. And there I saw three gates of heaven open in heaven; through each of them north winds go out; when they blow, *there is* cold, hail, hoar-frost, snow, dew and rain. And from one

3 gate it blows for good; but when they blow through the other two gates, it is with force and it brings torment over the earth, and they blow with force.

XXXV. And from there I went towards the west to the ends of the earth, and I saw there, as I saw in the east, three open gates – as many gates and as many outlets.

XXXVI. And from there I went towards the south to the ends of the earth, and there I saw three gates of heaven open; and the south

2 wind and dew and rain and wind come out from there. And from there I went towards the east of the ends of heaven, and there I saw the three eastern gates of heaven open, and above them *there were*

3 smaller gates. Through each of those smaller gates the stars of heaven pass and go towards the west on the path which has been

4 shown to them. And when I saw, I blessed, and I will always bless[1] the Lord of Glory who has made great and glorious wonders that he might show the greatness of his work to his angels and to the

---

¹ the angel . . . with me: Eth.I 'Uriel, the angel who *was* with me, the holy one'.
² Eth.I 'groups'.

¹ GQT'U 'a great and glorious plan'; D' 'the throne of the Great and Glorious One'.

¹ GMQT'UD'K 'And whenever I saw, I always blessed, and I will bless'.

souls of men,[2] that they might praise his work, and that all his creatures might see[3] the work of his power and praise the great work of his hands and bless him for ever.

XXXVII. The second vision which he saw, the vision of wisdom which Enoch, the son of Jared, the son of Malalel, the son of Cainan, the son of Enosh, the son of Seth, the son of Adam, saw.
2 And this *is* the beginning of the words of wisdom which I raised *my voice* to speak and say to those who dwell on the dry ground. Hear, you men of old, and see, you who come after, the words of the Holy
3 One[1] which I will speak before the Lord of Spirits. It would have been better to have said these things before, but from those who
4 come after we will not withhold the beginning of wisdom. Until now there has not been given by the Lord of Spirits such wisdom as I have received in accordance with my insight, in accordance with the wish of the Lord of Spirits by whom the lot of eternal life has
5 been given to me. And three parables were imparted to me, and I raised *my voice* and said to those who dwell on the dry ground,

XXXVIII. The first parable. When the community of the righteous appears, and the sinners are judged for their sins and are driven
2 from the face of the dry ground, and when the Righteous One[1] appears before the chosen righteous whose works are weighed by the Lord of Spirits, and *when* light appears to the righteous and chosen who dwell on the dry ground, where *will be* the dwelling of the sinners, and where the resting-place of those who have denied[2] the Lord of Spirits? It would have been better for them if they had
3 not been born. And when the secrets of the righteous are revealed, the sinners will be judged and the impious driven from the pre-
4 sence of the righteous and the chosen. And from then on those who possess the earth will not be mighty and exalted, nor will they be

---

[2] U[1] 'and to souls and to men'; GMQD' corrupt.
[3] and that all . . . see: GM 'and all his creation, that they might see'; QT[1]UD' corrupt.

[1] the words of the Holy One: so GMTD'FPB'; other MSS 'the holy words'.

[1] the Righteous One: GQTUD'A 'righteousness'.
[2] D' adds 'the name of'.

able to look at the face of the holy ones for the light of the Lord of
Spirits will have appeared on the face of the holy, the righteous and
5 the chosen. And the mighty kings will at that time be destroyed
6 and given into the hand of the righteous and the holy. And from
then on no one will *be able to* seek mercy from the Lord of Spirits, for
their life will be at an end.

XXXIX. And it will come to pass in these[1] days that the chosen and
holy children[2] will come down from the high heavens, and their
2 offspring will become one with the sons of men. In those days
Enoch received books of indignation and anger, and books of
tumult and confusion. And there will be no mercy for them, says
3 the Lord of Spirits. And at that time clouds and[3] a storm-wind
carried me off from the face of the earth, and set me down at the end
4 of heaven. And there I saw another vision, the dwelling of the
5 righteous and the resting-places of the holy.[4] There my eyes saw
their dwelling with the angels[5] and their resting-places with the
holy ones, and they were petitioning and supplicating and praying
on behalf of the sons of men; and righteousness like water flowed
before them and mercy like dew upon the ground. Thus it is among
6 them for ever and ever. And in those days my eyes saw the place of
the chosen ones[6] of righteousness and faith; and there will be
righteousness in their days,[7] and the righteous and chosen will be
7 without number before him for ever and ever. And I saw their
dwelling[8] under the wings of the Lord of Spirits, and all the
righteous and chosen shone[9] before him like the light of fire; and
their mouth was full of blessing, and their lips praised the name of
the Lord of Spirits. And righteousness will not fail before him, and
8 truth will not fail before him.[10] There I wished to dwell, and my

---

[1] GQTUD′ 'those'.   [2] GQT²U 'the children of the chosen and holy'.

[3] clouds and: GMQT¹UD′ om.

[4] righteous . . . holy: Eth.I 'holy . . . righteous'.

[5] GMQTU 'the angels of his righteousness'; D′ 'the holy angels'.

[6] GQT¹U 'And in that place my eyes saw the chosen one (Q 'chosen ones')';
MD′ 'And in those days my eyes saw the chosen one'; T² 'And in those days my eyes
saw the place of the chosen one'.

[7] GMQT¹UD′ 'his days'.   [8] GM 'his dwelling'; D′ 'the dwelling'.

[9] GQT¹UD′ 'were strong'.

[10] and truth . . . before him: some Eth.II MSS om.

soul[11] longed for that dwelling; there had my lot been assigned before, for thus it was decided about me before the Lord of Spirits.
9 And in those days I praised and exalted the name of the Lord of Spirits with blessing and praise, for he has destined me for blessing
10 and praise, in accordance with the wish of the Lord of Spirits. And for a long time my eyes looked at that place, and I blessed him and praised him, saying, Blessed is he, and may he be blessed from the
11 beginning and for ever! And in his presence there is no end. He knew before the world was created what the world would be,[12] even
12 for all the generations which are to come. Those who do not sleep bless you, and they stand before your glory and bless and praise and exalt, saying, Holy, holy, holy, Lord of Spirits; he fills the earth
13 with spirits. And there my eyes saw all those who do not sleep standing before him and blessing and saying, Blessed are you, and
14 blessed is the name of the Lord for ever and ever! And my face was transformed until[13] I was unable to see.

XL.   And after this I saw a thousand thousands and ten thousand times ten thousand, *a multitude* beyond number or reckoning, who
2 stood before the glory of[1] the Lord of Spirits. I looked, and on the four sides of the Lord of Spirits I saw four figures[2] different from those who were standing;[3] and I learnt their names, because the angel who went with me made known to me their names, and
3 showed me all the secret things. And I heard the voices of those
4 four figures as they sang praises before the Lord of Glory.[4] The first
5 voice blesses[5] the Lord of Spirits for ever and ever. And the second voice I heard blessing the Chosen One and the chosen who depend
6 on the Lord of Spirits. And the third voice I heard as they petitioned and prayed[6] on behalf of those who dwell on the dry
7 ground and supplicate in the name of the Lord of Spirits. And the

---

[11] GMTU 'my spirit'.

[12] what the world would be (lit. 'is'): GMQT'UD' 'what is for ever'.

[13] GMQT'UD' 'for'.

---

[1] the glory of: some MSS om.

[2] figures: lit. 'faces' (and so in verses 3, 8; lxiv. 1).

[3] M 'who sleep'; GQT¹(?)UD' 'who do not sleep'.

[4] DYB' 'of Spirits'.   [5] D' adds 'the name of'.

[6] as they . . . prayed: so Eth., but perhaps emend to 'petitioning and praying'.

fourth voice I heard driving away the satans, and not allowing them to come before the Lord of Spirits to accuse those who dwell
8 on the dry ground. And after this I asked the angel of peace who went with me and showed me everything which is secret,[7] Who are these four figures whom I have seen and whose words I have heard
9 and written down? And he said to me, This first one is the holy[8] Michael, the merciful and long-suffering; and the second, who *is* in charge of all the diseases and in charge of all the wounds of the sons of men, is Raphael; and the third, who *is* in charge of all the powers, is the holy[8] Gabriel; and the fourth, who *is* in charge of the repentance *leading* to hope[9] of those who will inherit eternal life, is[10]
10 Phanuel. And these *are* the four angels of the Lord Most High;[11] and the four voices I heard in those days.

XLI. And after this I saw all the secrets of heaven, and how the kingdom is divided, and how the deeds of men are weighed in the
2 balance. There I saw the dwelling of the chosen and the resting-places[1] of the holy; and my eyes saw there all the sinners who deny the name of[2] the Lord of Spirits being driven from there, and they dragged them off,[3] and they were not able to remain because of the
3 punishment which went out from the Lord of Spirits. And there my eyes saw the secrets of the flashes of lightning and of the thunder, and the secrets of the winds, how they are distributed in order to blow over the earth, and the secrets of the clouds and of the dew; and there I saw whence they go out in that place, and *how* from
4 there the dust of the earth is saturated. And there I saw closed storehouses from which the winds are distributed, and the storehouse of the hail,[4] and the storehouse of the mist, and the

---

[7] Some Eth.II MSS add 'and I said to him'.

[8] the holy: Eth.I om.

[9] the repentance *leading* to hope: some Eth.II MSS 'the repentance and hope'; Q corrupt.

[10] GMQT¹UD' 'is named'.   [11] Eth.I 'the Lord of Spirits'.

[1] of the chosen and the resting-places: some Eth: MSS 'of the chosen and the dwelling(s)'; UN 'of the chosen and'; QC' om.; D' 'of the sinners and the communities'.

[2] the name of: ADXY om.   [3] GQD' 'and being dragged off'.

[4] Eth.I HOB' add 'and of the winds'.

storehouse of the clouds;⁵ and its cloud remained over the earth
5 from the beginning of the world. And I saw the chambers⁶ of the
sun and the moon, whence they go out and whither they return,
and their glorious return, and how one is more honoured than the
other, and their magnificent course, and *how* they do not leave the
course, neither adding *anything* to, nor omitting *anything* from their
course, and *how* they keep faith with one another, observing *their*
6 oath. And the sun goes out first and completes its journey at the
command of the Lord of Spirits – and his name endures for ever
7 and ever. And after this *begins* the hidden⁷ and visible journey of the
moon, and it travels the course of its journey in that place by day
and by night. One stands opposite the other before⁸ the Lord of
Spirits, and they give thanks, and sing praises, and do not rest,
8 because their thanksgiving is rest for them. For the shining⁹ sun
makes many revolutions, for a blessing and for a curse, and the
path of the journey of the moon *is* for the righteous light, but for the
sinners darkness, in the name of the· Lord¹⁰ who has created *a
division* between light and darkness, and has divided the spirits of
men, and has established the spirits of the righteous in the name of
9 his righteousness. For no angel hinders,¹¹ and no power¹² is able to
hinder, because the Judge sees them all and judges them all before
himself.

XLII. Wisdom found no place where she could dwell, and her
2 dwelling was in heaven. Wisdom went out in order to dwell among
the sons of men, but did not find a dwelling; wisdom returned to
3 her place and took her seat in the midst of the angels. And iniquity
came out from her chambers; those whom she did not seek she
found, and dwelt among them, like rain in the desert, and like dew
on parched ground.

⁵ and the storehouse of the clouds: so APX; GU²D′ om.; many MSS 'and of the
clouds'.
⁶ Lit. 'storehouses'. ⁷ U 'And after this I saw the hidden'.
⁸ MT¹UD′ add 'the glory of'. ⁹ GQT¹UD′ om.
¹⁰ D′ adds 'of Spirits'. ¹¹ GT¹D′Y 'is able'.
¹² D′ 'and no satan'.

XLIII.   And again I saw flashes of lightning and the stars of heaven,
and I saw how he called them all[1] by their names, and they obeyed

2   him. And I saw the balance of righteousness, how they are weighed
according to their light, according to the width of their areas and
the day of their appearing, and *how* their revolutions produce
lightning;[2] and *I saw* their revolutions according to the number of

3   the angels, and *how* they keep faith with one another. And I asked
the angel who went with me and showed me what was secret, What

4   *are* these? And he said to me, Their likeness has the Lord of Spirits
shown to you; these are the names of the righteous[3] who dwell on
the dry ground and believe in the name of[4] the Lord of Spirits for
ever and ever.

XLIV.   And other things I saw in regard to lightning, how some of
the stars rise and become lightning, but cannot loose their form.[1]

XLV.   And this *is* the second parable about those who deny the
name of the dwelling of the holy ones and of the Lord of Spirits.[1]

2   They will not ascend into heaven, nor will they come upon earth:
such will be the lot of the sinners who deny[2] the name of the Lord of
Spirits, who will thus be kept for the day of affliction and distress.

3   On that day the[3] Chosen One will sit on the throne of glory, and
will choose[4] their works, and their resting-places will be without

---

[1] GMQD′ om.
[2] and *how* . . . lightning: so Eth.I; T² Eth.II 'and their revolution, *and how*
lightning produces lightning'.
[3] Eth.I 'the holy'.
[4] and believe in the name of: D′ 'and do not believe in'.

[1] loose their form: D′ 'stay with them'.

[1] the name . . . Spirits: so T² Eth.II, but T²B′ read 'community' for 'dwelling';
GMQT¹U 'the name of the dwelling of the holy ones and the Lord of Spirits' (M
om. 'the name of'); D′N 'the name of the Lord of Spirits and of the community (N
'*and* the dwelling') of the holy ones'.
[2] GQTU 'have denied'.   [3] GQT¹UD′ 'my'.
[4] So all Eth. MSS (perhaps a mistranslation of an Aramaic word which can mean
both 'to choose' and 'to test').

number; and their spirits[5] within them will grow strong when they see my Chosen One[6] and those who appeal to my[7] holy and[8]
4 glorious name. And on that day I will cause my Chosen One to dwell among them,[9] and I will transform heaven and make it an
5 eternal blessing and light. And I will transform the dry ground and make it a blessing, and I will cause my chosen ones to dwell upon
6 it; but those who commit sin and evil will not tread upon it. For I have seen, and have satisfied with peace, my righteous ones, and have placed them before me; but for the sinners my judgement[10] draws near before me,[11] that I may destroy them from the face of the earth.

XLVI.   And there I saw one who had a head of days, and his head *was* white like wool; and with him *there was* another, whose face had the appearance of a man, and his face *was* full of grace, like one of
2 the holy angels. And I asked one of the holy angels[1] who went with me, and showed me all the secrets, about that Son of Man,[2] who he was, and whence he was, *and* why he went with the Head[3] of Days.
3 And he answered me and said to me, This is the Son of Man who has righteousness, and with whom righteousness dwells; he will reveal all the treasures of that which is secret, for the Lord of Spirits has chosen him, and through uprightness his lot has surpassed all[4]
4 before the Lord of Spirits for ever. And this Son of Man whom you have seen will rouse the kings and the powerful from their resting-places, and the strong from their thrones, and will loose the reins of
5 the strong, and will break the teeth of the sinners. And he will cast down the kings from their thrones and from their kingdoms, for

---

[5] Eth.I 'souls'.   [6] Some Eth. MSS 'my chosen ones'; D' corrupt.
[7] C' 'his'.   [8] holy and: GMQT¹UD' om.
[9] C 'I will cause him to dwell among my chosen ones', and so in effect G; QUD'Y¹ read 'my chosen ones', but in other respects are corrupt or defective.
[10] T² and some Eth.II MSS 'but for the sinners judgement'; GMQT¹U 'but the judgement of the sinners'.
[11] D'(?) 'but the sinners draw near before me *in* judgement'.

[1] Eth.I and BCDP¹ 'one of the angels'; C' 'the angel of peace'.
[2] D' 'about the one who was born from men'.
[3] P¹ 'the Ancient'.
[4] Lit. 'his lot has conquered all'; GMT¹UD'EFH¹K 'his lot has been victorious'; CDY 'he has surpassed all'; Q defective.

they do not exalt him, and do not praise him, and do not humbly
6 acknowledge whence *their* kingdom was given to them. And he will
cast down the faces of the strong, and shame will fill them, and
darkness will be their dwelling, and worms will be their resting-
place; and they will have no hope of rising from their resting-
7 places, for they do not exalt the name of the Lord of Spirits. And
these are they who judge the stars of heaven, and raise their hands
against the Most High, and trample upon the dry ground, and
dwell upon it; and all their deeds show iniquity,[5] and their power
rests on their riches, and their faith is in the gods which they have
made with their hands, and they deny the name of the Lord of
8 Spirits.[6] And they will be driven from the houses of his congregation,[7] and of the faithful who depend on the name of[8] the Lord
of Spirits.

XLVII.   And in those days the prayer of the righteous and the blood
of the righteous[1] will have ascended from the earth before the Lord
2 of Spirits. In these days the holy ones who dwell in the heavens
above will unite with one voice, and supplicate, and pray, and
praise, and give thanks, and bless in the name of[2] the Lord of
Spirits, because of the blood of the righteous which has been
poured out, and *because of* the prayer of the righteous, that it may
not cease[3] before the Lord of Spirits, that justice may be done to
3 them, and *that* their patience may not have to last for ever. And in
those days I saw the Head[4] of Days sit down on the throne of his

---

⁵ So UEN²: QB′ 'and all their deeds *are* iniquity'; all other MSS, although
differing in detail, have a double reading, e.g. GMD′ 'and all their deeds show
iniquity, and all their deeds *are* iniquity'.

⁶ and they deny . . . Spirits: C′ om.; G om. 'the name of'.

⁷ GT¹ 'And they persecute the houses of his congregation'; MU have an impossible combination of both readings; D′ 'And they will desire the congregation of his
houses'.   ⁸ the name of: D′ om.

¹ and the blood of the righteous: here all MSS except MQ have 'the righteous' in
the singular, but the form is to be understood as a collective (cp. verse 4); M does
have 'the righteous' in the plural; Q om. 'the blood' and reads 'and of righteousness'. The preceding and following occurrences of 'the righteous' in verses 1f. are all
in the plural.

² in the name of: U om.; GMQD′ABCE 'the name of'.

³ Or 'that it may not be in vain'.   ⁴ C′ 'the Ancient'.

glory, and the books of the living were opened before him, and all his host, which *dwells* in the heavens above, and his council were standing before him. And the hearts of the holy ones were full of joy that the number of righteousness[5] had been reached,[6] and the prayer of the righteous[7] had been heard, and the blood of the righteous[8] had been required before the Lord of Spirits.

XLVIII. And in that place I saw an inexhaustible spring of right-eousness, and many springs of wisdom surrounded it, and all the thirsty drank from them and were filled with wisdom, and their dwelling *was* with the righteous and the holy and the chosen. And at that hour that Son of Man was named in the presence of the Lord of Spirits, and his name *was named* before the Head of Days. Even before the sun and the constellations were created, before the stars of heaven were made, his name was named before the Lord of Spirits. He will be a staff to the righteous and the holy,[1] that they may lean on him and not fall, and he *will be* the light of the nations, and he will be the hope of those who grieve in their hearts. All those who dwell upon the dry ground will fall down and worship before him, and they will bless, and praise, and celebrate with psalms the name of[2] the Lord of Spirits. And because of this he was chosen and hidden before him before the world was created, and for ever. But the wisdom of the Lord of Spirits has revealed him to the holy and the righteous, for he has kept safe the lot of the righteous, for they have hated and rejected this world of iniquity, and all its works and its ways they have hated in the name of the Lord of Spirits; for in his name they are saved, and he is the one who will require their lives.[3] And in those days the kings of the earth and the strong who possess the dry ground will have downcast faces because of the

[5] MD′ 'of the righteous' – the form is in the singular, but is to be understood as a collective (cp. below and verse 1).

[6] Eth.I 'had drawn near'.

[7] of the righteous: QC′ 'of the holy' – in both cases the forms are plural.

[8] of the righteous: the form is singular, but is to be understood as a collective (cp. above and verse 1).

[1] and the holy: GMQT¹UD′ om. [2] the name of: GTU om.

[3] and he . . . their lives: G(?) 'and according to his wish has it been in regard to their lives'; Q corrupt; D′OYB′ 'and his wish has been for their lives'.

works of their hands, for on the day of their distress and trouble
9 they will not save themselves. And I will give them into the hands
of my chosen ones; like straw in the fire, and like lead in water, so
they will burn before the righteous,[4] and sink before the holy,[5] and
10 no trace will be found of them. And on the day of their trouble there
will be rest[6] on the earth, and they will fall down before him[7] and
will not rise; and there will be no one who will take them with his
hands and raise them, for they denied the Lord of Spirits and his
Messiah. May the name of the Lord of Spirits be blessed!

XLIX.   For wisdom[1] has been poured out like water, and glory will
2 not fail[2] before him for ever and ever. For he *is* powerful in all the
secrets of righteousness, and iniquity will pass away like a shadow,
and will have no existence;[3] for the Chosen One stands before the
Lord of Spirits, and his glory *is* for ever and ever, and his power for
3 all generations. And in him dwells the spirit of wisdom, and the
spirit which gives understanding,[4] and the spirit of knowledge and
4 of power, and the spirit of those who sleep in righteousness. And he
will judge the things that are secret, and no one will be able to say
an idle word before him, for he *has been* chosen[5] before the Lord of
Spirits, in accordance with his wish.

L.   And in those days a change will occur for the holy and the
chosen; the light[1] of days will rest upon them, and glory and
2 honour will return to the holy. And on the day of trouble calamity
will be heaped up[2] over the sinners, but the righteous will conquer

---

[4] GQTUD' 'the holy'.   [5] GMQTU 'the righteous'.
[6] D' 'a stumbling block'.   [7] Eth.I C' 'before them'.

[1] BCX 'the spirit of wisdom'.
[2] D' 'will be inexhaustible' (lit. 'will be uncountable' or 'will be immeasurable').
[3] Lit. 'no place to stand'.
[4] So GQUBPXC': other MSS 'and the spirit of the one who gives
understanding'.
[5] G 'dedicated' or 'devoted'.

[1] T 'the Ancient'.
[2] calamity will be heaped up: G 'on which calamity will have been heaped up';
MT¹U corrupt; Q 'calamity will have been heaped up'; D' 'he will have heaped up
calamity'.

in the name of the Lord of Spirits; and he will show *this* to others
3 that they may repent and abandon the works of their hands. And
they will have no[3] honour before[4] the Lord of Spirits, but in his
name they will be saved; and the Lord of Spirits will have mercy on
4 them, for his mercy *is* great. And he *is* righteous in his judgement,
and before his glory iniquity will not *be able to* stand at his judge-
5 ment: he who does not repent before him will be destroyed. And
from then on I will not have mercy on them, says the Lord of
Spirits.

LI. And in those days the earth will return that which has been
entrusted to it, and Sheol will return that which has been entrusted
to it, that which it has received,[1] and destruction will return what it
2 owes. And he will choose the righteous and holy from among them,
3 for the day has come near that they must be saved. And in those
days the Chosen One[2] will sit on his[3] throne, and all the secrets of
wisdom will flow out from the counsel of his mouth, for the Lord of
4 Spirits has appointed him and glorified him. And in those days the
mountains will leap like rams, and the hills will skip like lambs
5 satisfied with milk, and all will become angels in heaven. Their
faces will shine with joy, for in those days the Chosen One will have
risen; and the earth will rejoice, and the righteous will dwell upon
it, and the chosen will go and walk upon it.

LII. And after those days, in that place where I had seen all the
visions of that which is secret – for I had been carried off by a
2 whirlwind, and they had brought me to the west – there my eyes
saw the secrets of heaven, everything that will occur on earth:[1] a

---

[3] no: U and some Eth.II MSS om.   [4] GMQT¹UD′ 'in the name of'.

[1] the earth . . . has received: so Eth.II, and Q is all but identical; G 'the earth will
return those who are stored up in it, and Sheol will return that which it has
received'; M 'the earth and Sheol will return that which has been entrusted to it,
that which it has received'; TUD′ 'Sheol will return that which has been entrusted
to it, (T² adds 'and the earth') that which it has received'.
[2] QT¹ 'And in those days my Chosen One'; D′ 'and chosen. In those days he'.
[3] GMQT¹UD′ 'my'.

[1] GMQTU 'all the secret *things* of heaven that will occur (QT² add 'on earth')';
D′ 'all the secrets of heaven and what will occur'.

mountain of iron, and a mountain of copper, and a mountain of
silver, and a mountain of gold, and a mountain of soft metal, and a
3 mountain of lead. And I asked the angel who went with me, saying,
4 What are these *things* which I have seen in secret? And he said to
me, All these *things* which you have seen serve the authority of his
5 Messiah, that he may be strong and powerful on the earth. And
that angel of peace answered me, saying, Wait a little, and you will
see,[2] and everything which is secret, which the Lord of Spirits has
6 established,[3] will be revealed to you. And these mountains which
you have seen,[4] the mountain of iron, and the mountain of copper,
and the mountain of silver, and the mountain of gold, and the
mountain of soft metal, and the mountain of lead – all these before
the Chosen One will be like wax before fire, and like the water
which comes down from above on[5] these mountains, and they will
7 become weak under[6] his feet. And it will come to pass in those days
that neither by gold, nor by silver, will men save themselves; they
8 will be unable to save themselves or[7] to flee. And there will be
neither iron for war, nor material[8] for a breast-plate;[9] bronze will
be of no use, and tin will be of no use and will count for nothing,
9 and lead will not be wanted. All these will be wiped out and
destroyed from the face of the earth, when the Chosen One appears
before the Lord of Spirits.

LIII.   And there my eyes saw a deep valley, and its mouth *was*
open;[1] and all those who dwell upon the dry ground and the sea
and the islands will bring gifts and presents and offerings to him,

---

  [2] and you will see: Eth.I om.

  [3] GQT'UD'(?) 'which surrounds the Lord of Spirits'.

  [4] GMQTU 'your eyes have seen'; D' 'you have seen with your eyes'.

  [5] on: D' om.   [6] Many MSS 'before'.

  [7] to save themselves or: GMQD' om.

  [8] material: lit. 'clothing, covering'; for the noun 'material' QD', although corrupt, have verbal forms which may point to an original text 'nor will men put on a
breast-plate'. After 'material' (or its equivalent) GMQT add by dittography 'for
war, nor material'.

  [9] nor material for a breast-plate: U 'nor a coat of mail for the breast'.

---

  [1] So Eth.II: D' is partially corrupt, but reads 'deep valleys, and their mouth(s)
were open'; GMQTU also read 'their mouths' (QT 'their mouth'), but otherwise
have an awkward or corrupt text.

2 but that deep valley will not become full. And their hands commit
evil, and everything at which *the righteous* toil, the sinners evilly
devour;[2] and *so* the sinners will be destroyed from before the Lord
of Spirits, and will be banished from the face of his earth, un-
3 ceasingly,[3] for ever and ever. For I saw[4] the angels of punishment
4 going[5] and preparing all the instruments of Satan. And I asked the
angel of peace who went with me, and I said to him,[6] These
instruments – for whom are they preparing them? And he said to
5 me,[7] They are preparing these[8] for the kings and the powerful of
6 this earth, that by means of them they may be destroyed. And after
this the Righteous and Chosen One will cause the house of his
congregation to appear; from then on, in the name of the Lord of
7 Spirits, they will not be hindered. And before him[9] these mountains will not[10] be *firm* like the earth, and the hills will be like a
spring of water; and the righteous will have rest from the ill-
treatment of the sinners.

LIV. And I looked and turned to another part of the earth, and I
2 saw there a deep valley with burning fire. And they brought the
3 kings and the powerful and threw them into that[1] valley. And there
my eyes saw how they made instruments for them – iron chains of
4 immeasurable weight. And I asked the angel of peace who went
with me, saying, These chain-instruments – for whom are they
5 being prepared? And he said to me, These are being prepared for
the hosts of Azazel, that they may take them and throw them into

----

[2] and everything . . . devour: so Eth.II, but the text is difficult and possibly corrupt; the Eth.I MSS do not provide a better text.

[3] Lit. 'and they will not cease'; T¹D' 'and they will cease' (i.e. 'and they will perish').

[4] Eth.I N add 'all'.

[5] Eth.I and some Eth.II MSS 'remaining'.

[6] and I said to him: so NP²; all other MSS om.

[7] D' 'And he answered me'; GMTD' add 'saying'.

[8] They are preparing these: QU om.; GMT om. 'They are preparing', but read 'these' in the accusative.

[9] before him (lit. 'before his face'): GT¹UD' 'before his righteousness'; M. corrupt.

[10] D'BCXC' om.

[1] Q and some Eth.II MSS 'the'; many MSS add 'deep'.

the lowest part of Hell; and they will cover their jaws with rough
6 stones, as the Lord of Spirits commanded. And Michael and
Gabriel, Raphael[2] and Phanuel – these will take hold of them on
that great day, and throw them[3] on that day into the furnace of
burning fire,[4] that the Lord of Spirits may[5] take vengeance on
them[6] for their iniquity, in that they became servants of Satan and
7 led astray those who dwell upon the dry ground. And in those days
the punishment of the Lord of Spirits will go out, and all the
storehouses of the waters which *are* above the heavens[7] . . . and
8 under the earth[8] will be opened,[9] and all the waters will be joined
with the waters[10] which *are* above the heavens.[11] The water[12] which
is above heaven is male, and the water[13] which *is* under the earth is
9 female. And all those who dwell upon the dry ground and those
10 who dwell under the ends of heaven will be wiped out. And because
of this[14] they will acknowledge[15] their iniquity which they have
committed on the earth, and through this[16] they will be destroyed.

LV. And after this the Head of Days repented and said, I have
destroyed to no purpose all those who dwell upon the dry ground.
2 And he swore by his great Name, From now on I will not act like
this[1] towards all those who dwell upon the dry ground; and I will

² Gabriel, Raphael: MTUD′ 'Raphael, Gabriel'.

³ and throw them: QD′ om.; GM om. 'throw them'.

⁴ GMT¹UD′ 'into the burning furnace'; QY 'into the burning fire'.

⁵ D′ 'for the Lord of Spirits will'.   ⁶ on them: G om.

⁷ All MSS except B′ add 'and in addition to the springs which are under the
heavens' or similar.

⁸ and under the earth: QU 'and the springs which *are* under the earth'; GM
corrupt; D′ om.

⁹ and all the storehouses . . . will be opened: GT¹U 'and will open all the
storehouses . . .'; M 'and all the storehouses . . . will have been opened'; D′ 'and he
will open all the storehouses . . .'.

¹⁰ with the waters: T¹UN om.; Q corrupt.

¹¹ which *are* above the heavens: Eth.I N om.

¹² The water: GMT¹UN 'That'.   ¹³ and the water: D′ 'and that'.

¹⁴ Q 'Because of this'; TUE 'And because'; D′ 'because'.

¹⁵ D′ 'they have not acknowledged'.

¹⁶ and through this: so MT¹U; Q Eth.II 'and because of this'; T² 'and because of
this through this'; G 'and this'; D′ 'and through it'; C′ om.

¹ like this: GMT¹UD′X om.

put a sign in heaven, and it will be a pledge of faith between me and
3 them for ever, so long as heaven *is* above the earth. And this will be
in accordance with my command;[2] when I want to take hold of
them by the hand of the angels on the day of distress and pain in the
face of this my anger and my wrath,[3] my wrath and my anger will
4 remain upon them,[4] says the Lord,[5] the Lord of Spirits. You
powerful kings, who dwell upon the dry ground, will be obliged to
watch my Chosen One[6] sit down on the throne of my glory,[7] and
judge, in the name of the Lord of Spirits, Azazel and all his
associates and all his hosts.

LVI. And I saw there the hosts of the angels of punishment as they
2 went, and they were holding[1] chains of iron and bronze. And I
asked the angel of peace who went with me, saying, To whom are
3 those who are holding *the chains* going? And he said to me, Each to
his own chosen ones and to his own beloved ones,[2] that they may be
4 thrown into the chasm in the depths of the valley. And then that
valley will be filled with their chosen and beloved ones, and the
days of their life will be at an end, and the days of their leading
5 astray will no longer be counted. And in those days the angels will
gather together,[3] and will throw themselves towards the east upon
the Parthians and Medes; they will stir up the kings, so that a
disturbing spirit will come upon them, and they[4] will drive them
from their thrones; and they will come out like lions from their
6 lairs, and like hungry wolves in the middle of their flocks. And they

---

[2] So GT[1]: M 'And this is my command'; Q corrupt; D' 'And it will be in
accordance with my command'; T[2]U Eth.II 'And after this it will be in accordance
with my command'.

[3] Eth.I 'my wrath and my anger'.

[4] my wrath . . . upon them: some Eth.II MSS 'my anger and my wrath will
remain upon them'; UD om. (hmt.); Q 'will remain upon them'; GMT[1]D' 'I will
cause my wrath and my anger to remain upon them'.

[5] the Lord: GMD'BCXB' om.

[6] D' 'my chosen ones'.

[7] GMT[1]UD' 'on the throne of glory'; CH[1]OB' 'at the right hand of the throne of
my glory'.

[1] and they were holding: T[1] om.; Q om. 'and'; MUD' om. 'they were holding'.

[2] GMQT[1]UD' 'To their chosen and their beloved ones'.

[3] GQ 'will return'.   [4] DY 'it'.

will go up and trample upon[5] the land of my[6] chosen ones, and the
land of my[7] chosen ones will become before them a tramping-
7 ground and a beaten track. But the city of my righteous ones will be
a hindrance to their horses, and they will stir up slaughter amongst
themselves, and their *own* right hand will be strong against them;
and a man will not admit to knowing his neighbour or[8] his brother,
nor a son his father or[9] his mother, until through their death[10] there
are corpses enough, and their punishment – it will not be in vain.[11]
8 And in those days Sheol will open its mouth, and they will sink into
it; and their destruction[12] – Sheol will swallow up the sinners
before the face of the chosen.

LVII. And it came to pass after this that I saw another host of
chariots, with men riding on them, and they came upon the wind[1]
2 from the east and from the west to the south. And the sound of the
noise of their chariots was heard,[2] and when this commotion
occurred, the holy ones observed *it* from heaven, and the pillars of
the earth were shaken from their foundations, and *the sound* was
heard from the ends of earth to the ends of heaven[3] throughout one
3 day.[4] And all will fall down and worship the Lord of Spirits. And
this is the end of the second parable.

LVIII. And I began to speak the third[1] parable about the righteous
2 and about the chosen. Blessed *are* you, the righteous and chosen,

---

[5] T[1]U 'and cover'.   [6] my: so D'; GQT[1] 'his'; MT[2]U Eth.II 'their'.
[7] my: so D'; GMQT[1]U and most Eth.II MSS 'his'; T[2]CX 'their'.
[8] his neighbour or: GMQT[1]UD' om.
[9] his father or: MT[1]UD' om.
[10] through their death: G om.; M corrupt; D'(?) 'among them'; Q corrupt in
entire passage 'until . . . in vain'.
[11] GMUD' 'and their punishment shall not be in vain' (D' om. 'and').
[12] G adds 'will cease', and MQT[2]U make similar additions. But in no case do the
additions provide an entirely satisfactory text.

[1] MQTUD' 'winds'; G corrupt.
[2] BCX om. 'the sound of'; MT[1]UD' om. 'was heard'.
[3] D' from the ends of heaven to the ends of earth'; GMTU 'from end to end of
heaven'; Q 'from the ends of heaven'.   [4] D' 'hour'.

[1] the third: D' 'another' *or* 'the second'.

3 for your lot *will be* glorious! And the righteous will be in the light of
the sun, and the chosen in the light of eternal life; and there will be
no end to the days of their life, and the days of the holy will be
4 without number. And they will seek the light, and will find righteousness with the Lord of Spirits. Peace *be* to the righteous with[2] the
5 Lord of the world![3] And after this it will be said to the holy that they
should seek in heaven[4] the secrets of righteousness, the lot of faith;
for it has become bright as the sun[5] upon the dry ground, and
6 darkness has passed away. And there will be ceaseless light, and to
a limit of days they will not come, for darkness will have been
destroyed previously; and the light will endure before the Lord of
Spirits, and the light of uprightness will endure before the Lord of
Spirits for ever.

LIX. And in those days my eyes saw the secrets of the flashes of
lightning, and the lights,[1] and the regulations governing them;[2]
and they flash for a blessing or for a curse, as the Lord of Spirits
2 wishes. And there I saw the secrets of the thunder, and *how* when it
crashes in heaven above, the sound of it is heard; and they[3] showed
me the dwellings of the dry ground,[4] and the sound of the thunder
for peace and for blessing, or for a curse, according to the word of[5]
3 the Lord of Spirits. And after this all the secrets of the lights and of
the flashes of lightning were shown to me; they flash to bring
blessing and satisfaction.

LX. In the five hundredth year, in the seventh month, on the
fourteenth *day* of the month in the life of Enoch. In that parable I

---

  [2] GQT'U 'in the name of'; D' 'in the peace of'.
  [3] B 'the Lord of Spirits'; D' 'the Lord for ever'.
  [4] GMTUD' 'to the holy in heaven that they should seek'.
  [5] MD'B 'for the sun has become bright'.

  [1] GMTUE 'and of the lights'; Q 'of the lights'.
  [2] Lit. 'and their regulation', but could also be translated 'and their judgement'.
  [3] So some Eth.II MSS: U corrupt; all other MSS 'he'.
  [4] and they . . . ground: the text makes no sense and is probably an interpolation
(although it is just possible that an original Aramaic 'and they showed me the
dwellings of the lightning' was misread by the translator).
  [5] according to the word of: G 'before'.

saw how the heaven of heavens was shaken violently, and the host
of the Most High and the angels, a thousand thousands and ten
2 thousand times ten thousand, were extremely disturbed. And then
I saw the Head of Days sitting[1] on the throne of his glory, and the
3 angels and the righteous were standing around him. And a great
trembling seized me, and fear took hold of me,[2] and my loins
collapsed and gave way, and my whole being[3] melted,[4] and I fell
4 upon my face. And the holy Michael sent another holy angel, one
of the holy angels,[5] and he raised me; and when he raised me,[6] my
spirit[7] returned, for I had been unable to endure the sight of that
5 host, and the disturbance, and the shaking of heaven. And the
holy[8] Michael said to me, What sight has disturbed you like this?
Until today has the day of his mercy lasted, and he has been
merciful and long suffering towards those who dwell upon the dry
6 ground. And when the day, and the power, and the punishment
and the judgement come, which the Lord of Spirits has prepared
for those who worship[9] the righteous judgement,[10] and for those
who deny the righteous judgement,[11] and for those who take his
name in vain — and that day has been prepared, for the chosen a
7 covenant, but for the sinners a visitation. And on that day two
monsters[12] will be separated[13] from one another; a female monster,

[1] GMT¹UD′ 'And the Head of Days was sitting' (M om. 'And'); Q 'Then I saw
the Head of Days sit'.
[2] MT¹UD′ om. 'took hold of me'; Q 'And trembling seized me, and great fear
seized me and took hold of me'.
[3] and my whole being: DY om. 'and'; FNX 'and my mind'.
[4] and my loins . . . melted: G 'and my loins gave way, and my whole being fell';
MQD′ 'and my loins gave way, and my (M om. 'my') mind'; T 'and my loins
collapsed and gave way, and my whole being'; U 'and my loins collapsed, and my
whole being gave way'.
[5] GMTUD′ 'And Michael sent another angel from among the holy ones'; Q
'And the holy angel Michael, one of the holy ones, was sent'. Some Eth.II MSS read
'one of the holy ones' for 'one of the holy angels'.
[6] and when he raised me: GMQT¹U om. (hmt.).
[7] Q 'soul'.   [8] the holy: Eth.I om.
[9] U 'who do not worship'.
[10] judgement: so all Eth. MSS, but possibly a mistranslation of an original
'judge'.
[11] and for those . . . judgement: UDE om. (hmt.); Q 'and for those who deny it
(? 'him')'.   [12] DOY 'two lions'; D′ 'two tigers'; G 'two large monsters'.
[13] M 'were separated'.

whose name *is* Leviathan, to dwell in the depths of the sea above
8 the springs of the waters; and the name of the male *is* Behemoth,
who occupies with his breast an immense desert[14] named Dendayn,[15]
on the east of the garden where the chosen and righteous dwell,[16]
where my great-grandfather[17] was received,[18] who was[19] the
seventh from Adam, the first man whom the Lord of Spirits made.
9 And I asked that[20] other angel to show me the power of those
monsters, how they were separated on one[21] day and thrown, one
into the depths of the sea, and the other onto the dry ground of the
10 desert. And he said to me, Son of Man, you here wish to know what
11 is secret. And the other angel spoke to me,[22] *the one* who went with
me and showed me what *is* secret, what *is* first and last in heaven, in
the heights, and under[23] the dry ground, in the depths, and at the
ends of heaven, and at the foundations of heaven, and in[24] the
12 storehouses of the winds;[25] and how the spirits[26] are distributed,
and how they are weighed, and how the springs and the winds[27] are
counted according to the power of *their* spirit;[28] and the power of
the light of the moon[29] . . . and the divisions of the stars according to
13 their names, and *how* all the divisions are made; and the thunder[30]
according to the places where it falls; and all the divisions that are
made in lightning that it may flash, and its hosts, how they quickly
14 obey; for the thunder has fixed intervals *which* have been given to

---

[14] an immense desert: lit. 'a desert that cannot be seen'. In the light of the LXX of Gen. i.2 perhaps to be translated 'a waste desert'.

[15] GTUD' 'Dundayn' or similar; Q 'Yendayn'.

[16] MT'UD' 'where the chosen and righteous *are*'.

[17] B 'your great-grandfather'; C' 'my great-grandfather Enoch'.

[18] where my . . . received: D' 'where the man was transformed'.

[19] who was: GMT'UD' om.   [20] GMT'UD'N 'the'; DHOB' 'this'.

[21] D' 'that'.   [22] to me: D' om.; GQT'U 'to him'.

[23] So GMD': all other MSS 'on'.   [24] in: G om.

[25] GQT 'of the spirits' (but here and in the next verse it is possible that the common word 'spirit' has the meaning 'wind'); D' 'of the Lord of Spirits'.

[26] Or 'the winds'; U om.

[27] the springs and the winds: so Eth.II; Eth.I (U corruptly) 'the springs of the spirits (or 'winds')', but possibly a mistake for 'the gates of the winds'.

[28] Or 'according to the power of the wind'.

[29] All MSS add 'and how *there is* a power of righteousness' (or 'and according to the power of righteousness'). The words are unintelligible, but are possibly a gloss on 'according to the power of *their* spirit'.

[30] D' 'and *how* all the divisions are made in the thunder'.

its sound for waiting; and the thunder and the lightning are not
separate, and *although* not one, through a spirit the two of them
15 move inseparably; for when the lightning flashes, the thunder
utters its voice, and the spirit at the proper time[31] causes *it* to rest,
and divides equally between them; for the storehouse of the times
for their occurrence is *like* that of the sand, and each of them at the
proper time[32] is held by a rein, and turned back by the power of the
spirit, and likewise driven forward, according to the number of the
16 regions of the earth. And the spirit of the sea is male and strong,
and according to the power of its strength *the spirit* turns it back
with a rein, and likewise it is driven forward and scattered amongst
17 all the mountains of the earth. And the spirit of the hoar-frost is its
18 *own* angel; and the spirit of the hail is a good angel. And the spirit of
the snow has withdrawn because of its power, and it has a special
spirit; and that which rises from it is like smoke, and its name *is*
19 frost. And the spirit of the mist is not associated with them[33] in
their storehouses, but has a special storehouse; for its course *is*
glorious[34] both in light and in darkness, and in winter and in
20 summer, and in its storehouse is an angel.[35] The spirit of the dew
has its dwelling at the ends of heaven, and it is connected with the
storehouses of the rain; and its course *is* in winter and in summer,
and its clouds and the clouds of the mist are associated, and one
21 gives to the other. And when the spirit of the rain moves from its
storehouse, the angels come and open the storehouse, and bring it
out; and when it is scattered over all the dry ground, it joins with all
the water that *is* on the dry ground; and whenever it joins with the
22 water that *is* on the dry ground,[36] . . . for the waters are for those
who dwell upon the dry ground, for *they are* nourishment for the dry
ground from the Most High who is in[37] heaven; therefore there is a

---

[31] at the proper time: or 'immediately'.
[32] at the proper time: GMTUD′ om.
[33] is not . . . them: Q 'joins with it'; D′ 'does not dwell with them'.
[34] Lit. 'in glory' or 'possesses glory', but the meaning is obscure.
[35] and in its storehouse . . . angel: so T¹U; T² 'and in its storehouse is light';
GMQD′ 'and its storehouse is an angel'; Eth.II 'and its storehouse *is* light, and it is
its angel'.
[36] and whenever . . . dry ground: QADOYB′C′ om. (probably a dittograph). If
not, the apodosis of the sentence has been lost.
[37] Some Eth. MSS 'from'.

23 fixed measure for the rain, and the angels comprehend it. All these
24 things I saw towards the Garden of Righteousness. And the angel
of peace who was with me said to me, These two monsters, prepared in accordance with the greatness of the Lord,[38] will be fed[39]
that the punishment of the Lord[40] . . . in vain. And children will be
25 killed[41] with their mothers, and sons[42] with their fathers. When the
punishment of the Lord of Spirits rests upon them, it will remain
resting that the punishment of the Lord of Spirits may not come in
vain[43] upon these. Afterwards the judgement will be according to
his mercy and his patience.

LXI. And in those days I saw long cords given to those[1] angels,
and they acquired wings for themselves, and flew, and went to-
2 wards the north. And I asked the angel, saying[2] Why did these take
the long[3] cords and go? And he said to me, They went that they
3 may measure.[4] And the angel who went with me said to me, These
will bring the measurements of the righteous and the ropes of the
righteous to the righteous,[5] that they may rely on the name of the
4 Lord of Spirits for ever and ever. The chosen will begin to dwell

---

[38] D′ 'prepared for the great day of the Lord'.

[39] G(?)D′ 'will provide food' (but could be impersonal with a passive sense 'will
be fed'); Q corrupt, but perhaps 'will feed them'.

[40] Eth.I 'the Lord of Spirits'. BCXC′ add 'may not be'; E adds 'may not come'.
D′ (probably correctly) continues for the remainder of the chapter, 'may rest upon
them that the punishment of the Lord of Spirits may not come in vain. And it will
kill children with their mothers and children with their fathers, when the punishment of the Lord of Spirits rests upon all. Afterwards the judgement etc.' In the
other MSS the words 'may rest upon them that the punishment of the Lord of
Spirits may not come' seem to have been omitted by mistake. The correction of the
mistake led to the text printed above, but the overfull text of GMQ (cp. note 43)
supports D′.

[41] GQTU 'And it will kill children'.   [42] GMTU 'children'.

[43] As part of their correction GMQ repeat here 'And it will kill children with
their mothers and children with their fathers when the punishment of the Lord of
Spirits rests' (cp. D′, note 40).

[1] those: Q 'the two'.
[2] GTUD′ 'saying to him'; M 'who was with me'.
[3] GMQT′UD′ om.
[4] And he said . . . may measure: QEH om.; MUD om. 'they went'.
[5] to the righteous: M Eth.II (except N) om.

with the chosen, and these measurements will be given to faith,
5 and will strengthen righteousness.[6] And these measurements will
reveal all the secrets of the depths of the earth, and those who were
destroyed by the desert, and those who were devoured by the fish of
the sea and by animals,[7] that they may[8] return and rely on the day
of the[9] Chosen One; for no one will be destroyed before the Lord of
6 Spirits, and no one can be destroyed. And all those in the heavens
above received a command, and power[10] and one voice and one
7 light like fire were given to them.[11] And him, before everything,[12]
they blessed and exalted and praised in wisdom; and they showed
8 themselves wise in speech and in the spirit of life. And the Lord of
Spirits set the Chosen One on the throne of his[13] glory, and he will
judge all the works of the holy ones[14] in heaven above, and in the
9 balance he will weigh their deeds.[15] And when he lifts his face to
judge their secret ways according to the word of the name of the
Lord of Spirits, and their path according to the way of the righteous
judgement of the Lord Most High,[16] they will all speak with one
voice, and bless, and praise, and exalt and glorify[17] the name of the
10 Lord of Spirits. And he[18] will call all the host of the heavens, and all
the holy ones above, and the host of the Lord, the Cherubim, and
the Seraphim and the Ophannim, and all the angels of power, and
all the angels of the principalities, and the Chosen One, and the
other host which *is* upon the dry ground and[19] over the water, on
11 that day, and they will raise one voice, and will bless, and praise,

---

[6] So Eth.I: Eth.II (by a mistake) 'the word of righteousness'.

[7] by the fish . . . by animals: TU 'by animals and those who were devoured by the fish of the sea'; GMD' 'by storehouses and those who were devoured by the fish of the sea'; Q 'by the fish of the sea'.

[8] D' adds 'all'.   [9] T 'my'.

[10] BCX 'and one power'; C om. 'and one voice'.

[11] were given to them: so BCXC'; all other MSS om. For the whole verse U D' have 'And those in the heavens above (D' add. 'and all the hosts') received a command and one voice and one light like fire'.

[12] Lit. 'before a word' (i.e. before uttering any other word).

[13] Eth.I om.   [14] Q 'the righteous'.

[15] G 'they will weigh their deeds'; MQUD'B' 'will their deeds be weighed'.

[16] Eth.I 'of the Lord of Spirits' (but U om. by hmt. 'and their path . . . judgement of the Lord of Spirits').

[17] Eth.I N 'hallow'.   [18] MD' 'they'.

[19] So some Eth.II MSS: all other MSS om.

and glorify[20] and exalt[21] *him*, in the spirit of faith, and in the spirit of wisdom and of patience,[22] and in the spirit of mercy, and in the spirit of justice and of peace, and in the spirit of goodness; and they will all say with one voice, Blessed is he, and blessed be[23] the name
12 of the Lord of Spirits for ever and ever. All those who do not sleep in heaven above will bless him; all his[24] holy ones who *are* in heaven will bless him, and all the chosen ones who dwell in the Garden of Life, and every spirit of light which is able to bless, and praise, and exalt and hallow your holy[25] name, and all flesh which beyond *its*
13 power will praise and bless your name for ever and ever. For great *is* the mercy of the Lord of Spirits, and *he is* long-suffering; and all his works and all his forces, as many as he has made,[26] he has revealed to the righteous and the chosen in the name of the Lord of Spirits.

LXII. And thus[1] the Lord commanded the kings and the mighty and the exalted, and those who dwell upon the earth,[2] and said, Open your eyes, and raise your horns,[3] if you are able to acknow-
2 ledge the Chosen One. And the Lord of Spirits sat[4] on the throne of his glory, and the spirit of righteousness was poured out on him, and the word of his mouth kills all the sinners and all the lawless,
3 and they are destroyed[5] before him. And on that day all the kings and the mighty and the exalted, and those who possess the earth,[6] will stand up; and they will see and recognise how he sits on the

---

[20] and glorify: Eth.I om.   [21] and exalt: G om.

[22] and of patience: so some Eth.II MSS; JLA' 'and in the spirit of patience'; other MSS 'and in patience'.

[23] and blessed be: D'P¹ 'and they will bless'.

[24] Eth.I BXYC' 'the'.   [25] Eth.I 'blessed'.

[26] and all his forces . . . made: so Eth.II; M 'and the whole extent of his works'; T¹ 'and everything that he has made'; T² 'and all his forces and everything that he has made'; GQD' corrupt; U defective.

[1] D' 'And after this'.

[2] Q 'who dwell upon the dry ground'; D' 'who possess the earth'.

[3] and raise your horns: U om.; D' 'and raise your eyelids'.

[4] So all MSS, but often emended to 'set him'.

[5] GQTU 'and all the lawless are destroyed' (U om. 'all'); MDY 'and all the lawless; they are destroyed'.

[6] Some Eth.II MSS 'dry ground'.

throne of his glory, and the righteous are judged in righteousness[7]
4 before him, and no idle word is spoken before him. And pain will
come upon them as *upon* a woman in labour for whom giving birth
is difficult, when her child enters the mouth of the womb, and she
5 has difficulty in giving birth. And one half of them will look at the
other, and they will be terrified, and will cast down their faces, and
pain will take hold of them, when they see that Son of a Woman[8]
6 sitting on the throne of his glory. And the mighty kings,[9] and all
those who possess the earth, will praise and bless and exalt him
7 who rules everything which is hidden.[10] For from the beginning the
Son of Man was hidden, and the Most High kept him in the
8 presence of his power, and revealed him *only* to the chosen; and the
community of the holy and the chosen will be sown, and all the
9 chosen will stand before him on that day. And all the mighty
kings,[11] and the exalted, and those who rule the dry ground, will
fall down before him on their faces and worship; and they will set
their hope upon that Son of Man, and will entreat him, and will
10 petition for mercy from him. But that Lord of Spirits will then[12] so
press them that they will hasten to go out from before him, and
their faces will be filled with shame, and the darkness will grow
11 deeper on their faces. And the angels of punishment will take
them,[13] that they may repay them for the wrong which they did to
12 his children[14] and to his chosen ones.[15] And they[16] will become a
spectacle to the righteous[17] and to his[18] chosen ones; they will

---

[7] and the righteous . . . righteousness: NOB' om. 'in righteousness'; GMQD' 'and righteousness is judged'; T 'and righteousness does not fail'; U defective.

[8] GQTUD' 'Son of Man'.

[9] GMQU 'And the kings and the mighty'.

[10] Or (less plausibly) 'who rules everything, who was hidden'.

[11] GMQTD'KN 'And all the kings and the mighty'; EH 'And all the mighty'; BX 'And all the kings'.

[12] GMTUD' om.

[13] M 'And the angels will take them for punishment' (and so probably intended by T²); T¹ 'And they will hand them over to the angels for punishment'; GQD' make no sense; U defective throughout verses 11f.

[14] to his children: QOB' om.

[15] and to his chosen ones: OB' om.; Q 'to his Chosen One'.

[16] QD'OB' 'it'.

[17] and to his chosen ones . . . to the righteous: some Eth.II MSS om.

[18] D' 'my'.

rejoice over them, for the anger of the Lord of Spirits will rest upon them, and the sword of the Lord of Spirits will be drunk with them.

13 And the righteous and the chosen will be saved on that day, and they will never see the face of the sinners and the lawless from then

14 on. And the Lord of Spirits will remain over them, and with that Son of Man they will dwell, and[19] eat, and lie down, and rise up for

15 ever and ever. And the righteous and chosen will have risen from the earth, and will have ceased to cast down their faces, and will

16 have put on the garment of life.[20] And this will be a garment of life[21] from the Lord of Spirits; and your garments will not wear out, and your glory will not fail before the Lord of Spirits.

LXIII. In those days the mighty kings[1] who possess the dry ground[2] will entreat the angels of his punishment[3] to whom they have been handed over that they[4] might give them a little respite, and[5] that they might fall down and worship before the Lord of

2 Spirits, and confess their sin before him. And they will bless and praise the Lord of Spirits, and say, Blessed be the Lord of Spirits and the Lord of kings, the Lord of the mighty and the Lord of the

3 rich,[6] and the Lord of glory and the Lord of wisdom! And everything secret is clear before you,[7] and your power *is* for all generations,[8] and your glory for ever and ever; deep, and without number, are all your secrets, and your righteousness is beyond

4 reckoning.[9] Now we realise that we ought to praise and bless the

5 Lord of kings and the one who is king over all kings. And they will say, Would that we might be given a respite, that we might praise and thank and bless him,[10] and make our confession before his[11]

---

[19] dwell and: GMQTUN[1] om.; D' '. . . Son of Man, and they will eat'.

[20] Eth.I and JNP[1](?)C' 'glory'.

[21] GMTUD' 'And this shall be your garment, the garment of life'.

[1] Eth.I 'the kings and the mighty'; AEHKNC' 'the kings'.

[2] QDY 'the earth'.   [3] QT 'of punishment'; U 'of his anger'.

[4] So H²C': all other MSS 'he'.   [5] Eth.I om.

[6] U 'exalted'.   [7] before you: so C'; all other MSS om.

[8] GQTD' 'And in everything secret your power shines for all generations'; M corrupt; U defective.

[9] C' 'deep are all your secrets, and your righteousness is beyond measure'.

[10] praise . . . him: GMTUD' 'sing praises and give thanks'; Q 'praise and thank him'.   [11] GQTUD' 'your'.

6 glory. And now we long for a little respite, but do not find *it*; we are driven off, and do not obtain *it*; and the light has passed away from

7 before us, and darkness *will be* our dwelling for ever and ever. For we have not made our confession before him, and we have not praised the name of the Lord of kings,[12] and we have not praised the Lord[13] for all his works,[14] but our hope has been on the sceptre

8 of[15] our kingdom and of our glory.[16] And on the day of our affliction and distress he does not save us, and we find no respite to make our confession that our Lord is faithful in all his doings, and in all[17] his judgements and his justice, and *that* his judgements show no

9 respect for persons. And we pass away from before him because of

10 our works, and all our sins have been counted exactly. Then they will say to them, Our souls are sated with possessions gained through iniquity, but they do not prevent our going down into the

11 flames[18] of the torment of Sheol. And after this their faces will be filled with darkness and shame before that Son of Man, and they will be driven from before him, and the sword will dwell[19] among

12 them before him. And thus says the Lord of Spirits, This is the law and the judgement for the mighty and the kings and the exalted, and for those who possess the dry ground, before the Lord of Spirits.

1, 2 **LXIV.** And I saw other figures hidden in that place. I heard the voice of the angel saying, These are the angels who came down from heaven[1] onto the earth, and revealed what is secret to the sons of men, and led astray the sons of men so that they committed sin.

---

[12] GD'EFC' 'the name of the Lord of Spirits (D' adds 'and of kings')'; Q 'the Lord of spirits and his name'; M 'the name of the Lord of lords'.

[13] GMQTD' 'our Lord'; U defective.

[14] for all his works: GMQT'UD' om.

[15] the sceptre of: so some MSS; other MSS 'the throne of', or 'the sceptre of the throne of', or 'the throne of the sceptre of'; BCX om.

[16] and of our glory: UD' om.; GM 'and on our glory'; Q 'and of our glory and of our riches'.

[17] in all: GMTUD' om.; Q corrupt.

[18] the flames: D' om.; GQU 'the heart'.

[19] D' 'may the sword dwell'.

[1] from heaven: GMQUD' om.

LXV.   And in those days Noah[1] saw that the earth had tilted, and
2 that its destruction was near. And he[2] set off from there, and went
to the ends of the earth, and cried out to his[3] great-grandfather
Enoch; and Noah said[4] three times in a bitter voice, Hear me, hear
3 me, hear me! And he[5] said to him, Tell me what it is that is being
done on the earth that the earth is so afflicted and shaken, lest I be
4 destroyed with it. And immediately there was a great disturbance
on the earth, and a voice was heard from heaven, and I fell upon
5 my face. And my great-grandfather Enoch came and stood by me,
and said to me, Why did you cry out to me with such bitter crying
6 and weeping? And a command has gone out from before the Lord
against those who dwell upon the dry ground that this must be
their end, for they have learnt all the secrets of the angels, and all
the wrongdoing of the satans, and all their secret power, and all
the power[6] of those who practise magic arts, and the power of
enchantments, and the power[7] of those who cast molten images for
7 all the earth; and further[8] how silver is produced from the dust of
8 the earth, and how soft metal occurs on the earth; for lead and tin
are not[9] produced from the earth like the former; there is a spring
which produces them, and an angel who stands in it, and that
9 angel distributes *them*. And after this my great-grandfather Enoch
took hold of me with his hand,[10] and raised me, and said to me, Go,
for I have asked the Lord of Spirits about this disturbance on the
10 earth. And he said to me, Because of their iniquity their judgement
has been completed, and they[11] will no longer be counted before

---

[1] T 'I Noah'.   [2] T 'I'.   [3] T 'my'.

[4] T 'and I said'; QD′ 'and Noah said to him'.

[5] GMQT′UD′ 'I'.

[6] and all their secret power, and all the power: GTD′ 'and all their power, the
most secret secrets, and all the power'; M(?) 'and all the power of the most secret
secrets, and all the power'; QUAEHN¹ 'and all the secret power' (QAN¹ om.
'secret').

[7] of enchantments and the power: BX om.; Q 'of those who practise enchantments and the power'.

[8] GTUD′ om.   [9] D′ om.

[10] GQD′ 'by my hand'.

[11] So M: all other MSS have verb in singular. But the text appears to be corrupt
and may represent a mistranslation of an original Aramaic 'their judgement has
been completed and will not be withheld before me'.

me; because of the **sorceries**[12] which they have searched out and learnt, the earth[13] and those who dwell upon it will be destroyed.
11 And for these there will be no place of refuge for ever, for they showed to them what is secret, and they have been condemned;[14] but not so for you,[15] my son; the Lord of Spirits knows that you *are*
12 pure and innocent of this reproach concerning the secrets. And he has established your name among the holy, and will keep you from amongst those who dwell upon the dry ground; and he has destined your offspring in righteousness[16] to be kings[17] and for great honours, and from your offspring will flow out a spring of the righteous and holy without number for ever.

LXVI.   And after this he showed me the angels of punishment who were ready to come and release all the forces of the water which is under the earth in order to bring judgement and destruction on all
2 those who reside and dwell[1] upon the dry ground. And the Lord of Spirits commanded the angels who were *then* coming out not to raise *their* hands, but to keep watch; for those angels were in charge
3 of the forces of the waters. And I came out from before Enoch.

LXVII.   And in those days the word of the Lord came to me, and he said to me, Noah, behold[1] your lot has come up before me, a lot
2 without reproach, a lot of love and of uprightness. And now the angels are making[2] a wooden *structure*, and when the angels come out[3] for that *task*, I will put my hand on it, and keep it safe, and from it will come the seed of life, and a change shall take place that

---

[12] sorceries: all MSS 'months'. But the text makes little sense, and 'months' has commonly been taken as a mistranslation of the Hebrew and Aramaic word for 'sorceries'.

[13] and learnt, the earth: so GTU; MQ Eth.II 'they have learnt that the earth'; D' corrupt.

[14] D' 'for they showed what is secret to those who have been condemned'.

[15] GQTUD' 'but as for you'.   [16] Eth.I 'your righteous offspring'.

[17] Q (and so probably T) 'both for kingship'; GMUD' corrupt.

[1] who reside and dwell: Q 'who dwell'; UBX 'who reside'.

[1] GMQT¹UD' om.   [2] Eth.I X 'have made'.

[3] come out: so T Eth.II; GMQUD' have a different verb (in various forms), but their text does not make sense.

3 the dry ground may not remain empty.[4] And I will establish your
offspring before me for ever and ever, and I will scatter those who
dwell with you over the face of the dry ground;[5] I will not *again* put
them to the test on the face of the earth,[6] but they will be blessed and
4 will increase on the dry ground in the name of the Lord. And they[7]
will shut up those angels who showed iniquity in that burning
valley which my great-grandfather Enoch had shown to me previously, in the west, near the mountains of gold and silver and iron
5 and soft-metal and tin. And I saw that valley in which *there was* a
6 great disturbance, and a heaving of the waters. And when all this
happened, from that fiery molten metal and the disturbance which
disturbed *the waters* in that place a smell of sulphur was produced,
and it was associated with those waters. And that valley of the
7 angels who led *men* astray burns under the ground; and through the
valleys of that same *area* flow out rivers of fire where those angels
will be punished who led astray those who dwell upon the dry
8 ground. And in those days those waters will serve the kings and the
mighty and the exalted, and those who dwell upon the dry ground,
for the healing of soul and body,[8] but *also* for the punishment of the
spirit. And their spirits[9] are *so* full of lust[10] that they will be
punished in their bodies, for they denied the Lord of Spirits. And
they see their punishment every day, yet they do not believe in his
9 name. And the more their bodies are burnt, the more a change will
come over their spirits for ever and ever; for no one can speak an
10 idle word before the Lord of Spirits. For judgement will come upon
them, for they believe in the lust[11] of their bodies, but deny the
11 spirit of the Lord. And those same waters will undergo a change in
those days; for when those angels are punished in those days,[12] the
temperature of those springs of water will change, and when the
angels come up *from the water*, that water of the springs will change
12 and will become cold. And I heard the holy[13] Michael answering

---

[4] and a change . . . empty: so QEC′; other MSS probably to be translated 'and
the dry ground shall undergo a change that it may not remain empty'.

[5] over the face of the dry ground: so CFP²BDOXYB′; other MSS om.

[6] So EFHP²: other MSS 'dry ground'. BDOXYB′ om. by hmt. 'I will not again
. . . face of the earth (dry ground)'.   [7] Eth.I F 'he'.

[8] of soul and body: GQUD′ 'of the body'.   [9] D′ 'souls'.

[10] GQU 'desire'.   [11] GQUD′ 'desire'.

[12] Eth.I 'waters'.   [13] the holy: Eth.I om.

and saying, This judgement with which the angels are judged is a testimony for the kings and the mighty who possess the dry ground. For these waters of judgement *serve* for the healing of the bodies of the **kings**,[14] and for the lust[15] of their bodies; but they do not see and do not believe that these waters will change, and will become a fire which burns for ever.

LXVIII.   And after this my great-grandfather Enoch gave me the explanation[1] of all the secrets in a book and the parables which had been given to him; and he put them together for me in the words of the Book[2] of the Parables. And on that day the holy[3] Michael answered Raphael, saying,[4] The power of the spirit seizes me **and makes me tremble**[5] because of[6] the harshness of the judgement of the secrets, the judgement of the angels.[7] Who can endure the harshness of the judgement which has been executed,[8] and before which they melt *with fear*? And the holy[3] Michael answered Raphael again, and said to him,[9] Who would not soften his heart[10] over it, and *whose* mind would not be disturbed by this word? Judgement has gone out[11] against them, upon[12] those whom they have led out like this. But it came to pass, when he[13] stood before the Lord of Spirits, that the holy[3] Michael spoke as follows to Raphael, I will not take their part under the eye of the Lord, for the Lord of Spirits is angry with them, for they act as if they were the Lord. Because of

13

2

3

4

5

[14] for the healing . . . of the kings: so all MSS except BCXY, although the MSS have 'angels' instead of 'kings'. But it seems likely that 'angels' is a mistranslation. BX 'for their healing'; C 'for the healing of the angels'; Y defective.
[15] So M: GQTUD′ 'desire'; Eth.II 'death'.

[1] D′ 'teaching'.
[2] G 'in the book of the words'.   [3] the holy: Eth.I om.
[4] GQUD′ 'answered me, saying to Raphael'.
[5] and makes me tremble: all MSS (except D′) 'and makes me angry', but it seems likely that the wrong meaning of the underlying Aramaic word was followed. D′ 'and makes me go up'.
[6] Q Eth.II (except Y) 'and because of'.
[7] of the angels: GMTUD′ om.   [8] Eth.II adds 'and remains'.
[9] GQU 'answered me again, and said to Raphael'.
[10] T² 'Whose heart would not be softened'; GMQT¹U 'Whose heart would not feel convicted'; D′ 'Whose heart has not felt convicted'.
[11] GQD′ 'by this word of judgement which has gone out' (GQ om. 'which').
[12] Or 'from', or 'because of'.   [13] D′ 'they'.

this the hidden judgement[14] will come upon them for ever and ever; for neither any *other* angel, nor any man, will receive their lot, but they alone have received their judgement for ever and ever.

LXIX.   And after this judgement they will terrify them and make them tremble, for they have shown this[1] to those who dwell upon
2 the dry ground. And behold[2] the names of those angels. And these are their names: the first of them *is* Semyaza, and the second Artaqifa, and the third Armen, and the fourth Kokabiel, and the fifth Turiel, and the sixth Ramiel, and the seventh Daniel, and the eighth Nuqael, and the ninth Baraqiel, and the tenth Azazel, the eleventh Armaros, the twelfth Batriel, the thirteenth Basasael, the fourteenth Ananel, the fifteenth Turiel, the sixteenth Samsiel, the seventeenth Yetarel, the eighteenth Tumiel, the nineteenth Turiel,
3 the twentieth Rumiel, the twenty-first Azazel. And these are the chiefs of their angels, and the names of their[3] leaders of hundreds,
4 and their leaders of fifties and their leaders of tens. The name of the first *is* Yequn, and this *is* the one who led astray all the children of the holy[4] angels; and he brought them down onto the dry ground,
5 and led them astray through the daughters of men. And the name of the second *is* Asbeel: this one suggested[5] an evil plan to the children of the holy angels,[6] and led them astray, so that they
6 corrupted their bodies with the daughters of men. And the name of the third *is* Gadreel: this is the one who showed all the deadly blows to the sons of men; and he led astray Eve, and he showed the weapons of death to the children of men, the shield and the breastplate and the sword for slaughter, and all the weapons of
7 death to the sons of men. And from his[7] hand they have gone out

---

[14]   the hidden judgement: Eth.I 'everything which is hidden'.

[1]   T om.; Q 'this judgement'.
[2]   behold: D' adds 'I will name'; GM apparently add corruptions of 'I will name'.
[3]   and the names of their: Eth.I EH 'and their names, and their'.
[4]   holy: GMQUD' and some Eth.II MSS om.: it is possible that the text derives from a false translation of 'all the (holy) children of God' (i.e. 'all the (holy) angels). N 'all the children of the angels of the Lord'.
[5]   QD' 'recommended'.
[6]   Possibly a false translation of 'to the holy children of God' (cp. note 4).
[7]   QD' 'their'.

against those who dwell upon the dry ground, from that time[8] and
8 for ever and ever. And the name of the fourth *is* Penemue: this one
showed the sons of men the bitter and the sweet, and showed them
9 all the secrets of their wisdom. He taught men the art of writing
with ink and paper, and through this many have gone astray from
10 eternity to eternity, and to this day. For men were not created for
this, that they should confirm their faith like this with pen and ink.
11 For men were created no differently from the angels, that they
might remain righteous and pure,[9] and death, which destroys
everything, would not have touched them; but through this
knowledge of theirs they are being destroyed, and through this
12 power it[10] is consuming me.[11] And the name of the fifth *is*
Kasdeyae: this one showed the sons of men all the evil blows of the
spirits and of the demons, and the blows *which attack* the embryo in
the womb so that it miscarries, and the blows *which attack* the soul,
the bite of the serpent and the blows which occur at midday, the
13 son of the serpent who is . . . strong.[12] And this is the **task**[13] of
Kesbeel, the chief of the oath, who showed *the oath* to the holy ones
14 when he dwelt on high in glory, and its[14] name *is* Beqa. And this
one told the holy[15] Michael that he should show him[16] the[17] secret
name, that they might mention it in the oath,[18] so that those who
showed the sons of men everything which is secret trembled before
15 that name and oath. And this *is* the power of this oath, for it is

[8] GMTUD′ 'day'.

[9] GMTUD′ 'pure and righteous'; Q 'pure and holy'.

[10] i.e. death.

[11] D′ 'us'.

[12] The text is awkward; in full it reads 'whose name is Tabaet'. I have omitted
'name' (which could easily have come in by mistake) and take 'Tabaet' as the word
meaning 'male' or 'strong'. But the passage remains obscure.

[13] Eth. 'number', but Charles's suggestion that the translation is based on a
misreading of an original 'task' is very plausible.

[14] Or 'his'.

[15] the holy: Eth. I om.

[16] So GMTUD′: Q om.; Eth.II 'them'.

[17] MTD′ENC′ 'his'.

[18] that they . . . the oath: so GQ; T 'that they might mention that secret name';
MUD′ 'that they might mention that (M 'evil and') secret name, that they might
mention it in the oath'; Eth.II 'that they might see that secret name, that they might
mention it in the oath'.

powerful and strong; and he placed this oath Akae[19] in the charge
16 of the holy[15] Michael. And these are the secrets of this oath ... and
they are strong[20] through his oath, and heaven was suspended[21]
17 before the world was created and for ever. And through it the
earth[22] was founded upon the water, and from the hidden *recesses* of
the mountains[23] come beautiful waters[24] from the creation of the
18 world and for ever. And through that oath the sea was created, and
as its foundation, for the time of anger, he placed for it the sand,
and it does not go beyond *it* from the creation of the world and for
19 ever. And through that oath the deeps were made firm, and they
stand and do not move from their place from *the creation of* the world
20 and for ever. And through that oath the sun and the moon complete
their course and do not transgress their command from *the creation
21 of* the world and for ever.[25] And through that oath the stars
complete their course, and he calls their names,[26] and they answer
22 him[27] from *the creation of* the world and for ever; and likewise the
spirits of the water, of the winds, and of all the breezes, and their
23 paths, according to all the groups of the spirits. And there are kept
the storehouses of the sound of the thunder and of the light of the
lightning;[28] and there are kept the storehouses of the hail and the
hoar-frost,[29] and the storehouses of the mist, and the storehouses of

[19] Since verses 13f. and verses 15–25 appear to deal with two different oaths, it is
possible that the obscure name 'Akae' (so all MSS except QD') is a corruption of
the word 'other', viz. 'and he placed this other oath ...' Q(?) 'this engraved oath';
D' 'this evil oath'.

[20] and they are strong (or 'and they were made firm'): so MT Eth.II; but the text
is not entirely intelligible as it stands and it is possible that something like 'All
things were created' has dropped out from before 'and they are strong' (but see note
21). GQU 'and *it* is strong'; D' 'and its strength'.

[21] QH 'And these are the secrets of this oath, and they are (Q 'it is') strong:
through his oath heaven was suspended', and other MSS perhaps to be translated
similarly.

[22] GMTU 'through it, and the earth'.

[23] Some Eth. MSS 'the hidden mountains'.

[24] beautiful waters: ULYA' 'waters for the living'; BCX 'beautiful waters for the
living'.

[25] from the creation ... for ever: M om.; GTU om. 'and for ever'.

[26] D' 'and they call their names'; Q 'they are called'.   [27] D' 'them'.

[28] the storehouses ... lightning: Eth.I 'the sound of the thunder and the light of
the lightning'.

[29] Eth.I 'and the storehouses of the hoar-frost'.

24 the rain and dew. And all these make their confession and give
thanks before the Lord of Spirits and sing praises with all their
power; and their food consists of all their thanksgiving, and they
give thanks and praise and exalt in the name of[30] the Lord of Spirits
25 for ever and ever. And this oath is strong over them, and through it
they are kept safe, and their paths are kept safe, and their courses
26 are not disturbed. And they had great joy, and they blessed and
praised and exalted because the name of that Son of[31] Man had
27 been revealed to them. And he sat on the throne of his glory, and
the whole judgement[32] was given to the Son of Man,[33] and he will
cause the sinners to pass away and be destroyed from the face of the
28 earth.[34] And those who led astray the world will be bound in
chains, and will be shut up in the assembly-place of their destruction, and all their works will pass away from the face of the earth.
29 And from then on there will be nothing corruptible,[35] for that Son
of Man has appeared and has sat on the throne of his glory, and
everything evil will pass away and go from before him; and the
word of that Son of[36] Man[37] will be strong[38] before the Lord of
Spirits. This is the third[39] parable of Enoch.

LXX. And it came to pass after this *that*, while he was living, his
name was lifted from those who dwell upon the dry ground to the
presence of that Son of Man and[1] to the presence of the Lord of
2 Spirits. And he[2] was lifted on the chariots of the spirit, and his[3]

[30] in the name of: D′ om.; QN om. 'in'.
[31] Son of: MTUD′ om.
[32] Lit. 'and the sum of the judgement'.
[33] And he sat . . . Son of Man: D′ om.
[34] and he will cause . . . the earth: D′ 'and he will not pass away nor be destroyed
from the face of the earth'; GMTU 'and he (? 'it') will pass away and be destroyed
from the face of the earth'; Q 'and the sinners of the earth have passed away from
before his face'.
[35] D′ 'there will not be this corruption'.
[36] Son of: B om.   [37] Man: GN 'a woman'.
[38] and the word . . . be strong: so T and some Eth.II MSS; other MSS 'and they
(AD′ 'he') will speak to that Son of Man, and he will be strong'.
[39] EFHNP² om.

[1] So GQTD′: other MSS om.   [2] T 'his name'.
[3] So MQD′YC′: other MSS 'the'.

3   name vanished among them. And from that day I was not counted[4]
    among them, and he placed me between two winds,[5] between the
    north and the west, where the angels took the cords to measure for
4   me the place for the chosen and the righteous. And there I saw the
    first fathers and the righteous who from *the beginning of* the world
    dwelt in that place.

LXXI.   And it came to pass after this that my spirit was carried
off, and it went up into the heavens. I saw the sons of the holy
angels[1] treading upon flames of fire, and their garments *were* white,
2   and their clothing, and the light of their face *was* like snow. And I
saw two rivers of fire, and the light of that fire shone like hyacinth,
3   and I fell upon my face before the Lord of Spirits. And the angel
Michael, one of the archangels, took hold of me by my right hand,
and raised me, and led me out to all the secrets of mercy and the
4   secrets of righteousness.[2] And he showed me all the secrets of the
ends of heaven and all the storehouses of all the stars and the lights,
5   from where they come out before the holy ones. And the spirit
carried Enoch off to the highest heaven,[3] and I saw there in the
middle of that light something built of crystal stones, and in the
6   middle of those stones tongues of living fire. And my spirit saw a
circle of fire which surrounded that house; from its four sides *came*
7   rivers full of living fire, and they surrounded that house. And
round about *were* the Seraphim, and the Cherubim and the
Ophannim; these are they who do not sleep, but keep watch over
8   the throne of his glory. And I saw angels who could not be counted,
a thousand thousands and ten thousand times ten thousand, sur-
9   rounding that house; and Michael and Raphael[4] and Gabriel and

---

⁴ So G QTD′J¹; M Eth.II 'included'; U 'praised'.
⁵ Or 'quarters', 'regions'.

¹ Possibly a false translation of 'the holy sons of God' (cp. chap. lxix, n. 4). Some
Eth.II MSS om. 'holy'.
² to all ... righteousness: D′ 'to all the secrets of mercy, and he showed me all the
secrets of righteousness'; GMQTU 'to all the secrets, and he showed me all the
secrets of mercy, and he showed me all the secrets of righteousness'.
³ GQU 'And he carried off my spirit, and Enoch *was* in the highest heaven'; TD′
'And he carried off my spirit, and I, Enoch, *was* in the highest heaven'; M 'And he
carried off my spirit, says Enoch, in heaven was I'. In all Eth.I mss. 'he carried off
my spirit' is grammatically anomalous.   ⁴ and Raphael: QU om.

Phanuel, and the holy angels who *are* in the heavens above, went in
and out of that house. And Michael and Raphael and Gabriel[5] and
Phanuel,[6] and many holy angels without number, came out from
10 that house; and with them the Head of Days,[7] his head white and
11 pure like wool, and his garments indescribable. And I fell upon my
face, and my whole body melted, and my spirit was transformed;
and I cried out in a loud voice in the spirit of power, and I blessed[8]
12 and praised[9] and exalted. And these[10] blessings which came out[11]
13 from my mouth were pleasing before that Head of Days. And that
Head of Days came with Michael and Gabriel, Raphael[12] and
Phanuel,[13] and thousands and tens of thousands of angels without
14 number. And that angel[14] came to me, and greeted me with his
voice, and said to me, You are the Son of Man who was born to[15]
righteousness, and righteousness remains over you, and the right-
15 eousness of the Head of Days will not leave you. And he said to
me, He proclaims peace to you in the name of the world which is to
come, for from there peace has come out from the creation of the
16 world; and so you will have it for ever and for ever and ever. And
all[16] will walk[17] according to your way, inasmuch as righteousness
will never leave you; with you will be their dwelling, and with you
their lot, and they will not be separated from you, for ever and ever
17 and ever. And so there will be length of days with that Son of Man,
and the righteous will have peace, and the righteous will have an
upright way[18] in the name of the Lord of Spirits for ever and ever.

[5]   MQUEHN 'and Gabriel and Raphael'; BCOXA' 'and Gabriel, Raphael'.
[6]   and Phanuel: GMQTUA om.
[7]   EHP[2] 'of the oath'.   [8]   Q adds 'him'.
[9]   QFP[2] add 'him'.   [10]   Eth.I 'those'.
[11]   came out: D' jumps from this word to lxxviii.8b, but begins again with lxxii.1
after reaching lxxxii.20.
[12]   QTUX 'and Gabriel and Raphael'; GM 'and Raphael and Gabriel'.
[13]   After 'Phanuel' GMQT go back by mistake to 'Phanuel' in verse 8 and repeat
all (so G) or parts of the intervening text.
[14]   that angel: U om.; GMT 'that one' or 'he'.
[15]   Some MSS 'in'.
[16]   Eth.II adds 'will be and' (ALB' 'who will be and').
[17]   Q 'dwell'.
[18]   and the righteous will have an upright way: so C'; QC om. (hmt.); all other
MSS om. 'will have'. Eth.II (except C') 'his upright way' instead of 'an upright
way'.

LXXII. The book of the revolutions of the lights of heaven, each as it is, according to their classes, according to their *period of* rule and their times, according to their names and their places of origin, and according to their months, which Uriel, the holy angel who was with me and is their leader, showed to me; and he showed me all their regulations exactly as they are, for each year of the world and for ever, until the new creation shall be made which will last for

2 ever. And this is the first law of the lights. The light the sun, its rising *is* in the gates of heaven which *are* towards the east, and its

3 setting *is* in the western gates of heaven. And I saw six gates from which the sun rises, and six gates in which the sun sets, and the moon *also* rises and sets in those gates, and the leaders of the stars together with those whom they lead; *there are* six in the east and six in the west, all exactly in place, one next to the other; and *there are*

4 many windows to the south and north[1] of those gates. And first there rises the greater light, named the sun, and its disk *is* like the disk of heaven, and the whole of it *is* full of a fire which gives light

5 and warmth. The wind blows the chariots on which it ascends, and the sun goes down from heaven and returns through the north in order to reach the east and is led so that it comes to the appropriate

6 gate, and shines *again* in heaven. In this way it rises in the first month in the large gate, namely it rises through the fourth of those

7 six gates which *are* towards the east. And in that fourth gate, from which the sun rises in the first month, there are twelve window-openings[2] from which, whenever they are opened, flames come

8 out. When the sun rises in heaven, it goes out through that fourth gate for thirty days, and exactly in the fourth gate in the west of

9 heaven it goes down. And in those days the day grows daily longer, and the night grows nightly shorter, until the thirtieth morning.

10 And on that day the day becomes longer than the night by a double *part*,[3] and the day amounts to exactly ten parts, and the night

11 amounts to eight parts. And the sun rises from that fourth gate, and sets in the fourth gate, and returns to the fifth gate in the east for thirty mornings; and it rises from it, and sets in the fifth gate.

---

[1] Lit. 'to the right and left'.   [2] Lit. 'open windows'.
[3] by a double *part*: i.e. by two parts. GQUD' add 'by nine parts' (QUD' possibly 'by a ninth part').

12 And then the day becomes longer by two parts, and the day amounts to eleven parts, and the night becomes shorter and
13 amounts to seven parts. And the sun returns to the east, and comes to the sixth gate, and rises and sets in the sixth gate for thirty one
14 mornings[4] because of its sign. And on that day the day becomes longer than the night, and the day becomes double the night; and the day amounts to twelve parts, and the night becomes shorter
15 and amounts to six parts. And the sun rises up that the day may grow shorter, and the night longer; and the sun returns to the east, and comes to the sixth gate, and rises from it and sets for thirty
16 mornings. And when thirty mornings have been completed, the day becomes shorter by exactly one part; and the day amounts to
17 eleven parts, and the night to seven parts. And the sun goes out from the west through that sixth gate, and goes to the east, and rises in the fifth gate for thirty mornings; and it sets in the west
18 again, in the fifth gate in the west. On that day the day becomes shorter by two parts, and the day amounts to ten parts, and the
19 night to eight parts. And the sun rises from that fifth gate, and sets in the fifth gate in the west, and rises in the fourth gate for thirty
20 one mornings because of its sign,[5] and sets in the west. On that day the day becomes equal with the night, and is *of* equal *length*; and the
21 night amounts to nine parts, and the day to nine parts. And the sun rises from that gate, and sets in the west, and returns to the east, and rises in the third gate for thirty mornings, and sets in the west
22 in the third gate. And on that day the night becomes longer than the day, and the night grows nightly longer,[6] and the day grows daily shorter until the thirtieth morning;[7] and the night amounts to
23 exactly ten parts, and the day to eight parts. And the sun rises from that third gate, and sets in the third gate in the west, and returns to the east; and the sun rises in the second gate in the east for thirty mornings, and likewise it sets in the second gate in the west of
24 heaven. And on that day the night amounts to eleven parts, and the

---

[4] GTUD′ 'thirty mornings'; Q corrupt; M defective.
[5] GMQT add 'in the fourth gate in the east'; U adds 'in the east'; D′ adds 'in the fourth gate'.
[6] and the night grows nightly longer: so GQTUD′; M 'and on that day the night grows longer'; Eth.II 'until the thirtieth morning'.
[7] morning: Q om.; Eth.II (except EFLN) 'day'.

25 day to seven parts. And the sun rises on that day from that second
gate, and sets in the west in the second gate, and returns to the east,
to the first gate,[8] for thirty one mornings,[9] and sets in the west in
26 the first gate.[10] And on that day the night becomes longer, and
becomes double the day; and the night amounts to exactly twelve
27 parts, and the day to six parts. And *with this* the sun has completed
the divisions of its journey,[11] and it turns back again along these[12]
divisions of its journey;[13] and it comes through that *first* gate[14] for
28 thirty mornings, and sets in the west opposite it. And on that day[15]
the night becomes shorter in length by one part[16] . . . , and amounts
29 to eleven parts, and the day to seven parts. And the sun returns, and
comes to the second gate in the east, and it returns along those
divisions of its journey[17] for thirty mornings, rising and setting.
30 And on that day the night becomes shorter in length, and the night
31 amounts to ten parts, and the day to eight parts. And on that day
the sun rises from that second[18] gate, and sets in the west, and
returns to the east, and rises in the third gate for thirty one
32 mornings, and sets in the west of heaven. And on that day the night
becomes shorter, and amounts to nine parts, and the day amounts
to nine parts, and the night becomes equal with the day. And the
33 year amounts to exactly three hundred and sixty four days. And
the length of the day and the night, and the shortness of the day
and the night – they are different because of the journey of that sun.
34 Because of it,[19] its journey becomes daily longer, and nightly

---

[8] to the first gate: D' 'and rises in the first gate'.

[9] B²X add 'because of its sign'.

[10] in the west in the first gate: M 'in the west in the sixth gate'; GQ 'in it on the first day in the west of heaven'; TUD' 'on that day in the west of heaven'.

[11] the divisions of its journey: D'(?) 'its appearances'.

[12] Eth.I JP¹ 'those'.

[13] divisions of its journey: D'(?) 'appearances'.

[14] M 'those gates'; QTUD' 'all the gates'; G 'all its gates'.

[15] day: U om.; GQD'F 'night'.

[16] by one part: M om.; GQUD' 'by nine parts' (UD' possibly 'by a ninth part'). All MSS add 'that is one part', a gloss apparently intended to explain that the word 'əd, used here with the meaning 'part', is the equivalent of the word kəfəl.

[17] divisions of its journey: D'(?) 'appearances'.

[18] GMQUD'¹ om.

[19] i.e. to this end, to bring about the difference in the length of day and night.

35 shorter. And this is the law and the journey of the sun, and its
    return, as often as it returns; sixty times it returns and rises, that is
    the great eternal light[20] which for ever and ever is named the sun.
36 And this which rises is the great light, which is *so* named after its
37 appearance,[21] as the Lord commanded. And thus it rises and
    sets;[22] it neither decreases, nor rests, but runs day and night in *its*
    chariot.[23] And its light is seven times brighter than that of the
    moon, but in size the two are equal.

LXXIII.   And after this law I saw another law, for the smaller light
2 named the moon. And its disk *is* like the disk of the sun,[1] and the
    wind blows its chariot on which it rides, and in fixed measure light
3 is given to it. And every month its rising and its setting change, and
    its days *are* as the days of the sun, and when its light is uniformly
4 *full*, it is a seventh part of the light of the sun. And thus it rises, and
    its first phase[2] *is* towards the east; it rises on the thirtieth morning,
    and on that day it appears and becomes for you the first phase[2] of
    the moon, on the thirtieth morning,[3] together with the sun in the
5 gate through which the sun rises. And a half[4] . . . with a seventh
    part, and its entire disk *is* empty, without light, except for a seventh
6 part, a fourteenth part[5] of its *total* light. And on the day it receives a
    seventh part and a half[6] of its light, its light amounts to a seventh-

---

   [20] as often as . . . eternal light: GQTUD' 'as often as – sixty times – that great
light returns and rises' (QTUD' om. 'sixty times'); M 'as often as it returns; it
returns and rises, that is the great light'.
   [21] D' 'And this is the one which rises according to its appearance'.
   [22] GD' 'As it rises, so it sets'; M 'Thus it rises and sets'; QT 'Thus it rises and
thus it sets'; U 'And thus it sets'; ANX 'And thus it sets and rises'.
   [23] in *its* chariot: GMQT'UD' om.

   [1] So M and some Eth.II MSS: other MSS 'heaven'.
   [2] first phase: lit. 'beginning'.
   [3] Eth.I 'day'.
   [4] All MSS except D'C'F add 'is distant', but this makes no sense. We expect a
verb meaning 'to rise', 'to appear'.
   [5] a fourteenth part: so QUD', but D' adds 'of its light, a seventh part'; G corrupt;
MT Eth.II 'from the fourteen parts'.
   [6] GQD'OA'B' (with several ungrammatical variations) 'a seventh part of a
half'.

7 and-seventh part and a half.[7] It sets with the sun,[8] and when the sun rises, the moon[9] rises with it, and receives a half of one part of light; and on that night at the beginning of its morning, at the beginning of the moon's day, the moon sets with the sun, and is

8 dark on that night in six and seven[10] parts and a half. And it rises on that day with exactly a seventh part, and goes out, and recedes from the rising of the sun, and becomes bright on the remainder of its days in *the other* six and seven[11] parts.

LXXIV. And another journey and *another* law I saw for it, in that

2 according to this law it makes its monthly journey. And Uriel, the holy angel who is the leader of them all, showed me everything,[1] and I wrote down their positions as he showed *them* to me; and I wrote down their months, as they are, and the appearance of their

3 light until fifteen days have been completed. In seventh parts it makes all its darkness full,[2] and in seventh parts it makes all its

4 light full, in the east and in the west.[3] And in certain months it changes *its* setting, and in certain months it follows its own indi-

5 vidual course. In two months it sets with the sun in those two gates

6 which *are* in the middle, in the third and in the fourth gate. It goes out for seven days, and turns back, and returns again to the gate from which the sun rises; and in that *gate*[4] it makes all its light full,

---

[7] GMQUD'D 'a seventh part and a half' (but QD' om. 'and'); T(?) 'a seven-and-sixth part and a half'. The numbers are hard to interpret and no MS provides a text that makes much sense. In the Aramaic fragments a much fuller table of the phases of the moon has survived, and the Ethiopic appears to be a rather garbled summary of this.

[8] GMQUD' 'And the sun sets'.

[9] the moon: GQUD' 'it'.

[10] six and seven: so MQTD'JLB'C'; other MSS 'seven and seven'.

[11] six and seven: so Eth.I NC'; other MSS 'seven and seven'.

[1] Eth.I 'And all this Uriel, the holy angel who is the leader of them all, showed me'; GMQD' add 'and their positions'.

[2] D' 'makes its darkness full to the fifteenth day'.

[3] it makes all its darkness full . . . west: so some Eth.II MSS and (basically) D'; GMQT'UA 'it makes all its light full, in the east and in the west'; T[2] and other Eth.II MSS 'it makes all its light full in the east, and in seventh parts it makes all its darkness full in the west'.

[4] in that *gate*: GMQT'UD' om.

and it recedes from the sun, and comes in eight days to the sixth
7 gate from which the sun rises. And when the sun rises from the
fourth gate, *the moon* goes out for seven days until it rises from the
fifth *gate*; and again it returns in seven days to the fourth gate, and
makes all its light full, and recedes, and comes to the first gate in
8 eight days. And again it returns in seven days to the fourth gate
9 from which the sun rises. Thus I saw their positions, how the
10 moons rose and the sun set in those days. And if[5] five years are
added together, the sun has an excess of thirty days; but all the
days *which* accrue to it for one year of those five years, when they
11 are complete, amount to three hundred and sixty four days. And
the excess of the sun and the stars comes to six days; in five years,
six *days* each *year*, they have an excess of thirty days, and the moon
12 falls behind[6] the sun and the stars by thirty days.[7] And the moon
conducts[8] the years exactly, all of them according to their eternal
positions; they are neither early nor late even by one day, but
change the year[9] . . . in exactly three hundred and sixty four days.
13 In three years *there are* one thousand and ninety two days, and in
five years one thousand eight hundred and twenty days, so that in
eight years there are two thousand nine hundred and twelve days.
14 For the moon alone the days in three years come to one thousand
and sixty two days,[10] and in five years it is fifty days behind[11] . . .
15 And there are one thousand seven hundred and seventy days in

[5] how the moons . . . And *if*: so GMT[1]D'; U defective; QT[2] 'according to the law
of their months the sun rising and setting in those days. And *if*'; Eth.II 'according to
the law of their months the sun rising and setting. And in those days *if*'.

[6] GMQT[1]U 'and they fall behind'; D' 'and it falls behind'.

[7] by thirty days: QU om.; GM add 'behind the sun and behind the stars'; T[1] adds
'behind the sun and the stars'; D' adds 'behind the sun and the moon and the stars'.

[8] D' 'And they conduct'.

[9] All Eth. MSS add 'precisely' which looks like an alternative rendering of
'exactly'.

[10] GQUD' (by mistake) 'one thousand and thirty days'; D' adds 'and in three
years it is sixty two (a mistake for 'thirty') days behind'. D' continues 'In five years
there are one thousand seven hundred and seventy days, *and* in five years it is fifty
days behind, so that for the moon . . .'.

[11] All MSS except D' add here 'for to its sum is to be added sixty two days (C
margin 'one thousand and sixty two days')'. This appears to be a corrupt gloss
whose insertion has seriously disrupted the text; D' (see note 10) seems to preserve
the text in a better state.

16 five years, so that for the moon the days in eight years amount to two thousand eight hundred and thirty two days. For the differ-
17 ence in eight years *is* eighty days, and all the days which *the moon* is behind in eight years *are* eighty days. And the year is completed exactly in accordance with their positions[12] and the positions of the sun, in that *sun and moon* rise from the gates from which *the sun* rises and sets for thirty days.

LXXV. And the leaders of the heads of thousands who *are* in charge of the whole creation and in charge of all the stars *have to do* also with the four *days* which are added, and are not separated from their position,[1] according to the whole[2] reckoning of the year. And these serve on the four days which are not counted in the reckoning
2 of the year. And because of them men go wrong in them, for these lights really serve in the stations of the world, one in the first gate, and one in the third gate,[3] and one in the fourth gate, and one in the sixth gate; and the exact harmony of the *course of the* world is completed[4] in the separate three hundred and sixty four stations of
3 the world. For the signs and the times and the years and the days the angel Uriel showed to me, whom the Lord of eternal glory has placed[5] in charge of all the lights of heaven, in heaven and in the world, that they might rule on the face of heaven, and appear over the earth, and be the leaders of day and night, *namely* the sun, and the moon, and the stars, and all the serving creatures who revolve
4 in all the chariots of heaven.[6] Likewise Uriel showed to me twelve gate-openings[7] in the disk of the chariot of the sun in heaven from which the rays of the sun come out; and from them heat[8] comes out over the earth, when they are opened at the times which are

---

[12] GQTUD' 'their world-positions'.

[1] GMT'U 'from their office'.
[2] Eth.I om.   [3] Eth.I adds 'of heaven'.
[4] G 'and with exactness the *course of the* world is completed'; D' 'the year is completed exactly'; Q 'and the exactness of the year he completes' (TU also have the active 'he completes').
[5] GMTUL 'whom the Lord of Glory has for ever placed'; Q 'whom the Lord of Spirits has for ever placed'; D' defective.
[6] in . . . heaven: Q 'with all the armies of heaven'.
[7] Lit. 'open gates'.   [8] MQB' 'death'.

5 appointed for them. And *there are such* for the winds and for the spirit of the dew, when they are opened[9] at the *appointed* times,[10]
6 open in heaven at the ends.[11] I saw twelve gates in heaven,[12] at the ends of the earth, from which the sun, and the moon, and the stars
7 and all the works of heaven go out in the east and in the west. And *there are* many window-openings[13] to the north and to the south[14] – and each window at its *appointed* time sends out heat[15] – corresponding to those gates from which the stars go out in accordance with his command to them, and in which they set according to
8 their number. And I saw chariots in heaven, running through the world above and below[16] those gates, in which the stars which
9 never set rotate. And one is bigger than all *the others*, and it goes round through the whole world.

LXXVI. And at the ends of the earth I saw twelve gates open to all the winds,[1] from which the winds come out and blow over the
2 earth. Three of them *are* open in the front of heaven, and three in the west, and three on the right of heaven, and three on the left.
3 And the three first *are* those which *are* towards the east, and three *are* towards the north, and the three after these[2] on the left *are*
4 towards the south, and three *are* in the west. Through four of them come winds of blessing and peace, and from those eight come winds of punishment; when they are sent, they bring devastation to the whole earth, and to the water which *is* on it, and to all those

---

[9] And *there are such* . . . opened: translation and meaning uncertain.

[10] at the *appointed* times: GMQT[1]UD′ om.

[11] open in heaven at the ends: D′ om. and probably copied by mistake from verse 6 (for 'open' cp. D′ in note 12).

[12] I saw twelve gates in heaven: GMQT[1]U 'When they are opened, *there are* twelve gates in heaven' ('When they are opened' repeated by mistake from verse 5); D′ ungrammatical, but probably '*There are* twelve gates open in heaven'.

[13] Lit. 'open windows'.

[14] Lit. 'to the left and to the right'.

[15] QA′ 'death'.

[16] and below: Eth.I and some Eth.II MSS om.

---

[1] Or 'to all directions' (in both Ethiopic and Aramaic the word for 'wind' can also have the meaning 'quarter, direction').

[2] after these: so GM; T Eth.II 'opposite (lit. 'at the back of') those'; QUD′ differ slightly.

who dwell upon it, and to everything which is in[3] the water and on
5 the dry ground. And the first wind from those gates, called the east
wind, comes out through the first gate which *is* towards the east, *the
one* which inclines to the south; from it comes devastation, drought,
6 and heat,[4] and destruction.[5] And through the second gate in the
middle comes what is right, and from it come rain,[6] and fruitful-
ness, and prosperity and dew; and through the third gate, which *is*
7 towards the north, come cold and drought. And after these the
winds towards the south come out through three gates. First,[7]
through the first of the gates, *the one* which inclines towards the
8 east, comes a hot wind.[8] And through the middle gate, which *is*
next to it, come pleasant fragrances, and dew, and rain, and
9 prosperity and life. And through the third gate, which *is* towards
10 the west, come dew, and rain, and locusts and devastation. And
after these the winds towards the north[9] . . . From the seventh
gate,[10] which *is* towards the east,[11] . . . come dew and rain, locusts
11 and devastation. And through the middle gate exactly come rain,
and dew, and life[12] and prosperity.[13] And through the third gate,
which *is* towards the west,[14] . . . come mist, and hoar-frost, and
12 snow, and rain, and dew and locusts. And after these[15] . . . the

---

[3] EFHP[2] 'on'.   [4] QFJNA' 'death'; D' 'punishment'.

[5] U 'force'.

[6] And through . . . rain: so all MSS (with minor variations) except GUD'J; GJ
'And through the second gate in the middle, from it come rain' (omission by hmt.);
D' 'And through the second gate exactly in the middle, from it come rain'; U
corrupt. 'What is right' is awkward, and D', although itself possibly defective, gives
better sense.

[7] So GMT Eth.II and Aram.: QUD' om.

[8] MTU 'hot winds'; A'B' 'a wind of death'; GD' corrupt.

[9] All Eth. MSS add a gloss 'named the sea' (for a Palestinian the sea is the west,
not the north).

[10] From the seventh gate: so I correct Eth. which in all its various forms appears
corrupt. GQTUD' 'and which came out (D' 'come out') from the seventh gate'; M
'and which came out from the great seventh gate'; Eth.II 'From three, the seventh
gate' or 'From, thirdly, the seventh gate'.

[11] All Eth. MSS add here a gloss – thus Q adds 'the south', GTUD' add 'towards
the south', M Eth.II add 'which inclines towards the south'.

[12] rain . . . life: Eth.I 'life, and rain, and dew'.

[13] and prosperity: GD' om.

[14] All Eth. MSS add here by mistake 'which inclines towards the north'.

[15] All Eth. MSS add here a gloss 'fourthly'.

winds towards the west. Through the first gate, which inclines towards the north, come dew, and rain,[16] and hoar-frost, and cold, and snow and frost. And from the middle gate come dew and rain, prosperity and blessing. And through the last gate, which *is* towards the south, come drought and devastation, burning and destruction. And *thus* the twelve gates of the four **quarters**[17] of heaven are complete. And all their laws, and all[18] their punishments and all their benefits[19] I have shown to you, my son Methuselah.

13

14

LXXVII. They call the first quarter eastern, because it is the first; and they call the second the south, because there the Most High descends,[1] and there especially[2] the one who is blessed for ever descends. And the western quarter is called waning, because there all the lights of heaven wane and go down. And the fourth quarter, named the north, is divided into three parts.[3] And the first of them *is* the dwelling-place for men; and the second *contains* seas of water, and the deeps, and forests, and rivers, and darkness and mist; and the third[4] part *contains* the Garden of Righteousness. I saw seven high mountains which were higher than all the mountains which *are* on the earth, and from them snow comes. And days and times and years pass away and go by.[5] I saw seven[6] rivers on the earth larger than all the *other* rivers; one of them comes from the east *and* pours out its water into the Great Sea. And two of them come from the north to the sea and pour out their water into the Erythraean sea in the east. And the remaining four flow out on the side of the north to their sea, ⟨two to⟩[7] the Erythraean sea, and two into the

2
3

4

5

6

7

---

[16] and rain: Eth.I om.

[17] So Aram.: Eth. by mistake repeats 'gates'.   [18] QU om.

[19] and all their benefits: Q and many Eth.II MSS om. 'all'; D′ 'and their benefits and everything'.

[1] So Eth., but often thought to be corrupt for 'dwell' which Aram. now attests.

[2] D′ 'and especially because there'.

[3] Aram. has a much fuller text than Eth. in verses 2–3a. Apart from other differences Aram. explains the name of the northern quarter and provides a second explanation of the name of the eastern quarter.

[4] GQTUD′ 'second'.

[5] and go by: GMTUD′ om.   [6] Eth.I om.

[7] two to: required for the sense, although omitted by all MSS (D′ alone has 'to').

Great Sea, and[8] they discharge themselves there, but some say:
8 into the wilderness. And I saw seven large islands in the sea and on the land: two on the land, and five in the Great Sea.[9]

LXXVIII.   The names of the sun *are* as follows: the first Oryares, and
2 the second Tomases. The moon has four names: the first name *is* Asonya, and the second Ebla, and the third Banase, and the fourth
3 Era'e. These are the two great lights; their disk *is* like the disk of
4 heaven, and in size the two *are* equal.[1] In the disk of the sun *are* seven parts of light which are added to it more than to the moon, and in fixed measure *light* is transferred *to the moon* until a seventh
5 part of the sun is exhausted. And they set, and go into the gates of the west, and go round through the north, and rise through the
6 gates of the east on the face of heaven. And when the moon rises, it appears in heaven and has a half of a seventh part of light; and on
7 the fourteenth day it makes all its light full.[2] And fifteen parts of light are transferred to it, until on the fifteenth day its light is full, according to the sign of the year, and amounts to fifteen parts. And
8 the moon comes into being by halves of a seventh part. And in its waning on the first day it decreases to fourteen parts of its light, and on the second to thirteen parts, and on the third to twelve parts, and on the fourth to eleven parts, and on the fifth to ten parts, and on the sixth to nine parts, and on the seventh to eight parts, and on the eighth to seven parts, and on the ninth to six parts, and on the tenth to five parts, and on the eleventh to four parts, and on the twelfth to three, and on the thirteenth to two,[3] and on the fourteenth to half of a seventh part, and all the light that remains

[8] Eth.II om.
[9] two . . . Sea: some Eth.II MSS 'two and five in the Great Sea'; M 'two on the land and five in the Erythraean sea'; GQTUD' 'seven and two in the Erythraean sea'.

[1] U 'and the size of the disk of both is equal'; GMQTD' 'and the size of the disk of both – like the disk of heaven – *is* equal'.
[2] GMQTD' text uncertain, perhaps 'it appears in heaven with a half of a seventh part; the light becomes whole in it; on the fourteenth day it makes its light full'; U corrupt.
[3] GMQUD'D'a 'to a half'.

9 from the total disappears on the fifteenth day.[4] And in certain
months the moon has twenty nine days in each *month*, and once
10 twenty eight. And Uriel showed me another law, *namely* when light
is transferred to the moon, and on which side it is transferred from
11 the sun. All the time that the moon is increasing in its light, it
transfers *light to itself* opposite the sun until, in fourteen days, its
light is full in heaven;[5] and when it is all ablaze, its light is full in
12 heaven. And on the first day it is called the new moon, for on that
13 day light rises on it. And *its light* becomes full exactly on the day the
sun goes down into the west, and it rises from the east at night. And
the moon shines through the whole night until the sun rises oppo-
14 site it, and the moon is seen[6] opposite the sun. And on the side on
which the light of the moon appears, there again it wanes until all
its light disappears, and the days of the moon come to an end, and
15 its disk remains empty, without light. And for three months, at its
proper time, it achieves thirty days, and for three months[7] it
achieves in each *month* twenty nine days, during which it completes
its waning, in the first *period of* time and in the first gate, in one
16 hundred and seventy seven days. And in the time of its rising for
three months it appears in each *month* for thirty days, and for three
months it appears in each *month* for twenty nine days. By night, for
twenty days each time,[8] it looks like a man, and by day like heaven,
for there is nothing else in it except its light.

LXXIX. And now, my son Methuselah,[1] I have shown you every-
2 thing, and the whole law of[2] the stars of heaven is complete. And he

[4] GMUD′a (with some corruptions and variations) 'and on the fourteenth to a
half and a seventh part of all its light, and on the fifteenth day what remains from the
total disappears'; QD′ 'and on the fourteenth to a half, and with a seventh part all
its light decreases, and on the fifteenth day what remains from the total disappears';
T partially corresponds to Eth.II and partially to GMUD′a.
[5] in heaven: Eth.I om.   [6] GQUD′aA 'is equal'.
[7] And for three months . . . three months: GMTD′D′a (with some corruptions
and variations) 'And for three months it achieves . . . days (numeral is missing, and
text corrupt; only T[2] has 'thirty'), and at its proper time, when it completes its
waning, for three months'; QU unintelligible, but similar to GM etc.
[8] for twenty days each time: D′ om.

[1] GMQUD′D′a om.
[2] U 'all the laws of'; GMQTD′a 'the law of all'; D′ 'the law and all'.

showed me the whole law for these, for every day, and for every time, and for every *period of* rule,[3] and for every year, and for the end thereof, according to its command for every month and every
3 week; and the waning of the moon which occurs in the sixth gate, for in that sixth gate its light becomes full, and after that it is the
4 beginning of the month; and[4] the waning which occurs in the first gate, at its proper time, until one hundred and seventy seven days are complete (reckoned according to weeks: twenty five *weeks* and
5 two days); and how[5] it falls behind the sun, according to the law of the stars, by exactly five days in one *period of* time, and when this
6 place which you see has been traversed. Such *is* the appearance and the likeness of[6] every light which Uriel, the great angel who is their leader, showed to me.

LXXX. And in those days Uriel[1] answered me and said to me, Behold I have shown you[2] everything, O Enoch, and have revealed everything to you, that you may see this sun, and this moon, and those who lead the stars of heaven, and all those who turn them,
2 their tasks, and their times[3] and their rising. But in the days of the sinners the years will become shorter, and their seed will be late on their land and on their fields, and all things on the earth will change, and will not appear at their proper time. And the rain will
3 be withheld, and heaven will retain *it*.[4] And in those times the fruits of the earth will be late and will not grow at their proper time, and
4 the fruits of the trees will be withheld at their proper time. And the moon will change its customary practice, and will not appear at its
5 proper time. But in those days it will appear in heaven,[5] and come
. . .[6] on top[7] of a large chariot in the west, and shine with more than

---

[3] and for every *period of* rule: D′ om.; GMQT(U)D′a 'which *is* for ruling'.
[4] the month; and: so Eth.II, but possibly corrupt for 'the waning; and'; Eth.I om.
[5] and how: GMQUD′D′a om; C′ om. 'how'.   [6] Lit. 'from'.

[1] Uriel: Q om.; GMTD′ 'the angel Uriel'; D′a defective.
[2] GTUD′ 'I will show you'.   [3] GMTD′D′a add 'and they turn them'.
[4] GQT'UD′a 'will stand still'.
[5] it will appear in heaven: so GTUD′D′a; all other MSS 'heaven will appear (or 'will be seen')'.
[6] Text unintelligible; I have omitted the word 'drought' which all MSS read here ('and drought will come').   [7] on top: possible meaning, but text obscure.

6 normal brightness. And many heads of the stars in command will go astray,[8] and these will change their courses and their activities, and will not appear at the times which have been prescribed for 7 them. And the entire law of the stars will be closed to the sinners, and the thoughts of those who dwell upon the earth[9] will go astray over them, and they will turn from all their ways, and will go 8 astray, and will think them gods. And many evils will overtake them,[10] and punishment will come upon them to destroy them all.

LXXXI. And he said to me, O Enoch, look at the book of the tablets of heaven, and read what is written upon them, and note 2 every individual fact. And I looked at everything in[2] the tablets of heaven, and I read everything which was written, and I noted everything. And I read the book and everything which was written in it, all the deeds of men, and all[3] who will be born of flesh on the 3 earth[4] for the generations of eternity. And then[5] I immediately blessed the Lord,[6] the eternal king of glory,[7] in that he has made all the works of the world, and I praised the Lord because of his 4 patience, and I blessed *him* on account of[8] the sons of Adam.[9] And at that time[10] I said, Blessed is the man who dies righteous and good, concerning whom no book of iniquity has been written, 5 and against whom no guilt has been found.[11] And these three[12]

---

[8] in command (lit. 'of command') will go astray: Q² 'will go astray in regard to the command'; GQ¹D′OB′ corrupt. [9] GMQT¹UD′D′a 'of those on the earth'.

[10] Lit. 'And evil will increase over them'.

[1] O Enoch . . . the book of the: Eth.I 'Look, O Enoch, at these (D′ 'the')'.

[2] everything in: MQTUD′D′a om.

[3] GD′a 'the book, all the deeds of men, and all'; MT 'the book of all the deeds of men, and of all'; D′ 'that book, and all the deeds of men, and all'; U defective.

[4] who will . . . earth: lit. 'the children of flesh who *will be* on the earth'.

[5] GMTUD′D′a om.   [6] Eth.I 'the great Lord'.

[7] BCX 'the king of glory'; GMTUD′D′a 'the king of glory for ever'; Q 'the king, the Lord of glory for ever'.

[8] blessed *him* on account of: D′ 'wept on earth because of'.

[9] Some Eth.II MSS 'the children of the world'.

[10] GMQT¹UD′a 'And after this'; D′ 'After this'.

[11] Q 'and against whom no guilt will be found'; GT¹UD′a 'nor will be found on the day of judgement'; M 'nor has been found on the day of judgement'; T² 'and *against whom* no guilt has been found on the day of judgement'; D′(?) 'and *against whom* judgement has not been found on that day'.   [12] Eth.I 'seven'.

holy ones brought me and set me on the earth before the door of my house, and said to me, Tell everything to your son Methuselah, and show all your children that no flesh is righteous before the Lord, for he created them. For one year we will leave you with your
6 children,[13] until you have regained your strength,[14] that you may teach your children, and write *these things* down for them, and testify to all your children. And in the second year they will take
7 you from among them. Let your heart be strong, for the good will proclaim righteousness to the good, the righteous will rejoice with
8 the righteous, and they will wish each other well. But the sinner will die with the sinner, and the apostate will sink with the
9 apostate. And those who practise righteousness will die[15] because of the deeds of men, and will be gathered in[16] because of the deeds
10 of the impious. And in those days they finished speaking to me, and I went to my family, as I blessed the Lord of the ages.[17]

LXXXII.   And now, my son Methuselah, all these things I recount to you and write down for you;[1] I have revealed everything to you[2] and have given you books about all these things. Keep, my son Methuselah,[3] the books from the hand of your father, that you may
2 pass *them* on to the generations[4] of eternity. I have given wisdom to you and to your children,[5] and to those who will be your children, that they may give *it* to their children for all the generations for
3 ever[6] – this wisdom *which is* beyond their thoughts.[7] And those who

[13] GMQTUD′ 'son'.
[14] until . . . strength: so MT Eth.II (possibly to be translated 'until you have given your last commands again', but in this case 'again' is a little strange); U om.; GD′D′a corrupt; Q 'until you have again comforted him'.
[15] D′D′a² 'will not die'.
[16] and . . . in: D′ 'they will be gathered in'; D′a(?) 'but they will be hidden'.
[17] GMTUD′D′a 'of the world'.

[1] for you: GMTD′a om.
[2] I have . . . to you: some Eth.II MSS om.; D′ om. 'everything'; U om. 'everything to you'; D′a 'I will reveal everything to you'.
[3] GMQD′D′a om.   [4] G 'children'.
[5] T 'and to your son'; G corrupt; M adds a second 'and to your children'.
[6] C′ 'for eternal generations'; Q and some Eth.II MSS 'for the generations for ever'; GMTUD′a 'for generations'; D′ 'and for generations'.
[7] that they may give . . . their thoughts: D′D′a (with some corruptions and

understand it will not sleep, but will incline their ears that they
may learn this wisdom, and it will be better for those who eat *from it*
4 than good food. Blessed are all the righteous, blessed are all those[8]
who walk in the way of righteousness, and do not sin like the
sinners in the numbering of all their days in which the sun journeys
in heaven, coming in and out through the gates for thirty days with
the heads over thousands of this[9] order of stars, *and* with the four
which are added and divide[10] between the four parts of the year,
5 which lead them and appear with them on four days. Because of
them men go wrong, and they do not[11] reckon them in the reckoning of the whole *course of the* world;[12] for men go wrong in respect of
6 them, and do not know them exactly. For they belong in the
reckoning of the year,[13] and are truly recorded *therein* for ever, one
in the first gate, and one in the third, and one in the fourth and one
in the sixth. And the year is completed in three hundred and sixty
7 four days.[14] And the account of it *is* true, and the recorded reckoning of it *is* exact, for the lights, and the months, and the feasts, and
the years, and the days Uriel showed me, and he inspired me – he
to whom the Lord of the whole created world gave commands
8 about the host of heaven for me. And he has power in heaven over
night and day to cause light to shine on men: the sun, and the
moon, and the stars, and all the powers of heaven which rotate in
9 their orbits. And this is the law of the stars which set in their places,
10 at their times, and at their feasts, and in their months. And these
are the names of those who lead them, who keep watch that they
appear[15] at their times,[16] and in their orders, and at their proper

variations) 'that they may give this wisdom to their children for generations, and all
the wise will sing praises, and wisdom will lie upon your thoughts'.

[8]   blessed are all those: GY om.; M 'blessed are all the righteous'; Q 'blessed then
are all those'; D'D'a 'blessed are those'; U defective.

[9]   GTD'D'a 'the'; MQU corrupt.

[10]   GMUD'aNOB' 'are divided'.

[11]   do not: D'B om.

[12]   the whole *course of the* world: U 'the *course of the* world'; D' 'the year'; B 'all men'.

[13]   P² 'the world'; U 'the world and the year'.

[14]   Eth.I 'And the year of three hundred and sixty four days is completed'.

[15]   Lit. 'who keep watch and they appear'; U 'who appear'; D' 'who appear and
they set'.

[16]   GMQTD'D'a add 'who lead them in their places'; U adds 'who lead them'.

times, and in their months, and in their periods of rule, and in their
11 positions. Their four leaders who divide the four parts of the year
appear first; and after them the twelve leaders of the orders who
divide the months and the years into three hundred and sixty four
days, with the heads[17] over thousands who separate the days; and
for the four *days* which are added to them there are the leaders who
12 separate the four parts of the year. And as for these heads over
thousands, one is added between the leader and the led[18] behind a
13 position, but their leaders make the separation. And these *are* the
names of the leaders who separate the four appointed parts of the
14 year: Melkiel, Helemmelek, Meleyal and Narel. And the names of
those whom they lead *are* Adnarel, Iyasusael and Iylumiel; these
three follow behind the leaders of the orders, and *each* one follows
behind the three leaders of the orders who follow behind those
leaders of positions who separate the four parts of the year. In the
15 beginning of the year[19] Melkiel rises first and rules, *the one* who is
called **the southern sun**;[20] and all the days of his period of rule during
16 which he rules *are* ninety one. And these *are* the signs of the days
which are to be seen on earth in the days of his period of rule: sweat,
and heat,[21] and **calm**;[22] and all the trees bear fruit, and leaves
appear on all the trees, and the wheat harvest, and rose flowers,
and all the flowers bloom[23] in the field, but the trees of winter[24] are
17 withered. And these *are* the names of the leaders who *are* under
them:[25] Berkeel, Zelebsael, and another one who is added, a head
over a thousand named Heloyaseph. And the days of the period of

---

[17] and the years . . . with the heads: GMQUD′D′a (with some corruptions and
variations) 'and for the three hundred and sixty *days* there are the heads'; T 'and the
three hundred and sixty four *days*, with the heads'.
[18] between . . . the led: GMUD′D′a 'between leader and leader'; QT′D defective. The meaning of this verse is rather obscure.
[19] of the year: GQTUD′D′a om.
[20] Eth. has 'Tama'ayni and sun' (the word for 'southern' was transliterated, not
translated, and 'and' was introduced by mistake).
[21] B′ 'death'.
[22] and calm: so U, but with a small correction; all other MSS 'and sorrow'.
[23] and all . . . bloom: GQTD′D′a 'and all the flowers which come out'; MU
defective.
[24] D′a 'of the field'.
[25] So all MSS except U (but we expect 'him'): U om. 'who are under them'.

18 rule of this one are complete. The second leader after him[26] is Helemmelek whom they call the shining sun; and all the days of
19 his light *are* ninety one. And these are the signs of the days[27] on earth: heat, and drought; and the trees bring their fruit to ripeness and maturity, and make their fruit dry;[28] and the sheep mate, and become pregnant; and men gather all the fruits of the earth, and everything which is in the fields, and the vats of wine. And *these*
20 *things* occur in the days of his period of rule. And these are the names and the orders and the leaders[29] . . . of these heads over thousands: Gedaeyal, Keel and Heel;[30] and the name of the head over a thousand who is added to them *is* Asfael. And the days of his period of rule are complete.

LXXXIII. And now, my son Methuselah, I will show you all the[1]
2 visions which I saw, recounting *them* before you. Two visions I saw before I took a wife, and neither one was like the other. For the first time when I learnt the art of writing, and for the second time before I took your mother, I saw a terrible vision; and concerning them I
3 made supplication to the Lord. I had lain down in the house of my grandfather Malalel, *when* I saw in a vision *how* heaven was thrown
4 down and removed, and it fell upon the earth. And when it fell upon the earth, I saw how the earth was swallowed up in a great abyss, and mountains were suspended on mountains, and hills sank down upon hills, and tall trees were torn up by their roots,[2]
5 and were thrown down, and sank into the abyss. And then speech

---

[26] So GTUD′D′a: other MSS 'them'.

[27] the signs of the days: MT 'the days of his sign'; GQUD′D′a corrupt or defective.

[28] and maturity . . . dry: GMQTD′D′a (with some corruptions and omissions) 'and produce all their fruit ripe and mature'; U defective.

[29] All MSS except GQUD′a add 'who *are* under them', but the text is awkward, and I omit with GQ. 'Who *are* under him' would be easier, but the text is still confusing. D′a 'and the leaders of those who *are* under these heads'; U defective.

[30] Keel and Heel: GMQUD′a om. 'and Heel'; D′ 'Helyael and Kiel'.

---

[1] GMQ 'my'. From the beginning of chapter lxxxiii onwards there are so many omissions and corruptions in U that it has not been thought worth recording them except in a few special cases.

[2] Lit. 'from their roots' or 'from their trunks'.

fell into my mouth, and I raised *my voice*[3] to cry out and said, The
6 earth is destroyed! And my grandfather Malalel roused me, while I
lay near him, and said to me, Why do you cry out so, my son, and
7 why do you moan so? And I recounted to him the whole vision
which I had seen, and he said to me, A terrible thing you have seen,
my son! Your dream-vision concerns[4] the secrets of all the sin of the
earth;[5] it is about to sink into the abyss, and be utterly destroyed.
8 And now, my son, rise, and make supplication to the Lord of Glory
– for you are faithful – that a remnant may be left on the earth, and
9 that he may not wipe out the whole earth.[6] My son, from heaven all
this will come upon the earth, and upon the earth there will be
10 great destruction. And then I rose, and prayed, and made supplication,[7] and wrote my prayer down for the generations of eternity,
11 and I will show everything to you, my son Methuselah. And when
I went out below, and saw heaven, and the sun rising in the east,[8]
and the moon setting in the west, and some stars, and the whole
earth,[9] and everything as he knew it at the beginning, then I
blessed the Lord of Judgement, and ascribed majesty to him, for he
makes the sun come out from the windows of the east so that it
ascends and rises[10] on the face of heaven, and sets out and goes in
the path which has been shown to it.

LXXXIV. And I raised my hands in righteousness, and I blessed
the Holy and Great One, and I spoke with the breath of my mouth,
and with the tongue of flesh which God has made for men born of
flesh,[1] that they might speak with it; and he has given them breath,

[3] G 'and I rose'; TN 'and I began'.
[4] Your dream-vision concerns (lit. 'is heavy with'): D' 'A hard vision you have
dreamed with regard to'; GMQT unintelligible.
[5] the secrets . . . earth: C' 'the secrets of all the sin; the earth'; G 'the sin of all the
sin; the earth'; M (corrupt?) 'the sin of all the sin of the earth'; QD' 'the sin of all the
earth'.
[6] and that . . . earth: GMQ om.
[7] GMTD' add 'and petitioned'.
[8] GMQ add 'and the sun'.
[9] and the whole earth: T and some Eth.II MSS om.
[10] Lit. 'and it ascends and rises'.

[1] Lit. 'for the children of the flesh of men'; some Eth.II MSS 'for the children of
men'; Q 'for the children of men of flesh'.

and a tongue and a mouth, that they might speak with them.
2 Blessed *are* you, O Lord King, and great and powerful in your majesty, Lord of the whole creation of heaven, King of Kings, and God of the whole world! And your kingly authority, and your sovereignty and your majesty will last for ever, and for ever and ever, and your power for all generations. And all the heavens *are* your throne for ever, and the whole earth your footstool for ever,
3 and for ever and ever. For you made, and you rule[2] everything, and nothing is too hard for you, and no wisdom escapes you; it does not turn away from your throne,[3] nor from your presence. And you know and see and hear everything, and nothing is hidden from
4 you, for you see everything. And now the angels of your heaven are doing wrong, and your anger rests upon the flesh of men until the
5 day of the great judgement. And now, O God and Lord and Great King, I entreat and ask that you will fulfil my prayer to leave me a posterity on earth, and not to wipe out all the flesh of men and
6 make the earth empty, so that there is destruction for ever. And now, my Lord, wipe out from the earth the flesh which has provoked you to anger, but the flesh of righteousness and uprightness establish as a seed-bearing plant for ever. And do not hide your face from the prayer of your servant, O Lord.

LXXXV. And after this I saw another dream, and I will show it all[1]
2 to you, my son. And Enoch raised *his voice*[2] and said to his son Methuselah, To you I speak, my son. Hear my words, and incline
3 your ear to the dream-vision of your father. Before I took your mother Edna, I saw in a vision on[3] my bed, and behold a bull came out of the earth, and that bull was white; and after it a heifer came out, and with the heifer[4] came two bullocks,[5] and one of them was

---

[2] Some Eth.II MSS 'fill'.

[3] So Q: all other MSS except U have a corrupt dittograph 'from her life, your throne'; U defective.

[1] it all: G 'the whole dream'.
[2] Q 'rose'; TD′NC′ 'answered'.   [3] GMTD′ 'of'.
[4] Lit. 'and with it (fem.)'; MTD′EFHP[1] 'and with it (masc.)'; Q 'with it (masc.)'.
[5] two bullocks: so GNC′; other MSS have an ambiguous phrase perhaps to be translated 'other bullocks'.

4 black, and the other red. And that black bullock struck the red one, and pursued it over the earth, and from then on I could not see that
5 red bullock. But that black bullock grew, and a heifer went with it; and I saw that many bulls came out from it which were like it and
6 followed behind it.[6] And that cow, that first one, came from the presence of that first bull, seeking that red bullock, but did not find
7 it; and thereupon it moaned bitterly,[7] and continued to seek it. And I looked until that first bull came to it and calmed it, and from that
8 time it did not cry out. And after this she bore another white bull,[8]
9 and after it she bore many black bulls and cows. And I saw in my sleep that white bull, how it likewise grew and became a large white bull, and from it came many white bulls, and they were like
10 it. And they began to beget many white bulls which were like them, one following another.[9]

LXXXVI. And again I looked with my eyes as I was sleeping, and I saw heaven above, and behold a star fell from heaven, and it arose
2 and ate and pastured amongst those bulls. And after this I saw the large and the black bulls, and behold all of them changed their pens and their pastures and their heifers, and they began to moan,[1]
3 one after another.[2] And again I saw in the vision and looked at heaven, and behold I saw many stars, how they came down and were thrown down[3] from heaven to that first star, and amongst those heifers and bulls; they were with them, pasturing[4] amongst
4 them. And I looked at them and saw, and behold all of them let out their private parts like horses and began to mount the cows of the bulls, and they all became pregnant and bore elephants and
5 camels and asses. And all the bulls were afraid of them and were terrified before them, and they began to bite with their teeth, and

---

[6] GMTD' 'them'.
[7] GQD' 'and it moaned bitterly over it (G 'in respect of it')'.
[8] GQD' 'two white bulls'.
[9] GMQTD' 'many following, one after another'.

[1] G 'to live'.
[2] Eth.II 'one with another'.
[3] Or 'and threw themselves down'.
[4] and amongst . . . pasturing: GMQD' 'and amongst those heifers they became bulls, and with them they pastured'; T unintelligible.

6 to devour, and to gore with their horns. And so they began to
devour those bulls, and behold all the children of the earth began
to tremble and shake before them, and to flee.[5]

LXXXVII. And again I saw them, how they began to gore one
another and to devour one another, and the earth began to cry out.
2 And I raised my eyes again to heaven and saw in the vision, and
behold there came from heaven beings who were like white men;
3 and four[1] came from that place, and three *others* with them.[2] And
those three who came out last took hold of me by my hand, and
raised me from the generations of the earth, and lifted me onto a
high place, and showed me a tower high above the earth, and all
4 the hills were lower.[3] And one[4] said to me, Remain here until you
have seen everything which is coming upon these[5] elephants and
camels and asses, and upon the stars, and upon all the bulls.[6]

LXXXVIII. And I saw one of those four who had come out first, how
he took hold of that first star which had fallen from heaven, and
bound it by its hands and its feet, and threw it into an abyss; and
2 that abyss was narrow, and deep, and horrible[1] and dark. And one
of them drew his[2] sword and gave *it* to those elephants and camels[3]
and asses, and they began to strike one another, and the whole
3 earth shook because of them. And as I looked in the vision, behold
one of those four who had come out cast from heaven and gathered
and took[4] all the large stars whose private parts *were* like the private
parts of horses, and bound them all by their hands and their feet,
and threw them into a chasm of the earth.

  [5] GMD′ add 'from them'.

  [1] So Eth.I: Eth.II 'one'.			[2] So M: other MSS 'him'.
  [3] So T Eth.II: GMQ 'built'(?); D′ 'firmly fixed'(?).
  [4] Q and many Eth.II MSS 'they'.
  [5] Eth.I 'those'.
  [6] GMQTD′ 'and upon the bulls and all of them'.

  [1] D′ 'and enclosed'; GMT(?) 'and desolate'; Q(?) 'and worm-infested'.
  [2] Eth.I 'a'.				[3] and camels: GMQD′ om.
  [4] cast . . . and took: so T Eth.II, but N reads 'cast a sword from heaven' etc., and
T reads 'and he cast from heaven' etc. The text is awkward, but the Eth.I variants
(some or all – so D′ – of the verbs in the plural) do not give better sense.

LXXXIX. And one of those four went to a white bull[1] and taught him[2] a mystery, trembling as he was.[3] He was born a bull, but became a man, and built for himself a large vessel and dwelt on it, and three bulls dwelt with him in that vessel, and they were
2 covered over.[4] And I again raised my eyes to heaven and saw a high roof, with seven water-channels on it, and those channels
3 discharged much water into an enclosure. And I looked again, and behold springs[5] opened on the floor of that large enclosure, and water began to bubble up and to rise above the floor; and I looked
4 at that enclosure until[6] its whole floor was covered by water. And water and darkness and mist increased on it; and I looked at the height of that water, and that water had risen above that enclosure and was pouring out over the enclosure, and it remained on the
5 earth. And all the bulls of that enclosure were gathered together until I saw how they sank and were swallowed up and destroyed in
6 that water. And that vessel floated on the water, but all the bulls and elephants and camels and asses sank to the bottom, together with all the animals, so that I could not see them. And they were unable to get out, but were destroyed and sank into the depths.
7 And again I looked in the vision until those water-channels were removed from that high roof, and the chasms of the earth were
8 made level,[7] and other abysses were opened. And the water began to run down into them until the earth became visible, and that vessel settled on the earth; and the darkness departed, and light
9 appeared. And that white bull who became a man went out from that vessel, and the three bulls with him. And one of the three bulls was white, like that bull, and one of them *was* red as blood, and one

---

[1] a white bull (or 'that white bull'): so M; Aram. 'one of the bulls'; other Eth. MSS 'those white bulls'.

[2] B²NXC' 'them'.

[3] B²NX 'trembling as they were'; GQ 'without him trembling'.

[4] and they were covered over: GMQ om. 'and'; D' (but with a minor mistake) 'and this vessel was closed over them'; Aram. 'and the vessel was closed and covered [over them]'.

[5] Aram. 'chambers'; D' 'chasms' (cp. verse 7).

[6] and I looked . . . until: so GT(U); Eth.II 'and made that enclosure invisible until'; MQD' corrupt; Aram. '[and] I looked until'.

[7] and the chasms . . . level: Aram. '] the chambers were stopped'.

10   *was* black;[8] and that white bull passed away from them. And they
     began to beget wild-animals and birds, so that there arose from
     them every kind of species: lions, tigers, wolves, dogs, hyenas,
     wild-boars, foxes, badgers, pigs, falcons, vultures, kites, eagles and
11   ravens. But amongst them was born a white bull. And they began
     to bite one another; but that white bull which was born amongst
     them begat a wild ass and a white bull with it, and the wild asses[9]
12   increased. But that bull which was born from it begat a black
     wild-boar and a white sheep; and that wild-boar[10] begat many
13   boars, and that sheep begat twelve sheep. And when those twelve
     sheep had grown, they handed one of their number over to the
     asses, and those asses in turn handed that sheep over to the wolves;
14   and that sheep grew up amongst the wolves. And the Lord brought
     the eleven sheep to dwell with it and to pasture with it amongst the
15   wolves, and they increased and became many flocks of sheep. And
     the wolves began to make them afraid,[11] and they oppressed them
     until they made away with their young, and they threw their young
     into a river with much water; but those sheep began to cry out
16   because of their young, and to complain to their Lord. But a sheep
     which had been saved from the wolves fled and escaped to the wild
     asses. And I saw the sheep moaning and crying out, and petition-
     ing their Lord with all their power, until that Lord of the sheep
     came down at the call of the sheep from a high room,[12] and came to
17   them, and looked at them.[13] And he called that sheep which had
     fled from the wolves, and spoke to it about the wolves that it should
18   warn them that they should not touch the sheep. And the sheep
     went to the wolves in accordance with the word of the Lord, and
     another sheep met that sheep[14] and went with it; and the two of
     them together[15] entered the assembly of those wolves, and spoke to
     them, and warned them that from then on they should not touch
19   the sheep. And after this I saw the wolves, how they acted even
     more harshly towards the sheep with all their power, and the sheep

---

[8] and one *was* black: Eth.I om.   [9] Some Eth.II MSS 'and the wild ass'.
[10] and that wild-boar: MQTD′ 'and the former' (lit. 'and that one'); G defective.
[11] Some Eth. MSS 'to fear them'.
[12] TD′B 'from the room of the Most High'.
[13] Or 'and pastured them'.   [14] GMQD′ 'met it'.
[15] GMQD′ add 'went and'.

20 cried out. And their Lord came to the sheep, and began[16] to beat those wolves; and the wolves began to moan, but the sheep became
21 silent, and from then on they did not cry out. And I looked at the sheep until they escaped from the wolves; but the eyes of the wolves were blinded, and those wolves went out in pursuit of the sheep with all their forces. And the Lord of the sheep went with them as
22 he led them, and all his sheep followed him; and his face *was* glorious, and his appearance terrible and magnificent.[17] But the
23 wolves began to pursue those sheep until they met them by a
24 stretch of water. And that stretch of water was divided, and the water stood on one side and on the other before them; and their
25 Lord, as he led them, stood between them and the wolves. And while those wolves had not yet seen the sheep, they went[18] into the middle of that stretch of water; but the wolves pursued the sheep,
26 and those wolves ran after them into that stretch of water. But when they saw the Lord of the sheep, they turned to flee before him; but that stretch of water flowed together again and suddenly resumed its natural form, and the water swelled up and rose until it
27 covered those wolves. And I looked until all the wolves which had
28 pursued those sheep were destroyed and drowned. But the sheep escaped from that water and went to a desert where there was neither water nor grass; and they began to open their eyes and to see; and I saw the Lord of the sheep pasturing them and giving
29 them water and grass, and that sheep going and leading them. And that sheep went up to the summit of a high rock, and the Lord of
30 the sheep sent it to them. And after this I saw the Lord of the sheep standing before them, and his appearance *was* terrible and ma-
31 jestic,[19] and all those sheep saw him and were afraid of him. And all of them were afraid and trembled before him; and they cried out after that sheep with them[20] which was in their midst,[21] We cannot

---

[16] GQTD′ 'and they began'; M corrupt.

[17] and his appearance . . . magnificent: GMTD′ 'and magnificent and terrible to see'; Q 'and terrible to see'.

[18] D′ (in part corruptly) 'had not yet seen him, the sheep went'.

[19] terrible and majestic: so Eth.II; Eth.I 'great and terrible and majestic'; Aram. 'strong and great and['.

[20] with them: so G; MQ 'with them to the other sheep'; D′ '*which* led them and the other sheep'; T Eth.II 'which was with him to the other sheep'.

[21] D′ adds 'and said'.

32 stand before our Lord, nor look at him. And that sheep which led
    them again went up to the summit of that rock; and the sheep
    began to be blinded and to go astray from the path which it had
33 shown to them, but that sheep did not know. And the Lord of the
    sheep was extremely angry with them, and that sheep knew, and
    went down from the summit of the rock, and came to the sheep,
    and found the majority of them with their eyes blinded and going
34 astray from his path.[22] And when they saw it, they were afraid and
    trembled before it, and wished that they could return to their
35 enclosure. And that sheep took some other sheep with it, and went
    to those sheep which had gone astray, and then began to kill
    them;[23] and the sheep were afraid of it. And that sheep brought
    back those sheep which had gone astray, and they returned to their
36 enclosures. And I looked there at the vision[24] until that sheep
    became a man, and built a house for the Lord of the sheep, and
37 made all the sheep stand in that house. And I looked until that
    sheep which had met that sheep which led the sheep[25] fell asleep;
    and I looked until all the large sheep were destroyed and small
    ones rose up in their place, and they came to a pasture, and drew
38 near to a river of water. And that sheep which led them, which had
    become a man, separated from them and fell asleep; and all the
39 sheep sought it and cried out very bitterly over it. And I looked
    until they left off crying for that sheep and crossed that river of
    water; and there arose all the sheep which led them in place of
40 those which had fallen asleep, and they led them. And I looked
    until the sheep came to a good place and a pleasant and glorious
    land, and I looked until those sheep were satisfied; and that house
41 *was* in the middle of them in the pleasant land. And sometimes
    their eyes were opened, and sometimes blinded, until another
    sheep rose up and led them, and brought them all back,[26] and their
42 eyes were opened. And the dogs and the foxes and the wild-boars
    began to devour those sheep[27] until the Lord of the sheep raised up

----

[22] from his path: GMQTD' om.
[23] and then . . . kill them: GMQD' 'killing them'.
[24] there at the vision: GMTD' 'in this vision'; Q 'in that vision'.
[25] GMQD' 'which led them'.
[26] D' 'and they all came back'.
[27] Gk.ᵛ 'And the dogs began to devour the sheep, and the wild-boars and the foxes devoured them'.

43 a ram²⁸ from among them²⁹ which led them. And that ram began to
   butt those dogs and foxes and wild-boars, on one side and on the
44 other, until it had destroyed them all.³⁰ And the eyes of that sheep
   were opened, and it saw that ram³¹ in the middle of the sheep, how
   it renounced its glory³² and began to butt those sheep, and *how* it
45 trampled on them and behaved unbecomingly.³³ And the Lord of
   the sheep sent the sheep to another sheep³⁴ and raised it up to be a
   ram, and to lead the sheep³⁵ in place of that sheep³⁶ which had
46 renounced its glory.³⁷ And it went to it, and spoke with it³⁸ alone,
   and raised up that ram, and made it the prince and leader of the
47 sheep;³⁹ and during all this those⁴⁰ dogs oppressed the sheep. And
   the first ram pursued that⁴¹ second ram, and that second ram rose
   and fled⁴² before it. And I looked until those dogs made the first
48 ram fall.⁴³ And that second ram rose up and led the small⁴⁴ sheep,
   and that ram begat many sheep and fell asleep; and a small sheep
   became ram in place of it, and became the prince and leader of
49 those sheep.⁴⁵ And those⁴¹ sheep grew and increased; but all the⁴⁶

---

²⁸ until the Lord . . . a ram: so C' Gk.ᵛ and similarly N; all other Eth. MSS corrupt.

²⁹ Gk.ᵛ 'from the sheep' and om. 'which led them'.

³⁰ Gk.ᵛ 'to butt and to pursue with *its* horns, and to hurl itself against the foxes, and after them against the wild-boars; and it destroyed many wild-boars, and after them [it injure]d the dogs'.

³¹ Gk.ᵛ 'And the sheep (plur.) whose eyes were opened looked at the ram'.

³² how . . . its glory: Gk.ᵛ 'until it left its way'.

³³ and began . . . unbecomingly: Gk.ᵛ 'and began to walk off the way'.

³⁴ the sheep to another sheep: Gk.ᵛ 'this lamb to another lamb'.

³⁵ and raised . . . the sheep: Gk.ᵛ 'to appoint it as the ram in command of the sheep'.

³⁶ D 'that ram' (lit. 'that male sheep').

³⁷ Gk.ᵛ 'in place of the ram which had left its way'. In notes 32, 33, and 37 a small fragment of Aram. appears to support the originality of Gk.ᵛ 'way'.

³⁸ Gk.ᵛ adds 'secretly'.

³⁹ and raised up . . . the sheep: Gk.ᵛ 'and raised it up to be the ram and leader and prince of the sheep'; GMQD' corrupt.

⁴⁰ GMQTD' Gk.ᵛ 'the'.

⁴¹ Gk.ᵛ 'the'.

⁴² and that second . . . fled: Gk.ᵛ 'and it fled'.

⁴³ Gk.ᵛ 'Then I looked at the first ram until it fell before the dogs'.

⁴⁴ small: Gk.ᵛ om.

⁴⁵ and that ram . . . those sheep: Gk.ᵛ om.

⁴⁶ So some Eth.II MSS Gk.ᵛ: other Eth. MSS 'those'.

dogs and foxes and wild-boars[47] were afraid and fled from it,[48] and that ram butted and killed all the animals, and those animals did not again prevail amongst the sheep and did not seize anything
50 further from them. And that house became large and broad, and for those sheep a high tower was built on that house[49] for the Lord of the sheep; and that house was low, but the tower was raised up and high; and the Lord of the sheep stood on that tower, and they
51 spread a full table before him. And I saw those sheep again, how[50] they went astray, and walked in many ways, and left that house of theirs; and the Lord of the sheep called some of the sheep and sent
52 them to the sheep, but the sheep began to kill them. But one of them was saved and was not killed, and it sprang away and cried out against the sheep, and they wished to kill it; but the Lord of the sheep saved it from the hands of[51] the sheep, and brought it up to
53 me, and made it remain *there*. And he sent many other sheep to
54 those sheep to testify *to them* and to lament over them. And after this I saw how when they left the house of the Lord of the sheep[52] and his tower, they went astray in everything, and their eyes were blinded; and I saw how the Lord of the sheep wrought much slaughter among them in their pastures until those sheep *themselves*
55 invited that slaughter and betrayed his place. And he gave them into the hands of the lions and the tigers and the wolves and the hyenas, and into the hands of the foxes, and to all the animals; and
56 those wild animals began to tear those sheep in pieces. And I saw how he left that house of theirs and their tower and gave them all into the hands of the lions, that they might tear them in pieces and
57 devour them, into the hands of all the animals. And I began to cry out with all my power, and to call the Lord of the sheep,[53] and to represent to him with regard to the sheep that they were being
58 devoured by all the wild animals. But he remained still, although he saw *it*, and rejoiced that they were devoured and swallowed up

---

[47] and wild-boars: Gk.[v] om.

[48] were afraid . . . from it: Gk.[v] 'fled from it and feared it' (Gk.[v] ends here).

[49] and for . . . house: so many Eth.II MSS; all other MSS (except GQU) have two versions of this. Later this double reading was shortened, in Eth.II probably deliberately, in GQU probably by accident.

[50] GMT most Eth.II MSS add 'again'.

[51] the hands of: GMD′ om.

[52] of the sheep: GMQTD′ om.   [53] GMQD′ 'of the lions'.

and carried off, and he gave them into the hands of all the animals
59 for food. And he called seventy[54] shepherds and cast off those
sheep[55] that they might pasture them; and he said to the shepherds
and to their companions, Each one of you from now on is to pasture
60 the sheep, and do whatever I command you. And I will hand *them*
over to you duly numbered and will tell you which of them are to be
destroyed, and destroy them. And he handed those sheep over to
61 them. And he called another and said to him, Observe and see
everything that the shepherds do against these sheep, for they will
destroy from among them more than I have commanded them.
62 And write down all the excess and destruction which is wrought by
the shepherds, how many they destroy at my command, and how
many they destroy of their own volition; write down against each
63 shepherd individually all that he destroys. And read out before me
exactly how many they destroy of their own volition,[56] and how
many are handed over to them for destruction,[57] that this may be a
testimony for me against them, that I may know all the deeds of the
shepherds, in order to hand them over *for destruction*, and may see
what they do, whether they abide by[58] my command which I have
64 commanded them, or not. But they must not know *this*, and you
must not show *this* to them, nor reprove them, but *only* write down
against each individual in his time all that the shepherds destroy
65 and bring it all up to me. And I looked until those shepherds
pastured at their time, and they began to kill and to destroy more
than they were commanded, and they gave those sheep into the
66 hands of the lions. And the lions and the tigers devoured and
swallowed up the majority of those sheep, and the wild-boars
devoured with them; and they burnt down that tower and de-
67 molished that house. And I was extremely sad about the tower,
because that house of the sheep had been demolished; and after
that I was unable to see whether those sheep went into that house.
68 And the shepherds and their companions handed those sheep over
to all the animals that they might devour them; each one of them at
his time received an exact number, and *of* each one of them after

---

[54] GMQ 'seven'.   [55] GQD′ add 'to them'.
[56] of their own volition: GMQTD′ and many Eth.II MSS om.
[57] Or 'and how many they hand over for destruction'.
[58] D′ 'act according to'.

the other there was written in a book how many of them he
69 destroyed[59] . . . And each one killed and destroyed more than was
prescribed, and I began to weep and to moan very much[60] because
70 of those sheep. And likewise in the[61] vision I saw that one who
wrote, how every day he wrote down each one which was destroyed
by those shepherds, and *how* he brought up and presented and
showed the whole book to the Lord of the sheep, everything that
they had done, and all that each one of them had made away with,
71 and all that they had handed over to destruction. And the book was
read out before the Lord of the sheep, and he took the book in[62] his
72 hand, and read it, and sealed it, and put it down. And after this I
saw how the shepherds pastured for twelve hours, and behold,
three of those sheep returned and arrived and came and began to
build up all that had fallen down from that house; but the wild-
73 boars hindered them so that they could not. And they began again
to build, as before, and they raised up that tower, and it was called
the high tower; and they began again to place a table before the
74 tower, but all the bread on it *was* unclean and was not pure. And
besides all *this* the eyes of these sheep were blinded so that they
could not see, and their shepherds likewise; and they handed yet
more of them over to their shepherds for destruction, and they
75 trampled upon the sheep with their feet and devoured them. But
the Lord of the sheep remained still until all the sheep were
scattered abroad and had mixed with them,[63] and they did not save
76 them from the hand of the animals. And that one[64] who wrote the
book brought it up, and showed it, and read *it* out in the dwelling of
the Lord[65] of the sheep; and he entreated him on behalf of them,
and petitioned him as he showed him all the deeds of their[66]

---

[59] and *of* each . . . he destroyed: so Eth.II, although the text is a little awkward
and perhaps should be emended to read 'and *of* each one of them the other (cp. verse
61) wrote in a book . . .'; Eth.I MSS offer litle sense. All MSS (except U) repeat some
words at the end of the verse by mistake.

[60] very much: GMQTD′ om.   [61] D′ 'my'.

[62] GMTD′ 'from'; Q corrupt.   [63] i.e., apparently, with the animals.

[64] GMQT 'this one'; D′ 'the one'.

[65] and read . . . the Lord: so MQT²(?) Eth.II; G 'and read *it* out before the Lord';
T¹ 'and read out the great things to the Lord'; D′ 'and read out the great things of
the Lord'.

[66] GMQD′ 'the'.

77 shepherds, and testified before him against all the shepherds. And he took the book, and put it down by him,[67] and went out.

XC. And I looked until the time that thirty-seven[1] shepherds had pastured *the sheep* in the same way, and, each individually, they all completed their time like the first ones; and others received them into their hands to pasture them at their time, each shepherd at his
2 own time. And after this I saw in the vision[2] all the birds of heaven coming: the eagles, and the vultures, and the kites, and the ravens; but the eagles led all the birds; and they began to devour those
3 sheep, and to peck out their eyes, and to devour their flesh. And the sheep cried out because their flesh was devoured by the birds, and I cried out[3] and lamented in my sleep on account of that shepherd
4 who pastured the sheep. And I looked until those sheep were devoured by the dogs and by the eagles and by the kites, and they left on them neither flesh nor skin nor sinew until only their bones remained; and their bones fell upon the ground, and the sheep
5 became few. And I looked until the time that twenty three shepherds[4] had pastured *the sheep*; and they completed, each in his
6 time, fifty eight times. And small lambs[5] were born from those white sheep, and they began to open their eyes, and to see, and to
7 cry to the sheep. But the sheep did not cry to them and[6] did not listen to what they said to them,[7] but were extremely deaf, and
8 their eyes were extremely and excessively blinded.[8] And I saw in the vision how the ravens flew upon those lambs, and took one of those lambs, and dashed the sheep in pieces and devoured them.
9 And I looked until horns came up on those lambs, but the ravens

[67] D′ adds 'in the same way'.

[1] So all MSS except M (QD′ corruptly), but a mistake for 'thirty-five': M om.
[2] GQT 'in my vision';D′ 'with my eyes'.
[3] GQ 'and I looked'; M 'and I saw'.
[4] GMQD′ om.
[5] GMQTD′ 'And behold, lambs'.
[6] D′L²N 'And the sheep cried to them, but they'; GOB′ 'But they did not cry to them and'; M 'But they oppressed them and'; Q 'And they cried to them, but they'; T 'But they did not hear them and'.
[7] what they said to them: GMQTD′N 'their words'.
[8] and excessively blinded: so T Eth.II; GMQ 'blinded and heavy'(?), but the text is of uncertain meaning; D′ corrupt.

cast their horns down;[9] and I looked until a big horn grew on[10] one
10 of those sheep, and their eyes were opened.[11] And it looked at them,
and their eyes were opened, and it[12] cried to the sheep, and the
11 rams saw it, and they all ran to it. And besides all this those eagles
and vultures and ravens and kites were still continually tearing the
sheep in pieces and flying upon them and devouring them; and
12 the sheep were silent, but the rams lamented and cried out. And
those ravens battled and fought with it, and wished to make away
13 with its horn, but they did not prevail against it. And I looked at
them until the shepherds and the eagles and those vultures and
kites came and cried to the ravens that they should dash the horn of
that ram in pieces; and they fought and battled with it, and it
14 fought with them and cried out that its help might come to it.[13] And
I looked until that man who wrote down the names of the
shepherds and brought *them* up before the Lord of the sheep came,
and he helped that ram and showed it everything, *namely that* its
15 help was coming down.[14] And I looked until that[15] Lord of the
sheep came to them in anger, and all those who saw him fled, and
16 they all fell into the[16] shadow before him. All the eagles and
vultures and ravens and kites gathered together and brought with
them all the wild sheep,[17] and they all came together and helped
17 one another in order to dash that horn of the ram in pieces. And I
looked at that man who wrote the book at the command of the Lord
until he opened that book of the destruction which those twelve last
shepherds had wrought, and he showed before the Lord of the
sheep that they had destroyed even more than *those* before them.
18 And I looked until the Lord of the sheep came to them and took in
his hand the staff of his anger and struck the earth; and the earth

---

⁹ D' 'broke their horns'.

¹⁰ So GC': all other MSS om ('one of those sheep' will then be in apposition to 'a
big horn').

¹¹ GMT add 'and their eyes saw'.

¹² GQT 'they'.   ¹³ to it: GMQTD' om.

¹⁴ G 'and he helped it, and saved it, and showed it everything; he had come down
for the help of that ram'.

¹⁵ GTD' 'the'; M corrupt.

¹⁶ So GMD': other MSS 'his'.

¹⁷ Some Eth.II MSS 'and brought with them all the wild asses'; GQD' (QD' in
part corruptly) 'and all the wild sheep came with them'.

was split, and all the animals and[18] the birds of heaven fell from
those sheep and sank in the earth, and it closed over them. And I
looked until a big sword was given to the sheep, and the sheep went
out against all the[19] wild animals to kill them, and all the animals
and the birds of heaven fled before them. And I looked until a
throne was set up in the pleasant land, and the Lord of the sheep
sat on it; and they took all the sealed books and opened[20] those
books before the Lord of the sheep. And the Lord called those
men,[21] the seven first white ones, and commanded *them* to bring
before him the first star[22] which went before those stars whose
private parts *were* like the private parts of horses[23] . . . and they
brought them all before him.[24] And he said to that man who wrote
before him, who was one of the seven white ones[25] – he said to
him,[26] Take those seventy shepherds to whom I handed over the
sheep, and who, on their own authority, took and killed more than
I commanded them. And behold I saw them all bound, and they
all stood before him. And the judgement was held first on the stars,
and they were judged and found guilty; and they went to the place
of damnation, and were thrown into a deep *place*, full of fire,
burning and full of pillars of fire. And those seventy shepherds
were judged and found guilty, and they also were thrown into that
abyss of fire. And I saw at that time how a similar abyss was
opened in the middle of the earth which was full of fire, and they
brought those blind sheep, and they were all judged and found
guilty and thrown into that[27] abyss of fire, and they burned; and
that[28] abyss was on the south[29] of that house. And I saw those

19
20
21

22

23
24

25

26

27

---

[18] GMQTD′ add 'all'.

[19] all the: TX 'the'; some Eth.II MSS 'these'.

[20] took . . . opened: the verbs are in the singular (TD′ have the second one in the
plural), but I take them to be used impersonally.

[21] Eth.II om.

[22] the first star: so GL; all other MSS 'beginning with the first star' (lit. 'from the
first star'), and the text has commonly been emended to read 'beginning with the
first star which led the way, all the stars whose . . .'.

[23] All MSS add a dittograph 'and the first star which fell (G 'went out') first'.

[24] and they brought . . . before him: C′ 'they brought it before him'.

[25] MQTD′ 'one of those seven white ones'; G 'from those white ones'.

[26] GQD′HOXB′ 'to them'.   [27] G 'this'.

[28] Some Eth. MSS 'this'; M corrupt.   [29] Lit. 'right'.

28 sheep burning, and their bones were burning. And I stood up to look until he folded up[30] that old house, and they removed all the pillars, and all the beams and ornaments of that house were folded up with it; and they removed it and put it in a place in the south[29] of

29 the land. And I looked until the Lord of the sheep brought a new house, larger and higher than that[31] first one, and he set it up on the site of the first one which had been folded up; and all its pillars *were* new,[32] and its ornaments *were* new and larger than *those of* the first one, the old one which he had removed. And the Lord of the sheep

30 *was* in the middle of it.[33] And I saw all the sheep which were left, and all the animals on the earth and all the birds of heaven falling down and worshipping those sheep, and entreating them and

31 obeying them[34] in every command. And after this those three who were dressed in white and had taken hold of me by my hand, the ones who had brought me up at first – they, with the hand of that ram also holding me, took me up and put me down in the middle of

32 those sheep before the judgement was held. And those sheep were

33 all white, and their wool thick and pure. And all those which had been destroyed and scattered and all the wild animals and all the birds of heaven gathered together in that house, and the Lord of the sheep rejoiced very much because they were all good and had

34 returned to his house. And I looked until they had laid down that sword which had been given to the sheep, and they brought it back into his[35] house, and it was sealed before the Lord; and all the

35 sheep were enclosed in[36] that house, but it did not hold them. And the eyes of all of them were opened, and they saw well, and there

36 was not one among them that did not see. And I saw that that

37 house was large and broad and exceptionally full. And I saw how a white bull was born, and its horns *were* big, and all the wild animals and all the birds of heaven were afraid of it and entreated it

38 continually. And I looked until all their species were transformed, and they all became white bulls; and the first one among them

[30] folded up: so NP(Y); D' 'changed'; M corrupt; other MSS 'submerged'.

[31] MQTD' 'the'.

[32] TD'B²NX add 'and its beams *were* new'.

[33] So M and some Eth.II MSS (M om. 'And'): all other MSS 'And all the sheep were within it' (G om. 'And').

[34] and obeying them: GQ om.

[35] G 'the'.   [36] G 'invited into'.

was[37] a **wild-ox**,[38] and that **wild-ox** was[37] a large animal and had big black horns on its head. And the Lord of the sheep rejoiced over

39 them and over all the bulls. And I was asleep in the middle of them;

40 and I woke up and saw everything. And this is the vision which I saw while I was asleep, and I woke up and blessed the Lord of

41 righteousness and ascribed glory to him. But after this I wept bitterly, and my tears did not stop until I could not endure it: when I looked, they ran down[39] on account of that which I saw, for everything will come to pass and be fulfilled; and all the deeds of

42 men in their order were shown to me. That night I remembered my[40] first dream, and because of it I wept and was disturbed, because I had seen that vision.

XCI. And now, my son Methuselah, call to me all your brothers and gather to me all the children of your mother,[1] for a voice calls me, and a spirit has been poured out over me, that I may show to

2 you everything that will come upon you for ever. And after this Methuselah went and called all his brothers[2] to him and gathered

3 his relations. And he spoke about righteousness to all his sons[3] and said, Hear, my children, all[4] the words of your father and listen properly to the voice of[5] my mouth, for I will testify to you and

4 speak to you, my beloved.[6] Love uprightness and walk in it. And do not draw near to uprightness with a double heart, and do not associate with those of a double heart,[7] but walk in righteousness, my children,[8] and it will lead you in good paths, and righteousness

---

[37] Or 'became'.

[38] All Eth. MSS have 'word' (*nagar*): in all probability this derives ultimately from a transliteration of the Aramaic word for 'wild-ox'.

[39] when I . . . ran down: G 'when I looked, for these ran down'; M corrupt; QT¹D' 'but they ran down'.   [40] GMQTD 'the'.

[1] G 'call to me all the children of your mother and gather to me all your brothers'.

[2] GMTD' add 'and called'.

[3] about righteousness . . . his sons: GQD'YB' 'to all the sons of righteousness'; M corrupt; T 'about his righteousness to all his sons'.

[4] GQT¹ 'you children of Enoch, all'; MD' 'all you children of Enoch'.

[5] the voice of: MQTD' om.   [6] GMQTD' 'O beloved'.

[7] and do not associate . . . double heart: GU om.; D' 'and do not associate with those who walk with a double heart'.

[8] in . . . children: G 'in uprightness and in righteousness'.

5 will be your companion. For I know that the state of wrongdoing will continue on the earth, and a great punishment will be carried out on the earth, and an end will be made of all iniquity, and it will

6 be cut off at its roots, and its whole edifice will pass away. And iniquity will again be complete on the earth, and all the deeds of iniquity and the deeds[9] of wrong and of wickedness will prevail[10]

7 for a second time.[11] And when iniquity and sin[12] and blasphemy and wrong and all kinds of *evil* deeds[13] increase, and *when* apostasy and wickedness and uncleanness increase, a great punishment[14] will come from heaven upon all these, and the holy Lord will

8 come[15] in anger and in wrath to execute judgement on the earth. In those days wrong-doing will be cut off at its roots, and the roots of[16] iniquity together with deceit will be destroyed[17] from under

9 heaven. And all the idols of the nations will be given up; *their* towers will be burnt in fire, and they will remove them from the whole earth; and they will be thrown down into the judgement of fire and will be destroyed in anger and in the severe judgement which *is* for

10 ever. And the righteous will rise from[18] sleep, and wisdom will rise

11 and will be given to them. And after this the roots of iniquity will be cut off, and the sinners will be destroyed by the sword; from the blasphemers they will be cut off in every place, and those who plan wrongdoing and those who commit blasphemy will be destroyed

12 by the sword.[19] And after this there will be another week, the eighth, that of righteousness, and a sword will be given to it that

9 the deeds: M om.

10 and all the deeds . . . will prevail: QT 'and it will contain all the deeds of iniquity and of wrong and of wickedness', and similarly D'; G corrupt.

11 Or 'to a double extent'.

12 GMQTD' 'sin and iniquity'.

13 GMT 'in all kinds of deeds'; D' corrupt.

14 And when . . . increase, and *when* apostasy . . . increase, a great punishment: MT 'And after this . . . will increase, and apostasy . . . will increase, and a great punishment'.

15 G adds 'upon earth'.

16 the roots of: GQ om. (Q also om. 'and').

17 will be destroyed: so some Eth.II MSS; GQ om.; other MSS 'and they will be destroyed'.

18 GMQD'X add 'their'.

19 For verse 11 Aram. has 'And they will uproot the foundations of wrongdoing and the works of deceit in it in order to carry out [the judgement]'.

the righteous judgement may be executed[20] on those who do
wrong, and the sinners will be handed over into the hands of the
13 righteous.[21] And at its end they will acquire houses because of their
righteousness,[22] and a house will be built for the great king in glory
14 for ever. And after this in the ninth week the righteous judgement
will be revealed to the whole world,[23] and all the deeds of the
impious will vanish from the whole earth; and the world will be
written down for destruction,[24] and all men will look to the path of
15 uprightness.[25] And after this in the tenth week, in the seventh part,
there will be the eternal judgement which will be executed on the
Watchers, and the great eternal heaven which will spring from the
16 midst of the angels.[26] And the first heaven will vanish and pass
away, and a new heaven will appear, and all the powers of heaven
17 will shine for ever[27] *with* sevenfold light. And after this there will be
many weeks without number for ever[28] in goodness and in right-
18 eousness, and from then on sin will never again be mentioned. And
now I tell you, my children, and show you the paths of righteousness and the paths of wrongdoing; and I will show you[29] again that

---

[20] to it . . . be executed: so GD; D′ 'to it that the judgement may be executed in
righteousness'; all other Eth. MSS 'to it that judgement and righteousness may be
practised'; Aram. 'to all the righteous to execute a righteous judgement'.

[21] on those . . . the righteous: Aram. 'on all the sinners, and they will be given into
their hands'.

[22] houses . . . righteousness: Aram. 'riches in righteousness'.

[23] Aram. 'to all the children of the whole earth'.

[24] and the world . . . for destruction: so M Eth.II; GQ corrupt; TD′ 'and he will
write *them* down for destruction for ever' (or perhaps 'he will write the world down
for destruction'); Aram. 'and they will cast into the pit['.

[25] Aram. 'the path of eternal righteousness'.

[26] there will be . . . the angels: so most Eth.II MSS; TD′J 'there will be the eternal
judgement which will be executed on the Watchers of the eternal heaven, the great
judgement which will spring from all (J 'the midst of) the angels'; G 'there will be the
great eternal judgement which will spring from the midst of the angels'; M 'there
will be the great eternal judgement in which he will take vengeance among the
angels', and similarly the corrupt Q. 'Spring' is a simple corruption of 'take
vengeance'; TD′ Eth.II appear to derive from a combination of alternative versions
of the text represented by M.

[27] for ever: GAHK om., but something equivalent is present in Aram.

[28] GD′ 'And after this *there will be* many weeks without number for ever, and they
will all be (D′ 'and it will be')'.

[29] GQTD′ 'and I have shown you'.

19 you may know what is to come. And now listen,[30] my children,
and[31] walk in the paths of righteousness, and do not walk in the
paths of wrongdoing; for all those who walk in the path of iniquity
will be destroyed for ever.

XCII. Written by Enoch the scribe – this complete wisdom
teaching,[1] praised by all men and a judge of the whole earth – for
all my sons who dwell upon the earth and for the last generations
2   who will practise uprightness and peace. Let not your spirit be
saddened because of the times, for the Holy[2] Great One has
3   appointed days for all things. And the righteous man[3] will rise from
sleep,[4] will rise and will walk in the path of righteousness, and all
his paths and his journeys *will be* in eternal goodness and mercy.
4   He will show mercy to the righteous man[5] and to him give eternal
uprightness and *to him* give power; and he will live[6] in goodness and
5   in righteousness and will walk[7] in eternal light. And sin will be
destroyed in darkness[8] for ever and from that day will never again
be seen.

1, 2 **XCIII.**   And after this Enoch began to speak[1] from the books. And
Enoch said, Concerning the sons of righteousness and concerning
the chosen of the world[2] and concerning the plant of righteousness
and uprightness[3] I will speak these things to you and make *them*
known[4] to you, my children, I Enoch, according to that which

---

[30] G om.; M corrupt; QTD′ 'listen to me'.   [31] G om.

[1] Written . . . wisdom teaching: so Eth.II; G 'The book written by Enoch. Enoch
indeed wrote this complete wisdom explanation and teaching'; MQTD′ unintelligible.
[2] Some Eth. MSS add 'and'.
[3] the righteous man: G 'wisdom'; M 'righteousness'.
[4] MD′ 'from his sleep'; G defective.   [5] GQ 'to righteousness'.
[6] Lit. 'be'; TD′ 'judge'.   [7] GQ(D′) 'and they will walk'.
[8] D′ 'And sin and darkness will be destroyed'.

[1] Enoch began to speak: so Eth.II; MTD′ 'Enoch was speaking'; G 'Enoch gave
and Enoch began to speak'; Q unintelligible; U 'Enoch gave'.
[2] of the world: C′ 'for ever'.
[3] righteousness and uprightness: GMTD′ 'uprightness'; Q 'righteousness'.
[4] MTD′ 'and have made *them* known'.

appeared to me in the heavenly vision, and *which* I know from the words of the holy angels and understand from the tablets of
3 heaven. And Enoch[5] then[6] began to speak from the books and said, I was born the seventh in the first week, while justice and righteous-
4 ness still lasted.[7] And after me in the second week great wickedness will arise, and deceit will have sprung up; and in it there will be the first end, and in it a man will be saved. And after it has ended,
5 iniquity will grow, and he will make a law[8] for the sinners. And after this in the third week, at its end, a man will be chosen as the plant of righteous judgement; and after him will come the plant of
6 righteousness[9] for ever. And after this in the fourth week, at its end, visions of the holy and righteous[10] will be seen, and a law[11] for all
7 generations and an enclosure will be made for them. And after this in the fifth week, at its end, a house of glory and of sovereignty will
8 be built for ever. And after this in the sixth week all those who live in it *will be* blinded, and the hearts of all, lacking wisdom, will sink into impiety. And in it a man will ascend; and at its end the house of sovereignty[12] will be burnt with fire, and in it the whole race of
9 the chosen root[13] will be scattered. And after this in the seventh week an apostate[14] generation will arise, and many *will be* its deeds,
10 but all its deeds *will be* apostasy. And at its end the chosen righteous from the eternal plant of righteousness will be chosen,[15] to whom will be given sevenfold teaching concerning his whole creation.[16]
11 For is there any man who can hear the voice of the Holy One, and not be disturbed? And who is there who can think his thoughts?
12 And who is there who can look at all the works of heaven?[17] And how should there be anyone who could[18] understand the works of

[5] MQTD' 'he'.   [6] C' om.
[7] Or 'while judgement and righteousness held back'.
[8] Or 'covenant'; QNC' 'and a law will be made'; GM corrupt.
[9] and after him . . . righteousness: so Eth.II; G om. (hmt.); MQTD' of uncertain meaning.
[10] G 'a vision of the holy and righteousness'; TC' 'holy and righteous visions'.
[11] Or 'covenant'.   [12] E 'the house of the sanctuary'.
[13] chosen root: M(Q)T 'root of power'.   [14] GM om.
[15] Some Eth.II MSS 'rewarded'; Aram. adds 'to be witnesses of righteousness'.
[16] GQD' 'property'.   [17] MD'DFP² 'of goodness'.
[18] G adds 'look at heaven, and who is there who can'; MT add 'look at (T 'understand') heaven, and how should there be anyone who could'; Q defective, but based on a similar text.

heaven and see a soul[19] or a spirit[20] and could tell *about it*,[21] or ascend and see all their ends and comprehend them or make
13 *anything* like them? And is there[22] any man who could know what is the breadth and the length of the earth? And to whom have all its
14 measurements[23] been shown? Or is there any man who could know the length of heaven, and what is its height, and on what it is fixed, and how large is the number of the stars, and where all the lights rest?

XCIV. And now I say to you, my children, love righteousness and walk in it; for the paths of righteousness are worthy of acceptance,
2 but the paths of iniquity will quickly be destroyed and vanish. And to certain men from a *future* generation the paths of wrongdoing and of death will be revealed, and they will keep away from them
3 and will not follow them. And now I say to you, the righteous: do not walk in the wicked path, nor *in* wrongdoing,[1] nor in the paths of
4 death, and do not draw near to them, lest you be destroyed. But seek[2] and choose for yourselves righteousness and a life that is pleasing, and walk in the paths of peace, that you may live and
5 prosper. And hold my words firmly in the thoughts of your heart, and let *them* not be erased from your heart, for I know that sinners will tempt men to debase wisdom,[3] and no place will be found for
6 it, and temptation will in no way decrease. Woe to those who build iniquity and wrongdoing and found deceit, for they will quickly be
7 thrown down and will not have peace. Woe to those who build their houses with sin, for from their whole foundation they will be thrown down, and by the sword they will fall; and those who acquire gold and silver will quickly be destroyed in the judgement.
8 Woe to you, you rich, for you have trusted in your riches, but from your riches you will depart, for you did not remember the Most

---

[19] So GMQD′XY: other MSS 'his soul'.
[20] So MTD′XY: GQ corrupt; other MSS 'or his spirit'.
[21] GMQ 'and could make *them*'; D′ 'and could remain'.
[22] MQTD′ 'And how should there be'.
[23] all its measurements: so T; other MSS 'the measurements of all of them'.

[1] nor *in* wrongdoing: GMQTD′ om.
[2] But seek: G 'like those who seek wickedness'.
[3] Lit. 'to make wisdom bad'.

9 High in the days of your riches. You have committed blasphemy and iniquity and are ready for the day of the outpouring of blood and for the day of darkness and for the day of the great judgement.

10 Thus I say and make known to you that He who created you will throw you down, and over your fall there will be no mercy, but

11 your creator will rejoice at your destruction. And your[4] righteous in those days will be a reproach to the sinners and to the impious.

XCV. Would that my eyes were a cloud of water that I might weep over you and pour out my tears like a cloud of water, so that I

2 might have rest from the sorrow of my heart! Who permitted you to practise hatred and wickedness? May judgement come[1] upon you,

3 the sinners! Do not be afraid of the sinners, you righteous, for the Lord will again deliver them into your hands that you may execute

4 judgement upon them as you desire. Woe to you who pronounce anathemas that you cannot loose;[2] healing *will be* far from you

5 because of your sin. Woe to you who repay your neighbours with

6 evil, for you will be repaid according to your deeds. Woe to you, lying witnesses, and to those who weigh out iniquity, for you will

7 quickly be destroyed. Woe to you, you sinners, because you persecute the righteous, for you yourselves will be handed over and persecuted, you men of iniquity,[3] and their yoke[4] will be heavy upon you.

XCVI. Be hopeful,[1] you righteous, for the sinners will quickly be destroyed before you, and you will have power over them as you

2 desire. And in the day of the distress of the sinners your young will mount up and rise[2] like eagles, and your nest will be higher than *that of* vultures; and you will go up and like badgers enter the crevices of the earth and the clefts of the rock for ever before the

---

[4] your: Eth.II has plural, GMQTD′ singular.

[1] GMQT(D′)C′ 'Judgement will come'.
[2] M² 'that cannot be loosed'; GM¹QD′ 'that can be loosed'.
[3] GM(Q)D′ 'because of iniquity'; P corrupt.
[4] GMQD′ 'its yoke'.

[1] TU 'Rejoice'.
[2] D′ 'and be revealed'; GTU 'and be thrown down'.

lawless, but they will groan and weep because of you, like satyrs.
3 And do not be afraid, you who have suffered, for you will receive
healing, and a bright light will shine upon you, and the voice of rest
4 you will hear from heaven. Woe to you, you sinners, for your riches
make you appear righteous, but your hearts prove to you that you
are sinners; and this word will be a testimony against you as a
5 reminder of *your* evil deeds. Woe to you who devour the finest of the
wheat and drink the best of the water and trample upon the
6 humble through your power. Woe to you who drink water all the
time, for you will quickly be repaid and³ will become exhausted
7 and dry,⁴ for you have left the spring of life. Woe to you who
commit iniquity and deceit and blasphemy; it will be a reminder
8 against you for evil. Woe to you, you powerful, who through power
oppress the righteous, for the day of your destruction will come; in
those days many good days will come for the righteous – in the day
of your judgement.

XCVII.   Believe, you righteous, that the sinners will become an
2 object of shame and will be destroyed on the day of iniquity. Be it
known to you *sinners* that the Most High remembers your destruc-
3 tion, and *that* the angels¹ rejoice over your destruction. What will
you do, you sinners, and where will you flee on that day of judge-
4 ment, when you hear the sound of the prayer of the righteous? But
you will not be² like them, *you* against whom³ this word will be a
5 testimony, You have been associated with the sinners. And in
those days the prayer of the holy⁴ will come before the Lord, and
6 for you will come the days of your judgement. And all the words of
your iniquity will be read out before the Great and⁵ Holy One, and
your faces will blush with shame,⁶ and every deed which is founded

---

³ will quickly be repaid and: MQTD′ om. 'will be repaid and'.
⁴ and dry: BCX 'and you do wrong'.

¹ GMQTD′N add 'of heaven'.
² GQD′ 'will be'.
³ GD′ 'like those against whom'; T 'like them, for against you'; C′ 'like them, but against you'.
⁴ So G and some Eth.II MSS: other MSS 'righteous'.
⁵ GGaMQN Gk.ᵐ om.
⁶ and your faces . . . shame: Gk.ᵐ 'before your faces'.

7 upon iniquity will be rejected. [7] Woe to you, you sinners, who *are* in the middle of the sea and on the dry ground; their memory *will be*

8 harmful to you. [8] Woe to you who acquire silver and gold, [9] but not in righteousness, and say, We have become very rich and have

9 possessions and have acquired everything that we desired. [10] And now let us do what we planned, [11] for we have gathered silver and filled our storehouses, and *as* many as water are the husbandmen of

10 our houses. And like water your lie will flow away, [12] for your [13] riches will not stay with you, [14] but will quickly go up from you; for you acquired everything in iniquity, and you will be given over to a great curse.

XCVIII.   And now I swear to you, the wise and the foolish, [1] that you

2 will see many things [2] on the earth. For you men will put on yourselves more adornments than a woman and more coloured *garments* than a girl [3] in sovereignty and in majesty and in power; and silver [4] and gold and purple and honour and food will be

3 poured out like water. Because of this they will have neither knowledge nor wisdom, [5] and through this they will be destroyed

---

[7] GQTD′ 'and he will reject every deed which is founded upon iniquity'; Ga corrupt; Gk.[m] 'Then he will remove all the works which have shared in iniquity'.

[8] their memory . . . harmful to you (lit. 'evil against you'): Gk.[m] '*there is* an evil record against you'.

[9] GaH Gk.[m] 'gold and silver'.

[10] and have possessions . . . desired: Gk.[m] 'and have got and have acquired possessions'.

[11] And now . . . planned: GM corrupt; Ga 'And now let us do all that we planned'; Q 'And now let us do what we desired'; Gk.[m] 'And let us do all that we desire'.

[12] for we have gathered . . . flow away: so Eth., but text appears corrupt in several respects; Gk.[m] 'for we have stored up silver in our storehouses and many goods in our houses, and like water **they have been poured out** (probable reading; text corrupt). You have been deceived'.

[13] So (U)D′ Gk.[m]: other Eth. MSS om.   [14] with you: Gk.[m] om.

[1] GGaQT Gk.[m] 'and not to the foolish'.   [2] Gk.[m] 'iniquities'.

[3] Gk.[m] 'For men will put on beauty like women, and fair colour more than girls'.

[4] and silver: so GaMQTD′; other Eth. MSS 'and in silver'.

[5] and silver . . . nor wisdom: Gk.[m] 'They will have silver and gold for food, and in their houses they will be poured out like water [because] they ⟨have⟩ neither knowledge, nor insight'.

together with their possessions and with all their glory and their
honour;[6] and in shame and in slaughter and in great destitution
4 their spirits will be thrown into the fiery furnace.[7] I swear to you,
you sinners, that *as* a mountain has not, and will not, become a
slave, nor a hill a woman's maid, so sin was not sent on the earth,
but man of himself created it, and those who commit it will be
5 subject to a great curse. And barreness[8] has not been given to a
woman,[9] but because of the deeds of her hands[10] she dies without
6 children. I swear to you, you sinners, by the Holy and[11] Great One,
that all[12] your evil deeds are[13] revealed in heaven, and *that* your
7 wrongdoing is not covered or hidden.[14] And do not think in your
spirit,[15] nor say[16] in your heart that you do not know and do not see
that every sin[17] is written down[18] every day in heaven[19] before the
8 Most High. From now on you know[20] that all your wrongdoing
which you do[21] will be written down every day until the day of[22]
9 your judgement. Woe to you, you fools, for you will be destroyed
through your folly; and you do not listen to[23] the wise, and good

---

[6] and through this . . . honour: Gk.[m] 'so you will be destroyed together with all
your possessions and all your glory and your honour' (remainder of verse 3 and
verse 4 severely damaged).

[7] into the fiery furnace: MQTD' om.

[8] G(Ga)MQN[1] 'an excuse'; D' corrupt; Gk.[m] om. (but 'childlessness' possibly to
be supplied).

[9] Gk.[m] 'to a barren woman'.

[10] Gk.[m] adds what appears to be an alternative version of verses 4f., 'For it was
not determined that a slave should be a slave; from above it was not given, but it
came about through oppression. Likewise iniquity was not given from above, but *it
came about* from transgression. Likewise a woman was not created barren, but
because of her own misdeeds she was reproached with childlessness'.

[11] GQTD' Gk.[m] om.   [12] P[1] Gk.[m] om.

[13] Gk.[m] 'will be'.

[14] and *that* your . . . hidden: Gk.[m] 'No unrighteous deed of yours will be hidden'.

[15] Gk.[m] 'soul'.   [16] Gk.[m] 'think'.

[17] D' 'all our sin'.

[18] that you do not . . . down: C' 'They do not know and do not see all our sin, for it
is written down'; Gk.[m] 'that they do not know and do not see, and *that* your
misdeeds are not observed, nor written down'.

[19] every day in heaven: Gk.[m] om.   [20] you know: Gk.[m] imperative.

[21] which you do: GaN Gk.[m] om.   [22] the day of: Gk.[m] om.

[23] GGa 'and you act impiously against'; D' 'and you do not act impiously
against'; M 'and you do not know'; Q 'and you do not see'.

10 will not come upon you.[24] And now know that you are ready for the day of destruction. And do not hope that you will live,[25] you sinners; rather you will go and die, for you know no ransom, for[26] you are ready for the day of the great judgement and for the day of

11 distress and great shame for your spirits. Woe to you, you stubborn of heart who do evil and eat blood. Whence do you have good things to eat and to drink and to be satisfied? From all the good things which our Lord, the Most High,[27] has placed in abundance

12 on the earth: *therefore* you will not have peace. Woe to you who love deeds of iniquity. Why do you hope for good for yourselves? Know[28] that you will be given into the hand of the righteous, and they will cut your throats and[29] kill you and will not have mercy on

13 you.[30] Woe to you who rejoice in the distress of the righteous, for

14 graves will not be dug for you.[31] Woe to you who declare the words

15 of the righteous empty,[32] for you will have no hope of life.[33] Woe to you who write lying words and the words of the impious,[34] for they write their lies that *men* may hear and not forget *their* folly;[35] and they will not have peace, but will die a sudden death.[36]

---

[24] Gk.[m] adds 'but evil [will befall] you'.

[25] that you will live: Gk.[m] 'to be saved'.

[26] for you know no ransom, for: so Ga Eth.II; G 'for you know a ransom, and'; M 'for you know no ransom'; T obscure; QD' 'for you know that'; Gk.[m] 'knowing [that]' (remainder of verse 10, verse 11, and the beginning of verse 12, severely damaged).

[27] our Lord, the Most High: GGaMQTD' 'the Lord Most High'.

[28] Gk.[m] 'Now be it known to you'.

[29] cut your throats (lit. 'necks') and: Gk.[m] om.

[30] Gk.[m] 'not spare you'.

[31] GGaD' 'for no grave of yours will be seen'; Gk.[m] 'no grave will be dug for you'.

[32] Gk.[m] uncertain, possibly 'Woe to you who wish to make of no effect the words of the righteous'.

[33] Gk.[m] 'of salvation'.

[34] and the words . . . impious: Gk.[m] 'and words of error'.

[35] for they write . . . folly: so Eth.II; GMQT 'for they write their lies (M om. 'their lies') that *men* may hear *them* and act impiously against their neighbour'; GaD' corrupt; Gk.[m] 'they write *them* and will lead many astray through their lies. You yourselves have gone astray'.

[36] and they . . . sudden death: Gk.[m] 'and you have no joy, but will quickly be destroyed'.

XCIX. Woe to you who do impious deeds and praise and honour lying words;[1] you will be destroyed and will not have a good life.[2]
2 Woe to you who[3] alter the words of truth, and they distort the eternal law[4] and count themselves[5] as being without sin; they[6] will
3 be trampled under foot on the ground.[7] In those days[8] make ready, you righteous, to raise[9] your prayers as a reminder, and lay them[10] as a testimony before the angels that they may lay[11] the sin of the
4 sinners before the Most High[12] as a reminder. In those days the nations will be thrown into confusion, and the races of the nations
5 will rise[13] on the day of destruction.[14] And in those days those who are in need will go out and seize their children and cast out their children;[15] and their offspring will slip from them,[16] and they will cast out their children while they are sucklings[17] and will not return to them[18] and will not have mercy on[19] their beloved ones.
6 And again I swear to you, the sinners, that sin is ready for the day

[1] Gk.[m] 'Woe to you who cause errors and by your false deeds gain honour and glory'; the Eth. MSS confuse second and third person forms in this verse and only T consistently has the second person.

[2] C' 'you will be destroyed and will have no hope of life'; Gk.[m] 'you are destroyed, you have no salvation for good'.

[3] GGaM 'Woe to those who'.   [4] Or 'covenant'.

[5] C' Gk.[m] 'Woe to you who alter the words of truth, and distort the eternal law (Gk.[m] 'pervert the eternal covenant'), and count yourselves'.

[6] C' 'you'.

[7] Gk.[m] 'they will be swallowed up in the earth'.

[8] In those days: Gk.[m] 'Then'.   [9] to raise: Gk.[m] 'and offer'.

[10] and lay them: so GT; other Eth. MSS corrupt; Gk.[m] 'give them'.

[11] T(D')Gk.[m] 'bring'.   [12] Gk.[m] adds 'God'.

[13] Gk.[m] 'And then they will be thrown into confusion, and they will rise'.

[14] QD' 'of the destruction of the sinners'; MT 'of the destruction of sin'; Gk.[m] 'of the destruction of wrongdoing'.

[15] And in . . . their children: so Eth., but GGaMQTD' 'and cast them out' for 'and cast out their children'; Gk.[m] 'At that very time those who give birth will cast out and **remove** and abandon their infants'.

[16] and their offspring will slip from them: i.e. in premature birth; Gk.[m] 'and those who are with child will [. . .]'.

[17] Eth.II 'and while they are sucklings they will cast them out'; Gk.[m] 'and those who suckle will cast out their children'.

[18] to them: Gk.[m] 'to their infants, nor to their sucklings'.

[19] have mercy on: Gk.[m] 'spare' (the remainder of verse 5, verse 6, and beginning of verse 7, has not survived).

7   of unceasing bloodshed. And they worship stone, and some carve
    images of gold and of silver and of wood and of clay,[20] and some,
    with no knowledge,[21] worship unclean[22] spirits and demons and
8   every *kind of* error,[23] but no help will be obtained from them. And
    they will sink into impiety[24] because of the folly of their hearts,
    and their eyes will be blinded through the fear of their hearts and
9   through the vision of their dreams.[25] Through these they will
    become impious and fearful, for they do all their deeds with lies
    and worship stones, and they will be destroyed at the same
10 moment.[26] And in those days blessed *are* all those who accept the
    words of wisdom and understand them,[27] and follow the paths[28] of
    the Most High, and walk in the path of righteousness,[29] and do not
11 act impiously with the impious, for they will be saved.[30] Woe to you
    who extend evil to your neighbours, for you will be killed in Sheol.
12 Woe to you who lay foundations of sin and deceit,[31] and *to those* who
    cause bitterness[32] on the earth, for because of this an end will be
13 made of them.[33] Woe to you who build your houses with the toil of
    others,[34] and all their building materials *are* the bricks and stones of

[20]   and some carve . . . clay: Gk.ᵐ '[. . .] and those who carve images of silver and of
gold, of wood [. . .] and of clay'.

[21]   with no knowledge: so GQTD'; Ga corrupt; M 'but not in the temples'; Eth.II
'in the temples'.

[22]   GGaMQTD' 'evil'.

[23]   and some, with . . . error: Gk.ᵐ 'and worship phantoms and demons [. . .] and
evil spirits [and] all errors, with no knowledge'.

[24]   Gk.ᵐ 'And they will go astray'.

[25]   and their eyes . . . dreams: Gk.ᵐ 'and the visions of *their* dreams will lead you
astray'.

[26]   Through these . . . same moment: Gk.ᵐ obscure, 'you and your lying works
that you have made and wrought of stone, and together you will perish'.

[27]   Gk.ᵐ 'And then blessed *are* all those who hear the words of the wise and will
learn them'.

[28]   and follow the paths: Gk.ᵐ 'in order to fulfil the commands'.

[29]   GGaMQD' 'in the path of his righteousness'; T Gk.ᵐ 'in the paths of his
righteousness'.

[30]   and walk . . . saved: Gk.ᵐ 'and they will walk in the paths of his righteousness,
and will not go astray with those who go astray, and will be saved'.

[31]   GQD'J¹ 'who make false and deceitful measures'; GaM corrupt.

[32]   cause bitterness: GQD' 'know'; Ga 'advise'.

[33]   Gk.ᵐ om. verses 11f.

[34]   Gk.ᵐ 'Woe *to those* who build their houses not ⟨by⟩ their own toil'.

14 sin;[35] I say to you, You will not have peace.[36] Woe to those who
    reject the measure[37] and the eternal inheritance of their fathers[38]
    and cause their souls to follow after error,[39] for they will not have
15 rest.[40] Woe to those[41] who commit iniquity and help wrong and kill
16 their neighbours until the day of the great judgement, for[42] he will
    throw down[43] your glory and put evil into your hearts[44] and rouse
    the spirit of his anger that he may destroy[45] you all with the sword;
    and all the righteous and holy[46] will remember your sin.

C.   And in those days[1] in one place fathers and sons will strike one
     another, and brothers will together fall in death until there flows of
2   their blood as it were a stream. For a man will not in mercy[2]
     withhold his hand from his sons, nor from his sons' sons,[3] in order
     to kill them, and the sinner will not withhold his hand from his
     honoured brother;[4] from dawn until the sun sets they will kill one
3   another.[5] And the horse will walk up to its chest in the blood of
4   sinners, and the chariot will sink up to its height.[6] And in those

---

[35] Gk.[m] 'and from stones and from bricks you make every building'.

[36] I say . . . peace: Gk.[m] uncertain, but different from Eth.

[37] Q 'the leaders'; D' 'the foundation'.

[38] Gk.[m] 'Woe *to those* who despise the foundation and the inheritance of their fathers which is from eternity'.

[39] Ga(M) 'and whose souls follow after error'; GQT(D') 'and follow after the soul of error'; Gk.[m] 'for the spirit of error will pursue you'. (Eth. 'soul' might also be translated 'spirit'.)

[40] GMQTD' 'for you will not have rest'; Gk.[m] 'There is no rest for you'.

[41] GMQTD' Gk.[m] 'you'.   [42] Gk.[m] adds 'then'.

[43] throw down: Gk.[m] uncertain, possibly 'destroy'.

[44] and put . . . hearts: Gk.[m] om.

[45] GM 'and rouse his anger and his spirit; he will destroy'; QT 'and rouse his anger, and his spirit will destroy'; D' 'and rouse the anger of his spirit, and will destroy'; Gk.[m] 'and rouse [his] anger [against] you; he will destroy'.

[46] GGaMQD' 'holy and righteous'; Gk.[m] probably only 'righteous'.

[1] Gk.[m] 'And then' (remainder of verse severely damaged).

[2] in mercy: GGaMQD'Gk.[m] om.

[3] GMT 'sons, nor from his son's son'; GaQ corrupt; Gk.[m] 'son, nor from his beloved'.

[4] and the sinner . . . brother: Gk.[m] 'and the sinner from the honoured man, nor from his brother'.

[5] Gk.[m] 'they will be killed together'.

[6] Gk.[m] 'sink down to its axles'; GGaQTD' corrupt.

days[7] the angels will come down[8] into the hidden places and gather together in one place all those who have helped[9] sin,[10] and the Most High will rise on that day[11] to execute the great judgement on
5 all the sinners.[12] And he will set guards from the holy angels over all the righteous and holy, and they will guard them[13] like the apple of an eye until an end is made of[14] all evil and all sin;[15] and even if
6 the righteous sleep a long sleep, they have nothing to fear.[16] And the wise men will see the truth,[17] and the sons of the earth will understand all the words of this book,[18] and they will know that their riches will not be able to save them in the overthrow of their
7 sin.[19] Woe to you, you sinners, when you afflict the righteous on the day of severe trouble and burn[20] them with fire;[21] you will be repaid
8 according to your deeds. Woe to you, you perverse of heart,[22] who watch to devise evil; fear will come upon you, and there is no one
9 who will help you. Woe to you, you sinners,[23] for[24] on account of the words of your mouth, and on account of the deeds of your hands which you have impiously done,[25] you will burn in blazing
10 flames of fire. And now know that the angels will inquire in heaven[26] into your deeds from[27] the sun and the moon and the

---

[7] Gk.[m] 'And on that day'.   [8] Gk.[m] adds 'descending'.

[9] GGaMQ 'who brought down'.

[10] and gather . . . sin: Gk.[m] uncertain, but apparently '(and) those who have helped unrighteousness will be gathered together into one place'.

[11] (G)Ga(M)Q(D') 'on that day of judgement'; Gk.[m] 'on the day of judgement'.

[12] GGaMQ 'amongst the sinners'; Gk.[m] 'on all'.

[13] Gk.[m] 'will be guarded'.   [14] GGaMQ[2] 'he makes an end of'.

[15] Gk.[m] 'until evils and sin come to an end'.

[16] Gk.[m] 'and from that *time* the pious will sleep a sweet sleep, and there will no longer be anyone to make them afraid'.

[17] the truth: so (Q)T Eth.II; GGaMD' unintelligible.

[18] Gk.[m] 'Then the wise among men will see, and the sons of the earth will pay attention to these words of this epistle'.   [19] Gk.[m] 'of unrighteousness'.

[20] Q 'save'; Gk.[m] 'keep', but probably corrupt for 'burn'.

[21] Gk.[m] adds 'for'.   [22] GGaMQTD' Gk.[m] 'you stubborn of heart'.

[23] Gk.[m] 'all you sinners'.   [24] GMQTD' Gk.[m] om.

[25] which you . . . done: GM 'which your impiety has wrought'; GaQ 'which *are* the works of your impiety'; TD' 'because of the works of your impiety'; Gk.[m] 'for you [have] gone astray ⟨from⟩ holy deeds' (remainder of verse 9, verse 10, and majority of verse 11, severely damaged).

[26] GGaMQTD' 'that from the angels he will inquire in heaven (G 'from heaven')'.   [27] GGaMQTD' 'and from'.

stars, *that is* into your sins, for on earth you execute judgement on
11 the righteous. And all the clouds and mist and dew and rain will
testify against you,[28] for they will all be withheld from you so that
12 they do not fall on you, and they will think[29] about your sins. And
now[30] give gifts to the rain that it may not be withheld from falling
on you, and that the dew, if it has accepted gold and silver from
13 you, may fall.[31] When[32] hoar-frost and snow with their cold and all
the snow-winds with all their torments fall on you, in those days[33]
you will not be able to stand before them.[34]

CI. Contemplate heaven, all[1] you sons of heaven, and all the
works of the Most High,[2] and fear him and do not do evil before
2 him.[3] If he closes the windows of heaven, and withholds the rain
and the dew so that it does not fall on the earth[4] because of you,
3 what will you do? And if he sends his anger upon you and upon all
your deeds,[5] will you not entreat him?[6] For you speak[7] proud and
hard *words* against his righteousness,[8] and you will not have peace.[9]
4 And do you not see the kings[10] of the ships, how their ships are

---

[28] And all . . . against you: so G(Ga)QD′P²; other Eth. MSS 'And he will call to
testify against you all the clouds and mist and dew and rain'.

[29] and they will think: so GQY; Ga defective; TB 'and they will not be'; other
Eth. MSS 'and they will not think'.

[30] Gk.ᵐ 'Therefore'.

[31] and that . . . may fall: so Eth. (MQ 'may not fall'; some Eth.II MSS om. 'that'
and 'may fall'); Gk.ᵐ uncertain, apparently 'and to the dew and [clouds] and mist;
pay gold that they may fall'.

[32] Gk.ᵐ 'For if'.   [33] in those days: Gk.ᵐ om.

[34] Gk.ᵐ 'before cold and their torments'.

[1] GGaMQT¹D′ om.

[2] Gk.ᵐ 'Consider therefore, you sons of men, the works of the Most High'.

[3] Gk.ᵐ 'and fear to do evil before him'.   [4] on the earth: Gk.ᵐ om.

[5] T Gk.ᵐ 'and upon your deeds'; GaM 'because of (Ga adds 'all') your deeds';
GQD′ defective.

[6] will you not entreat him?: so EHLC′ Gk.ᵐ; other Eth. MSS 'you will not be able
to entreat him'.

[7] Gk.ᵐ 'Why do you speak with your mouth?'

[8] Gk.ᵐ 'majesty'.   [9] and you . . . peace: Gk.ᵐ om.

[10] So all Eth. MSS, but a mistake, deriving from a misreading of the Aramaic for
'sailors'.

tossed by the waves and rocked by the winds, and are in distress?[11]
5 And because of this they are afraid,[12] for all their good possessions
go out on the sea with them,[13] and they think nothing good in their
hearts, *namely* that[14] the sea will swallow them up, and *that* they will
6 be destroyed in it. Is not all the sea and all its waters and all its
movement[15] the work of the Most High, and did he not seal all its
7 doings[16] and bind it all with sand?[17] And at his rebuke it dries up
and becomes afraid,[18] and all its fish[19] die and everything that is in
8 it; but you sinners who *are* on earth do not fear him. Did he not
make heaven and earth and everything that is in them? And who
gave knowledge and wisdom[20] to all the things that move on the
9 ground and[21] in the sea? Do not those kings[22] of the ships fear the
sea?[23] Yet sinners do not fear the Most High.[24]

CII. And in those days if he brings a fierce fire upon you,[1] whither
will you flee, and where will you[2] be safe? And when he utters his
2 voice against you, will you not be terrified and afraid?[3] And all the
lights will shake with great fear, and the whole earth will be
3 terrified and will tremble and quail. And all the angels will carry
out their commands and will seek to hide before the one who is

[11] Gk.[m] 'You [see] the sailors who sail the sea, their ships tossed by the waves and
storm'.
[12] Gk.[m] 'And beaten by the storm they are all afraid'.
[13] Gk.[m] 'and cast out into the sea [all] their [goods] and possessions'.
[14] and they think . . . that: so Eth.II; GGaMQTD' unintelligible; Gk.[m] 'and they
suspect in their hearts that'.   [15] and all its movement: Gk.[m] om.
[16] and did . . . its doings: so Eth.II, except E; E 'and did he not establish (or
perhaps 'prescribe') all its doings'; GGaMQTD' unintelligible; Gk.[m] 'and did he
not establish their [limits]'.   [17] Gk.[m] 'and bind it, and fence it with sand?'
[18] dries up . . . becomes afraid: GMQTD'X Gk.[m] transpose; Ga om. 'and
becomes afraid'.
[19] Gk.[m] 'and the fish' (the remainder of verse 7 and beginning of verse 8 has not
survived).
[20] and wisdom: Gk.[m] om.   [21] on the ground and: Gk.[m] om.
[22] So all Eth. MSS, but corrupt for 'sailors' (cp. note 10).
[23] Gk.[m] 'The sailors fear the sea'.
[24] Yet . . . Most High: Gk.[m] om. by hmt.

[1] Gk.[m] 'And when he throws out against you the waves of the fire of your
burning'.
[2] where will you: Gk.[m] om.   [3] Gk.[m] adds 'at the great sound'.

great in glory,[4] and the children of the earth will tremble and
shake;[5] and you sinners *will be* cursed for ever and will not have
4 peace.[6] Do not be afraid, you souls of the righteous, and be hopeful,
5 *you* who have died[7] in righteousness.[8] And do not be sad that your
souls have gone down[9] into Sheol in sadness, and *that* your bodies[10]
did not obtain during your life *a reward* in accordance with your
goodness,[11] but on the day on which you became as sinners and on
6 the day of cursing and punishment . . .[12] But when you die, the
sinners say about you,[13] As we die, the righteous have died,[14] and
7 of what use to them were their deeds? Behold, like us they have
died in sadness and in darkness,[15] and what advantage do they
8 have over us?[16] From now on we are equal, and what will they
receive,[17] and what will they see for ever? For, behold, they too
9 have died, and from now on they will never again see light.[18] I say
to you, you sinners, You are content to eat and drink, and strip
men naked and steal and sin,[19] and acquire possessions and see

[4] GGaMQT(D') 'before the great glory'.

[5] And all the lights . . . will tremble and shake: Gk.[m] in part corrupt and
apparently out of order, 'And the whole earth *will be* shaken and trembling and
thrown into confusion and the angels *will be* carrying out that which has been
commanded them, and heaven and the lights *will be* shaken, and all the children of
the earth *will be* trembling'.

[6] Gk.[m] 'and you, you sinners accursed for ever, there is no joy for you'.

[7] *you* who have died: some Eth.II MSS 'on the day you die'; GQT 'they who have
died'; GaD' 'the souls of those who have died'.

[8] Gk.[m] 'Be courageous, *you* souls of the righteous dead, of the righteous and the
pious'.

[9] T Eth.II add 'into great distress and crying and groaning and'.

[10] Gk.[m] 'and *that* the body of your flesh'.

[11] Gk.[m] 'holiness'.

[12] but on . . . punishment . . .: so Eth., but corrupt; Gk.[m] 'for the days which you
lived were days of sinners and accursed *men* on the earth'.

[13] Gk.[m] 'When you die, then the sinners will say'.

[14] Gk.[m] 'The pious have died according to *their* fate'.

[15] Gk.[m] 'And they like us have died. See then how they die in grief and darkness'.

[16] over us: QTD' Gk.[m] om.

[17] GGaQD' 'From now on we are equal, and how will they rise'; Gk.[m] 'From now
on let them rise and be saved'.

[18] and what will they see . . . light: Gk.[m] 'and they will for ever see **us** (Gk.[m] 'you')
eating and drinking well'.

[19] GMQTD' 'and steal and sin and strip men naked'.

10 good days.²⁰ But you saw²¹ the righteous, how their end was
peace,²² for no wrong was found in them until the day of their
11 death.²³ But they were destroyed²⁴ and became as though they had
not been, and their souls²⁵ went down into Sheol in distress.

CIII. And now I swear to you, the righteous, by his great glory and
his honour, and by his magnificent sovereignty¹ and by his majesty
2 I swear to you that I understand this² mystery. And³ I have read
the tablets of heaven and seen the writing of the holy ones,⁴ and I
3 found written and engraved in it⁵ concerning them⁶ that all good⁷
and joy and honour have been made ready and written down for
the spirits of those who⁸ have died in righteousness, and *that* much
good will be given to you in recompense for your toil, and *that* your
4 lot *will be* more excellent than the lot of the living. And the spirits of
you⁹ who have died in righteousness will live,¹⁰ and their spirits
will rejoice and be glad,¹¹ and the memory of them *will remain*¹²

---

²⁰ I say . . . good days: Gk.ᵐ 'Then ⟨you do well to eat and drink and⟩ steal and
sin and steal clothes and acquire *possessions* and see good days'.
²¹ But you saw: so D'P²; MT¹ and some Eth.II MSS 'You saw'; T² and some
Eth.II MSS 'Have you seen'; other Eth. MSS 'I saw'.
²² peace: GGaMQTD' om.   ²³ GTD' 'until they died'; MQ corrupt.
²⁴ But you saw . . . destroyed: Gk.ᵐ 'See therefore, they who justify themselves,
how their end was, for no righteousness was found in them until they died and were
destroyed'.
²⁵ GMQTD' 'spirits'.

¹ by his great . . . sovereignty: so Eth.II; G 'by the glory of the One who is great
and honoured and mighty in sovereignty'; QTD' 'by the glory of the Great One and
by his magnificent sovereignty'; other Eth.I MSS differ slightly. Most of verse 1 has
not survived in Gk.ᵐ.
² this: GGaMQ om.   ³ Gk.ᵐ 'for'.
⁴ (G)Q(T) 'the holy writing'; D' corrupt; Gk.ᵐ 'the writing of authority'.
⁵ GMQTD' 'them'.
⁶ and I found . . . them: Gk.ᵐ 'I learned what was written and engraved on them
[concerning] you'; D' also has 'concerning you'.
⁷ all good: Gk.ᵐ 'good things'.
⁸ GQD' 'for your spirits which'; Ga corrupt; Gk.ᵐ 'for the s[ouls] of those who'.
⁹ MT¹D' 'of those'.
¹⁰ and that much good . . . will live: Gk.ᵐ om. by hmt.
¹¹ and be glad: G(Ga) 'and be glad and will not be destroyed'; M corrupt; QTD'
Gk.ᵐ 'and will not be destroyed'.
¹² GMQT'D' Gk.ᵐ 'nor *will* the memory of them *be destroyed*'.

before the Great One for all the generations of eternity. Therefore
5 do not fear their abuse. Woe to you, you sinners,[13] when you die
in[14] your sin, and those who are like you say about you, Blessed
6 were the sinners; they saw all their days.[15] And now they have died
in prosperity and wealth; distress and slaughter they did not see[16]
during their life, but they died in glory, and judgement was not
7 executed on them during their life. Know[17] that their souls[18] will be
made to go down into Sheol, and they will be wretched, and[19] their
8 distress *will be* great;[20] and in darkness and in chains and in
burning flames your spirits[21] will come to the great judgement, and
the great judgement will last[22] for all generations for ever.[23] Woe to
9 you, for you will not have peace.[24] Do not say to the righteous and
good who were alive,[25] In the days of our[26] affliction we toiled
laboriously and saw every affliction and met many evils;[27] we were
10 spent and became few, and our spirit small. We were destroyed,[28]
and there was no one who helped us with words or deeds; we were
11 powerless and found nothing.[29] We were tortured and destroyed,
and did not expect to see life from one day to the next.[30] We hoped

---

[13] GGaMQTD' 'Woe to you, you sinners who are dead'; Gk.[m] 'And you, you
who are dead of the sinners'.

[14] GGaMTD' add 'the wealth of'.

[15] Gk.[m] 'when you die they will say about you, Blessed *were the* sinners all the
days that they saw'.

[16] And now . . . not see: Gk.[m] om. by hmt.

[17] BCXC' 'Do you know'; Gk.[m] 'You yourselves know'.

[18] T 'their spirits'; GQD' 'your spirits'; Gk.[m] 'your souls'.

[19] So D'CC': other Eth. MSS om.

[20] and they . . . great: Gk.[m] 'and there they will be in great distress'.

[21] your spirits: Gk.[m] 'and your souls'.

[22] and the great . . . last: Gk.[m] om.

[23] GGa(M)QTD' 'for all (Ga(M) om. 'all') the generations of eternity'; Gk.[m] 'in
all the generations of eternity'.

[24] Gk.[m] 'Woe to you, there is no joy for you'.

[25] Gk.[m] 'For do not say, you who were righteous ⟨and⟩ holy in your life'.

[26] M Gk.[m] om.; GGaQT'D' 'their'; Ga continues with the third person throughout verses 9–13 and in part in verses 14f.

[27] and saw . . . many evils: Gk.[m] om.

[28] and our spirit . . . destroyed: Gk.[m] om.

[29] and there was no one . . . found nothing: G(Ga)MQD' 'and did not find
anyone to help us even with a word'; Gk.[m] 'and we did not find a helper'.

[30] Gk.[m] 'and gave up hope of knowing safety again day by day'.

to become the head, but became the tail. We toiled and laboured, but were not masters of the fruits of our toil;[31] we became food for the sinners, and the lawless made[32] their yoke heavy upon us.
12 Those who hated us and those who goaded us[33] were masters of us,[34] and to those who hated us we bowed our necks, but they did
13 not have mercy on us.[35] We sought to escape from them that we might flee and be at rest,[36] but we found no place where we might
14 flee and be safe from them. We complained about them to the rulers in our distress and cried out against those who devoured us,[37] but they took no notice of our cry[38] and did not wish to listen
15 to our voice. And they helped those who plundered us and devoured us and those who made us few,[39] and they concealed their wrongdoing and did not remove from us the yoke of those who[40] devoured us and scattered us and killed us;[41] and they concealed our slaughter and did not remember that they had raised their hands against us.[42]

CIV. I swear to you, you righteous,[1] that in heaven the angels remember you for good before the glory of the Great One, and *that*

[31] Gk.[m] corrupt, apparently 'of our wages'.
[32] GGaMQTD' 'for the sinners and the lawless, and (GaMQTD' om. 'and') they made'.
[33] and those who goaded us: Q 'and those who hated us and goaded us'; D' 'and those who goaded us and surrounded us'.
[34] Those who . . . masters of us: Gk.[m] 'Those who rule *us*, our enemies, goad us and surround us'.
[35] and to those . . . mercy on us: Gk.[m] om.
[36] that we might . . . rest: Gk.[m] 'that we might be refreshed' (the remainder of verse 13 and beginning of verse 14 has not survived).
[37] Gk.[m] 'against those who struck us down and inflicted violence on us'.
[38] Gk.[m] 'and they did not receive our petitions'.
[39] Gk.[m] 'And they did not help us, not finding *anything* against those who inflicted violence on *us* and devoured us, but they harden against us them ⟨who⟩ killed us and made *us* few'.
[40] the yoke of those who: so GGaMFOB'C'; other Eth. MSS 'their yoke, but they'.
[41] and they concealed their . . . killed us: Gk.[m] om.
[42] and they concealed our . . . against us: Gk.[m] 'and they bring no charge concerning those of us who have been murdered, and concerning ⟨the⟩ sinners they do not remember their sins'.

[1] you righteous: GGaMQT'D' Gk.[m] om.

your names are written down before the glory of the Great One.[2]
2 Be hopeful! For you were formerly put to shame through[3] evils
and afflictions, but now[4] you will shine like the lights of heaven[5]
3 and will be seen, and the gate[6] of heaven will be opened to you. And
persevere in your cry for judgement, and it will appear to you, for
justice will be exacted from the rulers for all your distress,[7] and from
4 all those who helped those who plundered you.[8] Be hopeful, and do
not abandon your hope, for you will have great joy like the angels of
5 heaven.[9] What will you have to do?[10] You will not have to hide on
the day of the great judgement, nor will you be found to be
sinners.[11] The eternal judgement will be upon you for all the
6 generations of eternity.[12] And now[13] do not be afraid, you righteous,
when you see the sinners growing strong and prospering in their
desires,[14] and do not be associated with them, but keep far away
from their wrongdoing,[15] for you shall be associates of the host[16] of
7 heaven.[17] For you sinners say, None of our sins will be inquired
into[18] and written down! – *but* they will write down all your sins
8 every day.[19] And now I show to you that light and darkness, day
9 and night, see all your sins. Do not be impious[20] in your hearts, and

[2] and that your . . . Great One: AHKN[1] Gk.[m] om.

[3] Gk.[m] 'Be courageous, for you have grown old in'.

[4] but now: Gk.[m] om.   [5] GGaM(Q)T add 'you will shine'.

[6] GM 'and the gates'; Gk.[m] 'the windows'.

[7] Gk.[m] 'And your cry will be heard, and your judgement for which you cry will appear against everything which will help (against) you in respect of your affliction'.

[8] and from . . . plundered you: Gk.[m] 'and *it will be executed* on all who took part with those who inflicted violence on *you* and devoured you'.

[9] Gk.[m] om. verse 4.

[10] So GGaMQE: other Eth. MSS 'As for what you will have to do'.

[11] What . . . be sinners: Gk.[m] defective and reconstruction uncertain, but the text clearly differed from Eth – at least in the first part. After 'sinners' Gk.[m] adds 'you will be troubled and' (It is likely that something like 'But as for you sinners' has dropped out of the text before this: cp. note 12).

[12] The eternal . . . eternity: this only makes sense as an address to the sinners, and perhaps it was so originally.

[13] And now: Gk.[m] om.   [14] GGaMQTD' Gk.[m] 'ways'.

[15] Gk.[m] 'all their misdeeds'.   [16] GMQT(D') 'the good ones'.

[17] for you shall . . . heaven: Gk.[m] om.

[18] will be inquired into: so NC'; other Eth. MSS corrupt.

[19] Gk.[m] in verse 7 obscure and incomplete, but apparently similar to Eth.

[20] Gk.[m] 'Do not go astray'.

do not lie, and do not alter the words of truth, nor say that the words of the Holy and[21] Great One are lies, and do not praise your idols, for all your lies and all your impiety lead not to right-

10 eousness,[22] but to great sin. And now I know this mystery, that many sinners will alter and distort the words of truth,[23] and speak evil words,[24] and lie, and concoct great fabrications, and write

11 books in their *own* words.[25] But when they write out all my[26] words exactly in their languages, and do not alter or omit *anything* from my words, but write out everything exactly, everything[27] which I

12 testified about them before – *then* I know[28] another mystery, that books[29] will be given to the righteous[30] and wise *which will be the*

13 *source of* joy and truth and much wisdom.[31] And books will be given to them,[32] and they will believe in them and rejoice over them; and all the righteous who have learnt from them all the ways of truth will be glad.[33]

CV. And in those days, says the Lord, they shall call and testify to the sons of the earth about the wisdom in them.[1] Show *it* to them, for you *are* their leaders, and the rewards *which are to come* over all

2 the earth. For I and my son will join ourselves with them for ever in

---

[21] GQT om.; Gk.^m om. 'and Great'.

[22] Remainder of verse 9 and beginning of verse 10 lost in Gk.^m.

[23] many . . . truth: G(GaM)TP¹ 'the sinners will alter and distort the words of truth in many ways' (or perhaps 'the sinners will alter the words of truth and pervert many'); Gk.^m 'the sinners alter and write against [the words] of truth and lead astray (lit. 'change') the many'.

[24] and speak evil words: Gk.^m om.

[25] and write books in their own words (or 'concerning their words'): GGaMQD' 'and write out my books in their *own* words'; Gk.^m 'and write out the scriptures in their *own* names'.

[26] GGaMQD' 'the'.   [27] Q om.

[28] But when . . . know: Gk.^m 'And would that they would write out all my words exactly in their names, and not omit or change *anything* in these words, but write out exactly all the things which I testify to them. And again I know'.

[29] Gk.^m 'my books'.   [30] Gk.^m adds 'and holy'.

[31] *which . . . wisdom*: Gk.^m 'for joy of truth'.

[32] And books . . . them: Gk.^m om.

[33] Gk.^m 'and all the righteous will be glad to learn from them all the ways of truth'; in Eth. for 'be glad' many MSS have 'be rewarded'.

[1] the wisdom in them: i.e. in the books (lit. 'their wisdom').

the paths of uprightness during their lives, and you will have peace. Rejoice, you sons of uprightness! Amen.[2]

CVI. And after *some* days my son Methuselah took for his son
Lamech a wife,[1] and she became pregnant by him and[2] bore[3] a son.
2 And his body was white like snow and red like the flower of a rose,
and the hair of his head *was* white like wool[4] . . . and his eyes were
beautiful;[5] and when he opened his eyes, he made the whole house
bright like the sun so that the whole house was exceptionally
3 bright.[6] And when he was taken[7] from the hand of the midwife,[8] he
4 opened his mouth and spoke to the Lord of Righteousness.[9] And
his father[10] Lamech was afraid of him and fled and went to his
5 father Methuselah. And he said to him, I have begotten a strange
son; he is not like a man, but is like the children of the angels of
heaven, of a different type, and not like us. And his eyes *are* like the
6 rays of the sun, and his face glorious. And it seems to me that he is
not sprung from me, but from the angels,[11] and I am afraid lest
something extraordinary should be done[12] on the earth in his days.
7 And now,[13] my father, I am entreating you and petitioning you to
go[14] to our father Enoch, and[15] learn from him the truth, for his

---

   [2] Gk.[m] om. chap. cv, but from the fragments that have survived it is clear that Aram. had material corresponding at least to verse 1 and perhaps to the end of verse 2.

   [1] Gk.[m] 'And after *some* time I took a wife for my son Methuselah, and she bore a son and called his name Lamech; righteousness was brought low until that day. And when he came of age, he took a wife for himself'.
   [2] became pregnant by him and: Gk.[m] om.
   [3] Gk.[m] adds 'to him'.
   [4] All Eth. MSS add what seems to be a gloss, 'and his hair'; Gk.[m] 'And when the child was born, *his* body was whiter than snow and redder than the rose, *his* hair all white, and like white wool, and curly and glorious'.
   [5] and his eyes . . . beautiful: Gk.[m] om.
   [6] he made . . . exceptionally bright: Gk.[m] 'the house shone like the sun'.
   [7] Ga 'And thereupon he rose'; Gk.[m] 'And he rose'.
   [8] Ga Gk.[m] add 'and'.
   [9] and spoke . . . Righteousness: Gk.[m] 'and blessed the Lord'.
   [10] his father: Gk.[m] om.   [11] Gk.[m] 'an angel'.
   [12] Gk.[m] 'and I fear him lest something should occur'.
   [13] now: Gk.[m] om.   [14] to go: Gk.[m] 'Go'.
   [15] Remainder of verse 7 and beginning of verse 8 has not survived in Gk.[m].

8 dwelling is with the angels. And when Methuselah heard the words of his son, he came to me at the ends of the earth, for he had heard that I was there.[16] And he cried out,[17] and I heard his voice and went to him. And I said to him,[18] Behold, I am *here*, my son, for
9 you have[19] come to me.[20] And he answered me[21] and said, Because of a great matter[22] have I come to you,[23] and because of a disturb-
10 ing vision have I come near.[24] And now hear me, my father, for[25] a child has been born to my son Lamech whose form and type are not like the type of a man; his colour is whiter than snow and redder than the flower of[26] a rose, and the hair of his head is whiter than white wool, and his eyes *are* like the rays of the sun; and he opened
11 his eyes and made the whole house bright.[27] And he was taken from[28] the hand of the midwife and opened his mouth and blessed
12 the Lord of Heaven.[29] And his father Lamech[30] was afraid and fled to me. And he does not believe that he *is sprung* from him, but thinks him *to be*[31] from the angels[32] of heaven. And behold I have come to
13 you that you may make known to me the truth. And I, Enoch, answered and said to him,[33] The Lord will do new things on the earth, and this I have already seen in a vision and made known to you,[34] for[35] in the generation of my father Jared some from the

---

[16] for . . . there: Gk.ᵐ 'where he [saw] that I was then'.

[17] And he cried out: Gk.ᵐ 'And he said to me, [My] father, hear my voice and come [to] me'.

[18] to him: Gk.ᵐ om. [19] Gk.ᵐ 'Why have you'.

[20] Gk.ᵐ adds '*my son*'. [21] me: Gk.ᵐ om.

[22] GGaMTD' Gk.ᵐ 'need'. [23] to you: Gk.ᵐ 'here, father'.

[24] and because . . . near: Gk.ᵐ om. [25] hear me . . . for: Gk.ᵐ om.

[26] the flower of: Gk.ᵐ om.

[27] and he opened . . . bright: Gk.ᵐ om.

[28] And he was taken from (or perhaps 'rose from'): so GBCEL²C'; other Eth. MSS 'And he rose in'; Gk.ᵐ 'And he rose from'.

[29] Gk.ᵐ 'of Eternity'. [30] Gk.ᵐ 'And my son Lamech'.

[31] but thinks him *to be*: GGaMH 'but *that* his form *is*'.

[32] Gk.ᵐ 'And he does not believe that he is his son, but that *he is* from the angels' (after this one line of text seems to have dropped out and what remains of the verse is corrupt).

[33] Gk.ᵐ 'Then I answered, saying'.

[34] Gk.ᵐ in part obscure, 'The Lord will make a new command on the earth, and in the same way (?), *my* son, I have seen and made *it* known to you'.

[35] for: in Eth. could also be translated 'that'.

14 height of heaven transgressed the word of the[36] Lord.[37] And behold, they commit sin and transgress the law,[38] and have been promiscuous with women and commit sin with them, and have
15 married some of them, and have begotten children by them.[39] And there will be great destruction over the whole[40] earth,[41] and there will be[42] a deluge, and there will be great destruction for one year.
16 But this child who has been born to you[43] will be left on the earth,[44] and his three sons will be saved with him;[45] when all the men[46] who
17 *are* on the earth die, he and his sons will be saved.[47] They will beget on the earth giants, not of spirit, but of flesh, and there will be great wrath on the earth,[48] and the earth will be cleansed from all
18 corruption.[49] And now make known to your son Lamech[50] that the one who has been born is truly his son.[51] And call his name Noah, for he will be a remnant for you,[52] and he and his sons will be saved from the destruction which is coming on the earth because of all the sin and all the iniquity which will be committed on the earth in his
19 days. But after this there will be yet greater iniquity than that which was committed on the earth before. For I know the

[36] GGaQD'T[2] and some Eth.II MSS 'my'.

[37] some . . . Lord: N 'the angels of heaven transgressed the word of my Lord'; D Gk.[m] 'they transgressed the word of the (D' 'my') Lord, *departing* from the covenant of heaven'.

[38] Gk.[m] 'custom'.

[39] by them: GaQAN om.   [40] GaEHKNC' om.

[41] and have begotten . . . earth: Gk.[m] 'and they bear *children* not like spirits, but of flesh. And there will be great wrath on the earth' (cp. verse 17).

[42] there will be: Gk.[m] om.

[43] to you: Gk.[m] om.   [44] on the earth: Gk.[m] om.

[45] with him: Gk.[m] om.   [46] all the men: Gk.[m] 'those'.

[47] he and his sons will be saved: GGaQD' Gk.[m] om. (probably repeated by mistake). GGa also om., but by hmt., 'They will beget on the earth'. For Gk.[m] cp also note 48.

[48] They will beget . . . wrath on the earth: Gk.[m] om., but has a very similar passage at the end of verse 14 and the beginning of verse 15 (cp. note 41). Verse 17a in Eth. is probably an alternative version of the end of verse 14 and the beginning of verse 15 which has been introduced into the text in the wrong place.

[49] Gk.[m] 'and he will calm the earth from the corruption that is on it'.

[50] Gk.[m] 'And now tell Lamech'.

[51] that . . . his son: Gk.[m] 'He is your son in truth and holiness'.

[52] Gk.[m] adds 'whereby you will have rest' (after this there appears to be a lacuna and the text of the remainder of the verse is obscure).

mysteries of the holy ones, for that Lord[53] showed *them* to me and made *them* known to me, and I read *them* in the tablets of heaven.

CVII. And I saw written on them[1] that generation upon generation will do wrong[2] until a generation of righteousness shall arise, and wrongdoing shall be destroyed, and sin[3] shall 'depart from the
2 earth, and everything good shall come upon it.[4] And now, my son, go,[5] make known to your son Lamech that this child who has been
3 born is truly his son, and *this* is no lie. And when Methuselah had heard the words of his father Enoch – for he showed everything[6] to him which is secret[7] – he returned, having seen him,[8] and called the name of that child Noah; for he will comfort the earth after all the destruction.[9]

CVIII. Another book which Enoch wrote for his son Methuselah and for those who should come after him and keep the law in the
2 last days. You who have observed *it*[1] and are waiting[2] in these days until an end shall be made of those who do evil, and an end shall be
3 made of the power of the wrongdoers, do[3] indeed wait until sin

---

[1] And I saw . . . them: so Eth. Aram.; Gk.[m] 'Then I saw what was written on them'.

[2] that . . . wrong: Gk.[m] 'that one generation [will be] wor[se] than another'; Aram. 'that [generation] upon generation will do wrong in [. . .] and wrong will be ['; Gk.[m] adds 'and then I saw' (perhaps a duplicate version of the beginning of the verse).

[3] Aram. 'violence'.

[4] and everything . . . upon it (Ga 'upon the earth'): Gk.[m] 'and good things will come to them upon the earth'; Aram. damaged, but did apparently have 'to them'.

[5] Gk.[m] 'run'.

[6] Gk.[m] om.

[7] which is secret: GGaMQTD' Gk.[m] 'in secret'.

[8] he returned, having seen him: GaQ Gk.[m] om.; D' om. 'having seen him'; M 'he returned and showed *them* to him', and similarly G (which is defective).

[9] Gk.[m] 'And his name was called Noah, comforting the earth after the destruction'.

[1] GGa 'You who have done good'.

[2] and are waiting: GGaMQD' 'will wait'.

[3] GGaMQTD' 'And do'.

shall pass away; for their names will be erased from[4] the books of the holy ones,[5] and their offspring will be destroyed for ever, and their spirits will be killed, and they will cry out and moan in a chaotic[6] desert place, and will burn[7] in fire, for there is no earth

4 there. And there I saw something like a cloud which could not be discerned, for because of its depth I was not able to look up at it; and the flames of a fire I saw burning brightly, and *things* like bright

5 mountains revolved and shook from side to side. And I asked one of the holy angels who *were* with me and said to him, What is this bright *place*? For there is no heaven, but only the flames of a burning fire and the sound of crying and weeping and moaning

6 and severe pain. And he said to me, This place which you see – here will be thrown[8] the spirits of the sinners and of the blasphemers, and of those who do evil, and of those who alter everything which the Lord has spoken[9] by the mouth of the prophets about the things

7 which shall be done. For there are books and records about them in heaven above, that the angels may read them and know what is to come upon the sinners, and upon the spirits of the humble,[10] and of those who afflicted their bodies and were recompensed by God,

8 and of those who were abused by evil men; who loved[11] God, and did not love gold, or silver, or any worldly good, but gave up their

9 bodies to torment; who, from the moment they existed, did not desire earthly food, but counted themselves as a breath which passes away, and kept *to* this; and the Lord tested them much, and

10 their spirits were found pure that they might bless his name. And all their blessings I have recounted in the books; and he has assigned them their reward, for they were found to be such as loved

---

[4] GGa add 'the book of life and from'; Q adds 'from the books of the living and from'; MTD' add 'the book and from'.

[5] the books of the holy ones: MQTD'EB'C' 'the holy books'; G 'the book of the Holy One (or 'holy ones')'.

[6] chaotic: lit. 'that cannot be seen', but in the light of the LXX of Gen. i. probably to be translated 'chaotic'.

[7] will burn: so D'ABCXC'; other MSS 'have burnt'.

[8] GQD' 'led'.

[9] GGaQD' 'done'.

[10] Many Eth.II MSS 'the humble spirits'; D' 'the spirits of those who have gone astray'.

[11] So ABDEX: other MSS 'love'.

heaven more than their life in the world,[12] and even though they were trampled under foot by evil men, and had to listen to reviling and reproach from them and were abused, yet they blessed me.

11 And now I will call the spirits of the good *who are* of the generation of light, and I will transform those who were born in darkness, who in the flesh were not recompensed with honour, as was fitting to

12 their faith. And I will bring out into shining light those who love[13] my holy name, and I will set each one on the throne of his honour.

13 And they will shine for times without number, for righteousness *is* the judgement of God, for with the faithful he will keep faith in the

14 dwelling of upright paths. And they will see those who were born in

15 darkness thrown[14] into darkness, while the righteous shine. And the sinners will cry out as they see them shining, but they themselves will go where days and times have been written down for them.

---

[12] in the world: so Ga; all other MSS 'which *is* for ever'.
[13] GMQTD' 'loved'.
[14] GMQD' 'led'.

2 ENOCH

INTRODUCTION

2 Enoch, or 'Slavonic Enoch' (so-called to distinguish it from 'Ethiopian Enoch'), or 'The Book of the Secrets of Enoch' (a title based on the titles in some of the manuscripts), has been preserved only in Slavonic in two distinct recensions, each attested by more than one family of manuscripts.

Attention was first drawn to it in modern times by an extract contained in two MSS in the Synodal Library in Moscow printed by A. V. Gorsky and K. I. Nevostruev in their catalogue of MSS in that library, published in 1859.[1] The first edition of the work as a whole was that of A. N. Popov, who in 1880 printed the text from the Poltava MS (our P), written in 1679. In 1884 S. Novaković printed a much shorter text, with a number of obvious lacunae, from a 16th–17th cent. MS in the National Library in Belgrade (our N): this text is a Serbian redaction, but there are several clear indications that it was derived from a Russian original. Two years later M. I. Sokolov discovered another MS containing the work, also in Belgrade, and of the 16th cent., but in middle-Bulgarian (our R): the contents tallied much more closely with Popov's Poltava text than with that in the other Belgrade MS, and Sokolov concluded that this longer version represented the original and that the shorter text was an abbreviation of it.

The next few years witnessed fresh discoveries, both of MSS (including the earliest of all, that in the Uvarov collection, of the 15th cent. – our U) and of a number of fragments in the form of extracts and quotations preserved in other works. Despite the fact that the new evidence showed that the shorter version was known before the longer, and also that all the fragments were taken from it, Sokolov still maintained his opinion that the longer version was to be preferred, and accordingly chose as the basis for his edition of 1899 the Belgrade MS R, though his posthumous papers, edited

[1] See A. V. Gorsky and K. I. Nevostruev, *Opisanie slavyanskikh rukopisei Moskovskoi sinodal'noi (patriarshei) biblioteki*, II. ii (Moscow, 1859), pp. 626–7. The MSS are now in the Library of the State Historical Museum in Moscow.

by M. N. Speransky in 1910, show that he eventually relented to the extent of recognizing U as a witness to the existence of an 'intermediate version' from which the shorter version was derived.

The German scholar Bonwetsch, in the Introduction to his translation of 1922, denied the existence of this 'intermediate version' and argued that U is much better explained as a primary witness to the text of the shorter version; but he still followed Sokolov in maintaining the priority of the longer version. However, he made the point that the shorter version cannot reasonably be regarded as the abbreviation of the contents of any one of the existing 'longer' MSS. Nevertheless, all the MSS, wide as the divergences are, were (according to Bonwetsch) derived ultimately from the same original Slavonic translation.

Meanwhile, N. Schmidt had in 1921 argued cogently, in a brief article of only six pages, for the priority of the shorter version; and in this view he was supported by A. Vaillant in his full critical edition of 1952. But whereas Schmidt thought that the two Slavonic versions were traceable to two previously existing recensions in Greek, Vaillant, like Bonwetsch, preferred to think of them as Slavonic recensions and to trace them back to a single Slavonic translation, made probably in Macedonia in the 10th or 11th centuries. This translation, Vaillant thought, survives in all essentials in the 'short recension', attested by five MSS dating from the 15th to the 18th centuries (UBNVBa.), and by the fragments Mpr. Chr. Rum. and Tr. The 'long recension' in its pristine form (found only in the Belgrade MS R) Vaillant attributed to a reviser, who worked between the second half of the 13th cent. and the early part of the 16th – most probably towards the end of the 15th: this reviser was responsible for very many relatively minor corrections and alterations, and also for a number of substantial additions of new material. Finally, a second reviser, fairly soon afterwards, worked over his predecessor's text, paraphrased it sometimes rather freely, transposed an item here and there, and made a few more additions: this second reviser's activity is attested by the MSS J and P, both of which are unfortunately incomplete (as are also the MSS NVBa. of the 'short recension').

Vaillant's edition is therefore an edition of the 'short recension', his text being based on the oldest MS U. The variants of all the

MSS and the fragments are, however, cited in his apparatus with the exception of the putative additions of new material made by the first reviser: these are collected together in an appendix at the end (the text here being that of R, printed over an apparatus showing the variants in J and P).

Our translation is a translation of the text of the 'short recension' as given in Vaillant's edition. In the footnotes will be found a selection of the more important of the minor variations; but only occasionally, for obvious reasons, are the major variants of the 'long recension' either given in full, or, indeed, mentioned. When R appears in the footnotes, it is to be understood that it is supported by both J and P where extant, unless it is stated otherwise.

About the date, authorship, and original language of the work opinions have differed widely. At one extreme R. H. Charles concluded that it was written about the beginning of the Christian era, by an Alexandrian Jew, and in Greek (though certain parts of it 'were founded on Hebrew originals'). At the other extreme Mrs A. S. D. Maunder argued that it is a Bogomil work, written originally in Bulgarian, between the 12th and the 15th centuries. As a third, intermediate, view may be instanced that of Vaillant, who could refer to it as 'Christian Enoch' in contrast with 'Jewish Enoch' (i.e. 1 Enoch), though he was in no doubt that the author was a *Jewish* Christian, who was concerned to produce a Christian counterpart to the well-known Jewish Enoch, and wrote in Greek, probably in the second or early third century AD.

There is no certain indication, however, that 2 Enoch, even in the short recension, was known to any of the Greek or Latin Fathers. For example, it is customary to explain 'I saw all material things', quoted and attributed to Enoch both by Clement of Alexandria[2] and by Origen[3] in the light of several passages in 2 Enoch xiii.[4] But there are two difficulties here. In the first place, both in Clement and in Origen the words appear as an exact quotation ('when Enoch said, I saw . . .'), whereas not one of the suggested passages from 2 Enoch xiii is verbally identical; and secondly, Origen not only ascribes the quotation to Enoch, but

---

[2] Clem.-Alex. *Ecl. proph.* ii. 1.   [3] Orig. *Princ.* IV. iv. 8.
[4] xiii. 5–8, 14–15, 20–22, 23–26, 27.

also says that it was 'written in the same book' as another of
Enoch's sayings he has just quoted, and which appears to be taken
from 1 Enoch xxi. 1. What the answer is we do not know. It may be
that the words 'I saw all material things' did in fact stand in the
Greek copy of 2 Enoch xiii used by Clement and Origen, and the
Slavonic translator either omitted them or paraphrased them – in
which case Origen will have been guilty of a lapse of memory in
saying that they occured in the same book as 1 Enoch xxi. 1.
Alternatively it may be that Origen was correct and that they did
once stand in some texts of 1 Enoch, though they are not found
today in any known text of that work. Or it may be that the words
were not intended originally as an exact quotation at all, but
merely as a loose reference (to 1 Enoch xix. 3, for instance), and
Origen may have remembered them from his reading of Clement,
or both may have been familiar with them independently from
some collection of Enoch's sayings circulating in Alexandria or
from contemporary oral traditions about Enoch. And there are a
number of other possibilities. What we cannot have is certainty.
And there is a similar uncertainty about all the other suggested
patristic quotations.

But quite apart from the question whether or not 2 Enoch was
known to the Fathers, it is highly probable, if we are to argue from
analogy, that there was at one time a Greek text, of which the
earliest Slavonic text was a translation. It is also highly probable
that this Greek text was the original: there are a number of
linguistic pointers in this direction; and the Septuagint, rather
than the Hebrew, seems to have been the author's Bible. However,
this by itself tells us very little about him. Some of the names, found
only in 2 Enoch, such as Adoil[5] and Sofonima,[6] suggest at the very
least a Jewish background. The author, then, may well have been a
Jew of Alexandria (as Charles maintained) or of some other city of
the Dispersion, who spoke and wrote in Greek, and who quite
naturally regarded the Septuagint as his Bible. And yet there are
no specifically Jewish features anywhere: Enoch's admonitions
about gifts and offerings,[7] for instance, and the descriptions of the

---

[5] xi. 7.   [6] xxiii. 1, 2, etc.
[7] ii. 2–4; xiii. 46–47; xv. 6–7, 17–20; xvii. 7.

priestly functions and activities of Methuselah[8] and Nir,[9] are all very general, and they exhibit no points of contact in detail either with the sacrificial requirements of the Pentateuch or with any known Temple practices.

The case for a Christian origin depends partly on general considerations, partly on the lack of specifically Jewish features just mentioned, partly on alleged influence from the books of the New Testament (Charles's list of parallels can just as easily be explained as echoes of the New Testament in 2 Enoch as they can as echoes of 2 Enoch in the New Testament), but more particularly on how we understand the Melchizedek story in chap. xxiii at the very end.

According to this story Melchizedek is born, without the agency of a human father, from the body of Sofonima after her death: he has on his breast 'the seal of the priesthood',[10] and Nir is told that he will be 'a priest of priests for ever';[11] after the Flood the Lord will raise up another generation and Melchizedek will be 'chief priest' in that generation:[12] until then he is to be kept safe in the Garden of Eden. It is tempting to read this story as a development of what is said about Melchizedek in the Epistle to the Hebrews. In Hebrews Melchizedek appears 'without father, without mother, without genealogy',[13] and his priesthood is the type of the priesthood of Christ, who is described more than once both as 'a priest for ever'[14] and as 'the mediator' of a 'new (or 'better') covenant'.[15] If we read the story in 2 Enoch so, then 2 Enoch cannot be much earlier than the end of the first century A.D. and its origin must be Christian. On the other hand, the details in Hebrews and 2 Enoch that are alleged to correspond are not sufficiently close to establish anything like a water-tight case for dependence: we know from the evidence of Qumran that Jews, no less than Christians, were interested in Melchizedek; and there is, therefore, no reason to suppose that both a Jewish author and a Christian author could not have developed this interest independently, one in 2 Enoch and the other in Hebrews.

---

[8] xx. 1–2; xxi. 7–15.   [9] xxii. 15, 22–24.
[10] xxiii. 18.   [11] xxiii. 29.   [12] xxiii. 34.
[13] Heb. vii. 3.   [14] Heb. v. 6; vii. 21: cp. vii. 3.
[15] Heb. viii. 6; ix. 15; xii. 24: cp. vii. 22.

And there is the further difficulty that we cannot be sure that the Melchizedek story is an integral part of the original 2 Enoch. Chapters xxi–xxiii are missing altogether in Morfill's and Forbes's translations; and Bonwetsch relegated all three chapters to an appendix – the reason being that they are not included in the MSS N and Ba. of the short recension (both of which end with chap. xviii), while of the MSS of the long recension P ends with chap. xx and J at xxiii. 2. Vaillant, however, printed all of them as part of his text, following UB and two of the fragments (short recension) together with R (long recension); and as explained above, we, in our translation, have followed Vaillant.

Finally, a point of some interest in this connection has been made by A. Rubinstein. Enoch, in his admonitions about sacrifice at xv. 8–9 lays it down, 'And all you have for food, bind it by the four legs . . . The man who kills any beast without binding it – it is an evil custom'. For this binding of a victim before slaughter there is neither Biblical nor Rabbinic parallel. Yet later in 2 Enoch both Methuselah (at xxi. 9) and Nir (at xxii. 23) observe the provision. Chaps. xxi and xxii, therefore, even if not xxiii, have a very definite link with what goes before, although they are lacking in three of the MSS.

BIBLIOGRAPHY

EDITIONS

A. N. POPOV, *Bibliograficheskie materialy* (ii–viii) (= *ChOIDR*; Moscow, 1880, III. ix), pp. 89–139. [The text of P]

S. NOVAKOVIĆ, 'Apokrif o Enohu' in *Starine*, xvi (Zagreb, 1884), pp. 67–81. [The text of N]

M. I. SOKOLOV, *Materialy i zametki po starinnoi slavyanskoi literature*, III. vii: *Slavyanskaya kniga Enokha* (= *ChOIDR*; Moscow, 1899, IV. ii). [An edition of the text of R of the long recension, together with an apparatus recording the variants of U and P and also a Latin translation, followed by an edition of B of the short recension with an apparatus recording the variants of N and V.]

——, *Materialy i zametki po starinnoi slavyanskoi literature*, III. vii: *Slavyanskaya kniga Enokha pravednogo* (= *ChOIDR*; Moscow, 1910,

IV. ii. 1). [An edition of the texts of U and Ba of the short recension, together with a number of fragments.]

A. VAILLANT, *Le Livre des secrets d'Hénoch* (= *Textes publiés par l'Institut d'Études slaves*, IV; Paris, 1952 – reprinted 1976). [An edition of the short recension, with a full apparatus and a French translation – the major additions of the long recension are printed in an appendix, together with French translation.]

TRANSLATIONS

English

R. H. CHARLES and W. R. MORFILL, *The Book of the Secrets of Enoch: Translated from the Slavonic by* W. R. MORFILL, *and edited, with Introduction, Notes, and Indices, by* R. H. CHARLES (Oxford, 1896). [A translation of a text based on Popov's edition of P, though using also Novaković's edition of N and some readings supplied by Sokolov before publication.]

N. FORBES in R. H. CHARLES, *APOT* ii, pp. 425–469. [The long and the short recensions in parallel columns.]

French

A. VAILLANT, *Le Livre des secrets d'Hénoch* . . . [as above].

German

G. N. BONWETSCH, *Das slavische Henochbuch* (= *Abhandlungen der königlichen Gesellschaft der Wissenschaften zu Göttingen, Philologisch-historische Klasse*, N.F. i. 3; Berlin, 1896). [Both recensions, the longer above the shorter, with an Introduction.]

———, *Die Bücher der Geheimnisse Henochs: Das sogennante slavische Henochbuch* (= *TU* xliv. 2; Leipzig, 1922). [A translation, first of the long recension, and then of the short, with a full apparatus in each case, and an Introduction.]

P. REISSLER, *AjSaB²*, pp. 452–473. [Of the short recension.]

GENERAL

F. C. BURKITT, *Jewish and Christian Apocalypses* (London, 1914), pp. 75–76.

R. H. CHARLES, 'The Date and Place of Writing of the Slavonic Enoch' in *JTS* xxii (1921), pp. 161–163.

A.-M. DENIS, *IPGAT*, pp. 28–29.

O. EISSFELDT, *OTI*, pp. 622–623.

J. K. FOTHERINGHAM, 'The Date and Place of Writing of the Slavonic Enoch' in *JTS* xx (1919), p. 252.

——, 'The Easter Calendar and the Slavonic Enoch' in *JTS* xxiii (1922), pp. 49–56.

J.-B. FREY, art. 'Apocryphes de l'Ancien Testament' in *DBSup* i, cols. 448–453.

L. GINZBERG, *The Legends of the Jews*, i (Philadelphia, 1909), pp. 130–137 and v (Philadelphia, 1925), pp. 158–162.

K. LAKE, 'The Date of the Slavonic Enoch' in *HTR* xvi (1923), pp. 397–398.

E. LITTMANN, art. 'Enoch, Books of: II. Slavonic Enoch' in *JE* v (New York, 1903), pp. 181–182.

A. S. D. MAUNDER, 'The Date and Place of Writing of the Slavonic Enoch' in *The Observatory*, xli (1918), pp. 309–316.

J. T. MILIK, *The Books of Enoch: Aramaic Fragments of Qûmran Cave 4* (Oxford, 1976), pp. 107–116.

P. RIESSLER, *AjSaB²*, pp. 1297–1298.

L. ROST, *EATAP*, pp. 82–84.

A. RUBINSTEIN, 'Observations on the Slavonic Book of Enoch' in *JJS* xiii (1962), pp. 1–21.

N. SCHMIDT, 'The Two Recensions of Slavonic Enoch' in *JAOS* xli (1921), pp. 307–312.

E. SCHÜRER, *GjVZJC⁴* iii, pp. 290–294.

É. TURDEANU, 'Apocryphes bogomiles et apocryphes pseudo-bogomiles' in *Revue de l'histoire des religions*, cxxxviii (1950), pp. 181–187.

From the secret books of the taking up of Enoch the Just (in the Lord, O master, give a blessing), a wise man, a great man of letters, whom the Lord received that he might **be an eyewitness of**[1] the life above and of the most wise and great and unchangeable majesty of Almighty God, of the most great, many-eyed, and immoveable

[1] Emended on the basis of RJ ('that he might see').

throne of the Lord, of the most bright station of the servants of the Lord, and of the mighty, fire-born, ranks of the heavenly hosts, *and* of the ineffable harmony of a great multitude of elements, and of the varied aspect and inexpressible singing of the hosts of the cherubim, *and* to be the witness of immeasurable light.[2]

I. And at that time, said Enoch, when I had completed three hundred and sixty-five years,[1] in the first month, on a certain day[2] of the first month, I was in my house alone, weeping and sorrowing with my eyes. While I was resting on my bed, sleeping,[3] there appeared to me two men, very great, such as I had never seen on earth. Their faces were like the shining sun, their eyes burned like candles, out of their mouths came what looked like fire, and their clothing *was* **a diffusion of foam**, and their arms like golden wings at the head of my bed; and they called *me* by my name. I awoke from my sleep, and the two men were really standing by me.[4] And I made haste and got up and bowed down to them; and my face **was covered with frost** from fright. And the men said to me, Take courage, Enoch, do not be afraid: the eternal Lord has sent us to you; and behold, you shall go up with us today to heaven. And tell your sons[5] all they must do on earth, and in your house; and let no one look for you until the Lord returns you to them. And I obeyed them and went out. I called my sons Methusalom and Rigim[6] and I told them everything the men had said to me.

II. And *I said to them*, Behold, my children, I do not know where I am going or what will become of me. And now, my children, do not turn away from God, but live your lives in the Lord's presence, and

[2] Full title in URJP only.

[1] R has 'when my one hundred and sixty-fifth year was accomplished, I begot my son Methusalam. And after that I lived two hundred years: I completed all the years of my life, three hundred and sixty-five'.

[2] R adds 'the first day', which Vaillant explains as the first or seventh day of Easter (the 15th or 22nd of the month Nisan), a festal day which Enoch spends in retreat.   [3] U 'I slept'.

[4] R 'and I saw clearly the two men standing before me'.

[5] So U: BN etc. add 'and (R + 'all') your household'.

[6] R adds 'and Gaidad'.

keep his judgements; and do not refuse[1] the sacrifice of your
salvation, and the Lord will not refuse[2] the labour of your hands.

3 Do not deny the Lord his gifts, *and* the Lord will not deny *you* his
4 possessions in your storehouses. Bless the Lord with the firstborn
of your flocks *and* herds, and you will be the blessed of the Lord for

5 ever. Do not turn aside from the Lord, nor worship idols, who have
made neither heaven nor earth: may the Lord confirm your hearts

6 in the fear of him. And now, my children, let no one look for me
until the Lord returns me to you.

III.   And it came to pass, when I had spoken to my sons, the two
men called me and took me up on their wings; and they carried me

2 up into the first heaven and set me down there. And they brought
before me the elders, the masters of the ranks of the stars, and they
showed me their movement*s* and their displacements from year to

3 year. And they showed me two hundred[1] angels, who rule the stars
4 and the constellations[2] in heaven. And they showed me there a sea,
very great, much greater than the earthly sea; and angels were

5 flying with their wings. And they showed me the treasuries of the
6 snow and ice,[3] and terrifying angels guarding the treasuries. And
they showed me there the storehouses[4] of the clouds, from which

7 they rise[5] and go out. And they showed me the treasuries of the
dew, like the balm of olive trees, and the angels guarding their
treasuries; and their appearance[6] was like all the flowers of the
earth.

IV.   And those two men took me up into the second heaven and set
2 me down in the second heaven. And they showed me the prisoners,
under guard, of[1] the immeasurable judgement;[2] and there I saw

3 angels that had been condemned, weeping. And I said to the men
who *were* with me, Why are *these* in torment? The men answered

---

¹ B 'lessen'; R 'make odious'.   ² BR 'cut short'.

¹ two hundred = BNBaR: U 'in the light'.
² Lit. 'combinations'.   ³ So BNR: UBa 'cold'.
⁴ U 'the treasuries, and they showed me the storehouses'.
⁵ U 'go in'.   ⁶ NBa 'clothing'.

¹ R 'awaiting'.   ² So BBa, supported by NR: U is corrupt.

me, *These* are apostates from the Lord, who were not obedient to
4 the Lord's commands,[3] but took counsel with their own will.[4] And
I was *very* sorry for them. *And* the angels bowed low to me and said,
5 Man of God, *we ask you* that you would pray to the Lord for us. And
I answered them and said, Who am I, a mortal man, that I should
pray for angels; for who knows where I am going, or what will
become of me, or who will pray for me?

V.   And the men took me from there *and* led me up to the third
2 heaven, and set me in the midst of Paradise. And that place *is* more
beautiful than anything there is to see – all trees in full bloom, all
fruit ripe, every *kind of* food always in abundance, every breeze
3 fragrant. And *there are* four rivers flowing by in silent course: the
4 whole garden *is* good, producing *what is good* to eat.[1] And[2] the tree
of life *is* in that place, where the Lord rests, when he[3] goes into
Paradise; and that tree is indescribable for the quality of its
5 fragrance. And there is another tree nearby, an olive, which flows
6 ceaselessly with oil. And every tree *is* laden with good fruit: there is
7 no tree there without fruit; and the whole place is blessed.[4] And the
angels who guard Paradise *are* most glorious, *and* they serve God
8 continually[5] with unceasing voice *and* sweet singing. And I said,
9 How very blessed is this place. The men answered me, This place,
Enoch, is prepared for the righteous, who will endure hardships in
this life, and mortify themselves, and turn their eyes away from
unrighteousness, and execute true justice, to give bread to the
hungry, and to cover the naked with a garment, and to lift up
anyone who has fallen, and to help those who have been wronged,
10 who live their lives in the Lord's presence and serve him alone. For
them is this place[6] prepared as *their* eternal inheritance.
11   And those men took me from there and carried me up to the
north of the heaven and showed me there a very terrible place.

---

[3] Lit. 'voice'.
[4] R adds 'they deserted with their prince *and those* who are made fast in the fifth
heaven'.

[1] B 'producing every kind that is good to eat'.
[2] R adds 'in the midst'.   [3] U 'the Lord'.
[4] So BNBa: U 'sweet smelling'.
[5] Lit. 'throughout all days'.   [6] U om.

12   Every kind of torment and torture *is* in that place, and darkness
     and mist; and there is no light there, but a dark fire flaming up
     eternally in that place, and a river of fire rising up against all that
13   place. *And there are* cold *and* ice and prisons *in that place*, and fierce
     and cruel angels who carry weapons and inflict torments[7] without
14,15 mercy. And I said, How very terrible is this place. And the men
     answered me, This place, Enoch, is prepared for the impious, who
     do godless deeds on earth, who deal in spells and incantations[8] and
     boast of what they do, *who* steal the souls of men[9] secretly, who
16   loose the yoke that binds *them*, who grow rich from others' posses-
     sions through injustice, and have left the *man who is* hungry to die of
     starvation when they could have satisfied *him*, and have stripped
17   the naked when they could have clothed *them*, who did not
     acknowledge their creator, but worshipped idols and made
18   images, and bowed down to the work of *their own* hands. And for all
     these is this place prepared as *their* eternal inheritance.

VI.   And the men led me up from there and carried me up[1] to the
2   fourth heaven. And behold, they showed me there all the
3   movements[2] and all the rays of the sun and moon. And I measured
     their movement *and* compared their light; and I saw *that* the sun
     has a light seven times greater than the moon.[3] Their[4] path and the
     chariot on which each of them travels *is* like the wind in motion;
     and there is no rest for them as they go and return by day and
4   night. And *I saw* four great stars hanging on the right of the sun's
5   chariot *and* four on the left, which go with the sun eternally. And *I
     saw* angels going before the sun's chariot, flying spirits: twelve
     wings has each angel that draws the sun's chariot, carrying the
     dew and the heat, when the Lord commands *them* to go down to
     earth with the sun's rays.

6,7   And the men took me to the east of the heaven. And they showed
     me the doors through which the sun goes out according to the times
     appointed, and according to the circuits of the moon[5] of the whole

---

[7]   and inflict torments = B etc.: U is corrupt.
[8]   So NBaR: U 'calumnies'.   [9] U om. 'of men'.

[1]   from there . . . up = BNBa: U om.
[2]   BR add 'and displacements'.
[3]   U 'sun'.   [4] U 'its'.   [5] B 'months'.

year, and according to the shortening *and* lengthening[6] of the days
8 and of the nights.[7] *And they showed me* six doors, one open, **at a**
distance of thirty stades; and I tried to measure their size, but I
9 could not.[8] Through them the sun enters[9] and goes to the west.
10 Through the first door he goes out forty-two days, through the
second thirty-five days, through the third thirty-five days, through
the fourth thirty-five days, through the fifth thirty-five days,
11 through the sixth forty-two days. And again, returning through the
sixth door according to the circuit of the seasons, he goes in
through the fifth door thirty-five days, through the fourth door
thirty-five days, through the third door thirty-five days, through
12 the second thirty-five days. And the days of the year are ended
according to the cycle of the seasons.[10]

13 And the men led me up to the west of the heaven and showed me
there the six great doors, open according to the circuit of the
heavenly eastern *doors* opposite, through which the sun sets according to *his* entering[11] through the eastern doors and according to the
14 number of the days.[12] Thus he sets through the western doors; and
when he comes out from the western doors four angels take his
15 crown and carry it up to the Lord. But the sun turns his chariot and
16 goes without light; and there[13] they put the crown on him. They
showed me this numbering[14] of the sun and *of* the doors through
which he goes in and out; for these doors the Lord made, and he
appoints the sun to be the hour-keeper of the year.

17 And of the moon they showed me another numbering: they
showed me all her movements and all her circuits and her[15] doors.
18 They showed me twelve doors to the east: they showed me *the doors*
of the crown,[16] through which the moon goes in and out according

---

[6] So Ba: U is corrupt.   [7] and of the night*s* = B etc.: U om.
[8] Lit. 'and I measured their size and I could not comprehend their size'.
[9] N 'rises'.   [10] R 'the four seasons'.
[11] BNBa 'rising'.
[12] R adds 'three hundred and sixty-five and a quarter'.
[13] NBa add 'at the eastern doors'.
[14] So R: U reads 'waxing', which is in all probability a corruption of 'numbering'.
[15] and her = BN: U om.
[16] circuits . . . crown. The passage is corrupt. On the basis of the variants Vaillant
emends 'circuits, and they showed me her doors. They showed me twelve doors like
a crown to the east, and twelve such doors like a crown to the west'.

19 to the accustomed times. Through the first door to the east thirty-one[17] days certainly, and through the second thirty-five days certainly, and *through* the third thirty-one[18] days exceptionally, and through the fourth thirty days certainly, and through the fifth thirty-one[17] days extraordinarily, and through the sixth thirty-one days certainly, through the seventh thirty days certainly, through the eighth thirty-one days extraordinarily, and through the ninth thirty-one days precisely, and through the tenth thirty days certainly, through the eleventh thirty-one days exceptionally, through the twelfth door she enters twenty-two days[19] certainly.

20 And so also through the western doors, according to the cycle and number of the eastern doors: thus she goes in also through the western doors; and she completes the year with three hundred and

21 sixty-four[20] days. She goes into the year with four exceptional *quarter days*: for this reason they are excepted *and* set apart from the heaven and the year and are not counted in the number of the days; for they change[21] the seasons of the year, two new moons when she is waxing and a second two new moons when she is waning.[22]

22 When she finishes at the western doors, she returns *and* goes to the
23 eastern with her light: thus she goes day and night in a circle. Her orbit is like the sky; and the chariot on which she goes up *is* a wind in motion, and drawing her chariot *are* her flying spirits, each
24 angel having six wings. This is the numbering of the moon.

25 In the midst of the heaven I saw an armed host serving the Lord[23] on cymbals and organs *and* with a ceaseless voice; and I was enchanted as I listened to them.[24]

VII. And the men took me from there and carried me up to the
2 fifth heaven. And I saw there an immense host[1] – the Watchers.[2] Their appearance[1] *was* like men's appearance: in size they were

---

[17] B 'thirty'.   [18] BR 'thirty'.
[19] So R: U is corrupt.
[20] So BNBa: UR 'three hundred and sixty-five'.
[21] So BNBaR: U 'exceed'.
[22] and a second . . . waning = B: U om. The passage is obscure.
[23] So BNBaR: U 'God'.
[24] and I was . . . to them = BNBaR: U om.

[1] So B etc.: U corrupt.   [2] See 1 Enoch i.5, etc.

bigger than great giants, and their faces *were* sad and their mouths
3   silent;[3] and there was no service in the fifth heaven.[4] And I said to
the men who were with me, Why are they *so* very sad, and their
faces downcast, and their mouths silent, and *why* is there no service
4   in this heaven? And the men answered me, These are the
Watchers, who did not join their brothers,[5] two[6] princes and *the*
two hundred *others who* followed after them[7] and went down to
earth and broke their vow on the shoulder of mount Hermon to
defile themselves with human women; and because they defiled
5   themselves the Lord condemned them. And these are bewailing
their brothers and the punishment which was laid upon them.[8]
6   And I said to the Watchers, I have seen your brothers, and I have
heard what they did; and I know[9] their prayers, and I have prayed
7   for them. And behold, the Lord has condemned *them* below the
earth[10] until the heavens and the earth pass away: why then are
you waiting for your brothers, and *why* are you not serving in the
8   Lord's presence? Resume your previous services: offer *your* service
in the Lord's name,[11] in case you anger the Lord your God, *and* he
9   throws you down from this place. They listened to what I said and
10 were persuaded; and they stood in four ranks in the heaven. And
behold,[12] as I stood there, they began to blow together on four
trumpets, and the Watchers began to serve, as if with a single
voice, *and* their voice went up into the Lord's presence.

VIII.   And the men led me up from there and carried me up to the
sixth heaven. And I saw there seven angels in a group, bright and

---

[3] Lit. 'and the silence of their mouths (R adds 'perpetual')'.
[4] in the fifth heaven = BR: U om.
[5] Lit. 'who separated from themselves' (B 'who drove themselves out').
[6] So B: U 'two hundred'.   [7] after them = B: U om.
[8] punishment . . . upon them = B: U corrupt.
[9] So B: U corrupt.
[10] There is some confusion here. That the condemned angels were imprisoned
'below the earth' would seem to be part of a generally accepted tradition (e.g. Jub.
v. 6, 10; 1 Enoch lxxxviii. 3; 2 Pet. ii. 4), yet the angels Enoch is referring to would
seem to be those he has already met and talked with in the second heaven (see
chap. iv above).   [11] BR 'in the Lord's presence'.
[12] They listened . . . in the heaven. And behold = BR: U om.

2 very glorious; and their faces[1] shone like a ray of sunlight. There is
3 no difference *between them* in face or size or style of clothing.[2] These
   arrange *and* teach the right ordering of the world, the movement[3] of
   the stars, of the sun and of the moon, and of the angels, their
   guides, and of the heavenly voices;[4] and *they* bring harmony to all
4 the life of heaven. And they arrange also the regulation and order
   and execution[5] of the singing *and the offering of* all the praise and
   glory, and the angels[6] *who are* over the seasons and the years, and
   the angels *who are* over the rivers and over the seas, *and* the angels
   who are over the fruits and grass and all that grows, and the angels
5 of all the peoples. And these bear rule and record the deeds of all
6 living things in the presence of the Lord.[7] And among them *are*
   seven phoenixes and seven cherubim and seven six-winged
   angels,[8] speaking together and singing together in unison; and it is
7 impossible to describe their songs. And the Lord rejoices in his
   footstool.

IX.   And the men raised me up from there and carried me up to the
2 seventh heaven. And I saw *there* a great light, and all the fiery hosts
   of the incorporeal ones, the archangels, the angels, and the
3 brightness[1] of the ophannim;[2] and I was afraid and trembled. And
   the men took me into their midst, and they said to me, Take
4 courage, Enoch, do not be afraid. They showed me from afar the
   Lord sitting on his throne; and all the heavenly armies, grouped
   according to their rank, came forward and worshipped the Lord,
   and *then* they returned again and went to their places in joy and
5 gladness *and* in measureless light. And *there were* the glorious ones,
   who serve him by night and do not depart by day,[3] standing in the
6 Lord's presence *and* doing his will. And all the hosts of the

---

[1] So B etc.: U corrupt.
[2] So BNR (lit. 'or in the modification of *their* clothing'): U corrupt.
[3] So NBaR: U 'birth'.
[4] BNBa 'angels'.   [5] Lit. 'sweet voices'.
[6] Or '. . . praise and glory; and *these are* the angels . . .'
[7] Lit. 'And these rule and write all life before the face of the Lord'.
[8] So BNBaR: U 'and seven cherubim, six-winged creatures'.

[1] Lit. 'the bright station'.   [2] B 'seraphim'.
[3] So BNBaR: U 'to-day'.

cherubum[4] *were* around his throne, and did not depart *from it*, and the six-winged *angels* who cover his throne, singing in the Lord's

7 presence. And when I had seen all this, the two men departed from

8 me, and I saw them no more. They left me alone at the end of the heaven; and I was afraid *and* fell on my face.

9 And the Lord sent to me one of his glorious ones, Gabriel; and he said to me, Take courage, Enoch, do not be afraid. Get up, and

10 come with me, and stand in the presence of the Lord for ever. And I answered him and said, Alas, *my* lord, I am paralized by fear: call to me the men who brought me to this place; for I have confidence[5]

11 in them, and with them I will enter the Lord's presence. And Gabriel caught me up, just as a leaf is caught up[6] by the wind and

12 he swept me along and set me down in the Lord's presence. And I saw[7] the Lord – his face mighty and most glorious and terrible.

13 Who am I to describe[8] the proportions *of* his being,[9] *and* the Lord's face, mighty and most terrible, and his many-eyed and many-voiced choir,[10] and the Lord's immense throne, made without hands, or the company[11] assembled round it (the hosts of the cherubim and seraphim), or the unchanging *and* ineffable, never-

14 silent and glorious service *that is offered to him*? And I fell down on my face and worshipped the Lord.

15 And with his own mouth the Lord called me, Take courage, Enoch, do not be afraid: get up and stand in my presence for ever. And Michael, the Lord's great archangel,[12] raised me up and led

16 me into the Lord's presence. And the Lord made trial of his servants *and* said to them, Let Enoch come up to stand in my presence for ever. And the Lord's[13] glorious ones bowed down and

17 said, Let him come up. And the Lord said to Michael, Take Enoch and take off his earthly garments, and anoint *him* with good oil, and clothe *him* in glorious garments. And Michael took off from me my

18 garments and anointed me with good oil. And the appearance of

---

[4] BNBa add 'and the seraphim'.   [5] So B etc.: U corrupt.
[6] caught up = N supported by R: UBBa corrupt.
[7] So BR: U corrupt.   [8] U 'Who is to confess . . .'
[9] A probable translation. The MSS are corrupt. R has 'the incomprehensible being of the Lord'.   [10] So R.
[11] BR add 'of the choir'.   [12] So U: BNBaR 'archistratege'.
[13] Lord's = BNBa: U om.

the oil *was* more *resplendent* than a great light, and its richness like
sweet dew, and its fragrance like myrrrh, **shining like a ray of the**
19 **sun**.[14] And I looked at myself, and I was like one of the glorious
ones, and there was no apparent difference.

X. And the Lord called Vreveil,[1] one of his archangels, who was
wise and wrote down everything that the Lord did. And the Lord
2 said to Vreveil, Take the books from their storeplace, and give
3 Enoch a pen and dictate the books to him. And Vreveil made haste
and brought me the books, bright[2] with **smyrnium**,[3] and gave me a
4 pen from his own hand. And he told me all that happens in heaven[4]
and on the earth and in the sea, and the movements and courses[5] of
all the elements, and the changes of the years, and the movements
and mutations of the days, *and* the regulation and order and
execution[6] *of* the singing, and the going in of the clouds and the
going out of the winds, and all the words[7] of the songs[8] of the armed
5 host.[9] And all that it was proper that I should learn Vreveil
explained to me in thirty days and thirty nights: his lips were never
silent, as he went on speaking; and I, for my part, had no rest for
6 thirty days and thirty nights, as I made my notes.[10] And when I
had finished, Vreveil said to me, Sit down: write out everything I
have explained to you. And I sat down a second time for thirty days
7 and thirty nights; and I wrote out everything exactly. And I wrote
three hundred and sixty[11] books.

---

[14] Emended on the basis of U ('its ray, as it were, of the sun') and B ('like a
shining ray of the sun').

[1] Not only do the MSS vary considerably from one another in the spelling of this
name in each of the five instances in which it occurs in this chapter, but they also
differ individually from instance to instance. Thus, in the first instance BBa read
'Vreteil', N 'Vretil', and P 'Pravuil'; and B reads 'Vreteil' in the first instance, but
'Vreveil' in the others.

[2] So Ba: R 'decorated'; UBN are corrupt.
[3] So Vaillant, supposing a Gk. original σμυρνίον rather than σμύρνα ('myrrh').
[4] So BBa (lit. 'all the works of heaven'): U 'all the works of the Lord'.
[5] Lit. 'lives'.   [6] Lit. 'the sweet voice'.
[7] Lit. 'language'.   [8] So B: U 'of the new song'.
[9] Cp. vi. 25 above.   [10] Lit. 'writing all the signs'.
[11] RP 'three hundred and sixty-six'.

XI. And the Lord called me, and he set me on his left hand, nearer
2 than Gabriel; and I worshipped the Lord. And the Lord said to me,
All that you have seen, Enoch, *all* that is[1] and *all* that moves, and
all that has been created by me, I will reveal it to you, †before all
came to be from the first,†[2] all that I have created *and brought* from
non-existence into being, and from what is invisible into what is
3 seen. Not even to my angels have I revealed my secret, nor have I
told them how they themselves were formed, nor do they know how
my infinite and incomprehensible creation was accomplished; yet
4 I am revealing it to you to-day. *For* before what is visible was
brought into being, light appeared;[3] but I, *although* surrounded by
light, *was* like one of the invisible ones, *and* I journeyed[4] as the sun
5 journeys from east to west *and* from west to east. The sun will find[5]
6 rest; but I found no rest, for I was creating everything. Since I had
purposed to establish a foundation to form a visible creation, I
gave command to the depths that one of the invisible things should
7 rise up *and become* visible. *And* Adoil came out, immense in size; and
I looked at him, and behold, he had the great age[6] in his belly, and
I said to him, Open yourself, Adoil, and let what is visible be born
8 from you. And he opened himself, and the great age[6] came out of
him; and thus **was born the light** *from* him who bears the whole
9 creation which I purposed to create. And I saw that *it was* good;
and I set a throne for myself and sat upon it; but to the light I said,
Go up higher, and establish yourself, *and* be the foundation of the
10 things above. And above the light there is nothing else.

11   And I got up from my throne, and I looked[7] and called a second
time to the depths, and I said,[8] Let what is hard and visible come
12 out from the invisible. And Aruchaz came out, hard, heavy, and
13 very black.[9] And I saw that it was right;[10] and I said to him, Go
down below and establish yourself, and be the foundation of the

---

[1] Lit. 'stands'.
[2] I will . . . the first: corrupt. Vaillant translates 'moi je te l'expliquerai d'avant
qu'il ne soit apparu au début'.   [3] Lit. 'opened itself'.
[4] '*was* like . . . journeyed = NBa: U, supported by R, 'alone journeyed among the
invisible things'.   [5] B 'The sun found'; R 'The sun has'.
[6] So UB: NBa 'a very great stone'; R 'a great light'.
[7] So B: NBa 'I saw'; U 'I said'.
[8] So B etc.: U corrupt.   [9] R 'red'.
[10] Or 'that he was suitable'.

things below. And he went down and established himself, and was
14 the foundation of the lower things. And beneath the darkness there
is nothing else.

15   I encircled the ether with light, and I thickened it *and* stretched it
out over the darkness, and from the waters I built up great stones;
and I commanded the mists[11] of the abyss to become dry, and I
16 called[12] what fell back[13] the abyss. When I had gathered the sea
together into one place, I bound it with a yoke, *and* I set an eternal
boundary between the earth and[14] the sea, *so that* it should not be
burst by the waters: I fixed the vault of heaven and founded it
17 above the waters. And for all the heavenly host I formed the sun
from the great light, and I set it in the heaven that it might shine
18 over the earth. From the stones I struck a great fire; and from the
fire I created all the incorporeal host, and all the starry host, and
the cherubim, and the seraphim, and the ophannim (and all this I
19 struck from the fire). And I commanded the earth to make all kinds
of trees to grow, and all mountains,[15] and all life-giving plants, and
every kind of seed that is sown:[16] before I created living souls, I
20 prepared food for them. And I commanded the sea to produce its
fish, and all the reptiles that creep[17] over the earth, and all the birds
21 that fly. And when I had finished everything, I commanded my
wisdom to create man.[18]

22   And now, Enoch,[19] all I have told you, and all you have seen in
the heavens, and all you have seen on earth, and all *you* have
written in the books, *it was* by my wisdom *that* I planned to create it
23 all.[20] I created *it* from the lowest foundation to the highest and to
24 the farthest ends *of both*: I had neither counsellor nor helper. I alone
am eternal, not made by hands: my unchanging purpose is my

---

[11] BBa 'waves'.   [12] So BaR: U corrupt.
[13] what fell back = NBaR: U corrupt.
[14] between . . . and = BNBa: U om.
[15] Vaillant suggests 'all fruit', on the basis of Gen. i. 11.
[16] So BNBa: U 'all live seed which sows seed'.
[17] So BNR: U corrupt.
[18] R has a very much more extended account of the creation in this paragraph,
attributing God's separate works to separate days (as in Gen. i) and ending not only
with a reference to the blessing of the seventh day, but also to the appointment of the
'the eighth day' as 'the first'.   [19] So BNBaR: U om.
[20] to create it all = BNR: U 'it'.

counsellor, and my word is my deed, and my eyes watch over all things: if I turn away my face, all things perish; but if I look at all
25 things, they remain in being. Consider, Enoch, and realize who it is that is speaking to you; and take the books which *you* have written (and I give you Semeil and Rasuil,[21] who brought you up to me), and go down to earth, and tell your sons all I have said to you, *and*
26 all *you* have seen from the lowest heaven right up to my throne. (All the hosts have I created: there is not one *among them* who is opposed to me and is not subject *to me*: all are subject to my authority and
27 serve my might alone.) And give them the books which your hand has written,[22] and they will read *them* and recognize the creator,[23] and they will also understand that there is no other creator but me; and they will pass on the books your hand has written to their children, and *their* children to their children, and next-of-kin to
28 next-of-kin,[17] from one generation to another.[24] For I give you,
29 Enoch, *as* an intercessor,[25] Michael, Prince of my hosts. For what you have written, and what your fathers Adam and Seth[26] have written, will not be destroyed to the end of time; for I have commanded *my* angels Arioch[27] and Marioch,[28] whom I have set on the earth to guard it and to order temporal things, to preserve your fathers' writing, so that it is not destroyed in the flood which is to come, *and* which I shall bring upon the earth in your generation.[29]

30   I know the wickedness of man, that they will not bear the yoke that I have laid upon them,[30] nor do they sow the seed that I have
31 given them. But they have cast off my yoke, and they will take another yoke and will sow worthless seed, and they will worship idols and reject my authority, and the whole earth will sin[31] with
32 injustice and transgressions and adulteries *and* idolatries. Then will I bring a flood upon the earth; and the earth itself will perish in
33 a mighty swamp. And I will leave one righteous man of your stock

---

[21] R 'Raguil'.   [22] So BNBaR: U 'created'.
[23] U 'their creator' – i.e. the creator of the books.
[24] Lit. 'and generation to generation' (or 'and nation to nation').
[25] R 'curator'.
[26] So B etc.: U 'Joseph'.   [27] So UBBa: N Orioch,; RJ 'Ariuch'.
[28] So UBNBa: RJ 'Pariuch'.
[29] Or 'upon your nation'.   [30] Lit. 'raised up for them'.
[31] So UB: BaNR 'will be laden'.

with all his household, who will carry out[32] my wishes; and from their children will arise another[33] generation,[34] the last,[35] many in
34 number, and with great ambitions.[36] Then, in the course[37] of that generation,[34] the books you and your fathers have written will be revealed; for the guardians of the earth will show them to men of faith, and they will be explained to that generation[34] and come to be more highly thought of afterwards than they were before.

35 But now, Enoch, I am giving you a respite[38] of thirty days, so that you can spend it in your house and tell your sons *everything you have heard* from me, and your household, and everyone who keeps *my commands with all* his heart (let them read and understand that
36 there is none but me). And after thirty days I will send the angels for you, and they will take you[39] from the earth and from your
37 sons[40] to me. [41]For a place is prepared for you, and you shall live in my presence for ever and see my secrets; and you shall be my servants' scribe, for you shall write down everything that happens on earth and everything that is done by those who are on earth and in the heavens, and you shall act for me as a witness in the
38 judgement of the great age. All this the Lord said to me just as *if he were* a man speaking to his trusted friend.

XII.[1]

XIII. And now, my children, listen to what your father says and to all the commands I give you to-day: live your lives *as* in the Lord's presence,[1] *and see that* whatever you have to do[1] is in accordance

---

[32] U 'who did'.
[33] U om.
[34] Or 'nation'.
[35] the last = UBR: NBa 'afterwards'.
[36] Lit. 'and very insatiable'.
[37] R 'at the end'.
[38] So BNBaR: U corrupt.
[39] U adds 'to me'.
[40] U adds 'they will take you'.
[41] See note 1 to chap. xiii below.

[1] This chapter (found only in R) describes how Enoch is restored to earth, how he found Methusalam awaiting him, how he instructed him to assemble his household, and how, when they were assembled, he began the farewell address which follows in chap. xiii.

[1] The passage 'For a place (xi. 37) ... the Lord's presence' and the phrase 'you have to do' are found in U only, and Vaillant regards them both as interpolations.

2 with the Lord's will.[1] For I am sent to you by the Lord's command[2] to tell you everything that is and everything that will be to the day
3 of judgement. And now, my children, it is not from my own mouth that I am speaking to you to-day, but from the Lord's mouth, who
4 has sent me to you. For you hear my words from my mouth, *from the mouth of* a man fashioned just like you; but I have heard *the Lord's words* from the Lord's fiery mouth (for the Lord's mouth is a fiery furnace and his words a fiery flame that issues forth). You, my
5 children, see my face, *the face of* a man fashioned just like you; *but* I have seen the Lord's face, like *a piece of* iron heated in the fire that
6 scatters sparks. For you see a man's eyes, *the eyes of a man* fashioned just like you; but I have seen[3] the Lord's eyes, like the rays of the
7 shining sun that dazzles human eyes. You, my children, see my right hand motioning to you,[4] *the* hand of a man made just like you; but I have seen the Lord's right hand motioning to me[5] *and* filling
8 the heaven. You *can* see how large my body is, *that it is* just like yours; but I have seen how great the Lord is, *that he is* immeasur-
9 able, incomparable, and has no end. For you hear the words of my mouth; but I have heard the Lord's words, like[6] great thunder *with*
10 unceasing tumult of the clouds. And now, my children, listen to someone talking about an earthly king *and saying*, It is terrifying and perilous to stand before an earthly king, frightening and very
11 perilous,[7] for the king's will is death and the king's will is life. But to stand before the King of kings[8] – who can endure the infinite fear or
12 the great heat? But the Lord called *one* of his *angels* in charge of Tartarus[9] and set him by me; and the appearance of that angel was *like* snow, and his hands were ice, and he cooled my face (for I
13 could not endure the terror of the fiery heat). And so the Lord spoke all his words to me.

He supposes that the original passed without a break from the words of the Lord to those of Enoch, and that the additions, both in U and in R (i.e. chap. xii) are independent attempts to effect a smooth transition. He further explains 'whatever is in accordance with the Lord's will' as a chapter-heading incorporated into the text.

[2] Lit. 'from the mouth of the Lord'.

[3] U ' spoken'.   [4] Or, as BR, 'helping you'.

[5] Or, as BR, 'helping me'.   [6] U 'as of'.

[7] U om. 'and very perilous'.   [8] of kings = B: U om.

[9] *one* of his *angels* in charge of Tartarus (or 'the horror') = BNBa: UR 'one of his terrible elder angels'.

14   So now, my children, I know all things, some from the mouth of
the Lord, some my eyes have seen, from the beginning to the end
15 and from the end to the renewal. I know everything, and I have
written down *in* the books the extent of the heavens and all that is
in them: I have measured their movements and I know their hosts:
I have completed *the count* of[10] the stars, a great multitude without
16 number. What man can understand their revolutions[11] or their
movements or their returnings, or those that lead them or those
that are led? Not even the angels know their number; but I have
17 written down their names. And I have measured the circle of the
sun, and I have numbered *its* rays[12] and its goings in and its goings
18 out and all its movements: I have written down their names. And I
have measured the circle of the moon, and its movements every
day, the waning[13] of its light every day and hour; and I have
19 written out its names in the books.[14] The dwellings of the clouds
and their mouths and their wings and their rains and their drops
have I explored; and I have written *of* the rumbling of the thunder
20 and the wonder of the lightning. And they showed me their custodians *and* the passages measured out for them to go up *and down*[15]
(they go up bound and descend bound, lest with rude violence they
21 tear down the clouds and destroy everything that is on the earth). I
have written down the treasuries of the snow and the storehouses of
the ice and the cold airs:[16] I have observed how from time to time[17]
their custodians fill the clouds, yet the treasuries are not
22 exhausted. I have written down the resting-places of the winds: I
have looked and seen how their custodians bring their balances
and measures: first they put them on the balance,[18] and then in the
measure; and *they* let them out by measure over the whole earth,
lest with a rude breath they shake the earth.

23   From there I was taken down and came to the place of judgement; and I saw hell open, and I saw there a piece of level ground[19]

---

[10] BR 'I have written down'.
[11] Lit. 'the circuits of their changes'.
[12] So BR: U 'their faces'.
[13] the waning = BR: U corrupt.
[14] Cp. 1 Enoch lxxviii. 2.
[15] Lit. 'their passages where they go up by measure'.
[16] the cold airs: Ba 'cold air'; BN 'the air and cold'.
[17] Lit. 'how at times'.
[18] and measures . . . on the balance = BNBaR: U om.
[19] So B (lit. 'a certain plain'): U corrupt.

24 like a prison, a judgement-*place* without measure. And I descended and wrote *down* all the judgements of whose who were judged, and I saw[20] all their questionings; and I sighed and wept for the perdition of the impious, and I said to myself, Happy *the man* who was never born, or who after birth lived without sin in the Lord's eyes, so as not to come to this place or bear the yoke of this place.

25 And I saw the keepers of the keys of hell standing by the massive gates: their faces[21] were like *the faces of* great asps, their eyes like candles that had gone out, and their teeth were bared *and reached*

26 *down* to their chests. And I said to them openly, **Would that**[22] I had not seen you nor **caught sight**[22] of what you do: may none of my kinsmen *ever* come to you.

27 And from there I went up into the Paradise of the righteous; and I saw there a blessed place, and every creature is blessed, and all live in joy and gladness, and in measureless light, and in eternal

28 life. Then I said, my children (and now[23] I say *it again* to you), Happy *the man* who fears the name of the Lord, who will serve *him as though* in his presence always,[24] and make gifts, offerings of life,[25]

29 and who will live his life and die. Happy *the man* who will do what is just and right,[26] *and* clothe the naked with a garment and give

30 bread to the hungry. Happy *the man* who will champion[26] the orphan and widow, *and* who will help all who have been wronged.

31 Happy *the man* who will refuse[27] the unstable way, and who walks

32 in the paths of righteousness. Happy, too, *the man* who sows righte-

33 ous seed, for he shall reap it sevenfold. Happy *the man* in whom is

34 truth and *who* speaks the truth to his neighbour. Happy *the man* on

35 whose lips is true pity and gentleness. Happy *the man* who shall understand the works of the Lord and glorify him, and[28] through his works come to know him who made them.

36 And behold, my children, **after I had examined the things that**

---

[20] Vaillant emends 'I understood'.
[21] So BNBaR: U corrupt.
[22] So Vaillant. The MSS differ and are clearly all corrupt.
[23] and now = NBa: U om.
[24] Lit. 'who will serve before his face for ever'.
[25] Or 'will make gifts by offerings of life'.
[26] Lit. 'who will make a righteous judgement (to)'.
[27] BNBaR 'turn back from'.
[28] and glorify him, and: so the fragment Mpr: U om.

37 **have been ordained**[29] on earth, I wrote them down. I compared all
the years, and of the year I measured the months, and of the month
38 I counted the days, and of the day I counted the hours. I measured
the hours *and* wrote them out: I distinguished between the different
kinds of men[30] on earth; *and* I measured and proved every measure
39 and every honest balance, as [31]the Lord commanded me. And I
found a difference in these things: one year is more notable than
another year, one day than another day, one hour than another
40 hour.[31] So *also* one man is more notable than another man, one
because of *his* great possessions, another because of his wisdom,
another because of *his* intelligence, *his* skill, and his ability to keep
41 quiet.[32] But there is none greater than the man who fears the Lord;
for those who fear the Lord will be honoured[33] for ever.

42   The Lord created man with his own hands, and in the likeness of
43 his own face: small and great the Lord made *them*. He who reviles
the face of man, reviles the face of the Lord: he who detests the face
of man, detests the face of the Lord: he who despises the face of man
despises the face of the Lord: wrath and great judgement *are*
44 *appointed for those* who spit in the face of man. *But* happy *the man* who
turns his heart[34] towards every man, to help the man on trial,[35] to
raise up the fallen,[36] and to give to the needy; for in the day of[37] the
great judgement all men's deeds will be recalled by the record.[38]
45 Happy *the man* whose measure is honest and *his* weight honest and
his balance honest; for in the day of the great judgement every
measure and every weight and every balance will be on show, as if
in the market, and each *man* will know *the truth about* his measure
46 and receive his reward accordingly. The man who makes[39] an
offering before the Lord, the Lord will make his affairs to prosper:[40]

---

[29] So Vaillant: U 'leaving the countries (or 'limits')'.

[30] Lit. 'I distinguished every seed on earth'. The sequel in verses 40 and 41
below, as Vaillant points out, makes it clear that 'seed' is a metaphor as in
Ecclus. x. 19.

[31] the Lord . . . another hour = Mpr, supported by some MSS: U corrupt.

[32] Lit. 'and the silence of his mouth'.

[33] Or 'glorious'.   [34] his heart = Mpr etc.: U om.

[35] Lit. 'him who is judged'.   [36] Or 'the bruised'.

[37] in the day of = Mpr etc.: U om.   [38] Lit. 'the writing'.

[39] B 'He who hastens'; R 'He who hastens and makes'.

[40] Lit. 'will direct (R, supported by B, 'hasten') his acquisitions'.

47 the man who fills the lamp before the Lord with oil, the Lord will fill his barns with wheat.[41] Does the Lord need bread or candles or sheep or cattle? *Not at all*; but in this way the Lord tests the heart of

48 man. For then the Lord will send his great light, and in that[42] will the judgement be; and who, if there, can be hidden?

49 Now, my children, bear all this in mind, and pay attention to what your father is saying – to everything I am telling you as the

50 Lord instructed me.[43] Take these books, the books written by your father's hand, and read them, and learn from them the Lord's

51 works, that there is none but the Lord alone, who has set the foundations on the unknown, stretched out the heavens above the invisible, set the earth on the waters *and* founded it on the unstable, who alone made the countless *things in his* creation (*for* who has counted the dust of the earth or the sand of the sea, or the drops of

52 the clouds?), who has bound together the earth and the sea with indissoluble bonds, who has struck out from the fire the incomprehensible beauty of the stars[44] and has adorned the heaven, who has created all things so that what was invisible became visible,[45]

53 being himself invisible. And pass these books on to your children, and *see that your* children *pass them on* to their children, and *to* all your kin and all your generations,[46] to[47] those who have wisdom and fear the Lord; *and*[47] they will receive them and take more delight in them than in any choice food, and they will read *them* and hold

54 fast[48] to them. But the foolish and those who do not know the Lord will not receive *them*, but will repudiate *them*; for their yoke will

55 weigh them down. Happy *the man* who will bear their yoke *and* hold fast to it, for he will find *his recompense*[49] in the day of the great judgement.

56 For I swear to you, my children, that before man existed, a place of judgement was prepared for him; and a measure and a weight,

---

[41] Lit. 'the man who increases the lamp before the Lord, the Lord will increase his barns'.   [42] So BR Mpr: U 'in the darkness'.

[43] Lit. 'I am telling you from the Lord's mouth'.

[44] of the stars = B, supported by R: U om.

[45] Lit. '. . . all things from the invisible into the visible (so B; R 'into appearance'; U corrupt).   [46] Or 'nations'.

[47] So Vaillant: U reads '. . . generations: those who have wisdom . . . Lord will receive . . .'   [48] hold fast = BR: U corrupt.

[49] The probable sense: U reads 'he will find it'.

by which man will be tested, has been prepared there beforehand.

57 And I shall set down every man's deeds in writing, and no one will
58 be able to escape. So then, my children, live out your span of life in
patience and gentleness, so that you may inherit the eternal age
59 that is to come. And every blow and every wound and *scorching* heat
and every evil word, if it comes upon you[50] for the Lord's sake,
endure it; and though you may be able to retaliate, do not retaliate
upon your neighbour, for retaliation is the Lord's, and he will be
60 your avenger in the day of the great judgement. Suffer the loss of
your gold and silver for your brother's sake, so that you may
61 receive **heavenly**[51] treasure in the day of judgement. And stretch
out your hands to the orphan and the widow, and help the poor to
the utmost of your power; and they will be a protection[52] *in* the time
62 of trial. Every hard and heavy yoke,[53] if it comes upon you for the
Lord's sake, endure it,[54] and thus you will find your reward in the
63 day of judgement. In the morning and at noon and in the evening
of the day[55] it is good to go into the house of the Lord to glorify the
creator of all things.

64   Happy *the man* who opens his heart to praises, and who praises
the Lord: a curse *upon him who* opens his heart *to* reviling and to
slandering his neighbour.

65   Happy *the man* who opens his mouth to bless and glorify the
Lord: a curse on him who opens his mouth to curse and blaspheme
in the Lord's presence.

66   Happy *the man* who honours all the Lord's works: a curse upon
him who reviles the Lord's creation.

67   Happy *the man* who regards[56] the labours of his own hands to
establish them:[57] a curse upon him who looks *for an occasion* to
destroy the labours of others.

68   Happy *the man* who maintains the foundations of the fathers of

---

[50] upon you = BNBa: U om.
[51] **heavenly**: corrupt in all MSS: U 'which is of the flesh'; R 'which is full'; NBa Mpr 'not scanty'.
[52] B 'and you will find protection'.
[53] So BR Mpr: U corrupt.
[54] So B: U 'loosen it'; R 'endure all and loosen them'.
[55] of the day = BNBaR: U 'and to-day'.
[56] So BNBaR: U 'compares'.
[57] Lit. 'to raise them up'.

old:[58] a curse upon *him who* destroys his fathers' laws and boundaries.

59 Happy *the man* who sows peace: a curse upon him who destroys those who are at peace.

70 Happy *the man* who speaks peace, [59]and peace is with him: a curse upon him who does not speak peace[59] and there is no peace in his heart.

71 All this will be revealed in the measure *and* in the books in the day of the great judgement.[60]

72 So, my children, keep your hearts from all wickedness: †accord-
73 ing to the balance of light, be heirs†[61] for ever. You must not say, my children, *our* father is with the Lord and in answer to his
74 prayers we shall be forgiven our sin.[62] You see that I record all the deeds of every man; and no one *can* destroy what my hand has
75 written, for the Lord sees everything. So now, my children, listen to all your father's words, all that I am saying to you, so that they may
76 be an inheritance of peace for you. And the books that I have given you, do not hide them:[63] explain them to all who desire *to look into*
77 *them*, for they[64] may, perhaps, recognize the works of the Lord. For behold, my children, the day of the time appointed is drawing near, and the time appointed leaves me no choice: the angels who *are to* go with me are standing before me; and tomorrow I shall go
78 up to the highest heaven, to my eternal inheritance. This is why I command you, my children, to do the Lord's will in all things.

XIV. Mathusalom answered his father Enoch, What kind of food, father, would you like us to get ready for you, so that you can bless our dwellings, and your sons, and all your household, and glorify

---

[58] of old = BR Mpr: U corrupt.

[59] and peace . . . not speak peace = B, supported by NBaR: U om.

[60] So B etc.: U 'the judgement of the proud one'.

[61] The MSS are in confusion here. Vaillant translates 'in the balance inherit the light'. The idea seems to be that after Enoch's sons (or their hearts) had been weighed in the balance and approved they should inherit eternal light (cp. the illustrations in the Egyptian Papyrus of Ani of the weighing of Ani's heart in a balance and his subsequent introduction into the presence of Osiris).

[62] Lit. 'and he will pray us out of our sin'.

[63] So NBaR: U 'do not cast them aside'.

[64] So NBa: U 'you'.

2 your people, before you go away? And Enoch answered his son and
said, Listen, my child: from the day when the Lord anointed me
with the oil of his glory, I have had no food at all:[1] food is of no
3 consequence[2] to me; and I have no desire for any earthly food. But
call your brothers and all our[3] household and the elders of the
4 people, that I may speak to them and then depart. And
Methusalom made haste and called his brothers Regim and Ariim
and Achazuchan and Charimion[4] and all the elders of the people,
and he brought them to his father Enoch, and they bowed down to
5 **him.**[5] And Enoch received *them* and blessed them; and he answered
them and said,

XV. Listen, my children. In the days of your[1] father Adam, the
Lord came down to earth to visit it and all his creatures[2] that he
2 himself had made. *And* the Lord summoned all the cattle on the
earth and all the reptiles on the earth and all the birds with wings,
and he brought them to your[3] father Adam, so that he might give
3 names to everything on earth. And the Lord left them with him;
and he subjected everything to him as *his* inferior, and moreover
made it dumb;[6] that it should be submissive[7] and obedient to
4 man. For the Lord created man *and set him* over[8] all his possessions: there will therefore be no judgement for all living souls, but
5 for man only. There is one place in the great age for all the souls of
the cattle, and one fold and one pasture; for the soul of an animal
which the Lord has made will not perish[9] until the judgement, but

[1] anointed me . . . at all = BNBaR: U 'anointed my head with oil, and I was afraid'. [2] Lit. 'is not sweet'.
[3] So UN: BBaR 'your'. [4] R adds 'and Gaidad'.
[5] U 'to Enoch': R 'before his face'.

[1] So UBaR: BN Mpr 'our'. [2] Lit. 'his creation'. [3] BNBaR Mpr 'our'.
[4] R 'And the Lord set him as king over all things'.
[5] Lit. 'secondly'. [6] U 'deaf': R 'dumb and deaf'.
[7] that it should be submissive = B etc.: U corrupt.
[8] Mpr 'For he created man lord over . . .'.
[9] Lit. 'will not be shut off' in the sense of 'abandoned to death' (for the metaphor see Ps. lxxviii. 50 in the LXX – καὶ τὰ κτήνη αὐτῶν εἰς θάνατον συνέκλεισεν).

6 all souls *will* accuse man.[10] The man who feeds the soul of a beast[11] badly, transgresses against his own soul; but the man who offers a sacrifice of an animal without blemish – it is healing (he heals his

7 own soul).[12] And the man who offers a sacrifice of birds without

8 blemish – it is healing (he heals his own soul). And all you have for food, bind it by the four legs – it is healing (he heals his own soul).[12]

9 The man who kills any beast without binding it – it is an evil

10 custom[13] (he transgresses against his own soul). The man who does injury to a beast secretly – it is an evil custom[13] (he transgres-

11 ses against his own soul). The man who does injury to another man's soul injures his own soul; and there is no healing for him for

12 ever.[14] The man who commits murder kills his own soul; and there

13 is no healing for him for ever.[14] The man who pushes another man into a trap will be caught in it himself, *and* there is no healing for him for ever; and the man who drags another man into court,[15] his own judgement will not cease for ever.

14 Now, therefore, my children, keep your hearts from all unrighteousness which the Lord hates, and above all from every

15 living soul which the Lord made. Just as a man asks for his own soul from the Lord, so shall he do to every living soul; for in the great age there are many dwelling-places[16] prepared for man, *some*

16 very good houses, *and others*, evil houses without number. Happy *the man* who goes into the blessed houses, for in the evil ones there is

17 no *possibility of* conversion.[17] And if a man resolves in his heart to offer a gift to the Lord, and his hands do not do it, then the Lord will bring the labour of his hands to nothing, so that there is no

18 profit *from it*. If his hands do it, and his heart dissents,[18] even

---

[10] man = Mpr etc.: U corrupt.

[11] the soul of a beast = BNBa: U 'his own'.

[12] And the man who offers . . . his own soul = B supported by R: U om.

[13] Lit. 'law'.

[14] The man who commits . . . for ever = B Mpr: U om.

[15] Lit. 'pushes another man into judgement'.

[16] The normal word for 'barn' or 'refuge'. Vaillant translates 'retraites' and Morfill 'mansions' (though this is not the word used in the Slavonic at John xiv. 2).

[17] Or 'getting out of them'. The primary meaning of the word is 'asylum', but the secondary meaning 'conversion' is supported by BBaR 'return', 'turning back'.

[18] Lit. 'murmurs'.

though the doubt in his heart persists,[19] it will do him no harm.[2]

19 Happy the man who in his patience offers a gift to the Lord, for he
20 will find *his* recompense. And when a man promises that at a set
time he will offer a gift to the Lord, and does it, then he will find *his*
recompense; but if the time he has set goes by, *yet* he fulfils his
promise *afterwards*, it is *indeed* repentance, *though* he will not be
21 blessed,[21] for every delay is a cause of offence. And if a man clothes
the naked *and* gives bread to the hungry, he will find *his* recompense; but if his heart dissents,[18] he will be a loser and gain
22 nothing. **And when the poor man is satisfied, if his**[22] **heart is
arrogant,**[23] then he will lose all his well-doing and get no gain; for
the Lord detests an arrogant man.

XVI. And it came to pass, when Enoch had spoken to his sons and
to the princes of the people, all his people and all his neighbours
heard the Lord calling Enoch. And they agreed together, saying
2 Let us go and greet Enoch. And about two thousand[1] men assembled, and they came to the place Azuchan, where Enoch was and
3 his sons and the elders of the people. And they greeted Enoch,
saying, You, whom the Lord, the eternal king, has blessed, bless
now your people, and glorify *us* in the Lord's eyes, for the Lord has
chosen you [2]and appointed you to take away[2] our sins.

XVII. Enoch answered his people, saying, Listen, my children.
Before all things were, before all creation came into being, the Lord
appointed the age of creation: after that he created all his creation,
both what is visible and *what is* invisible; and after all that he made
man in his own image, and he set in him eyes to see and ears to hear

---

[19] Lit. 'and the pain of his heart does not cease'.
[20] Reading with B ('the murmuring profits nothing'): the other MSS diverge.
[21] So U: the other MSS differ. Vaillant proposes '. . . his promise, his repentance
will not be acceptable'.
[22] i.e. the heart of the giver.
[23] So Vaillant. U, supported by NBaR, reads 'And the poor man, when his heart
is satisfied, and he (i.e. the poor man) is arrogant'.

[1] So UR: BNBa 'four thousand'.
[2] and appointed . . . away (lit. 'to set you up as him who takes away') = B:
U corrupt.

2 and a heart to think and a mind to consider. Then the Lord arranged[1] the age for man's benefit, and he divided it into seasons[2] and into hours, that man might consider the changes[3] and ends of the seasons, the beginnings of the years and the ends of the months and the days and the hours, and that he might reckon the length of

3 his own life.[4] When the whole creation which the Lord has made comes to an end, and every man goes to the Lord's great judgement, then the seasons will perish, and there will be no years any more, nor will the months nor the days and hours be reckoned any

4 more, but there will be a single age. And all the righteous who escape the Lord's great judgement will be united with the great age, and the age[5] will be united with the righteous, and they shall

5 live eternally.[6] And they shall have no more labour nor suffering nor sorrow nor fear of persecution,[7] nor labour nor night nor darkness;[8] but they shall have *about them* a great light for ever and an indestructible wall, and *in* the great Paradise shall they have the

6 shelter of an eternal dwelling-place. Happy the righteous who escape the Lord's great judgement, for their faces will shine as brightly as the sun.

7 So now, my children, keep your souls from all unrighteousness; from all that the Lord hates. Live your lives as in the Lord's presence, and serve him alone, and bring him every offering *he has*

8 *ordained.* If you look up to heaven,[9] the Lord is there, for the Lord created the heavens:[10] if you look at the earth and the sea, and you consider[10] the things under the earth, the Lord is there also, for the

9 Lord created all things. Nothing you do can be hidden from the

10 Lord's eyes. *Let it be* in patience, in gentleness, and in the affliction of[11] your sorrows, *that you* leave this world of suffering.

---

[1] Lit. 'delivered'.
[2] into seasons = U: BNBa 'into years and into months'.
[3] So NR: U 'seasons'.
[4] U 'that he might give his life and death'.
[5] U om. 'and the age'.
[6] Lit. 'and they shall be eternally' (or 'and they shall be belonging to the age').
[7] Lit. 'nor expectation of violence'.
[8] nor labour . . . darkness: U 'and no labour neither of night nor of darkness'.
[9] So BR: U 'If he looks upward'.
[10] So BR: U 'if he looks . . . and he considers'.
[11] of: U 'and in' (but the case endings show that this is corrupt).

XVIII.   While Enoch was speaking to his people,[1] the Lord sent a blackness on the earth, and it was dark, and the darkness covered the men who were standing with Enoch. And the angels made haste, and the angels took up Enoch and led him up to the highest heaven; and the Lord received him, and he set him before him for ever. And the darkness departed from the earth and it was light, and the people saw and understood[2] how Enoch had been taken; and they glorified God and went to their own homes.[3]

XIX.[1]

XX.   And Methusalom made haste,[1] and his brothers, Enoch's sons, and they built an altar at the place Azuchan[2] where Enoch had been taken, and they took sheep and cattle and sacrificed before the Lord. And they called together all the people[3] who had come with them to the feast; and the people brought gifts to Enoch's sons, and they made merry and rejoiced for three days.[4]

XXI.   And on the third day, at sunset, the elders of the people spoke to Methusalom, saying, Go and stand before the Lord and before your people, [1]and before the altar of the Lord, and you will be glorified by[2] your people. And Methusalom answered his people,[1] The Lord, the God of my[3] father Enoch, he himself will raise up a priest over his people. And the people waited there the whole of that night in the place Azuchan;[4] and Methusalom stayed

---

[1]   At this point U inserts a title, 'Of the taking up of Enoch'.
[2]   So U: B etc. 'did not understand'.
[3]   NBa end with this chapter.

[1]   Chapter xix, which gives a summary of Enoch's activities, is found only in R and P.

[1]   So BR: U corrupt.
[2]   So U: BR 'Achuzan'.
[3]   called . . . people = BR: U corrupt.
[4]   Here, with a brief concluding formula, P ends.

[1-1]   and . . . people = BR: U om. (and in consequence, Methusalom's statement, which follows, is attributed to the elders).
[2]   Lit. 'in'.   [3]   So BR: U 'your'.
[4]   So UB: R 'Achuzan'.

by the altar and prayed to the Lord and said, Eternal Lord, the only God,[5] who hast chosen our[6] father Enoch, do thou, Lord, appoint[7] a priest for thy people, and give *their* hearts understanding
4 to fear thy glory and to do all things according to thy will. And Methusalom fell asleep, and the Lord appeared to him in a vision by night and said to him, Listen, Methusalom, I am the Lord, the God of your father Enoch: pay attention to what your people are saying, and stand before them and before my altar, and I will
5 glorify you before these my people all the days of your life. And Methusalom rose up from his sleep and blessed him[8] who had
6 appeared to him. And the elders of the people came to Methusalom in the morning; and the Lord God turned Methusalom's heart so that he listened to what the people said, and he said to them, The Lord our[9] God, let him do what he pleases to these his people.

7 And Sarsan and Charmis and Zazas[10] and the elders of the people made haste and arrayed Methusalom in a gorgeous robe and put a splendid crown on his head; and the people made haste and brought sheep and cattle and the kinds of birds that were appointed, so that Methusalom could sacrifice before[11] the Lord
8 and before[11] the people. And Methusalom went up to the altar of the Lord, like the morning-star when it rises, and all the people
9 followed after *him*. And Methusalom stood at the altar, and all the people *were* round about the altar. And the elders of the people took the sheep and the cattle and bound them by the four feet, and they laid them at the head of the altar; and the people said to Methusalom, Take your knife and slaughter these appointed
10 *victims* before the Lord. And Methusalom stretched out his hands to heaven and invoked the Lord, saying, Ah me, Lord! Who am I to stand at the head of thine altar *and* at the head of all thy people?
11 [12]And now, Lord, Lord, look upon thy servant, and on the head of all thy people,[12] and on all these who have been chosen, and give grace to thy servant before these people, that they may understand

---

[5] Lit. 'Lord of all the age, who art alone'.
[6] BR 'my'.   [7] So U (lit. 'show forth'): BR 'raise up'.
[8] So U: BR 'the Lord'.   [9] B 'your'.
[10] So UR: B 'And Sarsai and Charlis' (om. Zazas).
[11] R 'in the name of'.
[12-12] And now . . . people = B, supported by R: U om.

12 that thou hast ordained[13] a priest for thy people. And it came to pass, while Methusalom was praying, the altar trembled, and the knife rose up from the altar, and the knife leapt into Methusalom's

13 hands before all the people. And all the people trembled and glorified the Lord; and Methusalom was honoured before the Lord

14 and before all the people from that day onwards. And Methusalom

15 took[14] and slaughtered all that had come from the people.[15] And the people rejoiced and made merry before the Lord and before Methusalom on that day; and after that they went to their own homes.

XXII. But Methusalom stood at the head of the altar and at the

2 head of all the people from that day. In *the year* **1480** he explored[1] the whole earth and sought out all those who had believed in the Lord, and those who had fallen away:[2] he corrected and converted them; and no man was found, who had fallen away[2] from the

3 Lord's ways,[3] all the days that Methusalom lived. And the Lord blessed Methusalom in his sacrifices *and* his offerings and in all his ministry before the Lord.

4 And when Methusalom's days were near their end,[4] the Lord appeared to him in a vision by night and said to him, Listen, Methusalom, I am[5] the God of your father Enoch. I would have you know that the days of your life are at an end and the day of your

5 rest is approaching. Call Nir, your son Lamech's second son, and array him in your own holy robes and set him at my altar, and tell

6 him everything that will happen in his days. For the time is coming for the destruction of the whole earth and of every man and of

7 everything that moves on the earth. For in his days there will be great disorder on the earth, for man has become envious of man; and people will oppress[6] people, and nation will make war upon

---

[13] So BR: U 'that thou art: ordain'.   [14] R adds 'the knife'.

[15] BR 'all that had been brought by the people'.

[1] B 'In 482 he explored': U 'In 492 he inherited'; R recasts the passage, 'From that day for ten years, hoping for the eternal inheritance, he sought out . . .'. Vaillant's emendation is based on the number of years from the Creation according to the figures in the Septuagint.   [2] Lit. 'changed'.

[3] Lit. 'face'.   [4] Lit. 'And after the ending of the days of Methusalom'.

[5] BR add 'the Lord'.

[6] B 'threaten'; R 'behave themselves proudly against'.

nation: the whole earth will be filled with blood and with evil
8 disorder. Moreover, they will fall away from their Creator *and*
worship **what is fixed in heaven and what moves on earth**[7] and the
waves of the sea; and the adversary will magnify himself and
9 rejoice in what they do to my sorrow. The whole earth will change
its order, and all the fruits and all the grass will[8] change their
seasons,[9] for they will be waiting for the time of destruction; and all
10 nations on the earth will fall away,[10] and all I have desired.[11] And
then will I command the abyss *and* it will pour itself out on the
earth, and the treasuries of the waters of heaven will pour
themselves out on the earth, and all will be without form as it was
in the beginning;[12] and the whole structure of the earth will perish,
and the whole earth will tremble and lose its stability[13] from that
11 day onward. Then will I preserve Noe, your son Lamech's eldest
son; and I will raise up from his descendants another world, and
his descendants shall endure for ever.

12 And when he got up from his sleep, Methusalom was much
13 distressed about the dream. He called all the elders of the people,
and he told them everything the Lord had said to him and the
14 vision the Lord had revealed to him. And the people *too* were
distressed about his vision, and they answered him, The Lord has
power to do what he wills; so you must now do everything the Lord
15 has told you. Methusalom called Nir, Lamech's second son, and
arrayed him in the priestly robes before all the people, and he set
him at the head of the altar and taught him all that he had to do[14]
16 among the people. And Methusalom said to the people, Behold
Nir! Behold, he shall be your leader[15] from today *and* the guide of
17 the princes. And the people answered Methusalom, May the word
18 of the Lord be fulfilled on us as he promised you.[16] And while
Methusalom was speaking to the people, his spirit was troubled,

---

[7] All MSS corrupt. U 'the movement over the earth': BR 'the fixing in the heaven
and the movement of the earth'.

[8] will: U om.   [9] R 'seeds'.

[10] Lit. 'will change'.   [11] B 'to my sorrow'.

[12] Lit. '. . . on the earth, in matter as great as primitive matter'. The reference is to
the primaeval 'matter' out of which the world was made.

[13] So R: BU 'its strong one'.   [14] U 'all that he did'.

[15] Lit. 'he shall be before you'.

[16] So U: B and R have slightly longer variants.

and he fell on his knees and stretched out his hands to heaven and prayed to the Lord; and as he prayed, his spirit left him.

19 And Nir made haste, and all the people, and built a tomb for Methusalom; and they put there incense and sweet-cane and many
20 things to consecrate it.[17] And Nir and the people went, and they took up Methusalom's body and laid it in the tomb that they had
21 built for him and covered *it*.[18] And the people said, Blessed was
22 Methusalom before the Lord and before all the people. And afterwards[19] they assembled together, and Nir said to the people, Make haste today, and bring the sheep and the bullock and the turtledove and the pigeon, so that we may sacrifice before the Lord, and
23 he shall rejoice today;[20] and then go to your own homes. And the people listened to Nir the priest: they made haste and brought *the victims* and bound them at the head of the altar; and Nir took the
24 sacrificial knife and sacrificed before the Lord. And the people made haste and did what they had been told, and they made merry before the Lord the whole day: they glorified the Lord God, the
25 saviour[21] of Nir, before the people. From that day there was peace and order throughout the whole earth in Nir's days, for two hundred and two years.[22]
26 And after that the people fell away[23] from the Lord and began to be envious of one another; and people stood up against people and nation rose up against nation in strife, and there was great tumult.
27 And Nir the priest heard *about it*, and he was much distressed and said to himself, The time has come and the words *are fulfilled* that the Lord spoke to my grandfather Methusalom.

XXIII. And behold,[1] Sofonima, Nir's wife, was barren and had
2 borne Nir no child. And Sofonima was well on in years and very near her death; and she conceived, although Nir the priest had not

---

[17] So U: B 'many lights'; R has a longer conflate reading.

[18] So BR: U 'and set *it* down'.

[19] Lit. 'And from there'.   [20] B 'and rejoice today'.

[21] the saviour = U: B 'of heaven and'; R 'of heaven and earth and'.

[22] Vaillant suggests emending 202 to 2200 ($\sigma\beta'$ to $\beta\sigma'$), which would be the date of the generation preceding the flood.

[23] Lit. 'the people changed'.

[1] So BR Rum.: U om.

had intercourse with her since the day the Lord set *him* before the
3 people. ² Sofonima³ was ashamed and hid herself day after day, and
no one of the people knew; and the day came when she should give
4 birth. And Nir remembered his wife and called her to him in his
house to talk to her; and Sofonima went to her husband, and
5 behold, she was about to give birth.⁴ And when Nir saw her he was
very ashamed because of her, and he said to her, Why have you
done this, wife, and brought shame upon me before all the people?
6 And now, away from me: go where you have so shamefully conceived,⁵ in case I sully my hands on you and sin before the Lord.
7 And Sofonima answered her husband, saying, Behold, my lord, I
am well on in years⁶ and no youthful desires are left in me: I do not
8 know how in my innocence I have conceived. Nir did not believe
her, and he said to her a second time, Away from me, in case I
9 strike you and sin before the Lord. And it came to pass, while Nir
was speaking to his wife, that Sofonima fell down at Nir's feet and
died.

10 And Nir was greatly distressed and said to himself, Is it because
of what I said⁷ that this has happened to her? But now the eternal
11 Lord *is* merciful, for I lifted no hand against her.⁸ And Nir made
haste and shut⁹ the doors of his house and went to his brother Noe
12 and told him everything that had happened to his wife. And Noe
made haste and went to his brother's house; and his brother's wife
13 was clearly dead, and she was about to give birth.¹⁰ And Noe said
to Nir, Do not be distressed, Nir, my brother, for the Lord has
concealed our shame today, since no one of the people knows *about
this*; and now make haste,¹¹ let us bury her, and the Lord will

---

² Here J ends.
³ R 'When Sofonima realized that she had conceived, she'.
⁴ Lit. 'she had in her womb at the time of birth'.
⁵ Lit. 'you have conceived the shame of your womb'.
⁶ BR Rum. add 'and the day of my death (+ has come R)'.
⁷ Lit. 'Is it from my word (= B Rum.: R 'voice'; U 'Lord')'.
⁸ U adds here 'And the archangel Gabriel appeared to Nir and said to him, Do
not think your wife Sofonima died as a result of sin. This child that is born of her is
righteous fruit; and I will take him up to Paradise, so that you be not a father to a gift
of God'.   ⁹ So BR Rum.: U 'opened'.
¹⁰ Lit. 'and the aspect of his brother's wife *was* in death, and her womb at the time
of birth'.   ¹¹ BR Rum. 'let us make haste'.

14 conceal our disgrace.[12] And they laid Sofonima on a bed, and
    clothed her in black garments, and shut the door, *and went* and
    hollowed out tombs[13] secretly.
15   And when they had gone out to her **tomb,**[14] the child came out of
16 the corpse of Sofonima and sat on the bed. And Noe and Nir came
    in to bury Sofonima, and they saw the child sitting by the corpse,
17 and he had a garment on him.[15] And Noe and Nir were very
    frightened, for the child's body was perfect: he spoke with his
    mouth and blessed the Lord. Noe and Nir stared at him, saying,
18 This is the Lord's doing, my brother. And behold, the seal of the
19 priesthood *was* on his breast, and *he was* a joy to look at. And
    Noe said to Nir, Brother, behold, the Lord will restore the holy
20 tabernacle after us. And Nir and Noe made haste and washed the
    child and arrayed *him* in the priestly garments, and *they* gave him
    bread that had been blessed and he ate *it*; and they called him
21 Melchisedek. And Noe and Nir took Sofonima's body and took the
    black garments off her; and they washed her body and clothed her
    in splendid and exquisite garments. And they built her a tomb;[16]
    and Noe went, and Nir and Melchisedek, and they buried her with
22 honour openly. And Noe said to his brother, Keep the child
    secretly until the time *appointed*, for the people's wickedness has
    increased everywhere on earth, and if they see him, they will find
23 some way of killing him. And Noe returned home.
24   And behold, all *kinds of* iniquities increased greatly[17] everywhere
    on earth in Nir's days; and Nir was greatly distressed, the more so
25 for the child, saying, What can I do for him? Nir stretched out his
    hands towards heaven and invoked the Lord, saying, Alas, eternal
    Lord, all *kinds of* iniquities have increased greatly on earth in my
26 days, and I sense that our end is near. And now, Lord, what is the
    future of this child, and what his fate? What can I do for him, so
27 that he is not involved with us in this destruction? The Lord heard
    Nir *and* appeared to him in a vision at night and said to him,

---

12 R 'the disgrace of our shame'.
13 So U – no doubt assuming a separate tomb for the child: BR Rum. 'tomb'.
14 So Vaillant: U 'to her bed'; B Rum. 'to Nir's house'; R om.
15 So U Tr.: R Rum., supported by B, 'and wiping his garments'.
16 B Rum., suported by R, 'another house'.
17 increased greatly = B Rum., supported by R: U om.

Behold, Nir, the corruption on the earth is universal:[18] no longer
28 will I tolerate *it* or endure *it*. Behold, I intend very soon to bring a
great destruction on the earth; but have no worries about the child,
Nir, for after a little while I will send my archangel Gabriel,[19] and
29 he will take the child and put him in the Paradise of Eden. He will
not perish with those who are about to perish, for I have sent *him* as
a sign;[20] for he shall be to me a priest of priests for ever —
Melchisedek, and I will set him apart,[21] and I will make of him[22] a
great people who will honour me.

30   And Nir got up from his sleep and blessed the Lord who had
appeared to him, saying, Blessed *art thou*, Lord God of our[23]
fathers, who hast not let reproach fall on my priesthood or[24] the
priesthood of my fathers, for thy word has created a high priest in
31 the womb of my wife Sofonima. For I had no children, and this
child shall be[25] in place of my *own* children and become[26] my son;
and thou shalt count him with thy servants[27] [28]with Sonfi and
Onoch and Rusi and Milam and Seruch and Arusan, Nail and
Enoch and Methusalom and thy servant Nir;[28] and Melchisedech
32 shall be chief priest in another generation. For I know[29] that this
generation will end in turmoil and all will perish, and Noe my
brother will be preserved to another generation[30] to be its father;[31]
and from his family will spring a numerous people, and
Melchisedek will be chief priest among a people that is subject to
thee, O Lord, and serveth thee.

33   And it came to pass, when the child had been in Nir's house for
forty days, the Lord said to the archangel Gabriel,[32] Go down to
earth, to Nir the priest, and take the child Melchisedek that is with

[18] Lit. 'a great iniquity has already been on the earth'.
[19] Tr.R 'my archistratege Michael'.
[20] Lit. 'and I have shown *him* forth'.
[21] Lit. 'and I will sanctify him'.
[22] So U (lit. 'and I will change him into'): BR Tr. Rum. 'and I will set him up as'.
[23] So U: BR Rum. 'my'.   [24] Lit. 'in'.
[25] So B Rum.: UR 'and may this child be'.   [26] BR add 'as it were'.
[27] BR Rum. add 'and with thy priests'.
[28–28] So U: BR Rum. differ not a little.   [29] So BR: U corrupt.
[30] So UR: B Rum. 'in that day': R continues 'and the procreation will be from his
tribe, and there will be another people, and there will be another Melchisedek, chief
of the priests . . .'.
[31] Lit. 'for the procreation'.
[32] So U: BR Rum. 'to Michael'.

34 him[33] and put *him* in the garden of Eden to keep him safe. For the
time is now very near when I shall let loose all the waters over the
earth, and all that is on the earth shall perish; and I will give *him* a
place of honour in another generation, and Melchisedek shall be

35 chief priest in that generation. And Gabriel[34] made haste and flew
down by night; and that night Nir was asleep on his bed and
Gabriel[34] appeared to him *and* said to him, Thus says the Lord to

36 Nir, Let the child I entrusted to you come to me. And Nir did not
recognize who it was that was speaking to him, and he was much
troubled and said to himself, Can it be that the people know about
the child, and want to take him away and kill him? (For the
people's thoughts and inclinations were evil in the Lord's sight.)

37 And he answered Gabriel[34] and said, I have no child, neither do I

38 know who it is that is speaking to me. And Gabriel[35] answered him,
Have no fear, Nir, I am the archangel Gabriel:[36] The Lord has sent
me; and behold, I will take your child today and I will go with him

39 and put him in the Paradise of Eden. And Nir remembered his first
dream, and he believed and answered Gabriel,[34] Blessed be the
Lord who has sent you to me today; and now bless your servant
Nir, and take the child and do with him everything you have been

40 told to do. And Gabriel[34] took the child Melchisedek on his wings

41 that night and put him in the Paradise of Eden. And when Nir got
up in the morning and went into the house, he did not find the
child; and this was for Nir a cause both of great joy and of sorrow,[37]
for he had come to look upon the child as a son.[38]

---

[33] with him = BR Rum.: U om.   [34] So U: BR Rum. 'Michael'.
[35] So U: B Rum. 'Michael'; R 'he that spoke to me'.
[36] So U: BR Rum. 'I am the archistratege of the Lord'.
[37] So U: BR Rum. 'And Nir had great sorrow in place of joy'.
[38] U adds a doxology, 'Glory be to our God always, now and for ever, and to the
ages of ages. Amen'.
In B our apocryphon forms part of a series of Biblical stories and is followed
immediately by an account of the Flood.
R ends '. . . in place of joy, for he had no other son but him. So Nir died; and
afterwards there was no priest among the people. And from that time arose much
tumult on the earth'. Then follows a very much condensed account of the Flood and
Noah's subsequent history.
Rum. ends with the opening sentence of a Flood account, '. . . in place of joy, for he
had come to look upon the child as a son. But in that time all great tumult arose on
the earth. The Lord called Noe to the mountain Asir and told him to make an ark
speedily'.

THE APOCALYPSE OF ABRAHAM

Both the pseudo-Athanasian Synopsis and the Stichometry of Nicephorus include 'Abraham' in their lists of apocryphal books; but whether they are referring to our Apocalypse, or to our Testament, or to some other work bearing Abraham's name, it is impossible to say. Priscillian is similarly vague when he asks whether anyone has ever 'read a book of Abraham among the prophets of the established canon'.[1] Even more uncertain is the identity of the book (or books) 'of the Three Patriarchs' mentioned at the very end of the apocryphal list in the well known passage in *The Apostolic Constitutions* (VI. xvi. 3) – is one book being referred to here or are three? Are the 'three patriarchs' referred to Abraham, Isaac, and Jacob (as we should naturally expect)? Or is the fact that they occur at the very end of the list (after 'Isaiah' and 'David' and 'Elijah') significant, and are three later worthies therefore in mind?

Epiphanius, at first sight, is more definite. He records that among the apocryphal books used by the Sethians was one passing under the name of Abraham 'which also they assert to be a revelation'.[2] The obvious interpretation of this statement is that it is a reference to our Apocalypse. On the other hand, the Testament contains not a little apocalyptic material; and this is recognised, for example, in the title of the Testament in the Rumanian version ('The Life and Death of our Father Abraham, the Righteous, written according to the Apocalypse . . .'). So there could clearly be confusion between Apocalypse and Testament. The Sethians, about whom Epiphanius is writing, may have used either the Apocalypse or the Testament, or, perhaps, another work incorporating material in one, or the other, or both, or neither.

Even greater uncertainty surrounds the interpretation of a passage in the Prologue to Palladius's *Lausiac History*. In the traditional text of this passage Palladius refers to 'those who have written the lives of the Fathers, Abraham, Isaac, and Jacob, and

---

[1] Prisc. *Tract.* iii.
[2] Epiph. *Haer.* XXXIX. v. 1.

Moses also and Elijah, and those who came after them'.[3] But the standard modern text reads 'those who have written the lives of the Fathers, Abraham and those who came after him, Moses and Elijah and John'.[4] Whether or not Palladius knew three 'Lives' of all three patriarchs, or only a single 'Life' of Abraham, is for our present purposes immaterial. What is important to note is that the description 'Life' fits the Testament of Abraham just as well as it does the Apocalypse. Though it may well be that Palladius was referring to neither, but to a different work altogether, now no longer extant.

In modern times the Apocalypse has been preserved only in Slavonic. Two editions of the Slavonic text were published independently by N. S. Tikhonravov and I. I. Sreznevsky in 1863 from the 14th cent. Codex Sylvester (in which the Apocalypse appears as one item in a collection of lives of saints); and these two editions of the text were followed by the publication of a facsimile edition of the MS itself in 1891. The Apocalypse is also found in some of the MSS of the *Palaea interpretata*,[5] and the texts of several of these MSS have been edited.

Our translation is based on the Sylvester text (= S). This text, however, is in many places manifestly corrupt and not infrequently inferior to one or the other of the *Palaea* texts: in such cases the *Palaea* texts have been preferred. Three *Palaea* texts have been used: J = the 15th cent. MS of the *Palaea* in the Joseph Monastery at Volokolamsk (now in Moscow), edited by N. S. Tikhonravov; K = the 17th cent. MS originally in Solovetsk, transferred to Kazan, and edited by I. Ya. Porfir'ev; and R = the MS dated AD

---

[3] e.g. *PG* xxxiv. 1003–4 (reprinted from Ducaeus).

[4] Cuthbert Butler, *The Lausiac History of Palladius*, II (= *TS* VI. ii; Cambridge, 1904), p. 11.

[5] The *Palaea* is a compendium of miscellaneous items collected together primarily to show how the Old Testament was fulfilled in the New. Individual items vary not a little from MS to MS. The basic collection is thought to have been made in Greek in the 8th or 9th cents. and to have been translated into Slavonic in the 10th cent.: over the years it was much enlarged and expanded. Besides The Apocalypse of Abraham the *Palaea* has preserved, among other things, The Ladder of Jacob, a number of sagas about Cain, Abel, Lamech, and other Old Testament worthies, and, most important of all, the Slavonic version of The Testaments of the Twelve Patriarchs.

1494 in the Rumyantsev Museum (now the Lenin Library) in Moscow, edited by A. N. Pypin.

Most of the *Palaea* texts begin with a prologue not found in S: we have printed this prologue in full from R and K in the apparatus on p. 369. Some *Palaea* texts (and among them R and K) continue immediately with the opening words of chap. i, although this makes a very awkward connection; but others omit chaps. i–vi altogether and follow the prologue with the beginning of chap. vii ('And Abraham, having reasoned thus, came to his father, saying, Father Thara, fire is more honourable than images . . .'). R stops short at the end of chap. viii – i.e. it contains only the 'legendary' part of the Apocalypse and not the more specifically 'apocalyptic'. J and K agree in offering a more satisfactory conclusion, which is lacking in S; but, even here, J seems to be defective at the very end. And throughout there are many variants, omissions, additions, and displacements, by no means all of which are recorded in our apparatus. Also noteworthy is the vacillation between the use of the first and third persons in the narrative – the result of uncertainty in the tradition about whether Abraham himself is telling the story or someone else is telling it about him. Moreover, the work known as 'The Tale of the Just Man Abraham',[6] although it cannot be described as an 'abridgement' of the Apocalypse, nevertheless shows clear traces of dependence on the same tradition, and by its very existence provides an interesting illustration of how that tradition, in the Slavonic world at least, was being continually adapted and re-shaped.

Despite the wide variations in the extant Slavonic texts of the Apocalypse, and the consequent difficulty in tracing any part of it with any degree of certainty to a Greek or Semitic original, there can be no doubt at all that a very great deal of the material contained in it is ultimately Jewish. Thus, the tradition that Israel's ancestors in Mesopotamia 'even Terah, the father of Abraham, and the father of Nahor . . . served other gods' is attested as early as Josh. xxiv. 2. The Book of Jubilees relates how Abraham disputed with Terah about the folly of idol-worship and how he 'set fire to the idols' house' in Ur of the Chaldees, and then how later in

[6] Published most recently by P. A. Lavrov in *SORYaS* lxvii. 3 (St. Petersburg, 1899), pp. 70–81.

Haran, while observing 'the signs of the stars', he perceived at last the truth about the Creator, was thus led to forsake all kinds of false worship, and set out at the Divine command on his journey to Canaan[7]. And this account in Jubilees is repeated and developed in a variety of ways in later Jewish writings.

Yet this does not in itself prove that the author of the Apocalypse was a Jew. Christians read, not only their Bibles, but also Jubilees and other Jewish literature. They were also in touch in certain areas and at certain times with not a little Jewish oral tradition. There is clear evidence, from sources quite unconnected with the Apocalypse, that in this instance they knew some, at least, of the extra-Biblical Jewish traditions about Abraham.[8] And there are in the Apocalypse several passages which show signs of Christian influence, particularly towards the end (and pre-eminently chap. xxix). These passages may, of course, be Christian interpolations into an originally purely Jewish work. But not necessarily so.

A possible indication of date is the description of the burning and pillaging of the Temple by the heathen in chap. xxvii. This has been held to point to a date after AD 70. But chap. xxvii is in the second, 'apocalyptic', part of the book (ix–xxxi); so that for those who, like Ginzberg, think that the 'apocalyptic' part was originally independent of the 'legendary' (i–viii), chap. xxvii is only evidence for the date of the 'apocalyptic' part.

However, as the book stands, there are certainly connections between the two parts (chaps. xxv and xxvi make unambiguous references to the contents of i–viii). Consequently, even if the two parts were originally independent, they have not simply been joined together, but a definite attempt has been made to fuse them. And the fusion (if such it was) would seem to have been made by the middle of the 4th cent. at the latest, since the Clementine *Recognitions* refer to Abraham,

'who, since he was an astrologer, was able to recognise the Creator from the disposition and order of the stars, and understood that all things are

---

[7] Jub. xii. 1–8, 12, 16–28.
[8] See especially L. Ginzberg, 'Die Haggada bei den Kirchenvätern und in der apokryphischen Litteratur' in *Monatsschrift für Geschichte und Wissenschaft des Judenthums*, xliii (1899), pp. 486–490.

regulated by His providence. Whence also an angel standing by him in a vision, instructed him more fully about those things which he was beginning to perceive. But he shewed him also what was destined for his race and posterity, and promised that these places should not so much be given to them as restored'.[9]

Nothing is said in the *Recognitions* about the source of the writer's information about Abraham at this point. Furthermore, the 'legendary' interest of the passage is concentrated on Abraham's practice of astrology, rather than on his attack on idolatry, which is the main theme of the first part of the Apocalypse. Even so, what is significant is that in the *Recognitions* the 'legendary' and the 'apocalyptic' elements in the Abraham tradition are closely associated, and that the latter part of the passage quoted 'forms (as Box puts it) a good description of the second or apocalyptic part of our Book'.[10] In other words, *Recognitions*, i. 32, would seem to be evidence that the Apocalypse existed, at any rate in embryo, as early as *c.* 350, however much it may subsequently have been re-modelled, re-written, expanded, or interpolated, even perhaps as late as the 16th or 17th cents. (the date of our latest Slavonic MSS).

BIBLIOGRAPHY

EDITIONS

N. S. TIKHONRAVOV, *Pamyatniki otrechennoi russkoi literatury*, i (St. Petersburg, 1863), pp. 32–53 [= S], pp. 54–77 [= J].

I. I. SREZNEVSKY, *Drevnie pamyatniki russkogo pis'ma i yazyka: obshchee povremennoe obozrenie* (= *Izvěstiya Imperatorskoi akademii nauk po otdeleniyu russkogo yazyka i slovesnosti*, x (St. Petersburg, 1861–63), cols. 648–665) [= S].

——, *Drevnie . . .*, i (The above reissued in book form; St. Petersburg, 1866), pp. 247ᵇ–256ᵃ [= S].

---

[9] *Clem. Recogn.* i. 32 (Rufinus's translation of the *Recognitions* is to be dated *c.* AD 400).   [10] G. H. Box, *The Apocalypse of Abraham*, p. xvii.

I. Ya. PORFIR´EV, *Apokrificheskie skazaniya o vetkhozavetnykh litsakh i sobytiyakh po rukopisyam Solovetskoi biblioteki* (= *SORYaS* xvii. i (St. Petersburg, 1877), pp. 111–130) [= K].

A. N. PYPIN, *Lozhnye i otrechennye knigi russkoi stariny* (= ed. G. A. KUSHELEV-BEZBORODKO, *Pamyatniki starinnoi russkoi literatury*, iii (St. Petersburg, 1862), pp. 24–26) [= R].

[For the facsimile edition of S see *Otkrovenie Avraama* = *Obshchestvo lyubitelei drevnei pis´mennosti*, No. 99 (St. Petersburg, 1891).]

TRANSLATIONS

English

G. H. BOX (with the assistance of J. I. LANDSMAN), *The Apocalypse of Abraham: Edited, with a Translation from the Slavonic Text and Notes* (= S.P.C.K., *Translations of Early Documents*; London, 1918).

German

G. N. BONWETSCH, *Die Apokalypse Abrahams* (= *Studien zur Geschicte der Theologie und Kirche*, Bd. i, Heft 1 (Leipzig, 1897), pp. 1–70).

P. RIESSLER, *AjSaB²*, pp. 13–39.

B. PHILONENKO-SAYAR and M. PHILONENKO in *JSh-rZ* V. 5 (1982), pp. 415–460.

GENERAL

A.-M. DENIS, *IPGAT*, pp. 37–38.

L. GINZBERG, art. 'Abraham, Apocalypse of' in *JE* i (New York, 1901), pp. 91–92.

——, *The Legends of the Jews*, i (Philadelphia, 1909), pp. 209–213 and v (Philadelphia, 1925), pp. 217–218, 229–230.

P. RIESSLER, *AjSaB*,² pp. 1267–1269.

A. RUBINSTEIN, 'Hebraisms in the Slavonic Apocalypse of Abraham' in *JJS* iv (1953), pp. 108–115 and v (1954), pp. 132–135.

E. SCHÜRER, *GjVZJC⁴* iii, pp. 336–338.

É. TURDEANU, 'L'*Apocalypse d'Abraham* en slave' in *The Journal for the Study of Judaism*, iii (1972), pp. 153–180.

H. WEINEL in *EUX*, pp. 167–170.

The Book of the Revelation of Abraham, the son of Therin, the son of Nachor, the son of Seruch, the son of Roch, the son of Arphaxad, the son of Sim, the son of Noe, the son of Lamech, the son of Methusalam, the son of Enoch, the son of Ared.[1]

I.   One day, when I was planing the gods of my father Theran[1] and the gods of my brother Naoch,[2] when I was enquiring who in truth the Mighty God is, I, Abraham was doing my duty and devoting myself to the services *and* sacrifices of my father Thara to his gods of wood, stone, gold, silver, brass, and iron. And I went into their temple for the service; and I found the god Marumath by name, *who was* carved from stone, fallen down at the feet of the god Nachor,[3] *who was* of iron. And when I saw *it,* I was distressed. I was sure that I, Abraham, could not put him back in his place by myself, for he was a massive lump of stone *and* heavy. So I went and told my father; and he came in to help me.[4] And while we were lifting him to put him back in his place, his head fell off him; and I was still holding him by the head. And when my father saw that Marumath's head had fallen off, he said to me, Abraham. And I said, Here am I. And he said to me, Bring me the axes *and* pincers[5] from the house. And I brought *them* to him from the house. And he carved a second Marumath from a second stone without a head,

---

[1]   R has the title 'The Book about Abraham, forefather and patriarch'. RK begin 'Thara was Abraham's father, and Thara began to do what he saw done at his father Nahor's; and he worshipped idols and burned sacrifices before them, both calves and heifers, and did all that is pleasing to the devil. When Abraham saw this, he was very perturbed; and he said to himself, Behold, my father Thara is deceived by these gods of wood, for they have no souls (R om.) in them: they have eyes but they do not see, they have ears but they do not hear, they have hands but they do not feel, they have feet but they do not walk (R omits this clause), they have noses but they do not smell, and there is no voice in their mouths. So I think in very truth my father Thara is deceived. And Abraham, having reasoned thus' . . . (see above p. 365).

[1]   RJK 'Thara'.
[2]   my brother Naoch: RK 'Nahor'.
[3]   So J:RK 'Nachin'; S 'Naritsen'.
[4]   Lit 'came in with me'.
[5]   K om. '*and* pincers'.

and *he put on it* the head that had fallen off Marumath; but the rest of Marumath he destroyed.[6]

II.   And he made five other gods, and he gave them to me and told
2 me to sell them outside in the city street. And I saddled my father's
   ass and put them on it and went out onto the highway to sell them.
3 And behold, merchants from Fandana in Syria came with camels,
4 on their way into Egypt to trade. And I fell into conversation with
5 them.[1] One of their camels snorted, and the ass took fright, and ran
   away and upset the gods; and three of them were broken, and *only*
6 two remained *whole*. And when the Syrians saw I had gods, they
   said to me, Why did you not tell us you had gods? We would have
   bought them[2] before the ass heard the camel's snort,[3] and you
7 would not have had this loss. But *give* us the remaining gods, and
   we will pay you the proper price for the broken gods *as well as* for
8 the gods that remain *whole*.[4] (For I was worried how I should make
9 account[5] to my father.) And the three broken ones I threw into the
   water of the river Gur,[6] which was in that place; and they sank to
   the bottom and were *seen* no more.

III.   And as I went on my way a number of questions arose in my
2,5 mind which disturbed me.[1] And I thought,[2] Behold, Marumath

   [6] K 'And he cut the head from a second stone god and fastened it to the god
   Marumath, who had fallen down; and the head which had fallen off him, and the
   rest of the second god, he destroyed'.

   [1] RJK '. . . on their way into Egypt to buy there scarlet dye from the Nile. And I
   asked them, and they told me not (K om.), and I talked with them'. The word
   kokünilü here translated 'scarlet dye' is obscure. Landsman translates 'papyrus'. It
   seems more likely to be a corruption of Gk. κόκκινος ('scarlet colour') and to mean
   some kind of scarlet dye, possibly cochineal.
   [2] you had . . . bought them = RJK: S om.
   [3] Lit. 'voice'.
   [4] J 'But give us the remaining gods, and we will pay you a proper price. And I
   thought about it; and they paid the price of the broken gods *as well as* that for the
   remaining gods'.   [5] Lit. 'how I should bring the merchandise'.
   [6] R 'Tur'.

   [1] Lit. '. . . way, my heart was troubled and my thought strayed within me'.
   [2] RJK add verses 3 and 4. 'What is this evil that my father is doing? Is he not
   himself rather the god of his gods, since they owe their existence to his carving and

fell down and could not get up in his *own* temple, nor could I lift him up on my own, until my father came, and we both lifted him; and while we were unable to do this, his head fell off him, and my father[3] put it on another stone of a second god, which he had made without a head. And the other five gods, which were smashed *when they fell* off the ass, were not able either to save themselves, or to do harm to the ass because it had destroyed them; nor did their fragments come up out of the river. And I thought, If this be so, how then shall Marumath, my father's god, with a head made from one stone and a body made from another stone,[4] be able to save a man, or hear a man's prayer, and reward him?

IV. And as I pondered thus, I came to my father's house; and I watered the ass and put out hay for it. I took out the money and gave it into my father Thara's hands. When he saw it, he was glad *and* said, Blessed are you, Abraham, of my gods, for you have brought the price of the gods, so that my labour might not be in vain. And I answered and said to him, Listen, father Tera:[1] blessed are the gods of you, for you are their god, inasmuch as you have created them;[2] for their blessing is destruction and their might[3] is vain; and *since* they did not help themselves, how will they help you, or bless me? It is I who have done you service in this transaction, for by my astuteness I have secured you the money for the broken gods[4] *as well as for the others*. And when he heard what I said, he was furiously angry with me, because I had spoken disparagingly about his gods.

planing and skill? Would it not be rather better for them to worship my father since they owe their existence to his work? What is this delusion of my father in his works?'

[3] Lit. 'he'.

[4] Lit. 'having the head of a second stone, and made from a second stone'. The translation attempts to give a sense that is in accordance with what we are told at i.12.

[1] RJK here and subsequently read 'Thara'.

[2] blessed are the gods ... created them = RJK: S is here corrupt.

[3] J 'help'.   [4] Lit. 'broken ones'.

1,2 **V.** But I took note of my father's fury and went out.[1] He called me,
3   saying, Abraham; and I said, Here am I. And he said,[2] Collect the
     shavings of the wood, from which I was making gods of pine-wood
4   before you came, and take *them* and make me food for dinner. And
     while I was picking up the wood shavings I found among them a
     little god, lying in the shelter on my left; and on his forehead was
5   written, God Barisat. And I did not tell my father I had found the
6   wooden god Barisat among the shavings. And when I put the
     shavings on the fire to make food for my father, before I went away
7   to ask about the food, I stood Barisat by the fire *I had* made. And I
     gave him instructions and said, Barisat, look after the fire until I
     come back, so that it does not go out: if it is going out, blow on it, so
     that it burns up. I went away and did what I had intended. When I
8,9 came *back*, I found Barisat lying prostrate, his feet well into[3] the
10   fire, and terribly burnt. And I burst into laughter and said to
11   myself, Barisat, you can indeed make a fire and cook food! And as I
     was saying this in my mockery,[4] he was gradually burnt up by the
12   fire and reduced to ashes. And I took the food to my father, and he
13   ate it. And I gave him wine and milk, and he drank *it* and was
14   satisfied; and he blessed his god Marumath. And I said to him,
     Father Tera, do not bless your god Marumath, do not praise him:
     praise rather your god Barisat, for he, out of love for you, threw
15   himself into the fire to cook your food. And he said to me, Where is
16   he now? And I said, He has been reduced to ashes by the fury of the
17   fire and is become dust. And he said, Great is the might of Barisat:
     I will make another today; and tomorrow he shall make my food.

VI. But when I, Abraham, heard words like this from my father, I
     laughed in my mind, yet groaned in the grief *and* anger of my soul.
2   And I said, How can my father be served by what has been made
3   by him – *by* idols made *with his own hands*? Will he subject *his* body to

---

[1] R 'But I, because of my father's fury, went out'. RJK add 'And after I had gone
out'.
[2] And he said = RJK: S om.
[3] Lit. 'surrounded by'.
[4] RJK 'in my mind': K adds 'and laughed'.

his soul, and then the soul of the spiritual spirit to folly and
4 ignorance?[1] And I said, It is only right to suffer evil once: I will set
my mind on what is pure, and I will tell him plainly what I think.
5 And[2] I answered and said, Father Tera, whichever of these gods
6 you praise, you are deluded in your mind. See, the gods of your
brother Nachor,[3] which stand in the holy temple, are more honour-
7 able than yours. See too, Zuch, your brother Aron's god, is more
honourable than Marumath your god, for he is made of gold, *which
8 is* highly prized by men. And if he ages with the years, he can be
remade; but Marumath, if he is smashed[4] or broken, cannot be
9 restored, because he is of stone. And it is the same with the god
10 Avon who stands alongside Zuch. Barisat himself is burnt up in the
11 fire,[5] and is reduced to ashes, and is no more. And *yet* you say,
Today I will make another, and tomorrow he shall make my food.
12 He has perished utterly.[6]

VII. Fire, I say,[1] is more honourable than images; for even things
that are *otherwise* unsubdued are subdued by it, and it mocks what

---

[1] The obscurity here is probably due to dislocation in the text. JK read 'Will he
have subjected *his* body to his soul, and the soul to the spirit, and the spirit to folly
and ignorance?'

[2] S om.

[3] RK 'my brother Nachor'; J 'your father Nachor'.

[4] Lit. 'changed'.

[5] And it is the same . . . fire: RJK 'As for the god Joauv (R 'Jav'), who stands
alongside Zuch above the other gods – he is more worshipful than *your* god Barisat,
who is made of wood, for *he is* forged of silver: as there is adaptation for him also(?),
he is highly prized by men because of the brilliance (lit. 'show') of his appearance.
But Barisat, your god, when he was still not made, was rooted in the earth, great
and wonderful, with branches and blossoms and praises; and *then* you cut him with
an axe, and he was made into a god by your skill. And behold, now he is withered,
and his richness has perished (for this clause R reads 'and here is the stump'), and
from the height he is fallen to the ground, and from greatness has he come to
littleness, and his outward form has disappeared, and he is burnt up in the fire'.

[6] Lit. 'to destruction'.

[1] He has perished . . . I say: JK 'He has no might left, having perished utterly.
And Abraham, having reasoned thus, came to his father, saying, Father Thara, fire
. . .' (see above p. 365).

2 perishes *so* easily in its flames.[2] But more honourable still are the
3 waters, for they overcome fire and satisfy the earth. But neither
would I call them god, for they are subdued, and are inferior to[3] the
4 earth. But I call the earth more honourable still, since it overcomes
5 the substance and abundance of the **waters**.[4] But I would not call it
god, since it is dried up by the sun, and it is made for the use of
6 man. I would call the sun more worthy of worship than the earth,[5]
7 for with its rays it illumines the universe and the several airs. But I
would not account it god, for by night a cloud obscures its course.[6]
8 Nor, again, would I call the moon and stars god, for they too in
9 their season are darkened in their light at night. Listen, Tera, my
father, I will examine with you the question who is the God[7] who
10 created all these gods for whom we care. For who is he, or what is
he, who has made the heavens purple, who made the sun gold, *and*
11 who set light in the moon, and the stars with her? Who *is he who* has
made the dry land in between the many waters, and has given you
12 the power of speech?[8] Let God himself appear to us.[9]

[2] images; for . . . flames: RJK 'your gods of gold, silver, stone, and wood, for *the fire* burns your gods, and the gods it burns are subject to the fire, and the fire mocks them; and it has devoured your gods. But neither would I call it god, for it is subject to the waters'. [3] Lit. 'they are subdued, turning under'.

[4] SR 'the substance and abundance of the earth': JK 'the substance of water'.

[5] I would . . . earth = RJK: S om.

[6] for . . . course: RJK 'for when the night comes it is overcast with darkness'.

[7] So S: RJK 'I will tell you about the God'.

[8] Lit. 'and set you yourself in words': RJK add 'and has sought me out in the confusion of my thoughts'.

[9] RJK add a Christian gloss and then continue 'When his father Thara heard this, he looked at Abraham with bitter eyes, for what Abraham had said displeased him, *because* he loved the deceit handed down by his father Nachor. Abraham said to himself, I will test my father's gods *and see* whether they are able to help themselves. And Abraham took fire, and he set light to the temple where his father's gods were. When Aron (K 'Aran'), Abraham's brother, saw this (since he was devoted to the idols) he tried to save the idols from the fire; and so he himself was burned with his father's gods, and died before his father – for before this no son had died before his father, but the father *had always died* before the son; but after this men began to die before their fathers. And God loved Abraham, and God said to Abraham, Abraham, Abraham! You have sought the God of gods: leave now your father's house, and go into the land I will direct you to, and I will make you into a great nation, and all the generations of the earth shall be blessed from you'. Another Christian gloss follows, and then the text continues with the beginning of chap. viii ('While I was talking . . .').

VIII. And while I was talking[1] in this way to my father Tera in the
2 courtyard of my house, the voice of the Mighty One fell from
heaven in a deluge of fire, saying *and* calling *out*, Abraham,
3,4 Abraham! And I said, Here am I. And *the voice* said, You are
seeking God,[2] the Creator, by the understanding of your mind: I
5 am *he.* Leave your father, Tera, and leave *his* house, so that you do
6 not perish also in the sins of your father's house. And I went out.
7 And when I had gone out, before I could reach the outer door of the
court, a thunderbolt dropped from the sky,[3] and it burned him and
his house and all that was in his house to the ground, *all* forty cubits
of it.[4]

IX. Then came a voice saying to me twice, Abraham, Abraham!
2,3 And I said, Here am I. And *the voice* said, Behold, it is I: do not be
afraid; for I am the mighty God, who was before the world,[1] who in
4 the beginning[2] created the light of the world.[1] And I am your
5 shield, and I am your helper. Go *and* get me a calf of three years old,
and a she-goat of three years old, and a ram of three years old, and
6 a turtle-dove, and a pigeon, and set out a pure sacrifice for me. And
in that sacrifice I will set out *for you the secrets of* the ages, and tell you
hidden things; and you shall see great things, which you have not
seen; for you have loved *me* to seek me out, and I have called you
7 my friend.[3] But abstain from all cooked food,[4] and from drinking
8 wine, and from anointing *yourself* with oil for forty days. And then
set out the sacrifice for me, which I have commanded you, in the
9 place I will show you – on a high mountain. And there will I show
you the ages, which have been created and established, made and
renewed, by my word; and I will tell you the things that will come
to pass in them, on those who have done evil and *those who have done*
righteousness in the human race.

---

[1] Lit. 'reflecting'.   [2] RJK 'the God of gods'.
[3] Lit. 'a voice of thunder came': K adds 'and fire fell from heaven'.
[4] Here R ends.

[1] Lit. 'age' or 'aeon'.
[2] Lit. 'formerly'. K reads the clause 'who fomerly created heaven and earth and
then the first light of the world and the age'.
[3] Lit. 'lover': cp. 2 Chron. xx. 7; Isa. xli. 8; James ii. 23.
[4] Lit. 'food which comes from fire'.

X.   And when I heard the voice speaking words like this to me, I looked this way and that; and behold, there was no sign of anyone.[1]

2 And I was terrified: my senses left me; and I became like a stone

3 and fell down upon the ground.[2] And while I was still on my face on

4 the ground, I heard the voice saying, Go, Naoil,[3] and by virtue of my ineffable name sanctify that man to me, and strengthen him in

5 his terror. And the angel that he sent to me came, *and he was in* appearance like a man; and he took me by the right hand and set

6 me on my feet. And he said to me, Stand up, friend of God, who

7 loves you; and let no human terror hold you in its grip. For behold, I am sent to you to strengthen you, and to bless you in the name of

8 God, the creator of heaven and earth, who loves you. Take courage,

9 and come with me to meet him with all speed.[4] I am Iloil,[5] so named by him who shakes what is with me on the seventh expanse above the vault of heaven, a power by virtue of the ineffable name

10 that dwells in me. I am he who is appointed by his command to appease the strife the cherubic creatures have with one another, and to teach those who bear him the song[6] decreed for the seventh

11 hour of the human night. I am he who is ordained to restrain

12 Leviathan; for the attack and threat of every reptile are subdued by

13 me.[7] I am he who was commanded to set fire to your father's house

14 and to destroy him with it,[8] for he gave honour to dead things. *And* I am sent to you now to bless you and *to bless* the land which the Eternal One, whom you have invoked, has made ready for you;

15 and *it is* for your sake that I have made the journey to earth. Stand up Abraham: take courage and come: rejoice and be glad at heart; and I *will rejoice* with you; for eternal honour has been prepared for

16 you by the Eternal One. Come, carry through the sacrifice as you have been commanded; for behold, I am appointed *to be* with you

---

[1] Lit. 'no breath of man'.

[2] JK add 'for there was no strength in me to stand upon the ground'.

[3] JK 'Altez'.

[4] Lit. 'Take courage and hasten to him'.

[5] J 'Aol'; K 'Jaol'.

[6] those . . . song = JK: S is corrupt.

[7] JK add 'I am he who has been commanded to loosen hell and to destroy those who wonder (J 'him who wonders') at dead things'. Landsman translates '. . . destroy him who stareth at (or 'terrifieth') the dead'.

[8] Lit. 'to your father's house with him'.

17 and with the people who are to spring from you.[9] And with me
18 Michael gives you his blessing to eternity. Take courage: come.

XI.   And I got up and looked at him who had taken my right hand
2 and set me on my feet. And his body was[1] like sapphire, and his
face like chrysolite, and the hair of his head like snow; and *there was*
a linen band about his head, and it was like a rainbow, and the
robes he was wearing *were* purple, and *he had* a golden staff in his
3 right hand. And he said to me, Abraham; and I said, Behold, your
4 servant. And he said, Do not let what I look like or what I say
5 frighten[2] you: do not be upset; but come with me. And I *will* go
with you: you will be able to see me until the sacrifice, but after the
6 sacrifice you will see me no more.[3] Take courage: come.

XII.   And we went both together, forty days and nights; and I ate
no bread, nor did I drink water, for to look upon the angel who was
with me was food to me,[1] and his conversation with me was my
2,3 drink. And I[2] came to the glorious mountain of God, *to* Horeb. And
I said to the angel, Singer of the Eternal One, behold, I have no
sacrifice with me, nor do I know of any altar on the mountain; and
4,5 how shall I make a sacrifice? And he said, Look behind you. And I
looked behind me; and behold, following us were all the prescribed
victims for the sacrifice – a calf, a she-goat, and a ram, and a
6 turtle-dove, and a pigeon. And the angel said to me, Abraham; and
7 I said, Here am I. And he said, Slaughter all these, and
divide the animals into halves, and place each piece opposite its
8 corresponding piece,[3] but do not divide the birds. And give them to
the men, whom I will show you, *who will be* standing by you; for
they are the altar on the mountain, on which you must offer[4] the

---

[9] Lit. 'the people prepared from you'. Cp. xxii. 7.

[1] JK 'And the feet of his body were'.
[2] So JK: S is corrupt.
[3] you will be able . . . no more: lit. 'visible until the sacrifice, but after the sacrifice invisible for ever'.

[1] So JK: S adds 'and drink'.   [2] J 'we'; K 'they'.
[3] and place . . . corresponding piece: lit. 'one against another'.
[4] Lit '. . . mountain to offer (or 'bring')'.

9   sacrifice to the Eternal One. *But* the turtle-dove and the pigeon you must give to me; and I will go up on the wings of the birds to show you *what is* in heaven and on earth, and in the sea and the abysses, and in the lowest parts, and in the garden of Eden, and in its rivers, and in the fulness of the universe and its circle: you shall see it all.[5]

XIII. And I did everything the angel had commanded me. And I gave the divided animals to the angels who had come to us; but the

2,3 angel[1] took the birds. And I waited for the evening offering. And an unclean bird flew down upon the carcasses; and I drove it away.

4   And the unclean bird spoke to me and said, What are you doing, Abraham, on the sacred heights, where *men* neither eat nor drink, nor is there human food here: all these things will be consumed

5   with fire, and you will be burnt up *as well*. Leave the man who is with you and make your escape; for if you persist,[2] you will be

6   destroyed. And when I saw the bird speaking, I said to the angel,

7   What is this, my lord? And he said, This is Wickedness, Azazil; for

8   Abraham's lot is in the heavens, but yours on earth. He said to him, Shame upon you, Zazal;[3] for you have chosen and have loved

9   to live in your uncleanness[4] here. That is why the Eternal Ruler,

10 the Mighty One, has appointed you *to be* a dweller upon earth. And through you the evil *and* deceitful spirit *works among men*, and through you retribution[5] and misfortunes fall on the generations of

11 the unrighteous. Yet the Eternal Mighty God has not decreed that the bodies of the righteous should be in your hands: for them a

12 righteous life is assured, and perdition for wickedness. Listen,

13 fellow, be ashamed of yourself and go. For you were not appointed

14 to tempt all the righteous. Leave this man alone: you cannot beguile him for he is your enemy, and *the enemy* of those who follow

15 you and dote on what you want. The garment that of old was set apart in the heavens for you, is *now set apart* for him; and the corruption that was his has been transferred to you.

---

[5] Lit. 'see in all'.

[1] K adds 'Jaoil'.   [2] Lit. 'for if you go up into the height'.
[3] K 'Azazil': J om. 'He said . . . Zazal', and K places it before 'for Abraham's lot
. . .'.   [4] Lit. 'and have loved the dwelling-place of your uncleanness'.
[5] Lit. 'wrath'.

5 **XIV.** The angel said to Abraham,[1] Say to him, May you be a
burning coal of the earthly furnace. Azazil went into the inacces-
10 sible parts of the earth.[2] And the angel said to me, Do not answer
him, for God has given him power[3] over those who answer him.[4]
13 And however much he begged me to go down *with him*,[5] I did not
answer him.

XV. And as the sun was setting, behold, smoke as from a furnace.
2 And the angels who had the divided victims rose up from the top of
3 the smoking furnace. And the angel took me by the right hand, and
he set me on the right wing of the pigeon, and he himself sat on the
left wing of the turtle-dove – neither of which had been slaughtered
4,5 or divided. And he took me up to the edge of a fiery flame. And we
went up, as if *borne aloft* by many winds, to the heaven established
6 on the expanses. And I saw in the air, on the height to which we
7 went up,[1] a great light, which is indescribable. And behold, by that
light *I saw* a burning fire of people – many people, males all of
them, changing *their* appearance and *their* form,[2] running *hither and*

---

[1] JK "The angel said to me, Abraham; and I said, Here am I, your servant. [2]And
he said, By this will you know that the Eternal One, whom you have loved, has
chosen you. [3]Take courage, and do with vigour what I tell you against him who
maligns the truth. [4]Shall I not be able to reprove him who has betrayed the heavenly
secrets and taken counsel against the Mighty One?'

[2] Azazil ... earth: JK 'Go, Azazil, into the inaccessible parts of the earth. [6]For
your dominion is over those who are with you, with the stars and the clouds, who
give birth (K 'who are born') with the men whose lot is to judge you by your being
(K 'whose lot you are, and who exist to you by your being'); and righteousness is
your enemy (lit. 'enmity'). [7]For this reason, because your doom is sealed (lit. 'by
your perdition'), get out of my sight! [8]And I spoke the words that he had taught me.
[9]And he said, Abraham; and I said, Behold, your servant'.

[3] Lit. 'will'.

[4] JK add 'And he spoke to me a second time: and the angel said, Whatever he
says to you, do not answer, so that his power (lit. 'will') may not prevail over you.
[11]For the Mighty One, before the ages, gave him authority and power (lit. 'weight
and will'). [12] I did what the angel commanded me'.

[5] Lit. 'And however much he said to me that I should go down'. Landsman
translates simply 'And however much he spake to me', following Sreznevsky's
interpretation.

---

[1] And we went up ... we went up = JK: S 'And we went up on the height'.

[2] changing ... form = Sinod. 211: S is corrupt.

thither as they changed their form, and worshipping and crying out in a language[3] I did not know.

XVI. And I said to the angel, Why[1] have you brought me now to this place; for I cannot now see, my strength is gone, and I am at
2 the point of death.[2] And he said to me, Stay by me, and do not be afraid: he whom you will see coming straight towards us with a great and holy voice,[3] he is the Eternal One, who has set his love on
3,4 you. (But you will not actually see him[4]). Do not let your spirit fail,[5] for I am with you to strengthen you.

XVII. And while he was speaking, behold a fire round about, *and it was* coming towards us; and there was a voice in the fire like the
2 sound of rushing waters, like the roaring of the sea. And the angel
3 with me bowed *his head and* worshipped.[1] And I would have fallen prostrate on the ground; but the place on the height, where we were standing, at one moment lifted itself up[2] *and* at the next sank
4 back *again*. And he said, Only worship, Abraham, and sing the
5 song I have taught you (for there was no ground to fall on). And I
6 worshipped only, and I sang the song he had taught me. And he said, Sing without stopping; and I sang, and he himself also sang the song,[3]

7 Eternal One, Mighty One, Holy One, El, God, Monarch,
8 Self-begotten, incorruptible, unsullied, unborn, immaculate, immortal, self- perfect, self-illumined,
9 Without mother, without father, without birth, the High One, the Fiery One,[4]

[3] Lit. 'with a voice of words'.

[1] So JK: S 'whither'.
[2] Lit. 'I am already weakened, and my spirit is departing from me'.
[3] So J ('a great voice of holiness'): S is corrupt; K reads 'with a great voice, saying, Holy, holy, holy *is* the Lord'.
[4] Lit. 'But himself you will not see'.
[5] JK add 'for the shouting' (i.e. because of the paean of praise).

[1] So JK: S 'And the angel, bowing more, worshipped'.
[2] at one . . . up: S om.
[3] K adds 'the first song of Abraham, which the holy angel Jaoil taught him, going with him through the air'.   [4] JK add 'the Righteous One'.

10 Lover of man,[5] generous, bountiful, my defender, longsuffering, most merciful,

11 Eli (that is my God), eternal, mighty, holy, Sabaoth, most glorious, El, El, El, El, Jaoil.

12 Thou art he whom my soul hath loved, preserver, Eternal One, fire, Shining One, *whose* voice *is* like thunder,[6] *whose* aspect *is* like lightning, many-eyed, who receivest the prayers *of* those who honour thee.[7]

14 *Thou*, the Light, shinest before the light of morning on thy creation; and[8] in the heavenly dwelling places sufficient is the other light from the inexpressible dawn of the lights of thy face.

16 Receive my prayer,[9] and also the sacrifice which thou hast made
17 for thyself through me who sought thee. Receive me favourably, and show me, and teach me, and tell thy servant what thou hast promised me.

XVIII. And while I was still singing my song, the tongues[1] of fire on
2 the expanse rose up higher. And I heard a voice, like the roaring of
3 the sea; and it was not affected by the strength of the fire.[2] And as the fire rose up, soaring into the height, I saw beneath the fire a throne of fire, and, round about *it, a throng of* many-eyed ones singing the song, and, beneath the throne, four living creatures of
4 fire singing.[3] And they all looked the same: each one had four faces.
5 One face was like a lion's, another like a man's, another like an
6 ox's, *and* another like an eagle's — *each one had* four heads.[4] And each one had three *pairs of* wings,[5] *one pair* at their shoulders, and *another*

---

[5] JK add 'loving'.

[6] So JK: S '*whose* voice *is* not like thunder'.

[7] JK add 'and turning thyself from the prayers of those who importune thee with their importunities by their provocations. [13]Resolver of the confusions of the universe in the corruptible age, which are among the unclean and the unrighteous (K 'righteous'), renewing the age of the righteous'.

[8] JK 'and from thy face it is day on earth. [15]And'

[9] JK add 'and have pleasure in it'.

[1] Lit. 'lips'.

[2] Lit. 'and it did not cease because of the strength (JK 'great abundance') of the fire'.   [3] K adds 'beautifully and loudly'.

[4] JK add 'on their bodies, so that there were sixteen (J 'thirteen') faces to the four living creatures'.   [5] JK 'had six wings'.

7 at their sides,[6] and *another* at their loins. And with the wings at their shoulders they covered their faces, and with the wings at their loins they covered their feet, and the middle wings they stretched out 8 and flew forward with them. And when they had finished singing, 9 they looked at one another in a threatening manner.[7] And when the angel who was with me saw them threatening one another, he left me, and hurried towards them, and turned each[8] face of each living creature from the face opposite it, so that they could not see 10 each other's threatening faces. And he taught them the song of 11 peace which has its origin in the Eternal One. And while I was standing alone and looking, I saw behind the living creatures a 12 chariot with wheels of fire, each wheel full of eyes all round. And over the wheels was the throne that I saw; and it was covered with fire, and fire encircled it all round; and an ineffable light of a fiery 13 host surrounded *it*. And I heard their holy voices[9] like the voice of one man.

XIX. And the voice from the fire[1] came to me saying, Abraham, 2,3 Abraham! And I said, Here am I. And it said, Look now at the expanses which God set in order[2] underneath the firmament on which you are *now* standing; and see how on no expanse is there anyone else but him whom you have sought or has set his love on 4 you. And while he was still speaking, behold, the expanses parted, 5 and beneath me *lay* the heavens. And I saw on the seventh firmament, on which I was standing, a spreading fire, and light, and dew, and a multitude of angels, and a power of invisible glory from above; and I saw the living creatures, but I saw no one else 6 there. And I looked from the height where I stood to the sixth expanse; and there I saw a multitude of spiritual angels, without bodies – those, that is, who do the bidding of the fiery angels on the 7 **seventh**[3] firmament, on the heights of which I stood. And behold,

---

[6] and *another* at their sides: S om.
[7] So JK (Lit. '. . . another, and threatened one another'): S '. . . another, and deceived one another'.
[8] Lit. 'the'.
[9] Lit. 'the voice of their holiness'.

[1] JK 'And a voice from the midst of the fire'.
[2] Lit. 'which are to God'. [3] The MSS read 'eighth'.

there was no power on that expanse either, in any other form, but
8 only *that of the* spiritual angels. And the power which I saw on the
seventh firmament ordered the sixth[4] expanse to remove itself.
9 And I saw there, on the fifth *expanse*, the starry powers, and the
commands they are bidden to fulfil, and the elements of earth
which obey them.

XX. And the Eternal Mighty One said to me, Abraham. And I
1,2
3 said, Here am I. And he said,[1] Look down at those stars that are
4 below you: count them, and tell me how many there are. And I
5 said, How[2] can I, for I am *but* a man?[3] And he said to me, As the
number of the stars and their might, so will I appoint [for] your
descendants a race of people – a people set apart for me in my
6 heritage with Azazail. And I said, Eternal One, Mighty One, let
thy servant speak in thy presence, and may thy fury not be pro-
7 voked against thy chosen one. Behold, before thou didst raise me
up *here*, Azazail reviled me: so how now, when he is not before thee,
hast thou joined[4] thyself with him.[5]

XXI. And he said to me, Look now beneath your feet at the
expanse; and consider now the creation foreshadowed of old, the
creation on this expanse, and the things that are in it, and the age
2 prepared after it. And I looked at the expanse at my feet; and I saw
beneath *what is* on the third heaven and what is in it, and the earth
and its fruits,[1] and the things on it that move, and the things on it
that have breath, and the might of its men, and its spiritual
3 uncleanness, and its righteousness; and *I saw* its lowest parts and
4 the destruction that is in them, and the abyss and its torments.[2] I

---

[4] So JK: S 'third'.

[1] And he said = JK: S om.; K adds 'to me'.
[2] Lit. 'when'.
[3] J 'for I am *but* dust and ashes'; K 'for I am a man, *but* dust and ashes'.
[4] Lit. 'established'.　　　[5] So JK: S 'them'.

[1]JK 'and I saw beneath the likeness of a heaven (or 'under the seventh heaven') which was with it, and the earth there and its fruit'.
[2] JK 'and their righteousness, and the beginning of their works; [3]and *I saw* the abyss and its torments, and the lowest parts and the destruction which is in them'.

saw there the sea and its islands, and its cattle and its fish, and
Leviathan and his realm, and his bed and his caves, and the world
which lies above him, and his rollings and the destructions in the

5   world which he causes. I saw there the rivers and their risings and
6   their courses. And I saw there the garden of Eden, and its fruit, the
spring *and* the river that issues from it, and its groves and their

7,8 flowers, and those who do *what is* right. And I saw in it their food
9   and *their* peace. And I saw there a throng of people, men, women,
and children, and half of them *were* on the right side of the picture,
and half of them[3] on the left side of the picture.

XXII.   And I said, Eternal One,[1] Mighty One, what is this picture
2   of creation? And he said to me, This is my will *with regard* to what is
in the world, and I was pleased with it; and afterwards I gave
3   command to them by my word.[2] And everything I had planned to
be came into being: it was already pre-figured in this, for all *the
things and all the people* you have seen stood before me before they
4   were created. And I said, Mighty and Eternal Ruler, who then are
5   the people[3] in this picture on this side and on that? And he said to
me, Those on the left side are the many peoples which have existed
in the past, and after you are appointed,[4] some for judgement *and*
restoration, some for vengeance *and* perdition, until the end of the
6   age. And those on the right side of the picture, they are the people
7   set apart for me from the people with Azazil. These are the people
who are going to spring from you[5] and will be called my people.

XXIII.   Look further into the picture *and see* who it was that
beguiled Eve and what the fruit of the tree was, and you will learn
what will be and what will happen to your name among the people
2   as this age runs its course. Or, if you cannot understand *it*, I will

---

[3] on the right . . . half of them: S om.

[1] JK 'Pre-existent One'.
[2] Landsman translates 'This is my will with regard to those who exist in the
(divine) world-counsel, and it seemed well-pleasing before my sight, and then
afterwards I gave commandment to them through my Word'. *Svět* may mean either
'light' or 'world': *sovět* or *s^{u}vět* is the normal word for 'counsel'.
[3] Lit. 'who is this people'.   [4] Lit. 'prepared'.
[5] Lit. 'These are they whom I prepared to be born from you'. Cp. x. 16.

explain *it* to you (for I was pleased with it);[1] and I will tell you what
3 is determined.[2] And I looked into the picture, and my eyes ran to
4 the side of the garden of Eden. And I saw there a man, immensely
tall, alarmingly solid, such as I had never seen before,[3] who was
embracing a woman that was the man's equal *both* in *her* appear-
5 ance and *her* size. And they were standing under one of the trees in
Eden; and the fruit on that tree looked like a bunch of dates. And
behind the tree there stood what looked like a snake, with hands
and feet like a man's, and wings on its shoulders, three on its right
6 and three on its left.[4] And they held in their hands a bunch from the
7 tree; and they were **eating**[5] – the two I had seen embracing. And I
said, Who are these who are embracing each other? Who is it who
is between them? And what is the fruit they are eating, Mighty
8 Eternal One? And he said, This is the human world:[6] this is
9 Adam, and this is their desire upon earth: this is Eve. And what is
between them is the wicked path they started on towards perdi-
10 tion, namely Azazil. And I said, Eternal Mighty One, why hast
thou granted anyone like him the power to destroy in this way the
11 race of men through what they do on earth? And he said to me,
Listen, Abraham, I hate those who desire evil, because of what
they do; *and* I have granted him *authority* over them to rule and to be
12 loved by them. And I answered and said, Eternal Mighty One,
why hast thou willed that men should desire evil in their hearts?
13 For thou art angry with what thou hast willed thyself when a man
goes after the things that are of no substance in thy world.

XXIV. And he said to me, *It has been arranged* like this *as* **a wound to
the nations**[1] for your sake, and for the sake of the people of your race

   [1] what will happen . . . with it: JK 'what will happen to your descendants in the
course of the years. [2]And what you cannot understand, I tell you because I have
been pleased with you'.
   [2] Lit. 'and I will tell you the things laid up in my heart'.
   [3] Lit. 'incomparable in aspect'.
   [4] JK 'six wings on its right and six on its left'.
   [5] Or 'having intercourse'. All MSS are corrupt.
   [6] K 'the human counsel'.

   [1] Lit. 'near to the nations'. The emendation is obtained by reading *blizna rodom*
instead of *bliz narodom*. Landsman and Bonwetsch render 'Being angered at the
nations'.

who are set apart after you, *and* whose afflictions you will see in the
2 picture.[2] And I will tell you what will befall you, and what will
3,4 happen in the last days. Now look at the picture yourself. And I
looked, and I saw there the things in creation that were before me.
5 I saw what looked like Adam, and Eve with him, and with them the
wily adversary, and Cain who transgressed through the adversary.
6 *And I saw* the murdered Abel and the violence the transgressor
7 displayed against him.[3] I saw there fornication and those who lust
after it, and how abominable it is, and how devoted *to it* they are
who practice it; and *I saw too* the fire of their corruption in the lowest
8 parts of the earth. I saw there theft and those who are concerned in
9 it, and how they go to work.[4] I saw there naked men, with their
foreheads against each other, and their shame, and their passion
10 for one another; and *I saw* their retribution. I saw there Desire, and
in her hands the fount of every kind of lawlessness.[5]

XXV. I saw there what looked like the idol of Jealousy,[6] like one of
2 the carved wooden images my father made. Its body *was* of glitter-
ing brass; and before it *stood* a man worshipping it, and *there was* an
altar in front of it, with young men slaughtered on it before the idol.
3 And I said to him, What is this idol? What is this altar? Who are
4 the victims? Who is it that is sacrificing? And what is the temple,
which I see, so beautifully constructed? Its beauty *is* like thy[2] glory,
5 which is beneath the throne. And he said, Listen, Abraham: this
temple and the altar you have seen, and the fine craftsmanship, are
my idea of the sacredness of my glorious name, in which every
prayer of men rejoices, and *so too* the kings and prophets who will
arise, and whatever sacrifice I command them to make to me
6 among my people who will come from your race. But the idol you
have seen is my anger, with which my people, who will come from
7 you, will anger me. And the man you have seen sacrificing, he it is

---

[2] Lit. 'as you will see the afflictions on them in the picture'.
[3] Lit. 'and the destruction brought upon him and given through the transgressor'.
[4] JK add '*and I saw* their retribution *and* the judgement of the great **judgement**'.
[5] JK add 'and her silence (or 'scorn') and her waste, given over to destruction'.

---

[1] Cp. Ezek. viii. 3ff.
[2] So JK: S 'my'.

who angers me *with* murderous sacrifices, *which are* a witness to me of the judgement of the end, even at the beginning of creation.

XXVI. And I said, Eternal Mighty One, why hast thou ordained
2 that it should be like this? Canst thou not change thy mind?[1] And he said to me, Listen Abraham: take in what I am telling you; *and* give
3 me an answer to what I am about to ask you. Your father Tera — why did he not pay any attention to what you said and give up *his*
4 devilish idolatry until his whole house perished with him? And I said, Most Eternal, for no other reason than because he would not
5 listen to me; but I did not do as he did. And he said, Listen, Abraham, As was your father's light[2] in him, and as is your light[2] in you, so is the light[2] of my will in me: it is ready beforehand for the days that are to come. You will not know them, nor will you see with your own eyes what will happen in them: they are for your
6 descendants. Look in the picture.

XXVII. And I looked and I saw; and behold, the picture started to move. And a heathen people ran from the left side of it, and they
2 pillaged those on the right side, men, women, and children. And
3 some they killed,[1] and some they retained *as slaves*. I saw them running towards them for four generations;[2] and they burned the temple with fire, and they plundered the holy things that were in it.
4 And I said, Eternal One, behold, the hordes of the heathen are pillaging the people thou hast appointed *to be born* from me; and *some of them* they are killing, and some they are keeping to take into
5 exile; and they have burned down the temple with fire, and they
6 are stealing the works of art in it. Eternal Mighty One, if this be so, why hast thou saddened[3] my heart, and why must this be so? And he said, Listen Abraham. Everything you have seen must be

---

[1] Lit. 'turn back this revelation'. Landsman translates 'Wherefore hast thou established that it should be so, and then proclaim the knowledge thereof?'
[2] Or 'counsel' (so K).

[1] And some they killed: S om.
[2] *Skhod* (lit. 'descent', 'issue'; hence 'generation'). JK read *vkhod* ('entrance'). Landsman translates 'I saw them run towards them through four entrances'. In any case it is probable that the reference is to the four world empires – Babylon, Media, Greece, and Rome.   [3] K 'provoked'.

because your descendants will provoke my anger with the idol and
the murder you have seen in the picture – the *idol of* Jealousy in the
temple: everything you have seen must be. And I said, Eternal
Mighty One, let the evil *done* in ungodliness pass by, and ordain
punishments for them, *but show me* rather the righteous deeds of this
7 one;[4] for this thou canst do. And he said to me, The righteous
period will come first, through the holiness of *their* kings; and I will
judge truly those whom at the first I chose[5] to rule among them.
8 From them shall men come forth to care for them, as I have told
you and you have seen.

XXVIII.   And I answered and said, Mighty One, hallowed by thy
2 strength, be gracious to my request. *And* so tell me, thy beloved,
3,4 what I ask. Will what I have seen be upon them for long? And he
showed me a large group of his people and said to me, For four
generations,[1] as you have seen, they will provoke me; and during
those *generations* I will bring retribution upon them for what they
5 do. But in the fourth generation[2] of a hundred years, even[3] one
hour of the age (that is a hundred years), *they* will be held in
oppression among the heathen.[4]

XXIX.   And I said, Eternal One, and how long is an hour of the
2 age? And he said, For twelve years of this impious age have I
determined to keep *them* among the heathen, and all you have seen
shall come upon your descendants right up to the end of *that* time.[1]

⁴ This sentence is manifestly corrupt in S. JK read 'let the evil honour and the
deeds of those who have fulfilled the ordinances pass by rather than his righteous
deeds.' Landsman translates 'May the works of evil (wrought) in ungodliness now
pass by, but (show me) rather those who fulfilled the commandments, even the
works of his (?) righteousness'.

⁵ Lit. 'created'. JK read 'by the holiness of kings, to those who judge truly (K 'to'
those who are in truth'), whom I created from them at the first to rule among them'.

¹ *Skhod* (see above, chap. xxvii, n. 2).
² So S, reading *skhod*: JK read *vkhod* ('entrance'). Cp. Gen. xv. 16.
³ Lit. 'and'.
⁴ JK add 'but the hour is for their grace, even with reproaches among the
heathen'.

¹ to keep . . . time: Landsman translates 'to rule among the heathen and in thy
seed; and until the end of the times it shall be as thou sawest'.

3 Now make your calculations and your measurements, and look
4 into the picture. And I saw a man coming out from the left – *from*
the heathen side; *and* a great crowd of people, men, women, and
children, came out from the heathen side *also*, and they worshipped
5 him. And while I was still looking, *others* came out from the right
side; and some of them mocked that man, and some assaulted him,
6 but some of them worshipped him. I saw them worshipping him;
and Azazil ran up and worshipped, and, after kissing his face,
7 turned and stood behind him. And I said, Eternal Mighty One,
who is the man who has been mocked and assaulted, *but yet is*
8 worshipped by the heathen and[2] Azazil? And he answered and
said, Listen Abraham: the man you have seen mocked and
assaulted, and yet worshipped, he is the respite *granted* by the
heathen to the people who will come from you in the last days, in
9 this twelfth year of the ungodly age. But in the twelfth year of my
age of the end I will raise up this man you have seen from among
10 your descendants – from my *own* people. And they will all imitate
him, and **will realize** *he has been* called by me and change their
11 minds.[3] And those you have seen coming from the left side of the
picture and worshipping him – that is, many of the heathen will
12 trust in him. As you have seen *some* of your descendants on the right
side mocking and assaulting him, *and yet* some worshipping him –
13 many of them will find him a stumbling-block.[4] But those of your
descendants who worship him he will put to the test in the twelfth
14 hour at the end, so as to shorten the ungodly age. Before the new
growth of the righteous age begins to show, my judgement will be
accomplished on the lawless heathen through your descendants –
15 the people set apart for me. In those days I will bring ten plagues
upon all creatures on the earth; *and they will be afflicted* by mis-
16 fortunes and diseases, and groan in bitterness of soul. I will bring
all this on the generations of men who are upon it, because of the
17 corrupt practices by which they provoke my anger. And then will be
left the righteous from among your descendants, whose numbers are

---

[2] Lit. 'with'.
[3] The passage is obscure. The emendation is obtained by reading *pričiti* for *prituči*
(K *pritči*, J *pričti*). Bonwetsch and Landsman translate 'and such as are called by me
(will) join, (even) those who change in their counsels'.
[4] Or 'will be led astray by him'.

safe in my keeping, who press onward in the glory of my name to the place prepared for them beforehand, which you have seen laid waste

18 in the picture. And they will live by the established sacrifices and offerings of righteousness and truth in the righteous age, and they

19 will rejoice in me for ever. And they shall destroy those who destroyed them, and insult those who insulted them with *the words of*

20 their *own* blasphemies. They shall spit in the face *of those who are* reproved by me; and they shall gaze upon me, rejoicing with my

21 people as they rejoice, and welcoming those who turn to me.[5] You have seen, Abraham, what you have seen; and ponder[6] what you

22 have heard. Go to the place allotted you;[7] and behold, I am with you for ever.

1,2 **XXX.**   And while he was still speaking, I found myself on earth. And

3 I said, Eternal One! I am not now in the glory I was in above, and what my soul desired to understand with my heart I do not under-

4 stand. And he said to me, I will tell *you* what your heart desired: you desired to see the ten plagues I have prepared against the heathen *the plagues* I have prepared after the passing of the twelfth hour on

5 earth. Listen to what I *will* reveal to you. The first *plague* will be great

6 distress through want: the second, the burning of cities by fire: the third, destruction of cattle by pestilence: the fourth, universal starvation:[1] the fifth, destruction among rulers by the ravages of

7 earthquake and sword: the sixth, deluges of hail and snow: the seventh, lethal attacks by wild animals:[2] the eighth (to vary the mode of destruction), famine and pestilence: the ninth, retribution by the sword and flight in terror: the tenth, crashing thunder and destructive earthquakes.[3]

XXXI.   Then will I sound the trumpet from the air, and I will send

[5] Lit. 'and receiving those who turn to me'. JK 'and receiving and turning to me in repentance'.   [6] Lit. 'know'.
[7] Lit. 'Go to your lot'. JK read verses 21 and 22 'See, Abraham, what you have seen: hear what you have heard *and* what you have known. Go to my lot'. K then adds a brief summary of what has gone before.

[1] Lit. 'starvation of the world *and* their generation'.
[2] Lit. 'wild animals will be their grave'.
[3] Lit. 'the tenth, thunder and voices and earthquakes for destruction'.

2 my Elect One, with a full measure¹ of all my² power. And he shall
summon my people *who are* despised among the heathen; *and* those
who have reviled them and have had dominion over them in the
3 *present* age will I burn with fire. And I will give those who have
4 poured scorn on me to the scorn of the age to come. For I have
appointed them as food for the fire of hell *and to* fly through the air
unceasingly in the depths beneath the earth.³

¹ Lit. 'having in him an equal measure'.
² J 'his'.
³ Here S ends. J continues 'the worms' full womb. ⁵And those who have done
right, who have chosen *to do* my will, who have openly kept **my** commandments,
shall see *them* there', and K 'the wombs filled with the worms fruit. ⁵And those who
have openly kept my commandments shall see in them those who have done right,
who have chosen *to do* my will'. Both J and K continue further '⁶And they shall
rejoice with joy at the destruction of the remainder (lit. 'the men who remain'), who
pursued idols and murder. ⁷For they shall rot in the womb of the cunning worm
Azazil, and they shall burn in the fire of Azazil's tongue. ⁸For I hoped they might
come to me, but they would not; and they gave their praises to a foreigner and joined
themselves to him, for whom they were not intended, and forsook the mighty Lord
(lit. 'ruler'). XXXII. ¹*And* so, Abraham, listen and understand (lit. 'hear and see').
²Behold, your seventh generation will go out with you into a foreign land, and *a
foreign people* will enslave and afflict them, for one hour of the ungodly age. ³But the
people they will be subject to will I judge'. K then adds '⁴And the Lord said this
also, Listen, Abraham, to what I have told you about what will happen to your race
in the last days. ⁵And Abraham heard what God had said and pondered it'.

THE TESTAMENT OF
ABRAHAM

INTRODUCTION

The Testament is known from more than thirty Greek MSS, which contain a variety of legends, lives of saints, and other hagiographical material, and date from the 13th to the 17th cents. It is known also from several versions – Coptic (Bohairic), Arabic, Ethiopic, Slavonic, and Rumanian.

The Greek MSS are clearly divisible into two distinct recensions – the longer (= A) and the shorter (= B); and these recensions are distinct in the sense that they represent different arrangements of what is frequently different material, and there are no reasons for thinking either that B is an abridgement of A or that A is an expansion of B. The question to what extent the versions support one or other of these recensions admits of no easy answer. Thus, the Coptic follows neither exactly: it is on the whole much closer to B, but some details in it, which are absent from B, show resemblances to material contained in A. The Rumanian inclines towards A, although it is by no means identical with it. The Slavonic, on the other hand, inclines very definitely towards B, though the situation here is complicated by the fact that, as so often with Slavonic texts, a number of different 'inner-Slavonic' recensions have to be reckoned with. Of the Arabic and Ethiopic (which appears to have been made from the Arabic) there are no printed editions; but from what is known of the Arabic it would seem that it, like the Slavonic, also inclines towards B, though again with considerable variations. So also the Ethiopic.

James in his edition printed the Greek text of both recensions one after the other, using six MSS for A and three for B. Vassiliev printed only the text of the A recension, relying on a single MS (Cod. Vind. theol. 237 = James's E). The Greek text printed opposite Stone's English translation is a photographic reproduction of James's text of both recensions. Our own translation follows the A recension, except that four passages which are of more than

ordinary interest and which are lacking in A, have been added
from B. These passages will be found in chaps. vii, xi, xii, and xiii;
and they are distinguished by a heavy vertical line in the left-hand
margin.

About the date and place of origin of the Testament opinions
have varied. James styled it 'another fragment of early popular
Christian literature' and suggested that it was written as early as
the second century (probably in Egypt), that it embodied even
earlier legends, and that it received its present form perhaps in the
ninth or tenth cent.[1] On the other hand, Kohler, Ginzberg, and
Box, all stressed the essentially Jewish character of the work, and
argued in one way or another for a Semitic original, though Box
noted that our present Greek text does not read like a translation:
'The story in its original (Hebrew) form', he wrote, 'probably grew
up in the first half of the first century A.D. . . . This probably formed
the basis of a free Greek version, which was embellished with some
special features (e.g. in the description of the Angel of Death)
which owed their origin to Egypt'.[2] Against this, Schürer saw no
reason for thinking that the story was of Jewish origin, on the
ground that many such legends were invented by Christians.
Bousset-Gressmann were prepared to compromise and regarded
the Testament as an example of Christian adaptation of pre-
existing Jewish legend.[3] More recently, N. Turner has maintained
that James over-emphasized the Christian elements. For Turner
the Testament is Jewish in origin, but written in Greek – in all
probability in Egypt, though rather earlier than James suggested:
it subsequently passed into Christian hands and became very
popular in the Church from the fifth century onwards: Recension B
may reasonably be dated to the third century, while Recension A,
as it stands, cannot be earlier than the fifth or sixth century, and it
may well be very much later. Even more recently, M. Delcor has
argued along much the same lines: the traces of Christian
influence are much fewer and less definite than James and his
followers thought: the original Testament, which lies behind both

---

[1] James, p. 29.

[2] Box, pp. xxviii–xxix.

[3] W. Bousset – H. Gressmann, *Die Religion des Judentums im späthellenistischen Zeitalter*[3] (Tübingen, 1926), p. 45.

recensions, was a Jewish work incorporating a variety of traditions, some traceable to the Septuagint, some paralleled in the Palestinian Targum; and it was written in Egypt, perhaps by a member of the sect of the Therapeutae, about the beginning of the Christian era.

As was pointed out in the Introduction to the Apocalypse,[4] both the pseudo-Athanasian Synopsis and the Stichometry of Nicephorus mention 'Abraham' in their lists of apocryphal books; but whether they are referring to the Apocalypse, or to the Testament, or to some other work bearing Abraham's name and now lost, it is impossible to say. What patristic evidence there is is equally ambiguous. Of the nine MSS used by James, four definitely give 'The Testament of Abraham' as the title, and in three of the others the word 'Testament' occurs at some point in more elaborate titles; but of the remaining two MSS, one entitles the work 'The Narrative ($\Delta\iota\acute{\eta}\gamma\eta\sigma\iota\varsigma$) concerning the Life and Death of the righteous Abraham', and the other entitles it 'The Account ($\Lambda\acute{o}\gamma o\varsigma$) concerning the Death of Abraham'. Among the versions, the Slavonic calls it simply, 'The Death of Abraham', the Rumanian 'The Life and Death of our father Abraham', while the Coptic-Arabic-Ethiopic tradition (in which the Testaments of Abraham, Isaac, and Jacob, figure as a trilogy) introduces Abraham with a short preface explaining that what follows is an account of 'the going forth from the body of our holy fathers, the three patriarchs, Abraham, Isaac, and Jacob', and goes on to describe it as a 'homily' or 'discourse' of Athanasius, adding that Athanasius had discovered the substance of it in ancient apostolic writings.

In the light of these facts we cannot assume either that 'Testament' was the work's original title, or that it was widely known as a 'Testament' in the early Church. In any event, little attempt seems to have been made to make it look like one. The normal 'Testament' professes to be a record of its hero's last words of instruction and command, delivered in the first person to his family circle gathered round him. But the Testament of Abraham makes no such profession. Instead it provides a plain, factual,

---

[4] See above p. 363.

account of the events which led up to Abraham's death, written in the third person. In the circumstances, some such title as 'The Narrative of the Death of Abraham' would seem very much more suitable.

But whatever may have been the original title of the Testament and by whatever titles it may have been known subsequently, the existence of the versions is clear proof of its popularity in certain areas in the Church from the beginning of the mid-patristic period onwards. What is perhaps remarkable is that there is no clear testimony to its existence previously. The absence of a Latin version presumably indicates that it was not as popular in the West as it was elsewhere.

BIBLIOGRAPHY

EDITIONS

Greek

M. R. JAMES, *The Testament of Abraham: The Greek Text now first edited with an Introduction and Notes* (= *TS* II. ii (Cambridge, 1892), pp. 1–130).

A. VASSILIEV, *Anecdota Graeco-Byzantina*, i (Moscow, 1893), pp. 292–308.

Coptic

I. GUIDI, *Il testo copto del Testamento di Abramo* (= *Rendiconti della Reale Accademia dei Lincei: Classe di scienze morali, storiche e filologiche*, Ser. V, ix (Rome, 1900), pp. 157–180).

Slavonic

N. S. TIKHONRAVOV, *Pamyatniki otrechennoi russkoi literatury*, i (St. Petersburg, 1863), pp. 79–90.

G. POLIVKA, 'Die apokryphische Erzählung vom Tode Abrahams' in *Archiv für slavische Philologie*, xviii (1896), pp. 112–125.

Rumanian

M. GASTER, *The Apocalypse of Abraham: From the Roumanian Text, Discovered and Translated* (= *Transactions of the Society of Biblical Archaeology*, ix (London, 1893), pp. 195–226).

TRANSLATIONS

English

W. A. CRAIGIE, *The Testament of Abraham* (= *Ante-Nicene Christian Library, Additional Volume* (Edinburgh, 1897), pp. 183–201) – a translation of both Greek recensions arranged in parallel columns.

G. H. BOX, *The Testment of Abraham: Translated from the Greek Text with Introduction and Notes* (= S.P.C.K., *Translations of Early Documents*; London, 1927) – a translation of both Greek recensions.

M. E. STONE, *The Testament of Abraham: The Greek Recensions translated* (= *SBL Texts and Translations*, 2: *Pseudepigrapha Series*, 2; Missoula, 1972).

G. MACRAE, 'The Coptic Testament of Abraham' in *Studies on the Testament of Abraham* (ed. G. W. E. NICKLESBURG, Jr – as below), pp. 327–340.

W. E. BARNES, 'Extracts from the Testament of Abraham' in M. R. JAMES, *The Testament of Abraham* . . . (= *TS* II. ii (Cambridge, 1892), pp. 135–139) – from the Arabic.

W. LESLAU, 'The Testament of Abraham' in *Falasha Anthology: Translated from Ethiopic Sources with an Introduction* (= *Yale Judaica Series*, vol. vi (New Haven, 1951), pp. 92–102 and 176–180).

D. S. COOPER and H. B. WEBER, 'The Church Slavonic Testament of Abraham' in *Studies on the Testament of Abraham* (ed. G. W. E. NICKLESBURG, Jr. – as below), pp. 301–326.

M. GASTER, as above – from the Rumanian.

French

M. DELCOR, *Le Testament d'Abraham: Introduction, traduction du texte grec et commentaire de la recension grecque longue, suivi de la traduction des Testaments d'Abraham, d'Isaac et de Jacob d'après les versions orientales* (= *SVTP* 2; Leiden; 1973) – the translations of the two Greek recensions are by Delcor himself, the translation of the Coptic is by M. Chaîne, that of the Arabic by M. Chaîne and P. Marçais, and that of the Ethiopic by M. Chaîne and A. Caquot.

German

P. REISSLER, *AjSaB*[2], pp. 1091–1103 – a translation of the shorter Greek recension.

E. JANNSEN in *JSh-rZ* III.2 (1975), pp. 193–256 – a translation of both Greek recensions in parallel columns.

E. ANDERSSON, *Sphinx*, vi (Uppsala, 1903), pp. 220–236 – from the Coptic.

GENERAL

M. DELCOR, as above.

A.-M. DENIS, *IPGAT*, pp. 31–37.

C. W. FISHBURNE, 'I Corinthians iii. 10–15 and the Testament of Abraham' in *NTS* xvii (October 1970), pp. 109–115.

L. GINZBERG, art 'Abraham, Testament of' in *JE* i (New York, 1901), pp. 93–96.

—— , *The Legends of the Jews*, i (Philadelphia, 1909), pp. 299–306 and v (Philadelphia, 1925), pp. 266–267.

K. KOHLER, 'The Pre-Talmudic Haggada. II. The Apocalypse of Abraham and its Kindred' in *JQR* vii (1895), pp. 581–606.

G. W. E. NICKELSBURG, Jr, (ed.) *Studies on the Testament of Abraham* (= *SBL Septuagint and Cognate Studies*, 6; Missoula, 1976).

P. RIESSLER, *AjSaB*[2], pp. 1332–1333.

E. SCHÜRER, *GjVZJC*[4] iii, pp. 338–339.

É. TURDEANU, 'Notes sur la tradition littéraire du *Testament d'Abraham*' in *Silloge bizantina in onore di Silvio Giuseppe Mercati* (= *Studi Bizantini e Neoellenici*, ix; Rome, 1957), pp. 405–410.

N. TURNER, 'The "Testament of Abraham": Problems in Biblical Greek' in *NTS* i (1955), pp. 219–223.

H. WEINEL in *EUX*, pp. 170–172.

I. Now Abraham had lived out his life's span of nine hundred and
2 ninety-five years. All the years of his life he had lived in peace,
3 gentleness, and righteousness. He was, moreover, very hospitable;[1] for he pitched his tent at the crossroads by the oak of
Mamre and welcomed everyone, rich and poor, kings and rulers,
the maimed and the weak, friends and strangers, neighbours and
4 travellers. And the pious, all-holy, righteous, and hospitable Ab-
5 raham made them *all* welcome without distinction. But the bitter
cup of death, which is universal and inevitable, and life's uncertain
6 end, overtook even him. So it came about that the Lord God
summoned his archangel Michael and said to him, Prince
7 Michael! Go down to Abraham and tell him about his death, so
8 that he can set his affairs in order. For I have blessed him as the
stars of heaven and as the sand of the sea shore: throughout his life
and in his many business concerns he has prospered exceedingly;
9 and he is very rich indeed. He has been righteous beyond all men in
10 every good deed, hospitable and loving to the end of his days. Go,
archangel Michael, to Abraham, my well-loved friend, and inform
11 him about his death. Give him this assurance, You are going now
to leave this vain world: you are going to forsake *your* body, and
amid blessings[2] come to your Lord.

II. The Prince left God's presence and went down to Abraham at
2 the oak of Mamre. And he found the righteous Abraham in the
field nearby, assisting with the yokes of oxen that did the ploughing, together with the sons of Masek, and with others of his
3 servants, twelve in number.[1] The Prince Michael was approaching, when lo, Abraham saw him in the distance looking like a most
4 handsome soldier. So Abraham got up and went to meet him, as it
5 was his custom to go out and welcome every stranger. But the
Prince welcomed him first and said, Greetings, most honourable
father, God's righteous chosen one,[2] the Heavenly One's true
6 friend! Abraham said to the Prince, Greetings, most honourable

---

[1] Lit. 'The righteous one was very hospitable'.
[2] Or 'among the company of the good'. Lit. 'in good *things*' or 'in good *men*'.

[1] Recension B adds 'Abraham looked very old, and he was holding his son in his
arms'.   [2] Lit. 'soul'.

soldier, *whose face* shines like the sun and *whose form is* more handsome than any of the sons of men: you are welcome indeed!

7 But I must ask your Presence, what is the secret of your youthful

8 bloom? Tell me, I beg you,[3] where *do you come* from, what army *do you belong to*, and what is the purpose of your Grace's journey that

9 you have come here?[4] And the Prince replied, I come, righteous

10 Abraham, from a[5] great city. I have been sent by the great king *of that city* to arrange for the departure[6] of a true friend of his; for the

11 king is calling for him. And Abraham said, Come sir! Come with

12,13 me to my field. The Prince replied, I *will* come. They went to the

14 field where the ploughing was going on and sat down to talk. And Abraham said to his servants, the sons of Masek, Go to the stable.[7]

15 And fetch two good-natured and gentle horses, that have been

16 broken in, for me and this *our* guest to ride on. But the Prince said, No, my lord Abraham: let them not fetch horses, for I never ride on

17 a four-footed beast.[8] My king is indeed rich, with great commercial interests; and he has every kind of man and animal at his com-

18,19 mand. But I myself never ride on a four-footed beast.[8] So, righte-ous one,[2] let us make our way to your house, without fuss, on foot.

20 And Abraham said, Very well: so let it be!

III. And as they were going from the field towards his house, a cypress tree[1] by the roadside cried out with a human voice at God's bidding and said, Holy, Holy, Holy, is the Lord God who calls to

2 himself those who love him. Abraham said nothing,[2] supposing the

3 Prince had not heard the tree's voice. And when they came to the

4 house they sat down in the court. And Isaac saw the angel's face and said to Sarah his mother, My lady mother, the man sitting with my father Abraham is no member of the race that dwells on

---

[3] Lit. 'Tell me, your suppliant'.

[4] Lit. 'and from what road has your beauty arrived'.

[5] Lit. 'the'.

[6] Or 'to take the place'. Lit. 'to procure the succession'.

[7] Lit. 'the herd of horses'.

[8] Lit. 'because I refrain from this – *namely*, from ever sitting on a four-footed beast'.

[1] In Recension B the tree is 'like a tamarisk'.

[2] Lit. 'Abraham hid the mystery'.

5 earth. And Isaac ran out and welcomed him respectfully, falling at
6 the spirit[3]'s feet. The spirit[3] blessed him and said, The Lord God
   will graciously grant you his promise which he made to your father
   Abraham and his descendants, and he will also graciously grant
7 you your father's and mother's dear prayer. And Abraham said to
   his son Isaac, Isaac, my child, draw some water from the well and
   bring it to me in a basin, so that we can wash *our* guest's feet; for he
8 has come to us after a long journey and is tired. So Isaac ran to the
9 well, drew water in the basin, and brought it to them. Abraham got
   up and washed the Prince Michael's feet; and he[4] was much moved
10 and wept over the stranger. Isaac saw his father weeping, and he
11 wept too. And the Prince saw them weeping, and he also wept with
12 them. And the Prince's tears fell onto the basin, into the water of
13 the bowl, and became precious stones. When Abraham saw the
   wonder he was astonished, and he took the stones surreptitiously
   and said nothing[5] and kept the matter to himself.

IV. Then Abraham said to his son Isaac, Go, my beloved son, to
2 the dining-room and make it festive. Make up two couches for us
   there, one for me and one for this man, who is our guest to-day; and
   see that there is there a seat for two, a lamp-stand, and a table full
3 of good things. Make the room festive, my son: lay out the napkins
4 and the purple cloths and the silk. Burn every *kind of* costly and
   precious incense; and bring in sweet-smelling plants from the
5 garden and fill our house with them. Light seven oil lamps, so that
   we may make merry, because this guest of ours to-day deserves
   more honour than kings and governors: his very appearance is
6 superior to that of all other men. So Isaac set everything in excel-
7 lent order. And Abraham took the Prince Michael and went up to
8 the dining-room. Both of them took their seats on the couches, and
   Isaac[1] brought forward *the* table full of good things *and put it*
9 between them. Then the Prince got up and went outside, as if
   wanting to relieve himself; and he went up to heaven in the
10 twinkling of an eye. He stood before God and said to him,

---

[3] Lit. 'the incorporeal one'.
[4] Lit. 'Abraham'.   [5] Lit. 'and hid the mystery'.

[1] Lit. 'he'.

Sovereign Lord, thy Majesty must know that I cannot make
11 mention of *his* death to that righteous man. For I have never seen
upon earth a man like him – merciful, hospitable, righteous, trusty,
12 religious, *and* incapable of doing anything that is evil.[2] So now thou
13 knowest, Lord, that I cannot make mention of *his* death. But the
Lord replied, Go down, Prince Michael, to my friend Abraham;
14 and whatever he tells you, do it. Whatever he eats, eat *it* also with
15 him. I will send forth my Holy Spirit upon his son Isaac, and I will
put into Isaac's mind the thought[3] of his death, so that he sees his
16 father's death in a dream. Isaac will recount what he has seen and
17 you shall interpret *it*. And *then Abraham* himself will recognize that
18 his end *is near*. The Prince said, Lord, all heavenly spirits are
without bodies and neither eat nor drink, but this man has laid a
table for me with an abundance of every kind of earthly and
19 perishable dainty. What now, Lord, am I to do? How am I to see he
20 does not notice when I am sitting at the same table with him? The
21 Lord said, Go down to him, and have no anxiety on this score. For
while you are sitting with him I will send upon you an all-
devouring spirit, and it will consume from your hands and through
your mouth everything that is on the table; *and* make merry with
22 him in every way. Only you must interpret properly the meaning of
the vision, so that Abraham can recognize Death's reaping-hook
and life's uncertain end, and so make a settlement of all his goods.
23 For I have blessed him above the sand of the sea and as the stars of
heaven.

V.   The Prince then went down to Abraham's house and took his
2 seat with him at the table; and Isaac waited on them. When the
meal was over Abraham said his customary prayer, and the
3 archangel prayed with him. Each was resting upon his couch, and
Isaac said to his father, Father, I would like to stay[1] with you in this
room, to listen to your talk; for I think I should gain much profit
4 from what this excellent man has to say.[2] But Abraham said, No,

----

[2] Lit. 'abstaining from every evil deed'.
[3] Lit. 'mention' Cp. v. 6; vii. 22.

[1] Lit. 'rest'.
[2] Lit. 'for I love to hear the excellence of the conversation of this all-virtuous man'.

my son: go to your *own* room and rest on your *own* bed: we do not
5 want to be a burden to this man. Then Isaac, after being blessed by
them and having blessed them, went off to his own room and lay
6 down upon his bed. And God put the thought[3] of death into Isaac's
mind by means of dreams; and about the third hour of the night
7 Isaac woke up. He got up from his bed and went in great haste to
8 the room where his father and the archangel were sleeping. When
he got to the door he cried out, saying, Father Abraham, get up and
open *the door* for me quickly, so that I can come in and put my arms
9 round you and kiss you before they take you away from me. So
10 Abraham got up and opened *the door* for him. Isaac went in and put
11 his arms round him and began to weep loudly. Abraham was in
consequence much moved and wept loudly himself in sympathy.
2,13 When the Prince saw them weeping, he wept also. Now Sarah was
in her tent, and when she heard them weeping, she came running
14 to them and found them weeping in one another's arms. And Sarah
said with tears, My lord Abraham, what does this weeping mean?
Tell me, my lord: this brother, who is our guest to-day, has he
brought you news about your nephew Lot, that he is dead, and is
15 that why you are making this lamentation? The Prince replied and
said to her, No, sister Sarah, it is not as you say. Your son Isaac, I
think, had a dream, and he came to us weeping; and when we saw
him, we were much moved, and we wept too.

VI. And Sarah recognized something in the way the Prince spoke[1]
and realized immediately that the speaker was an angel of the
2 Lord. So Sarah made signs to Abraham to go outside the door;[2]
and she said to him, My lord Abraham, do you know who this
3,4 man is? Abraham said, I do not. And Sarah said, My lord, you
remember the three heavenly beings who were our guests in our
tent by the oak of Mamre, when you killed the calf without blemish
5 and prepared a meal for them? When the meat had been eaten, the
calf rose up again and joyfully sucked from its mother. You
remember, my lord Abraham, do you not, that they gave us the

---

[3] Lit. 'mention'. Cp. iv. 15; vii. 22.

[1] Lit. 'And Sarah heard the distinction of the Prince's conversation'.
[2] Lit. 'to go to the door outside'.

6 promise of a child, Isaac? This is one of those three holy men. And
Abraham said, What you say, Sarah, is true. Praise and glory be to

7 God the Father.[3] Indeed, when I was washing his feet in the bowl
of the washing-basin late this evening, I said to myself, These are

8 the feet of *one of* the three men that I washed then. And later on his

9 tears fell into the basin and turned into precious stones. And
Abraham took the stones[4] from the fold of his cloak and gave them

10 to Sarah saying, If you do not believe me, now look at these. And
Sarah took them and kissed *them*[5] and fondled *them*,[5] saying, Glory

11 be to God who shows his wonders to us. You may be certain, my
lord Abraham, that we are to receive a revelation about something,
whether for evil or for good.

VII. And Abraham left Sarah and went back inside the room, and

2 he said to Isaac, Come, dear son: tell me the truth. What was it that
you saw, and what happened to you that you came to us in such a

3 hurry? And Isaac made answer and began, *In my sleep* to-night, my

4 lord, I saw the sun and moon over my head. *The sun* encircled me

5 with its rays and gave me light.[1] And while I was looking on at this
and rejoicing at it, I saw heaven wide open; and I saw a brilliant[2]
man coming down out of heaven, who shone more brightly than

6 seven suns. And that man, who was like the sun, came and took the
sun away from my head, and he went back into the heavens, where
he had come from; and I was very upset, because he had taken the

7 sun from me. And after a little, while I was still upset and ill at ease,
I saw that man leave heaven a second time; and he took away the

8, 9 moon from my head as well. And I wept bitterly. And I implored
that brilliant man and said, No, my lord, please do not take my
glory from me: have pity on me and hear me! Even if you must take

10 the sun from me, at least leave me the moon. And he said, You
must let them be taken up to the King above, for he wills *to have*

11 them there. And he took them from me; but the rays he left upon
me.

---

³ Lit. 'Glory and praise from God and Father'.
⁴ Lit. 'And he took them'.   ⁵ Or '*him*'.

¹ Lit. '. . . the sun and the moon over my head, and encircling me with its rays and
giving me light'.   ² Lit. 'light-bearing'. Cp. xii. 7; xiv. 10; xvi. 16.

12 The sun and the moon and the stars mourned, saying, Do not
13 take away our glorious might. And that radiant man answered and
said to me, Do not weep because I have taken the light of your
house; for he has been removed from toils to rest, and from a
14 humble state to an exalted one. He is being lifted[3] from adversity
15 into prosperity: he is being lifted[3] from darkness into light. And I
16 said to him, I beg you sir, take the rays with him as well. And he
said to me, There are twelve hours in the day, and then *will* I take
17 all the rays. And while the radiant man was speaking I saw the sun
of my house going up into heaven; but I saw that crown no more.
And that sun was like you, father.

18 And the Prince said, Listen, rightous Abraham. The sun your
boy has seen is you, his father; and the moon, similarly, is his
mother Sarah. The brilliant man, who came down out of heaven,
he is a man sent from God, and he is about to take your righteous
19 soul away from you. For you must realize, most honoured
Abraham, that you are now about to leave your earthly life behind
20 *you* and depart to God. Then said Abraham to the Prince, This is
the most astonishing thing I have ever heard![4] So it is you, is it, who
21 are to take my soul away from me? The Prince said to him, I am
22 Michael, the Prince, who stands in the presence of God, I have
been sent to you in order to put into your mind the thought[5] of
23 death. After that I shall go back to him, as we were commanded.
24 And Abraham said, Now I know that you are an angel of the Lord
and you have been sent to take away my soul: yet I will not follow
25 you. But do whatever he commands.

VIII. And when he heard what Abraham said, the Prince at once
2 disappeared. And he went up to heaven and stood before God and
gave an account of everything he had seen in Abraham's house.
3 Furthermore, the Prince also told *his* Lord, Thy friend Abraham
also says this, I will not follow you; but do whatever he commands.
4 Is there then anything, Almighty Lord, that thy Glory and immortal
5 Majesty now commands? And God said to the Prince Michael, Go
6 down to my friend Abraham once again and tell him, Thus says the

---

[3] Lit. 'They are lifting him'.
[4] Lit. 'O, latest wonder of wonders'.
[5] Lit. 'mention'. Cp. iv. 15; v. 6.

Lord your God, who has brought you into the land of promise, who has blessed you above the sand of the sea and above the stars of heaven, and who granted you the child Isaac, born of the barren
7 Sarah, in your old age: I promise you I will bless you in every way
8 and make your descendants too many to be counted. I will give you everything you can ask of me; for I am the Lord your God and there
9 is none other but me. But why are you resisting me, and why are
10 you distressed? Tell me. And why are you resisting my archangel
11 Michael? Do you not know that all *men who are descended* from Adam
12 and Eve have died? Not one of the prophets has escaped death: no ruler has ever been immortal: none of your ancestors has escaped
13 death's mystery. All have died: all have been received in Hades: all
14 have been gathered by the reaping-hook of Death. But to you[1] I did
15 not send Death. I did not allow any deadly disease to come near you: I did not agree that Death's reaping-hook should visit you;
16 nor did I permit the nets of Hades to enfold you. I willed that no
17 evil should befall you at any time. Instead, I have sent you my Prince Michael for *your* good comfort, to inform you of your departure from the world, so that you can make arrangements about your house and all your goods, and so that you can pro-
18 nounce a blessing over your dear son Isaac. And you must know
19 that I have done this out of no desire to cause you pain. Why, then,
20 did you say to my Prince, I will not follow you? Why did you say
21 this? Are you not aware that if I were to allow Death to come to you, then I could indeed see whether you would come or not?

IX. After receiving the Lord's instructions the Prince went down
2 to Abraham. And when the righteous *man* saw him, he fell on his face to the ground as *if he were* dead; and the Prince told him
3 everything he had heard from the Most High. Then the pious and righteous Abraham got up and threw himself at the spirit'[1]s feet
4 and with many tears made supplication to him, saying, I implore you, Prince of the powers on high, since you yourself have deigned to come to me, your sinful and unworthy servant, I beg you now to
5 take a message for me yet once more to the Most High. Tell him,

---

[1] Lit. 'upon you'.

[1] Lit. 'the incorporeal one'.

Abraham thy slave has this to say, Lord, Lord, in every deed and
word when I besought thee, thou hast heard me and hast brought
6 to completion everything I planned. And now, O Lord, I would
not resist thy might, for I know indeed that I am not immortal but
7 must die. And so, just as all things yield to thine ordinance, and
shudder and tremble in the presence of thy power, I also am full of
8 fear. Yet one request I would make of thee; and now, O Sovereign
9 Lord, listen to my prayer. I would, while yet in this body, see the
whole earth and all created things, which thou didst establish by a
10 single word. When I have seen these, then will I depart from life
without regret.

1, 12   So the Prince went away again and stood before God. And he
told him everything, saying, Thy friend Abraham has this to say, I
13 would behold the whole earth in my life *here* before I die. And when
the Most High heard this he gave instructions to the Prince
14 Michael once again. And he said to him, Take a cloud of light and
15 the angels who are in command of the chariots. Then go down and
take the righteous Abraham *and set him* on the cherubim-chariot
and lift him up to the heights[2] of heaven, so that he may see the
whole earth.

X.   And the archangel Michael went down and took Abraham *and
set him* on the cherubim-chariot and lifted him up to the heights[1] of
heaven and acted as his guide on the cloud together with sixty
2 angels. And Abraham went up on the chariot over the entire earth;
3 and Abraham looked out on the world just as it was that day. *He
saw* some men ploughing, others driving wagons: in one place they
were looking after their sheep, elsewhere they were out in the fields,
dancing and making merry and playing the kithara: here they were
in conflict[2] and going to law with one another, there they were
4 weeping and then burying *their* dead. He saw too the newly-
5 married being escorted home. In a word, he saw everything that
6 was happening in the world, both good and evil. So, as Abraham
journeyed, he saw *a group of* swordsmen brandishing *their*
7 sharpened swords in their hands. And Abraham asked the Prince,

---

[2] Lit. 'upper air'.

[1] Lit. 'upper air'.   [2] Lit. 'they were wrestling'.

8 Who are these? And the Prince said, These are thieves, whose
intention it is to commit murder and steal and kill and destroy.
9 And Abraham said, Sir, could you not bid[3] wild beasts come out of
10 the wood and eat them up? And immediately, as he spoke, wild
11 beasts came out of the wood and ate them up. And in another place
he saw a man and a woman in fornication together; and he said,
12 Sir, bid the earth open and swallow them. And the earth was split
13 in two at once and swallowed them. In another place he saw men
breaking into a house and carrying off another man's property;
and he said, Sir, bid fire descend from heaven and consume them.
14 And immediately, as he spoke, fire descended from heaven and
15 consumed them. And there came at once a voice from heaven to the
Prince, saying, Prince Michael, bid the chariot stand still and stop
16 Abraham from seeing the whole of the earth. For if he sees all those
17 who are engaged in sin, he will destroy every living thing. For lo,
18 Abraham has not sinned, and he has no pity for sinners. But I have
made the world, and I have no wish to destroy any of the men I
have created;[4] but I put off the sinner's death until he turns again
19 and lives. Take Abraham up to the first gate of heaven, so that he
may view the judgements and the retributions there, and repent for
the sinners' souls he has destroyed.

XI.   Michael turned the chariot and brought Abraham eastwards
2 to the first gate of heaven. And Abraham saw two ways: the first
way was narrow and restricted and the second broad and spacious.
3 ⟨ And he saw there two gates: one broad gate⟩ across the broad
4 way, and one narrow gate across the narrow way. And outside the
5 two gates there, they saw a man seated on a golden throne. And the
man's appearance was terrifying, like *that* of the Sovereign *Lord*
6 *himself.*[1] And they saw many souls being driven along by angels
and herded through the broad gate; and they saw a few other souls
7 being taken by angels through the narrow gate. And whenever the
wondrous being who was seated on the golden throne saw a few
going in through the narrow gate and many through the broad one,

---

³ Lit. 'Sir, sir, hear my voice and bid'.
⁴ Lit. 'to destroy no one of them'.

¹ So A: D 'the Sovereign Messiah' (or 'Christ'); CE 'our Lord Jesus Christ'.

he[2] at once tore the hair of his head and his beard, and hurled
8 himself from his throne to the ground, weeping and wailing. But
whenever he saw many souls going in through the narrow gate,
then he got up from the ground and he took his seat on his throne
9 rejoicing and exulting with great gladness. And Abraham asked
the Prince, My lord Prince, who is this most wondrous man, who is
decked out with so great a glory, and who at one moment weeps
10 and wails, and at the next rejoices and exults? The spirit[3] made
answer, This is Adam, the first man to be made,[4] who is in so great
11 a glory. He surveys the world, inasmuch as all men owe their origin
12 to him. Whenever he sees many souls going in through the narrow
gate, then he gets up and sits on his throne, rejoicing and exulting
13 with gladness. For this narrow gate is *the gate* of the righteous,
14 which leads to life, and those who go in by it go to Paradise. That is
why the first man[4] Adam rejoices, because he sees souls being
15 saved. And when he sees many souls going in through the broad
gate, then he plucks at the hair of his head and hurls himself to the
16 ground, weeping and wailing bitterly. *It is* because the broad gate
is the gate of sinners, and it leads to destruction and eternal
17 punishment. That is why the first man[4] Adam throws himself[5]
from his throne and weeps and wails at the sinners' destruction,
because those who are perishing are many, whereas those who are
18 being saved are few. For in seven thousand there is scarcely to be
found a single soul who is being saved, *who is* righteous and
undefiled.

19 And Abraham said, He that cannot enter through the narrow
20 gate, can he not enter into life? Then Abraham wept and said, Ah
me! What shall I do? I am a big man,[6] and how can I enter through
the narrow gate, when a youth of fifteen could not get through it?
21 And Michael answered and said to Abraham, Do not be afraid,
father, and do not worry; for you will go through it without
hindrance, and so will all who are like you.

---

[2] Lit. 'that wondrous man'.
[3] Lit. 'The incorporeal one'.
[4] Lit. 'the first-formed'.
[5] Lit. 'Adam falls'.
[6] Lit. 'a man broad in body'.

XII. While he was still speaking,[1] lo, two angels *came*, fiery in
appearance, merciless in purpose, and relentless in expression,
and they were driving ten thousand souls along, beating them
mercilessly with fiery thongs; †and one soul the angel seized†.[2]
2 And they directed all the souls through the broad gate for destruc-
3 tion. So we also followed the angels and came inside that broad
4 gate. Now between the two gates stood a fearsome throne,[3] flashing
5 like fire. On it sat a wondrous man, bright as the sun, like a son of
God; and before him stood a table, all of gold and *covered with* the
6 finest linen, *which shone* like crystal. On the table lay a book, six
cubits thick and ten cubits broad, and on its right and on its left
7 were standing two angels holding paper and pen and ink. In front
of the table sat a brilliant[4] angel holding in his hand a pair of scales.
8 On his left sat a fiery angel, entirely without mercy and relentless,
and in his hand he held a trumpet that contained all-devouring fire
9 inside it, as a means of testing sinners. And while the wondrous
man who sat on the throne was giving his judgements and sentenc-
ing the souls, the two angels on his right and on his left were
10 recording. The *angel* on the right recorded the good deeds, the one
11 on the left the sins. And the angel in front of the table, who held the
pair of scales, weighed the souls, and the fiery angel, who held the
12 fire, put the souls to the test. And Abraham asked the Prince
13 Michael, What is it we are looking at? And the Prince replied,
What you are seeing, holy Abraham, is the judgement and retribu-
14 tion. And lo, the angel who held the soul in his hand *appeared*, and
15 he brought it before the judge. And the judge said to one of the

---

[1] So D. James's text ('While he was yet speaking these things to me') is a
reconstruction based on the untranslatable C. A has 'While he was yet speaking
these things to us' (cp. verse 3), and the Rumanian version 'And while they were
speaking'.

[2] So A. The other MSS vary considerably throughout the verse, though the
general sense is clear, apart from the details of this final clause. However, there can
be no doubt that something very like this must have stood, in the original
text because of the references back, both in verse 14 below and at xiv. 1. Furthermore, in
the parallel passage in the B recension only one angel figures as the driver instead of
two: he is driving sixty thousand souls (not ten thousand); and the soul he is holding
in his hand, whose good deeds and evil deeds are of equal weight, is that of a woman.

[3] So CDE: AB add 'that looked like fearsome crystal'.

[4] Lit. 'light-bearing'. Cp. vii. 5; xiv. 10; xvi. 16.

angels that were waiting on him, Open this book for me and find
16 me the sins of this soul. And when he had opened the book he found
17 that its sins and its good deeds balanced evenly. So he neither gave
it over to the torturers, nor *did he assign it a place among* those who
were being saved, but set it in the middle.

18   And Abraham said to Michael, Sir, is this the angel that takes
19 souls out of their bodies, or is it not? Michael answered and said,
This is Death; and he takes them away to the judgement-place for
20 the judge to pass judgement on them. And Abraham said, My
Lord, I beg you to take me up to the judgement-place, so that I can
21 see for myself how they are judged. Then Michael took Abraham
22 on a cloud and brought him to Paradise. And as he came near the
place where the judge was, the angel appeared and presented a
soul[5] to the judge; and the soul was saying, Have mercy on me,
23 lord. And the judge said, Why should I have mercy on you, when
you yourself had no mercy on your daughter that you had, your
24 own child?[6] Why did you murder her? And *the soul* made answer,
No lord! I am no murderer: my daughter has told lies about me.
, 26 The judge then ordered the writer of the records to come. And lo,
cherubim *came*, carrying two books, and with them was a man of
27 immense size. And he had on his head three crowns: one crown was
higher than the other two; and they were called Crowns of Witness.
28 In his hand the man had a pen of gold; and the judge said to him,
29 Let us have the details of the sin[7] of this soul. And the man opened
one of the books belonging to the cherubim, and he searched for the
30 sin of the woman's soul and found *it*. And the judge said, Wretched
soul! How *can* you say that you have done no murder? Did you not
after your husband's death, go and commit adultery with your
31 daughter's husband and kill your daughter?[8] And he convicted her
of other sins as well, all that she had committed since she was a
32 child. When the woman heard this she cried out, saying, Alas!
While I was in the world I forgot all the sins that I committed, but
33 here they are not forgotten. Then they took her and handed her
over to the torturers.

[5] Lit. 'that soul'.
[6] Lit. 'the fruit of your womb'.
[7] Lit. 'Substantiate the sins'.
[8] Lit. 'and kill her'.

XIII. And Abraham said, My lord Prince, who is this wondrous
judge, and who are these recording angels? And who is the angel
like the sun, who holds the scales, and who is the fiery angel who
holds the fire? And the Prince said, Most holy Abraham, do you see
the terrifying man who is sitting on the throne? He is the son of the
first man[1] Adam, and is called Abel, and he was killed by the
wicked Cain. He sits here to judge every creature,[2] examining both
righteous and sinners, because God has said, It is not I who judge
you, but by man shall every man be judged. For this reason he has
committed judgement to him, to judge the world until his *own* great
and glorious Coming. And then, righteous Abraham, will follow
the final judgement and retribution, eternal and unchangeable,
which no one will be able to dispute. For all men have their origin
from the first man;[1] and so by his son they are first judged here. At
the second coming they and every spirit and every creature[2] will be
judged by the twelve tribes of Israel.[3] At the third stage they will be
judged by the Sovereign God of all; and then at last will the whole
process reach its end.[4] The sentences will strike terror; and *there
will be* no one to rescind *them*. And so through three tribunals the
judgement of the world will be accomplished and *its* retribution.
(And that is why a matter cannot finally be settled on the evidence
of one or two witnesses but 'on the evidence of three witnesses
every fact[5] must be established'.) The two angels, one on the right
and one on the left, these record the sins and the good deeds. The
one on the right records the good deeds, the one on the left the sins.
The angel who is like the sun, who holds the scales in his hand, he is
the archangel Dokiel: he preserves an honest balance[6] and weighs
the good deeds and the sins with the justice of God. The fiery and
merciless angel, who holds the fire in his hand, he is the archangel
Pyruel, who has power over fire, and he tests men's deeds by fire. If
the fire burns up a man's deed, the angel of judgement takes him at

---

[1] Lit. 'the first-formed'.   [2] Or 'all creation'.

[3] So A: with variation in detail, CDE and the Rumanian read 'At the second
coming they and . . . will be judged by the twelve apostles': B combines both
readings ('At the second coming the twelve tribes of Israel and . . . will be judged by
the apostles').

[4] Lit. 'and then already the end of that judgement *is* near'.

[5] Lit. 'word' or 'thing'.   [6] Lit. '(Dokiel), the just weigher'.

once and carries him off to the sinners' place – a most disagreeable
19 place of punishment. If the fire tests a man's deed and does not
touch it, he is accounted righteous and the angel of righteousness
takes him and carries him up to be saved among the number of the
20 righteous. And so, most righteous Abraham, all things in all men[7]
are tested by fire and scales.

21   This one, who presents the souls is the teacher of heaven and
22 earth, the scribe of righteousness, Enoch. For the Lord sent them
here that the sins and the good deeds of each might be recorded.
23 And Abraham said, But how can Enoch take responsibility for[8] the
souls, since he has not *himself* experienced[9] death? How can he
24 pronounce sentence on all the souls? And Michael said, If he were
to pronounce sentence on them, *his sentence* would not stand. It is
not Enoch's function to sentence: it is the Lord who sentences; and
25 *Enoch's* only function is to write. For Enoch prayed to the Lord,
saying, Lord, I have no wish to sentence souls; in case I might be
26 harsh to any of them. Then said the Lord to Enoch, I shall bid you
write the sins of the soul that makes atonement, and it shall enter
27 into life. But if a soul makes no atonement and does not repent, you
will find its sins in writing, and *that soul* will be sent off to
punishment.

XIV. And Abraham said to the Prince, My lord Prince, the soul
that the angel was holding in his hand, how *is it that* it was
2 condemned to *be set in* the middle? And the Prince said, Listen,
righteous Abraham: *it was* because the judge found its sins and *its*
3 good deeds equal. So he consigned it neither to judgement nor to
4 salvation, until the Judge of all shall come. Abraham said to the
5 Prince, What more does the soul require to be saved? The Prince
answered, If it can come by one good deed more than its sins, it
6 attains salvation. And Abraham said to the Prince, Come, Prince
Michael and let us make intercession on this soul's behalf, and let
7 us see whether God will hear us. And the Prince said, Amen: so let
8 it be! And they made supplication and intercession on the soul's
behalf, and God heard them; and when they got up from their

---

[7] Or 'in every particular'.
[8] Lit. 'bear the burden of'.
[9] Lit. 'seen'.

9   prayer, they did not see the soul standing there. And Abraham said
    to the angel, Where is the soul you were keeping in the middle?
10 And the angel said, It has been saved by your righteous interces-
    sion; and lo, the brilliant[1] angel has taken it and carried it up into
11 Paradise. And Abraham said, I will glorify the name of God Most
12 High and his mercy that is without measure. And Abraham said to
    the Prince, I beg you, archangel, grant me my request, and let us
    beseech the Lord once more and throw ourselves on his compas-
13 sion. And let us entreat his mercy for the souls of the sinners I once
    cursed in malice and sent to their destruction — *those* that the earth
    swallowed up, and the wild beasts tore to pieces, and the fire
14 consumed, because of what I said. Now I realize that I sinned
15 before the Lord our God. Come, Michael, Prince of the powers on
    high: come, let us with tears beseech God to forgive me *my* sin and
16 grant them to me. And the Prince listened to him, and they made
17 supplication before God. When they had been praying for a long
    time, there came a voice from heaven, saying, Abraham,
    Abraham, I have heard your voice and your supplication; and I
18 forgive you *your* sin. And those, whom you imagine I destroyed, I
    have recalled and in my mercy[2] brought them *back* to life; because
19 for a time I have requited them in[3] judgement. But those whom I
    destroy while they are alive on earth, I will not requite in death.[4]

XV. The voice of the Lord said also to the Prince, Michael,
2   Michael, my minister, return Abraham to his house. For lo, his end
3   is near and the span of his life complete. He will thus be able to set
    everything in order; and after that, take him and bring him up to
4   me. And the Prince turned the chariot and the cloud and brought
5   Abraham to his house. And *Abraham* went into his dining-room
6   and sat upon his couch. And Sarah his wife came and flung her
    arms round the spirit's feet,[1] as if she were a suppliant, and said, I

---

[1]   Lit. 'light-bearing'. Cp. vii. 5; xii. 7; xvi. 16.
[2]   Lit. 'through *my* extreme goodness'.
[3]   Lit. 'into'.
[4]   The text is very uncertain at this point. A omits the last clause in verse 18
altogether and also has variants in verse 19: B reads almost completely differently
throughout.

[1]   Lit. 'the feet of the incorporeal one'.

thank you, sir, for bringing back my lord Abraham; for lo, we
7 thought he had been taken up from us. And his son Isaac also came
8 and put his arms round his neck. And so too all his male and female
slaves assembled about Abraham and embraced him, praising
9 God. And the spirit[2] said to him, Listen, righteous Abraham,
behold, your wife Sarah; and behold, your beloved son Isaac; and
10 behold, your men-servants and maid-servants all around you. Set
everything you have in order, because the day is at hand when you
11 are to leave *your* body and go once again to the Lord. And Abraham
12 said, Has the Lord said *this*, or are you saying it yourself? And the
Prince said, Listen, righteous Abraham: the Sovereign *Lord* has
13 commanded *it*, and I am telling you *so*. And Abraham said, I will
14 not follow you. And when the Prince heard that answer he left
Abraham immediately and went up into the heavens and stood
15 before God Most High. And he said, Lord Almighty, behold, I
have listened to everything thy friend Abraham has said to thee,
16 and I have granted his request. I have shown him *the extent of* thy
17 dominion, and all the land and sea that is under heaven. Judgement and retribution have I shown him by means of cloud and
19 chariot. And yet again he says, I will not follow you. And the Most
High said to the angel, Does my friend Abraham really say again, I
20 will not follow you? And the archangel said, Lord Almighty, this is
21 what he says. And I would not touch him because he has been thy
friend from the beginning and has done everything that is pleasing
in thy sight, and there is no man like him on earth, not even Job,
22 that wondrous man;[3] and that is why I would not touch him. So
may I have instructions, Immortal King, about what should now
be done?

XVI. Then the Most High said, Call Death here to me – *the one* who
2 is called The Shameless Face and the Pitiless Look. And Michael
the spirit[1] went away and said to Death, Come: the Sovereign of
3 creation, the Immortal King is calling for you. When Death heard

---

[2] Lit. 'the incorporeal one'.
[3] So D (and, it would seem, the original text). A reads 'Jacob' for 'Job': B omits
the negative: CE om. the entire clause.

[1] Lit. 'the incorporeal one'.

this he was much alarmed and shivered and shook; and he came with great trepidation and stood before the invisible Father, shivering, groaning, and trembling, as he awaited his Sovereign's

4 bidding. And the invisible God said to Death, Come, you *most*
5 bitter and savage name in *all* the world ! Hide your ferocity, cover up your corruption, put off your asperity[2] from you, and put on your beauty and all your glory, and go down to my friend
6, 7 Abraham. Take him and bring him to me. Yet I tell you now not to frighten him, but win him with gentle guile, for he is my own true
8 friend. Death listened and went out from the presence of the Most High; and he put on a most brilliant robe and made his face shine
9 like the sun. He appeared[3] more handsome and beautiful than any human, having assumed an archangel's form, and his cheeks
10, 11 flashed with fire. And so he went off to Abraham. Now the righteous Abraham had left his room and was sitting under the trees of Mamre, his chin on his hand, waiting for the archangel Michael to come *back*, when lo, there came in his direction a pleasant smell
12 and a flashing light. And Abraham turned round and saw Death
13 coming towards him in great glory and beauty. And Abraham got
14 up to meet him, for he thought he was God's Prince. And when Death saw him, he bowed to him and said, Greetings, honoured Abraham, righteous soul, true friend of God Most High, and
15 companion of the holy angels. And Abraham said to Death, Greet-
16 ings to you. You are like the sun, and you shine as does the sun:
17 most glorious helper, brilliant,[4] wondrous man! Whence comes
18 your Splendour to us? Who are you? And whence come you? Death said, Most righteous Abraham, lo, I tell you the truth: I am the
19 bitter cup of death. Abraham said to him, No: you are the world's paragon of loveliness: you are the glory and the beauty of angels and of men: you are more nobly formed than any form there is; and
20 *yet* you say you are the bitter cup of death. Should you not rather
21 say, I am more nobly formed than nobility itself?[5] And Death said, No: I am telling you the truth: *it is* that very name which God has
22 given me that I am telling you. And Abraham said, Why have you
23, 24 come here? And Death said, I have come for your holy soul. So

---

[2] Lit. 'bitterness'.   [3] Lit. 'He became'.
[4] Lit. 'light-bearing'. Cp. vii. 5; xii. 7; xiv. 10.
[5] Lit. 'than every good thing'.

Abraham said, I understand what you are saying; but I will not
25 follow you. And Death was silent and answered him not a word.

1, 2 **XVII.** Then Abraham got up and went into his house. But Death
3 followed him all the way. And Abraham went up to his room; but
4 Death also went up with him. And Abraham lay down on his
5 couch; and Death came and sat at his feet. And Abraham said, Go
6 away, go away from me; for I want to rest on my couch. Death said,
7 I will not go away until I take your spirit from you. Abraham said
to him, By God, who is immortal, I bid you tell me the truth: are
8 you Death? Death said to him, I am Death: I am the one who
9 destroys the world. And Abraham said, Since you are Death, I
pray you, tell me whether you come to all men in this way, in fine
10 form and glory and beauty like this? And Death said, No, my lord
Abraham: your righteous deeds and the boundless ocean of your
hospitality and the immensity of your love of God have become a
11 crown upon my head. I approach the righteous in beauty, and very
quietly, and with gentle guile; but sinners I approach, stinking of
corruption, with the greatest possible ferocity and asperity,[1]
12 and an expression that is both savage and without mercy. And
Abraham said, I pray you, listen to me, and show me your ferocity,
13 and all *your* corruption and asperity.[1] And Death said, You could
14 not see my ferocity, most righteous Abraham. And Abraham said,
Yes: I could see all your ferocity, because of the name of the living
15 God; for the power of my God who is in heaven is with me. Then
Death stripped himself of all his radiance and beauty, and all the
glory and sun-like appearance he had assumed, and he put on a
16 tyrant's robe. And he gave himself a threatening look, more savage
than any kind of wild beast and fouler than any foul thing known to
17 man.[2] He displayed to Abraham seven fiery dragons' heads and
18 fourteen faces of blazing fire and great ferocity – one dark-looking
face, one viper-like of the blackest kind, one a most horrible cliff,
one fiercer than an asp, one of a fearsome lion, and one of a horned
19 viper and a basilisk. And he displayed also the face of a fiery sword,
a face bearing a sword, a face of dreadful flashing lightning, and a
20 sound of fearful thunder. Moreover, he displayed another face of a

---

[1] Lit. 'bitterness'.
[2] Lit. 'fouler than all foulness'.

ferocious raging sea, and a fiercely boiling river, and a terrifying
21 three-headed dragon, and a cup of poisons mixed together. In
short, he displayed to him ferocity in plenty, asperity[1] beyond
endurance, and every kind of deadly disease – the smell of death
22 hung about it all.[3] And so great was the asperity[1] and ferocity
displayed that *the* men-servants and maid-servants died, in
23 number about seven thousand. And even the righteous Abraham
himself came to the brink of death,[4] and his spirit failed him.[5]

XVIII.　　And when the all-holy Abraham had seen all this in this
way, he said to Death, I beg you, all-destructive Death, hide your
ferocity, and put on the beauty and the form you had before.
2 Thereupon Death hid his ferocity and put on his beauty he had had
3 before. And Abraham said to Death, Why have you done this? You
have killed all my men-servants and maid-servants: did God send
4 you here to-day for this? And Death said, No, my lord Abraham, it
5 is not as you suggest:[1] it was because of you I was sent here. And
Abraham said to Death, And how then was it that these *servants*
6 died, if the Lord had not given word? And Death said, Believe *me*,
most righteous Abraham, the marvel is that you too were not taken
7 off along with them. I am only telling you the truth when I say that
if the right hand of God had not been with you in that hour, you too
8 would have had to depart this life. And righteous Abraham said, I
realize now that I have come to the brink of death,[2] and my spirit[3]
9 fails me. Nevertheless, I beg you, all-destructive Death, since my
servants have died before their time, come, let us beseech the Lord
our God to hear us and raise up those who perished before their
10, 11 time through your ferocity. And Death said, Amen: so let it be! So
Abraham got up and fell upon his face on the earth in prayer, and
Death with him; and God sent *the* spirit of life upon those who had

---

[3] Lit. '. . . death-bearing disease, as of the smell of death'.
[4] Or 'And righteous Abraham entered the faint of death'. Lit. '. . . came even to
the neglect of death'. Cp. xviii. 8; xx. 12.
[5] Or 'and his breathing began to fail'. Cp. xviii. 8.

[1] Lit. 'say'.
[2] Or 'that I have entered the faint of death'. Lit. '. . . the neglect of death'. Cp.
xvii. 23; xx. 12.
[3] Or 'breath'. Cp. xvii. 23.

12 died, and they were restored to life. So then the righteous Abraham ascribed glory to God.

XIX. And *Abraham* went up to his room and lay down to rest; but
2 Death came and stood before him. And Abraham said to him, Go
3 away from me: I want to rest; for I am exhausted.[1] And Death said,
4 I will not leave you until I take your soul. And Abraham, with a sullen face and angry look, said to Death, Who has ordered you to
5 say this? You are bluffing and saying this on your own; and I will not follow you until the Prince Michael comes to me, and *then* I will
6 go with him. And further,[2] if you want me to follow you, explain to
7 me all your changes of appearance – the seven fiery dragons' heads, and what the face of the cliff *means*, and the ruthless sword, and the great boiling river, and the turbid sea raging furiously.
8 Explain to me also the insufferable thunder and the terrifying lightning, and what the stinking cup of poisons mixed together
9 *means*: explain them all to me. And Death said, Listen righteous Abraham, for seven ages I create havoc in the world and bring all *men* down to Hades: kings and rulers, rich and poor, slaves and free men, I escort to the depths of Hades; and that is why I showed you
10 the seven dragons' heads. The face of fire I showed you because many are burned to death by fire, and *so it is* through the
11 face of fire *that* they see death. The face of the cliff I showed you because many men fall from the top of trees or fearful cliffs and disappear and perish; and *so it is* in the form of a fearful cliff *that*
12 they see death. The face of the sword I showed you because many are killed by the sword in wars; and they see death in *the form of* a
13 sword. The face of the great boiling river I showed you because many are carried off by inundations[3] and swept away by mighty rivers and die by drowning; and they see death before their time.
14 The face of the ferocious raging sea I showed you because many encounter violent storms at sea, are shipwrecked, and sink beneath
15 the waves; and they see death as the sea. The insufferable thunder and the fearful lightning I showed you because many men come to

---

[1] Lit. 'my spirit is invested with neglect'.
[2] Lit. 'But this also I say to you'.
[3] Lit. 'by the inrush of many waters'.

a time of wrath,[4] with insufferable thunder and fearful lightning,
16 and perish suddenly;[5] and that is the way they see death. I showed
you also poisonous creatures,[6] asps and basilisks, and leopards,
and lions, and cubs, and bears, and vipers, and, in short, the face of
every beast did I show you, most righteous one, because many men
are killed by beasts, and others die after being bitten[7] by poisonous
17 snakes, ⟨dragons, asps, horned vipers, basilisks⟩,[8] and the viper. I
showed you also deadly cups of poisons mixed together, because
many men are given poisons to drink by other men and without
apparent cause are carried off at once.

XX.   And Abraham said, Tell me, I pray you, is *the kind of* death
2 *that comes to a man* incalculable? Death said, I tell you truly, by
3 God's truth, there are seventy-two deaths. One *of these* is the
righteous death which has its appointed hour;[1] and many men
4 arrive at death and burial within a single hour. Lo, I have told you
5 everything you asked. Now I tell you, most righteous Abraham,
have done with all this discussing, and once and for all stop
6 questioning me. Come, follow me, even as God, the Judge of all has
7 directed me. But Abraham said to Death, Leave me yet a little
8 longer to rest on my couch, for I am very feeble.[2] From the moment
I set eyes upon you my strength failed: all my limbs seem like
9 lumps of lead; and I am very short of breath.[3] Go away for a little
10 while, for I must confess[4] I cannot bear the sight of you. And his
11 son Isaac came and fell upon his breast, weeping. And his wife
Sarah came too, and she flung her arms round his feet, wailing

----

⁴ i.e. the Divine wrath. Some emend to 'the time of death'.
⁵ Lit. 'and become in the taking away of men'.
⁶ Lit. 'beasts'.
⁷ Lit. 'having been made to swell'.
⁸ These words were inserted by James. They are found complete only in MS A,
where they follow immediately after 'wrath' in verse 15 and must be read there as
genitives depending on 'wrath'. A relic of the reading survives in B at the same point
in a jumble that makes no sense. Several other details in verses 15 and 16, both of
text and interpretation, are also far from certain.

¹ Lit. 'its limit'.
² Lit. 'for want of heart is great upon me'.
³ Or 'and my spirit is much distressed'.
⁴ Lit. 'for I have said'.

12 bitterly. And all his male and female slaves came as well, and they gathered round his couch; and Abraham came to the brink of
13 death.[5] And Death said to Abraham, Come, kiss my right hand; and may joy and life and power come to you (for Death was
14 deceiving Abraham). And *Abraham* kissed his hand, and
15 immediately his soul stuck fast to Death's hand. And at once the archangel Michael was at his side, with a host of angels, and they took his precious soul in their hands, in a sheet divinely woven.
16 And with divinely-scented myrrh and spices they tended righteous Abraham's body until the third day after his death; and they
17 buried him in the land of promise, at the oak of Mamre. And the angels escorted his precious soul and went up into heaven, chanting the Trisagion hymn to God, the Sovereign of all; and they
18 placed it where it could worship God the Father. And when the great hymn of praise and doxology to the Lord was ended, and when Abraham had worshipped, there came the clear voice of God the Father, saying, Take my friend Abraham to Paradise, where are the tents of my righteous ones and the resting-places of my
19 saints[, Isaac and Jacob in his bosom]. There is no toil there, no grief, no sighing, but peace and rejoicing and endless life.[6]

---

[5] Or 'and Abraham entered the faint of death'. Lit. '. . . came to the neglect of death'. Cp. xvii. 23; xviii. 8.

[6] The following addition is found in all the MSS:

'Let us also, my beloved brethren, imitate the patriarch Abraham's hospitality, and let us attain to his virtuous way of life; so that we may be worthy of life eternal, giving glory to the Father, and to the Son, and to the Holy Ghost. To him be glory and power for ever and ever. Amen'.

THE TESTAMENT OF ISAAC

INTRODUCTION

The Testament of Isaac has survived in Coptic, Arabic, and Ethiopic. Of the Coptic there are two versions, one in Sahidic and one in Bohairic, each extant in only a single MS. The Sahidic version is found as the second of four items in a MS in the Pierpont Morgan collection in New York (M 577, dated AD 894/5), and the Bohairic in Cod. Vat. Copt. 61 (dated AD 961/2) where it is grouped together with the Testaments of Abraham and Jacob as the fifth item in a series of ten. Both the Arabic and Ethiopic versions agree with the Bohairic in offering texts of all three Testaments and also in grouping them together.

Guidi, in the Introduction to his edition of the Bohairic text of the Testaments of Isaac and Jacob,[1] argued that both are imitations of the Testament of Abraham and that both were composed in Coptic. In this case the Arabic and Ethiopic versions will have been derived from the Coptic. And this hypothesis may be supported by the observation that the later versions follow the Bohairic, not only in grouping the Testaments of Abraham, Isaac, and Jacob, together as a unit, but also in attributing them in their present form to St. Athanasius.[2]

On the other hand, even if it be conceded that the two later Testaments are imitative, that is no reason why they should not have been composed in Greek, although the Greek originals have not as yet come to light. If the reference to the book, or books, 'of the three Patriarchs' in *The Apostolic Constitutions* (VI.xvi.3) is to our Testaments of Abraham, Isaac, and Jacob, then there must have been a Greek Isaac and a Greek Jacob as well as a Greek Abraham. Similarly, it might be argued that the enigmatic passage in Priscillian (*tract.* iii) shows that Priscillian knew a Latin version of all three Testaments,[3] and that this is further evidence in favour

---

[1] Guidi, p. 223. [2] See above p. 395.

[3] What Priscillian says (commenting on an Old-Latin rendering of Tobit iv. 12) is: '*Nos fili prophetarum sumus: Noe profeta fuit et Abraham et Isac et Iacob et omnes patres nostri qui ab initio saeculi profetaverunt. Quando in canone profetae Noe liber lectus est?*

of a Greek Isaac and a Greek Jacob. If there was, then various schemes of version descent are possible. But it would be idle to speculate on these possibilities when there are no Greek texts of either Isaac or Jacob actually available.

It would seem therefore, that, so far as date and place of origin are concerned, we can affirm even less about the Testaments of Isaac and Jacob than we can about the Testament of Abraham. The attribution of all three to St. Athanasius in the Coptic-Arabic-Ethiopic tradition must inevitably be suspect; and even if it were not, the further statement in the preface to the Testament of Abraham in the Bohairic that Athanasius 'found' them 'in ancient books of our holy fathers the apostles'[4] would be too vague to be of any real use (it looks far too much like a pious conjecture on the part of some editor or scribe). Even so, such evidence as there is points to Egypt as the place of origin – the name Athanasius, the geographical distribution of the extant texts, and the similarity of the Testaments of Isaac and Jacob to the Testament of Abraham, which in all probability was itself written in Egypt. This last point is of some importance. If the authors of the Testaments of Isaac and Jacob were not the same as the author or compilers of the Testament of Abraham, they must not only have known Abraham, but also have thought it worth while composing very passable imitations of it. However, it should be noted that although the pattern of the Testament of Isaac follows the pattern of Abraham closely, there is a new element introduced, viz. the moral and religious teaching attributed to Isaac; and it might well be argued that this new element is due to a Coptic author or redactor, since a strong practical and pastoral interest is one of the recurring features in all Coptic literature. The Testament of Jacob is much more imitative than is the Testament of Isaac, but it seems to imitate the Testament of Isaac rather than the Testament of Abraham directly. The outstanding characteristic of this Testament is its dependence throughout on the book of Genesis.

---

quis inter profetas dispositi canonis Abrahae librum legit? quis quod aliquando Isac profetasset edocuit? quis profetiam Iacob quod in canone poneretur audivit?'

[4] Cp. also Test. Jacob xi. 2 and xiii. 11.

In their present form the Testaments of Isaac and Jacob are certainly Christian. Yet it may be maintained, as it has been maintained in the case of the Testament of Abraham, that they contain Jewish legendary material, even if they were not themselves the work of Jewish authors. In the Testament of Isaac the explicitly Christian elements may have been superimposed, for they appear to be easily detachable. In the Testament of Jacob, on the other hand, they form a more integral part of the whole. But whatever be the truth here, there are signs that our existing texts have a long history behind them, although 'the violent treatment to which the *Testaments* (more especially the *Testament of Jacob*) have been subjected, lies a long way behind their present Coptic form.'[5]

The Sahidic text in the Pierpont Morgan MS has been chosen as the basis for the translation of the Testament of Isaac that follows, as being the most ancient text extant. The Bohairic was almost certainly made from the Sahidic, although as it has come down to us it does not always follow it exactly: it may, therefore, on occasion have preserved some features otherwise lost. In consequence, major divergences between Sahidic and Bohairic, which affect the subject-matter, have attention drawn to them in the notes.

BIBLIOGRAPHY

EDITIONS

Coptic (Sahidic)

K. H. KUHN, 'The Sahidic version of the Testament of Isaac' in *JTS* N.S. viii (1957), pp. 225–239.

Coptic (Bohairic)

I. GUIDI, *Il Testamento di Isacco e il Testamento di Giacobbe* (= *Rendiconti della Reale Accademia dei Lincei: Classe di scienze morali, storiche e filologiche*, Ser. V, ix (Rome, 1900), pp. 224–244).

---

[5] So Gaselee in G. H. Box, *The Testament of Abraham*, p. 56.

TRANSLATIONS

English

K. H. KUHN, 'An English Translation of the Sahidic Version of the Testament of Isaac' in *JTS* N.S. xviii (1967), pp. 325–336.

S. GASELEE, 'The Testament of Isaac' in G. H. BOX, *The Testament of Abraham . . . with an Appendix containing a Translation from the Coptic Version of the Testaments of Isaac and Jacob* (= S.P.C.K., *Translations of Early Documents*; London, 1927), pp. 57–75 – from the Bohairic.

W. E. BARNES, 'Extracts from the Testament of Isaac' in M. R. JAMES, *The Testament of Abraham . . .* (= *TS* II.ii (Cambridge, 1892), pp. 140–151) – from the Arabic.

French

M. CHAÎNE in M. DELCOR, *Le Testament d'Abraham . . .* (Leiden, 1973) – from the Bohairic (pp. 196–205), Arabic (pp. 252–261), and Ethiopic (pp. 224–233). The translations of the Arabic and Ethiopic, left only in draft by Chaîne, were revised and prepared for publication by P. MARÇAIS and A. CAQUOT respectively.

German

E. ANDERSSON, *Sphinx*, vii (Uppsala, 1903), pp. 77–94 – from the Bohairic.

P. RIESSLER, *AjSaB*[2], pp. 1135–1148 – from the Arabic(?).

GENERAL

M. DELCOR, *Le Testament d'Abraham . . .* (Leiden, 1973), pp. 78–83.

S. GASELEE [as above], pp. 55–56.

I. GUIDI [as above], p. 223.

M. R. JAMES, *The Testament of Abraham . . .* [as above], pp. 155–161.

P. NAGEL, 'Zur sahidischen Version des Testamentes Isaaks' in *Wissenschaftliche Zeitschrift der Martin-Luther-Universität Halle-Wittenberg*, xii. 3/4 (1963), pp. 259–263.

P. RIESSLER, *AjSaB²*, pp. 1334–1335.

H. WEINEL in *EUX*, p. 172.

This is the going forth from the body of Isaac the patriarch: he died on the twenty-fourth of Mesore,[1] in the peace of God. Amen.

I. Now Isaac the patriarch writes his testament and addresses his words of instruction to his son Jacob and to all those gathered round him. [2] The blessings of the patriarch will be on those who come after us, even those who listen to these words, to these words of instruction and these medicines of life, so that the grace of God [3] may be with all those who believe. This is the end of obedience, as it is written, You have heard a word, let it abide with you[1] – which [4] means that a man should strive patiently with what he hears.[2] God gives grace to those who believe: he who believes the words of God [5] and of his saints will be an inheritor of the Kingdom of God. God has been with the generations gone by, which have passed away, [6] because of their innocence and their faith towards God. He will be with the generations to come also.

II. Now it came to pass, when the time had come for the patriarch Isaac to go forth from the body, God sent to him the angel[1] of his [2] father Abraham at dawn on the twenty-second of Mesore. He said [3] to him, Hail, son of promise! (Now it was the daily custom of the [4] righteous old man Isaac to converse with the angels.) He lifted his

[1] i.e. 17 August. Boh. gives 21 August, which is confirmed as the commemoration day of all three patriarchs, Abraham, Isaac, and Jacob, at Test. Jacob xiii. 11.

[1] Probably an adaptation, or variant reading, of Ecclus. xix. 10.
[2] From here to the end of the chapter Boh. elaborates without adding anything essentially new.

[1] Boh. 'archangel Michael'.

face up to the face of the angel: he saw him assuming the likeness of
his father Abraham; and he opened his mouth *and* raised his voice
and cried out in great joy, I have seen your face like someone who
5 has seen the face of God. The angel said to him, Listen, my beloved
Isaac: I have been sent for you by God to take you to the heavens
and set you beside your father Abraham, so that you can see all the
saints; for your father is expecting you and is coming for you
6 himself. Behold, a throne has been set up for you close to your
father Abraham, and your lot and your beloved son Jacob's lot will
surpass that of all others in the whole of God's creation:[2] that is
why you have been given for evermore the name of Patriarch and
7 Father of the World. But the God-loving old man Isaac said to the
8 angel, I am astonished by you, for you are my father. The angel
answered, My beloved Isaac, I am the angel that ministers to your
9 father Abraham. But rejoice now, for I am to take you out of sorrow
10 into gladness, out of suffering to rest for ever. I am to transport you
from prison to a place where you can range at will – to a place of joy
and gladness: I am to take you to *where there is* light and merriment
11 and rejoicing and abundance that never fails. So then, draw up
your testament and a statement for your household,[3] for I am to
12 translate you to rest for all eternity. Blessed is your father who
begot you: blessed are you also: blessed is your son Jacob; *and*
blessed are your descendants that will come after you.

---

[2] Boh. adds the Trinitarian formula 'in the glory of the Father and the Son and
the Holy Spirit'.

[3] Since the word rendered 'testament' here can also mean 'will', the whole
sentence can quite properly be understood to mean 'make your will and set your
domestic affairs in order'; and this understanding of it is strengthened by the
observation that passages in the Testament of Abraham, where Michael is bidden
to instruct Abraham (and does instruct him) about what he is to do in preparation
for his death, must refer to the disposition of his worldly goods (T. Abr. i.7, viii. 17,
xv. 3, 10). On the other hand, T. Isaac x. 8, 15, 20 seem most naturally to refer to the
written 'Testament' of Isaac (cp. also i. 1) rather than to Isaac's 'will', just as
T. Jacob i. 2 seems to be an even clearer reference to the written 'Testament' of
Jacob (in a context and in language very similar to the context and the language of
our present passage). If, then, we are to believe, as many do, that T. Abr. served as a
model for the authors of the later Testaments, we have to assume also a shift in
understanding somewhere along the line: there can be little doubt about the
meaning of T. Jacob i. 2; but the meaning of T. Isaac ii. 11 is nothing like so certain.

III. Now Jacob heard them talking together, *but* he said nothing.

2 Our father Isaac said to the angel with a heavy heart, What shall I do about the light of my eyes, my beloved son Jacob? For I am

3 afraid of *what* Esau *might do to him* – you know the situation.[1] The angel said to him, My beloved Isaac, if all the nations on earth were gathered together, they would not be able to bring these

4 blessings *pronounced* over Jacob to nothing. When you blessed him, the Father and the Son and the Holy Spirit[2] blessed him; and Michael and Gabriel[3] and all the angels and all the heavenly ones and the spirits of all the righteous and your father Abraham *all*

5 answered, Amen. The sword,[4] therefore, shall not touch his body; but he shall be held in high honour and grow great and spread far

6 and wide, and twelve thrones shall spring from him. Our father Isaac said to the angel, You have given me much comfort, but do

7 not let Jacob know in case he is distressed. The angel said to him, My beloved Isaac, blessed is every righteous man who goes forth

8 from the body: blessed are they when they meet with God. Woe, woe, woe, three times *woe*, to the sinner, because he has been born into this world: great sufferings will come to him, Isaac, beloved of

9 God. Give these instructions, therefore, to your sons, and the

10 instructions your father has given you. Hide nothing from Jacob, so that he can write them as instructions for the generations that will come after you, and those who love God may live their lives in

11 accordance with them.[5] And take care that I am able to fetch you

12 with joy, without delay. The peace of my Lord that he has given me, I give to you, as I go to him who sent me.

IV. And when the angel had said this, he rose from the[1] bed on

2 which Isaac was sleeping. He went back to the worlds on high while our father Isaac watched him go, astonished at the vision he

3 had seen. And he said, I shall not see *day*light before I am sent for.

4 And while he was thinking this, behold, Jacob got up *and came to*

---

[1] Lit. 'you know the end of everything'.
[2] Boh. omits the reference to the Son and the Holy Spirit.
[3] Boh. omits the reference to Gabriel.
[4] Or 'Chains'.   [5] Lit. 'may work by them'.

[1] Lit. 'his' (i.e. Isaac's bed).

5 the door of the room. The angel had cast a sleep over him so that he should not hear them; and he got up and ran to where his father slept *and* said to him, My father, whom have you been talking to?
6 Our father Isaac said to him, You have heard, my son: your aged
7 father has been sent for to be taken from you. And Jacob put his arms round his father's neck *and* wept, saying, Ah me! My strength
8 has left me: to-day you have made me an orphan, my father. Our father Isaac embraced his son Jacob *and* wept; *and* both wept
9 together until they could weep no more.[2] And Jacob said, Take me
10 with you, father Isaac. But Isaac replied, I would not have it so, my
11 son:[3] wait until you are sent for, my loved one. I remember[4] on the day when the whole earth was shaken from end to end[5] talking to my lord *and* father Abraham, and I had no strength to do *anything*.
12 What god has ordained, he has ordained for each one by sure
13 authority: his ordinances are immutable. But I know, and I am glad that I am to go to God, and I am strengthened by a guiding[6]
14 spirit;[7] for this is a way that no one can escape. Listen, my son, Where is the first creation of the hands of God – our father Adam
15 and our mother Eve? Where is Abel,[8] and after him Mahalalel, and Jared, and our father Enoch, and Methuselah,[9] and our father
16 Noah, and his sons Shem, Ham, *and* Japheth? After these Arpachshad, and Cainan, and Shelah, and Eber, and Reu, and Serug, and Nahor, and Terah, and my blessed father Abraham,
17 and Lot his brother? All these experienced death except the perfect
18 one, our father Enoch.[10] After these, forty-two generations more[11]

[2] Lit. 'until they ceased'.

[3] Boh. adds 'but thanks be to God that you too are a father, my loved one'.

[4] Lit. 'I know myself'.

[5] Lit. 'when the extremity and the edge of the world was moved': alternatively 'when the capital and the pillar of the world was moved'. In Boh. the whole sentence runs 'I also remember a day when the high and flourishing cypress was moved . . .' (cp. T. Abr. iii. 1–2). In either version the argument seems to be that though creation and created matter may be shaken, yet God's ordinances are unshakeable.

[6] Or 'princely'.

[7] and I am strengthened . . . spirit: in Boh. Jacob is exhorted to be strong and to stop weeping.

[8] Boh. adds a reference to Seth and Enosh.

[9] Boh. adds a reference to Lamech.

[10] Boh. adds an explicit reference to Enoch's translation.

[11] Cp. Matt. i. 17. According to Boh., twelve generations.

shall pass until Christ comes, born of a pure virgin called Mary.[12]

9, 20 He will spend thirty years preaching in the world. At the end of all this, he will choose twelve men and reveal to them his mysteries and teach them about the archetype of his body and his true blood by means of bread and wine; and the bread will become the body of
21 God and the wine will become the blood of God. And then he will ascend the tree of the cross and die for the whole *creation*, and rise on the[13] third day and despoil hell, and deliver all mankind from the
22 enemy. The generations to come will be saved by his body and by
23 his blood until the end of time. The sacrifices of Christians will not cease until the end of time, whether *offered* secretly or openly; *and* the Antichrist will not appear so long as they offer up *their* sacrifice.
24 Blessed is every man who performs that service and believes in it, because the archetypal service[14] is in the heavens; and they shall celebrate with the Son of God in his kingdom.

V. While the God-loving old man, our father Isaac, was saying
2 this, all his household gathered round him and wept. His son told
3 all his relations, and they came to him in tears. Now our father Isaac had made for himself a bedroom in his house; and when his sight began to fail he withdrew into it and remained there for a hundred years, fasting daily[1] until evening, and offering for himself
4 and his household a young animal for their soul. And he spent half
5 the night in prayer and praise to God. Thus he lived an ascetic life
6 for a hundred years. And he kept three periods of forty days as fasts each year, neither drinking wine nor eating fruit nor sleeping on *his*
7 bed. And he prayed and gave thanks to God *continually*.

VI. Now when it became generally known that the man of God

---

[12] The rest of this chapter (on Christ's work and the Eucharist), together with v. 1–3a, is lacking in Boh.
[13] Lit. 'his'.
[14] Lit. 'the archetype, which is done'.

[1] Lit. '. . . in his house: when the light of his eyes was dim, he withdrew into it until the end of a hundred years, fasting daily'. It is here that Boh. rejoins our text, beginning 'And God was with him until he had completed a hundred years, and he fasted daily'.

had regained his sight,[1] people gathered to him from everywhere, listening to his words[2] of life; for they realized that a holy spirit of God was speaking in him. The great ones who came said to him, You can *now* see clearly *enough*: how comes it that after your sight had failed you have now regained it? The God-loving old man smiled and said to them, My sons and brothers, the God of my father Abraham has brought this about to comfort me in my old age. But the priest of God said to him, Tell me what I ought to do,[3] my father Isaac. Our father Isaac said to him, Keep your body holy, for the temple of God is set in it.[4] Do not engage in controversy with *other* men in case an angry word escapes your mouth. Be on your guard against evil-speaking, against vainglory,[5] *and* against uttering any thoughtless word;[6] and see that your hands do not reach out after what is not yours. Do not offer a sacrifice with a blemish in it;[7] *and* wash yourself with water when you approach the altar. Do not mix the thoughts of the world with the thoughts of God when you stand before him. Do your utmost to be at peace with everyone. When you stand before God[8] and offer your sacrifice,[9] when you come to offer it on the altar, you should recite privately[10] a hundred prayers to God and make this confession to God saying,

O God, the incomprehensible, the unfathomable, the unattainable, the pure treasure, purify me in love; for I am flesh and blood, and I run defiled to thee, that thou mayest purify me. I come burdened, *and I ask* that thou mayest lighten my burden: a fire will burn wood,[11] *and* thy mercy will take away mine iniquities. Forgive me, me that am a sinner: I forgive[12] the whole creation that thou

---

[1] Lit. 'the man of God saw clearly'.

[2] Lit. 'teachings'. [3] Lit. 'Tell me a word'.

[4] In Boh. the allusion to 1 Cor. iii. 16 is clearer and an exhortation to keep the flesh pure and holy is added.

[5] Boh. adds the warning not to speak alone with a woman.

[6] Boh. 'idle word'.

[7] Boh. 'when there is a blemish in you'. [8] Lit. 'him'.

[9] Boh. takes the equivalent of this clause with the preceding verse, which seems preferable. [10] Lit. 'by yourself'.

[11] Or 'matter'. In Boh., which elaborates this passage, the reference is unquestionably to created matter.

[12] Boh. 'do thou forgive' (imperative).

15 hast made. I have no complaint against anyone: I am at peace with
   all *that is made in* thine image: I am unmoved by all the evil
16 reasonings that have been brought before me. I am thy servant and
   the son of thy maidservant: I am the one who sins, thou art the one
   who forgives: forgive me and enable me to stand in thy holy place.
17 Let my sacrifice be acceptable before thee: do not reject me
   because of my sins; but receive me unto thee, in spite of[13] my many
18 sins, like a sheep that has gone astray. O God, who hast been with
   our father Adam, and Abel, and Noah, and our father Abraham,
   and his son Isaac, who hast been with Jacob, be thou with me also,
   and receive my sacrifice from my hand.
19 As you recite all this, take your sacrifice *and offer it*; and strive
   heavenwards because of the sacrifice of God, so that you do not
20 displease him. For the work of the priest is no small thing.

VII. Every priest to-day (and till the end of time) must be
temperate as regards his food and drink and sleep:[1] neither should
he talk about events connected with this world, nor listen to
2 anyone who is talking *about them*. Rather should he spend his whole
life occupied with prayer and vigils and recitation until our God
3 sends for him in peace. Every man on earth, be he priest or monk
(for after a long time they will love the life of holy retreat), must
renounce the world and all its evil cares and join in the holy service
4 the angels render in purity to God.[2] And they will be honoured
before God and his angels because of their holy sacrifices and their
angelic service, which is *like* the archetype that is rendered in the
5 heavens. And the angels will be their friends, because of their
perfect faith and their purity; and great is their honour before God.
6, 7 In a word, whether great or small, sinlessness is required of us. The
chief sins worthy of repentance are these: You shall not kill with the
8 sword; You shall not kill with the tongue either: You shall not
commit fornication with your body; You shall not commit fornication with your thoughts; You shall not go in to the young to defile

---

[13] Lit. 'because of'.

[1] In Boh. the list of prohibitions starts with wine and the reference to sleep is
omitted.
[2] Lit. 'and be in the holy service of the angels of the pure God'.

9 them: You shall not be envious; You shall not be angry until the
sun has set; You shall not be proud in dispositon; You shall not
10 rejoice over your neighbour's fall: You shall not slander; You shall
not look at a woman with a lustful eye; and, Do not readily listen to
11 slander.[3] We need to beware of these things, and of others like
them, till each one *of us* is secure from the wrath that shall be
revealed from heaven.

VIII. Now when the people gathered about him heard him, they
2 cried out aloud saying, *This is* meet and right: Amen. But the
God-loving old man was silent: he drew up his blanket: he covered
3 his face. And the people and the priest were silent, so that he could
4 rest himself a little. But the angel of his father Abraham came to
him *and* took him up into the heavens. He saw terrors and tumults
5 spread abroad on this side and on that; and it was a terror and a
6 tumult fearful to behold. Some had the face of a camel, others had
the face of a lion: some had the face of a dog, others had *but* one eye
7 and had tongs in their hands, three ells long, all of iron.[1] I looked,
and behold, a man was brought, and those who brought him went
8 with him.[2] When they reached the beasts, those who went with him
withdrew to one side: the lion advanced towards him, tore him
apart into little pieces, and swallowed him: it *then* vomited him up,
and he became like himself again; and the next *beast* treated him in
9 just the same way. In short, they passed him on from one to the
other:[3] each one would tear him into pieces, swallow him, and *then*
10 vomit him up; and he would become like himself again. I said to
the angel, What sin has this man committed, my lord, that all this
11 is done to him? The angel said to me, This man you are looking at
now had a quarrel with his neighbour,[4] and he died without their
12 being reconciled. See, he has been handed over to five chief[5]

---

[3] In this catalogue Boh. adds a reference to blasphemy and omits the last clause:
there are also other minor differences.

[1] In the list of animals Boh. adds hyenas and leopards and omits the reference to
tongs.
[2] Lit. 'and behold, one they brought him, they going with him'.
[3] Lit. 'they gave him into one another's hand'.
[4] According to Boh. the quarrel had lasted for five hours.
[5] Boh. has no equivalent for this word.

tormentors: they spend a year tormenting him for every hour[4] he
13 spent quarreling with his neighbour. The angel also said to me, My
beloved Isaac, do you think these are the only ones? Believe me,
Isaac, beloved of God, there are six hundred thousand[6] tormentors.
14 They spend a year tormenting a man for every hour that he spends
sinning – if he did not repent, *that is*, before he went forth from the
body.

IX. He led me on and brought me to a fiery river, the waves of
which were an ell[1] high, and its noise like the noise of heaven's
2 thunder. *And* I saw a host of souls submerged in it;[2] and those who
were in that river cried out and wept aloud, and there was a *great*
3 commotion and *much* groaning. But it is a discerning fire that does
not touch the righteous, yet burns up sinners and boils them in the
4 stench that surrounds them. I saw also the pit of the abyss, the
smoke of which went up in clouds:[3] I saw men sunk in it grinding
their teeth, crying out and wailing, and each one was groaning.
5, 6 The angel said to me, Look and see these others too. And when I
had looked at them, the angel said to **me**,[4] These[5] are those who
have committed the sin of Sodom: these are indeed in great distress.
7 I saw also pits full of worms that do not sleep: I saw Abdemer-
ouchos,[6] who is in charge of the punishments, made all of fire,
threatening the tormentors in hell and saying, Beat them until they
8 know that God is. I saw a house *built* of fiery stone,[7] and there were
9 grown men underneath it, crying out and wailing. The angel said
10 to me, Look with your eyes and contemplate the punishments. I
said to the angel, My eyes could not endure it:[8] for how long must

---

[6] Boh. 'seventy thousand'.

[1] Boh. 'thirty ells'.   [2] Boh. adds 'nine ells *deep*'.
[3] Lit. 'the smoke of which was very high'.
[4] So Boh.: Sah. 'him'.
[5] According to Boh. they were submerged in the cold.
[6] Boh. 'Abtelmolouchos'. Probably a corruption of the adjective τημελοῦχος
('care-taking'), applied to a 'tutelary' or 'guardian' angel, and then taken as an
individual angel's name. See M. R. James, *The Apocryphal New Testament* (Oxford,
1924), p. 507.
[7] Boh. 'I saw another abyss that was all fire'.
[8] Lit. 'behold them'.

11 these *punishments* go on? He said to me, Until the merciful God has pity.

X. After this the angel took me up into the heavens: I saw my
2 father Abraham and I made obeisance to him. He saluted me, with all the saints, and the saints honoured me because of my father:
3 they walked with me and took me to my Father. I worshipped him
4 with all the saints. Songs of praise rang out, Thou art holy, thou art holy, thou art holy, King, Lord Sabaoth: the heavens and the earth
5 are full of thy holy glory. The Lord said to my father from the holy place,[1] It is good that you have come, Abraham, you righteous root *and* faithful saint: it is good that you have come to our city.
6 Whatever you may want to ask now, make your requests in the name of your beloved son Isaac, and they shall be yours indeed.[2]
7 My father Abraham said, Thine is the power, O *Lord* Almighty.
8 The Lord said to Abraham, As for all those who are given the name of my beloved Isaac, let *each one of* them copy out his testament[3] and honour it, and feed a poor man with bread in the name of my beloved Isaac on the day of his holy commemoration: to you will I
9 grant them as sons in my kingdom. Abraham said, My Lord Almighty, if *a man* cannot copy out his testament,[3] can'st thou not in thy mercy accept him, for thou art merciful and compassionate?
10 The Lord said to Abraham, Let him feed a poor man with bread, and I will give him to you as a gift and *as* a son in my kingdom, and he shall come with you to the first hour of the thousand years.
11 Abraham said, Suppose he is poor and has no means of getting[4]
12 bread? The Lord said, Let him spend the night of my beloved Isaac'*s commemoration* without sleep, and I will give him to you as a
13 gift and an inheritor in my kingdom. My father Abraham said, Suppose he is weak and has no strength, can'st thou not in thy
14 mercy accept him in love. The Lord said to him, Let him offer up a little incense in the name of your beloved son Isaac, *and* I will give
15 him to you as a son in my kingdom. If he has no means of getting[4] incense, let him seek out *a copy of* his testament and read it on my

---

[1] Boh. adds 'Every man who shall give the name of my beloved Isaac to his son, my blessing shall be on his house for ever'.

[2] Lit. 'yours for a covenant'. Cp. xii. 10.

[3] Lit. 'write his testament'.   [4] Lit. 'has not found'.

16 beloved Isaac's day. If he cannot read it, let him go and listen to
17 others who can. If he is unable to do any of these things, let him go
   into his house and say a hundred prayers, and I will give him to
18 you as a son in my kingdom. But the most essential thing of all is
   that he should offer a sacrifice in my beloved Isaac's name, for his
19 body was offered as a sacrifice.[5] Yet not only will I give you
   everyone called by my beloved Isaac's name as a son in my
   kingdom: *I will give you* also everyone who does one of the things I
20 have mentioned. And *I will give you* everyone who concerns himself
   about Isaac's[6] life and his testament, or does any compassionate
   act, such as giving someone a cup of water to drink, or who copies
   out his testament[7] with his own hand, *and* those who read it with all
21 their heart in faith, believing everything that I have said. My
   power and the power of my beloved Son and[8] the Holy Spirit shall
   be with them, and I will give them to you as sons in my kingdom.
22 Peace to all of you, all my saints.

XI. Now when he had said this, songs of praise rang out, Thou art
   holy, thou art holy, thou art holy, King, Lord Sabaoth: the heavens
2 and the earth are full of thy holy glory. The Father said to Michael
   from the holy place, Michael, my steward, go quickly and gather
   together the angels and all the saints, so that they may come and
3 meet my beloved Isaac. And Michael sounded the trumpet at
4 once. All the saints gathered with the angels and came to the couch
   of our father Isaac:[1] the Lord mounted his chariot,[2] and the
5 seraphim went in front of him with the angels.[3] And when they
   came to our father Isaac's couch, our father Isaac beheld our
6 Lord's face immediately, *turned* towards him full of joy. He cried
   out, it is good that thou hast come, my Lord, and thy great
   archangel Michael: it is good that you have come, my father
   Abraham, and all the saints.

---

[5] Boh. omits the reference to the sacrifice of Isaac.
[6] Lit. 'his'.   [7] Lit. 'writes his testament'.
[8] Boh. omits 'my beloved Son and'.

[1] Boh. omits the references to Michael sounding the trumpet and to the
assembling of the saints and angels.
[2] Boh. 'the chariot of the cherubim' (cp. Ecclus. xlix. 8–also T. Abr. ix. 15 and
x. i).   [3] Boh. omits from here to the end of the chapter.

XII.   Now when he had said this, Jacob embraced his father: he
2 kissed his mouth and wept. Our father Isaac fixed his eyes on him[1]
3 and motioned to him to be silent.[2] Our father Isaac said to the
4 Lord, Remember my beloved Jacob. The Lord said to him, My
power shall be with him; and when the time comes and I become
man and die and rise from the dead on the third day, I will put your
name in everyone's mind, and they will invoke you as their father.[3]
5 Isaac said to Jacob, My beloved son, this is the last commandment
6 I give you to-day: keep a sharp eye on yourself. Do not dishonour[4]
the image of God; for what you do to the image of man, you do to
the image of God, and God will do it to you too in the place where
7,8 you will meet him. This is the beginning and the end. Now when he
had said this, our Lord brought his soul out of his body, and it was
9 white as snow. He greeted it: he set it on the chariot with him: he
took it up into the heavens, with the seraphim making music before
10 him, and all the angels and the saints. He freely granted him the
good things of his kingdom for ever, and all the requests our father
Abraham had asked of the Lord he freely granted him as a
covenant for ever.

XIII.   This is the going forth from the body of our father Isaac, the
2 patriarch, on the twenty-fourth of the month Mesore.[1] And the day
on which his father Abraham offered him as a sacrifice is the
3 eighteenth of Mechir.[2] The heavens and the earth were full of the
soothing odour of our father Isaac, like choice silver: this is the
4 sacrifice of our father Isaac the patriarch. When Abraham offered
him as a sacrifice to God, the soothing odour of Isaac's sacrifice
5 went up into the heavens. Blessed is every man who performs an
act of mercy in the name of these patriarchs, for they will be their
6 sons in the kingdom of the heavens. For our Lord has made with

---

[1] Lit. 'gave him a sign by winking with his eyes'.

[2] Boh. adds a request from Abraham asking the Lord to remember his son.

[3] Boh. omits the Christological reference and has a more detailed promise for
Jacob only.   [4] Lit. 'afflict'.

[1] See p. 427, n. 1. Boh. adds a reference to Abraham's death on the same day and
gives Isaac's age as a hundred and eighty years.

[2] i.e. 12 February.

them a covenant for ever, that everyone who performs an act of mercy on the day of their commemoration shall be given to them as
7 a son in the kingdom of the heavens for ever. And they shall come to the first hour of the thousand years, in accordance with the promise of our Lord, even our God and our Saviour Jesus Christ, through whom every glory is due to him and his good Father and the Holy Spirit, the giver of life to all *creation* and one in being with *the Father and the Son*, now and always, for ever and ever.[3] Amen.[4]

---

[3] Boh. has a less elaborate form of doxology with no reference to the Holy Spirit.
[4] In Boh. there follows a colophon asking prayer for the scribe, Macarius.

THE TESTAMENT OF JACOB

INTRODUCTION

The text of the Testament of Jacob here translated is the Coptic (Bohairic) text contained in Cod. Vat. Copt. 61. There are also versions extant in Arabic and Ethiopic. For particulars about these versions, their interrelationship, and for some views on the relationship of the Testament of Jacob to the Testaments of Abraham and Isaac, reference should be made to the prefatory remarks on the Testament of Isaac (above, pp. 423–425).

To what is said there only one further observation need be added. The distinguishing marks of the Testament of Jacob, i.e. its essentially derivative character (especially its dependence on the book of Genesis) and the impression that the Christian elements in it are less easily detachable than in the Testament of Isaac, coupled with the fact that no Sahidic text of it has been preserved (as is the case with the Testament of Isaac), might suggest an origin independent of both the Testaments of Abraham and of Isaac. It might be argued, for example, that the Testament of Abraham was written first, in Greek: that the Testament of Isaac came later as an independent work (though whether written in Greek, or Sahidic, or anything else, it is impossible to say); and that later still the Bohairic translator of these two Testaments put them together and himself composed (in Bohairic) a Testament of Jacob to make a trilogy.

At the other extreme, though perhaps with less cogency, it might be argued that the three Testaments were designed as a trilogy from the start, and that all three, therefore, were originally written in Greek. In this case, it will be pure accident that only the Testament of Abraham has survived in Greek, that there are no surviving Sahidic texts of either it or the Testament of Jacob, and that the Bohairic is the first extant text to group all three together.

And there are, of course, several intermediate possibilities, such as the view of Guidi already referred to.[1]

BIBLIOGRAPHY

EDITIONS

Coptic (Bohairic)

I. GUIDI, *Il Testamento di Isacco e il Testamento di Giacobbe* (= *Rendiconti della Reale Accademia dei Lincei: Classe di scienze morali, storiche e filologiche*, Ser. V, ix (Rome, 1900), pp. 245–261).

TRANSLATIONS

English

S. GASELEE, 'The Testament of Jacob' in G. H. BOX, *The Testament of Abraham . . . with an Appendix containing a Translation from the Coptic Version of the Testaments of Isaac and Jacob* (= S.P.C.K., *Translations of Early Documents*; London, 1927), pp. 76–89.

W. E. BARNES, 'Testament of Jacob (Abstract)' in M. R. JAMES, *The Testament of Abraham* . . . (= *TS* II. ii (Cambridge, 1892), pp. 152–154) – from the Arabic.

French

M. CHAÎNE in M. DELCOR, *Le Testament d'Abraham* . . . (Leiden, 1973) – from the Bohairic (pp. 205–213), Arabic (pp. 261–267), and Ethiopic (pp. 233–241). The translations of the Arabic and Ethiopic, left only in draft by Chaîne, were revised and prepared for publication by P. MARÇAIS and A. CAQUOT respectively.

German

E. ANDERSSON, *Sphinx*, vii (Uppsala, 1903), pp. 129–142 – from the Coptic.

[1] See above p. 423.

GENERAL

S. GASELEE [as above], pp. 55–56.

I. GUIDI [as above], p. 223.

M. R. JAMES, *The Testament of Abraham* . . . [as above], pp. 155–161.

This again is the going forth from the body of our father Jacob the patriarch, who is called Israel, on the twenty-eighth of the month Mesore,[1] in the peace of God. Amen.

I. Now it came to pass when the time had come for our beloved father Jacob the patriarch, the son of Isaac, the son of Abraham, to go forth from the body (and the God-loving Jacob was well on in 2 years), the Lord sent Michael the archangel to him. And he said to him, Israel, my beloved, you righteous root, write your words of instruction for your sons, and draw up your testament for them,[1] and concern yourself about those of your household, for the time has come *for you* to go to your fathers and rejoice with them for ever. 3 And when the God-loving Jacob heard this from the angel, he answered and said to him, My lord – for it was his daily custom to 4 talk to angels. He said to him, May the will of the Lord be done.

1,2 **II.** And God blessed our father Jacob. He made for himself a place apart, to which he withdrew and offered his prayers to God day and night, while the angels visited him and guarded him and kept 3 him safe and gave him strength in everything. God blessed him; and his people increased greatly in numbers in the land of Egypt. 4 For at the time he went down to Egypt to his son Joseph, his sight was failing as a result of continual weeping and worrying over his son Joseph; but after he arrived in Egypt and had seen his son 5 Joseph's face, he saw *everything* clearly *again*. And Jacob Israel flung

---

[1] i.e. 21 August.

[1] See note on T. Isaac ii. 11 (p. 428 above).

himself on[1] his son Joseph's neck: he greeted him with tears and said, Now let me die, for I have seen your face once more while you
6   are still alive, my beloved. And Joseph ruled over the whole of
7,8 Egypt. Jacob lived in the land of Gashen for seventeen years. He became very old and attained a great age: he kept all the commandments and *lived always in* the fear of the Lord; and his sight failed so that he could see no one because of extreme old age.

III. He lifted his eyes towards the radiance of the angel who was speaking to him, who was in appearance and in face like his father
2   Isaac: he was afraid and troubled. The angel said to him, Do not be afraid, Jacob: I am the angel who has been[1] with you from your
3   youth. I chose you to receive your father Isaac's blessing, and your
4   mother Rebecca's. I am with you, Israel, in everything you do and
5   everything you have seen. It was I who delivered you from Laban when he pursued you: I blessed you, and all your wives, and your
6,7 sons, and all your cattle. It was I too who rescued you from Esau. It was I too who brought you down into the land of Egypt, Israel; *and*
8   I have spread you out far and wide. Blessed is your father Abraham, for he became a friend of the Most High God because of
9   his hospitality. Blessed is your father Isaac who gave you life, for
10 his sacrifice was perfect *and* pleasing to God. Blessed are you too, Jacob, for you saw God face to face and beheld the host of the
11 angels of the Most High God. You saw the ladder set up on the
12 earth with its top reaching to heaven. You also saw the Lord set on
13 the top of it in power too great for words. You cried out saying,
14 This is the house of God, and this is the gate of heaven. Blessed are you, for you have found strength in God and *are* strong among men.
15,16 Now, therefore, do not be troubled, beloved of God. Blessed are you, Israel, and blessed are all your descendants, for you shall be called patriarchs until the end of this age; for you are my people,
17 and you are the root of the servants of God. Blessed is every nation which emulates your purity, and your virtues, and your righteous-
18 ness, and your good works. Blessed is the man who commemorates
19 you on your honoured festival. Blessed is he who does a charitable

---

[1] Lit. 'cast himself upon his face on'.

[1] Lit. 'walked'.

deed in your name, or gives a man a cup of cold water, or brings a perfect offering to your place,[2] or to any place, in your name, or receives a stranger, or visits the sick, or comforts an orphan, or

20 clothes someone who is naked, in your name. He shall lack no good thing in this world; and in the world to come ⟨he shall have⟩[3]

21 eternal life. And further, whoever writes an account of your life with its[4] labours, or whoever makes a copy of it[5] with his hands, or whoever reads it attentively, and whoever listens to it with faith and a resolute heart, and whoever emulates your manner of life – they shall be forgiven all their sins, and they shall be freely granted

22 you in the kingdom of the heavens. So get up now, for you are to exchange trouble and sorrow for eternal rest, and you are to be borne away to a repose that never ceases, to a rest that never ends, and to a light that never sets, and to pleasure and gladness and

23 spiritual joy. So now, give your commands to your sons, and peace be with you; for I am about to go to him who sent me.

IV. And when he had said this to him, the angel left him in peace

2 and returned to the heavens, while Jacob[1] gazed after him. And those who were in the house heard him giving thanks to the Lord

3 *and* glorifying him with praises. And all his sons gathered round him, from the youngest to the eldest of them, all in tears and in

4 great distress, saying, He is about to go away and leave us. And they said to him, What shall we do, beloved father, for we are aliens

5 in a foreign land? And Jacob said to them, Do not be afraid, for God appeared to me in Mesopotamia saying, I am the God of your fathers: do not be afraid: I am with you for ever, and with your descendants that shall come after you for ever: the land on which you are standing I will give to you and your descendants for ever.

6 And again he said to me, Do not be afraid to go down into Egypt: I will go with you down to Egypt; and I will increase your numbers, and your descendants shall flourish for ever, and Joseph shall lay

---

[2] Either Jacob's burial place, or (more probably) a shrine dedicated to him.

[3] These words were perhaps omitted under the influence of Mark x. 30 ‖ Luke xviii. 30.   [4] Or 'his'.

[5] Lit. 'whoever writes it'.

[1] Lit. 'he'.

7 his hands upon your eyes. And your people shall increase greatly in Egypt; and then they shall return to me here, and I will do them good because of you. But now you must leave this place.

V. And after this the time drew near for Jacob Israel to go forth
2 from the body. He called Joseph and spoke to him as follows, If I have found favour with you, then put your blessed hand upon my thigh and swear to me on oath before the Lord to lay my body in
3 my fathers' grave. And Joseph said to him, I will do as you ask, my
4 God-loving father. His father said to him, I would have you swear; and Joseph swore the oath to Jacob his father that he would take[1]
5 his body to his fathers' grave. And Jacob bowed himself upon his son's neck.

VI. Now after this it was reported to Joseph, Behold, your father is
2 in a sorry state. He took his two sons, Ephraim and Manasseh, and
3 came to his father Israel. When Israel saw them, he said to Joseph,
4 Who are these,[1] my son? Joseph said to his father Jacob Israel, These are my sons that God has given me in the land of my
5,6 humiliation. Israel said, Bring them near to me. Now Israel's sight
7 had failed because of his great age, and he could hardly see. And
8 Joseph[2] brought them close to him; *and* he kissed them. When Israel had embraced them, he said, God will add to your descend-
9 ants.[3] And Joseph made his two sons, Ephraim and Manasseh, do obeisance to him on the ground: Joseph put Manasseh under his
10 right hand and Ephraim under his left hand. But Israel changed his hands: he laid his right hand on Ephraim's head and his left

---

[1] Lit. 'And Joseph swore to Jacob his father according to these words to take'.

[1] Lit. 'these of yours'.

[2] Lit. 'he'.

[3] A rather abrupt and truncated echo of Jacob's words at Gen. xlviii. 11 in the Septuagint ('Behold, was I not *for a time* deprived of your person? And behold, *now* God has let me see your children too' – lit. 'God has shown me your seed also'). It is tempting to suppose there has been at some stage in the tradition some textual corruption, either through omission or misunderstanding – perhaps both. If we are to think in terms of misunderstanding, it may be that Sahidic *touo* ('show') has been confused with Bohairic *touho* ('add'), and that the sense originally intended was the same as that of the final clause in the Septuagint (i.e. 'God has let me see your children').

11 hand on Manasseh's head. And he blessed them: he gave them their patrimony, saying,

12
> The God who approved my fathers Abraham and Isaac,
> The God who has looked after me from my childhood till
>   to-day,
> The angel who rescues me from all my tribulations,
> Bless these lads who are my sons,
> With whom is left my name,
> And the name of my holy fathers Abraham and Isaac.
> They shall multiply: they shall increase:
> They shall become a great people on the earth.

13 Afterwards Israel said to Joseph, I am dying; but you[4] will return
14 to the land of your[4] fathers, and God will be with you.[4] Behold, you have been more favoured than your brothers, for I have taken the Amorites with my bow and my sword.

VII. Jacob called all his sons and said to them, Come to me, all of you, so that I can tell you what will happen to you, and also what
2 will happen to each one of you at the end of time. All Israel's sons
3 gathered round him, from the youngest to the eldest of them. Jacob Israel answered and said to his sons, Listen, sons of Jacob, listen to
4 Israel your father, from Reuben my first-born unto Benjamin. He told his sons what would happen to all twelve of them, name by
5 name and tribe by tribe, with heaven's blessing. Then all[1] kept silence so that he might rest a little.

VIII. He was taken up into the heavens to visit the resting-places.
2,3 And behold, a host of tormentors came out. The appearance of each one was different; and they were ready to torment the sinners – that is the fornicators, and the harlots, and the catamites, and the sodomites, and the adulterers, and those who have corrupted God's creation, and the magicians, and the sorcerers, and the unrighteous, and the idol-worshippers, and the astrologers, and
4 the slanderers and the double-tongued. In short, many are the

---

[4] Lit. 'you . . . your . . . you' (plural).

[1] Lit. 'the multitude of men'.

punishments for all the sins we have mentioned: the unquenchable fire, the outer darkness, the place where there shall be weeping and grinding of teeth, and the worm that does not sleep. And it is a terrible thing for you to be brought before the judge, and it is a terrible thing to come into the hands of the living God. Woe to all sinful men for whom these tortures and these tormentors are prepared. And again afterwards he took me and showed me the place where my fathers Abraham and Isaac were,[1] *a place* that was all light; and they were glad and rejoiced in the kingdom of the heavens, in the city of the beloved. And he showed me all the resting-places and all the good things prepared for the righteous, and the things that eye has not seen nor ear heard, and have not come into the heart of men, that God has prepared for those who love him and do his will on earth (for, if they end well, they do his will).

IX. After this, Jacob said to his sons, Behold I am about to be taken away and laid *to rest* with my people: lay my body with my people in the double grave in the field of Ephron the Hittite, where Abraham and his wife Sarah were buried, where Isaac was buried, in the path of the field and the grave that is in it, which was bought from the sons of Heth. And when Jacob had finished saying this, he drew his feet up on to his bed: he went forth from the body like every man. And the Lord came from heaven with Michael and Gabriel accompanying him, and many legions of angels singing before him. They took the soul of Jacob Israel to abodes of light with his holy fathers Abraham and Isaac. Such was[1] the life of Jacob Israel the patriarch. Joseph presented him to Pharaoh when he was a hundred and thirty years old, and he spent another seventeen years in Egypt: together this makes a hundred and forty-seven years. He went to his rest in a ripe old age, perfect in every virtue and spiritual grace; *and* he glorified God in all his ways, in the peace of God. Amen.

---

[1] Lit. 'the place where my fathers were, Abraham and my father Isaac'.

[1] Lit. 'Now these are the years of'.

X. Joseph threw himself upon his father, kissing him and weeping
2 for him. And Joseph instructed his servants, the embalmers, saying, Embalm my father in accordance with the best Egyptian
3 practice. They spent forty days embalming Israel; and when the
forty days of Israel's embalming were over, they spent another
4 eighty days mourning for him. And when the days of Pharaoh's
mourning were over (for he had been weeping for Jacob because of
his love for Joseph), Joseph spoke with Pharaoh's great ones and
5 said to them, If I may claim this favour from you, speak on my
behalf to Pharaoh the king saying, My father made me take an oath
when he was about to go forth from the body, saying, Bury my
6 body in my fathers' grave in the land of Canaan. So now I ask to be
allowed to go and[1] bury my father there and come back again.
7 Pharaoh the king said to Joseph the wise, Go in peace and bury
your father as he made you swear to do: take with you chariots and
wagons, and all the great ones of my kingdom, and as many of my
8 servants as you need. Joseph worshipped God in Pharaoh's
9 presence and went out from him. *And* Joseph set out to bury his
10 father. Many of[2] Pharaoh's servants went with him, and the elders
of Egypt, as well as all Joseph's household, and his brothers, and
11 the whole of Israel's household. And there went up with him
12 chariots and horsemen: they were a very great company. And they
stopped at the threshing floor of Gadad, which is on the bank on
13 the other side of Jordan. They mourned for him there with a great
and bitter mourning; and they mourned for him for seven days.
14 Those in the lowland heard the mourning at the threshing-floor of
Gadad, *and* they said, This great mourning is *a mourning* of the
Egyptians, so that that place is called 'The Mourning of Egypt' to
15 this day. They took Israel and buried him in the land of Canaan in
the double grave that Abraham had bought as a burial-place[3] for
16 silver from Ephron the Hittite, opposite Mamre. And Joseph
returned to Egypt together with his brothers and the party from
17 Pharaoh's household. After his father's death Joseph lived for
18 many more years and was king over Egypt. But Jacob Israel died
and was laid with his people.

[1] Lit. 'Now, therefore, let him bid me that I'.
[2] Lit. 'All'.   [3] Lit. 'property, possession'.

XI. Behold now, we have told *you* these things as best we could[1] in order to instruct you about the going forth from the body of our
2 father the patriarch Jacob Israel. [2]It is written in the divinely inspired scriptures and the ancient books of our fathers the apostles,
3 even I, Athanasius your father. If you want confirmation of this testament of the patriarch Jacob, take the *book* Genesis of the prophet Moses, the lawgiver, and read *what is* in it: your mind will
4 be enlightened: you will find this, and more, written about it. And again, you will find mention of God and his angels, for God[3] was a friend to the patriarchs[3] while they were yet in the body and spoke
5 with them many times in many passages of scripture. And you will find that he spoke too in many passages in scripture with the patriarch Jacob, saying, I will bless your descendants *and make them*
6 *as many* as the stars of heaven. And again, Jacob spoke with his son Joseph saying, My God appeared to me in the land of Canaan at Luz: he blessed me saying, I will bless you and make you too many to be counted, and peoples and nations shall spring from you: I will give this land to your descendants after you as a possession for all time.

XII. See, then, my beloved, we have heard these things about our
2 fathers the patriarchs. Let us therefore emulate their deeds and their virtues, and their love of God and their love of men, and their hospitality, that we may be worthy to become their sons in the kingdom of the heavens, and that they may pray for us to God that he may save us from punishments in hell which the holy patriarch Jacob spoke about in his words full of all sweetness, when he taught his sons about the punishments and called them the sword of the
3 Lord God. These are the river of fire that is prepared, and which engulfs sinners in *its* waves and those that have defiled themselves.
4 These are the things the patriarch Jacob revealed when he taught the rest of his sons, that those that love instruction should listen *to him* and do what is good at all times, and love one another, and

---

[1] Lit. 'according to the measure to which we have attained' (or 'we could attain').

[2] The sequence would be clearer if, with Andersson (n. 32), we were to supply some such verb as 'I have found' and continue 'it written . . ., even I, Athanasius your father'.   [3] Lit. 'he . . . them'.

5 strive after love and pity. For pity triumphs over judgement and love covers a multitude of sins;[1] and again, He who has pity on a poor man lends on usury to God.[2]

XIII. So now, my sons, let neither prayer nor fasting ⟨be lacking⟩, and persist in them continually; for they drive away the demons.
2 My sons, keep yourselves from fornication, and anger, and adultery, and every evil thing, and especially *from* violence, and
3 blasphemy, and theft. For no *man of* violence will inherit the kingdom of the heavens, neither *will any* fornicator, nor catamite, nor sodomite, nor blasphemer, nor covetous *man*, nor curser, nor
4 anyone who is defiled. In short, *these* and the others we have
5 mentioned will not inherit the kingdom of God. My sons, honour the saints, for it is they who pray for you, that your descendants may prosper[1] and that the land may be yours as an inheritance for
6 ever. My sons, be hospitable, that you may share the lot of our
7 father Abraham, the great patriarch. My sons, love the poor, that, as you do to the poor man here, so God may give you the bread of
8 eternal life in the heavens unto the end. He who feeds a poor man
9 with bread here, God will feed him from the tree of life. Clothe the poor man who is naked here on earth, that God[2] may put on you a robe of glory in the heavens, and so you may become a *true* son of our holy fathers the patriarchs, Abraham and Isaac and Jacob, in
10 the heavens for ever. Call to mind the word of God here and remember the saints, *and take care* that *copies of* their memoirs and their hymns are made[3] for the encouragement of those who hear them, so that your name also may be written in the book of life in the heavens, and you *too* may be numbered with the number of God's[4] saints who have pleased him in their generation, and take
11 part in the chorus with the angels in the land of the living. We commemorate the saints, our fathers the patriarchs, at this very

---

[1] Lit. 'covers their many sins'. Cp. Prov. x. 12; James v. 20; 1 Pet. iv. 8.
[2] Prov. xix. 17.

[1] Lit. 'may increase in numbers'.
[2] Lit. 'he'.
[3] Lit. '. . . saints, that they may write their memoirs and their hymns'.
[4] Lit. 'his'.

time every year: our father Abraham the patriarch on the twenty-eighth of Mesore, also our father Isaac the patriarch on the twenty-eighth of Mesore, and again our father Jacob on the twenty-eighth of this same month Mesore, as we have found it written in the ancient books of our holy fathers who were pleasing unto God. 12 Through their supplication and their prayers may all of us together be granted to share their lot in the kingdom of our Lord and our God and our Saviour Jesus Christ, through whom is the glory of the Father with him and the Holy life-giving Spirit now and always and for ever. Amen.

Remember me, that God may forgive me all my sins and give me understanding and give me stability without sin. Amen.[5]

---

[5] This last sentence is the scribe's colophon.

THE LADDER OF JACOB

The Ladder of Jacob is extant only in Slavonic, in two distinct recensions, preserved in several MSS of the *Palaea interpretata*.[1]

About its origin nothing whatever is known. According to Epiphanius[2] the Ebionites possessed an apocryphal work called Ἀναβαθμοὶ Ἰακώβου ('Jacob's/ James's Steps'); but the contents of the work as described by Epiphanius in no way correspond with the contents of the Ladder. Moreover, both the literary context in which Epiphanius places it ('. . . other Acts of apostles'), and the fact that he uses the declinable form of the proper name (Ἰάκωβος) strongly suggest that it was a New Testament apocryphon to which he was referring and that it was concerned with James, the Lord's brother.[3]

The central feature of the Ladder is Jacob's dream at Bethel. It begins as an amplification of Gen. xxviii. 10–12 after the manner of Jewish *haggada*. Then an angel appears, in typical apocalyptic style, to interpret Jacob's dream and goes on to prophesy his descendants' future suffering and their ultimate vindication.

That a Greek text lies behind the Slavonic is not only probable in itself, but it is also rendered more probable by certain points of contact between chap. vii in the 'longer' recension and one of the sources of the *Narrative concerning things done in Persia*, a 5th (?) cent. Greek work, first published in full in a critical edition by Bratke in 1899. If there was a Greek text of the Ladder, it will doubtless have formed part of the Greek *Palaea*; and since the Greek *Palaea* is usually dated in the 8th or 9th cents., a Greek Ladder must be pushed back into the 7th or 8th cents. at the latest, and it may well be very much earlier. There are no sound arguments for suggesting a Semitic original, though obviously such a possibility cannot be altogether excluded.

Since the Ladder is relatively brief it has been thought worthwhile to print translations of both the available Slavonic recen-

[1] On the *Palaea* see above, p. 364, n. 5.
[2] Epiph. *Haer*. XXX. xvi. 7.
[3] The normal Christian Greek for the patriarch Jacob is the indeclinable form, Ἰακώβ, following the Septuagint (e.g. John iv. 5; *Ep. Barn*. viii. 4).

sions one after the other. First is printed the 'shorter' recension from the *Palaea* in the Rumyantsev collection (= Rum. 453: AD 1494), published by A. N. Pypin in 1862, and designated by the symbol 'R'. Then follows a translation of the 'longer' recension from the *Palaea* of the Solovetski Library (= Sol. 431) published by I. Ya. Porfir´ev in 1877: this last MS is designated by the symbol 'S'; and in the apparatus are added certain readings from the *Palaea* of the Troitse-Sergieva monastery (no. 38), written in Kolomna in AD 1406, published by N. S. Tikhonravov in 1863, and designated 'K'. The chapter and verse numerations are so far as possible the same in both recensions.

The reader can thus study the differences between the recensions for himself and appreciate the problems that their existence raises. The 'longer' recension not only offers a more satisfactory opening, but also in chaps. v–vii goes into far greater detail about Israel's vindication (in particular there is a full description of the accompaniments of the coming of the 'man from the Most High', much of it, if not all, manifestly Christian). On the other hand, the 'shorter' recension offers in chap. ii a longer version of Jacob's prayer. And both recensions have suffered from having interpretations of the *Palaea* incorporated into the text (see especially the addition in chap. i). In these circumstances it would be hazardous to affirm simply that one recension is to be preferred and that the other is either an 'expansion' or an 'abbreviation'. And it would be equally hazardous to pick out passages here and there and stigmatize them as 'later additions' or 'interpolations' – unless, of course, they are very evidently pieces of *Palaea* interpretation. In a situation like this such terms as 'original' and 'interpolation' tend to lose their meaning. In both recensions, it seems, we are dealing with a document in an almost permanent state of literary flux.

BIBLIOGRAPHY

EDITIONS

A. N. PYPIN, *Lozhnye i otrechennye knigi russkoi stariny* (= ed. G. A. KUSHELEV-BEZBORODKO, *Pamyatniki starinnoi russkoi literatury*, iii (St. Petersburg, 1862), pp. 27–32). [= R]

N. S. TIKHONRAVOV, *Pamyatniki otrechennoi russkoi literatury*, i (St. Petersburg, 1863), pp. 91–95. [= K]

I. Ya. PORFIR´EV, *Apokrificheskie skazaniya o vetkhozavetnykh litsakh i sobytiyakh po rukopisyam Solovetskoi biblioteki* (= *SORYaS* xvii. 1 (St. Petersburg, 1877), pp. 138–149). [= S]

TRANSLATIONS

English

M. R. JAMES, *LAOT*, pp. 96–103. [A conflation of the two recensions based on Bonwetsch's German rendering.]

German

G. N. BONWETSCH, *Die apokryphe "Leiter Jakobs"* (= *Nachrichten von der Königl. Gesellschaft der Wissenschaften zu Göttingen. Philolog.-hist. Kl.*, 1900: Heft i; Göttingen, 1900, pp. 76–87.). [A translation of both recensions with a brief Introduction.]

GENERAL

A. VASSILIEV, *Anecdota Graeco-Byzantina*, i (Moscow, 1893), pp. xxx–xxxii.

E. BRATKE, *Das sogenannte Religionsgespräch am Hof der Sasaniden* (= *TU* N.F. iv. 3; Leipzig, 1899), pp. 101–6.

H. WEINEL in *EUX*, pp. 172–3.

———————

I. And behold, a ladder was set up on the earth, whose top reached to heaven; and the top of the ladder was in form like a man,
2 hewn out of fire. It had twelve steps to the top of the ladder, and on each step, up to the top, *were* two human forms, *one* on the right and *one* on the left: *there were* **twenty-four**[1] forms on the ladder, *visible* as
3 far as their breasts. But the central form, which I saw, *was* of fire as far as the shoulders and arms *and* much more terrifying than those
4 twenty-four forms. And while I was looking, behold, the angels of

[1] Emended in the light of verse 3 below: the MS reads 'four'. Cp. also the reading of K at i. 2 in the 'long recension' (p. 460 below).

God were ascending and descending on it; and the Lord had taken his stand upon it.

5   [2]For so it is to be understood, as when a man leans on his staff. Of
6 the angels we understand: those who were ascending are a figure of this – when the tree of the Cross was fixed in the earth at the Lord's passion, as the ladder was fixed in Jacob's sight, and the Lord received the heathen who were baptized, and they ascended into heaven; but those who were descending – *they are* the disobedient,
7 perverse ones. For Moses prefigured *this*, and said to them, Deceitful and perverse generation! Is this your thanksgiving to the Lord?
8 In this, then, we see the heathen ascending, but the Jews descending . . .[2]

9   . . .[3] on the highest form. And from there he called to me, saying,
10,11 Jacob, Jacob. And I said, Here am I, Lord! And he said to me, The land on which you are sleeping, to you will I give it, and to your descendants after you; and I will multiply your race as the stars of
12 heaven and as the sand of the sea. Through your descendants will the whole land be blessed, and those who live in it, until the last times, *even* the years of the end: my blessing, with which I have
13 blessed you, shall go forth from you to the last generation. And the East and West shall all be filled with your race.

II.   And as I heard *his voice* from the height, fear and trembling fell
2 on me. And I got up from my sleep; and while the voice was still *speaking*, and the word of God *was* in my ears, I said, How awesome is this place! this is none *other* but the house of God, and this is the
3 gate of heaven. And the stone, which had been my pillow, I set up *as* a pillar, and I poured oil[1] on the top of it; and I called the name of
4 that place the house of God . . .[2] O Lord God of Adam, thy . . .,[3] and Lord God of Abraham and Isaac my fathers, *who* were righteous in
5 all their ways before thee, who sittest in might upon the cherubim

---

[2-2] Obviously an interpretative Christian gloss.
[3] Lacuna in the MS.

[1] Oil from trees (not animal oil).
[2] Lacuna in the MS. We must supply at least 'And I prayed to God and spoke as follows' (or something similar) as in SK: cp p. 460 below.
[3] Lacuna in the MS: Pypin suggests 'creature'.

and on the fiery throne of glory and the many-eyed ones (as I saw
6 in my dream), *thou who* sustainest the four-faced cherubim,
who bearest also the many-eyed seraphim, who bearest the age of
7 all beneath thine arm and art supported by nothing; thou hast
established the heavens to the glory of thy name and stretched out
8 on the clouds of heaven the shining heaven beneath thee, that thou
mightest move the sun below it, and hide it in the night, that it
9 should not be taken for God. Thou hast set on them a course for the
moon and the stars: the former thou makest to wane and to wax;
and the stars thou commandest to pass by, that they too should not
10 be taken for gods. Of the face of thy glory the six-winged seraphim
are afraid; and they hide their feet and their faces with their wings.
11 And, as they fly with the others, they sing . . .[4] High One, with
twelve faces, many-named, Fiery One, in form like lightening,
Holy One, holy, holy, holy, Jao, Jaova, Jaoil, Sabakdos, Chabod,
12 Sabaoth, Omlelech, Ilabir, [5]Amis'mi, Barech,[5] Eternal King,
Strong One, Mighty One, Most Great, longsuffering, blessed, who
fillest the heavens and the earth and the sea and the abyss and all
13 the ages with thy glory. Hear my song which I have sung to thee,
and grant me my request which I shall ask of thee; and tell me the
interpretation of my dream, as thou art God, mighty, powerful,
and glorious, holy God, Lord of my fathers and my *God*.

III. And while I was still making my prayer, a voice spoke[1] before
my face, saying, Sarekl, elder of the joyful ones, *you* who are over
dreams, go and explain to Jacob the dream that he has seen, and
tell *him* everything that he has seen; but first give him a blessing.
2 And the archangel Sarekl came to me, and I looked *upon him*: there
3 was a face. . . .[2] But I was not afraid of his glance, for the face I had
seen in my dream[3] was more terrifying than this; and I was not
4 afraid of the angel's face. And the angel said to me, What is your
5,6 name? And I said, Jacob. *And he said*, Your name shall be called

---

[4] Lacuna in the MS.
[5-5] Bonwetsch 'Ame (?), S'me Barech'.

[1] Lit. 'saw': Bonwetsch translates 'appeared'.
[2] Lacuna in the MS.
[3] The MS adds *pritvanie* which appears to be both superfluous and corrupt.

7 Jacob no longer, but your name shall be like my name – Israel. And
   when I was coming from Fandana[4] in Syria to meet Esau my
   brother, he[5] came to me and blessed me and called my name Israel.
8 And he did not tell me his name until I adjured him; and then he
   told me, As you have prevailed.[6]

IV. *Then* he said to me, The ladder which you have seen, having
   twelve steps, *and* each step having two human forms *on it*, changing
2 their shape – the ladder is this age, and the twelve steps *are* the
3 times of this age; but the twenty-four forms are the kings of the
4 heathen tribes of this age. Under those kings . . .[1] of your *sons*. They
   will rise against the heathenness of your children's children; and he
   will lay waste this place through four generations[2] of the sins of
5 your children's children. And from the wealth of *their* forefathers
   will be built a sacristy in the temple to the name of your God and *the*
6 *God* of your fathers. And because of the provocation of your
   children it will lie waste until the fourth generation[3] of this age, for
7 you have seen four forms. The first – him *whom you saw* stumbling
   upon the step (the angels ascending and descending, and the forms
8 in the midst of the steps) – *that is*, the Most High will raise up a king
   from the descendants[4] of your brother Esau, and they will receive
   all the rulers of the races of the earth, who have done evil to your
9 descendants[5]. And they will be given into his hand; and *they* will
10 suffer *him* unwillingly. He will hold them by force and rule them;
   and they will not be able to resist him until the day he decides[6] *that*
11 *they should serve idols* . . .[7] *and sacrifice to dead things. And he will command*
12 *that all the people in his kingdom be forced to do this. And of those* who will

---

    [4] i.e. Paddan-aram (Gen. xxxv. 9).
    [5] i.e. the angel.
    [6] The MS reads *kop-zul*, which is unclear: the translation 'prevailed' is derived
from Gen. xxxii. 28. The remainder of the sentence has presumably been lost.

    [1] Lacuna in the MS: cp. the text of K in the 'long recension' at iv. 3.
    [2] Lit. 'ends', 'descents'.
    [3] Lit. 'end', 'descent'.
    [4] Lit. 'children's children'.   [5] Lit. 'seed'.
    [6] Lit. 'until the day when his intention goes out over them'.
    [7] Lacuna in the MS. The words in italics are taken from the *Palaea* interpreta-
tion, where they are quoted as coming from the text.

be guilty of such an offence, some *will serve* **the greatest**[8] of your race, and some Falkonagargail.[9]

V. And your descendants, Jacob, will be like strangers in a foreign land; and they will be ill-treated, and made slaves of, and flogged
2 daily. But the heathen, to whom they will be subject, God will judge. When a king shall rise up and execute judgement, then will there be a place for him: then will your descendants, Israel, be delivered from the oppression of the heathen, who have held them by force, and they will be free from every reproach of **their**[1] enemies; for the king will be *the* source[2] of all **vengeance**[3] and retribution upon those who have afflicted you, O Israel. And at the end of the age, those who have suffered bitterly[4] will rise up and cry out, and the Lord will hear them, and be moved,[5] and the Mighty One will feel
3 compassion for their suffering. For the angels and archangels pour
4 out their **prayers**[6] before him *for the* sparing [7]*of your tribe.*[7] Then will their women be fruitful; and then will the Lord protect your race.[8]

JACOB'S VISION OF A LADDER

I. Now Jacob was going to Laban his uncle; and he found a place and fell asleep there, having laid his head on a stone. Now the sun had gone down, and he saw there a dream; and behold, a ladder was fixed on the earth, and it reached to the heavens. And at its top
2 there was a form, like a man, hewn out of fire. Now it had twelve steps; and on every step there were two human forms, *one* on the

---

[8] R is here corrupt: the restoration is from S and K.

[9] Porfir´ev suggests this is a corruption of Greek χαλκός (a bronze statue) and Hebrew *Nergal* (the Mesopotamian idol mentioned at 2 Kings xvii. 30).

[1] So S and K in vi. 1 of the 'long recension' (below), where much of the material in this chapter is found in a different order: R reads 'your'.

[2] Lit. 'head'.

[3] Reading *m´štenie* for the *kreštenie* ('baptism') of the text as in S and K.

[4] Lit. '. . . the age, the bitter ones'.

[5] Lit. 'be entreated'.

[6] So S and K: R 'lightnings'.

[7-7] Lacuna in the MS: the words in italics are from the *Palaea* interpretation.

[8] Here follows the *Palaea* interpretation.

right and *one* on the left: *there were* twenty-four[1] forms on the ladder.
3 And the central form, which I saw, *was* of fire as far as the shoulders
   and the arms, *and* much taller than all *the others*: he was very
   terrifying, much more *terrifying* than the other twenty-four forms.
4-7 And while I was looking, behold, the angels of God were ascending
   and descending on it; *and* the Lord had taken his stand upon it.[2]
8,9 God stood, as it were, above the highest form. And from there he
10,11 called to me, saying, Jacob, Jacob, And I said, Here am I. And he
   said to me, The land on which you are sleeping, to you will I give it,
12 that it may be filled with your descendants. My blessing, with
   which I have blessed you, shall go from you to the last generation.
13 And the East and the West shall all be filled with your race.

II. And as I heard *his voice* from the height, trembling and terror
2 fell on me. [1]After getting up, *I*, Jacob, from my sleep, *I* said (the
3 voice was still in my ears) – after getting up, *I* said, to my feet, I
   prayed to God[1] and spoke thus, Lord, the Creator, Lord of all
4 Creation. And again I said, God of Abraham and of Isaac my
   father, and God of all who have walked before thee in righteousness: behold, I saw a terrifying vision, and trembling fell on me.
5 But remember, O Lord, Abraham my forefather, how he walked
   before thee in innocence and was perfect in all the ways of thy
6 commandments. So also my father, thy servant Isaac, did not
7 disobey thy commandments. Therefore, O Lord, look mercifully
   upon me also, on thy servant, and tell me *what is the interpretation of*
   this terrifying vision I have seen.

III. And while the voice and prayer were still on Jacob's lips,
   behold, an angel of God stood before him, saying, Jacob, I am sent
2 by the Creator of all to you to explain your dream to you. So pay
   attention to the explanation of your dream.

---

[1] So K: S 'two *and* four'.
[2] Here follows an interpretative gloss similar to that in R: see above (p. 456).

[1-1] There is obviously some confusion here about whether the narrative should
be in the first person or the third, and presumably also some dittography or
dislocation of the text.

IV. The ladder which you have seen, having twelve steps, and
2 each step having two human forms *on it*, changing their shape – the
ladder is this age, and the twelve steps are the times of this age, and
the twenty-four[1] forms are the rulers of the tribes of the heathen
3,4 age. By those tribes will your children's children[2] be tried. And
they will rise against the heathenness of your children's children,
and they will make this place desolate for four generations[3] of your
5 children's children. And in the name of *their* forefathers a temple
6 will be built in your name *and* that of your fathers. And the
provocation of your children will cause *it* to lie waste for four
7 generations[4] of this age, for you have seen four forms. The first,
8 who stumbled on the step – *that is*, there will be a ruler from your
9 kin, and he will do evil to your descendants; and he will be suffered
10 unwillingly by them. And he will hold them by force to rule them;
and they will not be able to resist[5] him; and he will decide[6] that
11 they should serve idols and sacrifice to dead things. And he will
command that all the people in his kingdom be forced to do *this*.
12 *And of those* who will be guilty of such an offence, some will serve the
greatest of your race, and some Falkonagargail.[7]

V. Know, Jacob, that your descendants will be strangers in a
foreign land; and they will be ill-treated, and made slaves of, and
2 flogged daily. But that people, whose slaves they are, the Lord will
judge; for the Mighty One will feel compassion for their suffering.
3 For the angels and archangels pour out their prayers before him for
the deliverance of your race, and that the Most High should have
4 mercy. Then will their women be fruitful; and after that the Lord
will defend your race with terrifying and mighty signs against
5 those who enslaved them. Their storehouses, which were full, will
be found empty of wine and of every kind of corn: their land will
seethe with reptiles and all kinds of deadly things; and there will be
many earthquakes and catastrophes.

[1] So K: S 'two *and* four'.
[2] K adds 'and the family of your sons'.
[3] Lit. 'ends', 'descents'.
[4] Lit. 'ends', 'descents'. Bonwetsch translates the whole phrase 'at the fourth end
of this age'.   [5] So K: S is corrupt.
[6] Lit. 'and his intention will go out upon them'.
[7] K 'Kalkonagargail'. See note 9 to chap. iv on p. 459 (above).

VI.   Then will the Most High execute judgement on that place and deliver your descendants from *their* servitude to those peoples who rule over them by force; and they will be saved from the reproach of

2 their enemies. For the king will be the source of vengeance, and will

3 rise up in bitterness against them. And they will cry out, and the Lord will hear them; and he will pour out his anger on Leviathan the sea-monster and kill the heathen Falkon[1] with the sword, for

4 against the God of gods he will exalt his pride. Then, Jacob, will come your vindication,[2] and *that* of your forefathers; and others,

5 too, will come after you and share also in your prosperity.[3] And then will your descendants blow the trumpet, and the whole kingdom of Edom will perish together with all the rulers and the tribes of the Moabites.

VII.   And as you saw angels[1] ascending on the ladder– *that is* in the last years there shall be a man from the Most High, and he will join

2 the higher things with the lower. Of him before[2] his coming shall

3 your sons and daughters prophesy and[3] see visions about him. And there shall be these signs at the time of his coming – a tree felled with the axe will drip blood: three-month old babies[4] will speak rationally: a child in his mother's womb will proclaim his way; *and*

4 a young man will be like an old man. And then will come the

5 Awaited One, whose path will be found by none.[5] Then will the earth rejoice, having received the glory of heaven; and what was

6 above will be below also. And from your descendants will sprout a kingly shoot;[6] and he will rise up and overthrow the power of evil.

7 He will be the saviour of *all* lands, peace to those who labour, and a

8 cloud protecting the whole world from the heat. Otherwise what was in disorder could not be *put into order*,[7] if he did not come:

---

[1] Or 'idol'. See iv. 12 and the note in the 'short recension' (p. 459 above).
[2] Lit. 'Then, Jacob, will your righteousness appear'.
[3] Lit. 'and after you there will be those who will go out in your righteousness'.

[1] K adds 'descending and'.   [2] So K: S om.
[3] K adds 'your young men'.
[4] So S: K 'a three-month old baby'.
[5] So S: K 'whose precursor you are'.   [6] Lit. 'root'.
[7] So S: K 'Otherwise the ordered will not be put in order'. Cp. the *Palaea* interpretation in R ('otherwise what was spoken would not be fulfilled').

9 otherwise the lower things could not be joined to the higher. When he comes the bulls of brass and stone and all the carved images will give tongue for three days and they will tell the news to certain wise men, *that they may* know what is to be on earth, and they will find their way to him by a star. On earth will they see him whom the

10 angels do not see. Then will the Almighty be found with a body on earth, and be embraced by mortal arms; and he will renew humankind and give life to Adam and Eve – dead through the fruit

11 of the tree. Then will the deceit of the impious be uncovered, and all idols will fall down and be put to shame before his face, clothed, as he will be, in splendour; for they thought only how they might deceive,[8] but they will be able to rule no longer, nor *will they be able*

12 *to* give prophecies. *Their* splendour will be taken from them, and they will be left without *their* glory; for he who is to come will take *their* power and *their* might from them, and he will give the truth to

13 Abraham, which he promised to him before. Then will he make all sharp things blunt and the rough smooth, and he will cast all unrighteousness into the depths of the sea and perform miracles in

14 heaven and on earth. And he will be wounded inside the house of the Beloved;[9] and when he is wounded, then comes salvation and

15 the end of all corruption. And those who have wounded him will receive a wound themselves, from which they will never be healed.

16 And all creation will bow down to the Wounded One, and many will put their trust in him; and everywhere, and in all lands, he will

17 be known. Those who have known his name will not be ashamed; and his power and years will never fail.

---

[8] Lit. S 'for they imagined in deceit': K 'for they are lying of imaginations'.
[9] Cp. Zech. xiii. 6.

JOSEPH AND ASENETH

INTRODUCTION

On two occasions Origen quotes from a work entitled 'The Prayer of Joseph'.[1] On the former occasion he describes it as 'one of the apocrypha current among the Hebrews'; and this would seem to identify it with 'The Prayer of Joseph' mentioned in the lists of apocryphal books.[2] Yet this work can hardly be identical with our Joseph and Aseneth inasmuch as: (1) neither of Origen's quotations (and the first is of some length) occur in any known recension of Joseph and Aseneth, and (2) the long prayer in the middle of Joseph and Aseneth (chaps. xii–xiii) is a prayer of Aseneth and not of Joseph.

The first certain notice of Joseph and Aseneth in the West is to be found in the *Speculum* of Vincent of Beauvais (*c.*1250). At the appropriate point in his narrative in the *Speculum Historiale*[3] Vincent gives a Latin version of the story, introducing it with the words 'Ex historia Assenech'. This Latin version was reprinted by Fabricius in the first volume of his *Codex Pseudepigraphus Veteris Testamenti*[4] and in his second volume[5] he added a fragmentary Greek text (corresponding to something like the first third of Vincent's Latin version), which had been copied for him by J.-C. Wolff from the mutilated Bodleian Cod. Gr. Barocc. 148.

To-day some twenty or more MSS containing the Greek text are known: they date from the 10th to the 19th cents; and in all of them Joseph and Aseneth appears as one of a number of miscellaneous items – mostly lives of saints and passions. Two quite distinct Latin versions have come to light, and it seems that Vincent's extract represents an abridgement of one of them. A Syriac version

---

[1] Orig. *Comm. in Ioann.* ii. 31 (on John i. 6); *Philoc.* xxiii. 15 (from the lost commentary on Genesis, quoted in Eus. *Praep. Evang.* VI. xi. 64).

[2] For a full discussion see Jonathan Z. Smith, 'The Prayer of Joseph' in *Religions in Antiquity: Essays in Memory of Erwin Ramsdell Goodenough* (= *Studies in the History of Religions: Supplements to* Numen, xiv; Leiden, 1968), pp. 251–294.

[3] ii (118–124).   [4] i, pp. 774–784.

[5] ii, pp. 85–102.

is preserved as the sixth chapter of the first book of the anonymous *Ecclesiastical History* attributed to Zacharias Scholasticus: there are Armenian, Slavonic, and Rumanian versions; and there was probably also at one time a version in Ethiopic, and perhaps versions in Coptic and Arabic as well, although these are no longer extant.

The titles given to the work in the different authorities vary a good deal. Thus, one Greek MS gives 'The Confession and Prayer of Aseneth, the daughter of Pentephres, the priest', another 'The wholesome Narrative concerning the corn-giving of Joseph, the all-fair, and concerning Aseneth, and how God united them', while the Syriac has more simply 'The History of Joseph the just and Aseneth his wife'. The popular modern title, 'Joseph and Aseneth', is found in none of the authorities.

Similarly, there is considerable variation between the authorities in text. Throughout the work the Greek MSS differ widely in their wording (as in the choice of synonyms, or whether an idea is expressed by a participle or by a main verb with 'and'): phrases, and sometimes whole clauses, appear in different places; and there are continual minor additions, or omissions, which sometimes affect the sense, but more often do not. In some cases these differences are confined to the Greek, in other cases they are reflected in one or other of the versions, or in one or more MSS of a version. From time to time the differences are more substantial: in chap. xix, for example, the dialogue between Joseph and Aseneth is much longer in some authorities than in others: between chaps. xxi and xxii some authorities have an additional prayer of Aseneth; and there are several different endings to the book, one of which gives a brief summary of the subsequent history of Joseph and Aseneth, and records their deaths, mainly in the form of an extract from Gen. l. 22–26. From all this it is clear that the text was treated with the greatest freedom, and it seems to have been so treated from the very beginning.

The first critical edition was Batiffol's, published in 1889–90. Batiffol used four Greek MSS – Vat. Gr. 803 (11th–12th cent: A), Vat. Palat. Gr. 17 (11th–12th cent.: B), Bodl. Gr. Barocc. 148 (15th cent.: C – the fragment published already by Fabricius), and Bodl. Gr. Barocc. 147 (15th cent.: D). Batiffol's text is based on A (with which C generally agrees where it is available) rather than on B (with which D generally agrees). A full conspectus of variants is given in the apparatus, together with the evidence of the Syriac (quoted from Oppenheim's Latin rendering). There is a 37-page Introduction. And at the end is printed, as an appendix, the text of one of the Latin versions from two Cambridge MSS which had been collated for Batiffol by M. R. James.

Philonenko's edition of 1968 contains not only a text with apparatus, but also a French translation, notes, and a very full Introduction. When one compares his edition with Batiffol's, one becomes aware how much of the material now available for the reconstruction of the text has only become available since Batiffol's day. But, in ordering and controlling it, Philonenko had the advantage of being able to profit from several critical studies which had appeared in the interval – notably Burchard's masterly *Untersuchungen zu Joseph und Aseneth*, published in 1965.

Following Burchard, Philonenko divided the Greek MSS into four groups (designated *a b c d*). But whereas Burchard had maintained that the most reliable text was to be found in the witnesses to *b*, and had held that *d* was an abbreviated text, *a* and *c* being in their different ways 'improved' texts, Philonenko preferred *d* ('the short recension') and explained *b c* and *a* as expansions of it ('the first long recension', 'the second long recension', and 'the third long recension', respectively). Batiffol's MSS A and C belong to the *a* group, his B and D to the *d* group. And among the versions, the Slavonic is allied with the *d* group and all the rest with the *b* group.

Accordingly, in contrast with Batiffol, whose edition was (in Philonenko's terms) an edition of 'the third long recension' (*a*), Philonenko himself set out to produce an edition of 'the short recension' (*d*). His primary authorities were the MSS B and D and the Slavonic version; and all the variants of B and D are recorded in his apparatus. In addition to these two MSS he used also five other MSS – A (Batiffol's primary authority), representing *a*; E (Athos Vatopedi 600: 15th cent.) F (Bucharest Gr. 966: 17th cent.) and G (Chillicothe, Ohio: 16th cent.), representing *b*; and H (Jerusalem, St. Sepulchre 73: 17th cent.), representing *c*. However, readings from AEFGH are only cited in the apparatus spasmodically. The result is that, while the reader is left in no doubt about Philonenko's views about what the true text of the short recension is, and the evidence on which those views are based, he gains little or no idea of the text of any of the three long recensions. For the text of the *a* recension he must still go to Batiffol: for the text of *b* he must rely on the versions (other than the Slavonic);[6] while so far as the text of *c* is concerned, he is left almost completely in the dark.

In spite of its limitations, however, it has been thought best to take Philonenko's text as the basis of the translation which follows. E. W. Brooks's translation, published in 1918 was, of course, based on Batiffol's text. Consequently, anyone who is so minded can, by the simple expedient of comparing the two translations, at least introduce himself in a rudimentary way, in English, to some of the textual complexities with which the work abounds.

As regards the origin of Joseph and Aseneth, the earliest fixed point is provided by the Syriac version. The Syriac, as already mentioned, is preserved in Pseudo-Zacharias's *Ecclesiastical History*, where we are told, not only that it was made from the Greek, but also that the Greek text used by the translator was found in 'a very ancient manuscript'. The *Ecclesiastical History* itself, on internal evidence, cannot have been put together later than AD 570. This would seem to carry back the date of the 'very ancient' Greek text to the mid-fifth century at the latest. And if Philonenko is right in thinking that the *b* recension (to which the Syriac belongs) is secondary, then the *d* recension, of which it is an expansion, must be still earlier.

But further back than this it is impossible to go with any degree of certainty. The work is patently a romance based on the three passing references to Aseneth at Gen. xli. 45, 50–52, and xlvi. 20. The Rabbinical literature shows that there were legends about Aseneth circulating in Jewish circles in the first centuries of the Christian era – in particular, a legend that she was only the foster-child of Potipherah, being in fact the daughter of Dinah, born after the rape by Shechem and spirited away to Egypt by an angel, and therefore not an Egyptian at all. But these legends have

---

[6] This is particularly unfortunate inasmuch as Burchard was of the opinion that *b* offered the best text of all.

no direct contact with Joseph and Aseneth in the form in which we know it.

Yet traces of Jewish influence and Jewish interests are clear enough – for example, the statement in chap. i that Aseneth 'was quite unlike the daughters of the Egyptians, but in every respect like the daughters of the Hebrews', and that her charms were similar to those of Sarah, Rebecca, and Rachel,[7] or, again, Joseph's expostulation in chap. viii, when Aseneth advanced to kiss him, that 'it is not right for a man who worships God . . . to kiss a strange woman. . . . So too it is not right for a woman who worships God to kiss a strange man, because this is an abomination in God's eyes'.[8] On the other hand, the description of 'the man who worships God' in the passage in chap. viii just quoted as one who 'eats the blessed bread of life and drinks the blessed cup of immortality and is anointed with the blessed unction of incorruption'[9] seems just as clearly to betray Christian interest and influence, and the same may be said about the incident of the angel and the honeycomb in chap. xvi.

According to Batiffol the work originated in Asia Minor in the 4th or 5th cent. AD, and the author was a Christian, though he was dependent for much of his subject-matter on Jewish traditions and legends. Burchard, representing a contrary point of view, was of the opinion that Batiffol and those who followed him had not merely over-emphasized the importance of the so-called 'Christian elements' in the work, but had also radically misunderstood them. For Burchard there is nothing in it, anywhere, that cannot quite satisfactorily be explained as Jewish; and Burchard took the view that the author was a Jew of the Dispersion, who wrote in Egypt, either in the last century BC or the first century AD. Other views have been that the author was a nationalist and orthodox Jew of Palestine (Aptowitzer), or that he was an Essene (Riessler), or that he belonged to the Therapeutae (K. G. Kuhn).

Philonenko, in the Introduction to his edition, attacked the problem in the light of his analysis of the textual evidence. The primary *d* recension, he argued, is unquestionably Jewish: it was

---

[7] i. 7–8.
[8] viii. 5–7.
[9] viii. 5; cp. xv. 4.

designed partly as a missionary tract, aimed at potential Gentile converts, and partly as a defence of mixed marriages between Jews and Gentiles, aimed at those Jews who were unable to see the obvious proselytizing possibilities in such marriages; and it is a product of the Dispersion in Egypt, written probably about AD 100–110. About the origin, date, and purpose, of the *b* recension Philonenko was more doubtful: it may have been made by a Jew much given to mystic speculation, or by a Gnostic Christian. But about the *c* and *a* recensions being due to Christians Philonenko had no doubts at all.

Whatever may be thought about the details of this exposition (and it would be a mistake to press the details), the great merit of it is that it takes into account, and considers together, all the separate issues involved – historical, theological, literary, and textual. If a generally agreed solution of the problem is ever arrived at, it is likely to be along the lines that Philonenko has laid down.

But one thing is certain: Joseph and Aseneth was written in Greek. The text of the Old Testament presupposed is that of the Septuagint, and the language and style are Septuagintal throughout. There are no grounds at all for regarding the Greek as a translation of either a Hebrew or an Aramaic original.

As previously indicated, the Greek text here translated is Philonenko's. The symbols for the MSS are his; and the majority of the variants recorded in his apparatus, which are capable of being differentiated in translation, have been noted.

BIBLIOGRAPHY

EDITIONS

Greek

P. BATIFFOL, *Le Livre de la Prière d'Aseneth* (= *Studia Patristica*, i–ii; Paris, 1889–90).

M. PHILONENKO, *Joseph et Aséneth: Introduction, Texte critique, Traduction, et Notes* (= *SPB* xiii; Leiden, 1968).

Latin

P. BATIFFOL, *Le Livre . . .* [as above], pp. 89–115.

Syriac

E. W. BROOKS, *Historia Ecclesiastica Zachariae Rhetori vulgo adscripta* (= *CSCO, Scriptores Syri,* III. v, *Textus*; Paris, 1919), pp. 21–55.

> Latin translations of the Syriac in:
> G. OPPENHEIM, *Fabula Josephi et Asenethae apocrypha e libro syriaco latine versa* (Berlin, 1886).
> E. W. BROOKS, *Historia Ecclesiastica . . .* [as above] (= *CSCO, Scriptores Syri,* III. v, *Versio*; Louvain, 1924), pp. 15–39.

Armenian

A. CARRIÈRE, 'Une version arménienne de l'Histoire d'Asséneth' in *Nouveaux Mélanges Orientaux* (=*Publications de l'École des Langues Orientales Vivantes,* IIᵉ Série, vol. xix; Paris, 1886), pp. 471–512. [The text of chaps. xxii–xxix only, followed by a French translation.]

S. HOVSEPHEANTZ, *A Treasury of Old and New Primitive Writers.* Vol. I (*Uncanonical Books of the Old Testament*; Venice, 1896), pp. 152–198.

> English translation of the Armenian in:
> J. ISSAVERDENS, *UWOT*[2], 79–128.

Slavonic

S. NOVAKOVIĆ, 'Srpsko-slovenski zbornik iz vremena despota Stefana Lazarevića: 10. Žitie Asenethi' in *Starine,* ix (Zagreb, 1877), pp. 27–42.

V. M. ISTRIN, 'Apokrif ob Iosife i Asenefe' in *Drevnosti: trudy Slavyanskoy komissii Imperatorskogo Moskovskogo arkheologicheskogo obshchestva,* iii (Moscow, 1898), pp. 146–199.

TRANSLATIONS

English

M. BRODRICK (Prepared by, from Notes supplied by the late SIR PETER LE PAGE RENOUF), *The Life and Confession of Asenath the Daughter of Pentephres of Heliopolis, narrating how the all-beautiful Joseph took her to Wife* (London, 1900).

E. W. BROOKS, *Joseph and Asenath: The Confession and Prayer of Asenath, Daughter of Pentephres the Priest* (= S.P.C.K., *Translations of Early Documents*; London, 1918).

French

M. PHILONENKO, *Joseph et Aséneth* . . . [as above].

German

P. RIESSLER, *AjSaB²*, pp. 497–538.

GENERAL

V. APTOWITZER, 'Asenath, the Wife of Joseph: A Haggadic Literary-Historical Study' in *HUCA* i (1924), pp. 239–306.

C. BURCHARD, *Untersuchungen zu Joseph und Aseneth: Uberlieferung-Ortsbestimmung* (= *Wissenschaftliche Untersuchungen zum Neuen Testament*, 8; Tübingen, 1965).

——, *Der dreizehnte Zeuge: Traditions-und kompositionsgeschichtliche Untersuchungen zu Lukas' Darstellung der Frühzeit des Paulus* (= *Forschungen zur Religion und Literatur des Alten und Neuen Testaments*, 103; Göttingen, 1970), pp. 59–86.

——, 'Zum Text von Joseph und Aseneth' in *Journal for the Study of Judaism*, i (1970), pp. 3–34.

——, 'Joseph et Aséneth: Questions actuelles' in *La littérature juive entre Tenach et Mischna: Quelques problèmes* (ed. W. C. VAN UNNIK; *Rech. Bib.* 9; Leiden, 1974), pp. 77–100.

A.-M. DENIS, *IPGAT*, pp. 40–48.

L. GINZBERG, *The Legends of the Jews*, ii (Philadelphia, 1910), pp. 170–178 and v (Philadelphia, 1925), pp. 374–375.

K. KOHLER, art. 'Asenath, Life and Confession or Prayer of' in *JE*
ii (New York, 1902), pp. 172–176.

K. G. KUHN, 'The Lord's Supper and the Communal Meal at
Qumran' in *The Scrolls and the New Testament* (ed. K. STENDAHL;
New York, 1957), pp. 74–77.

M. PHILONENKO, 'Joseph et Aséneth: Questions actuelles' in *La
littérature juive entre Tenach et Mischna: Quelque problèmes* (ed.
W. C. VAN UNNIK; *Rech. Bib.* 9; Leiden, 1974), pp. 73–76.

P. RIESSLER, 'Joseph und Asenath: Eine altjüdische Erzählung' in
Theologische Quartalschrift, ciii (1922), pp. 1–13.

——, *AjSAB²*, p. 1303–1304.

E. SCHÜRER, *GjVZJC⁴* iii, pp. 399–402.

I. It came to pass in the first year of the seven years of plenty, in
the second month, that Pharaoh sent out Joseph to go round the
2 whole land of Egypt. And Joseph came,[1] in the fourth month of the
first year, on the eighteenth day of the month,[2] into the district of
3 Heliopolis. And he was collecting all the corn of that land, as the
4 sand of the sea. Now there was in that city a man, a satrap of
Pharaoh; and this *man* was the chief of all Pharaoh's satraps and
5 lords.[3] And he[4] was very rich, and wise, and generous, and he was
Pharaoh's counsellor, and his name was Pentephres; and he was
6 the priest of Heliopolis.[5] And Pentephres had a virgin daughter of
about eighteen years of age, tall and beautiful and graceful, more
7 beautiful than any other virgin in the land.[6] And she was quite
unlike the daughters of the[7] Egyptians, but in every respect like the
8 daughters[8] of the Hebrews. And she was as tall as Sarah, and as
beautiful as Rebecca, and as fair as Rachel; and this virgin's name
9 was Aseneth. And the fame of her beauty spread through all that

---

[1] to go round . . . came: B om.
[2] in the fourth . . . month: Slav. om.
[3] and this *man* . . . lords: B om.
[4] Lit. 'this man'.
[5] B 'and Pentephres was the first man of Heliopolis'; D om.
[6] Or 'upon the earth'.
[7] d. of the: D om.
[8] but . . . daughters = HA: BD Slav. 'and'.

land, even to its remotest corners;[9] and all the sons of the lords and of the satraps and of the kings sought her hand in marriage, young

10 men all *of them*. And there was great rivalry between them because of her, and they began to fight among themselves[10] because of

11 Aseneth. And Pharaoh's eldest son heard about her, and he begged

12 his father to give her to him as *his* wife. And he said to him, Give me Aseneth the daughter of Pentephres the priest[11] of Heliopolis as *my* wife. And his father Pharaoh said to him, Why should you want a

13 wife of lower station than yourself? Are you not king[12] of all the

14 earth[13]? No! See now,[14] the daughter of King Joakim[15] is betrothed to you, and she is a queen and very beautiful indeed: take her as your wife.

II. Now Aseneth despised all men and regarded them with contempt; yet no man had ever seen her, for Pentephres had a tower in

2 his house, and it was large and very high. And the top storey had

3 ten rooms in it. The first room was large and pleasant; and it was paved with purple stones, and its walls were faced with precious

4 stones of different kinds. And the ceiling of that room was of gold; and within it[1] were ranged the innumerable gods of the Egyptians,

5 in gold and silver. And Aseneth worshipped all these; and she

6 feared them and offered sacrifices to them.[2] The second room contained all *the finery for* Aseneth's adornment and *her treasure-*

7 chests.[3] And there was much gold in it, and silver, and garments woven with gold, and precious stones of great price, and fine

8,9 linens. And all her girlish ornaments were there.[4] The third room contained all the good things of the earth;[5] and it was Aseneth's

[9] even to . . . corners: Slav. om.
[10] among themselves: B om.
[11] B 'the first man'.
[12] So D: BE 'king as you are'; G 'For you are king'.
[13] Or 'land'.
[14] See now: D om.
[15] So BD Slav.: FH 'of the king of Moab'; A 'of king Joachim of Moab'.

[1] Lit. 'that room'.   [2] FH add 'daily'.
[3] In this verse the authorities differ not a little among themselves over the details, though without any change in the general sense.
[4] Lit. 'And there was all the adornment of her virginity'.
[5] Or 'land'.

10 store-house. And seven virgins had the remaining seven rooms,
11 one each. And they used to wait on Aseneth, and were of the same
    age as she was, for they were all born on the same night as Aseneth;
    and they were very beautiful, like the stars of heaven, and no man
12 or boy had ever had anything to do with them. And Aseneth's large
13 room, where she spent her time,[6] had three windows. One window
    looked out over the courtyard to the east: the second looked to the
14 north, onto the street; and the third to the south. And a golden bed
15 stood in the room, facing the east. And the bed had a coverlet of
16 purple woven with gold, embroidered with blue, and fine linen. In
    this bed Aseneth used to sleep alone, and no man or woman ever[7]
17 sat upon it, except Aseneth only. And there was a great court all
    round the house, and a wall round the court, very high *and* built of
18 great rectangular stones. And there were four gates to the court,
    overlaid with iron; and eighteen strong young men-at-arms used to
19 guard each of them. And along the wall inside the court every kind
    of beautiful tree that produces fruit had been planted; and the fruit
20 on every one of them was ripe, for it was harvest time. And on the
    right of the court there was an ever-bubbling[8] spring of water, and
    beneath the spring a great cistern[9] that received the water from the
    spring *and* out of which a river flowed through the middle of the
    court and watered all the trees in it.

III. And it came to pass[1] in the fourth month, on the eighteenth[2]
    day of the month, that Joseph came into the district of Heliopolis.[3]
2   And as he approached the city, Joseph sent twelve men in front of
    him to Pentephres, the priest of Heliopolis, saying, May I be your
    guest to-day,[4] for it is near noon and time for the mid-day meal?
3   The sun's heat is overpowering, and I would enjoy some refresh-
4   ment under your roof. When Pentephres heard this, he was over-

---

[6] Lit. 'where her virginity was nurtured'.
[7] So BH Slav.: D om.
[8] Lit. 'rich': D om.
[9] Slav. adds 'of marble'.

[1] BH Slav. add 'in the first year of the seven years of plenty'.
[2] So H Slav. Syr. Arm. Lat.: BDFA 'twenty eighth'.
[3] B Slav. add 'and he was gathering the corn of that land' (Slav. + 'as the sand of the sea').   [4] Lit. 'I will stay with you to-day'.

5 joyed and said, Blessed be the Lord, the God of Joseph. And
6 Pentephres called his steward[5] and said to him, Make haste and
get my house into order, and prepare a great feast, because Joseph,
7 the mighty man of God, is coming to us to-day. And Aseneth heard
that her father and mother had come back from their family estate
8 in the country.[6] And she rejoiced and said, I will go and see my
father and my mother[7] for they have come back from our estate in
9 the country. And Aseneth hurried[8] and put on a fine linen robe of
blue woven with gold and a golden girdle round her waist, and she
put[9] bracelets round her hands and feet, and she put on golden
10 trousers and a necklace round her neck. And there were precious
stones all about her, with the names of the Egyptian gods inscribed
on them everywhere, on the bracelets and on the stones; and the
11 names of the idols were stamped on the stones. And she put a tiara
on her head and bound a diadem round her temples and covered
her head with a veil.

IV. And she hurried and came down by the staircase from her
storey at the top; and she came to her father and mother and
2 greeted them. And it gave Pentephres and his wife great joy to see
3 their daughter Aseneth adorned as the bride of God. And they took
out all the good things they had brought from their estate in the
4 country, and they gave them to their daughter.[1] And Aseneth
rejoiced at the good things, and at the fruit, the grapes and the
dates, and at the doves and at the pomegranates and the figs, for
5 they were all delightful. And Pentephres said to his daughter
Aseneth, *My* child: she said, Lo, *here* I *am, my* lord. And he said to
6 her, Sit down, please,[2] between us: I want to talk to you.[3] And
7 Aseneth sat down between her father and her mother. And her

---

[5] Lit. 'him who was over his house'.
[6] Lit. 'the field of their inheritance'. And so similarly at iii. 8, iv. 3, xvi. 2, xx. 5,
xxiv. 14, and xxvi. 1.
[7] and my mother: BF om.
[8] B adds 'into the room where her robes lay'.
[9] she put = Slav.: BD om.

[1] and they gave . . . daughter: B om.
[2] So BH: D om.
[3] Lit. 'and I will speak my words to you'.

father Pentephres[4] took her right hand in his right hand[5] and said
8 to her, *My* child; and Aseneth said, What is it, father?[6] And
Pentephres said to her, See, Joseph, the mighty man of God, is
coming to us to-day, and he is ruler of all the land of Egypt, for
Pharaoh has appointed him ruler of all our land;[7] and he is the
distributor of corn throughout the country and is to save it from the
9 famine that is to come upon it. And Joseph is a man that worships
God: *he is* discriminating, and a virgin (as you are to-day), and a
man of great wisdom and knowledge, and the spirit of God is[8] upon
10 him, and the grace of the Lord *is*[9] with him. So come, my child, and
I will give you to him as *his* wife: you shall be his bride, and he shall
11 be your bridegroom for ever. And when Aseneth heard what her
father said, a great red sweat came over her, and she was furious[10]
12 and looked sideways at her father.[11] And she said, Why should my
lord and my father speak like this and talk as if he would hand me
over like a prisoner to a man of another race, a *man who was a*
13 fugitive and was sold *as a slave*? Is not this the shepherd's son from
14 the land of Canaan, and he was abandoned by him? Is not this the
man who had intercourse with his mistress,[12] and his master threw
him into prison where he lay in darkness,[13] and Pharaoh brought
15 him out of prison, because he interpreted his dream? No! I will
16 marry the eldest son of the king, for he is king of all the earth.[14] On
hearing this, Pentephres thought it wiser to say no more to his
daughter about Joseph, for she had answered him arrogantly and
in anger.

V. And behold, one of the young men from Pentephres's retinue
2 burst in and said, Lo, Joseph is at the gates of our court. And

---

[4] So D: B om.
[5] in his right hand = B Slav.: D om.
[6] Lit. 'Let my lord and (B om. 'my lord and') my father speak'.
[7] of all our land: DF om.
[8] So FA: BD 'was'; EH om.
[9] BD 'was'.
[10] Lit. 'she was angry with a great wrath'.
[11] at her father: B om.
[12] Is not . . . mistress = D Slav.: B om.
[13] Lit. 'into the prison of darkness'.
[14] Or 'land': D adds 'of Egypt'.

Aseneth quickly left her father and her mother and ran upstairs and went into her room and stood at the big window that looked towards the east, so as to see *Joseph* as he came into her father's
3 house. And Pentephres and his wife and all his relations went out
4 to meet Joseph. And the gates of the court that looked east were opened, and Joseph came in, sitting in Pharaoh's viceroy's chariot.
5 And there were four horses yoked *together*, white as snow, with
6 golden reins; and the chariot was covered over[1] with gold. And Joseph was wearing a marvellous white tunic, and the robe wrapped round him was purple, made of linen woven with gold: *there was* a golden crown on his head, and all round the crown were[2] twelve precious stones, and above the stones twelve golden rays;
7 and a royal sceptre *was* in his right hand. And he held an olive
8 branch stretched out, and there was much fruit on it. And Joseph
9 came into the court, and the gates were shut. And strangers, whether men or women, remained outside, because the gate-
10 keepers had shut the doors.[3] And Pentephres came, and his wife, and all his relatives, except their daughter Aseneth; and they made
11 obeisance to Joseph with *their* faces to the ground. And Joseph got down from his chariot and extended his right hand to them.

VI. And Aseneth saw Joseph and she was cut to the quick, her stomach turned over,[1] her knees became limp, and her whole body
2 trembled. And she was much afraid and cried out and said, Where shall I go, and where can I hide myself from him? And how will Joseph, the son of God, regard me, for I have spoken evil[2] of him?
3 Where can I flee and hide myself, for he sees everything, and no secret is safe from him, because of the great light that is in him?
4 And now may Joseph's God be propitious to me[3] because I spoke
5 evil in ignorance. What can I hope for,[4] wretch that I am? Have I

---

[1] Lit. 'shaded over'. Is the reference to a golden awning over the chariot, or was the chariot itself overlaid with gold?
[2] the crown were: B om.
[3] D adds 'and all strangers were shut out'.

[1] Lit. 'and she was strongly pricked in the soul, and her inwards were broken'.
[2] D om.   [3] D 'have mercy on me'.
[4] Lit. 'What then shall I see (= DF: BA 'follow')'.

not spoken, saying, Joseph is coming, the shepherd's son from the land of Canaan? And now, behold, the sun is come[5] to us from
6 heaven in his chariot and has come into our house to-day. But I was foolish and reckless to despise him, and I spoke evil of him and
7 did not know that Joseph is the son of God. For who among men will ever father such beauty, and what mother[6] will *ever* bear such a light? Wretch that I am and foolish, for I spoke evil *of him* to my
8 father. Now let my father give me to Joseph[7] as a maidservant and a slave, and I will serve him for ever.

VII. And Joseph came into Pentephres's house and sat down on a seat; and he washed his feet, and he placed[1] a table in front of him separately, because he would not eat with the Egyptians, for this
2 was an abomination to him. And Joseph spoke to Pentephres and all his relations, saying, Who is that woman standing in the solar[2]
3 by the window? Tell her to go away.[3] (*This was* because Joseph was afraid she too might solicit him;[4] for all the wives and daughters of the lords and satraps of all the land of[5] Egypt used to solicit him to
4 lie with him.[6] And many of the wives and daughters[7] of the Egyptians suffered much, after seeing Joseph, because he was so handsome; and they would send emissaries to him with gold and
5 silver and valuable gifts.[8] And Joseph would reject them out of
6 hand,[9] saying, I will not sin before the God of Israel. And Joseph kept his father Jacob's face before his eyes continually,[10] and he remembered his father's commandments; for Jacob used to say to Joseph and his brothers, Be on your guard, my children, against the strange woman, and have nothing to do with her, for she is ruin

---

[5] B 'like the sun is he come'.
[6] Lit. 'what kind of womb'.
[7] to Joseph: B om.

[1] So BEA: D 'they placed'.
[2] So BD: EFHA 'top storey'.
[3] Lit. 'Let her leave this house'.
[4] she . . . him: D om.
[5] the land of: BF om.   [6] DE 'them'.
[7] D adds 'of the potentates'.
[8] gold . . . gifts: B 'many gifts'.
[9] Lit. 'would send them back with threats and insults'.
[10] DH Slav. om.

7 and destruction. That is why Joseph said, Tell that woman to go
8 away.[11]) And Pentephres said to him, *My* lord, the woman you
   have seen in the storey at the top is no stranger: she is our daughter,
   a virgin, who detests men; and no other[12] man has ever seen her,
9 apart from you to-day. And if you wish it, she shall come and speak
10 with you; for our daughter is your sister. And Joseph was overjoyed
11 because Pentephres said, She is a virgin who detests men. And
   Joseph answered Pentephres and his wife and said, If she is your
   daughter, then let her come, for she is my sister, and I will regard[13]
   her as my sister from to-day.

VIII. And Aseneth's mother went up to the top storey and brought
   Aseneth *down* to Joseph; and Pentephres said to his daughter
   Aseneth, Greet your brother, for he too is a virgin as you are
   to-day, and he detests all strange women just as you *detest* all
2 strange men. And Aseneth said to Joseph, May you have joy, *my*
   lord, blessed *as you are* of God Most High; and Joseph said to her,
3 May God, who has given all things life, bless you. And Pentephres
4 said to Aseneth, Come near and kiss your brother. And when she
   came near to kiss Joseph, Joseph stretched his right hand out, and
5 laid it against her breast, and said, It is not right for a man who
   worships God, who with his mouth blesses the living God, and eats
   the blessed bread of life, and drinks the blessed cup of immortality,
   and is anointed with the blessed unction[1] of incorruption, to kiss a
   strange woman, who with her mouth blesses dead and dumb idols,
   and eats of their table the bread of anguish,[2] and drinks of their
   libations the cup of treachery,[3] and is anointed with the unction of
6 destruction. A man who worships God will kiss his mother and his
   sister that is of his *own* tribe and kin,[4] and the wife that shares his
7 couch, who with their mouths bless the living God. So too it is not
   right for a woman who worships God to kiss a strange man,
8 because this is an abomination in God's eyes. And when Aseneth

---

[11] Lit. 'Let that (DFH 'the') woman leave this house'.
[12] B 'strange'.   [13] Lit. 'love'.

[1] of life . . . unction = HA: BD Slav. om.; cp. xv. 4.
[2] Lit. 'strangling': D 'shame'.
[3] Lit. 'ambush'.   [4] and kin: BE om.

heard what Joseph said, she was most distressed and cried out aloud; and she fixed her gaze on Joseph, and her eyes were filled 9 with tears. And Joseph saw her and his heart went out to her – for Joseph was tender-hearted and compassionate and feared the 10 Lord.[5] And he lifted up his right hand above her head and said,

> O Lord, the God of my father Israel, the Most High, the Mighty One,
> Who didst quicken all things, and didst call *them* from darkness into light,
> And from error into truth,[6] and from death into life;
> Do thou, O Lord, thyself quicken and bless this virgin,
> 11 And renew her by thy spirit,[7] and remould her by thy secret hand,
> And quicken her with thy life.
> And may she eat the bread of thy life,[8]
> And may she drink the cup of thy blessing,
> She whom thou didst choose before she was begotten,[9]
> And may she enter into thy rest, which thou hast prepared for thine elect.

IX. And Aseneth was filled with joy at Joseph's blessing, and she went up[1] in haste to her storey at the top and fell on her couch exhausted, because she felt *not only* happy, *but also* disturbed and very frightened;[2] and she had been bathed in perspiration from the moment she heard Joseph speaking[3] to her in the name of God 2 Most High. And she wept bitterly, and she repented of her gods she 3 used to worship; and she waited for evening to come. And Joseph ate and drank; and he said to his servants, Yoke the horses to the

[5] for Joseph . . . Lord: D om.
[6] And from . . . truth = HA: BD Slav. om.
[7] DA 'holy spirit'.
[8] and remould . . . thy life = F Lat.: BD Slav. om. (A om. 'and remould . . . hand').
[9] She . . . begotten = BD Slav.: FA 'And number her with thy people which thou didst choose before all things came into being'.

[1] So BEA Slav.: DFH 'away'.
[2-3] Lit. 'and a continual (D om.) sweat was poured about her (= D: BFA om. 'was poured about her') when she heard these words from Joseph who had spoken'.

chariot (for he said, I must depart and go round the whole city and
4 the district[4]). And Pentephres said to Joseph, Stay the night here,
5 my lord, and to-morrow go your way. And Joseph said, No! I must
be going *now*, for this is the day when God began his works: in eight
days time I will come back again[5] and stay the night here with
you.

X. Then Pentephres and his relations went away to their estate.
2 And Aseneth was left alone with the[1] virgins, and she was listless
and wept until sunset: she ate no bread and drank no water; and
3 while all slept she alone was awake. And she opened *the door* and
went down to the[1] gate; and she found the portress asleep with her
4 children. And Aseneth quickly took down the leather curtain from
the door, and she filled it with ashes and carried it up to the top
5 storey and laid it on the floor. And she secured the door and
fastened it with the iron bar from the side; and she groaned aloud
6 and wept. And the virgin that Aseneth loved most of all the
virgins[2] heard her mistress groaning, and she roused the other
7 virgins[3] and came[4] and found the door shut. And she listened to
Aseneth groaning and weeping and said, Why are you so
8 sorrowful, my lady? What is it that is troubling you? Open *the door*
for us, so that we can see you. And Aseneth said to them from
inside (shut in *as she was*), I have a violent headache and am resting
on my bed; and I have no strength left to open to you now,[5] for I am
9 utterly exhausted;[6] but go each of you to her room. And Aseneth
got up and opened her door quietly, and went into her second
room, where *her treasure*-chests *and the finery* for her adornment were,
and she opened her wardrobe and took out a black and sombre
10 tunic. (And this was her mourning tunic, which she had worn for
11 mourning when her eldest[7] brother died). And Aseneth took off her
royal robe and put on the black *one*, and she untied her golden

---

4 Lit. 'land'.
5 So D Slav.: BEFA om.

1 D 'her'.   2 most of ... virgins: D om.
3 and ... virgins = EFA: BDGH Slav. om.
4 B 'made haste'.   5 BF om.
6 Lit. 'for I am grown weak in all my limbs'.
7 So BDA Slav.: EFG 'younger'.

girdle and tied a rope round her waist *instead*, and she took her tiara
off her head and the diadem, and the bracelets from her hands.
12 And she took her best robe, just as it was,[8] and threw it out of the
13 window, for the poor. And she took all her innumerable gold and
silver gods and broke them up into little pieces, and threw[9] them
14 *out of the window* for the poor and needy.[10] And Aseneth took her
royal dinner, even the fatted beasts and the fish and the meat, and
all the sacrifices for her gods, and the wine-vessels for their
libations; and she threw them all out of the window as food for the
15 dogs. And after this she took the ashes and poured them out on the
16 floor. And she took sackcloth and wrapped it round her waist, and
she removed the fillet from her hair and sprinkled herself with
17 ashes; and she fell down upon the ashes. And she beat her breast
repeatedly with her two[11] hands and wept bitterly and groaned all
18 night until the morning. And in the morning Aseneth got up and
looked, and lo, the ashes underneath her were like mud because of
19 her tears. And again Aseneth fell down on her face upon the ashes
20 until sunset. And so Aseneth did for seven days; and she tasted
neither food nor drink.[12]

XI. And it came to pass on the eighth day that Aseneth[1] looked up
from the floor where she was lying (for she was losing the use of her
limbs as a result of her great affliction).

XII. And she[1] stretched her hands out towards the east, and her
eyes looked up to heaven,[2] and she said,

[8] Lit. 'all her chosen robe'. Is the reference to the 'royal robe' of verse 11 – as we
have assumed? Or ought we to take στολή ('robe') here in the more general sense of
'equipment' and translate 'all her choice apparel'? If so, the girdle, the tiara, the
diadem, and the bracelets, which Aseneth had just taken off, will also be included
(as the editors of the *a* recension distinctly state), and perhaps some other items as
well – though xiv. 15 and xviii. 3 make it clear that Aseneth did not empty her
wardrobe completely! [9] D 'gave'.

[10] and needy: D om. [11] B om.

[12] Lit. 'and she tasted nothing at all'.

[1] So D: B Slav. 'she'.

[1] D 'Aseneth'. B prefixes to this chapter the title 'Prayer and Confession of
Aseneth', which is found also in A between verses 1 and 2.

[2] looked up to heaven: BD Slav. om.

2 O Lord, God of the ages, that didst give to all the breath of
    life,
  That didst bring into the light the things unseen,
  That hast made all things and made visible what was
    invisible,

3 That hast raised up the heaven and founded the earth upon
    the waters,
  That hast fixed the great stones upon the abyss of water,
  Which shall not be submerged,
  But to the end they do thy will.[3]

4 O Lord, my God, to thee will I cry: hear my supplication;[4]
  And[5] unto thee will I make confession of my sins,
  And unto thee will I reveal my transgressions of thy law.

5 I have sinned, O Lord, I have sinned:
  I have transgressed thy law and acted impiously,
  And I have spoken things evil before thee.
  My mouth, O Lord, has beeen defiled by things offered to
    idols,
  And by the table of the gods[6] of the Egyptians.

6 I have sinned, O Lord, before thee; I have sinned and acted
    impiously,
  Worshipping idols, dead and dumb,
  And I am not worthy to open my mouth unto thee, wretch
    that I am.

7 I have sinned, O Lord, before thee,
  I, the daughter of Pentephres the priest,
  I, the haughty and arrogant *Aseneth*.
  To thee, O Lord,[7] I present my supplication, and unto thee
    will I cry:
  Deliver me from my persecutors, for unto thee[8] have I fled,
  Like a child to his father and *his* mother.

8 And do thou, O[9] Lord, stretch forth thy hands over me,

---

[3] D 'ordinance'.
[4] hear my supplication: B om.
[5] D om.
[6] to idols . . . the gods: D 'to the idols'.
[7] O Lord = D Slav.: B 'also'.
[8] will I cry . . . unto thee = B Slav.: D om.   [9] B 'my'.

As a father that loves his children[10] and is tenderly
    affectionate,[11]
And snatch me from the hand of the enemy.

9   For lo, the wild primaeval Lion pursues[12] me;
And his children are the gods of the Egyptians that
    I have abandoned and destroyed;
And their father the Devil is trying to devour me.

10 But do thou, O Lord, deliver me from his hands,
And rescue me from his mouth,
Lest he snatch me like a wolf and tear me,
And cast me into the abyss of fire, and into the tempest of the
    sea;
And let not the great Sea-monster swallow me.

11 Save me, O Lord, deserted *as I am*,
For my father and mother denied me,
Because I destroyed and shattered their gods;
And now I am an orphan and deserted,
And I have no other hope save in thee, O Lord;
For thou art the father of the orphans, and the champion of
    the persecuted,
And the help of them that are oppressed.

12 For[5] lo, all the gods[13] of my father Pentephres are but for a season
and uncertain; but the habitations of thine inheritance, O Lord,
are incorruptible and eternal.

XIII. Look upon my orphanhood, O Lord, for unto thee did I flee,
2 O Lord.[1] Lo, I took off my royal robe interwoven with gold and put
3 on a black tunic *instead*. Lo, I loosed my golden girdle and girt
4 myself with a rope and sackcloth. Lo, I threw off my diadem from
5 my head and sprinkled myself with ashes. Lo, the floor of my room
once scattered with stones of different colours and of purple, and

---

[10] over . . . children = B Slav.: D om.
[11] and is . . . affectionate = B: D Slav. om.
[12] the wild . . . pursues = B: D 'as a lion he pursues'.
[13] So B Slav.: DFH 'habitations'.

[1] O Lord . . . O Lord = D: B 'O Lord'; Slav. om. altogether.

besprinkled with myrrh,[2] is now sprinkled with my tears[3] and[4]
6 scattered with ashes.[5] Lo, Lord, from the ashes and from my tears
there is as much mud inside my room as there is on a public[6]
7 highway. Lo, Lord,[7] my royal dinner and my fatted beasts have I
8 given to the dogs.[8] And lo, for seven days and seven nights[9] I have
neither eaten bread nor drunk water; and my mouth is dry like a
drum, and my tongue like horn, and my lips like a potsherd, and
my face is shrunken, and my eyes are failing as a result of my
9 incessant tears.[10] But do thou, O Lord, pardon me, for in ignorance
did I sin against thee and uttered calumnies against my lord
10 Joseph. And I did not know, wretch that I am, that he is thy son, O
Lord; for they told me that Joseph was a shepherd's son from the
land of Canaan, and I believed them; but I was wrong, and I
despised Joseph, thine elect one, and I spoke evil of him, not
11 knowing that he is thy son. For what man ever was so handsome,
and who else is as wise and strong as Joseph? But to thee, my Lord,
12 do I entrust him; for I love him more than mine own soul. Preserve
him in the wisdom of thy grace, and give me to him as a servant, so
that I may wash his feet and serve him and be his slave for all[11] the
seasons of my life.

XIV.   And as Aseneth finished her confession to the Lord, lo, the
2 morning star rose in the eastern sky. And Aseneth saw it and
rejoiced and said, The Lord God has indeed heard me, for this star
3 is a messenger and herald of the light of the great day. And lo, the
heaven was torn open near the morning star and an indescribable
4 light appeared, And Aseneth fell on her face upon the ashes; and
there came to her a man from heaven[1] and stood at her head;[2] and

---

[2] and bespr. with m.: B om.   [3] with my tears: D om.

[4] BD om.; Slav. adds 'to-day'.

[5] scattered with ashes: D om.

[6] Lit. 'broad'.   [7] B 'my Lord'.

[8] So BA: DFH Slav. 'the strange dogs'.

[9] and seven nights: Slav. om.

[10] Lit. 'as a result of the inflammation of my tears'.

[11] B om.

[1] So FG: B 'a man of light from heaven'; D 'the man of God'.

[2] Lit. 'over her head'.

5 he called to her, Aseneth.[3] And she said, Who called me? For the
door of my room is shut and the tower is high: how then did anyone
6 get into[4] my room? And the man[5] called her a second time and said,
Aseneth, Aseneth; and she said, Here am I, my lord, tell me who
7 you are. And the man said, I am the commander[6] of the Lord's
house[7] and chief captain[8] of all the host of the Most High:[9] stand
8 up,[10] and I will speak to you. And she looked up and saw a man like
Joseph in every respect, with a robe and a crown and a royal staff.
9 But his face was like lightning, and his eyes were like the light of the
sun,[11] and the hairs of his head like flames[12] of fire, and his hands
10 and his feet like iron from the fire. And Aseneth looked *at him*, and
11 she fell on her face at his feet in great fear and trembling. And the
man said to her, Take heart, Aseneth, and do not be afraid; but
12 stand up,[13] and I will speak to you. And Aseneth got up, and the
man said to her, Take off the black tunic you are wearing and the
sackcloth round your waist,[14] and shake the ashes off your head,
13 and wash your face with water. And put on a new robe that you
have never worn before,[15] and tie your bright girdle round your
14 waist – the double girdle of your virginity. And *then* come back to
15 me, and I will tell you what I have been sent to you to say. And
Aseneth went into the room where *her treasure*-chests *and the finery for*
her adornment were;[16] and she opened her wardrobe and took *out* a
new, fine, robe, and she took off her black robe and put on the new
16 and brilliant *one*. And she untied the rope and the sackcloth round
her waist;[17] and she put on the brilliant double girdle of her

---

[3] So B: D Slav. om.

[4] Lit. 'and how did he come into' (= B Slav.: D 'and how did you come here
into').   [5] B 'And he'.

[6] So BD: A 'chief captain'; EFG 'ruler'.

[7] So BEF Slav.: G 'of the Lord': D 'of glory of the Lord'; A 'of the Lord God'.

[8] So D: EFGA 'and commander'.

[9] So GA Slav.: D 'of all the host of the Lord Most High'; F 'of all the heavenly
host'; B om. 'and chief . . . High' altogether.

[10] Lit. 'stand upon your feet' (D 'stand up from the floor').

[11] B 'his eyes like the sun'.   [12] Lit. 'a flame'.

[13] Lit. 'stand upon your feet' (D om. 'upon your feet').

[14] round your waist (lit. 'from your loins') = FGA: B 'from you'; D Slav. om.

[15] Lit. 'a new robe, undefiled'.

[16] where . . . were: B om.

[17] And . . . waist: D om.

virginity – one girdle round her waist and the other round her
17 breast. And she shook the ashes off her head, and washed her face
with pure water, and covered her head with a fine and lovely veil.

XV.   And she came *back* to the man; and when the man saw her he
said to her, Take now the veil off your head, for to-day you are a
2 pure virgin and your head is like a young man's. So she took it off
her head; and the man said to her, Take heart, Aseneth,[1] for lo,
3 Lord has heard the words of your confession. Take heart, Aseneth:[2]
your name is written in the book of life, and it will never be blotted
4 out. From to-day you will be made new, and refashioned, and
given new life; and you shall eat the bread of life and drink the cup
of immortality, and be anointed with the unction of incorruption.[3]
5 Take heart, Aseneth:[4] lo, the Lord has given you to Joseph to be his
6 bride, and he shall be your bridegroom. And you shall no more be
called Aseneth, but 'City of Refuge' shall be your name; for many
nations shall take refuge in you, and under your wings shall[5] many
peoples[6] find shelter,[7] and within your walls those who give their
7 allegiance to God in penitence will find security. For Penitence is
the Most High's daughter and she entreats the Most High on your
behalf every hour,[8] and on behalf of all who repent;[9] for he is the
father of Penitence[10] and she the mother of virgins, and every hour
she petitions him for those who repent; for[11] she has prepared a
heavenly bridal chamber for those who love her,[12] and she will look
8 after them for ever. And Penitence is *herself* a virgin, very beautiful

---

[1] BFHA Slav. add 'you pure virgin'.
[2] Take heart Aseneth: D om.; BA add 'you (A + 'pure') virgin'.
[3] The authorities differ not a little in detail here. All, however, refer to Aseneth's
eating of the bread and all except F to her drinking of the cup. Her anointing with
the unction appears in HGA Arm., but not in BDEF Slav. Cp. viii. 5.
[4] BA add 'you (A + 'pure') virgin'.
[5] under . . . shall: D om.
[6] B 'nations'; G om.
[7] find shelter (lit. 'shelter themselves') = EGH: B 'lodge and sh. th.'; D om.
[8] on your b. every hour: B om.
[9] and (B om.) on b. of all (BG om.) who r.: D om.
[10] for . . . Penitence: D om.
[11] she the mother . . . for: B om.
[12] B 'him'.

and pure and chaste and gentle; and God Most High loves her, and
9 all his angels do her reverence. And lo, I am on my way to Joseph,
and I will talk to him about you, and he will come to you to-day
and see you and rejoice over you; and he shall be your bridegroom.
10 So listen to me, Aseneth, and put on your wedding robe, the
ancient[13] robe,[14] the first[15] that was stored away in your room, and
deck yourself in all your finest jewellry, and adorn yourself as a
11 bride, and be ready to meet him. For lo, he is coming to you to-day;
12 and he will see you and rejoice. And when the man had finished
13 speaking Aseneth was overjoyed. And she fell at his feet and said to
him, Blessed be the Lord God[16] that sent you out to deliver me
from darkness and bring me into light; and blessed be his name for
14 ever. Let me speak now, *my* lord, if I have found favour with you: sit
down a little on the bed, and I will get a table ready and food for
you to eat;[17] and I will bring you good wine, of the finest flavour, for
you to drink;[18] and *then* you shall go your way.

XVI. And the man said to her, Bring me, please, a honeycomb too.
2 And Aseneth said, Let me send someone, *my* lord,[1] to my family
3 estate in the country, and I will get you a honeycomb. And the man
said to her, Go into your *inner* room and you will find a honeycomb
4 *there*. And Aseneth went into her *inner* room and found a honeycomb lying on the table; and the comb was as white as snow and
5 full of honey, and its smell was like the breath[2] of life. And Aseneth
took the comb and brought *it* to him; and the man said to her, Why
did you say, There is no honeycomb in my house? And lo, you have
6 brought me this. And Aseneth said, *My* lord, I had no honeycomb
in my house, but it happened just as you said: did it perchance
7 come out of your mouth, for it smells like myrrh?[3] And the man

[13] So BEFHA: D om.
[14] So BFA: DEH om.
[15] So BD: HA 'even the first'; EF om.
[16] B om.
[17] Lit. '. . . and bread, and eat' (imperative).
[18] Lit. 'wine, whose savour reaches to the heavens, and drink' (imperative).

[1] So D: B Slav. om.
[2] Lit. 'smell'.
[3] D adds 'from your mouth'.

stretched his hand out and placed it on her head and said, You are blessed, Aseneth, for the indescribable things[4] of God[5] have been revealed to you; and blessed *too* are those who give their allegiance

8 to the Lord[6] God in penitence, for they shall eat of this comb. The bees of the Paradise of Delight[7] have made this honey, and the

9 angels of God eat of it, and no one who eats of it shall ever die. And the man stretched his right hand out and broke off *a piece* of the

10 comb and ate it; and he put *a piece* of it[8] into Aseneth's mouth. And the man stretched his hand out and put his finger[9] on the edge of the comb that faced eastwards; and the path[10] of his finger became

11 like blood. And he stretched his hand out a second time and put his finger on the edge of the comb that faced northwards; and the

12 path[10] of his finger became like blood. And Aseneth was standing

13 on the left and watching everything the man was doing. And bees came up from the cells of the comb, and they were as white as snow, and their wings were *irridescent* – purple and blue and gold;[11] and they had golden diadems on their heads and sharp-pointed stings.

14 And all the bees flew in circles round Aseneth, from her feet right up to her head; and yet more bees,[12] as big as queens, settled on

15 Aseneth's lips. And the man said to the bees, Go, please, to your

16 places. And they all left Aseneth and fell to the ground, every one *of*

17 *them*,[13] and died. And the man said, Get up now, and go to your place; and they got up[14] and went, every one *of them*, to the court round Aseneth's *tower*.

XVII. And the man said to Aseneth, Have you observed this? And

---

[4] So BDH: G 'the hidden things'; F 'the mysteries'; A 'the indescribable mysteries'.

[5] So BDA: FGH 'the Most High'.

[6] BF add 'your'.

[7] i.e. the Garden of Eden (cp. the LXX at e.g. Gen. iii. 23 and Ezek. xxxi. 9).

[8] Lit. 'and he gave of the comb with his hand'.

[9] B Lat. 'his forefinger'.

[10] So D Lat.: B Slav. 'appearance'.

[11] Lit. 'and their wings were as purple, and hyacinth, and as threads of gold' (= B: A '. . . hyacinth, and as scarlet': D Slav. om. 'and as threads of gold').

[12] Aseneth . . . bees: D om.

[13] every one *of them* = B: D Slav. om.

[14] And they got up = BFG A Slav.: D om.

2 she said, Yes,[1] *my* lord, I have observed it all. And the man said, So
3 shall be the[2] words I have spoken to you. And the man touched the
comb, and fire went up from the table and burnt up the comb; and,
as it burned, the comb gave out a refreshing fragrance that filled
4 the room. And Aseneth said to the man, There are, *my* lord, seven
virgins with me, who have been brought up with me, and who wait
upon me: they were born in the same night as I was and I love
them: let me call them,[3] so that you can bless them as you have
5 blessed me. And the man said, Call *them*;[4] and Aseneth called
them, and the man blessed them and said, God,[5] the Most High,
6 will bless you[6] for ever. And the man said to Aseneth, Take this
table away; and Aseneth turned to move the table, and[7] the man
vanished out of her sight, and Aseneth saw what looked like a
7 chariot of fire being taken up into heaven towards the east. And
Aseneth said, Be merciful, O Lord, to thy maidservant, because it
was in[8] ignorance that I spoke evil[9] before thee.

XVIII. And while this was happening,[1] behold,[2] a young man, one
of Joseph's[3] servants, came and said, Lo, Joseph, the mighty man
2 of God is coming to you[4] to-day. And Aseneth called her steward[5]
and said, Get ready a special dinner for me, because Joseph, the
3 mighty man of God, is coming to us. And Aseneth went into her
room and opened her wardrobe, and she took out her finest[6] robe
4 that shone like lightning, and she put it on. And she tied a resplendent royal girdle round her waist – and this girdle was[7] of precious

---

[1] Lit. 'Lo'.   [2] B 'my'.
[3] Lit. 'Pray, I will call them = DGA: B om.
[4] And the man . . . *them* = BG: Slav. 'And he said, Call *them*'; D om.
[5] So DEFG Slav.: A 'the Lord God'; B om.
[6] E adds 'and you shall be seven pillars of the City of Refuge'.
[7] B adds 'immediately'.
[8] D adds 'my'.   [9] B 'this word'.

[1] So B: D Slav. 'and when Aseneth said this'; F 'and Aseneth was saying these
things to herself'; A 'and while Aseneth was yet saying these things to herself'.
[2] So B Slav.: D 'immediately'.
[3] So BDA Slav.: EFG 'Pentephres's'.
[4] So D Slav. (plural): B 'you' (sing.).   [5] Lit 'him who was over her house'.
[6] Lit. 'first'.   [7] and this g. was: B om.

5 stones. And she put golden bracelets round her hands, and golden
boots on her feet, and a costly necklace about her neck; and she put
a golden crown upon her head, and in the crown, in front, were the
6,7 costliest of stones. And she covered her head with a veil. And she
said to her maidservant, Bring me pure water from the spring. And
Aseneth bent down to the water in the basin [on the cockle-shell];[8]
and her face was like the sun, and her eyes like the rising morning
star.

XIX.   And a little slave came and said to Aseneth, Lo, Joseph is at
the gates of our court; and Aseneth went down with the seven
2 virgins to meet him.[1] And when Joseph saw her, he said to her,
Come to me, pure virgin, for I have had good news about you from
3 heaven, explaining everything about you.[2] And Joseph stretched
his hands out and embraced Aseneth, and Aseneth *embraced*
Joseph,[3] and they greeted each other for a long time and received
new life in their spirit.[4]

XX.   And Aseneth said to him, Come, *my* lord, come into my
house; and she took his right hand and brought him[1] inside her
2 house. And Joseph sat down on her father Pentephres's seat, and
she brought water to wash his feet; and Joseph said to her, Let one
3 of *your* virgins come, and let her wash my feet. And Aseneth said to
him, No, *my* lord, for my hands are your hands, and your feet my
feet,[2] and no one else shall wash your feet; and so she had her way

---

[8] Philonenko would exclude these words on the ground that they make no sense.
He interprets the verse as a description of a rite of divination (lecanomancy):
Aseneth, therefore, could not bend over both a basin and a shell at the same time. It
is worth noting, however, that Batiffol's much fuller text, not only makes no
mention of a shell, but also leaves no room for doubt that Aseneth's purpose in
sending for the water was 'to wash her face', and that it was only when she saw her
reflection in the water that she desisted ('Lest I wash off this great and welcome
beauty').

[1] So D: BFA 'Joseph'.   [2] from heaven . . . you: D om.
[3] and embraced As . . . Joseph = DA: B om.
[4] Or 'by their breath': D om. 'and rec. . . . spirit'.

[1] So B: D 'and hand in hand (lit. 'holding each other's right hands') they
entered'.   [2] So DFA Slav.: B 'my feet your feet'.

4 and washed his feet. And Joseph took her by the right hand and
5 kissed it,[3] and Aseneth kissed his head. And Aseneth's parents[4]
came back from their country estate, and they saw Aseneth sitting
with Joseph and wearing a wedding[5] robe; and they rejoiced and
6 glorified God, and they ate and they drank. And Pentephres said to
Joseph, To-morrow I will invite the lords and satraps of Egypt,
and I will celebrate your wedding, and you shall take Aseneth as
7 *your* wife. And Joseph said, First I must tell Pharaoh about
Aseneth, because he is my father; and he will give me Aseneth as *my*
8 wife himself. And Joseph stayed that day with Pentephres; and he
did not sleep with Aseneth, for he said, It is not right for a man who
worships God to have intercourse with his wife before their
marriage.

XXI.[1]   And Joseph got up early in the morning, and he went away
2 to Pharaoh and told him about Aseneth.[2] And Pharaoh sent and
3 called[3] Pentephres and Aseneth.[4] And Pharaoh was astonished at
her beauty and said, The Lord will bless you, *even* the God of[5]
Joseph,[6] who has chosen you to be his bride, for[7] he is the first-born
son of God, and[8] you will be called the daughter of the Most High,
4 and Joseph shall be your bridegroom for ever. And Pharaoh took
5 golden crowns and put them on their heads and said, God Most
6 High will bless you and prosper your family[9] for ever. And

---

[3] Or 'her'.
[4] B adds 'both her father and her mother'.
[5] So BA Slav.: D 'bright'.

[1] Philonenko's text of this chapter is for the most part a reconstruction from the
Slavonic, B and D having a number of omissions. A, on the other hand, agrees in the
main with the Slavonic apart from a few small variations, expansions, and additions.
[2] and told . . . Aseneth: BD om.
[3] And Phar. . . . called = Slav.: D 'And Phar. called'; B om.
[4] Pent. and As. = D: Slav. 'Pent. and his daughter'; B om.
[5] And Phar. . . . God of = (A) Slav.: BD om.
[6] So A: Slav. 'Israel'; BD om.
[7] who . . . for = (A) Slav.: BD om.
[8] he is . . . and = F(A) Syr.: BD Slav. om.
[9] Lit. 'and multiply you'.

Pharaoh turned them towards each other, and they kissed each other. And Pharaoh celebrated their wedding with a banquet and much merry-making[10] for seven days; and he invited all the chief
7 men in the land of Egypt.[11] And he issued a proclamation, saying,[12] Any[13] man who does any work during the seven days of Joseph and
8 Aseneth's wedding[14] shall die. And when the wedding was over and the banquet ended, Joseph had intercourse with Aseneth; and Aseneth conceived by Joseph and bore Manasseh and his brother Ephraim in Joseph's[15] house.

XXII. And after this the seven years of plenty came to an end, and
2 the seven years of famine began. And when Jacob heard about his son[1] Joseph, he came into Egypt, with all his family, in the second month, on the twenty-first *day* of the month; and he settled in the
3 land of Goshen.[2] And Aseneth said to Joseph, I[3] will go and see your father, because your father Israel is my father; and Joseph
4 said to her, Let us go together. And Joseph and Aseneth came into the land of Goshen, and Joseph's brothers met them[4] and made
5 obeisance to them upon the ground. And they came to Jacob and he blessed them and kissed them;[5] and Aseneth hung upon his
6 father[6] Jacob's neck and kissed him. And after this they ate and
7 drank. And Joseph and Aseneth went to their house, and Simeon and Levi escorted them, to protect them:[7] Levi was on Aseneth's
8 right hand and Simeon[8] on the left. And Aseneth took Levi's hand because she loved him as a man *who was* a prophet and a worshipper

---

[10] Lit. 'drinking'.
[11] you will be called . . . Egypt = (A) Slav.: BD om.
[12] And . . . saying = (D) (A) Slav.: B om.
[13] So BFGA Slav. (lit. 'every'): D 'if any' ('man does . . . he shall die').
[14] B Slav. add 'that man'.
[15] So DFA Slav.: BG 'Pharaoh's'.

[1] his son: Slav. om.
[2] So BA Slav.: D 'Egypt'.
[3] So BEFGA Slav.: D 'we'.
[4] into . . . them = BA Slav.: D 'and Joseph's brothers'; B adds 'in the land of Goshen'.   [5] and kissed them = B Slav.: D om.
[6] his father: D om.
[7] Lit. 'escorted them because their enemies were envious of them'.
[8] So B: DFA Slav. 'Joseph'.

of God and *a man who* feared the Lord. And he used to see letters written in the heavens, and he would read them and interpret them[9] to Aseneth privately; and Levi saw the place of her rest in the highest heaven.

XXIII. And as Joseph and Aseneth were passing by, Pharaoh's eldest son saw them[1] from the wall.[2] And when he saw Aseneth[1] he was driven to distraction by her because she was so beautiful; and Pharaoh's son sent messengers[3] and summoned Simeon and Levi to him, and they came to him and stood before him.[4] And Pharaoh's son said to them, I have heard[5] that you are better soldiers than any others there are on earth, and *that* with your *own* right hands you destroyed the city of Shechem and with your *own* two swords you cut to pieces thirty thousand fighting men.[6] I need your help: let us get together without delay;[7] and I will give you gold and silver in abundance, and menservants and maidservants, and houses and great estates.[8] Make a compact with me,[9] and shew kindness to me; for I was greatly wronged by your brother Joseph, because he married Aseneth although[10] she was originally pledged to me. And now come with me, and I will take up arms against Joseph and kill him with my sword, and I will marry Aseneth; and you shall be my brothers and[11] my friends for ever, But if you will not listen to me, I will kill you with my sword (and as he said this he bared his sword and showed it them). Now Simeon was a brave but impetuous man, and he drew his sword from its scabbard and made a rush at Pharaoh's son, as if to strike him. And Levi was

---

[9] So B (lit. 'he would reveal them'): D 'he would reveal all things'.

[1] D 'her'.
[2] from the wall = BEA: DFG Slav. om.
[3] So BFA Slav.: DG om.
[4] and stood before him = BFG: D Slav. om.
[5] Lit. 'I know'.
[6] Lit. 'thirty thousand men of war' (D om. 'of war').
[7] So Slav. (lit. 'I call you to my aid: make haste. Lo, I will take you as companions'): D 'I call you to my aid: make haste'; B 'And lo, I will take you to my aid this day'; A 'And I this day will take you to myself as companions'.
[8] Lit. 'inheritance'.
[9] So G: B 'swear to me'; D 'listen to me'; A 'strive together with me'.
[10] Lit. 'and'.   [11] my brothers and: D om.

aware of what Simeon was about to do, for Levi was a prophet and
foresaw everything that was to happen; and Levi trod hard on
9 Simon's right foot as a sign to him to curb his wrath. And Levi said
to him, Why so angry with him? For we are the children of a man
who worships God, and it is not right for a man who worships God
10 to repay his neighbour evil for evil. And Levi said to his neighbour,[12] Pharaoh's son, respectfully and in good humour, *My* lord,
why do you speak to us like this? For[13] we are men who worship
God, and our father is the servant of God Most High, and our
brother Joseph is loved by God: how could we do[14] anything so
11 wicked in God's eyes? And now, listen to ús, and be careful you
12 never repeat what you have just said about our brother Joseph. If,
however, you persist in this wicked plan, see, our swords are drawn
13 against you. And they[15] drew their swords from their scabbards
and said, Do you see these swords? It was with them that the
Lord[16] God avenged the outrage on the sons of Israel, which the
men of Shechem committed in the affair of our sister Dinah,
14 whom[17] Shechem, Hamor's son, defiled. And Pharaoh's son saw
their drawn swords, and he was afraid and trembled and fell on his
15 face to the ground at their feet. And Levi stretched his hand out
and lifted him up, saying, Do not be afraid: only be careful you say
16 nothing against our brother. And they went out from him, leaving
him trembling and afraid.

XXIV. And Pharaoh's son was in much affliction and torment
2 because of Aseneth, and he was greatly distressed. And his servants
whispered in his ear, Lo, the sons of Bilhah and Zilpah, the
maidservants of Leah and Rachel, Jacob's wives, hate Joseph and
Aseneth and are jealous of them, and they will do what you want.
3 And Pharaoh's son sent messengers[1] and summoned them, and
they came to him by night; and Pharaoh's son said to them, I have
4 heard[2] that you are good soldiers. And Gad and Dan, the elder

---

[12] his neighbour: D om.　　　　　[13] Lit. 'And'.
[14] Lit. 'and how (D om.) shall we do'.
[15] D 'Simeon and Levi'.
[16] the Lord: D om.　　　　　[17] BD Slav. add 'in'.

[1] So BGA Slav.: DF om.　　　　　[2] Lit. 'I know'.

brothers, said to Pharaoh's son, Let our lord tell his servants what
5 it is he wants, and we will do it.[3] And Pharaoh's son was overjoyed,
and he said to his servants, Go away and leave us alone, for I have
6 something to say to these men privately. And all the servants went
out; and Pharaoh's son told them lies, saying, I offer you a choice
between prosperity and death:[4] so choose prosperity[5] and not
7 death. I know that you are good soldiers, and *that* you will not die
as women *die*; but act like men and take vengeance on[6] your
8 enemies. I heard (he continued[7]) your brother Joseph say to my
father Pharaoh, Dan and Gad are the children of maidservants[8]
9 and are not my brothers. And I am only waiting for my father to die
to take action against them and all their progeny, so that they will
not share the inheritance with us, for they are the children of
maidservants, and it was they who sold me to the Ishmaelites.
10 When my father is dead I will repay them for the wrong they did
11 me. And my father Pharaoh commended Joseph and said to him,[9]
What you have said is quite right, *my* son; and now[10] take some of
my soldiers[11] and proceed against them as they did against you,
12 and I will help you. And when the men heard what Pharaoh's son
told them they were much[12] troubled and distressed, and they said
to him, We appeal to you, *our* lord, to help us; and whatever you tell
13 your servants to do, we will do it. And Pharaoh's son said to them,
To-night I will kill my father, for my father Pharaoh is like[13] a
father to Joseph; and[10] do you also kill Joseph,[14] and I will marry
14 Aseneth. And Dan and Gad said to him, We will do everything you
have told us to. We overheard Joseph say to Aseneth, Go to-
morrow to our country estate, for it is vintage-time; and he has
arranged for six hundred armed soldiers to go with her and fifty

---

[3] Lit. 'his (= B: DEGA Slav. 'your') will'.
[4] Lit. 'Blessing and death are before your face (= BFG(A): D Slav. 'before the face of God').   [5] Lit. 'the blessing'.
[6] and . . . on = DA Slav.: B 'and greet'.
[7] Lit. 'he says'.
[8] B 'a maidservant'.
[9] to him: B om.   [10] Lit. 'for the rest'.
[11] D Slav. add 'with you'.
[12] DF Slav. om.   [13] D om.
[14] and . . . Joseph = D Slav.: BF om.

15 outrunners.[15] And when Pharaoh's son heard this, he[16] gave the
four men five hundred men each and appointed them their officers
16 and commanders. And Dan and Gad said to him,[17] We will go by
night and lie in wait at the brook and hide in the woods on the
17 banks.[18] And as for you, take fifty men with you, archers on
horseback, and go on ahead,[19] some distance in front; and Aseneth
will come and fall into our[20] hands,[21] and we will cut down the men
18 who are with her.[22] And Aseneth will flee in her chariot and fall
into your hands and you will *be able to* deal with her as you wish.
19 And afterwards we will kill Joseph while he is fretting about
20 Aseneth; and we will kill his children before his eyes. And Pharaoh's
son was delighted when he heard this, and he sent two thousand
21 soldiers after them. And they came to the brook and hid in the
woods on the banks, and five hundred men took up their position in
front; and in between them was a highway.[23]

XXV. And Pharaoh's son went to his father's room to kill him; but
2 his father's guards would not allow him[1] to go in to him. And
Pharaoh's son said to them, I want to see[2] my father because I am
3 going off to gather the grapes from my newly planted vine.[3] And
the guards said to him, Your father is in pain, and he has been
awake all night; but he is resting *now*; and he said to us, Do not let
4 anyone in to me, not even my eldest son. And he went away in
anger; and he took fifty mounted archers, and he went in front of
5 them as Dan and Gad had told him to. And Naphtali and Asher[4]
said to Dan and Gad, Why must you plot[5] again against our father
Israel and against our brother Joseph? For God looks after him as if

---

[15] and fifty outrunners = (F)A Slav: BD om.
[16] when . . . he: D 'the son of Pharaoh'.
[17] D 'the son of Pharaoh'.
[18] Lit. 'in the wood of reed(s)' (and so subsequently at xxiv. 21; xxvii. 7; xxviii.
5, 7).   [19] BA add 'of her'.
[20] So EFA Slav.: B 'your' (plur.): DG 'your' (sing.).
[21] EF 'ambush'.
[22] who are with her: B om.
[23] Lit. 'a wide (B om.) road'.

[1] B adds 'to kill him or'.
[2] Lit. 'I will see'.   [3] D 'vineyard'.
[4] and Asher: B om.   [5] Lit. 'work evil'.

6 he were the apple of his eye. Did you not once sell Joseph *as a slave*, and to-day he is king of the whole earth,[6] and *its* saviour,[7] and gives

7 us corn? And now, if you make plots against him again, he will call upon the God of Israel,[8] and he will send fire from heaven,[9] and it will burn you up, and the angels of God will fight against you.[10]

8 And their elder brothers Dan and Gad were angry with them, saying, Are we then to die like women? God forbid! And they went out to encounter Joseph and Aseneth.

XXVI. And Aseneth got up early *in the morning* and said to Joseph, I am going to our estate in the country; but I am frightened because

2 you are not coming with me. And Joseph said to her, Take heart and do not be afraid, but go; for the Lord is with you and he will

3 keep you from all evil[1] as the apple of an eye. And I will go and distribute my corn, and give corn to all the men in the city,[2] so that

4 no one dies of famine in the land of Egypt.[3] And Aseneth departed

5 on her journey and Joseph to the distribution of the corn. And Aseneth came to where the brook was with *her* six hundred men; and suddenly[4] the men that were with Pharaoh's son leaped out from their ambush[5] and joined battle with Aseneth's soldiers, and they cut them down with their swords and killed all[6] Aseneth's

6,7 outrunners. And Aseneth fled[7] in her chariot. And Levi, the son of Leah, was informed about all this (for he was a prophet), and he told his brothers[8] about Aseneth's danger; and they took, each one

[6] BGA 'land of Egypt'.

[7] and *its* saviour: B om.

[8] the God of Israel = BD: A 'the Most High'; Slav. 'heaven' (cp. EG Syr. 'he will go up into heaven').

[9] from heaven: Slav. om.

[10] and the angels . . . you: Slav. om.

[1] B 'danger'.

[2] all . . . city = FA: BD 'those in the city'; Slav. 'all men'.

[3] So DA: Slav. 'in all the land'; B 'in Egypt, in all the land which is under it'.

[4] Slav. om.

[5] from their ambush: Slav. om.

[6] killed all: B om.

[7] And As. fled = EFGA Slav.: D 'And As. was distressed and fled'; B om.

[8] And Levi . . . brothers = B: D 'And Levi was informed about . . . told the men of *his* counsel'; Slav. 'And Levi told his brothers'.

of them,[9] his sword on his thigh, and their shields on their arms,[10] and their spears in their right hands,[11] and they went after Aseneth
8   with what speed they could.[12] And Aseneth fled, and lo, Pharaoh's son met her, and fifty men with him; and Aseneth saw him, and she was afraid and trembled.[13]

1,2   **XXVII.**   And Benjamin was sitting with her in the chariot. And Benjamin was a sturdy[1] lad, about eighteen years old, indescribably
3   handsome,[2] and as strong as a young lion; and he feared God. And Benjamin jumped down from the chariot, and he took a round stone from the brook and hurled it with all his might[3] at Pharaoh's son and hit him on his left[4] temple and wounded him severely,[5] and
4   he fell from his horse half-dead. And Benjamin clambered up on a rock and said to the driver of Aseneth's chariot, Give me fifty
5   stones from the brook; and he gave him fifty stones. And Benjamin hurled the stones and killed the fifty men that were with Pharaoh's
6   son; and the stones sank into the temples of each one of them. Then the sons of Leah, Reuben and Simeon, Levi and Judah, Issachar[6] and Zebulon, went after the men who had lain in ambush; and they fell upon them suddenly, and cut down[7] the two thousand men,
7   and the six of them[8] killed them. And their brothers, the sons of[9] Bilhah and Zilpah, fled; and they said, We have been ruined through our brothers;[10] and[11] Pharaoh's son is dead, killed by

[9] of them = BA Slav.: DEFG om.
[10] and . . . arms = DA Slav.: BF 'and their shields'.
[11] and . . . hands = EA Slav. (cp. F 'and their spears in their hands'): B 'and their spears on their arms'; D om.
[12] with what speed they could (lit. 'at a swift run') = EF(A) Slav.: BD om.
[13] A Slav. add 'and she called upon the name of (A + 'the Lord') her God'.

[1] So BA: the others vary not a little here.
[2] D adds 'beyond the nature of man'.
[3] Lit. 'filled his hand and hurled it': cp. 2 Kings ix. 24.
[4] BD om.
[5] Lit. 'and wounded him with a great and grievous wound' (= G Slav.: EFA 'and wounded him with a grievous wound'): BD om.
[6] Slav. om.   [7] D adds 'all'.
[8] Lit. 'the six (D add 'hundred') men'.
[9] the sons of: D om.
[10] Lit. 'We are perished from out of our brethren'.
[11] D 'for'.

Benjamin, and all those with him have perished at his hand:[12]
come now, let us kill[13] Aseneth [and Benjamin],[14] and let us make
8 for the woods. And they came, with their swords drawn, covered in
blood; and Aseneth saw them, and she said, O Lord my God, that
didst quicken me from death, that didst say to me, Thy soul shall
live for ever, deliver me from these men. And the Lord God heard
her voice, and immediately[15] their swords fell from their hands to
the ground and were reduced to dust.

XXVIII. And the sons of Bilhah and Zilpah saw the miracle that
had happened and they were afraid[1] and said, The Lord is fighting
2 for Aseneth against us. And they fell on *their* faces to the ground
and made obeisance to Aseneth, saying, Have mercy on us, your
servants, for you are our mistress and queen, and[2] we have done
3 you[3] a great wrong and our brother Joseph.[4] And now God has
brought retribution on us: we pray you, therefore, have mercy on
us, and deliver us from our brothers' hands,[5] for they will avenge
4 the outrage *done to* you and their swords will be against us. And
Aseneth said to them, Take heart and do not be afraid, for[6] your
brothers are men who worship God, and do not repay evil for evil[7]
5 to any man.[8] But retire to the woods until I can secure your pardon
and mollify their wrath; for what you have been trying to do to
6 them is indeed no trifling matter.[9] Take heart *though*, and do
7 not be afraid, for the Lord will see justice done between us.[10] And
8 Dan and Gad fled to the woods. And behold, the sons of Leah

[12] and all . . . hand: BD om.
[13] So EFGA Slav.: BD 'make war against'.
[14] So all MSS: Slav. om.
[15] she said . . . immediately = (A) Slav.: BD om.

[1] DG 'much afraid'.
[2] your servants . . . queen and = F(A): BD 'your servants, because'; Slav. 'our mistress'.   [3] D adds 'our lady'.
[4] and . . . Joseph: Slav. om.
[5] BD 'from our brothers'.
[6] And . . . for = EG(A) Slav.: D 'And . . . them, Do not fear for'; B 'And we know that'.   [7] for evil: B om.
[8] to any man: D om.
[9] Lit. 'for you have dared great things against them'.
[10] Lit. 'between me and you' (= EA Slav.: BD 'between you').

came, running like deers in pursuit of them; and Aseneth got down
9 from her chariot, and she greeted them with tears. And they made
obeisance to her on the ground and wept aloud; and they asked
about their brothers, the maidservants' sons, intending to kill
10 them. And Aseneth said to them, Spare your brothers and do them
no harm, for the Lord has shielded me and reduced the swords in
their hands to dust, and they melted away like wax before the fire.
11 Surely this is enough for us that the Lord is fighting for us: so[11]
12 spare your brothers. And Simeon said to Aseneth, Why should our
13 mistress plead[12] for her enemies? No! We will cut them down[13] with
our swords, because they have plotted evil against our father Israel
and against our brother Joseph[14] now on two occasions,[15] and *they*
14 *have plotted* against you to-day. And Aseneth said to him, No
brother, you must not repay evil for evil to your neighbour,[16] for
15 the Lord will avenge this outrage. And after this[17] Simeon bowed
to Aseneth;[18] and Levi came to her, and he kissed her right hand
16 and blessed her.[19] Thus Aseneth saved the men from their brothers'
wrath, so that they did not kill them.

XXIX. And Pharaoh's son lifted himself up from the ground and
sat up; and he spat blood from his mouth, because his blood was
2 running from his temple into[1] his mouth. And Benjamin advanced
upon him[2] and took hold of his sword[3] and drew it from its
3 scabbard (for Benjamin had no sword of his own with him). And as
he was about to strike Pharaoh's son, Levi rushed up and seized
him by the hand and said, No brother, you must not do this, for we

---

[11] Lit. 'for the rest'.

[12] Lit. 'Why does our mistress speak'.

[13] D adds 'limb from limb'.

[14] against our father . . . Joseph = Arm.: B 'concerning our brother Joseph and his father Israel'; D 'against our father Joseph'.

[15] So DF (lit. 'now this twice'): B om.

[16] evil for . . . neighbour = BA: FG 'evil for evil'; D 'your neighbour evil'.

[17] after this = B: D om.

[18] So B (lit. 'Simeon greeted Aseneth'): D 'Aseneth greeted Simeon'.

[19] and blessed her = B: D om.

---

[1] Lit. 'in'.

[2] upon him = BFA: D om.

[3] D adds 'to strike him'.

are men who worship God, and it is not right for a man who
worships God to repay evil for evil, or to trample upon a man who

4 has *already* fallen, or to harry his enemy to death. But come: let us
bind up[4] his wound; and if he lives, he will be our friend, and his

5 father Pharaoh will be our father. And Levi raised Pharaoh's son
up and washed the blood off his face and bound a bandage round
his wound; and he set him on his horse and took him to his father.

6,7 And Levi told him everything that had happened. And Pharaoh
got up[5] from his throne and made obeisance to Levi upon the

8 ground.[6] And on the third day Pharaoh's son died from the wound

9 of Benjamin's stone.[7] And Pharaoh mourned for his eldest son,[8]

10 and he was worn out with grief. And Pharaoh[9] died at[10] the age of

11 one hundred and nine; and he left his crown[11] to Joseph. And

12 Joseph was king in Egypt for[10] forty-eight years. And after this
Joseph gave the crown to Pharaoh's grandson; and Joseph was like
a father to him in Egypt.

---

[4] Lit. 'let us heal him from'.
[5] So BFGA: D 'And when Pharaoh heard he got up'.
[6] B adds 'and he blessed him.'
[7] So BFG: D 'his wound which Benjamin gave him'.
[8] for . . . son = BA: D 'and all the council of the palace'.
[9] So B Slav.: D 'he'.
[10] D adds 'about'.
[11] So BEGA: F 'the crown of his kingdom'; D '*his* dominion and his crown'.

THE TESTAMENTS OF THE
TWELVE PATRIARCHS

INTRODUCTION

The Testaments, as we know them, are a collection of the 'last words' of the twelve sons of Jacob. In the form in which they have been transmitted to us they are clearly the work of a single author or editor, inasmuch as each individual testament is constructed according to the same overall pattern. First, the patriarch gives his immediate family, assembled round his death-bed, details about his own early life and experiences: next he discourses at some length either on a particular virtue they should cultivate or on a particular vice they should avoid, charging them meanwhile to keep 'the law of the Lord' and live in obedience to 'the commands of the Most High': then he warns them (not infrequently on the basis of what he has read in 'the writing of Enoch') of the evils that will come upon them as a result of their moral deterioration, though he can usually assure them that 'in the last times' God will bring 'salvation', not only to Israel, but also to the Gentiles; and then, finally, he asks to be buried, not in Egypt, but in Canaan, at the family burial-place in Hebron – and it is recorded in each instance that this was done.

The earliest explicit reference to the existence of the Testaments in anything like their present form is in Rufinus's translation of Origen's *Homilies on Joshua*:[1] here Origen seems to be referring to the passage about 'the seven spirits of error' in T. Reub. ii and iii: he calls the work in which the passage occurs (according to Rufinus) 'a certain little book which is called The Testament (*sic*) of the Twelve Patriarchs'; and he notes that it is extra-canonical. Similarly, Jerome knew a 'Book of the Patriarchs', and adds that it is apocryphal:[2] he says he found in it a statement which is most naturally understood as a free quotation from T. Naph. ii. 8; so there can hardly be any doubt that it is to our Testaments he is referring. Later on, the 'Patriarchs' occur among the recognized

---

[1] Orig. *In Iesu hom.* xv. 6.
[2] Hieron. *Tract. de Ps.* xv. 7.

apocrypha in the List of Sixty Books, the pseudo-Athanasian Synopsis, and the Stichometry of Nicephorus, though not in the Gelasian Decree. Parallels between the Testaments and Christian writers earlier than Origen (especially Hermas, Irenaeus, Hippolytus, and Tertullian) have sometimes been noted and used to argue that these writers knew the Testaments and were influenced by them, but the evidence is in fact insufficient to prove dependence in either direction: what it suggests, rather, is the common use of the same popular contemporary ideas and phrases.

For the text of the Testaments we are dependent to-day upon twenty-six witnesses in all – nineteen continuous Greek manuscripts, three collections of extracts from the Greek text, and four versions (Armenian, Slavonic, Serbian, and 'New Greek'). A Latin version should also be mentioned, made in the thirteenth century, by Robert Grosseteste from the Greek manuscript now in the University Library at Cambridge (Ff. 1. 24: 10th cent.).

It was this Cambridge manuscript that J. E. Grabe used for his text in the first printed edition of the Testaments in 1698; and to it he appended a selection of variants from the Oxford MS. Bodl. Barocc. Gr. 133 (13th cent.). Grabe's text was reprinted by J. A. Fabricius in 1713 and by A. Gallandi in 1765 (= *PG* ii. 1025–1160). In 1869 R. Sinker provided the first genuinely critical edition: he printed a much more accurate reproduction of the Cambridge MS as his text and added a full conspectus of variant readings from the Oxford MS in his apparatus: ten years later he published an *Appendix* with collations of two more MSS.

To R. H. Charles belongs the distinction of having investigated for the first time the details and inter-relationship of all the evidence then available. In his edition of 1908 Charles used nine Greek MSS (designated by the letters *a* to *i*[3]) together with the Armenian and Slavonic versions. He divided the Greek MSS into two groups, α and β. α represented the agreement of *chi*: all other MSS belonged to the β-group, which in turn Charles divided into two smaller groups. The former of the smaller groups consisted of *aef*, to which the Slavonic version was related: the latter consisted of *bdg*, to which the Armenian version was related. Charles thought that in general the α-group was preferable to the β-group, and for

[3] In this designation Camb. Ff. 1. 24 = *b* and Oxf. Bodl. Barocc. 133 = *a*.

the construction of his text he relied chiefly, within the α-group, on c (= Vat. Cod. Gr. 731: 13th cent.).

The next development was M. de Jonge's *editio minor* of 1964. This was in no sense a rival edition to Charles's. It was, rather, an abridgement and simplification, the purpose of which was 'to assist scholars in using Dr. Charles's material to greater profit'. Its importance lies in its editor's radical dissent from Charles's preference for the α-group among the Greek MSS. Instead of reprinting Charles's α-type text based on c, de Jonge reverted to the practice of Charles's predecessors and printed as his own text a transcript of b (= Camb. Ff. 1. 24), which he regarded as the best representative of the preferable β-group. To his apparatus he admitted only corrections of obvious mistakes and corruptions in b, and also a small selection of other variants (taken from Charles) that he thought might have some claim to originality or were interesting on their own account. The only exception here was the inclusion of variants found in the extracts from the Testaments in Cod. Venet. Marc. Gr. 494 (13th cent.), published by M. R. James in 1927, and which he designated k.

Fourteen years later, in 1978, followed the promised *editio maior* – the joint work of de Jonge and three colleagues. A number of discoveries had been made since Charles's day, but their total effect on the new edition was not nearly as great as might have been expected. Of the ten additional continuous Greek MSS discovered eight turned out to be copies of MSS already known, and therefore of no independent value: of the three collections of Greek extracts only one (k) proved to be of any serious significance; and of the four versions, only the Armenian was thought worth citing regularly in the apparatus. So far as the text itself is concerned, Charles's division of the Greek MSS into the α and β groups was abandoned. Since all witnesses except b (k) exhibit common errors against b (k), and since b (k) exhibit common errors against all other witnesses, the true division was recognized to be between b (k) and the rest – between what were now called Fam. I and Fam. II. At the top of the stemma, as reconstructed, stands the archetype of the whole tradition, which in course of time was developed and debased: b (k) represent the earliest surviving direct derivatives from the archetype: other groupings spring from later developments and debasements. The text printed is therefore an 'eclectic' text, in which the readings of Fam. I $(b(k))$ are usually, though not invariably, preferred to variants from Fam. II.

Our translation follows very closely the text of de Jonge's *editio maior*, and the symbols in the notes are the symbols from its apparatus.

Attempts to determine the origin of the Testaments have occasioned no little controversy.

Grabe, recognizing that in their present form they embody both Jewish and Christian elements, suggested that they were written by a Jew and interpolated afterwards by a Christian. But his theory was not accepted before 1884, when F. Schnapp, using Sinker's new critical edition, revived and developed it. In the intervening period the Testaments were universally thought to be a Christian work, and argument centred on the question whether the author was a Jewish Christian or a Gentile Christian. Schnapp's analysis, however, was adopted by Schürer in the second edition of his *Geschichte* (1886) and thus became widely disseminated. Bousset accepted it in a modified form. And so did Charles.

When purged of their interpolations, Charles maintained, the Testaments are patently Jewish. Their original language was Hebrew; and they were written in the later years of John Hyrcanus (in all probability between 109 and 106 BC). The author was a Pharisee, who combined loyalty to the best traditions of his party with unbounded admiration for Hyrcanus, in whom the Pharisaic party had come to recognize the actual Messiah. Having dated the Testaments thus exactly, Charles went on to stress that their permanent value lies, not so much in the light they shed on movements within Judaism in the late second century BC, as in the influence they exercised on the authors of the New Testament. 'The main, the overwhelming value of the book', he wrote, 'lies . . . in its ethical teaching, which has achieved a real immortality by influencing the thought and diction of the writers of the New Testament, and even those of our Lord'.[4]

---

[4] R. H. Charles, *The Testaments of the Twelve Patriarchs, translated from the Editor's Greek Text*, p. xvii.

This account of the Testaments met with a ready welcome and soon found its way into the text-books, with the result that the Testaments became firmly established as an essential part of the 'background reading' required of all students of New Testament theology and ethics. In 1953, however, in his *The Testaments of the Twelve Patriarchs: A Study of their Text, Composition, and Origin*, de Jonge challenged the whole basis of Charles's position. So far from being an interpolated Jewish work, de Jonge argued, the Testaments were in origin a Christian work that incorporated and adapted traditional Jewish material. They were to be dated, in all probability, about AD 200. To use them as 'background' evidence for the understanding of the New Testament, except in the most general way, is therefore illegitimate. What they illustrate is not 'the preparation of Christianity' but 'the social and religious life of the early Christian Church'.[5]

De Jonge's challenge inevitably forced on all those interested in the Testaments a fundamental reconsideration of the question of their origin. From the ensuing debate it has become clear that neither hypothesis is tenable in its extreme form, and that many of the details in both require considerable modification if either is to be seriously maintained.[6] And a number of mediating hypotheses have been put forward – H. C. Kee, for example, after investigating the ethical background of the Testaments, suggested that they were produced in a Jewish environment that thought and spoke in Greek, possibly Egypt, about 100 BC. It has become apparent, too, that certain lines of demarcation can no longer be drawn as firmly and finely as was once assumed. For instance, the distinction between the terms 'Jewish' and 'Christian', so far as they are applicable to the contents of the Testaments, has become blurred: a very great deal of the material in them is neither specifically Jewish nor specifically Christian – to counsel love for the brethren is not necessarily Christian, nor is it necessarily Jewish to utter warnings about the dangers of fornication. Or again, although in

[5] M. de Jonge, *The Testaments of the Twelve Patriarchs . . .*, p. 128.

[6] It is perhaps worth remarking that in the progress of the debate de Jonge himself played a not inconspicuous part, both by weighing carefully and answering the criticisms levelled at him, and by modifying details where he thought it expedient.

theory the distinction between a hypothesis which postulates a Jewish original interpolated by Christians and an alternative which postulates a Christian original based on traditional Jewish material is plain enough, if the Christian interpolations are held to be numerous in the one case and the basic Jewish material to be extensive in the other, the difference between the two in practice is nothing like so great as might be supposed.

On the Jewish side, attention has been concentrated on the detailed examination of the contacts of the Testaments with post-Biblical Judaism. Especially striking are the parallels between some of the 'extra-canonical' items in the Testaments and the Book of Jubilees: thus, Judah's exploits in battle, recounted in T. Jud. iii–vii, fit naturally into the context of the wars of Jacob and his sons against the Canaanites described in Jub. xxxiv. 1–9, while T. Naph. i. 9–12 and Jub. xxviii. 9 agree in representing Zilpah and Bilhah as sisters. Such parallels might easily be explained, of course, by supposing that a Christian author of the Testaments had read Jubilees in Greek (for we know that there was a Greek version of Jubilees circulating in the Church). But this kind of explanation is by no means universally applicable. At T. Zeb. iii. 2, for instance, is found the rather odd piece of information that, after selling Joseph, his brothers took the money and bought sandals with it for themselves and their families. The statement is paralleled in the Targum of Pseudo-Jonathan to Gen. xxxvii. 28 and again in the Pirke de Rabbi Eliezer xxxviii. In such instances there can hardly be any doubt that the author of the Testaments was directly dependent on popular Jewish traditions, either oral or written.

Of special interest in this connection are the so-called 'Aramaic Levi' and 'Hebrew Naphtali'. Among the manuscripts discovered in the Genizah of the synagogue at Cairo, and published in the early years of this century, were some sizeable fragments of two hitherto unknown works. One was a text in Aramaic, which was most naturally interpreted as part of a Testament of Levi and exhibited a series of verbal parallels with our T. Levi viii–ix and xi–xiii: the other was a 'Testament of Naphtali' in Hebrew, complete, and which, although essentially very different from our T. Naph., nevertheless had a number of points of contact – particu-

larly in its far longer version of the two visions recorded in T.
Naph. v and vi. The manuscripts containing both works are to be
dated in the early mediaeval period. Subsequently (in the 1950s)
further fragments containing texts similar to the Cairo texts,
though by no means identical with them, came to light at Qumran.
We can thus be certain that in pre-Christian times there were in
existence a Testament of Levi in Aramaic and a Testament of
Naphtali in Hebrew, though what, if any, connection there was
between them we do not know. The fact that one was in Aramaic
and the other in Hebrew does not suggest any immediate connection. It may be, of course, that both derive ultimately from a
collection of twelve Testaments, written either in Hebrew or
in Aramaic, and the the preservation of the particular texts we
have is due to accident and no more. Yet, if so, it still remains true
that texts of Levi and Naphtali alone have been preserved for us,[7]
that two texts of both have been discovered quite independently in
two different places and in manuscripts of widely disparate dates,
and that both texts of Levi are in Aramaic and both texts of
Naphtali are in Hebrew. In any event, the ancient texts recovered
differ so markedly from the Levi and Naphtali we know as to
preclude the possibility that they were in either case the Semitic
original of which our Greek text is a translation.

On the other hand, as might be expected, our Greek Testaments
show the unmistakable influence of the Septuagint. A trivial
instance of this occurs at T. Jos. viii. 2, where Potiphar's wife
clutches at Joseph's 'garments' (in the plural, as in the Septuagint
of Gen. xxxix. 12), and not at his 'cloak' (in the singular, as in the
Hebrew). A more substantial instance in the same Testament is
the mention of 'the hippodrome' by Rachel's tomb.[8] Many of these
instances are explicable as changes made casually by copyists, or
as deliberate modifications introduced into the text by revisers.[9]
But not all. In his initial work on the Testaments de Jonge drew

[7] The fragments of Aramaic Levi at Qumran appear to come from no less than
four separate MSS, which makes the absence of texts of any other Testaments
(apart from Hebrew Naphtali) all the more significant.

[8] T. Jos. xx. 3, from the Septuagint of Gen. xlviii. 7.

[9] Thus, in the first instance just quoted 'cloak' is read by a number of the MSS in
preference to the 'garments' of our preferred text.

attention to the statement in T. Iss. iii. 1 that Issachar grew up to be a farmer, which reflects the Septuagint of Gen. xlix. 15 as against the Hebrew ('a slave in forced labour')[10]. Since there are allusions to farming all through the Testament, and Issachar's sons are also described as farmers, it follows that this is no freak rendering, ascribable to some translator of a Hebrew or Aramaic original, who, when he came to T. Iss. iii. 1 just substituted the Septuagint rendering from Genesis for what he found in the text in front of him. The Testament of Issachar as a whole must have been composed in Greek. And, if Issachar, then in all probability the other Testaments as well.

It was observed at the beginning of this Introduction that in their present form all twelve Testaments are constructed according to the same overall pattern, and therefore we must suppose they are the work of a single author or editor. Who it was that first conceived the idea of producing this collection of twelve Testaments from the material at his disposal we do not know. (The likelihood is that he was a Christian of the second century.) What does seem fairly certain is that the material at his disposal was considerable, that others before him had produced Testaments of individual patriarchs, and that others after him (to judge from the complexities of the textual problems raised by both the surviving manuscripts and the versions) had no scruples about continuing the tradition he had inherited by altering his text and introducing further modifications and additions of their own.

BIBLIOGRAPHY

EDITIONS

Greek

R. SINKER, *Testamenta XII Patriarcharum; ad fidem codicis Cantabrigiensis edita: accedunt lectiones cod. Oxoniensis* (Cambridge, 1869).

——— , Testamenta XII Patriarcharum: *Appendix containing a collation of the Roman and Patmos MSS and bibliographical notes* (Cambridge, 1879).

---

[10] M de Jonge, *The Testaments* . . ., pp. 77–78.

R. H. CHARLES, *The Greek Versions of the Testaments of the Twelve Patriarchs, edited from nine MSS, together with the variants of the Armenian and Slavonic Versions and some Hebrew fragments* (Oxford, 1908).

M. R. JAMES, 'The Venice Extracts from the Testaments of the Twelve Patriarchs' in *JTS* xxviii (1927), pp. 337–348.

M. DE JONGE, Testamenta XII Patriarcharum, *edited according to Cambridge University Library MS Ff 1. 24, fol. 203a–262b, with Short Notes* (= *PVTG* I. i; Leiden, 1964).

——— , in co-operation with H. W. HOLLANDER, H. J. DE JONGE, and TH. KORTEWEG, *The Testaments of the Twelve Patriarchs: A Critical Edition of the Greek Text* (= *PVTG* I. ii; Leiden, 1978).

Armenian

S. HOVSEPHEANTZ, *A Treasury of Old and New Primitive Writers.* Vol. I (*Uncanonical Books of the Old Testament*; Venice, 1896), pp. 27–151.

Slavonic

N. S. TIKHONRAVOV, *Pamyatniki otrechennoi russkoi literatury*, i (St. Petersburg, 1863), pp. 96–232.

TRANSLATIONS

English

R. SINKER, *The Testaments of the Twelve Patriarchs Translated* (= *Ante-Nicene Christian Library*, xxii. 2 (Edinburgh, 1871), pp. 5–79).

R. H. CHARLES, *The Testaments of the Twelve Patriarchs, translated from the Editor's Greek Text and edited, with Introduction, Notes, and Indices* (London, 1908).

——— , *APOT* ii, pp. 282–367.

——— , *The Testaments of the Twelve Patriarchs* (= S.P.C.K., *Translations of Early Documents*; London, 1917).

J. ISSAVERDENS, *UWOT²*, pp. 267–358 – from the Armenian.

German

F. SCHNAPP in E. KAUTZSCH, *APAT* ii, pp. 458–506.
P. RIESSLER, *AjSaB*², pp. 1149–1250.
J. BECKER in *JSh–rZ* III. 1 (1974), pp. 1–164.

GENERAL

J. BECKER, *Untersuchungen zur Entstehungsgeschicte der Testamente der Zwölf Patriarchen* (= *Arbeiten zur Geschicte des antiken Judentums und des Urchristentums*, 8; Leiden, 1970).
E. J. BICKERMAN, 'The Date of the Testaments of the Twelve Patriarchs' in *JBL* lxix (1950), pp. 245–260.
W. BOUSSET, 'Die Testamente der Zwölf Patriarchen' in *ZNW* i (1900), pp. 141–175, 187–209, 344–346.
F.-M. BRAUN, 'Les Testaments des XII Patriarches et le problème de leur origine' in *R Bibl* lxvii (1960), pp. 516–549.
C. BURCHARD, 'Zur armenischen Überlieferung der Testamente der zwölf Patriarchen' in (ed. W. ELTESTER) *Studien zu den Testamenten der Zwölf Patriarchen* (= *Beihefte zur ZNW*, xxxvi; Berlin, 1969), pp. 1–29.
F. C. CONYBEARE, 'On the Jewish Authorship of the Testaments of the Twelve Patriarchs' in *JQR* v (April 1893), pp. 375–398.
A.-M. DENIS, *IPGAT*, pp. 49–59.
O. EISSFELDT, *OTI*, pp. 631–636.
J.-B. FREY, art. 'Apocryphes de l'Ancien Testament' in *DB Sup* i, cols. 380–390.
J. W. HUNKIN, 'The Testaments of the Twelve Patriarchs' in *JTS* xvi (1915), pp. 80–97.
M. DE JONGE, *The Testaments of the Twelve Patriarchs: A Study of their Text, Composition and Origin* (Assen, 1953).
—— (ed.), *Studies on the Testaments of the Twelve Patriarchs: Text and Interpretation* (= *SVTP* 3; Leiden, 1975).
—— , 'The Main Issues in the Study of the Testaments of the Twelve Patriarchs' in *NTS* xxvi. 4 (July 1980), pp. 508–524.
H. C. KEE, 'The Ethical Dimensions of the Testaments of the XII

Patriarchs as a Clue to Provenance' in *NTS* xxiv. 2 (Jan. 1978), pp. 259–270.

K. KOHLER, 'The Pre-Talmudic Haggada I.A. The Testaments of the Twelve Patriarchs' in *JQR* v (April 1893), pp. 400–406.

—— , art. 'Testaments of the Twelve Patriarchs' in *JE* xii (New York, 1906), pp. 113–118.

E. PREUSCHEN, 'Die armenische Übersetzung der Testamente der zwölf Patriarchen' in *ZNW* i (1900), pp. 106–140.

K. H. RENGSTORF, 'Herkunft und Sinn der Patriarchen-Reden in den Testamenten der zwölf Patriarchen' in *La littérature juive entre Tenach et Mischna: Quelques problèmes* (ed. W. C. VAN UNNIK; *Rech. Bib.* 9, Leiden, 1974), pp. 29–47.

P. RIESSLER, *AjSaB²*, pp. 1335–1338.

L. ROST, *EATAP*, pp. 106–110.

F. SCHNAPP, *Die Testamente der zwölf Patriarchen untersucht* (Halle, 1884).

E. SCHÜRER, *HJPTJC* II. iii, pp. 114–124.

—— , *GjVZJC⁴* iii, pp. 339–356.

C. C. TORREY, *AL*, pp. 129–131.

É. TURDEANU, 'Les Testaments des Douze Patriarches en slave' in *Journal for the Study of Judaism*, i (1970), pp. 148–184.

THE TESTAMENT OF REUBEN, ABOUT IDEAS

I. A copy of the Testament of Reuben, which he gave as a command to his sons before he died, in the hundred and twenty-fifth year of his life.

2 When he was ill, two years after the death of Joseph, his sons and
3 grandsons met together to visit him. And he said to them, My
4 children, I am dying and going the way of my fathers. And seeing there Judah and Gad and Asher, his brothers, he said to them, Raise me up, *my* brothers, so that I can tell my brothers and my
5 children what lies hidden in my heart; for I am about to die. And he

got up and kissed them and said, weeping, Listen, my brothers, pay attention ⟨my sons⟩,[1] to Reuben your father, *and* to the

6 commands I give you. And behold, I call the God of heaven to witness against you to-day, so that you do not live your lives in the ignorance of youth and give yourselves up to fornication, as I did,

7 and defiled my father Jacob's bed. For I tell you, he struck me with a foul disease in my loins for seven months; and had not my father Jacob prayed for me to the Lord, ⟨I would have died⟩,[2] for[3] the

8 Lord was minded to destroy me. For I was thirty years old when I did *this* evil before the Lord; and for seven months I was

9 dangerously ill. And with determination I set myself for seven

10 years to repent before the Lord. I drank no wine nor strong drink, no meat entered my mouth, and I tasted no pleasant food at all, as I mourned over my sin (for it was great). May no such thing *ever again* happen in Israel!

II. And now listen to me, children, *and I will tell you* what I saw

2 concerning the seven spirits of error when I repented. Seven spirits were appointed[1] by Beliar against man, and they are responsible

3 for what he does when young.[2] [[3] Also seven spirits were given him

4 at the creation to be the means of his doing everything.[4] *The* first *is* the spirit of life, with which *man's* substance is created. *The* second

5 *is* the spirit of sight, with which comes desire. *The* third *is* the spirit of hearing, with which is given[5] teaching. *The* fourth *is* the spirit of

6 smell, with which taste is given to draw in air and breath. *The* fifth

7 *is* the spirit of speech, with which comes knowledge. *The* sixth *is* the spirit of taste, with which comes eating and drinking;[6] and by

---

[1] The restoration seems called for by Reuben's description of himself as 'your father': *lm* add 'and my children' and *chn* add 'and my sons' after 'my brothers', and *d* reads 'children' instead of 'my brothers'. Cp. T. Jos. i. 2.

[2] Cp. T. Jud. xix. 2; T. Gad v. 9.

[3] So *b ef*: *gldm a chi* om.

[1] Lit. 'given'.

[2] Lit. 'and they are the origin of the works of youth'.

[3] We follow Charles in bracketing ii. 3–iii. 2 as an interpolation: iii. 3 follows naturally on ii. 2.

[4] Lit. 'so that by them should be *done* every work of man'.

[5] So *ldm ef*: *bka chi* 'with which comes'.

[6] Lit. 'with which comes the eating of foods and drinks'.

them[7] *man's* strength is built up (for food is the foundation of
8 strength). *The* seventh *is* the spirit of procreation and sexual
9 intercourse, with which sin enters through love of pleasure. For
this reason it is last *in the order* of creation and first *among the desires* of
youth, because the truth about it goes unrecognized,[8] and it leads
the young man like a blind man to a pit, and like a beast over a
precipice.

III. Besides all these there is an eighth spirit of sleep, with which
were brought into being the deep sleep[1] of nature and the image of
2,3 death. With these spirits is mingled the spirit[2] of error.] *The* first,
the spirit of fornication, is seated in the nature and the senses: *the*
second, *the* spirit of insatiate desire, in the stomach: *the* third, *the*
4 spirit of fighting, in the liver and the gall. *The* fourth *is the* spirit of
obsequiousness and chicanery, so that by studied effort *a man* can
5 make a good impression. The fifth *is the* spirit of arrogance, so that
he can boast[3] and have a good opinion of himself. *The* sixth *is the*
spirit of lying, *which leads a man* to invent things in depravity and
envy, and to conceal things[4] from his family and the members of his
6 household. *The* seventh *is the* spirit of unrighteousness, with which
come theft and acts of rapacity, so that *a man* can satisfy his own
natural love of pleasure;[5] for unrighteousness works together with
7 the other spirits by a mutual give-and-take.[6] [And besides all these
the spirit of sleep, the eighth spirit, is combined with error and
8 phantasy.][7] And so every young man perishes and plunges his
mind into darkness away from the truth, inasmuch as he neither
understands the law of God nor takes note of his fathers' warnings
9 (as, indeed, happened to me in my youth). And now, children, love

---

[7] So *bl*: II-*l* (*d*) 'by it' (i.e. by the spirit of taste).
[8] Lit. 'because it has been filled with ignorance'.

[1] Or 'trance' or 'fear' (Gk. ἔκστασις: cp. Gen. ii. 21, xv. 12; 1 Sam xi. 7; etc.).
[2] So *bdm*: II-*dm* 'are mingled the spirits'.
[3] So II: *bk* 'so that he can be excited'.
[4] *b c* om. 'and to conceal things'.
[5] Lit. 'so that he can do the love of pleasure of his heart'.
[6] There are several different readings here, none of which is entirely satisfactory.
Charles preferred 'by the taking of gifts'.
[7] Cp. verse 1.

the truth and it will keep you safe. This is my advice to you.[8] Listen to your father Reuben.

10 Pay no attention to a woman's face, and never be alone with another man's wife, nor be too inquisitive about women's affairs.
11 For had I not seen Bilhah bathing in a secluded place I would not
12 have fallen into so great a sin.[9] For my mind was obsessed by the thought of *her* woman's nakedness and would not let me sleep until
13 I had done the abominable thing. For while our father Jacob was away on a visit to his father Isaac, when we were in Eder, near the house of Ephrath (*that is* Bethlehem),[10] Bilhah had been drinking; and she was lying asleep in her bedroom with nothing over her.
14 And I went in and saw her nakedness and did the wicked deed; and
15 I left her still asleep and went away. And immediately an angel of God told my father Jacob about my wickedness; and he came and mourned over me. And *as for Bilhah*, he had no further relations with her.

IV. Pay no attention, therefore, to women's beauty, neither bother your minds about their affairs; but live in simplicity of heart *and* in the fear of the Lord, persevering in *your* labours and devoting yourselves to learning and *the tending of* your flocks,[1] until the Lord gives you the wife he has chosen for you,[2] so that you do not suffer
2 as I did. Until[3] my father's death I had not the courage to look Jacob in the face, nor to speak to any of my brothers because of *their*
3 reproaches. And even now my conscience smites me because of my
4 sin. However, my father encouraged me, for he prayed to the Lord for me, that the Lord's anger might pass me by, even as the Lord showed me. And from then on I repented and[4] I have been very
5 careful and have not sinned. So, my children, observe all the
6 commands I give you and you will not sin. For fornication is

---

[8] Lit. 'I am teaching you'.
[9] Lit. 'into the great sin'.
[10] So *b*: *ldme* 'near Ephrath and Bethlehem'; *af nchi* 'near Ephrath in Bethlehem'.

[1] and devoting . . . flocks: lit. 'and wandering in letters and your flocks'.
[2] Lit. 'a wife whom he wills'.
[3] So *b*: II 'for until'.
[4] So *gld* Arm.: *b* 'from then on therefore'; *eaf* 'from then on even in *my* thoughts'; *chi* 'from then on until now'.

destruction to the soul: it separates from God and drives *those who indulge in it* to idols, inasmuch as it clouds the mind and understanding; and it leads young men down to Hades before their
7 time.[5] For fornication has ruined many; because, even though a man be old or of noble birth, it makes him an *object of* reproach and
8 a laughing-stock with *both* Beliar and his fellow men.[6] For it was because Joseph avoided women and kept his mind pure from all thoughts of fornication that he found favour with the Lord and
9 men. For the Egyptian woman did many things to him, and sent for magicians, and brought him love-potions; but he stood firm
10 against temptation.[7] And so the God of my fathers rescued him
11 from every visible and hidden death. For if fornication has not gained the mastery over the mind,[8] neither will Beliar gain the mastery over you.

V. Women are evil, my children: because they have no power or strength *to stand up* against man, they use wiles and try to ensnare
2 him by *their* charms;[1] and *man*, whom *woman* cannot subdue by
3 strength, she subdues by guile. For, indeed, the angel of God told me about them and taught me that women yield to the spirit of fornication more *easily* than a man *does*, and they lay plots in *their* hearts against men: by the way they adorn themselves they first lead their minds astray, and by a look they instil the poison, and
4 then in the act *itself* they take them captive – for a woman cannot
5 overcome a man by force. So shun fornication, my children, and command your wives and daughters not to adorn their heads and faces,[2] for every woman that uses wiles of this kind has been
6 reserved for eternal punishment. It was thus that they allured the Watchers before the flood; for, as a result of seeing them continually, the Watchers[3] lusted after one another, and they conceived the act in their minds and changed themselves into the shape of men and appeared to the women[4] when they were having inter-

---

[5] Lit. 'not in their time'.   [6] Lit. 'and the sons of men'.
[7] Lit. 'the inclination of his soul admitted no evil desire'.
[8] So *b a*: II-*a* 'your mind'.

[1] Lit. 'forms'.   [2] So *bk*: II adds 'to deceive the mind'.
[3] Lit. 'these'.   [4] Lit. 'them'.

7 course with their husbands. And the women,[3] lusting in their minds after their phantom forms, gave birth to giants (for the Watchers seemed to them tall enough to touch the sky).

VI. Beware, then, of fornication; and if you would be pure in mind,
2 guard your senses against every woman.[1] And command the women,[2] too, not to make close friends of men,[3] so that they also
3 may be pure in mind. For constant meetings, even though no sinful acts may be involved, are for women[2] a disease for which there is no
4 cure, and for us an eternal reproach of Beliar. For indulgence in fornication allows no scope for either understanding or godliness, and the lust that inspires it provides a home for every kind of
5 jealousy.[4] And so you will be jealous[5] of the sons of Levi and seek[5]
6 to be raised above them; but you will not succeed. For God will
7 avenge them, and you will die a cruel death. For to Levi the Lord gave the sovereignty – and to Judah (and with them also to me and
8 Dan and Joseph, that we should be rulers *too*). For this reason I command you to listen to Levi, for he will know the law of the Lord and interpret his precepts and offer sacrifice for all Israel until the
9 coming[6] of the anointed high priest,[7] of whom the Lord spoke. I charge you by the God of heaven to deal honestly, each one with his
10 neighbour, and to have love, each one for his brother.[8] And approach Levi with humility, so that you may receive a blessing
11 from his mouth. For he shall bless Israel and Judah, because the
12 Lord has chosen him to rule as king over all the peoples. And accord his sons their proper reverence[9] for they[10] will die in wars on our behalf (*in wars* seen and unseen), and he[10] will be among you an eternal king.

[1] Lit. 'female'.
[2] Lit. 'them'.
[3] Lit. 'not to associate with men as couples'.
[4] Lit. 'For fornication has neither understanding nor godliness in itself, and all jealousy dwells in its lust'.
[5] The tenses vary in the MSS: the future seems preferable in both places.
[6] Lit. 'until the consummation of the times'.
[7] Or 'of Christ, the high priest'.
[8] So II: *b* om 'and to have . . . brother'.
[9] Lit. 'And bow down before his seed'.
[10] Lit. 'it' (i.e. his seed).

VIII. And when he had given his sons these commands, Reuben
2 died. And they put him in a coffin until they carried him up from
Egypt and buried him in Hebron in the double cave where his
fathers were.

THE TESTAMENT OF SIMEON,
ABOUT ENVY

I. A copy of the words of Simeon, which he spoke to his sons before
he died, in the hundred and twentieth year of his life – the year in
2 which Joseph died. For they came to visit him when he was ill; and
he made an effort and sat up and kissed them, and he said to them,[1]

II. Listen, children, listen to Simeon your father, *and I will tell you*
2 what is[1] in my heart. I was my father Jacob's second son; and
Leah, my mother, called me Simeon because the Lord had heard
3 her prayer. I became a hardened warrior: no venture deterred me;
4 and I was afraid of nothing. For my heart was hard, my will[2]
5 inflexible, and my feelings[3] without compassion (for courage is a
gift to men from the Most High *and is manifest both* in *their* souls and
in *their* bodies).

6 And at that time I was jealous of Joseph, because our father
7 loved him. And I determined[4] to kill him, because the prince of
error sent the spirit of jealousy and blinded my mind, so that I did
not regard him as a brother, nor did I consider my father Jacob.
8 But his God and his fathers' God sent his angel and rescued him
9 from me. For when I had gone to Shechem to take ointment for the
flocks, and Reuben *had gone* to Dothan (where our stocks were, and
10 all our stores), our brother Judah sold him to the Ishmaelites. And
when Reuben came, he was upset, for he had intended to take him
11 back safely to his father. But I was angry with Judah because of

---

[1] So *b*: II om. 'to them'.

[1] Lit. 'what I have'.
[2] Lit. 'liver'.   [3] Lit. 'bowels'.
[4] Lit. 'I set my liver against him'.

this[5] (because he had let him go alive); and for five months I
12 continued so. But God[6] restrained me and withheld from me the
uśe of my hands; for my right hand was half withered for seven
13 days. And I realized, children, that it was because of Joseph that
this had happened to me; and I repented and wept, and I prayed to
the Lord that I might be restored[7] and keep myself from all
14 pollution and envy and from all wrong-doing.[8] For I realized that
what, in envy, I had planned to do to my brother Joseph was wrong
in the Lord's sight and my father Jacob's.

III. And now, my children, beware of the spirits of error and envy.
2 For envy dominates a man's whole mind and lets him neither eat
3 nor drink nor do anything that is good. It is continually suggesting
to him that he should kill the man that is envied; yet[1] the man that
is envied continues to flourish, while the man that envies wastes
4 away. For two whole years[2] I humbled myself with fasting in the
fear of the Lord; and I realized that deliverance from envy comes
5 from the fear of God. If[3] a man flees to the Lord for shelter, the evil
6 spirit runs away from him, and *the load on his* mind is lightened. And
from then on he feels sympathy for the man that is envied and
shows no prejudice against those who love him; and so he is
envious no more.

IV. And my father asked about me, because he saw that I was sad;
2 and I said, My heart is torn with anguish.[1] (For I mourned more
than all *my brothers*, because it was I who was responsible for selling
3 Joseph.) And when we went down into Egypt and he bound me as
4 a spy, I knew that I was suffering justly and was not put out. But
Joseph was a good man, and he had the spirit of God in him: he was

---

[5] So II: *b chi* om. 'because of this'.
[6] So *b*: II 'the Lord'.
[7] So *gl eaf*: *b* 'that he might restore my hand'; *dm chi* 'that my hand might be
restored'.   [8] Lit. 'folly'.

[1] Lit. 'and'.
[2] Lit. 'For two years of days'.
[3] So *bk*: II 'for if'.

[1] Lit. 'I am distressed in my liver'.

compassionate and merciful; and he bore me no grudge, but loved
5 me just as he did *his* other brothers. So beware, my children, of all
jealousy and envy, and live in sincerity of soul and with a good
heart, keeping in mind *the example of* your father's brother, so that
God may give you also grace and glory and blessing on your heads,
6 just as you saw in him. Never in all his days did he find fault with us
for what we did,[2] but he loved us as his own soul and honoured us
more than his sons,[3] and he bestowed riches and cattle and fruits
7 on all of us. So too each one of you, my beloved[4] children, must love
his brother with a good heart, and you must rid yourselves of the
8 spirit of envy. For this makes the soul savage and destroys the
body: it causes anger and conflict in the mind, and acts as a spur to
deeds of blood: it impairs a man's natural powers of thought and
paralyses his intelligence:[5] moreover, it deprives him of sleep,
9 causing confusion in *his* soul and trembling in *his* body. And even if
he gets some sleep,[6] some vicious passion deludes him and devours
him, and with evil spirits disturbs his soul, stirs up *his* body, and
ensures that he wakes up with his mind in turmoil; and he appears
in consequence to *other* men as someone possessed of an evil and
poisonous spirit.

V. The reason why Joseph was handsome and good-looking was
that no wickedness had found a home with him; for the face is an
2 index of the turmoil in the spirit.[1] And now, my children, set your
hearts on what is pleasing to the Lord, and follow a straight path
3 among men, and you will win favour with God and men. And
beware of committing fornication, for fornication is the mother of
all evils: it separates from God and drives *those who indulge in it* to
4 Beliar. For I have seen it recorded in the writing of Enoch that your
sons together with you[2] will be corrupted by fornication and turn

---

[2] Lit. 'concerning this thing'.
[3] So II: *b* reads '. . . soul, and more than his sons, and he honoured us'.
[4] So *b*: II om.
[5] Lit. 'it leads the thinking process to ecstasy and does not allow intelligence to
work in men'.   [6] Lit. 'And even in sleep'.

[1] Lit. 'for out of the distress of the spirit the face makes clear'.
[2] So *b*: II 'your sons after you'.

5 your swords against Levi.[3] But they will not be able to get the
better of Levi, for *it is* the Lord's war he will be fighting and he will
6 gain the victory over all your company. And your sons[4] will be few
in number, scattered in Levi and Judah;[5] and no one of you will
ever be chosen as a leader,[6] just as my father Jacob prophesied in
his blessings.

VI. Behold, I have told you everything beforehand, so that I may
2 not be answerable for the sin of your souls. If, then, you can rid
yourselves of envy and all stubbornness,

> As a rose shall my bones flourish in Israel,
> And as a lily my flesh in Jacob,
> And my fragrance shall be as the fragrance of Lebanon.
> And as cedars shall my faithful sons[1] be multiplied for ever,
> And their branches shall stretch afar off.

3 > Then shall perish the offspring of Canaan,
> And no remnant shall be left to Amelek,
> And all the Cappadocians shall perish,
> And all the Hittites shall be destroyed.

4 > Then shall fail the land of Ham,
> And all the people perish.
> Then shall the whole earth rest from trouble,
> And all that is under heaven from war.

5 > Then shall Shem be glorified,
> For the Lord, the great God of Israel, shall appear on earth as
>   man
> And shall save Adam through him.[2]

6 > Then shall all the spirits of error be trodden under foot,
> And men shall rule over the wicked spirits.

---

[3] Lit. 'do harm to Levi with the sword'.
[4] Lit. 'And they'.   [5] Cp. Gen. xlix. 7.
[6] Lit. 'will be for leadership'.

[1] Lit. 'holy men from me'.
[2] Lit. '. . . Israel, appearing on earth as man and saving Adam in him'. There is
uncertainty about the details of the text at this point, but all authorities are in
agreement about God's appearance on earth.

7   Then shall I arise in joy;
And I will bless the Most High because of his marvellous
    works,[3]
Because God took a body, and ate with men, and saved men.

VII.   And now, my children, submit to Levi, and through Judah[1]
you will gain your freedom; and do not set yourselves up against
these two tribes, because *it is* from them *that* God's salvation will
2   come[2] to you. For the Lord will raise up from Levi as it were a high
priest, and from Judah as it were a king, God and man: he[3] will
3   save all the Gentiles and the race of Israel. That is why I am giving
you all these commands, so that you also may command your
children to observe them generation after generation.

VIII.   And Simeon finished his commands to his sons; and he slept
2   with his fathers, being an hundred and twenty years old. And they
put him in a coffin *made* of wood that would not rot, to take his
bones up to Hebron; and they carried them up secretly during[1]
3   a war of the Egyptians. For Joseph's bones were kept by the
4   Egyptians with the royal treasures.[2] For the magicians told them
that if Joseph's bones were taken away,[3] there would be darkness
and gloom throughout all the land of Egypt[4] – a very great plague
for the Egyptians, so that they would not be able to recognize one
another *even* with *the aid of* a lamp.

IX.   And Simeon's sons wept for their father in accordance with
2   the law of mourning. And they were in Egypt until the day they left
Egypt under Moses.[1]

[3] Lit. 'in his marvellous works'.

[1] Lit. 'in Judah'.   [2] Lit. 'spring up, sprout'.
[3] So II (i.e. the king – reading οὗτος σώσει): *b* 'so he' (i.e. the Lord – reading
οὕτως σώσει).

[1] Lit. 'in'.
[2] Lit. 'in the treasure-houses of the kings (*b l* palaces)'.
[3] Lit. 'that at the exodus of Joseph's bones'.
[4] So II: *b* om. 'the land of'.

[1] Lit. 'until the day of their exodus from Egypt by the hand of Moses'.

THE TESTAMENT OF LEVI,
ABOUT THE PRIESTHOOD AND ARROGANCE

I. A copy of the words of Levi, which he left as a testament to his sons before his death,[1] about everything they would do, and what 2 was going to happen to them, till the day of judgement. He was in good health when he called them to him (for it had been revealed to him that he was about to die). And when they had met together he said to them,

II. I, Levi, was conceived in Haran and born there; and after that 2 I came with my father to Shechem. And I was a young man, about twenty, when, with Simeon, I took vengeance on Hamor *because* of 3 *what he had done to* our sister Dinah. And when we were[1] feeding the flocks in Abel-meholah a spirit of understanding from the Lord came upon me, and I observed all men's evil ways,[2] and that unrighteousness had built itself walls, and iniquity had entrenched 4 itself behind ramparts.[3] And I was grieved on man's behalf; and I 5 prayed to the Lord that I might be saved. Then sleep fell upon me, and I saw a high mountain – that is mount Aspis in Abel-meholah. 6 And behold, the heavens opened, and an angel of the Lord said to 7 me, Levi, come in. And I went from the first heaven into the 8 second; and I saw there water hanging between the two. And I saw[4] a third heaven, far brighter and more brilliant[5] than these 9 two, and infinite in height. And I said to the angel, Why is this? And the angel said to me, Do not stay wondering at these, for when you have gone up there, you will see four other heavens even more 10 brilliant and beyond comparison *with them*; for you will stand close to the Lord and be his minister, and you will declare his mysteries to men and be the herald *of the good news* about the one who is to

---

[1] So II-*a*: *ba* om. 'before his death'.

[1] So *bl*: II 'when I was'.
[2] Lit. 'all men having destroyed their way'.
[3] Lit. 'iniquity sat upon towers'.
[4] So *bk*: II adds 'yet'.
[5] So II: *bk* om. 'and more brilliant'.

11 come to set Israel free. And through you and Judah will the Lord appear among men and bring salvation through them[6] to all
12 mankind. And the Lord's portion will provide your livelihood; and he will be your field *and* vineyard, *your* fruits, *and your* gold *and* silver.

III. Hear, then, about the seven heavens. The lowest is the gloomiest because it witnesses[1] all the unrighteous deeds of men.
2 The second holds fire, snow, ice, ready for the day which the Lord has decreed[2] in the righteous judgement of God: in it are all the
3 spirits[3] of retribution for vengeance on the wicked. In the third are the warrior hosts appointed to wreak vengeance on the spirits of error and of Beliar at the day of judgement. But the *heavens down* to
4 the fourth above these are holy.[4] For in the highest of all the Great
5 Glory dwells, in the holy of holies, far above all holiness. And in the *heaven* next to it are the angels of the Lord's presence, who minister and make expiation to the Lord for all the sins committed unwit-
6 tingly by the righteous; and they offer to the Lord a soothing odour,
7 a spiritual and bloodless offering. And in the *heaven* below *it* are the angels who bear the answers to the angels of the Lord's presence.
8 And in the *heaven* next to it are thrones *and* powers, in which
9 praises,[5] are offered to God continually. And when the Lord looks upon us, all of us are shaken; and the heavens and the earth and the
10 abysses are shaken at the presence of his majesty. Yet men do not perceive these things, and they sin and provoke the Most High.

IV. But know[1] that the Lord will execute judgement on men, because when the rocks are being rent, and *the light of* the sun extinguished, and the waters dried up, and fire losing its power,[2]

---

[6] Lit. 'in them' (so *bk lm*): *g eaf* 'for himself'; *chi* 'in himself'; *d* om.

[1] So II: *b* 'it is near'; *k* 'it endures'.
[2] Lit. 'the day of the Lord's decree'.
[3] Or 'winds'.
[4] The text is difficult. There is clearly a division at this point between the three lower heavens, described already, and the four higher, which are now described in descending, instead of ascending, order. Charles proposed to emend 'And the four heavens above these are holy'. [5] Lit. 'hymns'.

[1] Lit. 'Now, therefore, know (pl.)' [2] Lit. 'cowering'.

and all creation in confusion, and the unseen spirits wasting away, and Hades despoiled through the suffering of the Most High, men will be unbelieving and persist in their iniquities; *and* on this

2 account will they be judged and punished.[3] But the Most High has heard your prayer: he will separate you from iniquity and make you his son[4] and servant and a minister of his presence.

3   A bright light of knowledge will make you to shine in Jacob,
    And like the sun will you be to the whole race[5] of Israel.
4   And a blessing shall be given to you and to all your sons,[5]
    Until the Lord looks upon all the Gentiles with the affection
       of his son for ever.

Nevertheless, your sons will lay hands on him to get him out of
5 their way.[6] And this is why wisdom and understanding have been
6 given you, that you may instruct your sons about him. For blessed shall he be who blesses him, and they who curse him shall perish.

V. And the angel opened to me the gates of heaven, and I saw the
2 holy temple, and the Most High *sitting* on a throne of glory. And he said to me, Levi, To you have I given the blessings of the priest-
3 hood until I come and dwell in the midst of Israel. Then the angel brought me down to earth; and he gave me a shield and a sword and said, Take vengeance on Shechem because of Dinah, and I will
4 be with you, for the Lord has sent me. (And it was at that time that I killed the sons of Hamor, as it is written in the heavenly tablets.)
5 And I said to him, Please, sir, tell me your name, so that I can call
6 on you in time of trouble. And he said, I am the angel that intercedes for the nation of Israel, so that no one may destroy them
7 completely, for every evil spirit is ranged against them.[1] And afterwards I woke up, and I blessed the Most High and the angel that intercedes for the nation of Israel and all the righteous.

VI. And when I was going to my father, I found a bronze shield

---

[3] Lit. 'in punishment will they be judged'.
[4] Lit. 'to separate you from iniquity and to become to him a son'.
[5] Lit. 'seed'.   [6] So *bk*: II 'to crucify him'.

[1] Lit. 'him'.

(hence the name of mount Aspis, which is[1] near Gebal to the south
2,3 of Abila). And I kept these things in mind. I urged my father and
my brother Reuben to tell the sons of Hamor they must be
circumcised – for I was furious at the abominable thing they had
4 done in Israel. And I killed Shechem first, and Simeon killed
5 Hamor. And afterwards *our* brothers came and put the city to the
6 sword. And our father heard about it and was angry, and he was
grieved that they had accepted circumcision and after that had
been put to death; and in his blessings he made an exception of us
7 among our brothers.[2] For we sinned because we had done this
8 against his will (he[3] was in fact unwell that day). But I saw that
God had pronounced sentence[4] on Shechem because they had
wanted to do to Sarah what they had done to our sister Dinah; and
9 the Lord prevented them. And so too they had persecuted our
father Abraham as a foreigner; and they trampled on[5] his flocks
when they were pregnant, and they shamefully ill-treated Jeblae,
10 who had been born in his household. And they behaved like this to
all foreigners: they took their wives away from them by force and
11 *then* sent them away. But retribution from the Lord[6] overtook them
at last.

VII. And I said to my father, Do not be angry, sir, for by you the
Lord will destroy the Canaanites and give their land to you and
2 your descendants after you. For from to-day Shechem will be
called a city of imbeciles; for as a man mocks a fool, so did we make
3 a mockery of them, because they had indeed committed an out-
4 rage[1] in Israel by defiling our sister. And we took our sister away
from there and departed and came to Bethel.

---

[1] So II: *b* 'for it is'.
[2] Lit. 'he did (or 'made') otherwise'. Whatever precisely this obscure expression
may mean, there can be no doubt that it refers to Gen. xlix. 7, where Simeon and
Levi are cursed by Jacob and told they will be 'scattered in Israel'.
[3] So *b c*: II-*c* 'I'.
[4] Lit. 'that there was a sentence of God for evils'.
[5] So *bl*: II-*l* 'they vexed' (*g* is absent).
[6] Lit. 'the Lord's wrath'.

[1] Lit. 'folly'.

VIII. And after we had been there seventy days, I had another
2 vision[1] just as I had had before. And I saw seven men clothed in
white saying to me, Get up, put on the robe of the priesthood, and
the crown of righteousness, and the breast-piece of understanding,
and the mantle of truth, and the rosette of faith, and the turban of
3 the sign, and the ephod of prophecy. And one by one they brought
these things and put *them* on me and said, From now on be a priest
4 of the Lord, you and your descendants for ever. And the first
5 anointed me with holy oil and gave me a staff of judgement. The
second washed me with pure water and fed me with bread and
wine (the holiest of holy things) and arrayed me in a holy and
6 glorious robe. The third clothed me with a linen vestment like an
7,8 ephod. The fourth put round me a girdle like purple. The fifth gave
9,10 me a branch of rich olive. The sixth put a crown on my head. The
seventh put round me[2] a diadem of priesthood; and they filled my
hands[3] with incense, so that I might serve as priest to the Lord.
11 And they said to me, Levi, by three functions will your descendants
be distinguished,[4] for a sign of the glory of the Lord who is to come.
12 And he who believed will be the first, and no office[5] shall be greater
13,14 than his.[6] The second will be the priesthood. The third will be
called by a new name, for a king shall arise out of Judah and
establish a new priesthood, after the fashion of the Gentiles, for all
15 the Gentiles. And his coming *will be* marvellous, as of a mighty
16 prophet,[7] of the stock of Abraham our father. Everything that is
desirable in Israel shall be yours and your descendants'; and you
shall eat of everything that delights the eye, and from the Lord's
17 table shall your descendants assign themselves a portion. And
some of them shall be high priests, and judges, and scribes; for by
18 their testimony[8] shall what is holy be preserved.[9] And when I woke

[1] Lit. 'again I saw a thing (*bk*: II 'a vision').
[2] So *g eaf chi* (*ldm* are missing): *bk* explicitly 'put on my head'.
[3] This is the technical Old Testament term for consecration to the priestly office
(see e.g. Exod. xxxii. 29; Judg. xvii. 5, 12; 1 Kings xiii. 33).
[4] Lit. 'into three beginnings thy seed will be divided'. Charles rendered 'thy seed
shall be divided into three offices'.
[5] Lit. 'lot'.   [6] Lit. 'it' or 'he'.
[7] So *bk*: II 'as of a prophet of the Most High'.
[8] Lit. 'their mouth'.
[9] Or 'shall the holy place be guarded'.

19 up I realized that this *vision* was like the other one. And I kept this one secret too, and I told it to nobody.

IX. And after two days Judah and I went up with our father to
2 Isaac. And my grandfather blessed me in words that recalled the
3 visions[1] I had seen; and he would not come with us to Bethel. But when we came to Bethel, my father Jacob saw in a vision about me
4 that I should be their priest before God. And he got up early in the morning and paid tithes to the Lord on everything through me.
5,6 And we went to Hebron to settle there. And Isaac sent for me repeatedly to instruct me in[2] the law of the Lord, just as the angel of
7 God had shown me. And he taught me the law of the priesthood, of sacrifices, of whole-offerings, of first-fruits, of freewill-offerings, *and*
8 of peace-offerings. And each day he continued instructing me and
9 busied himself on my behalf before the Lord. And he said, Beware, *my* son, of the spirit of fornication; for this will persist, and through
10 your descendants it will pollute the sanctuary.[3] So find yourself a wife while you are young, *a girl* without fault, not worldly minded,
11 and not of foreign[4] or of Gentile stock. And before you enter the sanctuary,[3] bathe; and when you offer the sacrifice, wash, and
12 when you finish the sacrifice, wash again. *Use only wood* from the twelve trees that always have leaves *to* present *your offerings* to the
13 Lord *by fire*, as indeed Abraham taught me.[5] And sacrifice to the
14 Lord only clean animals and birds. And offer[6] the choicest of all first-fruits and wine. And every sacrifice you must salt with salt.

X. Now, children, observe the commands I give you, for what I
2 have heard from my fathers I have told you. I am innocent of all your ungodliness and of the sin[1] you will commit at the end of time against the Saviour of the world, acting godlessly, leading Israel
3 astray, and stirring up against it great evils from the Lord. And together with the rest of Israel you will sin against the law, so that

[1] Lit. 'blessed me according to all the words of my visions'.
[2] Lit. 'to put me in remembrance of'.
[3] Lit. 'the holy things'.   [4] Or 'Philistine'.
[5] Cp. Jub. xxi. 12.   [6] So *b*: II adds 'to the Lord'.

[1] Lit. 'transgression'.

he will not bear with Jerusalem[2] because of your wickedness, but
4 will tear in two the temple veil[3] so as not to cover your shame. And
you will be scattered as captives among the Gentiles and be[4] a
5 reproach and a curse[5] and be trampled under foot. For the house
which the Lord will choose shall be called Jerusalem, as it stands
written in the book of the righteous Enoch.

XI.   When I married I was twenty eight years old, and my wife's
2 name was Melcha. And she conceived and bore *a son*, and she
called him Gershom because we were living as foreigners in our
3 land (for Gershom means[1] 'living as a foreigner'). And I saw *in a*
4 *vision* about him that he would not be in the front rank. And
5 Kohath was born in *my* thirty fifth year, towards sunrise. And I saw
in a vision that he was standing raised above the rest of the
6 congregation round about him (that is why I called him Kohath,
7 which is 'beginning of greatness' and 'reconciliation'[2]). And as a
third *son* she bore me Merari in my fortieth year; and it was a
difficult birth (that is why his mother called him Merari, which is
8 'my bitterness' – and his life too was in danger). And Jochebed was
born in my sixty fourth year, in Egypt; for by then I was much
esteemed among my brothers.

XII.   And Gershom married, and his wife bore him Libni and
2 Shimei. And Kohath's sons *were* Amram, Izhar, Hebron, and
3,4 Uzziel. And Merari's sons, Mahli and Mushi. And in my ninety
fourth year Amram married my daughter Jochebed, for they were
5 born the same day, he and my daughter. I was eight years old when
I went into the land of Canaan and eighteen when I killed
Shechem, and at nineteen I became a priest; and *I was* twenty eight
6 *when* I married and forty *when* I came into Egypt. And you, my
children, are a third generation. Joseph died in my hundred and
eighteenth year.

---

[2] Or 'so that Jerusalem will not bear *it*'.
[3] Lit. 'garment'.   [4] So *b*: II adds 'there'.
[5] So II-*gm*: *b gm* om. 'and a curse'.

[1] Lit. 'is written'.
[2] Lit. 'bringing together'.

XIII. And now, my children, I command you to fear the Lord with all your heart and live in sincerity in accordance with all his law.
2 And you too must teach your children how to read,[1] so that they may have understanding all their life *through* reading the law of
3 God continually. For everyone that knows the law of God will be
4 honoured and accepted wherever he goes. He will in fact find many more friends than his parents; and not a few will be anxious to do
5 him service and hear the law from his mouth. Do good works, my
6 children, on earth, so that you may find *your reward* in heaven. And sow good things in your souls, so that you may find them in your life; for if you sow evil things, you will reap every *kind of* trouble and
7 tribulation. Acquire wisdom in the fear of God with diligence; for even if exile comes, and cities and lands are devastated, and gold and silver and all possessions become a total loss, no one can take away the wise man's wisdom – only the blindness of ungodliness
8 and the disablement[2] *that comes* of sin. For wisdom[3] will be for him a shining *light* even among enemies, and in a strange country a
9 fatherland, and in the midst of foes she will be found a friend. If anyone teaches these things and acts on them, he will share a king's throne, as indeed Joseph our brother did.

XIV. And now, children, I understand from the writing of Enoch that at the end you will sin against[1] the Lord, and lay hands . . .[2] in all wickedness, and your brothers will be ashamed because of you,
2 and you will become[3] a laughing-stock among all the Gentiles. But our father Israel will not be held responsible for[4] the godlessness of the chief priests who will lay their hands upon the Saviour of the
3 world. The heaven is purer than the earth; and you *are* the lights of
4 heaven,[5] like sun and moon. What will all the Gentiles do, if you

---

[1] Lit. 'teach your children letters'.
[2] So *bg*: *dlm eaf chi* 'callousness'.
[3] Lit. 'she'.

[1] Lit. 'you will act godlessly towards'.
[2] An object is required here: *chi* have 'upon him'.
[3] So *kl eaf c*: *b gdm hi* 'and there will become'.
[4] Lit. 'will be pure from' (so *bkl*: II-*l* 'is pure from').
[5] So *bkl*: II-*l* 'Israel'.

are darkened by ungodliness and bring a curse upon our race, for whose sake the light of the law[6] *was given* (*for* what was given through you *was given* for the enlightenment of every man)? Him you will desire to kill; and you will teach commandments contrary
5 to the precepts of God. You will rob the Lord's offerings; from the portions alloted to him you will steal; and before sacrificing to the Lord you will take *for yourselves* the choicest *pieces* and share them
6 like common food[7] with whores. You will teach the Lord's commandments for your own personal gain. You will pollute married women and defile the virgins of Jerusalem,[8] and you will be united with prostitutes and adulteresses. You will take Gentile women as wives and purify them with a *form of* purification contrary to the law; and your unions will be like Sodom and Gomorrah in
7 ungodliness. And you will be full of self-importance on account of the priesthood and set yourselves up against *other* men; and not only so, but you will think yourselves of more importance even than the commandments of God, and you will mock at holy things[9] and make cheap jokes about them.[10]

XV.　And so the temple, which the Lord will choose, will be *laid* waste because of *your* uncleanness,[1] and you will be *carried off as*
2 captives by all the Gentiles. And you will be an abomination to them and bear the reproach and eternal shame of having been
3 condemned by the righteous judgement of God. And all who see
4 you will turn and run away from you. And if it were not because of Abraham, Isaac, and Jacob, our fathers, I should have no descendant left *alive* on earth.

XVI.　And now I understand in the book of Enoch that you will go astray and profane the priesthood and pollute the sacrifices for
2 seventy weeks. And you will set aside the law and discredit the words of the prophets: you will persecute righteous men with a

---

[6] So *gm eaf ch*: *bki* 'the light of the world'; *ld* 'the light of the world and the law'.
[7] Lit. 'and eat *them* in contempt'.
[8] So *b k*: II 'Israel'.　　　　　[9] Or 'the holy place'.
[10] and make . . . them: lit. 'jesting in contempt'.

[1] Lit. 'will be desolate in uncleanness'.

crazy determination and hate the godly *and* abhor the words of the
3 faithful. And you will brand as a deceiver a man who renews the
law in the power of the Most High, unaware of who he is,[1] and you
will finally kill him, as you suppose, and through *your* wickedness
4 bring innocent blood upon your heads. Because[2] of him your
sanctuary will be *laid* waste, *levelled* to the ground, *and* polluted.
5 And your land[3] will be unclean; and[4] a curse will rest upon you,
and you will be dispersed among the Gentiles until he comes to you
and once more receives you in pity through[5] faith and water.

XVII. And since I have told you about the seventy weeks, let me
2 tell you also[1] about the priesthood. For in each jubilee there will be
a priesthood. In[2] the first jubilee the first *priest* anointed to the
priesthood will be great, and he will speak to God as to a father;
and his priesthood will be perfect with the Lord,[3] and on his day of
3 joy he will stand up for the salvation of the world. In the second
jubilee the anointed *priest* will be conceived amid the distresses of
his people;[4] and his priesthood will be held in high honour and
4 esteem by all. And the third priest will be overcome by sorrow.
5 And the fourth will suffer anguish because unrighteousness will
make a determined assault upon him,[5] and Israelites[6] will hate one
6,7 another. The fifth will be overcome by darkness. And so also the
8 sixth and the seventh. And in the seventh *jubilee* there will be
pollution *of a kind* that I cannot speak of in the presence of the Lord
9 and men[7] (but they will know who do these things). Because of this
they will be taken as captives and plundered, and their land and
10 their possessions will be destroyed. And in the fifth week they will
return to their land in its desolation, and they will renew the house

---

[1] Lit. 'unaware of his majesty'.
[2] So *b k*: II 'And because'.   [3] Lit. 'place'.
[4] Lit. 'but'.   [5] Lit. 'in'.

[1] Lit. 'since you have heard . . . hear also'.
[2] So *b l*: II-*l* 'and in'.
[3] So II: *b* 'perfect with the fear of the Lord'.
[4] Lit. 'in the sorrow of the beloved ones'.
[5] Translation uncertain.
[6] Lit. 'and all Israel'.
[7] So *b*: II om. 'the Lord and'.

11 of the Lord. And in the seventh week will come priests, *who will be* idolaters, quarrelsome, money-lovers, arrogant, lawless, licentious, corrupters of children, and given to unnatural vice with animals.

XVIII. And after judgement has come upon them from the Lord, the priesthood will fail.

2 Then will the Lord raise up a new priest,[1]
   To whom all the words of the Lord will be revealed;
   And he will execute true judgement on earth for many days.
3 And his star will arise in heaven, as a king,
   Lighting up the light of knowledge **as the sun the day**;[2]
   And he will rank as great in the world until he is taken up.
4 He will shine forth like the sun on the earth,
   And dispel all darkness from under heaven;
   And there will be peace in all the earth.
5 The heavens will exult in his days,
   And the earth will be glad, and the clouds rejoice;
   And the knowledge of the Lord will be poured out on the earth,
   Like the water of the seas.
   And the angels of glory of the Lord's presence will be glad in him.
6 The heavens will be opened,
   And from the temple of glory will come his call to his sacred office[3]
   With the Father's voice, as from Abraham Isaac's father.
7 And the glory of the Most High will be uttered over him,
   And the spirit of understanding and holiness will rest upon him in the water.
8 He will declare[4] the majesty of the Lord to his sons in truth for evermore,

---

[1] So II: *b* '[1]And after . . . from the Lord, [2]then will the Lord raise for the priesthood a new priest'.
[2] The MSS vary here: none is entirely satisfactory.
[3] Lit. 'will come upon him the sacred thing'.
[4] Lit. 'give'.

And there will be no successor to him from generation to
generation for ever.

9 And in his priesthood the Gentiles will increase in knowledge
on the earth,
And be enlightened through the grace of the Lord;
But Israel will be weakened through ignorance,
And plunged into darkness by sorrow.[5]
In his priesthood will all sin come to an end,
And the lawless cease to do evil;
And the righteous will rest in him.

10 And he will open the gates of **Paradise**,
And destroy the power of the sword that threatened Adam.

11 And he will give the saints *the right* to eat from the tree of life,
And the spirit of holiness will be on them.

12 And Beliar will be bound by him,
And he will give power to his children to tread the evil spirits
underfoot.

13 And the Lord will rejoice over his children,
And[6] take pleasure in those who are dear to him for ever.

14 Then will Abraham and Isaac and Jacob shout in exultation,
And I will be glad,
And all the saints will be clothed with joy.

XIX. And now, my children, you have heard everything. Choose,
then, for yourselves either darkness or light, either the law of the
2 Lord or the ways[1] of Beliar. And we answered our father, saying,
In the Lord's presence we will live our lives in accordance with his
3 law. And our father said, The Lord is a witness, and his angels are
witnesses, and I am a witness, and you are witnesses, of what you
4 have said. And we said, *We are* witnesses. And with this Levi
brought his commands to his sons to an end; and he stretched out
his feet, and was gathered to his fathers, when he was a hundred
5 and thirty seven years old. And they put him in a coffin; and later
on they buried him in Hebron, by the side of Abraham, Isaac, and
Jacob.

[5] So II: *bk* om. 'And in his priesthood . . . sorrow'.
[6] So II: *b* (*k*) add 'the Lord'.

[1] Lit. 'works'.

THE TESTAMENT OF JUDAH, ABOUT COURAGE, AND LOVE OF MONEY, AND FORNICATION

I. A copy of the words of Judah that he spoke to his sons before he
2,3 died. They met together and came to him; and he said to them, I
was my father's fourth son, and my mother[1] called me Judah,
saying, I give thanks to the Lord because he has given me a fourth
4 son as well. I was agile and active in my youth; and I was obedient
5 to my father in everything. And I blessed[2] my mother and my
6 mother's sister. And when I grew up, my father Jacob promised
me,[3] saying, You will be a king and prosper in all things.

II. And the Lord showed me favour in everything I did, both out
2 in the country and at home – as I saw when[1] I raced a hind and
3 caught it and made *it into* a meal for my father. The gazelles I
would catch as they ran, and I could overtake anything on the
plains. A wild mare I overtook and caught *it* and tamed *it*; and I
4 killed a lion and rescued a kid from its mouth. I took a bear by its
paw and dashed it against a crag;[2] and any beast, if it turned on
5 me, I tore it apart like a dog. I raced the wild boar and grasped it as
6 I ran, and I tore it in pieces. A leopard in Hebron jumped out on *my*
dog, and I caught it by the tail and sent it flying and destroyed it.[3]
7 A wild ox, which was feeding in the fields near Gaza, I took by the
horns, and whirled *it* round and stunned *it* and threw *it* on the
ground and killed it.

III. And when the two kings of the Canaanites, armed with their
coats of mail, came against the flocks with all their forces, on my
own I fell upon the king of Hazor, seized him and struck him on the
2 greaves, and I dragged him down and so killed him. And the other,

[1] So *b*: II 'my mother Leah'.
[2] So *b*: II 'honoured'.
[3] So *b chi*: *gldm eaf* 'prayed for *God's blessing on* me'.

[1] So the probable text behind *b*: II 'I know that'.
[2] Lit. 'rolled it away into a crag'.
[3] Lit. 'and it was broken'.

the king of Tappuah, I killed as he was sitting on his horse; and so I
3 scattered all *his* people.[1] And when I killed king Achor[2] (one of the
giants who was shooting arrows in front *of him* and behind *him as he
sat* on *his* horse), I took aim with a stone weighing sixty pounds and
4 flung *it* at *his* horse and killed it. And I fought Achor for two hours,
5 and I killed him; and I cut his shield in two and cut off his feet. And
as I was stripping off his breastplate, eight comrades of his began
6 to fight with me. So I wound my garment round my hand and
threw stones at them; and I killed four of them, but the others fled.
7 And our father Jacob killed Beelisas, the leader of the kings,[3] a
8 giant in strength *and over* eighteen feet in height! And terror[4] seized
9 them, and they brought their war against us to an end. My father
10 had no anxiety, if there was a war, and I was with my brothers. For
he had seen in a vision about me that an angel of might always
followed me everywhere, so that I should not be overcome.

IV. And in the south we became involved in a more serious war
than the one in Shechem. And I took the field with my brothers;
and I went in pursuit of a thousand men, and I killed two hundred
2 men of them and four kings. And I went up against them on the
3 wall, and I killed two more kings. Also we set Hebron free and
liberated all the prisoners that had been taken by the kings.[1]

V. On the next day we set off for Aretan, a city strongly fortified,
2 inaccessible and menacing.[1] Gad and I approached from the east
3 of the city, and Reuben and Levi from the west.[2] And the men that

---

[1] So *b*: *l e hi* explicitly 'his people'; *gd af c* 'their people'.
[2] There is obviously some confusion here since only two kings are mentioned in
verse 1, but verse 3 introduces a third with a proper name. Charles argued, on the
basis of Rabbinic sources, that verses 3–5 originally described Judah's encounter
with the king of Tappuah and that the otherwise unknown name Achor arose as a
corrupt dittography of 'the other' (Heb. *'aḥer*) at the beginning of verse 2. He
accordingly bracketed the end of verse 2 and the beginning of verse 3 as an
interpolation.   [3] Lit. 'king of all the kings'.
[4] Lit. 'trembling'.

[1] Lit. 'and we took all the captivity of the kings'.

[1] Lit. 'promising death to us'.
[2] So II-*l*: *b l* add 'and on the south'.

4 were on the wall, thinking we were alone, were drawn away after us. And so the *rest of our* brothers, without being seen, climbed up the wall on the other two sides on ladders[3] and entered the city
5 while *the defenders* were unaware of it. And we took it and put it to the sword; and as for those who had taken refuge in the tower, we
6 set fire to the tower and took both it and them. And as we were going away the men of Tappuah set upon our prisoners; and we put these in charge of our sons,[4] and we fought with them as far as
7 Tappuah. And we killed them too and burned their city, and everything in it we carried off as spoil.

VI. And when I was at the waters of Cozeba, the men of Jobel took
2 the field against us. And we fought with them;[1] and we killed their
3 allies from Shiloh and gave them no opportunity to attack us.[2] And *the men* of Machir[3] came upon us on the fifth day to take our prisoners, and we advanced against them and got the better of them in a fiercely contested battle (for there were many seasoned warriors among them); and we killed them before they had gone up
4 the slope. But when we came to their city, their women rolled *down*
5 stones on us from the brow of the hill on which the city stood. And Simeon and I hid ourselves at the back; and we seized the heights and destroyed the whole city.

VII. And the next day we were told that *the men of* Gaash, the city of
2 the kings,[1] were coming against us with a massive force. So Dan and I pretended to be Amorites and gained entrance into their city
3 as allies. And at dead of night our brothers came, and we opened the gates for them; and we destroyed all the inhabitants[2] and their possessions, and we took as booty everything they had, and razed

---

[3] Lit. 'by stakes'.
[4] So *gdl eaf* (*m* is lacking): *b* 'and having taken these with us together with our sons'.

[1] So *b*: *gdl eaf* add 'and defeated them'.
[2] Lit. 'no passage to come in against us'.
[3] Or 'And from Machir they'.

[1] So (*e*) *af*: there is a bewildering variety of readings at this point.
[2] Lit. 'all of them'.

4 their three walls to the ground. And we approached Timnah, where all those were who had taken refuge from³ the warring kings.
5 Here⁴ they were abusive, and in my fury I rushed against them to the brow *of the hill on which the city stood.*⁵ And they kept slinging stones
6 and *throwing* darts at me. And had not my brother Dan fought with
7 me, they would have killed me. But so furious was our assault on them that they all fled; and they found their way to my father by a different route, and they pleaded with him, and he made peace
8 with them. And we did them no harm, but made a truce with them
9 and restored all *our* prisoners to them. And I rebuilt⁶ Timnah, and
10 my father rebuilt⁶ Rabael. I was twenty years old when this war
11 happened. And the Canaanites were afraid of my brothers and of me.

VIII. And I had a number of flocks and herds, and my chief
2 herdsman was Iran the Adullamite. When I went to *see* him I met¹ Barsam, king of Adullam. And he gave us a feast; and he invited
3 me and gave me his daughter Bathshua in marriage. She bore me Er and Onan and Shelah: two of them the Lord struck down childless; but Shelah was spared,² and you are his children.

IX. After we came out of Mesopotamia, from Laban, *into Canaan* our father¹ lived in peace with his brother Esau for eighteen years,
2 and his sons with us. And when eighteen years had gone by, in my own fortieth year, Esau, my father's brother, attacked us with a
3 large and powerful company. And he fell by the bow of Jacob and was taken up **wounded**² in the hill-country of Seir; and he died on
4 the road above Anoniram. And we went in pursuit of Esau's sons. Now they had a city with a wall of iron and gates of brass, and we could not get into it; and we encamped round about *it* and beseiged
5 them. And when after twenty days they had not opened *the gates*

³ Lit. 'where was all the refuge of'.
⁴ Lit. 'Then'.   ⁵ Cp. vi. 4.
⁶ Lit. 'built'.

¹ Lit. 'saw'.   ² Lit. 'lived'.

¹ So II-*d*: *b d* 'our father and ourselves'.
² Lit. 'dead'.

and were looking *at us*, I got a ladder, and, with my shield over my head, climbed up *it*, and was met with a shower of stones[3] *weighing* nearly three talents; and when I got to the top I killed four of their

6 warriors. And on the day following Reuben and Gad went in and
7 killed six[4] more. Then they asked us for terms of peace, and, after
8 consulting our father, we put them to forced labour. And they used to give us *each year* two hundred cors of wheat, five hundred baths of oil, and fifteen hundred measures of wine, until we went down into Egypt.

X. After this my son Er married Tamar,[1] a girl from
2 Mesopotamia, an Aramaean. And Er was wicked and had doubts about Tamar because she was not from Canaan; and an angel of
3 the Lord struck him on the third day in the night.[2] And he had not had intercourse with her as a result of his mother's crafty schem-
4 ing; for he did not want to have children by her.[3] While the wedding was still being celebrated,[4] I gave her Onan in marriage as a husband's brother; and he too was wicked and would not have intercourse with her, though he lived with her for a whole year.
5 And when I threatened him, he lay with her but spilled *his* seed on the ground, just as his mother had told him to; and he also died
6 through *his* wickedness. And I wanted to give Shelah to her as well, but my wife Bathshua would not agree to it; for she had set her face against Tamar, because she was not a Canaanite as she was herself.

XI. And I was well aware that the Canaanite stock was wicked,
2 but youthful passion blinded my mind. And when I saw her pouring out the wine at dinner,[1] I was led astray under the influ-
3 ence of the wine and spent the night with her. And she, while I was

---

³ Lit. 'and I went up accepting stones'.
⁴ So II-*l:b l* 'sixty'.

¹ According to Gen. xxxviii. 6 Judah himself was responsible for marrying Er to Tamar.   ² So *b*: *gdl eaf* 'on the third night'; *m* 'on the third day'; *chi* om.
³ Or 'she did not want *him* to have children by her'.
⁴ Lit. 'In the days of the bride-chamber'.

¹ Cp. xiii. 5–7.

4 away, went and found a wife for Shelah from Canaan. And when I
5 discovered what she had done, I cursed her in my distress. And she
died too through her sons' wickedness.

XII. And after this, while Tamar was a widow, she heard, two
years later, that I was on my way to shear my sheep; and she
adorned herself in bridal array and sat in the city of Enaim,[1] at the
2 gate. For it was a custom of the Amorites that *a girl* who was about
3 to marry should sit by the gate for seven days as a prostitute. I had
myself been drinking at the waters of Cozeba, and, fuddled as I was
with wine, I did not recognize her: moreover, the way she had
adorned herself made her seem the more desirable; and so I was
4 deceived. And I turned to her and said, Let me lie with you. And
she said, What will you give me? And I gave her my staff and my
belt and the diadem of the kingdom, and I lay with her; and she
5 conceived. And not knowing what she had done, it was my intention to kill her;[2] but she secretly sent me the pledges, and
6 humiliated me. And when I asked her to come and see me, she told
me[3] also what I had said to her privately while I was lying with her
in my drunken stupor; and *so* I could not kill her, for it was the
7 Lord's doing. And I thought[4] perhaps it was a trick and she had got
8 the pledges from someone else. But I never approached her again,[5]
because I had done something that all Israelites regard as an
9 abomination. And the people in the city said there had been no
prostitute[6] in the gate[7] (because she came from somewhere else
10 and sat in the gate for only a little while). And I thought that no one
11 knew that I had had intercourse with her. And after this we went
12 into Egypt, to Joseph, because of the famine. And I was forty-six;
and I lived there for seventy three years.

XIII. And now, my instructions to you.[1] Pay attention, my

---

[1] There are a number of variants here: *e* seems to give the original text.
[2] Cp. Gen. xxxviii. 24.
[3] Lit. 'I heard'.   [4] Lit. 'I said'.
[5] Lit. 'But I did not approach her any more until my death'.
[6] Lit. 'temple-prostitute'.
[7] So II-*l* (*d* is lacking and *chi* have a different text): *b l* 'in the city'.

[1] Lit. 'whatsoever things I command you'.

children, to your father,[2] and keep all my sayings, and conform to the ordinances[3] of the Lord, and obey the commandments of the

2 Lord God.[4] And do not follow after your natural desires, nor yield to the promptings of your own inclinations: do not be proud and overbearing;[5] and do not boast of your feats in youth, for this too is

3 evil in the Lord's eyes. I myself boasted that when at war no beautiful woman's face ever beguiled me, and I censured my brother Reuben because of *what he had done to* Bilhah, my father's wife; yet the spirit of pride[6] and fornication ranged itself against me until I had spent the night with Bathshua, the Canaanite, and with

4 Tamar, who had been married to my sons. And I said to my father-in-law, I will talk to my father about it, and *only* so will I take your daughter. And he showed me an immense hoard of gold that

5 was ear-marked for his daughter[7] (for he was a king). And he adorned her with gold and pearls and got her to pour out the wine

6 for us at dinner and display her beauty.[8] And the wine turned away

7 my eyes, and pleasure dulled my wits. And I became enamoured of her, and I spent the night with her and transgressed the Lord's

8 command and my father's also; and I married her. And the Lord rewarded me as I deserved, inasmuch as I had no joy of her children.

XIV. And now, my children, do not give way to drunkenness, for wine turns the mind away from truth, inflames *our* lustful inclina-

2 tions, and leads the eyes into error. For the spirit of fornication uses[1] wine as an instrument to give pleasure to the mind; and both

3 of these destroy a man's powers. For if a man drinks wine and makes himself drunk, it disturbs his mind with filthy thoughts *which lead him on* to fornication, and it heats his body to *hanker after* sexual intercourse; and if there is opportunity to gratify his lust, he

---

[2] So *b*: II 'to Judah your father'.
[3] So *b*: II 'all the ordinances'.
[4] So *bm*: II-*m* 'of God'.
[5] do not . . . overbearing: lit. 'in the haughtiness of your heart'.
[6] Or 'jealousy' (lit. 'zeal').
[7] that . . . daughter: lit. 'in his daughter's name'.
[8] Lit. '. . . at dinner in the beauty of women'.

[1] Lit. 'has'.

4 commits the sin and is not ashamed. Such is *the effect of* wine, my
5 children; for a man that is drunk has no respect for anyone. For
look how it made me go astray, so that although there were many
people in the city I was not ashamed to turn aside to Tamar before
them all; and I committed a great sin and brought shame on my
6 sons.[2] *Similarly,* after I had been drinking wine, I was not ashamed
to transgress the command of God, and I took a Canaanite woman *as*
7 *my wife.* So the man who drinks wine needs *to exercise* discretion, my
children; and discretion means drinking for only as long as one can
8 preserve one's self-respect.[3] Otherwise, if one goes beyond this
limit, the spirit of error gets into the mind and makes the drunkard
indulge in filthy talk and transgress and feel no shame, but rather
take pride in what is dishonourable and think it something good.

XV. The man who commits fornication has no inkling that he is
2 being damaged and no shame at being frowned upon. For even if
he is a king, if he commits fornication, he is stripped of his kingship
and goes away *naked*:[1] he has become the slave of fornication and
3 has been stripped, just as I *was* myself. For I gave away my staff
(that is the prop of my tribe) and my belt (that is *my* power) and *my*
4 diadem (that is the glory of my kingdom). And after I had repented
of it, I drank no wine nor did I eat any meat[2] until I was an old
5 man; and I took no part in any festivities. And God's angel showed
me that women hold sway over king and beggar alike, and that
6 they always will.[3] From the king they take away his glory, and from
the warrior his strength, and from the beggar *even* the little that
keeps him from utter destitution.[4]

XVI. So when you drink wine, my children, observe the limit; for
there are four evil spirits in it – lust, consuming *passion*, profligacy,

---

[2] Lit. 'and uncovered the covering of my sons' uncleanness'.
[3] Or 'respect for others'.

[1] In verses 1 and 2 *b* om. 'has no inkling . . . if he commits fornication' through
homioteleuton, and then adds a negative before 'goes away' to help the sense.
[2] Lit. 'wine and flesh I did not take'.
[3] Lit. 'for ever'.
[4] Lit. 'the smallest prop of his poverty'.

2 *and* money-grubbing. If you drink wine at a celebration,[1] *do it* with moderation[2] and in the fear of God;[3] for if you drink immoderately,[2] and the fear of God is lacking, drunkenness ensues and

3 shamelessness creeps in. But better still, do not drink at all,[4] so that you do not sin through violent talk and quarrelling and slander and transgression of the commands of God, and you perish before

4 your time. Moreover, wine reveals the secrets of God and men to foreigners (just as I revealed the commands of God and the secrets of my father Jacob to the Canaanite woman, Bathshua); and God

5 has told *us* not to reveal them to them. And wine, too, is a cause of strife[5] and confusion.

XVII. I warn you, my children, not to be lovers of money nor to focus your attention on women's beauty, because it was *her* money

2 and *her* beauty[1] that led me astray to Bathshua the Canaanite. For I well know that it is these two things that will lead my family into

3 wickedness: they will corrupt even the wise men among my sons; and they will be responsible for the decline of the kingdom of Judah, which the Lord gave me because of my obedience to my

4 father. For I never disobeyed[2] my father Jacob: whatever he told

5 me, I did. And Abraham, my father's father, gave me his blessing and said that I should be king in Israel; and Isaac again gave me a

6 similar blessing. And *so* I know that it is from me that the royal line will stem.[3]

XVIII. And I have also read in the books of the righteous Enoch

2 about the evils you will do in the last days. So be on your guard, my children, against fornication and the love of money: pay attention

3 to your father Judah. For these things separate *us* from the law of

---

¹ Or 'with a merry heart': lit. 'in gladness'.
² Lit. 'being respectful . . . not being respectful'.
³ *b* adds 'you will live' and so understands the sentence differently ('If you drink . . . with moderation . . . you will live').
⁴ *b* seems to be defective here: the other MSS differ widely, though they agree on the general sense.   ⁵ Lit. 'war'.

¹ Lit. 'shapeliness'.
² Lit. 'caused grief with regard to the word of'.
³ Lit. 'the royal thing will stand'.

God, and distract *our* thoughts,[1] and encourage arrogance, and
4 prevent *us* from showing mercy to one another. They rob a man's
soul of all goodness, and oppress him with toils and troubles, and
5 deprive him of his sleep, and devour his flesh. And he holds back
the sacrifices due to God,[2] and ignores his blessing, and pays no
heed to a prophet when he speaks, and is offended by even so much
6 as a mention of religion.[3] For the man who is a slave to two passions
that are contrary to God's commands cannot obey God, because
they have blinded him; and he walks about in broad daylight as if it
were night.

XIX. My children, the love of money is a sure path to idolatry,
because, when led astray by money, men call gods those that are no
2 *gods*,[1] and it drives to distraction whoever is in its grip. For the sake
of money I lost my children; and had I not repented and humbled
myself, and had not my father Jacob prayed for me, I should have
3 died childless. But the God of my fathers, the compassionate and
4 gracious one, pardoned *me*, because I did it in ignorance. For the
prince of error blinded me, and I was ignorant, being but a man
and *a creature made of* flesh, corrupted by *his* sins; and I came to
understand my own weakness when I had been thinking myself
invincible.

XX. Understand then, my children, that two spirits attend on
2 man, the *spirit* of truth and the *spirit* of error. And in between is the
spirit of rational understanding,[1] to incline *us* whichever way it
3 wills. And men's deeds of truth and deeds of error are written on
4 their hearts;[2] and the Lord knows each one of them. And there is no
time when men's deeds can be hidden, because they have been
5 written in his innermost heart[3] before the Lord. And the spirit of

---

[1] Lit. 'blind the inclination of the soul'.
[2] Lit. 'And he hinders the sacrifices of God'.
[3] Lit. 'by a word of godliness'.

[1] Or 'those that do not exist'.

[1] Lit. 'the *spirit* of the understanding of the mind'.
[2] Lit. 'And the things of truth and the things of error are written on the breast of
man'.   [3] Lit. 'in the breast of his bones'.

truth testifies to everything and accuses everyone; and the sinner is destroyed by fire on the evidence of[4] his own heart and cannot *even* raise his face to the judge.

XXI. And now, children, show Levi the respect due to him,[1] so that you may endure, and do not set yourselves up against him, or
2 you will be swept away completely. For the Lord gave me the kingdom and him the priesthood; and he made the kingdom
3 inferior to the priesthood. He gave me the things on earth, him the
4 things in heaven. As the heaven is higher than the earth, so is God's priesthood higher than the kingdom on earth, unless it falls away from the Lord through sin and becomes subservient to the earthly
5 kingdom.[2] For the Lord chose him rather than you,[3] to approach him, and to eat at his table, and *to offer* the first-fruits, the choice
6 *offerings*,[4] of the sons of Israel. But you will be king in Jacob;[5] and you will be like a sea for them.[6] For just as on the sea *both* upright and wicked are tossed about, and some are taken prisoner while others make their fortunes, so also *shall* every race of men *be* in you: some will be in danger and taken prisoner while others will grow
7 rich through plunder. For those who reign as kings will behave[7] like sea-monsters and gulp down men like fish: they will enslave sons and daughters that are free and plunder houses, lands, flocks,
8 and money. And in their wickedness they will feed the flesh of many to the ravens and the cranes;[8] and they will excel in *every kind*
9 *of* evil, spurred on by greed. And false prophets will appear like hurricanes and persecute all upright men.

XXII. But the Lord will divide them into opposing groups, and
2 there will be continual wars in Israel. And my kingdom will be

---

[4] Lit. 'is burned up out of'.

[1] Lit. 'love Levi'.
[2] *bd* om. 'unless . . . kingdom'.
[3] Lit. 'thee'. Note the abrupt change to second person singular (cp. T. Iss. v. 4–5): *chi* accordingly add 'the angel of the Lord said to me' before 'the Lord chose him'.　　　　　[4] So *b* (*l*): II-*l* 'the first-fruits of the choice *offerings*'.
[5] *b* om. 'But . . . Jacob'.
[6] So *ba*: II-*a* 'among them'.
[7] Lit. 'be'.　　　　　[8] Gr. 'ibises'.

brought to an end by men of another race before the salvation of Israel comes and the God of righteousness appears,[1] so that Jacob 3 and all the Gentiles may rest in peace. And he will preserve my sovereign rights[2] for ever; for the Lord swore to me on oath that my kingdom and my descendants' *kingdom* shall never fail to the end of time.[3]

XXIII. Now I am much grieved, my children, because of the licentious acts and meddlings in witchcraft and idolatries of which you will be guilty, contrary to the royal *law*, in running after 2 ventriloquists, omens, and the demons of error. You will turn your daughters into singing-girls and prostitutes and take part in the 3 abominable things the Gentiles do. Because of this the Lord will bring on you famine and pestilence, death and sword, unrelenting siege and vicious dogs[1] and taunts from friends, destruction and failure of eyesight, slaughter of children and abduction of wives, seizure of *your* possessions, *the* burning of *the* temple of God, *the* desolation of *your* land, *and* your own enslavement by the Gentiles. 4,5 And they will make some of you eunuchs for their wives. And when[2] you return to the Lord in purity of heart and repent and order your lives in accordance with God's commands, then the Lord will show you mercy and restore you from *your* captivity among your enemies.

XXIV. And after this a star will come forth for you out of Jacob in peace, and a man will arise from among my descendants like the sun of righteousness, living with men in meekness and righteousness, and no sin will be found in him.

2   And the heavens will be opened over him,
        To pour out the blessing of the spirit of the Holy Father;
        And he will pour out the spirit of grace upon you.
3   And you will be his sons in truth,

---

[1] Lit. 'until the salvation of Israel comes, until the appearing (Gk. παρουσία) of the God of righteousness'.   [2] Lit. 'the power of my kingdom'.
[3] So *b g*: the other MSS vary, but give much the same sense.

[1] Lit. 'and dogs for tearing enemies in pieces'.
[2] So *b g*: II-*g* 'until'.

And live in accordance with his commands from first to last.

4   This *is* the shoot of God Most High,
     And this the fountain that gives life to[1] all mankind.

5   Then will the sceptre of my kingdom shine forth,
     And from your root will come a stem.

6   And from[2] it will spring a staff of righteousness for the
         Gentiles,
     To judge and to save all that invoke the Lord.

XXV.   And after this Abraham and Isaac and Jacob will rise to life
again, and my brethren and I will be chiefs of our tribes in Israel:
Levi *will be* first, I second, Joseph third, Benjamin fourth, Simeon
2 fifth, Issachar sixth, and so all in order. And the Lord will bless[1]
Levi, the angels of the presence me, the powers of the glory Simeon,
the heaven Reuben, the earth Issachar, the sea Zebulon, the
mountains Joseph, the tabernacle Benjamin, the lights *of heaven*
Dan, Eden[2] Naphtali, the sun Gad, the olive[3] Asher.

3   And there will be one people of the Lord and one language;
     And there will be no spirit of error of Beliar any more,
     For he will be thrown into the fire for ever.

4   And those who have died in grief will rise again in joy,
     And those who *are* in penury for the Lord's sake will be made
         rich,
     And those who *are* in want[4] will eat their fill,
     And those who *are* weak will receive strength,
     And those who have been put to death for the Lord's sake will
         awake to life.[5]

5   And the harts of Jacob will run with gladness,
     And the eagles of Israel will fly with joy

---

[1] Lit. 'the fountain to *the* life of'.
[2] Or 'through' (lit. 'in').

[1] So *gdm ef*: *bl chi* 'the Lord blessed'; *kn* lacking.
[2] Lit. 'the delicacy' (= ἡ τρυφή, used a number of times in the Greek Old
Testament to render the Hebrew 'Eden').
[3] So *b* Arm. (cp. Deut. xxxiii. 24): others 'the moon'.
[4] So *b*: *dm ef* 'in hunger'; *l g a chi* lacking.
[5] Lit. 'in life'.

(But the ungodly will mourn and sinners weep),
And all the peoples will glorify the Lord for ever.

XXVI. And so, my children, observe the whole of the law of the
2 Lord, for there is hope for all who make straight **their** way.[1] And he
said to them, I am a hundred and nineteen years old, and I am to
3 die in the sight of you all this day. Do not bury me in expensive
clothes, nor tear my belly open (for this *is what* those who are kings
4 would do); and take me up to Hebron with you. And as he finished
speaking Judah fell asleep; and his sons did everything he had
commanded them, and they buried him in Hebron with his
fathers.

THE TESTAMENT OF ISSACHAR,
ABOUT SIMPLICITY

I. A copy of the words of Issachar.
He called his sons and said to them, Listen, children, to your
father, Issachar: listen carefully, you whom the Lord loves, to what
2 I say, I was born to Jacob as his fifth son as a result of the hire for
3 the mandrakes.[1] For Reuben[2] brought in mandrakes from the
4 country, and Rachel met him outside and took them. And Reuben
was in tears; and Leah, my mother, heard him *crying* and came out.
5 (Now these *mandrakes* were sweet-smelling apples that the land of
Aram used to produce on a piece of high ground underneath a
6 water-spring.) And Rachel said, I will not give them to you: I will
7 treasure them as if they were my children.[3] Now there were two
apples;[4] and Leah said, Surely it is enough for you to have taken
away the husband I married as a girl:[5] will you take these

[1] All the MSS read either 'his way' (*bl*) or 'his ways' (II-*l*): *chi*, in addition, have 'hold fast to' instead of 'make straight'.

[1] Lit. 'in hire of the mandrakes'.
[2] So II: *b* 'Jacob'.
[3] I will . . . children: lit. 'for they will be to me instead of children'.
[4] So *b*: II 'two of these apples'.
[5] Lit. 'the husband of my virginity'.

8   away too? And she said, Behold, Jacob shall be yours to-night in
9   exchange for your son's mandrakes. And Leah said to her, Do not
    be so superior and flatter yourself, for Jacob is mine, and I am the
10 wife of his youth. But Rachel said, How so? For he was pledged in
    marriage to me first, and *it was* for my sake he served our father
11 fourteen years. What should I do to you? For men's deceit and
    cunning are always on the increase, and on earth deceit prospers.
12 If it were not so, you would not be living with Jacob now.[6] For you
    are not his wife, but you were deceitfully foisted on him instead of
13 me. And my father deceived me and took me away that night, and
    would not let me see *what was going on*; for, if I had been there, this
14 would not have happened. And Rachel said, Take one mandrake,
15 and for the other[7] I will hire him out to you for one night. And
    Jacob slept with Leah, and she conceived and bore me; and on
    account of the hire I was called Issachar.

II.   Then an angel of the Lord appeared to Jacob, saying, Rachel
    shall bear two children, for she has declined intercourse with her
2   husband and chosen continence. And had not Leah, my mother,
    given up[1] the two apples in exchange for intercourse she would
    have borne eight sons: as it was, she bore *only* six, and Rachel bore
    the *other* two because the Lord looked favourably on her because of
3   the mandrakes.[2] For he saw that it was for children she wanted
4   intercourse with Jacob and not for pleasure. For on the very next
    day she gave Jacob up again to get the other mandrake also. And
5   so[3] the Lord took notice of Rachel because of the mandrakes.[4] For
    though she very much wanted to, she would not eat them, but
    dedicated them in the house of the Lord and presented them to the
    priest of the Most High who was *there* at that time.

III.   So when I grew up, my children, I lived an upright life, and I

---

[6] Lit. 'you would not be seeing the face of Jacob'.
[7] Lit. 'the one'.

[1] Lit. 'paid' (so *b*: II 'sold').
[2] Lit. 'looked upon her in the mandrakes'.
[3] So *b*: II om. 'And so'.
[4] Lit. 'listened to Rachel in the mandrakes'.

became the family's farmer[1] and brought in *the* fruits of the fields in
2 their season. And my father blessed me, for he saw that I lived
3 simply. And I was not a busybody in what I did, nor wicked[2] and a
4 slanderer of my neighbour. I never spoke evil of anyone, nor did I
5 censure any man's *style of* life, living simply myself.[3] And so I was
thirty when I married; for my labours exhausted my strength, and
the thought of pleasure with a woman hardly ever entered my
mind, for I used to be so worn out that sleep would get the better of
6 me *almost at once.* And my father always rejoiced in my simplicity;
for whatever it was I was labouring at, all the choice fruits and all
the firstfruits I would offer first through the priest to the Lord, then
7 to my father, and then I *would enjoy it*[4] myself. And the Lord
doubled my possessions;[5] and Jacob also knew that God was
8 assisting my simplicity. For I used to bestow the good things of the
earth on everyone that was poor and everyone that was oppressed
in simplicity of heart.

IV. And now, listen to me, my children, and live in simplicity of
2 heart;[1] for I have observed *that* it finds favour with the Lord.[2] The
simple-*hearted man* does not covet gold, is not jealous of his neighbour, is not concerned about variety in his food, is not *always*
3 wanting different clothes, makes no plans[3] for a long life, but waits
4 on the will of God alone. And the spirits of error have no power
over him, for he averts his eyes from a woman's beauty, so as not to
5 mislead or corrupt his mind. No envy will invade his thoughts:
malice does not subvert his soul; nor is his mind obsessed by
6 money-getting.[4] For he lives an upright life, and looks at everything simply, and gives no countenance to the wickedness that

[1] Lit. 'a farmer of my fathers and my brothers'.
[2] So *b l*: II-*l* 'envious'.
[3] Lit. 'walking in simplicity of eyes'.
[4] The addition 'would enjoy *it*' is in fact found in *g*: *d* (*m*) add 'would partake of
them'.   [5] Lit. 'the good things in my hands'.

[1] So *b*: II 'in the simplicity of your hearts'.
[2] Lit. 'for I have seen in it all the good pleasure of the Lord'.
[3] Translation uncertain.
[4] So *b* (lit. 'nor does he think of money-getting with insatiable desire'). For
'money-getting' (πορισμού) II reads 'distraction' (περισπασμόν).

results from the error of the world,[5] so as not to get a distorted view of any of[6] the Lord's commands.

V. So keep the law of God, my children, and try to live simply and in innocence; and do not be over-inquisitive about the Lord's 2 commands, nor about the affairs of *your* neighbour. But love the Lord and *your* neighbour, *and* show compassion for the poor and the 3 weak. Put your backs into your work as farmers: give yourselves up to your labours in the field of every kind; and offer gifts to the Lord 4 with thanksgiving. For with the first-fruits of the earth has the Lord blessed[1] you,[2] just as he has blessed all the saints from Abel until 5 now. For the share allotted you is no other than the richness of the 6 earth, whose fruits *are produced* by toil. For[3] our father Jacob blessed 7 me with blessings of the earth and of first-fruits. And Levi and Judah were honoured by the Lord among Jacob's sons; for the Lord gave them each their share,[4] and to the one he gave the 8 priesthood and to the other the kingdom. So then, obey them, and live simply like your father (for to Gad, too, it has been granted to destroy the raiders that are coming on Israel).

VI. I know, my children, that in the last times your sons will turn their backs on simplicity and become obsessed by greed:[1] they will abandon innocence and resort to cunning; and, forsaking the 2 Lord's commands, they will attach themselves to Beliar. And they will give up farming and follow their own wicked inclinations; and 3 they will be dispersed among the Gentiles and enslaved by their enemies. And tell your children this, so that, if they sin, they may 4 the more quickly return to the Lord; for he is merciful and will deliver them and restore *them* to their land.

---

[5] So *b* (lit. 'not accepting wickedness with *his* eyes from the error of the world'): II 'not accepting wicked eyes from the error of the world'.

[6] So *b*: II om. 'any of'.

[1] So *b*: II 'will the Lord bless'.
[2] So II: *b* om.   [3] So *b*: II 'For even'.
[4] Lit. 'cast lots among them'.

[1] Lit. 'and will cleave to insatiable desire'.

VII. I am a hundred and twenty two years old, and I am not aware
2 that I have committed any deadly sin. I have not had intercourse
with any other woman but my wife: I have not committed fornica-
3 tion through a lustful eye.[1] I have not drunk wine to be led astray
by it: I have not coveted any desirable thing that was my neigh-
4 bour's. My heart has harboured no deceit: no lie has ever passed
5 my lips. If anyone were in distress, I joined my sighs with his; and
with the poor have I shared my bread. I never ate alone. No
boundary-stone have I moved. I have been reverent and truthful
6 all my days. I have loved the Lord with all my strength; and in the
same way I have loved all men as though they were[2] my *own*
7 children. Do these things too, my children, and every spirit of
Beliar will turn and run, and nothing that wicked men can do will
prevail against you; and you will gain the mastery over[3] every wild
beast, since you have with you the God of heaven, sharing men's
8 company,[4] in simplicity of heart. And he commanded them to
carry him up to Hebron and bury him there in the cave with his
9 fathers. And he stretched out his feet and died (*Jacob's* fifth *son*),[5] in
a good old age, in full possession of all his faculties;[6] and with *his*
strength unimpaired he slept the eternal sleep.

THE TESTAMENT OF ZEBULON,
ABOUT COMPASSION AND MERCY

I. A copy of the words[1] of Zebulon, which he left as a testament to
his children, in the hundred and fourteenth year of his life, two[2]
years after the death of Joseph.
2 And he said to them, Listen to me, *you* sons of Zebulon, pay
3 attention to your father's words. I am Zebulon, a good gift to my

---

[1] Lit. 'by the uplifting of the eyes'.
[2] So *b*: II 'more than'.   [3] Lit. 'you will enslave'.
[4] Lit. 'walking with men'.   [5] So *b*: II om.
[6] Lit. 'having every limb healthy'.

[1] So *eaf chi*: *dlm* 'of the testament'; *b g* om.
[2] So II: *b* 'thirty-two'.

parents; for when I was born, the numbers of our father's flocks
and herds had been much increased by the share he had received

4 as a result of the strategem of the different coloured rods.[3] I am not
aware, my children,[4] that I have ever sinned, save only in thought.

5 Nor do I remember that I have done anything contrary to the law,
except for the part I played without knowing what I was doing *in
the conspiracy* against Joseph (for I promised my brothers[5] not to tell

6 my father what had happened). And I wept much[6] when I was on
my own, for I was afraid of my brothers, because they had all
agreed that if anyone betrayed the secret he should be put to the

7 sword. But when they wanted to kill him, I warned them solemnly
with tears against this wicked deed.

II. For Simeon and Gad were incensed against Joseph and made
an attack on him,[1] *intending* to kill him; and Joseph fell on his face

2 and said to them, Have mercy on me, brothers, pity our father
Jacob: do not raise your hands against me to shed innocent blood,

3 for I have not sinned against you. And if indeed I have sinned, then
punish me; but do not raise your hand *against me*[2] for our father

4 Jacob's sake. And as he was saying this, I felt pity *for him* and began

5 to weep, and I was overcome completely.[3] And Joseph too was
weeping, and I *wept* with him; and my heart was throbbing, and
the joints of my body refused to function,[4] and I could not stand.

6 And when he saw me weeping with him, and *the two of* them coming
on him to kill him, he took refuge behind me and begged them *for*

7 *mercy*. But Reuben stood up and said, Brothers, let us not kill him,
but let us throw him into one of these dry pits that our fathers dug

8 and found no water. (For that is why the Lord prevented water

9 from welling up in them, so that Joseph should be preserved. And
the Lord did so until they sold him to the Ishmaelites.)

---

[3] Lit. '. . . increased when in the different coloured rods he had *his* share'. Cp.
Gen. xxx. 25–43.   [4] So *b*: II om. 'my children'.

[5] Translation uncertain: *b g* (*l*) 'I covered for my brothers'; *dm eaf chi* 'I confirmed
to my brothers'.   [6] So *b*: II 'And I wept many days about Joseph'.

---

[1] Lit. 'For Simeon and Gad came against Joseph with (*b* om.) anger (*b* om.)'.

[2] 'Against me' is in fact added by *gdm* (ἐπ᾽ ἐμέ) and *eaf* (μοί).

[3] Lit. 'and my liver was loosened and all the substance of my bowels became
weak upon my soul'.   [4] Lit. 'and the joints of my body went out of place'.

III.   And I refused, *my* children, to take my share of the money that
2   was paid for Joseph. But Simeon and Gad and our six other
brothers took what was paid for Joseph and bought sandals for
3   themselves and for their wives and children, saying, We will not
buy food with it,[1] for it is our brother's blood-money, but let us
tread it well under foot, because he said he would be king over us;
4   and *so* let us see what will become of his dreams. (That is why it is
written in the writing of the law of Enoch that whoever will not
raise a child[2] for his brother, his sandal shall be taken off and his
5   face spat upon. Joseph's brothers had no wish for their brother to
6   live; and the Lord took off Joseph's sandal[3] from them. For when
they came into Egypt they had their sandals taken off[4] by Joseph's
servants as soon as they arrived at the gate, and so they made their
obeisance to Joseph, as was the custom at the Pharaoh's court.[5]
7   And not only did they make obeisance to him, but they were also
spat upon immediately they fell down in front of him; and so they
8   were put to shame before the Egyptians. For the Egyptians heard
afterwards how disgracefully we had treated Joseph.)

1,2   **IV.**   And then they sat down to eat.[1] But I ate nothing for two days
and two nights out of pity for Joseph; and Judah did not eat with
them *either*, but kept watch on the pit, for he was afraid that Simeon
3   and Gad might make off and kill him. And when they saw that I too
4   was not eating, they set me to guard him until he was sold. And he
spent three days and three nights in the pit; and so when he was
5   sold he was very hungry. And when Reuben heard that he had
been sold while he was away, he tore his clothes off and lamented,
6   saying, How shall I look my father Jacob in the face? And he took
the money and ran after the merchants, but did not find anyone;

---

[1]   Lit. 'We will not eat it'.   [2]   Lit. 'raise up seed'.
[3]   So *b*: II explains 'the sandal that they wore against their brother Joseph'.
[4]   Lit. 'they were taken off'.
[5]   Lit. 'according to the form prescribed by the Pharaoh (so *b g*: II-*g* 'by King
Pharaoh').

[1]   There are wide variations between the MSS here. The translation is based on *b*
('After these things they threw to eat').

for they had left the main road and gone off through *the country of the*
7 Trogolocolpites by a short cut. And Reuben ate nothing that day.
8 So Dan came to him and said, Do not weep or mourn, for I have
9 thought of[2] something we can tell our father Jacob. Let us kill a
he-goat, and dip Joseph's tunic *in its blood*, and say, Do you
recognize it? Is this your son's tunic? And this is what they did.[3]
10 For they had stripped Joseph of our father's tunic when they were
11 about to sell him and had put a slave's old coat on him. Now
Simeon had the tunic and would not give it up, and he wanted to
cut it in pieces with his sword, because he was angry *Joseph* was *still*
12 alive and he had not killed him. But we all stood up against him
together and said, If you will not give it up, we will say you did *this*
13 evil thing in Israel on your own. And so he gave it up; and they did
as Dan had suggested.

V. And now, my children, I appeal to you to keep the Lord's
commands, and to show mercy to your neighbour and be compassionate towards all men – and not only towards humans, but
2 towards animals too. For that was why the Lord blessed me, and
when all my brothers were taken ill, I escaped unharmed; for the
3 Lord knows each man's motives. So let mercy reign in your hearts,[1]
my children, because as a man treats his neighbour, so also will the
4 Lord treat him. For my brother's sons were being taken ill as well
as their fathers, and were dying, on account of Joseph, because they
had shown him no mercy; but my sons were preserved in perfect
5 health, as you well know. And when I was in Canaan, on the coast,
I used to catch fish for my father Jacob; and although many *other
people* were drowned in the sea, I survived unhurt.

VI. I was the first to make a boat to sail on the sea, for the Lord
2 gave me the necessary knowledge and skill.[1] And I fitted a rudder[2]
behind it and stretched a sail on an upright piece of wood in the

---

[2] Lit. 'I have found'.
[3] So II: *b* omits the whole clause.

[1] Lit. 'Have, therefore, mercy in your bowels'.

[1] Lit. 'gave me understanding and wisdom in it'.
[2] Lit. 'And I let down a piece of wood'.

3 middle of it. And I sailed it along the shores and caught fish for my
4 father's household until we came to Egypt. And[3] out of compassion
5 I gave some of my catch to[4] every man *that was* a foreigner. And if
   there was anyone who was foreign, or ailing, or aged, I boiled and
   dressed the fish and offered it to all men, as each had need, making
6 them my guests out of a fellow-feeling for them. And so the Lord
   gave me a rich catch of fish; for he who shares *what he has* with his
7 neighbour is repaid many times over by the Lord. I caught fish for
   five years; and I shared it with whoever I came across[5] and there
8 was *still* enough for my father's entire household. In the summer I
   caught fish, and in the winter I looked after the sheep with my
   brothers.

VII.   Now I will tell you what I did. I saw a man who was in distress
   because he had nothing warm to put on in winter,[1] and I had
   compassion on him; and I took a garment from my house without
2 anyone noticing and gave it to the man that was in distress. So you
   too, my children, must show compassion and mercy to all men
   without partiality, and give to every man with a good heart from
3 the things that God has given you. And if you have nothing at the
   time to give a man in need, have a fellow-feeling for him, and show
4 him compassion and mercy. I remember[2] I had nothing ready to
   hand *on one occasion* to give a needy man, so I accompanied him on
   his journey for seven furlongs in tears, and my heart went out to
   him in sympathy.

VIII.   And so, my children, be compassionate and merciful to every
   man, that the Lord may be compassionate and merciful to you too.
2 (Because, indeed, in the last days the Lord sends[1] his compassion
   on the earth, and wherever he finds a merciful heart,[2] he makes his
3 dwelling there.) For just in so far as a man has compassion on his

---

   [3] vi. 4–6, 7b ('and I shared . . . household') and vii. 1–viii. 3 ('. . . on him') are
found in *bgld* (*m*) only.   [4] So *b*: *gldm* 'I shared with'.
   [5] Lit. 'with every man I saw'.

   [1] Lit. 'in distress by nakedness of winter'.
   [2] Lit. 'I know'.

   [1] So *b d*: *kgl* (*m*) 'will send'.   [2] Lit. 'bowels of mercy'.

4   neighbour, so *has* the Lord[3] *compassion* on him. And when we went
    down to Egypt, Joseph bore no malice against us; and when he saw
5   me he had compassion.[4] Let him be an example to you and bear no
    malice either,[5] my children, and love one another,[6] and do not,
6   each of you, keep a record of his brother's wrongdoing. For this is a
    bar to unity and splits up any family, and is a source of confusion in
    the soul and destroys a man completely.[7] For the man that bears
    malice is devoid of mercy.[8]

IX.   See *what happens* to water; for when it flows all of it together *as a*
2   *single river* it sweeps along with it stones, wood, earth,[1] sand. But if
    it is divided into a number *of separate streams*, it disappears into the
3   ground and becomes of no account at all. So will you be too, if you
4   are divided. Do not let yourselves, therefore, be split in two, so that
    you have two heads,[2] for everything the Lord has made has *but* one
    head *only*: he has provided two shoulders, hands, *and* feet; but all
5   the limbs obey the one head. I understand from the writing of my
    fathers that in the last days you will forsake the Lord, and[3] you will
    be divided in Israel and follow two kings, and you will commit
6   every *kind of* abomination and worship every *kind of* idol. And your
    enemies will take you away as captives, and you will be oppressed
    by[4] the Gentiles and suffer every *kind of* indignity[5] and distress and
7   mental anguish.[6] And afterwards you will remember the Lord and
    repent; and he will bring you back again, for he is merciful and
    compassionate and has no evil designs on men, because *he knows*
    that they are flesh and *that* the spirits of error deceive them in
8   everything they do. And then shall the Lord himself, the light of

---

[3]   So *b k*: *gldm* add 'also'.
[4]   and when . . . compassion: found in *bgld* only.
[5]   So *b g* (*d*): others om. 'and bear . . . either'.
[6]   So *bg* (*d*): others add 'also'.
[7]   Lit. 'and destroys existence': so *ld eaf*; *bg* om. through homoioteleuton; *chi*
evidently secondary.   [8]   For . . . mercy: found in *bgld* only.

[1]   *bl* wrongly 'the' (sand) – reading τήν for γῆν.
[2]   Lit. 'split into two heads'.
[3]   in the last . . . Lord, and: found in *bgld* only.
[4]   So *gl eaf hi*: *bdc* 'you will be forced to live among'.
[5]   Lit. 'weakness'.
[6]   and mental anguish: found in *bgld* only.

righteousness, arise for you, and healing and compassion shall be in his wings:[7] he shall ransom mankind from their slavery to Beliar; and every spirit of error shall be trampled underfoot. And he shall convert all the Gentiles, so that they are filled with zeal for him.[8] And you shall see God[9] in human form *in the house*[10] which the Lord

9 will choose (Jerusalem is its name). And *then* by the wickedness of your doings[11] you will provoke him again, and you will be thrown out until the end of time.

X. And now, my children, do not be sad because I am dying, nor
2 cast down at my departure. For I shall rise again in the midst of you, as a ruler in the midst of his sons; and I shall rejoice in the midst of my tribe with as many as have kept the law of the Lord and
3 the commands of their father Zebulon. But upon the ungodly will the Lord bring eternal fire, and he will destroy them for all time.
4,5 Meanwhile,[1] I am going to my rest, as did my fathers. Do you fear the Lord your God with all your strength all the days of your life.
6 And when he had finished speaking, he slept the perfect[2] sleep; and
7 his sons put him in a coffin. And afterwards they carried him up to Hebron and buried him with his fathers.

THE TESTAMENT OF DAN,
ABOUT ANGER AND FALSEHOOD

I. A copy of the words of Dan, which he spoke to his sons in his last days, in the hundred and twenty-fifth year of his life.
2 He called his family together and said, Listen to my words, *you*
3 sons of Dan, and pay attention to what your father has to say.[1] I have found by experience all through my life that truth and just

---

[7] and healing . . . wings: found in *bkgldm* only.
[8] So *bkgl* (*d*): others 'And you shall return to your own land'.
[9] So *bkl*: *gdm eaf* 'the Lord' (with subsequent omission through homoioteleuton in *eaf*).   [10] Some such addition is needed: cp. T. Levi x. 5, xv. 1.
[11] *bk* 'words': II 'works'.

[1] So II-*g*: *bk* (*g*) om.   [2] Lit. 'good'.

[1] Lit. 'the words of your father's mouth'.

dealing are good and pleasing to God, and that falsehood and
4 anger are evil, because[2] they teach man every kind of wickedness. I
confess to you to-day, my children, that I was myself delighted
when it was suggested that we should kill Joseph,[3] although he was
5 a true and good man. And I was overjoyed when Joseph[4] was sold,
6 because his father loved him more than us. For the spirit of
7 jealousy and self-esteem said to me, You are his son as well. And
one of the spirits of Beliar egged me on,[5] saying, Take this sword
and kill Joseph with it, and your father will love you when he is
8 dead. (This spirit that tried to persuade me to thirst for Joseph's
9 blood, like a leopard for a kid's, is the spirit of anger.) But the God
of our[6] father Jacob would not let him fall into my hands, and he
prevented me from ever finding him alone to do that wicked deed
and thus destroy two tribes in Israel.

II. And now, my children, I am dying, and I assure you that
unless you keep yourselves from the spirit of falsehood and anger,
2 and love truth and patience, you will perish. Anger blinds a man,
3 my children, and the angry man can see no one as he truly is.[1] For
though it is *his own* father or mother, he treats them as enemies:
though it is *his* brother, he does not recognize *him*: though a prophet
of the Lord, he disobeys *him*: though a righteous man, he takes no
4 notice *of him*: *though* a friend, he does not acknowledge *him*. For the
spirit of anger wraps the nets of error round him and blinds his
natural eyes: through[2] falsehood it darkens his mind and gives him
5 its own *distorted* vision. And what does it blind[3] his eyes with? With
a bitter hatred;[4] and it makes him like itself,[5] so that he is envious of
his brother.

III. Anger is evil, my children, for it becomes *as it were* a soul to the

---

[2] So *b*: II om.
[3] Lit. 'that in my heart I was delighted about the death of Joseph'.
[4] So *b*: II 'he'.   [5] Lit. 'worked with me'.
[6] So *b*: II 'my'.

[1] Lit. 'There is blindness in anger, my children, and no (*b* adds 'angry') man sees
a face in truth'.   [2] So *b*: II 'and through'.
[3] Lit. 'wrap round'.   [4] Lit. 'With hatred of heart'.
[5] Lit. 'and it gives him its own heart'.

2 soul itself. And it makes the body of the angry man its own, and
gains the mastery over *his* soul, and motivates the body to commit
3 iniquity of every kind. And when it does *it*, the soul justifies what is
4 done,[1] because it does not see. Consequently, the man that is
angry, if he is a man of influence, has a threefold power in his
anger: first, through the power and[2] the help of his servants;
secondly, through his wealth, which enables him to exert pressure
and win the verdict, although he is in the wrong; and thirdly,
because he has the natural *power* of *his own* body and himself[3] does
5 the evil. And even if the man that is angry is a weakling, he
nevertheless has twice the power *that was given him* by nature; for
6 anger always helps trangressors. This spirit, together with *the spirit
of* falsehood stands[4] ever at Satan's right hand, so that by cruelty
and falsehood his ends may be achieved.

IV. Understand, then, how powerful anger is, and how deceptive
it is.[1] For first of all it provokes by word: then it strengthens the *man*
provoked by deeds, and creates disorder and makes havoc in his
3 mind;[2] and thus it goads his soul to fury. So when anyone criticizes
you, you must not[3] be moved to anger; and if anyone praises you as
good men, you must not be too elated – do not all of a sudden either
4 go into ecstacies or take offence. For first it delights the ear, and so
it alerts the mind to consider **what has been said in provocation**, and
5 then, in a fit of rage, *the man* thinks his anger justified. If any loss or
deprivation befalls you,[4] my children, do not lose your heads, for
this very spirit makes *a man* desire what he has been deprived of so
6 that he becomes angry through longing *for it*. If you suffer a loss
voluntarily,[5] do not grieve *about it*, for grief leads on to anger[6] with

---

[1] Or, possibly, 'And when it (i.e. 'the soul') does it, it justifies what is done'.
[2] So *b*: II om. 'the power and'.   [3] Lit. 'through himself'.
[4] Lit. 'goes' or 'lives its life'.

[1] Lit. 'that it is in vain' (the Gk. word μάταιος, usually rendered 'vain' or 'empty',
is in several passages in the Gk. Old Testament used to render the Heb. *kazabh*, 'lie,
falsehood' – e.g. Amos ii. 4; Ezek. xiii. 6).
[2] Lit. 'and disturbs his mind with bitter damages'.
[3] *b* om.   [4] So *b*: II 'If you fall into any loss or deprivation'.
[5] So *bl*: II-*l* add 'or involuntarily'.
[6] Lit. 'for from grief it causes to arise anger'.

7 falsehood. Anger with falsehood is a double evil, and each assists the other to stir up the mind; and when the soul is stirred up continually the Lord departs from it and Beliar has dominion over it.

V. So keep, my children, the Lord's commands and observe his law; and turn from anger and hate falsehood, that the Lord may
2 dwell in you and Beliar may flee from you. Speak the truth to each other, and you will be preserved from *the ill-effects of* pleasure[1] and from troubles; and[2] you will be at peace, since you will have *with you*
3 the God of peace, and contention will have no hold over you. Love the Lord throughout[3] your life, and one another with a true heart.
4 For I know that in the last days you will turn away from the Lord, and you will despise Levi and set yourselves up against Judah, but you will be powerless against them; for an angel of the Lord will
5 guide them both, because by them will Israel stand. And when you turn from the Lord, you will give yourselves up to every kind of evil, doing *all* the abominable things the Gentiles do and wantonly pursuing the women of the lawless, while the spirits of error work
6 in you every kind of wickedness. For I have read in the book of the righteous Enoch that your prince is Satan, and that all the spirits of fornication and arrogance will turn their attention to Levi[4] and constantly dog the footsteps of Levi's sons in order to make them sin against the Lord.

7 And my sons will associate themselves with Levi,
   And join with them in all their sins;
   And Judah's sons will be covetous,
   And plunder other men's goods like lions.
8 Because of this you will be carried captive with them,
   And there will you suffer all the plagues of Egypt,
   And all the evils of the Gentiles,
9 Yet,[5] when you return to the Lord,

---

[1] Lit. 'you will not fall into pleasure' (so *b*: II 'wrath').
[2] Lit. 'but'.
[3] Or 'with all' (lit. 'in all').
[4] Or 'will obey Levi' (lit. 'listen to Levi').
[5] Lit. 'And so'.

You will find mercy,
And he will bring you to his sanctuary,
Proclaiming to you[6] peace.

10 And there will arise to you from the tribe of Judah and *from* Levi
the Lord's salvation,
And he will make war against Beliar,
And avenge our fathers in a mighty victory.[7]

11 And he will set free the prisoners of Beliar[8]
(The souls, *that is*, of the saints);
And he will turn the hearts of the disobedient back to the
Lord again;
And he will give to them that call on him eternal peace.

12 And the saints will rest in Eden,
And in the new Jerusalem will the righteous rejoice,
And it will be to the glory of God for ever.

13 And no longer will Jerusalem lie in ruins,
Nor Israel endure captivity;
For the Lord will be in the midst of it,
Living together with men,
And the Holy One of Israel will reign[9] over them
In humility and poverty.
And he who has faith in him will reign in truth in the
heavens.

VI. And now fear the Lord, my children, and beware of Satan and
2 his spirits. Draw near to God and to the angel that intercedes for
you, for he is a mediator between God and men for the peace of
Israel; and he will[1] stand up against the kingdom of the enemy.
3 This is why the enemy is at such pains to overthrow all those that
4 invoke the Lord. For he knows that on the day that Israel puts its
5 faith in God[2] the enemy's kingdom will be brought to an end. The

---

[6] So *bk*: II 'And he will give you'.
[7] Lit. 'And he shall give a vengeance of victory to our fathers (*b* 'boundaries')'.
[8] Lit. 'And the captivity shall he take from Beliar'.
[9] Lit. '. . . Israel reigning'.

[1] So *b*: II '. . . God and men; and for the peace of Israel he will . . .'.
[2] Lit. 'Israel believes'.

angel of peace himself will strengthen Israel and preserve it from
6 the worst of evils. But in the time of Israel's lawlessness the Lord
will leave them and go to the Gentiles that do his will, for none of
7 the angels will be equal to him.[3] And his name shall be in every
8 place of Israel and among the Gentiles, *his name of* Saviour. Keep
yourselves, therefore, my children, from every wicked deed, and
turn your backs on anger and all falsehood, and love truth and
9 patience. And what you have heard from your father pass on to
your *own* children, so that the Saviour[4] of the Gentiles may accept
you; for he is true and patient, meek and lowly, and teaches the law
10 of God by what he does. Turn, then, from unrighteousness of every
kind and hold fast to the righteousness of the law of the Lord; and
11 your race will be kept safe for ever.[5] And bury me near my fathers.

VII. And after saying this, he kissed them and slept the eternal
2 sleep. And his sons buried him; and afterwards they carried up his
bones *and laid them* alongside *those of* Abraham and Isaac and Jacob.
3 Nevertheless, just as[1] Dan had prophesied to them (that they
would forget the law of their God and be alienated from their own
land and from the race of Israel and their family and kinsmen[2]), so
it came to pass.[3]

THE TESTAMENT OF NAPHTALI, ABOUT NATURAL GOODNESS

I. A copy of the Testament of Naphtali, which he left as a testament at the time of his death, in the hundred and thirty-second
year of his life.
2   When his sons were met together in the seventh month, on the
fourth[1] day of the month, while he was still in good health, he made

---

[3] So II: *b* '. . . leave them and go after him that does his will, for to none of the
angels will he be as to him'.   [4] So II-*l*: *bkl* 'Father'.
[5] So II: *b* omits this last clause.

[1] So *b*: II om. 'just as'.   [2] So II: *b* om. 'and kinsmen (lit. 'seed')'.
[3] So *b* (*d*): II (−*d*) om. the final clause.

[1] So *b*: II 'first'.

3 a feast for them[2] – in fact, a banquet. And after he had woken up
next morning he said to them, I am going to die. And they did not

4 believe him. And he blessed the Lord and insisted that after the

5 feast of the day before he would die. So he began to say to his sons,[3]
Listen, my children, you sons of Naphtali, listen to what your

6 father is saying. I was Bilhah's child; and because Rachel craftily
gave Bilhah to Jacob instead of herself and she bore me on Rachel's

7 thighs, I was consequently called Naphtali. And Rachel loved me
because I was born on her thighs; and as I was an attractive child,[4]
she would kiss me and say, May I *live to* see a brother of yours, from

8 my own womb, just like you. So it came about that Joseph was like

9 me in everything, in answer to Rachel's prayers. And my mother
was[5] Bilhah, the daughter of Rotheus, the brother of Deborah,
Rebecca's nurse, and she was born on the very same day as Rachel.

10 And Rotheus was of Abraham's stock, a Chaldaean, devout, free-

11 born, and well-bred. And he was taken as a prisoner and bought by
Laban, and he gave him Aina, his slave-girl, as his wife; and she
bore a daughter, and he called her Zilpah after the village where he

12 had been taken prisoner. And again[6] she bore **a daughter and he
called her** Bilhah,[7] saying, My daughter is one of those who are
always in a hurry to run after anything new;[8] for as soon as she was
born she was in a hurry to be suckled.

II. And since I was *as* light-footed as a deer, my father Jacob chose
me for all missions and messages; and as *if I were* a deer he gave me

2 his blessing. For just as the potter knows how much the vessel *he is
making* is to contain, and takes *the right amount of* clay for it, so too the

---

[2] So II: *b*'he made a supper himself'.

[3] So *b*: II om. 'to his sons'.

[4] So *b* (lit. 'being delicate in form'): II 'when I was still young' (lit. 'being still
delicate').

[5] Lit. 'is'.

[6] Lit. 'next'.

[7] The text in all the MSS is difficult here. Either we must assume that some
words have fallen out (hence our translation, which follows a reconstruction based
on the analogy of the previous verse), or we must emend the masculine participle
'saying' to the feminine in order to make Aina, and not Rotheus, the speaker (and so
the parent responsible for giving Bilhah her name).

[8] Lit. 'My daughter is a hurrier-after-novelty'.

Lord makes the body with a view to the spirit it is to contain,[1] and
3 he puts the spirit into *it* according to the body's capacity. And the
proportions of the two correspond perfectly,[2] for the whole
4 creation[3] of the Most High *has been fashioned* by weight and measure
and rule. And just as the potter knows what the use of each vessel
is, *and* what it is fit for, so also the Lord knows for how long the body
5 will persist in goodness and when it will turn to evil.[4] For there is
nothing that is made and no thought which the Lord does not
6 know, for he created every man in his own image. As *is* a man's
strength, so also *is* his work; and as his mind, so also his skill;[5] and
as his purpose, so also his achievement; and as his heart, so also his
mouth; and as his eye, so also his sleep; and as his soul, so also his
7 word, either in the law of the Lord or the law of Beliar. And as there
is a distinction between light and darkness, *and between* seeing and
hearing, so also there is a distinction between one man and
another, and between one woman and another; and it cannot be
8 said that one is like another either in face or in mind.[6] For God
made all things good in *their* order: *first* the five senses in the head
(and he joined[7] the neck to the head and the hair to give it glory[8]),
then the heart for understanding, the belly †for secretion of the
stomach†, the **windpipe** for health, the liver for anger, the gall for
bitterness, the spleen for laughter, and kidneys for shrewdness, the
muscles of the loins for power, the ribs to form a chest,[9] the loins for
9 strength, and so on. So then, my children, order your lives to do
what is right[10] in the fear of God, and do nothing that is not in
10 order, out of context, or not in season. For if you tell the eye to hear,
it cannot: so neither, if *your are* in darkness, will you be able to do
the deeds of light.

---

[1] Lit. 'with a view to the likeness of the spirit'.
[2] Lit. 'And there is no remainder, one out of the one, a third of a hair'.
[3] Or 'for every creature'.
[4] Lit. 'when it begins in evil'.
[5] So II: *b* wrongly repeats 'his work'.
[6] All the Gk. MSS. are more or less corrupt: the translation is based on a
reconstruction made with the help of Arm.
[7] So *b*: II 'and joining'.
[8] So *bl*: II-*l*ᶜ. . . to the head, adding also to it the hair to give *it* dignity and glory'.
[9] Or 'the sides for sleeping on'. Both text and translation are uncertain.
[10] *b* 'be in order to good things': II 'let all your works be in order to good things'.

III. Do not, then, be goaded into wrong-doing by covetousness,[1] neither deceive yourselves with empty words, because if you keep silent in purity of heart you will understand how[2] to hold fast God's
2 will and reject the devil's. Sun moon and stars do not change their order: so too you must not change the law of God by the disorderli-
3 ness of what you do. The Gentiles went astray and forsook the Lord and changed their order, and they went after stones and stocks, led
4 away by spirits of error. But you *will* not *be* so, my children: you have recognized in the vault of heaven, in the earth, and in the sea, and in all created things, the Lord who made them all, so that you should not become like Sodom which changed the order of its
5 nature. Similarly, the Watchers also changed the order of their nature, and the Lord cursed them also at the flood, and *it was* because of them *that* he made the earth a waste, without inhabitants or fruits.

IV. I am telling you this, my children, because I have read in the holy writing of Enoch that you yourselves also will forsake the Lord and do the same wicked things that the Gentiles do and behave like
2 the lawless men of Sodom.[1] And the Lord will bring captivity upon you, and you will be slaves there to your enemies and subjected to every *kind of* hardship and ill-treatment until the Lord has made an
3 end of you altogether. And after your numbers have diminished and your strength is exhausted, you will return and acknowledge the Lord your God; and in his great mercy he will bring you back
4 into your own land. And it shall be, when they have come into the land of their fathers, they will again forget the Lord and act
5 impiously. And the Lord will scatter them over the whole surface of the earth, until the Lord's compassion comes – a man that does righteousness and deals mercifully with all those who are far off and those who are near by.

---

[1] Lit. 'Be not eager, therefore, to corrupt your deeds through covetousness'.
[2] So II: *b* 'you will be able'.

[1] Lit. '. . . the Lord, walking according to all the wickedness of the Gentiles, and you will do according to all the lawlessness of Sodom'.

V. In the fortieth year of my life I had a vision[1] on the Mount of Olives[2] (on the east of Jerusalem), that the sun and the moon were
2 standing still. And behold, Isaac, my father's father, said to us, Run and take hold *of them*, each one *of you* as best he can, and whoever lays hands *on them*, to him will the sun and the moon
3 belong. And we ran, all of us together; and Levi took hold of the sun, and Judah was the first to lay hands on the moon, and both of
4 them were lifted up with them. And when Levi was as the sun, a young man gave him twelve palm branches; and Judah was
5 radiant like the moon, and under his feet were twelve rays. And Levi and Judah ran towards each other and took hold of one
6 another. And behold, a bull *appeared* upon the earth, having two great horns, and *there were* eagle's wings on its back; and we wanted
7 to lay hands on it, but we could not. For Joseph got hold of it first
8 and ascended up on high with it. And I looked[1] (for I was in *the* gardens[3]), and behold, a holy writing appeared to us, saying, Assyrians, Medes, Persians, Elamites, Galachians, Chaldaeans, Syrians, shall in turn take captive[4] the twelve tribes of Israel.

VI. And again, seven months afterwards, I had a vision of[1] our father Jacob standing by the sea of Jamnia, and we, his sons, *were*
2 with him. And behold, a ship came sailing by, full of salt fish,[2] *but* without sailors or steersman; and the ship was inscribed, The
3 Ship[3] of Jacob. And our father said to us, Let us get into our ship.
4 And when we had gone on board, a violent storm got up, and there was a great gust of wind, and our father, who was at the helm, was
5 blown away from us. And we drifted[4] storm-tossed; and the ship filled with water, *and it was* pounded by massive waves so that it

---

[1] Lit. 'I saw'.
[2] Lit. 'on the mountains of olive(s)'.
[3] So *gdlm* Arm.: others corrupt.
[4] Lit. 'shall inherit in captivity'.

[1] Lit. 'I saw'.
[2] In all probability 'full of salt fish' is a corrupt dittography of the following 'without sailors'.   [3] So II-*l*: *bl* om. 'The Ship'.
[4] Lit. 'we were carried over the sea'.

6　was broken up. And Joseph made his escape in a dinghy; and we
　　got away on ten planks (Levi and Judah were *on one plank* together).
7,8　And we were all scattered to the ends *of the earth.* But Levi, in
9　sackcloth prayed for us all to the Lord. And when the storm ceased,
　　the ship reached the land, just as if nothing unusual had hap-
10　pened.[5] And behold, our father Jacob came, and we all rejoiced
　　together.

VII.　I told the two dreams to my father, and he said to me, These
　　things must be fulfilled at their proper time, after Israel has
2　suffered much. Then my father said to me, I believe that Joseph is
　　alive, for I see that the Lord always includes him along with you.
3　And he said in tears, You are alive, Joseph, my child, though I am
　　unable to look on you, and you cannot see Jacob who begot you.
4　And he reduced us to tears as well by what he said; and I longed[1] to
　　tell *him* that *Joseph* had been sold, but I was afraid of my brothers.

VIII.　And behold, my children, I have shown you *what shall be in*
2　the last times, for all *these* things shall happen in Israel. Instruct
　　your children, therefore, that they keep united with Levi and
　　Judah; for through Judah will salvation come to Israel,[1] and in him
3　will Jacob be blessed. For through his tribe God will appear,
　　dwelling among men on the earth, to save the race of Israel; and he
4　will gather together the righteous of the Gentiles. If you do what is
　　good, my children, both men and angels will bless you; and God
　　will be glorified through you among the Gentiles, and the devil will
　　flee from you, and the wild animals will be afraid of you, and the
5　Lord will love you,[2] and the angels will keep close to you. For just
　　as a man who has brought up a child well is remembered as a
6　benefactor, so also a good work is a sure memorial before God.[3] But
　　who does not do what is good – men and angels will curse him; and

[5] Lit. 'as it were in peace'.

[1] Lit. 'I burned in my bowels'.

[1] Lit. 'will salvation sprout up for Israel'.
[2] So *gle*: all others om. 'and the Lord will love you' through homoioteleuton.
[3] Lit. 'For as when anyone has brought up a child well, he has a happy
remembrance, so also for a good work there is a happy remembrance before God'.

God will be dishonoured among the Gentiles through him, and the devil will use him as his own peculiar instrument, and every wild animal will gain the mastery over him, and the Lord will hate him. 7 For the commandments of the law are far from simple, and the 8 keeping of them requires some skill.[4] For there is a time to embrace one's wife, and there is a time to abstain, so that one can give 9 oneself to prayer. There are, then, two commandments; and, unless their proper order is maintained, the result is sin. And so too 10 it is with the other commandments. So be wise in God, and prudent; and understand the order of his commandments and the laws of every action, so that the Lord may love you.

IX. And when he had charged them with many such words, he asked them to take his bones to Hebron and bury them with his 2 fathers. And when he had eaten and drunk and made merry, he 3 hid[1] his face and died. And his sons did everything their father Naphtali had instructed them.

THE TESTAMENT OF GAD,
ABOUT HATRED

I. A copy of the Testament of Gad, which he gave[1] to his sons in 2 the hundred and twenty-seventh[2] year of his life, saying, I was the ninth[3] son born to Jacob, and I was a courageous keeper of the 3 flocks. I used to guard the flock at night, and whenever a lion came against the flock, or a wolf, or a leopard, or a bear, or any wild animal, I would go after it and get hold of it by the foot with my hand, and whirl it round *my head* and stun it and send it flying from 4 me,[4] and so kill it. Now Joseph had been feeding the flocks with us for about a month, and, delicate as he was, he was affected by the

---

[4] Lit. '. . . are double, and through skill must they be fulfilled'.

[1] Lit. 'covered'.

[1] Lit. 'spoke'.
[2] So *bl*: II-*l* 'fifth'.   [3] So II: *b* 'seventh'.
[4] Lit. 'and hurled it over two stades' – i.e. about a quarter of a mile!

5 heat and taken ill. And he returned to Hebron to his[5] father; and he
6 made him lie down near him, because he loved him. And Joseph
said to our father, Zilpah and Bilhah's sons are killing the best *of the
sheep*[6] and eating them without Judah and Reuben's knowledge.[7]
7 For he had seen that I had rescued a lamb out of a bear's mouth
and killed the bear, and I had destroyed the lamb because I was
worried that it would not live, and we had eaten it; and he told our
8 father.[8] And I held this against Joseph until the day he was sold
9 into Egypt. And the spirit of hatred was in me, and I did not want
either to see Joseph or to hear about him;[9] and he accused us to our
faces of eating the sheep without Judah *knowing it*. And whatever he
told our father, he believed him.

II. I confess my sin now, *my* children, how I often wanted to kill
him, because I cordially hated him and had no kindly feelings
2 towards him at all.[1] And I hated him even more because of his
dreams; and I would have licked him out of the land of the living,
3 just as a calf licks up the fresh green grass off the ground. That was
why Judah[2] and I sold him to the Ishmaelites for thirty pieces of
gold; and we hid ten of them[3] and showed the *other* twenty to our
4 brothers. And so through covetousness I was bent on killing him.
5 But[4] the God of my fathers saved him from me and prevented me
from committing an outrage in Israel.

III. And now, my children, listen to the truth:[1] do what is right and
keep the whole law of the Most High; and do not be led astray by the

---

[5] So *b*: II 'our'.
[6] Lit. '. . . killing the good things'.
[7] Or 'in defiance of Judah and Reuben' (lit. 'contrary to the opinion of Judah and Reuben').
[8] So *b*: II-*d* om. 'and he told our father'; *d* 'and having seen the lamb he spoke against us to Jacob'.
[9] Lit. 'and I did not wish either through eyes or through hearing to see Joseph'.

[1] Lit. 'because I hated him up to the soul and there was altogether no liver of mercy in me for him'.　　　　　　　　　　　　　　[2] So *b*: II 'Simeon'.
[3] Lit. 'we hid the ten'.　　　　[4] Lit. 'And'.

[1] Lit. 'listen to words of truth'.

2 spirit of hatred, for it corrupts all human relationships.[2] A man inspired by hatred takes exception to anything anyone does: if anyone keeps the law of the Lord he gets no praise: if anyone fears
3 the Lord and strives for what is right, he is not loved. *A man inspired by hatred* maligns the truth, envies the successful, welcomes backbiting, *and* loves arrogance; for hatred has blinded him.[3] And this is how I regarded Joseph.

IV. So beware of hatred, my children, because it is a sin[1] against
2 the Lord himself. For it refuses to listen to his commandments that
3 we should love our neighbours, and it sins against God. For if a brother stumbles,[2] it wants to publish it abroad immediately to everyone, and urges that he should be brought into court for it, and
4 punished, and put to death. And with a servant, it stirs him up against his master, and applies every *kind of* pressure,[3] in the hope
5 that it can somehow kill him. For hatred joins forces with envy against those who prosper: when it hears of their success, or sees it,
6 it is always dismayed.[4] For just as love would bring back the dead to life and revoke a death sentence, so hatred would kill those who are alive and allow no one to live who is guilty of even the smallest
7 crime. For the spirit of hatred co-operates with Satan in everything through faint-heartedness, and the result is men's death; but the spirit of love co-operates with the law of God by long-suffering, and the result is men's salvation.

V. Hatred is evil, for it invariably goes hand in hand with falsehood and speaks against the truth; and it makes small things out to be great, represents darkness as light, calls what is sweet bitter, and breeds[1] slander and wrath[2] and war and violence and a

---

[2] Lit. 'for it is evil in all the doings of men'.
[3] Lit. 'his soul'.

[1] Lit. 'it makes lawlessness'.
[2] So *b*: II 'falls'.
[3] So *bl*: II-*l* 'and rejoices over him in every affliction'.
[4] Lit. 'sickly'.

[1] Lit. 'teaches'.   [2] So II: *b* om. 'and wrath'.

craving for all kinds of evil things,[3] and it fills the heart with

2 devilish poison. And[4] I tell you this from *my own* experience, my children, so that you may turn your backs on hatred[5] and hold fast

3 to the love of the Lord. Righteousness gets rid of hatred: humility destroys hatred; for the righteous and the humble man is ashamed to do what is unrighteous, since he is rebuked, not by someone else, but by his own conscience,[6] because the Lord looks at his inten-

4 tions. He speaks no ill of anyone,[7] for the fear of the Most High[8]

5 overcomes hatred. Because he is afraid he might offend the Lord,

6 he will do no wrong at all to anyone, even in thought. I learned this myself in the end, after I had repented of my behaviour to Joseph.

7 For true repentance, as God understands it,[9] destroys ignorance,[10] drives out darkness, enlightens the eyes, gives knowledge to the

8 soul, and leads the mind to salvation. And what it has not learned

9 from men, it comes to know through repentance. For God afflicted me with a disease of the liver, and if it had not been for the prayers

10 of my father Jacob, I would in all probability have died.[11] For by the very same things by which a man transgresses, by them is he

11 punished. Consequently, since it was my liver that was set against Joseph without mercy, in my liver was I judged and suffered without mercy for eleven months – for just as long as I had nursed a grudge against Joseph until he was sold.

VI. And now, my children, love each one of you his brother, and put away hatred from your hearts, and love one another in deed

2 and word and thought.[1] For in my father's presence I would speak amicably to Joseph, and, when I had gone out, the spirit of hatred

3 would darken my mind and excite my soul to kill him. So love one

---

[3] Lit. 'and all covetousness of evil things'.
[4] So *b*: II om.
[5] So *b*: II 'so that you may drive out the hatred of the devil'.
[6] Lit. 'heart'.
[7] So *b* (lit. 'of a man'): II 'of a holy man'.
[8] So *bl*: II-*l* 'of God'.
[9] Lit. 'true repentance according to God'.
[10] So II: *b* 'disobedience'.
[11] Lit. '. . . Jacob, my spirit would almost have been lost from me'.

[1] Lit. 'and inclination of the soul'.

another from the heart. And if anyone sins against you, speak to him as a friend, having *first* got rid of the poison of hatred, and be
4 frank with him; and if he confesses and repents, forgive him. But if he denies *it*, do not get involved in a dispute with him, in case he
5 starts to swear and you become responsible for a double sin. Do not let another man hear your secret in an action at law:[2] if you do, he will hate you and become your enemy and do you serious harm;[3] for often enough when he talks to you deceitfully, or concerns himself in your affairs with evil intent, he has *only* caught the poison
6 from you. And if he denies *it*, and yet exhibits a sense of shame when reproved, desist:[4] do not provoke him *any further*, for *a man* who denies *something* may repent and not wrong you again: on the contrary, he may even do you honour, and be afraid *of you*, and live
7 at peace *with you*. But if he is shameless and persists in his wrong-doing, even so forgive him from the heart, and leave vengeance to God.

VII. If anyone is more prosperous than you are, do not distress yourselves; but pray for him, that he may have perfect prosperity,
2 for *to do* so, maybe, is for your own good.[1] And if he is even more successful, do not be envious: remember that everyone must die; and offer a hymn[2] to the Lord, who gives good and profitable
3 things to all men. Study the Lord's judgements, and he will not
4 forsake your mind, but give it peace.[3] And if a man gets rich by evil means, like Esau my father's brother, do not be jealous; but[4] wait
5 for the time appointed by the Lord.[5] For either he takes away what has been acquired by evil means, or he forgives those who repent,
6 or for the unrepentant he reserves punishment for ever. For the

---

[2] Or 'in a quarrel' (lit. 'in battle'). The alternative in the translation has been preferred because the author was evidently influenced here by Prov. xxv. 8–10.

[3] Lit. 'and commit a great sin against you'.

[4] So II (lit. 'keep quiet'): *b* has a passive form of the verb ('he is to be left undisturbed' (?)).

[1] Or 'for *to do* so is just as much for your own good'.

[2] So *bl*: II-*l* 'offer hymns'.

[3] A combination of the readings of *b* (which leaves out 'not') and of the prototype of II (which leaves out the emphatic 'he').   [4] So II: *b* 'for'.

[5] Lit. 'the limit of the Lord'.

man who is poor and free from envy, who gives thanks to the Lord in all things, is himself richer than all men,[6] because he avoids the
7 vexations of *other* men.[7] Have done, then, with hatred, and love one another in sincerity.[8]

VIII. And also, tell your children to honour Judah and Levi; for
2 from them will the Lord raise up a saviour[1] for Israel. For I know that at the last your children will turn away from them and be *involved* in all *kinds of* wickedness and oppression and corruption
3 before the Lord. And when he had rested a little, he said to them[2] again, My children, obey your father and bury me near my fathers. And he drew up his feet and fell asleep in peace. And five years afterwards they carried him up and buried[3] him in Hebron with his fathers.

THE TESTAMENT OF ASHER, ABOUT THE TWO ASPECTS[1] OF VICE AND VIRTUE

I. A copy of the Testament of Asher, which he gave[1] to his sons in the hundred and twenty-sixth[2] year of his life.
2 While he was still in good health he said to them, Listen, children of Asher, to your father, and I will tell you everything that
3 is right in the sight of God. Two ways has God appointed for mankind, and two impulses, and two kinds of action, and two

[6] So II: *b* 'rich among all men'.
[7] Or 'because he does not engage in the worthless toils of *other* men' (lit. 'because he has not the evil distraction of men' – cp. Eccl. i. 13; etc.).
[8] Lit. 'in uprightness of heart'.

[1] So *b*: *ldm eaf* 'arise as a saviour'; *k g chi* Arm. 'raise up salvation'.
[2] So *b*: II om. 'to them'.
[3] So II: *b* 'laid'.

[1] Lit. 'faces' – and so throughout this Testament.

[1] Lit. 'spoke'.   [2] So II: *b* 'hundred and twentieth'.

4   courses,[3] and two ends. Thus, all things are in twos, one over
5   against the other. There are two ways, of good and evil, and along
    with these are the two impulses in our breasts that make the
6   distinctions between them. So, if the soul is well disposed to what
    is good, its every action is in righteousness, and, if it sins, it
7   repents at once; for when a man's thoughts are set on things that
    are righteous and he rejects what is wicked, he upsets what is evil
8   immediately and uproots what is sinful. But if *the soul* inclines the
    impulse to wickedness, its every action is in wickedness: having
    spurned what is good, *such a man* takes to himself what is evil, and
    under Beliar's control, even if he does anything good, he turns it to[4]
9   wickedness; for whenever he begins as though to do good, the end
    of his action spurs him on to doing evil,[5] since the treasure-house of
    the impulse[6] is filled with the poison of an evil spirit.

II.   Someone, then, may say what is good[1] (he said) for the sake of
2   evil, and the end of what he does leads to evil. A man may[2] ⟨ . . . ⟩,[3]
    because he shows no compassion for his accomplice in evil: this
3   indeed has two aspects, but the whole is evil. A man may love a
    knave:[4] he is just as much *involved* in wickedness *as the other man*,
    because he would be willing even to die in evil because of him; and
    here too it is clear that there are two aspects, but the result as a
4   whole is evil. Though it is love, it is wickedness,[5] for it conceals
    what is evil: it may look good nominally,[6] but the end tends to evil.
5   Another *man* is a thief, a scoundrel, a robber, *and* a cheat, and yet
    has pity on the poor: this case also has two aspects, but the whole is
6   evil. By cheating his neighbour, he[7] angers God and swears falsely

---

[3] So II: *b* 'places'.   [4] Lit. 'in'.
[5] Or 'he forces the end of his action into doing evil'.
[6] So II: *b* 'of the devil'.

[1] Lit. 'There is, then, a soul saying the good'.
[2] Lit. 'There is a man' – and so subsequently.
[3] Comparison with verse 3 suggests that a clause is missing here.
[4] Lit. 'the wicked-doer'.
[5] So *b*: II 'it is in wickedness'.
[6] So II: *b* is corrupt.
[7] So *b*: II 'He who cheats his neighbour . . .'.

against the Most High, yet he pities the poor: the Lord, who commands the law, he flouts and treats with contempt, and yet to 7 the poor man he gives relief. He defiles the soul and makes the body glamorous: he destroys many and pities a few; and this also has two 8 aspects, but the whole is evil.[8] Another *man* commits adultery and fornicates, yet abstains from food: while he fasts he does evil, and by *his* power and wealth drags down many *others* with him, and yet in spite of *his* excessive wickedness he does what is commanded: 9 this also has two aspects, but the whole is evil. Such men are like 10 pigs *or* hares; for they are half clean, but in truth are unclean. For God has said so in the heavenly tablets.

III. So do not be like them, my children, men of two aspects, *one* good and *the other* evil; but cling to goodness only, for God[1] makes 2 his home in it and men strive after it. Turn away from evil and, destroy the devil by your good works; for those of two aspects do not serve God, but their own lusts, in order to please Beliar and men like themselves.

IV. For good men and those of a single aspect, though they may be thought sinners by those of two aspects, are righteous in God's 2 eyes. For many who kill the wicked do two things – a good thing through an evil one;[1] but the whole is good because *whoever does it* 3 has uprooted and destroyed what is evil. A man may hate the man who pities *the poor* and is unrighteous, and the man who commits adultery and fasts:[2] this also has two aspects, but the thing as a whole is good, because he follows the Lord's example in not accepting what seems good together with what is in truth evil. 4 Another *man* will not keep a festival[3] with profligates, in case he may defile his mouth[4] and pollute his soul: this also has two

[8] So II: *b* om. 'but . . . evil'.

[1] So *b*: II 'for even God'.

[1] So II-*g*: *b g* 'an evil thing through a good one'.
[2] So II: *b*, through corruption, has a slightly different text here with a completely different (and impossible) meaning.
[3] Lit. 'will not see a good day' (cp. Esther viii. 17; ix. 19, 22: also 1 Sam. xxv. 8).
[4] So *b*: II 'his body'.

5 aspects, but the whole is good. For[5] such men are like stags and
hinds because just like wild animals they seem to be unclean, but
they are altogether clean because they live their lives full of zeal for
God: in so far as they abstain from what God hates too, and forbids
by his commandments, they keep what is evil away from what is
good.

V. So you see, my children, how there are two in all things, the one
2 over against the other, and the one is hidden by the other.[1] Death
succeeds to life, dishonour to glory, night to day, and darkness to
light; but all things are under the day, and the things that are
righteous under life (that is why eternal life has to wait for[2] death).
3 And it cannot be said that truth is a lie, nor right wrong; for all
4 truth is under the light, just as all things are under God. All this
have I proved in my life, and I have not strayed from the path of
truth which the Lord marked out;[3] and I have examined the
commandments of the Most High and lived, so far as I could, with
a single aspect *directed* to what is good.

VI. Observe then, my children, the commandments of the Lord
2 yourselves, and follow the truth with a single aspect. For men of
two aspects receive a two-fold punishment.[1] Hate the spirits of
3 error that contend against men. Keep the law of the Lord, and do
not look on evil as if it were good; but concentrate your attention on
what is really good, and persevere in it along with[2] all the Lord's
commandments, and settle yourselves down in it[3] and take your

---

⁵ So *b*: II om.

¹ This short text is found in *b g*: *k* and *l* are lacking; *dm eaf chi* have various
additional clauses. Originally the (probably secondary) longer text may have read
'by the other: in a judgement is *hidden* partiality, in ownership greed, in feasting
drunkenness, in laughter sorrow, in marriage self-indulgence'.
² Lit. 'eternal life waits for'.
³ Lit. 'I have not wandered from the truth of the Lord'.

¹ Again *dm eaf ch* have an obviously secondary addition, 'for they both do what is
evil and applaud those that do it': subsequently *eaf ch* read 'following the example
of' instead of 'Hate'.   ² Lit. 'and keep it in'.
³ So II: *b* 'in him'.

4 rest in it.[3] For men's ends reveal their *progress in* righteousness, when they make the acquaintance of the angels of the Lord and *the*
5 *angels* of Satan. For if the soul departs *from the body* troubled, it is tormented by the evil spirit that it served in lusts and evil deeds.
6 But if *it departs* quietly *and* with joy, *that man* has already become acquainted with the angel of peace that will comfort him with[4] life.

VII. Do not, children,[1] be like Sodom, which did not recognize the
2 Lord's angels and perished for ever. For I know that you will sin and be handed over to your enemies, and your land will be desolated and your holy places destroyed,[2] and you will be scattered to the four corners of the earth and be dispersed and despised like water that is useless, until the Most High looks with favour on the
3 earth. And he will come himself as a man, eating and drinking with men and quietly breaking the head of the dragon through water: in this way he will save Israel and all the Gentiles – God playing the
4 part of man. Tell this, then, to your children, so that they do not
5 disbelieve him. For I have read in the heavenly tablets that you certainly will disbelieve him and you will undoubtedly treat him shamefully, and pay no attention to the law of God but only to the
6 commands of men.[3] Because of this you will be scattered like my brothers Gad and Dan, who will forget their own lands and tribe
7 and tongue. But the Lord will gather you together in faith because of the hope of his compassion *for you*, for Abraham and Isaac and Jacob's sake.

VIII. And when he had finished speaking to them he gave them instructions, saying, Bury me in Hebron. And he died and slept the
2 perfect sleep.[1] And afterwards his sons did as he had instructed them and carried him up and buried him with his fathers.

---

[4] Lit. 'in'.

[1] So *b*: II om.
[2] So II: *b* om. 'and your holy places destroyed'.
[3] So *b l a: gde* add 'carried away by wickedness of single aspect', a reading that probably underlies the variants in *f* and *chi*.

[1] Lit. 'And he died, having fallen asleep with a good sleep'.

THE TESTAMENT OF JOSEPH, ABOUT CHASTITY

I. A copy of the Testament of Joseph.

When he was about to die he called his sons and his brothers and
2 said to them, My children and brothers,

Listen to Joseph, Israel's loved one:
Listen carefully, *my* sons, to your father.

3   I have seen in my life envy and death,
But[1] I did not go astray in the truth of the Lord.

4   These my brothers hated me, but[1] the Lord loved me:
They wanted to kill me, but[1] the God of my fathers kept me
safe:
They let me down into a pit, but[1] the Most High brought me
up again.

5   I was sold into slavery, but[1] the Lord[2] set me free:
I was taken into captivity, but[1] his strong hand supported
me:
I was assailed by hunger, but[1] the Lord himself fed me:

6   I was alone, but[1] God gave me comfort:
I was ill, but[1] the Most High came to my help:
I was in prison, but[1] the Saviour showed me favour;
In bonds, and he released me;

7   Slandered, and he pleaded my cause;
Reviled by the Egyptians, and he delivered me;
Envied by *my* fellow-servants,[3] and he promoted me.

II. And thus it came about that Potiphar, the captain of Pharaoh's
2 bodyguard,[1] entrusted his household to me. And I had to struggle

---

[1] Lit. 'and'.

[2] So *b l*: II-*l* 'the Lord of all'.

[3] So II (lit. 'in envyings with *my* fellow-servants'): *b* 'envied and tricked' (lit. 'in envyings with tricks').

---

[1] Lit. 'Pharoah's chief-cook': already in the Gk. Old Testament the title seems to have changed its meaning (cp. especially Dan. ii. 14, in both the Septuagint and Theodotion's translation, with Josephus, *Ant.* X. x. 3 (§197)).

against a shameless woman, who was pressing me to transgress with her; but the God of my father Israel kept me[2] from the burning
3 flame. I was thrown into prison, I was beaten, I was mocked; but[3]
4 the Lord caused the jailer to take pity on me. For he will not forsake those who fear him, whether it be darkness they are in, or prison, or
5 distress, or need. For God is not ashamed as a man *is ashamed*, nor is he afraid like a mortal, nor is he weak or easily pushed out of the
6 way like an earth-born *human*. But in all places he is near at hand, and gives comfort in different ways, though for a little while he may
7 absent himself in order to test the disposition of the soul. By ten temptations he showed his approval of me, and in all of them I endured; for endurance is a first-rate[4] medicine, and fortitude bestows *on us* many excellent gifts.

III. How often did the Egyptian woman threaten me with death! How often did she give me over to punishment, and then call me back and threaten me, when I refused to have intercourse with her!
2 And she would say to me, You shall be my lord, and lord of all I possess, if you will give yourself to me, and you shall be as our
3 master. But I would remember the words of my father Jacob,[1] and
4 I would go into my room and pray to the Lord. And I used to fast during those seven years, but[2] I looked to the Egyptian[3] as if I were living on the fat of the land (for God grants those who fast for his
5 sake the gift of a healthy look[4]). And if he was away from home, I would not drink wine;[5] and for three whole days I would take my
6 food and give it to the poor and the sick. And I used to get up early to seek the Lord and weep for the Egyptian woman of Memphis, for she kept on pestering me – even during the night she would come to me under the pretence that she was concerned about me.

---

[2] So *b*: II 'delivered me'.
[3] Lit. 'and'.   [4] Lit. 'great'.

[1] The text here is very confused, the MSS varying between 'the words of my fathers' and 'the words of my father' (with or without 'Jacob'): *b* combines all possibilities and reads 'the words of the fathers *and* of my father Jacob' (cp. Jub. xxxix. 6): the text translated is found only in *d*.
[2] Lit. 'and'.   [3] i.e. to Potiphar.
[4] Lit. 'for those who fast for God's sake receive grace of face'.
[5] So II-*l d*: *b (l) d* (?) 'And if he gave me wine I would not drink it'.

7 And at first,[6] because she had no son,[7] she pretended to regard me
8 as a son; and so I prayed to the Lord, and she bore a son.[7] Thus,[8]
for a time it was as a son that she embraced me, and I did not
recognize *the truth*; but at last she tried to lure me[9] into fornication.
9 And when I realized it, I was ready to die with grief; and after she
had gone away, I came to myself, and I made a lamentation for her
for many days, because I was now aware of her wiles and *her* deceit.
10 And I repeated to her the words of the Most High, in the hope that
she might turn[10] from her evil lust.

IV. How often did she flatter me with words as a holy man, craftily
in her talk praising my chastity in her husband's presence, while
when we were alone she would do all she could to bring about my
2 downfall. She would laud me openly as chaste, but in secret say to
me, Have no fear of my husband, for he is convinced about your
chastity; and even if anyone told him about us, he would not
3 believe *it*. And because of all this[1] I would lie on the ground in
sackcloth and beseech God that the Lord would deliver me from
4 the Egyptian woman. But when she saw she had achieved nothing,
she came to me again under the pretence that she wanted to be
5 instructed and learn the word of the Lord. And she said to me, if
you want me to forsake idols, be persuaded by me,[2] and I will
persuade the Egyptian to give up idols *too, and both of us* will live as
6 the law of your Lord requires.[3] But I said to her, The Lord
requires[4] that his worshippers should not live unclean lives, nor
7 has he any use for adulterers. And she made no reply, still craving
8 for the satisfaction of her lust. And as for me, I gave myself even
more to fasting and to prayer that the Lord might deliver me from
her.

---

[6] So *b d*: II-*d* om. 'And at first'.
[7] Lit. 'male child . . . a male'.
[8] So *b*: II om.
[9] Lit. 'she lured me'.
[10] So *b*: II 'return'.

[1] Lit. 'In all these things'.
[2] So *b*: II 'lie with me'.
[3] Lit. '. . . give up idols, walking (pl.) in the law of your Lord'.
[4] So II (lit. 'wills'): *b* 'says'.

V. And again, on another occasion, she said to me, if you will not commit adultery, I will kill the Egyptian, and so take you as a
2 lawful husband. And I, when I heard this, rent my robe and said, Woman, show some respect for the Lord, and do not do such an evil thing:[1] if you do, you will destroy yourself; for I will let
3 everybody know of your impious plan. So she was frightened and
4 begged me not to tell anyone about her wickedness. And she went away and sent me all kinds of delectable gifts to mollify me.

1,2 **VI.** And she sent me food mixed with incantations. And when the eunuch that brought it came, I looked up and saw a frightening man presenting me with a sword together with the dish; and I realized that she had had recourse to magic[1] to lead *my* soul astray.
3 And when he had gone out, I wept; and I ate neither that nor any
4 other of her food. So then, a day later, she came to me, and noticing the food said to me, Why is it you have not eaten any of the food?
5 And I said to her, it is because you have filled it with death. Did
6 you not say, I will serve idols no more,[2] but the Lord only? So I can tell you now that the God of my father revealed your wickedness to me through an angel, and I have kept the food[3] as evidence against
7 you, in the hope that you might see it and repent. But so that you can learn that the wickedness of evil-doers has no power over those who worship God in chastity, (I took *some of the food* and ate *it* in front of her, saying,) The God of my fathers and the angel of
8 Abraham will be with me. And she fell on her face at my feet and
9 wept; and I lifted her up and admonished her. And she promised not to transgress again.

VII. But because her heart was set[1] on me and she was still hoping to seduce me,[2] she took to groaning and throwing herself to the

---

[1] Lit. 'this evil deed'.

[1] Or 'I realized that her scheme was'
[2] Lit. 'I do not approach idols'.
[3] Lit. 'kept it'.

[1] So *b*: II 'was still set'.
[2] Lit. '. . . set on me with a view to licentiousness'.

2 ground.[3] And when the Egyptian saw her, he said to her, Why are
you looking so sad?[4] And she said, I am pained at heart, and my
spirit's groanings distress me. And he took special care of her,
3 although there was nothing wrong with her. Then she rushed in to
me, while her husband was away from home,[5] and said to me, I
shall hang myself, or throw myself down a well, or over a cliff, if you
4 will not be persuaded by me.[6] And when I saw that the spirit of
5 Beliar was troubling her, I prayed to the Lord. And I said to her,
Why are you *so* troubled and distraught, and blinded by *your* sins?
Do not forget that if you kill yourself, Setho, your husband's
concubine, your rival, will ill-treat your children and obliterate
6 your memory from the earth. And she said to me, So then you do
love me! It is enough for me that you are concerned about my life
and my children's *lives*: I have a good hope that I shall attain my
7 end.[7] And she did not realize that it was because of my God I had
8 said this, and not because of her. For if a man has yielded to the
passion of an evil desire, and become a slave to it, as she had,
whatever good thing he hears about the passion he is overcome by,
he takes as a justification of his evil desire.[8]

VIII. I tell you, *my* children, it was about noon when she left me;
and I spent *the rest of* the day and all the night in prayer to the
Lord. And about dawn I got up in tears, begging to be rescued
2 from the Egyptian woman. In the end, she took hold of my clothes
3 and forcibly dragged me to her to have intercourse *with me*. And
when I saw that in her madness she was holding onto my clothes by
4 force, I fled naked. And she falsely accused me,[1] and the Egyptian
imprisoned me in his house; and next day he had me flogged and
5 sent me to Pharoah's prison.[2] And because I was now in fetters the

---

[3] So *b*: II 'and looking sad'.
[4] Lit. 'Why has your face fallen?'
[5] Lit. 'was still outside'.
[6] So *b*: II 'if you will not lie with me'.
[7] Lit. 'that I shall enjoy my desire'.
[8] Lit. 'he takes it towards an evil desire'.

[1] So II: *b* adds 'to her husband'.
[2] So II: *b* wrongly repeats 'the Egyptian sent me to the prison in his house'.

Egyptian woman was prostrate with grief; and she heard about me, how I was singing praises to the Lord, although[3] in the house of darkness, and rejoicing with a cheerful voice, and glorifying my God – for I had been at last set free from the Egyptian woman.[4]

IX.   And she sent to me frequently saying, If you will consent to grant me my desire, then I will release you from *your* bonds and set
2 you free from the darkness. But the idea of giving in to her never entered my head; for God prefers a man, who in a den of darkness fasts in chastity, to the man who lives in extravagance and wanton-
3 ness in his apartments in a palace.[1] (And the man who lives in chastity wants glory too, and if the Most High[2] knows that it is good *for him*, he bestows this on him also, even as he did on me.)
4 How often, although unwell, did she come down to me in the dead of night and listen to my voice as I prayed; but when I heard her
5 groanings I kept quiet. For when I was in her house she would bare her arms and breasts and legs to entice me into having intercourse with her; for she was more than ordinarily beautiful, and she adorned herself especially to beguile me. But the Lord protected me from her devices.

X.   So you see, my children, what great things fortitude can do,
2 together with prayer and fasting. And you too – if you strive for chastity and purity in fortitude and humility of heart, the Lord will
3 dwell in you, for he loves chastity. And wherever the Most High dwells, even though a man encounters envy, or slavery, or slander, or darkness,[1] the Lord who dwells in him, because of his chastity, not only rescues him from the evils, but also exalts *him* and glorifies
4 him, even as *he did* me. For in every way man is under constraint, in
5 deed and word and thought. My brothers know how my father

---

[3] So *b* (lit. 'being'): II om.
[4] Lit. '– only that by the occasion I had been set free. . . .'

[1] So *l* (lit. 'in the inner rooms of palaces'): *gm eaf* (with a one-letter difference in the Gk.) 'in the inner rooms of kings'; *b* 'in inner rooms'.
[2] So *b*: II 'And if the man . . . too, and the Most High . . .'

[1] So II: *b* om. 'or darkness'.

loved me, and yet I did not set myself above them in my heart:[2] although but a child, I had the fear of God in my mind,[2] for I knew
6 that all things will pass away. And I knew my proper place, and I honoured my brothers; and out of respect for them[3] I kept quiet when I was being sold, so that I did not tell the Ishmaelites my race, *or* that I was a son of Jacob, a great and powerful man.

XI. You too, then, must have the fear of God before your eyes[1] in everything you do,[2] and honour your brothers; for everyone that
2 keeps the law of the Lord will be loved by him. And when I came to the Indocolpitae with the Ishmaelites, they questioned me, and I said, I am their home-born slave, so as not to shame my brothers.
3 And the senior among them said to me, You are no slave: only to look at you makes that clear enough. And he threatened me with
4 death. But I said, I am their slave. And when we came into Egypt they began to quarrel over me, *about* which *of them* should pay
5 money *for me* and take me *as his own.* However, it was agreed that I should be *left* in Egypt with one of their retailers until they came
6 back again with *more* goods for sale.[3] And the Lord made the retailer well-disposed towards me, and he entrusted his household
7 to me. And the Lord blessed him through me, so that he became
8 richer and richer.[4] And I was with him three months and five days.

XII. *It was* at that time *that* the Memphian woman, the wife of Petephris, passed in a chariot[1] with a great display, and she cast her eyes in my direction, for the eunuchs had told her about me.
2 And she said to her husband with reference to the retailer, He has got his riches through a young Hebrew; and they say that he was
3 stolen out of the land of Canaan. Now then, see that justice is done

[2] So *b*: II '. . . in my mind . . . in my heart'.
[3] Lit. 'and because of fear of them'.

[1] So II: *b* om. 'before your eyes'.
[2] So II: *b* 'in what you do'.
[3] Or 'with the profits of their trading'.
[4] Lit. 'and he multiplied him in silver and gold'.

[1] So II-*g*: *b g* om. 'in a chariot'.

to him and take the youth away to be your steward; and the God of the Hebrews will bless you, for the favour of heaven[2] is on him.

XIII. And Petephris was persuaded by what she said, and he ordered the retailer to be brought; and he said to him, What is it that I hear, that you steal people[1] out of the land of the Hebrews[2]
2 and sell them as slaves? But the retailer fell on his face and implored him, saying, Please, my lord, I do not understand what
3 you are saying. But he said, Where then, did you get your Hebrew servant from? And he said, The Ishmaelites put him in my charge
4 until they came back. And he did not believe him but ordered him to be stripped and beaten. And when he persisted in his statement[3]
5 Petephris said, Let the young man be brought. And when I was brought in, I did obeisance to the chief eunuch (for he was third in rank beside Pharoah and in charge of all the eunuchs, with a wife
6 and children and concubines). And he took me apart from him and
7 said to me, Are you a slave or a freeman? And I said, A slave. [4]And
8 he said [to me], Whose [slave are you]? And I said [to him], The Ishmaelites'. And [again] he said to me, How did you become their slave? And I said, They bought me out of the land of Canaan.[5]
9 And he did not believe me and said,[6] You are lying. And he ordered me to be stripped and beaten.

XIV. But the Memphian woman was looking out of the window while I was being beaten, and she sent to her husband, saying, What you are doing[1] is unjust, for you are punishing a free man
2 that has been stolen as if he were an evil-doer. And when, after being beaten, I made no change in what I said, he ordered me to be
3 imprisoned, Until, he said, the boy's owners come. And his wife

---

[2] Lit. 'for favour from heaven'.

[1] Lit. 'souls'.
[2] So *b*: II 'the land of Canaan'.
[3] So II: *b* om. 'in his statement'.
[4] The bracketed words in verses 7 and 8 are not found in II.
[5] So II: *b* 'out of Canaan'.
[6] And he did not . . . said: so *b*; II 'And he said to me'.

[1] Lit. 'Your judgement'.

said to him, Why are you keeping him under arrest? *He came here* as
a captive and is a well-bred boy: far better set him free and make
4 him one of your servants. (For she wanted to see me as a result of
5 her sinful yearning; and I was completely unaware of it.) But he
said to the Memphian woman, It is not *the custom*[2] of the Egyptians
6 to take away what belongs to others before proof is given. This he
said with reference to the retailer; and about me *he said* that I must
be kept in prison.[3]

XV.   And twenty-four days afterwards the Ishmaelites came. And
2 they had heard that my father Jacob was mourning for me. And
they said to me, How was it that you said you were a slave? We
have discovered that you are the son of a great man in the land of
3 Canaan,[1] and your father is in mourning[2] in sackcloth. And again I
could have wept,[3] but I restrained myself so as not to shame my
4 brothers. And I said, I do not know *anything about that at all*: I am a
5 slave. Then they made up their minds to sell me in case I should be
found in their possession. For they were afraid that Jacob might
6 wreak a savage vengeance on them; for it was reported[4] that he was
7 a great one with the Lord and with men.† Then the retailer said to
them, Release me from the judgement of Petephris. And they came
and asked me, saying, He was bought by us with money. And he
set us free.[5] †

XVI.   And the Memphian woman told her husband to buy me, For
2 I hear (said she) they are selling him. And she sent a eunuch to the
Ishmaelites and asked them to sell me. And the chief of the

---

² This is implied in all MSS and added explicitly in *g l d m* Arm.
³ So *b*: II 'and the boy, *he said*, must be kept in prison'.

¹ So II: *b* 'in Canaan'.
² So *b*: II adds 'for you'.
³ So *b* (lit. 'And again I wanted to weep'): II 'And I wanted very much to weep'.
⁴ So *b*: II 'for they heard'.
⁵ Or 'And he sent us away'. The text of verses 6 and 7 is clearly in disarray. In
verse 7 there are wide variations between the MSS, from no one of which, when
taken by itself, is it possible to construct a consistent sense, nor, when all are taken
together, is it possible to reconstruct a hypothetical original with any degree of
probability. The translation offered is a fairly literal rendering of what is found in *b*.

bodyguard summoned the Ishmaelites and *also* asked them to sell
3 me.[1] And as he was not able to come to an agreement with them,[2]
he withdrew. But the eunuch who had been sounding them out
told his mistress, They are asking an enormous price for the boy.
4 And she sent another eunuch, saying, Even if they want two minas
in gold, do not worry or be sparing with the gold: only buy the boy
5 and bring him. And he paid them eighty pieces of gold for me, but
he told the Egyptian woman that a hundred had been paid for me.
6 And although I had seen *it*,[3] I kept quiet, so that the eunuch should
not be called to account.[4]

XVII. You see, my children, how much I had to put up with in
2 order not to shame my brothers. So you too must love one another
3 and by *your* endurance hide one another's faults. For God delights
in brotherly concord and in the inclination of a heart directed to
4 love. And when my brothers came into Egypt, when they discovered that I had returned their money to them, and I did not
5 reproach them but rather welcomed them, and *when*, after Jacob's
death, I showed even more love towards them and did even more
6 than he had told me to, they were astonished.[1] For I would not let
them suffer even the most trivial hardship: indeed, I gave them
7 everything I had. Their sons *were* my sons, and my sons as their
slaves: their life[2] *was* my life,[2] and all their suffering *was* my
suffering, and every weakness of theirs my own feebleness: my land
8 *was* their land, their will my will.[3] And I did not arrogantly exalt
myself among them because of my worldly glory, but I was among
them as one of the least.

---

[1] So most MSS. In *b g d c* there is an omission through homioteleuton resulting in
the whole verse appearing as 'And he (she?) sent a eunuch to the Ishmaelites and
asked them to sell me'.
  [2] So *b*: II om. 'to come to an agreement with them'.
  [3] So *b*: II 'And although I knew *it*'.
  [4] Or 'tortured'. So *b*: II 'put to shame' (*g d m* have an obviously secondary form of
the sentence, 'so that I should not shame the eunuch' – cp. xi. 2, xv. 3, xvii. 1).

  [1] So *b*: II om. 'they were astonished'.
  [2] Lit. 'soul'.
  [3] So II: *b* 'my will their will'.

XVIII. So if you too, my children, live in accordance with the
Lord's commands, he will exalt you here,[1] and he will bless you
2 with what is good for ever.[1] And if anyone tries to harm you, treat
him well and pray for him, and you will be delivered[2] by the Lord
3 from every evil. For you know well enough[3] that it was because of
my endurance that I married a daughter of my masters; and a
hundred talents of gold were given me with her, for the Lord made
4 them *as if they were* my slaves. And he gave me beauty also, like a
flower, surpassing the beauties of Israel; and he preserved me into
old age in strength and in splendour, because I was like Jacob in
everything.

1,2 **XIX.** Listen, my children, also to the visions[1] that I saw. There
were twelve stags feeding, and nine of them were dispersed and
8 scattered[2] over the earth,[3] and so also *were* the *other* three[4]. . . . And I
saw that from Judah was born a virgin wearing a linen robe, and
from her came forth a lamb without blemish; and on his left hand

---

[1] Or 'in this world . . . in eternity'.
[2] Lit. 'redeemed'.   [3] Lit. 'For behold, you see'.

[1] So *b c*: all other witnesses, including Arm., read singular.
[2] So *bkl* (*g*?): all others, including Arm., om. 'dispersed and'.
[3] So *bk*: II 'over all the earth'; Arm. om.
[4] For 'and . . . three' Arm., reads 'but three were saved; and on the next day they
too were scattered'. For verses 3–7 only Arm. is extant: whether it has preserved the
original Gk. text, either as a whole or in part, is not clear: the following is M. E.
Stone's translation in his *The Armenian Version of the Testament of Joseph: Introduction,
Critical Edition, and Translation* (*S.B.L. Texts and Translations Series*, 6: *Pseudepigrapha
Series*, 5; Missoula, Montana, 1975, pp. 53–55):

3 And I saw that the three stags became three lambs and they cried out to the
Lord and he brought them forth out of darkness into light and he brought them
4 to a green and watered place. And there they cried out to the Lord until the
nine stags were gathered to them and they became like twelve sheep, and after
a little they increased and became many flocks.
5   After this I saw and, behold, twelve bulls which were sucking the one cow
which, through the vast amount of her milk, was making a sea. And the twelve
6 flocks and the innumerable herds were drinking from it. And the horns of the
fourth bull were elevated up to the heavens and became like a wall for the flocks
7 and another horn flowered between the horns. And I saw a calf which circled it
twelve times and became an aid to the bulls altogether.

there was as it were a lion; and all the animals made an assault on
him, but[5] the lamb overcame them and destroyed them and tramp-
9 led them underfoot. And the angels rejoiced because of him, and
10 men *rejoiced also*, and the whole earth.[6] And these things shall come
11 to pass at their proper time, in the last days. So you must, my
children, observe the Lord's commands, and honour Judah and
Levi, for from them shall come[7] to you the Lamb of God, who by
12 grace will save all the Gentiles and Israel. For his kingdom is an
eternal kingdom, that shall not be shaken. But my kingdom among
you shall come to an end like a watchman's hut in a fruit-garden,
for after the summer it will disappear.

XX. I know that after my death the Egyptians will oppress you,
but God will avenge you and will bring you **into the land he promised
2 to your fathers.**[1] But you must take my bones up with you; for while
my bones are on the way, the Lord will be with you in light, and
3 Beliar will be in darkness with the Egyptians. And take up your
mother Zilpah *also*, and bury her near Bilhah,[2] by the hippo-
4 drome,[3] close to Rachel. And when he had finished speaking, he
5 stretched out his feet and slept the eternal sleep. And all Israel
6 mourned for him, and all Egypt, with a great mourning; for he had
felt for the Egyptians as if they were part of himself,[4] and he had
helped them and stood by them in all *their* undertakings and plans
and business matters.

---

[5] Lit. 'and'.

[6] In verses 8 and 9 Arm. has a number of variants which are not likely to be
original. Nevertheless the Armenian text of these verses is given (for information) in
Stone's translation:

> 8 And I saw among the horns a virgin who had a many-coloured garment and
> from her a lamb went forth. And from its right side all wild beasts and creeping
> 9 things attacked and the lamb overcame them and destroyed them. And the
> bulls and the cow and the three horns were glad because of it and rejoiced with
> it.

The variants in Arm. in verses 10–12 (mainly omissions) have not been thought
worth recording.   [7] Lit. 'arise'.

[1] *bk* 'into the promise of your fathers'; *glefc* 'into the promises of your fathers';
d 'into the land of the promise of your fathers'; *mahi* are lacking.
[2] Cp. Jub. xxxiv. 16.   [3] Cp. Gen. xlviii. 7 (LXX).
[4] Lit. 'as for his own limbs'.

THE TESTAMENT OF BENJAMIN,
ABOUT A PURE MIND

I. A copy of the words of Benjamin, which he left as a testament to his sons after he had lived a hundred and twenty-five years.[1]

2 And after he had kissed them he said, As Isaac was born to
3 Abraham in his hundreth year, so also was I to Jacob. And since Rachel died in giving me birth, I had no milk: so I was suckled by
4 Bilhah, her slave-girl. For Rachel was barren for twelve years after she had borne Joseph; and she prayed to the Lord and fasted for
5 twelve days, and *afterwards* she conceived and bore me. For our father loved Rachel very dearly and was longing to have two sons
6 by her.[2] That was why I was called Son of days (that is Benjamin).

II. Now when I went into Egypt and my brother Joseph recognized me, he said to me, What did they tell my father when they
2 sold me? And I said to him, They spattered your tunic with blood, and sent it and said, Do you recognize this as your son's tunic?
3 [1]And he said to me, Yes, brother; for when the Ishmaelites took me, one of them stripped off my tunic, gave me a loincloth, and
4 flogged me, and told me to run off. But when he went away to hide
5 my coat, a lion met him and killed him. And so his companions were frightened and sold me to *some* others of them.

III. So you, my children, must love the Lord, the God of heaven, and keep his commandments, and follow the example of the good
2 and holy man Joseph. And let your mind be set on what is good, just as you know mine is:[1] *the man* who has his mind so set[2] sees all

---

[1] So II: *b* 'a hundred and twenty years'.
[2] Lit. 'to see two sons from her'.

[1] In ii. 3 – iii. 5 the Armenian has a very different text. There is no reason to suppose it original despite the somewhat inconsequential nature of the Greek as preserved.

[1] Lit. 'be towards the good, as also you know me'.
[2] Lit. 'he who has the mind good'.

3 things rightly. Fear the Lord, and love *your* neighbour; and even if the spirits of Beliar claim you, *and afflict you* with every *kind of* evil and hardship,[3] yet no evil or hardship[3] will gain the mastery over

4 you, even as *they did* not over my brother Joseph. How many there were that wanted to kill him! But God protected him; for a man who fears God and loves his neighbour cannot be struck down by the spirit of the air (*that is* the spirit of Beliar), because he is

5 protected by the fear of God. Nor can he be overcome by anything that men or animals contrive against him, for he is helped by the

6 love of the Lord, which he has towards his neighbour. For Joseph begged our father[4] to pray for *his* sons,[5] that the Lord would not

7 hold them accountable for their wicked plots against him. And it was because of this that Jacob cried out, *My* child Joseph, you good child,[6] you have won your father Jacob's heart.[7] And he embraced

8 him and kissed him for two hours, and said, In you shall be fulfilled the prophecy of heaven about the Lamb of God and the Saviour of the world – that one without blemish shall be offered up on behalf of sinners, and one without sin shall die on behalf of the ungodly, in the blood of the covenant, for the salvation of the Gentiles and of Israel, and he shall destroy Beliar and those who serve him.

IV. You saw, children, how that good man was rewarded in the end.[1] Imitate, therefore,[2] his compassion in sincerity,[3] so that you

2 also may wear crowns of glory. The good man has not an eye that cannot see;[4] for he shows mercy to all men, sinners though they

3 may be, and though they may plot his ruin. This *man*, by doing good,[5] overcomes evil, since he is protected by the good; and he

4 loves the righteous as his own soul. If anyone is honoured, he does

---

³ Lit. 'evil of tribulation'.

⁴ So II: *b* 'for I begged our father Jacob'.

⁵ So II (*ldm* 'for his sons'): *b* 'for our brothers'.

⁶ So probably the original text: *b* om. 'you good child'; *l eaf c* om. '*My* child Joseph'.

⁷ Lit. 'You have conquered the bowels of your father Jacob'.

¹ Lit. 'You saw, children, the end of the good man'.

² So II: *b* om.   ³ Lit. 'in good purpose'.

⁴ Lit. 'has not a dark eye'.

⁵ So II (lit. 'This *man* who does good'): *b* 'Thus *the man* who does good'.

not envy him: if anyone is rich, he is not jealous: if anyone is brave, he applauds him: the man who is chaste he trusts and sings his praises: on the poor man he has mercy: on the sick compassion; *and*
5 the praises of God are ever in his mouth. Whoever fears God he defends: whoever loves God he helps:[6] if anyone repudiates the Most High, he admonishes him and reclaims him; and whoever has been blessed with a good spirit he loves as dearly as he loves himself.

V. If, then, your minds are predisposed to what is good, children,[1] wicked men will live at peace with you, the profligate will reverence you and turn towards the good, and the money-grubbers will not only turn their backs on the things they have been striving for, but even give what they have got by their money-grubbing to those
2 who are in distress. If you do good, the unclean spirits will keep away from you, and even the wild animals will be afraid of you.[2]
3 For where there is *the* light of good works[3] in *a man's* mind, darkness
4 flees from him. For if anyone insults a holy man, he repents; for the holy man shows mercy on the man that has reviled him and says
5 nothing in reply. And if anyone betrays a righteous man,[4] and the righteous *man* prays *about it*, though he may be humiliated for a little while, not long afterwards he appears in far greater splendour, as my brother Joseph did.

VI. The good man's impulse is not in the power of the error of the
2 spirit of Beliar, for the angel of peace acts as a guide to his soul. And he does not look with greedy eyes on the things that perish, nor
3 does he pile up riches and delight in them. He takes no delight in pleasure: he causes *his* neighbour no pain: he does not overload himself with luxuries:[1] nor is he led astray by a lustful eye;[2] for the

[6] So *b*: II 'he agrees with' (lit. 'runs together with').

[1] So *b l*: II-*l* om.
[2] So II: *b* 'will run away from you in fear'.
[3] So II: *b* 'reverence for good works'.
[4] Lit. 'soul'.

[1] So II: *b* 'food' (with one letter different in the Gk.).
[2] Lit. 'he does not go astray by uplifting of eyes'.

4 Lord is all in all to him. His[3] good impulse acknowledges neither honour nor dishonour from men, neither does it countenance any deceit, or lie, *or* strife, or reviling; for the Lord dwells in him and lights up his soul and gives him joy in the face of all men always.

5 His good mind will not let him speak with two tongues,[4] *one* of blessing and *one* of cursing, *one* of insult and *one* of compliment, *one* of sorrow and *one* of joy, *one* of quietness and *one* of tumult, *one* of hypocrisy and *one* of truth, *one* of poverty and *one* of wealth; but it has a single disposition only, simple and pure, that says the same

6 thing to everyone.[5] It has no double sight or hearing; for whenever *such a man* does, or says, or sees anything,[6] he knows that the Lord is

7 looking into his soul in judgement. And he purifies his mind so that he is not condemned by God and men. But everything that Beliar does is double and has nothing single about it at all.

VII. Be wary, therefore, my children, of Beliar's malice; for to

2 those who trust it he gives a sword. But the sword is the mother of seven evils. To start with, the mind conceives through Beliar, and the first *child* is envy, secondly *comes* destruction, third oppression,

3 fourth exile, fifth famine, sixth tumult, seventh desolation.[1] And this is why Cain was given over to seven vengeances by God; for the

4 Lord brought one plague on him every hundred years. After two hundred years[2] he began to suffer, and in the[2] nine hundredth year he was destroyed[3] at the flood, because of the righteous Abel, his brother. By the seven evils[4] was Cain judged, but Lamech by

5 seventy times seven. For those who like Cain are inspired by envy to hate their brothers will always be judged with the same punishment.

---

[3] Lit. 'The'.
[4] Lit. 'The good mind has not two tongues'.
[5] Lit. '. . . pure, concerned with all men'.
[6] Lit. 'for everything he does or says or sees'.

[1] Or 'destruction' (cp. verse 4).
[2] Or 'when he was two hundred years old . . . in his'.
[3] Lit. 'desolated' (cp. verse 2).
[4] So *gldm* Arm.: *b f* 'in the seven hundred years'; *e* 'in (by) the seven hundred'; *a* 'by (in) the seven'; *c* 'by (in) all the evils'.

VIII. And so you, my children, must turn your backs on malice, envy, and hatred of your brothers, and take your stand with
2 goodness and love. A man with a pure mind, *who is well-grounded* in love, never looks at a woman with a view to fornication; for there is
3 no defilement in *his* heart, because God's spirit rests upon him. For as the sun is not defiled when it shines on[1] manure and mud, but rather dries both up and drives away the unpleasant smell, so also the pure mind, though surrounded by the defilements of the earth, rather becomes a source of strength,[2] but itself is not defiled.

IX. But I gather from the words of the righteous Enoch that you will give yourselves up to evil practices.[1] For as *the men of* Sodom committed fornication, so also will you, and all but a few of you will perish. And you will renew *your* wanton relations with women; and the Lord's kingdom will not remain[2] among you, for he himself will
2 take it away *from you* immediately. But God's temple will be in your portion, and the last will be more glorious than the first;[3] and the twelve tribes will be gathered together there, and all the Gentiles, until the Most High sends forth his salvation by the visitation of an
3 only-begotten prophet.[4] And he will enter into the first temple, and there the Lord will be insulted and treated with contempt[5] and
4 lifted up on a tree. And the curtain of the temple will be torn apart; and God's spirit will pass to[6] the Gentiles, like a fire poured out.
5 And he will come up from Hades and ascend[7] from earth to heaven. (And I know how humble he will be on earth, and how glorious in heaven.)

X. And when Joseph was in Egypt, I longed to see what he was

[1] Lit. 'when it turns towards'.
[2] Lit. 'rather builds up'.

[1] Lit. 'that there will be also doings among you that are not good'.
[2] Lit. 'will not be'.
[3] So *gld*: *bk* are corrupt and *eaf* incomplete.
[4] So II: *bk* om. 'prophet'.
[5] So *bk*: II om. 'and treated with contempt'.
[6] So II-*d*: *bkd* 'will descend on'.
[7] So *bk*: II 'pass'.

like, and what his face looked like; and through the prayers of my
father Jacob I did see him, while I was awake in the daytime,
2 exactly as he was. You must realize, my children, that I am dying.
3 Deal honestly, therefore, each one *of you* with his neighbour, and do
what is right and just to encourage mutual trust,[8] and keep the law
4 of the Lord and his commands. For these things, I tell you, are of
greater value than anything else I can bequeath to you:[9] you too,
then, must give them to your children as an eternal possession; for
5 so did Abraham and Isaac and Jacob. They left all these things to
us as a heritage, saying, Keep God's commands until the Lord
6 reveals his salvation to all the Gentiles. Then will you see Enoch,
Noah, and Shem, and Abraham, and Isaac, and Jacob, rising on
7 the right hand in gladness. Then shall we also rise, each one over
our tribe, and worship the king of heaven, who appeared on earth
in the guise of a humble man; and all those who believed him on
8 earth will rejoice with him. Then, too, all men will rise, some to
glory and some to disgrace. And the Lord will judge Israel first for
the wickedness done to him; for when he appeared as God in the
9 flesh, as a deliverer, they did not believe him. And then he will
judge all the Gentiles, everyone of them who did not believe him
10 when he appeared on earth. And he will convict Israel through the
chosen ones of the Gentiles, just as he convicted Esau through the
Midianites, who **refused** to become their brothers because of *their*
fornication and idolatry,[10] and they were estranged from God and
11 had no place among those who fear the Lord.[11] But if you live in
holiness in the Lord's presence, you will again dwell in security
with[12] me, and all Israel will be gathered to the Lord.

XI. And I shall be called a ravening wolf no longer because of your
ravages, but a worker of the Lord, who provides food for those who
2 do what is good. And in the last times there will appear from
among my descendants a *man* beloved by the Lord, who will hear

---

[8] Lit. 'Do, therefore, truth and righteousness, each one with his neighbour, and judgement to assurance'.

[9] Lit. 'For these things I teach you instead of all inheritance'.

[10] None of the extant readings in this clause is intelligible.

[11] Lit. '. . . from God, becoming not children in the portion of those who fear the Lord'.

[12] Lit. 'in'.

his voice on earth, and do his will and pleasure,[1] and enlighten all the Gentiles with new knowledge: *he will be* a light of knowledge bursting in on Israel with[2] salvation, ravaging them[3] like a wolf, and giving *what he has snatched from them* to the synagogue of the
3 Gentiles. And until the end of time his fame will endure[4] in the synagogues of the Gentiles, and among their rulers, like a musical
4 tune that is in everyone's mouth. And both his deeds and his words will find a place in the sacred books,[5] and he will be one of God's
5 chosen ones for ever. And it was to him that my father Jacob was referring when he said to me, He will compensate for the deficiencies of your tribe.

XII. And when he had got to the end of what he had to say, he said, I charge you, my children, carry my bones up out of Egypt, and
2 bury me in Hebron, near my fathers. And Benjamin was a hundred and twenty-five years old when he died, having achieved a ripe old
3 age;[1] and they put him in a coffin. And in the ninty-first year after the **entry**[2] of the sons of Israel **into**[2] Egypt their children[3] took the bones of·their fathers up secretly, during the war with Canaan,[4]
4 and buried them in Hebron, at their fathers' feet. And they returned from the land of Canaan and lived in Egypt until the day of their departure from the land of Egypt.

---

[1] Lit. '. . . Lord, hearing on earth his voice, and doing the good pleasure of his will': so *d eaf*; *c* '. . . Lord, hearing . . . and doing . . . of his mouth'; *b g l* om. 'and doing . . . of his will'.   [2] Lit. 'in'.

[3] *b* 'him'.   [4] Lit. '. . . time, he shall be'.

[5] Lit. 'And in the sacred books he will be written up, both *his* work and his word'.

[1] Lit. '. . . died, in a good old age'.

[2] All MSS read 'exodus . . . from', which must be wrong in the light of verse 4: Jub. xlv. 1 and xlvi. 9, when taken together, support the emendation that this happened ninety-one years after the entry.

[3] Lit. 'they and their brothers'.

[4] So II (lit. 'in the war of Canaan'): *b* 'in a place called Canaan'.

THE ASSUMPTION OF MOSES

INTRODUCTION

The Assumption is preserved only in an incomplete Latin version, which has survived as the underwriting on a single quire of a 6th or 7th cent. palimpsest in the Ambrosian library at Milan (Cod. C73 Inf.). This palimpsest contains on other quires the Latin fragments of Jubilees and also fragments of an anonymous heretical commentary on St. Luke. The text was published by Ceriani in 1861 in the first fascicle of his *Monumenta Sacra et Profana*. Although the first three lines of the Assumption are unfortunately wanting, it seems that the work started at the beginning of the quire. But at the end the text breaks off in mid-sentence, and there are no means of knowing how much has been lost.

The MS itself gives the work no title. The common title, 'The Assumption of Moses', was inferred by Ceriani from the fact that Gelasius of Cyzicus, in his Collection of the Acts of the Council of Nicaea, quotes i. 14 and explicitly attributes it to the Assumption,[1] a work independently proved to have been known in the early Church from references in other patristic writers and from the ancient lists of apocryphal books.

Nevertheless, the identification is not certain. The lists mention a 'Testament' of Moses as well as an 'Assumption'; and 'Testament' is a description that fits the contents of our fragment very well. Moreover, the lists all place the Testament before the Assumption. A variety of possibilities is therefore opened up. Three of them may be stated: (1) that our fragment is indeed the Assumption, as Ceriani inferred, and that the Testament either has been lost or is Jubilees under another name (this last hypothesis will explain why the fragments of Jubilees were found in such close proximity to our fragment in the same palimpsest); (2) that our fragment is the Testament and not the Assumption, and that Gelasius's ascription of i. 14 to the Assumption is due to confusion on his part between the two (in this case it is the Assumption which

[1] Gelasius, *Hist. Conc. Nic,* II. xvii. 17.

has been lost); and (3) that the Testament and the Assumption, originally two distinct works, were at an early date combined and subsequently circulated as the 'Assumption', and that it is the opening of this combined work which has been preserved in our fragment (this was Charles's view).

But whatever the true solution may be it is worth observing that Gelasius attributes two further quotations to the Assumption, and that neither of them is found in our fragment. Both concern a dispute between the archangel Michael and the Devil:

'In the Book of the Assumption of Moses', Gelasius writes, 'Michael the archangel, disputing with the Devil, says, For from his Holy Spirit we all were created. And again he says, From God's presence went forth his Spirit, and the world came into being'.[2]

More details about this dispute may be gleaned from other Fathers, some of whom explicitly name the Assumption as their source. The earliest reference to the legend is to be found in the Epistle of Jude in the New Testament. There we are told that the dispute was 'about the body of Moses', and Michael is quoted as having said to the Devil 'May the Lord rebuke you!'; but there is no mention of any source.[3]

Problems of date and origin, though by no means simple, are not intractable. Ostensibly the Assumption supplies details which are lacking in Moses's final charge to Joshua as recorded in Deut. xxxi. In fact it is an apocalypse, which sketches the history of Israel from the time of Moses's death to the final consummation (i. 18). In vi. 2 ff. Moses predicts the succession of 'an insolent king . . . who will not be of priestly stock . . . and he will treat them ruthlessly . . . for thirty-four years'. This king is clearly Herod the Great, who succeeded the Maccabaean priest-kings in 37 BC and reigned till 4 BC. Moses goes on to predict that this king will have sons, 'who will succeed him and rule for shorter periods': 'a powerful king of the west' will come and 'take them captive and burn a part of their temple with fire, and crucify some of them round their city'; and then the End will come (vii. i).

---

[2] Gelas. *Hist. Conc. Nic.* II. xxi. 7.   [3] Jude 9.

Charles argued that this reflects a situation soon after Herod's death and before any of his sons had reigned as long as their father – i.e. the period between 3 BC and AD 30. According to this view, the 'powerful king of the west' is Varus, the Roman governor of Syria, who in 4 BC suppressed a Jewish rebellion and crucified two thousand Jews after the troops of his lieutenant Sabinus had set fire to the roof of the Temple. And this view has been very generally accepted.

Another, very different, view has been proposed by J. Licht and adopted and developed by G. W. E. Nickelsburg. According to this view the Assumption was originally written during the persecution of Antiochus Epiphanes, near the beginning of the fourth decade of the second century BC (that is, roughly about the same time as the apocalyptic parts of Daniel – perhaps even earlier), and it was subsequently interpolated and updated in Herodian times. In this case, there are two distinct strata in the text as we have it, and we have to deal both with an original author and with at least one editor.

At the other extreme, G. Hölscher and others, accepting the unity of the work, have connected it with the second-century AD revolt in Hadrian's time. Hölscher himself identified the 'powerful king of the west' with Titus, and explained what this king is said to do against the background of the events of AD 70; and he suggested AD 130 as the date at which the author wrote – just before the Second Revolt began. On the other hand, K. Haacker, who attributed the work to a Samaritan, would date it after the Second Revolt – at any time between AD 135 and the end of the century.

In any event the author was not a revolutionary. Charles described him as 'a Pharisaic Quietist'; though it must be admitted that there is no sound reason for connecting him so unambiguously with the Pharisees. Nor do there seem any sound reasons for connecting him with any other Jewish sect or party of which we have any definite knowledge – least of all with the Zealots, as Schürer proposed! But there can be no doubt whatever about his belief that the passive obedience exhibited by the Hasidim, rather than the militancy displayed by the Maccabees, was the attitude that would earn God's final vindication (ix. 6–x. 10). And in this connection we should note that the figure of the Levite Taxo, who is to appear at the end (ix. 1) and exhort his seven sons to retire to a cave and die rather than transgress the commandments, is manifestly modelled on elements in the stories of the scribe Eliezer and the seven sons of a mother, who die rather than eat pork in 2 Macc. vi. 18–vii. 42, and of the faithful who were cut to pieces in their hiding-places rather than profane the Sabbath in 1 Macc. ii. 29–38 and 2 Macc. vi. 11.

There are no discernible traces of Christian influence anywhere.

The text of the fragment is very corrupt and its Latin debased. It is clearly a version translated from Greek, for a number of Greek words have been transliterated, and many of the curiosities in the Latin may be explained as Greek phrases and idioms that have been translated over-literally. Also, the patristic evidence strongly supports the existence at one time of a Greek version. And behind the Greek, in all probability, lay a Semitic original, though whether that original was in Hebrew or Aramaic is an open question.

The translation which follows is a revision of Charles's translation: a number of his emendations have been dispensed with, however, when the text can be made to yield a tolerable sense as it stands.

BIBLIOGRAPHY

EDITIONS

A. M. CERIANI, *Monumenta sacra et profana*, I. i (Milan, 1861), pp. 55–64. [Ceriani's text is reproduced, not only by Charles, but also by Volkmar and by Laperrousaz – see below.]

A. HILGENFELD, *Novum Testamentum extra canonem receptum*, fasc. i (Leipzig, 1866), pp. 93–116.

R. H. CHARLES, *The Assumption of Moses, translated from the Latin sixth-century MS, the unemended Text of which is published herewith, together with the Text in its restored and critically emended form, edited with Introduction, Notes, and Indices* (London, 1897).

C. CLEMEN, *Die Himmelfahrt des Mose* (= *Kleine Texte für theologische Vorlesungen und Übingen*, 10; Bonn, 1904–2nd edit. 1924).

TRANSLATIONS

English

R. H. CHARLES, *The Assumption of Moses, translated* . . . [as above]
(London, 1897).

———, in *APOT* ii, pp. 407–424.

W. J. FERRAR, *The Assumption of Moses, translated with Introduction
and Notes* (= S.P.C.K., *Translations of Early Documents*; London,
1917).

French

E.-M. LAPERROUSAZ, *Le Testament de Moïse (généralement appelé
'Assomption de Moïse'): Traduction avec introduction et notes* (= *Semitica*,
xix; Paris, 1970).

German

G. VOLKMAR, *Mose Prophetie und Himmelfahrt: Eine Quelle für das
Neue Testament zum ersten Male deutsch herausgegeben* (Leipzig,
1867).

C. CLEMEN in E. KAUTZSCH, *APAT* ii., pp. 311–331.

P. RIESSLER, *AjSaB*[2], pp. 485–495.

E. BRANDENBURGER in *JSh-rZ* V. 2 (1976), pp. 57–84.

GENERAL

F. C. BURKITT, *Jewish and Christian Apocalypses* (London, 1914),
pp. 19 and 37–40.

A.-M. DENIS, *IPGAT*, pp. 128–141.

O. EISSFELDT, *OTI*, pp. 623–624.

J.-B. FREY, art. 'Apocryphes de l'Ancien Testament' in *DB Sup* i,
cols. 403–409.

K. HAACKER, 'Assumptio Mosis – eine samaritanische Schrift?'
in *TZ* xxv (1969), pp. 385–405.

G. HÖLSCHER, 'Über die Entstehungszeit der "Himmelfahrt
Moses" in *ZNW* xvii (1916), pp. 108–127 and 149–158.

M. R. JAMES, *LAOT*, pp. 42–51.

J. LICHT, 'Taxo, or the Apocalyptic Doctrine of Vengeance' in *JJS*
xii (1961), pp. 95–103.

G. W. E. NICKELSBURG, JR. (ed.),*Studies on the Testament of Moses* (= *SBL Septuagint and Cognate Studies*, 4; Cambridge Mass., 1973).

P. RIESSLER, *AjSaB*², pp. 1301–1303.

F. ROSENTHAL, *Vier apokryphische Bücher aus der Zeit und Schule R. Akiba's* (Leipzig, 1885), pp. 1–38.

L. ROST, *EATAP*, pp. 110–112.

E. SCHÜRER, *HJPTJC* II. iii, pp. 73–83.

———, *GjVZJC*⁴ iii, pp. 294–305.

C. C. TORREY, *AL*, pp. 114–116.

S. ZEITLIN, 'The Assumption of Moses and the Revolt of Bar Kokba' in *JQR* N.S. xxxviii (July, 1947), pp. 1–45.

I. ⟨The Testament of Moses – the instructions he gave in the one
2 hundred and twentieth year of his life,⟩[1] that is the two thousand
3 five hundredth year from the creation of the world (or according to
   oriental reckoning ⟨the two thousand seven hundredth), and the
4 four hundredth⟩ after the departure from Phoenicia, when the
   people had gone out after the Exodus,[2] under the leadership of
5 Moses, to Amman beyond the Jordan [, in the prophecy that was
6 made by Moses in the book Deuteronomy]. Moses[3] called to him
7 Joshua the son of Nun, a man approved by the Lord to be the
   minister[4] of the people and of the Tabernacle of the Testimony
8 with all its holy things, and to bring the people into the land given
9 **to their fathers**, so that it might be given them in accordance with
   the covenant and the oath, *by* which he had declared in the Taber-
10 nacle that he would give *it them* by Joshua. And Moses said to
   Joshua,[5] Promise[6] to do with all diligence everything you have

   [1] Three lines are wanting at the beginning of the MS. The translation is of Charles's restoration, based on the model of The Testaments of the Twelve Patriarchs.

   [2] Lit. 'after the departure'.   [3] Lit. 'who'.

   [4] Lit. 'successor'. The Lat. *successor*, which occurs again at x. 15, is in all probability a rendering of an underlying Gk. διάδοχος, used in several passages in the Gk. Bible, and elsewhere, in the sense of 'minister' (cp. especially Ecclus. xlvi. 1).

   [5] Lit. '(. . . give *it them* by Joshua), saying to Joshua this word'.

   [6] Text 'And promise'. A verb seems to have fallen out: Charles conjectured '⟨Be strong⟩ **and of a good courage**' on the basis of Deut. xxxi. 7.

11 been commanded, so that **you may be** blameless **before** God. So says
12 the Lord of the world. For he created the world for his people's
13 sake. But he did not reveal this purpose in creation at the world's
foundation, so that the Gentiles might thereby be convicted, and
might by their arguments with one another, to their own humilia-
14 tion, convict themselves. Accordingly, he chose and appointed
me,[7] and prepared me from the foundation of the world, to be the
15 mediator[8] of his covenant. And **now** I warn you that my span of life
is near its end and that I am about to pass on to sleep with my
16 fathers, even in the presence of all the people. So study this writing
carefully, so that you may know how to preserve the books that I
17 entrust you with. Set them in order and anoint them with cedar-oil
and store them away in jars of earthenware in the place the Lord
intended[9] from the beginning of the creation of the world *as the place*
18 *where* men should invoke his name till the Day of Repentance, when
he will look on them with favour at the final consummation.[10]

II. ⟨And now⟩ under your leadership[1] they shall enter the land
which he determined to give *them* and promised to their fathers.
2 You shall bless *them* and give to each one of them *a portion* in it, and
confirm their inheritance **in it**,[2] and establish for them a kingdom;
and you shall **appoint** local magistrates for them,[3] in accordance
3 with their Lord's design, in justice and in righteousness. . . . But
after they enter their land . . . years; and afterwards they shall be
ruled by chiefs and kings for eighteen years, and *for* nineteen years
4 . . . .[4] For two[5] tribes will go down and transfer the **Tabernacle of the**
5 **Testimony**.[6] Then the God of heaven **will** make *there* the court of his

---

[7] Lit. 'he thought out and invented me'.
[8] Lat. *arbiter* (and so also at iii. 12).
[9] Lit. 'in the place he made'.
[10] Lit. '. . . in the respect with which the Lord will respect them in the consummation of the end of the days'.

[1] Lit. 'through you'.   [2] Text 'in me'.
[3] Lit. 'and you shall send out offices of places for them'.
[4] The text here is untranslatable (*et ·xviiii· annos abrumpens tib· x·*). Charles
suggested either 'the ten tribes will be apostates' or 'the ten tribes will break away'.
[5] So text. Charles emended to 'twelve' and saw here a reference to 2 Sam. vi. 1–2.
[6] Lit. 'the testimony of the tabernacle'.

tabernacle and the **tower** of his sanctuary, and the two holy tribes shall be established *there* (but the ten tribes will establish kingdoms

6 for themselves according to their own arrangements). And they

7 will offer sacrifices for twenty years. And seven will surround *the place* with walls,[7] and I will protect[8] nine, and ⟨four⟩ shall **transgress** the Lord's covenant and profane the **oath** the Lord made with

8 them. And they will sacrifice their sons to foreign gods, and they

9 will set up idols in the sanctuary and serve them. And in the Lord's house they will commit all kinds of abominations and carve *representations of* every kind of animal *all round the walls*.

III. ⟨And⟩ in those days a king from the east will come against

2 them and his cavalry will cover their land. And he will burn their city[1] with fire, together with the Lord's holy temple, and he will

3 carry off all the holy vessles. And he will drive out the whole population and take them to his own country; and the two tribes he

4 will take along with him. Then will the two tribes call **indignantly** on the ten tribes, like a lioness on the dusty plains, hungry and thirsty.

5 And they will cry out aloud, Righteous and holy is the Lord, for because you have sinned, we too, in just the same way, have been

6 carried **off** with you, together with our children.[2] Then the ten tribes will mourn, when they hear the reproaches of the two tribes,

7 and they will say, What can we do for you, brothers: has not this

8 misery come to all the house of Israel? And all the tribes will mourn

9 and cry to heaven saying, God of Abraham, and God of Isaac, and God of Jacob, remember thy covenant which thou didst make with them, and the oath which thou didst swear to them by thyself, that they should never lack descendants in the land which thou didst

10 give them. Then will they remember me in that day, tribe saying to

11 tribe, and *one* man *saying* to[3] another, Is not this what Moses said would happen to us[4] in his prophecies – *Moses* who suffered much in Egypt and in the Red Sea and in the wilderness for forty years?

[7] Lit. 'surround the walls'. Cp. iv. 7.
[8] Lit. 'go round', 'encircle'.

[1] Lit. 'colony'. Cp. v. 6; vi. 8.
[2] In the text 'together with our children' follows 'thirsty' at the end of verse 4.
[3] Lit. 'about'.
[4] Lit. 'Is not this what Moses was testifying to us'.

12 He warned us[5] (and summoned heaven and earth to witness
against us) not to transgress God's[6] commandments, of which he
13 was *himself* the mediator to us. These things have happened to us
after his death, just as he said they would and as he warned us[7] at
the time; and his prophecies have been fulfilled,[8] even to our being
14 carried off as captives into eastern lands. And they will be kept in
slavery for some seventy-seven years.

IV. Then one of those *set* over them will go into *his house* and
spread out his hands and fall on his knees and pray for them,
2 saying, Lord of all, king *who sittest* on the lofty throne, who rulest
the world, and dost will that this people should be thy chosen
people: then didst thou will that thou shouldest be called their
God, according to the covenant thou didst make with their fathers.
3 And they have gone as captives into another land with their wives
and their children, and *they are living* among[1] foreign peoples and
4 where there is much **idolatry**.[2] Look upon *them* and have pity on
5 them, O Lord of heaven. Then will God remember them because of
the covenant that he made with their fathers, and he will show his
6 pity at that time also. And he will put it into the mind of a king to
pity them; and he will send them back to their *own* land and
7 country. Then some from the tribes[3] will go up and come to their
8 appointed place and once again surround the place *with walls*. And
the two tribes will continue in the faith appointed for them, in
sadness and lamentation because they will be unable to offer
9 sacrifices to the Lord of their fathers. And the ten tribes will be
fruitful and **increase** among the **Gentiles** during the time of their
captivity.[4]

[5] Lit. 'he testified'. Cp. Deut. iv. 25–27.
[6] Lit. 'his'.   [7] Lit. 'he testified to us'.
[8] Lit. 'and which things have come to pass'.

[1] Lit. 'and around the gate of'.
[2] Text 'great majesty'. The translation offered is based on Charles's emendation
'great vanity' ('vanity' in the Old Testament is not infrequently associated with
idols).
[3] Lit. 'some parts of the tribes'.
[4] After 'And the ten tribes will be fruitful' the text becomes more than usually
uncertain.

V. And when the day of reckoning[1] draws near and retribution
2 comes through kings who share their guilt and punish them, they
3 themselves also will be divided as to truth – hence **the sayings**, They
will abandon righteousness and turn to iniquity, and, They will
defile with *their* **pollutions** the house of their worship, and, They will
4 turn wantonly to foreign gods. For they will not follow the truth of
God; but some *of them* will pollute the altar with the ⟨very⟩ gifts
they offer to the Lord, who are not priests but slaves *and* sons of
5 slaves. And those who are *their* masters, *that is* their teachers at that
time, will show favour to **the rich** and **take** bribes and sell judge-
6 ments in return for **presents**. And so *their* city[2] and their whole land[3]
will be filled with acts of lawlessness and deeds of evil; and their
judges will be ungodly men, **who have turned their backs** on the Lord,
and are ready to give judgements **for money** as each man wants.[4]

VI. Then shall arise kings to rule over them, and they shall be
called priests of the Most High God (they will be responsible for
2 much ungodliness in the holy of holies). And an insolent king will
succeed them, who will not be of priestly stock, an arrogant and a
3 shameless man; and he will judge them as they deserve. And he
will put their leaders to death with the sword, and **bury** them
4 secretly so that no one should know where their bodies are. He will
5 kill *both* old and young and spare no *one*. He will be the object of
6 universal dread and detestation.[1] And he will treat them ruthlessly, as the Egyptians treated them, for thirty-four years, and
7 make their lives unbearable. And he will produce children, who
8 will succeed him and **rule** for shorter periods. Into their **parts** will

[1] Lit. 'the times of censuring'.
[2] Lit. 'colony'. Cp. iii. 2; vi. 8.
[3] Lit. 'and the borders of their dwelling'.
[4] Lit. 'as each may wish'. The text of verses 5 and 6 is very corrupt, although the
general sense is plain. In verse 5 Charles excised *'that is* their teachers' and 'in return
for **presents**' as explanatory glosses, and he preferred the emendation 'pervert
judgement' for the 'sell judgements' of the MS. In verse 6 six lines of text are
repeated in the MS with a number of variations: the second version is, on the whole,
the better, and this has been followed, so far as it can be made to yield any
consecutive sense at all.

[1] Lit. 'Then the fear of him will be bitter unto them in their land'.

come **the cohorts** and a powerful king of the west, **who** will conquer them, and take them captive, and burn a part of their temple with fire, *and* crucify some *of them* round their city.[2]

VII. And after this the times shall come to an end, **in a moment** the
2 . . . course shall ⟨come to an end⟩: the four hours shall come. They
3 will be forced . . .[1] And in their time[2] pestilential and impious men
4 will bear rule, alleging that they are righteous. And these will stir up their minds to anger,[3] for they will be crafty men, self-indulgent, hypocritical, ready for a party at any hour of the day, gluttons,
5,6 guzzlers, . . .,[4] who devour the goods of the ⟨poor⟩ on the pretext of
7 **justice, but** *in reality* **to destroy them**, grumblers, deceitful *people* who hide themselves away in case they should be recognized, impious,
8 full of *every* vice and villany, who say from sunrise to sunset, Let us[5] have feasts and revels, eating and drinking; and let us behave like
9 princes.[6] And although their hands and minds are occupied with things unclean, they will make a fine show in words, even saying,[7] Do not touch ⟨me⟩, lest you pollute me in the place where. . . .[8]

VIII.[1] . . . And there shall come upon them ⟨a second⟩ retribution and wrath, such as has not befallen them from the beginning until that time, when he will stir up against them the king of the kings of the earth, **a man who rules** with great power, who will crucify those

[2] Lit. 'colony'. Cp. iii. 2; v. 6.

[1] At the beginning of this chapter the MS is so defective as to be virtually untranslatable.
[2] Or 'And from among these'.
[3] Lit. 'stir up the anger of their minds'.
[4] MS again defective.   [5] Lit. 'We shall'.
[6] Lit. 'and we shall esteem ourselves as though we shall be princes'.
[7] Lit. 'and moreover they will say'.   [8] MS defective.

[1] According to Charles, chaps. viii and ix reflect the period of Antiochus Epiphanes and the Maccabees so closely that in their present context they must be out of place: originally, Charles thought, chaps. viii and ix stood between v and vi, and they were transposed 'by the final editor'. Granted the truth of Charles's observation, however, it may well be (in view of the chaotic state of the existing text) that their present position is due to some accident in the textual tradition rather than deliberate transposition.

2 who confess their circumcision. And those who **deny** *it*[2] he will
3 torture and put in chains and imprison. And their wives will be
given to the gods among the Gentiles, and their young sons will be
operated on by the doctors **to look as though they had not been**
4 **circumcised**. And others among them will suffer punishment by
torture and fire and sword; and they will be forced to carry round
their idols publicly, polluted things, just like *the shrines* that house[3]
5 them. And in the same way they will be forced by those who torture
them to enter their inmost sanctuary and forced with goads to
blaspheme and insult **the Name**,[4] and, as if that were not enough,[5]
the laws as well by having **a pig** upon the altar.

IX.   Then in that **day there will be** a man of the tribe of Levi, whose
2 name will be Taxo, and he will have seven sons. And he will ask
them, saying, See, *my* sons, a second cruel and unclean retribution
has come upon the people and a punishment without mercy and **far**
3 **worse than** the first. For what nation or what region or what people
among those who do not worship **the Lord**, who have done many
atrocious things, have suffered as great calamities as have befallen
4 us? So now, *my* sons, listen to me: you know well enough[1] that
neither the fathers nor their forefathers provoked God by trans-
5 gressing his commandments. For you know that our strength lies
6 here, and let us act accordingly.[2] Let us fast for three days; and on
the fourth day let us go out to a cave in the country, and let us die
rather than transgress the commandments of the Lord of lords, the
7 God of our fathers. For if we do this and die, our blood will be
avenged before the Lord.

X.   And then shall his kingdom appear throughout all his
        creation;
        And then shall the Devil meet his end,

[2] Reading *negantes* for the *necantes* of the text. Charles suggested *celantes* ('those
who conceal it'). Another suggestion is *secantes* or *circumsecantes* ('those who circumcise' – cp. 1 Macc. i. 61).
[3] Lit. 'contain'.   [4] Text 'the Word'.
[5] Lit. 'finally after these things'.

[1] Lit. 'see and know'.
[2] Lit. 'For you know that these things are strength to us and this will we do'.

And sorrow shall depart with him.

2 Then shall be consecrated[1] the angel who has been
    appointed chief,
Who will immediately avenge them of their enemies.

3 For the Heavenly One will ⟨ arise⟩ from his royal throne,
And go forth from his holy dwelling-place
With wrath and anger because of his sons.

4 And the earth will tremble:
It will be shaken to its farthest bounds;
And high mountains will collapse
And **hills** be shaken and fall.[2]

5 And the sun will not give *its* light;
And the horns of the moon will be turned into darkness,
And they will be broken,
And it will be turned wholly into blood;
And the orbit of the stars will be disturbed.

6 And the sea will retire into the abyss,
And the fountains of waters will fail,
And the rivers **dry up**.

7 For the Most High will arise, the Eternal God alone,
And he will appear to punish the Gentiles,
And he will destroy all their idols.

8 Then happy will you be, Israel;
And you will trample upon *their* necks [and the wings of an
    eagle],[3]
For the time allotted them will have run its course.[4]

9 And God will exalt you,
And set you in heaven above the stars,[5]

---

[1] Lit. 'Then shall be filled the hands of'. Cp. Exod. xxviii. 41, xxix. 9; Lev. xxi. 10.
[2] Text reads 'And high mountains will be brought low and shaken and valleys
will fall'.
[3] The first two lines of this verse are clearly inspired by Deut. xxxiii. 29 as read in
the Septuagint and other versions ('Happy *are* you Israel, . . . and you shall trample
(lit. 'go upon') their neck(s)'). Hence the words in square brackets are likely to be a
gloss, presumably added by someone who took the original 'go upon' in the sense of
'mount' or 'ride upon', and had either Exod. xix. 4 or Isa. xl. 31 in mind.
[4] Lit. 'And they will be ended' (Lat. *et inplebuntur*). Cp. Luke xxi. 24 (Lat. *donec
impleantur tempora nationum*).
[5] Lit. 'And make you abide in the heaven of the stars'.

In the place where **he** dwells **himself.**[6]

10   And you **will look** from on high and see your enemies on earth,[7]

And you will recognize them and rejoice,

And give thanks and confess your Creator.

11 And as for you, Joshua, *son of* Nun, take heed of what is written in
12 this book.[8] For from *my* death [, *that is my* assumption,][9] until his
13 advent there shall be two hundred and fifty times.[10] And this is the course of these ⟨times⟩, which they will pursue until they are
14,15 complete. But I am about to depart to sleep with my fathers. So then, Joshua, *son of* Nun, **Be strong**: God has chosen you to be the minister in my place of the same covenant.

XI.   And when Joshua had heard what Moses had written in his writing and all he had foretold,[1] he rent his clothes and threw
2 himself at the feet of Moses. And Moses comforted him and wept
3 with him. And Joshua answered him and said, What kind of **consolation** is it that you give me, *my* lord Moses, and how can I be
4 **consoled** when **you** tell me something so distressing? When you say that you are about to leave this people, tears and laments are
5,6 bound to be. ⟨But now⟩, where will you be buried?[2] Or what shall
7 be the sign that marks *your* burial place? Or who shall dare to move your body **from it** as *if it were that of an ordinary* man from place
8 to place? For all men when they die have their burial-places corresponding to the age *in which they live*[3] on earth, but your burial-place is from the rising to the setting sun, and from the south to the confines of the north: the whole world is your burial-place.

---

[6] Text 'In their (masc.) dwelling-place'.

[7] Charles would read 'in Gehenna', supposing that Lat. *in terram* was a rendering of Gk. *en ge*, and that the Gk. *ge* here was a transliteration of Heb. *ge* ('valley'), used absolutely for *ge-Hinnom* as in Jer. ii. 23 (cp. vii. 31, 32).

[8] Lit. 'keep these words and this book'.

[9] According to Charles, an addition by the editor who combined the 'Assumption' with the 'Testament'.

[10] i.e. weeks of years.

[1] Or 'said previously'.

[2] Lit. 'what place will receive you?'   [3] Or 'corresponding to *their* age'.

,10 *My* lord, **you are about to go away**; and who shall feed this people? Or
11 who is there to pity them, and who shall guide them on the way? Or
who shall pray for them day by day,[4] so that I may be able to lead
12 them into the land of *their* **forefathers**?[5] How, then, am I to **look after**
this people as a father *looks after his* only son, or as a mother[6] *her*
virgin daughter, who is being brought up **to be given** the husband
she will revere (*for the mother* will shield her body from the sun and
13 *take care* she does not run about without her shoes)? ⟨And how⟩
shall I supply them with food and drink according to their needs?[7]
14 For they number some **six** hundred thousand ⟨men⟩,[8] and they
15 have become so many through your prayers, lord Moses. And
what wisdom or understanding have I that I should either give
16 judgement or answer by word in the house ⟨of the Lord⟩? And the
kings of the Amorites also, when they hear we are attacking *them*,
and believing that there is no longer **among them** *that* sacred spirit
worthy of the Lord, made up of many parts and beyond all understanding, the lord of the word, faithful in all things, the divine
prophet throughout the earth, the most perfect teacher in the
world – *believing* that he is no longer among them, **they will** say, Let
17 us go against them. If only once *our* enemies have done what is
wrong against the Lord, they have no advocate[9] to offer prayers for
them to the Lord, as did Moses the great messenger, who hour by
hour, day and night, prayed without ceasing *for them*,[10] looking to
him who rules the **whole** world with mercy and justice, *and* remind-
ing *him* of the covenant *made with their* fathers and propitiating the
18 Lord with an oath. For they will say, He is not with them: so let us
19 go and wipe them off the face of the earth. What then shall become
of this people, *my* lord Moses?

XII. And when Joshua had finished speaking, he threw himself to
2 the ground again at the feet of Moses. And Moses took his hand

---

[4] Lit. '. . . for them not **omitting** a single day'.

[5] Text *araborum*. The emendation supposes *atavorum*: another possibility is *amorr-
eorum* – cp. verse 16.

[6] Lit. 'lady'.

[7] Lit. 'according to the will of their will'.

[8] Text '⟨. . .⟩ for of them there were a hundred thousand'. Cp. Exod. xii. 37.

[9] Lit. 'defender'.

[10] Lit. 'had his knees fixed to the earth praying'.

3 and lifted him up into the seat in front of him. And he answered
   and said to him, Joshua, do not belittle **yourself**, but take courage
4 and listen to me, God has created all the nations on the earth, and
   he has created us: he has foreseen *what will happen to both* them and us
   from the beginning of the creation of the earth to the end of the age;
   and nothing has been overlooked by him, not even the smallest
   detail, but he has foreseen everything and **brought everything about**.
5 ⟨And⟩ everything that is to be on this earth the Lord has foreseen,
6 and lo, it is **brought** ⟨into the light. . . . The Lord⟩ has appointed me
   ⟨to pray⟩ for them and for their sins and ⟨to make intercession⟩ for
7 them. For it was not because of any virtue or **steadfastness** on my
   part, but because he willed it so,[1] that his pity and patience took
8 hold of me. And I tell you, Joshua, it is not because of this people's
9 godliness that you are to destroy the nations. All the pillars of the
   heaven *and* the earth have been made **and** approved by God and are
10 under **the signet ring** of his right hand. Thus, those who keep and
11 observe **God's** commandments will increase and prosper. But those
   who sin and ignore the commandments will be denied the blessings
   that have been mentioned, and they will be punished with many
12 torments by the nations. Yet it is impossible that he should wholly
13 destroy them and forsake them. For God has gone forth, he who
   has foreseen everything to the end, and his covenant has been
   established; and by the oath which . . .[2]

---

[1] Lit. 'but by careful arrangement'. If Charles was right the original will have
meant 'but of his good pleasure'.
[2] The MS breaks off in mid-sentence.

THE TESTAMENT OF JOB

INTRODUCTION

If the 'liber qui appellatur Testamentum Job, apocryphus' mentioned in the Gelasian Decree refers to our Testament, there would seem to have been a Latin version of it circulating in the West in the fifth and sixth centuries. But apart from this possibility, there is no reference to the Testament, or certain quotation from it, anywhere in antiquity.

The Testament was first introduced to the modern world by A. Mai, who in 1833 printed a Greek text in the seventh volume of his *Scriptorum Veterum Nova Collectio*. Mai did not disclose the source of his text, since identified as the 13th century Vatican MS Vat. gr. 1238. In 1890 M. R. James 'was able to examine a MS of the Testament at Paris': this was B.N. gr. 2658 (11th century), containing also the Testaments of the Twelve Patriarchs as well as the well-known 'Interpretation of Hebrew Names' and the 'Questions and Answers' attributed to Anastasius of Sinai; and it was this MS that was used by James as the foundation of his edition in 1897, the variants of Mai's text, which are often considerable, being set out in full in the apparatus. The only other MS known to James was Paris B.N. gr. 938 (16th century), which was obviously a transcript of B.N. gr. 2658 and therefore negligible. In 1911 the collation of a fourth MS (Messina San Salvatore 29; AD 1307), made against James's text, was published by A. Mancini.[1]

Meanwhile, the existence of a version in Slavonic had been brought to light. In 1878 S. Novaković published the first text of this version from a MS in Belgrade; and thirteen years later Gj. Polívka produced a critical edition, printing the text of a Šafařík MS as his basic text and adding the variants of the Belgrade MS and another from Moscow in his apparatus. For text-critical purposes, however, the Slavonic version has not proved of much assistance; it is exceedingly periphrastic and there are many (obviously deliberate) abbreviations and expansions.

[1] A. Mancini, 'Per la critica del "Testamentum Iob" (= *Rendiconti della Reale Accademia dei Lincei*, Ser. V, xx (1911), pp. 479–502).

The Greek text in S. P. Brock's edition of 1967, as in James's edition, is basically that of the Paris MS (= P); though where P is manifestly corrupt preference is given to the readings of either the Vatican MS (= V), or the San Salvatore MS (= S), or both. Because of its internal complications reference is made in the apparatus to the Slavonic version only when it clearly confirms a Greek variant.

The American Society of Biblical Literature Pseudepigraha Group edition, which was published seven years after Brock under the editorship of R. A. Kraft, had of necessity to rely on the same Greek MSS. However, as might be expected in an attempt at what was described as 'a step towards an eclectic text', P assumes rather less prominence than previously. Moreover, the traditional verse divisions were not a little modified.

About the origin and date of the Testament nothing whatever is known. Nevertheless, several widely differing opinions have been expressed. For example, Kohler, in the introduction to his translation, published in 1897, declared himself in favour of an Essene origin for the work and a pre-Christian date. On the other hand, James, in the introduction to his edition, published in the same year, maintained that the author was 'a Jew by birth, a Christian by faith', and that he lived in Egypt in the second or third century AD. Subsequently, Kohler seems to have modified his views somewhat, for in his *Jewish Encyclopaedia* article of 1904 there is no mention of the Essenes, and he refers simply to the Testament being 'one of the most remarkable productions of the pre-Christian era, explicable only when viewed in the light of ancient Hasidean practise'. Another strong supporter of the Testament's Jewish origin was Torrey, who characteristically saw beneath the extant Greek 'texts' an underlying original in Aramaic, which he dated to the first century BC.

What is indisputable, however, is that the author of the Testament *as it now stands* knew and used the canonical Job in the Greek Septuagint version and not in the Hebrew original or any other version: this means that he wrote in Greek and that he was not translating from Aramaic or anything else – the Septuagint words and phrases are throughout so much part of the texture of the work that they could not possibly be due to a translator. In other words, the Testament is a Hellenistic work through and through. Hence Philonenko, for instance, looked to Egypt and went on to suggest a possible origin among the Therapeutae there during the first century AD.

Further, there is much to be said for the view that the author was familiar with the New Testament as well as with the Old – such expressions as ἀπροσωπόληπτός ἐστιν [ὁ Κύριος], ἀποδιδοὺς ἑκάστῳ (iv. 8: cp. 1 Pet. i. 17; Rom. ii. 6 . . .), σκωληκόβρωτος (xx. 8: cp. Acts xii. 23), and εἰς τὸ διηνεκές (xxxiii. 7: cp. Heb. vii. 3, x. 1, 12, 14) tell strongly in favour of it; and it may also be argued that the 'patience' or 'endurance' of Job (i. 5) and his final vindication (lii–liii) are presented as a type of the sufferings and 'end' of Christ (cp. James v. 11). If this be so the author must have been a Christian, although he seems to have made no conscious attempt to 'Christianize' the details of his material, and his contacts with the New Testament look much more like unconscious reminiscences than deliberate allusions.

Beyond this it is difficult to go. He may have known a Hebrew Midrash on Job or an Aramaic Targum: he may have been familiar with stories about Job from contemporary Jewish folk-lore; or he may have been dependent on his own creative imagination, except in so far as it was inspired by the contents of the canonical Job in the Septuagint, and modified by such scraps of Jewish tradition as that Job's wife was named Dinah – a tradition which appears both in the Targum to Job and in Pseudo-Philo (who clearly identified her with the daughter of Jacob[2]), although it is to be observed that in the Testament Job marries twice and Dinah is his second wife (i. 6). In any case, the Septuagint Job emerges as the only 'source' that can be certainly identified.

Finally, if the author was a Christian and familiar with the New Testament, he cannot have written before the second century. His vocabulary contains some 'late' words – 'late' either in occurrence or in the meaning he attaches to them; and this fact should make us pause before assigning the earliest possible date to the Testament.

---

[2] Pseudo-Philo, *Liber Antiquitatum Biblicarum*, viii. 8.

Our translation is based on Brock's edition and for the most part follows his text.

BIBLIOGRAPHY

EDITIONS

Greek

A. MAI, *Scriptorum Veterum Nova Collectio*, vii (Rome, 1833), pp. 180–191.

M. R. JAMES, 'The Testament of Job' in *Apocrypha Anecdota*, ii (= *TS* V. i; Cambridge, 1897), pp. lxxii–cii and 103–137.

S. P. BROCK, *Testamentum Iobi* (= *PVTG* ii (Leiden, 1967), pp. 1–60).

R. A. KRAFT, with HAROLD ATTRIDGE, RUSSELL SPITTLER, and JANET TIMBLE, *The Testament of Job: Greek Text and English Translation* (= *SBL Texts and Translations* 5, *Pseudepigrapha Series* 4; Missoula, 1974).

Slavonic

S. NOVAKOVIĆ, 'Apokrifna prica o Jovu' in *Starine*, x (Zagreb, 1878), pp. 157–170.

Gj. POLÍVKA, 'Apokrifna prica o Jovu' in *Starine*, xxiv (Zagreb, 1891), pp. 135–155.

TRANSLATIONS

English

K. KOHLER, 'The Testament of Job: An Essene Midrash on the Book of Job, re-edited and translated with Introductory and Exegetical Notes' in G. A. KOHUT (ed.), *Semitic Studies in memory of Rev. Dr. Alexander Kohut* (Berlin, 1897), pp. 264–338 – the text is a reprint of Mai's.

R. P. SPITTLER in R. A. KRAFT, *The Testament of Job* . . . [as above].

French

M. PHILONENKO, *Le Testament de Job: Introduction, traduction et notes*
(= *Semitica*, xviii; Paris, 1968).

German

P. RIESSLER, *AjSaB²*, pp. 1104–1134.
B. SCHALLER in *JSh-rZ* III. 3 (1979), pp. 301–387.

GENERAL

M. DELCOR, 'Le Testament de Job, la prière de Nabonide et les
traditions targoumiques' in S. WAGNER (ed.), *Bibel und Qumran*
(Berlin, 1968), pp. 57–74.
A.-M. DENIS, *IPGAT*, pp. 100–104.
J.-B. FREY, art. 'Apocryphes de l'Ancien Testament' in *DB Sup* i,
col. 455.
L. GINZBERG, *The Legends of the Jews*, ii (Philadelphia, 1910), pp.
225–242 and v (Philadelphia, 1925), pp. 381–390.
K. KOHLER, art. 'Job, Testament of' in *JE* vii (New York, 1904),
pp. 200–202.
M. PHILONENKO, 'Le Testament de Job et les Thérapeutes' in
Semitica, viii (1958), pp. 41–53.
D. RAHNENFÜHRER, 'Das Testament des Hiob und das Neue
Testament' in *ZNW* lxii (1971), pp. 68–93.
P. RIESSLER, *AjSaB²*, pp. 1333–1334.
B. SCHALLER, 'Das Testament Hiobs und die Septuaginta-
Übersetzung des Buches Hiob' in *Biblica*, lxi, fasc. 3 (1980),
pp. 377–406.
E. SCHÜRER, *GjVZJC⁴* iii, pp. 406–407.
F. SPITTA, 'Das Testament Hiobs und das Neue Testament' in
Zur Geschichte und Litteratur des Urchristentums, III. 2 (Göttingen,
1907), pp. 139–206.
W. B. STEVENSON, *The Poem of Job* (London, 1947), pp. 78–80.
C. C. TORREY, *AL*, pp. 140–145.

I. The Book of the Words of Job, who was called Jobab.

2 On the day when he was taken ill and about to bring his stewardship to an end, he called his seven sons and his three

3 daughters *to him*. Their names were Tersi, Choros, Huon, Nike, Phoros, Phiphe, Phrouon, Hemera, Cassia, and Amaltheias-keras.

4 And when he had called his children, he said, Gather round, my children, gather round me, so that I can describe to you what the

5 Lord did to me and everything that has happened to me. For I am your father Job, who has endured much; and you are a chosen,

6 honoured, race, of the stock of Jacob, your mother's father. For I am of the sons of Esau, Jacob's brother; and your mother Dinah, through whom I became your father, was Jacob's daughter[1] – my former wife, with ten other children, died a bitter death. So listen to me, *my* children, and I will tell you what befell me.

1,2 **II.** I was Jobab before the Lord gave me the name of Job. When I was called Jobab, I used to live at that time very near a much-

3 venerated idol's temple.[1] And as I looked continually at the whole

4 burnt-offerings offered to it, I thought to myself, Can this really be the God who made the heaven and the earth and the sea and us ourselves? How can I know?[2]

III. And in the night, while I was asleep, there came to me a loud

2 voice with a very great light, saying, Jobab, Jobab. And I said, Here am I; and it said, Get up and I will show you who it is you

3 want to know. He to whom they bring the whole burnt-offerings and pour out drink-offerings is not God but the power of the Devil,

4 by whom human nature is[1] deceived. And when I heard *this*, I fell

5 down on my bed in worship. And I said, My lord, who hast come

6 for the salvation of my soul; I beg thee, if this is the sanctuary[2] of

---

[1] Lit. 'For I am of the sons of Esau, brother of Jacob, of whom is your mother Dinah, from whom I begot you'.

[1] V has a much fuller text in this chapter and reads here 'near my house there was a certain idol (lit. 'an idol of someone') that was worshipped by the people'.
[2] So PS: V adds 'what is true'.

[1] Lit. 'will be'.   [2] Lit. 'place'.

Satan, by whom men are[1] deceived, give me authority to go out
7 and cleanse his sanctuary,[2] so that I can put an end to his drink-
offerings – and who is there to stop me, seeing I am king of this
land?

IV. And the light answered me and said, You can indeed cleanse
this sanctuary;[1] but I *must* let you know everything the Lord has
2 commanded me to tell you. And I said, Everything he has com-
3 manded me, his servant, I will listen to and do. And again he said,
4 This is what the Lord says, If you do attempt to cleanse Satan's
sanctuary,[1] he will turn against you in anger and fight against you;
but although he will afflict you with many calamities, he will not be
5 able to kill you. He will take your possessions away: he will destroy
6 your children. But if you endure, I will make your name famous
7 among all generations on earth till the end of time. And I will
return your possessions to you, and double shall be restored to you,
8 so that you may know that the Lord[2] has no favourites and richly
9 repays everyone who obeys *him*. And you will be raised up at the
10 resurrection; for you will be like a boxer in the games[3] who keeps
11 the struggle up and gains *his* crown. Then you will know that the
Lord is just, true, and strong, and gives strength to his elect.

V. And I, my children, made answer to him, To death will I
2 endure, and I will not yield. And after I had been sealed by the
angel, he departed from me; *and* then, my children, the next night I
got up and took fifty servants with me and set out for the shrine of
3 the idol's temple and razed it to the ground. And this done, I went
back into my house, with orders that the doors were to be securely
fastened.

VI. And you will be astonished, my children, when you hear what
2 happened next.[1] For as soon as I had gone into my house and had
3 secured my doors, I gave orders to my door-keepers, If anyone
comes for me to-day, do not tell me about it, but say, He is not

---

[1] Lit. 'place'.　　　[2] Lit. 'he'.
[3] Lit. 'like an athlete boxing'.

[1] Lit. 'Hear, my children, and marvel'.

4 available; for he is indoors dealing with urgent business. And while
I was indoors, Satan disguised himself as a beggar and knocked at
5 the door. And he said to the girl at the door, Tell Job I want to see
6,7 him. The girl came in and told me this. And she was instructed to
make it clear that I was not at the moment available.

VII. When Satan heard *this*, he went away and put an assalion[1] on
his shoulders, and he came and spoke to the girl at the door and
2 said, Say to Job, Give me of your bounty[2] a loaf of bread, so that I
3 may *have something to* eat. And I gave the girl a loaf that had been
4 burnt to give him; and I sent a message to him,[3] Do not expect to
5 eat of my bread again, for you have become my enemy. And the girl
at the door was ashamed to give him the loaf that was burnt and
6 ashy (for she did not know that he was Satan); so she took a good
7 loaf of her own and gave him. He took it, and, knowing what had
happened, said to the girl, Go back, you good-for-nothing servant,
8 and fetch the loaf that was given you to give me. And the girl was
most upset, and she said in tears, You are quite right to say I am a
good-for-nothing servant. If I had not been, I would have done as
9 my master told me. And she went back and brought him the burnt
10 loaf, and said to him, My lord says, You shall not eat of my bread
11 again, because I have become your enemy: yet I have given you
this so that I cannot be accused of refusing an enemy who asked of
12 me. When Satan heard this, he sent the girl back to me, saying,
Just as this loaf is burnt through and through, so too will I make
your body; for I go my way, and within a single hour I will make
13 you desolate. And I answered him again, Do what you will, and if
you are determined to afflict me,[4] I am ready to bear whatever you
lay upon me.

VIII. When he had left me, he went away *and roamed to and fro*
2 beneath the vault of heaven. And he got the Lord to promise him

---

[1] A word of doubtful meaning, which does not occur elsewhere in Greek. Kohler (*Semitic Studies* . . ., p. 316) declares that it is for ἄσιλλα (= אסילא), and, appealing to Kohut's *Arukh* (s.v. אסל), translates it as 'basket'; but this word in both Hebrew and Greek means 'yoke'. V adds the adj. 'ragged': hence Kohler's translation, 'an old torn basket'.   [2] Lit. 'from your hands'.

[3] Lit. 'and I said to him'.

[4] Lit. 'Do what you are doing; for if you wish to bring something on me'.

authority over my possessions. And then, when he had been given the authority, he came and took away all my wealth.

IX. So listen, for I will tell you everything that happened to me
2 and what was taken from me. For I had a hundred and thirty
3 thousand sheep; and I set apart seven thousand of them to be shorn
4 for the clothing of orphans, widows, the poor, and the helpless. I
5 had a pack of eight hundred dogs that guarded my flocks; and I had another two hundred dogs that guarded[1] my house. I had nine thousand camels; and from them I selected three thousand and set them to work in various cities;[2] and I loaded them with goods, and I sent them off into the cities and villages with instructions to go and distribute to the helpless and to those in want and to all the
6 widows. I had a hundred and forty[3] thousand asses in the pastures; and I set apart five hundred of them and gave orders that their foals[4] should be sold and the proceeds given to the poor and needy.
7 And the poor[5] from all countries used to come and seek me out;[6]
8 and the four doors of my house were ever open. And I would give my servants orders that these should be kept open: my aim was to ensure that no one should come asking for charity and see me sitting at the door, and turn away out of nervousness, and get nothing. *My aim was* rather that whenever people saw me sitting at one door, they should go in by another and get as much as they needed.

X. There were thirty tables set up in my house, available at all
2 hours, for the exclusive use of strangers: I had also twelve other
3 tables laid for widows; and if any stranger appeared asking for charity, he had to be fed at table before being given what he needed
4 – for I would not allow *anyone* to leave my door empty-handed.[1]
5 And I had three thousand five hundred yoke of oxen; and from

---

[1] So SV Slav.: P om. 'my flocks . . . that guarded'.
[2] Lit. 'three thousand to work in every city'.
[3] So SV Slav.: P 'thirty'.   [4] Lit. 'offspring'.
[5] So V Slav.: PS 'And all'.   [6] Lit. 'come to meet me'.

[1] Lit. 'with an empty bosom'. Not infrequently 'bosom' was used metaphorically for the fold of the garment above the girdle in which valuables were stowed (e.g. Prov. xvii. 23; Luke vi. 38): hence the natural meaning here is what we mean by the

them I picked out five hundred yoke and allocated them to plough-
6 ing in any field of anyone who could use them; and what they
7 produced[2] I set apart for the poor at their table. And I had fifty
bake-houses, from which I provided *what was necessary* for the
service of the beggars' table.

XI. And there were also some strangers who saw my goodwill and
2 were anxious to help in the service themselves. And there were
some others who were at the time without the wherewithal and so
were unable to contribute anything,[1] and they would come and
appeal to me, saying, Might we also share in this service,[2] although
3 we have nothing? As a favour to us, lend us money, so that we can
go off and trade in cities far away, and so be able to render service
4,5 to the poor. And afterwards we can repay you what is yours. And
when I heard this, I was glad that they would actually take *money*
6 from me to care for the beggars. And I would eagerly accept the
7 bond and give them as much as they wanted. And I took no
8 security from them, apart from just the written record. And so they
9 would trade with what was mine. And sometimes they would be
successful in their trading and *make enough to* give to the beggars.
10 Sometimes, again, they would be robbed; and they would come
and appeal to me, saying, Be patient with us, we beg you, while we
11 see[3] how we can pay you back. And when I heard this, I would feel
sympathy for them and bring out their note of hand and read it in
their presence and tear it up and release them from their debt,[4]
saying, Inasmuch as I trusted you in the cause of the poor, I will

phrase 'with his pockets empty'. However, it is just possible that in this particular
context the sense intended was 'with an empty stomach', though such an extended
meaning for 'bosom' would be unusual, if not unparalleled. In any case we are
dealing with an exact quotation from Job xxxi. 34 in the Septuagint version, which
understands the whole passage rather differently from what is implied by the
Hebrew original.

   [2] Lit. 'and their fruit'.

   [1] Lit. 'unable to spend'.

   [2] Lit. 'We beg you, can we also perform this service?'

   [3] SV Slav. 'that we may see': P 'let us see'.

   [4] And when I heard ... debt: so V; PS obscure.

12 take nothing from you. And I would not accept anything from any debtor.[5]

XII. And if ever any well-intentioned man[1] came to me and said, I have not myself the means to aid the poor, yet I would gladly serve

2 the beggars to-day at your table, permission would be granted, he would do his service, and he would be given his own meal; and when evening came and he was leaving to go off home, he would be

3 made take something from me, for I would say, I know you are a working-man, who expects and looks for your wages: you must take something. And I would not allow the hireling's wages to remain with me in my house.

XIII. Quite spent were those who milked the cows, for the milk[1] streamed on the mountains; and the butter was spread over my

2 paths. And my cattle were so numerous that they were folded

3 among the rocks and the mountains because of those in labour. So it was that the mountains were drenched with milk and became

4 like solid butter. My slaves who cooked the widows' food grew

5 weary. And, with scant regard for the poor, they called down curses on me, saying, Would God we were full of his meats –

6 whereas I was being more than ordinarily kind.

1,2 **XIV.** I had six **harps**[1] and a ten-stringed lyre. And every day, after the widows had been fed, I would get up and take the lyre and play

3 it for them, and they would sing. And with the harp I would

4 remind them of God, so that they might glorify the Lord. And if ever my slave-girls started complaining, I would take the harp up

5 and sing of the wages of recompense; and I would put an end to their fault-finding[2] and complaints.

[5] Lit. 'from my debtor'.

[1] Lit. 'any man of a cheerful heart'.

[1] So SV: P om. 'the milk'. V has several significant divergences, both here and elsewhere, in this chapter.

[1] Reading ψαλτήρια for ψαλμούς: cp. Job xxi. 12 (LXX).
[2] So SV: P adds 'of the psalm, that is'.

XV. And every day, when the ministry of service was over, my
2 sons would have their dinner. And they would go to their eldest
3 brother's house to dine with him; and they would take with them
their three sisters and their attendant maidservants[1] (for when my
4 sons were at table they had male slaves waiting on them). And I
would get up early and offer sacrifices on their behalf according to
their number, three hundred pigeons, fifty he-goats, and twelve
5 sheep. All this, after what was needed for the actual sacrifices had
been set aside,[2] I would order to be got ready for the beggars; and I
would say to them, Take this, which is over and above what is
6 needed for the sacrifices,[3] so that you can pray for my children. It
may be that my sons have sinned in the Lord's sight by boasting,
7 saying superciliously, We are this rich man's children and these
8 goods are ours. Why then should we do service too? – because pride
9 is an abominable thing in the sight of God. And again would I offer
on God's altar a choice bullock, in case my sons had plotted evil in
their heart before God.

XVI.[1] And I had been doing this for seven years after the angel's
2 message to me. Then Satan, after he had been given authority, at
3 last came down without pity. He burned up the seven thousand
sheep appointed for the clothing of the widows and the three
thousand camels and the five hundred asses and the five hundred
4 yoke of oxen. All this he destroyed himself, since he had been given
5 authority to take action against me. And the rest of my beasts were
6 taken off by my fellow-countrymen. They had always been well
treated by me; but now they rose against me and took off my
7 remaining animals for themselves. And I was told about the loss of
my possessions; and I gave praise to God and did not blaspheme.

XVII. Then the Devil, when he saw my reaction,[1] contrived a plot

---

[1] Lit. 'and the things laid upon the maidservants'.
[2] Lit. 'after the arrangement'.
[3] Lit. 'which is superfluous after the arrangement'.

[1] V has a different (and shorter) text for this chapter.

[1] Lit. 'having come to know my heart'.

2 against me. He disguised himself as the king of the Persians, appeared before my city, and assembled all the rogues that were in
3 it. And he addressed them in a threatening manner and said, This man Jobab has squandered all the good things of the earth until there is nothing left, and he has shared them out among the needy,
4 the blind, and the lame. He has also destroyed the shrine of the great God and laid waste the place of libation, and for this I will bring retribution on him – for what he has done to the house of God. So get together, and despoil him yourselves of all his animals
5 and whatever else he has on earth. And they answered and said to him, He has seven sons and three daughters: suppose they flee for protection to other lands and lodge complaints against us for behaving like tyrants, and then, they might raise a force against us
6 and kill us. And he said to them, Have no fear at all: the greater part of his possessions I have already destroyed by fire, the rest I have taken from him, behold,[2] I will destroy[3] his children also.

XVIII. When he had said this, he went off and brought down the
2 house upon my children and killed them. My fellow-countrymen, when they saw that what he said had really happened, turned on me suddenly and drove me out and started to lay their hands on
3 everything in my house. I saw with my own eyes worthless and
4 disreputable men *sitting* at my tables and on my couches. And I was unable to utter a word, for I was exhausted like a woman in
5 labour, whose loins are weakened by the intensity of the pains. But I was especially mindful of what the Lord had foretold to me through his angel about the campaign *there was to be against me*, as well as the panegyrics *that were to follow*, about which he had spoken
6 to me too. And I became like someone who wants to go into a city to
7 see its wealth and inherit a part of its glory – like ⟨someone with⟩ a cargo on board a sea-going ship, who, when out in mid-ocean, sees the rising swell and adverse winds, and flings the cargo into the sea, saying, I am prepared to lose everything provided I can get
8 into this city to inherit better things than chattels and ship. In this way I thought of my possessions as nothing when compared with that city the angel had spoken to me about.

---

[2] So SV: P 'now'.
[3] So SV: P om. 'I will destroy'.

XIX. When the final messenger came and informed me of the loss
2 of my children, I was greatly distressed. And I rent my robe and
3 said to the man who brought the message, How was it then that
you escaped? And then, when I understood what had happened, I
cried out and said,

4 The Lord gave, the Lord has taken away:
As it pleased the Lord, so has it come to pass.
Blessed be the name of the Lord.

XX. So, when all that I had was lost, Satan realized that he could
2 not turn me into a mocker. And he went off and begged my body
3 from the Lord, so that he might strike me with diseases. Then the
Lord handed me over to him to do with my body as he would, but
4 over my life[1] he gave him no authority. And he came to me as I was
5 sitting on my throne, mourning the loss of my children. And he was
like a great hurricane and overturned my throne, and I spent
6 three hours in my throne, unable to get out.[2] And he struck me with
7 a cruel disease from head to foot. And in great agitation and
8 distress I went outside the city and sat on a dunghill. My body was
eaten by worms, and I drenched the earth with moisture: pus
9 streamed from me, and[3] many were the worms in my body. And if
ever a worm crawled out, I would pick it up and put it back[4] in the
same place, saying, Stay in the same place where you were put, till
instructions are given by him who gave you your orders.

XXI. And I spent forty-eight years on the dunghill outside the city,
2 diseased as I was. With my own eyes, my children, I saw my first
wife carrying water to some fine fellow's house like a maidservant,
3 so that she might get bread and bring it to me. And cut to the quick
I would say, O, the pretentious arrogance of the rulers of this city!
4 How can they treat my wife like a slave-girl? And then I would
resume my patient musings.

---

[1] Or 'soul'. Gk. ψυχή as in the LXX at Job ii. 6 for the Hebrew *nephesh*.
[2] So PS: V '. . . three hours lying on the ground'.
[3] So V (reading καὶ ἰχῶρες τόν σώματός μου ἔρρεον καί): PS om. ἔρρεον καί.
[4] So V: PS 'bring it near'.

XXII. And after eleven years they prevented even the bread from being brought to me, scarcely allowing my wife[1] to have her own
2 food. And when she got it, she would share it out between herself and me, saying in her grief, Woe is me! Soon there will not even be
3 bread for him to eat. And she had no hesitation in going out into the market-place to beg bread from the breadsellers, so as to bring it to me to eat.

XXIII. And Satan, when he heard about this, disguised himself as
2 a breadseller. And, quite by chance, my wife went to him and
3 asked for bread, thinking he was human. And Satan said to her,
4 Put down the purchase-money, and take what you want. She answered him and said, Where am I to get money from? Do you
5 not know about the evils that have come upon us? Have pity, if you
6 can: if not, then let it be.[1] And he answered her, saying, Had you
7 not deserved your ills, they would not have come upon you.[2] But now, if you have no money with you, leave the hair of your head with me as a pledge and take three loaves: maybe you will be able
8 to live *on them* for three days *more*. Then she thought, Well, what is the hair of my head to me compared with my hungry husband?
9 And so with scant respect for her hair, she said to him, Very well,[3]
10 take it. Then with a pair of scissors he cut her hair off and gave her
11 three loaves, publicly. She took them and came and brought them to me; and Satan followed her along the road, but so as she should not see him,[4] and led her heart astray.

XXIV. As soon as my wife came near me, she cried out, wailing, and said to me, Job, Job, how long will you go on sitting on the dunghill outside the city, thinking it will only be for a little while
2 longer, and waiting and hoping for your deliverance? As for me, I wander about from place to place, a vagabond serving-maid; and[1]

---

[1] Lit. 'allowing her'.

[1] Lit. 'but if not, see *to it* yourself'.
[2] Lit. 'you would not have received them'.
[3] Lit. 'Arise and'.　　　　[4] Lit. 'walking secretly'.

[1] P 'wherefore': SV 'for already' – cp. Job ii. 9 b (LXX).

your memorial has vanished from the earth – that is, the sons and daughters that I bore and endured the pains of labour for, all to no
3 purpose. You yourself sit stinking and infested with worms, and
4 you spend the night under the open sky. And I, again, utterly wretched, work by day and suffer at night to get bread to bring you.
5 For it is difficult enough now to get my own food,[2] and I share it out
6 between us; for I do not think it right that you should be racked
7 with pain and at the same time have nothing to eat. That is why I made up my mind to go out shamelessly into the market-place.
8 And when the breadseller said to me, Pay me the money and you
9 can take the bread,[3] I told him about our poverty. And I heard him say, If you have no money, woman, let me have the hair of your head, and take three loaves; maybe you will *be able to* live *on them* for
10 three days *more*. And I lost heart and said to him, Very well,[4] cut it off. And[5] so he got up and dishonoured me by cutting off my hair with a pair of scissors in the market-place, while a gaping crowd stood by.

XXV. *And they said,*

2 Who is not amazed that this is Sitidos, the wife of Job, she who used to have fourteen curtains to protect her sitting-room, and a door inside *the other* doors so that only someone who was of real importance could gain access to her?
3 Now she exchanges her hair for bread!
4 Her camels loaded with good things used to carry *them* abroad for beggars,
   Yet now she gives her hair in return for bread!
5 Lo! She who at home had seven tables that were never moved, at which the beggars and every stranger used to eat,
   Yet now she sells her hair for bread!
6 See! She who had a basin to wash her feet in, made of gold and silver,

---

[2] So (it seems) P: SV Slav. have a longer text.

[3] The text here is in considerable confusion. The MSS differ widely and several conjectural restorations have been proposed. Our translation is based on V, which offers a sense that is reasonably consecutive, even if not perfect.

[4] Lit. 'Arise and'.

[5] So SV Slav.: P om. 'Very well . . . And'.

But now she goes barefoot,[1] and even gives her hair in exchange for bread!

7 Lo! This is she who had clothing of fine linen embroidered with gold,

But now she is dressed in rags and gives her hair in exchange for bread!

8 See her that had gold and silver couches,

But is now selling her hair for bread!

9,10 Once for all, Job,[2] to cut a long story short,[3] I tell you straight, My will is broken and my strength is gone:[4] get up, take the loaves, and satisfy your hunger; and *then* curse[5] the Lord and die; and I, at least, shall be spared the exhaustion that comes from *my concern for* your body's pain.

XXVI. And I answered her, Lo, I have been afflicted by diseases for seventeen years, and I have submitted patiently to the worms in 2 my body. But I have never been so dispirited by the pains as by the 3 words you have just uttered, Curse[1] the Lord and die. This is a burden we both of us bear together – the loss of our children and possessions: would you have us now curse[1] the Lord and so deprive 4 ourselves of[2] the great wealth *that is to be*? Why is it you do not remember the great benefits we once enjoyed? If, then, we have received good at the Lord's hand, should we not also endure evil? 5 But let us be patient till the Lord is moved with pity and shows us 6 mercy. Do you not see the Devil standing behind you and turning what goes on in your mind upside down, so that he can lead me astray as well? For he wants to cast[3] you as one of those brainless women who subvert their own husbands' integrity.

---

[1] Lit. 'she treads the ground with *her* feet'.
[2] So SV Slav.: P 'Job, Job'.
[3] Lit. 'many things there are that have been said'.
[4] Lit. 'Because of the weakness of my heart my bones are broken'. In Hebrew 'bones' in the plural are not infrequently used for the whole personality: for the parallelism 'heart . . . bones' cp. Isa. lxvi. 14.
[5] Lit. 'speak a work against'.

[1] Lit. 'Speak a word against'.
[2] Lit. 'and so be alienated from'.
[3] Lit. 'show'.

XXVII   And I turned backwards towards Satan, who was behind
my wife, and I said, Come out into the open. Stop hiding yourself.
Does a lion display his strength in a cage? Does a bird fly away
2   when in a basket? Come out and do battle with me. Then he came
out from behind my wife and stood and lamented, saying, Lo, Job,
I am exhausted, and I give in to you, though you are human and I
am a spirit: you are smitten by disease, but I am in great distress *as*
3   *well*. For it is as if two athletes were wrestling,[1] and one threw the
other; and the one that was on top silenced the one underneath by
4   filling his mouth with sand and twisting his every limb. But the one
underneath bore it all with patient endurance, and did not give in[2],
5   and it was the one on top that *at last* shouted out *that he was beaten*. So
you too, Job, were underneath, and smitten by disease; but you
have overcome my wrestling tricks that I employed against you.
6,7   Then Satan went away from me in shame for three whole years. So
now, my children, you too must be patient whatever happens to
you; for patience is better than anything.

1,2   **XXVIII.**   And after I had been smitten for twenty years, the *neigh-
bouring* kings heard what had happened to me, and they set out and
came to me, each one from his own country, to visit me and console
3   me. When they were some distance off, they did not recognize me;
but they cried out aloud and lamented, and they rent their robes
4   and sprinkled themselves with earth. And they sat down by me for
seven days and seven nights, and not one of them said a word to
5   me. And it was not because they were being patient with me that
they waited without speaking: it was because they had known me
before these evils in my wealthy days, when I would display[1] to
them *my* precious stones, and they would look on with amazement
and clap their hands, and say, If all that we three kings possess
were brought together into a single place, there would be no

---

[1]   A free translation of an uncertain text.
[2]   Or 'and did not faint'. So SV: if we read without the negative, as in P, the sense
would seem to be 'though much weakened'. Again, the text in this verse is very
uncertain.

[1]   Lit. 'when I would begin to bring up'.

6 comparison with the splendid stones of your kingdom. For I was
7 the leading nobleman of the East. And when they came to *the land of*
Ausitis, they asked in the city, Where is Jobab, who is the king of all
8 Egypt?[2] And people told them about me, He is sitting on the
dunghill outside the city, for he has not come up inside the city for
9 twenty years. They asked again about my possessions and it was
explained to them what had happened to me.

XXIX. And when they heard *it*, they left the city in company with
2 the citizens, and my fellow-citizens pointed me out to them. But
3 they contradicted *them*, saying that I was not Jobab. While they
were still in open disputation, Eliphaz, the king of the Temanites,
4 turned towards me and said, Are you Jobab, our fellow-king? I
wept and sprinkled earth upon my head, and by nodding I made it
plain to them that I was.

XXX. And when they saw me nod my head, they fell to the ground
2 in a faint. And their armies were alarmed at the sight of the three
kings lying prostrate on the ground (*for they remained there* for three
3 hours, like corpses). Then they got up and said to one another, It is
4 he. And finally they sat for seven days, discussing my affairs,
reckoning up my cattle and possessions, *and* saying, We were
aware, were we not, of the many good things that were sent by him
to the villages and cities round about for distribution to the
beggars, besides what was given away[1] in his house? How is it that
he is now reduced to this corpse-like condition?

XXXI. After they had discussed the matter in this way for seven
days, Elihu[1] answered and said to his fellow-kings, Let us go closer
to him and examine him carefully to see whether it is really he or
2 not. Now they were about a hundred yards away, because of the
3 stench from my body. And they got up and came closer to me with

---

[2] So all MSS. Perhaps an early copyist's slip for 'Ausitis'. V adds 'and of this country'.

[1] So V: PS 'lying about'.

[1] So all MSS. See note at xxxiii. 1.

perfumes in their hands, while their soldiers, accompanying them, burned[2] incense all round me, so that they could come near me.

4,5 Three days they spent burning[3] incense. And when they came up to me, Elihu took up the tale[4] and said to me, Are you Jobab, our fellow-king? Are you the man who once was held in great esteem? Are you the man who was like the day's sun throughout the earth? Are you the man who was like the moon and the stars shining at

6,7 midnight? And I said to him, I am. And at this he raised a great

8 lament and lifted up his voice in a royal dirge, while the other kings and their armies made response.

XXXII. Hear, then, the lament of Elihu, declaring to his servants the wealth of Job:

2   You are the man who mustered the seven thousand sheep for
         the clothing of the beggars!
     Where then is the glory of your throne?
     You are the man who mustered the three thousand camels
         for the carriage of goods for the poor!
     Where then is the glory of your throne?

3   You are the man who mustered the three thousand cattle for
         the poor man's ploughing!
     Where then is the glory of your throne?

4   You are the man who had the golden couches, but are now
         sitting on a dunghill!
     Where now is the glory of your throne?

5   You are the man who had the throne of precious stones, but
         are now sitting in ashes![1]
     Where now is the glory of your throne?

6   For who was like you in the midst of your children? For you
         blossomed together like a fragrant apple-tree!
     Where now is the glory of your throne?

7   You are the man who established the sixty tables set apart for
         the beggars!
     Where now is the glory of your throne?

---

² Lit. 'threw'.   ³ Lit. 'supplying'.
⁴ Lit. 'answered'.

¹ So S (= ἐν σποδῷ): P 'in a roadway' (= ἐν ὁδῷ). V om. verses 5 and 6.

8   You are the man who had the censers for the sweet-smelling
       assembly,[2] but now you live in a stench!
       ⟨Where now is the glory of your throne?⟩[3]
9   You are the man who had the golden lamps upon the silver
       lampstands, but now you wait for the light of the moon!
       Where then is the glory of your throne?
10   You are the man who had the ointment *made with resin* from
       the frankincense-tree, but now you are in want.[4]
       Where then is the glory of your throne?
11   You are the man who laughed the wrong-doers and sinners
       to scorn, but now you *yourself* have become a jest!
       Where now is the glory of your throne?
12   You are Job, who had great glory!
       Where now is the glory of your throne?

XXXIII. Elihu[1] went on with his lament, and his fellow-kings made
2 response, so that there was a great disturbance. And when the
noise ceased, Job said to them, Silence!

       Now will I show you my throne,
       And *its* glory and *its* splendour that is among the saints.
3   My throne is in the realms above the world,
       And its glory and *its* splendour at the right hand of the
            Father.[2]
4   The whole world will pass away and its glory be destroyed,
       And those who are attached to it will perish with it;
5   But my throne is in the holy land,
       And its glory is in the world of changelessness.
6   The rivers will dry up,
       And the pride of their waves will go down to the depths of the
            abyss;
7   But the rivers of my land, where my throne is,

---

² So PS: V 'the censers for song *made* of *precious* stones'.
³ P omits this line altogether: SV insert it between '. . . assembly' and 'but now
. . .' above.
⁴ So PS (= ἐν ἀπορίᾳ): V 'in rottenness' (= ἐν σαπρίᾳ).

¹ So PS: V 'Eliphaz'. 'Eliphaz' would seem to be required all through chaps.
xxxi–xxxiii.   ² So P: S 'God'; V 'the Saviour'; Slav. 'the heavenly king'.

Do not dry up, nor will they disappear,
But they will last for ever.

8 These kings will pass away, and the leaders will pass on,
And their glory and *their* boast will be like *a reflection* in a
mirror.[3]

9 But my kingdom is for ever,
And *its* glory and its splendour are among the Father's
chariots.

XXXIV. And as I said this to them to silence them, Eliphaz said
angrily to his friends, What use is there in our having come to him
as we have, with our armies, to console him? Lo! he even casts
aspersions on us as well: let us, therefore, go back to our own lands.
He himself sits in misery, eaten by worms and smelling horribly,[1]
and yet he exalts himself against us – Kingdoms pass away and
their governments, he says, but my kingdom[2] will last for ever!
Much disturbed Eliphaz got up and turned away from them in
high dudgeon, saying, I am going; for we have come to console
him, and yet he has rebuffed us in the presence of our own soldiers.

XXXV. Then Bildad took hold of him, saying, You must not speak
like this to a man who is in mourning *for his children* and is suffering
under many other afflictions too. We are in the best of health, and
yet, because of the stench, we were not able to get near him without
the help of many perfumes. Have you forgotten altogether, Eliphaz,
what you were like when you were ill yourself for *only* two days. So
let us now be patient and try to find out[1] what his condition really
is. It may be, may it not, that his mind has gone? It may be, may it
not, that he remembers his former good fortune and has been
driven mad by it? For who would not be put out of his mind and
driven mad when beset with *such* plagues? But let me approach him
and try to find out what his condition is.

[3] So SV: P 'like a mirror'.

[1] Lit. 'in distress of worms and (in) stenches'.
[2] So SV Slav.: P 'and lo, ours'.

[1] So SV Slav.: P om. 'and try to find out'.

XXXVI. Then Bildad got up and approached me, saying, Are you
2 Job? And I said to him, Yes. And he said, Are you in your right
3 mind? And I said, My mind is not set on earthly things (for the
earth is transient and *so are* they that dwell on it), but my mind[1] is
set on heavenly things, because there is no disturbance in heaven.
4 Bildad answered and said, We know that the earth is transient,
since from time to time it changes: sometimes it is directed rightly,
and sometimes it is at peace, and then at other times it is at war.
5 But about heaven we hear that it enjoys tranquillity. If you are
6 really sane I will ask you a question. If you answer me sensibly to
begin with, I will ask you a second question. And if you answer me
satisfactorily *again*, we shall know for certain that your mind is in
no way impaired.

XXXVII. And again he said *to me*, In whom do you put your trust?[1]
2,3 And I said, In the living God. And again he said to me, Who took
4 away your possessions and brought these misfortunes on you? And
5 I said, God. And again he answered and said to me, So you put
your trust in God. **Was he not unjust** (**it is for you to judge**)[2] in
bringing these misfortunes on you or taking your possessions
6 away? If he gave and took away, he ought not to have given
anything at all – no king will ever humiliate his own soldier, his
trusty guardsman (though who is there that can ever comprehend
the depths *of the mysteries* of the Lord and of his wisdom?). Or should
7 we presume[3] to attribute injustice to the Lord? Answer me this,
8 Job. And again I say to you, If you are in your right mind, show *me*
(if you understand) how it is we see the sun rise in the east and set
in the west, yet when we get up again in the morning, we find the
same *sun* rising in the east? Explain this to me, if you are God's
servant.

XXXVIII. And to this I said, I do have understanding, and my
mind is sane enough. Why, then, should I not speak of the Lord's

[1] Lit. 'but it'.

[1] Or 'On what do you pin your hopes?'
[2] Following James: all MSS are corrupt.
[3] Lit. 'Or does anyone presume'.

mighty works? Should my mouth fail altogether in its duty to my
2 Master? God forbid! For who are we to pry into heavenly things,
3 seeing we are mortal and our portion dust and ashes? So, in order
to prove to you that I am sane, listen to a question I will put to you.
Food enters *the body* through the mouth, and through the same
mouth water too is drunk, and it passes down the same throat; but
when both go lower still,[1] they are separated from one another.
4,5 Who, then, makes the separation? Bildad said, I do not know. I
answered and said to him, If, then, you do not comprehend the
working of the body, how can you comprehend celestial things.
6 And Zophar, answering, said, We are not conducting an enquiry
into what is beyond our powers: what we want to know is whether
you are in your right mind; and in fact we have discovered that
7 your powers of thought have not deserted you. What, then, would
you have us do for you? For, see, **we have brought with us**[2] the
physicians of our three kingdoms. Will you be treated by them, and
8 so, perhaps, find relief? But I answered and said, My healing and
my treatment are from the Lord, who is the creator even of
physicians.

XXXIX. And as I was saying this to them, my wife Sitidos came in
2 her rags. She had run away from the master, to whom she was in
service, because she had been prevented from going out in case my
3 fellow-kings should see her and take her off. And when she came,
she flung herself at their feet, and she wailed and said, Do you
4 remember me, Eliphaz and your two friends? *Do you remember* what
I used to be like among you and how *gorgeously* I used to be arrayed?
5,6 But now, see how I am dressed when I go out! Then they set up a
great wailing, till they became doubly weary and grew silent.
7 Eliphaz took hold of his purple cloak to tear it off and throw it
8 round my wife. And she begged them saying, Bid your soldiers, I
ask you, to dig in the ruins of the house that collapsed over my
children, so that their bones may be preserved as a memorial *of*
9 *them*.[1] For we have not been able *to do it ourselves*[2] because of the

---

[1] Lit. 'go into the drain'.
[2] Following Brock's restoration: all MSS are corrupt.

[1] Or 'for a commemoration *of them*', or 'for a tomb'.
[2] may be preserved . . . able: so S(V) Slav.; P corrupt.

10 expense: we shall at least then be able to look upon their bones. Am I only a wild beast or have I the womb of a brute that my ten
11 children are dead, and not one of them have I buried? And they were going off to dig, but I restrained them, saying, Do not labour
12 in vain. You will not find my children, because they have been
13 taken up into heaven by their maker *and their* king. Then again they answered me and said, Who now will not say you are out of your mind and mad to say, My children have been taken up into heaven? Show us how this can be true.

XL. I answered and said to them, Lift me up, so that I can stand.
2 So they lifted me up and supported my arms on either side. And
3 then, standing up, I gave thanks to the Father.[1] And after my prayer I said to them, Lift up your eyes to the east and see my children with crowns *on their heads* beside the glory of the Heavenly
4 One. When my wife Sitidos saw *them*, she fell to the ground in worship and said, Now I know that I have a memorial with the Lord. I will get up and go into the city and shut my eyes a little and
5 refresh myself for my menial tasks. And she set off to the city, and she went into the byre where her own cattle were that had been
6 seized by the rulers whose slave she was. And beside a manger she
7 fell asleep and died content. The ruler, who owned her, searched
8 for her without success. In the evening he went into the cattle-byre
9 and found her prostrate corpse. All who saw her cried out, lowing and wailing over her,[2] and the noise was heard throughout the city.
,11 Then they rushed in to find out what had happened. And they found her dead, and the animals standing round and wailing for
12 her. So they carried her out and buried her; and they laid her in *the*
13 *ruins of* the house that had collapsed over her children. And the beggars in the city made a great lamentation, saying,

See! This is Sitidos, the wife to boast about and glory in!
She was not thought worthy of a proper burial!

14 And the dirge made over her you will find in the Paraleipomena.

---

[1] So P: S Slav. 'first (om. Slav.) to the Lord and to God'; V 'to God first'.
[2] Of this incident James wrote (*TS* V. i, p. c): 'The sense of the original . . . is I think this, that when the employer of Sitis found her dead in the stable, *all the beasts* cried out over her μετὰ μυκήματος κλαυθμοῦ: and the noise they made attracted the citizens, who rushed in and found her dead, and the beasts weeping over her'.

XLI. Eliphaz and the rest sat down beside me after this, arguing
2 and saying many fine things against me. After twenty seven days
3 they got up to go to their own country.[1] And then Elihu made them
swear an oath, saying, Stay with me till I have made things plain to
him, for you have spent far too many days listening patiently to
4 Job's boasting about his righteousness. For my part I will not put
up with it. For from the beginning I, like you,[2] have kept up the
lament for him, remembering his former good fortune; and he has
only used it for self-glorification. High-sounding and presump-
5 tious are his words, saying, he has his throne in heaven. But listen
6 to me, and I will show you that he has no portion *there*.[3] Then
Elihu, inspired by Satan, launched into a scurrilous attack upon
me, as is recorded in the Paraleipomena of Eliphaz.[4]

XLII. After he had ceased his fine words, the Lord appeared to me
2 and spoke through whirlwind and clouds. And he censured Elihu,
making it clear to me that he who had been speaking by him was
3 not a man but a beast. And while the Lord was speaking to me
through the cloud, the four kings also heard his voice as he spoke.
4 And after the Lord had finished speaking to me, he said to Eliphaz,
5 What now Eliphaz? You have sinned and your two friends *also*; for
6 you were wrong in what you said about my servant Job. So bestir
yourselves and get him to offer sacrifices on your behalf, that your
sin may be removed; for had it not been for him, I would have
7 destroyed you. And they brought me the materials for sacrifice.
8 And I took them and offered them on their behalf; and the Lord
accepted *the sacrifice* and forgave them their sin.

XLIII. Then Eliphaz, Bildad, and Zophar perceived that the Lord
had forgiven them their sin (though he had not deemed Elihu
2,3 worthy). And Eliphaz was inspired and sang a hymn. And his

---

[1] So PS: V has a much longer text in these first two verses, giving the substance of
the friends arguments against Job.
[2] Lit. 'I also'.
[3] So PS: V 'what his portion is'.
[4] So the MSS. Should we read 'Elihu'? Cp. note on xxxiii. 1.

other friends and the armies made response to him near the altar.

4   His hymm was this:[1]

> Banished are our sins, and buried is our wickedness.
5   Elihu, Elihu, the only wicked one, will have no memorial
>   among the living:
>   His lamp is quenched, its light has failed:[2]
6   The brilliance of his torch will turn to judgement on himself;
>   For he is the *child* of darkness and not of light,
>   And the door-keepers of darkness will inherit his glory and
>   *his* splendour.
7   His kingdom has passed away: his throne has crumbled into
>   dust;
>   And the honour of his dwelling-place[3] is in Hades.
8   He has loved the serpent's beauty and the dragon's scales:
>   Its venom and its poison shall be **his food**.[4]
9   Never has he sought the Lord's favour,[5] nor has he feared
>   him,
>   And even those who are honoured by him he has provoked.
10 The Lord has forgotten him, and the saints[6] have abandoned
>   him;
11 And anger and passion shall be his dwelling-place.[3]
12 He has no pity in his heart, nor peace in his **mouth**:[7]
>   The poison of asps he has on his tongue.
13 Righteous is the Lord: true are his judgements.
>   With him is no favouritism: he will judge us all alike.
14 Lo, the Lord is at hand: lo, the saints[6] have been made ready,
>   While crowns with panegyrics lead the way.
15 Let the saints[6] rejoice, let them be joyful in heart,
16 For they have obtained the glory for which they hoped.
17 Done away is our sin, cleansed is our wickedness.
>   But wicked Elihu has no memorial among the living.

---

[1] Lit. 'Thus Eliphaz spoke'.
[2] Lit. 'he (it) has put out its light'.
[3] Lit. 'tabernacle'.
[4] Reading εἰς βοράν: PSV Slav. εἰς βορράν ('to the north').
[5] Lit. 'He has not gained the Lord for himself'.
[6] Or 'holy ones' (i.e. 'angels').
[7] Reading ἐν τῷ στόματι αὐτοῦ: P ἐν τ. σώματι αὐ. ('in his body'); SV Slav. om.

XLIV. After Eliphaz had finished the hymn, while all made response to him and circled round the altar, we got up and went
2 into the city where we now have our home. And we held great festivities and took our delight in the Lord; and once again I did my
3 best to help the beggars. And all my friends came to me, and those
4 who knew *how* to do good.[1] And they asked me, saying, What do you ask of us now? And I, with the beggars in mind, to do them good again, asked *them* and said, Give me, each one of you, a lamb
5 to clothe the beggars' nakedness with. And then each of them brought me a lamb apiece and a tetradrachm of gold. And the Lord blessed everything I had and doubled it.

XLV. And now, see, my children, I am about to die. Never forget
2 the Lord. Do good to the beggars, *and* do not neglect the helpless.
3,4 *And* do not marry wives *that are daughters* of foreigners. And now, my children, I will divide[1] among you everything I have, so that each one of you may be in complete control of the portion that is his.[2]

XLVI. And they brought what was to be divided to the seven
2 boys.[1] And he set aside nothing from the property for the girls[2] *at all*. And they were hurt and said to their father, Our lord and father, are we not also your children? Why have you not given us a
3 share in your property? Job said to the girls,[2] Do not be distressed,
4 my daughters, for I have not forgotten you. In fact I have provided for you[3] an inheritance better than that of your seven brothers.
5 Then he motioned to his daughter called Hemera, and he said to her, Take this[4] ring and go to the strong-room and fetch the three
6 little golden urns, so that I may give you your inheritance. She
7 went away and fetched them. And he opened them and took out

---

¹ So P: SV 'those who knew that I was doing good'.

¹ Lit. 'Behold, therefore, my children, I divide'.
² With these words Job ends his personal testimony, and at the beginning of the next chapter the narrative, with which the work opened, is resumed. It appears from li. 4 that the narrator is Nereos, Job's brother.

¹ Lit. 'males'.   ² Lit. 'females'.
³ Lit. 'I sent to you'.   ⁴ Lit. 'the'.

three cords of many colours, such as no man could possibly
8 describe; for they were not of earth but of heaven, flashing with
9 sparks of fire like the rays of the sun. And he gave one cord each to
his daughters,[5] saying, Take them and gird them round you, that
they may keep you safe all the days of your life and fill you with
every good thing.[6]

XLVII. The other daughter, called Cassia, said to him, Father is
this the inheritance you were saying was better than our brothers'?
What is the use of these strange cords? How can we live on them?
2 And their father said to them, Not only will you be able to live on
3 them; but these cords will lead you to the greater world — to life in
4 the heavens. Surely, children, you cannot be unaware of the value
of these ropes? The Lord thought me worthy of them on the day
when he willed to have mercy on me and to cure my body of the
5 diseases and the worms. He called to me and supplied me with
these three cords, saying to me, Arise, gird up your loins like a
6 man: I will question you, and do you answer me. I took *the cords* and
girded myself; and immediately, from that very moment, the
worms disappeared from my body, and so too did the diseases.
7 And after that my body received strength through the Lord, as
8 though it had not suffered anything at all. And I even forgot my
9 distress of mind. And the Lord spoke to me in power, showing me
10 what has been and what will be. Consequently, my children, with
these *cords* you will never now have the Enemy arrayed against you
nor even his thoughts in your hearts, because it is the Father's[1]
11 amulet. Get up, then, and gird them round you before I die, so that
you may be able to see those who are coming for my soul and
marvel at God's creatures.

XLVIII. Accordingly, the one called Hemera got up and wound her
2 rope about her, just as her father had said. And she assumed
3 another heart, no longer minding earthly things. And she gave

[5] So SV: P om. 'each to his daughters'.
[6] So V: PS 'Take them about your breast, that it may be well (P om.) with you all
the days of your life'.

[1] So P: SV Slav. 'the Lord's'.

utterance in the speech of angels, sending up a hymn to God after the pattern of the angels' hymnody; and the Spirit let the hymns she uttered be recorded on her robe.

XLIX.   And then Cassia girded herself, and she *too* experienced a change of heart, so that she no longer gave thought to worldly

2 things. And her mouth took up the speech of the *heavenly* powers,

3 and she lauded the worship of the heavenly sanctuary.[1] So if anyone wants to know about the worship that goes on in heaven,[2] he can find it in the hymns of Cassia.

L.   And the remaining one, the one called Amaltheias-Keras, put on her girdle; and she *likewise* gave utterance with her mouth in the

2 speech of those on high. Her heart too was changed and withdrawn from worldly things; and she spoke in the language of the cherubim,

3 extolling the Lord of Virtues, and proclaiming their glory. Anyone who would pursue the Father's glory any further will find it set out in the prayers of Amaltheias-Keras.

1,2 **LI.**[1]   After the three had finished singing *their* hymns, I, Nereos,

3 Job's brother, sat down beside him as he lay *upon his bed*; and I listened to my brother's three daughters as they discussed together

4 the *heavenly* mysteries[2]. And I wrote down this book, except for the hymns and the signs of the word, for these are the mysteries[2] of God.

LII.   So Job lay[1] ill in bed, yet without pain and suffering, for pain

---

[1] Lit. 'she lauded the work of the High Place'.
[2] Lit. 'to know the work of the heavens'.

[1] The translation in this chapter follows V, which yields a reasonably consistent sense. P and S are both difficult and in varying degrees very evidently corrupt.
[2] Lit. 'the great things'.

[1] So V. P and S are corrupt and add 'And after three days' at the beginning (by dittography from the next verse).

was no longer able to affect him because of the sign of the girdle
2 that he wore. And after three days he saw the holy angels[2] who
3 came for his soul. And he got up immediately and took a lyre and
4 gave it to his daughter Hemera: to Cassia he gave a censer: to
5 Amaltheias-Keras he gave a tambourine; that they might give
6 praise to those who had come for his soul. And as they took them,
7 they saw the shining chariots which had come for his soul. And
8 they gave praise and honour, each in her special tongue. And after
9 this, he who sat in the great chariot got out and greeted Job (this
the three daughters saw, as did also their father, but no one else).
10 He took Job's soul, went off with it in his arms, and placed it in the
11 chariot and journeyed to the east. But Job's body was made ready
12 for burial and carried to the grave. His three daughters led the
way, with their girdles round them, singing hymns of praise to the
Father.[3]

LIII. And I Nereos, his brother, and the seven boys,[1] together with
2 the poor and orphans and all the helpless, made lamentation. And
they said, Woe to us to-day, double woe, for to-day the strength of
3 the helpless has been taken away, the light of the blind has been
taken away, the father of the orphans has been taken away, he who
received strangers has been taken away, he who clothed the
4 widows[2] has been taken away. Who, then, will not mourn for the
5 man of God? No sooner had they brought the body near the grave
than all the widows and orphans gathered round and prevented his
6 being put in it.[3] But after three days they laid him in the grave,

---

[2] So V: PS om. 'the holy angels'.
[3] So P (lit. 'singing praise in hymns of the Father'): SV Slav. 'singing praise to God in hymns'.

[1] Lit. 'male children'.
[2] Lit. 'the clothing of the widows'. So P: the other MSS have some additional clauses in the catalogue.   [3] Lit. 'in the grave'.

sleeping peacefully as he was, having won for himself a name to be honoured in every succeeding generation. Amen.[4]

[4] So P Slav.: SV om. 'Amen'. Then S Slav. adds:

'And Job lived after the plague (Slav. + 'and his sufferings') one hundred and seventy years, and the whole span of his life *was* two hundred and forty-eight years. And he saw his children's children (Slav. 'children and grandchildren and great grandchildren') *to the* fourth (Slav. 'third') generation'.

V adds:

'He left seven sons and three daughters; and there were not found under heaven any fairer than Job's daughters. Job was formerly named Jobab; but his name was changed to Job by the Lord. He lived before the plague for eighty-five years; and after the plague he received double of all things, including also his years, one hundred and seventy. So he lived altogether two hundred and forty-eight years. And he saw his children's children to the fourth generation. It is written also that he rose with those whom the Lord raised. To God be glory'.

THE PSALMS OF SOLOMON

INTRODUCTION

The Psalms of Solomon are neither quoted nor referred to explicitly by any of the Fathers. The earliest mention of them is in the catalogue of contents in the *Codex Alexandrinus* of the Bible in the British Library (5th cent.) where 'eighteen Psalms of Solomon' are listed right at the end, after the two Epistles of Clement, which in turn follow the 'Apocalypse of John'. Presumably *Alexandrinus* contained a text of the Psalms, but it does so no longer: its last leaves have been lost, and the text breaks off rather more than half-way through 2 Clement. Later on, the Psalms occur in the List of Sixty Books, as also in the pseudo-Athanasian Synopsis and the Stichometry of Nicephorus. In the last two, however, they are joined together with the Odes – 'Psalms and Ode(s) of Solomon'. They are not mentioned in the Gelasian Decree.

The text of the Psalms is preserved in some ten Greek manuscripts (two of them defective), one Greek fragment (consisting of xvii. 2–xviii. 14),[1] and also in two defective Syriac manuscripts and two Syriac fragments (both, oddly enough, containing xvi. 6–13). The Greek MSS date from the late 10th or early 11th cent. to the early 15th, and in all of them the Psalms appear as one among a number of other works, some Biblical and some ecclesiastical. In the two Syriac MSS, however, the Psalms are preceded by the Odes, but there is no distinction between them: the Psalms follow immediately on the Odes without a break: all are given the title 'Psalms'; and they are numbered consecutively from the beginning of the Odes – thus, Psalm i in our numeration becomes Psalm xliii in the Syriac, and so on up to lx. Neither Syriac MS contains any other work. One of them (Rylands Cod. Syr. 9; 16th cent.) is deficient at the beginning of the Odes and also from Ps. xvii. 38 to the end: the other (B.L. Addit. 14538; 9th or 10th

---

[1] See W. Baars, 'A New Fragment of the Greek Version of the Psalms of Solomon' in *VT* xi (1961), pp. 441–444.

cent.) contains only Odes xvii. 7–xlii. 20 and Pss. i.i–iii. 5 and x. 4–xviii. 5.

The combination of Odes and Psalms in a single series known as 'Psalms' in the Syriac tradition raises the question, Was this a peculiarity of the Syriac-speaking church or was it also known elsewhere? As we have seen, both the pseudo-Athanasian Synopsis and the Stichometry of Nicephorus list the 'Psalms and Ode(s) of Solomon' together. It is possible that there is evidence here that the Psalms and Odes were combined in some Greek MSS – though in the reverse order, it would seem, from the order in the Syriac. It is possible, too, that when *Alexandrinus* and the List of Sixty Books mention the 'Psalms' only they are referring to a similar combination.[2] But all this is mere hypothesis. The facts are that only ten Greek MSS of the Psalms are known, all of which have preserved the Psalms without the Odes; and these, together with the Syriac, are the only evidence there is for the text of the Psalms.

It is now generally agreed that the Psalms were originally written in Hebrew. The Greek will accordingly be a version from the Hebrew. It has been suggested that the Syriac is also a version from the Hebrew; but this suggestion has found few supporters, and most regard the Syriac as a secondary version made from the Greek.

There are no obviously Christian passages in the Psalms nor any that look as if they had been worked over by Christian editors. The Psalms are Jewish through and through and breathe the atmosphere of the canonical Psalms of David, in conscious imitation of which they were doubtless written.

The writer himself belongs to the circle of 'the righteous' (iii. 3–8), or God's 'holy ones' (ix. 3), or 'those who fear the Lord' (xv. 13), as against their opponents 'the unrighteous' (xv. 4–13), or 'sinners' (ii. 34–35), or 'lawless ones' (xiv. 6). These latter are charged, not merely with general misbehaviour, immorality, and ungodliness (e.g. iv. 1–22), but specifically with having set up a non-Davidic monarchy (xvii. 4–6) and with having profaned the Temple and its sacrifices (ii. 3; viii. 11–12). The writer and his

---

[2] Though this is most unlikely in the case of *Alexandrinus*, since the text, as it stands, refers explicitly to 'eighteen' Psalms.

circle abhor such lawless deeds (xii. 1–4): they pride themselves that they 'walk in the righteousness of [God's] ordinances, in the law which he commanded' (xiv. 2); and they await in patience the advent of the legitimate Davidic Messianic King (xvii. 21–35: cp. xviii. 5–9).

It is not difficult to see here a reflection of the opposition between the Pharasaic and Sadducaean parties sometime during the first century BC. References to a foreign conqueror in three of the Psalms enable us to fix the date of these three, at least, more exactly. The foreign conqueror came 'from the end of the earth' (viii. 15) and sent off his captives 'to the west' (xvii. 12) – so from the west he presumably came. At first he was welcomed by some of the nation, and the way was left open for him to approach Jerusalem (viii. 16–18). Later, it seems, he encountered resistance and used battering-rams to breach the walls (ii. i). Having captured Jerusalem, he was responsible for a general massacre (viii. 19–21) and introduced his soldiers into the Temple where they contemptuously 'trampled' the altar (ii. 2). Ultimately he was murdered in Egypt, and his body lay exposed for lack of burial (ii. 26–27). These details correspond very closely with what is recorded elsewhere of the details of Pompey's capture of Jerusalem in 63 BC and his death in Egypt in 48 BC.

Whether the Psalms were all the work of a single author or not we have no means of knowing. Nor can we tell how close in date the other Psalms are to the three which refer to Pompey. Many moderns think of a 'school' as having produced the Psalms rather than a single author, and most would connect it with the Pharisees – hence the popular (but quite unofficial) title 'Psalms of the Pharisees'. Some, however, would dispute this connection, partly on the ground that the Psalms themselves provide only the most general evidence for it, and partly on the ground that we know as yet far too little about the various movements and parties within Judaism in the 1st cent. BC to make certainty possible – in particular, it seems likely that there was in fact a much greater variety in the groupings and factions at the time than the conventional Pharisee–Sadducee–Essene categorization suggests (in which case the authors of the Psalms may well have belonged to one of these otherwise 'unknown' groups).

But in any case, there is no need to suppose that all the Psalms were written at once. Schüpphaus, for example, has maintained that two separate 'clusters' of Psalms can be identified, which, he claimed, represent two separate stages in the development of a single community (though it was for Schüpphaus a Pharisaic community): one cluster stems from the time of the Roman invasion in 63 BC, the other from somewhere between 48 and 43/2 BC.

On any hypothesis, however, the Psalms are patently Palestinian; and the probability is that they were written in Jerusalem.

The translation which follows is based on Gray's. The verse numeration is that of von Gebhardt (with Gray's numeration in brackets).

BIBLIOGRAPHY

EDITIONS

Greek

H. E. RYLE and M. R. JAMES Ψαλμοὶ Σολομῶντος: *Psalms of the Pharisees, commonly called The Psalms of Solomon. The Text newly revised from all the MSS, Edited with Introduction, English Translation, Notes, Appendix, and Indices* (Cambridge, 1891).

O. VON GEBHARDT, Ψαλμοὶ Σολομῶντος: *Die Psalmen Salomo's zum ersten Male mit Benutzung der Athoshandschriften und des Codex Casanatensis herausgegeben* (= *TU* xiii. 2; Leipzig, 1895).

J. VITEAU and F. MARTIN, *Les Psaumes de Salomon. Introduction, texte grec et traduction . . . avec les principales variantes de la version syriaque* (= *Documents pour l'étude de la Bible*; Paris, 1911).

H. B. SWETE, *The Old Testament in Greek*[4], iii (Cambridge, 1912), pp. 765–787.

——, *The Psalms of Solomon with the Greek Fragments of the Book of Enoch* (Cambridge, 1899), pp. 1–23. [Reprinted from the above.]

A. RAHLFS, *Septuaginta*[5], ii (Stuttgart, 1952), pp. 471–489.

Syriac

J. RENDEL HARRIS, *The Odes and Psalms of Solomon, now first published from the Syriac version* (Cambridge, 1909; 2nd ed. 1911).

J. RENDEL HARRIS and A. MINGANA, *The Odes and Psalms of Solomon, re-edited for the Governors of the John Rylands Library*. Vol. i: *The Text with Facsimile Reproductions* (Manchester, 1916).

W. BAARS, *Peshiṭta*, Part IV, fasc. 6 (Leiden, 1972), pp. i–vi, 1–27.

TRANSLATIONS

English

H. E. RYLE and M. R. JAMES, Ψαλμοὶ Σολ. . . . [as above].

G. B. GRAY in R. H. CHARLES, *APOT* ii, pp. 625–652.

J. RENDEL HARRIS, *The Odes and Psalms of Solomon, now first published from the Syriac version* (Cambridge, 1909; 2nd ed. 1911).

J. RENDEL HARRIS and A. MINGANA, *The Odes and Psalms of Solomon, re-edited for the Governors of the John Rylands Library*. Vol. ii: *The Translation with Introduction and Notes* (Manchester, 1920) . . . [from the Syriac].

French

J. VITEAU and F. MARTIN, . . . [as above].

German

A. HILGENFELD, 'Die Psalmen Salomo's, deutsch übersetzt und auf Neue untersucht' in *Zeitschrift für wissenschaftliche Theologie* (Leipzig, 1871), pp. 383–418.

R. KITTEL in E. KAUTZSCH, *APAT* ii (Tübingen, 1900), pp. 127–148.

P. RIESSLER, *AjSaB*², pp. 881–902.

S. HOLM-NIELSEN in *JSh-rZ* IV. 2 (1977), pp. 49–112.

GENERAL

J. BEGRICH, 'Der Text der Psalmen Salomos' in *ZNW* xxxviii (1939), pp. 131–164.

A.-M. DENIS, *IPGAT*, pp. 60–64.

O. EISSFELDT, *OTI*, pp. 610–613.

W. FRANKENBERG, *Die Datierung der Psalmen Salomos* (= *Beihefte zur ZAW*, i; Giessen, 1896).

J.-B. FREY, art. 'Apocryphes de l'Ancien Testament' in *DBSup* i, cols. 390–396.

K. G. KUHN, *Die älteste Textgestalt der Psalmen Salomos, inbesondere auf Grund der syrischen Übersetzung neu untersucht* (= *Beiträge zur Wissenschaft vom Alten und Neuen Testament*, IV. Folge, 21. Heft; Stuttgart, 1937).

J. O'DELL, 'The Religious Background of the Psalms of Solomon (Re-evaluated in the light of the Qumran Texts)' in *Revue de Qumran*, III. 2 (1961–1962), pp. 241–257.

P. RIESSLER, *AjSaB²*, pp. 1322–1323.

L. ROST, *EATAP*, pp. 89–91.

J. SCHÜPPHAUS, *Die Psalmen Salomos: Ein Zeugnis jerusalemer Theologie und Frömmigkeit in der Mitte des vorchristlichen Jahrhunderts* (= *ALGhJ* 7; Leiden, 1977).

E. SCHÜRER, *HJPTJC* II. iii, pp. 17–23.

——, *GjVZJC*⁴ iii, pp. 205–212.

C. C. TORREY, *AL*, pp. 106–108.

C. H. TOY, art. 'Psalms of Solomon, The' 'in *JE* x. (New York, 1905), pp. 250–251.

R. B. WRIGHT, 'The Psalms of Solomon, the Pharisees and the Essenes' in *SCS* 2 (ed. R. A. KRAFT; Missoula, 1972), pp. 136–154.

I

1   I[1] cried to the Lord in my utter affliction,
    To God when sinners assailed.

2   Suddenly there was heard the clamour of war before me:
    I said, He will listen to me, for I am full of righteousness.

3   I considered in my heart that I was full of righteousness
    When I prospered and was rich in children;

4   Their wealth was spread over the whole earth,
    Their glory reached the extremity of the earth.

5   They were raised up to the stars:
    Men said, They will never fall.

6   But they became insolent in their prosperity,
    And have no understanding.[2]

---

[1] Jerusalem is speaking.
[2] So Syr.: Gk. has 'and they brought not (καὶ οὐκ ἤνεγκαν)', which may be a corruption of καὶ οὐκ ἔγνωκαν, presupposed by Syr.

7   Their sins were in secret,
      And I knew *it* not.

8   Their lawless deeds *went* beyond those of the heathen before
      them;
      They utterly profaned the sanctuary³ of the Lord.

II

A Psalm.   Of Solomon.   Concerning Jerusalem.

1   When the sinner became proud he cast down fortified walls
      with a battering-ram,
      And thou didst not restrain *him*.

2   Foreign nations went up to thine altar,
      In pride they trampled *it* with their sandals;

3   Because the sons of Jerusalem had defiled the sanctuary¹ of
      the Lord,
      Had profaned the offerings to God with lawless deeds.

4   Wherefore he said, Cast them far from me,
      I take no pleasure in them.²

5   *Her*³ glorious beauty was held of no account before God,
      It was utterly dishonoured.

6   *Her* sons and *her* daughters were in grievous captivity,
      Their neck bears a seal-ring, a mark⁴ among the nations:

7   He dealt with them in accordance with their sins;

---

³ Lit. 'holy things'.

¹ Lit. 'holy things'.

² Following Hilgenfeld's emendation (οὐκ εὐδοκῶ ἐν αὐτοῖς for οὐκ εὐώδωκεν
αὐτοῖς in the MSS). If the reading (and punctuation) of the MSS be followed, verses
4–5 will run:
      'Wherefore he said, Cast them far from me.
        Her glorious beauty did not prosper them,
      It was held of no account before God,
        It was utterly dishonoured'.

³ i.e. Jerusalem's (cp. verse 20). So M: others 'his'.

⁴ Lit. 'Their neck in (with) a seal, in (with) a mark . . .'. Prisoners had a thong or
rope around their necks, fastened with a seal.

For he abandoned them into the hands of those who
prevail.

8 He turned away his face from pitying them,
Young and old and their children together;

9 For they did evil together in not listening.

9 (10) And heaven abhorred *them* and the earth detested them,

(11) For no man upon it had done what they did.

10 (12) And the earth shall recognise all thy righteous judgements,
O God.

11 (13) They set the sons of Jerusalem to be mocked because of the
harlots in her:
Every passer by entered in in the full light of day.

12 (14) They used to make mock with their lawless deeds, as they
themselves used to do:
In the full light of day they paraded their iniquities.

13 And the daughters of Jerusalem were profane according to
thy judgement,

(15) Because they had defiled themselves in unnatural
intercourse.

14 I am pained in my bowels and my inward parts at these
things.

15 (16) I will justify thee, O God, in uprightness of heart,
For in thy judgements *lies* thy righteousness, O God.

16 (17) For thou hast rendered to the sinners according to their
deeds,
And according to their sins, *which were* very wicked.

17 (18) Thou hast uncovered their sins, that thy judgement might be
manifest:

(19) Thou hast blotted out the memory of them from the earth.

18 God is a righteous judge, and will respect no one.

19 (20) For the nations reviled Jerusalem, trampling it down:
Her beauty was dragged down from the throne of glory.

20 (21) She girded on sackcloth instead of fine raiment,
A rope about her head in place of a crown.

21 (22) She removed the diadem of glory which God had set upon
her:

(23) In dishonour was her beauty cast upon the ground.

22 (24) And I saw, and entreated the Lord and said,

Long enough, Lord, hath thy hand been heavy on Jerusalem
with the onset of the nations.

23 (25) For they have mocked, and spared not, in wrath and
implacable anger;

(26)   For they[5] will be utterly destroyed, unless thou, Lord,
rebuke them in thy wrath.

24 (27) For it was not out of zeal that they acted, but in lust of soul,

(28)   So as to pour out their wrath upon us in plunder.

25 (29) Delay not, O God, to bring recompense upon their heads,
To **change**[6] the pride of the dragon into dishonour.

26 (30) And I did not wait long before God showed me his **body**,[7]
Stabbed, on the mountains of Egypt,
Esteemed of less account than the least on land and sea –

27 (31) His body, carried about on the waves in great ignominy,
With none to bury *him*, because he[8] had rejected him in
dishonour.

28   He did not consider that he was man,

(32)   Nor did he consider the end.

29 (33) He said, I will be lord of land and sea;
And he did not recognise that God is great,
Mighty in his great strength.

30 (34) He is king in the heavens,
And judges kings and dominions.

31 (35) It is he who raises me up to glory,
And lays low the proud in eternal destruction, in
dishonour,
Because they knew him not.

32 (36) And now behold, princes of the earth, the judgement of the
Lord,
For he is a great king, and righteous, judging *the earth* that
is under heaven.

---

[5] i.e. the people of Jerusalem. The passive in the Gk. may, however, rest on a mistranslation.

[6] Gk. 'say', due to a misinterpretation of an underlying Heb. *lmr* (for *lhmr*), taken as *l'mr*.

[7] Gk. 'his insolence', due to a misinterpretation of an underlying Heb. *gwtw* (for *gwytw*), taken as *g'wtw*. The allusion is in all probability to the details of the assassination of Pompey in the neighbourhood of Mount Cassius, near Pelusium in Egypt, in 48 BC.

[8] i.e. God.

33 (37) Bless God, you who fear the Lord with understanding,
>   For the mercy of the Lord is on those who fear him, in
>   judgement;

34 (38) So as to distinguish between righteous and sinner,
>   To recompense sinners for ever according to their deeds;

35 (39) And to have mercy on the righteous, *delivering him* from the
>   affliction of the sinner,
>   And to recompense the sinner for what he has done to the
>   righteous.

36 (40) For the Lord is good to those who call on him in patience,
>   Acting according to his mercy towards his holy ones,
>   Setting *them* continuously before him in strength.

37 (41) Blessed *be* the Lord for ever before his servants.

III

A Psalm.   Of Solomon.   Concerning the Righteous.

1   Why do you sleep, *my* soul, and *why do you* not bless the Lord?

1 (2)   Sing a new song to God who is worthy of praise.

2   Sing and be wakeful in vigilance for him,
>   For pleasing to God is a psalm from a glad heart.

3 (3)   The righteous remember the Lord continually,
>   With thanksgiving and justification, the Lord's
>   judgements.

4 (4)   The righteous *man* will not be heedless when chastened by
>   the Lord,
>   His good pleasure is always before the Lord.

5 (5)   The righteous *man* stumbled, and *yet* held the Lord righteous;
>   He fell, and watches what God will do for him,

(6)   He gazes eagerly *towards the source* whence his deliverance
>   will come.

6 (7)   The steadfastness of the righteous is from God their saviour.
>   In the righteous *man's* house sin has no permanent
>   lodging[1]:

---

[1] Lit. 'In the righteous *man's* house there does not lodge sin upon sin': cp. verse
10(12).

7 (8)　The righteous *man* continually searches his house,
　　　　So as to remove unrighteousness arising from unwitting
　　　　　sin.

8 (9)　He made atonement for *sins of* ignorance by fasting and
　　　　　affliction of his soul;

　(10)　And the Lord purifies every man that is holy together with
　　　　　his house.

9 (11)　The sinner stumbled, and he curses his life,
　　　　The day of his birth, and *his* mother's travail.

10 (12)　He has added sins to sins in his lifetime.

　(13)　He fell – how[2] grievous his fall! And he shall not rise up.

11　　　The destruction of the sinner is for ever,

　(14)　And *God*[3] will not remember him when he visits the
　　　　　righteous.

12 (15)　This is the portion of sinners for ever;

　(16)　But they that fear the Lord shall rise to life eternal,
　　　　And their life *shall be* in the light of the Lord, and shall
　　　　　come to an end no more.

IV

Conversation of Solomon with the men-pleasers.

1　　　Why do you sit, godless man, in the council of the holy,
　　　　When[1] your heart is far removed from the Lord,
　　　　Provoking with transgressions the God of Israel?

2　　　Extravagant in speech, extravagant in appearance above all
　　　　　men,
　　　　Is the man severe in speech when he condemns sinners in
　　　　　judgement.

3　　　And his hand is first upon him as *if* in zeal,
　　　　While[1] he is himself guilty of manifold sins and of
　　　　　intemperance.

[2] Gk. 'because': the underlying Heb. *ky*, however, was probably exclamatory.
[3] Gk. 'he'.

[1] Gk. 'and'.

4   His eyes are upon every woman without discrimination;
        His tongue is lying when he makes a contract with an oath.

5   At night and in secret he sins as if he were not seen:
        With his eyes he speaks to every woman in evil agreement:

5 (6)   He is quick to enter every house cheerfully as though
            without guile.

6 (7)   May God destroy those who live in hypocrisy in the company
            of the holy:
        With corruption of his flesh and with penury *may God
        destroy* his life.

7 (8)   May God reveal the works of the men-pleasers:
        With mockery and derision *may God reveal* his works.

8 (9)   And may the holy vindicate the judgement of their God,
        When sinners are destroyed from the presence of the
            righteous –

  (10) The man-pleaser who proclaims the law[2] with deceit.

9 (11) And their eyes are upon the house of the man *who is* in
            security,
        That like a serpent they may destroy each other's[3] wisdom
            with transgressors' words.

10 (12) His words are deceptions for the accomplishment of an
            unrighteous desire:

  (13) He did not cease until he had succeeded in scattering
            families as *if* in bereavement:

11   He laid waste a house for the sake of a lawless desire.

  (14) He deceived with words, *saying*, There is no one who sees and
            judges.

12 (15) At this he was filled with lawlessness,
        And his eyes *turned* to another house,
        To destroy *it* with high-flown words;

13   *Yet* his soul, like Sheol, is not sated with all these.

14 (16) May his portion, Lord, be dishonoured before thee;
        May he go forth groaning, and return home cursed.

15 (17) May his life be *spent* in anguish and penury and want, O
            Lord:

[2] Lit. 'who speaks law'.
[3] each other's: so the Gk., but probably corrupt, though no satisfactory suggestion has been put forward.

16 (18)   May his sleep be *beset* with grief, and his waking with
                anxiety.
            May sleep be taken from his eyelids at night:
            May he fail dishonourably in every work he undertakes.[4]

17 (19) May he enter his house empty-handed,
            And may his house be void of everything wherewith to
                satisfy his appetite.

18 (20) May his old age right up to his death[5] *be spent* in loneliness
            without children.

19 (21) May the flesh of the men-pleasers be torn apart by wild
                beasts,
            And may the bones of the lawless *lie* dishonoured in the
                sight of the sun.

20 (22) May ravens pluck out the eys of hypocrites,
    (23)   For they have laid waste many houses of men
                dishonourably,
            And have scattered *them* in *their* lust;

21 (24) And they were not mindful of God,
            Nor did they fear God in all these things;
    (25)   And they provoked and aroused God's anger.

22   May he destroy them from the earth,
            Because with deceit they have beguiled the souls of the
                innocent.

23 (26) Blessed are those who fear the Lord in their innocence:
    (27)   The Lord will deliver them from deceitful men and
                sinners,
            And he will deliver us from every snare of the lawless.

24 (28) May God destroy those who insolently work every kind of
            unrighteousness,
            For a great judge, and mighty, is the Lord our God in
                righteousness.

25 (28) May thy mercy, Lord, be upon all those who love thee.

---

[4] Lit. 'work of his hands'.
[5] Lit. 'to his being taken up' (cp. Luke ix. 51).

V

A Psalm.   Of Solomon.

1   O Lord God, I will praise thy name with joy,
    In the midst of those who have knowledge of thy righteous
      judgements.

2   For thou art good and merciful, the refuge of the poor:

2 (3)   When I cry unto thee, do not disregard me in silence.

3 (4)   For no one will take spoil from a mighty man;

  (5)   And who shall take of all that thou hast made, unless thou
      thyself give it?

4 (6)   For man and his portion *lie* before thee in the balance:
    He cannot make increase beyond what is prescribed by
      thee,[1] O God.

5 (7)   When we are afflicted we will call upon thee for help,
    And thou wilt not turn back our prayer,
    Because thou art our God.

6 (8)   Make not thy hand heavy upon us,
    Lest, from distress,[2] we sin.

7 (9)   And if thou dost not restore us, *yet* we will not keep away,
    But unto thee will we come.

8 (10)   For if I hunger, I will cry unto thee, O God;
    And thou wilt give to me.

9 (11)   Thou dost feed the birds and the fish,
    When thou givest rain to the steppes that green grass may
      spring up,

10   So as to provide[3] fodder on the steppe for every living
      thing;

  (12)   And if they hunger, they lift their face to thee.

11 (13)   Kings and rulers and peoples dost thou nourish, O God,
    And who is the hope of the poor and the needy, unless it be
      thou, Lord?

12 (14)   And thou wilt listen (for who is good and kind but thou?),

---

[1] Lit. 'beyond thy judgement'.

[2] Or 'under restraint'.

[3] So the MSS. Von Gebhardt conjectured 'Thou hast provided'.

Making glad the soul of the humble by opening thy hand
in mercy?

13 (15) Man's goodness is grudging and . . .;[4]

And if he repeat *it* without murmuring, that too is marvellous.

14 (16) But thy gift is great in goodness and generous;

And he whose hope is in thee will not be sparing in giving.

15 (17) Thy mercy, Lord, is upon the whole earth, in goodness.

16 (18) Happy is the man whom God remembers and supplies with
what he needs in moderation.[5]

(19) If man has an excess, *then* he sins.

17 (20) Sufficient are moderate means with righteousness,

And in this the blessing of the Lord becomes abundance
with righteousness.

18 (21) **May** those that fear the Lord **rejoice**[6] in prosperity,

And *let* thy goodness *be* upon Israel in thy kingdom.

19 Blessed *is* the glory of the Lord, for he *is* our king.

VI

In Hope. Of Solomon.

1 Happy the man whose heart is set to call upon the name of
the Lord;

2 When he makes mention of the name of the Lord, he will
be saved.

2 (3) His ways are guided by the Lord,

And the works of his hands are protected by the Lord his
God.

3 (4) His soul will not be disturbed with the sight of evil dreams:

(5) When he crosses rivers, and when the seas toss, he will not
be dismayed.

4 (6) He arose from his sleep and blessed the name of the Lord:

---

[4] Gk. 'and the morrow' (similarly Syr., expanded), which cannot be right.
Possibly the underlying Heb. was *bmḥr* ('at a price').

[5] Lit. 'remembers in due proportion of sufficiency'.

[6] May . . . rejoice: MSS 'rejoiced'.

(7) In peacefulness of heart he sang to the name of his God;
5 And he entreated the Lord for all his household.

(8) And the Lord hears[1] the prayer of everyone *who is* in fear of God:

The Lord grants every request of the soul that hopes upon him.

(9) Blessed *is* the Lord who acts mercifully to those who love him in truth.

VII

Of Solomon. Of turning.[1]

1 Remove not thy habitation from us, O God,
Lest those that hate us without cause assail us.

2 For thou hast rejected them, O God:
Let not their foot trample upon thy holy inheritance.

3 Do thou chasten us in thy good pleasure;
Yet give *us* not over to the nations.

4 For if thou sendest death,
Thou thyself givest it charge concerning us;

5 For thou art merciful,
And wilt not be angry and destroy us utterly.

6 (5) While thy name dwells in our midst, we shall find mercy,

(6) And no nation will prevail against us;

7 For thou art our protector,

(7) And we shall call upon thee, and thou wilt hear us;

8 (8) For thou wilt pity the race of Israel for ever,
And wilt not reject *us*;

9 And we *shall be* under thy yoke for ever,
And under the lash of thy chastening.

10 (9) Thou wilt guide us in the time that thou helpest us,
Showing mercy to the house of Jacob on the day thou didst promise them.

---

[1] Lit. 'heard'.

[1] The Gk. could mean 'conversion' or 'restoration'. Neither, however, is very suitable in the light of the contents of the psalm itself.

VIII

Of Solomon. For victory.

1 Distress and the sound of war has my ear heard,
    The noise of the trumpet sounding out slaughter and
      destruction,

2 The sound of much people as of a great and howling wind,[1]
    As a hurricane with mighty fire sweeping through the
      wilderness.

3 And I said in my heart, Where, then, will God's judgement
      be?[2]

4 I heard the sound at Jerusalem, the holy city:

4 (5) My loins were broken at hearing *it*,

5 (6) My knees tottered, my heart was afraid,
    My bones were shaken like flax.

6 (7) I said, They establish their ways in righteousness.

7 I considered the judgements of God since the creation of
      heaven and earth:
    I held God righteous in his judgements which have been
      from of old.

8 (8) God laid open their sins to the sun,
    All the earth came to know the righteous judgements of
      God.

9 (9) In hidden places beneath the earth *were* their iniquities
      performed in provocation:

 (10) They committed incest, son with mother, and father with
      daughter;

10 (11) They committed adultery, every man with his neighbour's
      wife.
    They made agreements under oath with one another
      concerning these things.

---

[1] Lit. 'of an exceedingly great wind'.

[2] Lit. 'Where, then, will God judge him?' – i.e. Israel. It is possible, however, that through a simple misunderstanding on the part of the Gk. translator, two pronouns have been confused – hence the suggested emendation, 'Where, then, will God judge **us**?'

11 (12) They plundered the sanctuary[3] of God,
         As though there was no heir to redeem.[4]

12 (13) They trampled the altar of the Lord, *coming straight* from all
              kinds of uncleanness,
              And with menstrual blood they defiled the sacrifices as
              though they were common flesh.

13 (14) They left no sin undone, wherein they did not surpass the
              heathen.

14 (15) Therefore God mixed for them a spirit to mislead *them*,
              And gave them to drink a cup of undiluted wine to *make
              them* drunk.

15 (16) He brought *the man* that is from the end of the earth, *the man*
              whose lash is ruthless:[5]

   (17)   He determined upon war against Jerusalem and her land.

16 (18) The rulers of the land went to meet him with joy,
              They said to him, Welcome is your journey! Come, enter
              in with peace.

17 (19) They levelled out the rough ways before his entering in,
              They opened the gates to Jerusalem, they crowned its
              walls.

18 (20) He entered, as a father *enters* his sons' house, in peace:
              He set down his feet with great assurance.

19 (21) He took possession of her fortified towers, and of the wall of
              Jerusalem;

   (22)   For God led him on in assurance, while they went astray.

20 (23) He put to death their rulers, and every man wise in counsel:
              He poured out the blood of the inhabitants of Jerusalem
              like unclean water:

21 (24) He led away their sons and daughters, whom they had
              begotten in defilement.

22 (25) They did according to their uncleanness, as their fathers *had
              done*:

   (26)   They defiled Jerusalem and the things consecrated to the
              name of God.

---

[3] Lit. 'the holy things'.
[4] i.e. to recover what had been taken away.
[5] Lit. 'him who smites mightily'.

23 (27) God is shown righteous in his judgements among the nations
      of the earth;

(28)   And the holy ones of God are like lambs innocent in their
      midst.

24 (29) Worthy to be praised is the Lord who judges the whole earth
      in his righteousness.

25 (30) Behold now, O God, thou hast shown us thy judgment in thy
      righteousness:

(31)   Our eyes have seen thy judgements, O God.

26   We have justified thy name that is honoured for ever;

(32)   For thou art the God of righteousness, who judges Israel
      with discipline.

27 (33) Turn, O God, thy mercy upon us,
      And have pity on us:

28 (34) Gather together the dispersion of Israel with mercy and
      goodness,

(35)   For thy faithfulness *is* with us.

29   And we stiffened our neck;
      And thou art our chastener.

30 (36) Disregard us not, O our God,
      Lest the nations swallow us up, as though there were none
      to deliver.

31 (37) But thou art our God from the beginning;
      And upon thee is our hope, O Lord.

32 (38) And we shall not be distant from thee,
      For thy judgements upon us *are* good.

33 (39) Upon us and our children *is thy* good will for ever:
      O Lord our Saviour, we shall never more be moved.

34 (40) Worthy of praise for his judgements *is* the Lord by the mouth
      of his holy ones;
      And Israel *is* blessed by the Lord for ever.

IX

Of Solomon.   For rebuke.

1   When Israel was led away in captivity to a foreign land,
      When they fell away from the Lord who redeemed them,

1 (2)   They were cast out from the inheritance which the Lord
             had given them.

2   The dispersion of Israel *was* among every nation, according
             to the word of God,

   (3)   That thou mightest be justified, O God, in thy
             righteousness by reason of our transgressions;

   (4)   For thou art a just judge over all the peoples of the earth.

3 (5)   For no one who does evil shall be hidden from thy knowledge,

   (6)   And the righteous deeds of thy holy ones *are* before thee, O
             Lord;
             And where shall man hide himself from thy knowledge, O
             God?.

4 (7)   Our actions[1] *are* subject to our own choice and freedom of
             will,
             To do right or wrong in the works of our hands;

   (8)   And in thy righteousness dost thou visit the sons of men.

5 (9)   And he who does right lays up life for himself with the Lord,
             And he who does wrong is responsible for his own
             destruction;

   (10)   For the judgements of the Lord *are given* in righteousness
             for each man and *his* house.

6 (11) Unto whom wilt thou show kindness, O God, if it be not to
             them that call upon the Lord?

   (12)   He will purify a soul in sin when confession *and*
             acknowledgement *is made*;

   (13)   For shame is upon us and upon our faces on account of all
             these things.

7 (14) And to whom will he forgive sins, if it be not to those who
             have sinned?

   (15)   Thou shalt bless the righteous and not call *them* to account[2]
             for the sins they have committed;
             And thy goodness is upon sinners when they repent.

8 (16) And now, thou art *our* God, and we are the people whom thou
             hast loved:

---

[1] Lit. 'works'.
[2] The sense of the verb is uncertain – possibly 'and wilt thou not guide *them* (in
cases where they have sinned)?'

Look and show pity, O God of Israel, for we are thine;
And remove not thy mercy from us, lest they assail us.

9 (17) For thou didst choose the seed of Abraham above all the
nations,
And didst set thy name upon us, O Lord;

(18) And thou wilt never cast us off.[3]

10 Thou didst make a covenant with our fathers concerning us;

(19) And we shall hope in thee, as our souls turn *to thee*.
The mercy of the Lord *be* upon the house of Israel for ever
and ever.

X

A Hymn.   Of Solomon.

1 Happy is the man whom the Lord remembers by *giving* a
reproof,
And who is fenced off[1] from the evil road by a whip,
That he may be cleansed of sin, so as not to multiply *it*.

2 He who prepares his back for lashes shall be purified;
For the Lord *is* good to those who endure *his* discipline.

2 (3) For he will make straight the ways of the righteous, and not
turn *them* aside by discipline;

3 (4) And the mercy of the Lord *is* upon those who love him in
truth.

4 And the Lord will remember his servants in mercy;

(5) *For* the testimony *is* in the law of the everlasting covenant,
The testimony of the Lord for the ways of men at *his*
visitiation.

5 (6) Just and holy is our Lord in his judgements for ever,
And Israel shall praise the name of the Lord with gladness.

6 (7) And the holy ones shall give thanks in the assembly of the
people;

[3] Lit. 'And thou wilt not rest (or 'cease') for ever': von Gebhardt, by conjecture,
'and thou wilt not reject *us* for ever'.

[1] Lit. 'encircled': Syr. (by emending the Gk.) 'restrained'.

And upon the poor shall God have mercy, to the joy of
Israel.

7 (8) For God *is* eternally good and merciful,
And the congregations of Israel shall glorify the name of
the Lord.

8   The salvation of the Lord *be* upon the house of Israel for
everlasting joy.

XI

Of Solomon.   For expectation.

1   Sound in Sion the trumpet to summon the saints,

1 (2)   Proclaim in Jerusalem the voice of him who brings good
tidings
That the God of Israel has shown mercy in his visitation of
them.

2 (3) Stand upon the height, O Jerusalem, and behold your
children,
From the east and the west, gathered together by the Lord.

3 (4) From the north they come in the joy of their God:
From the islands far away has God gathered them.

4 (5) High mountains has he made low to *make* a plain for them:
   (6)   The hills fled at their approach.

5   The woods gave them shade as they passed by:
   (7)   God caused to spring up for them every *kind of* sweet-
scented tree;

6   That Israel might pass by at the visitiation of the glory of
their God.

7 (8) Put on, O Jerusalem, the garments of your glory:
Make ready the robe of your consecration;
For God has spoken good *concerning* Israel, for ever and
ever.

8 (9) May the Lord perform what he has spoken concerning Israel
and Jerusalem:
May the Lord raise up Israel by his glorious name.

9   The mercy of the Lord *be* upon Israel for ever and ever.

XII

Of Solomon.   Against the tongue of lawless men.

1   O Lord, deliver my soul from the lawless and wicked man,
      From the tongue that is lawless and slanderous,
      And which utters lies and deceit.

2   Infinitely agile are the words of the tongue of the wicked man,
      Like fire burning up stubble on a threshing-floor.[1]

3   *The purpose of* his sojourn is to fill households with a lying tongue,
      To cut down the trees of the joy that sets the lawless on fire,[2]

3 (4)   To confound households[3] in warfare by means of slanderous lips.

4   May God remove far from the innocent the lips of the lawless by *bringing them to* want;
      And may the bones of slanderers be scattered *far* from those who fear the Lord:

(5)   May the slanderous tongue perish in flaming fire *far* from the holy.

5 (6)   May the Lord preserve the quiet soul that hates the unjust;
      And may the Lord guide the man who makes peace in the home.

6 (7)   The salvation of the Lord *be* upon Israel his servant for ever;
      And may sinners perish altogether at the presence of the Lord;
      And may the holy ones of the Lord inherit the promises of the Lord.

---

[1] So one MS (H), though this may be a secondary conjecture to make sense of the difficult reading of the other MSS and Syr. ('like fire among the people burning up its beauty').

[2] Both text and interpretation of this verse are very uncertain. 'The trees of joy' are probably the righteous: 'on fire' – *sc.* with envy?

[3] Text, 'lawless households'; but the adjective is probably by dittography from the preceding line.

XIII

Of Solomon.   A Psalm.   Comfort for the righteous.

1   The right hand of the Lord sheltered me,
       The right hand of the Lord spared us:

2   The arm of the Lord saved us from the sword that passes
       through,[1]
       From famine and the death of sinners.

3   Evil beasts rushed upon them:
       With their teeth they tore their flesh,
       With their fangs they crushed their bones.

4 (3) But from all these the Lord delivered us.

5 (4) The **godly**[2] man was troubled on account of his errors,
       Lest he should be taken away along with the sinners;

6 (5) For the overthrow of the sinner is terrible,
       But not one of these things shall touch the righteous.

7 (6) For the chastening of the righteous *for sins done* in ignorance
       And the overthrow of the sinners are not alike:

8 (7) The righteous is chastened with circumspection,
       So that the sinner may not rejoice over the righteous;

9 (8) For he will admonish the righteous as a beloved son,
       And his chastisement is that of a firstborn;

10 (9) For the Lord will spare his holy ones,
       And will wipe out their errors by *means of* discipline.

11   For the life of the just *is* for ever,
 (10)   But sinners shall be taken away into destruction,
       And their memorial shall be found no more.

12 (11) But upon the holy is the mercy of the Lord,
       And upon those who fear him his mercy.

---

[1] *Sc.* the land (cp. Ezek. xiv. 17).
[2] So Wellhausen, by an easy emendation: MSS 'ungodly'.

XIV

A Hymn.   Of Solomon.

1   Faithful is the Lord to those who love him in truth,
    To those who endure his discipline,

2 (1)   To those who walk in the righteousness of his ordinances,
    In the law which he commanded us that we might live.

3 (2)   The Lord's holy ones shall live by it for ever:
    The garden of the Lord, the trees of life, are his holy ones.

4 (3)   Their planting is rooted for ever:
    They shall not be pulled up all the days of heaven;

5   For the portion and the inheritance of God is Israel.

6 (4)   But not so are the sinners and lawless ones,
    Who preferred a day in the companionship of their sin:

7   Their desire was for the briefness of corruption,
    (5)   And they remembered not God.

8   For the ways of men are known before him at all times,
    And he knows the secrets[1] of the heart before they come to
    pass.

9 (6)   Therefore their inheritance *is* Sheol and darkness and
    destruction,
    And they shall not be found in the day when the righteous
    obtain mercy.

10 (7)   But the Lord's holy ones shall inherit life with joy.

XV

A Psalm.   Of Solomon.   With a Song.

1   When I was in distress I called upon the name of the Lord,
    I hoped for the help of the God of Jacob, and was saved;

1 (2)   For thou art the hope and the refuge of the poor, O God.

---

[1] Lit. 'store-houses'.

2 (3)   For who, O God, is strong, except to give thanks to thee in
        truth?

(4)   And how can a man show his power,[1] except in giving
        thanks to thy name?

3 (5)   A new psalm with song in gladness of heart,
        The fruit of the lips together with the tongue in harmony,[2]
        The first-fruits of the lips from a holy and righteous heart—

4 (6)   He who performs these things shall never be shaken by evil:
        The flame of fire and the wrath against the unrighteous
        shall not touch him,

5 (7)   When it goes forth from before the Lord against sinners,
        To destroy all the substance of sinners;

6 (8)   For the mark of God is upon the righteous for salvation.

7   Famine and sword and death *shall be* far from the righteous,

(9)   For they shall flee from the holy as men pursued in **war**;[3]

8   But they shall pursue sinners and overtake *them*,
        And those who act lawlessly shall not escape the
        judgement of the Lord:

9   As by enemies skilled *in war* shall they be overtaken,

(10)   For the mark of destruction is upon their forehead.

10 (11)   And the inheritance of sinners *is* destruction and darkness,
        And their iniquities shall pursue them to Sheol below:

11 (12)   Their inheritance shall not be found by their children,

(13)   For sins shall devastate the houses of sinners;

12   And sinners shall perish for ever on the day of the Lord's
        judgement,

(14)   When God visits the earth with his judgement.

13 (15)   But those who fear the Lord shall find mercy on it,
        And shall live by the compassion of their God;
        But sinners shall perish eternally.

---

[1] Lit. 'And wherein is a man mighty'.
[2] Lit. 'The fruit of the lips with a well-tuned instrument of the tongue'.
[3] The MSS read 'famine'.

XVI

A Hym.   Of Solomon.   For Help to the Holy.

1   When my soul slumbered, away from the Lord, I almost
        slipped
        In the lethargy of the sleep **of those**[1] far from God –

2   My soul was almost poured out to death,
        Close to the gates of Sheol, alongside the sinner,

3   With my soul separated from the Lord God of Israel –
        Had not the Lord succoured me in his everlasting mercy.

4   He goaded me, as a horse is spurred, to awaken me to him,
        My saviour and helper at all times saved me.

5   I will give thanks to thee, O God, for thou didst help me, to
        save *me*,
        And thou didst not reckon me among sinners for
        destruction.

6   Remove not thy mercy from me, O God,
        Nor mindfulness of thee from my heart until death.

7   Hold me back[2] from wicked sin, O God,
        And from every wicked[3] woman who causes the foolish to
        stumble;

8   And let not the beauty of a woman who acts lawlessly beguile
        me,
        Nor that of any useless thing which takes its origin in sin.

9   Direct the works of my hands **before** thee,[4]
        And preserve my footsteps in the mindfulness of thee.

10 Keep my tongue and my lips in words of truth:
        Anger and unreasoning wrath remove far from me.

11 Complaint and faint-heartedness in affliction keep far from
        me,
        When, if I sin, thou chastenest me to turn *me* back.

---

[1] Reading τῶν for τῷ.
[2] Lit. 'prevail over me'.
[3] Possibly read πορνείας ('of unchastity') for πονηρᾶς ('wicked').
[4] MSS 'in thy place'.

12 But confirm my soul with good will and cheerfulness:
    When thou strengthenest my soul, what is given *me* will
        suffice me.
13 For if thou strengthenest not,
    Who will endure chastisement in penury?
14 When a man is rebuked because of his corruption,
    Thy testing *of him* is in his flesh and in the affliction of
        penury.
15 If the righteous endures in all these, he shall receive mercy
        from the Lord.

XVII

A Psalm.   Of Solomon.   With Song.   Of the King.

1 O Lord, thou art our king for ever and ever,
    For in thee, O God, shall our soul glory.
2 What is the duration of man's life upon earth?
    As are his days, so is his hope set upon them.
3 But we will hope in God our saviour;
    For the might of our God *is* for ever with mercy,
3 (4) And the kingdom of our God *is* for ever over the nations in
        judgement.
4 (5) Thou, Lord, didst choose David as king over Israel,
    And thou didst swear to him concerning his posterity for
        ever,
    That his kingdom would not fail before thee.
5 (6) But, for our sins, there rose up against us sinners:
    They assailed us and thrust us out (*they* to whom thou didst
        give no promise),
   (7) They took possession with violence, and did not praise thy
        honourable name.
6 They set up in splendour a kingdom in their pride,[1]
   (8) They laid waste the throne of David in the arrogance of
        their fortune.[2]

---

[1] The sense of the Gk. is uncertain: possibly 'as a result of their elevation'.
[2] Lit. 'change' (i.e. of fate).

7   And thou, O God, wilt overthrow them and wilt remove their
                offspring from the earth,
  (9)   When there rises up against them a man that is foreign to
                our race.
8 (10) According to their sins wilt thou recompense them, O God,
                That it may befall them according to their works.
9 (11) God will show them no pity.
                He sought out their offspring, and let not one of them go.
10 (12) Faithful is the Lord in all his judgements which he performs
                on earth.
11 (13) The lawless one laid waste our land so that none inhabited it:
                They destroyed young and old and their children together.
12 (14) In the wrath of his **anger**[3] he sent them off to the west,
                And the rulers of the land *he exposed* to derision without
                mercy.
13 (15) In *his* foreign ways the enemy acted arrogantly,
                And his heart was alien from our God.
14 (16) And everything he did in Jerusalem
                Was in accordance with what the heathen *do* in their **strong**
                cities.[4]
15 (17) And the children of the covenant ruled over them among
                peoples of mixed origin:
                There was not among them one who dealt honestly and
                faithfully in the midst of Jerusalem.
16 (18) Those who loved the assemblies of the holy fled from them,
                As sparrows scattered from their nest.
17 (19) They roamed about in deserted places that their souls might
                be preserved from harm;
                And precious in the eyes of those who lived abroad was any
                that escaped alive from them.
18 (20) Over the whole earth were they scattered by lawless men.
  (21)   For the heavens withheld the rain from dropping upon the
                earth:

[3] Gk. 'beauty', which can hardly be right. Perhaps an original Heb. 'פיו ('his
anger') was misread as יפיו ('his beauty'), or alternatively the Gk. κάλλους
('beauty') may be a corruption of καπνοῦ ('smoke' – i.e. 'in his smoking anger', cp.
Isa. lxv. 5).
[4] MSS 'in their cities to their gods'.

19   *The* perennial springs from the deeps were stopped up, *and the streams* from *the* high mountains *stayed*;

    For there was none among them who dealt righteously and justly.

20   From their ruler to the lowest of the people, *they were* utterly sinful:

(22)   The king was a transgressor, and the judge disobedient, and the people sinful.

21 (23) Behold, O Lord, and raise up for them their king, the son of David,

    For the time which thou didst *fore*see, O God, that he may reign over Isrel thy servant.

22 (24) And gird him with strength, that he may shatter unrighteous rulers;

(25)   *And* purify Jerusalem of the nations which trample *her* down in destruction.

23 (26) In wisdom, in righteousness, may he expel[5] sinners from *the* inheritance:

    May he smash[5] the sinner's arrogance like a potter's vessel.

24   With a rod of iron may he break[5] in pieces all their substance:

(27)   May he destroy[5] the lawless nations by the word of his mouth,

25   So that, at his rebuke, nations flee before him;

    And may he reprove[5] sinners by the word of their *own* hearts.

26 (28) And he shall gather together a holy people, whom he shall lead in righteousness,

    And he shall judge the tribes of the people which has been sanctified by the Lord his God.

27 (29) And he shall not permit unrighteousness to lodge any more in their midst,

    Nor shall there dwell with them any man with knowledge of wickedness;

(30)   For he shall know them, that they are all sons of their God.

---

[5] These verbs could be taken as infinitives rather than optatives (i.e. following on 'gird him . . . that . . .').

28　And he shall divide them up by their tribes over the land:

(31)　　Neither settler nor alien shall live among them any more.

29　He shall judge peoples and nations in the wisdom of his
　　righteousness. Selah.

30 (32)　And he shall have the peoples of the Gentiles to serve him
　　under his yoke;

　　And he shall glorify the Lord at the centre[6] of all the earth,

(33)　　And he shall purify Jerusalem, making it holy as of old;

31 (34)　So that nations shall come from the ends of the earth to see
　　his glory,

　　Bringing as gifts her sons who had fainted,

(35)　　And to see the glory of the Lord, with which God glorified
　　her.

32　And he *shall be* a righteous king, taught by God, over them,

(36)　　And there shall be no unrighteousness in his days in their
　　midst,

　　For all shall be holy, and their king the anointed Lord.

33 (37)　And he shall not put his trust in horse and rider and bow,

　　Nor shall he increase his store of gold and silver for war,

　　Nor shall he concentrate *his* hopes on numbers for the day
　　of battle.

34 (38)　The Lord himself *is* his king, the hope of him who is strong in
　　the hope of God;

　　And he shall have mercy on all the nations *that stand* before
　　him in fear.

35 (39)　For he will smite the earth with the word of his mouth for
　　ever:

(40)　　He will bless the people of the Lord with wisdom and joy;

36 (41)　And he himself *is* pure from sin, so that he may rule a great
　　people,

　　That he may rebuke rulers, and remove sinners by the
　　might of *his* word.

37 (42)　And during his days he shall not be weakened, *relying* on his
　　God;

---

[6] Lit. 'mark' (*i.e.* navel). Others take the phrase as 'conspicuously before'; but it
is doubtful whether the Gk. can bear this meaning.

For God created him strong in the holy spirit,
And wise in prudent counsel, together with strength and
righteousness;

38 (43) And the blessing of the Lord *is* with him providing[7] strength,
And he shall not be weakened.

39 (44) His hope *is* upon the Lord:
Who then can prevail against him –

40   Strong in his works, and mighty in the fear of God,
(45)   Shepherding the flock of the Lord faithfully and righteously?
And he will not let any among them languish in their
pasturing.

41 (46) And he shall lead them in equity;
And there shall be no arrogance among them that any of
them should be oppressed.

42 (47) This *is* the majesty of the king of Israel, of which God has
knowledge,
So as to raise him up over the house of Israel, to educate
them.

43 (48) His words *are* refined more than the very choicest gold:
In the assemblies he will administer justice to the tribes of
a people that has been sanctified:
(49)   His words *are* as the words of holy *men* amidst sanctified
peoples.

44 (50) Blessed *are* they who shall be in those days,
Seeing the good things of Israel which God shall accomplish
in the gathering of the tribes.

45 (51) May God hasten his mercy upon Israel,
May he deliver us[8] from the uncleanness of profane
enemies.

46   The Lord *is* our king for ever and ever.

---

[7] Gk. 'in'.
[8] Gk. 'he will deliver us'.

XVIII

A Psalm. Of Solomon. Again of the Anointed of the Lord.[1]

1   Lord, thy mercy is over the works of thy hands for ever:
       Thy goodness is over Israel with a rich gift.

2   Thine eyes look upon them, and not one of them is[2] in want:
2 (3)   Thine ears listen[2] to the hopeful prayer of the poor.

3   Thy judgements *extend* over the whole earth in mercy,
  (4)   And thy love *is* upon Abraham's children, the sons of Israel.

4   Thy discipline *is* upon us as on a first-born, an only son,
  (5)   So as to turn the obedient soul away from ignorant stupidity.

5 (6) May God purify Israel for the day of mercy and blessing,
      For the day of election, at the **manifestation**[3] of his anointed one.

6 (7) Blessed *are* they who shall be in those days,
      Seeing the good things of the Lord which he will perform for the generation that is to come,

7 (8) Under the rod of discipline of the Lord's anointed in the fear of his God,
      In wisdom of spirit, and of justice and of might,

8 (9) So as to direct *every* man in works of righteousness in the fear of God,
      So as to establish them all before the Lord,

9 (10) A generation excellent in the fear of God in the days of *his* mercy. Selah.

10 (11) Great is our God and glorious, dwelling in the highest,
  (12)   He who established the luminaries in *their* course for the determining of seasons from year to year,
      And they have not turned aside from the path which he appointed them.

[1] Or 'anointed Lord' (cp. xvii. 32).
[2] Gk. 'shall be . . . will listen'.
[3] Following Manson's conjecture of ἀναδείξει for ἀνάξει in the MSS – a word otherwise unknown.

11 (13) Their path each day is in the fear of God,
        From the day God created them unto eternity:
12 (14) They have not gone astray from the day he created them,
        From the generations of old they have not turned aside
           from their paths,
        Except *when* God ordered them through the command of
           his servants.

THE ODES OF SOLOMON

INTRODUCTION

For the text of the Odes we are dependent on two Syriac MSS (both defective), supplemented by a Greek text of one of the Odes and also by a Coptic version of five of them preserved in the well-known Gnostic work *Pistis Sophia*.

The two Syriac MSS are: (1) Rylands Cod. Syr. 9 (16th cent.: = H) in the John Rylands Library at Manchester, which contains all the Odes except i, ii, and the beginning of iii; and (2) B.L. Addit. 14538 (9th or 10th cent.: = B), which has a much greater deficiency at the beginning, but is complete from the middle of xvii. 7 to the end. The text of the single ode which has survived in Greek (Ode xi) is one of a number of items in a 3rd century papyrus codex in the Bodmer collection at Geneva (Pap. Bod. XI).[1] The five odes preserved in Coptic in the *Pistis Sophia* are i, v, vi, xxii, and xxv. Ode ii is thus unattested by any authority, as is also the beginning of Ode iii.

Ode i is extant only in Coptic and our translation of it has been made by Dr. K. H. Kuhn from Schmidt's text of the *Pistis Sophia*. Otherwise the translation is from the Syriac. It follows mainly the text of H, although from xvii. 7 onwards B has been preferred occasionally: all differences between H and B, however, have been recorded in the footnotes, as well as the Coptic and Greek variants where they occur.

If we take the Odes as they stand, there can be no doubt at all that they are Christian. Christ is mentioned by name: there are references to events in the Gospels (e.g., to the Baptism in xxiv);

---

[1] The remaining items in the codex are a miscellaneous collection – two psalms from the Old Testament, Jude and the two Epistles of Peter from the New Testament, the apocryphal correspondence of St. Paul with the Corinthians, the Nativity of Mary (The Apocalypse of James), the *Apology* of Phileas, and Melito's *Homily on the Pasch*.

and the prevailing atmosphere is Christian throughout (e.g., the opening of xix could not have been written by anyone who was not a convinced Trinitarian). Nevertheless, several theories of redaction and interpolation have been put forward, the most influential being that of Harnack, who maintained that Odes iv and vi were Jewish in origin (on the basis of the references to the Temple, which Jesus had said was to be destroyed), that xix and xxvii were purely Christian, and that the rest were originally Jewsish odes later interpolated by a Christian. But none of these theories has met with any general acceptance.

From a rather different point of view it has been argued that the Odes betray Gnostic influence. In particular, H. Schlier has suggested that they stem from a syncretistic Baptist sect, which in some respects had similar beliefs and practices to the Mandaeans. Yet there is no evidence in the Odes either of the characteristic Gnostic doctrine of emanations from a distant God, or of a radical dualism between matter and spirit: on the contrary, Ode xvi witnesses to a doctrine of Creation which would have been impossible for any thoroughgoing Gnostic. Ultimately, of course, the evaluation of such Gnostic affinities as there are in the Odes depends on the general theory held of the nature of Gnosticism and the date of its rise. But this much is certain, that, while the Odes may very well have been composed in an area where Gnostic (or proto-Gnostic) speculations were current, and their theology affected accordingly, they show no trace of any developed, or logically formulated, Gnostic system.

If, then, we are thinking in terms of a single author (and there is no sound reason for suggesting a plurality of authors) the most that the evidence will permit us to say is that he was a Christian. In all probability he was a Jewish Christian. And, if we are prepared to stress certain parallels between the Odes and the Qumran literature, and at the same time accept the view that the members of the Qumran community were Essenes, we can go on to suppose (with J. H. Charlesworth) that the author either had been himself an Essene before his conversion, or at least subjected to very strong Essene influences.

But whatever the truth, from very early days the Odes were ascribed to Solomon. No claim to Solomonic authorship is made in the text and there is little to suggest it. It may be that the belief that Solomon was the author arose because of the association of the Odes with the Psalms. This association obtains not only in the Syriac tradition, but also in the Coptic and the Greek. In the two available Syriac MSS both Odes and Psalms are arranged as a single collection with the Odes first: the individual pieces are numbered consecutively i–lx (i.e. 42 Odes + 18 Psalms); and all of them seem to have been known as 'Psalms'. Where our Ode i is quoted in the Coptic *Pistis Sophia* it is described as 'the nineteenth Ode', which is clear enough evidence that in the tradition known to the author of *Pistis Sophia* the Psalms and the Odes were also combined (but in the reverse order to that found in the Syriac), and also that the whole collection was known to the Copts as 'Odes'. The two Greek lists of Biblical books, the pseudo-Athanasian Synopsis and the Stichometry of Nicephorus, both refer to the 'Psalms and Ode(s) of Solomon'. This last phrase is most naturally understood as a reference to two distinct collections, with two separate titles, although it can be interpreted as the title of a single collection – especially as the Stichometry very obviously treats the two together and assigns them in all 2100 *stichoi*. However, in either case, Psalms and Odes are very closely related.

But whether the Odes were composed in the first instance as an entirely independent work or were designed as a Christian supplement to the Psalms, there can be no doubt about the antiquity of the title 'Odes'. Not only is 'Odes' the title of the combined work in the tradition represented by the author of the *Pistis Sophia* (3rd century?): the Greek text of Ode xi, preserved in Bodmer Papyrus XI (also 3rd century), is prefaced by the heading 'Ode of Solomon'; and the Latin apologist Lactantius (*c*.240–*c*.320) quotes from Ode xix in such a way as to make it quite clear that he was familiar with a collection of 'Odes' which were numbered as ours are ('Solomon in ode undevicesima ita dicit: *Infirmatus est uterus Virginis . . .*').[2] The

---

[2] Lactantius, *Div. Inst.* IV. xii. 3 (One MS reads 'psalmo' in place of 'ode'). Whether Lactantius was quoting from an independent collection of Odes or from a combined collection of Odes and Psalms cannot, of course, be determined; but if the latter, the Odes will have preceded the Psalms, as in our two Syriac MSS. Nor can we know whether Lactantius was quoting from a Latin version or making his own translation (presumably from the Greek).

title 'Odes' would thus appear to be very ancient indeed, if not original; and it was in all probability inspired by the summary of Solomon's achievements in 1 Kings iv. 32 ('And he uttered three thousand proverbs: and his songs [Sept. 'odes'] numbered a thousand and five').

The quotation of the Odes by Lactantius as if they were Scripture, and also by the author of the *Pistis Sophia*, together with the evidence of the Bodmer papyrus, suggests that they were known and respected over a wide geographical area by the end of the third century at the latest. Comparison with other early writers, however, yields little of any real value. There are possible literary connections between the Odes on the one hand, and Cyril of Jerusalem, the Acts of Thomas, and Ephraem Syrus, on the other. Yet the evidence is far from conclusive. More compelling than any are a number of rather striking similarities between the Odes and Ignatius of Antioch: some of these may be accidental, but there are too many to be entirely so; and, although insufficient to prove literary dependence one way or the other, they leave no doubt that both the author of the Odes and Ignatius were products of the same environment. On the whole, therefore, a date for the Odes *c.*AD 100–200 is the most probable and Syria and its neighbourhood the most likely place of origin. But when, where, and in what circumstances they were first combined with the Psalms it is impossible to say.

There remains the question of the original language. The fact that the text of the Odes has come down to us in Syriac, Coptic, Greek, and Latin (albeit in a solitary quotation), suggests Greek as the common denominator; and there is no lack of scholars who have argued forcefully for a Greek original. Yet the mere existence of a Greek text, from which Syriac, Coptic, and Latin versions may have been derived, is no guarantee of its originality. From an entirely different angle attention has been drawn to certain Semitic features in the Odes – notably to the regular use of parallelism, and to the occurrence from time to time of indubitably Semitic constructions (e.g. 'He richly blessed me' at xxviii. 4); and arguments have been advanced accordingly in favour of Hebrew, Aramaic, or Syriac originals. Since the author was a Christian, however, he is unlikely to have written in either Hebrew or Aramaic at the date suggested above, so that, if we are to suppose a Semitic original, Syriac is the most probable. On the other hand, it is claimed that the Semitic features can quite adequately be accounted for by supposing that the author was writing in Greek, but in a consciously 'Biblical' style, and taking as his model the poetical books of the Septuagint. The discovery of the Greek text of Ode xi and its publication in 1959 gave a fresh impetus to the discussion in that it was now at last possible to set the Greek side by side with the Syriac and compare them, even if over a very limited area. But the comparison has resulted in no firmer conclusions than formerly. M. Testuz, who edited the Greek text of Ode xi, declared himself definitely in favour of a Greek original, while freely admitting Semitic influences. However, J. A. Emerton, in 1967, at the end of a very full discussion of all the arguments brought forward to date, could sum up, 'The most probable conclusion to be drawn is that the Odes of Solomon were composed in Syriac'; and J. H. Charlesworth, to judge from the notes in his edition of 1973, would seem inclined to agree.[3]

BIBLIOGRAPHY

EDITIONS

Greek

M. TESTUZ, *La Onzième Ode de Salomon* in *Papyrus Bodmer*, X–XII (Geneva, 1959), pp. 47–69.

M. LATTKE, *Die Oden Salomos* . . . [as below], vol. 1.

---

[3] A technical point is perhaps worth noting in this connection. In the Odes, the third person preformative of the imperfect begins with *n*-(rather than *y*-). From the evidence of the Syriac inscriptions it seems that the change took place round about AD 200 (see E. Jenni, 'Die altsyrischen Inschriften, 1.–3. Jahrhundert n. Chr.' in *TZ* xxi (1965), pp. 371–385). We cannot, of course, be precise in such matters, and there may well have been a time lag between the change in popular speech in some places and its appearance in inscriptions. Nevertheless, this suggests that we can scarcely date the present Syriac text of the Odes much before AD 200 – though inevitably, in itself, it gives us no help in deciding whether that text is the author's original, or an edited version of the original, or a translation from Greek!

J. H. CHARLESWORTH, *Papyri and Leather Manuscripts* . . . [as below], pp. 7 – 12.

Syriac

J. RENDEL HARRIS, *The Odes and Psalms of Solomon, now first published from the Syriac version* (Cambridge, 1909; 2nd edit. 1911).

J. RENDEL HARRIS and A. MINGANA, *The Odes and Psalms of Solomon, re-edited for the Governors of the John Rylands Library.* Vol. i: *The Text with Facsimile Reproductions* (Manchester, 1916).

J. H. CHARLESWORTH, *The Odes of Solomon, edited with Translation and Notes* (Oxford, 1973).

——, *Papyri and Leather Manuscripts of the Odes of Solomon* (= *The Dickerson Series of Facsimiles of Manuscripts Important for Christian Origins*. Vol. 1; Durham N. C., 1981), pp. 21 – 89.

M. LATTKE, *Die Oden Salomos in ihrer Bedeutung für Neues Testament und Gnosis*. 3 vols. (= *Orbis Biblicus et Orientalis*, XXV. 1, 1a, 2; Fribourg and Göttingen, 1979/80. [The Syriac text is printed in Estrangela in vol. 1a, and there is a transliterated version of it facing the translation in vol. 1. Vol. 2 contains Greek, Syriac, and Coptic concordances.]

Coptic

C. SCHMIDT, Pistis Sophia *neu herausgegeben, mit Einleitung nebst griechischem und koptischem Wort-und Namenregister* (= *Coptica* II; Copenhagen, 1925). [For the text of Odes i, v, vi, xxii, and xxv.]

M. LATTKE, *Die Oden Salomos* . . . [as above], vol. 1.

J. H. CHARLESWORTH, *Papyri and Leather Manuscripts* . . . [as above], pp. 13 – 20.

TRANSLATIONS

English

J. RENDEL HARRIS, *The Odes and Psalms of Solomon, now first published from the Syriac Version* (Cambridge, 1909; 2nd edit. 1911).

J. RENDEL HARRIS and A. MINGANA, *The Odes and Psalms of Solomon, re-edited for the Governors of the John Rylands Library.* Vol. ii: *The Translation with Introduction and Notes* (Manchester, 1920).

J. H. BERNARD, *The Odes of Solomon* (= *TS* VIII. iii; Cambridge, 1912).

J. H. CHARLESWORTH, *The Odes of Solomon* . . . [as above].

G. HORNER, *Pistis Sophia* (London, 1924). [Of Odes i, v, vi, xxii, and xxv, from the Coptic.]

French

J. LABOURT, 'Les Odes de Salomon' in *R Bibl* N.S. vii (Oct. 1910), pp. 484–500 and N.S. viii (Jan. 1911), pp. 5–21. [Reprinted in J. LABOURT and P. BATIFFOL *Les Odes de Salomon: Une œuvre chretieńne des environs de l'an 100–120* (Paris, 1911), pp. 5–38.]

German

J. FLEMMING and A. HARNACK, *Ein jüdisch-christliches Psalmbuch aus dem ersten Jahrhundert, aus dem syrischen übersetzt* (= *TU* xxxv. 4; Leipzig, 1910).

W. BAUER, 'Die Oden Salomos' in E. HENNECKE and W. SCHNEEMELCHER, *Neutestamentliche Apokryphen in deutscher Übersetzung*[3], ii (Tübingen, 1964), pp. 576–625.

C. SCHMIDT, *Koptisch-gnostische Schriften. I. Die Pistis Sophia, usw.* (= *GCS* 13(45); Leipzig, 1905–3rd ed. 1959). [Of Odes i, v, vi, xxii, and xxv, from the Coptic.]

M. LATTKE, *Die Oden Salomos* . . . [as above], vol. 1.

GENERAL

E. A. ABBOTT, 'The Original Language of the Odes of Solomon' in *JTS* xiv (April 1913), pp. 441–445 and xv (Oct. 1913), pp. 44–45.

A. ADAM, 'Die ursprüngliche Sprache der Salomo-Oden' in *ZNW* lii (1961), pp. 141–156.

P. BATIFFOL, 'Les Odes de Salomon' in *R Bibl* N.S. vii (Oct. 1910), pp. 483–484, N.S. viii (Jan. 1911), pp. 21–59, and N.S. viii (April 1911), pp. 161–197. [Reprinted in J. LABOURT and P. BATIFFOL, *Les Odes de Salomon: Une œuvre chrétienne des environs de l'an 100–120* (Paris, 1911), pp. 39–115.]

W. BAUER, 'The Odes of Solomon' in *NTA* ii, pp. 808–810. [A translation, by R. McL. WILSON, of the Introduction to Bauer's German translation of the Odes (see above).]

J. CARMIGNAC, 'Les affinités Qumrâniennes de la onzième Ode de Salomon' in *Revue de Qumran*, III. i (1961–1962), pp. 71–102.

——, 'Recherches sur la langue originelle des Odes de Salomon' in *Revue de Qumran*, IV. iii (1963), pp. 429–432.

H. CHADWICK, 'Some Reflections on the Character and Theology of the Odes of Solomon' in *Kyriakon: Festschrift Johannes Quasten*, i (ed. P. GRANFIELD and J. A. JUNGMANN; Münster, 1970), pp. 266–270.

J. H. CHARLESWORTH 'The Odes of Solomon – Not Gnostic' in *CBQ* xxxi (1969), pp. 357–369.

——, 'Les Odes de Salomon et les manuscrits de la Mer Morte' in *R Bibl* lxxvii (Oct. 1970), pp. 522–549.

R. H. CONNOLLY, 'The Odes of Solomon: Jewish or Christian?' in *JTS* xiii (Jan. 1912), pp. 298–309.

——, 'Greek the original Language of the Odes of Solomon' in *JTS* xiv (July, 1913), pp. 530–538, and xv (Oct. 1913), pp. 45–47.

A.-M. DENIS, *IPGAT*, pp. 65–66.

J. DE ZWAAN, 'The Edessene Origin of the Odes of Solomon' in *Quantulacumque: Studies presented to Kirsopp Lake* (ed. R. P. CASEY, S. LAKE and A. K. LAKE; London 1937), pp. 285–302.

H. J. W. DRIJVERS, 'Die Oden Salomos und die Polemik mit den Markioniten im syrischen Christentum' in *Symposium Syriacum 1976* (= *Orientalia Christiana Analecta*, 205; Rome, 1978), pp. 39–55.

——, 'The 19th Ode of Solomon' in *JTS* N.S. xxxi (1980), pp. 337–355.

J. A. EMERTON, 'Some Problems of Text and Language in the Odes of Solomon' in *JTS* N.S. xviii (Oct. 1967), pp. 372–406.

R. M. GRANT, 'The Odes of Solomon and the Church of Antioch' in *JBL* lxiii (1944), pp. 362–377.

H. GUNKEL, 'Die Oden Salomos' in *ZNW* xi (1910), pp. 291–328.

G. KITTEL, *Die Oden Salomos, überarbeitet oder einheitlich?* (= *Beiträge zur Wissenschaft vom Alten Testament*, xvi; Leipzig, 1914).

H. SCHLIER, 'Zur Mandäerfrage' in *Theologische Rundschau*, N.F. v (1933), pp. 1–34 and 69–92.

W. H. WORRELL, 'The Odes of Solomon and the *Pistis Sophia*' in *JTS* xiii (Oct. 1911), pp. 29–46. [Contains an English translation of the five Coptic odes.]

I[1]

1   The Lord is upon my head like a wreath,
     And I shall not leave him.
2   The wreath of truth has been plaited for me,
     And it has let thy branches bud within me;
3   For it is not like a withered wreath that does not bud:
4   But thou art alive upon my head,
     And thou hast budded upon me.
5   Thy fruits are full and perfect:
     They are full of thy salvation.

II

This ode is not extant.

III

1   . . . I clothe.
2   And his[1] limbs are with him,
     And I hang on them, and he loves me;
3   For I should not have known how to love the Lord,
     If he had not loved me.
4   Who can understand love,
     But he who is loved?
5   I love the Beloved One, and my soul loves him;
     And where his rest is, there too am I.
6   And I shall not be a stranger,
     Because there is no grudging[2] with the Most High and merciful
       Lord.

---

[1] Extant only in Coptic.

[1] There is some confusion in the MS between the readings 'his' and 'my'.
[2] Or 'envy'.

7 I was united *to him*, because the lover has found the Beloved One,
   Because I love that Son, **I shall** become a son;[3]
8 For he who is joined to him that does not die,
   He too will become immortal,
9 And he who takes pleasure in life[4]
   Will become a living one.
10 This is the guileless Spirit of the Lord,
   That teaches men to know his ways.
11 Be wise, and understand, and be attentive.
   Hallelujah.

IV

1 No man changes thy holy place, O my God,
   And there is no one who will change it and set it in another place,
2 For none has authority over it;[1]
   For thou didst purpose thy sanctuary before thou madest places:
3 What[2] is older will not be changed by those that are younger than
      it.[3]
   Thou has given thy heart, O Lord, to thy faithful ones:
4 Thou wilt never be ineffectual,
   Nor wilt thou be fruitless;
5 For one hour of thy faithfulness[4]
   Is better than all days and years.
6 For who will put on thy grace and be rejected?
7 Because thy seal is ⟨kn⟩own,
   And thy creatures are known to it,
8 And ⟨the⟩ hosts ⟨h⟩old it,
   And the elect archangels are clothed in it.
9 Thou hast given us communion with thee:[5]

---

[3] Text 'Because I shall love that Son, in order that I may become a son'.
[4] Differently pointed, the consonants could mean 'the living one'.

[1] Or 'Because there is no authority over it'.
[2] Or 'He who'.   [3] Or 'he'.
[4] Or 'faith in thee'.
[5] Or 'thy fellowship'.

It was not that thou wast in need of us, but that we were in need of thee.

10 Sprinkle upon us thy dews,
And open thy rich springs which flow with milk and honey for us.

11 For there is no regret with thee,
That thou shouldest feel regret for anything that thou hast promised;

12 And the end was manifest to thee.

13 For what thou hast given thou hast given freely,
So that thou shouldest not take them **back** henceforth;[6]
For everything was manifest to thee, as God,

14 And was prepared from the beginning before thee;
And thou, O God, hast made all.

15 Hallelujah.

V

1 I thank thee, O Lord,
Because I love thee.

2 O Most High, do[1] not forsake me,
Because thou art my hope.

3 Freely I received thy grace:
I shall live by it.

4 My persecutors will come, but will not see me:

5 A cloud of gloom will fall ⟨upon⟩ their eyes,
And a mist of obscurity will bring darkness upon them;

6 And they will not have light to see,
That they may not seize me.

7 Their plan will become stupidity,[2]
And what they have plotted will come back upon their own heads;

8 For they have thought out a plan,
But it will not come to anything for them;

---

[6] Text 'So that thou shouldest not henceforth pull and take them'.

[1] This verb may also be translated as an indicative. Conversely, verses 5–7 may express wishes rather than statements.
[2] Lit. 'swellings'.

9 They have wickedly made preparations,
But they have been found to be in vain.

10 For my hope is in the Lord,
And I shall not be afraid;

11 And because the Lord is my deliverance,
I shall not be afraid.

12 And he is on my head like a crown,
And I shall not be shaken;

13 And even if everything is shaken,
I *shall* remain;

14 And even if everything that is visible perishes,
I shall not die:

15 Because the Lord is with me, and I am with him.
Hallelujah.

VI

1 As the ⟨wind⟩[1] moves over the harp, and the strings speak,

2 So does the Spirit of the Lord speak in my members, and I speak by his love.

3 For he destroys anything foreign,
And everything is of the Lord.

4 For so it was from the beginning,
And will be to the end;

5 That nothing might withstand him,
And nothing might rise up against him.

6 The Lord has multiplied the knowledge of himself,[2]
And has been zealous that the things should be known which, by his grace, have been given us.

7 And he has given us his praise for his name:
Our spirits praise his Holy Spirit.

8 For a stream went out, and became a great and broad river,
For it overwhelmed everything, and broke it up, and carried it to the temple;[3]

[1] The word supplied also means 'spirit'.
[2] Or 'his knowledge'.
[3] Or 'and broke up and carried away the temple'.

9 And the restraints of men were not able to restrain it,
 Nor the skill of those who restrain water;

10 For it came upon the face of the whole earth,
 And filled everything;

11 And all the thirsty on earth drank,
 And *their* thirst was brought to an end and quenched;

12 For the drink was given by the Most High.

13 Blessed, therefore, are the ministers of that drink,
 Those who have been entrusted with his water:

14 They have refreshed the dry lips,
 And have raised up the will that was paralysed;

15 And souls that were near to expiring
 They have held back from death;

16 And limbs that were fallen
 They have straightened and raised up:

17 They have given strength to their coming,
 And light to their eyes;

18 For everyone has known them in the Lord,
 And by means of the waters they lived eternal life.[4]
 Hallelujah.

VII

1 Like the course of anger over wickedness,
 So is the course of joy over the Beloved One;
 And he[1] brings in of its fruits without hindrance.

2 My joy is the Lord, and my course is towards him:
 This my path is beautiful;

3 For I have a helper to the Lord.
 He made himself known to me, without grudging,[2] in his
   generosity;
 For in his kindness he set aside his majesty.[3]

---

[4] Or 'And they lived by means of the eternal living waters'.

[1] Or 'it' (i.e. the course).
[2] Or 'as one without envy'.
[3] Lit. 'For his kindness made little his greatness'.

4   He became like me, in order that I might accept him:
    In appearance he seemed like me, in order that I might put him on.

5   And I did not tremble when I saw him,
    Because he had pity on me.

6   He became like my nature, in order that I might learn *to know* him,
    And like my form, in order that I might not turn away from him.

7   The Father of knowledge
    Is the Word of knowledge:

8   He who created Wisdom
    Is wiser than his works;

9   And he who created me before I came into being
    Knew[4] what I should do when I came into being.

10 Therefore he had pity on me in his great pity,
    And granted me to ask of him, and to receive of his sacrifice;

11 Because he is incorruptible,
    The completion of the ages and their Father.

12 He granted him to appear to those who are his,
    In order that they might recognize him who made them,
    And that they might not think that they had come into being of
        themselves.

13 For to knowledge he set his way:[5]
    He made it broad and long, and brought it to all perfection;

14 And he set upon it the footprints of his light,
    And it[6] went from the beginning to the end;

15 For by him was he served,[7]
    And he was well pleased with the Son.

16 And because of his deliverance he will take hold of everything;
    And the Most High will be known in his saints,

17 To proclaim to those who have psalms of the coming of the Lord,
    That they may go out to meet him, and may sing to him,
    With joy and with the harp of many sounds.

18 The seers will go before him,
    And be seen before him;

19 And they will praise the Lord in his love,

---

    [4] MS 'knows'.
    [5] Or 'For he appointed knowledge as his way'.
    [6] Some prefer to point the consonants so as to read 'I'.
    [7] Or 'was it made'.

Because he is near and sees.
20 And hatred will be taken away from the earth,
And will be drowned together with jealousy;
21 For ignorance has been destroyed,
Because the knowledge of the Lord has come.
22 Those who sing will sing of the grace of the Lord Most High,[8]
And will offer their psalms;
23 And their heart will be like the day,
And the sound of their voices like the great beauty of the Lord.
And there will be nothing that lives
That is either ignorant or **dumb**;[9]
24 For he has given a mouth to his creation,
To open the voice of the mouth to him, and to praise him.
25 Praise his power, and proclaim his grace.
Hallelujah.

VIII

1 Open, open your hearts to the exultation of the Lord,
And let your love overflow[1] from the heart to the lips,
2 To bring forth fruits to the Lord, even a holy life,
And to speak with watchfulness in his light.
3 Arise and stand up,
You who once were brought low:
4 You who were in silence,
Speak, for your mouths have been opened:
5 You who were despised,
From henceforth be raised up, for your righteousness has been
raised up;
6 For the right hand of the Lord is with you,
And he is your helper,
7 And peace was prepared for you

---

[8] Or 'Those who sing of the grace of the Lord Most High will sing'.
[9] Lit. 'And there will be nothing with life,
Nor with ignorance, nor with sorcery'.

[1] Lit. 'increase'.

Before your war began.

8 Hear the word of truth,
And receive the knowledge of the Most High.

9 Your flesh will not know what I am saying to you,
Nor your clothing what I am declaring to you.

10 Keep my secret, you who are kept by it:

11 Keep my faith, you who are kept by it;

12 And know my knowledge, you who know me in truth.

13 Love me with affection,
You who love.

14 For I do not turn my face from those that are mine,
Because I know them;

15 And before they came into being
I perceived them;
And on their faces I set my seal.

16 I fashioned their members;
And my breasts I prepared for them,
That they might drink my holy milk, that they might live by it.

17 I was well pleased with them,
And I am not ashamed of them;

18 For they are my own work,
And the power of my thoughts.

19 Who, therefore, will stand against my work,
Or who is he that is not subject to them?

20 I willed and formed mind and heart,
And they are mine;
And I set my chosen ones at my right hand.

21 And my righteousness goes before them;
And they will not be separated from my name,
Because it is with them.

22 Pray and continue earnestly in the love of the Lord,
And, you who are beloved, in the Beloved One;
And, you who are kept, in him who lived *again*;
And, you who are delivered, in him who was delivered;

23 And you will be found incorruptible in all ages because of the name
   of your Father.
Hallelujah.

IX

1 Open your ears,
And I will speak to you:

2 Give me yourselves,[1]
That I too may give you myself,[2]

3 The word of the Lord, and his will,
The holy purpose which he planned concerning his Christ.

4 For in the will of the Lord is your life,
And your perfection is incorruptible.

5 Become rich in God the Father,
And receive the mind of the Most High:
Be strong, and be delivered in his grace.

6 For I proclaim peace to you, his pious ones,
That none of those who hear may fall in the war,

7 And that those also who have known him may not perish,
And that those who receive *him* may not be ashamed.

8 Truth is an eternal crown
(Blessed are those who set it on their heads),

9 A stone of great price;
For the wars are on account of the crown;

10 And righteousness took it
And gave it to you.

11 Put on the crown in the true covenant of the Lord;
And all those who have been victorious will be written in his book;

12 For their book is the victory that is yours;
And she[3] sees you before her, and wills that you may be delivered.
Hallelujah.

X

1   The Lord directed my mouth by his word,
And opened my heart by his light,

---

[1] Lit. 'your souls'.
[2] Lit. 'my soul'.
[3] i.e., victory.

2 And caused his immortal life to dwell in me,
And granted me to tell of the fruit of his peace,

3 To restore the souls of those who wish to come to him,
And to lead a goodly band of captives back to freedom.

4 I became strong and powerful and led the world captive,
And it became to me to the glory of the Most High, even of God my
Father.

5 And the peoples who were scattered were gathered together,
And I was not defiled by my sins,[1]
Because they praised[2] me in high places.

6 And the footprints of light were set on their hearts,
And they walked in my life and were delivered,
And became my people[3] for ever and ever.
Hallelujah.

XI[1]

1 My heart was circumcised,[2] and its flowers appeared,
And grace sprouted up in it;
And it bore fruit to the Lord.[3]

2 For the Most High circumcised[2] me with his Holy Spirit,
And laid bare my kidneys towards himself;
And filled me with his love.

3 And his circumcision[4] became my deliverance;
And I ran in the way in his peace,
In the way of truth:

4 From the beginning to the end
I received his knowledge.[5]

---

[1] A slight change of the pointing would render possible the translation 'by my love'.　　　　　　　　　　　　　　　　　　　　　　　　　[2] Or 'confessed'.

[3] Or 'And were with me'.

[1] Ode xi is extant in Greek as well as in Syriac, and all but minor ways in which the former differs from the latter are recorded in the notes. Some obvious errors in the Greek are ignored.　　　　　　　　　　　　　　　　　　　　　[2] Or 'cut'.

[3] Gk. 'God'.　　　　　　[4] Or 'incision'.

[5] Or 'knowledge of him'.

5   And I was firmly established on the rock of truth,[6]
     Where he set me;

6   And speaking waters touched my lips
     From the Lord's spring[7] without grudging;[8]

7   And I drank, and was intoxicated
     By the living,[9] immortal, waters;

8   And my intoxication was not without knowledge,
     But I[10] abandoned vanities,

9   And turned[10] towards the Most High, my God,
     And became rich through his gift;

10   And I abandoned folly, which is cast over the earth,[11]
     And I stripped it off and cast it from me;

11   And the Lord renewed me with his clothing,
     And possessed me[12] with his light,

12   And gave me incorruptible refreshment from above,[13]
     And I became like the ground which sprouts and rejoices in its
       fruits.

13   And the Lord is like the sun
     Upon the face of the ground:

14   He enlightened my eyes,[14]
     And my face received[15] the dew;

15   And my breath took pleasure
     In the pleasant fragrance[16] of the Lord;

16   And he brought me to his paradise,
     Where are the riches of the pleasure of the Lord.[17]

[6] Gk. 'a firm rock'.   [7] Gk. adds 'of life'.
[8] Or 'From the spring of the Lord who is without envy'.
[9] Gk. om. 'living'.   [10–10] Gk. 'I turned from vanities'.
[11] Or 'folly lying on the ground' – so Gk.
[12] Gk. 'revived me', or 'regained me for himself'.
[13] Gk. 'And brought me to life again with his incorruption'.
[14] Or 'my eyes shone' – so Gk.   [15] Gk. 'was besprinkled with'.
[16] Gk. 'the fragrance of the kindness'.
[17] Gk. adds, 'I beheld trees, beautiful and bearing fruit,
     And their crown was a natural growth;
     Their branches sprouted, and their fruits laughed;
     Their shoots *came up* from an immortal land.
     And the river of joy watered them,
     And *flowed* round their land of eternal life.'
(The word translated 'shoots' usually means 'roots'.)

17   And I worshipped the Lord because of his glory:
18   And I said, Blessed, O Lord,
      Are those who have been planted in thy ground,
      And those who have a place in thy paradise,
19   And grow up in the growth of thy trees,
      And have moved from darkness to light.
20   Behold, all thy labourers are excellent,
      [18]Who perform good works,
21   And turn from wickedness to thy pleasantness,
      And have turned the bitterness of the trees away from them,
      When they were planted in thy ground.[18]
22   And everything has become like a relic of thee,[19]
      And an eternal remembrance of thy faithful servants.
23   For there is much room in thy paradise,
      And there is nothing that is unprofitable;
      But everything is full of[20] fruits.
24   Praise be to thee, O God, [21]the pleasure that is in the eternal
          paradise.[21]
      Hallelujah.

XII

1   He filled me with the words of truth,
     In order that I might speak it;
2   And truth flowed from my mouth like the flow of waters,
     And my lips declared its[1] fruits.
3   And he[1] made his[1] knowledge abound in me,
     Because the mouth of the Lord is the true Word,
     And the gate of his light.
4   And the Most High gave him[1] to his worlds,

[18-18] Gk. 'They make good transformations
              From wickedness to kindness;
              The bitterness of the plants is changed in thy land.'
[19] Gk. 'becomes like thy will'. It then adds 'Blessed are the ministers of thy
waters'.   [20] Gk. 'bears'.
[21-21] Gk. 'in the paradise of eternal delight'.

[1] These pronouns can be translated into English as either masculine or neuter.

The interpreters of his beauty,
And the narrators of his glory,
And the confessors of his thought,
And the preachers of his mind,
And the sanctifiers (?) of his works.

5 For the swiftness of the Word cannot be told,
And like its[2] telling, so too are its[2] swiftness and its[2] speed,
And his course is without limit:

6 He never falls, but stands fast,
And he knows not his descent, nor his way.[3]

7 For as is his work, so is his expectation;[4]
For it is the light and sunrise of thought.

8 And by him the worlds spoke one to another,
And those that were silent acquired speech;

9 And by him friendship and agreement came into being,
And they spoke one to the other what they had *to say*;

10 And they were goaded on by the Word;
And they knew him who made them,
Because they were in agreement;

11 For the mouth of the Most High spoke to them,
And through him his explanation had free course.

12 For the habitation of the Word is a man,[5]
And his truth is love.

13 Blessed are those who have understood everything through him,[1]
And have known the Lord in his truth.
Hallelujah.

XIII

1 Behold, the Lord is our mirror:
Open your eyes and see them in him;
2 And learn how your face is,

[2] i.e. of the swiftness: a slight change in the pointing would render possible the translation 'his'.
[3] With a slight emendation, 'And his descent and his way are unknown'.
[4] The form is anomalous but very close to the word for 'his expectation'.
[5] Or 'man': or 'the Son of man'.

And utter praises to his Spirit;

3   And wipe the **filth**[1] from your face,
And love his holiness and put it on;

4   And you will be without blemish all the time with him.
Hallelujah.

XIV

1   Like the eyes of a son on his father,
So are my eyes, O Lord, continually towards thee;

2   Because with thee are my breasts and my pleasure.

3   Turn not thy compassion away from me, O Lord,
And take not thy kindness from me.

4   Stretch out thy right hand to me continually, O my Lord,
And be a guide to me until the end because of thy good pleasure.

5   I shall[1] be pleasing before thee because of thy glory,
And because of thy name I shall[1] be delivered from the evil one;

6   And thy gentleness, O Lord, will[1] abide with me,
And the fruits of thy love.

7   Teach me the psalms of thy truth,
That I may bear fruits in thee;

8   And open to me the harp of thy Holy Spirit,
That I may praise thee, O Lord, with every melody.

9   And according to the abundance of thy compassion, so mayest
thou grant me;
And make haste to grant our requests.

10   And thou art sufficient for all our needs.
Hallelujah.

XV

1   As the sun is a joy to those who seek its day,
So my joy is the Lord;

---

[1] The Syriac word here is otherwise unknown.

[1] These verbs may be optative rather than indicative.

2   Because he is my sun,
And his rays roused me,
And his light dispelled all the darkness from my face.

3   I obtained eyes by him,
And saw his holy day:

4   Ears became mine,
And I heard his truth.

5   The thought of knowledge became mine,
And I delighted myself through him.

6   I forsook the way of error,
And I went to him and received from him deliverance without
    grudging;[1]

7   And according to his gift he gave to me,
And according to his great beauty he made me.

8   I put on incorruption through his name,
And I put off corruption by his grace.

9   Death was destroyed from before my face,
And Sheol was brought to nothing at my word.

10   And immortal life rose up in the land of the Lord,
And it became known to his faithful ones,
And was given unsparingly to all those who trust in him.
Hallelujah.

XVI

1   As the work of the ploughman is the ploughshare,
And the work of the helmsman is the steering of the ship,
So, too, my work is the psalm of the Lord in his praises.

2   My craft and my occupation are in his praises,
Because his love nourished my heart,
And it brought up his fruits to my lips.

3   For my love is the Lord,
Therefore I will sing to him;

4   For I am made strong by his praises,
And I have faith in him.

[1] Or 'received deliverance from him that is without envy'.

5   I will open my mouth,
And his Spirit will proclaim in me
The glory of the Lord and his beauty,

6   The work of his hands,
And what his fingers have made,

7   For the multitude of his mercies,
And for the might of his Word.

8   For the Word of the Lord searches out what is unseen,
And perceives his thought;

9   For the eye sees his works,
And the ear hears his thought.

10   He spread out the earth,
And set the waters in the sea:

11   He stretched out the heavens,
And set in order the stars;

12   And set in order the creation and established it;
And he rested from his works.

13   And the created things run in their courses,
And perform their tasks,
And know not how to stand still and be idle;

14   And the hosts are subject to his Word.

15   The treasury of the light is the sun,
And the treasury of the darkness is the night;

16   And he made the sun for the day that it might be bright,
And night brings darkness upon the face of the earth.

17   And they take over, the one from the other;
They proclaim[1] the beauty of God.

18   And there is nothing that is apart from the Lord,
Because he was before anything came into being.

19   And the worlds came into being by his Word,
And by the thought of his heart.

20   Glory and honour be to his name.
Hallelujah.

---

[1] Or 'complete'.

XVII

1 I was crowned by my God,
And my crown is the Living One;

2 And I was justified by my Lord,
And my deliverance is incorruptible:

3 I was released from vain things,
And I am not a man condemned:

4 My bonds were severed by **his**[1] hands:
I received the face and likeness of a new person;
And I walked in him[2] and was delivered,

5 And the thought of truth led me;
And I went after it and did not go astray.

6 And all who saw me were amazed,
And I seemed to them to be a stranger.

7 And he who knew and **brought** me **up** is the Most High in all his
perfection;
And he held me in honour[3] in his kindness,
And he raised my mind to the height of truth.

8 And thence he gave me the way of his steps,
And I opened the gates that were shut;

9 And I broke in pieces the bars of iron;
But my fetters[4] grew hot and melted before me.

10 And nothing seemed to me to be shut,
Because I was the opening of everything;

11 And I went to all my[5] prisoners to release them,
That I might leave no man bound and[6] binding.

12 And I gave my knowledge without grudging,[7]
And my prayer *was* in my love.

13 And I sowed my fruits in hearts,
And I transformed them in myself.

14 And they received my blessing and lived,

---

[1] The removal of a point gives this translation instead of the 'her' in the MS.
[2] Or 'I entered into it'.
[3] So H: B 'And he is glorified'.
[4] Lit. 'my own iron'.   [5] So H: B 'the'.
[6] So H: B 'or'.   [7] Or 'envy'.

And were gathered to me and delivered,
15 Because they became my members,
And I am their head.
16 Glory be to thee, our head, O Lord Christ.
Hallelujah.

XVIII

1 My heart was raised up by the love of the Most High and was
enlarged,
That I might praise him through my name.
2 My members were strengthened,
That they might not fall from his power:
3 Diseases departed far from my body,
And it[1] stood up for the Lord by his will,
Because his kingdom is firm.
4 O Lord, because of those who lack *the knowledge of thee*,
Wilt thou take away[2] thy word from me?
5 Neither, because of their works,
Wilt[3] thou withhold from me thy perfection.
6 The light will not be conquered by darkness,
Nor will truth flee from falsehood.
7 Thy right hand will make our deliverance victorious,
And thou wilt receive from every place,
And wilt preserve, everyone who is held by evil.[4]
8 Thou art my God: falsehood and death are not in thy mouth,
But thy will is perfection;
9 And thou knowest not vanity,
Because it, too, knows not thee;
10 And thou knowest not error,
Because it, too, knows not thee.
11 And ignorance appeared as fine dust,

---

[1] So H: B 'they'.
[2] So H: B 'cast'.
[3] The verbs in verses 5–7 may be optative.
[4] Or 'by misfortunes'.

And as the scum of the sea.

12 And vain people thought concerning it that it was great:
They,[5] too, came to resemble it and became vain.

13 And those who have knowledge understood[6] and thought,
And were not defiled in their thoughts;

14 Because they were in the mind of the Most High,
And they laughed at those who were walking in error:

15 But they spoke the truth
From the inspiration which the Most High breathed into them.

16 Glory and great honour[7] be to his name.
Hallelujah.

XIX

1 A cup of milk was offered to me,
And I drank it in the sweetness of the kindness of the Lord.

2 The Son is the cup,
And he who was milked is the Father,
And the Holy Spirit milked him;[1]

3 Because his breasts were full,
And it was not desirable that his milk should be emitted without
reason;

4 The Holy Spirit opened her[2] bosom,
And mixed the milk of the two breasts of the Father,

5 And gave the mixture to the world without their knowing;
And those who receive *it* are in the fulness of the right hand.

6 The womb of the Virgin embraced[3] *it*,
And she conceived and bore;

7 And the Virgin became a mother with great compassion;

---

[5] So H: B 'And they'.
[6] Lit. 'knew'.
[7] Lit. 'beauty'.

[1] So H: B 'And she who milked him is the Holy Spirit' (The Syriac word for
'Spirit' is feminine).
[2] Cp. note[1]. If a point were removed, 'his' (i.e. the Father's) could be read.
[3] Or 'caught'.

8   And she was in labour, and bore a Son without feeling pain,
     Because it did not happen without a reason;
9   And she did not seek a midwife,
     Because he delivered[4] her.
10   She bore as it were a man by the will *of God*,[5]
     And bore *him* and made *him* known,[6]
     And obtained *him* in great power;
11   And she loved *him* in deliverance,
     And guarded *him* in kindness,
     And made *him* known in greatness.
     Hallelujah.

XX

1   I am a priest of the Lord,
     And to him I minister as priest,
2   And to him I offer the offering of his thought.
3   For not as the world,
     Nor as the flesh, is his thought,
     Nor as those who serve in a fleshly way.
4   The offering of the Lord is righteousness,
     And purity of heart and lips.
5   Offer your[1] kidneys without blemish,
     And let not your bowels afflict *another's* bowels,
     And let not your soul afflict *another's* soul.
6   You shall not acquire a stranger by the blood of your soul,
     Nor shall you seek to defraud your neighbour,
     Nor shall you deprive him of the covering of his nakedness.
7   But put on the grace of the ungrudging Lord;[2]
     And come to the[3] paradise, and make yourself a garland from his
          tree,

---

[4] Or 'kept alive'.
[5] Or 'by *her own* will'.
[6] Lit. 'And bore *him* in showing forth'.

[1] So H: B 'my'.
[2] Or 'the Lord who is without envy'.
[3] So H: B 'his'.

8   And put *it* on your head, and delight *in it*,
    And recline on his serenity.
9   And his glory will go before you,
    And you will receive of his kindness and of his goodness,[4]
    And grow fat in the glory of his holiness.
10 Glory and honour be to his name.
    Hallelujah.

XXI

1   I raised my arms[1] on high
    To the pity of the Lord,
2   Because he cast away my bonds from me;
    And my helper raised me up to his pity and his deliverance.
3   And I put off darkness,
    And put on light.
4   And my soul acquired members
    In which is no[2] pain,
    Neither distress, nor sufferings.
5   And supremely helpful to me became the thought of the Lord,
    And his incorruptible fellowship.
6   And I was raised up in his light,
    And I passed[3] before his face;
7   And I came near to him,
    Praising and thanking him.
8   He made my heart overflow, and it was found in my mouth,
    And it appeared on my lips;
9   And the exultation of the Lord and[4] his praise lit up[5] my face.
    Hallelujah.

---

[4] So H: B 'grace'.

[1] So H: B 'arm'.
[2] So B: H om. 'no'.
[3] So B: H 'worked'. The only difference is the position of a point.
[4] So H: B 'in'.
[5] Lit. 'became great upon'.

XXII

1   He who brought me down from the height,
    And raised me up from the lower regions,

2   And he who gathered the things that were in the middle
    And laid them[1] low for me,

3   He who scattered my enemies,
    And my adversaries;

4   He who gave me power over bonds,
    That I might loose them;

5   He who overthrew by my hands the seven-headed dragon,
    (And thou didst set me over his roots,[2] that I might destroy his
        seed) –

6   *It is thou*:[3]
    Thou wast there and didst help me,
    And in every place thy name was blessed by me.[4]

7   Thy right hand destroyed his evil venom;[5]
    And thy hand made the way level for those who believe in thee,

8   And chose them from the graves,
    And set them apart from the dead:

9   It took dead bones,
    And covered them with bodies;

10 And they were motionless,
    And it gave them help[6] for life.

11 Thy way and thy person[7] were incorruptible:
    Thou didst bring thy world to corruption,
    That everything might be dissolved and renewed,

12 And that the foundation for everything might be thy rock;
    And upon it thou hast built thy kingdom;

---

[1] So B: om. H.
[2] So H: B 'root'.
[3] The syntactical relationship of this verse to verses 1–5 is difficult.
[4] So H: B 'was encircling me' (and similarly the Coptic).
[5] So H: B 'the venom of evil'.
[6] So H: B 'energy'.
[7] According to the punctuation of the MSS 'thy person' goes with the next line to give 'And thou didst bring thy person into the world, even into corruption'.

And thou didst become[8] the dwelling-place of the saints.
Hallelujah.

XXIII

1 Joy belongs to the saints,
And who will put it on but they alone?

2 Grace belongs to the elect,
And who will receive it but those who have trusted in it from the
beginning?

3 Love belongs to the elect,
And who will put it on but those who have possessed it from the
beginning?

4 Walk in the knowledge of the Most High,[1]
And you will know the grace of the Lord[2] without grudging,[3]
His exultation and the perfection of his knowledge.

5 And his thought was like a letter,
His[4] will came down from on high;

6 And it was sent like an arrow from a bow,
That is shot with force;

7 And many hands rushed upon the letter,
To snatch it and take it and read it;

8 And it fled from their fingers;
And they were afraid of it and of the seal which was upon it,

9 Because they were not allowed to loose his[5] seal,
For the power that was upon the seal was greater than they.

10 But those who saw it went after the letter,
That they might know where it would stop,
And who would read it,
And who would hear it.

---

[8] So H: B 'And it became'.

[1] So H: B 'of the Lord'.
[2] 'And you will know . . . Lord': om. H.
[3] Or 'who is without envy'.
[4] So H: B 'And his'.
[5] So H: B 'its'.

11 But a wheel received it,
    And it came upon it;
12 And with it was a sign
    Of kingship and of government.
13 And everything that was moving the wheel
    It mowed and cut down;
14 And it gathered a multitude of adversaries;
    And it covered up rivers;
15 And it crossed over and uprooted many woods,[6]
    And made a broad path.
16 The head came down to the feet,
    Because as far as the feet[7] ran the wheel,
    And what was coming[8] on it.
17 The letter was one of command,[9]
    Because[10] all places were gathered together.
18 And on his[5] head appeared the head that was revealed,
    And the Son of truth from the Most High Father.
19 And he took possession of everything and received it;
    And the thoughts of many came to nothing.
20 And all who led astray **escaped**[11] and fled,
    And those who persecuted were extinguished and blotted out.[12]
21 But the letter became a great tablet,
    Which was written completely by the finger of God;
22 And the name of the Father was upon it,
    And of the Son, and of the Holy Spirit,
    To reign for ever and ever.
    Hallelujah.

---

[6] So H: B 'peoples'.

[7] So B: H 'foot'.

[8] So H: B 'had come'. If the word were differently pointed the line might be translated 'And that which was the sign upon it'.

[9] So H: B 'It was a letter and a command'.

[10] So H: B 'And because'.

[11] Text 'were bold'.

[12] So B: H 'irritated'.

XXIV

1. The dove flew upon the head of our Lord[1] Christ,
   Because he was her head.

2. And she sang over him,
   And her voice was heard.

3. And the inhabitants feared,
   And the settlers trembled.

4. The birds[2] forsook their wings,[3]
   And all the reptiles died in their holes.

5. And the depths were opened and were covered *again*,
   And they sought the Lord like those in travail;

6. But he was not given to them for food,
   Because he was not theirs.

7. But the depths were immersed in the immersion of the Lord,
   And those who existed from of old perished in that thought;

8. For they became corrupt[4] from the beginning,
   And the completion of their corruption[5] was life.

9. And every one of them that was lacking perished,
   Because they were not permitted to utter a word[6] in order to remain.

10. And the Lord destroyed the thoughts
    Of all those with whom the truth was not;

11. For they lacked wisdom,
    Those who were proud of heart.

12. And they were rejected,
    Because the truth was not with them,

13. Because the Lord made his way manifest,
    And enlarged his grace.

14. And those who perceived it
    Know his holiness.
    Hallelujah.

---

[1] the head of our Lord: om. H.   [2] So H: B 'It flew *and*'.
[3] The exact meaning of these three words is uncertain: the translation 'took to flight' has also been suggested.   [4] Or 'travailed'.
[5] This is the usual meaning. But the cognate verb can mean 'travailed' (cp. note[4]), and so perhaps this noun means 'travail'.
[6] Or 'Because they had no word to utter'.

XXV

1   I escaped from my bonds,
     And to thee I fled, O my God,

2   Because thou hast been a right hand of deliverance,
     And my helper.

3   Thou hast restrained those who rose up against me,
     And I shall not see him again,[1]

4   Because thy person was with me,
     Which saved me in thy grace.[2]

5   But I was despised and rejected in the eyes of many,
     And I was in their eyes as lead.

6   And strength from thee was given me,
     And help.

7   Thou didst set a lamp for me on my right hand and on my left,
     And there will be[3] nothing in me without light.

8   And I was covered with the covering of thy Spirit,
     And I removed from myself[4] the[5] garments of skins,

9   Because thy right hand raised me up,
     And caused sickness to pass away from me.

10   And I became mighty in the[6] truth,
     And holy in thy righteousness.

11   And all who were opposed to me were afraid of me,
     And I became the Lord's, in the name of the Lord.

12   And I was justified in his kindness;
     And his rest is for evermore.
     Hallelujah.

XXVI

1   I poured forth praise to the Lord,
             Because I am his.

---

[1] So H: B 'And they were not seen again'.   [2] So H: B 'goodness'.

[3] So H: B 'That there might be'; and, similarly, the Coptic.

[4] The consonants might be pointed to read 'Thou didst remove from me'.

[5] So H: B 'my'.   [6] So H: B 'thy'.

2   And I will utter his holy psalm,
    Because my heart is with him;

3   For his harp is in my hands,
    And the psalms of his rest will not be silent.

4   I will cry to him with all my heart:
    I will praise and exalt him with all my members;

5   For from the east to the west
    Praise is his,

6   And from the north to the south
    Thanksgiving is his,

7   And from the top of the heights to their furthest part
    Perfection[1] is his.

8   Who can write the psalms of the Lord,
    Or who can recite them?

9   Or who can instruct his soul for life,
    That his soul may be delivered?

10 Or who can rest upon the Most High,
    That he may speak from his mouth?

11 Who is able to interpret the wonders of the Lord?
    For he who interprets will be destroyed,
    And what is to be interpreted will remain.

12 For it is enough to know and rest;
    For the psalmists remain in rest,

13 Like a river that has an abundant spring,
    And flow for the help of those who seek it.
    Hallelujah.

XXVII

1   I spread out my hands,
    And sanctified my Lord;

2   Because the stretching out of my hands is his sign,[1]

3   And my spreading out[2] is the upright wood.
    Hallelujah.

[1]   Or perhaps, 'whole-offering'.

[1]   So H: B 'was hindered'.
[2]   The word often means 'simplicity'.

XXVIII

1   Like the wings of doves over their young
(And the mouths[1] of their young are towards their mouths)
So, too, are the wings of the Spirit over my heart.

2   My heart is delighted and leaps for joy,
Like the babe who leaps in the womb of his mother.

3   I believed: therefore[2] I was at rest,
Because he is faithful in whom I believed.

4   He richly blessed me,
And my head is towards him;
And no sword shall separate me from him,
Nor blade;

5   Because I was made ready[3] before destruction came,
And I was placed on his incorruptible wings,[4]

6   And immortal life came forth,[5]
And kissed me.

7   And from it is the Spirit in[6] me,
And she[7] cannot die for she is living.[8]

8   Those who saw me wondered,
Because I was persecuted;

9   And they thought that I was swallowed up,
Because I appeared to them as one of those that perish.

10   But my oppression
Became my deliverance.

11   And I became an abomination to them,
Because there was no envy in me:

12   Because I did good to every man,
I was hated;

---

[1] So B: H 'mouth'.
[2] So H: B 'therefore, also'.
[3] So H: B 'I made ready' or 'I was made ready'.
[4] Or 'the wings of incorruption'.
[5] So H: B 'embraced me'.
[6] So H: B 'who is in'.
[7] See note[1] at Ode xix. 2.
[8] So H: B 'life'.

13 And they surrounded me like mad dogs,
    Who ignorantly attack their masters,

14 Because their intelligence is corrupted,
    And their intellect perverted.

15 But I was holding waters in my right hand,
    And I endured[9] their bitterness by my sweetness;

16 And I did not perish, because I was not their brother,
    Nor was my birth like theirs.[10]

17 And they sought my death, but were not successful,
    Because I was older than their memory,
    And in vain did they attack[11] me.

18 And those who were after me[12]
    Sought in vain to destroy
    The memory of him who was before them;

19 Because the mind of the Most High is not to be forestalled,
    And his heart is better than all wisdom.
    Hallelujah.

XXIX

1 The Lord is my hope:
   I shall not be ashamed in him.

2 For according to his glory he made me;
   And according to his goodness,[1] so he gave to me;

3 And according to his compassion he raised me up;
   And according to his great beauty he exalted me;

4 And he brought me up from the depths of Sheol,
   And from the mouth of death he drew me.

5 And I laid low my enemies,
   And he justified me in his grace;

6 For I believed in the Lord's Christ,

[9] So H: B 'forgot'.
[10] So H: B 'Nor did they recognize my birth'.
[11] So H: H[mg.] and B 'cast lots upon'.
[12] So H: B om. 'me'.

[1] So H: B 'grace'.

And it was plain to me that he was the Lord.

7 And he showed me[2] his sign,
And led me in his light;

8 And he gave me the rod of his strength,
That I might subdue the thoughts of peoples,
And lay low the power of mighty men;

9 To make war by his word,
And to gain the victory by his might.

10 And the Lord cast down my enemy by his word,
And he became like the chaff which the wind carries away.

11 And I gave praise to the Most High,
Because he made great his servant and the son of his handmaid.
Hallelujah.

XXX

1 Draw yourselves water from the living spring of the Lord,
Because it has been opened to you.

2 And come, all you who thirst, and take a draught,
And rest by the spring of the Lord,

3 Because it is excellent and pure,
And gives rest to the soul.

4 For its waters are far pleasanter than honey,
And the honeycomb of bees is not to be compared with it;

5 Because it comes out from the lips of the Lord,
And from the heart of the Lord is its name.

6 And it came unhindered and unseen,
And until it was set in their midst men did not know it.

7 Blessed are those who drank from it,
And were refreshed by it.
Hallelujah.

[2] So B: H 'him'.

XXXI

1 The depths melted before the Lord,
And darkness was destroyed by his appearance:

2 Error erred and perished before him,[1]
And folly[2] became inactive,[3] and it sank because of the truth of the Lord.

3 He opened his mouth and spoke grace and joy,
And spoke a new song of praise to his name;

4 And he lifted up his voice to the Most High,
And he presented to him those sons who had come into being through him;[4]

5 And his person was justified,
Because his holy Father had granted him that it should be so.

6 Come forth, you who have been oppressed,
And receive joy;

7 And take possession of your souls through grace,
And take to yourselves immortal life.

8 And they condemned me when I stood up,
Me, who was uncondemned;

9 And they divided my spoil,
Although nothing was owing to them.

10 But I endured, and was silent and quiet,
That I might not be moved by them;

11 But I stood without moving, like a firm rock,
Which is buffeted by the waves and *yet* endures;

12 And I bore their bitterness because of humility,
In order that I might deliver my people and take possession of them,

13 And that I might not render void the promises to the patriarchs,
Whose seed I promised to deliver.[5]
Hallelujah.

---

[1] Lit. 'from him'.
[2] So B: H 'contempt'.
[3] Lit. 'received (so B: H 'gave') immobility'.
[4] Or 'who were in his hands' (so H: B 'hand').
[5] Or 'For the deliverance of whose seed I was promised'.

XXXII

1   The blessed have joy from their heart,
    And light from him who dwells in them,
2   And the Word from the truth who was[1] from[2] himself;
3   Because he became strong in the holy power of the Most High,
    And will remain unmoved for ever and ever.
    Hallelujah.

XXXIII

1   But again grace[1] ran and left corruption,
    And came down upon him to bring him to nothing.
2   And he destroyed destruction[2] from before him,
    And spoiled all his work.
3   And he stood upon a high peak and uttered his voice,
    From one end of the earth to the other;
4   And he drew to himself all those who obeyed him,
    And he did not appear as an[3] evil one.
5   But a perfect virgin stood,
    Proclaiming, and crying out, and saying,
6   Turn, you sons of men,
    And you, their daughters, come,
7   And leave the ways of this corruption,
    And draw near to me.
8   And I will enter into you,
    And bring you out from destruction,
    And make you wise in the ways of truth.
9   Do not be corrupted,
    And do not perish.

[1] Or 'came into being'.
[2] B om.

[1] 'Grace' is fem.: 'corruption' is masc.
[2] Or 'wrought complete destruction'.
[3] Or 'the'.

10   Hear me and be delivered,
      For I proclaim among you the grace of God;
11   And by me you will be delivered and become blessed:
      I am your judge.
12   And those who have put me on will not be rejected,
      But will obtain incorruption in the new world.
13   O my elect ones walk in me!
      And I will make my ways known to them that seek me,
      And cause them to trust in my name.
      Hallelujah.

XXXIV

1   There is no difficult way where there is a simple heart,
      Nor a barrier[1] in upright thoughts,
2   Nor a storm in the depth of an enlightened thought.
3   Where the man who is virtuous is surrounded on every side,
      There is in him nothing discordant,[2]
4   The likeness of what is beneath.
      He is what[3] is above;
5   For everything is above,
      And beneath is nothing,
      But there is believed to be something by those who have no
         knowledge.
6   Grace was revealed for your deliverance:
      Believe, and live, and be delivered.
      Hallelujah.

XXXV

1   The dew[1] of the Lord overshadowed me in rest,[2]
      And he set up a cloud of peace above my head,

[1] Or 'offence': the word usually means 'wound'.
[2] Or 'doubtful' (lit. 'divided').
[3] Or attaching verse 4a to 4b instead of to 3b, read 'Is he who'.

[1] Or 'shower'.   [2] So H: B 'gentleness'.

2   Which kept me continually,
     And became my deliverance[3].

3   All *things*[4] were shaken and agitated,
     And smoke and judgement[5] went out from them;

4   And I was at peace in the legion[6] of the Lord,
     And he was to me more than dew[7] and more than a foundation.

5   And I was carried as a child by his mother,
     And he gave me as milk the dew of the Lord;

6   And I grew up according to his gift,
     And I rested in his perfection;

7   And I spread out my hands in the ascent of my soul,
     And stood erect[8] towards the Most High,
     And was delivered with[9] him.
     Hallelujah.

XXXVI

1   I rested on the Spirit of the Lord,
     And she[1] raised me on high;

2   And she made me stand on my feet on the Lord's heights,
     Before his perfection and his glory,
     While I was praising[2] *him* in the composition of his psalms.[3]

3   She bore me before the face of the Lord;
     And although I was a son of man,
     I was named the Shining[4] One, the Son of God,

4   While I was praised[2] among those who are praised,[5]

[3] So B: H 'And was mine in deliverance'.
[4] H might also be translated 'all *people*' or even 'everyone'.
[5] So H: B 'a judge'.   [6] Or 'precept'.
[7] The words 'dew' here and in verse 5, 'overshadowed' in verse 1, and 'child' in verse 5 all come from similar roots. Here the word might be 'shade', written defectively.
[8] Or 'was directed'.   [9] Or 'towards' as in 7b.

[1] See note[1] at Ode xix. 2.
[2] The participle could be either active or passive.
[3] B connects this line with the next verse.
[4] Or 'enlightened'.   [5] So B: H 'who praise'.

And was great[6] among the great ones;

5 For according to the greatness of the Most High, so she made me,
And according to his renewal he renewed me.

6 And he anointed me from his perfection,
And I became one of those near to him.

7 And my mouth was opened like a cloud of dew,
And my heart gushed forth like[7] a fount of righteousness;

8 And my access to him was in peace,
And I was established in the Spirit of providence.
Hallelujah.

XXXVII

1   I spread out my hands towards my[1] Lord,
And towards the Most High I lifted up my voice;

2   And I spoke with the lips of my heart,
And he heard me when my voice reached[2] him.

3   His word came to me,
That gave me the fruits of my labours,

4   And gave me rest in the grace of the Lord.
Hallelujah.

XXXVIII

1   I went up into the light of Truth as if into a chariot,[1]
And Truth led me and brought me,

2   And took me across chasms and rifts,[2]
And delivered me from crags and valleys;[3]

3   And he became to me a harbour of deliverance,
And placed me on the arms[4] of immortal life;

---

[6] Or 'the greatest'.   [7] B om.

[1] So H: B 'the'.   [2] Lit. 'fell to'.

[1] Or, perhaps, 'ship'.   [2] So H: B 'empty rifts'.
[3] Or 'waves'.   [4] So H: B 'stair'.

4 And he went with me and gave me rest, and did not let me err,
Because he was[5] Truth.

5 And I was in no danger, because I walked with him,
And I erred in nothing, because I obeyed him;

6 For Error fled from him,
And did not meet him.

7 But Truth went along a straight path;
And everything which I did not know
He showed me,

8 Even all the drugs of Error,
And all the scourges of death[6] which are thought[7] to be sweetness.

9 And the corruptor of corruption
I saw while the bride who is corrupted[8] was adorning herself,
Even the bridegroom who corrupts and is corrupted;

10 And I asked Truth, Who are these? And he said to me,
This is the Deceiver,[9] and *that is* Error;

11 And they imitate the Beloved One and his bride,
And cause the world to err, and corrupt it;

12 And they invite many to a banquet,
And give them to drink the wine of their intoxication,

13 And they cause them to vomit their wisdom and understanding,
And they render them[10] irrational;

14 And then they abandon them,
But they go about raving[11] and corrupting,[12]
Because they are without understanding,
For neither do they seek it.

15 And I acted wisely, so that I did not fall into the hands of the
Deceiver.[13]
And I congratulated myself, because Truth had gone with me.

[5] So H: B 'was and is'.
[6] Or 'of death' may go with 'sweetness'. The word translated 'scourges' could also be rendered 'attractions'.
[7] So B: H 'which men suppose'.
[8] So H: B has a participle which could be active or passive.
[9] Lit. 'This is he who causes to err'.
[10] So H: the fem. sing. pronoun in B presumably refers to wisdom.
[11] So B: H 'entreating' or 'commanding'.
[12] Or 'corrupted'.
[13] So H: B plural. See also note[9] on verse 10.

16 And I became strong, and lived, and was delivered,
And my foundations were laid near[14] the Lord;
Because he planted me.

17 For he set the root,
And watered it, and made it firm, and blessed it;
And its fruits will be for ever.

18 It went deep, and grew tall, and spread out,
And became full and large.

19 And the Lord alone was praised
For his planting and for his cultivation,

20 For his care and for the blessing of his lips,
For the beautiful planting of his right hand,

21 And for the discovery[15] of his planting,
And for the intelligence of his mind.
Hallelujah.

XXXIX

1 Mighty rivers are the power of the Lord,
Which carry headlong
Those who despise them,

2 And twist their steps,
And ruin their fords,

3 And seize their bodies,
And destroy their souls;

4 For they are swifter than lightning[1]
And faster.

5 But those who cross them in faith
Will not be shaken,

6 And those who walk on them without blemish
Will not be perturbed;

7 Because the Lord is a sign in them,

---

[14] Or 'on the hand of'.
[15] Some emend to 'splendour'.

[1] So H: B 'lightnings'.

And the sign becomes the path of those who cross in the name of
the Lord.

8   Put on, therefore, the name of the Most High, and know him,
And you will cross without danger,
Because the rivers will be obedient to you.

9   The Lord bridged them by his Word,
And walked, and crossed them on foot;

10 And his footprints remain on the waters, and have not been
obliterated,
But are like a piece of wood which is firmly[2] fixed:

11 On this side and that the waves are lifted up,
But the footprints of our Lord Christ remain,

12 And are not effaced,
Or obliterated;

13 And a path has been established for those who cross after him,
And for those who follow in the steps of his faith,
And worship his name.
Hallelujah.

XL

1   As honey drips from the honeycomb of bees,
And milk flows from the woman who loves her children,

2   So, too, is my hope on thee, O my God.
As a spring brings forth its waters,
So my heart brings forth the praise of the Lord,
And my lips utter praise to him.

3   And my tongue is sweet ⟨in⟩ his anthems,[1]
And my members grow fat in[2] his psalms;

4   And my face[3] rejoices in his exultation,
And my spirit exults in his love,

---

    [2] Or 'in truth'.

    [1] Or '⟨in⟩ intimacy with him'.
    [2] So B: H om. 'is sweet . . . fat in', . . . though 'in' was probably read before 'his
psalms' and later erased.
    [3] B 'also'. The following verse could be construed with the subject of 3b.

And my soul shines in him.

5 And he who is fearful will trust in him,
And deliverance will be established in him;

6 And his gain is immortal life,
And those who receive it are incorruptible.
Hallelujah.

XLI

1 All[1] his children will[2] praise the Lord,
And they will[3] receive the truth of his faith;

2 And his sons will be known to him:[4]
Therefore let us sing in his love.

3 We live[5] in the Lord by his grace,
And we receive life through his Christ.

4 For a great day has shone upon us,
And marvellous is he who gave us[6] of his praises.

5 Let us all, therefore, join together in the name of the Lord,
And let us honour him in his goodness;

6 And let our faces shine in his light,
And let our hearts meditate in his love,
By night and by day:

7 Let us exult on account of the exultation of the Lord.

8 All those who see me will marvel,
Because I am of another race;

9 For the Father of truth remembered me –
He who possessed me from the beginning;

10 For his wealth gave me birth,
And the thought of his heart.

11 And his Word is with us all along our way,
The deliverer who gives new life *to us* does not reject our souls –

12 The man who was brought low,

[1] So H: B 'All of us'.
[2] The verbs in this verse could express a wish.
[3] So H: B 'we shall'.
[4] B originally read 'And they will be known to his sons'.
[5] So H: B 'rejoice'.   [6] B om. 'us'.

And was raised up in his righteousness.

13 The Son of the Most High appeared
   In the perfection of his Father;

14 And the light dawned from the Word,
   That was[7] beforehand in him.

15 The Christ is one in truth,
   And was known from before the foundation of the world,

16 That he might give new life to souls for ever in the truth of his
   name.
   Let there be a new song of praise to the Lord from those who love
   him.
   Hallelujah.

XLII

1 I spread out my hands, and drew near to my Lord,
  Because the stretching out of my hands is his sign,

2 And my spreading out[1] is the outspread[1] wood,
  Which was set up on the way of the Upright One.

3 And I became useless
  To those [2]who knew me,
  In order that I might be hidden from those[2]
  Who did not take hold of me;

4 And I will be with those
  Who love me.

5 All my persecutors died;
  And they who trusted in me sought me, because I am alive;

6 And I arose and am with them,
  And I will speak through their mouths.

7 For they rejected those who persecute them,
  And I have laid upon them the yoke of my love.

8 As the arm of the bridegroom upon the bride,
  So is my yoke upon those who know me;

---

[7] Or 'came into being'.

[1] These two words could be translated 'simplicity' and 'simple' respectively.
[2-2] So B: H om.

9   And as the bed that is spread in the bridal chamber,
    So is my love upon those who believe in me.

10 I was not rejected, even though I was thought to be,
    And I did not perish, even though they supposed it of me.

11 Sheol saw me and was grieved,
    And Death disgorged me, and many with me:

12 I was vinegar and bitterness to him,
    And I went down with him as far as his depth extended;

13 And he let feet and head hang loose,[3]
    Because they[4] could not endure my face.

14 And I made an assembly of living men among his dead,
    And I spoke to them with living lips,
    In order that my word might not be without effect.

15 And those who had died ran to me,
    And cried and said, Have pity on us, Son of God!

16 And deal with us according to thy kindness,
    And bring us out of the bonds of darkness,

17 And open for us the gate,
    That by it we may come out with thee,
    For we see that our death does not touch thee.

18 May we too be delivered with thee,
    Because thou art our deliverer.

19 And I heard their voice,
    And set their faith in my heart,[5]

20 And I set[6] my name on their heads,
    Because they are free men[7] and are mine.
    Hallelujah.

---

[3] Or 'let go of feet and head'.
[4] So H: B 'he'.
[5] H omits this line.
[6] So B: H unintelligible.
[7] Lit. 'they are sons of free men'.

THE TESTAMENT OF SOLOMON

INTRODUCTION

The Testament, which is extant only in Greek,[1] relates how Solomon discovered that his building operations on the Temple were being frustrated by the demon Ornias: how in answer to prayer he was given authority, not only over Ornias but also over all the demons, to 'confine' them and use them as builders; and how, in the exercise of this authority, he summoned them before him one by one and set each a particular task until the Temple was completed. Ostensibly, the Testament is Solomon's warning to Israel against the dangers of apostasy, idolatry, and demon-worship, written shortly before his death and as a result of his own bitter experience (chaps. xv and xxvi). In fact, it is an essay in popular demonology and magic.

We are thus introduced by the Testament to that area of beliefs and practices which is probably best illustrated by the contents of the Hellenistic magical papyri. But we catch glimpses of it also in a variety of sources – for instance, in the incidental allusion in the Gospels, Acts, and Pauline Epistles to 'the rudiments' (or 'elements') of the world,'[2] to 'devils' (or 'demons') as the cause of disease,[3] and to the 'casting out'[4] of them and cures[5] by 'exorcists'.[6]

In view of the widespread acceptance of these ideas in the ancient world it is hardly surprising that Jews, who reflected on the accounts of the nature and extent of Solomon's wisdom recorded in 1 Kings iv. 29–34 and Wisd. vii. 17–22, should assume that he knew as much about demons as he did about the other departments of nature, and that he had been given power to control them. Josephus, at all events, is a witness to this belief. In his description of Solomon he writes:

[1] G. Graf (*Geschichte christ. arab. Literatur*, I. (= *Studi e Testi*, 118; Vatican, 1944), p. 210) has, however, drawn attention to the existence of a Syriac MS in Paris (B.N. Fonds Syriaque 194; 16th cent.) and an Arabic MS in the Vatican (Vat. ar. 448; 17th cent.), both of which seem to contain texts of the Testament.

[2] Gal. iv. 3; Col. ii. 8.

[3] Matt. xii. 22.   [4] Mark iii. 15, 22.

[5] Luke ix. 42.   [6] Acts xix. 13.

'And God granted him knowledge of the art used against demons for the benefit and healing of men. He also composed incantations by which illnesses are relieved, and left behind forms of exorcisms with which those possessed by demons drive them out, never to return'.[7]

And Josephus goes on to record how he himself had seen a certain Jew, named Eleazar, exorcise a demon in the presence of the Roman Emperor Vespasian and his retinue. Eleazar held under the possessed man's nose a ring 'which had under its seal one of the roots prescribed by Solomon', and then, as the man smelled it, Eleazar dragged the demon out through the man's nostrils. The man immediately fell to the ground. Eleazar then solemnly forbade the demon to re-enter the man, using the name of Solomon and pronouncing over him one of the Solomonic incantations. Josephus does not say explicitly in this passage that Solomon wrote down the 'incantations', and 'forms of exorcism' which he composed. But that he did so is a natural inference. At a later date, Origen certainly knew of exorcists who used 'adjurations written by Solomon'.[8]

But the Testament is very far from being a collection of Solomon's magic formulae. As a 'testament' it belongs to an established literary category – a category, moreover, which it seems was originated by Jews. Further, its main motif (that Solomon acquired power over the demons and used them to build the Temple) reappears in the Talmud.[9] This means that the Testament's framework, at least, is firmly fixed within Judaism. On the other hand, despite many features in the body of the work that are unmistakeably Jewish (such as the name of the demon Asmodeus in chap. v and the phrase quoted at iii. 5 from Wisd. ix. 4), there are many more that are attributable to pagan, and particularly Gnostic, influence. A good illustration here is the summary in chap. xviii of 'the thirty-six elements': these are the well-known *decani* of the Zodiac circle, which are described, for example, by Celsus,[10] though in less detail than in the Testament. And there are, too, a number of distinctively Christian features. Thus,

[7] Jos., *Ant.* VIII. ii. 5. (§ 45: Loeb Library translation).
[8] Orig. *Matt. comm. ser.* 110.
[9] T. B. *Giṭṭin* 68a–b.
[10] Orig. *c. Cels.* viii. 58.

Christ's power over the demons is referred to several times.[11] It is true that Christ is not mentioned by name, but the references to his Virgin Birth and Crucifixion are unmistakeable.[12] Most interesting of all in this connection is the passage in chap. xi describing the 'legion of demons' subordinate to the 'Lionbearer', who is inhibited 'by the name of him that endured after many sufferings at the hands of men, whose name is Emmanuel, who even now has enchained us and will come to plunge us from a cliff under the water'. This is a clear allusion to the story of the healing of the Gerasene demoniac as recorded in Mark v. 1–20 and Luke viii. 26–39.[13]

Fleck, the first editor of the Testament, regarded it as a Byzantine work of the Middle Ages. Bornemann dated it early in the 4th century on account of the resemblances between its demonology and the demonology of the *Institutes* of Lactantius. Conybeare suggested that an original Jewish document of uncertain date was worked over by a Christian, possibly as early as AD 100. Schürer simply described the Testament as 'Christian' and suggested no date.

In his edition of 1837 Fleck printed the text of a single 16th cent. Paris MS (B.N. Anciens fonds grecs, no. 38 – Colbert 4895). For his edition of 1922 McCown had access to no less than twelve additional MSS (all 15th or 16th cent.) which represent four different recensions (ABCD). As the basis of the Testament McCown postulated an initial Jewish tale, beginning with Solomon's birth and continuing with stories of his dealings with demons and his building of the Temple, roughly similar to what is now found in Recension D, though very far from identical with it. The Testament was an adaptation of this nucleus by a Greek Christian, who wrote, perhaps in Asia, perhaps in Egypt, but more probably in Galilee, somewhere between AD 200 and AD 250 – in any case the Testament must have been in existence by AD 400 at the latest, because it is quoted as 'his (i.e. Solomon's) Testament', in *The Dialogue of Timothy and Aquila*.[14] Recension A differs little from the

---

[11] xi. 6; xv. 10, 11; xvii. 4; xxii. 20.   [12] xii. 3; xv. 10; xxii. 20.

[13] The parallel version in Matt. viii 28–34 does not mention the name 'Legion'.

[14] Cp. F. C. Conybeare. *The Dialogues of Athanasius and Zacchaeus and of Timothy and Aquila* (= *Anecdota Oxoniensia*, Classical Series, Part viii; Oxford, 1898), p. 70.

original, though it is obviously secondary at the beginning and shows signs of expansion at the end. Recension B, which is independent of A, fills out the details about individual demons and is also inclined to expand the Christian passages: it is to be dated in the fourth or the fifth century. Finally, perhaps as late as the twelfth or thirteenth century, came Recension C, a further recension of Recension B.

Fleck's Paris MS belongs to Recension B, and so both Bornemann's German translation and Conybeare's English translation follow this recension. The text in McCown's edition, however, is based mainly on Recension A; and it was this text that was adopted by Riessler for his German translation in 1927. The text published by Delatte is that of the Paris MS B.N. 2011 (18th cent.): it is a similar, though substantially longer, version of the material in McCown's Recension D. Our own translation is based on McCown.

BIBLIOGRAPHY

EDITIONS

F. F. FLECK, *Wissenschaftliche Reise durch das südliche Deutschland, Italien, Sicilien und Frankreick*, II. iii (Leipzig, 1837), pp. 111–140. [Fleck's text is readily available in the reprint in *PG* cxxii. 1315–1358, together with accompanying Latin translation.]

C. C. McCOWN, *The Testament of Solomon, edited from manuscripts at Mount Athos, Bologna, Holkham Hall, Jerusalem, London, Milan, Paris and Vienna, with Introduction* (= *Untersuchungen zum Neuen Testament*, Heft 9; Leipzig, 1922).

A. DELATTE, *Anecdota Atheniensia*, Tome I (= *Bibliothèque de la Faculté de philosophie et lettres de l'Université de Liége*, fasc. xxxvi; Liége and Paris, 1927), pp. 211–227.

TRANSLATIONS

English

F. C. CONYBEARE in *JQR* xi (Oct. 1898), pp. 1–45. [Translation with Introduction]

German

F. A. BORNEMANN in *Zeitschrift für die historische Theologie*, N.F., Bd. VIII, Heft iii (1844), pp. 9–56. [Translation with Introduction]

P. RIESSLER, *AjSAB²*, pp. 1251–1262.

GENERAL

F. A. BORNEMANN, 'Conjectanea in Salomonis Testamentum' in *Biblische Studien von Geistlichen des Königreichs Sachsen*. II. Jahrgang (1843), pp. 45–60, IV. Jahrgang (1846), pp. 28–69.

A.-M. DENIS, *IPGAT*, p. 67.

J.-B. FREY, *DBSup* i, cols. 455–456.

L. GINZBERG, *The Legends of the Jews*, iv (Philadelphia, 1913), pp. 149–154 and vi (Philadelphia, 1928), pp. 291–293.

P. RIESSLER, *AjSAB²*, pp. 1338–1339.

E. SCHÜRER, *HJPTJC* II. iii, pp. 151–155.

——, *GjVZJC⁴* iii, pp. 407–414, 418–420.

C. H. TOY, art. 'Solomon, Testament of' in *JE* xi (New York, 1905), pp. 448–449.

A. LUKYN WILLIAMS, 'The Cult of the Angels at Colossae' in *JTS* x (April 1909), pp. 424–425.

Blessed art thou, O Lord God, who didst give to Solomon this authority; to thee be glory and might for ever. Amen.

I. And behold, while the temple of the city of Jerusalem was being
2 built and the craftsmen were at work on it, the demon Ornias used to come at sunset and take half the pay of the young overseer[1] and half his rations. And he used to suck the thumb of his right hand every day. And the young man, whom I loved dearly, was wasting away.

3 Now I, Solomon, questioned the young man one day and said to him, Did I not think more of you[2] than all the craftsmen that work

---

[1] Gk. πρωτομαῖστωρ: the meaning is unknown.
[2] Lit. 'love you more'.

in the temple of God and grant you double pay and rations? How is
4 it that you are wasting away day by day? But the young man said,
Let me tell you, O king, what has happened to me. After we are
dismissed from work on the temple of God at sunset, while I am
resting, an evil demon comes and takes away half my pay and half
my rations, and takes hold of my right hand and sucks my thumb.
And behold, my soul is in torment and my body is wasting away
day by day.

5   When I heard this, I, king Solomon, went into the temple of God
and prayed him with all my soul, praising him day and night, that
the demon might be delivered into my hands and that I might have
6 authority over him. And it came to pass, as I was praying to the
God of heaven and earth, that a little ring with a seal carved from a
precious stone was given me from the Lord Sabaoth by the arch-
7 angel Michael. And he said to me, Take, Solomon, son of David, a
gift sent you by the Lord Sabaoth, the Most High God, and you
will be able to confine all the demons both female and male, and,
through their agency, build Jerusalem while you wear this seal of
God.

8   And with very great joy I began to praise and glorify the Lord of
heaven and earth. And the next day I ordered the young man to
9 come to me and gave him the seal and said to him, At whatever
hour the demon comes upon you throw this ring at the demon's
chest and say to him, Solomon summons you to him; and *then* come
to me quickly, and do not be frightened or alarmed.[3]

10   And behold, at the usual hour came Ornias, the cruel demon,
like burning fire, to take the young man's wages as was his custom.
11 But the lad, according to Solomon's orders, threw the ring at the
demon's chest, saying to him, Solomon summons you to him; and
12 he went off in haste to Solomon. The demon cried out aloud and
said to the young man, Why did you do this? Take the ring and give
it to Solomon, and I will give you all the silver and gold there is in
13 the earth; only do not take me away to Solomon. And the young
man said, As the Lord lives, the God of Israel, I cannot cope with
14 you unless I take you away to Solomon. And the young man came
and said to Solomon, King Solomon, I have brought you the

---

[3] Lit. 'taking no thought of what is likely to frighten you.'

demon, as you told me to, and behold, he is standing in front of the gates outside, bound, and crying out in a loud voice that he will give me all the silver and gold there is in the earth to prevent me bringing him to you.

II. And when I, Solomon, heard this, I got up from my throne and saw the demon shivering and trembling; and I said to him, who are you, and what is your name? The demon said, I am called Ornias.

2 And I said to him, Tell me what sign of the zodiac you lie under. And the demon answered and said, The Water-pourer; and I suffocate those who lie under the Water-pourer, who because of

3 *their* lust for women have called upon the sign of the Virgin. I also appear in sleep, changing into three forms: sometimes *I am* like a man lusting for the beauty of young girls not yet fully grown, and at my touch they are in great pain: sometimes I take wings to

4 heavenly regions: sometimes I take on the appearance of a lion. I am an offspring of the archangel, the Power of God, but I am

5 inhibited by the archangel Uriel. When I, Solomon, heard the name of the archangel I prayed and glorified the God of heaven and earth; and when I had sealed the demon I set him to work at stone-cutting, to cut the stones of the temple that were lying by the

6 sea shore and had been brought through the Arabian sea. And he was afraid to touch the cutting tools,[1] and he said to me, I pray you, king Solomon, set me free and I will bring all the demons up to you.

7 Since he refused to be subject to me, I prayed the archangel Uriel to come to my aid; and immediately I saw the archangel Uriel

8 coming down to me from heaven. And he ordered great fish to come up out of the sea, and he dried up their province, and cast his portion upon the ground; and in that way and this he subjected the great demon Ornias so that he cut the stones and contributed to the construction of the temple which I, Solomon, was building.

9 And again I glorified the God of heaven and earth; and I ordered Ornias to go round to his portion, and I gave him the seal and said, Be off! And bring me here the ruler of the demons.

III. Ornias took the ring and went off to Beezebul and said to him,

2 Solomon summons you to him. Beezebul said to him, Tell me, who

---

[1] Lit. 'to touch iron.'

3 is this Solomon you speak of? Ornias threw the ring at Beezebul's
4 chest, saying, King Solomon summons you. And Beezebul cried
out as if at a great burning flame of fire, and he got up and followed
5 him of necessity and came to me. And when I saw the ruler of the
demons, I glorified God and said, Blessed art thou, O Lord God
Almighty, who didst give to thy servant Solomon wisdom that sits
beside thy throne,[1] and didst make subject to me all the power of
6 the demons. And I questioned him and said, Tell me, who are you?
7 The demon said, I am Beezebul, the leader of the demons. I
commanded that he should stay close beside me and make
arrangements for the demons to appear before me. He himself
promised to bring to me all the unclean spirits in chains. And I
again glorified the God of heaven and earth, giving thanks to him
at all times.

IV. I enquired of the demon whether there was a female among
2 the demons. When he said there was, I asked to see her.[1] And
Beezebul went off and fetched Onoskelis[2] for me to see.[3] She was
very beautiful in form, and had the body of a fair-skinned woman,
3 but the shanks of a mule. When she came to me I said to her, Tell
4 me who you are. She said, I am called Onoskelis, a spirit in bodily
form, who lurks in holes on earth, for I have my dwelling in caves;
5 but my ways are varied. Sometimes I choke a man: sometimes I
pervert them from their nature. My most frequent dwellings are
6 cliffs, caves, chasms. Often, too, I have intercourse with men, since
they consider me a woman – most often with the olive-skinned,
because they share my star, for these worship my star *both* secretly
and openly, and then do not realize that they harm themselves and
stimulate me to more mischief. For they want through the recollec-
7 tion *of it* to get money. But I supply little *even* to those who worship
me well.
8 I asked her whence she was born. And she said, From an
unseasonable noise, the so-called echo of the sky when it emits a

---

[1] Cp. Wisd. ix. 4.

---

[1] Lit. 'I wished to know'. Some MSS, however, read 'I wished to see'.
[2] This could be translated 'Donkey Shanks'. She was a well-known Hellenistic
demon.   [3] Lit. 'And going away Beelzebul showed me Onoskelis'.

9 leaden noise, was I born in a wood. I said to her, Under what star
do you pass? And she said, Under the full moon, because it is under
the moon that I travel for the most part. I said, What is the angel
10 that inhibits you? And she said, The very same as in you, O king.
11 Thinking that this was a piece of foolery, I ordered a soldier to hit
her; but she cried out and said, I tell you, O king, by the wisdom of
12 God that is given to you. And I blessed[4] the name of the Holy One
of Israel; and I ordered her to spin hemp for the ropes of the work of
the temple of God. Thus sealed and bound she was inhibited, so
that I made her stand spinning hemp night and day.

V. And I ordered another demon to be brought to me. And he
2 brought me Asmodeus,[1] the evil demon, bound. I asked him, Who
3 are you? And he, with a threatening look, said, And who are you? I
said to him, Under punishment, as you are, do you *dare* answer me
like this? And he fixed me with the same look and said, How should
I answer you? You are a man's son, and I an angel's (though born[2]
of a man's daughter), so that no word *from a member* of the heavenly
4 race to an earthborn is overbearing. My star lurks in heaven and
men call me the Waggon,[3] others Snakefooted. For this reason
smaller stars too take their position along with my star, for my
5 father's dignity and throne is in heaven to this day. Do not ask me
many questions, Solomon, for your kingdom also in due time will
be torn in pieces: this glory of yours is transient, you have *but* a short
time to torment us; and *then* we shall again have free range over
mankind, that they may worship us as gods (for they do not know
6 the names of the angels that are appointed over us). When I,
Solomon, heard this, I bound him with greater precaution, and I
ordered him to be flogged and to confess what he was called and
7 what was his function. The demon said, I am called renowned
Asmodeus. I increase men's evil-doing throughout the world. I
plot against the newly-wed: I mar the beauty of maidens and
8 estrange their hearts. I said to him, Is this your only function? He

---

[4] Lit. 'spoke'.

[1] Cp., Tobit iii. 8, 17. In Hebrew (e.g. T. B. *Giṭṭin* 68a–b) he is Ashmedai.
[2] Lit. 'and I was born'.
[3] Another name of the Great Bear.

replied, Through the stars I spread madness among women, and then *it spreads itself* in great waves; and I have killed up to seven.

9 And so I adjured him by the name of the Lord Sabaoth, Fear God, Asmodeus; and tell me what angel you are inhibited by. The demon said, Raphael, who stands in the presence of God: I am also driven away by the liver of a fish along with its gall smoked over

10 saffron ashes. I questioned him again, saying, Do not hide anything from me, because I am Solomon the son of David, and tell me the name of the fish you reverence. And he said, The name is called sheat-fish: it is found in the rivers of Assyria, for there only is it

11 produced, because I too am found in those parts. And I said to him, Nothing else from you, Asmodeus? And he said to me, The power of God, who through his seal bound me with unbreakable bonds, knows that what I told you is true. But I beg you, king

12 Solomon, do not condemn me to water. But I smiling said, As the Lord lives, the God of my fathers, you *shall* have iron to wear, and you shall make clay for the construction of the temple. And I ordered that there should be ten water-pots and that they should be heaped upon him. And with a terrible groan the demon began to carry out his orders. Asmodeus did this because he had fore-

13 knowledge also. And I, Solomon, glorified God, who had given me this authority. The liver of the fish and the gall along with a piece of white storax I burnt over Asmodeus, because of his strength; and his voice was inhibited and his tooth full of sharpness.

VI. And I ordered Beezebul to stand before me again, and I sat him beside me, and I thought it fit to ask him, Why are you the only

2 ruler of the demons? He said to me, Because I am the only one of the heavenly angels left remaining. For I was a leading heavenly

3 angel called Beezebul. And with me was a second impious one whom God cut off, and now confined here he rules my folk that are imprisoned in Tartarus: he gets his food in the Red Sea, and in his

4 own time will come to triumph. And I said to him, What are your functions? And he said to me, I too destroy through tyrants, and cause the demons to be worshipped among men, and excite holy priests, *who have been* chosen *by God*, to lust; and I bring about

5 jealousies in cities and murders, and I bring on wars. And I said to him, Bring me the one you mentioned, who feeds in the Red Sea.

But he said, I will not bring up anyone to you *myself*; but one called Ephippas shall come, who will bind him and bring him up from the
6 depth. And I said to him, Tell me how he comes to be in the depth of the Red Sea and what his name is. He said, Do not ask me: you cannot learn *it* from me; for he himself will come to you because I
7 too am with you. I said to him, Tell me, what star are you associated with? He said, What is called the Evening Star among
8 men. I said, Tell me what angel you are inhibited by. He said, By the all-powerful God: he is called among the Hebrews Patike (he that came down from on high); but he is *the* Emmanuel of the Greeks. And I am afraid of him and tremble before him.[1] If anyone
9 adjures me by Eloi,[2] his great name of power, I disappear. When I, Solomon, heard this, I commanded him to saw Theban marbles. When he began to saw, all the demons shouted with a loud voice
10 because of their king Beezebul. I, Solomon, questioned him, saying, If you want to obtain *your* release, tell me about heavenly things. And Beezebul said, Listen, O king. If you burn gum and incense and sea-bulbs, nard and saffron, and light seven lamps in an earthquake, you will make your house secure. But if (that is, if you are pure) you light them in the early morning sunlight, you will see how the heavenly serpents wind along and draw the
11 chariot of the sun. When I, Solomon, heard this, I rebuked him and said, Be quiet, and saw the marbles I told you to.

Chaps. VII to XVIII all follow the same pattern. Demons are summoned, questioned as to their names and functions and the angel by whom each is inhibited, and finally assigned to work on the temple. The contents are summarised.

VII. Lix Tetrax,[1] who carries his face high in the air, but the rest of his body winding like a snail. He raises a violent dust storm to frighten Solomon. He is busiest in summer, causing colics and fires and semitertian fever, and is inhibited by the archangel Azael. He is ordered to throw stones to the craftsmen on top of the temple.

[1] Lit. 'I fear him with trembling'.
[2] Cp. Mark xv. 34.

[1] An emendation of McCown. These terms occur in the magical formulae known as *Ephesiaca grammata*.

VIII. Seven intertwined comely demons,[1] the seven elements, world-rulers of darkness, Guile, Strife, Clotho, Storm, Error, Power, Worst: this last one foretells Solomon's succumbing to love. They are set to dig the foundations of the temple.

IX. A headless demon, Murder, seeing through his breasts, continually severing and devouring men's heads, inhibited by the fiery lightning. For the moment he is ordered to remain with Beezebul.

X. A demon like a great dog, called Rod, mastering men's minds through the throat and destroying them, inhibited by Briathus. He offers to show Solomon's servant a green stone in a mountain and Solomon agrees. When he brings it Solomon decrees that he and the headless demon, Murder, should be bound and carry the stone round like a lamp day and night to the craftsmen at work. Later they too are set to work cutting marble.

XI. An Arabian demon like a lion rampant, called Lionbearer. He has a legion of demons subordinate to him; and, when Solomon asks by whom he is inhibited, replies, 'By the name of him that endured after many sufferings at the hands of men, whose name is Emmanuel, who even now has enchained us and will come to plunge us from a cliff under the water.' Solomon orders the legion to carry wood, and the demon to saw it up fine with his nails and feed the furnace.

XII. A three-headed serpent, called Serpent's Crest, inhibited by 'the place of the skull,[1] for there the Angel of the Great Council fore-ordained that I should suffer, and now openly he will dwell upon a cross.' He tells Solomon that there is much gold hidden in the foundation of the temple. Solomon finds this and orders him to make bricks.

XIII. A female demon with long dishevelled hair, called Obyzuth, attacking women and children, inhibited by the angel Raphael, whose name written on a scrap of paper is a protection against her for women in childbirth. Solomon orders her to be bound by the hair and hung up in front of the temple that the children of Israel can see her and glorify God.

---

[1] Probably the Pleiades: the third, Clotho, the Spinster, was the name of one of the three Greek fates.

[1] Lit. 'the brain'.

XIV.   A demon with the face and feet of a man and the limbs of a serpent, with wings on its back, called Winged Serpent, who causes abortions in pregnancy among beautiful women. He threatens Solomon, and burns up with his breath the forests of Lebanon, the timber destined for the temple. Solomon invokes the angel who inhibits him, Bazazath, and condemns him to saw marbles.

XV.   A three headed female demon, called Enepsigus, who is also 'called by countless names'.[1] She has connections with the moon and can be brought down by enchantment, inhibited by Rathanael. She prophecies to Solomon the division of his kingdom and the destruction of the temple, when the jars in which he has enclosed the demons will be broken and they will be dispersed over the world again, until the son of God should be stretched upon a tree, he whose number is 644 – i.e., Emmanuel.[2] Solomon does not believe her until his death, when he writes the Testament to warn the children of Israel about the demons. He orders her to be fettered with unbreakable bonds.

XVI.   A demon like a horse in front and a fish behind, living in the sea and causing shipwrecks, who also transforms himself into a man, called Cynopegus,[1] inhibited by Iameth. He is beginning to faint without water, so Solomon puts him in a jar with ten measures of sea water, smears the mouth with asphalt, pitch, and tow, seals it with the ring, and orders it to be stored in the temple.

XVII.   An anonymous lascivious spirit of a giant slaughtered in the time of the giants, who lives in tombs and causes men to become demoniacs, inhibited by 'the Saviour that is to descend'. He is confined with the rest.

XVIII.   The thirty-six elements, man-shaped, bull-shaped, bird-faced, animal-faced, sphinx-faced, serpent-shaped. Most of them cause physical

---

[1] Reminiscent of Artemis, who had three forms, being also the moon and, as Hecate, a goddess of the underworld. The epithet μυριώνυμος recalls Isis, who also had connections with the moon.

[2] If the Greek letters of Emmanuel are taken as numerical symbols they add up to 644, though, of course, 644 would normally be expressed by the three letters χμδ̄ (as it is here).

[1] The name appears to be a compound of 'dog' and 'fountain', and the demon probably has a connection with Poseidon.

troubles, and often charms and remedies are given for these. They are set to draw water.

XIX. And I, Solomon, was honoured by all men under heaven. I was building the temple of God, and my kingdom was prospering.
2 All the kings used to come to me to see the temple of God which I was building, and they used to bring me gold and silver and offer bronze and iron and lead and timber for the construction of the
3 temple. Among them also came Sheba, queen of the South, who was an enchantress of great skill, and she did obeisance to me.

XX. And behold, an aged man, one of the craftsmen, threw himself down before me saying, King Solomon, son of David, have pity on my old age. And I said to him, Tell me, old man, what it is you
2 want. He said, I appeal to you, O king. I have an only son, and every day he makes some kind of attack on me; for he has hit me in the face and on the head and threatens to murder me. This is why I
3 have come to you so that you may avenge me. When I heard this, I gave orders that his son should be brought to me. When he came, I
4 said to him, Is this the truth about you? And he said, O king, I must have been out of my mind to frighten my father in the way I have.[1] Be merciful to me, O king, for such irregular behaviour
5 makes a sorry story.[2] So when I, Solomon, had heard the young man, I urged the old man to think it over. But he was unwilling to and said, He should be put to death.
6   And when I saw that the demon Ornias laughed, I was very angry at his laughing in my presence; and I put the other aside and ordered Ornias to come, and I said to him, Accursed one, *how dare*
7 *you* laugh at me? He said, I appeal to you, O king. It was not because of you that I laughed, but because of the unfortunate old man and the wretched youth, his son; for in three days he will be dead, and behold, the old man wants to put him to a painful death.
8,9 And I said, Is this really so? The demon said, Yes, O king. And I ordered the demon to stand aside, and the old man and his son to

---

[1] Lit. 'I have been full mad to make my father quake through my hand.'
[2] Lit. 'for *it would be* contrary to what is established to hear such a parable and distress'.

10 come, and I ordered them to become friends. And I said to the old
man, In three days bring your son to me here. They did obeisance
and departed.

11   And I gave orders that Ornias should be brought to me again,
and I said to him, Tell me how you know this, that in three days the
12 young man will be dead. And he said , We demons mount upon the
vault of heaven and fly amid the stars, and we hear the decrees that
13 come forth from God and that relate to the lives of men. Then we
go, and whether by force of influence, or by fire, or by sword, or by
14 mishap, we disguise ourselves and destroy. And I asked him, Tell
me, then, how is it that you demons are able to go up into heaven.
15 He said to me, Whatever is done to perfection in heaven, so also is
it upon earth; for the rulers and authorities and powers fly above
16 and are thought worthy of entrance to heaven. But we demons get
exhausted, for we have no foothold for ascending or resting, and we
fall away like leaves from trees, and the men that see *it* think stars
17 are falling from heaven. It is not so, O king: we fall because of our
weakness; and, because we have no support from any quarter, we
fall down like lightnings upon the earth, and burn up cities, and set
fields on fire. But the stars of heaven are secure in the vault *of*
18 *heaven*. When I, Solomon, heard this, I ordered the demon to be
kept under guard for five days.

19   After the five days were over I summoned the old man, and he
was unwilling to come. Then he came, and I saw he was broken
20 and miserable. And I said to him, Where is your son, old man? He
said, I am now childless, O king, and I, without hope, keep watch
21 by my son's tomb. When I, Solomon, heard this, and knew that
what had been told me by the demon was true, I glorified the God
of heaven and earth.

XXI.   And Sheba, the queen of the South, was astonished when she
saw the temple I was building, and she gave ten thousand shekels
2 of bronze. She went into the temple and saw the altar, and the
cherubim and seraphim overshadowing the mercy seat, and the
two hundred precious stones of the lamps flashing with different
3 colours, lamps of emerald and hyacinth stones and sapphire. And
she saw the vessels of silver and bronze and gold, and the bases of
the pillars entwined with bronze wrought like chains. She saw also

4 the brazen sea with its base[1] and the thirty-six bulls. And they were all working in the temple of God – for the wage of one gold talent, except for the demons.

XXII. Now Adarces, king of the Arabians, sent a letter which ran as follows,

Adarces, king of the Arabians, to king Solomon greeting. Behold, we have heard of the wisdom that has been given you and that, man as you are, understanding has been given you from the Lord in respect of the spirits of the air and earth and under the

2 earth. There is a spirit in Arabia; for at dawn there comes a wind which blows until the third hour, and its blast is terrible, and it kills men and cattle, and nothing that breathes can live before the

3 demon. I beg you, therefore, since the spirit is like a wind, to devise something wise in accordance with the wisdom that has been given you by the Lord your God, and deign to send a man able to arrest

4 it. And behold, we will be yours, king Solomon, both I and all my people; and all my land, even all Arabia, will be at peace, if you can

5 bring about this deliverance[1] for us. Wherefore we beg you, do not ignore our supplication, and become our lord for all time, for ever. May my lord fare well always, continually.

6 I Solomon, when I had read this letter, folded it and gave it to my slave, saying to him, After seven days remind me of this letter.

7 Jerusalem had been built, and the temple was being completed. And there was a great corner-stone, that I wanted to put into place

8 as the main corner-stone, to complete the temple of God. And all the craftsmen and all the demons that were co-operating with them came together to bring the stone and set it on the pinnacle of the

9 temple; but they were not strong enough to lift it. But after seven days I remembered the letter of the king of the Arabians; and I

10 called my slaveling and said to him, Load up your camel, and take a wine-skin and this seal, and go to Arabia, to the place where the evil spirit blows, and hold the wine-skin and the ring in front of the

11 mouth of the wine-skin. And when the wine-skin is inflated, you will find that it is the demon who inflates it. Then quickly tie the

---

[1] The meaning of ἐπιστάθόν is uncertain. See 1 Kings vii. 23–25; 2 Chron. iv. 2–4.

[1] Lit. 'vengeance'.

wine-skin up tightly, and, when you have sealed it with the ring, load it onto your camel and bring it here. So go, and fare you well.

12 Then the slave did as he was ordered and journeyed to Arabia. And the people there were doubtful whether he would after all be
13 able to arrest the evil spirit. And at daybreak the servant got up and stood in front of the spirit's blast; and he put the wine-skin on the ground, and on it he put the ring also. And it entered the
14 wine-skin and inflated it. But the slave stood and tied the wine-skin tightly at the mouth, in the name of the Lord Sabaoth; and the
15 demon was kept a prisoner[3] in the wine-skin. The slave, too, remained for three days to see that all was well;[4] and the spirit no longer blew, and the Arabians recognised that he had safely con-
16 fined the spirit. Then he loaded the wine-skin onto his camel. The Arabians sent the slave on his way with gifts and honours, praising God (for they now had peace). But the slave brought the spirit and set it on top of the temple.

17 On the next day I, Solomon, went into the temple; and I was worried about the main corner-stone. And the wine-skin, standing up, walked seven paces, and stood on its mouth and did obeisance
18 to me. And amazed that, although *tied up* in the wine-skin, it still was able to walk, I told it to stand up. The wine-skin stood up, and
19 stood inflated on its feet. And I questioned him, saying, Who are you? The spirit inside said, I am a demon called Ephippas, the
20 Arabian. And I said to him, What angel are you inhibited by? He said, By him who is to be born of a virgin, since angels worship him, and who is to be crucified by the Jews.

XXIII. I said to him, Tell me, what can you do? He said, I can
2 move mountains and transport houses and throw down kings. And I said to him, If you can, lift this stone up to the highest point of the corner of the temple. He said, Not only will I lift this stone up, O king, but with the help of the demon in the Red Sea *I will lift up also* the airy pillar that is in the Red Sea, and you can set it where you
3 will. And, saying this, he slipped in underneath the stone, and he lifted it, and mounted the steps carrying the stone, and placed it at

---

[3] Lit. 'the demon remained'.
[4] Lit. '. . . for three days as a demonstration'.

4 the top of the entrance to the temple. I, Solomon, said in elation, Truly now has been fulfilled the scripture that says, The stone that the builders rejected, this became the head of the corner – and so on.

XXIV. And again I said to him, Go, and bring me the pillar in the Red Sea you spoke of. Ephippas went off and brought up the
2 demon and the pillar, both *of them* carrying it from Arabia. But I, because these two spirits were able to shake the whole world in a single moment, cleverly outwitted them by sealing them around on
3 this side and that, and I said, Keep careful watch. And they have remained supporting the pillar in the air to this day, as a demon-
4 stration of the wisdom that was given me. The pillar, of an enorm-ous size, was hanging in the air, supported by the spirits; and from
5 below the spirits supporting it looked as if they were air. When we looked carefully, the base of the pillar seemed slightly askew; and it is so to this day.

XXV. And I asked the other demon, the one who came up from the sea with the pillar, Who are you, and what are you called, and
2 what is your function, for I have heard much about you? And the demon said, I, king Solomon, am called Abezethibu, and once I
3 used to dwell in the first heaven, which is named Ameluth. I, then, am a malevolent winged spirit, with a single wing, who plots against everything that breathes under heaven. I was present when Moses went in to Pharaoh, king of Egypt; and I hardened his
4 heart. I am he whom Jannes and Jambres invoked, when they withstood Moses in Egypt. I am he who wrestled against Moses
5 with wonders and signs. So I said to him, How was it then that you
6 were found in the Red Sea? He said, At the exodus of the sons of Israel I hardened Pharaoh's heart; and I stirred up Pharaoh and his servants and caused them to pursue after the sons of Israel. And Pharaoh followed close *upon them* and *so did* all the Egyptians. I was there then, and we followed close; and we all came to the Red Sea.
7 And it came to pass that when the sons of Israel had crossed, the water turned back and covered the entire Egyptian army. I was with them then, and I too was covered by the water; and *so I*
8 remained in the sea, kept under the pillar, until Ephippas came. I,

Solomon, charged him solemnly to support the pillar till the end of
9 time. And with God's help I adorned his temple with all seemli-
ness. And I continued to rejoice and glorify him.

XXVI. Now I took wives without number from every land and
kingdom. And I was on a visit to the king of the Jebusites; and I
saw a woman in their kingdom, and fell violently in love, and
2 wanted to add her to my wives. And I said to their priests, Give me
this Shumanite (*sic*), because I have fallen violently in love with
her. They said to me, If you have fallen in love with our daughter,
3 worship our gods, great Raphan and Moloch, and take her. But I
4 refused to worship and said, I do not worship a foreign god. But
they made the girl promise, saying, If it should happen that you go
into Solomon's kingdom, say to him, I will not sleep with you,
unless you do what my people do:[1] take five locusts and slaughter
5 them in the name of Raphan and Moloch. I, because I loved the
damsel (for she was very beautiful), and because I was without
understanding, thought nothing of the blood of the locusts; and I
took them under my hands and sacrificed in the name of Raphan
and Moloch. And I took the girl into my royal palace.

6 And the spirit of God was taken away from me, and from that
day onwards what I said seemed like nonsense. And she forced me
7 to build temples to idols. So I, miserable wretch, did what she told
me; and the glory of God departed from me altogether, and my
spirit was plunged in darkness, and I became a laughing-stock to
idols and to demons.

8 That is why I have written this my Testament, so that you, who
hear may pray, and give heed to the last things and not the first, *and*
so may find a full measure of grace for ever and ever. Amen.

---

[1] Lit. 'unless you become like my people'.

THE APOCALYPSE OF ELIJAH

INTRODUCTION

Among the Coptic Biblical fragments from Akhmim, acquired for the Bibliothèque Nationale in Paris by G. Maspero in the early 1880s, were fourteen papyrus leaves in the Akhmimic dialect and seven in the Sahidic. These proved on examination to be the remains of two distinct codices. The texts were previously unknown, though undoubtedly of an apocryphal work or works. There was a considerable overlap between them so that it was frequently possible to restore gaps in the Akhmimic from the Sahidic and *vice versa*. The presumption, therefore, was that they were, at least in part, two versions in different dialects of the same original(s).

The first editor (U. Bouriant in 1885) took the view that only a single work was involved; and from the fact that Zephaniah appeared as the speaker on one of the Sahidic leaves he concluded that the work was the lost Apocalypse of Zephaniah, known to have existed from its mention in the List of Sixty Books. A similar view was taken by L. Stern in the following year. However, in 1888 a further eight leaves, recently acquired by the Berlin Museum, were identified as belonging to the same codex as the fourteen Akhmimic leaves in the Bibliothèque Nationale; and at the end of the text on one of these leaves (it would seem the last in the codex) was the colophon 'The Apocalypse of Elijah'. Consequently, the codex must have contained more than one work. The question was (and is), How many?

An answer depends partly upon the order in which the loose leaves from both codices are arranged, and partly upon what is presumed to be the relationship between the two codices. The codices certainly overlapped. But that does not necessarily mean that their contents were precisely the same. And Bouriant and Stern had each arranged the Paris leaves in a different order.

In the Introduction to his edition of the texts in 1899 G. Steindorff examined this question in detail and concluded that three works were involved: (1) an apocalypse of Elijah; (2) an apocalypse of Zephaniah; and (3) an 'Anonymous' apocalypse. This interpretation was decisively rejected by Schürer some ten years later, who maintained not only that there were no adequate grounds for distinguishing the 'Anonymous' from Zephaniah, but also that there were none for distinguishing a separate Elijah apocalypse either. Elijah, he pointed out, was referred to in the text of the alleged separate apocalypse twice, together with Enoch, in the third person;[1] but if Elijah were in fact being represented by the author as the recipient of the revelations and as himself recording them, he might naturally be expected to refer to himself in the first person. Thus, in spite of the colophon at the end of the Akhmimic text, we have to do (so Schürer argued), not with three works, but with one only, and that the Apocalypse of Zephaniah.

Although many subsequent students have been doubtful about Steindorff's 'Anonymous', few, if any, have been prepared to treat the final colophon as cavalierly as did Schürer, especially since the publication in 1912 by E. A. Wallis Budge in his edition of B. L. Or. 7594 (an uncial MS of the mid 4th cent., containing Sahidic texts of Deuteronomy, Jonah, Acts, and Revelation) of what he called 'the opening part of a short composition', written in a cursive hand at the end of Acts. This 'opening part' of Budge's 'short composition' was identified by C. Schmidt in 1925 as the beginning of the Elijah apocalypse isolated by Steindorff;[2] and so an additional argument was produced in favour of Steindorff's analysis, at least so far as his isolation of the Elijah apocalypse is concerned and his definition of its contents.

The final vindication of Steindorff's view was provided by the discovery of yet another Sahidic text in the Chester Beatty collection in Dublin (P. Chester Beatty 2018). This text had been known to exist since the 1950s, but no details became generally available until A. Pietersma and S. T. Comstock published their edition of it in the autumn of 1981.

The manuscript consists of ten leaves, of which the first five are virtually complete, while the remainder are rather more fragmentary. Quite apart from the fragmentary nature of these last

---

[1] At iii. 25 and 91.   [2] i.e. i. 1–15.

leaves, however, the manuscript comes to an abrupt end at iii. 72. On palaeographical grounds the editors argued that this was not due to accidental loss or mutilation, but to the copy that the scribe had before him having ended similarly. Yet, whether or not we are prepared to accept the editors' arguments in their entirety, the fact is that P. Chester Beatty 2018 begins and (for practical purposes) ends with the Elijah apocalypse, and there is no indication that it ever contained anything else: in this respect it differs markedly from the primary Akhmimic and Sahidic texts discovered in the 1880s. It should also be noted that in those texts, complementary as they otherwise were, there was a gap between ii. 13 and ii. 23, caused by the absence of a single leaf of the Akhmimic, where there was no complementary Sahidic: this gap (i.e. ii. 14–22) was covered by the Chester Beatty manuscript, with the result that it at last became possible to read through the text of the apocalypse from beginning to end as a single continuous whole.

In these circumstances no excuse is needed for treating 'Elijah' as a separate entity here, and for leaving 'Zephaniah' and the 'Anonymous' for independent treatment later.

There can be no doubt that the early Church knew of at least one apocryphal work bearing Elijah's name. Origen, in his *Commentary on Matthew* (according to the Latin translation) attributes St. Paul's quotation at 1 Cor. ii. 9 to 'the Secrets of Elijah the Prophet'.[3] Ambrosiaster refers it to 'the Apocalypse of Elijah'.[4] Jerome, in denying this and explaining the quotation as a free paraphrase of Isa. lxiv. 4, nevertheless admits the existence of an 'Apocalypse of Elijah', from which some said St. Paul was quoting.[5] Similarly, Epiphanius explains Eph. v. 14 as a quotation from 'Elijah'.[6] An apocryphal 'Elijah' (without further definition) is mentioned in *The Apostolic Constitutions*;[7] a work 'Of Elijah the

---

[3] Orig. (*Matt. com. ser.* 117): 'in nullo enim regulari libro hoc positum invenitur, nisi in secretis Eliae prophetae'. The Gk. original is, of course, no longer extant.

[4] Ambrosiast. (*in I Cor.* ii. 9): 'hoc scriptum est in Esaia profeta aliis verbis (est in apocalypsi Heliae in apocryfis)'.

[5] Hieron. (*Ep.* lvii. 9; *in Esai.* lxiv. 4–5).

[6] Epiph. (*Haer* XLII. xii. 3); 'τοῦτο δὲ ἐμφέρεται παρὰ τῷ Ἠλίᾳ'.

[7] *Const. Apost.* VI. xvi. 3.

prophet' is listed in the pseudo-Athanasian Synopsis and the Stichometry of Nicephorus; and an 'Apocalypse of Elijah' occurs in the List of Sixty Books. But the only ancient reference, which gives any serious indication of contents, is a passage in the apocryphal Epistle of Titus, published from an 8th cent. Würzburg MS by Dom Donatien de Bruyne in 1925.[8] The passage, which presumably comes from the Elijah apocryplon mentioned previously in the Epistle,[9] runs as follows:

'And then the prophet Elijah witnesses to what he saw: "The angel of the Lord", he says, "showed me a deep valley, which is called Gehenna, burning with sulphur and pitch. And in that place are many souls of sinners, and they are tortured there with torments of different kinds. Some suffer through hanging by their genitals, others by their tongues, some by their eyes, and yet others hanging upside down; and women will be tortured through hanging by their breasts, and young men by their hands: some girls are roasted on the gridiron, and some souls are impaled and in perpetual pain. By these different punishments is proclaimed what each one has done: those that suffer through their genitals are the adulterers and pederasts: those that are suspended by their tongues are the blasphemers and false witnesses: those that are **hung up** by their eyes are those who have caused their own fall through what they see, gazing in concupiscence on the guilty deeds of others: those that were hanging upside down, these are those who hated the righteousness of God, men of evil counsel (no one of them is in agreement with his brother) – rightly, therefore, do they endure the punishment decreed for them. And as for the women that are ordered to be tormented in their breasts, these are those who gave their bodies to men in wantonness; and the men also will be close by them in their torments, hanging by their hands for this very reason." '[10]

[8] D. de Bruyne, 'Epistula Titi, discipuli Pauli, De Dispositione Sanctimonii' in *R Bén* xxxvii (1925), pp. 47–72. A useful discussion of the epistle, especially of its quotations of Biblical and apocryphal texts, was almost immediately afterwards published by A. von Harnack, 'Der apokryphe Brief des Paulusschülers Titus "De dispositione sanctimonii" ' in *Sitzungsberichte der preussischen Akademie der Wissenschaften, Jahrg. 1925: phil.-hist. Kl.* (Berlin, 1925), pp. 180–213. Harnack assigned the Epistle to the 5th cent. and argued that it was Priscillianist.

[9] de Bruyne, op. cit., pp. 54–55: . . . 'O divina dei meditacio ut ante praevideret de futuro saeculo, ut Enoch iustus de primo populo reputato constituitur scribere gesta hominum priora, et Helias sanctus huius plebis serotinae novae conscriberet acta . . .'.   [10] de Bruyne, op. cit., p. 58.

Such descriptions of the torments of Hell are not uncommon in apocalyptic literature, especially in the later literature (cp., for example, Apoc. Esdras iv. 7–v. 6 – below, pp. 935–7). But nothing like it is to be found in our Coptic apocalypse.[11] Nor are St. Paul's alleged quotations at 1 Cor. ii. 9 and Eph. v. 14 to be found there either, although it is possibly not without significance that the first of them does occur at the very beginning of the apocryphal Titus, where it appears to be cited as if it were a well-known 'word of the Lord'. From the evidence available, therefore, it looks as if there were several apocrypha, bearing the name of Elijah, circulating in the early centuries. They may have been different recensions of the same basic material: they may have been completely independent. We have no means of knowing.

But about our Coptic apocalypse two things may be said with little fear of contradiction: (1) it is of some respectable antiquity; and (2) if not entirely Christian in origin, whatever Jewish sources it may have had have been so thoroughly Christianized as to be virtually unrecognizable.

To take the first point first. The two main MSS containing the Sahidic text (i.e. Steindorff's and the Chester Beatty) are dated either in the late 4th cent. or in the early 5th, and that containing the Akhmimic in the 4th. The cursive hand which made the addition corresponding to the opening verses of the Akhmimic text at the end of Acts in B. L. Or. 7594 is dated to *c.* AD 350; so that this text must have come into existence in the earlier half of the 4th cent. at the latest. Most Coptic texts of this kind are translations from Greek; and that our apocalypse is no exception was made as certain as can be by the publication by E. Pistelli in 1912 of a small 4th cent. papyrus fragment, the verso of which contains (though in a very mutilated state) the Greek text of iii. 90–92. If we are to allow time for the Greek text to become generally known, to be translated into Coptic, and then to become known in Coptic, it would seem that we must push back the date of composition into the 3rd cent. or even earlier.

The Christian elements in the apocalypse are undeniable, es-

[11] The nearest approach is the very general statement at iii. 86–87 (cp. also 'Anon.' Apoc. i. 6, ii. 4, iii. 12–16 – below, pp. 920, 922, 924).

pecially the many apparent reminiscences of the New Testament. It is possible to discount some of the contacts with Revelation (such as 'they shall neither hunger, nor shall they thirst' at i. 10 – cp. iii. 61, or 'they will give them the right to eat from the tree of life and to wear white garments' at iii. 60)[12] as no more than part of the common stock-in-trade of apocalyptic literature, whether Jewish or Christian. But it is not so easy to apply this explanation to the description of the Antichrist as 'the Son of Perdition' and 'the Lawless One' at ii. 33–34:[13] the warning against believing in the Antichrist's claims at iii. 1–2 looks very much as if it derived from Our Lord's words as recorded at Matt. xxiv. 5, 23; and the injunction 'Love not the world nor the things in the world' at i. 2 seems to be an exact quotation of 1 John ii. 15. Furthermore, according to iii. 3, when the Christ comes, he will be preceded by 'the sign of the cross'; and at i. 6–7 there is an unmistakeable statement of the Doctrine of the Incarnation ('That is why the God of glory took pity on us: he sent his Son into the world to deliver us from *our* slavery. When he came to us, he told neither angel nor archangel nor any power; but he assumed the form of a man when he came to us to save us').[14] What is uncertain is whether these Christian elements are an original part of the apocalypse or were superimposed by a Christian editor who re-wrote and expanded a Jewish source (as has been argued by several scholars, notably by Steindorff himself, Bousset, and Rosenstiehl).

In 1897 M. Buttenwieser published from a Munich MS a Jewish Apocalypse of Elijah, which records a revelation made by the archangel Michael to Elijah on Mount Carmel concerning the times of the End. From the historical references in it Buttenwieser thought that the original apocalypse had been written soon after AD 260 and that it had been edited and expanded in the 6th and 7th cents. There are indubitably contacts between this Jewish apocalypse and our Coptic apocalypse, particularly in the historical section in chap. ii of our apocalypse, though none of them are very close. According to Rosenstiehl, our apocalypse, as it now

---

[12] Cp. Rev. ii. 7, vii. 9, 16.
[13] Cp. 2 Thess. ii. 3, 8.
[14] Cp. *Ep. ad Diognetum*, vii. 2–4.

stands, dates from the 3rd cent. of our era; and it is the work of an author who refashioned material composed in the 1st cent. BC by a Jew with Essene learnings, who lived in Egypt.

The possibility of a Jewish base must consequently be left open. However, it is worth noting that if that base was in its essentials the same as the nucleus that Buttenwieser discerned in his apocalypse, and he was right in dating that nucleus after AD 260 (a date with which Bousset concurred), then our apocalypse cannot have been the 'Secrets of Elijah' known to Origen (since Origen died *c.* 250). Likewise, Rosenstiehl's 3rd cent. date for the apocalypse as it now stands would seem to suggest the same conclusion. But, as was remarked previously, there were probably several 'Elijahs' circulating in the early centuries in various languages, some of which were only distantly related to one another, if related at all.

The translation which follows is based on the Akhmimic text as printed in Steindorff's edition, the Sahidic texts, when available, being used to fill the gaps in the Akhmimic, whether these gaps be of only a word or two, or more extensive (the minor gaps are indicated by the sign ' ⟨ ⟩ ', others by '. . .'). Occasionally, too, a Sahidic reading has been preferred to the Akhmimic as representing a better text. But in any case, all significant textual variants, or any that might be thought of any special interest, have attention drawn to them in the notes.

The chapter and verse divisions are those adopted by Rosenstiehl; but for convenience Steindorff's page-numeration, according to his ordering of the individual leaves, has been inserted in brackets in the translation where applicable – thus, '(A 19)' indicates page 19 in the Akhmimic codex as reconstructed by Steindorff, to be found on pp. 66–67 of his edition, and '(Sa^{St} 6)' indicates page 6 of his Sahidic text, to be found in his edition on pp. 120–125. Similarly in the notes, 'A' and 'Sa^{St}' indicate Steindorff's Akhmimic and Sahidic respectively, 'Sa^{CB}' indicates the Chester Beatty Sahidic, and 'Sa^{Sch}' indicates the Sahidic fragment from the beginning of the apocalypse as edited by Schmidt.

Thus, apart from the Greek fragment from iii. 90–92, the texts available are:

A: i. 1–ii. 13 ('. . . saying'); ii. 23 ('The cities . . .')–iii. 19 ('. . . all the saints'); iii. 33 ('Shameless One . . .')—iii. 69 ('. . . perish in'); iii. 84 ('A righteous judgement . . .')—iii. 99.

Sa^CB: i. 1—iii. 72 ('. . . passed me by').

Sa^St: i. 23 ('because . . .')—ii. 13 ('. . . saying'); iii. 7 ('the sky . . .')—iii. 84 ('. . . give tongue'.)

Sa^Sch: i. 1—9 ('. . . for you thrones'); i. 12 ('of the earth . . .')—15 ('. . . the Evil One').

BIBLIOGRAPHY

EDITIONS

Coptic

U. BOURIANT, 'Les papyrus d'Akhmim (Fragments de manuscrits en dialectes bachmourique et thébain)' in *Memoires publiés par les membres de la mission archéologique française au Caire*, tom. i, fasc. 2 (Paris, 1885), pp. 242–304.

G. STEINDORFF, *Die Apokalypse des Elias, eine unbekannte Apokalypse, und Bruchstücke der Sophonias-Apokalypse: koptische Texte, Übersetzung, Glossar* (= *TU* xvii (N.F. ii) 3a; Leipzig, 1899).

E. A. WALLIS BUDGE, *Coptic Biblical Texts in the Dialect of Upper Egypt* (London, 1912), pp. lv–lvii and 270–271.

C. SCHMIDT, 'Der Kolophon des MS orient 7594 des Britischen Museums: eine Untersuchung zur Elias-Apokalypse' in *Sitzungsberichte der preussischen Akademie der Wissenschaften, Jahrg. 1925: phil.-hist. Kl.* (Berlin, 1925), pp. 312–321.

A. PIETERSMA and S. T. COMSTOCK, with H. W. ATTRIDGE, *The Apocalypse of Elijah based on P. Chester Beatty 2018* (*SBL: Texts and Translations 19, Pseudepigrapha Series 9*; Scholars Press, Chico, California, 1981).

Greek

E. PISTELLI, *Papiri greci e latini*, i (Florence, 1912), pp. 16–17 (no. 7).

C. WESSELY, 'Les plus anciens monuments du christianisme écrits sur papyrus: textes édités, traduits et annotés' in *PO* xviii. 3 (Paris, 1924), pp. 487–488.

A.-M. DENIS, *Fragmenta Pseudepigraphorum quae supersunt Graeca* (= *PVTG* iii; Leiden, 1970), p. 104.

A. PIETERSMA and S. T. COMSTOCK, *The Apocalypse of Elijah* ... [as above], pp. 90–94.

TRANSLATIONS

English

H. P. HOUGHTON, 'The Coptic Apocalypse' in *Aegyptus*, xxxix (1959), pp. 179–210.

French

U. BOURIANT, 'Les papyrus ...' [as above].

J.-M. ROSENSTIEHL, *L'Apocalypse d'Élie: Introduction, Traduction et Notes* (= *Textes et Études pour servir à l'histoire du judaïsme inter-testamentaire*, i; Paris, 1972).

German

L. STERN, 'Die koptische Apocalypse des Sophonias, mit einem Anhang über den untersahidischen Dialect' in *Zeitschrift für ägyptische Sprache und Alterthumskunde* (Leipzig, 1886), pp. 115–135.

G. STEINDORFF, *Die Apokalypse des Elias* ... [as above].

C. SCHMIDT, 'Der Kolophon ...' [as above].

P. RIESSLER, *AjSaB²*, pp. 114–125.

W. SCHRAGE in *JSh-rZ* V. 3 (1980), pp. 193–288.

GENERAL

W. BOUSSET, 'Beiträge zur Geschichte der Eschatologie, I: Die Apokalypse des Elias' in *Zeitschrift für Kirchengeschichte*, xx (Gotha, 1899), pp. 103–112.

M. BUTTENWIESER, *Die hebräische Elias-Apokalypse und ihre Stellung in der apokalyptischen Litteratur des rabbinischen Schrifttums und der Kirche* (Leipzig, 1897).

A.-M. DENIS, *IPGAT*, pp. 163–169.

J.-B. FREY, art 'Apocryphes de l'Ancien Testament' in *DBSup* i, cols. 456–458.

M. R. JAMES, *LAOT*, pp. 53–61.

P. RIESSLER, *AjSaB²*, p. 1272.

W. SCHNEEMELCHER, 'Spätere Apokalypsen' in E. HENNECKE and W. SCHNEEMELCHER, *Neutestamentliche Apokryphen³*, ii. (Tübingen, 1964), p. 534. [Translated, by E. BEST, in *NTA* ii, p. 752.]

E. SCHÜRER, *GjVZJC⁴* iii, pp. 361–369.

H. WEINEL in *EUX*, pp. 164–167.

I. (A 19) The word of the Lord came to me, saying, Son of man,[1] say to this people, Why do you[2] pile sin upon sin and provoke the
2 Lord God who has made you to wrath? Love not the world nor the things in the world, for the boastfulness of the world is of the devil
3 and its destruction. Remember that the Lord of glory,[3] who has made all things, has taken pity on you to deliver us from the slavery
4 of this *present* age. For time and time again the Devil has desired to stop the sun from shining on the earth, and to stop the earth from
5 bearing *its* fruit, and wanted to devour men like the fire that runs (A 20) among the stubble,[4] wanting to devour them like water.
6 That is why the God of glory took pity on us: he sent[5] his Son into
7 the world to deliver us from *our* slavery. When he came to us, he told neither angel nor archangel nor any power;[6] but he assumed
8 the form of a man when he came to us to save us.[7] For this reason
9 ⟨you will⟩ be his sons, since he is your father. Remember he has prepared for you thrones and crowns in heaven, saying, All who obey me shall receive thrones and crowns from what is mine (said the Lord); for I will write my name upon their forehead and seal
10 their (A 21) right hand. They shall neither hunger, nor shall they thirst, nor shall the Son of Lawlessness have his way with them, nor shall thrones hinder them; but they shall walk with angels to

---

[1] Sa^CB and Sch om. 'Son of man'.
[2] Sa^CB and Sch 'Why do you sin and'.
[3] Sa^CB and Sch om. 'of glory'.
[4] So Sa^CB and Sch: A 'that runs with a voice' (i.e. noisily).
[5] Sa^CB 'he will send'.
[6] Sa^CB and Sch om. 'nor any power'.
[7] Sa^CB adds '⟨from the⟩ flesh'.

11 my city. But sinners shall be put to shame: they[8] shall not pass beyond the thrones; but the thrones of death will hold them back and rule over them, because the angels do not acknowledge them[9] *and* they have become strangers to God's[10] dwelling-places.

12   Listen, wise men of the earth, and be on your guard against[11] the
13 deceivers, of whom there will be many at the end of time. For they will have doctrines that are not of God: they will reject the law of God – men who have made (A 22) their belly their god,[12] saying,
14 Fasting has no substance and God did not create it. They make themselves strangers to the covenant ⟨of God⟩[13] and rob themselves of the glorious promises. Such men are never established in
15 firm faith. So do not let them lead you astray. Remember ⟨that⟩ the Lord created fasting when he made the heavens, for men's profit, because of the passions and desires[14] that are at war with you, so
16 that the Evil One may not burn you up.[15] But I have created a pure
17 fasting, said the Lord. The man who fasts always (A 23) will not sin
18,19 through jealousy or strife.[16] Let the man who is pure fast. But the man who fasts, and is not pure provokes the Lord and the angels also; and he harms his own soul, laying up for himself a store of
20 retribution for the day of retribution. But I have[17] created a pure
21 fasting with a pure heart and pure hands. It forgives sins: it heals diseases: it drives out demons: it is efficacious at the throne of God, like a sweetener, like a fragrance, for the forgiveness of sins[18] by
22 pure prayer. What respectable workman among you will go out into the fields without (A 24) his tools? Or who will go out to fight
23 in war without a breastplate? Will he not be killed if he is found,
24 because he has despised the king's service? So, too, it is impossible
25 for anybody to come to the holy place and doubt. The man who

---

[8] Sa[CB] om. 'shall be put to shame: they'.
[9] Lit. 'do not agree with them'.
[10] Lit. 'his'.
[11] Lit. 'Listen, wise men of the earth, concerning'.
[12] Slightly emended on the basis of Sa[CB and Sch].
[13] So Sa[CB and Sch].
[14] Sa[CB] adds 'of different kinds'.
[15] Sa[CB] 'may not deceive you'.
[16] Lit. 'sin with jealousy and strife in him'.
[17] Sa[CB] 'But the Lord has'.
[18] So Sa[CB]: A is slightly defective here.

doubts – his prayer is . . . in himself;[19] neither do the angels
26 acknowledge him.[20] Be then of one mind always in the Lord,[21] so
that you may *be able to* interpret all things.[22]

II. But as for the Assyrian kings and the destruction of the heaven
and the earth and the things under the earth[1] – from now on they
shall not prevail over ⟨those who are mine⟩, said the Lord; and
2 those who are mine[2] shall not be afraid (A 25) in the war. When
they ⟨see a king⟩ appearing in the north, ⟨they will call him⟩ the
3 ⟨Assyrian⟩ king ⟨and⟩ the King of Unrighteousness. ⟨He will make
endless⟩ wars on Egypt and *be the cause of* many disturbances: there
will be groaning throughout the land, for your children will be
4 carried away. Many will seek death in those days, but death will
5 elude them.[3] And a king will arise in the lands of the west, who will
6 be called the King of Peace. He will run upon the sea like a roaring
7 lion; *and* he will kill the King of Unrighteousness. He will take
8 vengeance on Egypt with much fighting and bloodshed. (A 26) *And*
it will come to pass in those days that †the orders ⟨peace⟩ from
9 ⟨Egypt⟩ and an ⟨empty⟩ gift.† ⟨He will give⟩ peace to the ⟨saints,
10 saying⟩, The name of ⟨God⟩ is one. ⟨He will⟩ do honour to the
11 priests of God[4] and exalt[5] the places of the saints.[6] He will give
†empty† gifts to the house of God: he will wander about in the
12 cities of Egypt in secret and without their knowledge. He will count
the holy places: he will weigh the idols of the Gentiles: he will count
13 their riches: he will set up priests for them. He will order the wise
men of the land and the great men of the people to be arrested and
taken to the metropolis that is by the sea, saying, There is but one
14 single language. And when you hear, There is peace and joy . . .

---

[19] Sa[St] 'He who doubts in his prayer is dark in himself' (and similarly Sa[CB]).
[20] Lit. 'agree with him'.
[21] Sa[CB] adds 'be wise in the time'.
[22] So Sa[CB and St]: A 'every hour' or 'at every hour'.

[1] Sa[CB and St] om. 'and the things under the earth'.
[2] Lit 'and they'.
[3] Sa[CB and St] om. 'but death will elude them'.
[4] So[CB and St]: A 'to the saints'.
[5] Or 'erect'.
[6] Sa[CB and St] 'the holy places'.

(Sa^{CB} 7) behold, I will tell you what is distinctive about him,[7] so
15 that you can recognize him. For he has two sons, one on his right
and one on his left. Now, the one on his right will look like a devil,
and he will defy the name of God (for four kings come from that
16 king). But in his thirtieth year he will come down[8] to Memphis, *and*
17 he will build a temple in Memphis then. His own son will rise up
against him and kill him: the whole land will be in turmoil on that
18 day. He will issue an edict throughout the whole land that the
priests of the land and all the saints be arrested, saying, All the gifts
and all the good things my father gave you, (Sa^{CB}8) you shall give
19 back twice over. He will shut up the holy places: he will take away
20 their houses:[9] he will make captives of their children. He will give
orders that they offer sacrifices *which are* abominations and *bring*
deep distress upon the land: he will appear beneath the sun and the
21 moon on that day. The priests of the land will rend their garments.
22 Woe to you, rulers of Egypt, in those days, for your day has passed:
the violence done to the poor will redound on you; and your
23 children will be carried off as spoil. (A 27) The cities of Egypt will
groan in those days, for they will not hear the voice of the seller nor
24 *the voice of* the buyer. The market-places of the cities of Egypt will
gather dust: those in Egypt will weep together: they will seek
25 death, *but* death will elude them and pass them by. In those days
they will run up onto the rocks and jump off, saying, Fall down
26 upon us; and still they will not die.[10] Two further afflictions will
27 come upon the whole land in those days. The king will give orders
that all women with children at the breast be arrested and brought
before him bound, and that they suckle dragons, (A 28) and that
28 their blood be squeezed out of their breasts, and that it be used as
29 poison for arrows.[11] Because of the need *for soldiers* for the wars[12] he
will also order that all children of twelve and under be taken and
30 made to learn how to shoot with bow and arrow. *Every* midwife in

---

[7] Lit. 'I will tell you his signs'.
[8] Or 'up'.
[9] Lit. 'their house'.
[10] Sa^{CB} adds 'but death will elude them'.
[11] Lit. 'and that it (or 'they') be given to the poison of the arrows'.
[12] So Sa^{CB} (lit. 'the need of the wars'): A 'the need of (i.e. 'the famine in') the
cities'.

the land will mourn; *and* the woman who has children will raise her eyes to heaven, saying, Why ever did I sit on the birth-stool to bring children into the world? The childless and the virgin will

31 rejoice, saying, Now is the time for us to rejoice because we have no children upon earth: our children are in the heavens.

32 In those days three (A 29) kings will arise among the Persians and will take the Jews that are in Egypt, and transport them to

33 Jerusalem; and they will inhabit it and dwell there. Then if you hear, Safety is[13] in Jerusalem, *then* rend your garments, you priests of the land, for the coming of ⟨the⟩ Son of Perdition will not long be

34 delayed. The Lawless One will appear in those days in the holy places.

35 The kings of the Persians will flee in ⟨those⟩ days to Hrearit[14]

36 with the Assyrian kings. Four kings will fight with three. They will spend three years in that place until they can lay their hands upon the riches of the temple[15] there.

37 In those days (A 30) blood will flow from Kos to Memphis. The river of Egypt will turn into blood, and no one will be able to drink

38 from it for three days. Woe to Egypt and those who live there!

39 In those days a king will appear in the city called the City of the Sun; [16]and the whole land will be in turmoil. He will hurry

40 up to Memphis in the sixth year of the Persian kings. He will start a rebellion[17] in Memphis: he will kill the Assyrian kings; *and*

41 the Persians will wreak vengeance on the land. He will order the slaughter of all the Gentiles and the lawless: he will order the temples of the Gentiles to be plundered and their priests destroyed: he will order the temples of the saints to be (re)built; *and* he will

42 give double gifts (A 31) to the house of God. He will say, The name

---

[13] Sa[CB] 'Safety and security are'.

[14] Obscure: perhaps a place-name, or alternatively a verb of unknown meaning.

[15] Sa[CB] om. 'of the temple'.

[16] The translation of verses 39b–42 follows Sa[CB], which seems to give a better sense in the context. A reads '. . . and the whole land will be in turmoil ⟨and⟩ flee up to Memphis. In the sixth year the Persian kings will start a rebellion in Memphis. They will kill the Assyrian king; *and* the Persians will wreak vengeance on the land and order the slaughter of all the Gentiles and the lawless. They will order the holy temples to be (re)built: they will give double gifts (A 31) to the house of God. They will say. The name of God is one'.

[17] Lit. 'he will act treacherously'.

43 of God is one. The whole land will worship the Persians; and the remnant which has survived the onslaught will say, The Lord has sent us a righteous king so that the land might not become a desert.
44 †He will command not to give any king †[18]for three years and six months. The land will be full of good things in great abundance.
45 The living will turn towards the dead and say, Rise up and share with us this life of peace.[19]

III. In the fourth year of that king, the Son of Lawlessness will
2 appear, saying, I am the Christ[1] (though he is not). Do not believe
3 him. When the Christ comes, he will come (A 32) encircled by angels, like a flock of doves circling round their dove-cote:[2] he will walk[3] on the clouds of heaven, with the sign of the cross preceding
4 him. The whole world will see him, like the sun that shines from the eastern regions to the western: thus will he come,[4] with all his
5 angels round him. The Son of Lawlessness will also try to stand in
6 the holy places. He will say to the sun, Fall; and it will fall: he will
7 say, Shine; and it will: he will say, Be darkened; and it will.[5] He will say to the moon, Turn into blood; and it will. He will go with them
8 through the sky. He will walk upon the sea and (A 33) on the rivers as if on the dry land.[6] He will make the lame walk: he will make the deaf hear: he will make the dumb speak: he will make the blind see:
9 he will make the lepers clean: he will heal the sick; *and* he will cast out demons from those possessed by them. He will do many signs
10 and wonders in the sight of everyone. He will do everything[7] that

---

[18] A possible emendation might be '. . . any**thing to the** king' (i.e. 'He will command that nothing be given to the king'). Pietersma and Comstock rendered Sa[CB] 'He will command that no king be given them'.

[19] Lit. 'and be with us in this rest'.

[1] Note that in Coptic Χριστός always has the article, whether it is used as a title ('the Christ', 'the Anointed One') or as a proper name ('Christ').

[2] Lit. 'he comes like a dove-cote, with a crown of doves surrounding him'.

[3] Lit. 'he walks'.

[4] Lit. 'thus he comes'.

[5] Sa[CB] reverses the order of the last two commands to the sun and omits the following command to the moon.

[6] Sa[CB] and St convert the following sentence into a command introduced by 'He will say, Walk . . .', with further variants between the two authorities.

[7] Lit. 'the works'.

11 the Christ will do,[8] except only the raising of the dead. By this you
will know that he is the Son of Lawlessness, for he has no power
12 over the soul. Behold, I will tell you what his distinguishing
13 features are, so that you may be able to recognize him. He is a
spare,[9] weedy,[10] man, tall,[11] thin-legged, with a patch of grey hair
at the front of his head, (A 34) *but otherwise* bald, with his
eyebrows[12] reaching to his ears, and with leprous sores on the tips
14 of his fingers.[13] He will transform himself in front of those who look
at him:[14] he will become a child: he will become an old man:[15] he
will transform all his features; but what distinguishes his head
15 cannot be changed. By this you may be certain that he is the Son of
Lawlessness.

16   The virgin, whose name is Tabitha, will hear that the Shameless
17 One has appeared in the holy places. And she will put on her linen
18 garment and pursue him up into Judaea; and she will reproach
19 him all the way to Jerusalem, *crying out*, O Shameless One, O Son of
Lawlessness, O you who have been an enemy of all the saints.

20   (Sa^St 6) Then the Shameless One will turn in fury upon the
21,22 virgin. He will pursue her to the west. He will suck her blood at
eventide, and throw it[16] on the temple; and it[16] will become the
23 salvation of the people. She will arise in the morning, alive, and
will reproach him, saying, Shameless One, you have no power over
24 my soul, nor over my body; for I live in the Lord always. (Sa^St 7)
And she will say also, My blood you have thrown on the temple has
become the salvation of the people.

25   Then, when Elijah and Enoch hear that the Shameless One has
appeared in the holy place, they *will* come down to fight against
him, saying, Are you then not ashamed to cling to the saints,[17] for
26 you are a stranger, always? You have been an enemy of what is in

---

[8] So Sa^St: A 'has done', and so apparently Sa^CB.
[9] Lit. 'little'.
[10] Meaning doubtful.
[11] So Sa^St: A 'young': Sa^CB is defective at this point.
[12] Sa^CB 'eyelids'.
[13] Lit. 'there being bareness of leprosy at the front of his hands'.
[14] Sa^CB and St 'in front of you'.
[15] Sa^CB and St reverse the order ('. . . old man . . . child').
[16] Text 'her' . . . 'she' (cp. verse 24).
[17] Sa^CB om. 'to cling to the saints'.

27 heaven and what is on the earth: you have been an enemy of the
28 thrones and of the angels, You are a stranger always. You fell from
29 heaven like the morning stars. You abandoned your proper
30 home:[18] you were alienated from your tribe.[19] Are you then not
ashamed to cling to God, for you are the Devil?

31 The Shameless One will hear *it* and be furious, and he will fight
with them in the market-place of the great city; and he will spend
32 seven days fighting with them.[20] And they will lie dead in the
market-place for three and a half days; and all the people will see
33 them. But on the fourth day they will arise and reproach him,
saying, O (A 35) Shameless One, O son of Lawlessness,[21] are you
then not ashamed to lead astray the people of God, for whom you
34 have not suffered? Do you not know that we live in the Lord, so that
we can reproach you continually when you say, Over these have I
35 prevailed?[22] We will lay aside the flesh of the body[23] and kill you,
36 since you *will* have no power to speak on that day. For we are
strong[24] in the Lord always; but you are ever an enemy of God.[25]
37 The Shameless One will hear *it* and be furious and fight with them;
38 and the whole city will gather round them. On that day they will
shout aloud to heaven, shining *like the stars*, and all the people[26] and
39 the whole world will see them. The Son of Lawlessness will not
40 prevail over them. (A 36) He will vent his fury on the land[27] and set
41 himself to sin against the people. He will hunt down all the saints,
and they will be brought *to him* as prisoners with the priests of the
42 land. He will kill them and destroy them . . .,[28] and their eyes will
43 be put out with iron spikes. He will peel off their skins from their

---

[18] Lit. 'you changed'.
[19] So SaSt (lit. 'the tribe became darkness for you'): Sa^{CB} is fragmentary here, but it certainly read 'your tribe'.
[20] Sa^{CB} adds 'and kill them'.
[21] So A: Sa$^{CB and St}$ om. 'O Son of Lawlessness'.
[22] So Sa$^{CB and St}$: in A the last half of this verse is manifestly corrupt.
[23] So SaSt: A 'spirit'; Sa^{CB} is defective at this point.
[24] SaSt 'for we live': Sa^{CB} is defective.
[25] Sa$^{CB and St}$ om. 'of God'.
[26] Sa$^{CB and St}$ om. 'and all the people'.
[27] So Sa$^{CB and St}$: A 'He will go to the land'.
[28] This lacuna in A cannot be filled from Sa, since both Sa^{CB} and SaSt om. verse 41 and verse 42 as far as here.

44 heads:[29] he will pull out their nails one by one. He will order
45 vinegar and lye to be put in their noses. Those who are unable to
   endure the tortures of that king will take *their* money and flee on
46 ferries to desert places.[30] When they die they will be like men
47 asleep.[31] The Lord will receive to himself their spirits and their
   souls. Their (A 37) flesh will be *as permanent as* rock:[32] no wild beast
48 shall eat them until the last day of the great judgement. *Then* will
   they rise up and find a place of rest; but they will not share in the
49 kingdom of the Christ like those who have endured. For the Lord
   said, I will grant them to sit on my[33] right hand. They will obtain
50 grace for others.[34] They will be victorious over the Son of Lawlessness: they will see the destruction of heaven and earth: they will
51 obtain the thrones of glory and the crowns. Sixty righteous will be
   chosen in those days, who are prepared:[35] they will arm themselves
   with the breastplate of God, and run to Jerusalem, and fight with
52 the Shameless One, saying, All the mighty works (A 38) which the
   prophets did from the beginning, you have done; *but* you could not
53 raise the dead, for you have no power over the soul. By this we
54 have recognized that you are the Son of Lawlessness. He will hear
   it and be furious, and order fires to be lit on the altars[36] and the
55 righteous to be bound and put on them and burned. And on that
   day many will change their minds and desert him, saying, This is
   not the Christ: the Christ does not kill the righteous: he does not
   pursue honest men: does he not rather seek to persuade them by
   signs and wonders?[37]
56   In those days the Christ will take pity on his own. He will send

---

[29] Sa[CB] om. 'He . . . heads'.

[30] Sa[CB and St] 'flee to the ferries (Sa[St] 'rivers'), saying, Ferry us to the desert'.

[31] Lit. 'They will sleep like men asleep'.

[32] Sa[St], wrongly, 'Their flesh tastes like ham (i.e. πέρνα for πέτρα)': Sa[CB] is
defective.   [33] So Sa[CB and St]: A 'their'.

[34] Sa[CB and St] om. this sentence.

[35] So Sa[St]: A Sa[CB] 'Sixty righteous who are prepared for this hour will hear'
(Sa[CB] adds 'in those days').

[36] Lit. 'and order altars to be kindled'. Sa[CB and St] om. the reference to the
kindling of the altars, though the righteous are burned on them.

[37] So Sa[St]: A, obviously corruptly, 'he does not pursue men while he will seek, but
he persuades them by signs and wonders'. Sa[CB] is defective but appears to agree
substantially with Sa[St].

his angels from heaven, in number six hundred and four
57 thousand,[38] each one of them having six (A 39) wings. Their voice
will shake heaven and earth as they bless and glorify *their Lord*.
58 Those upon whose forehead the name of Christ is written, and
59 upon whose[39] hand is the seal, both small and great, they will set
60 upon their wings and protect[40] them from his wrath. Then will
Gabriel and Uriel be a pillar of light to lead them[41] into the holy
land; and they will give them the right to eat from the tree of life,[42]
and to ⟨wear white⟩ garments, and to be guarded ⟨by angels⟩.
61 ⟨They shall⟩ not ⟨thirst⟩,[43] nor ⟨shall⟩ the Son of ⟨Lawlessness⟩
62 have power over them. ⟨But⟩ on ⟨that day⟩ the land will be in
turmoil ⟨and the sun be⟩ darkened: peace and the spirit will be
removed from the earth:[44] the trees will be uprooted and fall: the
63 wild beasts and the cattle will die in confusion. (A 40) The birds
will fall dead upon the ground:[45] the earth will be dry;[46] *and* the
64 waters of the sea will be dried up. The sinners on the earth will
groan, saying, What have you done to us, Son of Lawlessness, by
65 saying, I am the Christ, though you are the Devil? You have no
66 power to save yourself: how can you save us? You have performed[47]
⟨signs⟩ before us and[48] estranged ⟨us⟩ from the Christ who made
67 us.[49] ⟨Woe⟩ to us ⟨that we have⟩ listened to you. ⟨Behold, now we⟩
68 shall die of famine.[50] ⟨Where⟩ now is there the vestige of a ⟨right-
eous man that we may⟩ reverence **him**?[51] Or where is there ⟨a
69 teacher⟩ that we can appeal to ⟨him⟩? Now we shall perish in ⟨Sa[St]

---

[38] Sa[CB and St] 'sixty-four thousand'.
[39] Sa[CB and St] add 'right'.
[40] Lit. 'take'.
[41] Sa[CB and St] add 'until they bring them'.
[42] On the restorations from here to the end of A 39 see Schmidt, *Der Kolophon . . .*, p. 321.   [43] Sa[CB and St] 'They shall not hunger nor thirst'.
[44] Lit. 'They will carry the ⟨peace⟩ from upon the earth and the spirit'. The 'spirit', which is to be 'removed from the earth', is presumably the Divine spirit, which was active initially at the creation (Gen. i. 2) and subsequently 'filled the whole world' (Wisd. i. 7).   [45] Cp. Anon. Apoc. iii. 26 (below, p. 925).
[46] Sa[CB] om. 'the earth will be dry'.
[47] Sa[CB and St] add 'empty'. On the restorations from here to the end of A 40 see Schmidt, *Der Kolophon . . .*, p. 321.   [48] Lit. 'until you'.
[49] So A Sa[St]: Sa[CB] 'everyone'.
[50] Sa[CB and St] add 'and tribulation'.
[51] A 'it': Sa[CB] 'you' (i.e. 'thee'); Sa[St] leaves the pronoun unexpressed.

70 13)⁵² *the day of* wrath, for we have disobeyed God. We went to the
71 deep places in the sea; *but* we found no water. We dug in the rivers
72 *to a depth of* sixteen cubits; *but* we found no water. Then **will** the
    Shameless One **weep**⁵³ on that day, saying, Woe is me that my time
73,74 has passed me by. I said my time would not pass me by. My years
    have become months, my days have vanished like dust driven by
75 the wind: now I shall perish with you. Run out, therefore, into the
76 desert; lay hands upon the brigands, *and* kill them. Bring the saints
77 up; for it is because of them (Sa^{St} 14) that the earth bears fruit. For
    it is because of them that the sun shines upon the earth. For it is
78 because of them that the dew comes down upon the earth. The
    sinners will weep, saying, You have made us enemies of God. ⟨If⟩
    you can, ⟨get up⟩ and pursue ⟨them⟩.

79   Then will he spread his fiery wings and fly forth after the saints.
80,81 He will fight with them again. The angels will hear *of it*, and they
82 will come down and fight with him in a war with many swords. On
    that day the Lord will hear and order the heaven and the earth in
83 great anger to send forth fire. And the fire will overwhelm the earth
    to an extent of seventy-two cubits: it will devour the sinners and the
84 devils like stubble. (A 41) A righteous judgement will there be on
85 that day: the mountains of the earth will give tongue.⁵⁴ The paths
    will speak with one another, Did you hear to-day the sound⁵⁵ of ⟨a⟩
    man walking, who did not come to the judgement of the Son of
    God?

86   The sins of each will stand against him in the place where they
    were committed – those committed in the day as well as those
87 committed in the night. The **righteous**⁵⁶ and the . . . will see the
    sinners in ⟨their⟩ punishments, both those who have persecuted
88 them and those who have handed them over to death. Then the
    sinners . . . will see the place of the righteous, and thus will they be
89 favoured.⁵⁷ In those days what the ⟨righteous⟩ (A 42) ask for many

---

⁵² One folio of A is missing here; but Sa^{St} is available until A resumes at verse 84,
as is also Sa^{CB} as far as the end of verse 72.

⁵³ Text 'Then the Shameless One wept'.

⁵⁴ So Sa^{St}: A has '. . . in a righteous judgement. On that day will the mountains
and the earth give tongue'.

⁵⁵ Lit. 'voice'.

⁵⁶ Text 'unrighteous'.

⁵⁷ Lit. 'and thus there will be grace'.

90 times will be given them. On that day will the Lord judge heaven
and earth. He will judge those who have transgressed in heaven
and those who have done the same on earth. He will judge the
shepherds of the people. He will ask them about the sheep; and
they will be given him, unencumbered by wickedness and lies.[58]

91 Then *will* Elijah and Enoch descend. They *will* lay aside *their*
92 worldly flesh and take on spiritual flesh. They *will* pursue the Son
93 of Lawlessness and kill him without his being able to speak. On
94 that day he will melt before them like (A 43) ice melted by fire. He
95 will perish like a dragon that has no breath. He will be told, Your
time has passed you by: now you are to perish together with those
96 who believe in you. They will be flung into the pit of the abyss, and
it will be shut over them.

97 On that day the Christ, the King, with all the saints, will come[59]
98 from heaven. He will burn[59] the earth, and spend[59] a thousand
years upon it; for the sinners had taken possession of it. He will
make a new heaven and a new earth, no devil . . . will be[60] in them.
99 He will reign with the saints, going up ⟨and⟩ down; and they will be
with the (A 44) angels always, and with the Christ a thousand
years.

The Apocalypse of Elijah

---

[58] Lit. 'there being no deadly deceit in them'.
[59] Lit. 'comes . . . burns . . . spends'.
[60] Lit. 'is'.

THE ASCENSION OF ISAIAH

INTRODUCTION

A tradition that Isaiah was 'sawn in two' by Manasseh was known by both Jews and Christians. Most early Christian writers give no details,[1] although some specify that the saw used was made of wood.[2] The Talmud, however, is more explicit. In one version Isaiah is brought to trial before Manasseh: at the conclusion of the hearing Isaiah pronounces the Name and is immediately swallowed up by a cedar-tree: the cedar is sawn in two, and 'when the saw reached his mouth he died'.[3] In another Talmudic version Manasseh resolves to kill Isaiah: Isaiah hears of it and flees and hides himself inside a cedar-tree: unfortunately a piece of his garment sticks out and betrays him: so Manasseh orders the cedar to be cut through; and it is this crime which is alluded to particularly at 2 Kings xxi. 16 ('Manasseh shed so much innocent blood, that he filled Jerusalem with it up to the brim').[4] Yet another variant of the same story is to be found in a fragment preserved as a gloss attached to Isa. lxvi (the last chapter in the book) in two MSS of the Targum of Jonathan on the Prophets – *Codex Reuchlinianus* and Cod. Vat. Ebr. Urbin. 1: according to this account, Isaiah, outraged by Manasseh's profanation of the Temple, prophesied its destruction by Nebuchadrezzar: when Manasseh heard of it he was filled with fury,

> 'He said to his servants, Run after him, seize him! They ran after him. He fled from before them, and a carob tree opened its mouth and swallowed him. They brought saws [+ of iron *Cod. Reuch.*] and cut through the tree until Isaiah's blood flowed like water.'[5]

The first indication of the existence of a separate apocryphal

[1] e.g. Tert. (*pat.* 14; *scorp.* 8).
[2] e.g. Justin (*Tryph.* cxx. 14–15).
[3] T. B. *Yebamoth*, 49 b.   [4] T. J. *Sanhedrin*, x. 2.
[5] See P. de Lagarde, *Prophetae Chaldaice* (Leipzig, 1872), p. xxxiii; P. Grelot, 'Deux tosephtas targoumiques inédites sur Isaïe LXVI' in *R Bibl* lxxix (1972), pp. 515–518.

work concerned with this incident is found in Origen. 'It is clear', Origen writes, 'that tradition relates that Isaiah the prophet was sawn asunder and the circumstances are recorded in a certain apocryphon.'[6] In a similar passage he names this apocryphon 'the Isaiah apocryphon'.[7] And in yet another passage (in Jerome's translation) he mentions a tradition that Isaiah was condemned for blaspheming Moses and the Law;[8] and the terms in which Origen states this charge have obvious points of contact with Balchira's accusation in Ascension iii. 6–10.

In the century after Origen, Didymus the Blind, when describing the details of Isaiah's martyrdom in the course of his comment on Ps. xxxv. 15, mentions a second charge as having been brought against Isaiah also – that he had described his contemporaries as 'rulers of Sodom' and 'a people of Gomorrah';[9] and it is to be noted that precisely the same second charge follows immediately on the heels of the blasphemy charge in Ascension iii. 10. Again, when commenting on Eccl. xi. 6, Didymus refers to Christ's journeying through the heavens and adds that his source is the description 'by Isaiah . . . in the Ascension' (a clear allusion to Ascension x. 20–31).[10] Epiphanius, too, about the same time (end of 4th cent.), refers twice to 'The Ascension of Isaiah' as accepted and used by heretics: the Archontici used it:[11] the Egyptian heretic Hieracas appealed to it for confirmation of his doctrine of the Spirit; and in this last connection Epiphanius cites Ascension ix. 35–36 in full.[12]

In the early 5th cent. Jerome provides three pieces of evidence:

(1) He records that contemporary Jewish opinion gave two reasons for Isaiah's condemnation – first, Isaiah had offended all classes in Jerusalem by addressing them as 'rulers of Sodom' and 'a people of Gomorrah' (Isa. i. 10); and second, whereas God himself had laid it down through Moses, 'No man may see me and live'

---

[6] *Ep. ad Afric.* 9.

[7] *Comm. in Matt. tom. X.* 18 (on Matt. xiii. 56); cp. *Matt. comm. ser.* 28 (on Matt. xxiii. 37–39).   [8] *In Es. hom.* i. 5.

[9] *Comm. in Pss.* 218[3–14] (= M. Gronewald, *Papyrologische Texte und Abhandlungen,* viii (Bonn, 1969), pp. 354–357).

[10] *Comm. in Eccl.* 329[21–23] (= G. Binder and L. Liesenborghs, *Pap. Texte und Abh.* ix (Bonn, 1969), pp. 66–67).   [11] *Haer.* XL. ii. 2.

[12] *Haer.* LXVII. iii. 4.

(Exod. xxxiii. 20), Isaiah had dared to claim 'I saw the Lord' (Isa. vi. 1). The same two charges, as we have seen, are found in conjunction both in the mouth of Balchira at Ascension iii. 6–10 and in Didymus: Jerome, however, has them in the reverse order, influenced, perhaps, by the order of the passages in the canonical Isaiah.[13]

(2) Two interpretations of Isa. lvii. 1–2, Jerome says, are possible. Either the passage can be taken generally as a reference to all those whose 'innocent blood' Manasseh shed, or it can be taken as a prophecy by Isaiah of his own martyrdom. Both interpretations are allowed by the Jews of Jerome's day, and the tradition that Isaiah was 'sawn in two by Manasseh with a wooden saw' is 'a very firmly established tradition among them'.[14]

(3) In commenting on Isa. lxiv. 4–5 Jerome remarks that these verses are paraphrased by St. Paul at 1 Cor. ii. 9: he then adds 'The Ascension of Isaiah and the Apocalypse of Elijah also quote this passage'. The quotation is found (in its Pauline form) in the Latin and in the Slavonic versions at Ascension xi. 34, though not in the Ethiopic.[15]

In the mid-sixth century the unknown author of the Pseudo-Chrysostom *Opus imperfectum in Matthaeum* gives an account of an interview of Hezekiah with Manasseh and Isaiah, which is not only generally very similar to the scene described in Ascension i, but also exhibits many detailed points of contact.[16] But since Pseudo-Chrysostom mentions no source, it is impossible to say whether he was dependent upon the Ascension as we know it, or (possibly) upon a source of the Ascension, or whether he derived his information independently from tradition.

And finally, in the eleventh century, Georgius Cedrenus says that Isaiah prophesied the coming of the Antichrist, the duration of the Antichrist's rule on earth and his being cast into 'Tartarus', the coming of Christ, and the resurrection to judgement of both good and evil, 'in the Testament of Hezekiah King of Judah'[17] – a

---

[13] *Comm. in Es.* i. 10.
[14] *Comm. in Es.* lvii. 1–2.   [15] *Comm. in Es.* lxiv. 4–5.
[16] *Op. imperf. in Matt.* Hom. i (= *PG* lvi. 626).
[17] *Historiarum Compendium* (= *Corp. scr. hist. Byz.* (ed. I. Bekker; Bonn, 1838, vol. i, pp. 120–121: also *PG* cxxi. 152).

work whose existence is otherwise unattested. If Cedrenus had not named his source so distinctly, it would naturally be assumed that he was alluding to Ascension iv. 12–18. Was Cedrenus, then, guilty of a slip in naming his source? Or was 'The Testament of Hezekiah' a recognised alternative title for the Ascension? Or was it, perhaps, the title of one of the Ascension's constituent parts, which may still have survived in the eleventh century as a separate work?

The complete text of the Ascension here translated is preserved only in Ethiopic. Three Ethiopic manuscripts are available: A (Bodl. Aeth. d. 13 – formerly Huntington 626; 15th cent.), B (B. L. Or. 501; 15th cent.), and C (B. L. Or. 503; 18th cent.). For comparison with the Ethiopic there are also available: (1) seven leaves of a papyrus codex of the 5th–6th centuries in the Amherst Collection (now part of the Pierpont Morgan Library in New York), giving a Greek text of ii. 4–iv. 4 with some lacunae, first published by B. P. Grenfell and A. S. Hunt in 1900; (2) two Latin fragments from a Vatican MS (Vat. lat. 5750; 5th–6th cent.), containing ii. 14–iii. 13 and vii. 1–19, first published by A. Mai in 1828; (3) a Latin text of vi–xi, first printed by Antonius de Fantis in 1522 from an unknown MS and subsequently reprinted from de Fantis by J. K. L. Gieseler, C. F. A. Dillmann, and R. H. Charles ('with certain corrections'); and (4) a Slavonic text of vi–xi, now known from six MSS, first published by A. N. Popov in 1879. All these texts will be found conveniently assembled in parallel columns in Charles's edition (pp. 83–139).[18]

As further authorities may be listed: (5) two very fragmentary leaves of a mid-to-late 4th century papyrus codex giving the Sahidic text of iii. 3–6, 9–12, and xi. 24–32, 35–40; (6) thirteen even less well preserved fragments of a papyrus roll giving scraps of an Akhmimic text extending from the very beginning of the book to very near the end, and probably also dating from the 4th cent.; (7) the so-called 'Greek Legend', published by O. von Gebhardt in 1878 from a 12th century Paris MS (B. N. Gr. 1534), which

[18] It is to be observed that Charles printed the Slavonic text in a Latin translation made by Bonwetsch.

contains a number of legends of saints commemorated between 1 March and 31 May – the Isaiah legend seems to be based on at least some knowledge of the contents of the Ascension, and Charles, in reprinting from von Gebhardt the major part of it in his edition (pp. 141–8), has picked out the possible literary parallels by the use of heavy type; and (8) another Slavonic text published by L. Stojanović in 1890.

The translation which follows is a translation of the Ethiopic; and in the apparatus all the more important variants of the three Ethiopic manuscripts are recorded. Similarly recorded are all important variants in the Amherst Greek text (= 'Gk'), in the Latins (Vat. Lat. 5750 = 'L': de Fantis = 'L²'), in the Sahidic (= 'Sah'), in the Akhmimic (= 'Akh.') and in Popov's Slavonic (= 'Slav'). On a few occasions the evidence of the Greek Legend has been cited (= 'Gk^L').

As it now stands in Ethiopic, the Ascension divides naturally into two parts — i–v and vi–xi. The first part describes the events that led up to the death of Isaiah and the details of his martyrdom at the hands of Manasseh: the second part takes the reader back to 'the twentieth year of the reign of Hezekiah' and describes a vision which Isaiah saw in that year, preceded by the title 'The vision which Isaiah the son of Amoz saw'. And this twofold division in the Ethiopic is supported by both L² and Slav., which are not fragments, but versions of the vision *and no more* (i.e. of vi–xi only); and they also both have the title at the beginning 'The vision . . .' Chapters vi–xi, therefore, circulated independently of the rest of the work. It is possible of course that some late editor of the Ascension detached from it the last six chapters and so turned them into a separate work which he called 'The Vision'. Nevertheless the fact that the Ethiopic also has the title before vi makes it much more likely that these chapters were originally separate and that it was only later that they were joined on to i–v because they also were about Isaiah. In any case, vi–xi show clear signs of Christian authorship (e.g. ix. 12–17 and xi. 1–22), whether we are prepared to leave it at that or prefer to particularize further and attribute their origin to 'Christian–Gnostic circles' (so Helmbold).

Chapters i–v raise more difficult questions. Not only is the story of Isaiah's martyrdom rooted firmly in Judaism, but there are in the story as it is told in these chapters not a few features that suggest a Jewish origin for them (e.g. the statement at ii. 2 that Balchira was a Samaritan). On the other hand, there is even more evidence of a Christian origin (e.g. i. 7 and iii. 13–20). At the very beginning there is some confusion about whether Hezekiah's purpose in summoning Manasseh was to give him 'commands' (i. 6; ii. 1) or to 'deliver to him' the written records of his own vision in his fifteenth year and of Isaiah's vision in his twentieth year (i. 2–6). And the progress of the narrative between iii. 12 and v. 1 is very awkwardly interrupted by the details of another vision of Isaiah, in which are discussed the Incarnation, the Crucifixion, the Resurrection, the early history of the Church, the events leading up to the End, and the Last Judgement.

The generally agreed solution of these difficulties is that the basis of i–v is a document recounting Isaiah's martyrdom, probably Jewish in origin, into which a Christian editor has inserted a Christian apocalypse (iii. 13–iv. 22) and made also a number of other additions and adaptations. Whether or not it was this same editor who at the same time added vi–xi to i–v it is impossible to say. Certain it is that, inasmuch as i. 5 looks forward to vi–xi, this verse at any rate is unlikely to have been added until very near the final stage in the Ascension's history.

That this final stage was reached by the mid-fourth century at the latest is proved by the Sahidic fragments. These fragments represent two leaves from a single codex: they preserve sections of text from opposite ends of the book; and they are to be dated *c.* AD 350–375. If we are prepared to allow a reasonable margin for the circulation of the work in Sahidic before our particular MS was copied, for its translation into Sahidic from Greek, and for its circulation in Greek after final editing, we are taken back to AD 350 as the latest possible date.[19] And the actual date is in all probability very much earlier. Indeed, Charles committed himself to a date in 'the latter half of the second century' and went on to claim that the

---

[19] If we can rely on the approximate 4th cent. date suggested for the Akhmimic fragments, they will, of course, support this conclusion.

three 'constituents . . . circulated independently as early as the first century'.[20]

Charles may very well be right. What is important to remember is that Origen's 'Isaiah apocryphon' may have been no more than the section recording the martyrdom, and, further, that although Epiphanius and Jerome refer explicitly to 'The Ascension of Isaiah' as the source of quotations from chaps. ix and xi, this is no clear proof that they knew the book in its final form – 'The Ascension of Isaiah' may have been their name for vi–xi only. This last possibility is, however, unlikely. Whatever Origen's 'apocryphon' may have contained, the likelihood (especially in view of the evidence of the Sahidic fragments) is that 'The Ascension' known to Didymus, Epiphanius, and Jerome, was the Ascension as we know it to-day.

If the section recounting the martyrdom was of Jewish origin, a good case can be made for its having had a Hebrew or Aramaic original, which was later translated into Greek. But the original language of the other two sections was undoubtedly Greek (as was the language of the complete book). And, to judge from the evidence of the surviving Greek fragments, the Ethiopic is a very faithful translation.

BIBLIOGRAPHY

EDITIONS

Ethiopic

R. Laurence, *Ascensio Isaiae Vatis, Opusculum pseudepigraphum, multis abhinc seculis, ut videtur, deperditum, nunc autem apud Aethiopas compertum, et cum versione Latina Anglicanaque publici iuris factum* (Oxford, 1819).

C. F. A. Dillmann, *Ascensio Isaiae Aethiopice et Latine, cum prolegomenis, adnotationibus criticis et exegeticis, additis versionum Latinarum reliquiis* (Leipzig, 1877).

[20] R. H. Charles, *The Ascension of Isaiah* (London, 1900), pp. xi–xii.

R. H. CHARLES, *The Ascension of Isaiah, translated from the Ethiopic version, which, together with the new Greek fragment, the Latin versions and the Latin translation of the Slavonic, is here published in full. Edited with Introduction, Notes, and Indices* (London, 1900).

Greek

B. P. GRENFELL and A. S. HUNT, *The Amherst Papyri, being an account of the Greek papyri in the collection of the Right Hon. Lord Amherst of Hackney.* Part I (London, 1900), pp. 1–22.

O. VON GEBHARDT, 'Die Ascensio Isaiae als Heiligenlegende' in *Zeitschrift für wissenschaftliche Theologie*, xxi (1878), pp. 330–353.

Coptic

L. TH. LEFORT, 'Coptica Lovaniensia' in *Le Muséon*, li (1938), pp. 1–32.

——, 'Fragments d'Apocryphes en Copte – Akhmîmique' in *Le Muséon*, lii (1939), pp. 1–10.

——, *Les manuscrits coptes de l'Université de Louvain*, i (*Textes Littéraires*; Louvain, 1940), pp. 72–78.

P. LACAU, 'Fragments de l'Ascension d'Isaïe en Copte' in *Le Muséon*, lix (1946), pp. 453–467.

Latin

A. MAI, *Scriptorum Veterum Nova Collectio e Vaticanis codicibus edita*, III. ii (Rome, 1828), pp. 238–239.

Slavonic

A. N. POPOV, *Opisanie rukopisei i katalog knig tserkovnoi pechati biblioteki A. I. Khludova* (Moscow, 1872), pp. 414–419.

——, *Bibliograficheskie materialy*, i (= *ChOIDR*; Moscow, 1879 I. vii), pp. 13–20.

L. STOJANOVIĆ, 'Stare srpske hrisovulje, akti, biografije, letopisi, tipici, pomenici, zapisi i dr.' (= *Spomenik Srpske Kraljevske Akademije*, iii (Belgrade, 1890), pp. 190–194).

A. A. SHAKHMATOV and P. A. LAVROV, *Sbornik XII veka Moskovskogo Uspenskogo sobora*, i (= *ChOIDR*; Moscow, 1899 II. ii. 1), pp. 129–136. [Reproduced photographically with an Introduction by D. ČIŽEVSKIJ, The Hague, 1957.]

I. IVANOV, *Bogomilski knigi i legendi* (Sofia, 1925), pp. 134–149.

TRANSLATIONS

English

R. LAURENCE, *Ascensio Isaiae Vatis . . .* [as above. The English version was reprinted under the title *The Ascension of Isaiah the Prophet, translated from the Ethiopic*; Glasgow, 1889.]

R. H. CHARLES, *The Ascension of Isaiah . . .* [as above].

——, 'The Martyrdom of Isaiah' in *APOT* ii, pp. 155–162 [A translation of i. 1–iii. 12 and v. 1–14 only].

——, *The Ascension of Isaiah* (= S.P.C.K., *Translations of Early Documents*; London, 1919).

D. HILL, 'The Ascension of Isaiah' in *NTA* ii, pp. 642–663. [An English version of the German translation of J. FLEMMING and H. DUENSING below.]

French

R. BASSET, *Les Apocryphes Éthiopiens traduits en français*. III. *L'Ascension d'Isaïe* (Paris, 1894).

E. TISSERANT, *Ascension d'Isaïe: Traduction de la version éthiopienne avec les principales variantes des versions grecque, latines et slave: Introduction et notes* (Paris, 1909).

German

G. BEER in E. KAUTZSCH, *APAT* ii, pp. 119–127 [A translation of ii. 1–15, iii. 1–12, and v. 2–14 only].

J. FLEMMING and H. DUENSING 'Die Himmelfahrt des Jesaja' in E. HENNECKE and W. SCHNEEMELCHER, *Neutestamentlliche Apokryphen in deutscher Übersetzung*[3], ii (Tübingen, 1964), pp. 454–468.

P. RIESSLER, *AjSaB*[2], pp. 481–484 [A translation of i. 1–2, ii. 1–iii. 12, and v. 1–14 only].

E. HAMMERSHAIMB in *JSh-rZ* II. 1 (1973), pp. 1–34 [A translation of i. 1–iii. 12 and v. 1–14 only].

GENERAL

G. H. BOX, Introduction in *The Ascension of Isaiah* (trans. R. H. CHARLES; S.P.C.K., *Translations of Early Documents*; London, 1919), pp. vii–xxvi.

F. C. Burkitt, *Jewish and Christian Apocalypses* (London, 1914), pp. 45–48 and 72–74.

J. Daniélou, *The Theology of Jewish Christianity* (= *The Development of Christian Doctrine before the Council of Nicaea*, I. Translated and edited by J. A. Baker; London, 1964), pp. 12–14.

A.-M. Denis, *IPGAT*, pp. 170–176.

O. Eissfeldt, *OTI*, pp. 609–610.

D. Flusser, 'The Apocryphal Book of *Ascensio Isaiae* and the Dead Sea Sect' in *Israel Exploration Journal*, iii (1953), pp. 30–47.

J.-B. Frey, art. 'Apocryphes de l'Ancien Testament' in *DBSup* i, cols. 409–411.

L. Ginzberg, *The Legends of the Jews*, iv (Philadelphia, 1913), pp. 277–279 and vi (Philadelphia, 1928), pp. 370–375.

A. K. Helmbold, 'Gnostic Elements in the "Ascension of Isaiah" ' in *NTS* xviii (Jan. 1972), pp. 222–227.

E. Littmann, art. 'Isaiah, Ascension of', in *JE* vi (New York, 1904), pp. 642–643.

W. Lüdtke, 'Beiträge zu slavischen Apokryphen: 3. Zur *Ascensio Isaiae*' in *ZAW* xxxi (1911), pp. 222–226.

M. Philonenko, 'Le *Martyre d'Ésaïe* et l'histoire de la secte de Qoumrân' in *Pseudépigraphes de l'Ancien Testament et manucrits de la mer Morte*, i (Paris, 1967), pp. 1–10.

P. Riessler, *AjSaB*², pp. 1300–1301.

L. Rost, *EATAP*, pp. 112–114.

E. Schürer, *HJPTJC* II. iii, pp. 141–146.

——, *GjVZJC*⁴ iii, pp. 386–393.

C. C. Torrey, *AL*, pp. 133–135.

É. Turdeanu, 'Apocryphes bogomiles et apocryphes pseudo-bogomiles' in *Revue de l'histoire des religions*, cxxxviii (1950), pp. 213–218.

A. Vaillant, 'Un apocryphe pseudo-bogomile: La Vision d'Isaïe' in *Revue des études slaves*, xlii (1963), pp. 109–121.

I. And it came to pass in the twenty-sixth[1] year of the reign of Hezekiah, king of Judah, that he summoned Manasseh his son (his

2 only son). And he summoned him in the presence of Isaiah the son

---

[1] Gk.ᴸ 'twenty-fifth'; Akh. 'sixteenth'.

of Amoz, the prophet, and in the presence of Josab Isaiah's son, in
3 order to deliver to him the truths[2] the king himself had seen about[3]
the eternal judgements,[4] and the torments of Gehenna, and what
concerns **the prince of this world**[5] and his angels and his sovereign-
4 ities and his powers, and the expectations for the coming of the
Beloved,[6] which he himself had seen in the fifteenth year of his
5 reign during his illness. And he delivered to him the written
records that Samnas the scribe had made,[7] and also those that
Isaiah the son of Amoz had given to him and to the prophets,[8] so
that they might write out and store up with him what he himself
had seen in the king's house[9] about the judgement of the angels and
the destruction of this world, and about the garments of the saints
and their[10] going forth, and about their[10] transformation, and the
6 persecution and ascension of the Beloved. In the twentieth year of
Hezekiah's reign Isaiah had seen the words of this prophecy, and
7 he had delivered them to Josab his son. And while Hezekiah[11] was
giving *his* commands, *and* Josab, Isaiah's son, *was* standing by,
Isaiah said to king Hezekiah (thus Manasseh was not the only
other person who heard what Isaiah said[12]), As the Lord lives,
whose Name has not been entrusted to this world, and as the
Beloved of my Lord lives, and as the Spirit that speaks in me lives,
all these commands and all these precepts[13] will be repudiated by
your son Manasseh, and I myself will be tortured by him and so

---

[2] Lit. 'words of truth'.

[3] Lit. 'and'.

[4] So A : BC 'the judgements of this world'.

[5] So Dillmann: A reads 'the place of eternal punishment' and BC read 'the place of punishment of this world'.

[6] Lit. 'and the words of faith in the Beloved'.

[7] Lit. 'the written words . . . had written'.

[8] A 'that Isaiah the son of Amoz and the prophets also had given to him'.

[9] A 'what the king alone had seen'.

[10] Charles regarded these pronouns as 'all but certainly wrong': in his judgement the 'going forth' and the 'transformation' are the Messiah's. Cp. iii. 13.

[11] Lit. 'he'.

[12] Lit. 'but not in the presence of Manasseh only did he say to him'. Could the original here possibly have meant that Manasseh was *not* present at this stage of the proceedings – i.e. that when the essential business had been concluded Manasseh disappeared and only Josab was left, in addition to Hezekiah, to hear Isaiah's oracle?

[13] Lit. 'words'.

8 depart *this life*. And **Balchira will serve Sammael before Manasseh,**[14] and will carry out all his designs; and Manasseh[11] will become a
9 disciple of Beliar rather than of me. And many there are in Jerusalem and in Judaea that he will turn away from the true faith; and Beliar will make his abode in Manasseh, and by his hands I
10 shall be sawn in two. When he heard these words Hezekiah wept very bitterly, and he rent his garments and put earth upon his head
11 and fell on his face. But Isaiah said to him, The design of Sammael against Manasseh is accomplished *already*: there is nothing you
12 can do. And Hezekiah determined there and then to kill his son
13 Manasseh. But Isaiah said to Hezekiah, The Beloved has frustrated your plan, and your purpose will not be achieved; for to this end[15] have I been called, and I shall inherit what the Beloved has in store for me.[16]

II. And after Hezekiah died and Manasseh became king, he did not remember his father Hezekiah's commands, but forgot them; and Sammael made his abode in Manasseh and clung fast to him.
2 And Manasseh abandoned the service of his father's God and
3 served Satan and his angels and his hosts. And he turned away his father Hezekiah's household from the pursuit of wisdom[1] and from
4 the service of God. And Manasseh turned away his own heart to serve Beliar – for the angel of lawlessness, who is the ruler of this world, is Beliar, whose name is Matanbukus. And he delighted in Jerusalem because of Manasseh and supported him in his leading
5 *Judah* astray, and in the lawlessness prevalent in Jerusalem. Magic and sorcery and divination and augury and fornication and adultery[2] increased, as also the persecution of the righteous by Manasseh and Balchira[3] and Tobiah the Canaanite and John of

[14] Eth. reads 'And Sammael Malchira will serve Manasseh', which suggests that Malchira is a sort of surname of Sammael's. The emendation assumes that Malchira is a corruption of the Balchira or Belchira, who appears at ii. 12, iii. 1, etc. (or, perhaps, the original form of the name).
[15] Lit. 'for with this calling'.
[16] Lit. 'inherit the inheritance of the Beloved'.

[1] Lit. 'And he turned away the house of his father which had been before the face of Hezekiah (from) the words of wisdom'.　　[2] Gk. om. 'and adultery'.
[3] Gk. om. 'and Balchira'.

6 Anathoth, and by Zadok[4] the chief of the works. And the rest of what happened is recorded in the book of the kings of Judah and Israel.

7 And when Isaiah, the son of Amoz, saw the lawlessness that was common practice in Jerusalem, and the worship of Satan and his wantonness, he left Jerusalem and settled in Bethlehem of Judah. 8 And there too there was much lawlessness, so that he left Beth- 9 lehem and settled on a mountain in a desert place. And Micaiah the prophet, and the aged Ananias, and Joel, and Habakkuk, and his son Josab, and many of the faithful who believed in the ascension into heaven, *also* left *where they were* and settled on the moun- 10 tain. They were all clothed with garments of hair,[5] and they were all of them prophets: they had nothing with them, but were naked; and they all lamented with a great lamentation because of the 11 apostasy of Israel. And they had nothing to eat but only the wild herbs that they gathered on the mountains; and they cooked them and lived on them together with the prophet Isaiah. And they remained on the mountains and on the hills for two years.

12 And after this, while they were in the desert, there was in Samaria a certain man named Balchira,[6] of the family of Zedekiah, the son of Chenaanah, the false prophet, whose home was in Bethlehem. (Now Zedekiah,[7] the son of Chenaanah, was Balchira's[8] father's brother, and in the days of Ahab king of Israel he had been the master of the four hundred prophets of Baal, and had himself hit Micaiah, the son of Amada, the prophet, and 13 abused him. And Micaiah had also been abused by Ahab and put in prison with the prophet Zedekiah. They were with Ahaziah, son 14 of **Ahab, king of Samaria**.[9] And Elijah the prophet from Thebon[10] in Gilead was reproving Ahaziah and Samaria; and he prophesied about Ahaziah that he would die upon a bed of sickness, and that

---

[4] So Gk. only: Eth. has no name.

[5] They . . . hair: B om. (perhaps because of the succeeding statement that they were naked).

[6] So BC here: A 'Belchira'; Gk. 'Belicheiar'. There is considerable variation between the authorities at other occurrences of the name. We print regularly 'Balchira'.	[7] So Gk.: Eth. 'Hezekiah'.

[8] Lit. 'his'.

[9] Charles's restoration of a text which is a jumble, both in Eth. and Gk.

[10] So A: BC 'Zebon'.

Samaria would be delivered into the hands of Shalmaneser,[11]
15 because he had slaughtered the prophets of God. And when the
false prophets who were with Ahaziah, the son of Ahab, and their
master Jalerjas of mount Ephraim[12] – he[13] was Zedekiah's brother
– heard *it*, they persuaded Ahaziah, king of Gomorrah,[14] and he
killed[15] Micaiah).

III. And Balchira[1] was well acquainted with the place where
Isaiah and the prophets who were with him were, and he had seen
it, for he himself lived near Bethlehem; and he was an adherent of
Manasseh. And he prophesied lies in Jerusalem; and many of the
people in Jerusalem attached themselves to him, though he was a
2 Samaritan. (For when Shalmaneser,[2] king of Assyria, attacked
and captured Samaria and took away the nine and a half[3] tribes as
captives and carried them off to the mountains[4] of the Medes and
3 the rivers of Gozan,[5] this *Balchira*, while still a youth, got away and
came to Jerusalem in the days of Hezekiah, king of Judah; but he
did not follow the way of life of his Samaritan father, for he was
4 afraid of Hezekiah. And in Hezekiah's time he was found making
5 seditious statements[6] in Jerusalem. And Hezekiah's servants
accused him, and he made his escape to the neighbourhood of
6 Bethlehem. And they persuaded . . .[7]) And Balchira accused Isaiah
and the prophets who were with him, saying, Isaiah and those who
are with him are prophesying against Jerusalem and against the

[11] Eth. 'Leba Nasr'; Gk. 'Alnasar'.
[12] So L¹: Eth. 'Joel' or 'Ijoel'; Gk. 'Islal' (corrupt for 'Israel'?).
[13] So L¹: Eth. 'Ibchira'; Gk. 'Becheira'.
[14] So Gk. and L¹: Eth. 'Aguaron'. Gomorrah is a contemptuous reference to
Samaria (cp. Isa. i. 10; Jer. xxiii. 13–14).
[15] So L¹: Gk. 'they killed'; Eth. om.

[1] So Gk. L¹: Eth. 'And to Belchira'.
[2] Eth. 'Alagar Zagar'; Gk. 'Algasar'; L¹ 'Salmanassar'.
[3] So Gk. and L¹: Eth. om. 'and a half'.
[4] So Gk.: L¹ 'mountain'; Eth. 'boundaries'.
[5] So Gk. L¹: Eth. 'Tazon'.
[6] Lit. 'speaking words of lawlessness'.
[7] There appears to be a gap in the text at this point. Gk. reads 'And they
persuaded' and then carries straight on: similarly Eth. and Sah. with 'And he
persuaded'; L¹ om. 'And (t)he(y) persuaded' altogether.

cities of Judah, *saying* that they will be laid in ruins, and against the sons of Judah and Benjamin[8] that they will go into captivity, and against you, *my* lord king, that you will go *too*, *loaded* with hooks and

7 iron chains. But they prophesy falsely against Israel and Judah.

8 And Isaiah himself has said, I see more than the prophet Moses.

9 For Moses said, No man can see God and live; but Isaiah has said,

10 I have seen God, and behold I am *still* alive! You must know, o king,[9] that he is a liar.[10] Furthermore, he has called Jerusalem Sodom and addressed the princes of Judah and Jerusalem[11] as people of Gomorrah. And Balchira[12] brought many charges

11 against Isaiah and the prophets before Manasseh. Now Beliar had taken up his abode in the heart of Manasseh, and in the hearts of the princes of Judah and Benjamin, and the king's eunuchs and

12 counsellors. And what Balchira said pleased Manasseh[13] greatly, and he sent and had Isaiah arrested.

13 For Beliar was especially furious with Isaiah because of *his* vision, and because of his exposure of Sammael, and because it was through him that the going forth of the Beloved from the seventh heaven had been made known, and his transformation, and his descent *to earth*, and the likeness into which he would be transformed (*that is* the likeness of a man), and the persecution to which he would be subjected, and the torments the sons of Israel would inflict on him, and the calling and instruction[14] of his twelve disciples, and that before the sabbath he would be crucified upon

14 the tree,[15] and that he would be crucified with wicked men, and that he would be buried in the tomb, and the twelve who had been with him would have their faith in him shaken, and the guards who

15 would guard the tomb, and the descent of the angel[16] of the

---

[8] So L¹: Eth. om 'against the sons of Judah and'; Gk. om. 'that they will be laid . . . sons of Judah'.

[9] Lit. 'O king, know'.

[10] So Gk. L¹: Eth. 'that they are prophets of lies'.

[11] So Eth. L¹: Gk. Sah. 'Israel'.

[12] A Gk. Sah. L¹ 'he': BC 'they'.

[13] Lit. 'him'.

[14] So Eth. (lit. 'and the presence (or 'advent') and teaching'): Gk. 'and the teaching' only.

[15] Gk. om. this clause.

[16] So A Gk.: BC 'angels'.

Christian church which is in the heavens (whom he will summon
16 in the last days), and *that* ⟨Gabriel⟩,[17] the angel of the Holy Spirit,
and Michael, the prince of the holy angels, would on the third day
17 open the tomb, and the Beloved himself, sitting upon their
shoulders,[18] would come forth and send out his twelve disciples.
18 And they will teach all nations and every language *about* the
resurrection of the Beloved; and those who believe in his cross and
in his ascension to the seventh heaven (where he came from) will
19 be saved. And many who believe in him will speak by the Holy
20 Spirit. And many wonders and miracles will be performed in those
21 days. And afterwards, before he comes again,[19] his disciples will
forsake the teaching of the twelve apostles and their faith[20] and
22 their love and their purity. And there will be much strife before he
23 comes.[21] In those days many there will be who love office, even
24 though they are devoid of wisdom. And there will be many lawless
elders and shepherds who oppress their flocks; and they will ravage
25 *them*, because they have not holy shepherds.[22] And many will
exchange the honour of the garments of the saints for the garments
of money-lovers; and there will be much respect of persons in those
26 days, and many friends of this world's pomp. And there will be
much backbiting and empty ambition before the Lord comes,[19]
27 and the Holy Spirit will turn away from many; and there will be
only a few in those days, whether prophets or any others[23] whose
28 words can be trusted[24] – just one here and one there in different
places, because of the spirit of error and fornication and empty

[17] There is a lacuna in the Gk. at this point: the suggestion that it was filled by 'Gabriel' is due to Grenfell and Hunt. 'The angel of the Holy Spirit' appears several times in the Ascension (e.g. iv. 21, vii. 23): cp. especially xi. 4.

[18] So BC Gk.: A 'upon the shoulders of the seraphim'.

[19] Lit. 'when he (the Lord) draws near'.

[20] A Gk. 'the Faith'.

[21] So Gk.: Eth. 'much strife at his coming and when he draws near'.

[22] Eth. is hopelessly corrupt after 'and they will ravage'. Gk. has a lacuna and resumes with what appears to be the end of a passive participle ('. . . ed because they have not pure shepherds'). Our translation follows Charles in combining elements from both Eth. and Gk. and assumes that 'pure' in Gk. (ἀγνούς) is a corruption of an original (ἀγίους) preserved in Eth.

[23] So Eth.: Gk. 'and there will not be in those days many prophets'.

[24] Lit. 'whose words are strong'.

ambition and love of money[25] in those who will be called the
29 servants of the Beloved[26] and have received him.[26] Shepherds and
30 elders will hate one another. For in the last days there will be great
jealousies, because each one will proclaim what he himself thinks is
31 right. And they will ignore the prophecies of the prophets that were
before me, and these my visions[27] also they will repudiate in order
to give free expression to their own lusts.

IV. And now, Hezekiah, and son Josab, at the **consummation** of the
2 world it will happen like this.[1] At the consummation[2] Beliar, the
great prince, will come down, the king of this world, who has had
dominion over it since it first came into being: he will come down
from his abode in the vault of heaven[3] in the form of a man, *as* a
3 lawless king *and* a matricide. And this king[4] will persecute the plant
which the twelve apostles of the Beloved have planted; and one of
4 the twelve will be delivered into his hand. Beliar[5] will come in the
form of that king,[6] and all the powers of this world will come with
5 him, and they will do whatever it is he wants. At his command the
sun will rise during the night, and he will make the moon appear at
6 mid-day. And he will have his own way in the world over everything: he will act and speak like[7] the Beloved and will say, It is I
7 who am the Lord, and before me there has been no other. And all
8 the people in the world will believe in him. And they will sacrifice
to him and serve him, saying, This is the Lord, and beside him
9 there is no other. And he will turn away the greater part of those

[25] Gk. has a lacuna from here to the end of verse 30.
[26] Lit. 'that one'.
[27] B 'the visions'.

[1] Lit. 'these are the days of the **consummation** of the world'. For 'consummation'
Eth. has an unusual form, which might be rendered 'calling', but in any case it can
hardly be right. Gk. has been imperfectly preserved, though there is little doubt that
the word here was 'filling' or 'filling up'.
[2] Lit. 'After it is consummated'.
[3] Lit. 'from his firmament'.
[4] The translation here offers a slightly abbreviated version of both Eth. and Gk.
texts, neither of which in its present form gives an entirely satisfactory sense.
[5] C Gk. 'this prince': AB 'this prince Beliar'.
[6] So BC Gk.: A '*even* this king will come'.
[7] So AC: B 'he will make himself like'.

10 who have been united to receive the Beloved after him. And the effect of his miracles will be *felt* in every city and in every place.
11,12 And he will set up an image of himself in every city. And he will
13 rule for three years and seven[8] months and twenty-seven days. And of the faithful and of the saints who saw him in whom they hoped (him who was crucified, *that is* Jesus, the Lord Christ) – after that I, Isaiah, had seen him who was crucified and ascended[9] – and of those too who have believed in him *without seeing him*, few will be left as his servants in those days. They will flee from one desert place to another as they await his coming.

14 And after ⟨one thousand⟩ three hundred and thirty-two[10] days the Lord with his angels and with the hosts of the holy ones[11] will come from the seventh heaven with the glory of the seventh heaven, and
15 he will take Beliar and his hosts away to Gehenna. And he will give rest to the godly that he finds still in the flesh in this world [while the sun will be ashamed[12]] and to all who through faith in him have
16 cursed Beliar and his kings. But the saints will come with the Lord, with their garments that are *now* stored up on high in the seventh heaven: with the Lord will come those whose spirits are reclothed, *and* they will come down and will be in the world; and he will strengthen those found in the flesh together with the saints, in the garments of the saints, and the Lord will minister to those who
17 have kept watch in this world. And after that, they will change into their garments *from* on high, and their flesh will be left behind in
18 this world. Then will the voice of the Beloved rebuke the heaven and the earth[13] in anger, and the mountains and the hills, and the cities and the desert, and the trees, and the angel of the sun[14] and *the angel* of the moon,[15] and everything Beliar has used to publicize

---

[8] So AC: B 'three'.

[9] Charles thought this parenthesis 'an editorial addition made to adapt the Testament of Hezekiah to its present context'.

[10] A reads 'three hundred and thirty and two' (without 'one thousand'); BC 'thirty times one hundred and thirty-two'.

[11] Or 'saints'.   [12] Cp. Isa. xxiv. 23.

[13] So A: B 'the heaven and that which is of the earth'; C 'that which is in the heaven and that which is of the earth'. Charles, by a slight emendation, 'the things of heaven and the things of earth'.

[14] B om. 'and the angel of the sun'.

[15] So BC: A 'and the moon'.

himself and his activities in this world. Then will come the resurrection and the judgement; and the Beloved will send fire among them,[16] and it will burn up all the ungodly, and they will be as though they had never been.

19 And the rest of the details[17] of the vision is written in the vision of
20 Babylon. And the rest of the vision of the Lord, behold, it is written in the parables I have written down in the book which contains my
21 public prophecies. And the descent of the Beloved into Sheol, behold, it is written in the place[18] where the Lord says, Behold, my son will understand.[19] And all these things are written in the Psalms,[20] in the parables of David, the son of Jesse, and in the Proverbs of Solomon his son, and in the words of Korah and of Ethan the Israelite, and in the words of Asaph, and also in the other psalms which the angel of the Spirit has inspired (*that is* in
22 those[21] which have no name attached to them), and in the words of my father Amos, and of the prophet Hosea, and of Micah, and of Joel, and of Nahum, and of Jonah, and of Obadiah, and of Habakkuk, and of Haggai, and of Zephaniah, and of Zechariah,[22] and of Malachi, and in the words of Joseph the just, and in the words of Daniel.

V. Then Beliar's anger was roused against Isaiah because of these visions, and he took up his abode in Manasseh's heart; and he
2 sawed Isaiah in two with a **wood**-saw.[1] And while Isaiah was being sawn, his enemy Balchira stood by, and all the false prophets stood
3 by, laughing and rejoicing at what was happening to Isaiah. And Balchira, inspired by Mechembechus,[2] came near to Isaiah,[3]

---

[16] Lit. 'will cause a fire to go up from him'.
[17] Lit. 'words'.   [18] So AC: B 'the psalms'.
[19] i.e. Isa. lii. 13 (LXX).
[20] Charles thought 'the Psalms' a gloss, added to explain 'the parables of David'.
[21] So BC: A 'and in those'.
[22] So AC: B 'and of Zechariah, and of Zephaniah'.

[1] The 'wooden saw' of the MSS and the tradition is due, according to Charles, to a misunderstanding of an original Hebrew phrase, 'a saw of wood', which was intended to mean 'a saw for sawing wood', presumably made of metal – indeed, in one passage in Gk.[L] (iii. 14–15) it is specifically said to be 'an iron saw'.
[2] Lit. 'in M.': Dillmann emended 'and M.' to accord with the verbs in the rest of the verse which are plural.   [3] Lit. 'stood up before Isaiah'.

4 laughing and making fun[4] *of him*. And Balchira[5] said to Isaiah, Say,
I have been wrong[6] in everything I have said: what Manasseh does
5 is good and right. And what Balchira and those with him do is also
6 good. And this he said to him when they started sawing him in two.
7 But Isaiah was in a vision of the Lord: his eyes were open but he did
8 ⟨not⟩ see them. And Balchira said to Isaiah, Say what I tell you to,
and I will make them change their minds; and I will make Manasseh
and the princes of Judah and the people and all Jerusalem fall
9 down before you. And Isaiah answered and said, All I can say is,
May you be accursed and damned, you and all your powers and all
10 your house.[7] For you can take nothing *from me* but only the skin off
11 my body. Then they took Isaiah, the son of Amoz, and sawed him
12 in two with a **wood**-saw. And Manasseh and Balchira and the false
13 prophets and the princes and the people all stood looking on. But
before he was sawn in two he had said to the prophets who were
with him, Make your escape into the region of Tyre and Sidon,
14 because God has mixed this cup for me alone. And while he was
being sawn in two Isaiah neither cried out nor wept; but he went on
15 speaking by the Holy Spirit until he was sawn right through. This
Beliar did to Isaiah using Balchira and Manasseh as his agents; for
Sammael had been furious with Isaiah since the days of Hezekiah,
king of Judah, because of the vision he had seen about the Beloved,
16 and because of *the vision about* the destruction of Sammael he had
seen through the Lord, when Hezekiah his[8] father was still king.
And he[9] acted in accordance with the will of Satan.

The Vision which Isaiah, the son of Amoz, saw.

VI.   In the twentieth year of the reign of Hezekiah, king of Judah,
Isaiah the son of Amoz, and Josab, Isaiah's son, came from Gilgal[1]
2 to Hezekiah in Jerusalem. And Isaiah sat down on the king's
couch; and they brought him a seat, but he would not sit on it.[2]
3 And Isaiah began to talk to king Hezekiah about what was certain

---

[4] So C: AB 'laughing, making fun'. Charles omitted 'laughing' as a doublet.
[5] So B: AC 'Beliar'.   [6] Lit. 'I have lied'.
[7] So B: A and C have several small variations.
[8] i.e. Manasseh's.   [9] i.e. Manasseh.

[1] So C, supported by G^L: AB 'from Galilee'; L^2 Slav. om.
[2] and they brought . . . on it: L^2 Slav. om.

and sure, and all the princes of Israel and the eunuchs and the king's counsellors were seated *round him;*[3] and there were forty[4] prophets and sons of the prophets who had come from the villages and the mountains and the plains, when they heard that Isaiah

4 had come from Gilgal[5] to Hezekiah. And they had come to greet
5 him, and to hear what he said. And *they hoped* he would lay his hands on them, and that they might prophesy and he would listen to their prophecy;[6] and all of them were *assembled* before Isaiah.
6 And while Isaiah was talking about what was sure and certain[7] to Hezekiah,[8] they all heard a door opened and the voice of the Holy
7 Spirit.[9] And the king gathered together all the prophets and all the people that could be found there, and they came; and Micah and the aged Hananiah and Joel and Josab[10] were sitting on his right.[11]
8 And when they all heard the voice of the Holy Spirit, all of them worshipped *and fell* on their knees and glorified the God of truth, the Most High – he who is in the world above, the Holy One, who
9 sits on high, and who takes his rest among the saints.[12] And they gave praise to him who had thus given to a man a door into an
10 unknown world.[13] And while he was speaking in the Holy Spirit in the hearing of all, he *suddenly* became silent, and his spirit was caught up into heaven,[14] and he no longer saw the men who were
11 standing in front of him. But his eyes were open although his lips
12 were silent, and the spirit of his body was taken up from him.[15] And

---

[3] L²Slav. 'were standing before him'.

[4] L²Slav. om.

[5] So BC L² Slav.: A 'Galilee'.

[6] So AC: B 'and that he might prophesy and that they might listen to his prophecy'. L² and Slav. have the whole passage differently ordered and slightly abbreviated, though it is clear that they support AC in that it was the prophets who were to prophesy and not Isaiah (as in B).

[7] Lit. 'was speaking words of truth and of faith' (and similarly in verse 3).

[8] So AC: B om. 'to Hezekiah'; L² Slav. om. 'and of faith to H.'

[8–9] L² Slav. 'the Holy Spirit came upon him, and all saw and heard the words of the Holy Spirit'.   [10] L² Slav. om. 'and Josab'.

[11] L² Slav. add 'and on his left'.

[12] Or 'holy ones'. L² Slav. abbreviate '. . . knees and sang to the Most High God, who takes . . . saints'.

[13] Lit. 'who thus has given a door in an unknown world, has given *it* to a man': L² Slav. differ here.   [14] and . . . heaven: L² Slav. om.

[15] and . . . from him: L² Slav. om.

13 only his breath remained in him,[16] for he was in a vision. And the angel that was sent to explain things to him in the vision[17] was not of this world,[18] nor was he one of the angels of glory of this world,
14 but had come from the seventh heaven. And, apart from the circle of the prophets, the people who were there did ⟨not⟩[19] believe that
15 the holy Isaiah had been caught up *into heaven.* For the vision that the holy Isaiah saw was not *a vision* of this world, but of the world
16 that is hidden from man.[20] After Isaiah had seen this vision he gave an account *of it* to Hezekiah and to his son Josab [21]and to the other
17 prophets who had come. But the magistrates and eunuchs and the people did not hear *it,* but only Samnas the scribe, and Joachim, and Asaph[22] the secretary of state; for they were men who did what is right and were approved of by the Spirit.[23] And the people did not hear *it either,* for Micah and his son Josab had sent them away when the wisdom of this world had been taken from him, and he was left looking like a corpse.

VII. And Isaiah related the vision he had seen to Hezekiah, and to his son Josab, and to Micah, and to the other prophets:
2   When I was prophesying and you were listening to me, I saw a glorious angel, whose glory was not like that of the angels I had been in the habit of seeing; for he had a glory and a dignity[1] *of a kind*
3 so great that I cannot describe the splendour of this angel.[2] And I was looking *at him* when he took me by the hand;[3] and I said to him,

---

[16] L[2] 'sed inspiratio sancti spiritus erat cum illo', and similarly Slav. without 'sancti'. Both L[2] and Slav. om the end of this verse and verse 13.

[17] Lit. 'sent to make him see'.   [18] Lit. 'firmament'.

[19] Supplied from L[2] Slav.: Eth. has no negative.

[20] Lit. 'from his (i.e. man's) flesh'. So AC: B 'whilst he (i.e. man) is in the flesh'; L[2] Slav. 'from all flesh'.

[21] and to the other . . . vii. 1 his son Josab: L[2] Slav. om.

[22] We should probably emend 'Joachim, son of Asaph' (see 2 Kings xviii. 18, 37, and par.).

[23] Lit. 'and had upon them the soothing odour of the Spirit'.

[1] Lit. 'order': L[2] Slav. 'light'; L[1] 'holy' (i.e. 'a great and holy glory').

[2] L[2] Slav. 'which (i.e. the light) I cannot make known'; L[1] 'which glory I cannot describe'.

[3] L[1] 'And he approached and took me by the hand'; L[2] Slav. 'And he took me by the hand and raised me on high'.

Who are you? What is your name? And where are going to take me?
4 (For the power to talk to him had been given to me.) And he said to me, When I have taken you up and shown you the vision I have been sent to show you, then you will understand who I am, but my name you shall not know,[4] because you are to return again to your
5 flesh. But in the place where I am to take you,[5] you will see *a vision*,
6 for I have been sent for this very purpose.[6] And I was overjoyed
7 because he spoke gently to me. And he said to me, Are you then overjoyed because I have spoken gently to you? And he said, One who is greater than I am will you see, and he will speak to you
8 gently and graciously. And the Father of the One who is greater *than I am* will you also see,[7] for I have been sent from the seventh
9 heaven to explain all this to you. And we went up, he and I, into the vault of heaven, and there I saw Sammael and his hosts; and there was much strife there, for the angels[8] of Satan were all jealous of
10 one another. And as it is on high, so also is it on earth: what happens in the vault of heaven happens similarly here on earth.
11 And I said to the angel, ⟨What is this strife and⟩[9] why this jealousy?
12 And he said to me, It has been like this since the world was made till now;[10] and this strife *will continue* until the One you are to see comes and destroys him.

13 After this he took me up ⟨into the *regions*⟩[11] above the vault,
14 which is the first[11] heaven. And there I saw in the middle of it a
15 throne;[12] and on its right and on its left were angels. And the angels on the left[13] were not like those on the right; but those on the right had a greater glory and they all sang praises together.[14] The throne

---

[4] So Eth. L² Slav.: L¹ 'I will not tell you'.

[5] L¹L² Slav. 'But when I have taken you up'.

[6] L² Slav. om. 'for I . . . purpose'.

[7] There is not a little variation in detail between the authorities here.

[8] So L¹ (and by implication L² Slav., which have a substantially different text): Eth. 'words' (reading λόγοι for ἄγγελοι).

[9] Supplied from L¹: L² Slav. 'What is this strife and jealousy and conflict?'

[10] It has been . . . now: L² Slav. 'this is the Devil's strife'.

[11] Supplied from L² Slav.

[12] L² Slav. add 'and on it there sat an angel in great glory'.

[13] So L¹: Eth. om. 'And the angels on the left'; L² Slav. om. 'And the angels . . . left . . . right'.

[14] Lit. 'with one voice'.

was in the middle, and they sang praises.[15] And those on the left sang praises after them, but their voices were not like the voices of those on the right and their praises were not like the others' praises.
16 And I asked the angel who was accompanying me and said to him,
17 To whom is this praise addressed? And he said to me, **To the glory of him who is in**[16] the seventh heaven, to him who takes his rest in the holy world,[17] and to the Beloved, from whom I have been sent to you.[18]

18   And again he took me up – into the second heaven (now the height of this heaven is the same as *the distance* from the heaven to
19 the earth[19]). And ⟨there, as⟩[20] in the first heaven, *were* angels on the right and on the left, and a throne in the middle, and the praises of the angels in the second heaven; and the one who was seated on the throne in the second heaven had greater glory than all *the rest*.[21]
20 And great was the glory in the second heaven, and their praises
21 were not like the praises of those in the first heaven.[22] And I fell on my face to worship him; but the angel who was accompanying me[23] would not permit it and said to me, You must not worship any throne or angel that is in the six heavens[24] (that is why[25] I have been sent to accompany you[26]), but *you shall worship* only *him* whom
22 I shall tell you to in the seventh heaven.[27] For your throne, your garments, and your crown, which you will see *later*, are set above
23 all these heavens and their angels. And I rejoiced greatly because

[15] The throne . . . praises: L[2] Slav. om.; L[1] om. 'and they sang praises'.
[16] Eth. 'In the glory of'. The emendation is based on L[1]L[2] Slav., but more particularly on L[1].
[17] So A: the other authorities vary. Charles thought them all corrupt and suggested as a possible original 'to him who inhabits eternity'.
[18] Eth. adds 'thither is it sent'.
[19] So BC L[1]: L[2] Slav. 'from the first heaven to the earth'; A 'from the earth to the heaven'; then Eth. L[1] add 'and to the vault'.
[20] Supplied on the basis of L[1]L[2] Slav. 'And I saw there as' (L[1] + 'I had seen').
[21] and a throne . . . all *the rest*: L[2] Slav. om.; L[1] breaks off at 'middle'.
[22] L[2] 'And the glory of these angels and their song were more excellent than those of the first angels'; and similarly Slav.
[23] L[2] Slav. 'instructing me'.
[24] So Eth.: L[2] 'in that heaven'; Slav. 'from heaven'.
[25] So L[2] Slav.: Eth. 'whence'.
[26] L[2] Slav. 'to instruct you'.
[27] L[2] Slav. om. 'in the seventh heaven'.

those who love the Most High and his Beloved will in the end be taken up there by the angel of the Holy Spirit.

24 And he took me up into the third heaven; and, as before, I saw *angels* on the right and on the left, and there also a throne was set in the middle,[28] but the memory of this world had no place there.[29]

25 And I said to the angel who was with me (for my face was becoming brighter and brighter[30] as I went up from heaven to heaven), Has nothing, then, of that vain world any place here?[31]

26 And he answered and said to me, Nothing *of that world* has any place[32] because of its frailty, yet nothing is hidden here of what is

27 done there.[33] And I asked[34] how it is known, and he answered, saying, When I have brought you up to the seventh heaven, from which I was sent, *that is* to *the heaven* which is above these *heavens*, you will understand that nothing is hidden from the thrones and from those who live in the heavens and from the angels. And great were the praises which they sang and the splendour of the one who was seated on the throne; and the glory of the angels on the right and on the left was greater than that of the heavens beneath them.[35]

28 And again he took me up—into the fourth heaven; and the height from the third to the fourth heaven was greater than that from the

29 earth to the vault of heaven. And there I saw again angels on the right and *angels* on the left, and one seated on a throne in the

30 middle;[36] and there too they sang praises. And the praises and the splendour of the angels on the right were greater than those of *the*

31 *angels* on the left. So also the splendour of the one who was seated on the throne was greater than that of the angels on the right, yet their glory was greater than *the glory* of those who were below.

[28] So B: AC add 'and one who sat'; L²Slav. invert '. . . I saw a little throne and angels on the right and on the left'.
[29] Lit. 'of this world was not named'.
[30] Lit. 'for the glory of my face was being transformed'.
[31] Lit. 'Is nothing . . . world named here?'
[32] Lit. 'is named'.
[33] So Slav.: Eth. L² 'and nothing is hidden there of what is done'.
[34] Lit. 'And I desired to understand'.
[35] Both L² and Slav. have much shorter texts in this verse.
[36] L² Slav. 'And there I saw a throne and angels on the right and on the left'. L² om. from here to the end of verse 30.

32,33   And he took me up into the fifth heaven. And again I saw *angels*
on the right and on the left, and one seated on a throne, more
34 glorious than those of the fourth heaven. But the glory of *the angels*
35 on the right was greater than *the glory* of those on the left.[37] And the
splendour of the one who was seated on the throne was greater
36 than that of the angels on the right. And their praises were more
37 glorious than those of the fourth heaven. And I praised him who
cannot be named, and the only-begotten Son who dwells in the
heavens, whose name has not been revealed to any man,[38] who has
given such great glory to the angels and even greater glory still to
the one who is seated on the throne.[39]

VIII.   And he took me up into the air of the sixth heaven and I
beheld a glory I had not seen in the five heavens while I was being
2,3 taken up, and angels[1] resplendent in great glory.[2] And the praises
4   there were sublime[3] and wonderful.[4] And I said to the angel who
5   was accompanying me, What is it that I see, my lord? And he said
6   to me, I am not your lord but your companion.[5] And again I asked
him and said to him, Why are there no companions for the angels
7   *on the right*?[6] And he said, From the sixth heaven and above it there
are no more *angels* on the left, nor is there a throne set in the middle,
but ⟨they have their direction⟩[7] from the power of the seventh
heaven, where he dwells that cannot be named, and the Elect One,
whose name has not been revealed, and whose name none of the
8   heavens can learn.[8] For it is to his voice alone that all the heavens

[37] Eth. adds 'from the third to the fourth *heaven*'.

[38] Lit. 'flesh'.

[39] L[2] Slav. diverge widely from Eth. in their description of the fifth heaven: verses
32–34 are much abbreviated, 35 is lacking, and 37 is altogether different.

[1] Charles emended '. . . five heavens. For I saw angels . . .' on the basis of L[2] Slav.

[2] Both L[2] and Slav. have an additional clause here about the angelic powers.

[3] Lit. 'holy'.

[4] So L[2] Slav.: Eth. reads *manbar* ('throne'), presumably a corruption of *manker*.

[5] So Eth.: probably a rendering of an original σύνδουλος ('fellow-servant'), from
which, through a corruption, L[2] Slav. got 'counsellor' (σύμβουλος).

[6] L[2] Slav. om. this verse.

[7] Supplied on the basis of L[2] 'they have *their* arrangement' and Slav. 'they are
administered'.

[8] L[2] 'where is the precious Son of God' and Slav. similarly.

and the thrones respond; and I have been empowered and sent to
9   bring you up here so that you may behold this glory, and so that
you may see the Lord of all these heavens and of these thrones,
10 transforming himself until he becomes like you in form and in
11 appearance.[9] And I tell you, Isaiah, no man who is to return into a
body of that world has *ever* come up *here* and seen what you see,
12 what you have seen, and what you will see.[10] For you have been
permitted to come up here *because you are to share* in the lot of the
13 Lord.[11] And I glorified and praised my Lord, because through
14 *sharing in* his lot I was to go up there. And he said to me, Hear then
this again from your companion.[12] When by the angel of the Spirit
you have been taken up there from that alien body *of yours*,[13] then
will you receive the garment[14] that you will see, and you will *also*
15 see other garments numbered and stored up *there*. And then will
16 you become equal to the angels of the seventh[15] heaven. And he
took me up into the sixth heaven, and there were no *angels* on the
left nor *was there* a throne in the middle, but all *the angels* looked the
17 same and their praises were equal. And I was allowed to sing
praises with them too, and also the angel who was accompanying
18 me,[16] and our praises were like theirs. And they glorified the Father
of all,[17] and his Beloved,[18] the Christ, and the Holy Spirit, all
19 together.[19] And *the voices of these angels* were not like the voices of the
20 angels in the five heavens,[20] nor like their words; but the voices
21 were different there, and there was much light there. And then,

[9] L[2] Slav. om. verse 10. The reference is to the successive transformations
described in detail in x. 17ff.

[10] The translation of this verse follows Charles's lead in a slight re-arrangement
of the details.

[11] Eth. adds first 'in the lot of the cross' and then 'and thence comes the power of
the sixth heaven and of the air'.

[12] Hear . . . companion: L[2] Slav. om.

[13] So AC: B 'when God the Spirit has taken you up in an alien body'; L[2] Slav.
follow a text which is different.

[14] L[2] 'your garment'; Slav. 'a garment'. Both om. the rest of the verse.

[15] L[2] 'sixth'.

[16] Lit. 'and with that angel'.

[17] So L[2] Slav.: Eth. 'And they all named the first (C om.) Father'.

[18] So A: BC 'the Beloved'; L[2] Slav. 'his beloved Son' and om. 'the Christ'.

[19] Lit. 'all with one voice'.

[20] L[2] Slav. 'the fifth heaven' and om. 'nor like their words'.

when I was in the sixth heaven, I thought the light I had seen in the
22 five heavens[21] was darkness. And I rejoiced and gave praise to him
who had bestowed such lights on those who await his promise.[22]
23 And I besought the angel who was accompanying me[23] that I
24 might not *have to* return from there to the world of the flesh. (For
truth to tell, Hezekiah and son Josab and Micah,[24] there is great
25 darkness here.) And the angel who was accompanying me[23]
realized what I was thinking and[25] said, If you rejoice in this light,
how much more will you rejoice in the seventh heaven when you
26 see the lights where are the Lord and his Beloved,[26] and also the
garments and the thrones and the crowns stored up for the righteous,
for those, *that is*, who believe in that Lord who will descend in your
human form (for great and marvellous is the light that is there).[27]
27 But as for your not returning to your body – the time has not come
28 for your coming here. And when I heard *this* I was much troubled;
but he said, Do not be troubled.[28]

IX. And he took me up into the air of the seventh heaven, and
again[1] I heard a voice: it said, How far may anyone go up who lives
2 among aliens?[2] And I was afraid and trembled. And[3] as I trembled,
behold there came a second voice which said, The holy Isaiah is
3 permitted to come up here, for here is his garment.[4] And I asked
the angel who was with me and said, Who was it who forbade me to
4 go up, and who was it **who permitted**[5] me? And he said to me, He

----

[21] L² Slav. 'the fifth heaven'.
[22] L² Slav. 'mercy'.   [23] L² Slav. 'instructing me'.
[24] Hezekiah . . . Micah: L² Slav. om.
[25] realized . . . and: L² Slav. om.
[26] So Eth.: L² Slav. 'where sits the heavenly Father and his only-begotten Son';
Eth. then adds 'whence I have been sent, who is to be called Son in this world. Not
yet has he been manifested, he who shall be in the corruptible world'.
[27] for those . . . there: L² Slav. om.
[28] but . . . troubled: L² Slav. om.

[1] L² Slav. om. 'again'.
[2] So Eth.: L² Slav. 'who wills to live in the flesh'.
[3] Eth. adds 'he said to me'.
[4] L² Slav. vary in the details of this verse.
[5] Eth. 'turned to': L² Slav. 'commanded'. The emendation is derived from
ὁ ἐπιτρέπων μοι in Gk.[L] ii. 24.

who forbade you is he **who is over**[6] the praises of the sixth heaven.
5 And he **who permitted**[5] you is your Lord,[7] the Lord of the world, the
Lord Christ, who will in the world be called Jesus;[8] but his name
you cannot hear until you have left your body.

6   And he took me up into the seventh heaven, and I saw there a
7 marvellous light and angels innumerable. [9]And I saw there all the
8 righteous from the time of Adam. And I saw there the holy Abel
9 and all the righteous. And I saw there Enoch and all who were with
him,[10] stripped of the garments of the flesh; and I saw them in their
garments of the world above, and they were like angels,[11] standing
10 there in great glory. But they were not seated on their thrones, and
11 their crowns of glory were not upon them. And I asked the angel
who was with me,[12] Why have they received the garments, but not
12 the thrones and crowns? And he said to me, They *will* not receive
either *their* crowns or *their* thrones of glory (although they see and
know *now* which of them will have the thrones and which the
crowns) until the Beloved descends in the form in which you will
13 see him descend. He will indeed descend into the world in the last
days – the Lord who will be called Christ after he has descended
and become like you in form;[13] and they will think he is flesh and a
14 man.[14] And the prince[15] of that world will stretch out **his hand
against the Son**,[16] and they will hang him on a tree and will kill
15 him,[17] not knowing who he is. And his descent, as you will see, will

---

[6] Eth. 'on whom is': L[2] Slav. read the verse '. . . is the angel who is over the angels
(Slav. om. 'the angels') of the sixth heaven who sing praises'.

[7] So AB: C 'is our Lord'; L[2] Slav. 'is the Son of God'.

[8] L[2] Slav. om. 'the Lord of the world . . . Jesus'.

[9–10] L[2] Slav. 'And I saw certain of the righteous'.

[11] L[2] Slav. om. 'like angels'.

[12] who was with me: L[2] Slav. 'and I said'.

[13] like you in form: B 'as you will see'.

[14] Eth. L[2] and Slav. differ widely in verses 12 and 13, and all three are difficult.
Charles suspected a displacement in Eth. and would transfer the clause within
brackets in verse 12 to follow 'Christ' in verse 13 ('. . . called Christ, although they
see . . . crowns after he has descended . . .').   [15] So L[2] Slav.: Eth. 'god'.

[16] Eth. 'by the hand of his Son'; L[2] 'his hand against the Son of God (cp. Slav. '. . .
on account of his Son will stretch out his hands against him').

[17] (**the Son**) and they . . . kill him: Eth. 'and they will lay their hands upon him and
will hang him on a tree'; L[2] 'and he will kill him and will hang him on a tree and will
kill *him*'; Slav. 'and they will hang him on a tree and he will kill him'.

be hidden even from the heavens, so that it will not be known who
16 he is. And when he has plundered the angel of death, he will ascend
on the third day (and he will have been in the world for five
17 hundred and forty-five days).[18] Then will many of the righteous
ascend with him, whose souls do not receive their garments until
18 the Lord Christ ascends and they ascend with him.[19] Then will
they receive their [garments and their][20] thrones and their crowns,
19 when he has ascended into the seventh heaven. And I asked him
20 what I had already asked him in the third[21] heaven. And he said to
21 me, Everything that happens in that world is known here. And
while I was still talking to him, one of the angels that stood nearby,
who was even more glorious than the angel who had brought me
22 up from earth, showed me a book[22] and opened it, and the book
had writing in it,[23] but not like *the writing in* the books of this world.
And he gave *it* to me, and I read it; and behold, the deeds of the
sons of Israel[24] were written in it, and also the deeds of others
23 whom you do ⟨not⟩ know,[25] my son Josab.[26] And I said, There is
indeed nothing that happens in this world that is hidden in the
24 seventh heaven.[27] And I saw there many garments stored up, and
25 many thrones and many crowns. And I said to the angel, Whose
26 are these garments, and thrones, and crowns? And he said to me,
These *are the* garments *which* many from the world will receive,[28]

---

[18] Charles was persuaded that this clause was not part of the original, though he thought that the Eth. translator found it in his Gk. text since the idea is Gnostic. Both L[2] and Slav., however, omit it, although they have a much fuller text of verses 15 and 16 containing a clear reference to the Descent into Hell.

[19] whose . . . with him: L[2] Slav. 'and he will send out his preachers into all the world and will ascend into the heavens'.

[20] L[2] Slav. om. 'garments and their'.

[21] L[2] Slav. 'first' (but see vii. 27).

[22] Eth. 'books' (and plurals similarly throughout this verse).

[23] Lit. 'the book was written'.

[24] the sons of Israel: L[2] Slav. 'Jerusalem'.

[25] Eth. 'whom you know'; Slav. 'whom I do not know'; L[2] 'concerning which I also was'.   [26] L[2] Slav. om. 'my son Josab'.

[27] L[2] Slav. have an additional question at this point about the identity of the 'more glorious' angel, who is named in the answer as Michael (cp. verses 29 and 42).

[28] So Eth.: L[2] 'lose'; Slav. 'be robbed of'. Both L[2] and Slav. require that 'the one' later in the verse be taken as a reference to the Antichrist.

who believe in the words of the One who is to be named,[29] as I told you; and they will observe these things[30] and will believe in them,[31] and they will believe in his cross – for them are **these garments** stored
27 up.[32] And I saw One standing, whose glory surpassed that of all the
28 others, and his glory was great and wonderful. And when I saw him,[33] all the righteous I had seen, and the angels also I had seen, approached him, and Adam and Abel and Seth and all the righteous came near him and worshipped him and praised him with one voice; and I too sang praises with them, and my praises were as
29 theirs. And then all the angels came near and[34] worshipped and
30 sang praises. And I[35] was transformed again[36] and became like an
31 angel. Then the angel who was accompanying me said, Worship
32 him; and I worshipped and sang praises. And the angel said to me,
33 This is the Lord of all the splendours you have seen. And while he[37] was still speaking I saw another glorious One like him, and the righteous came near him and worshipped and sang praises, and I[38] sang praises with them; but **my**[39] glory was not transformed so that
34 I looked like them.[40] Then the angels came near and worshipped
35 him. And I saw the Lord and a second angel, and they were
36 standing. But the second that I saw was on my Lord's left. And I asked, Who is this? And *the angel who was accompanying me* said to me, Worship him, for this is the angel of the Holy Spirit, who *is* upon
37 you, and who has spoken also in the other righteous.[41] And the eyes of my spirit were open, and I saw the Great Glory; but I could not

[29] L² Slav. om. 'who is to be named'.

[30] So AC: B 'observe his commandments'.

[31] So A: BC 'him'.

[32] AC 'but for them are stored up'; B 'which for them are stored up'. L² Slav. om. 'and they will observe . . . stored up'.

[33] And I saw One . . . I saw him: L² Slav. 'And being turned I saw the Lord in great glory, and I feared exceedingly. And'.

[34] L² Slav. 'And then Michael came near and worshipped and with him all the angels' (cp. verses 23 and 42).

[35] So L² Slav.: Eth. 'he'.

[36] So L² Slav.: Eth. om. 'again'.

[37] So Slav.: Eth. 'I' (L² om. 'while . . . speaking').

[38] So Eth.: L² Slav. 'he'.

[39] Eth. 'his', supported by L² Slav. 'and he transformed not himself'.

[40] Lit. 'transformed after the manner of their appearance'.

[41] L² Slav. '. . . Holy Spirit, who speaks in you and in all the righteous'.

then look upon *him*, nor could the angel who was with me, nor any
38 of the angels I had seen worshipping my Lord. Yet I saw the
39 righteous gazing intently upon the Glory.[42] And my Lord (and the
angel of the Spirit too) came near me and said, Privileged indeed
you are to have been allowed to see God, and privileged also,
40 because of you, is the angel who is with you.[43] And I saw how my
Lord worshipped, and the angel of the Holy[44] Spirit too, and both
41 together gave praise to God.[45] And then all the righteous came
42 near and worshipped, and the angels came near and worshipped;
and all the angels sang praises.[46]

X.   And I heard then the voices and the praises that I had heard in
2 each of the six heavens – that I had heard as I ascended. And all *the
voices and the praises* were addressed to that Glorious One,[1] whose
3 glory I could not look upon. And I heard and saw the praises *which
4 were being sung* to him. And the Lord and the angel of the Spirit were
5 hearing and seeing everything.[2] For all the praises which come up
6 from the six heavens are not only heard but seen. And I heard the
angel, who was accompanying me, *speaking to me*; and he said, This
is the Most High, who sits enthroned above the heavenly hosts,[3]
who dwells in the holy world and rests among his holy ones, who
will be called by the Holy Spirit through the lips of the righteous
7 the Father of the Lord.[4] And I heard the voice of the Most High,
the Father of my Lord, saying to my Lord the Christ, who will be
8 called Jesus,[5] Go and descend through all the heavens: descend to

[42] So L²: Eth. 'upon that One's glory'; Slav. 'upon his glory'.

[43] Lit. 'See how it is given to you to see God, and because of you power (B adds 'of
coming here') is given to the angel who is with you'.

[44] BC om. 'Holy'.

[45] [39]came near . . . to God: L² Slav. 'came near (Slav. + 'to them') and they
worshipped (L² + 'him') and sang praises both together'.

[46] There are a number of minor variations in verses 41 and 42. L² Slav. again
have a reference to Michael (cp. verses 23 and 29).

[1] And all . . . Glorious One: L² Slav. 'And all were glorifying him'.

[2] L² Slav. om. verses 3 and 4.

[3] Lit. 'the Most High of the high ones'.

[4] L² Slav. express the details of this verse rather differently: instead of 'will be
called' they have 'is praised', and they omit 'the Father of the Lord'.

[5] L² Slav. 'the voice of the Eternal saying to the Lord Son'.

the vault of heaven and to the world:[6] descend to the angel in Sheol;
9   but to Haguel you shall not go.[7] And you must transform yourself
10 so as to be like all those who are in the five heavens. And you must
    take care to transform yourself so as to be like the angels of the
11 vault of heaven *as well*, and the angels also who are in Sheol.[8] And
    so none of the angels of the world will know that you are Lord with
12 me of the seven heavens and of their angels. And they will not know
    that you are with me **until** with a **loud** voice I call *to* the heavens and
    their angels and their lights, right up to the sixth heaven, so that
    you may judge and destroy the princes and the angels and the gods
    of that world and the world *itself* over which they exercise
13 dominion.[9] For they have denied me and have said, We alone are,
14 and who is there apart from us? And afterwards you will ascend
    from the **angels** of death to your *appointed* place;[10] and you will have
    no need to transform yourself as you go up,[11] for you will ascend in
15 glory to sit on my right hand. Then the princes and powers of the
16 world[12] will worship you. And I heard the Great Glory[13] giving
    these commands to my Lord.
17   And so it was that when he had left the seventh heaven, I saw my
18 Lord in the sixth heaven.[14] And the angel who had accompanied
    me[15] from this world was with me, and he said to me, Understand
    this, Isaiah, and watch,[16] so that you may see[17] the transformation
19 and descent of the Lord. And I looked,[18] and when the angels saw

---

[6] descend to the vault of heaven and to the world: so A; BC 'descend to the vault
of the heaven of the world'; L² Slav. 'and you will be in the world'.

[7] but . . . go: L² Slav. om.   [8] who are in the five . . . Sheol: L² om.

[9] The Eth. MSS differ in this verse and an agreed text is highly uncertain. L²
Slav. have a much shorter and simpler text both in verse 11 and in verse 12.

[10] And afterwards . . . place: AC 'And afterwards . . . from the gods of death . . .
place'; B 'and when you have died and risen you will ascend to your *appointed* place';
Slav. 'and when you are raised from the earth'; L² om.

[11] Lit. 'and you shall not transform yourself in each heaven'.

[12] L² Slav. expand the details here.

[13] So BC: A 'him of the great glory'.

[14] L² Slav. 'And then the Lord went out from the seventh heaven and descended
into the sixth heaven'.

[15] L² Slav. 'who was instructing me', and then om. 'from this . . . and he'.

[16] Lit. 'see'.

[17] So AC: B 'so that you may know'; L² Slav. 'what is'.

[18] L² Slav. om. 'And I looked' (and so similarly at the beginning of verse 20).

him, those in the sixth heaven gave him glory and praised him (for he had not been transformed so as to look like the angels there);

20 and they praised him, and I also praised *him* with them. And I saw that when he descended into the fifth heaven and transformed himself in the fifth heaven to look like the angels there, they did not

21 praise him, for his form was like theirs. And then he descended into the fourth heaven and transformed himself to look like the angels

22 there; and when they saw him, they neither gave him glory nor did

23 they praise him, for his form was like their form. [19]And I saw again that when he descended into the third heaven he transformed himself to look like the angels in the third heaven. And those who

24 kept the gate of the *third* heaven demanded the password, and the Lord gave *it* to them, so that he might not be recognized; and when they saw him, they neither gave him glory nor did they praise him,

25 for his form was like their form. And again I saw[20] that when he descended into the second heaven, there again he gave the password, for those who kept the gate demanded *it* and the Lord gave *it*

26 *to them*. And I saw that when he was made like the form of the angels in the second heaven, they saw him and did not praise him,

27 for his form was like their form. And I saw him again, when he descended into the first heaven, and there too he gave the password to those who kept the gate; and he made himself like the form of the angels who were on the left of the throne there, and they neither gave him glory nor did they praise him, for his form was like their

28 form. But as for me, no one questioned me because of the angel who

29 was accompanying me. And again he descended into the vault of heaven where dwells the prince of this world,[21] and he gave the password to those on the left; and his form *was* like theirs, and they did not praise him there – instead, they were all jealous of one another and were fighting one another (such is the power of evil

30 there and of jealousy about things that do not matter[22]).And I saw

---

[19] L[2] Slav. summarize verses 23–28 ('And he came into the third heaven and into the second and into the first, transforming himself in each of them, so that they neither sang praises to him nor worshipped him, for he looked like them. And he showed the signs to the guardians of the gates *as he passed* through each of the heavens').   [20] So A: BC add 'him'.

[21] where ... world = Eth. Slav.: L[2] om.

[22] So AC: B om. 'about ... matter'; L[2] Slav. om. 'instead ... matter'.

that when he descended and made himself like the angels of the air,
31 he looked just like one of them. And he gave no password, for each
one of them was *busy* cheating and doing violence to his
neighbour.[23]

XI.   And after this I looked, and the angel who was talking with
me, who was accompanying me,[1] said to me, Understand *this*,
2 Isaiah, son of Amoz, for this is why I have been sent by God.[2] And I
saw clearly a woman of the family of the prophet David, whose
name was Mary, and she was a virgin; and she was betrothed to a
man whose name was Joseph, a carpenter (and he too was of the
stock and family[3] of the righteous David, of Bethlehem in Judah;
3 and he had received her as his wife by lot[4]). And when she was
betrothed she was found to be with child; and Joseph the carpenter
4 was minded to repudiate her. But the angel of the Spirit[5] appeared
in this world; and after that Joseph did not repudiate her, but kept
5 Mary and told no one anything about it. And he did not approach
Mary but kept her as a holy virgin, though a child was in her
6,7 womb. And he did not live with her *for* two months. And two
months afterwards Joseph was in his house and Mary his wife;[6]
8 and they were alone together. And while they were alone, Mary
9 looked up and saw a little child; and she was frightened. And at

---

[23]   So Eth.: Slav. 'for they did not ask him *for one*'; L[2] 'and they sang no praises'.

[1]   L[2] Slav. om. 'who was talking . . . accompanying me'.
[2]   So Eth. Slav.: L[2] 'the Lord'. L[2] Slav. then give verses 2–22 only in summary
('. . . sent by God) to show you all things, for no man before you has seen, nor will
any man after you be able to see, what you have seen and heard. And I saw one like a
son of man, and he lived with men in the world, and they did not recognize him').
[3]   B om. 'and family'.
[4]   Lit. 'and he entered into possession of his lot'. This curious statement is
explicable in the light of the tradition that appears in the *Protevangelium* of James (ix.
1, xix. 1) that Mary had been brought up in the Temple, and that when she was
twelve years old, all the widowers in the neighbourhood were assembled in the
Temple, each bringing a rod, so that a sign from heaven through the rods might
indicate which of the widowers should be her husband. When, after prayer,
Joseph's rod was handed back to him, a dove flew out of it and settled on his head.
[5]   So AC: B 'Holy Spirit'.
[6]   So AC (though in A it has been almost completely erased): B 'betrothed'.

that very moment[7] her womb was found[8] as it had been before she
10 had conceived. And when her husband[9] Joseph said to her, What is
it that has frightened you?, his eyes were opened and he saw the
infant and praised the Lord, because *he realized that* God had come
11 into what was his.[10] And there came a voice to them, Tell no one
12 about this vision. Yet the story of the infant spread through Beth-
13 lehem. There were some who said, Mary the virgin has borne a
14 child less than two months after she was married. And many said,
She has not borne a child, for no midwife has attended *her*, and we
have heard no cries of *labour* pains. And they were all kept from
recognizing who he was: they all knew about him; but they did not
15 know where he came from. And they[11] took him and went to
16 Nazareth in Galilee.[12] And I saw, Hezekiah and son Josab (and I
say this also to the other prophets who are standing by[13]) – *I saw*
that *the whole of this* was hidden from all the heavens and from all
17 the princes and from all the gods of this world.[14] And I saw how as
a babe at Nazareth he sucked the breast like any other babe,[15] in
18 order not to be recognized. And when he was grown up, great were
his marvels and wonders in the land of Israel and at Jerusalem.
19 And then the Enemy, in a fit of jealousy, roused the sons of Israel
against him (not knowing who he was), and they handed him over
to the king and crucified him; and he descended to the angel *of*
20,21 *Sheol*.[16] In Jerusalem then I saw him hanging upon a cross. And so
also after the third day *I saw him* rise again and remain *on earth* for
several days.[17] (And the angel who was accompanying me said,
22 Understand *this*, Isaiah.) And I saw him when he sent out the
23 twelve apostles and ascended. And I saw him, and he was in the
vault of heaven,[18] but he had not transformed himself; and all the

---

[7] Lit. 'And after she was frightened'.
[8] So A: BC 'she found her womb'.
[9] her husband = AC (but erased in A): B om.
[10] Lit. 'into his portion'.   [11] i.e. Joseph and Mary.
[12] B om. 'in Galilee'.   [13] Lit. 'who are there'.
[14] So AC: B 'and from him who is of this world'.
[15] Lit. '. . . breast, and it was according to custom'.
[16] Descent 'to the angel of Sheol' is mentioned in G^L ii. 39.
[17] So AB: C 'for forty days'. Cp. ix. 16.
[18] And I saw him (BC om.) . . . vault of heaven: L^2 Slav. 'And I saw *him* ascending into the vault of heaven'.

angels of the vault and Satan[19] saw him, and they worshipped.[20]
24 And there was much lamentation there as[21] they said, How was it
that our Lord descended **into our midst**[22] and we did not perceive
the glory which was upon him *and* which we see has been upon him
25 from the sixth heaven? And he ascended into the second heaven;[23]
26 and he did not transform himself. But all the angels who were on
the right and on the left and the throne in the middle both worshipped him and praised him; and they said, How was it that our Lord
was hidden from us while he was descending and we did not
27 perceive *his glory*?[24] And so too he ascended into the third heaven;
28 and they praised *him* and said the same. And in the fourth heaven
29 and also in the fifth they said precisely the same. But now they
could all see him in his true glory, for he did not transform
30 himself.[25] And I saw that when he ascended into the sixth heaven
31 they worshipped him and praised him. And in every heaven the
32 praises increased. And I saw how he ascended into the seventh
heaven and all the righteous and all the angels[26] praised him; and
then I saw him sit down on the right hand of the Great Glory,[27]
33 whose glory I told you I was not able to look upon.[28] And I saw also
34 the angel of the Holy Spirit[29] sitting on the left hand. And this angel
said to me, Isaiah, son of Amoz, I set you free;[30] for you have seen

---

[19] L² Slav. om. 'and Satan'.

[20] and they worshipped = AC: B om.; L² Slav. 'and they feared greatly and worshipped'.   [21] L² Slav. om. 'there was . . . as'.

[22] Eth. 'upon us'; L² in our midst'; Slav. 'in the midst'. Both L² and Slav. continue 'and we did not recognize the king of glory' (omitting 'which . . . heaven').

[23] L² Slav. 'And from the first heaven he ascended more glorious'; Sah. '*And he*] ascended into the fir[*st heaven*'.

[24] L² Slav. 'How did you pass through us, Lord, and we did not see (Slav. 'recognize') you, nor did we worship you?' Both then summarize verses 27–30 ('And thus he ascended into the second and the third and the fourth and the fifth and the sixth heaven'). Sah. agrees substantially with L² Slav. against Eth. as far as 'the fifth heaven' in the summary in verse 29, but after this it approximates rather more closely to Eth.

[25] Lit. 'But there was but a single glory, and from it he did not change himself'.

[26] So Eth. Sah.: L² Slav. add 'and all the powers'.

[27] So B Sah. Slav.: AC 'of him'; L² om. 'and then I saw . . . Glory'.

[28] So Eth. Sah.: L² Slav. 'upon whom ('which'?) I was not able to look'.

[29] So Eth.: Slav. 'the angel of the Spirit'; L² 'a marvellous angel'.

[30] So Eth.: L² Slav. 'it is enough for you'; and then Eth. adds 'for these are great things'.

35 what no mortal man has *ever* seen *before*.[31] Yet you must return to
your garments *of the flesh* until your days are completed. Then will
you come up here.

36   These things Isaiah saw and told them[32] to all who were in
37 attendance, and they sang praises.[33] And he spoke to king
38 Hezekiah and said, Thus have I spoken. And[34] the end of the world
39 and all this vision will be fulfilled in the last generations.[35] And
Isaiah made him swear that he would neither tell the people of
40 Israel nor give[36] these words to any man to transcribe. . . . And
then shall you read *them*.[37] And keep watch in the Holy Spirit, so
that you may receive your garments and thrones and crowns of
glory, which are stored up *for you* in the seventh heaven.[38]

41   It was because of these visions and prophecies that Sammael
Satan sawed Isaiah, the son of Amoz, the prophet, in two, using
42 Manasseh as his agent. And Hezekiah entrusted all these things to
43 Manasseh in the twenty-sixth year.[39] But Manasseh did not remember them, nor did he take any notice of them; and so, by
becoming the servant of Satan, he was destroyed.

    Here ends the vision of Isaiah the prophet together with his
ascension.[40]

---

[31] L² Slav. add Isa. lxiv. 4 as quoted by St. Paul at 1 Cor. ii. 9: they then continue 'And he said to me, Return . . .'.

[32] So L² Slav.: Eth. 'These things I saw, and Isaiah told them' (which would seem to be supported by Sah.).

[33] So Eth.: L² Slav. 'and when they heard these marvellous things they (L² + 'all') sang praises and glorified God who shows such favour to men'.

[34] L² Slav. om. 'and said . . . spoken. And'.

[35] B 'at the last day'.

[36] L² Slav. 'And he forbade them to tell . . . and to give'.

[37] There must be a lacuna here since Isaiah is obviously speaking. The transla-tion follows AC. L² and Slav. both have long and interrelated texts; but they do not help since both are corrupt.

[38] L² Slav. 'in the heavens': they then add 'And he finished speaking and went out from king Hezekiah' and om. verses 41–43. Sah. would seem to have ended similarly, although it certainly read 'in the seventh heaven'.

[39] B adds 'of his reign'.

[40] So AC: B om. altogether; L² 'Here ends the vision of Isaiah the prophet'; Slav. has a doxology instead.

THE PARALEIPOMENA OF
JEREMIAH

INTRODUCTION

The fact that texts of this work have survived in Greek, in Ethiopic, in at least three different Armenian recensions, and in more than one Slavonic recension, suggests that it was known in antiquity over a wide area and enjoyed considerable popularity. Yet it seems never to have been either quoted or referred to by any of the Fathers. Neither, apparently, does it occur in any of the Greek lists of apocryphal books.[1] It does, however, find a place in both the Armenian and the Slavonic lists.

As a title, 'The Paraleipomena of Jeremiah' represents an abbreviation of what, to judge from the manuscripts, was the popular Greek title – 'The Paraleipomena of Jeremiah the Prophet'. And so similarly the Armenian and the Slavonic traditions. 'Paraleipomena' (i.e. 'things left out'), used absolutely, was the recognized title for the Books of Chronicles in the Greek Old Testament; and, as a result, the term gained a wider currency and came to be used, especially among those concerned with Biblical apocrypha, to describe a new edition of a work already in existence, or, more often, a supplement to it – for example, in The Testament of Job the reader is referred for further details about a more than ordinarily 'scurrilous attack' upon Job to 'the Paraleipomena of Eliphaz'.[2]

As we have seen, the Greek, Armenian, and Slavonic traditions agree in calling our work 'The Paraleipomena of Jeremiah' (or something similar), but the Ethiopic tradition prefers as a title 'The Rest of the Words of Baruch'; and, since it was in its Ethiopic version that the book first became known to the modern world, it

---

[1] There is no reason to suppose that the 'Baruch pseudepigraphon', which figures towards the end of the lists in Pseudo-Athanasius and Nicephorus, was intended to refer to the Paraleipomena. No number of *stichoi* is indicated; and if a reference to a work now extant was intended, it is far more likely to have been to the Greek Apocalypse of Baruch.

[2] Test. Job xli. 6: cp. xl. 14 (see above pp. 642 and 641).

was only natural that it should initially be grouped among the Baruch books. Yet manifestly the book is primarily about Jeremiah and not Baruch: Baruch is an important, but subsidiary, figure; and his importance lies in his function as scribe (as in the canonical Jeremiah). Furthermore, when numbers began to be assigned to the different Baruch books (1 Baruch, 2 Baruch, 3 Baruch, 4 Baruch), there was inevitably confusion about which book was which, and particularly between the last two. If one came across a reference in an author to '4 Baruch' without further explanation, was it to be understood that the reference was to the Paraleipomena of Jeremiah or to the Greek Apocalypse of Baruch? Or, to put the question the other way round, if one wanted to refer to the Paraleipomena should one call it '3 Baruch' (with M. R. James[3]) or '4 Baruch' (with R. H. Charles[4])? In consequence, it has become increasingly common to distinguish the two works by reverting to the use of the titles found in the ancient Greek manuscripts, even though we cannot be sure in either case that these titles are original. (And it may be noted, too, that it has also become much more common than once it was to speak of 'The Syriac Apocalypse of Baruch' rather than '2 Baruch').

The attention of the modern West was first drawn to the Paraleipomena by C. F. A. Dillmann's article on the Old Testament pseudepigrapha in the first edition of Herzog's *Real-Encyklopädie für protestantische Theologie und Kirche* which appeared in 1860.[5] Dillmann there described it as 'a Christian apocryphon'. Six years later he himself published an edition of the Ethiopic text, which was translated into German by F. Prätorius in 1872, and again by E. König in 1877; and so it became generally available.

An edition of the Greek text was published by A. M. Ceriani in 1868 on the basis of a single 15th cent. MS from Bra in Piedmont, supplemented by evidence from some of the Menaea MSS of the Eastern Church for 4 November (when the Fall of Jerusalem was commemorated). These Menaea MSS preserve only portions of the text in an abbreviated and less pure form, so that, despite the

[3] M. R. James, *Apocrypha Anecdota*, ii (= *TS* V. i (Cambridge, 1897), pp. liii and lxxi).   [4] R. H. Charles, *APOT* ii, p. 471.

[5] J. J. Herzog, op. cit., vol. xii, p. 314.

fact that there are additions here and there, they represent what would normally be called a 'short recension': the title in them is usually either 'Narrative about the Capture of Jerusalem and the Lamentation of the Prophet Jeremiah and concerning the Trance of Abimelech' or a variant version of it.[6]

J. Rendel Harris's edition of 1889 provided a critically constructed Greek text (of the 'long recension'), with an apparatus and full Introduction. In constructing his text Harris relied on three Greek MSS (a = Cod. Braidensis A. F. ix. 31, 15th cent. – Ceriani's MS; b = Cod. S. Sepulcri 34, 11th cent.; and c = Cod. S. Sepulcri 6, 10th cent.), the evidence of several of the Menaea ('short recension') MSS, and also of the Ethiopic version for which he professed a high regard.

Since Harris's day a number of other manuscripts have come to light belonging to both recensions; but few of them have as yet been adequately examined. Moreover, the relationship between the two recensions (if, indeed, there are only two), and the versional material in its various recensions, is more than ordinarily complex, and little detailed work has so far been done to unravel the complexity. However, in the brief introductory matter to their pilot edition of 1972 R. A. Kraft and A.-E. Purintin gave a convenient list of all known and 'suspected' witnesses up to that date, together with a suggested classification. With a commendable honesty they emphasized that 'all the materials presented here are in every way provisional'. And it is clear that this statement is intended to cover not only their list of available witnesses and their suggested classification of them, but their eclectic Greek text of the 'long recension' as well.

The scene of the Paraleipomena is set in Jerusalem both at the beginning and the end of the Babylonian exile. Jeremiah goes with the exiles to Babylon: Baruch stays near Jerusalem, lamenting its desolation; and Abimelech (i.e. the Ebed-melech of Jer. xxxviii. 7–13), having been sent to gather figs so that he may not see the

---

[6] A fair specimen of this 'short recension' text will be found in A. Vassiliev, *Anecdota Graeco-Byzantina*, i (Moscow, 1893), pp. 308–316. The text is from Vat. Barberini 3 (*a.* 1497).

impending destruction of the city, falls into a miraculous sleep which lasts for sixty-six years. Since the Lord proclaims 'I will shelter him there until I bring the people back to the city' (iii. 10), the sixty-six years of Abimelech's sleep are presumably of significance in determining the date of the Return.

So, at any rate, Harris, who by identifying the destruction of Jerusalem by Nebuchadnezzar in 586 BC with its sack by the Romans in AD 70, and adding 66, arrived at the date AD 136. The author, Harris argued, was clearly a Christian, and in his opinion a Jewish Christian, who was writing a Tract for the Times. After the Second Jewish Revolt had been finally crushed in AD 135, Jerusalem, which had been a ruin for more than sixty years, was rebuilt and renamed Aelia Capitolina. It was to be peopled exclusively by Gentiles, and an imperial edict prohibited Jews from entering on pain of death. The Paraleipomena points out that Jews can evade this edict by forsaking Babylon (i.e. Judaism) and entering their rightful city (i.e. the Christian Church). The book is therefore 'the Church's Eirenicon to the Synagogue, at the time of the Hadrianic edict'.[7]

This view, accepted in its essentials by a number of subsequent scholars, notably by P. Bogaert in the Introduction to his translation of the Syriac Apocalypse of Baruch, has not gone unchallenged. E. Schürer, for example, drew attention to a number of what would seem to be distinctively Jewish features in the work; and later, G. Delling emphasized the fundamental concern with the fate of Jerusalem and the future of the Jewish people, the references to the need for social purity (vi. 13–14, viii. 2–5) being especially significant in this respect. So, according to Delling, it is 'a book for edification', stressing the importance for Jews of the Holy City, the Temple, and the regular life of praise and prayer; and it is to be dated at any time in the first third of the second century AD.

If we take this last view we shall, of course, have to explain the Christian elements in the book as later additions. There is no difficulty in explaining ix. 10–32 in this way (as does Delling): ix. 10–32 gives a circumstantial account of how Jeremiah was re-

---

[7] J. R. Harris, *The Rest of the Words of Baruch*, p. 14.

stored to life three days after his natural death, how he prophesied the advent of Christ and what followed from it (including the explicit reference to 'the Son of God who awakens us out of sleep, Jesus Christ'), and how this prophecy provoked the Jews to stone him; and it may well have been added as a suitable tail-piece in order to Christianize an otherwise purely Jewish work.

But is the work, apart from ix. 10–32, purely Jewish? There are, in particular, several apparent reminiscences of the New Testament, such as 'Jerusalem which is above' (v. 34; cp. Gal. iv. 26), 'teaching them to keep themselves from the pollutions of the Gentiles' (vii. 32; cp. Acts xv. 19–20), and 'the true Light which lighteth me' (ix. 3; cp. John i. 9). Are these examples to be explained as genuine reminiscences of Christian writings on the part of a Christian author? Or, are they Christian intrusions into a Jewish document? Or, are they, perhaps, mere verbal coincidences?

If we are prepared to accept the book as a unity and regard it as Christian throughout, the original language is likely to have been Greek. If it was Jewish, apart from the later Christian modifications, then it may have been written originally either in Greek, or in Hebrew or Aramaic. The mention of 'Zar' as a god's name at vii. 25 has sometimes been held to point to a Hebrew original, inasmuch as *zar* is the common Hebrew word for 'strange(r)' or 'foreign(er)'. But this argument is not conclusive. It cannot be supposed that the hypothetical translator into Greek did not know what *zar* meant and therefore transliterated, since in the very next verse he refers to Jeremiah's grief because his contemporaries 'were invoking a foreign god' (vii. 26). Nevertheless, 'thou god Zar' is undoubted proof that the Greek text had a Semitic background, even if it was not a translation from Hebrew. And another piece of evidence that tells in the same direction is the use of ὁ Ἱκάνος for 'the Almighty' at vi. 3, which accords with the practice of the later translators of the Old Testament (i.e. Aquila, Symmachus, and Theodotion), who normally render the Hebrew *shaddai* in this way, though usually without the article.

Finally, a number of contacts with the other apocryphal Jeremiah or Baruch books deserve notice. Thus, the account of Jeremiah's hiding of the Temple vessels at iii. 7–8 is paralleled or echoed, not only in 2 Macc. ii. 4–5, but also in Syr. Apoc. Bar. vi.

7–10, in the apocryphal Life of Jeremiah in *The Lives of the Prophets*,[8] and in the Garshuni 'Jeremiah Apocryphon' edited by A. Mingana in the first volume of the *Woodbrooke Studies* in 1927.[9] Again, the story of Abimelech and his long sleep reappears in the 'Jeremiah Apocryphon',[10] and it is also apparently referred to in the Prologue to Gk. Apoc. Bar. (*v.* 2). Especially important are the dozen or so parallels with Syr. Apoc. Bar., the more striking of which occur in the same relative order in both books (e.g. Par. Jer. i. 1–2 ‖ Syr. Bar. ii. 1–2; Par. Jer. iv. 3–4 ‖ Syr. Bar. x. 18; Par. Jer. vii. 8–12 ‖ Syr. Bar. lxxvii. 19–26). Theoretically it is possible to explain these parallels either by supposing that the author of the Paraleipomena knew and used the Syriac Apocalypse, or that the author of the Syriac Apocalypse knew and used the Paraleipomena, or that both authors knew and used a common source. Among those who have discussed the question, P. Bogaert preferred the first alternative,[11] and G. W. E. Nickelsburg the third.[12]

It is perhaps also worth noting that the statement of the people after Jeremiah's prophecy of the advent of Christ at ix. 20 ('These are the very same words that were spoken by Isaiah, the son of

[8] Life of Jeremiah, 9–12 (See C. C. Torrey, *The Lives of the Prophets* (= *JBL Monograph Series*, i; Philadelphia, 1946), pp. 22 and 36).

[9] A. Mingana, *Woodbrooke Studies*, i (Cambridge, 1927), pp. 125–138 and 148–233 (= *Bulletin of the John Rylands Library*, xi (Manchester, 1927), pp. 329–342 and 352–437): see especially pp. 171–173 (= *Bulletin . . .*, pp. 375–377). The apocryphon had previously been translated into French by E. Amélineau in his *Contes et romans de l'Égypte chrétienne*, ii (Paris, 1888), pp. 97–151, under the title 'Histoire de la captivité de Babylone'. Another edition of the text, together with a French translation, was published by L. Leroy and P. Dib under the title 'Un apocryphe carchouni sur la captivité de Babylone', in *Revue de l'Orient chrétien*, xv (Paris, 1910), pp. 255–274, 398–409 and xvi (Paris, 1911), pp. 128–154. To what extent this apocryphon should be regarded as a completely separate work, and not just another (though widely divergent) recension of the Paraleipomena, is debateable.

[10] A. Mingana, op. cit., pp. 167 and 185–187 (= *Bulletin . . .*, pp. 371 and 389–391).

[11] As had previously, for example, R. H. Charles, *The Apocalypse of Baruch* (London, 1896), p. xviii.

[12] Nickelsburg rightly points out in this connection that the author of 2 Maccabees claims to be dependent for his story of Jeremiah and the Temple furnishings on an extant written source (2 Macc. ii. 4), so that presumably there were written Jeremiah-Baruch traditions in circulation which antedated the Syriac Apocalypse.

Amoz, when he said, I beheld God and the Son of God') shows acquaintance with a detail in the tradition of Isaiah's martyrdom which reappears elsewhere in Origen,[13] in Jerome,[14] and in the apocryphal Ascension of Isaiah.[15]

Our translation is, in all essentials, a translation of the text as printed by Harris, which, as explained above, represents the 'long recension'.

BIBLIOGRAPHY

EDITIONS

Greek

A. M. CERIANI, *Monumenta sacra et profana*, V. i (Milan, 1868), pp. 9–18.

J. RENDEL HARRIS, *The Rest of the Words of Baruch: A Christian Apocalypse of the year 136 AD* (Cambridge, 1889).

R. A. KRAFT and A.-E. PURINTUN, *Paraleipomena Jeremiou* (= *SBL Texts and Translations* 1, *Pseudepigrapha Series* 1; Missoula, 1972).

Ethiopic

C. F. A. DILLMANN, *Chrestomathia aethiopica* (Leipzig, 1866), pp. viii–x and 1–15.

Armenian

S. HOVSEPHEANTZ, *A Treasury of Old and New Primitive Writers*. Vol. I (*Uncanonical Books of the Old Testament*; Venice, 1896), pp. 349–377.

Slavonic

N. S. TIKHONRAVOV, *Pamyatniki otrechennoi russkoi literatury*, i (St. Petersburg, 1863), pp. 284–297 and 273–284.

[13] Orig. *In Es. hom.* i. 5.
[14] Hieron. *Comm in Es.* i. 10.
[15] Asc. Isa. iii. 8–9 (see above p. 789).

A. N. POPOV, *Opisanie rukopisei i katalog knig tserkovnoi pechati biblioteki A. I. Khludova* (Moscow, 1872), pp. 406–413.

S. NOVAKOVIĆ, 'Apokrifi jednoga srpskog ćirilovskog zbornika XIV. vieka' in *Starine*, viii (Zagreb, 1876), pp. 40–48.

TRANSLATIONS

English

R. A. KRAFT and A.-E. PURINTUN [as above].

J. ISSAVERDENS, *UWOT*[2], pp. 193–232 [Separate translations of three of the Armenian versions].

French

R. BASSET, *Les Apocryphes Éthiopiens traduits en français*. I. *Le Livre de Baruch et la Légende de Jérémie* (Paris, 1893).

German

F. PRÄTORIUS, 'Das apokryphische Buch Baruch im Äthiopischen' in *Zeitschrift für wissenschaftliche Theologie*, xv (1872), pp. 230–247.

E. KÖNIG, 'Der Rest der Worte Baruchs. Aus dem Aethiopischen übersetzt und mit Anmerkungen versehen' in *Theologische Studien und Kritiken*, l (1877), pp. 318–338.

P. RIESSLER, *AjSaB*[2], pp. 903–919.

GENERAL

P. BOGAERT, *L'Apocalypse Syriaque de Baruch*, i (= *Sources chrétiennes*, no. 144; Paris, 1969), pp. 177–221.

G. DELLING, *Jüdische Lehre und Frömmigkeit in den Paralipomena Jeremiae* (= *Beihefte zur ZAW*, 100; Berlin, 1967).

A.-M. DENIS, *IPGAT*, pp. 70–78.

J.-B. FREY, art. 'Apocryphes de l'Ancien Testament' in *DBSup* i, cols. 454–455.

L. GINZBERG, *The Legends of the Jews*, iv (Philadelphia, 1913), pp. 318–321 and vi (Philadelphia, 1928), pp. 409–411.

K. KOHLER, 'The Pre-Talmudic Haggada, I. B. The Second Baruch or rather the Jeremiah Apocalypse' in *JQR* v (April 1893), pp. 407–419.

G. W. E. NICKELSBURG, JR., 'Narrative Traditions in the Paralipomena of Jeremiah and 2 Baruch' in *CBQ* xxxv (1973), pp. 60–68.

P. RIESSLER, *AjSaB*[2], p. 1323.

E. SCHÜRER, *GjVZJC*[4] iii, pp. 393–395.

M. E. STONE, 'Some Observations on the Armenian Version of the Paralipomena of Jeremiah' in *CBQ* xxxv (1973), pp. 47–59.

I. It came to pass, when the Israelites were taken captive by the king of the Chaldaeans, God spoke to Jeremiah *saying*, Jeremiah, my chosen one, get up and leave this city, you and Baruch, for I am about to destroy it because of the many sins of those who live in it. 2 For your prayers are like a solid pillar in the middle of it, and like a 3 wall of adamant around it. Get up now, *both of* you, and leave *it*, 4 before the army of the Chaldaeans surrounds it. And Jeremiah answered, saying, I beseech thee, Lord, permit thy servant to speak before thee. And the Lord said to him, Speak, Jeremiah, my 5 chosen one. And Jeremiah spoke, saying, Lord Almighty, wilt thou deliver the chosen city into the hands of the Chaldaeans, so that the king can boast, together with his hosts, and say, I have prevailed 6 against the holy city of God? No, my Lord: if it is thy will, let it be 7 destroyed by thine own hands. And the Lord said to Jeremiah, Since you are my chosen one, get up and leave this city, you and Baruch, for I am about to destroy it because of the many sins of 8 those who live in it. For neither the king nor his army will be able to 9 enter it, unless I first open its gates. So get up, and go to Baruch, 10 and tell him what I have said. And then, get up *both of* you at midnight,[1] and go onto the city walls, and I will show you that 11 unless I first destroy the city they will not be able to enter it. And when he had said this, the Lord left Jeremiah.

II. And Jeremiah rent his clothes and put dust upon his head; and 2 he went in to the sanctuary of God. And when Baruch saw him with dust sprinkled on his head and his clothes rent, he cried out

---

[1] Lit. 'at the sixth hour of the night'.

aloud, saying, Father Jeremiah, What is the matter with you?[1]

3 What sin have the people committed *now*? (*And he said this* because, whenever the people sinned, Jeremiah would sprinkle dust on his

4 head and pray for the people, that their sin might be forgiven. *That is why* Baruch asked him, saying, Father, what is the matter with

5 you?[1]) And Jeremiah said to him, See that you *too* rend your clothes, but rather let us rend our hearts; and let us not draw water for the drinking-troughs, but rather let us weep and fill them with

6 tears, for the Lord will have no mercy on this people. And Baruch

7 said, Father Jeremiah, what has happened? And Jeremiah said, God is delivering the city into the hands of the king of the

8 Chaldaeans, to take the people captive to Babylon. And when Baruch heard this, he too rent his clothes and said, Father

9 Jeremiah, who has told you this? And Jeremiah said to him, Stay with me *here* a little longer, until midnight,[2] and you will learn that

10 what I have told you is true. So they remained by the altar weeping.

III. And when midnight came[1] Jeremiah and Baruch went up together onto the city walls in accordance with the Lord's instruc-

2 tions to Jeremiah. And behold, a trumpet-blast sounded, and angels came forth from heaven with torches in their hands; and

3 they stood on the city walls. And when Jeremiah and Baruch saw them, they wept, saying, Now we know indeed that what we were

4 told is true. And Jeremiah pleaded with the angels, saying, Do not destroy the city yet, I beg you, before I have had an opportunity to say something to the Lord. And the Lord said to the angels, Do not destroy the city before I have spoken with Jeremiah, my chosen one. And *Jeremiah* said, Lord, I pray *thee*, bid me speak before thee. And the Lord said, Speak, Jeremiah, my chosen one. And

5,6 Jeremiah said, Behold, Lord, now we know that thou art delivering thy city into the hands of its enemies, and they will carry off the

7 people to Babylon. What should we do with the sacred things *in thy temple* and the vessels used in thy service? What wouldest thou have

---

[1] Lit. 'What is it to you?'
[2] Lit. 'until the sixth hour of the night'.

[1] Lit. 'And when the hour of the night came'.

8 us do with them? And the Lord said to him, Take them and consign them to the earth,[2] saying, Listen, O earth, to the voice of him who created you in the abundance of the waters, who sealed you with seven seals in seven periods of time, and who will afterwards receive your beauty: guard the vessels of the service till the coming
9 of the Beloved One. And Jeremiah said, I beseech thee, Lord, show me *too* what I should do about Abimelech the Ethiopian, for he has done many kindnesses to the people, and to thy servant Jeremiah (for it was he who hoisted me up out of the muddy pit), and I would not wish him to see the city's destruction and desolation, and be
10 distressed about it. And the Lord said to Jeremiah, Send him to the vineyard of Agrippa by the mountain *road*; and I will shelter him
11 there until I bring the people back to the city. And the Lord *also* said to Jeremiah, Go with your people to Babylon, and stay with
12 them and preach to them,[3] until I bring them back to the city. But
13 leave Baruch here until I speak to him. And when he had said this,
14 he left Jeremiah and went up into heaven. And Jeremiah and Baruch went into the sanctuary and consigned the vessels of the service to the earth,[4] as the Lord had instructed them, and the earth swallowed them instantly; and the two of them sat down and
15 wept. And in the morning early, Jeremiah sent Abimelech away, saying, Take *your* basket and go to Agrippa's farm by the mountain road: fetch a few figs, and give *them* to those of the people who are ill: on you *be* joy from the Lord, and *may his* glory *rest* upon your
16 head. And Abimelech went off *and did* as he had been told.

IV. And in the morning early, behold, the army of the Chaldaeans surrounded the city; and the great angel blew the trumpet, saying, Enter the city, army of the Chaldaeans, for behold, the gate has
2 been opened for you. So the king entered with his host and took all
3 the people captive. And Jeremiah took the keys of the temple, and went outside the city and threw them *up* in the face of the sun, saying, I tell you, sun, take the keys of God's temple, and guard them until the day when the Lord tells you what to do with them;
4 because we have proved unworthy guardians of them and faithless

---

² So *ab*: *c* Eth. add 'and to the altar'. Cp. verse 14.
³ Lit. 'stay with them evangelizing them'. Cp. v. 21.
⁴ So *ab* Eth.: *c* adds 'and to the altar'. Cp. verse 8.

5 stewards. *And* while Jeremiah was still weeping for the people, *he*
6 *and* they were dragged off to Babylon. But Baruch put dust on his
head, and sat down and uttered this lament, saying,

> Why is Jerusalem desolated?
> Because of the sins of the beloved people
> She is delivered into the enemies' hands,
> Because of our sins and *the sins* of the people.

7 > But let not the lawless ones boast and say,
> We have been able to take God's city by our own strength.
> You have indeed prevailed against her;
> But it was because of our sins that we were delivered up.

8 > And our God will have pity on us,
> And he will restore us to our city:
> But as for you, you will not endure.[1]

9 > Blessed are our fathers, Abraham, Isaac, and Jacob,
> For they departed from this world
> And did not see the destruction of this city.

10 And when he had said this, he went out weeping and saying, O
11 Jerusalem, I leave you, mourning for you. And he remained,
sitting on a tomb, while the angels came and told him in detail
about everything.

V. Now Abimelech had gone to fetch the figs and was bringing
them back in the midday heat;[1] and he came upon a tree, and sat
down in its shade to rest awhile. And he leaned his head on the
fig-basket and fell asleep; and he slept soundly for sixty-six years
2 without waking up. And afterwards, when he did wake up, he said,
It is a pity I did not sleep a little bit more: I feel very drowsy,[2]
3 because I have not had enough sleep. Then he took off the cover
4 over the fig-basket and found the figs oozing sap. And he said, I
5 would have liked a bit more sleep, because I feel so drowsy.[2] But I
am afraid that if I do go to sleep, I might not wake up for sometime,
and my father Jeremiah will be put out; for if he had not been in a

---

[1] Lit. 'you will not have life'.

[1] Lit. 'And Abimelech fetched the figs in the heat'.
[2] Lit. 'my head is weighed down'.

6 hurry, he would not have sent me out to-day at daybreak. So I will
get up, and go on in the heat – **would that I could find somewhere**
7 **where there is no heat and daily toil!**[3] He got up accordingly, and
picked up the fig-basket and put it on his shoulders, and made his
way into Jerusalem; and he did not recognize it, neither *his* house,
nor the district where he lived,[4] nor *could he find* any of his relations.[5]
8 And he said, Blessed be the Lord, for I must be in a trance: this is
9 not the city. I am lost, for I came by the mountain road after I woke
10 up from my sleep. And because I was drowsy[6] through not having
11 had enough sleep, I must have lost my way. *It would be* absurd to
12 tell Jeremiah that I got lost. And he went out *some distance* from the
city; and, looking at it, he saw the city's landmarks and said, This
13 is indeed the city, but I am lost. And he went back again inside the
city, and searched, and discovered no single person that he knew.[7]
14 And he said, Blessed be the Lord, for a mighty trance has fallen on
15 me. And he went outside the city again, and remained there in
16 deep distress, not knowing where to go. And he put the basket
down, saying, I will sit here until the Lord takes this trance away
17 from me. And while he was sitting *there*, he saw an old man coming
in from the country; and Abimelech said to him, Tell me, old man,
18 what city that is? And he said to him, Jerusalem. And Abimelech
said to him, Where is Jeremiah the priest, and Baruch the scribe,
and all the people of this city, because I have not been able to find
19 them? And the old man said to him, Surely you must be from this
20 city yourself: otherwise why should you be thinking about
Jeremiah to-day and asking about him such a long time after he
21 went away? Jeremiah is in Babylon with the people; for they were
taken captive by king Nebuchadnezzar, and Jeremiah is with them
22 preaching to them and instructing them.[8] And as soon as
23 Abimelech heard what the old man told him, he said *to him*, No one
should insult anyone who is older than he is himself, and if you
were not an old man, I would laugh at you and call you mad to tell

---

[3] Harris's reconstruction on the basis of *a* and *b*: *c* om.; Eth. is clearly corrupt.
[4] Lit. 'nor place'.
[5] Lit. 'nor his own stock'.
[6] Lit. 'And my head being heavy'.
[7] Lit. 'no one of his own people'.
[8] Lit. 'to evangelize them and instruct them in the word'. Cp. iii. 11.

24 me that the people have been taken captive to Babylon. Even if the
cataracts of heaven[9] had descended on them there would not yet
25 have been time for them to reach Babylon. For how long is it since
my father Jeremiah sent me to Agrippa's farm for a few figs to give
26 to those of the people who are ill? I went off and fetched them, and
on the way back in the heat I came to a tree, and I sat down to rest a
bit, and leaned my head on the basket, and went to sleep; and when
I woke up, I took off the cover over the fig-basket, as I thought I
have been rather a long time, and I found the figs oozing sap, as if I
had just picked them. Yet you tell me the people have been taken
27 captive to Babylon. So that you may know *that I am telling you the*
28 *truth*, come, look at the figs. And he took off the cover of the
29,30 fig-basket for the old man. And he *too* saw them oozing sap. And
when the old man saw them he said, My son, you are a righteous
man, and God would not let you see the city's destruction; for it is
God who has brought this trance upon you. For, behold, it is
sixty-six years to the very day since the people were taken captive
31 to Babylon. And so that you may understand that this is true, my
child, look out on the countryside, and see how much progress the
crops have made, and you will realize that it is not yet the time for
32 figs.[10] Then Abimelech cried out aloud, saying, I will bless thee,
Lord God of heaven and earth, the repose of the souls of the
33 righteous in every place. And he said to the old man, What month
34 is it? And he said, Nisan; **and it is the twelfth of Nisan**.[11] And
Abimelech picked out some of the figs, and gave them to the old man,
and said to him, God will light your way to the city of Jerusalem
which is above.

VI. After this Abimelech went outside the city and prayed to the
Lord. And lo, an angel of the Lord came and led him back to where
2 Baruch was; and he found him sitting on a tomb. And when they
saw each other, they both wept and kissed each other. And Baruch

---

[9] See Gen. vii. 11, viii. 2; 2 Kings vii. 2, 19; Mal. iii. 10 — in the LXX.

[10] Both text and interpretation here are uncertain; but the translation attempts
to give the sense that seems to be required.

[11] *ab* 'Nisan, which is the twelfth month'; *c* 'Isaac is this month'; Eth. 'the twelfth
of the month Nisan, which is Mijazja'.

looked up and saw the figs covered up in the basket; and he lifted
his eyes up to heaven and prayed, saying, It is God who rewards
3 his saints. Prepare yourself, my heart, and make merry, and rejoice
while you are in your body[1] – that is, in your house of flesh; for your
sorrow has been turned into joy. For the Almighty is coming, and
4 he will take you out of your body, for there is no sin in you. Revive,
5 my virgin faith, and believe that you will live. Look at this basket of
figs; for lo, they are sixty-six years old and they have not gone
6 mouldy, nor do they smell at all, but they are oozing sap. So will it
be with you, my flesh, if you do what you are commanded by the
7 angel of righteousness. He who has preserved the basket of figs, he
8 will preserve you again by his power. And then Baruch said to
Abimelech, Get up, and let us pray to the Lord and ask him to
show us how we can send word to Jeremiah in Babylon *and tell him*
9 about how you have been protected. And Baruch prayed, saying,
O Lord our God, our Strength, the chosen Light which came forth
from his mouth, I beg thee and beseech thee by thy goodness, the
10 great Name no man can know, hear the voice of thy servant, and let
there be knowledge in my heart. What wouldest thou that we
11 should do? How can I send *word* to Jeremiah in Babylon? While
Baruch was still praying, behold, an angel of the Lord came and
12 said to Baruch, Baruch, counsellor of light, have no anxiety about
how you are to send *word* to Jeremiah; for to-morrow, at dawn, an
eagle will come to you, and you can send him as a messenger to
13 Jeremiah. And write a letter, saying, Speak to the Israelites *and say
to them*, The stranger that is among you, let him be separated *from
you*, and let this continue for fifteen days; and after this I will bring
14 you to your city, says the Lord. Whoever does not separate himself
from Babylon, Jeremiah, shall not enter the city; and I will punish
them, so that they are not received back again by the Babylonians,
5,16 says the Lord. And after saying this, the angel left Baruch. And
Baruch sent to the Gentiles' Market[2] and got some paper and ink,
and wrote a letter as follows,

17   Baruch, servant of God, to Jeremiah, who is of the captivity that
is in Babylon, greeting. Rejoice that God has not allowed us to

---

[1] Lit. 'tent, tabernacle'. Cp. 2 Cor. v. 1, 4.
[2] So *c: ab* 'to the Diaspora of the Gentiles'; Eth. 'to the street (or 'market')'.

leave this body in mourning for the city's desolation and humilia-
18 tion. *Rejoice* because the Lord has had compassion on our tears and
remembered the covenant he made with our fathers, Abraham,
19 Isaac, and Jacob. For he sent me his angel and spoke these words
20 to me that *now* I send to you. These, then, are the words the Lord
God of Israel has spoken, who brought us out of the land of Egypt,
21 out of the mighty furnace. Because you did not keep my precepts,
but were arrogant and obstinate, I was furious and delivered you
22 in anger to the furnace in Babylon. If, then, you will listen to me,
says the Lord, and do as my servant Jeremiah tells you,[3] – whoever
listens I will bring back from Babylon, but whoever will not listen
23 shall become a stranger *both* to Jerusalem and to Babylon. You
shall test them by the water of Jordan, *and* whoever will not listen
will be obvious enough: this is the sign of the great seal.

1,2 **VII.** And Baruch got up and left the tomb.[1] And the eagle
answered in a human voice and said, Hail, Baruch, steward of the
3 faith. And Baruch said to him, Chosen you are, you who now
speak, out of all the birds of heaven; for this is plain from the light
4,5 in your eyes. Tell me, then, what you are doing here. And the eagle
said to him, I was sent here so that you could send any message you
6 wanted by me. And Baruch said to him, Can you take this message
7 to Jeremiah in Babylon? And the eagle said to him, This is why I
8 was sent. And Baruch picked up the letter, and fifteen figs from
9 Abimelech's basket, and tied them round the eagle's neck. And he
said to him, I tell you, king of birds, go in peace, and carry my
10 message safely. Do not be like the raven, which Noah sent out, and
which never returned to him in the ark again; but be like the dove,
which on the third occasion brought back a message to that good
11 man. So do you too take this message of encouragement[2] to
Jeremiah and those with him, and fare you well: take this letter[3] to
12 the chosen people of God. Even if all the birds of heaven gather

---

[3] Lit. '. . . Lord, by the mouth of my servant Jeremiah'.

[1] So *ab* Eth.: *c* adds 'and he found the eagle sitting outside the tomb'. Clearly
something has dropped out at some stage.
[2] Lit. 'this good message'.
[3] Lit. 'this piece of paper'.

round you, and all the enemies of truth set themselves in array against you, fight them; *and* may the Lord give you strength. Fly straight as an arrow, without deviating either to right or to left, in
13 the strength of God. Then the eagle flew off with the letter and made his way to Babylon, and he alighted on a tree outside the city
14 in an unfrequented spot. And he stayed there in silence until Jeremiah came by, accompanied by some others of the people, coming out to bury a man who had died. (For Jeremiah had asked Nebuchadnezzar, saying, Give me a place where I can bury my
15 people's dead. And he had given him one.) So they were coming out *of the city* and weeping over the dead man, and they came up to where the eagle was; and the eagle cried out, saying, I tell you, Jeremiah, God's chosen one, go and gather together all the people, and bring them here to hear the good news I have brought you
16 from Baruch and Abimelech. When Jeremiah heard this, he gave praise to God; and he went off and gathered the people together, with the women and the children, and came where the eagle was.
17 And the eagle flew down upon the man that was dead, and he came
18 to life again (this happened so that they should believe). And all the people were amazed at what had happened, saying, Is not this the God who appeared to our fathers in the wilderness through Moses? Did he not then refer to himself as if he were an eagle?[4] Has
19 he not now appeared to us through this great eagle here?[5] And the eagle said to Jeremiah, Come, untie this letter, and read it to the
20 people. So he untied the letter and read it to the people. And when
21 the people heard *it*, they wept and put dust on their heads. And they said to Jeremiah, Help us, and tell us what we must do to
22 regain our city. And Jeremiah answered and said to them, Do everything you have been told to do in the letter, and God will
23 bring us to our city. And Jeremiah also wrote a letter to Baruch as follows,

Do not neglect, my dear son, to make petition for us in your prayers that God may prosper our way till we escape from the control of this lawless king; for you were found righteous before him and he did not let you come here with us, so that you might not

---

[4] Cp. Exod. xix. 4; Deut. xxxii. 10–11.

[5] Lit. '. . . Moses, and he made himself in the form of an eagle, and appeared to us through this great eagle?'

see the affliction that has befallen the people at the hands of the
24 Babylonians. For just as anyone who is anxious to do what he can
for a father, whose only son has to undergo punishment, will put
something over the father's face so that he cannot see the son
actually being punished and thus be mortified even more than he
was before, so God had pity on you and did not let you come to
Babylon, so that you might not see the people's affliction; for since
we came to this city we have been afflicted continuously, for
25 sixty-six years to the very day. For often enough when I have come
out of doors I have found some of the people about to be hanged by
king Nebuchadnezzar, and they would be in tears, saying, Have
26 mercy upon us, thou god Zar.[6] When I heard this I was distressed
and made a double lamentation, not only because they were being
hanged, but *also* because they were invoking a foreign god, saying,
27 Have mercy on us. And I would remember the feast days we kept
in Jerusalem before we were made captives. And when I remembered them, I would groan and turn back to my house in
28 anguish and in tears. So now make petition in[7] the place where you
are, you and Abimelech, on this people's behalf, that they may
listen to me and the instructions that I give them, and that we may
29 escape from here. For I tell you, the whole time we have been here
the Babylonians[8] have pestered us and said, Sing us one of the
songs of Zion, even the song of your God. And we would answer
them, How can we sing to you, seeing we are in a foreign land?

30   And after this *Jeremiah* tied the letter to the eagle's neck, saying,
31 Go in peace, and may the Lord watch over both *of them*. And the
eagle flew off, and carried the letter, and gave it to Baruch. And
Baruch untied it, and he read it and kissed it, and when he heard
32 about the distresses and afflictions of the people he wept. And
Jeremiah took the figs and distributed them among the people who
were ill. And he remained *there* teaching them to keep themselves
from the pollutions of the Gentiles of Babylon.

---

   [6] So *a* and *b*. 'Zar' is a transliteration of the common Hebrew word *zar* =
'strange' or 'foreign' (for its use in the phrase 'strange god' see Pss. xliv. 20 and
lxxxi. 9). *c* reads 'Sabaoth'. The Eth. MSS vary between 'Zar', 'Sorot', and 'Sarot'.
   [7] Lit. 'to' (acc.).
   [8] Lit. 'they'. Cp. Ps. cxxxvii. 3.

VIII. And the day came when God led the people out of Babylon.
2 And the Lord said to Jeremiah, Get up, *both* you and the people,
and make your way to Jordan; and say to the people, He that is for
the Lord, let him leave behind what was done in Babylon – the men
who married Babylonian[1] wives and the women who married
3 Babylonian[1] husbands. And let those who listen to you cross over,
and bring them to Jerusalem; but those who will not listen to you,
4 do not bring into it. And Jeremiah told them this; and they got up
and came to Jordan to cross over, and he repeated to them what the
Lord had told him. And half of those who had married Babylonians[1]
refused to listen to Jeremiah, but said to him, We will never leave
5 our wives behind: let us take them back with us to our city. So they
crossed the Jordan and came to Jerusalem. And Jeremiah stood
up, and Baruch, and Abimelech, and said, No one with a Babylo-
6 nian partner shall enter this city. And they said to them, Let us
then return to Babylon where we belong.[2] And they went away.
7 But when they came to Babylon, the Babylonians came out to meet
them, saying, You shall not enter our city because in your hatred
for us you left secretly: you shall not return to us for that reason.
For we have bound ourselves by oath, in the name of our god, not
to receive either you or your children, because you left us secretly.
8 And when they heard this, they turned back and came to a deserted place some distance from Jerusalem; and they built a city for
9 themselves and called it Samaria. And Jeremiah sent *a message* to
them, saying, Repent, for the angel of righteousness is coming and
will lead you to your place on high.

IX. And those who were of Jeremiah's party rejoiced and offered
2 sacrifice on the people's behalf continuously for nine days. On the
3 tenth day Jeremiah alone offered sacrifice. And he prayed, saying,
Holy, holy, holy, the Incense of the living trees, the true Light which
4 lighteth me till I am taken up to thee, beyond the sweet voice of the

---

[1] Lit. 'married from them'. After 'Babylonians' in verse 4 the text of *c* breaks off
and concludes with a collection of historical scraps, mostly derived from 1 and 2
Esdras (LXX).

[2] Lit. 'to Babylon, to our place'.

two seraphim, and beyond the sweet smell of the incense of the
5 cherubim.[1] Michael, the archangel of righteousness, is my con-
6 stant delight till he brings the righteous in.[2] I beseech thee,
Almighty Lord of all creation, the Unbegotten and the Incomprehensible, in whom all judgement was hidden before these
7 things came into being . . . And as Jeremiah was saying this,
standing at the altar with Baruch and Abimelech, he sank into a
8 death-like swoon.[3] And Baruch and Abimelech stayed *there* weeping and crying out aloud, Jeremiah our father, the priest of God,
9 has left us and gone away. And all the people heard their wailing,
and they all ran to them and saw Jeremiah lying dead upon the
ground; and they rent their clothes and put dust on their heads and
10 made a bitter lamentation. And afterwards they made prepara-
11 tions to bury him. And lo, a voice came, saying, Bury not a man
who is still alive, because his soul is coming *back* into his body
12 again. And when they heard the voice they did not bury him, but
remained round his body[4] for three days discussing, but not know-
13 ing, when he would rise up. And after three days his soul came *back*
into his body, and he raised his voice in the middle of them all and
said, Glorify God, glorify God, all of you, and *also* the Son of God
who awakens us out of sleep, Jesus Christ, the Light of all the ages,
14 the unquenchable Lamp, the Life of faith. After four hundred and
seventy-seven years from now, he will come[5] to earth; and the Tree
of Life, which was planted in the middle of Paradise will make all
trees that are barren bear fruit, and they will grow and sprout.[6]
15 And as for those that have sprouted and boast and say, We have
thrust out our topmost branches to the sky[7] – the Tree that is firmly
rooted will make them wither, tall though they are, and will bend
16 their branches *to the earth*. And it will make scarlet white like wool:

---

[1] So Eth.: *ab* 'I beseech thee beyond another sweet smell of incense'.
[2] So *ab*: Eth. 'I beseech thee that Michael, skilled in song (the angel of righteousness is he), may hold open the gates of righteousness till they enter in'.
[3] Lit. 'he became like one of those delivering up his soul'.
[4] Lit. 'his tabernacle'. Cp. 2 Cor. v. 1, 4.
[5] Lit. 'There are, after these times, other four hundred and seventy-seven years,
and he comes'.
[6] So *ab*: Eth. adds 'and their fruit will dwell with the angels'.
[7] Lit. 'We gave our end to the air'.

snow will be turned black; *and* sweet water will become salt,[8] in the
17 great light of the gladness of God. And he will bless the islands, so
18 that they bear fruit by the word of the mouth of his Christ. For he
will come and go out and choose for himself twelve apostles to
preach the gospel among the Gentiles (I have seen him adorned by
his Father and coming into the world on the mount of Olives); and
19 he will feed the hungry souls. While Jeremiah was saying this
about the coming of the Son of God into the world, the people
20 became incensed and said, These are the very same words that
were spoken by Isaiah, the son of Amoz, when he said, I beheld
21 God and the Son of God. Come then: let us kill him, but not in the
22 same way as we killed Isaiah: let us rather stone him to death. *And*
Baruch and Abimelech were much distressed by this madness,
especially because they were anxious for a full account of the
23 mysteries that he had seen. And Jeremiah said to them, Make no
move,[9] and do not weep, for they will not kill me until I have told
24 you everything that I saw. And he said to them, Bring me a stone.
25 And he set it up and said, Light of the ages, make this stone become
,27 like me. And the stone assumed the likeness of Jeremiah. And they
28 stoned the stone, thinking that it was Jeremiah. And *meanwhile* he
delivered all the mysteries he had seen to Baruch and Abimelech.
29 Then, with the firm intention of bringing his stewardship to an
30 end, he *went and* stood in the middle of the people. And the stone
shouted out, saying, You foolish Israelites, why are you stoning
me, under the impression that I am Jeremiah? Lo, Jeremiah is
31 standing in the middle of you. And when they saw him, they bore
down upon him at once with many stones. And his stewardship
32 was fulfilled. And Baruch and Abimelech came and buried him;
and they took the stone and set it up as a memorial to him, and
inscribed these words upon it, This is the stone that came to the aid
of Jeremiah.[10]

[8] Eth. adds 'and salt water will become sweet'.
[9] Lit. 'Be silent'.
[10] *a* and *b* add 'And the rest of the words of Jeremiah, and all *his* might, behold, are they not written in the Epistle of Baruch?'

THE SYRIAC APOCALYPSE
OF
BARUCH

INTRODUCTION

References and quotations in patristic writers make it clear that
several other books, either attributed to, or connected with,
Baruch were known in antiquity in addition to the Baruch of our
Apocrypha and the books translated in the present collection.
Thus, we hear of: (1) a book of 'Baruch', to which three MSS of
Cyprian's *Testimonia* ascribe an otherwise unknown quotation of
some twelve lines, which appears (in these MSS only) at *Test*. iii.
29: (2) a book, from 'near the end of which' an alleged prophecy of
Christ's birth, mode of dress, death, and resurrection, is quoted in
the *Altercatio legis inter Simonem Iudaeum et Theophilum Christianum* of
the monk Evagrius;[1] and (3) a Gnostic book which is quoted and
discussed at length by Hippolytus.[2] But about these books we have
no further information. As books they have disappeared completely.

The Syriac Apocalypse only narrowly escaped a similar fate. For
reasons at which we can but guess, it seems to have been especially
popular in the Syriac-speaking churches of the East and on occasion to have been included in the Syriac Bible. Normally, however,
only chaps. lxxviii–lxxxvi were included in the Bible; and these
chapters appeared as an independent work, with the title 'The
Epistle of Baruch', or something similar, and with no hint that they
were an extract. It thus came about that, although the 'Epistle'
was well known to the modern world because it was found in a

---

[1] See *CSEL* xlv (Vienna, 1904), p. 19. The possibility that this book is to be
identified with The Paraleipomena of Jeremiah (which has a prophecy of the
coming of Christ in the middle of the final chapter: see Par. Jer. ix. 13–18) would
seem to be ruled out by the fact that the words quoted by 'Theophilus' are not found
there. However, the whole section Par. Jer. ix. 10–32 is easily detachable (see above
pp. 816–7), and it may be that 'Theophilus' was quoting from a different recension.

[2] Hippolyt. *Philosoph.* v. 24–27.

number of Syriac Biblical MSS, the book as a whole was lost until
A. M. Ceriani discovered it in the mid-nineteenth-century in the
now famous sixth-century MS of the Bible in the Ambrosian
Library at Milan (Cod. B. 21 Inf.). Ceriani published first a Latin
translation in 1866,[3] and then the Syriac text itself in 1871. A
photo-lithographic facsimile of the complete Ambrosian MS followed in 1876–1883. Another edition of the text of the Apocalypse
only was published by M. Kmosko in 1907 (with a Latin Introduction and translation), and yet another, by S. Dedering, in 1973.

The title of the book in the MS states that the Syriac was
translated from the Greek. Whether this statement goes back to the
translator, or was inserted by a later copyist or editor, it is impossible to say. But there is no reason to doubt its truth. All the internal
evidence is in favour of it; and the discovery at Oxyrhynchus in
1897 of a fragmentary leaf from a fourth or fifth-century Greek
codex, containing xii. 1–xiii. 2 and xiii. 11–xiv. 3, proves the
existence at one time of at least a Greek version.[4]

The earlier critics all assumed that Greek was the language in
which the book was written. R. H. Charles questioned this assumption and argued in favour of a Hebrew original; and his arguments
were for many years very widely accepted. Subsequently, however,
P. Bogaert questioned Charles's arguments: none of the suggested
instances of mistranslation, Bogaert maintained, on which Charles
had mainly relied to support his case, are at all compelling; and for
Bogaert the hypothesis of an original in Greek, addressed in all
probability to the Jewish Dispersion is equally plausible.

And similarly with regard to the unity of the book. Charles
claimed to have identified no less than six separate sources, some
taking an optimistic view of Israel's future in the world and some
the reverse, while some presupposed that Jerusalem was still
standing (and were therefore to be dated before AD 70) and some

---

[3] In *Monumenta sacra et profana*, I. ii, pp. i–iv and 73–98.

[4] So far as the possible existence of versions in other languages is concerned, P. S.
van Koningsveld ('An Arabic Manuscript of the Apocalypse of Baruch' in *The
Journal for the Study of Judaism*, vi (1975), pp. 205–207) has drawn attention to the
existence of an Arabic version in a Mt. Sinai MS (no. 589 in A. S. Atiya's hand list),
which is especially interesting because it is clearly not a direct translation of the
Syriac text as given in the Ambrosian MS.

presupposed that it had already been destroyed (and were therefore to be dated after AD 70). These six sources, Charles suggested, were assembled, and in many respects radically altered, by an editor who worked round about AD 100. Bogaert, on the other hand, was impressed by the evidence of an underlying plan in the book, and in consequence was concerned to stress its literary unity. Inconsistencies there certainly are: it is also possible that some of them may be accounted for by the use of different sources, some belonging to the years before AD 70 and some after; but that these sources can be identified with that degree of precision which Charles claimed, and the history of the composition of the book reconstructed in such detail, is unlikely.

However, Charles's final date for the book as it stands (*c.* AD 100) is probably not far wide of the mark. B. Violet put it a little later – *c.* AD 115, and thought it not impossible that F. Rosenthal was right in seeing the author as a member of the circle gathered round Rabbi Akiba at Jamnia. Bogaert particularized even further and suggested as a possibility the name of Rabbi Joshua ben Hananiah (*c.* AD 40–125).

At all events, the author was not a Christian; for the book shows no trace of Christian influence of any kind. He was unmistakeably a Jew, who was living in the difficult times following the destruction of Jerusalem in AD 70, whose general outlook was essentially traditional, and whose main concern was to give his dispirited co-religionists, whether in Palestine, or scattered among the Gentiles, a message of hope. Observance of the Law is his constant refrain – 'Look at what has befallen Zion, and what has happened to Jerusalem . . . If you endure and persevere in the fear of him, and do not forget his law, the times will change for your good, and you will see the consolation of Zion':[5] the whole world will be transformed, the dead raised, and 'those who have now been justified by obedience to my law' will be glorified and attain 'the world which does not die'.[6] Moreover, the End is at hand, 'for the youth of the world is past . . . the times have run their course and the end is very near: the pitcher is near the cistern, the ship to port, the traveller to the city, and life to *its* consummation'.[7]

---

[5] xliv. 5, 7.   [6] li. 3.   [7] lxxxv. 10.

Attention should be drawn to a number of parallels with the Ezra Apocalypse (4 Ezra in the Vulgate and 2 Esdras in our Apocrypha) and also with *The Biblical Antiquities* of pseudo-Philo.[8] These parallels have usually been explained by theories of literary dependence on the part of the authors, either on one or both of the other works as we know them, or on their sources. This may be so. But all three works seem to reflect the same background and they are probably roughly contemporary. There is, therefore, no need to suppose that any one of them was directly dependent on the others. All three were presumably written under the influence of the same traditions, ideas, and aspirations, and several authors may quite independently have given expression to them in very much the same words.[9]

Furthermore, it has been suggested that the words quoted from 'another prophet' at *Ep. Barn.* xi. 9 are in fact a quotation from Syr. Apoc. lxi. 7. If this is so the quotation will be the earliest piece of evidence there is for the existence of the Syriac Apocalypse. Unfortunately the date of The Epistle of Barnabas is, if anything, even less certain than are the dates of the Ezra Apocalypse, of *The Biblical Antiquities*, and of the Syriac Apocalypse itself!

The translation which follows is Charles's translation revised.

BIBLIOGRAPHY

EDITIONS

Syriac

A. M. CERIANI, *Monumenta sacra et profana*, V. ii (Milan, 1871), pp. 113–180.

[8] The parallels with the Ezra Apocalypse will be found conveniently set out in G. H. Box, *The Ezra-Apocalypse* (London, 1912), pp. lxix–lxx, and those with pseudo-Philo in M. R. James, *The Biblical Antiquities of Philo* (S.P.C.K., *Translations of Early Documents*; London, 1917), pp. 46–54. Parallels with The Paraleipomena of Jeremiah are discussed above on pp. 817–8, those with The Greek Apocalypse of Baruch are discussed below on pp. 900–1.

[9] On the figure of Baruch generally in Jewish tradition and the legends attached to his name see L. Ginzberg, *The Legends of the Jews*, iv (Philadelphia, 1913), pp. 322–325 and vi (Philadelphia, 1928), pp. 411–413.

———, *Translatio Syria Pescitto Veteris Testamenti ex codice Ambrosiano sec. fere vi, photolithographice edita* (Milan, (1876–1883),foll. 257a–267a.

R. H. CHARLES, *The Apocalypse of Baruch, translated from the Syriac* . . . (London, 1896), pp. 125–167. [An edition of the text of 'The Epistle of Baruch' only – see below.]

M. KMOSKO, *Patrologia Syriaca* I. ii (Paris, 1907), coll. 1056–1306.

S. DEDERING, *Peshiṭta*, Part IV, fasc. 3 (Leiden, 1973), pp. i–iv and 1–50.

Greek

B. P. GRENFELL and A. S. HUNT, *The Oxyrhynchus Papyri*, iii (London, 1903), pp. 3–7 (no. 403).
reprinted in

R. H. CHARLES, *APOT* ii, pp. 487–490.

B. VIOLET, *Die Apokalypsen des Esra und des Baruch* . . . [as below], pp. 219–220 and 222–223.

A.-M. DENIS, *Fragmenta Pseudepigraphorum quae supersunt Graeca* (= *PVTG* iii; Leiden, 1970), pp. 118–120.

P. BOGAERT, *L'Apocalypse syriaque de Baruch* . . . [as below], i, pp. 40–43.

TRANSLATIONS

English

R. H. CHARLES, *The Apocalypse of Baruch translated from the Syriac, Chapters I–LXXVII from the sixth cent. MS in the Ambrosian Library of Milan, and Chapters LXXVIII–LXXXVII – the Epistle of Baruch – from a new and critical text based on ten MSS and published herewith. Edited, with Introduction, Notes, and Indices* (London, 1896).

———, *APOT* ii, pp. 470–526.

———, *The Apocalypse of Baruch* (= S.P.C.K., *Translations of Early Documents*; London, 1918).

French

P. BOGAERT, *L'Apocalypse syriaque de Baruch, introduction, traduction du syriaque et commentaire*, 2 vols. (= *Sources chrétiennes*, nos. 144–5; Paris, 1969).

German

V. RYSSEL in E. KAUTZSCH, *APAT* ii, pp. 402–446.

B. VIOLET, *Die Apokalypsen des Esra und des Baruch in deutscher Gestalt*
(= *GCS* Bd. 32; Leipzig, 1924), pp. 203–336.

P. RIESSLER, *AjSaB*², pp. 55–113.

A. F. J. KLIJN in *JSh-rZ* V 2 (1976), pp. 103–191.

GENERAL

W. BAARS, 'Neue Textzeugen der syrischen Baruchapokalypse' in
VT xiii (1963), pp. 476–478.

A.-M. DENIS, *IPGAT*, pp. 182–186.

O. EISSFELDT, *OTI*, pp. 627–630.

J.-B. FREY, art. 'Apocryphes de l'Ancien Testament' in *DBSup* i,
cols. 418–423.

L. GINZBERG, art. 'Baruch, Apocalypse of (Syriac)' in *JE* ii (New
York, 1902), pp. 551–556.

L. GRY, 'La date de la fin des temps selon les révélations ou les
calculs du Pseudo-Philon et de Baruch' in *R Bibl* xlviii (1939),
pp. 337–356.

J. HADOT, 'La Datation de *l'Apocalypse syriaque de Baruch*' in
Semitica, xv (1965), pp. 79–95.

J. RENDEL HARRIS, *The Rest of the Words of Baruch* (London,
1889), pp. 6–9.

M. R. JAMES, 'Notes on Apocrypha' in *JTS* xvi (April 1915),
pp. 403–405.

A. F. J. KLIJN, 'The Sources and the Redaction of the Syriac
Apocalypse of Baruch' in *The Journal for the Study of Judaism*, i
(1970), pp. 65–76.

G. W. E. NICKLESBURG, JR., 'Narrative Traditions in the
Paralipomena of Jeremiah and 2 Baruch' in *CBQ* xxxv (1973),
pp. 60–68.

W. O. E. OESTERLEY, Introduction in R. H. CHARLES, *The
Apocalypse of Baruch* (= S.P.C.K., *Translations of Early Documents*;
London, 1918), pp. vii–xxxiii.

P. RIESSLER, *AjSaB*², pp. 1270–1272.

F. ROSENTHAL, *Vier apokryphische Bücher aus der Zeit und Schule Akiba's* (Leipzig, 1885), pp. 72–103.

L. ROST, *EATAP*, pp. 94–97.

E. SCHÜRER, *HJPTJC* II. iii, pp. 83–93.

——, *GjVZJC*[4] iii, pp. 305–315.

C. C. TORREY, *AL*, pp. 123–126.

B. VIOLET, *Die Apokalypsen* . . . [as above], pp. lvi–xcvi.

F. ZIMMERMANN, 'Textual Observations on the Apocalypse of Baruch' in *JTS* xl (1939), pp. 151–156.

The Book of the Revelation of Baruch, the son of Neriah:
Translated from the Greek into Syriac.

I. And it came to pass in the twenty-fifth year of Jeconiah, king of Judah, that the word of the Lord came to Baruch, the son of 2 Neriah, and said to him, Have you seen all that this people are doing to me, that the evils which these two tribes that remained have done are greater than *those of* the ten tribes that were carried 3 away as captives? For the former tribes were forced by their kings to commit sin, but these two *tribes* have of themselves been forcing 4 and compelling their kings to commit sin. For this reason I am about to bring ruin on this city and on its inhabitants, and for a time it shall be taken away out of my sight; and I will scatter this people among the Gentiles, that they may do good to the Gentiles. 5 And my people shall be chastened; but the time will come when they will seek prosperity once more.

II. I have told you this so that you may tell Jeremiah, and all those 2 that are like you, to leave this city. For your deeds are like a solid pillar to this city, and your prayers like an impregnable wall.

III. And I said, O Lord, my lord, have I come into the world for no other purpose than to see the evils of my mother? Surely not, my 2 lord. If I have won thy favour, take my life away first, so that I 3 may join my fathers and not witness my mother's destruction. I am caught in a dilemma: I cannot resist thee; and yet I cannot bear to

4 watch the ruin[1] of my mother. But one thing I will ask of thee,[2] O
5 Lord. What is to happen after this? For if thou destroyest thy city
   and dost deliver up thy land to those that hate us, how will the
6 name of Israel again be remembered? How will anyone proclaim
7 thy praises? To whom will what is in thy law be explained? Is the
   universe[3] to return to its original state and the world to revert to
8 primeval silence? Is the human race[4] to be **destroyed** and mankind
9 to be blotted out?[5] And what is to become of all thou didst say to
   Moses about us?

IV.   And the Lord said to me, This city shall be given up for a time,
   and for a time the people shall be chastened; yet the world will not
2 be consigned to oblivion. Do you think that this is the city about
3 which I said, On the palms of my hands have I engraved you? This
   building, which now stands in your midst, is not the one that is to
   be revealed, *that is* with me *now*, that was prepared beforehand here
   at the time when I determined to make Paradise, and showed it to
   Adam before he sinned (though when he disobeyed *my* command-
4 ment it was taken away from him, as was also Paradise). And after
   this I showed it to my servant Abraham by night among the
5 divided pieces of the victims. And again I showed it also to Moses
   on mount Sinai when I showed him the pattern of the tabernacle
6 and all its vessels. And now it is preserved with me, as is also
7 Paradise. Go, then, and do as I command you.

V.   And I answered and said,

>   So, then, I am to be held responsible for Zion,[1]
>   For thine enemies will come to this place,
>   And they will pollute thy sanctuary,
>   And they will lead thine inheritance into captivity

---

[1] Lit. 'to see the evils'.
[2] Lit. 'I will say before thee'.
[3] Text 'ornament', doubtless through a misunderstanding of the Gk. κόσμος.
[4] Lit. 'the multitude of souls'.
[5] Lit. 'and the nature of man not again be named'.

[1] Lit. 'So, then, I am to be guilty for Zion', Charles emended 'So, then, I am
destined to **grieve** for Zion'.

And make themselves masters of those whom thou hast
  loved;
And they will depart again to the place of their idols,
And they will boast before them.
And what wilt thou do for thy great name?

2 And the Lord said to me,

My name and my glory are to all eternity;
And my judgement will maintain its right in its own time.
And you will see with your eyes
3 That the enemy will not overthrow Zion,
Nor shall they burn Jerusalem,
But they shall be the ministers of the Judge for a time.

4 But go and do what I have told you to.

5 And I went and took Jeremiah, and Iddo, and Seriah, and Jabish,
and Gedaliah, and all the nobles of the people, and I led them out
to the Kidron valley; and I repeated to them everything that had
6,7 been told me. And they cried out aloud, and all of them wept. And
we sat there and fasted until the evening.

VI. And on the next day the Chaldaean army surrounded the city;
and when evening came, I, Baruch, left the people, and I went and
2 stood by the oak.[1] And I was grieving over Zion and lamenting
3 over the captivity that had come upon the people. And suddenly a
powerful spirit[2] lifted me up and carried me over the wall of
4 Jerusalem. And I saw four angels standing at the four corners of
5 the city, each of them holding a fiery torch in his hands. And
another angel began to descend from heaven; and he said to them,
6 Keep hold of your lamps, and do not light them till I tell you. For I
am sent first to speak a word to the earth and to put in it what the
7 Lord, the Most High, has commanded me. And I saw him descend
into the Holy of Holies, and take from it the veil, and the holy **ark**,[3]
and *its* cover, and the two tablets, and the holy vestments of the

---

[1] Cp. lxxvii. 18.
[2] Or 'a strong wind'.
[3] Text 'ephod'.

priests, and the altar of incense, and the forty-eight precious stones with which the priest was adorned, and all the vessels of the
8 tabernacle. And he cried to the earth in a loud voice,

> Earth, earth, earth, hear the word of the mighty God,
> And receive what I commit to you.
> And guard them until the last times,
> So that, when you are ordered, you may restore them,
> And strangers may not get possession of them.
9   For the time has come when Jerusalem also will be delivered
>   for a time,
> Until it is said that it shall be restored again for ever.

10 And the earth opened its mouth and swallowed them up.

VII. And after this I heard that angel saying to the angels that held the lamps,

> Destroy and throw down the wall to its foundations,
> So that the enemy cannot boast and say,
> We have thrown down the wall of Zion,
> And we have burnt the place of the mighty God.

2 **And the spirit restored me to**[1] the place where I had been standing before.

VIII. Then the angels did as he had comanded them; and when they had broken up the corners of the walls, a voice was heard from the interior of the temple, after the wall had fallen, saying,

> 2   Enter, you enemies *of Jerusalem*,
>   And let *her* adversaries come in;
>   For he who kept the house has abandoned it.

3,4 And I, Baruch, went away. And after this the Chaldaean army entered and took possession of the house and all that was round
5 about it. And they carried the people off as captives: some of them they killed; and they put Zedekiah the king in fetters and sent him to the king of Babylon.

---

[1] Conjectural reading based on vi. 3. Text 'And you have seized'.

IX. And I, Baruch, came, together with Jeremiah, whose heart was found pure from sins, *and* who had not been captured when the
2 city was taken. And we rent our clothes and wept, and we mourned and fasted seven days.

X. And after seven days the word of God came to me and said to
2 me, Tell Jeremiah to go to Babylon and support the people in their
3 captivity *there*. But you must remain here to share in Zion's deso-
4 lation;[1] and I will show you afterwards what is to happen at the end
5 of days. And I passed on to Jeremiah the Lord's commands. And he went away with the people; but I, Baruch, returned and sat in front of the gates of the temple and made this lament over Zion and said,

6   Happy the man who was never born,
     Or the child who died at birth.[2]
7   But as for us who are alive, woe to us,
     Because we see the afflictions of Zion,
     And what has happened to Jerusalem.
8   I will summon the sirens from the sea, *and say*,
     Come you night-demons from the desert,
     And you, demons and jackals from the forests:
     Awake and prepare yourselves for mourning,
     And take up with me the dirges,
     And make lamentation with me.
9   Sow not again, you farmers;
     And why, earth, should you yield your crops at harvest?
     Keep to yourself your goodly fruits.
10   And why any longer, vine, should you produce your wine?
     For no offering of it will again be made in Zion,
     Nor again will they offer first-fruits from it.
11   And you, heavens, withhold your dew,
     And open not the treasuries of rain.
     And you, sun, withhold the brightness of your rays,

---

[1] Lit. '. . . here amid the desolation of Zion'.
[2] Lit. 'Or he, who having been born, has died'.

12   And you, moon, conceal the brilliance of your light;
       For why should any light again be seen
       Where the light of Zion is darkened?

13   And you, bridegrooms, go not into *the bridal chamber*,
       And let not the **brides**[3] adorn themselves with garlands;
       And let not the *married* women pray for children,

14   For the barren shall rejoice above all,
       And those who have no sons will be glad,
       And those who do have sons will be in anguish.

15   For why should they bear *children* in pain,
       Only to bury *them* in grief?

16   Or why, again, should men have sons,
       Or why any more should a human infant[4] be given a name,
       Where this mother is desolate
       And her sons are carried away as captives?

17   Speak not henceforth of beauty,
       Nor talk of comeliness.

18   And you, priests, take the keys of the sanctuary,
       And throw them *up* to the heaven above,
       And give them to the Lord and say,
       Guard thy house thyself,
       For we have been found false stewards.

19   And you, virgins, who weave fine linen
       And silk with the gold of Ophir,
       Take quickly all *these* things and throw *them* into the fire,
       That it may bear them up to him who made them,
       And the flame carry them to him who created them,
       Lest the enemy get possession of them.

XI.   And I, Baruch, say this against you, Babylon,
              If you had prospered
              And Zion had dwelt in her glory,
              Great would have been our grief
              That you should be equal to Zion.
2   But now *our* grief is infinite

---

[3] Text 'virgins', who first (rightly) occur in verse 19.
[4] Lit. 'the seed of their kind'.

And *our* lamentation measureless;
For lo, you are prosperous
And Zion desolate.

3 Who will be the judge concerning these things?
Or to whom shall we complain about what has befallen us?
O Lord, how hast thou borne *it*?

4 Our fathers went to *their* rest without suffering,
And the righteous sleep in the earth in peace;

5 For they did not know of this present distress,
And had heard nothing about what has befallen us.

6 Would that you had ears, o earth,
And that you had a heart, o dust,
So that you could go and announce in Sheol,
And say to the dead,

7 You are happier than we who are alive!

XII. But I will tell you what is in my mind,
And I will speak against you, prosperous land.

2 The noonday does not always burn,
Nor do the sun's rays constantly give light:

3 Do not expect [and hope] that you will be always prosperous
and joyful;
And be not proud and domineering.

4 For without doubt in its own good time
The *divine* wrath will awake against you,
Which now is restrained by patience
As if by reins.

5 And when I had so said, I fasted seven days.

XIII. And after this, I, Baruch, was standing on mount Zion, and
2 lo, a voice came from on high and said to me, Stand up, Baruch,
3 and hear the word of the mighty God. Because you have been
dismayed at what has happened to Zion you shall be kept safe and
4 preserved until the consummation of the times. And you shall
serve as witness, so that if ever those prosperous cities say, Why
5 has the mighty God brought this retribution on us?, you can say to
them (you and those like you who have seen this evil), ⟨This is the

evil) and retribution which has come on you and on your people in its *appointed* time, so that the nations may be thoroughly chastened. And they will be waiting for *the end of it*.[1] And if they say at that time, When *will the end of it be*?, you shall say to them,

6,7

8

You who have drunk the wine that has been strained,
Drink also of its dregs,
This is the judgement of the Exalted One,
Who has no favourites.

9 For this very reason he once had no mercy on his own sons,
But afflicted them as if they were his enemies,
Because they sinned:

10 Thus were they chastened then,
That they might be sanctified.

11 But now, you peoples and nations, you are guilty,
Because you have always trodden down the earth,
And treated the creation shamefully;
For I have always showered my gifts upon you,
And you have always been ungrateful for them.

XIV. And I answered and said, Lo, thou hast shown me the course of the times and what is to be after these things; and thou hast explained to me that retribution, which thou hast described to me, shall come upon the nations. And now I know that there have been many sinners, and they have lived in prosperity and departed from the world; but there will be few nations left in those times, to whom what thou hast said can be repeated. What advantage is there in this? What worse *evils* than those we have seen come upon us are we to expect to see?

4,5 Once again will I speak in thy presence. How have they profited, who were men of understanding in thy sight, and did not pursue paths that led nowhere like the rest of the nations, and never said to dead *idols*, Give us life, but always feared thee and followed thy ways? Lo! They have been carried off; nor because of them hast thou had mercy on Zion. Even if others did evil, was it not due to Zion that she should be forgiven because of the good things that

2

3

6

7

---

[1] Lit. 'they will be expecting'.

they did, instead of being overwhelmed because of the evil things
8 the others did? But who, O Lord, my Lord, can comprehend *the
workings of* thy judgement? Or who can search out the depths of thy
9 way? Or who can trace the profundity of thy path? Or who can
describe thy unfathomable counsel? Or what man that has ever
been born has ever discovered either the beginning or the end of
,11 thy wisdom? For we all have been made like a breath. For as *our*
breath comes up from inside *us*, and does not return, but disappears, so it is with men:[1] they do not depart *this life* as and when
they would,[2] nor do they know what will happen to them in the
12 end. The righteous quite rightly look forward to *their* end, and they
leave their dwelling here without fear, because they have a store of
13 *good* works laid up in thy treasuries. So they leave this world
without fear, and trust that they will attain the world which thou
14 hast promised them. But as for us, our lot is hard:[3] we suffer injury
15 and insult now, and we can only look forward to *further* evils. But
thou knowest truly what thou hast done[4] on behalf of[5] thy servants;
for we cannot understand what is good as thou, our creator, canst.

16 And yet again I will speak in thy presence, O Lord, my lord.
17 When of old there was no world, and no one to inhabit it, thou didst
make thy plan, and thou didst utter thy word, and immediately the
18 works of creation stood before thee. And thou didst say that thou
wouldest make man for thy world to be the administrator of thy
works, so that it might be known that he was not made because of
19 the world, but the world because of him. And now it would seem
that[6] the world which was made because of us remains, but we, for[7]
whom it was made, disappear.

XV. And the Lord answered and said to me, You are quite rightly
perplexed about the disappearance of man, but you are wrong in
2 what you think about the evils that come upon sinners. When you

---

[1] Lit. 'with the nature of men'.
[2] Lit. 'according to their own will'.
[3] Lit. 'woe to us'.
[4] Or 'made'.
[5] Or 'by means of'.
[6] Lit. 'And now I see that'.
[7] Lit. 'because of'.

said, The righteous are carried off, and the wicked are prospered;
3 and again, when you said, Man cannot comprehend *the workings of*
4 thy judgement – listen, and I will tell you: pay attention, and I will
5 explain to you. Man would have had excuse for not understanding
my judgement, if he had not been given the law, and I had not
6 instructed him in understanding. But now, because he has transgressed with his eyes open, on this ground alone (that he knew) he
7 must be punished. And as regards what you said about the righteous,
that it was because of them that this world came into being, so also
8 **shall** that which is to come **come into being** because of them. For this
world is for them a *place of* strife, and weariness, and much trouble;
but that which is to come *will be* a crown with great glory.

XVI.   And I answered and said, O Lord, my lord, our years here[1]
are few and evil, and who is able in so brief a **time** to acquire what
cannot be measured.

XVII.   And the Lord answered and said to me, With the Most High
2 it does not matter whether a man's life be long or short.[1] For what
profit was it to Adam that he lived nine hundred and thirty years,
3 and yet transgressed the command that had been given him. The
length of time that he lived did not profit him, but brought death
4 and shortened the lives of his descendants. Or in what way was
Moses the loser in that he lived only a hundred and twenty years,
and yet, inasmuch as he obeyed his creator, brought the law to the
sons of Jacob and lit a lamp for the nation of Israel?

XVIII.   And I answered and said, He that lit *the lamp* took *advantage*
2 of *its* light;[1] but there are few who have done as he did. Many of
those to whom he has given light have preferred[2] Adam's darkness
and have not rejoiced in the light of the lamp.

---

[1] Lit. 'the years of this time'.

[1] Lit. 'With the Most High account is not taken of much time nor of a few years'.

[1] Or 'He that lit *the light* received *it* from the Light' (so Bogaert).
[2] Lit. 'have taken from'.

XIX. And he answered and said to me, That is why he established a covenant for them at that time and said, Behold I have set before you life and death; and he summoned heaven and earth to witness

2 against them. For he knew that his time was short, but that heaven

3 and earth would endure for ever. Yet after his death they sinned and transgressed, though they knew that they had the law against *them*, and the light which nothing could deceive, and the *celestial*

4 spheres to add their testimony, and also me. Now so far as the present state of things is concerned, it is for me to pass judgement, so do not worry about them nor distress yourself because of what

5 has happened. For it is now the end of time that should be con-sidered (whether *it is a matter* of business, or of prosperity, or of

6 misfortune) and not the beginning of it. Because though a man may have been prosperous when he was young, if misfortune comes upon him in his old age, he will forget all his former

7 prosperity. Conversely, though a man may have been the victim of misfortune when he was young, if at the end of his life he becomes

8 prosperous, he will not remember his former misfortunes. Further-more, even if, from the day on which death was decreed against transgressors, every single man had been prosperous all through his life,[1] and in the end had been destroyed, it would all have been in vain.

XX. Behold, the time is coming when the days will speed on more swiftly than of old, and the seasons will succeed one another more rapidly than in the past, and the years will pass by more quickly

2 than they do now. That is why I have now taken Zion away, so that

3 I may the more speedily punish the world at its appointed time. So now hold fast in your heart everything that I command you and

4 seal it in the recesses of your mind. And then will I show you the

5 judgement of my might, and my ways that are unfathomable. Go, therefore, and purify yourself for seven days: eat no bread, drink no

6 water, and speak to no one. And afterwards come to this place,[1] and I will reveal myself to you, and tell you hidden truths, and give

---

[1] Lit. 'all that time'.

[1] Lit. 'that place'. Presumably mount Zion (cp. xiii. 1 and xxi. 2).

you instruction about the course of the times; for they are coming, and there will be no delay.

XXI. And I went away and sat in a cave in the hillside in the Kidron valley, and I purified myself there, and though I ate no bread I was not hungry, and though I drank no water I was not thirsty; and I was there till the seventh day, as he had commanded 2 me. And afterwards I came to the place where he had spoken with 3 me. And at sunset my mind was beset by many thoughts, and I 4 began to speak in the presence of the Mighty One. And I said, O thou who hast made the earth, hear me, thou who hast fixed the vault of heaven **by thy word**[1] and hast made fast the height of it by thy spirit, thou who hast called *into being* from the beginning of the world things which did not previously exist, and they obey thee. 5 Thou who hast commanded the air by thy nod, and hast seen the 6 things which are to be as the things which **have been already**. Thou who rulest in *thy* great design the hosts that stand before thee, *and* dost control, as with a rod of iron,[2] the countless holy beings whom thou didst make from the beginning, of flame and fire, which stand 7 around thy throne. To thee only does it belong to do at once 8 whatever thou dost wish. Thou makest the rain to fall drop by drop upon the earth, and thou alone knowest the end of the times before 9 they come: have respect unto my prayer. For thou alone art able to sustain all who are, and those who **have passed away**, and those who 10 are to be, those who sin, and those who **are righteous**.[3] For thou alone dost live, immortal and past finding out, and thou knowest 11 the number of mankind. And if in the course of time many have sinned, yet others, not a few in number, have been righteous.

12 Thou knowest *the place* which thou hast reserved for the end of those who have sinned, and the destiny of the others who have been 13 righteous. For if there were this life only, which belongs to all men, 14 nothing could be more bitter than this. For what gain is strength that turns to weakness, or plenty that turns to famine, or beauty

---

[1] Text 'in its fulness': cp. Ps. xxxiii. 6.

[2] Lit. 'control in anger'.

[3] Text 'who are justified'. The text then adds 'as living *and* being past finding out' – clearly a dittograph of the opening clause of the next verse.

15 that turns to ugliness? For the nature of man is always changing.
16 For what we once were, now we no longer are, and what we now
17 are, we shall not long remain. For if a term had not been set for all,
18 their beginning would have been in vain. But do thou inform me
about everything that comes from thee, and enlighten me about
everything I ask thee.

19   For how long will what is corruptible endure, and for how long
will mortals thrive on earth,[4] and the transgressors[5] in the world
20 continue in their pollutions and corruptions? In thy mercy issue
thy command and bring to pass everything thou saidst thou
wouldst, that it may be made known to those who think thy
21 patience is but weakness. And show to those who do not know **that**
everything that has happened to us and to our city up till now **has
been** in accordance with the patience of thy power, because for thy
22 name's sake thou hast called us a beloved people. **So bring mortality
23 to an end now**.[6] Restrain the angel of death, and let thy glory appear
and the might of thy beauty be known: let Sheol be sealed so that
from now onwards it may not receive the dead; and let the
24 treasuries of souls restore those that are held fast in them. For there
have been many years of desolation since the days of Abraham and
Isaac and Jacob, and of all those like them who sleep in the earth,
25 on whose account thou didst say thou didst create the world. And
now show thy glory quickly, and do not put off what thou hast
promised.

26   And when I had finished this prayer I was completely exhausted.

XXII.   And after this, behold, the heavens opened, and I saw *a
vision*, and strength was given me, and a voice was heard from on
2 high, and it said to me, Baruch, Baruch, why are you troubled?
3 What comfort is there for a man if he sets off on a journey by road
and never reaches his journey's end, or if he goes by sea and never
4 arrives at the port he was making for? Or if he promises to give
someone else a present and never does, is it not *equivalent* to

---

[4] Lit. 'will the time of mortals be prospered'.
[5] Or 'those who pass away': cp. verse 9.
[6] Text 'Every nature, from now onwards, is mortal'.

5 robbery? Or if he sows seed in the earth, but does not reap the fruit
6 from it in its season, does he not suffer a total loss? Or if he plants a
plant, can he expect any fruit from it before the regular time for
7 fruit? Or if a pregnant woman bears a still-born child, is she not the
8 *unwitting* cause of her infant's death? Or if a man builds a house and
does not finish it by putting a roof on it, can it *properly* be called a
house? Tell me that first.

1,2 **XXIII.**   And I answered and said, Indeed, no, O Lord, my lord. And
he answered and said to me, Why then are you troubled about
what you do not know, and upset by things you do not understand.
3 For just as you have not forgotten the people who now are, and
those who have passed away, so I remember those who are to
4 come.[1] Because when Adam sinned and death was decreed against
those who were to be born *from him*, then the number of those to be
born was fixed, and for that number a place was prepared where
the living might live out their lives and the dead might be kept in
5 security. Thus, until that number is reached, no creature will live
6 again (since my spirit is the creator of life) and Sheol will receive
7 the dead. And again, you are to be privileged to hear what is to
come after these times. For my redemption is near and is not as far
away as once it was.

XXIV.   For behold, the time is coming when the books will be
opened in which are written the sins of all who have sinned, and
also the treasuries in which are stored *the records of* the righteous
2 deeds of all created beings who have been righteous. And then you
will appreciate[1] (and many with you) the patience of the Most
High in every generation; for he has been ever patient with all men,
3 both with those who sin and with those who are righteous. And I
answered and said, But behold, Lord, no one knows how many are
the things that are already past, nor how many there are that are
4 yet to come. For I know only too well what has happened to us, but
what will happen to our enemies I do not know; nor do I know
when thou wilt visit thy works.

[1] Text 'so I remember those who are remembered and those who are to come'.

[1] Lit. 'see'.

XXV. And he answered and said to me, You too will be preserved
till the time of *the coming of* the sign which the Most High will
2 provide for those on earth at the end of days. And this shall be the
3 sign – when a stupor seizes those on earth and they are assailed by
4 all kinds of misfortune and adverse circumstances. And when they
say as a result of their sufferings, The Mighty One has no longer
any interest in the earth, then, when they have given up hope, the
time will come.[1]

XXVI. And I answered and said, Will the period of suffering that is
to be continue for long, and will the ordeal last many years?

XXVII. And he answered and said to me, That time will be divided
into twelve separate periods,[1] and each one of them will have its
2 own special characteristics.[2] The first period will see the beginning
3 of the troubles. In the second period will occur assassinations of the
4 great ones *of the earth.* In the third period the annihilation of many
5,6 by death. In the fourth period destruction by the sword.[3] In the
7 fifth period famine and lack of rain.[4] In the sixth period earth-
8,9 quakes and terrors . . .[5] In the eighth period *the appearance of* many
10 spectres and attacks by demons. In the ninth period the falling of
11 fire *from heaven.* In the tenth period every kind of havoc and
12 oppression. In the eleventh period *much* wickedness and impurity.
13 And in the twelfth period chaos resulting from the mixing together
14 of all these things. For *although* each of the periods of that time will
be marked off from the rest by its special characteristics, they will
15 *ultimately all* be mixed together and reinforce one another.[6] For

---

[1] Lit. 'the time will awake'.

[1] Lit. 'twelve parts' (and similarly subsequently).
[2] Lit. 'each one of them is reserved for that which is appointed for it'.
[3] Lit. 'the sending of the sword'.
[4] Lit. 'withholding of rain'.
[5] 'In the seventh period . . .' is omitted in the MS.
[6] Charles thought verses 14 and 15 not only 'obscure' but also 'possibly corrupt'.
He translated 'For †these parts of that time are reserved, and† shall be mingled one
with another and minister one to another. For some shall **leave out** some of their own,
and receive *in its stead* from others, and some complete their own and that of others,
so that those . . .'.

some will **fall short**[7] in the calamities they bring and have their deficiency made up by others, while some will supply their full tale themselves and also make up for what is lacking in others, so that those on earth in those days may not understand that this is the final consummation.

1,2 **XXVIII.** Nevertheless, whoever is wise then will understand. For the measure and reckoning of that time are two parts – weeks of
3 seven weeks.[1] And I answered and said, It is good for a man to come to that time and see *what happens then*: yet it is surely better
4 that he should not come in case he fails. [But I will ask[2] this also.
5 Will the Incorruptible despise what is corruptible and *not care about* what happens to the corruptible, and concern himself only with
6 what is not corruptible?][3] But if, Lord, what thou hast foretold to me will assuredly come to pass, reveal this also to me, if I have
7 indeed found favour with thee. Will these things happen in one place or in *just* one area[4] of the earth, or will the whole earth experience them?

XXIX. And he answered and said to me, Whatever happens then will happen to the whole earth; so that all who are alive will
2 experience *it*. For at that time I will protect only those who are
3 found in those days in this land. And it shall be that when all is accomplished that was to come to pass in the *twelve* periods *before the end*,[1] the Messiah shall then begin to be revealed. And
4 Behemoth shall appear from his place and Leviathan shall ascend

---

[7] Sense required by the context: text 'increase'.

[1] So literally. Charles thought interpretation 'impossible'. On various possibilities see M. R. James's note in *The Biblical Antiquities of Philo* (London, 1917), pp. 131–132.   [2] Lit. 'say'.
[3] Verses 4 and 5 break the connection of thought, and no account is taken of them in the context, although some sort of answer appears to be given to the question in xliii. 2.   [4] Lit. 'or in one of the parts'.

[1] Lit. 'in those parts'. We have taken the reference here to be to the twelve divisions of the time of the Messianic woes (described in detail in chap. xxvii): however, the reference could possibly be to the 'parts of the earth' mentioned in xxviii. 7.

from the sea — those two great monsters I created on the fifth day of
creation and have kept until then; and then they shall serve as food
5 for all that survive. The earth also shall yield its fruit ten thousand-
fold; and on each vine there shall be a thousand branches, and each
branch shall produce a thousand clusters, and each cluster produce a thousand grapes, and each grape produce a cor of wine.
6 And those who have been hungry will rejoice; and, also, they shall
7 see marvels every day. For winds shall go forth from me bearing
the scent of aromatic fruits every morning, and, at the close of day,
8 clouds distilling a health-giving dew. And at that time the storehouse of manna shall descend from on high again; and they shall
eat of it in those years, because it is they who have come to the final
consummation.

XXX. And it shall come to pass after this, when the time of the
presence[1] of the Messiah *on earth* has run its course, that he will
return in glory *to the heavens*: then all who have died and have set
2 their hopes on him will rise again. And it shall come to pass at that
time that the treasuries will be opened in which is preserved the
number of the souls of the righteous, and they will come out, and
the multitude of souls will appear together in one single assembly;
and those who are first will rejoice, and those who are last will not
3 be cast down. For each one of them will know[2] that the pre-
4 determined end of the times has come. But the souls of the wicked,
5 when they see all this, will be the more discomforted.[3] For they will
know that their torment is upon them and that their perdition has
arrived.

XXXI. And after this I went to the people and said to them,
2 Summon all your elders to me, and I will speak to them. And they
3 all assembled in the Kidron valley. And I answered and said to
them,

Hear, O Israel, and I will speak to you,
And give ear, you sons of Jacob, and I will instruct you.

---

[1] Or 'advent' (Gk. παρουσία).
[2] Lit. 'For he knows'.
[3] Lit. 'will waste away the more'.

4   Forget not Zion,
     But keep in remembrance the anguish of Jerusalem.
5   For behold, the time is coming,
     When everything that is shall become the prey of corruption,
     And be as though it had never been.

XXXII. But as for you, if you prepare your hearts, and sow in them
the fruits of the law, it will be a protection to you when the Mighty
2   One shakes the whole creation. For after a little while the building
3   of Zion will be shaken so that it may be built again. But that
building will not endure, but will after a time be razed to the
4   ground,[1] and it will remain desolate until the *appointed* time. And
afterwards it must be renewed in glory and be made perfect for
5   evermore. We should not, therefore, **be distressed**[2] so much over the
6   evil which has come now as over what is still to be. For there will be
a greater trial than either of these two tribulations when the
7   Mighty One renews his creation. And now, do not come near me
8   for a few days, and do not seek me out until I come to you. And
when I had said all this to them, I, Baruch, went my way; and
when the people saw me going they cried out in dismay,[3] saying,
9   Where are you going, Baruch, are you going to desert us, as a
father might desert his children, and leave them orphans?

XXXIII. Are these the orders your companion, the prophet
2   Jeremiah, gave you when he said to you, Look after this people
while I go and support the rest of *our* brothers in Babylon, who
3   have been sentenced to be held as captives there? If now you are
going to desert us too, it were better for all of us to die while you are
still with us,[1] and that only then should you go away.

XXXIV. And I answered and said to the people, God forbid that I
should desert you or leave you. I am only going to the Holy of
Holies to inquire of the Mighty One about you and about Zion, in

---

    [1] Lit. 'be rooted out'.
    [2] Text has the active 'cause grief'.
    [3] Lit. 'they lifted up their voice and lamented'.

    [1] Lit. 'to die before you'.

the hope that I may get some further understanding. After this I will come back to you.

XXXV. And I, Baruch, went to the holy place and sat down amid the ruins, and I wept and said,

2   Would that mine eyes were springs *of water*,
    And mine eyelids a fountain of tears;
3   For how shall I lament for Zion,
    And how shall I mourn for Jerusalem?
4   Because in the very place where I now lie prostrate,
    The high priest of old offered holy sacrifices,
    And burned incense of fragrant odours.
5   But now our pride has turned to dust,
    And our hearts' desire to ashes.

XXXVI. And when I had said this I fell asleep there; and I saw a
2   vision in the night. And lo, a forest of trees planted on a plain, with high mountains and steep cliffs all round it; and the forest covered
3   most of the plain. And lo, alongside it there grew up a vine, and
4   from underneath it issued a softly-flowing stream. And when the stream reached the forest it became a raging torrent, and its waves submerged the forest and in a moment uprooted nearly all *the trees that were in* the forest and undermined the mountains that were
5   round about it. And the topmost branches of the forest were laid low, and the peaks of the mountains crumbled;[1] and *the waters from* the stream increased more and more, so that nothing was left of
6   that great forest but a single cedar. And when they had beaten down and destroyed and uprooted all the other *trees that were in* the forest, so that nothing was left of it, nor could the place where once it had been be recognized, then the vine came with the stream, very quietly and unobtrusively, to a place not far from where the cedar
7   was *lying*; and the stricken cedar found itself close to the vine.[2] And I looked, and lo, the vine opened its mouth and spoke and said to the cedar, Are you not the cedar that was left of the forest of wickedness, by whose means wickedness persisted and flourished

---

[1] Lit. 'were laid low'.
[2] Lit. 'and they brought the cedar that had been cast down to it'.

8 all those years, and goodness never? You kept conquering what was not yours, and you showed no pity towards what was not yours: you kept extending your power over those who were far distant from you, and those who were near you, you held fast in the toils of your wickedness; and always you carried yourself proudly 9 as if you could never be uprooted. But now your time has gone by 10 and your hour is come. So, cedar, go the way of the forest, which has gone before you, and be reduced to dust like it, and let all your 11 ashes be mingled together. Recline now in anguish and take your ease in torment till your last hour comes, when you will come back again and be tormented even more.

XXXVII. And after this I saw the cedar burning, and the vine flourishing; and all around it the plain was full of unfading flowers. And I awoke and got up.

XXXVIII. And I prayed and said, O Lord, my lord, thou dost 2 always enlighten those whose guide is understanding. Thy law is 3 life and thy wisdom the true guide. Explain to me, therefore, what 4 this vision means. For thou knowest that I have always followed the path of thy law, and from my earliest days I have never turned away from thy wisdom.

XXXIX. And he answered and said to me, Baruch, this is the 2 interpretation of the vision you have seen. You saw the great forest with high and rugged mountains round it – the meaning is this: 3 Behold, the time is coming when this kingdom, which once destroyed Zion, will itself be destroyed, and it will be made subject by 4 another that will come after it. And then, after a time, that *kingdom* also will be destroyed, and yet another, a third, will arise; and that also will have the sovereignty for its time, and *then* it will be 5 destroyed. And after this a fourth kingdom will arise, which will prove far more tyrannical and savage than any of those that went before it; and it will extend its rule[1] like the forests on the plain, and it will hold sway for many years[2] and exalt itself even more than the

---

[1] Lit. 'and it will rule many times'.
[2] Lit. 'for times'.

6 cedars of Lebanon. Truth will be hidden by it, and all those who are polluted by iniquity will take refuge in it, just as evil beasts take

7 refuge and creep into the forest. And when the time for its end has come, and its fall is imminent, then will be revealed my Messiah's **kingdom**,[3] which is like the stream and the vine; and when that is

8 revealed, it will destroy[4] the hosts that are gathered round it. And as for the lofty cedar that you saw,[5] the sole survivor of the forest, and what you heard the vine saying to it, the meaning is this:

XL. The last leader of that time will be left alive after the rest of his hosts have been destroyed, and he will be put in fetters and taken up to mount Zion; and my Messiah will charge him with all his iniquities, and will enumerate all the evils his hosts have

2 perpetrated, and will confront him with them. And afterwards he will put him to death; and he will preserve the remnant of my

3 people, gathered in the place that I have chosen. And his **kingdom**[1] shall stand for ever, until this world of corruption comes to an end

4 and the times appointed are fulfilled. This is your vision, and this is what it means.

XLI. And I answered and said, Who will take part in this, and how many of them will there be? And who will be judged worthy of a

2 place in that world?[1] For I will declare to thee my thoughts and ask

3 about what is in my mind. For I see many of thy people who have

4 rejected thy covenant and thrown off the yoke of thy law. But again, I have seen others who have abandoned their vanities and

5 fled for refuge beneath thy wings. What is to happen to them, and

6 what will be their lot at the end? Can it be that everything they have done throughout their lives[2] will be weighed, and they will be judged as the balance tips?

---

[3] Text 'beginning' (probably through a misunderstanding of an underlying Gk. ἀρχή = either 'beginning, origin' or 'first place, sovereignty').

[4] Lit. 'uproot'.

[5] Or 'And as for the cedar you saw lying on the ground' (cp. xxxvi. 6).

[1] See n.[3] to the previous chapter.

[1] Lit. 'worthy to live at that time'.

[2] Lit. 'Or perhaps the time of these'.

XLII. And he answered and said to me, I will explain these things
2 to you as well. You asked, Who will take part in this, and how
many of them will there be? Believers will receive the good things
3 they have been promised and scoffers the reverse. And you asked
about those who have embraced the covenant and those who have
4 abandoned it.[1] The answer is this. Those who were at one time
subject *to the covenant*, and afterwards went off and mingled with
foreigners of mixed descent – their former manner of life will count
5 for nothing. And those who started in ignorance but afterwards
found the secret of life, and joined the **people**[1] set apart from other
peoples – their former manner of life will count for nothing either.[2]
6 And time will succeed to time, and season to season, and one will
recive from another; and then, at the end, everything will be
compared[3] according to the measure of the times and the hours of
7 the seasons. For corruption will claim those who belong to it, and
8 life those who belong to it. And the dust will be summoned and
told, Give up what is not yours, and surrender everything you have
guarded until its *appointed* time.

XLIII. But you, Baruch, must apply your mind to what has been
said to you, and understand *the visions* that have been shown you;
2 for many eternal consolations await you. For you will depart from
here, and leave behind you the scenes now so familiar to you; and
you will forget these corruptible things and have no recollection of
3 what happens among mortals. So go and give your people their

---

¹ Lit. 'those who have drawn near and those who have gone away'.

¹ Text 'the peoples'.
² The whole of this passage is obscure and verses 4 and 5 are peculiarly difficult.
We have taken our cue from Bogaert, whose translation not only makes good sense,
but also has the merit of being in line with the doctrine of retribution formulated by
Ezekiel. Charles rendered the verses, 'As for those who were before subject, and
afterwards withdrew and mingled themselves with the seed of mingled peoples, the
time of these was the former, and was accounted as something exalted. And as for
those who before knew not but afterwards knew life, and mingled *only* with the seed
of the **people** which had separated itself, the time of these *is* the **latter**, and is
accounted as something exalted' (= *APOT* ii, p. 502: his earlier version in *The
Apocalypse of Baruch*, pp. 67–68, has several significant differences).
³ So Charles: Bogaert rendered 'toutes choses deviendront égales'.

orders, and come back to this place; and afterwards fast seven days, and then I will come to you and speak to you.

XLIV. And I, Baruch, went and came to my people; and I called my eldest son and **Gedaliah, my friend**,[1] and seven of the elders of the people, and I said to them,

2   Behold, I go to my fathers,
     And tread the way[2] of all the earth.

3   Do not forsake the way of the law,
     But guard and guide the people that are left,
     Lest they forsake the commandments of the Mighty One.

4   For you can see that he whom we serve is just,
     And that our creator has no favourites.

5   Look at what has befallen Zion,
     And what has happened to Jerusalem.

6   For the judgement of the Mighty One will be made known
        thereby,
     And his ways, which though unfathomable, are right.

7   For if you endure and persevere in the fear of him,
     And do not forget his law,
     The times will change for your good,
     And you will see the consolation of Zion.

8   Because whatever is now, is nothing,
     But what is to be will be very great.

9   For everything corruptible will pass away,
     And everything mortal will disappear:
     No memory of it will endure,
     For it is defiled with evils.

10   What makes good progress now will end in vanity,
     And what prospers now will shortly fall
     And be reduced to dust.

11   What is to be will become the object of desire,
     And on what is to come will we set our hopes,
     For it is a time that does not pass away.

---

[1] Text 'the Gedaliahs, my friends'.
[2] Lit. 'According to the way'.

12   The age[3] is coming, which abides for ever,
          And the new world which does not turn to corruption
          Those who own its sway:[4]
          It has no pity for those on the road to torment,
          And leads not to perdition those who live in it.

13   For these are they who will inherit the time that has been
            spoken of,
          And theirs is the inheritance of the time that has been
            promised.

14   These are they who have won for themselves treasuries of
            wisdom,
          And with whom are found stores of understanding,
          And have not turned their backs on mercy,
          And have held fast to the truth of the law.

15   To them will be given the world to come;
          But the dwelling-place of the rest (and there are many of
            them)
          Will be in the *abyss of* fire.

1,2   **XLV.** So instruct the people as best you can: that is our task. For if you teach them, you may preserve them.

XLVI. And my son and the elders of the people answered and said to me, Does the Mighty One wish to chasten us so much that he is
2   prepared to take you from us so soon? Then we shall really be in darkness, and there will be no light *at all* for the people who are left.
3   For where again shall we look for *instruction in* the law, or who will
4   show us the difference between death and life? And I said to them, I cannot resist the will[1] of the Mighty One: nevertheless, Israel shall never want a wise man, nor the race of Jacob a son of the law.
5   Only make up your minds to obey the law; and be subject to those who, in fear, are wise and understanding, and determine that you
6   will never depart from them. For if you do this, the good things I told you about before will come to you; and you will escape the

---

[3] Lit. 'hour'.
[4] Lit. 'those who walk in its beginning'. See n.[3] to chap. xxxix.

[1] Lit. 'throne'.

7 punishment, about which I warned you. But I said nothing about my being taken up,[1] either to them or to my son.

XLVII. And I dismissed them and went away, and I said to them as I went, I am going to Hebron, for the Mighty One has sent me
2 there. And I came to the place where I had been told to go; and I sat there, and I fasted seven days.

XLVIII. And after the seventh day I prayed before the Mighty One and said,

2   O my Lord, thou dost summon the times to come *to thee*,
    And they stand before thee:
    Thou dost cause the power of the ages to pass away,
    And they do not resist thee:
    Thou dost arrange the course of the seasons,
    And they obey thee.
3   Thou alone knowest for how long the generations will
        endure,
    And thou revealest not thy mysteries to many.
4   Thou makest known the might of fire,
    And thou weighest the lightness of the wind.
5   Thou dost explore the limit of the heights,
    And scrutinize the depths of darkness.
6   Thou dost decree the number *of those* who pass away and *of*
        those who are preserved,
    And thou preparest an abode for those who are to be.
7   Thou dost remember the beginning thou hast made,
    And forgettest not the destruction that is to be.
8   With frightening and formidable signs thou dost command
        the flames,
    And they change into spirits.[1]

[1] Lit. 'taken'. This would most naturally be understood simply as a reference to Baruch's impending death, had he not already announced this in no uncertain terms at xliv. 2. The probability is that what is intended here is an 'ascension' or 'translation' (as also at xlviii. 30), a sense well attested in the Old Testament (Gen. v. 24; 2 Kings ii. 5, 9; Pss. xlix. 15, lxxiii. 24; Ecclus. xlviii. 9).

[1] Or 'winds'.

And with a word thou dost quicken that which was not,
And with *thy* mighty power thou holdest back that which not
   yet has come.

9   Thou dost instruct created things by thy understanding,
    And thou teachest the spheres to minister in their orders.

10 Armies innumerable stand before thee,
    And minister in their orders quietly at thy nod.

11 Hear thy servant,
    And give ear to my petition.

12 For we are born to live only for a little while,
    And very soon we go away.

13 But with thee hours are like an age,
    And days as generations.

14 Be not therefore angry with man, for he is nothing,
    And take no account of our deeds, for what are we?

15 For lo, it is by thy gift that we come into the world,
    And we do not leave it by our own decision.

16 For we said not to our parents, Give us birth,
    Nor did we send to Sheol and say, Receive us.

17 How then can our strength withstand thy wrath,
    Or how can we endure thy judgement?

18 Protect us in thy compassion,
    And in thy mercy help us.

19 Behold the little ones that are subject to thee,
    And save all those that draw near to thee;
    And destroy not the hope of our people
    And cut not short the times of our aid.

20 For this is **the nation**[2] thou hast chosen,
    And these are the people without equal in thine eyes.

21 But I now will speak before thee,
    And tell thee what is in my mind.

22 In thee do we trust, for lo, thy law is with us,
    And we know we shall not fall so long as we keep thy statutes.

23 For all time are we blessed in this at least,
    That we have not mingled with the Gentiles.

24 For we are all one famous people,

[2] Text 'until'.

Who have received one law from the only One;
And the law which is with us will help us,
And the matchless wisdom which is in our midst will sustain
us.

25 And after I had prayed and said these things I was much exhausted.

26 And he answered and said to me,

Your prayer has been plain enough, Baruch,
And all your words have been heard.

27 But my judgement claims what is due to it,
And my law exacts its rights.

28 In accordance with your own words will I answer you,
And in accordance with your prayer will I speak to you.

29 For the truth is, he that has become corrupt is not at all:[3] he has done evil so far as he could do anything; and he has neither 30 pondered[4] my goodness nor understood[4] my patience. But you will 31 indeed be taken up,[5] as I have *already* told you. And that time I have *also* told you about will come, and the time of distress begin: it will come and pass by with a sudden fury, creating havoc through 32 the vehemence of its onset. And in those days all the inhabitants of the earth will lean upon one another,[6] because they are unaware that my judgement has come upon them.

33 For there will not be found many wise at that time,
And the prudent will be but few;
And even those possessed of knowledge will keep silent.

34 And there will be many rumours and numerous idle tales,
And uncanny things will be seen to happen,
And not a few predictions will pass from mouth to mouth:
Some of them *will prove* unfounded,
And some *will be* confirmed.

35 And honour will be turned to shame,

---

[3] Charles described the text here as 'unintelligible'.
[4] Lit. 'remembered . . . accepted'.
[5] See n.[1] to chap. xlvi.
[6] Lit. 'rest against each other'. Charles would emend '**be moved** one against another'.

And strength fall into disrepute:
Confidence will disappear,
And beauty will become an object of contempt.

36 And many will say to others at that time,
Where has discretion hidden itself,
And where has wisdom fled for refuge?

37 And while they are meditating on these things,
Those who had thought nothing of themselves will be seized
    by envy,
And the even-tempered man will become a prey to passion:
Many will be stirred up by anger to their mutual hurt,
And they will raise up armies to shed *each others'* blood,
And in the end they will perish all together.

38 And it will come to pass at that very time,
That it will be apparent to all that the times are changing,
Because in all those times they polluted themselves
And oppressed *the poor*;
And each one of them went his own way,
And remembered not the law of the Mighty One.

39 Therefore a fire shall consume their thoughts,
And in the flame shall the plans they have made be tested;
For the Judge will come and will not delay.

40 Each one of the earth's inhabitants knew when he was
    sinning,
But because of their pride they would not recognize[7] my law.

41 But many will then weep bitterly
Over the living more than over the dead.

42 And I answered and said, O Adam, What was it that you did to all
your posterity? And what should be said to Eve who first listened to
43 the serpent? For all this multitude is going to corruption: innumerable are those whom the fire will devour.

44,45   Yet again I will speak in thy presence. Thou, O Lord, my Lord,
46 knowest what is in thy creature. For thou didst of old command the
dust to produce Adam; and thou knowest the number of those who
have been born from him, and how much they have sinned before
thee — those who have been born and have not confessed thee as

---

[7] Lit. 'they did not know'.

47 their creator. And, so far as all these are concerned, their end will convict them, and thy law, which they have transgressed, will requite them on thy day.

48 But now let us leave aside the wicked and inquire about the
49 righteous. And I will recount their blessedness and proclaim[8] the
50 glory that is reserved for them. For without question, just as in this transitory world in which you live, you have for a little while endured much toil, so in that world, to which there is no end, you will receive great light.[9]

XLIX.   But I will again ask of thee, O Mighty One, and beg mercy
2 from him who made all things. In what form will those live who live
3 in thy day, and what will they look like afterwards?[1] Will they then resume their present form and put on these entrammelling members, which are now involved in evils and are the instruments of evils; or wilt thou perhaps transform what has been in the world, as also the world itself?

L.   And he answered and said to me, Listen, Baruch, to what I say,
2 and keep a record in your mind of everything you learn. For the earth will certainly then restore the dead it now receives so as to preserve them: it will make no change in their form, but as it has received them, so it will restore them, and as I delivered them to it,
3 so also will it raise them. For those who are then alive must be shown that the dead have come to life again, and that those who
4 had departed have returned. And when they have recognized those they know now, then the judgement will begin,[1] and what you have been told already will come to pass.

---

[8] Lit. 'and not be silent in celebrating'.
[9] According to Charles verses 48–50 are a fragment of an address delivered by Baruch to the people, and not to God. He found another fragment of this same address (originally preceding 48–50 here) in liv. 16–18, and yet another (following 48–50) in lii. 5–7.

[1] Lit. 'and how will the appearance (or 'splendour') of those after that time continue?'

[1] Lit. 'will grow strong'.

LI. And after the appointed day is over, the **appearance**[1] of those
who have been condemned will be changed, as will also be the
2 glory of those who have been justified. For the appearance of the
3 evil-doers will go from bad to worse, as they suffer torment. Again,
the glory of those who have now been justified through[2] *their
obedience to* my law, who have had understanding in their life, and
who have planted in their heart the root of wisdom – their faces will
shine even more brightly and their features will assume a luminous
beauty,[3] so that they may be able to attain and enter the world
4 which does not die, which has been promised to them then. For
over this, more than over anything else, will the *others* who come
then lament that they rejected my law, and stopped up their ears,
5 so that they might not hear wisdom or receive understanding. For
they will see those who are now their inferiors in a far better and
more glorious state than they are – for these will be transformed so
that they look like angels, while they can only contemplate in
6 horror the decaying shadows of their former selves.[4] For they will
see *all this* first; and afterwards they will depart to their torment.

7   But those who have been saved by their works,
         Whose hope has been in the law,
         Who have put their trust in understanding,
         And their confidence in wisdom,
         Shall see marvels in their time.
8   For they shall behold the world which is now invisible to
              them,
         And realms[5] now hidden from them,
9   And time shall no longer age them.

---

[1] So, by the change of a single diacritical point: text 'pride'.

[2] Or 'in'.

[3] Lit. 'their appearance (or 'splendour') will be glorified in changes and the form
of their face will be turned into the light of their beauty'.

[4] That the initial punishment of the wicked is not only to witness the transformation of the righteous, but also to appreciate to the full the serious deterioration in
their own condition, would seem to be the sense required in this most difficult
passage. Charles (perhaps over-literally) rendered 'they shall yet more waste away
in wonder at the visions and in the beholding of the forms'.

[5] Lit. 'the time'.

10   For in the heights of that world shall they dwell,
And they shall be made like the angels,
And be made equal to the stars;
And they shall be changed into whatever form they will,
From beauty into loveliness,
And from light into the splendour of glory.

11 For the extent of Paradise will be spread before them, and they will be shown the majestic beauty of the living creatures that are beneath the throne, and all the armies of the angels, who are now kept back by my word lest they should reveal themselves, and are restrained by *my* command, so that they may keep their places until

12 *the moment of* their advent comes. Then shall the splendour of the

13 righteous exceed even the splendour of the angels. For the first shall receive the last, those whom they were expecting, and the last those of whom they had heard that they had passed away.[6]

14   For they will then have been delivered from this world of misery
And laid down the burden of sorrow.

15   For what then have men lost their life,
And for what have those who were on earth exchanged their soul?

16   For then they chose for themselves this time,
Which cannot pass without sorrow:
They chose for themselves this time,
Whose issues are full of lamentations and evils,
And they denied the world which ages not those who come to it,
And rejected that time and the glory *of it*,
So that they cannot share in the triumphs about which I have told you.

LII.   And I answered and said, How can **we** forget those whose
2 future is punishment? And why, again, do we mourn for those who

---

[6] The distinction here seems to be not between the angels and the righteous, but between the righteous who have already died and those who would not join them until after the resurrection: cp. 2 Esdras v. 42; 1 Thess. iv. 15 – also xxx. 1–3 (above).

3   die, and weep for those who depart to Sheol? Far better, *surely*, keep
    our lamentations for the beginning of that torment which is to be,
4   and reserve *our* tears for *the* destruction when it comes. But on the
5   other hand – the righteous: what should they do now? I would say,[1]
6   Rejoice in the suffering you now endure: why concern yourselves
7   about[2] the downfall of your enemies? Make yourselves ready for
    what is reserved for you, and prepare yourselves for the reward laid
    up for you.[3]

LIII.   And when I said this I fell asleep there, and I saw a vision;
and lo, a very great cloud was coming up out of the sea. And I kept
looking at it. And lo, it was full of waters, white and black; and
there were many colours in those waters, and what looked like
2   flashes of lightning appeared at the top of it. And I watched the
3   cloud as it moved, and it quickly covered all the earth. And after
this, the cloud began to pour the waters that were in it on the earth.
4   And I saw that the waters that descended from it were not all the
5   same. For at first, for a time, they were all black; but afterwards I
saw that the waters became bright (though there were fewer of
them); and after this again I saw black *waters*, and then again
6   bright; and again black, and again bright. This happened twelve
7   times; but there were always more black waters than bright. And
when the end of the cloud came, lo, it rained black waters, darker
than all that had been before, with fire mixed with them; and
where those waters descended they left a trail of devastation and
8   destruction. And after this I saw the lightning I had seen at the
9   top of the cloud take hold of it and hurl it to the earth. And the
lightning shone so brilliantly that it lit up the whole earth, and it
restored those regions where the last waters had descended and left
10 such devastation. And it took hold of the whole earth and subjected
11 it to its control. And after this I looked and I saw twelve rivers
coming up out of the sea; and they began to surround the lightning
12 and become subject to it. And I woke up in terror.

---

[1] The rendering of verses 4 and 5 here given represents a slight re-ordering of the
text in an attempt to make some sense. Charles rendered 'But even in the face of
these things will I speak. And as for the righteous, What will they do now?'
[2] Lit. 'Why do you look for?'
[3] See n.[9] to chap. xlviii.

The Prayer of Baruch.

LIV. And I besought the Mighty One and said,

Thou alone, O Lord, knowest beforehand the secrets[1] of the world,

And what happens in its time thou dost bring about by thy word;

And in the light of what is done by[2] those on earth

Thou wilt speed up the beginnings of the times,

And the end of the ages thou alone knowest.

2   For thee nothing is too hard,

Thou doest everything easily by a nod.

3   To thee the depths come as the heights,

And the beginnings[3] of the ages are obedient to thy word.

4   Thou revealest to those who fear **thee** what is prepared for them,

And so dost thou comfort them.

5   Thou showest wonders to the ignorant:

Thou dost break down the dividing wall for those who do not know;

And thou dost light up what is dark

And reveal what is hidden to the pure,

Who in faith have submitted to thee and to thy law.

6   Thou hast shown thy servant this vision:

Reveal to me also its interpretation.

7   For I know that when I have besought thee, thou hast answered me,

And when I have made request, thou hast made response to me.

Thou didst reveal to me with what language[4] I should praise thee,

And with which of my members I should offer *my* praises and hallelujahs to thee.

---

[1] Lit. 'the heights' (i.e. the inaccessible things).
[2] Lit. 'And against (or 'according to') the works of'.
[3] Or 'princes' (i.e. angels).
[4] Lit. 'voice'.

8   For if *all* my members were mouths, and the hairs of my head
         voices,
     Even then I could not praise or magnify thee as I should,
     Nor could I recount thy praise nor tell the glory of thy
         beauty.

9   For what am I among men,
     And why am I reckoned among those of far more worth than
         I,
     That I should have heard all these marvellous things from
         the Most High,
     And numberless promises from him who created me?

10   Happy my mother among those that bear children,
     And worthy of praise among women is she who gave me
         birth!

11   For I will not cease to praise the Mighty One,
     And with a thankful voice I will recount his wonders.

12   For who can do wonders like thine, O God,
     Or who can understand thy purpose in creation?[5]

13   For with thy counsel thou dost govern all the creatures
     Which thy right hand has created,
     And thou hast established every source of light beside thee,
     And the treasuries of wisdom thou hast prepared beneath thy
         throne.

14   Justly do they perish who have not loved thy law:
     The torment of judgement awaits those who have not sub-
         mitted to thy power.

15   For though Adam first sinned and brought untimely death upon
     all men, yet each one of those who were born from him has either
     prepared for his own soul *its* future torment or chosen for himself
16   the glories that are to be (for without doubt he who believes will
17   receive his reward). But now, as for you, you wicked that now are,
     prepare to meet[6] destruction: your punishment will come quickly,
     because you have rejected the understanding of the Most High.
18   For what he has done has not taught you, nor has the craftsman-
19   ship revealed perpetually in his creation persuaded you.[7] Thus

---

[5] Lit. 'thy deep thought of life'.
[6] Lit. 'turn to'.   [7] See n.[9] to chap. xlviii.

Adam was responsible for himself only:[8] each one of us is his own
20 Adam. But do thou, O Lord, explain to me the things thou hast
revealed to me, and give me an answer to the questions that I
21 asked. For at the consummation retribution will fall on those who
have done evil for[9] the evil they have done, and thou wilt make
22 glorious the faithful for[9] their faithfulness. For those who are
among thine own thou rulest, and those who sin thou dost root out
from among thine own.

LV. And when I had finished this prayer, I sat down there under a
2 tree, to rest in the shade of *its* branches. And as I considered it, I
was astonished and amazed at the immensity of the goodness that
sinners on earth have rejected, and the scale of the torment they
have despised, although they were very well aware that they would
3 be tormented for their sins. And while I was pondering these and
similar things, lo, the angel Ramiel, who presides over genuine
4 visions, was sent to me; and he said to me, Why are you so
5 distraught, Baruch, and why so troubled in mind? For if you are so
moved ⟨when⟩ you have only heard about the judgement, what *are*
6 *you going to be like* when you see it happening before your eyes? And
if you are so overwrought at the prospect of the coming of the day of
7 the Mighty One, what *will you be like* when it actually arrives? And
if you are so upset by what you have been told about the torment of
the evil-doers, how much more *so will you be* when the complex
8 details are disclosed?[1] And if you are distressed about what you
have heard is to happen then (things both good and bad), how *will*
it be with you when you see what the *Mighty One in his* majesty will
reveal, when he convicts some and gives others cause for rejoicing?

LVI. However, you have asked the Most High to reveal to you the
interpretation of the vision you have seen, and I have been sent to
2 tell you. For the Mighty One has indeed made known to you the
sequence of the times that have passed and of those that are yet to
be in the world, from the beginning of its creation right up to its

[8] Lit. 'Thus Adam is not the cause, but of his own soul only'.
[9] Lit. 'according to'.

[1] Lit. 'when the work ('event') reveals marvels'.

3 consummation – times of falsehood and times of truth. You saw a
great cloud coming up out of the sea that went on and covered the
earth: this *cloud* is the duration of the age of the world, which the
4 Mighty One determined when he decided to make the world. And
so it was that when the world had gone out from his presence, the
duration of the world came into being, something of small account,
established according to the richness of the understanding of him
5 who sent it. And you saw at the top of the cloud black waters
descending first upon the earth – this is the transgression of the first
6 man, Adam. For when he transgressed untimely death appeared:
sorrow came to be, and suffering was produced and pain created,
and toil became the rule: pride reared its head:[1] Sheol insisted on
being renewed by blood: the conception of children was brought
about and the passion of parents roused: man's whole status
7 received a blow; and goodness languished. What could be blacker
8 or darker than all this? This is the beginning of the black waters
9 that you saw. And from these black waters again *other* black *waters*
10 were derived, and even greater darkness[2] was produced. For the
man who was a danger to himself became a danger even to the
11,12 angels. For at the time he was created they enjoyed freedom. And
some of them came down *to earth* and had intercourse with women.
13,14 And those who did so then were tormented in chains. But the rest
15 of the **in**numerable[3] host of angels restrained themselves. And
those who lived on earth perished all together through the waters
16 of the flood. These are the first black waters.

LVII.   And after these you saw bright waters: these *represent* the
fount of Abraham and his family, and the coming of his son and of
2 his grandson, and of those like them. For at that time the unwritten
law was observed by[1] them and the provisions[2] of the commandments were then fulfilled: then originated belief in the coming
judgement: hope for a world to be renewed was then established;

---

[1] Charles rendered '**disease** began to be established'.
[2] Lit. 'and the darknesses of darknesses'.
[3] The text has no negative.

[1] Lit. 'was named among'.
[2] Lit. 'works'.

and the promise of a life to come hereafter was implanted *in men's*
3 *hearts*. These are the bright waters that you saw.

LVIII. And the black third waters that you saw – these *represent* the mixture of all the sins of the nations that followed the death of those righteous men, and the wickedness of the land of Egypt in subject-
2 ing their sons to such cruel servitude. However, these in their turn had their day.

LIX. And the bright fourth waters that you saw *represent* the com-ing of Moses and Aaron and Miriam and Joshua, the son of Nun,
2 and Caleb and all those like them. For at that time the lamp of the eternal law shone on all those in darkness, giving to believers the promise of their reward, and warning unbelievers about the tor-
3 ment of fire reserved for them. At that time, too, the heavens shook, and what was beneath the throne of the Mighty One trembled,
4 when he was taking Moses to himself. For he showed him many other things together with the ordinances of the **law**[1] – the consum-mation of the **times**[1] (just as he has also shown you), and similarly the pattern of Zion and its dimensions, as it was to be constructed,
5 **and** the pattern of the sanctuary, as it now is. Then he showed him also the dimensions of the fire, the depths of the abyss, the weight of
6 the winds, and the number of the drops of rain; and the mastery of
7 anger, the dignity[2] of patience, and the truth of judgement; and the root of wisdom, the riches of understanding, and the fount of
8 knowledge; and the height of the air, the extent of Paradise, the consummation of the ages, and the beginning of the day of judge-
9 ment; and the number of the offerings, and the countries which
10 were as yet unknown;[3] and the mouth of Gehenna, the abode of
11 vengeance, the home of faith, and the dwelling-place of hope; and the vision of the future torment, the throng of innumerable angels, the flaming hosts, the splendour of the lightning, the sound of the thunder, the orders of the **archangels**,[4] the treasuries of light, the
12 changes of the seasons,[5] and the careful study of the law. These are the bright fourth waters that you saw.

---

[1] Text 'laws . . . time'.   [2] Lit. 'abundance'.
[3] Lit. 'and the earths (i.e. 'lands') which had not yet come'.
[4] Text 'chief (sing.) of the angels'.   [5] Lit. 'times'.

LX. And the black fifth waters you saw coming down as rain are what the Amorites did, their spells and incantations, the evils of their mysteries, and the contaminating effect[1] of their pollutions.
2 For even Israel was then polluted and went astray in the days of the judges,[2] although they witnessed many signs given them by their creator.

LXI. And the bright sixth waters that you saw – this is the time
2 when David and Solomon were born. And at that time Zion was built, and the sanctuary dedicated; and much blood of the nations that had sinned then was shed, and many offerings were offered at
3 the dedication of the sanctuary. And peace and tranquillity
4 reigned at that time. *The voice of* wisdom was heard in the assembly, and the riches of understanding were prized in the congregations.
5 And the holy festivals were celebrated enthusiastically[1] and with
6 much joy. The rulers' judgements were then seen to be unbiased, and the justice of the precepts of the Mighty One was maintained
7 in truth. And because the land enjoyed *God's* favour[2] at that time, and because those who lived there did not sin, it was made more glorious than any other land; and the city of Zion became the ruler
8 of all lands and countries. These are the bright waters that you saw.

LXII. And the black seventh waters that you saw *represent* the perversion *brought about* by Jeroboam's plan to make two golden
2 calves; and all the iniquities of the kings after him; and the curse of
3 Jezebel,[1] and the idol-worship that Israel practised at that time;
4 and the withholding of the rain, and the famines that followed until
5 women even ate their own children; and the captivity that overtook

---

[1] Lit. 'and the mingling'.
[2] Text 'judgement'.

[1] Lit. 'in goodness'.
[2] Lit. 'the land was beloved'.

[1] So literally: it is unclear whether the reference is to the curse pronounced upon Jezebel and its fulfilment (1 Kings xxi. 23; 2 Kings ix. 10, 30–37), or to the curse which Jezebel was in herself and consequently to Israel (2 Kings ix. 34).

6 the nine and a half tribes because of their many sins (for Shalmaneser, king of Assyria, came and carried them off as cap-
7 tives). And so far as the Gentiles are concerned, there is no need to stress how they always did what was sinful and wicked, and never
8 what was righteous. These are the black seventh waters that you saw.

LXIII. And the bright eighth waters that you saw – these are the integrity and honesty of Hezekiah, king of Judah, and the grace
2 that was accorded him.[1] For when Sennacherib was stirred up to destroy himself, and his anger maddened him into leading to their destruction also the motley collection of peoples that were with
3 him: when, moreover, king Hezekiah heard what the king of Assyria was plotting, to come and destroy his people (the two and a half tribes that were left – and he wanted to lay waste Zion too): then Hezekiah, in trust and reliance on his righteousness, spoke
4 with the Mighty One and said, Behold, Sennacherib is ready to destroy us; and he will boast when he has laid Zion waste and take
5 credit to himself. And the Mighty One heard him, for Hezekiah was wise, and he listened to his prayer, because he was righteous.
6 And the Mighty One then gave instructions to his angel Ramiel
7 (*the angel* who is speaking to you *now*). And I went and destroyed the whole host of them – the number of the officers alone was a hundred and eighty-five thousand, and each one of them had an
8 equal number *under his command*. And on this occasion I burned their bodies inside, but their outer clothing and their armour I preserved intact, so that what the Mighty One had done might seem still more wonderful, and that as a result his name might be
9 spoken of throughout the entire earth. Thus Zion was saved and
10 Jerusalem delivered: Israel too was freed from *its* distress. And all those who were in the holy land rejoiced, and the name of the
11 Mighty One was glorified so that it was spoken of *everywhere*. These are the bright waters that you saw.

LXIV. And the black ninth waters that you saw – these *represent* all the wickedness there was in the days of Manasseh, Hezekiah's son.

---

[1] Lit 'and his grace'.

2 For he did very many wicked things: he killed the righteous: he perverted judgement: he shed the blood of the innocent: he violated and polluted married women; and he demolished the altars and destroyed their offerings, and drove out the priests so that they 3 could not minister in the sanctuary. And he made an image with five faces, four of them looked to the four winds, and the fifth at the top of the image *was there* to provoke the jealousy of the Mighty 4 One. At that time *a sentence of* wrath went out from the presence of the Mighty One that Zion should be rooted up (and it has hap- 5 pened in your days). And also against the two and a half tribes there went out a decree that they too should be carried off as 6 captives (as you have now seen). And to such lengths did the impiety of Manasseh go that the glory of the Most High departed 7 from the sanctuary. For this reason Manasseh was even in his own 8 day called 'The Impious', and his final lodging was in the fire. For though the Most High at last heard his prayer when he was shut up in[1] the bronze horse, and the horse was melting, and a sign was 9 given to him then, his life was far from perfect, and all he deserved 10 was to know by whom he would be tormented in the end.[2] For he who is able to do good is also able to punish.

LXV. Thus Manasseh did many wicked things, and he thought that in his time the Mighty One would not inquire into them. 2 These are the black ninth waters that you saw.

LXVI. And the bright tenth waters that you saw – these are the faithfulness of the generation of Josiah, king of Judah, who was the only one at the time who submitted himself to the Mighty One with 2 all his heart and soul. And he purged the land of idols, and hallowed all the vessels that had been polluted, and restored the offerings to the altar, and lifted up the heads[1] of the holy, and exalted the righteous, and honoured men of wisdom and understanding, and brought back the priests to their ministry, and destroyed and removed the magicians and soothsayers and

---

[1] Lit. 'when he was thrown into'.
[2] 'Text corrupt' (Charles).

[1] Lit. 'the horn'.

3 necromancers from the land. And not only did he kill the impious that were still alive, but he also had the bones of the dead taken
4 from their graves and burnt. And the festivals and the sabbaths he restored with their proper rites:[2] he burned those who were polluted: he burned also the lying prophets that had deceived the people; and the people that had listened to them he threw alive into
5 the brook Kidron, and raised a heap of stones over them. And he devoted himself heart and soul to the Mighty One; and he was remarkable in his day for his strict observance of the law,[3] so that during his life-time no one that was uncircumcised was left any-
6 where in the land, nor any evil-doer. He will indeed receive an eternal reward, and he will be more honoured by the Mighty One
7 than many at the last time. For it was because of him, and those like him, that the honours and the glories you were told about
8 before were created and prepared. These are the bright waters that you saw.

LXVII. And the black eleventh waters that you saw – these are the
2 calamity that has now overtaken Zion. Do you imagine that the angels in the presence of the Mighty One experience no pain that Zion should be so delivered up, and when they see the Gentiles boasting in their hearts, and crowds before their idols saying,

> She is now trodden down, she who so often trod *others* down,
> And she has been reduced to servitude, she who reduced
> *others*?

3 Do you imagine the Most High rejoices at this, or that his name is
4 thereby glorified? How will it serve towards his righteous judge-
5 ment? Yet after this, great troubles will afflict those who are dispersed among the Gentiles, and wherever they may be living
6 they will be humiliated. So long as Zion is delivered up and Jerusalem laid waste, idols will prosper in the Gentile cities; and *while* the sweet smoke of the incense of the righteousness which is according to the law no longer ascends in Zion, it will be replaced

---

[2] Charles rendered 'he established in their sanctity', although the last word is plural.

[3] Lit. 'and he alone was firm in the law at that time'.

everywhere in Zion's neighbourhood by the smoke of godlessness.[1]
7 And the king of Babylon, who has now destroyed Zion, will exalt
   himself, and he will make great claims in the Most High's pre-
8,9 sence. But he also will come to grief at last. These are the black
   waters.

LXVIII. And the bright twelfth waters that you saw – this is the
2 meaning *of them*. After all this, a time will come when your people
   will be in such a sorry state that there is a risk of their perishing
3 altogether. Even so, they will be saved, and their enemies will fall
4,5 before them. And for a time they will have much joy. And then,
   after a short interval, Zion will be rebuilt, and its offerings will be
   restored again, and the priests will return to their ministry, and the
6 Gentiles also will come and acclaim it.[1] However, things will not be
7 as they were in former times. And after this, disaster will strike
8 many nations. These are the bright waters that you saw.

LXIX. The last[1] waters that you saw, darker than all that had been
   before them – those *waters* that came after the gathering together of
2 the twelve other waters concern the whole world. For the Most
   High made a separation at the beginning,[2] because he alone knows
3 what will happen. As for the enormities and impious deeds that
4 would be committed before him, he foresaw six kinds of them. And
   as for the good deeds of the righteous to be done before him, he
   foresaw six kinds of them *also*, apart from what he himself would do
5 at the consummation of the age. That is why there were not black
   waters *mixed* with black, nor bright with bright;[3] for it is the
   consummation.

   ¹ Lit. '. . . in Zion, and in the place of Zion everywhere, lo, there is the smoke of
   godlessness'.

   ¹ Lit. 'come to glorify it'.

   ¹ Lit. 'other'.
   ² The phrases 'gathering together' and 'make a separation' recall the language of
   Gen. i. 7 and 10.
   ³ This, as it stands, is obscure. What is clear, however, is that the black waters of
   the 'consummation' and the bright waters that follow are to be understood as
   distinct from the previous alternations of black and bright waters in the course of
   world history.

LXX. Hear then the interpretation of the last black waters which
2 are to come after the *other* black *waters*: this is the meaning. Behold,
the days are coming, and when the time of the age has ripened, and
the harvest[1] of its evil and its good seeds has come, the Mighty One
will bring upon the earth and its inhabitants, and upon its rulers,
3 trepidation of spirit[1] and consternation of mind. And they will hate
one another, and provoke one another to fight; and obscure men
will have dominion over men of reputation, and the lowly born will
4 be exalted above the nobles. And the many will be delivered into
the hands of the few, and those who were nothing will rule over the
strong, and the poor will have much more than the rich, and the
5 impious will set themselves up against the brave. And the wise will
be silent, and *only* fools will speak: neither the designs of *ordinary*
men, nor the plans of the powerful,[2] will come to anything, nor will
6 any hopes for the future prove well-founded.[3] And when what has
been predicted has happened, then will confusion descend upon all
men: some of them will fall in battle: some of them will perish in
anguish, and some of them will be **destroyed**[4] by their own people.
7 Then will the Most High reveal those peoples whom he has prepared beforehand, and they will come and make war with the
8 leaders that then are left. And whoever escapes in the war will die
by earthquake, and whoever escapes the earthquake will be
burned by fire, and whoever escapes the fire will be **destroyed**[5] by
9 famine. And whoever, whether of the victors or the vanquished,
escapes all these things, and comes safely through them, will be
10 delivered into the hands of my servant, the Messiah. For the whole
earth will devour those who live on it.

LXXI. But the holy land will have mercy on its own, and will
2 protect those who are living there at that time. This is the vision
3 that you saw, and this is the interpretation of it. And I have come to
tell you this because your prayer has been heard by the Most High.

[1] Plural in the MS.
[2] Singular in the MS.
[3] Lit. 'nor will the hope of those who hope be confirmed'.
[4] Text 'be hindered'.
[5] Text 'will add'.

LXXII.   Listen now also *to what I have to tell you* about the bright
waters[1] that are to come at the consummation after these black
2 *waters*: this is the meaning *of them*. After the signs have appeared,
which you were told about before, when the nations are in confusion, and the time of my Messiah is come, he will call all the nations
together, and some of them he will spare, and some of them he will
3 destroy. This is what will happen to the nations spared by him.
4 Every nation that has not **exploited**[2] Israel and has not trampled
5 the race of Jacob underfoot will be spared. And this will be because
6 some out of all the nations will become subject to your people. But
all those who have had dominion over you, or have **exploited**[2] you,
will be given over to the sword.

LXXIII.   And when he has brought low everything that is in the
world, and has sat down in peace for ever on the throne of his
kingdom,

> Then shall joy be revealed,
> And rest made manifest.
2 And then shall healing descend as dew,
> And disease shall disappear;
> And anxiety and anguish and lamentation shall pass from
> men,
> And gladness spread through all the earth.
3 And never again shall anyone die before his time,
> Nor shall any adversity suddenly befall.
4 And law suits[1] and accusations and contentions and
> revenges,
> And murder[2] and passions and envy and hatred,
> And all things like these shall be done away
> And go to their condemnation.

---

[1] Both here and at lxxiv. 4 Charles substituted 'lightning' for 'waters' to accord
with the details of the vision as given in liii. 8–10.
[2] Text 'known'.

[1] Lit. 'judgements'.
[2] Lit. 'blood'.

5   For it is these things that have filled this world with evils,
    And it is because of these that the life of man has been so
        troubled.

6   And wild beasts shall come from the forest
    And minister to men,
    And asps and dragons shall come out of their holes
    To submit themselves to a little child.

7   And women shall no longer have pain when they bear
        children,
    Nor shall they suffer agony when they yield the fruit of the
        womb.

LXXIV.   And in those days the reapers shall not grow weary,
    Nor those that build be toilworn;
    For both works and workers together
    Will prosper in complete accord.

2   For that time marks the end of what is corruptible
    And the beginning of what is incorruptible.

3   Thus, what was predicted will be fulfilled in it:
    It is beyond the grasp of evil men,
    Accessible only to those who will not die.[1]

4 These are the bright waters[2] that came after the last dark waters.

LXXV.   And I answered and said,

    Who can be compared with thee, O Lord, in thy goodness?
    For it is beyond us altogether.

2   Or who can search out thine infinite compassion?

3   Or who can comprehend thine understanding?

4   Or who is able to describe the workings of thy mind?

5   Who among mortals can hope to come near *doing any of* these
        things,
    Unless he is one of those to whom thou art merciful and
        gracious?

---

[1] So, strictly, the Syriac, which has masculines for 'evil' and 'those who will not die'. It is possible, however, to take the Syriac masculines as a misunderstanding of original neuters – as Charles ('It is far away from evils, and near to those things which die not').

[2] See note on lxxii. 1.

6   For if thou didst not have compassion upon man,
        Those who are under thy right hand
        Could not achieve these things –
        Only those who are called to be among the number thou hast
            determined.[1]
7   But if we, who are alive, know for what reason we have
            come,[2]
        And submit ourselves to him who brought us out of Egypt,
        We shall come again[3] and remember what is past,
        And rejoice in what has been.
8   But if we do not know for what reason we have come[2]
        And do not recognize the sovereignty of him who brought us
            out of Egypt,
        We shall come again[3] and regret[4] what has been now,
        And grieve over what is past.

LXXVI.   And he answered and said to me, Since the interpretation
of this vision has been given you as you asked, Listen to what the
Most High has to say, so that you may know what is to happen to
2 you after this. For you must certainly leave this world, yet you will
not die, but you will be preserved until the consummation[1] of the
3 times. So go up to the top of that mountain, and you will get a view
of the entire land and be able to distinguish its various features[2] –
the tops[3] of the mountains, the bottoms[3] of the valleys, the depths
of the seas, and the many rivers, so that you can see what you are
4 leaving behind and where you are going. This shall be in forty days
5 time from now. But now go and spend these days teaching the
people as best you can, so that they may understand what will lead
to death and what to life in the last times.[4]

---

    [1] Lit. 'who are able to be called in the numbers named'.
    [2] i.e. 'we have been born'.
    [3] i.e. at the resurrection.
    [4] Lit. 'desire'.

    [1] Text 'but to the preservation'. Cp. xiii. 3 and xxv. 1.
    [2] Lit. 'and all the regions of the land shall pass before you and the figure of the
world'.   [3] Singular in the MS.
    [4] Lit. 'so that they may learn so as not to die in the last times, but may learn in
order that they may live in the last times'.

LXXVII. And I, Baruch, went away; and I came to the people, and
2 I called them together, high and low alike. And I said to them,
Listen, you sons of Israel: see how many there are of you who have
3 survived, out of the twelve tribes of Israel. For *it was* to you and to
4 your fathers *that* the Lord gave the law, and not to all peoples. And
because your brothers disobeyed the Most High's commandments
he brought retribution both on you and on them: he did not spare
the one, and he caused the others to be led away as captives and left
5,6 none of them behind. But you are here with me. If, then, you direct
your ways aright, you will not go as your brothers went; but they
7 will come to you. For he whom you worship is merciful, and he in
whom you hope is gracious; and he can be relied on to do good and
8,9 not evil. You have seen, have you not, what happened to Zion? Do
you think, perhaps, that it was the place that sinned, and that it
was because of this that it was overthrown? Or *again*, that the land
had committed some outrage, and that was why it was delivered
10 up? Are you not aware that it was because of you, who had sinned,
that *the city*, which had not sinned, was overthrown, and that it was
because of *you* evil-doers that *the land*, which had done no evil, was
11 delivered up *to its* enemies? And the whole people answered and
said to me, So far as we can recall the good things the Mighty One
has done for us, we do recall them; and what we do not remember,
12 he in his mercy knows. But do this for us, your people: write to our
brothers in Babylon a letter on a scroll, *a letter* of instruction and
encouragement, to reassure them also before you leave us.

13   For the shepherds of Israel have perished,
       And the lamps that gave light have gone out,
       And the fountains have held back their streams,
       From which we used to drink.
14   And we are left in darkness,
       Amid the trees of the forest, and in the thirst of the
            wilderness.

15   And I answered and said to them,

       Shepherds and lamps and fountains come from the law;
       And though we depart, yet the law remains.
16   If, then, you respect the law and turn your hearts to wisdom,

A lamp will not be wanting and a **shepherd**[1] will not fail,
And no fountain will dry up.

17 But, as you asked me, I will write *a letter* to your brothers in Babylon, and I will send it by the hands of men; and I will write also *a* similar *letter* to the nine and a half tribes, and send it by

18 means of a bird. And on the twenty-first day of the eighth month, I, Baruch, came and sat down under the oak[2] in the shade of its

19 branches, and no one was with me – I was alone. And I wrote two letters: one I sent by an eagle to the nine and a half tribes; and the other I sent to those that were in Babylon by the hands of three

20,21 men. And I called the eagle and said to it, The Most High created

22 you to be the king of[3] all the birds. Go now: stop nowhere *on your journey*: neither look for any roosting-place,[4] nor settle on any tree, till you have crossed the broad waters of the river Euphrates, and come to the people that dwell there, and laid this letter at their feet.

23 Remember how, at the time of the flood, a dove brought Noah back

24 an olive,[5] when he had sent it out from the ark. Ravens, too, waited on Elijah, and brought him food, as they had been commanded.

25 Solomon also, when he was king, whenever he wanted to send a message or find out anything, would give instructions to a bird,

26 and it obeyed his instructions. And now, never mind how tired you are: do not stray from your course, either to right or left, but fly straight there; and carry out the instructions of the Mighty One, as I have explained them to you.

The Letter of Baruch, the son of Neriah, which he wrote to the Nine and a Half Tribes.

LXXVIII. This is the letter[1] that Baruch, the son of Neriah, sent to the nine and a half tribes, which were across the river Euphrates, in which these things were written.

2   Baruch,[2] the son of Neriah, to his brothers in captivity, Mercy

---

[1] Text 'mind'.   [2] Cp. vi. 1.
[3] Lit. 'to be higher than'.   [4] Lit. 'neither enter a nest'.
[5] Lit. 'the fruit of an olive'.

[1] Lit. 'These are the words of the letter'.
[2] Lit. 'Thus says Baruch'.

3 and peace *to you*. I can never forget, my brothers, the love of him who created us, who loved us from the beginning and never hated
4 us, but rather subjected us to discipline. Nor can I forget that all we of the twelve tribes are united by a common bond, inasmuch as we
5 are descended from a single father. Hence my concern to leave you in this letter, before I die, some words of comfort amid the evils that have come upon you, *in the hope* that you may also be moved to share in your brothers' grief at the evil that has befallen them, and, again, that you may accept as just the sentence *the Most High* passed upon you, namely, that you should be carried off as captives (even though what you have suffered is scarcely in proportion to what you did), in order that in the last times you may be found
6 worthy of your fathers. For if you realize that what you now suffer is for your good, so that you may not in the end be condemned and tormented, then you will receive eternal hope – if, that is, you have purged your minds of the vanities and errors that were the cause of
7 your being taken away. For if you do this, he will remember you continually, he who always promised on our behalf to those who were far superior to ourselves, that he will never forget us or forsake us, but in the greatness of his mercy will gather together again those who have been dispersed.

LXXIX. Now, my brothers, hear first what happened to Zion, how
2 Nebuchadnezzar, king of Babylon, made an attack on us. (For we had sinned against him who created us and had not kept the commandments he gave us, although he did not chasten us as we
3 deserved.) And so we feel far greater sympathy for you since what happened to you happened also to us.[1]

LXXX. And now, my brothers, I tell you that when the enemy had surrounded the city, the angels of the Most High were sent, and *it was* they *who* threw down the fortifications of the strong wall and destroyed the firm iron corners, which could not be dislodged.
2 But they hid **all** the vessels[1] of the sanctuary, so that they should not

---

[1] Both text and translation here are very uncertain.

[1] Text 'But they hid the vessels of the vessels'.

3   be polluted by the enemy.[2] And when they had done this, they
    surrendered to the enemy the wall that had been thrown down, the
    plundered house, the burnt temple, and the people who were
    overcome because they had been surrendered, so that the enemy
    could not boast and say, By our prowess in battle have we been
4   able to lay waste even the house of the Most High. Your brothers,
    too, were put in chains and taken away to Babylon and made to
5   live there. But we have been left here; and there are very few of us.
6,7 This is the wretched situation I am writing to you about. For I
    know full well what a consolation it was for you when Zion was
    inhabited: the knowledge that it prospered was a major consola-
    tion for the suffering you endured in being exiled from it.

1,2 **LXXXI.**   But as to consolation, I should tell you this.[1] I was mourn-
    ing for Zion, and I prayed the Most High for mercy, and I said,

3   Will things continue for us as they are to the end?[2]
        And will these evils come upon us always?
4   And the Mighty One responded[3] in the fullness of his mercy,
        And he spoke to me by way of revelation,[4]
        So that I might receive consolation;
        And he showed me visions,
        So that I should suffer no more anguish;
        And he made known to me the mystery of the ages,
        And the advent of the times he showed me.

    LXXXII.   And so, my brothers, I am writing to you, so that you may
2   find consolation in the midst of your many troubles. Do not doubt
    that our creator will avenge us on all our enemies, in accordance
    with what each one of them has done to us: above all, *have no doubt*
    that the consummation which the Most High has appointed is very
    near, and his mercy that is coming; and the consummation of his
    judgement is not far off.

    ---

    [2] Charles emended 'lest the enemy should **get possession of them**'.

    [1] Lit. 'hear the word'.
    [2] Or (according to other MSS) 'How long will these things continue for us'.
    [3] Lit. 'acted'.
    [4] Lit. 'And he revealed to me the word'.

3   For lo, we see now the Gentiles in great prosperity,
       Though their deeds are impious;
       But they shall be like a breath of wind *that dies away*.

4   And we behold the extent of their power,
       Though what they do is wicked;
       But they shall become like a drop *from a bucket*.

5   And we see the strength of their might,
       Though they resist the Mighty One every hour;
       But they shall be treated like spittle.

6   And we consider their glory and grandeur,
       Though they do not observe the Most High's statutes,
       But they shall disappear like smoke.

7   And we reflect on their beauty and their gracefulness,
       Though they are soaked in pollutions;
       But as grass that withers shall they fade away.

8   And we consider their brutality and cruelty,
       Though they give no thought to *their* end;[1]
       But as a passing wave shall they be broken.

9   And we remark the boastings of their might,
       Though they deny the beneficence of the God who gave *it*
           them;
       But as a passing cloud shall they pass away.

LXXXIII.   For the Most High will assuredly speed up his
       times,
       And he will assuredly bring on his seasons.

2   And he will assuredly judge those who are in his world,
       And will truly punish all men,[1]
       In accordance with their hidden[2] works.

3   And he will assuredly examine *their* secret thoughts,
       And what is stored away in the innermost recesses of their
           being,[3]
       And he will expose and censure *them* openly.

---

[1] Or 'to the end *of it*'.

[1] Lit. 'all things'.
[2] Another reading is 'sinful'.
[3] Lit. 'in the chambers which are in all the limbs of man'.

4   Do not, then, worry yourselves about these present things,[4] but
    rather look to the future, because what has been promised to us will
5   come. And let us not now fix our attention upon the delights the
    Gentiles enjoy in the present *age*, but let us remember what has
6   been promised to us in the end. For set times and seasons,[5] and all
7   that goes with them,[6] will assuredly pass away. And then the
    consummation of the age will reveal the great might of its ruler,
8   when all things come to judgement. So prepare yourselves for *the
    coming of* what you have believed in in the past, so that you do not
    find yourselves the losers in both worlds, by having been carried off
9   as captives here, and being tormented there. For in what is now, or
    in what has been, or in what is to come, in all these things, the evil
    is not entirely evil, nor, again, is the good entirely good.

10 For all the health that now is is turning into disease.
11 And all the strength that now is is turning into weakness,
    And all the might that now is is turning into impotence.
12 And all the energy of youth is turning into old age and
        dissolution,
    And all the beauty and gracefulness that now are are turning
        into decay and ugliness.
13 And all the proud dominion that now is is turning into
        humiliation and shame.
14 And all praise of the splendour that now is is turning into the
        shame of speechlessness,
    And all the luxury and pomp that now are are turning into
        silent ruin.
15 And all the delight and joy that now are are turning to worms
        and corruption.
16 And all acclaim of the pride that now is is turning into dust
        and stillness.
17 And all heaping-up of riches that now is is turning only into
        Sheol.
18 And all the spoils of passion that now are are turning into
        inexorable death,

----

[4] Lit. 'Let none of these present things, therefore, go up into your hearts'.
[5] Lit. 'For the limits of the times and of the seasons'.
[6] Lit. 'and all that is in them'.

And all passion of the lusts that now is is turning into a
    judgement of torment.

19 And all artifice and craftiness that now are are turning into a
    proof of truth.

20 And all sweet-smelling ointments that now are are turning
    into judgement and condemnation.

21 And all love of falsehood is turning into well-earned
    degradation.

22 Since, then, all these things are happening now, can anyone be-
23 lieve that vengeance is far off?[7] The consummation of all things will
result in truth.

LXXXIV. Behold, I have informed you about these things while I
am still alive, and I am telling you *about them* so that you may
understand what is worth pursuing;[1] for the Mighty One has
commissioned me to instruct you, and I will, *therefore*, remind you
2 of some of the precepts he has given us[2] before I die. Remember
how Moses at one time summoned heaven and earth to witness
against you and said, If you transgress the law you will be scat-
3 tered, but if you keep it you will be firmly planted[3] *in your land*. And
other things, too, he told you when you, the twelve tribes, were
4 together in the wilderness. But after his death you rejected them;
5 and so there came upon you what had been predicted. Moses told
you beforehand, so that it might not happen to you; and it hap-
6 pened to you,[4] because you forsook the law. And now I also tell
you, after you have suffered, that if you take note of what you have
been told, you will receive from the Mighty One whatever has been
7 appointed and reserved for you. Furthermore, may this letter
stand as a witness *between us* (between you and me), so that you
may remember the commandments of the Mighty One, and that I
8 also may have a defence before him who sent me. Remember the

---

[7] Lit. 'that they will not be avenged?'

[1] Lit. 'that you may learn the things that are excellent'.
[2] Lit. 'and I will set before you some of the commandments of his judgement'.
[3] Another reading is 'you will be kept'.
[4] Or 'Moses told you before it happened to you, and it happened to you'.

law and Zion, the holy land and your brothers, and the covenant of
9   your fathers; and do not forget the festivals and the sabbaths. And
hand on this letter and the traditions of the law to your sons after
10 you, just as your fathers handed *them* on to you. Be always regular
in your prayers, and pray diligently with all your heart that the
Mighty One may restore you to his favour, and that he may not
take account of your many sins, but remember the faithfulness of
11 your fathers. For if he is not to judge us in the fullness of his mercy,
woe to all of us poor mortals![5]

LXXXV.   Consider, too, that in days gone by and in the generations
of old our fathers had to help them[1] righteous men and holy
2   prophets. Moreover, we were in our own land; and they helped us
when we sinned, and, relying on their merits,[2] interceded for us
with our creator, and the Mighty One heard their prayer and
3   forgave us. But now the righteous have been gathered *to their
fathers*, and the prophets have fallen asleep, and we also have been
exiled from *our* land: Zion has been taken from us, and nothing is
4   left us now save the Mighty One and his law. But if we direct and
dispose our hearts *aright*, we shall retrieve everything that we have
lost, and *gain* many more and much better things than we have lost.
5   For what we have lost was subject to corruption, but what we shall
6   receive is incorruptible. (And I am writing also to our brothers in
Babylon in the same terms, to assure them about these things.)
7   Keep everything you have been told constantly in mind, because
so long as the breath is in our bodies we are still free to choose.[3]
8   Once again, the Most High is patient with us here: he has shown us
what is to be and has not hidden from us what is to happen in the
9   end. Before, then, the judgement demands its own, and the truth
what is its due, let us prepare ourselves to take possession, and not
be taken possession of, to hope and not be put to shame, and to
have rest with our fathers and not be in torment with our enemies.
10 For the youth of the world is past, and the strength of the creation

---

[5] Lit. 'all of us who have been born!'

[1] Lit. 'had helpers'.
[2] Lit. 'because they trusted in their works'.
[3] Lit. 'because we are still in the spirit and the power of our liberty'.

already exhausted: the times have run their course and the end is very near: the pitcher is near the cistern, the ship to port, the
11 traveller to the city, and life to *its* consummation. And yet again, prepare yourselves, so that when you have finished your journey and leave the ship, you may find rest and may not be condemned
12 when you go away. For when the Most High brings all these things to pass, there will be there no further opportunity for repentance, no set times[4] nor appointed seasons,[5] no *possible* change in ways *of life*,[6] no place for prayer nor offering[7] of petitions, no acquiring of knowledge nor giving of love, no place of repentance for the soul nor supplication for offences, no intercession by the fathers nor
13 prayer by the prophets nor help from the righteous. But there will be there the sentence of destruction, the way of fire and the path
14 that leads to Gehenna. That is why there is one law, *given by one*
15 *man*, one world and an end for all who are in it. Then will *the Mighty One* preserve those he can forgive, and at the same time destroy those who are polluted by *their* sins.

LXXXVI.   So when you receive this letter that I have written, see
2 that you read it in your congregations. And think about it, es-
3 pecially on your fast-days. And may this letter serve as a means of your remembering me, as I also have remembered you in *writing* it, and always *do remember you*.

LXXXVII.   And when I had finished this letter, and had written it carefully to the very end, I folded it, and sealed it as a safeguard, and tied it to the eagle's neck, and despatched it and sent it off.

Here ends the Book of Baruch, the son of Neriah

---

[4] Lit. 'no limit to the times'.
[5] Lit. 'no length for the seasons'.
[6] The text is uncertain here owing to variations in the MSS.
[7] Lit. 'sending'.

THE GREEK APOCALYPSE
OF BARUCH

INTRODUCTION

There can be little doubt that this apocalypse is 'the book of Baruch the prophet' known in Origen's day and said by him to contain 'very clear information about the seven worlds or heavens'.[1]

The credit for its discovery in modern times belongs to Dom Cuthbert Butler, who found a Greek text of it in 1896 among a collection of apocryphal and ecclesiastical items in a late fifteenth century paper manuscript in the British Library (B.L. Addit. 10073). This Greek text was published by M. R. James in the following year. It mentions, however, only five heavens.

Ten years before Butler's discovery S. Novaković had published the text of a Slavonic version, preserved in a fifteenth century Serbian manuscript; and James printed an English translation of it, by W. R. Morfill, immediately after his own edition of the Greek. This Slavonic text would seem to be even less complete than the Greek, inasmuch as it mentions only two heavens.

Meanwhile, unknown to James, there had been published (in 1894) N. S. Tikhonravov's text of a second Slavonic version contained in a Moscow manuscript, also of the fifteenth century. Subsequently other MSS of both Slavonic versions have come to light, as well as another Greek manuscript. The complications arising from these discoveries, particularly so far as the Slavonic versions are concerned, both in their mutual relationship to one another and in their joint relationship to the Greek, have not been resolved; and it was for this reason that J.-C. Picard, in his edition of 1967, ignored the Slavonic versions altogether, except for several pages devoted to the statement and discussion of some of the problems in his Introduction. However, Picard did make full use of the other Greek MS (Andros, Monastery of the Hagia, 46; 15th

---

[1] Orig. *De princ.* II. iii. 6.

cent.), which he had discovered himself; but unfortunately it is so closely allied to the British Library MS that it is of little help in establishing a critical text.

It is possible that there was at one time a Latin version as well as a Slavonic, which was in circulation at least in the north-western area of Spain in the seventh century. But the evidence here is only indirect. There are no surviving Latin texts or fragments of text.[2]

About the date and origin of the Greek Apocalypse opinions differ. James took the view that it is 'a Christian Apocalypse of the second century'. There are some passages that could have been written only by a Christian. The author betrays knowledge, not only of the Pauline epistles, but also of certain of the apocryphal writings – notably of the Paraleipomena of Jeremiah, which (on Harris's dating) is assignable to AD 136. Yet the Greek Apocalypse was known to Origen. It must accordingly be dated *c*. AD 140–200.

In opposition to James, L. Ginzberg was of the opinion that the book was almost wholly Jewish. 'Only one passage', he maintained, 'can with certainty be considered a Christian interpolation; and that is the one concerning the vine . . . in ch. iv'. The author, moreover, betrays signs of both Indian and Gnostic influence. He was, therefore, a Jewish Gnostic, who wrote 'about the beginning of the second century, when gnosis was at its height among both Jews and Christians'.[3]

H. M. Hughes, in the Introduction to his translation in R. H. Charles's *Apocrypha and Pseudepigrapha*, trod a middle road between these two extremes. For Hughes the framework of the apocalypse was characteristically Jewish, and a number of features mark it out as a work of Jewish origin. But 'the hand of a Christian redactor can be traced in certain interpolations'. These interpolations are not confined to the passage about the vine in chap. iv: they are, in fact, 'most evident in the concluding chapters'. The original (Jewish) apocalypse, according to Hughes, is to be dated somewhere near the beginning of the second century, and the Christian redactor 'soon after AD 136'. The book in its present form is thus

---

[2] See M. R. James in *JTS* xvi (1915), p. 413.
[3] L. Ginzberg in *JE* ii (1902), p. 551.

roughly contemporary with Jeremiah's Paraleipomena (on Harris's dating), a product of the same circumstances, and inspired by the same motives – i.e. 'the conversion of Jews and Ebionites'.

Any ultimately acceptable solution to this question will thus obviously depend on what answers are given to the two subsidiary, but related, questions: (1) How compelling in themselves are the alleged Christian elements, and how integral are they to the work as a whole?; and (2) How significant are the parallels with the other Baruch literature, and how are these parallels best explained?

The passage concerning the vine in chap. iv is universally admitted to be Christian, though, if we are thinking of it as a Christian interpolation, opinions may differ about the actual extent of the interpolation (iv. 15 is in fact the only verse in the passage that is incontrovertibly Christian). At xiii. 4 the mention of the renegades 'in *the* church' (ἐν ἐκκλησίᾳ) and of '*their* spiritual fathers' sounds Christian enough: on the other hand at xvi. 4 the reference to those who 'despised my commandments and my assemblies (τῶν ἐκκλησίων μου), and insulted the priests who proclaimed my words to them', though it may be Christian, is more naturally taken as Jewish; and our judgement in either case is likely to depend on whether we translate ἐκκλησία as 'church' or 'assembly'. Similarly, the catalogues of vices at iv. 17, viii. 5 and xiii. 4, may be echoes of such New Testament passages as Matt. xv. 19 ‖ Mark vii. 21–22 and Gal. v. 19–21; or they may equally well be explained as no more than part of the stock-in-trade of any ancient writer who was concerned with morals, whether pagan, Jewish, or Christian.[4] Evidence of this kind is unfortunately indecisive.

Of far more significance is the occurrence of the rather curious word translated 'smite' at xvi. 3 (διχοτομήσατε: lit. 'cut in two'). This word also occurs in an almost identical context at Matt. xxiv. 51 ‖ Luke xii. 46, where it is usually remarked on by the commentators and not infrequently explained as a misunderstanding of an Aramaic original on the part of the Greek translator of one of

[4] Cp. e.g. Diog. Laert. vii. 110–114 (Zeno); Dead Sea *Man. Disc.* iv. 9–11; Wisd. xiv. 25–26; Philo, *De post. Cain.* xv; *Ep. Barn.* xx. 1–2.

the Gospel sources. What makes the use of the word at Gk. Apoc. xvi. 3 even more significant is the fact that it is found only three verses after a very clear reminiscence of Matt. xxv. 21 (one of the three passages bracketed by Hughes as indubitably Christian interpolations). Add to this two phrases found elsewhere ('no living creature would be preserved', viii. 7; and 'God . . . shortened its days', ix. 7), compare them with 'And except the Lord had shortened the days, no flesh would have been preserved; but for the sake of the elect . . . he shortened the days' (Mark xiii. 20 || Matt. xxiv. 22); and it is difficult to escape the conclusion that we are dealing in the Greek Apocalypse with an author who is writing with the Lord's Discourse concerning the End in mind, and, moreover, with someone who knew it in its Markan form as well as its Matthaean.[5] And we might take the point even further by arguing that the whole idea of the three classes of angels, some of whom offer Michael baskets full of flowers, others baskets only partially full, and yet others nothing at all (the idea worked out in detail in chaps. xii–xvi) was inspired from the same Gospel source – i.e. by the scene at the end of the Parable of the Talents, where one servant offers his master five talents gained by trading, another two, but a third nothing (Matt. xxv. 14–30).

All this means that we cannot account satisfactorily for such a complicated situation either by suggesting that it is accidental or just by positing 'Christian interpolation' and leaving it at that. The final redactor, or editor, or author, whoever he may have been, was undoubtedly a Christian. Whatever Jewish material he may have used he certainly re-phrased and very thoroughly recast. He was not a mere interpolator.

The parallels with the other Baruch literature can be dealt with more briefly, since there are no verbal parallels other than those which arise naturally out of the narrative setting. In verse 2 of the Prologue Baruch is introduced, located beside a river, 'weeping over the captivity of Jerusalem': this corresponds generally to the contents of Syr. Apoc. v. 5–6 and vi. 2, and Par. Jer. iv. 6–10. The statement in the next verse that 'he was sitting at the beautiful

---

[5] To appreciate the full force of this argument the relevant texts should be compared in Greek in each instance.

gates, where the Holy of Holies lay', can be compared with Syr. Apoc. x. 5 and xxxiv. 1–xxxv. 1.[6] The particularly noteworthy feature in this verse is the reference to Abimelech and his being 'preserved by the hand of God at Agrippa's farm', which plainly refers to the contents of Par. Jer. iii. 9–10, 15, v. 1–vi. 1, even if not to the text.[7] And then immediately, at the beginning of chap. i, the statement that Baruch was weeping over Jerusalem's captivity is repeated (though this time in the first person), with the additional information that this was made the occasion for an angelic visitation: we may compare again Syr. Apoc. vi. 2 and Par. Jer. iv. 6–10 with the addition of Syr. Apoc. vi. 3–4 and Par. Jer. iv. 11.

It is thus evident that the Greek apocalypse belongs squarely within what may be called 'the Baruch tradition', so far as its narrative setting is concerned. But there are few, if any, contacts outside this setting. If we are prepared to take the text of the opening verses as they stand, we can argue equally well either that the author knew both the Syriac Apocalypse and the Paraleipomena much as we know them to-day, or, alternatively, that he had access to much the same sources and traditional material that their authors had. If, however, we are doubtful about whether the Prologue is an original part of the book (on the ground that it refers to Baruch in the third person, whereas the rest of the book purports to have been written by Baruch himself in the first person), the case for direct knowledge of the Syriac Apocalypse and the Paraleipomena on the part of our author is very much weaker, inasmuch as the most telling contacts are to be found in the Prologue only. But in either case it is tempting to see the Greek Apocalypse as a later apocalyptist's amplification of the situation described so neatly at Par. Jer. iv. 11 ('And he [i.e. Baruch] remained, sitting on a tomb, while the angels came and told him in detail about everything'). In no case are there grounds for positing dependence in the reverse direction. The Greek Apocalypse may be later than the other two works, or it may be contemporary with them: it is unlikely to be earlier.

---

[6] At Par. Jer. iv. 11 (cp. vi. 1 and vii. 1) Baruch sits on a tomb.

[7] Agrippa's property is described as a χωρίον ('farm'–lit. 'place', 'estate') at Gk. Apoc. prol. 2 and Par. Jer. iii. 15, v. 25, but as an ἀμπελών ('vineyard') at Par. Jer. iii. 10.

There remains the question of the identity of our present book with 'the Book of Baruch, the prophet' known in Origen's day. Origen says that his book gave information about seven heavens (the usual number when a plurality of heavens is mentioned), whereas our book treats of only five. Is our surviving text an abbreviated recension of the original? Was Origen suffering from a lapse of memory when he specified seven heavens? If he was not familiar with the contents of the book himself, had he been mis-informed about the details? Or was he referring to a different book altogether?

Since the translation which follows has been based on that of Hughes, it has been thought best to retain the square brackets which Hughes inserted to identify what he thought were the more noteworthy Christian interpolations.

BIBLIOGRAPHY

EDITIONS

Greek

M. R. JAMES, 'The Apocalypse of Baruch' in *Apocrypha Anecdota* ii (= *TS* V. i (Cambridge, 1897), pp. li–lxxi and 83–94).

J.-C. PICARD, *Apocalypsis Baruchi Graece* (= *PVTG* ii (Leiden, 1967), pp. 61–96).

Slavonic

S. NOVAKOVIĆ, 'Otkrivenje Varuhovo' in *Starine*, xviii (Zagreb, 1886), pp. 203–209.

N. S. TIKHONRAVOV, *Apokrificheskie skazaniya* (= *SORYaS* lviii. 4 (St. Petersburg 1894), pp. 48–54).

M. I. SOKOLOV, 'Apokrificheskoe Otkrovenie Varukha' in *Drevnosti: trudy Slavyanskoi komisii Imperatorskogo Moskovskogo arkheologicheskogo obshchestva*, iv, 1 (Moscow, 1907), pp. 201–258.

I. IVANOV, *Bogomilski knigi i legendi* (Sofia, 1925), pp. 193–200.

TRANSLATIONS

English

H. M. HUGHES in R. H. CHARLES, *APOT* ii, pp. 527–541.

W. R. MORFILL, 'The Apocalypse of Baruch: Translated from the Slavonic' in *Apocrypha Anecdota* ii (= *TS* V. i (Cambridge, 1897), pp. 95–102).

German

V. RYSSEL in E. KAUTZSCH, *APAT* ii, pp. 446–457.

P. RIESSLER, *AjSaB²*, pp. 40–54.

W. HAGE in *Jsh-rZ* V. 1 (1974), pp. 1–44.

N. BONWETSCH, 'Das slavisch erhaltene Baruchbuch' in *Nachrichten von der Königl. Gesellschaft der Wissenschaften zu Göttingen, Philolog.-hist. Klasse* (1896: Heft i; Göttingen, 1896, pp. 91–101). [Of the Slavonic.]

GENERAL

A.-M. DENIS, *IPGAT*, pp. 79–84.

O. EISSFELDT, *OTI*, pp. 630–631.

L. GINZBERG, art. 'Baruch, Apocalypse of (Greek)' in *JE* ii (1902), pp. 549–551.

M. R. JAMES, 'Notes on Apocrypha vi: Traces of the Greek Apocalypse of Baruch in other writings' in *JTS* xvi (1915), pp. 410–413.

W. LÜDTKE, 'Beiträge zu slavischen Apokryphen: 2. Apokalypse des Baruch' in *ZAW* xxxi (1911), pp. 219–22.

P. RIESSLER, *AjSaB²*, pp. 1269–1270.

L. ROST, *EATAP*, pp. 86–88.

E. SCHÜRER, *GjVZJC⁴* iii, pp. 313–314.

É. TURDEANU 'Apocryphes bogomiles et apocryphes pseudo-bogomiles' in *Revue de l'histoire des religions,* cxxxviii (1950), pp. 177–181.

——, L'*Apocalypse de Baruch* en slave' in *Revue des Études slaves,* xlviii (1969), pp. 23–48.

Prologue

A narrative and revelation of Baruch concerning those ineffable things which he saw by command of God. May the Lord add his blessing.[1]

2   A revelation of Baruch, who was beside the river Gel[2] weeping over the captivity of Jerusalem, when also Abimelech was pre-
3   served by the hand of God at Agrippa's farm. And he was sitting at the beautiful gates, where the Holy of Holies lay.

I.   I, Baruch, was weeping in my mind and **sorrowing**[1] on account of the people, and because Nebuchadnezzar the king had been
2   permitted by God to destroy his city, saying, Lord, why didst thou set on fire thy vineyard and lay it waste? Why didst thou do this? And why, Lord, didst thou not punish us in some other way, but didst deliver us to nations such as these, so that they reproach *us*
3   and say, Where is their God? And behold, as I was weeping and saying such things, I saw an angel of the Lord coming and saying to me, Listen Baruch,[2] *for you are a man* much beloved: do not be so distressed about the condition of Jerusalem – so says the Lord, the
4   Almighty. For he has sent me to you to make known and to show
5   you all the things of God. For your prayer has been heard by him
6   and has reached the ears of the Lord God. And when he had said this to me, I was silent. And the angel said to me, Argue with God no more, and I will show you other mysteries, greater than these.
7   And I, Baruch, said, As the Lord God lives, if you will show me and I hear from you, I will say nothing more: may God hold it against
8   me[3] in the day of judgement if I do say more! And the angel of the powers said to me, Come and I will show you the mysteries of God.

II.   And he took me and brought me where the vault of heaven was set, and where there was a river that no man can cross, nor any

---

[1] Lit. 'Bless thou, O Lord'.
[2] James suggested 'Kidron', an original *ΚΕΔ[ΡΩΝ]* having been corrupted into *ΓΕΛ*: cp. Syr. Apoc. v. 5, xxi. 1, xxxi. 2.

[1] Reading πενθῶν for ἔχων.
[2] Lit. 'Understand, O man'.
[3] Lit. 'God shall add judgement to me'.

2 alien creature[1] from any of those that God created. And he took me
and brought me to the first heaven and showed me a door of great
size; and he said to me, Let us go in through it. And we went in as if
we were being carried along on wings, about a thirty days' journey.
3 And he showed me a plain inside the heaven; and there were men
living on it with the faces of oxen, and the horns of stags, and the
4 feet of goats, and the hind-quarters of lambs. And I, Baruch, asked
the angel, Tell me, pray, what is the extent of the heaven in which
we journeyed, what are its dimensions, and what is the plain, so
5 that I also may tell my fellow men? And the angel, whose name was
Phamiel,[2] said to me, This door that you see is *the door* of the
heaven, and the extent of *the heaven* is as great as the distance from
earth to the heaven; and again, the length of the plain you saw is as
6 great as *the distance* ⟨from north to south⟩. And again the angel of the
powers said to me, Come and I will show you greater mysteries.
7 But I said, I pray you show me what these men are. And he said to
me, These are *the men* who built the tower of strife against God, and
the Lord banished them.

III.   And the angel of the Lord took me and brought me to a second
heaven and showed me there also a door like the first and said, Let
2 us go in through it. And we went in, carried on wings, about a sixty
3 days' journey. And he showed me a plain there too, and it was full
4 of men; and they looked like dogs, and *their* feet *like* stags' feet. And
5 I asked the angel, *My* lord, I pray you tell me who these are? And
he said, These are *the men* who planned the building of the tower;
for *the men* you see deported multitudes of both men and women to
make bricks (and no woman who was making bricks was allowed
to stop, even when about to give birth to a child, but had to
produce her child while she was still making the bricks, and
6 support her child in *her* apron, and go on making the bricks). And
when they had built the tower to *a height* of four hundred and
sixty-three cubits the Lord appeared to them and confused their

---

[1] Or 'breeze'.
[2] A corruption, either of 'Phanuel', which is supported by the Slavonic here (cp.
1 Enoch xl. 9, liv. 6, lxxi. 8, 9, 13), or of 'Remiel' (cp. Syr. Apoc. lv. 3: also 1 Enoch
xx. 8 and 2 Esdras iv. 36).

7 speech. And they took a drill and tried to bore through the heaven,
saying, Let us see *whether* the heaven is made of clay, or of brass, or
8 of iron. When God saw this he would not allow them to, but struck
them with blindness and confusion of speech, and made them as
you see.

IV. And I, Baruch, said, Behold, *my* lord, you have shown me *some*
great and wonderful things; and now show me all things for the
2 Lord's sake. And the angel said to me, Come let us go through *it*.[1]
⟨And I went⟩ with the angel from there about a hundred and
3 eighty-five days' journey. And he showed me a plain and a serpent,
which appeared to be two hundred plethra in length.[3] And he showed
4 me Hades; and it looked dark and god-forsaken. And I said, Who is
5 this dragon, and who is the cruel *creature* round him? And the angel
said, The dragon is the one who eats the bodies of those who live
6 wicked lives, and he depends on them for sustenance. And this is
Hades, which itself is very like him, in that it drinks about a cubit
out of the sea, and *yet the level of the sea* does not go down at all as a
7 result. Baruch said, And how *is this*? And the angel said, Listen, the
Lord God made three hundred and sixty rivers, of which the most
important are Alphias, Abyrus, and the Gericus; and it is because
8 of these *that the level of* the sea does not go down. And I said, Show
me, I pray you, which tree it was that led Adam astray. And the
angel said to me, It was the vine, which the angel **Sammael**[3]
planted, and the Lord God was angry about it and cursed him and
his plant; and for this reason he forbade Adam to touch it, and that
was why the devil was roused to envy and deceived him through
9 his vine. [And I, Baruch, said, Since then the vine has been the
cause of so much evil, and is under the judgement of the curse of
God, and *brought about* the destruction of the first created man, how
10 is it that it is now so useful? And the angel said, A good question.
When God brought the flood upon the earth, and destroyed all
mankind[4] and four hundred and nine thousand giants, and the

---

[1] It would seem that the entry to the third heaven is to be located here, but that
the descriptive details have somehow fallen out of the text. Cp. n[1] to chap. x.
[2] Reading ὡς ὁράσεως πλέθρα σ´ for ὡς ὡράσεως πέθρας (i.e. nearly four miles).
[3] Text 'Samuel': cp. ix. 7.   [4] Lit. 'flesh'.

water rose fifteen cubits above the highest *mountains, then* the water
entered Paradise and destroyed every flower *there*; but it dislodged
the vine[5] from its place inside Paradise altogether and thrust it out.

11 And when the earth appeared out of the water, and Noah came out
12 of the ark, he began to plant some of the plants he found. And he
found a shoot of the vine[6] and picked it up and asked himself, What
13 is it? And I came and told him about it. And he said, Shall I plant
it, or what *shall I do*? If Adam was destroyed because of it, I have no
desire to incur God's anger through it. And so saying he prayed
14 that God would reveal to him what to do about it. He prayed
earnestly and wept for forty days; and when he had finished his
prayer he said, Lord, I entreat thee to reveal to me what to do
15 about this plant. And God sent his angel Sarasael and said to him,
Up, Noah, and plant the shoot, for these are the Lord's words,

> Its bitterness shall be changed into sweetness,
> And its curse shall become a blessing,
> And what is produced from it shall become the blood of God.

And as it was through it that the human race was condemned, *so*
again through Jesus Christ, the Immanuel, will they be restored in
16 him and gain entry into Paradise.] But you must realize, Baruch,
that just as it was through this very tree that Adam was condemned and divested of the glory of God, so men who now **drink**[7]
the wine that comes from it without moderation are worse transgressors than Adam, and are far from the glory of God and on the
17 road to eternal fire. For ⟨no⟩ good comes out of it. Those who drink
to excess are led astray in all sorts of ways:[8] brother has no pity for
brother, nor father for son, nor children for parents: from **drinking**[9]
wine come all *evils* – murders, adulteries, fornications, perjuries,
thefts, and such like; and nothing good is achieved by it.

V. And I, Baruch, said to the angel, Let me ask you one thing, *my*
2 lord. You told me that the dragon drinks a cubit out of the sea: tell

---

[5] Lit. 'the shoot of the vine'.
[6] Lit. 'the shoot'.
[7] Reading πίνοντες for δρῶντες.
[8] Lit. '. . . excess do these things'.
[9] Reading πόσεως for πτώσεως.

3 me also how big is his belly? And the angel said, His belly is Hades;
and it extends about as far as three hundred men can throw a
plummet.[1] But come, so that I may show you even greater
wonders[2] than these.

VI.   And he took me and brought me to where the sun starts out *on*
2 *its daily journey*. And he showed me a chariot and four, under which
burned a fire; and in the chariot a man was sitting, wearing a
crown of fire, *and* the chariot *was* drawn by forty angels. And
behold, a bird *was* circling before the sun, about nine . . . away.[1]
3 And I said to the angel, What is this bird? And he said to me, This
4 is the guardian of the world. And I said, *My* lord, how is it the
5 guardian of the world? Explain to me. And the angel said to me,
This bird flies beside the sun, and, as it stretches out its wings, it
6 catches *the sun's* fiery rays. If it did not catch them, the human race
would not be preserved, nor any other living creature. God
7 appointed this bird *to do this*. And *the bird* stretched out its wings,
and I saw on its right wing some very large letters indeed, *as large* as
the area of a threshing-floor – about four thousand modii; and the
8 letters were of gold. And the angel said to me, Read them. And I
read *them*, and they said this, Neither earth nor heaven brought me
9 to the birth, but wings of fire brought me to the birth. And I said,
10 What is this bird, *my* lord, and what is its name? And the angel said
11 to me, Its name is Phoenix. And ⟨I said⟩, What does it eat? And he
12 said to me, The manna of heaven and the dew of the earth. And I
said, Does the bird excrete? And he said to me, It excretes a worm,
and the excrement of the worm is cinnamon, which kings and
13 princes use. But wait and you shall see the glory of God. And while
he was talking with me there came a thunder-clap, and the place
was shaken where we were standing. And I asked the angel, What
is this noise, *my* lord? And the angel said to me, The angels are now
opening the three hundred and sixty-five gates of heaven, and the
14 light is being separated from the darkness. And a voice came,

---

[1] Lit. 'and as far as a plummet is thrown ⟨by⟩ three hundred men, so big is his
belly'.   [2] Lit. 'works'.

[1] The text reads ὡς ὄρει ἐννέα, for which no satisfactory emendation has yet been
proposed.

15 which said, Lightgiver, give brightness to the world. And when I
16 heard the bird's cry I said, What is this cry, *my* lord? And he said,
This is *the bird* that wakes up the cocks on earth. For just as **others do
through their mouths**,[2] so too does the cock proclaim his message to
those who are in the world in his own way. For the sun is made
ready by the angels, and the cock crows.

VII. And I said, And where does the sun begin its labours after the
2 cock crows? And the angel said to me, Listen, Baruch. All the
things I showed you are in the first and second heaven; and in the
third heaven the sun passes through and gives brightness to the
3 world. But wait and you shall see the glory of God. And while I was
talking with him, I saw the bird, and it appeared in front, and it
4 grew smaller and smaller, and *then* returned to its full size. And
behind *the bird*[1] I saw the shining sun, and the angels with it
drawing *it*, and a crown on its head – a sight too brilliant for our
5 eyes to look upon. And as soon as the sun shone the phoenix
stretched out its wings. And when I beheld such great glory I was
reduced to abject terror, and I backed away and hid in the wings of
6 the angel. And the angel said to me, Do not be afraid Baruch: only
wait and you shall see their setting also.

VIII. And he took me and brought me to the west. And when the
time of the setting came, I again saw the bird coming in front, and
the sun coming with the angels; and as soon as it came I saw the
2 angels, and they took the crown off its head. But the bird stood
3 exhausted and with its wings folded. And when I saw this I said,
Why did they take the crown off the sun's head, *my* lord, and why is
4 the bird so exhausted? And the angel said to me, The sun's crown,
when it has been through the day, four angels take it and carry it up
to heaven and renew it, because its rays have been defiled on earth;
5 and so it is renewed in this way each day. And I, Baruch, said, And
why, *my* lord, are its rays defiled on earth? And the angel said to
me, Because it beholds the lawlessness and unrighteousness of men
– *their* fornications, adulteries, thefts, extortions, idolatries,

---

[2] Reading τὰ διὰ στόματος for τὰ δίστομα.

[1] Lit. 'this'.

carousals, murders, quarrels, jealousies, slanders, wranglings, gossipings, divinations, and so forth, which are not pleasing to
6 God: that is why it is defiled, and that is why it is renewed. And *you asked* about the bird, how it gets exhausted. It keeps the suns rays under control through the fire and burning heat of the entire day,
7 and it gets exhausted by it. For, as we said before, unless its wings acted as a screen to the sun's rays, no living creature would be preserved.

IX.   And when they had gone away, the night fell, and with it *came*
2 **the chariot**[1] of the moon, together with the stars. And I, Baruch, said, *My* lord, show me this also, I beg you, how it goes out, where
3 it goes from, and in what form it moves along. And the angel said, Wait, and you shall see this also shortly. And on the next day I saw it in the form of a woman, sitting in a wheeled chariot. And in front of it were oxen, and there were lambs in the chariot, and a multi-
4 tude of angels likewise. And I said, What are the oxen and the
5 lambs, *my* lord? And he said to me, They also are angels. And again I asked, Why is it that at one time it waxes, but at another wanes?
6 ⟨And he said to me,⟩ Listen, Baruch, What you are looking at now was intended by God to be the most beautiful of all the things he
7 made.[2] And when the first Adam sinned, it was near Sammael when he took the serpent as a garment. And it did not hide itself away; and God was angry with it and punished it, and shortened
8 its days. And I said, And how is it that it does not shine always, but only in the night? And the angel said, Listen: as courtiers cannot speak freely in the presence of a king, so the moon and the stars cannot shine in the presence of the sun; for the stars are always suspended *in their places*, but they are overpowered[3] by *the light of* the sun, and the moon, although it is not injured, is worn out by the sun's heat.

X.   And when I had learned all these things from the archangel, he

---

[1] Reading τὸ ἅρμα for μετὰ καί.
[2] Lit. 'this (fem.) which you are looking at was written by God beautiful as no other (fem.)'.
[3] Lit. 'dispersed'.

2 took *me* and brought me into a **fourth**[1] heaven. And I saw a level
3 plain, and in the middle of it a pool of water. And there were in it
many flocks of birds of all kinds, but not like those here *on earth*; for
the crane I saw *was as big* as great oxen, and all *the birds* were much
4 bigger than those in the world. And I asked the angel, What is the
plain, and what is the pool, and what are the many flocks of birds
5 round it? And the angel said, Listen, Baruch: the plain that has the
pool in it and other wonders is *the place* where the souls of the
righteous come whenever they meet together in groups to talk to
6 one another. But the water is what the clouds receive and rain
7 upon the earth and cause *its* fruits to grow.[2] And I said to the angel
of the Lord again, And the birds? And he said to me, They are
8 those which sing the Lord's praises continually. And I, Baruch,
said, *My* lord, how is it that men say that the water which descends
9 as rain is from the sea? And the angel said, What descends as rain is
from the sea, and also from the waters on earth; but what makes
10 the fruits grow is from the latter source. You must understand that
this is where what is called the dew of heaven comes from.

XI. And the angel took me and brought me from there to a fifth
2 heaven. And the gate was shut. And I said, *My* lord, cannot this
gateway be opened[1] for us to go in? And the angel said to me, We
cannot go in until Michael comes, who holds the keys of the
kingdom of heaven: only wait and you shall see the glory of God.
3 And there was a great noise, like thunder. And I said, What is this
4 noise, *my* lord? And he said to me, Prince Michael is now coming
5 down to receive the prayers of men. And behold, a voice came,
saying, Let the gates be opened! And they were opened;[2] and there
6 was a roar, as of thunder. And Michael came, and the angel who

---

[1] The text reads 'third'. But Baruch is conducted into 'a fifth heaven' at xi. 1;
hence we must presume that the events recorded in chaps. iv–ix happened in the
third heaven, despite the absence of any explicit indication to that effect at iv. 1–2.
Cp., however, vii. 2: also n.[1] to chap. iv.
[2] Lit. 'and the fruits grow'.

[1] Lit. 'is not this gateway opened'.
[2] Lit. 'And they (impersonal) opened *them*'.

was with me met him and made obeisance to him and said,
7 Greetings, my prince, and *prince* of all our order. And Prince
Michael said, Greetings to you also, our brother and the inter-
8 preter of the revelations to those who live good lives. And after
saluting one another in this way, they stood still. And I saw that
Prince Michael had in his hands an enormous bowl: it was as deep
as *the distance* from heaven to earth, and as wide as *the distance* from
9 north to south. And I said, *My* lord, what is it Prince Michael is
holding? And he said to me, This is where the merits of the
righteous enter, and such good works as they do, which are carried
in it into the presence of the God of heaven.

XII. And as I was talking with them, behold, angels came with
2 baskets full of flowers; and they gave them to Michael. And I asked
the angel, Who are these, *my* lord, and what are they bringing with
3 them? And he said to me, These are the angels *who are* over the
4 **righteous.**[1] And the archangel took the baskets and emptied them
5 into the bowl. And the angel said to me, These flowers are the
6 merits of the righteous. And I saw other angels carrying baskets
that were ⟨neither⟩ empty nor full.[2] And they began to lament and
would not come near because what they had to offer was imperfect.[3]
7 And Michael cried out and said, Come here, you angels, and bring
8 *me* what you have brought as well. And Michael was very sad (as
was also the angel who was with me) because they did not fill the
bowl.

XIII. And there came in the same way other angels weeping and
wailing, and saying in fear, See, lord, how worn out we are,[1] for we
2 were allotted to evil men, and we want to get away from them. And
Michael said, You cannot get away from them, or the Enemy will
3 win the victory in the end; but tell me what you are asking for. And
they said, We beg you, Michael, our prince, transfer us away from
them, for we cannot remain attached to wicked and foolish men,

---

[1] Reading δικαίων for ἐξουσιῶν.
[2] Reading οὔτε κενὰ οὔτε γέμοντα for κενὰ οὐ γέμοντα.
[3] Lit. 'because they had not the prizes complete'.

[1] Lit. 'how blackened we are'.

for there is nothing good in them, but *only* every kind of un-
4 righteousness and greed. For we have never seen them devoting
themselves [in *the* church either to *their* spiritual fathers or] to any
one good thing,[2] but where there is murder, there are they in the
middle of it, and where there are fornications, adulteries, thefts,
slanders, perjuries, envyings, carousals, quarrels, jealousies,
wranglings, idolatry, divination, and so forth, there are they doing
things like this, and others worse. So we beg you to let us be quit of
5 them. And Michael said to the angels, Wait till I have been told by
the Lord what is to happen.

XIV. And Michael departed immediately, and the doors were
2 shut; and there was a noise like thunder. And I asked the angel,
What is the noise? And he said to me, Michael is now presenting
the merits of men to God.

XV. And then Michael came down *again*, and the gate was
2 opened; and he was carrying oil. And *he went to* the angels with the
baskets *that had been* full; and he filled them with oil, saying, Take *it*
away, reward our friends a hundred times over – those who have
toiled in patience and done good things; for those who have sowed
3 generously shall also reap generously. And he said also to those
who had brought the baskets that were not full, Come here as well:
take the reward that is due for what you brought, and distribute *it*
4 among the race of men. [Then he said both to those who had
brought the full *baskets* and to those *who had brought the baskets that
were* not full, Go and bless our friends and say to them, So the Lord
says, You have been[1] faithful in a **few things**,[3] he will put you in
control of many things: come and share the joy of your Lord.]

XVI. And he turned round and said to those who had brought
nothing, The Lord says *to you*, Do not be gloomy and weep; and do

---

[2] Lit. 'For we did not see them enter in church ever either into spiritual fathers or
into one good thing'. The syntax here is very difficult and it may well be that the
original text has been tampered with.

[1] Lit. 'You are'.

[2] Reading ἐπὶ ὀλίγα for ἐπὶ ὀλίγῃ.

2 not leave the race of men alone. But inasmuch as they angered me by what they did, go and make them jealous and angry and embittered against *a people that is* no people, against a people that 3 has no understanding. And more – afflict them with caterpillar and maggot, and rust and locust, ⟨and⟩ hail with flashes of lightening and wrath, and smite them[1] with sword and with death, and their 4 children with demons. For they did not heed my voice, neither did they observe my commandments nor do *them*; but they despised my commandments and my assemblies,[2] and insulted the priests who proclaimed my words to them.

1,2 **XVII.** And as he spoke the door was shut, and we withdrew. And the angel took me and restored me to *where I was* at the beginning. 3 And when I came to myself I ascribed glory to God, who had 4 accounted me worthy of so great an honour. And do you, *my* brothers, who have been granted such a revelation, ascribe glory to God also yourselves, so that he too may glorify you now and always, even to all eternity. Amen.

---

[1] Lit. 'cut them in two'. See Introduction (pp. 899–900 above).
[2] Or 'and my churches' (Gk. καὶ τῶν ἐκκλησίων μου).

THE APOCALYPSE OF ZEPHANIAH
AND
AN ANONYMOUS APOCALYPSE

INTRODUCTION

The details of the discovery of the Coptic MSS containing the text of these apocalypses, the problems involved in the arrangement of the individual leaves in some sort of intelligible order, and the opinions of the editors and other scholars who have worked on them, have already been treated in the Introduction to The Apocalypse of Elijah.[1]

According to Steindorff three distinct works are preserved in these leaves, in varying degrees of completeness: (1) an apocalypse of Zephaniah, of which only a very small portion has been preserved on one side of one of the Sahidic leaves,[2] and to the text of which there is no parallel in the Akhmimic; (2) an apocalypse of Elijah, contained on the last thirteen Akhmimic leaves in the order in which Steindorff arranged them, and also on the remaining six Sahidic leaves, which offer (with gaps) a parallel text to a considerable portion of the Akhmimic text; and (3) an 'Anonymous' apocalypse contained in the first nine of the Akhmimic leaves.

Nearly all subsequent authorities have followed Steindorff to the extent of distinguishing the first two apocalypses – the passage on the single Sahidic leaf where Zephaniah speaks in the first person ('Truly I, Zephaniah, saw') has been generally regarded as conclusive evidence that on this leaf, at least, we have before us part of the text of a Zephaniah apocalypse, while the colophon at what appears to be the end of the Akhmimic codex ('The Apocalypse of Elijah') was usually taken to be sufficient proof that what immediately precedes it was the text of an Elijah apocalypse, even before the publication of the much fuller Sahidic text of this apocalypse contained in P. Chester Beatty 2018 left no doubt at all about its separate identity.

[1] See above, pp. 753–5.
[2] The text on the other side of this leaf is illegible.

But beyond this there has been less unanimity. The first nine
leaves of the Akhmimic codex (according to Steindorff's arrangement) are so markedly different in subject-matter from the last
thirteen (i.e. the Elijah apocalypse) that they must belong to a
different work. The question is, Is that 'different work' yet a third,
independent, apocalypse (for about its being an apocalypse there
can be no doubt at all), or is it part (indeed, the major part) of the
Zephaniah apocalypse?

As we have seen, Steindorff preferred the former alternative; and
he called his third apocalypse 'The Anonymous Apocalypse', because in the portion of its text that has been preserved the seer is
not named. But this further distinction of Steindorff's has been
challenged from more than one angle. It has been pointed out that
the fact that there is no Akhmimic parallel to the single Sahidic
'Zephaniah' leaf, whereas there are Akhmimic parallels to the
remaining six Sahidic leaves, is almost certainly accidental: the
majority of the surviving Akhmimic leaves have no Sahidic parallels; and there is no reason to suppose that the coverage is likely to
be complete on one side rather than the other. In any case, the
Akhmimic text of the presumed 'Anonymous' is itself far from
complete: we do not know, for instance, how much is missing at the
beginning; and the Sahidic 'Zephaniah' fragment may well belong
there, or in the gap in the middle, or, even, at the end. Moreover,
there are some very evident contacts in subject-matter between the
'Zephaniah' leaf and the 'Anonymous': both are concerned with
the torments of Hell; and there are several coincidences of
language, the most obvious being concentrated in Apoc. Zeph. 6–7
and 'Anon.' Apoc. i. 11–12. All this tells in favour of their not being
two independent works, but one and the same.

A further complication was introduced into the debate by the
publication in 1940 by L. Th. Lefort[3] of a very small, and for the
most part illegible, fragment, which may have some bearing on
the problem. As reconstructed by Lefort, the text of the fragment
ends with the words '⟨Truly I Ze⟩phaniah saw ⟨these things⟩',
followed by the colophon '⟨The Apocalypse of Ze⟩phan⟨iah⟩'. If we

---

[3] L. Th. Lefort, *Les manuscrits coptes de l'Université de Louvain*, i (= *Textes Littéraires*;
Louvain, 1940), pp. 79–80.

are to trust Lefort's reconstruction, and if there is any relationship at all between the new fragment and the previously known 'Zephaniah' leaf, it would seem that the first lines on the 'Zephaniah' leaf, as far as 'Truly I, Zephaniah, saw and took note of these things', are the conclusion of the Zephaniah apocalypse, and that what follows (from 'And the angel of the Lord . . .') belongs to something else – unless, of course, 'Truly I, Zephaniah, saw these things' was a kind of refrain, occurring regularly throughout the apocalypse at the end of each section, and then, finally, at the very end. However, in view of the fact that on Lefort's fragment only very few complete words are legible, it would be unwise to pursue the possibilities here.

For these reasons it has been thought best to treat the whole of the 'Zephaniah'-'Anonymous' material together and print the translations of the Sahidic and Akhmimic texts one after the other. Those who follow Steindorff can then read them, as he did, as fragments of two separate works. Those who do not can either read them as fragments of the same work (i.e. as all belonging to the Apocalypse of Zephaniah), or alternatively indulge in whatever re-ordering of the individual leaves and identification of their contents they please.

A Zephaniah apocalypse was certainly known in the early Church, since one is mentioned in the List of Sixty Books; and this apocalypse is in all probability the same work as 'The Book of the Prophet Zephaniah' mentioned by pseudo-Athanasius and the Stichometry of Nicephorus. An indication of contents may perhaps be found in a solitary quotation in Clement of Alexandria. The passage in Clement runs as follows:

> 'Are not these statements like those of Zephaniah the prophet? "And the spirit took me, and brought me up to the fifth heaven, and I beheld angels called lords; and their diadem had been set upon them by the Holy Spirit; and each of them had a throne seven times brighter than the light of the rising sun; and they dwelt in temples of salvation, and they hymned the ineffable Most High God." '[4]

But Clement's quotation has no parallel, either in the Sahidic

[4] Clem.-Alex. *Strom.* V. xi. 77.

'Zephaniah' fragment or in what remains of Steindorff's 'Anonymous'; nor is there any obvious gap anywhere into which it might suitably be fitted.

The Sahidic 'Zephaniah' fragment affords no clue as to the origin of its text: that text might be Jewish in origin: it might be Christian; and it might equally well be a re-working by a Christian of an originally Jewish source. On the other hand, most agree that the 'Anonymous' was in origin Jewish, but that the Jewish original has been reworked by a Christian, though far less drastically than the associated Apocalypse of Elijah: there are in the 'Anonymous' no unequivocally Christian passages or phrases, but there are several apparent reminiscences of the New Testament.[5]

As in the Apocalypse of Elijah, the translation is based on the texts as edited by Steindorff and his page numeration has been inserted in brackets where applicable, in order to facilitate reference.[6] 'Sa' = 'Sahidic' and 'A' = 'Akhmimic'.

BIBLIOGRAPHY

EDITIONS

Coptic

U. BOURIANT, 'Les papyrus d'Akhmim (Fragments de manuscrits en dialectes bachmourique et thébain)' in *Mémoires publiés par les membres de la mission archéologique française au Caire*, tom. i, fasc. 2 (Paris, 1885), pp. 242–304.

G. STEINDORFF, *Die Apokalypse des Elias, eine unbekannte Apokalypse, und Bruchstücke der Sophonias-Apokalypse: koptische Texte, Übersetzung, Glossar* (= *TU* xvii (N.F. ii) 3a; Leipzig, 1899).

TRANSLATIONS

English

H. P. HOUGHTON, 'The Coptic Apocalypse' in *Aegyptus*, xxxix (1959), pp. 40–91.

[5] e.g., with i. 3 cp. Matt. xxiv. 40–41 ‖ Luke xvii. 34–35; with ii. 10–12 cp. Rev. i. 13, 15, ii. 18, xix. 10, xxii. 8–9; and with iii. 18 cp. 1 Cor. xv. 38.

[6] See above p. 759.

French

U. BOURIANT, 'Les papyrus d'Akmim . . . [as above].

German

L. STERN, 'Die koptische Apocalypse des Sophonias, mit einem
  Anhang über den untersahidischen Dialect' in *Zeitschrift fur
  ägyptische Sprache und Alterthumskunde* (Leipzig, 1886), pp. 115–
  135.
G. STEINDORFF, *Die Apokalypse des Elias . . .* [as above].
P. RIESSLER, *AjSaB*², pp. 168–177.

GENERAL

A.-M. DENIS, *IPGAT*, pp. 192–193.
J.-B. FREY, art. 'Apocryphes de l'A.T.' in *DBSup* i, cols. 456–458.
M. R. JAMES, *LAOT*, pp. 72–74.
P. RIESSLER, *AjSaB*², pp. 1274–1275.
W. SCHNEEMELCHER, 'Spätere Apokalypsen' in E. HENNECKE
  and W. SCHNEEMELCHER, *Neutestamentliche Apokryphen*³, ii
  (Tübingen, 1964), pp. 533–534. [Translated, by E. BEST, in
  NTA ii, pp. 751–752.]
E. SCHÜRER, *GjVZJC*⁴ iii, pp. 367–369.
H. WEINEL in *EUX*, pp. 162–164.

THE APOCALYPSE OF ZEPHANIAH

(Sa 1)⟨I saw⟩ a soul, five thousand angels set over it ⟨and⟩ guarding
it, taking ⟨it⟩ to the east, and carrying it to the west, striking . . .
2 giving it hundred (?) . . . scourges each one daily. I was afraid: I
3 threw myself on my face, for my knees were weak. The angel gave
me his hand. He said to me, Be victorious that you may be
victorious, and be strong that you may be victorious over the
4 accuser and may come up from hell.[1] And when I got up, I said,

---

[1] Cp. Anon. Apoc. iii. 1, 6–7 (pp. 923 and 924 below).

5 And who is this they are set over? He said to me, This is ⟨a⟩ soul whose lawless doings were no secret;[2] and before it succeeded in
6 repenting, it was visited and taken out of its body. Truly I, Zephaniah, saw and took note of these things.[3]

7   And the angel of the Lord walked with me. I saw a wide open place, with thousands upon thousands surrounding it on the left and myriads upon myriads on the right.[4] The nature of each one was different, their hair all loose like women's hair, ⟨their⟩ teeth like the teeth of . . . .[5]

AN ANONYMOUS APOCALYPSE

I.   (A 1) . . . dies, we will bury him like every man: if he dies, we will carry him out, and play the lyre before him, and sing our songs over his body.
2   But I went with the angel of the Lord. He took me over my whole
3 city. There was no one to be seen. Then I saw two men walking together on the same road: I saw ⟨them talking⟩. And I saw also two women grinding at a mill together; and I saw them talking. And I saw ⟨also⟩ two on ⟨one⟩ couch, ⟨both of them taking⟩ their
4 ⟨rest(?)⟩ on their couch. ⟨And I saw⟩ the whole world ⟨suspended⟩ like a drop of ⟨water, hanging from a bucket⟩ (A 2) that comes up
5 ⟨from⟩ a well.[1] I said to the angel of the Lord, Is there no darkness nor night in this place? He said to me, No; for where the righteous and the saints are, in that place there is no darkness, but they are
6 always in the light. And I saw all the souls of men who were undergoing punishment. And I cried out unto the Lord Almighty, ⟨How long⟩ wilt thou abide with the saints and be patient with the
7 world ⟨and⟩ these souls which are undergoing punishment? The

    [2] Lit. 'a soul which was found in its lawlessness'.
    [3] Lit. 'saw, seeing these things'. For the possibility that these words mark the end of the apocalypse see the Introduction (pp. 916–7 above).
    [4] Cp. Anon. Apoc. i. 11.
    [5] Cp. Anon. Apoc. i. 12, ii. 7.

    [1] Cp. Isa. xl. 15. The text is restored following P. Lacau ('Remarques sur le manuscrit akhmimique des Apocalypses de Sophonie et d'Élie' in *Journal asiatique*, ccliv (1966), pp. 169–195).

angel of the Lord said to me, Come and I will show you . . . of
righteousness. And he took me up onto mount Seir; *and* he ⟨showed
me⟩ three men, (A 3) with whom two angels were walking, happy
8 and rejoicing over them. I said to the angel, Who[2] are these? He
said to me, These are the three sons of Joatham the priest, who did
not keep their father's commandment, nor did they observe the
statutes of the Lord. Then I saw two more angels weeping over the
9 three sons of Joatham the priest. I said ⟨to⟩ the angel, Who are
these? He said, These are the angels of the Lord Almighty, who
write down all the good works of the righteous upon **their**[3] roll,
while they ⟨sit⟩ at the gate of heaven. But I take them from them
and bring them ⟨up⟩ (A 4) before the Lord Almighty for him to
10 write their name in the book of the living. And the other angels of
the accuser, who is on the earth, also write down all the sins of men
upon their roll; and they too sit at the gate of heaven and read them
out to the accuser for him to write them down on his roll, so that he
11 can accuse them when they come out of the world down below. I
then walked *further* with ⟨the⟩ angel of the Lord, *and* I looked in
front of me: I saw a place there . . . thousand and myriads upon
12 myriads of angels walking through ⟨it.[4] Their⟩ face was like a
panther's, their tusks protruded from their mouths ⟨like⟩ a wild
boar's, their eyes (A 5) were bloodshot, their hair all loose like
13 women's hair,[4] and they had scourges of fire in their hands. And
when I saw them, I was afraid; *and* I said to that angel who was
14 walking with me, Who[5] are these? He said to me, These are the
attendants upon the whole creation, who come to the souls of the
ungodly and take them and put them here. They spend three days
going round with them in the air before they take them and hurl
15 them into their eternal punishment. I said, I pray you, *my* lord, give
16 them no authority to come to me. The angel said, Have no fear: I
will not allow them to come to ⟨you⟩, for you are holy before (A 6)
the Lord: I will not allow them to come to you, for the Lord
17 Almighty has sent me to you, for ⟨you are⟩ holy before him. Then
he signalled to them, and they turned back and kept their distance
from me.

---

[2] Lit. 'What sort'.   [3] Text 'his'.
[4] Cp. Apoc. Zeph. 7.
[5] Lit. 'What sort'.

II.   But I walked with the angel of God. I looked in front of me; *and*
I saw gates. Then, when I approached them, I found they were
gates of copper. The angel touched them *and* they opened before
2   him. I went in with him. I found myself in what seemed to be the
main street of[1] ⟨a⟩ beautiful city. I walked down the middle of it.
Then the angel of the Lord transformed himself beside me there.
3   And I looked and I saw[2] gates of copper with bolts of copper and
bars of iron. (A 7) And they closed against me there. I saw in front
of me the gates of copper breathing out fire *to a distance of* about fifty
4   stades. Again I turned;[3] *and* I saw a great sea. And I thought it was
a sea of water. I found it was a whole sea of fire, like a marsh, that
breathed out fire continually, and its waves burned with sulphur
5   and pitch. They began to come near me. I thought therefore that
the Lord Almighty had come to visit me. When I saw ⟨him⟩,[4] I fell
6   on my face before him to worship him. I was very much afraid. I
implored (A 8) him to save me from this torment. I cried out,
saying, Eloi, Lord Adonai Sabaoth, I entreat thee to save me from
this torment that has come upon me.

7   Then[5] I stood *up*. I saw a great angel in front of me, his hair flying
out *round his head* like the lionesses, his teeth *showing* outside his
mouth like a bear's, his hair flying out like women's,[6] while his
8   body was like serpents who wanted to swallow me. And when I saw
him, I was so afraid of him that every limb in my body was
9   paralysed. I fell down on my face: I was not able to stand. I prayed
before (A 9) the Lord Almighty, *I pray thee that* thou wilt save me
from this torment, thou who didst deliver Israel from Pharaoh,
king of Egypt, thou who didst deliver Susanna out of the hand of
the unrighteous elders, thou who didst deliver the three saints,
Shadrach, Meshach, *and* Abednego, out of the fiery blazing
furnace, I pray thee that thou wilt save me from this torment.

10   Then I got up *and* stood *upon my feet*. I saw a great angel standing

---

[1] Lit. 'I found its whole street like that of'.

[2] Lit. 'And I looked at them, and I found that they were'.

[3] Here follows a word (lit. 'they will walk') which seems to have no place in the
context.   [4] So Lacau

[5] Lit. 'In that same hour'.

[6] Cp. Apoc. Zeph. 7 (p. 920 above).

in front of me: his face shone like the **rays**[7] of the sun in its glory: his face was like the face of a man filled with its glory; and he had what looked like a golden girdle round his breast, *and* his feet were like
11 brass (A 10) refined by fire. And when I saw him, I rejoiced, for I thought the Lord Almighty had come to visit me. I fell on my face:
12 I worshipped him. He said to me, It is God you must pay homage to:[8] you must not worship me. I am not the Lord Almighty; but I am the great angel Eremiel, who*se place* is *in the world* below, *and I have been appointed* over the abyss and hell, in which all souls have been imprisoned from the end of the flood, which was upon the
13 earth, until to-day.[9] Then I asked the angel, What is the place I
14 have come **down**[10] to? He said to me, This is hell. I then asked him, Who is this great angel I have seen, who is standing as he is? He said, This is the one who accuses men before the Lord. Then ⟨I⟩ looked: I saw he had a roll (A 11) in his hand, *and* he began to
15 unfold it. And when he had spread it out, I read it in my own language. I found all the sins I had committed written down by him, from my childhood till to-day, all written on that roll of mine
16 without a mistake anywhere. If I had not been to visit ⟨a⟩ sick person or a widow, I found it ascribed to me as a failure on my roll: an orphan I had not visited I found[11] ascribed to me as a failure on
17 my roll. *If there had been* a day when I did not fast, when I did not pray at the hour of prayer, I found it ascribed to me as a very bad thing indeed on my roll; (A 12) and *if there had been* a day when I had not visited the sons of Israel, I found it ascribed to me as a failure
18 on my roll. So I fell down on my face and prayed before the Lord Almighty, May thy mercy reach as far as me and wipe my roll clean; for thy mercy is everywhere and fills every place.

III. Then I got up *and* stood *upon my feet*. I saw a great angel in front of me, saying to me, Be victorious, be strong; for you have been strong, you have been victorious over the accuser, you have come up from hell and the abyss,[1] you shall now cross at the ferry-place.

---

[7] Text 'gifts'.   [8] Lit. 'Devote yourself to him'.
[9] Cp. 1 Enoch xx. 7 (Gk.^a²); 2 Esdras iv. 36.
[10] Text 'up'.   [11] Text 'was found'.

[1] Cp. Apoc. Zeph. 3 (p. 919 above).

2 Again he brought another roll, written by hand: he began to unfold
it. I read in it. I found it was written in my own language . . . *2 pages*
3 *missing* . . . (A 13) They helped me: they set me upon that boat: they
were singing praises before me, namely thousands upon thousands
and myriads upon myriads of angels. I also put on an angelic
4 garment. I saw all those angels praying. I too prayed together with
5 them: I knew their language that they spoke with me. (This, my
sons, is the trial that has to be – that the good and evil *deeds of every*
6 *man* are weighed in a balance.) Then a great angel came out with a
golden trumpet in his hand. He sounded it three times over my
head, saying, Be victorious, *he* who has been victorious, be (A 14)
7 strong, *he* who has been strong. For you have been victorious over
8 the accuser, you have escaped from the abyss and hell.[1] You shall
now cross at the ferry-place; for your name has been written in the
9 book of the living. I wanted to exchange greetings with him; *but* I
10 could not, so great was his glory. Then he hurried off to all the
righteous, to Abraham, and Isaac, and Jacob, and Enoch, and
Elijah, and David. He talked with them like a friend with friends,
while they themselves were in conversation with one another.
11 Then the great angel came to me, the golden trumpet in his hand.
He sounded it up to heaven; *and* the heaven opened from east to
12 west, from north to south. I saw the sea I had seen (A 15) down in
hell: its waves rose up to the clouds. I saw all the souls submerged
in it. I saw some bound with their hands to their necks, and fetters
13 on their hands and feet. I said, Who are these? He said to me,
These are those who **search men out**[2] and give them gold and silver
to lead the souls of men astray.

14   And I saw others covered with fiery mats. I said, Who are these?
He said to me, These are those who lend money on interest and
15 take interest on interest. And I saw others, blind men crying out. I
was astonished when I had seen·all these works of God. I said, Who
16 are these? (A 16) He said to me, These are those who were under
instruction and heard the word of God, but were weak and fell
17 away.[3] But I said to him, Have they no *opportunity for* repentance?
He said, Yes. I said, How long for?[4] He said to me, Until the day

---

[2] Text 'who carry them along'.
[3] Lit. 'but were not perfect in the thing which they heard'.
[4] Lit. 'Until what day?'

18 when the Lord will judge *the world*. And I saw others with their hair on them. I said, Are there hair and body in this place? He said, Yes: the Lord gives them body and hair as he pleases.

19 And I saw very many others *also*: he brought them out, and they looked at all these punishments. They cried out in prayer before the Lord Almighty, saying, We beseech thee (A 17) for those who suffer all these punishments, that thou wouldest have mercy on

20 them all. But when I saw them, I said to the angel who was talking with me, *Who are these*? He said, Those who are interceding with the

21 Lord are Abraham and Isaac and Jacob. At the same time each day they come with the great angel. He sounds the trumpet up to heaven and another fanfare over the earth. All the righteous hear

22 the fanfare. They come running, praying daily to the Lord

23 Almighty for these who suffer all these punishments. And again the great angel comes with the golden trumpet in his hand and sounds it over the earth. It is heard from east to west and from south to north. Again he sounds the trumpet (A 18) up to heaven; *and* his trumpet-call[5] is heard.

24 I said, *my* lord, why did you not let me see them all? He said to me, I have no authority to show them to you, until the Lord Almighty arises in his wrath to destroy the earth and the heavens.

25 They will see *what is happening* and be troubled, and all will cry out, saying, All men[6] who belong to thee, we will give *them* all to thee on

26 the day of the Lord. Who will be able to stand before him when he arises in his wrath to ⟨destroy⟩ the earth and ⟨the heavens⟩? All trees that grow upon the earth will be uprooted with their roots and fall down. And all high towers and the birds that fly ⟨over them⟩ [down and all high towers] will fall ⟨to the ground⟩.[7]

---

[5] Lit. 'sound'.
[6] Lit. 'flesh'.
[7] The text is restored following Lacau. Cp. Apoc. Elijah iii. 62–63 (p. 771 above).

THE APOCALYPSE OF ESDRAS

INTRODUCTION

Apart from the canonical Book of Ezra in the Old Testament, several apocryphal books bearing Ezra's name have been at one time or another known and esteemed in the Church.

In the MSS of the Greek Bible the book entitled 'Esdras A' represents a parallel version of the material contained in the canonical 2 Chron. xxxv–xxxvi, Ezra, and Nehemiah: there are two substantial omissions, one noteworthy addition, and a variety of minor variations both in order and in detail. There is no reason for thinking that Esdras A was derived directly from the canonical Ezra-Nehemiah, either in Hebrew or in Greek: in all probability it was a fresh Greek translation of a different recension of the Hebrew. In the Latin Bible it appears as 'III Ezra' (or Esdras), and it is now usually printed an an appendix after the New Testament. In the English Apocrypha it stands first as '1 Esdras'.[1]

'2 Esdras', which stands next in our Apocrypha, is a completely independent work with complications of its own. In the Latin Bible it is identified as 'IV Ezra' (or Esdras), and in the modern editions follows 'III Ezra' in the appendix. The central part of the book (chaps. iii–xiv) is preserved not only in Latin, but also in not less than seven Oriental versions; and it is evident from quotations in the Fathers that there was at one time a Greek version as well. Most scholars regard chaps. iii–xiv (which are in form an apocalypse) as the original core, written by a Jew in either Hebrew or Aramaic about the end of the first cent. AD, to which were added subsequently chaps. i–ii as an introduction and chaps. xv–xvi as a conclusion. These additions now survive only in Latin, although a 4th cent. fragment of a Greek text of xv. 57–59 is known, having-been published in 1910.[2] It is not uncommon, following the lead of

---

[1] 'Esdras B' of the Greek Bible is the translation of the canonical Ezra-Nehemiah (reckoned as a single book). In the Latin tradition, however, it became the custom to distinguish them: hence in Latin Bibles 'I Ezra' (or Esdras) = the canonical Ezra and 'II Ezra' (or Esdras) = the canonical Nehemiah.

[2] Pap. Oxyr. 1010. Published by A. S. Hunt in *The Oxyrhynchus Papyri*, vii (1910), pp. 11–15.

some of the Latin MSS, to refer to these additions as 'V Ezra' (or Esdras) and 'VI Ezra' respectively.

Standing in the same tradition as 2 Esdras, of which they are plainly later developments, are the three Ezra books translated in this collection – viz. The Apocalypse of Esdras, The Vision of Esdras, and The Apocalypse of Sedrach. Other Ezra books which have not been included in the collection, but which may be mentioned, are: (1) a Syriac apocalypse, edited and translated into German by Baethgen in 1886, which is chiefly concerned with the duration of the rule of Islam;[3] (2) an Ethiopic apocalypse, edited and translated into French by Halévy in 1902,[4] which reviews the whole course of human history from the days of Adam, dividing it into 'weeks', and assigning to Ethiopia and 'the Son of the Lion' a prominent place in the events just before the End; and (3) the Armenian 'Inquiries made by the prophet Esdras of the Angel of the Lord concerning the Sons of Men', the Armenian text of which was printed by Hovsepheantz in 1896[5] and an English translation by Issaverdens in 1901.[4] This last has in general more in common with our three works than either the Syriac or Ethiopic apocalypses, in that in it Esdras enquires (and is informed) about what God has prepared for the righteous and for sinners 'at the end of time', but there are no points of contact in detail.

The Apocalypse of Esdras, with which we are immediately concerned, is known from two MSS. The first (Paris B.N. gr. 929; 15th cent.) contains a text in very poor condition. It was this text that C. Tischendorf used as the basis for his edition of 1866, it being then the only text available. Subsequently a second text in another Paris MS (B.N. gr. 390; 16th cent.) was brought to light, but inasmuch as this text appears to have been copied directly

[3] See F. Baethgen, 'Beschreibung der syrischen Handschrift "Sachau 131" auf der Königlichen Bibliothek zu Berlin' in *ZAW* vi (1886), pp. 199–210.

[4] J. Halévy, 'Te'ezâza Sanbat (Commandements du Sabbat)', accompagné de six autres écrits pseudo-épigraphiques' (= *Bibliothèque de l'École des Hautes Études: section des sciences historiques et philologiques*, fasc. cxxxvii (Paris, 1902), pp. xviii–xxii, 57–79, and 178–195).

[5] S. Hovsepheantz, *A Treasury of Old and New Primitive Writers*. Vol. I (*Uncanonical Books of the Old Testament*; Venice, 1896), pp. 300–304.

[6] J. Issaverdens, *UWOT*[2], pp. 503–509.

from that in the earlier MS its critical value is minimal. Both, of course, were used by O. Wahl in his edition of 1977.

The similarities between our apocalypse and what may be regarded as its model, 2 Esdras, are numerous. Both works grapple with the problem of evil and seek to justify the ways of God to man in the form and language of apocalyptic. God's justice is questioned, and his treatment of the righteous is contrasted with his treatment of the unrighteous. The fundamental question is asked, why was Adam allowed to sin? Man's state under judgement is claimed to be worse than that of the brute beasts. Deep concern is shown for sinners and Esdras pleads for them, that they may be spared, have time and opportunity to repent, and so gain the reward of their repentence. (In the Apocalypse, this concern is emphasised by the incident at the end, where Esdras refuses to surrender his soul and enjoy the eternal life which is promised him until he is satisfied about the fate of these who are being punished for their sins.)

On the other hand, there are few exact verbal parallels between the two works, so that it can hardly be maintained that the writer of the Apocalypse was using 2 Esdras as a source in the accepted sense of that word. The closest parallels are the dating of Esdras's vision in the Apocalypse in 'the thirty-second year' (i. 1; cp. 2 Esdr. iii. 1), the instruction to him to fast (i. 3–5; cp. 2 Esdr. v. 13, vi. 31, 35), the description of Adam as the work of God's hands followed by the details of how he was set in Paradise and there transgressed the Divine command (ii. 10–16; cp. 2 Esdr. iii. 5–7), and the repeated assertion that it were 'better for man not to have been born than to come into the world' (i. 6, 21, v. 9, 14; cp. 2 Esdr. iv. 12, vii. 116). Especially instructive in this connection is such a passage as Apoc. v. 12–13. Here a comparison is made between the 'farmer' who 'sows wheat seed in the earth' and 'man' who 'sows his seed in the field of a woman', and then the process of growth till the time of birth is described in detail. The passage, though intelligible, does not help the argument, and it is difficult to see why it has been placed where it is. The parallel at 2 Esdr. viii. 41, however, is in form a parable ('The farmer sows many seeds in the ground . . ., but not all the seeds sown come up . . . So too in the world of men: not all who are sown will be saved'). There the point is clear enough, the argument is illuminated, and the comparison fits the context admirably. We are left with the impression that the parable in 2 Esdras is primary and that somehow, in the tradition as it has been handed on by the author of the Apocalypse, the original point has been lost, although certain key-words have been preserved.

The Apocalypse as it stands is patently Christian, and, although attempts have been made to explain it as a fundamentally Jewish work with extensive Christian interpolations,[7] they can hardly be said to have been successful. There can be little doubt that the author was a Christian, since Christian features are discernible on almost every page. For instance, Esdras pleads three times for 'the race of Christians', at i. 6, ii. 7, and v. 1: Paul and John are mentioned at i. 19, 'all the apostles' at ii. 1, and 'Peter and Paul and Luke and Matthew' in between 'Enoch and Elias and Moses' and 'all the righteous and the patriarchs' at v. 22: Mark xiii. 7–8, 12–13, 28–29, is clearly the source of iii. 12–13, while 1 Cor. xv. 52 is quoted in part at iv. 36.

There is a presumption, therefore, that our Greek text is not a translation but (apart from its corruptions) what the original author wrote. With this accords the close agreement of vii. 5–7 with the Septuagint Greek text of Isa. xl. 12 and Ps. cxxxvi. 25.

Various dates have been suggested. James, for instance, thought the Apocalypse as late as the 9th cent. AD.[8] Others have dated it earlier.[9] All that can safely be said is that if it stands in the same tradition as 2 Esdras and is indeed a later development of it, then the Apocalypse cannot be dated before *c.* AD 150 at the earliest. Against such an early date is the fact that there are no certainly identifiable quotations from the Apocalypse in any Father; nor is there any certain reference to it in any of the Scriptural lists (the 'Apocalypse of Esdras' mentioned at the very end of the Old Testament items in the List of Sixty Books may be to our

---

[7] Thus, Riessler distinguished: (1) the Jewish base (i. 1–iii. 10; iii. 16–iv. 8; iv. 16–21; v. 6–vi. 2) and (2) the Christian interpolations (iii. 11–15; iv. 9–15; iv. 22–v. 5; vi. 3–vii. 16).

[8] M. R. James, *Apocrypha Anecdota* (= *TS* II. iii; Cambridge, 1893), p. 113.

[9] e.g. P. Batiffol (art. 'Apocalypses apocryphes' in F. Vigouroux *Dictionaire de la Bible*, I. ii (Paris, 1892), col. 765) suggested the 5th–8th cents.

Apocalypse, but it is much more probably a reference to 2 Esdras).

The translation which follows is made from the text as printed by Wahl. And in this connection it is worth observing that the late Greek style in which the Apocalypse is written has combined with the unsatisfactory condition of the MSS to make it extremely difficult in many passages to coax the text into yielding anything approaching a tolerable sense.

BIBLIOGRAPHY

EDITIONS

C. TISCHENDORF, *Apocalypses Apocryphae* (Leipzig, 1866), pp. 24–33.

O. WAHL, *Apocalypsis Esdrae. Apocalypsis Sedrach. Visio Beatae Esdrae* (= *PVTG* iv; Leiden 1977), pp. 25–35.

TRANSLATIONS

English

A. WALKER, *Apocryphal Gospels, Acts, and Revelations* (= *Ante-Nicene Christian Library*, xvi; Edinburgh, 1870), pp. 468–476.

German

P. RIESSLER, *AjSaB²*, pp. 126–137.

U. B. MÜLLER in *JSh-rZ* V. 2 (1976), pp. 85–102.

GENERAL

A.-M. DENIS, *IPGAT*, pp. 91–96.

M. R. JAMES, *The Testament of Abraham* (= *TS* II. ii; Cambridge, 1892), pp. 64–65.

——, in R. L. BENSLY, *The Fourth Book of Ezra* (= *TS* III. ii; Cambridge, 1895), pp. lxxxvi–lxxxix.

P. RIESSLER, *AjSaB²*, p. 1273.

C. TISCHENDORF, 'Einleitung in die Offenbarung des Johannes usw.' in *Theologische Studien und Kritiken* (Hamburg, 1851), pp. 423–431.

B. VIOLET, *Die Esra-Apokalypse* (*IV Esra*) (= *GCS* xviii; Leipzig, 1910), pp. l–lix.

A word and revelation of the holy prophet Esdras, even God's beloved.
May *our* Father add his blessing.[1]

I. It came to pass in the thirty-second year and on the twentieth
2 *day* of the month I was in my house. And I cried out, saying to the
3 Most High, Lord, grant me the privilege to see[2] thy mysteries. And
when it was night there came an angel, Michael the archangel, and
he said to me, From to-morrow, Esdras,[3] you must abstain *from*
4 *food* for seventy *days*. And I fasted as he told me. And Raphael, the
5 prince, came and gave me an incense stick. And I fasted for twice
6 **five**[4] weeks; and I saw God's mysteries and his angels. And I said to
them, I would plead with God for the race of Christians: *it were*
better for man not to have been born than to come into the world.
7 So I was taken up into heaven. And I saw in the first heaven a great
8 company of angels; and they led me to the judgements. And I
heard a voice saying to me, Have mercy on us, Esdras, God's
9 chosen one. Then I began to say, Woe to the sinners, when they see
the righteous above angels, and they themselves are in the fires of
10 hell.[5] And Esdras said, Have mercy on the works of thy hands, thou
11 *who art* full of compassion and mercy: pass sentence on me rather
than on the souls of the sinners; for it is better to punish one soul
12 than to bring the whole world to destruction. And God said, I will
13 give rest to the righteous in Paradise; and I am *indeed* merciful. And
14 Esdras said, Lord, why dost thou favour the righteous? For just as

[1] Lit. 'Bless, Father'.
[2] Lit. 'Lord, give the glory that I may see'.
[3] Lit. 'the prophet Esdras'.
[4] So Walker (thus making seventy days in all): the MSS read 'sixty'.
[5] Lit. 'into the Gehenna of fire'.

a hired servant[6] who has served his time and goes away, and *then* comes again into the service of his *former* master as a slave **by a lucky chance**,[7] so also is the righteous *man who has* received his reward[6] in

15 heaven. But have mercy on the sinners, for we know that thou art
16 merciful. And God said, I do not see how I can have mercy on
,18 them. And Esdras said, They cannot endure thy wrath. And God
19 said, They have brought it on themselves.[8] And God said, I would
20 have you as Paul and John: you offer me freely, uncorrupt, the inviolable treasure, the precious jewel of **virginity**,[9] the rampart of
21 men. And Esdras said, *It were* better for man not to have been born,
22 better not to be alive: the irrational creatures are better when compared with man, because they have *to endure* no punishment.
,24 But thou hast fashioned us, and given us over to judgement. Woe to sinners in the world to come, for their judgement is interminable and *their* flame unquenchable.

II. While I was talking thus with him, Michael came, and Gabriel,
2,3 and all the apostles, and said, Hail, faithful man of God. ⟨And
4 Esdras said,⟩ Up, Lord, and come with me to judgement. And God said, Behold, I give you[1] my covenant, mine and yours,[1] for your[2]
5,6 acceptance. And Esdras said, Let us plead in thine ear. And God said, Ask Abraham your father how a son should plead with a
7 father,[3] and *then* come *and* plead with **me**.[4] And Esdras said, As the Lord lives, I will not cease pleading with thee on behalf of the race
8 of Christians. Where are thy ancient mercies, Lord? Where is thy
9 patience? And God said, As I made night and day, I made the righteous and the sinner, and *the sinner* should have lived as the

---

[6] Gk. μίσθιος ('hired servant') . . . μισθόν ('reward'). Both translation and sense in this verse are far from certain.

[7] Reading ἐπιτυχῶς for ἐπιτυχεῖν.

[8] Lit. 'These things *are* of such men'.

[9] Reading παρθενίας for παρθένου.

[1] Singular.   [2] Plural.

[3] Lit. '. . . your father what sort of son pleads in a father'. (The occurence here of the rare δικάζεσθαι ἐν should be noted, which, if the B text of the LXX at Judg. vi. 32 is any guide, should mean 'plead against': in this case the reference could conceivably be to Gen. xxii rather than to Gen. xviii).

[4] MSS 'us'.

10 righteous. And the prophet said, Who made the first-formed
11 Adam, the first *man*? And God said, My unsullied hands. And I set
12 him in Paradise to keep the pasture of the tree of life. But he then
13 set his mind on disobedience and transgressed. And the prophet
14 said, Was he not guarded by an angel? And was he not watched
over by the cherubim in *this* life *so that he might come* to the world that
15 has no end? How then was it that he who was watched over by
angels was deceived? Thou didst specifically command him to take
16 heed and to conform to what **thou** didst say to him.[5] Yet if thou
hadst not given **him** Eve, the serpent would not have deceived him.
17 **As for thee**, whom thou willest thou dost save, and whom thou
18 willest thou dost destroy. And the prophet said, Let us pass over,
19 my Lord, to a second judgement. And God said, I cast fire upon
20 Sodom and Gomorrah. And the prophet said, Lord, thou dost
21 reward us as we deserve.[6] And God said, Your sins exceed the
22 limits of my tolerance.[7] And the prophet said, Remember the
Scriptures, my Father, **who** didst measure out Jerusalem and set it
23 up: have mercy, Lord, on sinners: have mercy on thy creation:
24 have pity on thy works. Then God remembered what he had made,
25 and he said to the prophet, How can I have mercy on them? They
gave me vinegar and gall to drink, and **not even then** did they
26 repent. And the prophet said, Reveal thy cherubim, and let us go
27 together to judgement; and show me what the day of judgement is
28,29 like. And God said, You are wrong, Esdras; for the day of judgement is like a day on which there is no rain upon the earth:
30,31 compared with that **day**[8] it is a merciful judgement. And the
prophet said, I will not cease pleading with thee, unless I see *that*
32 final day.[9] ⟨And God said,⟩ Count the stars and the sand of the sea;
and if you can count them, you can also plead with me.

III.   And the prophet said, Lord, thou knowest that I am but

---

[5] The text in verses 12–15 is very badly preserved. In consequence, the translation offered is highly questionable.
[6] Lit. 'worthily dost thou bring *it* upon us'.
[7] Lit. 'exceed my kindness'.
[8] Reading ἡμέραν for ἑσπέραν.
[9] Lit. 'the day of the consummation'.

2 human,[1] and how can I count the stars of heaven and the sand of
3 the sea? And God said, My prophet, my chosen one, no man may
   know that great day and the manifestation that must precede the
4 judgement of the world.[2] For your sake, my prophet, I have told
5 you the day, but the hour I have not told you. And the prophet
6 said, Lord, tell me also the years. And ⟨God said,⟩ If I see that the
   world's righteousness has increased, I will be patient with them.
   But if not, I will stretch my hand out and take hold of the world by
   the four corners, and I will collect all *the peoples* into the valley of
   Jehoshaphat, and I will wipe out the race of men, and the world
7 will be no more. And the prophet said, How then can thy right
8,9 hand be glorified? And God said, I am glorified by my angels. And
   the prophet said, Lord, if thou didst purpose so, why didst thou
10 fashion man? Thou didst say to Abraham our father, I will greatly
   multiply your descendants *until they are as numerous* as the stars of
   heaven and as the sand on the sea shore. Where, then, is thy
11 promise? And God said, First I will make earthquakes and bring
12 ruin on beasts and men. And when you see that brother betrays
   brother to death, and children turn against parents, and a wife
13 leaves her own husband, and when nation makes war upon nation,
14 then you will know that the end is near. Then brother will have no
   mercy on brother, nor man on wife, nor children on parents, nor
15 friends on friends, nor slave on master. For the Adversary of men
   himself will ascend from Tartarus and make a great display before
16 men. What shall I do with you, Esdras; and why do you plead with
   me?

IV.   And the prophet said, Lord, I will not cease to plead with thee.
2,3 And God said, Count the flowers on the earth. If you can count
4 them, you can also plead with me. And the prophet said, Lord, I
   cannot count *them*: I am but human;[1] but in spite of this I will not
5 cease *my* pleading with thee. I would, Lord, see also the lower parts
6,7 of Tartarus. And God said, Come down and see. And he gave me
8 Michael and Gabriel and thirty-four other angels. And I went

---

[1] Lit. 'I wear human flesh'.
[2] Lit. 'the manifestation which holds back to judge the world'.

[1] Lit. 'I wear human flesh'.

down eighty-five steps; and they took me down *another* five hundred
9 steps. And I saw a fiery throne, and upon it an old man *was* sitting,
10 and his judgement was merciless. And I said to the angels, Who is
11 this, and what *was* his sin? And they said to me, This is Herod who
for a short spell was a king, and ordered the slaughter of the babes
12,13 from two years old and under. And I said, Alas for his soul. And
again they led me down *a further* thirty steps, and I saw there a
14 seething fire, and in it a multitude of sinners; and I heard their
15 voices, but their forms I did not see. And they led me down many
16 steps lower still, which I could not count. And I saw there aged
men, and red-hot lengths of metal were being screwed[2] into their
17,18 ears. And I said, Who are these, and what *is* their sin? And they
19 said to me, These were[3] eavesdroppers. And they led me down
20 again another five hundred steps. And I saw there the worm that
21 does not sleep, and the fire that consumes the sinners. And they led
me down to the bottom of *the pit of* destruction, and I saw there the
22 twelve plagues of the abyss. And they led me away towards the
south, and I saw there a man hanging by his eyelids, and the angels
23 were scourging him. And I asked, Who is this, and what *was* his
24 sin? And Prince Michael said to me, This man committed incest
with his mother: as a punishment for his miserable lust[4] he was
25 ordered to be hanged. And they led me away towards the north,
26 and I saw there a man held down by iron bars. And I asked, Who is
27 this? And he said to me, This is *the man* who says, I am the son of
28 God, and who made **stones**[5] bread and water wine. And the
prophet said, Lord, tell me what he looks like, and I **will** instruct[6]
29 mankind not to believe him. And he said to me, His face is like a
wild beast's. His right eye is like the Daystar,[7] and the other does
30 not move:[8] his mouth *is* a cubit *across*: his teeth *are each* a span long:
31 his fingers *are* like pruning-hooks: his footmarks *measure* two spans;

---

[2] Lit. 'and burning pivots were turning'.
[3] Lit. 'are'.
[4] Lit. 'having accomplished his little will'.
[5] Reading λίθους for πλήθους.
[6] Reading παραγγελῶ for παραγγέλλω.
[7] Lit. 'like a star that rises early'. Cp. Isa. xiv. 12; Rev. ii. 28, xxii. 16.
[8] Gk. ἀσάλευτος – the Greek Bible rendering for the 'phylactery' which was to be worn 'between the eyes' (at Exod. xiii 16 and Deut. vi. 8, xi. 18).

32 and on his forehead *is* an inscription, 'Antichrist'. He has been
33 exalted to heaven: to hell shall he descend.[9] At one time he will
34 become a child, at another an old man. And the prophet said,
Lord, how canst thou permit *it*,[10] and *meanwhile* the human race is
35 led astray? And God said, Listen, my prophet: he becomes both a
child and an old man, and *yet* no one believes him, that he is my
36 beloved son. And after this a trumpet will sound,[11] and the tombs
37 will be opened, and the dead will be raised incorruptible. Then the
Adversary, when he hears the fearful threat, will hide himself
38 outside in the darkness. Then will the heaven and the earth and the
39 sea be destroyed: then will I burn the heaven *to the extent of* eighty
40 cubits and the earth *to the extent of* eight hundred cubits. And the
41 prophet said, And what sin has the heaven committed? And God
42 said, When ⟨. . .⟩ there is the evil.[12] And the prophet said, Lord, and
43 what sin has the earth committed? And God said, When the
Adversary, after hearing my fearful threat, has hidden himself, and
because of this, I will melt the earth in a furnace and with it the
rebel of the human race.

V. And the prophet said, Have mercy, Lord, on the race of Christ-
2 ians. And I saw a woman hanging, and four wild beasts *were*
3 sucking her breasts. And the angels said to me, This woman *not only*
begrudged to give her milk, but she also threw *her* infants into the
4 rivers. And I saw grim darkness and night without stars or moon.
5 And there is there neither young nor old, nor brother with brother,
6 nor mother with child, nor wife with husband. And I wept and
7 said, Sovereign Lord, have mercy on the sinners. And while I was
saying this a cloud came and took hold of me and carried me away
8,9 again to heaven. And I saw there many judgements. And I wept
bitterly and said, Better *were it* for a man not to have come out of his
10 mother's womb. And those who were undergoing punishment
cried out saying, Since you came here, you holy *man* of God, we
11 have found little respite. And the prophet said, Blessed are they
12 that weep for their sins. And God said, Listen *my* beloved Esdras,

[9] Cp. Isa. xiv. 13–15; Matt. xi. 23 ‖ Luke x. 15.
[10] Or '*him*'.
[11] So B: A om. 'will sound'.
[12] God's answer here is clearly incomplete.

Just as a farmer sows wheat seed in the earth, so also a man sows
13 his seed in the field of a woman. *During the* first *month* it remains as it
was,[1] *in the* second it **increases in size**,[2] *in the* third it grows hair, *in the*
fourth it grows nails, *in the* fifth it takes milk for food,[3] *in the* sixth it
becomes **ready**[4] and receives *its* soul, *in the* seventh it prepares
itself,[5] *and in the* ninth the doors of the woman's womb[6] are opened
14 and it is born safe and sound upon the earth. And the prophet said,
15 Lord, better were it for the man not to have been born. Woe to the
16 human ⟨race⟩ then, when thou comest[7] to judgement. And I said to
the Lord, Lord, why didst thou fashion man and deliver him to
17 judgement? And God said with some vehemence,[8] I will not have
18 mercy on those who disregard my covenant. And the prophet said,
19 Lord, where is thy goodness? And God said, I created all things for
20 man's sake, and man does not keep my commandments. And the
21 prophet said, Lord, show me the judgements and Paradise. And
the angels led me away towards the east, and I saw the tree of life.
22 And I saw there Enoch and Elijah and Moses and Peter and Paul
and Luke and **Matthew**[9] and all the righteous and the patriarchs.
23 And I saw there the †punishment†[10] of the air and the blowing of
the winds and the stores of crystals and the everlasting judge-
24,25 ments. And I saw there a man hanging by his head. And they said
26 to me, This man moved boundary-stones. And I saw there some
cruel judgements.[11] And I said to the Lord, Sovereign Lord, what
27 man is there who has ever been born *and* has not sinned? And they
led me down lower in Tartarus, and I saw the sinners all mourning
28 and weeping, and ⟨lamenting⟩ *their* evil lot.[12] And I wept also when
I saw the human race being punished so.

[1] Lit. 'it is all together'.
[2] Reading ὀγκοῦται for οἰχοῦτε.
[3] Lit. 'it becomes milky'.
[4] Reading ἕτοιμον for αἴτιμον.
[5] Here the eighth stage is omitted.
[6] Lit. 'gate-house'.
[7] So MS (ἔλθῃς). Perhaps we should read 'it comes' (ἔλθῃ).
[8] Lit. 'with a lofty proclamation'.
[9] Reading Ματθαῖον for Ματθείαν (Matthias).
[10] Gk. κόλασιν.
[11] Lit. 'And I saw there great judgements'.
[12] So A: B om 'and ⟨lamenting⟩ *their* evil lot'.

VI. Then God said to me, Do you know, Esdras, the names of the
2 angels at the consummation – Michael, Gabriel, Uriel, Raphael,
3 Gabuthelon, Aker, Arphugitonos, Beburos, and Zebulon? Then
came a voice to me, Come die, Esdras my beloved, and give up
4 what was entrusted to you. And the prophet said, And how will
5 you get at my soul to take it away? And the angels said, We can get at
6 it and expel it through your mouth. And the prophet said, Mouth
to mouth I spoke with God, and it shall not come out[1] from there.
7,8 And the angels said, Let us take it through your nostrils. And the
9 prophet said, My nostrils have savoured the glory of God. And the
10 angels said, Let us get it and take it through your eyes. And
11 the prophet said, My eyes did see the back parts of God. And
the angels said, Let us get it and take it through the top of your
12 head. And the prophet said, I walked together with Moses on the
13 mountain-*top*, and it shall not come out[1] from there. And the angels
14 said, Let us take it and expel it through your toes. And the prophet
15 said, My feet also walked at the altar. And the angels went away
16 without success, saying, Lord, we cannot take his soul. Then he
said to his only-begotten Son, Go down, my beloved Son, with a
17 great host of angels, and take the soul of my beloved Esdras. And[2]
the Lord took a great host of angels and *went down and* said to the
prophet, Give up to me what was entrusted to you – what I
18 entrusted to you: the crown has been made ready for you. And the
prophet said, Lord, if thou takest my soul from me, who will
19 remain to plead with thee on behalf of the human race? And God
said, Since you are mortal and of the earth you *should* not plead
20 with me. And the prophet said, I will not stop *my* pleading with
21 thee. And God said, Even so, give up now what has been entrusted
22 to you: the crown has been made ready for you. Come die, so that
23 you may obtain it. Then the prophet began to weep and say, O
Lord, what have I gained *from my* pleading with thee, if I am now to
24 sink down into the earth? Alas, alas, for I am to be consumed by
25 worms. Weep for me all saints and righteous men; *for* I pleaded
26 much. Weep for me all saints and righteous men, for I have entered
the depths of hell.[4]

---

[1] Lit. 'it does not come out'.
[2] Lit. 'For'.   [3] Lit. 'the dish of Hades'.

VII. And God said to him, Listen, Esdras my beloved. I, although immortal, endured a cross; I tasted vinegar and gall: I was buried
2 in a tomb; and I raised up my chosen ones. Adam I called forth from hell, that the human race might have no cause to be afraid of
3 death. For that *part of man* which is of me, that is *his* soul, departs to heaven; that *part of him* which is of the earth, that is *his* body,
4 departs to the earth from which it was taken. And the prophet said,
5 Alas, alas, What shall I do? How shall I fare? I do not know. And then the blessed Esdras began to say,

> O eternal God, the creator of all that is,
> Who didst measure the heaven with thine outstretched hand,
> And dost hold the earth in *thy* grasp,
> 6 Who ridest upon the cherubim,
> Who didst take up the prophet Elijah to heaven
> In a chariot of fire,
> 7 Who givest food to all flesh,
> Whose power all things fear,
> And before whose face they tremble;[1]
> 8 Give ear to me and my constant pleading with thee,
> 9 And grant to all who transcribe this book,
> And *to all who* have *charge of* it,
> And remember my name and preserve my memory,
> Grant to them blessing from heaven.
> 10 And bless all **their**[2] concerns
> As thou didst also bless the end of Joseph,
> 11 And remember not **their**[2] former sins
> In the day of **their**[2] judgement.
> 12 But as many as do not believe this book
> Will be utterly consumed,
> As *were* Sodom and Gomorrah.

13 And there came to him a voice saying, Esdras, my beloved, what-
14 ever you have asked I will grant to each one. And immediately he surrendered his precious soul with much honour, in the month of

---

[1] Lit. 'at whom all things shudder and tremble before the face of thy power'.
[2] MSS. 'his'.

15 October on the eighteenth *day*. And they buried him with due ceremony;[3] and his honoured and holy body is a perpetual source of strength, *both* of soul and body, to those who are moved to come
16 to him. To Him to whom it belongs *be* glory, power, honour, and worship, to the Father, and to the Son, and to the Holy Spirit, now and always, world without end. Amen.

---

[3] Lit. 'with incense and psalms'.

THE VISION OF ESDRAS

INTRODUCTION

The Vision of Esdras, like The Assumption of Moses, is extant only in Latin; and when G. Mercati published his edition in 1901 he had to rely on a single MS (Vat. lat. 3838; 12th cent.). Seventy years later, by the time O. Wahl came to prepare his edition of all three of the Esdras apocrypha translated in the present collection, a second MS of the Vision had also become available (Linz, Bibliothek des Priesterseminars A I/6; 10th or 11th cent.). This second MS raised unexpected complications. When a second MS of the Apocalypse of Esdras was discovered, as we have seen,[1] the effect was minimal, since the newly discovered MS was no more than a copy of the one already known. Not so with the new MS of the Vision. In the Vision there are several noteworthy divergencies in basic subject-matter between the two MSS towards the end of the text (additional classes of sinners appear in the Linz MS which are absent from the Vatican): there are continual differences in wording throughout (especially in the order of words, even when the same words are used); and further, whereas in the Vatican MS the narrative refers consistently to Esdras in the third person, in the Linz MS Esdras almost invariably speaks of himself in the first. A specimen will serve to illustrate these last two points:

Vatican MS	*Linz MS*
4 Veniebant viri fortissimi et transiebant flammam,	4 Veniebantque per se viri magni et transiebant flammam eius,
5 et non tangebat eos. Et dixit Esdras: Qui sunt isti, qui tam securi procedunt?	5 et non eos tangebat. Et interrogavi angelos, qui me ducebant: Qui sunt isti, qui cum tanto gaudio procedunt?

How are these differences to be accounted for? If the Vision was originally written in Latin, did some later worthy tamper with, or 'improve', the author's text? Or, if Latin was not the original

---

[1] Above, pp. 928–9.

language, are we to suppose there were two independent translations of the same (presumably Greek) original? Or were there two (not necessarily independent) translations of two different recensions of the original? Wahl ventilated possibilities of this kind in his Introduction but, understandably, did not pursue them; and in the body of his work he printed the text of both MSS in parallel columns.

Wahl's typescript was ready for the Press when there came to his notice a further text of the Vision tucked away at the end of the first book of the Magnum Legendarium Austriacum in a late 12th cent. MS from Lower Austria (Heiligenkreuz, cod. 11), which had, in fact, already been edited by A. Mussafia as long ago as 1871.[2] Fortunately, this additional evidence necessitated no serious rearrangement of his book as it then stood. The Heiligenkreuz codex aligned itself very definitely with Mercati's Vatican MS, though it was far from identical with it, so that all Wahl needed to do was to record its variants at the foot of his 'Vatican' column.

In the absence, therefore, of any established critical edition, and of any clear indication as to how such an edition might be established, it seemed that the wisest course for us was to base our own translation unreservedly on the Vatican MS (= V). From time to time, however, attention is drawn in the footnotes to any variants offered by either the Linz (= L) or Heiligenkreuz (= H) MSS that might either be important for the understanding of the document as a whole or be of interest in the interpretation of any particular passage.

That the Vision is related in some way to the Apocalypse of Esdras is clear enough. In both Vision and Apocalypse Esdras is taken on a tour of the nether regions to inspect the torments of the damned and conducted down a series of steps by angels.[3] In both he asks the angels who the particular individuals are that are undergoing particular punishments: he receives answers in the form 'These are . . .'; and he then beseeches God for mercy on each particular class of sinner. Some of the punishments described in

---

[2] A. Mussafia, *Sulla visione di Tundalo* (= *Sitzungsberichte der phil.-hist. Classe der Kaiserlichen Akademie der Wissenschaften*, Band 67 (Vienna, 1871), pp. 202–206).

[3] Vis. Esdr. 2, 12, 58: cp. Apoc. Esdr. iv. 8, 13, 15, 19.

both books are, of course, similar, as is inevitable in this type of literature, and so also are some of the sinners; but especially significant for the relationship between the Vision and the Apocalypse are the descriptions in each of King Herod seated on 'a fiery throne',[4] and the descriptions of the punishment of the incestuous – it is to be noted that in both Vision and Apocalypse this particular punishment is inflicted in 'the south'.[5] Attention may also be drawn to the passage at the end of the Vision, where Esdras refuses the angels' first offer to take him to heaven, where he compares man's lot on earth unfavourably with that of the animals, and where God replies 'I fashioned man in my own image and I commanded them that they should not sin, and they did sin: that is why they are in torments'. There are parallels here, not only in the Apocalypse, but also in the Apocalypse of Sedrach and in 2 Esdras.[6]

None of these last parallels (nor, indeed, any of the others) are sufficiently close to demand direct literary dependence. They suggest rather that the Vision stands squarely in the Ezra apochryphal tradition and that it is essentially an independent re-working of some of the same material that found its way also into the Apocalypse (chaps. iv and v). When the Vision as a whole is compared with the other Ezra apocrypha, it looks very much as if the author was concerned to concentrate on one element only in the tradition – namely, the details of the torments of the damned. No doubt he has himself elaborated it and developed it. But the result has been that all the other elements in the tradition are virtually ignored. That is why, for instance, the fundamental question why God created man and then arranged things so that he suffers as he does (a question which is discussed at some length in the other Ezra apocrypha) gets in the Vision only a very cursory mention, and then only at the very end.

That the author was a Christian can hardly be denied. It is true that he is less obviously Christian than the author of the

---

[4] Vis. Esdr. 37–39: cp. Apoc. Esdr. iv. 9–12.
[5] Vis. Esdr. 19–21: cp. Apoc. Esdr. iv. 22–24.
[6] With Vis. Esdr. 56–57 cp. Apoc. Esdr. vi. 3–15 and Apoc. Sedr. ix. 1–3: with Vis. Esdr. 62 cp. Apoc. Esdr. i. 22 and 2 Esdr. vii. 65–66, viii. 29–30: with Vis. Esdr. 63 cp. Apoc. Esdr. ii. 10–12, Apoc. Sedr. iv. 4–6, and 2 Esdr. iii. 5–7.

Apocalypse. He makes no mention of Christians as such, or of Christian worthies; and there are no explicit references in the Vision to the New Testament (other than to Herod 'who in Bethlehem of Judaea killed young children because of the Lord'). On the other hand, there are references to 'the Lord's Day' (10), to 'baptism' (46), to the 'Mass' (10 LH), to 'confession' (26 VH, 36 VH, 64), and to 'penance' (36 VH, 64). And with this agrees the author's concentration on the torments in Hell. The Apocalypse of Peter (? 2nd cent.) provides a very early example of Christian interest in these matters, and the Apocalypse of Paul (xxxi–xliv) another, rather later (4th cent.).

About the date of the Vision it is impossible to say very much. If it was written in Latin, it could be as late as the 10th cent. (the date of the earliest MS). If, on the other hand, our Latin text is a translation of a Greek original, any date between the 5th and 9th centuries is possible.[7]

BIBLIOGRAPHY

EDITIONS

G. MERCATI, *Note di letteratura biblica e cristiana antica* (= *Studi e Testi*, V; Rome, 1901), pp. 61–73.

O. WAHL, *Apocalypsis Esdrae. Apocalypsis Sedrach. Visio Beati Esdrae* (= *PVTG* iv; Leiden, 1977), pp. 49–61.

TRANSLATIONS

German

P. RIESSLER, *AjSaB²*, pp. 350–354.

[7] In his edition Mercati drew attention to the fact that the phrase 'because of the Lord' (*propter dominum*), which occurs at the end of the description of Herod (38), is found also in one of the antiphons set in some breviaries for use at Lauds on Holy Innocents' Day. Does this mean that the author of the Vision wrote in Latin and was influenced by the Liturgy, or that a translator from Greek was so influenced, or that the phrase was added by a later copyist?

GENERAL

A.-M. DENIS, *IPGAT*, p. 93.
P. RIESSLER, *AjSaB²*, p. 1291.

Esdras prayed to the Lord, saying, Give me, Lord, faith so that I
2 may not fear when I see the judgements of the sinners. And seven
angels of Tartarus were given him, who carried him down[1] seventy
3 steps into the nether regions. And he saw the fiery gates; and in
these gates he saw two lions lying, from whose mouths and nostrils
4 and eyes fierce *tongues of* flame protruded. And strong men were
coming and passed through the flame; and it did not touch them.
5 And Esdras said, Who are those who walk *through the flame* with such
6 confidence?[2] The angels said to him, Those are the righteous
7 whose fame has reached to heaven, those who have done great
works of mercy, *who* have clothed the naked, *and* whose thoughts
8 and inclinations have been always good.[3] And others were coming,
and tried to go in *through* the gates; and the **lions**[4] mauled them, and
9,10 the fire burned them. And Esdras said, Who are those? The angels
said, Those are they who denied the Lord, and on the Lord's Day[5]
11 sinned with women. And Esdras said, Lord, spare the sinners.
12 And they led him a further fifty steps lower down; and he saw
13 there men standing and undergoing punishment. Some angels
were piling fire upon them in front, and others were beating them
14 with fiery whips. And the earth was crying out, saying, Beat *them*,
and do not spare them, because *it was* upon me *that* they did their
15 wicked deed. And Esdras said, Who are those who are daily
16 punished so severely? The angels said, Those are they who had
17 intercourse with married women. The married women are *women*
who adorned themselves, not for their own husbands, but to please

---

[1] Lit. 'over': L 'down in'.
[2] L 'who walk with such great joy'.
[3] Lit. '*and* desired a good desire'.
[4] All three MSS read 'dogs'.
[5] LH add 'before Mass'.

18 others (and so yielded to their evil inclinations).[6] And Esdras said,
Lord, spare the sinners.

19 And again they *took him and* set him down[7] at the south; and he
saw a fire, and poor *people* hanging up, *both* men[8] and women, and[9]

20 angels were beating them with fiery cudgels. And Esdras said,[10]

21 Who are those? And the angels said, These (*sic*) are they who had
intercourse with their mothers, and yielded to their evil incli-

22 nations.[11] And Esdras said, Lord, spare the sinners.

23 And they led him down *further* into the nether regions;[12] and he
saw a caldron of burning[13] sulphur and pitch, and *the level of* it rose

24 and fell like a wave of the sea. And some righteous were coming,
and they were walking in the middle of it, over the waves of fire,
praising the name of the Lord, just as if they were walking over dew

25 or cool water. And Esdras said, Who are those? The angels said,

26 Those are they who to their profit daily made confession in the
presence of God and of his holy priests, by doing works of mercy,

27 *and* by resisting sins.[14] And some sinners came, wanting to cross
over, and angels of Tartarus came and plunged them into the

28 burning fire. And they cried out from the fire, saying, Lord, have

29 mercy on us; but[15] he showed them[16] no mercy. *Their* voices could
be heard, but they themselves could not be seen[17] because of the

30,31 fire and torment. And Esdras said, Who are those? The angels
said, Those were covetous *men* and thieves[18] all their days: no

32 stranger did they take in, no work of mercy did they do. They took
for themselves unjustly what belonged to others: they followed

33 their evil inclinations;[19] and that is why they are in torments. And
Esdras said, Lord, spare the sinners.

---

[6] Lit. 'desiring an evil desire'.

[7] L 'And they took me down and set *me* down'.

[8] V om.   [9] LH add 'four'.

[10] V adds 'Lord, spare the sinners' – obviously in error.

[11] Lit. 'desiring an evil desire'.

[12] So VH: L specifies that he was taken down what would seem to be an
impossible number of steps ('II quingentos').   [13] V om. 'burning'.

[14] L 'Those are they who did many works of mercy and clothed the naked'.

[15] Lit. 'and'.   [16] V om. 'them'.

[17] Lit. 'A voice was heard and no flesh was seen'.

[18] Or 'slanderers' (so VH, Lat 'detractores'): L 'robbers' (Lat. 'raptores').

[19] Lit. 'they had (L 'desired') an evil desire'.

34 And he walked on further, and he saw in a dark place the worm
35 that does not die[20] – its size he could not measure. And in front of its
mouth were standing many sinners; and when it drew in a breath
they were sucked into its mouth[21] like flies, but when it breathed
36 out they all came out *again* with a different colour. And Esdras said,
Who are those? And the angels said, Those were full of every evil,
and they passed over without confession and penance.[22]

37 And he saw[23] a man sitting on a fiery throne, and from the fire *his*
servants ministered to him on every side, and his counsellors stood
38 round about him in the fire. And Esdras said, Who is that? And the
angels said, That man was a king for many years, Herod by name,
who in Bethlehem of Judah killed[24] young children because of the
39 Lord. And Esdras said, Lord, thou hast pronounced a proper
judgement.

40 And he walked *on further* and saw men bound, and angels of
41 Tartarus were stabbing them in the eyes with thorns. And Esdras
said, Who are those? The angels said, *Those* who showed the lost
42 wrong ways. Esdras said, Lord, spare the sinners.

43 And he saw girls coming with shackles weighing five hundred
44 pounds towards the west. And Esdras said, Who are those? And
the angels said, Those are *the girls* who violated *their* virginity before
their marriages.

45 And he saw[25] a collection of old men lying *on the ground*, and over
them was being poured molten iron and lead; and he said, Who are
46 those? The angels said, Those are the doctors of the law who
confused baptism and the law of the Lord, because they used to
teach with words *only and* not follow up *their words* with deeds;[26] and

[20] Lit. 'the immortal worm' (cp. Isa. lxvi. 24; Mark ix. 48).
[21] Lit. 'they entered its mouth'.
[22] So VH: L om. 'and they . . . penance'. Then LH add 'And he walked on further
still and saw a fiery river and a great bridge over it. And some righteous men came
and crossed over *it* with joy and exultation. And some sinners came, and the bridge
was reduced to the thinnest thread. And they fell into the river confessing their sins,
and saying, We have done every evil thing there is *to do*, and that is why we are being
punished in this way. And they were begging for mercy; but no mercy was granted
them'.   [23] So V: LH 'And he walked on further and saw'.
[24] V om.
[25] V om. 'he saw'.
[26] Lit. 'were not filling out in deed'.

47 they are judged in this *way*. And Esdras said, Lord, spare the sinners.

48 And he saw over against the setting of the sun a smelting-furnace of enormous size burning with fire, into which were being thrown
49 many kings and princes of this world. And many thousands of the poor *were* accusing them and saying, Those are the ones who made use of their power to oppress us, and turned free men[27] into slaves.

50 And he saw another furnace burning with pitch and sulphur, into which were being thrown sons who had laid hands upon their parents, and done them injury with their mouth.[28]

51 And in a very dark place he saw another furnace burning, into which many women were being thrown; and he said, Who are
52 those? The angels said, Those are they who conceived[29] children in
53 adultery and killed them. And the little ones themselves were accusing them, saying, Lord, the souls thou gavest us, they have
54 destroyed.[30] And he said, Who are those? The angels said, Those
55 are the women who killed their children.[31] And Esdras said, Lord, spare the sinners.

56 Then came Michael and Gabriel and said to him, Come to
57 heaven.[32] And Esdras said, *As* my Lord lives, I will not come before I see all the judgements of the sinners.[33]

58 And they led him down into the nether regions a further fourteen steps. And he saw lions and little dogs[34] lying round a flame of fire; and the righteous were passing through them and crossing over
59 into Paradise. And he saw many thousands of the righteous; and their dwellings were very splendid and enduring.[35]

[27] Or 'turned *our* children'.

[28] LH add 'And into it were also being thrown those who had denied God and had not paid *their* hired servants the wages due to them'.

[29] Lit. 'had'.

[30] LH add 'And he saw other women hanging in the fire, and serpents sucking their breasts'.

[31] LH add 'And did not give their breasts to others *who were* orphans'.

[32] L adds 'that we may celebrate the Pasch'.

[33] LH add 'And he saw further some men who were being mauled by wild beasts. And he said, Who are those? And the angels said, Those are men who altered boundary-marks and gave false witness. And he said, Lord, spare the sinners'.

[34] LH 'lions and camels'.

[35] LH add 'Light is there, *and* joy, and prosperity. And every day they have manna from heaven, because they did many deeds of mercy while on earth. And

60   And after he had seen these things he was taken up into heaven;[36] and a host of angels came and said to him, Intercede with the Lord for the sinners. And they set him down in the Lord's presence.

61   And he said, Lord, spare the sinners. And the Lord said, Esdras, let them receive what is due to them from the record of their deeds.

62   And Esdras said, Lord, thou hast dealt more leniently with the animals than with us: they feed on grass and render thee no praises: they die and have no sin; but us thou dost torment *both*

63   *when* living and *when* dead. And the Lord said, Esdras, I fashioned man in my own image, and I commanded them that they should

64   not sin, and they did sin: that is why they are in torments. But the elect[37] will go to eternal rest by virtue of confession and penance[38]

65   and the abundance of *their* works of mercy. And Esdras said, Lord,

66   what is it that the righteous do so that they escape judgement? And the Lord said to him, The slave who has done well for his lord will receive *his* freedom: so also the righteous the kingdom of heaven. Amen.

there are many there who did not do *them*, because they had not the wherewithal (L+ 'they were inhibited by *their* small means'). Nevertheless they enjoy a similar rest because of the goodwill they had. And so they praise the Lord our God, who has *always* loved righteousness'.

[36] L specifies that Esdras was taken up into the seventh heaven.

[37] Lit. 'And those who are chosen'.

[38] So VH: L 'by virtue of penance and prayer and confession'.

THE APOCALYPSE OF SEDRACH

INTRODUCTION

This work is extant only in Greek and was edited by M. R. James from a single MS in the Bodleian Library at Oxford (Bodl. Cod. Misc. gr. 56; 15th cent.), in which it occurs as the final item. The text, even more than the text of the Apocalypse of Esdras, is in many places very corrupt, with the result that the sense is often far from clear: particularly is this so in chap. xi, where Sedrach utters a lamentation over the various members of his body. Moreover, the original opening of the work seems at some stage to have been lost. The text as it now stands in the MS begins with a three-and-a-half page homily on love, which is obviously a separate piece and in all probability to be attributed to Ephraem Syrus. James printed only the opening and closing sections of this homily, and an abbreviated version of these sections has been included in our translation (chap. i).

The title 'The Apocalypse of Sedrach' is due to James. The title in the MS is 'The Word of . . . Sedrach', though whether or not this was the author's own title it is impossible to say – it may well be due to a later editor or scribe. But in any case the work is not an apocalypse as the term 'apocalypse' is usually understood; for, although Sedrach, like St. Paul, is caught up into 'the third heaven' (ii. 4: cp. 2 Cor. xii. 2), no revelation in the strict sense is made to him.[1] Instead, there follows a dialogue between Sedrach and God in which Sedrach questions God about His purposes in Creation and God defends himself against any charges of injustice and cruelty in His treatment of man.

The name 'Sedrach' also present a problem. 'Sedrach' appears in the Greek versions of the Book of Daniel as the equivalent of the Hebrew and Aramaic 'Shadrach' – i.e. it is the recognised Greek form of the name given to Daniel's friend Hananiah by the chief of

---

[1] It is also worth noting that, although the title explicitly states that the work is about 'the second coming of our Lord Jesus Christ' as well as 'love and repentance and orthodox Christians', there is no mention of the Second Coming in it anywhere.

the eunuchs at the Babylonian court (Dan. i. 7, etc.); and it may well be that our author had Shadrach-Hananiah in mind when he wrote. On the other hand, it is much more probable that James's conjecture is correct and that 'Sedrach' represents the corruption of an original 'Esdras'.

The main reason for thinking this is that the work is undoubtedly related both to 2 Esdras and to The Apocalypse of Esdras — it stands firmly, that is, within the apocryphal Esdras tradition. Not only is the theme of the justification of God's ways to man, so prominent in Sedrach, treated at length in both these other works: there are also a number of often very close parallels between Sedrach and one or other of them, or both. As examples of such parallels may be given: (1) God's particular choices — 'among animals the sheep, . . . among rivers the Jordan, among cities Jerusalem' (Sedr. viii. 3: cp. 2 Esdras v. 23–27); (2) Sedrach's reluctance to surrender his soul immediately he is asked to do so and, when he finally agrees, his question about what limb it would be taken out through (Sedr. ix–x: cp. Apoc. Esdras vi. 3–vii. 3); and (3) Sedrach's observation that 'it were better for man if he had not been born', his fundamental question why did God make man in the first instance if He would not have mercy on him, and God's reply that man's present condition is due to his disobedience in Paradise (Sedr. iv: cp. 2 Esdras iv. 12 and Apoc. Esdras i. 6, 21, v. 9, 14; 2 Esdras vii. 116–126 and Apoc. Esdras iii. 9; 2 Esdras iii. 5–7 and Apoc. Esdras ii. 10–17).

By way of contrast, there is little obvious contact between Sedrach and The Vision of Esdras. What parallelisms there are are few and insubstantial: they are confined to the section at the very end of the Vision;[2] and each of them is shared with the other Esdras books. All in all, the general impression created is that the author of the Vision selected for amplification from the elements in the tradition that found a place in the Apocalypse the details about the torments of the damned (i.e. Apoc. Esdras iv–v), while the author of Sedrach chose to concentrate on the more fundamental theme of

---

[2] They are: (1) the prophet's reluctance to surrender his soul (Sedr. ix–x: cp. Vision 56–57); (2) his questioning of God about the reasons for man's present evil lot (Sedr. iv: cp. Vision 62–63); and (3) his final entry into heaven (Sedr. xvi. 9: cp. Vision 60).

the justice of God's dealings with His creatures. If the question be asked why it should be thought that Sedrach represents a later stage in the tradition than the Apocalypse rather than *vice versa*, the answer is that a close study of the parallels suggests it. For instance, at Sedr. ix. 1 God's 'only-begotten Son' is very awkwardly introduced without warning as the agent chosen to demand Sedrach's surrender of his soul, whereas at Apoc. Esdras vi. 1–17 a band of angels is selected for this task and the only-begotten is only commissioned to lead them on a second attempt after their first attempt on their own had failed; and, in the same context, the argument with the angels that follows Esdras's question about which limb his soul should be taken out through at Apoc. Esdras vi. 5–14 makes much better sense than God's distinctly obscure reply to Sedrach's similar question at Sedr. x. 1–4. There should be no difficulty here in deciding which version is primary and which secondary.

If James's date for the Apocalypse of Esdras in the 9th cent. be acceptable, then the likelihood is that Sedrach will be 10th or 11th cent., though both may be very much earlier.[3] In favour of a late date is the fact that the language of Sedrach abounds in neo-Greek forms and constructions and not infrequently (as James rather unfortunately put it) 'degenerates into modern Greek'. Nor is Sedrach mentioned in any of the lists of apocryphal books. Some scholars have claimed to be able to detect at various points evidence for the use of Jewish sources, which, it seems, were not used by the authors of the other Esdras books;[4] but whatever justification there may, or may not, be for this claim, there is no gainsaying the evidence of such incontrovertibly Christian features as the introduction of Christ himself as the speaker at xii. 1, the references to 'apostles', 'gospels', 'services', and 'my holy churches' at xiv. 10–12, and the knowledge of books of the New Testament displayed at vi. 5, vii. 7–8, xiv. 5–6, and xv. 3, 6–7.

---

[3] See above p. 930

[4] e.g. R. Meyer, art. 'Sedrach-Apokalypse' in *Religion in Geschichte und Gegenwart*,[3] v (1961), col. 1631.

BIBLIOGRAPHY

EDITIONS

M. R. JAMES, *Apocrypha Anecdota* (= *TS* II. iii; Cambridge, 1893), pp. 127–137.

O. WAHL, *Apocalypsis Esdrae. Apocalypsis Sedrach. Visio Beati Esdrae.* (= *PVTG* iv; Leiden, 1977), pp. 37–48.

TRANSLATIONS

English

A RUTHERFORD, *The Apocalypse of Sedrach* (= *Ante-Nicene Christian Library, Additional Volume* (Edinburgh, 1897), pp. 175–180).

German

P. RIESSLER, *AjSaB*[2], pp. 156–167.

GENERAL

A.-M. DENIS, *IPGAT*, pp. 97–99.

M. R. JAMES, *The Testament of Abraham* (= *TS* II. ii; Cambridge, 1892), pp. 31–33, 66.

G. MERCATI, 'The Apocalypse of Sedrach' in *JTS* xi (1910), pp. 572–3.

P. RIESSLER, *AjSaB*[2], p. 1274.

B. VIOLET, *Die Esra-Apokalypse (IV Esra)* (= *GCS* xviii; Leipzig, 1910), pp. 1–lix.

The word of the holy and blessed Sedrach concerning love and repentance and orthodox Christians and concerning the second coming of our Lord Jesus Christ. Lord, give thy blessing.

I. Beloved, let us prefer nothing before unfeigned love. . . . There is no greater love than that a man lay down his life for his friends.

II.   And an unseen voice sounded in his ears *saying*, Come, Sedrach, since you desire so earnestly to speak with God and to ask him to reveal what you would enquire about. And Sedrach said, Why *so*, my lord? And the voice said to him, I am sent to you to bring you up here into heaven. And he said, I would *indeed* speak face to face[1] with God; *but* I am not worthy, lord, to go up into the heavens. And stretching out his wings the angel took him, and went up into the heavens, and set him down in the third heaven. And the flame of the Godhead rested upon him.

III.   And the Lord said to him, It is well you have come, my beloved Sedrach. What is it that you would plead before the God who formed you, for you said, I would speak face to face[1] with God? Sedrach said to him, I would indeed plead before thee, as a son with his father.[2] Why, my Lord, didst thou make the earth? The Lord said to him, For the sake of man. Sedrach said, And why didst thou make the sea? Why didst thou sow every good thing upon the earth? The Lord said, For the sake of man. Sedrach said to him, If thou didst these things, why didst thou *then* destroy him? The Lord said, Man is my work, and what my hands have fashioned, and I discipline him[3] as I find *necessary*.

IV.   Sedrach said to him, Thy discipline[1] is punishment and fire: they are bitter, my Lord. It were better for man if he had not been born. Why then didst thou make *him*, my Lord? Why didst thou weary thy unsullied hands with toil and fashion man, since thou wouldest not have mercy on him? God said to him, I made the first-formed Adam, and I set him in Paradise where grew[2] the tree of life; and I said to him, *You may* eat of all the fruits, only keep away

---

[1] Lit. 'mouth to mouth'.

[1] Lit. 'mouth to mouth'.
[2] Lit. 'Yes: the son has a cause me the father'.
[3] Or 'I educate him'.

[1] Or 'education'.
[2] Lit. '. . . Paradise, in the midst of'.

6 from the tree of life, for if you eat of it, you will most surely die. And he disobeyed my command and was deceived by the devil and ate of the tree.

V. Sedrach said to him, It was in accordance with thy will, my
2 Lord, that Adam was deceived. Thou didst command thine angels to worship Adam; and the first of the angels who disobeyed thy
3 command and did not worship him, thou didst banish, **because he transgressed**[1] thy command and refused to approach what thy
4 hands had fashioned. If thou didst love man, why didst thou not
5 kill the devil, who devises *every kind of* wickedness? Who can fight an invisible spirit? He enters the hearts of men like smoke ⟨and⟩
6 teaches them every sin. He even fights against thee, the immortal
7 God. What then can wretched man do against him? But have mercy, Lord, and remit *thy* punishments: or else, count[2] me also
8 among the sinners. If thou hast no mercy upon sinners, where are thy mercies, where *is* thy compassion, Lord?

VI. God said to him, You must understand that I gave Adam[1]
2 dominion over all things. I made him wise and heir of heaven and
3 earth, and I put all things under him. And every *other* living thing
4 runs away from him and *avoids* his presence. But although he had received my *gifts*, he became estranged *and* an adulterer and a
5 sinner. What father *is there*, tell me, who after giving his son his share of his estate, and *the son*, after taking what was *now* his, left his father, and went away into a foreign land and became the slave of a
6 foreign master — what father is there,[2] seeing that his son has
7 deserted him, will not be furious,[3] and go after him and take his property back, and disown his son,[4] because he deserted his father?
8 How *then should it be otherwise with me*? I, the terrible and jealous God, gave Adam[1] all things, and he, after he had received them, became an adulterer and a sinner.

[1] MS 'Why did he transgress . . .?'
[2] Lit. 'receive'.

[1] Lit. 'him'.
[2] Lit. 'and the father'.
[3] Lit. 'his heart is smoking'.
[4] Lit. 'and banish him from his glory'.

VII. Sedrach said to him, Thou, Lord, didst fashion man. Thou knowest of what kind his inclinations were, and of what kind our knowledge is, and *yet* thou dost plead man *himself* as the excuse for

2 his punishment. But cast him out – surely I alone will not *be*

3 *sufficient to* fill the heavenly places? ⟨If not,⟩ save man also, Lord; *for*

4 wretched man has sinned, Lord, against thy will. ⟨God said to him,⟩ Why do you waste words on me, Sedrach? I fashioned Adam and his wife and the sun ⟨and the moon⟩, and I said, Look at one another, *and see* how bright the other[1] is (for the sun and Adam had

5 the same stamp upon them[2]). The wife of Adam is more radiant in

6 beauty than the moon; and he gave her life.[3] Sedrach said, And

7 what does beauty profit if it wastes away in the earth? How *was it that* thou didst say, Lord, Do not repay evil for evil? How is it,

8 Lord? The word of thy Godhead never lies: so why dost thou

9 reward man *thus*? Dost thou not will evil for evil? I know that among the animals no one of them is more contrary than the mule.

10,11 Yet we force it *to go* where we want it to with a bridle. Thou hast angels: send them as guardians;[4] and when man takes a step in the direction of sin, let them take hold of one of his feet so that he does not go where he would.

VIII. God said to him, If I were to take hold of his foot, he would *only* say, Thou didst show me no kindness in the world. So I left him

2 to his will because I loved him. That is why I sent my righteous

3 angels to guard him night and day. Sedrach said, I know, Lord, that among thy creatures thou didst love man first, among animals the sheep, among trees the olive, among fruits the grape, among winged creatures the bee, among rivers the Jordan, among cities

4,5 Jerusalem. And all these things man also loves, my Lord. God said

---

[1] Lit. 'how bright he' or 'how bright it'.

[2] Lit. 'the sun and Adam were one stamp'.

[3] This passage is more than usually obscure. From the text as it stands it is unclear whether the comparison is between Adam and Eve on the one side and the sun and moon on the other, or between Adam and the sun on the one side and Eve and the moon on the other. However, in either case, not a little must have disappeared from the original text. Perhaps, also, we should emend the final clause to read 'and I gave her life'.

[4] Lit. 'send *them* to guard them'.

to Sedrach, I *will* ask you one question, Sedrach. If you can answer
me, I can rightly take your part, although you have been cross-
6 examining him who fashioned you. Sedrach said, What is the
7 question,[1] *my* Lord God. ⟨The Lord God said to him,⟩ Since *the day
that* I made all things, how many men have been born, how many
8 have died, how many will die, and how many hairs have they? Tell
me, Sedrach, since the heaven and the earth were created, how
many trees have there been on the earth, how many have fallen,
how many will fall, how many will there be, and how many leaves
9 have they? Tell me, Sedrach, since I made the sea, how many
waves have risen up, how many have fallen back again, how many
10 will rise up, and how many winds blow on the seashore? Tell me,
Sedrach, since the creation of the ages of the earth, when it rains,
how many drops have fallen on the earth, and how many will fall?
11 And Sedrach said, Thou alone, Lord, knowest all these things:
12 thou alone hast understanding of all these things. Only, I pray
thee, set man free from punishment; otherwise, I too must go to
punishment and not be separated from our race.

IX. And God said to his only-begotten Son, Go, take the soul of my
2 beloved Sedrach, and set it down in Paradise. The only-begotten
Son said to Sedrach, ⟨Give up what was entrusted to you⟩,[1] what
our Father deposited in your mother's womb, in the holy tabernacle
3 *of* your *body* before you were born. Sedrach said, I will not give my
4 soul to thee. **The Son**[2] said to him, Why then was I sent and came
5 here, and you make excuses to me? For I was ordered by my Father
not to take your soul by force:[3] so then, give me your soul which he
desires so much.

X. And Sedrach said to God, And how wilt thou take my soul?
2 From what limb? And God said to him, Do you not know that your

---

[1] Lit. 'Sedrach said, Say'.

[1] Not in the MS: supplied from Apoc. Esdr. vi. 3 (see above, p. 939).

[2] Reading ὁ υἱός for ὁ Θεός. What follows immediately leaves no doubt that it is
the Son who is speaking here, though there is some confusion later on (cp. especially
x. 1 and xii. 1). A parallel ambivalence, if not necessarily a confusion, may be
observed at Apoc. Esdr. vi. 16, 17, 19, and 21.

[3] Lit. 'shamelessly'.

soul is centred in your lungs and your heart ⟨and⟩ is dispersed
3 through all your limbs? It is brought up through throat and larynx
and the mouth. And when the time comes for it to come out, it is
first of all collected and gathered together from the toes and all the
4 *other* limbs, and *then* it has to be separated from the body and parted
5 from the heart. When Sedrach had heard all this, and thought
6 about the reference to death, he was much disturbed. And Sedrach
said to God, Grant me, Lord, a little **respite**[4] so that I can weep; for I
have heard ⟨that⟩ tears are a most powerful and effective medicine
for the weak body that thou hast fashioned.

XI.   And he began to say with tears and lamentation,

> O head, *so* marvellous *and* adorned like heaven,
> Bright as the sun that lights the heaven and earth!
2 Your hairs are wiser guides than Teman,
> Your eyes than Bozrah,
> Your ears than thunder,
> Your tongue than a trumpet.[1]
3 And your brain is *but* a tiny creature;
> *Yet the* head controls the whole body's movement.
> O fairest and most beloved of all *my members*,
4 Now must **you**[2] sink into the earth and be forgotten.

5 O hands, *so* gentle, docile, and hard-working,
> Through which the body[3] receives its food!
6 O hands, *so* well adapted to provide domestic needs.[4]
7 O fingers embellished and adorned with gold and silver!
> Great works are wrought by the fingers.
8 The three joints unite the palms
> And enhance their beauty.
> And now you must become strangers to this world.

---

[4] Reading ἄνεσιν for ἴασιν (cp. Apoc. Esdr. v. 10).

[1] Lit. 'Those who know *are* your hairs from Teman, your eyes from Bozrah, your ears from thunder, your tongue from a trumpet'. (For Edom as the traditional home of wisdom cp. Jer. xlix. 7–22, where both Teman and Bozrah are specifically mentioned.)   [2] Text 'it'.
[3] Lit. 'the vessel'.
[4] Lit. 'O hands, most apt of all, which heaping up, you equipped the houses'.

9　　O feet that walk so well, that run of your own accord,
　　　Most agile, that cannot be restrained![5]

10　　O knees, *so* joined that without you the body[3] does not move!

11　　The feet run *by the light of* sun and moon,
　　　By night and by day:
　　　They provide everything to eat and drink,
　　　And give the body[3] food.

12　　O feet **most swift**[6] and nimble, that stir up the dust of the earth,
　　　To stock houses with every good thing!

13　　O feet that carry the whole body,
　　　That run to the holy places to do penance[7] and entreat the saints!
　　　Now must you stay motionless.

14　　O head and hands and feet,
　　　Now no longer may I keep you.[8]

15　　O soul, what sent you into my lowly and wretched body?

16　　Now must you be separated from it
　　　And go up where the Lord calls you,
　　　And the wretched body go away to judgement.

17　　O body beautified: hair flowing like the stars:
　　　Head embellished *and* adorned like heaven!

18　　O face, fragrant with ointment:
　　　Eyes that give light:

19　　Voice *like* the sound of a trumpet: tongue most gentle:
　　　Beard most handsome: hair like stars:
　　　Head reaching up towards the sky:
　　　Body most beautifully adorned, light-giving, **elegant**,[9] all-knowing!

---

[5]　Lit. 'Most swift, exceedingly invincible'.
[6]　Reading ὠκύτατοι for ἀνθύτατοι.
[7]　Or '. . . holy places in penitence'.
[8]　Lit. 'until now have I kept you'.
[9]　Reading γλαφυρόν for γλεύφορον.

20   Now must you sink into the earth,
       And **beneath the earth**[10] your beauty disappear.

XII. Christ said to him, Enough, Sedrach. How long will you shed tears and moan? Paradise has been opened for you, and by dying 2 you will live. Sedrach said to him, Yet once again will I speak to thee, Lord. How long have I to live before I die? Do not refuse me 3,4 my request. The Lord said to him, Speak, Sedrach. ⟨Sedrach said,⟩ If a man lives eighty ⟨or⟩ ninety years, or *even* a hundred, and lives them as a sinner,[1] and then turns again and lives in penitence, for how many days must he have lived in penitence *before* thou dost 5 forgive his sins? God said to him, If a man lives a hundred ⟨or⟩ eighty years, and *then* turns and repents for three years and has fruits of righteousness to show, and then death overtakes him, I will not remember any of his sins.[2]

XIII. Sedrach said to him, Three years are a long time, my Lord: suppose death overtakes him before he has completed his *three years* 2 *of* penitence. Have mercy, Lord, upon thine image, and have 3 compassion, for three years are a long time. God said to him, If a man lives a hundred years and then remembers his death and makes his confession[1] before men and I find him, after a time I will 4 forgive all his sins. Sedrach said again, Lord, yet again I implore 5 thy compassion ⟨for⟩ thy creature's sake. The time is long: suppose 6 death overtakes him and snatches him away at once. The Saviour said to him, I will put one question to you, Sedrach, my beloved: then shall you put yours to me.[2] If the sinner repents for forty days, I will remember none of the sins that he committed.

XIV. And Sedrach said to the archangel Michael, Hear me, powerful advocate, and help me, and act as *my* ambassador, *and*

---

[10] Reading ὑπὸ γῆς for ὕπαγε.

[1] Lit. 'lives them in sins'.
[2] Lit. 'all his sins'.

[1] Or 'confesses *me*' (cp. Matt. x. 32 ‖ Luke xii. 8).
[2] Something seems to be missing from the text here, since God asks no question, nor does Sedrach reply with another question or repeat his previous one.

2 *plead* that God have mercy on the world. And falling down on their faces *together* they prayed to God and said, Lord, teach us how man is to be saved. What kind of penitence is necessary, and what in

3 particular must he do? ⟨God said,⟩ Man is saved by acts of penitence, by intercessions, by services in church, by floods of tears, *and*

4 by fervent lamentations. Do you not know that my prophet David *was saved* by tears? And the rest too – do you *not* know that they were

5 saved, *each of them*, at one critical moment? Do you *not* know, Sedrach, that there are Gentiles who, though they have not the

6 law, ⟨yet⟩ fulfil ⟨the requirements⟩ of the law?[1] For ⟨even though⟩ they are unbaptised, yet my divine spirit has entered into them, and they are converted to my baptism, and I receive them with my

7 righteous ones in Abraham's bosom. And there are some, who have been baptized with my baptism and have been anointed with my holy[2] oil, who yet turn their backs on it altogether and show no

8 sign of a change of mind. But with deep compassion and an unfailing wealth of mercy I wait for their repentance, although they do what my Godhead hates and pay no attention to the wise

9 man's saying, No sinner is ever acquitted.[3] Do you really not know that Scripture says, And those who repent shall not see punish-

10 ment? And ⟨they pay no attention either to the⟩ apostles, nor to my

11 word in the gospels; and they make my angels sad. And more, in my assemblies and services they do not respect my messenger.[4]

12 Neither do they **keep quiet**[5] in my holy churches, but instead of falling on their knees in fear and trembling, they stand up and make fine speeches, which I do not accept myself, neither *do* my angels.

---

[1] Lit. '⟨yet⟩ do ⟨the things⟩ of the law'.

[2] Lit. 'divine'.

[3] Lit. 'In no wise do we justify a sinner'.

[4] Meaning obscure (Gk. οὐ προσεύχουσιν τὸν ἄγγελόν μου). The occurrence of προσεύχειν in the active is unusual, to say the least. Furthermore, who is the ἄγγελος – Christ, or the angel presumed to be in attendance at the service, or the Christian minister in charge?

[5] Reading καθίστανται for ἵστανται though the corruption is probably more deep-seated. It is possible that the details here have been suggested by the parable in Luke xviii. 9–14. (I owe this last observation to Dr. A. M. Allchin, who has kindly assisted me over some of the other liturgical passages in this document. Ed.)

XV. Sedrach said to God, Lord thou alone art sinless and of
2 infinite compassion, and hast mercy and pity upon sinners. Yet thy
Godhead said, I came not to call the righteous but sinners to
3 repentance. And the Lord said to Sedrach, Do you not know,
Sedrach that the robber was saved at one critical moment when he
4 repented?[1] Do you not know that my **apostle**[2] and evangelist was
5 also himself saved at one critical moment? ⟨But sinners are not so
saved,⟩ because their hearts are like a decaying stone – these are
those who follow unholy paths and are to be destroyed with
6 Antichrist. Sedrach said, My Lord, thou didst also say, My divine
spirit entered into the Gentiles, who though they have not the law
7 ⟨yet⟩ fulfil ⟨the requirements⟩ of the law.[3] As with the robber, and
the apostle and evangelist, and the others who have **attained to**[4]
8 thy kingdom, my Lord, so also, Lord, pardon those who have
sinned at the last, for life is full of hardship and offers little
opportunity for repentance.

XVI. The Lord said to Sedrach, I made three periods in man's
2 life.[1] When he is a youth I overlook his failures because they are *the
failures* of a youth: when later *he becomes* a man, I keep watch over
his thoughts; and when later *still* he grows old, I watch over him
3 also, in the hope that he may repent. Sedrach said, Lord, thou
knowest all these things and understandest *them*: only be compas-
4 sionate towards sinners. The Lord said to him, Sedrach, my beloved, I promise to be compassionate; and I will reduce the forty
5 days to twenty.[2] And whoever makes mention of your name shall
not see the place of punishment, but shall be with the righteous in a
6 place of refreshment and rest. And if anyone records this admir-
able discussion[3] in writing, his sin shall never be reckoned *against*

---

[1] Lit. 'was saved . . . to repent'.
[2] Reading ἀπόστολος for ἀπόστολοι.
[3] Lit '⟨yet⟩ do ⟨the things⟩ of the law'.
[4] Reading φθάσαντες εἰς for πταίσαντες.

[1] Lit. 'I made man in three orders'.
[2] Lit. '. . . compassionate even from below the forty days as far as twenty'.
[3] Or 'saying'.

7 *him*. And Sedrach said, Lord, if anyone brings illumination to thy
8 servant, deliver him, Lord, from every evil. And Sedrach, the
9 servant of God, said, Now take my soul, Lord. And God took him
and set him in Paradise with all the saints. To whom be glory and
might for ever and ever. Amen.

INDEX OF SCRIPTURAL REFERENCES

OLD TESTAMENT

APOCRYPHA

NEW TESTAMENT

971

INDEX OF ANCIENT AUTHORS
AND WORKS

974

INDEX OF MODERN AUTHORS

INDEX OF SUBJECTS

866; the existing world was created for man's sake 849, for Israel's sake 607, or for the sake of the righteous 850, 853; it will be transformed or renewed and the new c. will last for ever 13, 227, 257, 293, 858, 864, 870, 876.

Cup, the: of (God's) blessing 481; of immortality 480, 488; of life 488.

Daughter: a younger must not be given in marriage before her elder sister 88.

Day, the (= the d. of the Lord, when he will destroy the earth and the heavens, 925): that great d. 234; the d. of the great consummation 205; the (great) d. of (the great) judgement 25, 72, 212, 276, 312, 527, 904, etc.; the d. of cursing and punishment 308; the d. of darkness 297; the d. of destruction 301–2; the d. of distress 184, 235, 301; the d. of iniquity 298; the d. of repentance 607. See Judgement.

Dead, the: the abode of 210–12.

Death: the spirit sent by God to claim the soul of Abraham 406, 415–21 – cp. 411; his reaping-hook 402, 406; the angel of d. 853.

Devil, the: originally an angel driven out of heaven because he refused to worship Adam 150, 958.

Dispersion, the: Israel is dispersed among the Gentiles 532, 535, 554, 581, 592, 668, 881; a prayer for their gathering together again 667; God will gather them 670, 889.

Eden. See Paradise, also Garden.

Elect (Chosen) One, my: title applied to Joseph 486, Jeremiah 821, 822, 829, and Esdras 935; my (the) El. One = the Messiah 223, 226, 227, 230, 231, 232, 233, 235, 242, 243, 391, 800.

Elect (chosen) ones: the el. of Israel 14; more generally 481; and especially in 1 Enoch as a synonym for the righteous 184, 236–37, etc.

Emmanuel: title of Christ 743, 744, 745. See Immanuel.

End. See Consummation.

Enoch: the scribe (of righteousness) 198, 203, 294, 413 – cp. 342; the first man on earth to write 22–3 – cp. 274; his writings listed 23; his writings quoted or referred to 68, 317, 328 – especially in Test. XII. Pat. 523, 532, 533, 546, 557, 564, 569, 598; they describe what is in the heavens 344, and what is to happen on earth 756; some 360 of his books were written at the dictation of the archangel Vreveil 338, 340, 341, 344; all are to be carefully preserved for the benefit and profit of future generations 271, 313, 341, 342, 347, 349; he did not die 413, 430, but was translated 254–55, 342; 354; in Eden he keeps the records of men's deeds till the Day of Judgement 23–4 – cp. 42, 342, 348, 349; he will descend with Elijah on the Day and destroy the Antichrist 773, and he will function as a witness at the Judgement 42, 342.

Error: the prince of er. 521; the spirit of er. 790; the spirits of er. 524, 527, 561, 569, 580; the seven spirits of er. 516–17.

Eternal life: 196, 221, 224, 237, 345, 353, 445, 659 – cp. eternal rest 428, etc.

Fasting: created when God made the heavens 763.

Tabernacles. *See* Feasts.

Tablets: two sets of t., one of clay and the other of stone, recording the lives of Adam and Eve, made by Seth 160–161; 'the heavenly t.' are the heavenly original of the levitical laws 19, 21, 24, 26, 29, 30, 31, 56, 59, 63, 88, 93, 100, 101, 103, 135, 579, record good men's names and deeds 57, 64, 95, 99, 270, 309, 528, and predict the events of the future 77, 80, 295, 317, 581.

Tartarus: 208, 777, 935, 938, 947, 948, 949.

Taxo: 603–4, 612.

Terah: is a worshipper of idols, Abraham argues with him, and sets fire to his idols' house 47–48; he is not only an idolater but also a craftsman who makes and sells idols, Abraham argues with him, and his house is destroyed by act of God 369–75.

Throne(s): the throne of God 164, 202, 207, 214, 289, 329, 336, 337, 339, 341, 381–82, 609, 613 – cp. 'the throne of (his) glory' 226, 228, 235, 238, 242, 243, 244, 254, 255, 457, 528; thrones are prepared in heaven for the patriarchs 428, for Job 637, 642, and for the righteous 762, 770, 802, 803, 804, 812.

Torments of the damned, the. *See* Punishment.

Treasuries, heavenly: tr. where the righteous have a store of good works laid up 849, 854; tr. in which their souls are preserved after death 857 – cp. 853.

Tree(s): the tree of knowledge in Eden 154, 156, was variously a fig-tree 164, or a date-palm 385, or a vine 906 – cp. 'the tree of wisdom' 219; the tree of mercy from which flows the oil of life 157, 158; the tree of life 163, 164, 166, 331, 451, 537, 771, 832, 957–58 (eaten by Adam) – cp. 213–15 (a date-palm); God's 'holy ones' are 'trees of life' 673.

Trinity, the: 429, 437, 709, 714, 801, 806, and in doxologies 439, 452, 941.

Trisagion hymn, the: 421.

Unction: 964, 'the unction of incorruption', 480, 488.

Unleavened Bread. *See* Feasts.

Vessels of the Temple, the: carried away by Nebuchadnezzar 608; consigned to the earth to prevent this happening, by Jeremiah 823, by an angel 843–44, 889.

Vine, the: as the human race was condemned through the v., so it will be restored (through the Eucharist) 907.

Watchers (= archangels): 198, cp. 208, 223, 243, 255, also 335.
        (= fallen angels): 22 (?), 23, 33, 36, 41, 184, 195, 198, 200, 203, 204, 205, 293, 334–35, 519, 569. *See* Angels (fallen).

Ways, the two: 577, 578 – cp. 291, 294, 296, also 408–10.

Weeks. *See* Feasts.

Weighing of souls at the Judgement: 224, 242, 349, 410, 412, 924.

Wisdom: God's agent in creation 340; from heaven she sought a dwelling-place on earth and did not find it 225.

Wood: regulations about the w. to be used in sacrifices 69.

Word (of God), the: 47, 702, 703, 706, 722, 729, 730, 852(?).

Worship God: men (or women) who w. G. 477, 480, 493, 494–95, 496, 501, 503, 585.

Writing(s): Seth makes two sets of tablets, one of clay, the other of stone, recording the lives of Adam and Eve 160–61; the writings of Adam and Seth are to endure to the end of time 341 – cp. 342; the angel Penemue taught men the art of writing with ink and paper, through which many have been led astray 252; Enoch was the first among men to write 22–3 – cp. 274; Vreveil dictates the books to Enoch 338, and Enoch is to give them to his children as a permanent legacy for future generations 341–42; Kainam finds and transcribes an ancient inscription on a rock, containing the teaching of the Watchers 36; Noah writes a medical treatise and leaves everything he had written to Shem 42; Abraham transcribes and studies his fathers' books 49, and commends them to Isaac (i.e. 'the words of Enoch' and 'the words of Noah') 68; Jacob reads from 'the words of Abraham' 116, and passes on the ancestral books to Levi 129; Levi used to see 'letters written in the heavens' and read and interpret them to Aseneth 495; Zebulon refers to 'the writing of my fathers' 560.